Lecture Notes in Computer Science 1349

Edited by G. Goos, J. Hartmanis and J. van Leeuwen

Springer
Berlin
Heidelberg
New York
Barcelona
Budapest
Hong Kong
London
Milan
Paris
Santa Clara
Singapore
Tokyo

Michael Johnson (Ed.)

Algebraic Methodology and Software Technology

6th International Conference, AMAST'97
Sydney, Australia, December 13-17, 1997
Proceedings

Volume Editor

Michael Johnson
Macquarie University
School of Mathematics, Physics, Computing, and Electronics
Sydney NSW 2109, Australia
E-mail: mike@mpce.mq.edu.au

Cataloging-in-Publication data applied for

Die Deutsche Bibliothek - CIP-Einheitsaufnahme

Algebraic methodology and software technology : 6th international conference ; proceedings / AMAST '97, Sydney, Australia, December 13 - 17, 1997. Michael Johnson (ed.). - Berlin ; Heidelberg ; New York ; Barcelona ; Budapest ; Hong Kong ; London ; Milan ; Paris ; Santa Clara ; Singapore ; Tokyo : Springer, 1997
(Lecture notes in computer science ; Vol. 1349)
ISBN 3-540-63888-1

CR Subject Classification (1991): F.3-4, D.2, C.3, D.1.6, I.2.3, H.2.1-4

ISSN 0302-9743
ISBN 3-540-63888-1 Springer-Verlag Berlin Heidelberg New York

Typesetting: Camera-ready by author
SPIN 10652702 06/3142 – 5 4 3 2 1 0 Printed on acid-free paper

Preface

The sixth international Algebraic Methodology and Software Technology Conference (AMAST'97) was held in Sydney, Australia, between December 13 and December 17, 1997. Previous AMAST conferences had been held in Iowa (1989 and 1991), in Twente (1993), in Montreal (1995), and in Munich (1996).

Over the years AMAST has developed into a wide ranging initiative with a number of workshops held each year in addition to the now annual AMAST conference. For me the outstanding feature of AMAST, present again this year, is its mix of serious mathematical development of formal methods in software engineering with practical concerns, tools, case studies, and industrial involvement. The annual conference is a special opportunity for theoreticians, practitioners, and industrial participants to share their experiences in advancing software technology, programming methodology, and their algebraic and logical foundations.

AMAST'97 attracted an unusually large number of submissions resulting in extraordinary workloads for this year's programme committee: V.S. Alagar (Canada), Egidio Astesiano (Italy), Didier Begay (France), R. Buckland (Australia), J. Cannon (Australia), Kokichi Futatsugi (Japan), Armando Haeberer (Brazil), Paola Inverardi (Italy), Michael Johnson (Australia), Rocco De Nicola (Italy), Anton Nijholt (Holland), Fernando Orejas (Spain), Mehmet Orgun (Australia), John Plaice (Australia) John Potter (Australia),R. Ramanujam (India), Charles Rattray (Great Britain), T. Rus (USA), T. Sakabe (Japan), Giuseppe Scollo (Holland), R.K. Shyamasundar (India), Andrzej Tarlecki (Poland), R.F.C. Walters (Australia), and M. Wirsing (Germany).

The programme committee also needed to call on a large number of additional referees including: A. Arnold, Marek Bednarczyk, Michele Boreale, Tomasz Borzyszkowski, Pietro Cenciarelli, Maura Cerioli, Corina Cirstea, Flavio Corradini, Eva Coscia, Maarten Fokkinga, Thom Fruehwirth, Stefania Gnesi, James Harland, A.W. Heerink, David Janin, Joost-Pieter Katoen, Alexander Knapp, Anton Koelbl, Beata Konikowska, Anna Labella, Diego Latella, Huimin Lin, Chuchang Liu, Kamal Lodaya, P. Madhusudan, Alfio Martini, Scott McCallum, Chiara Meo, Stephan Merz, Ugo Montanari, Carlo Montangero, Madhavan Mukund, Tohru Naoi, K. Narayan Kumar, Monica Nesi, Geoff Outhred, Catuscia Palamidessi, Paritosh Pandya, Joachim Parrow, Mannes Poel, Corrado Priami, Rosario Pugliese, N. Raja, Gianna Reggio, Bernhard Reus, Michael Richmond, Ken Robinson, Robert Rosebrugh, Igor Shparlinski, G. Sivakumar, Masahiko Skai, P.S. Subramanian, Pim van den Broek, Axel Wabenhorst, Uwe Wolter, Shinichirou Yamamoto, Shoji Yuen, Xiaogang Zhang, Elena Zucca, Job Zwiers.

The systems and tools demonstrations committee was chaired by Richard Buckland and consisted of Richard Buckland, Ken Robinson, and Jon Tidswell. Local arrangements were coordinated by Vicki Carruthers.

The organisers are grateful for the support of Macquarie University and its Department of Computing, the Microsoft Research Institute, the Joint Research Centre for Advanced Systems Engineering and the Australian Research Council.

October 1997 Michael Johnson

Table of Contents

Systems and Tools Demonstrations

Software Configuration with Information Systems

Slim Ben Lamine[1] and John Plaice[2]

[1]Département d'informatique, Université Laval, Sainte-Foy (Québec) Canada.
Email: benlamin@ift.ulaval.ca

[2]School of Computer Science and Engineering,
University of New South Wales, Sydney 2052, Australia.
Email: plaice@acm.org

1 Introduction

There is no aspect of software engineering that does not require versions. Software is versioned, individual components are versioned, so is documentation. Although the presence of versions at all levels complicates the builds of large systems, these must be handled correctly, because software *will* evolve.

Software configuration designates the building of a system from its components. This process might be single-layered, in which a complete system is built directly from atomic components, such as source, text or graphics files; or multi-layered, in which case subsystems are successively built up from component subsystems, which have themselves already been configured.

At each level, each system or component—hereafter called a *module*—can have several versions. We call the set of *conceptual* (possible) *versions*—those that can be imagined or "thought of"—of that module its *conceptual version space*, and the set of *physical versions* of that module its *physical version space*.

Key to successful, automated software configuration management is the structure of these version spaces. In particular, we need a model for constructing version spaces where the following issues are considered to be fundamental.

Succinctness Designating a version should be done with as few words as possible. A system that requires lengthy version expressions to designate any particular version is likely to be unwieldy.

Approximability One should be able to designate what features are required of a system, allowing the configuration management system to find the version that best approximates what was actually requested. If need be, regression tests can be applied to the built system to ensure that the desired features are in fact supplied.

Encapsulation The entire life cycle of any given module is unlikely to be of interest to those that use that particular module. For example, the sequence of edits to a source file is unlikely to be of any use to someone running a build of a company's major software products. Similarly, when releases are being made, untested versions of components should not even be considered for inclusion. Therefore, it should be possible, at any moment, to only consider a subset of a module's version space.

Concurrency It is not uncommon to have several people working simultaneously on a particular module, each making changes to different aspects of that module. The version space model should be flexible enough to allow the many different kinds of common concurrent work.

Interoperability Any significant software system typically includes work done by many teams, which may be geographically removed, possibly in different companies or organizations. It is unrealistic to assume that the same version spaces are going to be used by all of these teams. But for configuration management of the entire project to be successful, there must be meaningful interaction between the version spaces of the systems being built by different teams. In practice, this means that some form of translation from one version space to another is required.

Scalability At different levels, version spaces will be quite different. For example, the versions for a stack class will not resemble the versions for a multilingual typesetting system. Nevertheless, the same general approach should be applicable at all levels of software development.

Repeatability The same query for a version of a module should always give the same results, even if new information has been added to the software database. This property is absolutely fundamental for proper support for released versions, as it allows one to verify bug reports and to correct those bugs properly. We assume of course that nothing has been *removed* from the software database, otherwise repeatability would be unachievable.

If these desired properties give an idea of what is necessary of version spaces, they elide the question "What is a version?" A version of a module is the culmination of a series of edits, changes or additions to that module. New versions are produced by *refining* or *recombining* previous versions.

This notion of refinement has already been studied in the field of denotational semantics. In particular, Dana Scott's *information systems* [7] can be used to define domains. Unlike the topological approaches used for presenting semantics, information systems are based on the notion of repeatedly *adding* information, similar to the notion of *delta* or *change* regularly used in software configuration.

An information system is a set of tokens, along with a definition for *consistent sets* and an *entailment relation.* The maximal consistent sets are called *elements.* Subsets of the token sets can be used to define *sub-information systems.* Entire information systems can be related through *approximable mappings*, which preserve consistency.

In this paper, we present a model for building version spaces, using information systems. In our approach the tokens are the deltas or attributes making up a version and the versions are the elements. Hence an attribute space is a partial order $\sqsubseteq$ with certain properties guaranteeing consistency, while a version space is the set of elements. Sub-information systems are used for encapsulation purposes. Approximable mappings are used to define the interoperation between different version spaces with different definitions of consistency. Once the problem is framed in this manner, it is easy to specify version selection and software configuration, along with such useful concepts as personal workspaces.

The whole model is based on the concept of *information refinement.* The refinement between versions ($\sqsubseteq$) facilitates the designation of versions. The refinement between version spaces, using approximable mappings, simplifies the passage from one version space to another.

The rest of the paper is organized as follows. Section 2 begins with a survey of the literature. Section 3 provides the intuition for our model of attributes and versions. Section 4 gives the key definitions and results for information systems, along with the analogies to version spaces. Section 5 defines a simple class of version spaces that subsumes most of the literature. Section 6 explains how the same module may have several version spaces associated with it. Section 7 defines a more complex class of version spaces to support concurrent work. Section 8 shows how software configuration takes place using a single conceptual space, assuming the variant substructure principle of Plaice and Wadge [5]. Section 9 does the same in the presence of several different conceptual spaces. We conclude in Section 10 with a discussion of future work.

2 Key concepts in the literature

In existing configuration management systems, the most common version space is the tree. This approach, first used in the SCCS [6] and RCS [8] systems, and still used in many commercial systems, supposes that a version of a component can be designated by a string of numbers, as in `4.1.3.2`, corresponding to a node in a tree. That version subsumes all of the modifications, usually called deltas, that led to that particular version. The deltas composing a version are not independent, as they are partially (usually totally) ordered: each delta depends on the previous ones.

The success of the tree approach is two-fold. First, the causal relationship between successive deltas is retained, thereby allowing important historical information to be stored in a succinct manner, which is fundamental to software process support. Second, versions can be quickly designated, using just a few words, as not all of the deltas leading to each version need be enumerated.

However, the tree approach is ill-suited to concurrent development, since merges require a directed acyclic graph, not a tree, to be properly modeled. In addition, the tree approach is not well suited to expressing orthogonal properties of variants, as is required for combining, say, different user interface languages (English, French, Japanese, ...) and platforms (Unix, Windows NT, OS/2, ...) See [5] for further discussion.

In addition, the numeric approach used to designate versions is simply too low-level. When one is building a particular version of a large system, one needs automatic support for the selection of the appropriate versions of tools and components needed for the build, and numbered versions are just too limited, since different systems and components evolve at different rates and according to different needs. For example, is no reason to suppose that version `4.1.3.2` of the C compiler has anything to do with version `4.1.3.2` of the Unix link editor;

hence, if one wishes to compile a C program, one cannot simply request version `4.1.3.2` and expect everything to work.

There have been several approaches [2,4,5,9] to naming versions symbolically in such a way that versions are considered to apply uniformly to all components of a system: these approaches are collectively known under the term *uniform versioning*. A version is defined through a logical formula or through an expression designating an element in a partial order. Version selection is greatly simplified when builds of large systems are effected, as one just demands the same version from every component.

These methods can be divided into two categories. In the Change-Oriented Versioning (COV) model [4] and Zeller's Feature Logic model [9], versions are designated by logical formulas that combine the different attributes making up a version, where the attributes are all at the same level. For a given component, a particular version is chosen if it satisfies the logical formula used to request a version. This top-down approach is much more abstract than the SCS-RCCS approach, in the sense that variants are considered primary, and is much more suitable for building large systems.

Nevertheless, the logical approach ignores the two aspects that actually made the standard version/variant graph successful: causality between different versions is lost, since all attributes are considered to be at the same level. Furthermore, it is difficult to designate versions in a succint manner, as all of the deltas need to be enumerated.

In Plaice and Wadge's [5] and Heidenreich's [2] partial order approaches, it is assumed that there exists a partial order between versions, and that different components do not all exist in the same set of versions. However, when a particular version of a system is requested, the most relevant or best approximation of that version is requested of each component, using the partial order. This bottom-up approach, called the *variant substructure principle*, greatly simplifies version selection. And, unlike in the logical approaches, a causal relationship still exists between different versions. However, the long names that occur when designating versions are still a problem.

Despite the work mentioned above, to the best of our knowledge, no current model allows one to define the interoperation of different configuration management systems, each with its own mode of version space. That is precisely the object of this paper, which not only addresses this question, but also synthesizes the fundamental ideas mentioned above into a coherent whole. As a result, several key aspects of software configuration management are simplified. We retain the COV idea that a version is a set of attributes: in fact, a version is *defined* to be the set of attributes making it up. We also retain the partial order from Plaice and Wadge's work, as well as the variant substructure principle. However, the attributes are ordered, like the deltas in the RCS-like systems, in such a way that versions can be designated without enumerating all of the attributes making up a version.

3 Attributes, descriptions and versions

For the purposes of this paper, we will suppose that we are creating versions of *modules*. For the moment, we will not look at questions of module structure; we will come back to this subject in Section 8.

We will also assume that the relevant differences between different versions of a module are all *explicit*. In other words, what links the versions of a given module are implicit features, while what differentiates them are explicit features.

These explicit features can come about in many different ways. Some will be changes resulting from straight-forward linear development. Others will designate choices or variants, for such concepts as interface languages or host implementations. Given the variety of these features, we choose to call them *attributes* and we will assume that a version is completely defined by its *description*, which is the set of attributes of which it is composed.

For example, the description of the initial version of a one-module program for drawing geometric figures might just be {base}. Once it has been used, this version might be independently transformed into two other versions, {base, optimized} for an optimized version, and {base, graphic} for a graphic version using a bitmapped screen. Combining the features of these two versions would require additional work, thereby resulting in description {base, optimized, graphic, graph_opt}.

From this example it should be clear that there is typically a causal relation between attributes. In fact, the graphic attribute implies the base attribute, since the graphic attribute is tied to the original version, which has the base attribute. Furthermore, the graph_opt attribute implies the graphic, optimized and base attributes. These causal relationships define a partial order, written as follows:

$$\begin{aligned} \texttt{base} &\sqsubseteq \texttt{optimized} \\ \texttt{base} &\sqsubseteq \texttt{graphic} \\ \texttt{optimized} &\sqsubseteq \texttt{graph\_opt} \\ \texttt{graphic} &\sqsubseteq \texttt{graph\_opt} \end{aligned}$$

Once the order on attributes is defined, it is no longer necessary to specify all of the attributes to designate a version. For example, the set {graph_opt} unambiguously designates version {base, optimized, graphic, graph_opt}. Similarly, {graphic} designates version {base, graphic}. We will use the term *partial description* for those sets that unambiguously designate descriptions, even if they are not themselves full descriptions.

In both of the examples in the previous paragraph, the partial description consisted of the greatest attribute in the complete description. What happens if the greatest attribute is not included, for example, with {graphic, optimized}? Intuitively, this means that a version that offers both the graphics and optimized capabilities is requested. This means that the two must be combined. So the greatest lower bound—with respect to the partial order—of these two attributes is sought. Hence, {graphic, optimized} should also designate version {base, optimized, graphic, graph_opt}.

Therefore, to create a description from a partial description, all that is required is to compute the downward closure of the least upper bound of the partial description. Section 5 will define a class of information systems that formalizes these ideas.

4 Information systems

The concepts of attribute, description and version can all be formalized using information systems. This section provides the basic definitions. First are the information systems.

Definition 1. An *information system* is a structure $\mathcal{A} = (A, \mathrm{Con}, \vdash)$, where A is a countable set *(the tokens)*, is a non-empty subset Con *(the consistent sets)* of $\mathrm{Fin}(A)$ and $\vdash$ *(the entailment relation)* is a subset of $(\mathrm{Con}\backslash\{\emptyset\}) \times A$ that satisfy the following axioms:

IS 1. $X \subseteq Y \in \mathrm{Con} \Rightarrow X \in \mathrm{Con}$,
IS 2. $a \in A \Rightarrow \{a\} \in \mathrm{Con}$,
IS 3. $X \vdash a \Rightarrow X \cup \{a\} \in \mathrm{Con}$,
IS 4. $X \in \mathrm{Con} \wedge a \in X \Rightarrow X \vdash a$,
IS 5. $(X, Y \in \mathrm{Con} \wedge \forall b \in Y \,.\, X \vdash b \wedge Y \vdash c) \Rightarrow X \vdash c$.

The analogy to be drawn is that tokens are the attributes making up versions, consistent sets are the partial descriptions, and the entailment relation defines what attributes can be added to a partial description to form another partial description.

The first axiom ensures that every subset of a partial description is itself a partial description. The second axiom states that every attribute belongs to at least one version description. The third axiom guarantees that the adjunction of an entailed attribute to a partial description yields another partial description. The fourth ensures that the entailment relation is reflexive, i.e. all attributes belonging to a partial description are themselves entailed by that description. The fifth axiom guarantees transitivity, i.e. the set of entailed attributes does not entail more attributes.

The last condition is important, as it ensures that an entailed attribute adds no more information than was implicitly implied in the consistent attribute set. In other words, adding the entailed attribute does not change the approximated version.

If the consistent sets correspond to the partial descriptions, then the maximal consistent sets correspond to full descriptions, i.e. they are the versions. These sets are called *elements*.

Definition 2. The *elements* $|\mathcal{A}|$ of an information system $\mathcal{A} = (A, \mathrm{Con}, \vdash)$ are those subsets x of A that are:

EL 1. non-empty: $x \neq \emptyset$,
EL 2. consistent: $X \subseteq^{\text{fin}} x \Rightarrow X \in \text{Con}$,
EL 3. $\vdash$-closed: $X \subseteq x \wedge X \vdash a \Rightarrow a \in x$.

Of course, versions should be buildable from incomplete but consistent descriptions. This is done by computing the *closure* of a partial description.

Definition 3. The *closure* of a consistent set X, written $\overline{X}$, is the set of all tokens a such that $X \vdash a$.

In other words, the version corresponding to a partial description is simply the closure of that description, assuming of course that the partial description was consistent.

As is standard when introducing mathematical structures, there are substructures for information systems as well as morphisms between information systems. These are defined below and will be used in future sections. In the definitions that manipulate several information systems, they will be written as $\mathcal{A} = (A, \text{Con}_A, \vdash_A)$, $\mathcal{B} = (B, \text{Con}_B, \vdash_B)$, etc.

In the introduction, the need for encapsulation of version spaces—for abstraction, security, personal workspaces—was specified. These *version subspaces* will be defined using *sub-information systems.*

Definition 4. Let $\mathcal{A} = (A, \text{Con}_A, \vdash_A)$ and $\mathcal{B} = (B, \text{Con}_B, \vdash_B)$ be information systems. Then $\mathcal{A}$ is a sub-information system of $\mathcal{B}$, written $\mathcal{A} \trianglelefteq \mathcal{B}$, if and only if:

SIS 1. $A \subseteq B$,
SIS 2. $X \in \text{Con}_A \Leftrightarrow X \subseteq A \wedge X \in \text{Con}_B$,
SIS 3. $X \vdash_A a \Leftrightarrow X \subseteq A \wedge a \in A \wedge X \vdash_B a$.

The second axiom states that a consistent set X in $\mathcal{B}$ remains consistent in $\mathcal{A}$. The third axiom states that those tokens that were entailed by X in $\mathcal{B}$ are still entailed by X in $\mathcal{A}$. As a result, $\overline{X}$ will be an element both in $\mathcal{A}$ and in $\mathcal{B}$.

The introduction also specified the need for interoperability between different version spaces. This feature is provided by *approximable mappings*, which relate different information systems. To define approximable mappings, we must extend the entailment relation to sets. We will therefore write $X \vdash Y$, meaning $X \vdash a$ for all $a \in Y$.

Definition 5. Let $\mathcal{A}$ and $\mathcal{B}$ be two information systems. An *approximable mapping* $f\colon \mathcal{A} \longrightarrow \mathcal{B}$ is a binary relation between the two sets Con_A and Con_B such that for all u, $u' \in \text{Con}_A$ and v, $v' \in \text{Con}_B$,

AM 1. $\emptyset f \emptyset$,
AM 2. $ufv \wedge ufv' \Rightarrow uf(v \cup v')$,
AM 3. $u' \vdash_A u \wedge ufv \wedge v \vdash_B v' \Rightarrow u'fv'$.

Simply put, f must carry consistent sets to consistent sets.

5 A simple class of version spaces

The concepts of attribute, partial description and version now all have formal definitions, respectively, as token, consistent set and element. Furthermore, the transformation of a partial description into a full description is simply the closure of the partial description.

This section defines a simple class of version spaces as information systems, based on the intuitive discussion in Section 3. This class is shown below to be sufficiently general to describe several version spaces from the literature.

Suppose there exists a partially ordered set of attributes $(A, \sqsubseteq)$. Section 3 showed how version descriptions could be built from partial descriptions, by taking the least upper bound of a partial description, then adding to that description all of the tokens that were less than than maximal element. It would be useful to define an information system $\mathcal{A}$, based on A, that would be in keeping with this intuition.

Since the partial descriptions should be the consistent sets, the consistent sets X of A should be those that have a least upper bound $\sqcup X$. Similarly, $X \vdash a$ should mean that $a \in \downarrow\sqcup X$, where $\downarrow y = \{x \mid x \sqsubseteq y\}$ is the *downwards closure* of y.

It turns out, however, that this is not sufficient to define an information system, as axiom (IS1) is not respected. As an example, consider the attribute space in Figure 1 (a). Set $\{a, b, c, e, f, g\}$ might be considered to be a version, as it has a least upper bound. However, axiom (IS1) states that every subset of that set should be consistent, i.e. have a least upper bound. But this is not the case, since set $\{a, b\}$, although bounded above, does not have a *least* upper bound.

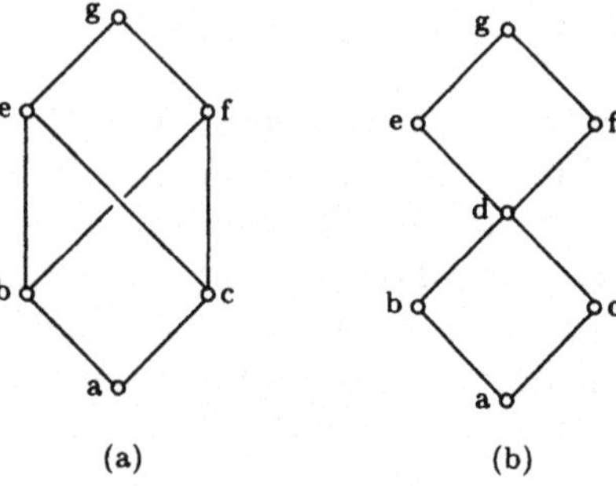

Fig. 1. Factorization of an attribute space

In fact, this example shows the kind of problems that can occur when concurrent engineering is taking place. Attributes e and f each play two roles: first as join of b and c, second as their own additional deltas. But the join of b and c does not exist on a standalone basis, despite the fact that it is required for both e and f. One way to handle this situation is to factor out the common changes to e and f, namely the join of b and c, then to create the necessary changes to reach e and f. The new order would then be the one presented in Figure 1 (b). In the next section, a more flexible alternative will be presented.

An additional condition is therefore imposed on A: every subset bounded above must have a least upper bound. This condition ensures that A defines an information system.

Definition 6. A ***simple attribute space*** is a partially ordered set $(A, \sqsubseteq)$ such that every subset bounded above has a least upper bound.

Theorem 7. *Let* $(A, \sqsubseteq)$ *be a simple attribute space. Define* Con *to be all those sets of* A *that are bounded above. Define* $\vdash \in \text{Con} \times A$ *by* $X \vdash a$ *if and only if* $a \in \downarrow \sqcup X$. *Then* $\mathcal{A} = (A, \text{Con}, \vdash)$ *is an information system.*

Proof Trivial.

Definition 8. Let $(A, \sqsubseteq)$ be a simple attribute space. The information system $\mathcal{A}$ derived from A is called a ***simple version space.***

Now that a class of version spaces as information systems has been defined, these must be related to the version spaces that are found in the literature.

The most common version space is the *tree.* Used by such the original version control tools, such as RCS [8] and SCCS [6], trees are still used in many commercial configuration tools, such as Adele [1] and ClearCase [3]. Tree spaces have the advantage of retaining the causal relationship between successive deltas, thereby allowing important historical information to be stored in a succinct manner. Since two points in a tree are only comparable if they are on the same branch, each subset bounded above is a subset of a branch, hence has an upper bound. Therefore a tree is a simple attribute space.

If trees are well suited for successive revisions or for designating divergent variants, they are not well-suited for explaining the merger of previous work. To do that requires some form of directed acyclic graph. For work in multidimensional variants, lattices have been proposed as a model. For example, the Change Oriented Versioning model [4] designates versions through propositional formulas over a set of attributes. Therefore, the version space forms a lattice, which of course has the least upper bound property. Hence it is a simple attribute space.

The literature also includes "hybrids" of trees and lattices, as in the work of Plaice and Wadge [5] and Zeller [9], which attempt to combine the advantages of both systems.

Zeller's model uses ***feature logics*** to designate versions, where a feature is a ***name:value*** pair. The basic syntax of the language designating versions is

$$V ::= a \mid \top \mid \bot \mid f : V \mid f : \top \mid V \sqcap V' \mid V \sqcup V' \mid \neg V$$

Here $\top$ means the empty version (no information), $\bot$ means the inconsistent version (too much information), $f : V$ designates a feature, $f : \top$ introduces a name and the Boolean operations are clear. For a given set of named attributes X, a partial order can be generated using this language. Since the conjunction operator computes the least upper bound of its arguments, this partial order is also a simple attribute space.

Hence, many version spaces in the literature are simple version spaces. However, in the discussion above, nowhere was it mentioned whether each version in a version space is actually *inhabited*, i.e. for a given module M, does version V appearing in a version space actually exist? Here we encounter the notion of *conceptual versions*, which can be imagined or thought of, or *physical versions*, which actually exist.

Some of the most difficult problems in software configuration come from the interaction between conceptual versions and physical versions: a user might request a conceptual version, and an appropriate physical version would then have to be selected, even though the exact physical version might not be available. It is this kind of issue that will be discussed in the sections below.

6 Version subspaces of a single module

The presentation up to now has been referring to a single version space, and has focused on the kinds of version space that can be conceived, given our precept of versions as sets of attributes. It is obvious that different modules do not necessarily have the same version spaces, but there can in fact be several version spaces for a single module. In this section, we will consider the different kinds of version spaces that a single module M might have.

In the introduction, a distinction was made between *conceptual* and *physical* versions. Conceptual versions are those versions that "can be thought of", whether or not they actually exist, while physical versions do actually exist. We call the set of conceptual (resp. physical) versions of M the *conceptual* (resp. *physical*) *version space*, written $\mathcal{C}(M)$, (resp. $\mathcal{P}(M)$).

If both of these spaces are information systems, what should be their relationship? In that case, $\mathcal{C}(M)$ (resp. $\mathcal{P}(M)$) would require a *conceptual* (resp. *physical*) *attribute space*, written $C(M)$, (resp. $P(M)$). Because only a single module M is being considered, there is no ambiguity in writing C, P, $\mathcal{C}$ and $\mathcal{P}$.

Now what is the relationship between C and P and between $\mathcal{C}$ and $\mathcal{P}$? Simply put, the three following properties must hold:

1. Physical attributes are also conceptual attributes: $P \subseteq C$.
2. Physical partial descriptions are also conceptual partial descriptions: $X \in \mathrm{Con}_P \Leftrightarrow X \subseteq P \wedge X \in \mathrm{Con}_C$.
3. If a physical attribute is entailed by a physical partial description, it is still entailed within the conceptual attribute space. $X \vdash_P a \Leftrightarrow X \subseteq P \wedge a \in P \wedge X \vdash_C a$.

In other words, $\mathcal{P}$ must be a sub-information system of $\mathcal{C}$, i.e. $\mathcal{P} \trianglelefteq \mathcal{C}$.

Intuitively, the conceptual space must include everything in the physical space, and, furthermore, must not contradict it. For example, in the case of a simple attribute space, the maximal token in a description in the physical space must necessarily be included in the corresponding description in the conceptual space.

The spaces $\mathcal{C}(M)$ and $\mathcal{P}(M)$ are examples of ***version subspaces*** of M. Given that the conceptual space $\mathcal{C}(M)$ contains all versions that "can be thought of", it is the largest subspace of M. All other subspaces will be included in $\mathcal{C}(M)$.

There is no limit to the kinds of subspaces that one might wish to consider. Depending on the tasks that are considered to be important, one might define subspaces for personal workspaces, for different levels of confidence in the code, for different levels of visibility within an organization, for different levels of visibility of the development process, etc. As for the physical space, these subspaces should be information systems, and hence should all be sub-information systems of the conceptual space.

Of course, for each of these subspaces, there is a conceptual subspace and a physical subspace. Consider, for example, the personal subspaces for worker a, C_a for the conceptual one and P_a for the physical one. Then the following relationship should hold.

$$\begin{array}{ccc} C & \trianglerighteq & P \\ \trianglerighteq & & \trianglerighteq \\ C_a & \trianglerighteq & P_a \end{array}$$

When dealing with orthogonal attributes, such commuting diagrams should be the norm with respect to subspaces. When dealing with simple attribute spaces, it is easy to ensure that these diagrams do in fact commute. For this example, $P_a = C_a \cap P$. For more complex spaces, such as the concurrent attribute spaces presented in the next section, then the definitions for the different subspaces must be done with care to ensure that such desirable properties are in fact respected.

7 Concurrent software development

Simple attribute spaces are useful for many problems, but they are limited in their capacity to support finegrain concurrent development. Consider, for example, two programmers simultaneously working on the same source file. Because of a tight production schedule, each is making updates to the file, and periodically taking into account the work of the other, ensuring that there are no inconsistencies being developed along the way. As a result, a sort of Eiffel tower development process takes place, as shown in Figure 2.

The process being developed here is clearly *not* a simple version space. Nevertheless, it can be made consistent by considering a version to be complete if it includes, recursively, all of the attributes that are immediately greater than pairs of attributes in the partial description that generated it.

Formalizing this notion requires a new operator on partially ordered sets.

Definition 9. Let $X \subseteq A$ be a set. Then $\uparrow X$ is the set containing $\downarrow X$ and all those attributes immediately greater than pairs of attributes in $\downarrow X$:

$$\uparrow X = \downarrow X \cup \left\{ z \in A \;\middle|\; \exists x, y \in \downarrow X \; \left(z > x \wedge z > y \wedge \neg \exists w < z \; (w > x \vee w > y)\right)\right\}.$$

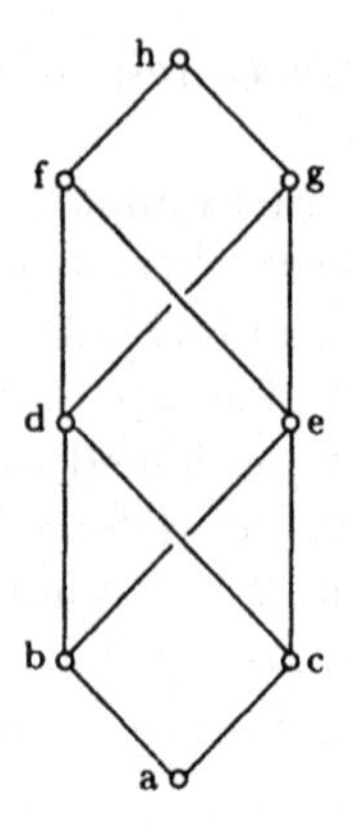

Fig. 2. Concurrent attribute space

This operator can be iterated, so $\uparrow^{n+1}X = \uparrow(\uparrow^n X)$, where $\uparrow^0 X = X$.

Now a *concurrent attribute space* can be defined.

Definition 10. A *concurrent attribute space* is a partial order $(A, \sqsubseteq)$ such that for every bounded subset $X \subseteq A$, $\uparrow^\omega X$ has a maximal element.

Theorem 11. *Let* $(A, \sqsubseteq)$ *be a concurrent attribute space. Define* Con *to be all those sets of* A *that are bounded above. Define* $\vdash \in \text{Con} \times A$ *by* $X \vdash a$ *if and only if* $a \in \uparrow^\omega X$. *Then* $\mathcal{A} = (A, \text{Con}, \vdash)$ *is an information system.*

Proof Trivial.

With the concurrent development space, the physical space as a whole does not always remain an information system. Some parts may be inconsistent for a temporary period. However, the way the development took place, the individual physical spaces *did* remain consistent: as soon as an inconsistency was found, a new node was added.

This section was designed to show that it is possible to create very complex version spaces that allow a high degree of flexibility while still retaining a formal basis. Clearly, concurrent version spaces are only an example.

8 Uniform versioning of hierarchical modules

Normally, software configuration does not deal with a single module. Rather, many modules use each other, either directly or indirectly, and the task of software configuration is to build a particular version of a complete system from the appropriate versions of the appropriate components.

In this section, we discuss how software configuration takes place, assuming that the *same* conceptual space is being used for all modules, although they may differ in their physical spaces, as the development process will be different for each module. This approach is called ***uniform versioning*** [4], and does not correspond to the standard model used by industry, which is based on ***change sets***, in which each version of a given module states explicitly what versions of the modules it uses must be selected.

In the model presented here, each module's version is requested separately, and the best approximation to the requested version is selected for that module. These modules are then put together, using the appropriate build operations. The build operations are themselves versioned, and fit in the same framework. At each point, when a module is built from components, it is tagged with the version that was actually built, rather than with the version that was requested. Doing so increases reusability of intermediate components, as multiple physical copies of the same module are not created. This approach, called the ***variant substructure principle***, was first presented in [5].

For the purposes of the presentation below, we suppose that there is a database $B : M \rightarrow V \rightarrow D$ containing versioned modules, where M is a module name, V is a version and D is the expression defining version V of module M. We will suppose that D is either of the form c, meaning some kind of atomic module; or $[c, M_0, \ldots, M_n]$, meaning that module M is composed of atomic module c, along with modules M_0 through M_n. Module M_0 is assumed to be the build function to be applied to create a module, while list $[M_1, \ldots, M_n]$ is M's ***import list.***

We are now ready to define version selection, given the above assumptions. Here is the basic algorithm:

$$
\begin{array}{l}
\texttt{select}(B, M, p) = \\
\texttt{let } (D, V) = \texttt{get}(B, M, p) \\
\texttt{in}\,\texttt{case } D \texttt{ of } \quad c : (c, V) \\
\qquad [c, M_0, ..., M_n] : \texttt{let } \ (E_i, V_i) = \texttt{select}(B, M_i, p), i \in 0..n \\
\qquad\qquad\qquad\qquad\quad \texttt{in } \left(E_0(c, E_1, ..., E_n), \overline{(V \cup V_0 \cup \cdots \cup V_n)}\right)
\end{array}
$$

A request is made that module M be created, using partial description p. For each module, the appropriate definition, tagged with a version, is selected, using the **get** function (explained below). If that version of the module is atomic, it is simply returned with the same version tag. Otherwise, the same request is made that the component modules $M_0, \ldots, M_n$ be created, using partial description p. Then the module is created, and the new version is the closure of the union of the component versions.

The **get** function must take the partial description p, compute the version within the ***conceptual*** version space, and then translate that version into a version in the ***physical*** space. Since B has been defined so that $\mathcal{P}(M) = \mathrm{dom}(B(M))$, **get** can be defined as follows.

$$
\begin{array}{l}
\texttt{get}(B, M, p) = \\
\quad \texttt{let } V = \texttt{closure}_{\mathcal{P}(M)}(\overline{p} \cap \mathcal{P}(M)) \\
\quad \texttt{in } (B(M)(V), V)
\end{array}
$$

The get function assumes that the physical space associated with each module is a sub-information system of the conceptual space. Using this approach, we can refer to version V of *any* module, whether or not any changes have been made to that module to actually create V. If a less refined version is sufficient, it will be returned, along with a tag of the lesser version.

9 Software configuration with multiple version spaces

If a single conceptual space might be feasible for small systems, it certainly is not for large ones. Most likely, there will be different conceptual spaces for different needs, be they modules, module libraries, programming teams or companies.

In this section, we consider a simple case of multiple version spaces, in which different parts of the software database use different conceptual spaces. To do this, a new form of module expression is given, $\langle M, C\rangle$, which means module M using conceptual space C. In this situation, the conceptual space in which configuration takes place must become a parameter of functions `select` and `get`.

When there are several conceptual spaces, the key problem is what to do when passing from one to the other. The answer is that there must be an *approximable mapping* from one to the other. If we wish to retain the variant substructure principle, there must in fact be approximable mappings in both directions. In the presentation below, we write $\mathrm{aa}(C, C')$ to designate an approximable mapping from C to C'. There might be several possible, we assume here that just one is chosen.

$$
\begin{array}{l}
\texttt{select}(B, M, C, p) = \\
\quad \texttt{let } (D, V) = \texttt{get}(B, M, C, p) \\
\quad \texttt{incase } D \texttt{ of } \quad c : (c, V) \\
\qquad\qquad \langle M, C'\rangle : \texttt{let } \ (E, V') = \texttt{select}\big(B, M, C', \mathrm{aa}(C, C')(p)\big) \\
\qquad\qquad\qquad\qquad \texttt{in } \ \big(E, \mathrm{aa}(C', C)(V')\big) \\
\qquad [c, M_0, ..., M_n] : \texttt{let } \ (E_i, V_i) = \texttt{select}(B, M_i, C, p), i \in 0..n \\
\qquad\qquad\qquad\qquad \texttt{in } \ \Big(E_0(c, E_1, ..., E_n), \overline{(V \cup V_0 \cup \cdots \cup V_n)}\Big)
\end{array}
$$

According to this approach, when a new conceptual space C' is encountered, the version description must be translated into something understandable in C'. The resulting version must then be translated *back* into something understandable in C, hence the two approximable mappings. Should an approximable mapping only be available in the C to C' direction, then the resulting version would simply be V.

As for the get function, it just has to make the conceptual space explicit when a closure is being undertaken.

$$
\begin{array}{l}
\texttt{get}(B, M, C, p) = \\
\quad \texttt{let } V = \texttt{closure}_{\mathcal{P}(M)}\big(\texttt{closure}_C(p) \cap \mathcal{P}(M)\big) \\
\quad \texttt{in } \big(B(M)(V), V\big)
\end{array}
$$

In this section, nowhere was it specified what different conceptual spaces might be used for. They might be global or local, they might correspond to third-party software spaces, they might correspond to poorer spaces that contain mainly information about high-level variants while other richer spaces might contain detailed information about revisions or bug fixes. There are no limits.

10 Conclusion

This paper has developed a general model for software versioning and configuration, based on information systems. The set of versions of a module, called its version space, should form an information system. Depending on the development process of that module, different kinds of version space can be defined, and approximable mappings can be used to relate the different version spaces of a single module as well as the version spaces of different modules.

Much work remains to be done. Many categories of version space could be defined to support specialized aspects of software development. In particular, we must develop version spaces and approximable mappings that allow modifications to previously released code but that do not make more complex access to the code through the highest-level variant spaces.

References

1. J. Estublier. A configuration manager: The Adele data base of programs. In *Proceedings of the Workshop on Software Engineering Environments for Programming-in-the-Large*, pages 140–147, Harwichport, Massachusetts, June 1985.
2. Georg Heidenreich and Mark Minas andDetlef Kips. A new approach to consistency control in software engineering. In *Proceedings of the 18th International Conference on Software Engineering (ICSE-18 '96)*, pages 289–297, September 1996.
3. David B. Leblang. The CM challenge: Configuration management that works. In Walter Tichy, editor, *Configuration Management*, pages 1–38. John Wiley and Sons, Ltd., Baffins Lane, Chichester, West Sussex PO19 1UD, England, 1994.
4. Bjorn P. Munch, Jens-Otto Larsen, Bjorn Gulla, Reidar Conradi, and Even-Andre Karlsson. Uniform versioning: The change-oriented model. In *Proceedings of the 4th International Workshop on Software Configuration Management (Preprint)*, pages 188–196, Baltimore, Maryland, May 1993.
5. John Plaice and William W. Wadge. A new approach to version control. *IEEE Transactions on Software Engineering*, 19(3):268–276, March 1993.
6. Marc J. Rochkind. The source code control system. *IEEE Transactions on Software Engineering*, SE-1(4):364–370, December 1975.
7. D. Scott. Domains for denotational semantics. *LNCS*, 140:577–613, 1982. Automata, Languages and Programming.
8. Walter F. Tichy. Design, implementation, and evaluation of a revision control system. In *Proceedings of the 6th ACM/IEEE International Conference on Software Engineering*, pages 58–67, Tokyo, Japan, September 1982.
9. Andreas Zeller and Gregor Snelting. Handling version sets through feature logic. In Wilhelm Schäfer and Pere Botella, editors, *Proceedings of the 5th European Software Engineering Conference*, volume 989 of *Lecture Notes in Computer Science*, pages 191–204. Springer-Verlag, September 1995.

Head-Tactics Simplification

Yves Bertot

INRIA Sophia Antipolis

Abstract. Tactics are commands used to guide goal-directed proofs in interactive proof environments. This paper presents various possible simplifications on tactic expression and provides a justification for these simplifications, based on a precise description of the way tactics operate. In particular, this paper introduces a class of *head-oriented* tactics that are especially suited for simplification. Most of these simplifications have been developed in an simplifier coupled with a tactic generator based on mouse interaction.

1 Introduction

The work described in this paper deals with tools for interactive proof environments on the computer. The help that computers could bring in the development of proofs has been recognized for a long time. Two main domains have developed from this recognition. The first area is that of proof automation. In this domain, interactivity is considered harmful and researchers attempt to make the computer find complex proofs on its own. In this domain, one has to fight with incompleteness and complexity theorems, that express that there is no algorithm that will successfully detect true formulas, and, that even in domains where algorithms exist, these algorithms may often be useless because of the time they require to reach a solution. The second area is that of interactive proof development. In this domain, one still relies on a human operator to describe the main steps of the proof and the research goal is to make human operators as efficient as possible in their work to provide the proof steps.

Interactive proof development tools often contain two kinds of formal languages. The first one is used to represent the logical formulas, the second one is used to change the state of the proof environment, in order to progress towards a state where the validity of some formulas has been ascertained and mechanically checked. An important mode of operation is *goal-directed proof*, where one states a logical formula to prove and applies commands to reduce this command into simpler formulas. The commands that one applies in this mode are usually called *tactics*. The tactics form a sub-language of the command language of proof environments, with control and composition operators.

Recent studies in the user-interface of theorem proving tools [22] have shown that the characteristics of modern computer workstations could be used efficiently to improve the usage of proof environments. With features like *Proof-by-pointing* [2], it is possible to interpret simple tokens of information, like the position of the mouse with respect to a logical formula, to produce complex tactics. In this paradigm, mouse interaction is considered a high-level language, compiled into the tactics language, considered as a low-level language. In different words, the proof-by-pointing algorithm is just a compiler, used thousands of times in one interactive session with the proof environment.

The results of the proof-by-pointing algorithm need to be simplified. The simplification is different from thue usual optimization phase of a compiler. Here the efficiency will vary little between the original expression and the simplified one. On the other hand, readability will be a significant criterion, since the aim of tools like proof-by-pointing is to construct commands that the user could have written by hand. Another important feature of this work is that the new expressions produced by the simplifier are semantically different from the original expressions, in ways that are justified by practical experience.

This simplifier is what we describe in this paper. In the second section, we give a short description of proof representation in type theory and use this framework to show how tactics operate, to present a few tactic composition constructs, and to introduce a class of tactics we call *head-oriented tactics*. In the third section, we describe several simplification rules on tactic expressions. The first simplification rule concerns only a composition construct. The next group of rules concern the tactics used to handle implication and *forall* quantification. The last rules concern the interaction of these tactics with head-oriented tactics. All these simplification rules are used in a user-interface we are developing for the Coq proof system [13].

1.1 Related work

In the study of proof systems, very little attention has been devoted to the language used to advance proof description, with one notable exception: the ML programming language [17,19]. This functional language has now evolved into a general-purpose programming language, but it was originally intended as the command language for the Edinburgh LCF proof system. Its formal semantics have been thoroughly studied, as have the ways to compile and to execute it. The language is still evolving, and it is increasingly being used outside the proof community.

In the specific domain of tactics and tactic composition, precise descriptions of tactics are given in [7], [18], and [11], each time as an instanciation for their specific proof systems. A more abstract account of *tactic trees* was done in [12]. This account represents quite faithfully the notions of tactics that are used in this paper. The work described in [9] also contains an interesting study of tactics and their interaction with metavariables (called existential variables in this paper).

The presentation of proof systems described in this paper draws very much from the area of type theory, where proof checking is viewed as a generalization of program type-checking. This domain has been initiated by work of Martin-Löf [16] and has led to many implementations of proof systems [7,13–15].

Work on proof-by-pointing is the initial incentive for this work on tactic simplification. Proof-by-pointing, where commands are generated from an interpretation of locations selected by the user, has been formally described in [2] and [4]. It has been implemented in several experiments of proof environments, based on a variety of proof systems: Isabelle [20], HOL [21], a theorem prover developped in λ-prolog [8], and Coq [13], all using a structure editor [22,5] to facilitate the input of mouse location information. Although the initial algorithm is intended for "common" logics, extensions of this notion have also been studied for modal logic [10]. On the implementation side, the importance of structure editors for mouse interaction has also been studied and an experiment using the Lego proof system [14] and Emacs [6] have shown that this coupling could be lessened [3].

2 Domain of study

In this section we first describe how proof assistants can use the Curry-Howard paradigm to represent proofs and how this model can be used in uniform tactics.

2.1 The Curry-Howard isomorphism and head-oriented tactics

This section introduces the concepts of type theory and tactics to help understand the context of our work.

Types for proof assistants The Curry-Howard isomorphism relies on the strong similarity that there is between typing a program and checking a proof. It establishes a link between types and logical propositions on one side and programs and proofs on the other side. The most typical example revolves around the arrow, used in one case to represent function types and in the other case to represent implication. This correspondance is quite easy to understand intuitively: *a proof of $A \Rightarrow B$ maps any proof of A to a proof of B*, exactly in the same manner that a total function of type $A \rightarrow B$ maps any element of A to an element of B.

For an expressive formalism, it is necessary to go beyond the types regularly found in programming languages. For instance, a universally quantified formula $\forall x \in \mathcal{N}.P(x)$ also corresponds to a function type for functions that map any object n of type $\mathcal{N}$ to a proof of $P(n)$. One sees immediately that this function takes all its arguments in the same type $\mathcal{N}$ and maps them to *different* types: here the result type depends on the value of the argument, and not only on the argument type as one is accustomed to with polymorphic functional languages. It is possible to generalize the recursive data-structures found in functional languages to capture logical phenomena. For instance, a conjunction is very much akin to a pair type, while a disjunction is akin to a sum type.

Proving a theorem boils down to exhibiting an object whose type is the theorem's statement. Here, the two methods of forward proving and backward proving, as already known in the context of other logical systems like HOL or Isabelle are also available. When performing forward proving, you simply construct by hand a term with the right type. This is very often difficult because the type information that is requested by the proof system is very cumbersome to provide. Backward proving is also possible: first state the goal logical formula, then provide a function that might return an object of that type, if it were applied to arguments of the right type, then consider these new types as new subgoals and proceed recursively.

Backward proving proceeds by constructing terms with typed holes. At the beginning, there is only one hole and its type is the goal. When the user attempts to fill this hole in with a function whose arguments are undetermined new holes are created, presumably with simpler types, corresponding to simpler goals. This is top-down construction. This top-down construction is very well presented in Alf [15].

Beyond the idea of manipulating proof terms with typed holes, one might want to consider having holes in the types themselves, leading to situations where the exact statement of what needs to be proved will be decided as the proof goes on. The idea is quite appealing, especially for automatic proofs and when the proof of a statement depends on the existence of a term verifying some specific property. The holes are often referred to as *existential* variables and these holes are usually filled in using some form of unification (higher order unification in Isabelle for instance [20]). However, such existential variables usually end up occurring in several goals, that is, in the type of several holes and this breaks some form of regularity in the proving process: the proof of two distinct goals in a given incomplete proof term is not independent if these two goals share an existential variable. In the rest of this paper we will not consider proof term development with existential variables, so that the property that two subgoals can be proved independently holds.

Understandably, tactics-based proving is also available [18]. *Tactics* are functions that take a goal as argument and return a new list of subgoals and a validation, with the intended meaning that the validation makes it possible to construct a proof of the goal as soon as it is given a list of proofs for the subgoals. Here the validation simply needs to be an incomplete proof term, that will have the type of the goal as soon as one provides the subterms corresponding to its holes.

Tactics operation

Introduction and elimination of $\forall$ and $\Rightarrow$ Many theorems have a statement in a *functional* form, that is, a universally quantified statement of the form $\forall x : A.B$ or an hypothetical statement of the form $A \Rightarrow B$. The natural form of proofs for these statements is that of a function, which takes an element of the given type as argument (here A in both cases) and has a body where this element can be used to construct an object of type B. It is natural to have a local context attached to each goal and a tactic, named `Intro`, that takes a goal of the form given above and produces a new goal with the statement B and a new declaration $x : A$ (meaning we have an object x of type A) in the local context. For the proof term construction, this corresponds to expressing that the proof will have the form of a lambda abstraction $\lambda x : A.M$ where M is the new hole.

In this framework, introducing a *cut* in the proof simply corresponds to introducing a β-redex. There are three possible forms of tactics that make this kind of manipulation possible:

1. There is a `Cut` tactic. When applied to a goal B, the tactic `Cut A` introduces two new goals $A \Rightarrow B$ and A. The proof term constructed has the form $M(N)$, where M must have type $A \Rightarrow B$ and N must have type A.
2. There is a `Generalize` tactic. When applied to a theorem `thm` of type A for a goal B, it introduces a goal of the form $A \Rightarrow B$. The proof term constructed has the form $M($`thm`$)$. This may look useless, but it will be used to make instances of universally quantified theorems appear (the operation named $\forall$-elimination) as follows: if the goal is C and if `thm` has the statement $\forall x : A.B(x)$ and if a has the type A, then `Generalize thm(`a`)` produces a goal of the form $B(a) \Rightarrow C$.
3. There is an `LApply` tactic. When applied to a theorem `thm` of type $A \Rightarrow B$ for a goal C, it produces the two goals $B \Rightarrow C$ and A. The proof term constructed has the form $M($`thm`$(N))$ where M must have type $B \Rightarrow C$ goal and N must have type A.

In some respect, the `Cut` tactic and the `Generalize` and `LApply` tactics do not live in the same world, as they can be distinguished by the kind of arguments they take. The argument of the `Cut` tactic is a logical formula (a type) while the argument of the two other tactics is a proof term. From a practical point of view this difference is important: logical formulae tend to grow large while proof terms will more often consist in a single identifier (a theorem name) applied to a limited number of arguments.

Tacticals Tactics can be composed in several ways, for instance with repetitive statements, or conditionally, depending on the failure of previous tactics. In this section, we will only refer to constructions for sequence compositions.

The first sequencing construction corresponds to the `THEN` tactic of LCF-style provers. In our presentation it will be noted `tac`$_1$`; tac`$_2$. The behavior of this construction is to apply `tac`$_1$ on the goal at hand and then apply `tac`$_2$ on all the goals produced by `tac`$_1$. This construction is very supple with respect to the number of produced goals, but the user has to be sure that `tac`$_2$ will operate successfully on all of them.

The second sequencing construction corresponds to the `THENL` tactic of LCF-style provers. In our presentation it will be noted `tac;[tac`$_1$`; ...;tac`$_n$`]`. The behavior of this construction is to apply `tac` on the goal at hand, to verify that it produces n goals G_1, ..., G_n and to apply `tac`$_1$, ..., `tac`$_n$ respectively to these goals. This construction is more rigid, as it expects a specific number of new subgoals, but the user can apply different tactics for different subgoals.

Paradoxically, a useful tactic that is complementary to the `THENL` tactical is a tactic that does nothing. When several goals are produced, it is important to be able to express that one will do something specifically on one of the subgoals, and nothing on the others. We shall name `Idtac` a tactic that succeeds on any goal and produces exactly the same goal.

Head oriented tactics As we already mentionned, theorems whose statement is an implication have a functional form. After applying one such theorem to the right number of arguments, one reaches a derived theorem whose statement is a plain subterm of the initial statement. In terms of proof term construction, this corresponds to filling a hole of type B with a theorem of type $A_1 \Rightarrow \cdots \Rightarrow A_n \Rightarrow B$ applied to the n holes $A_1, \ldots, A_n$. A head-oriented tactic is a tactic that incorporates directly this behavior in its mode of operation.

Definition *A tactic* `tac` *is* head-oriented *if for any two theorems* $\mathtt{thm}_1$ *and* $\mathtt{thm}_2$ *with types B and $A \Rightarrow B$ respectively,* $\mathtt{tac}\ \mathtt{thm}_1$ *and* $\mathtt{tac}\ \mathtt{thm}_2$ *can be applied successfully whenever the other one can, and if $G_1, \ldots, G_n$ are the goals generated by the tactic* $\mathtt{tac}\ \mathtt{thm}_1$ *then A, $G_1, \ldots, G_n$ are, in this order, the goals generated by* $\mathtt{tac}\ \mathtt{thm}_2$.

Formally, the *head* and *depth* of a logical formula can be recursively described as follows:

1. The head of $\forall x : A.B$ is the head of B, the depth of $\forall x : A.B$ is the depth of B plus one,
2. the head of $A \Rightarrow B$ is the head of B, the depth of $A \Rightarrow B$ is the depth of B plus one,
3. if A does not fit in the previous patterns, the head of A is A, its depth is 0.

The head-oriented behavior can be extended to cope with *dependent* functional types (that is, universal quantification). The first means of extension appears when there is a way to know which specific instance of the head is expected and when the universally quantified variable occurs in the theorem head. A second means of extension comes with the possibility of providing to the tactic the value to instanciate variables with, using a syntax of the form:

$$\mathtt{tac\ thm\ with\ x_1\ :=}\ val_1\ \mathtt{x_2\ :=}\ val_2\,.$$

While only certain head-oriented tactics have a way to infer the exact instance of the head that is needed and can apply the first method, all head-oriented tactics can be augmented to provide the second method.

The main example of head-oriented tactics in the Coq system [13] is `Apply`. For a goal C and a theorem `thm` whose head is B and whose depth is n, partitionned in m universal quantifications and p implications, this tactic will detect if the m universally quantified variables occur in B, if C is an instance of B for some assignment of values to these variables, and produce p new goals. The initial hole will be replaced by a term $\mathtt{thm}\ a_1 \cdots a_n$ where the a_i's are values for the universally quantified variables or holes corresponding to instances of the left-hand sides of implications.

For instance, let us consider the current goal of interest is the following statement:

$$P(a_1, \ldots, a_{k-1}, b_k, a_{k+1}, \ldots, a_n)$$

and let us suppose the theorem `thm` has the following statement (i.e., it has the following type):

$$\forall x \in A.Q_1(x) \Rightarrow \cdots \Rightarrow Q_m(x) \Rightarrow P(a_1,\ldots,a_{k-1},x,a_{k+1},\ldots,a_n).$$

In this situation, the tactic `Apply thm` will infer that the theorem can be applied, that it must be applied to the term b_k and to proofs of $Q_1(b_k)$, ..., $Q_m(b_k)$.

Using the `with ...:= ...` construct to specify the value of some variables does not preclude relying on matching to infer the other values. For instance if the theorem has the following statement:

$$\texttt{le\_trans} : \forall x,y,z : \texttt{nat}.\ x \leq y \Rightarrow y \leq z \Rightarrow x \leq z$$

then the tactic `Apply le_trans with y := some_value` will apply successfully whenever `some_value` is defined and the goal has the form $a \leq b$.

3 Tactic simplification rules

In this section we shall review the various "equivalences" that can be used to simplify tactics. We put the word between quotes because strict equivalence will not always be respected, in the sense that we will also consider transformations where a tactic is replaced with a tactic that does not perform exactly the same operations.

One could view these simplifications as optimizations. It is then sensible to describe what are the optimization criteria. Paradoxically, the main criterion is not the efficiency of the produced code tactic code: this efficiency varies little between the original and simplified expressions. The main criterion is conciseness. All the simplifications we will propose reduce the size of the manipulated tactics, where the size is the number of nodes in the tree structure representing th tactics (this tree structure is an abstract syntax tree).

3.1 Flattenning sequences

The `THEN` operator accepts arbitrary tactics as children. For this reason a `THEN` operator can itself appear as child of another `THEN` operator. From an abstract point of view, one may want to consider the algebraic properties of the `THEN` operator, when considered as a binary operator on an abstract space. The first interesting property is that the `THEN` operator is associative.

To understand a justification of this property, one needs to recall the intuitive interpretation of tactics as proof term constructors, where the only input is a subgoal, that is a subterm type. The proof term can be abstractly understood as a tree, where each node is decorated with a goal. It is possible to partition the proof tree construction obtained by the successful execution of a tactic of the form:

$$\texttt{tac}_1\texttt{;(tac}_2\texttt{;tac}_3\texttt{)}$$

The goals produced by $\texttt{tac}_1$ are then handled by applications of the tactic $\texttt{tac}_2\texttt{;tac}_3$. This construction can be represented the following way:

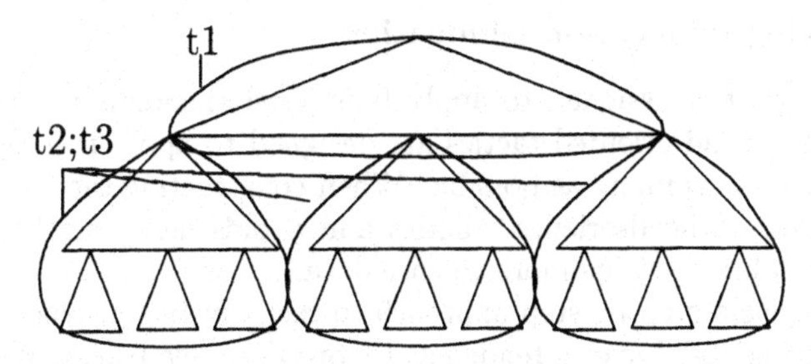

It is also possible to partition the structure of the proof term differently, with a divide placed between applications of $\mathtt{tac}_2$ and applications of $\mathtt{tac}_3$, as represented in the following figure:

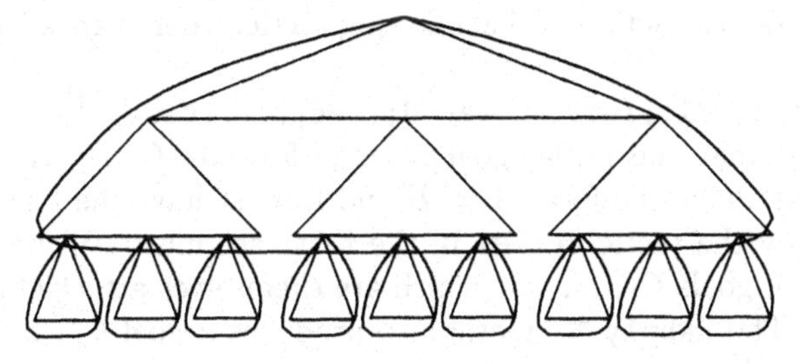

Thus, the same proof tree can be viewed as the result of the following tactic:

$$(\mathtt{tac}_1;\mathtt{tac}_2);\mathtt{tac}_3.$$

Based on this remark, the THEN operator is an operator with a list arity: it can accept an arbitrary number of children. With this approach, the associativity property gives the following simplification rule:

$$\mathtt{tac}_1;\ldots;\mathtt{tac}_n;(\mathtt{tac}'_1;\ldots;\mathtt{tac}'_p) \rightarrow \mathtt{tac}_1;\ldots;\mathtt{tac}_n;\mathtt{tac}'_1;\ldots;\mathtt{tac}'_p \quad (1)$$

3.2 Interactions between THEN and THENL in the Coq system

The use of the same separator ";" for the THEN and THENL tactics gives a special meaning to the question of how the THEN constructor associates: in the presence of a tactic construction of the form:

$$\mathtt{tac};\ \mathtt{tac}';[\mathtt{tac}_1 \mid \ldots \mid \mathtt{tac}_n],$$

one may wonder how the set of tactics $\mathtt{tac}_1$, ..., $\mathtt{tac}_n$ should be adapted to tac and tac′. The solution that is used as a reference in this paper, which corresponds to the implementation in Coq, is that n has to be the number of goals produced by the tactic tac; tac′ as a whole. This is imposed by the parser, which naturally binds on the left.

On the implementation side, the structure parsed when recognizing the given text has a tree structure that does not use a THENL node, but only a special kind of element in THEN sequences, to represent the $[\mathtt{tac}_1 \mid \ldots \mid \mathtt{tac}_n]$, which we shall call a PARALLEL node. As an unfortunate side effect, the associativity rule is broken. The simplification rule number (1) given in the previous section can only apply if $\mathtt{tac}'_p$ is not a PARALLEL node.

3.3 Removing implication elimination

The tactic `LApply` is designed to apply functional theorems to one argument at a time, while head-oriented tactics are designed to apply theorems to many arguments, in fact, as many as possible. When constructing tactics, one usually prefers using direct head-oriented tactics and avoids using the `LApply` tactic, since the first solution yields more concise data.

Tools that use a step-by-step approach to recursively construct tactics (like proof-by-pointing [2]) have a tendency to privilege sequences of uses of the `LApply` tactic. In this section we will study the patterns using compositions of `LApply` and head oriented tactics that can be replaced with simple uses of head oriented tactics.

Let us consider the action of the following tactic, where `tac` is a head-oriented tactic:

$$\texttt{LApply H1;[Intro H;tac H;[tac}_1\texttt{|...|tac}_n\texttt{] | tac']}$$

Let us suppose that the initial goal is some formula C. By the definition of `LApply`, `H1` must have the form $A \Rightarrow B$ and `H` must have the form `B`. Also, the goal attacked by the tactic `tac H1` in the first case must still be C. Now, `tac H` will produce n goals $C_1, \ldots, C_n$,which are themselves attacked by the tactics $\texttt{tac}_1$ to $\texttt{tac}_n$. The `LApply H1` tactic also produces a goal `A`, which is attacked by the tactic `tac'`.

Now if we consider the action of the following tactic on the same goal:

$$\texttt{tac H1;[tac'|tac}_1\texttt{|...|tac}_n\texttt{]}$$

By the definition of head-oriented tactics, the tactic `tac H1` should succeed and produce the $n+1$ goals $A, C_1, \ldots, C_n$, which are attacked by `tac'`, $\texttt{tac}_1, \ldots, \texttt{tac}_n$. Everything should work smoothly, except that in the first case the tactics $\texttt{tac}_1, \ldots, \texttt{tac}_n$ work in a context where there exists a local `H1` with type B, while no such object is present in the context in the second case. Aside from these differences, this leads us to a simplification rule with the following form:

$$\begin{array}{l}\texttt{LApply } H\texttt{;[Intro } H_1\texttt{;}\\ \quad \texttt{tac } H_1\texttt{;[}tac_1\texttt{|...|}tac_n\texttt{]}\\ \qquad\qquad\qquad\qquad \texttt{|}tac'\texttt{]}\\ \qquad\qquad\qquad\qquad\qquad \rightarrow \texttt{tac } H\texttt{;[}tac'\texttt{|}tac_1\texttt{|...|}tac_n\texttt{]}\end{array} \quad (2)$$

The two sides of the rule are not strictly equivalent in the following two ways:

1. The goals produced by the two tactics are not produced in the same order in both cases.
2. The context available in new subgoals is not the same in both case.

These discrepancies limit the conditions in which the simplification rule can be applied. Because of the first one, the simplification cannot be applied on a tactic if this tactic is in a context where the order of produced goals is important. For instance, this simplification should not be used to clean a script composed of a sequence of tactics, where each tactic is applied to a goal given by its rank (the usual form of proof scripts in systems like Isabelle, HOL, PVS, Coq, etc.).

Because of the second one, the simplification should not be used without a global check that the cancelled proof term will not be used in sub-tactics. It is not only necessary to check that the cancelled name does not occur again, but also that no tactic that does a systematic search in the local context is used.

In the case of tactics generated using an interactive tool, these constraints on the applicability of the simplification rule can be relaxed for two reasons. First, the generated tactic is usually the last one of the script at that moment so that there is no problem of coherence with respect with the order of new subgoals. Second, the interactive tool may be designed so that names introduced using `LApply` and `Intro` are used only once, thus ensuring that the cancelled name is not used somewhere else (for instance, proof-by-pointing is designed in this manner).

3.4 Compacting *forall* elimination

Forall elimination denotes the process to go from a context containing a formula $\forall x.P(x)$ to a context containing a formula $P(a)$ for some a. If `H` is a proof term having the first formula as type, forall elimination can be performed using the following tactic:

$$\texttt{Generalize (H } a\texttt{);Intro H1}$$

Now, if $P(a)$ is yet another universally quantified formula, one could perform a second forall elimination by putting a second instance of the same pattern behind the `Intro H1` tactic, with a new value b. However, one should notice that `(H a)` is itself a proof term having $P(a)$ as type and the two successive forall eliminations could also be performed correctly by the following tactic:

$$\texttt{Generalize (H } a\ b\texttt{);Intro H2}$$

This explanation can be generalized to an arbitrary number of successive forall eliminations, thus yielding the following simplification rule:

$$\begin{array}{l} \texttt{Generalize (}H\ a_1\ \ldots a_n\texttt{);} \\ \quad\quad \texttt{Intro } H_1\texttt{;} \\ \texttt{Generalize (}H_1\ a_{n+1}\texttt{);} \\ \quad\quad \texttt{Intro } H_2 \rightarrow \texttt{Generalize (}H\ a_1 \ldots a_n\ a_{n+1}\texttt{);} \\ \quad\quad\quad\quad \texttt{Intro } H_2 \end{array} \tag{3}$$

Of course, the general applicability is not granted for this rule, as the same constraints as above appear for names that have been cancelled.

3.5 Mixing $\forall$ and $\Rightarrow$ elimination with head-oriented tactics

Since head-oriented tactics also take a proof term as argument, rule number (3) is directly adaptable to each head-oriented tactic `tac`:

$$\begin{array}{l} \texttt{Generalize (}H\ a_1\ \ldots a_n\texttt{);} \\ \quad\quad \texttt{Intro } H_1\texttt{;} \\ \quad\quad\quad \texttt{tac } H_1 \rightarrow \texttt{tac (}H\ a_1 \ldots a_n\texttt{)} \end{array} \tag{4}$$

Obviously, the tactic `tac H1` on the left hand side may itself result from the compaction of implication eliminations, as performed using rule number (2). So rules (2) and (4) can be used to compact uses of head-oriented tactics, implication eliminations, and forall eliminations in one command. But this only works if the forall quantifications are outside the implications.

A pattern where an implication is outside a forall quantification like $A \Rightarrow \forall x.B$ yields a tactic pattern with the following form:

```
LApply H;[Intro H1; tac (H1 a1)|Idtac]
```

It is not possible to replace this tactic with an instance of `tac` applied directly to some proof term. This proof term would have to contain a complete proof of A. However, there is one feature we have described in head-oriented tactics that we have not yet exploited: the possibility to give explicitly variables values, value by value. In the case above, the relevant tactic is:

```
tac H1 with x := a1
```

This remark does not carry over very well into a simplification rule. Not all the data present in the simplification result appears in the reduced expression: the variable name `x` is produced only when one knows that the forall quantification in the statement (the type of `H`) introduces a variable of that name. We are confronted with the fact that the tactic pattern which we use to perform forall elimination does not contain this name and the information is lost.

To cope with this issue, we assume that the algorithm that produces the tactic expression is capable of annotating the generated tactics with variable names. From now on, we will consider forall-elimination patterns of the following form, indicating that the forall quantification introduced a variable named `x`:

$$\texttt{Generalize (H } \mathtt{a}^{x}\texttt{);Intro H1}$$

With this approach, rule number (3) should be replaced with the following rule:

$$\begin{array}{l}\texttt{Generalize }(H\ a_1^{x_1}\ \ldots a_n^{x_n})\texttt{;}\\ \qquad\texttt{Intro }H_1\texttt{;}\\ \quad\texttt{Generalize }(H_1\ a_{n+1}^{x_{n+1}})\texttt{;}\\ \qquad\texttt{Intro }H_2 \rightarrow \texttt{Generalize }(H\ a_1^{x_1}\ldots a_n^{x_n}\ a_{n+1}^{x_{n+1}})\texttt{;}\\ \qquad\qquad\texttt{Intro }H_2\end{array} \tag{5}$$

Rule number (4) should also be modified accordingly.

Now the following rule makes it possible to switch from a simple use of head-oriented tactics to a more elaborate one:

$$\texttt{tac }(H\ a_1^{x_1}\ a_n^{x_n}) \rightarrow \texttt{tac }H\texttt{ with }x_1\texttt{ := }a_1\ldots x_n\texttt{:=}a_n \tag{6}$$

The right hand side of this rule is arguably less concise than its left hand side, so it should be used with care. In fact, it should be used only when it makes it possible to use the following rule, corresponding to an implication elimination preceding an arbitrary mixture of forall and implication eliminations and a head-oriented tactic.

$$\texttt{LApply }H\texttt{;[Intro }H_1\texttt{;}$$

$$\texttt{tac}\ H_1\ \texttt{with}\ x_1 := a_1 \quad \ldots \quad x_n := a_n \quad \texttt{|Idtac]} \rightarrow \texttt{tac}\ H\ \texttt{with}\ x_1 := a_1 \ldots x_n := a_n \qquad (7)$$

There is a similar rule for a forall elimination preceding an arbitrary mixture of forall and implication eliminations and a head oriented tactic.

$$\texttt{Generalize (}\ H\ a^x\texttt{);}\ \texttt{[Intro}\ H_1\texttt{;}\ \texttt{tac}\ H_1\ \texttt{with}\ x_1 := a_1 \quad \ldots \quad x_n := a_n \quad \texttt{|Idtac]} \rightarrow \texttt{tac}\ H\ \texttt{with}\ x := a\ x_1 := a_1 \ldots x_n := a_n \qquad (8)$$

4 Conclusion

The work described in this paper presents a few classes of tactics and tactic constructors (tacticals) and simplification rules between tactic patterns. These simplifications are used as the formal basis for an simplifier that has actually been implemented in a proof environment composed of a user-interface with graphical features [1], where tactics can be edited by hand or produced mechanically from mouse-clicks issued by the user. Adding this simplifier to the command generator is very well perceived by the user, even though the optimized commands are not strictly equivalent to the original ones. One positive feature is that generated commands look like hand-crafted ones: this makes them more readable.

The work presented here has some limitations. First, we have deliberately avoided a setting where logical formulas can contain holes (existential variables). In such a context, many of the simplifications we have presented become very fragile. For instance, our simplifications rely on the fact that direct subgoals can be attacked in any order. This is no longer true in the presence of existential variables.

In this paper, we have chosen to only introduce informally the semantics of each tactical and the characteristics of the class of head-oriented tactics. To completely justify the validity of our simplification, one would need a much more formal description of tactics. This could be a complementary area of research, which we have started with an abstract description of tactics and tacticals, developed directly in the proof system. Thus, we may even be able to prove mechanically the validity of our simplifications.

Another area of possible work is to understand whether the THEN and THENL constructs provide the better set of basic constructs for writing complex tactics. In some respect, it seems that a variant, mixing the semantics the two constructs could make it easier to write shorter tactics. For example a composition tactical could differentiate the new subgoals in two sets: those corresponding to the tactic applied to the head (principal subgoals, in some —etymological— sense) and those corresponding to implication antecedents due to head-oriented behavior (side goals).

Acknowledgements

The work on proof-by-pointing, which initiated this one, was started with Laurent Théry and Gilles Kahn, it also was their adamant pressure for better usage that led to these simplifications. The work described in this paper is the explanation of algorithms implemented in the CtCoq system. I would like to thank the other developers of this system, Janet Bertot and Francis Montagnac for their help in this development.

References

1. Janet Bertot and Yves Bertot. CtCoq: A system presentation. In *Automated Deduction (CADE-13)*, volume 1104 of *Lecture Notes in Artificial Intelligence*, pages 231–234. Springer-Verlag, July 1996.
2. Yves Bertot, Gilles Kahn, and Laurent Théry. Proof by pointing. In *Theoretical Aspects of Computer Software*, volume 789 of *Lecture Notes in Computer Science*, pages 141–160, 1994.
3. Yves Bertot, Thomas Schreiber, and Dilip Sequeira. Proof by pointing in a weakly structured context. ftp://ftp.dcs.ed.ac.uk/pub/lego/pbp/main.ps.
4. Yves Bertot and Laurent Théry. A generic approach to building user interfaces for theorem provers. To appear in Journal of Symbolic Computation.
5. Patrick Borras, Dominique Clément, Thierry Despeyroux, Janet Incerpi, Gilles Kahn, Bernard Lang, and Valérie Pascual. Centaur: the system. In *Third Symposium on Software Development Environments*, 1988. (Also appears as INRIA Report no. 777).
6. Debra Cameron and Bill Rosenblatt. *Learning GNU Emacs*. O'Reilly & Associates, Inc., 1991.
7. Robert Constable, S. F. Allen, H. M. Bromley, W. R. Cleaveland, J. F. Cremer, R. W. Harber, D. J. Howe, T. B. Knoblock, N. P. Mendler, P. Panangaden, J. T. Sasaki, and S. F. Smith. *Implementing mathematics with the Nuprl proof development system*. Prentice-Hall, 1986.
8. Amy Felty. *Specifying and Implementing Theorem Provers in a Higher-Order Logic Programming Language*. PhD thesis, University of Pennsylvania, 1989.
9. Amy Felty and Douglas Howe. Tactic theorem proving with refinement-tree proofs and metavariables. In *Automated Deduction(CADE-12)*, volume 814 of *Lecture Notes in Computer Science*. Springer-Verlag, June 1995.
10. Amy Felty and Laurent Théry. Interactive theorem proving with temporal logic. To appear in Journal of Symbolic Computation.
11. Michael Gordon and Thomas Melham. *Introduction to HOL : A theorem proving environment for higher order logic*. Cambridge University Press, 1993.
12. Timothy Griffin. *Notational definition and top-down refinement for interactive proof development systems*. PhD thesis, Cornell University, 1988.

13. INRIA. *The Coq Proof Assistant Reference Manual*, December 1996. Version6.1.
14. The LEGO World Wide Web page. url `http://www.dcs.ed.ac.uk/home/lego`.
15. Lena Magnusson and Bengt Nordström. The ALF proof editor and its proof engine. In *Types for Proofs and Programs*, volume 806 of *Lecture Notes in Computer Science*, pages 213–237. Springer-Verlag, 1994.
16. Per Martin-Löf. *Intuitionistic type theories.* Bibliopolis, 1984.
17. Robin Milner, Mads Tofte, and Robert Harper. *The Definition of Standard ML.* MIT Press, 1990. ISBN 0-262-63132-6.
18. Lawrence C. Paulson. *Logic and computation, Interactive proof with Cambridge LCF.* Cambridge University Press, 1987.
19. Lawrence C. Paulson. *ML for the working programmer.* Cambridge University Press, 1991.
20. Lawrence C. Paulson and Tobias Nipkow. *Isabelle : a generic theorem prover*, volume 828 of *Lecture Notes in Computer Science.* Springer-Verlag, 1994.
21. Laurent Théry. A proof development system for the HOL theorem prover. In *Higher Order Logic theorem proving and its applications*, volume 780 of *Lecture Notes in Computer Science.* Springer-Verlag, August 1993.
22. Laurent Théry, Yves Bertot, and Gilles Kahn. Real Theorem Provers Deserve Real User-Interfaces. *Software Engineering Notes*, 17(5), 1992. Proceedings of the 5th Symposium on Software Development Environments.

Iteration 2-theories: *Extended Abstract*

Stephen L. Bloom*

Zoltán Ésik**

Anna Labella ***

Ernest G. Manes

Stevens Institute of Technology
Department of Computer Science
Hoboken, NJ 07030
bloom@cs.stevens-tech.edu

A. József University
Department of Computer Science
Szeged, Hungary
esik@inf.u-szeged.hu

Dept. of Computer Science
University of Rome "La Sapienza"
Via Salaria 113
00198 Rome, Italy
labella@dsi.uniroma1.it

Dept. of Mathematics
University of Massachusetts
Amherst, MA
USA
manes@math.umass.edu

Abstract. The axioms of iteration 2-theories capture the equational properties of iteration in conjunction with horizontal and vertical composition in all algebraically complete categories. We give a concrete representation of the free iteration 2-theory generated by a 2-signature.

1 Introduction

Algebraically complete categories [Fre91, Fre92] are important for computer science. These are exactly those categories in which one may define recursive data types in a canonical way as initial solutions of recursive functorial equations corresponding to data type specifications. Let $\mathcal{C}$ be a category with a given collection $\mathcal{F}$ of functors $\mathcal{C}^{n+p} \longrightarrow \mathcal{C}^n$, $n, p \geq 0$, which contains the projections $\mathcal{C}^n \longrightarrow \mathcal{C}$, $n \geq 1$, and which is closed under composition and target tupling. Suppose that for each $F : \mathcal{C}^{n+p} \longrightarrow \mathcal{C}^n$ in $\mathcal{F}$ and each $\mathcal{C}^p$-object y, there is an initial F_y-algebra $(F^\dagger y,\ \mu_{F,y})$, where F_y denotes the endofunctor $F(-, y) : \mathcal{C}^n \longrightarrow \mathcal{C}^n$. It is well-known, see e.g. [BE93], that the assignment $y \mapsto F^\dagger y$ is the object map of a unique functor $F^\dagger : \mathcal{C}^p \longrightarrow \mathcal{C}^n$ such that $\mu_F = (\mu_{F,y})_{y \in \mathcal{C}^p}$ is a natural transformation (in fact, a natural isomorphism) $F \cdot \langle F^\dagger, \mathbf{1}_p \rangle \longrightarrow F^\dagger$. (Here, $\mathbf{1}_p$ stands for the identity functor $\mathcal{C}^p \longrightarrow \mathcal{C}^p$.) Borrowing terminology from [Fre91], we call the pair $(\mathcal{C}, \mathcal{F})$ an *algebraically complete category* if $F^\dagger$ is in $\mathcal{F}$ whenever F is. (In [Fre91], only functors in one variable are discussed.)

The definition of an algebraically complete category implicitly specifies a dagger operation $F \mapsto F^\dagger$ on the functors $F : \mathcal{C}^{n+p} \longrightarrow \mathcal{C}^n$ in $\mathcal{F}$. Given this operation, and the natural transformations μ_F, there is a canonical way to extend the definition of dagger to any natural transformation $\tau : F \longrightarrow G$ between functors $F, G : \mathcal{C}^{n+p} \longrightarrow \mathcal{C}^n$ in $\mathcal{F}$ to obtain a natural transformation $\tau^\dagger : F^\dagger \longrightarrow G^\dagger$ such that $\mu = (\mu_F)$ is itself natural in F. Thus, viewing the functors in $\mathcal{F}$ and their natural transformations as a 2-theory, i.e., a 2-category with cartesian structure, we obtain a dagger operation defined on all 2-cells. This dagger operation, defined both on functors and on natural transformations, or more generally, on horizontal and vertical morphisms, interacts smoothly with the categorical and cartesian structure. *The study of this interaction is the topic of the present paper.* Building on results in [EL96], we give an axiomatic treatment. We introduce a new concept, **iteration 2-theories**, that

* Partially supported by the US-Hungarian Joint Fund under grant number 351.

** Partially supported by a grant of the National Foundation for Scientific Research of Hungary, the Alexander von Humboldt Foundation, and by the US-Hungarian Joint Fund under grant number 351.

*** Partially supported by the EEC–HCM project EXPRESS.

generalizes (ordered) iteration theories [BE93, Esia]. By describing explicitly the structure of the free iteration 2-theories, we show that the axioms of iteration 2-theories capture precisely the equational properties of the dagger operation in algebraically complete categories. Our description involves regular trees. An indication of some applications to computer science of iteration 2-theories and the results of this paper is given in Section 11.

In this abstract, we will omit most proofs.

For each nonnegative integer n, the set $\{1, 2, \ldots, n\}$ is denoted $[n]$; the set of all positive integers is $[\omega]$. The composite of two functions $f : X \to Y$, $g : Y \to Z$, and, more generally, two morphisms in any category, is written in diagrammatic order as either $fg : X \to Z$ or $f \cdot g : X \to Z$.

2 Theories and 2-theories

2.1 Theories

A (Lawvere) **theory** T is a category whose objects are the nonnegative integers in which n is a coproduct of 1 with itself n times; more precisely, T contains n "distinguished morphisms" $i_n : 1 \to n$, $i \in [n]$, for each $n \geq 0$, with the following coproduct property: for any family of n morphisms $g_i : 1 \to p$ in T there is a unique morphism $g : n \to p$ in T such that for each $i \in [n]$,

$$i_n \cdot g = g_i.$$

This uniquely determined morphism g is denoted $\langle g_1, \ldots, g_n \rangle : n \to p$, and is called the **tupling** of the morphisms g_i. In particular, the tupling of the empty family produces a unique morphism $0_p : 0 \to p$, for each $p \geq 0$. Any tupling of distinguished morphisms is called a **base morphism**. We assume always that for any $f : 1 \to p$, $\langle f \rangle = f$.

For example, the theory **Tot** has all total functions $[n] \to [p]$ as morphisms $n \to p$, $n, p \geq 0$, with function composition as the category composition. Every morphism is base in this theory.

If T and T' are theories, a **theory morphism** $T \to T'$ is a functor which preserves the objects and distinguished morphisms.

A theory is *trivial* if each hom-set $T(n, p)$ has at most one morphism. If T is not trivial, there is a unique injective (faithful) theory morphism from **Tot** to T, which takes the function $f : [n] \to [p]$ to the base morphism

$$\langle 1f_p, 2f_p, \ldots, nf_p \rangle$$

and we usually assume without comment that **Tot** is a subtheory of every theory.

As is the case with any category with binary coproducts, we may introduce two derived operations on any theory T: *pairing*, which is a function

$$T(n,p) \times T(m,p) \to T(n+m,p)$$
$$f, g \mapsto \langle f, g \rangle$$

for all $n, m, p \geq 0$, and *separated sum*, which is an operation

$$T(n,p) \times T(m,q) \to T(n+m,p+q)$$
$$f, g \mapsto f \oplus g.$$

The definitions are the expected ones. For example, $i_{n+m} \cdot \langle f, g \rangle = i_n \cdot f$, if $i \in [n]$.

A **preiteration theory** is a theory T equipped with a unary operation $^\dagger : T(n, n+p) \to T(n,p)$, called a "dagger operation", for each $n, p \geq 0$. This operation need not satisfy any particular properties. A **morphism of preiteration theories** is a theory morphism which preserves the dagger operation.

Example 2.1 Suppose that $(A, \leq)$ is an ω-complete poset with a least element. Then every ω-continuous function $A \longrightarrow A$ has a least fixed point, and more generally, when the powers of A are ordered pointwise, for each ω-continuous function $f : A^{n+p} \longrightarrow A^n$, and each $a \in A^p$ there is a least $x = af^\dagger$ such that

$$x = f(x, a).$$

Thus, $f^\dagger$ is a function $A^p \longrightarrow A^n$, and it is easy to check that $f^\dagger$ is also ω-continuous. Thus the ω-continuous functions on the powers of A form a preiteration theory in which $f^\dagger$ is given as above.

Definition 2.2 *A preiteration theory T is an* **iteration theory** *if T satisfies all identities true in all theories of ω-continuous functions.*

In particular, we mention the the *fixed point identity*,

$$f^\dagger = f \cdot \langle f^\dagger, 1_p \rangle,$$

all $f : n \longrightarrow n + p$, and the *pairing identity*, which shows that the dagger operation is determined by its value on morphisms with source 1.

$$\langle f, g \rangle^\dagger = \langle f^\dagger \cdot \langle h^\dagger, 1_p \rangle,\ h^\dagger \rangle,$$

all $f : n \longrightarrow n + m + p$, $g : m \longrightarrow n + m + p$, where

$$h = g \cdot \langle f^\dagger, 1_{m+p} \rangle : m \longrightarrow m + p.$$

An axiomatic definition of iteration theories can be found in [Esi80], and [Esib].

2.2 2-theories

If C is a 2-category (see [KS74, Bor94]), we use the notation $(f, u, g) : x \longrightarrow y$ to denote a 2-cell with horizontal morphisms $f, g : x \longrightarrow y$ and a vertical morphism $u : f \longrightarrow g$. When $f = g$ and u is the identity vertical morphism $f \longrightarrow f$, we will usually write just f for both the vertical identity morphism and for the 2-cell $(f, f, f) : x \longrightarrow y$. (When necessary, we write $\mathbf{I}_f : f \longrightarrow f$ for the identity vertical morphism.) The horizontal composite of $(f, u, g) : x \longrightarrow y$ with $(f', u', g') : y \longrightarrow z$ is denoted either by $(f \cdot f', u \cdot u', g \cdot g')$ or by $(ff', uu', gg') : x \longrightarrow z$, and the vertical composite of $(f, u, g) : x \longrightarrow y$ with $(g, u', h) : x \longrightarrow y$ is written $(f, u \star u', h) : x \longrightarrow y$.

We let $\mathbf{Cell}\, C$ denote the category whose objects are the 0-cells of C and whose morphisms $x \longrightarrow y$ are the 2-cells $x \longrightarrow y$ in C. Composition in $\mathbf{Cell}\, C$ is horizontal 2-cell composition in C.

We recall from [BE93] that a **2-theory** is a 2-category T such that both the horizontal structure in T as well as $\mathbf{Cell}\, T$ are theories; the distinguished morphisms $1 \longrightarrow n$ in $\mathbf{Cell}\, T$ are the 2-cells $i_n = (i_n, i_n, i_n) : 1 \longrightarrow n$, $i \in [n]$. Thus, for any 2-cells $(f_i, u_i, g_i) : 1 \longrightarrow p$ in T, $i \in [n]$, there is a unique 2-cell $(f, u, g) : n \longrightarrow p$ such that

$$(f_i, u_i, g_i) = (i_n f, i_n u, i_n g),$$

for each $i \in [n]$ We denote this uniquely determined 2-cell by

$$(\langle f_1, \ldots, f_n \rangle,\ \langle u_1, \ldots, u_n \rangle,\ \langle g_1, \ldots, g_n \rangle).$$

Thus, for any collection of 2-cells $\alpha_i : 1 \longrightarrow p$. $i \in [n]$, there is a unique 2-cell $\alpha : n \longrightarrow p$ such that $i_n \cdot \alpha = \alpha_i$, for each $i \in [n]$. We write

$$\alpha = \langle \alpha_1, \ldots, \alpha_n \rangle.$$

Note in particular, that vertical composition in 2-theories is pointwise: if $\alpha = (f, u, g)$ and $\beta = (g, v, h)$ are 2-cells $n \longrightarrow p$, then

$$\alpha \star \beta = (f,\ \langle u_1 \star v_1, \ldots, u_n \star v_n \rangle,\ g),$$

where $u_i : i_n \cdot f \longrightarrow i_n \cdot g$ and $v_i : i_n \cdot g \longrightarrow i_n \cdot h$, for each $i \in [n]$.

Each theory may be regarded as a 2-theory all of whose vertical morphisms are vertical identities. This observation allows us to define all subsequent notions only for 2-theories.

Example 2.3 The basic example of a 2-theory is the 2-theory of functors and natural transformations over a category $\mathcal{C}$. The horizontal morphism $n \longrightarrow p$ are the functors $\mathcal{C}^p \longrightarrow \mathcal{C}^n$, and the vertical morphisms the natural transformations. Horizontal and vertical composition have their usual meaning.

Definition 2.4 *If T_0 and T are 2-theories, we say T_0 is a* **sub 2-theory** *of T if for each $n, p \geq 0$, $T_0(n,p) \subseteq T(n,p)$ and the 2-theory operations of T_0 are the restrictions of those of T.*

If T, T' are 2-theories, a **2-theory morphism** $\varphi : T \longrightarrow T'$ assigns to each horizontal arrow $f : n \longrightarrow p$ in T a horizontal arrow $f\varphi_H : n \longrightarrow p$ in T' and to each vertical 2-cell $(f, u, g) : n \longrightarrow p$ in T a 2-cell $(f,u,g)\varphi = (f\varphi_H, u\varphi_V, g\varphi_H) : n \longrightarrow p$ such that base morphisms are assigned themselves, horizontal and vertical compositions and identities are preserved. In detail, when the expressions are meaningful, the following identities hold:

$$((f,u,g) \star (g,v,h))\varphi = (f\varphi_H,\ u\varphi_V \star v\varphi_V,\ h\varphi_H)$$
$$((f,u,g) \cdot (f',u',g'))\varphi = (f,u,g)\varphi \cdot (f',u',g')\varphi$$
$$(f,\ \mathbf{I}_f,\ f)\varphi = (f\varphi_H,\ \mathbf{I}_{f\varphi_H},\ f\varphi_H)$$
$$i_n\varphi = i_n, \quad i \in [n].$$

We sometimes drop the subscripts H, V on φ, and write $(f,u,g)\varphi = (f\varphi, u\varphi, g\varphi)$.

2.3 Horizontally and vertically pointed 2-theories

Suppose that T is a 2-theory and $\perp : 1 \longrightarrow 0$ is a horizontal morphism in T. Write $\perp_{1,p}$ for the horizontal composite $\perp \cdot 0_p$ as well as for the corresponding 2-cell $(\perp_{1,p}, \perp_{1,p}, \perp_{1,p})$.

A **horizontally pointed 2-theory** T is just a 2-theory with a distinguished horizontal morphism $\perp : 1 \longrightarrow 0$. Identifying this morphism with the identity 2-cell $(\perp, \perp, \perp) : 1 \longrightarrow 0$, it follows that for any $n \geq 0$ and any 2-cell $\alpha : n \longrightarrow p$,

$$\perp_{1,n} \cdot \alpha = \perp_{1,p}.$$

A **morphism of horizontally pointed 2-theories** is a 2-theory morphism which preserves the point.

The vertical notion has more substance.

Definition 2.5 *A* **vertically pointed 2-theory** *is a 2-theory T having a distinguished horizontal morphism $\perp : 1 \longrightarrow 0$ such that for each horizontal $f : 1 \longrightarrow p$ there is a unique 2-cell $(\perp_{1,p}, \perp_f, f)$.* **A morphism of vertically pointed 2-theories** *is a 2-theory morphism which preserves the point $\perp$ and hence the vertical morphisms $\perp_f : \perp \longrightarrow f$:*

$$(\perp_{1,p}, \perp_f, f)\varphi = (\perp_{1,p}, \perp_{f\varphi}, f\varphi).$$

It follows that in a vertically pointed 2-theory there is a unique vertical morphism

$$\perp_f : \langle \perp_{1,p}, \ldots, \perp_{1,p} \rangle \longrightarrow f,$$

for each horizontal $f : n \longrightarrow p$. (Thus, when $f = \langle f_1, \ldots, f_n \rangle$, $\perp_f = \langle \perp_{f_1}, \ldots, \perp_{f_n} \rangle$.)

Example 2.6 Each preiteration theory considered as a 2-theory is a naturally pointed 2-theory, where the horizontal point is $1_1^{\dagger}$.

If T is an ordered theory, see [BE93], page 233, then T is a 2-theory which has a vertical morphism $f \longrightarrow g$, for $f, g : n \longrightarrow p$, exactly when $f \leq g$. In particular, for each poset A, the theory whose morphisms $n \longrightarrow p$ are the monotonic functions $A^p \longrightarrow A^n$ is ordered. If A has a least element, this theory is vertically pointed. More generally, if T is a strict ordered theory (see [BE93], page 244), then T is a vertically pointed 2-theory.

Let A be a set of action symbols. The 2-theory of synchronization trees over A with vertical morphisms the synchronization tree homomorphisms, is a vertically pointed 2-theory. The point $\perp$ is the tree which has only one vertex (see [BE93], chapter 13). Synchronization trees over A with simulations as vertical morphisms also form a vertically pointed 2-theory. (For the definition of simulation, see [Park81].)

Let C be a category with initial object. The functor 2-theory over C has morphisms $n \longrightarrow p$ the functors $C^p \longrightarrow C^n$. The vertical morphisms are the natural transformations. When C has an initial object, this 2-theory is vertically pointed with point the constant functor determined by the initial object.

3 Some 2-theories of trees

We will be concerned with 2-theories in which both horizontal and vertical morphisms are labeled trees. The labeling of both kinds of trees will be determined by a "categorical 2-signature".

A 1-signature Σ is an ω-sequence of pairwise disjoint sets Σ_n.

Definition 3.1 *A* **categorical 2-signature** $\Sigma = (\Sigma_0, \Sigma_1, \ldots)$, *2-signature, for short, is an ω-sequence of (small) categories.*

The collection of all categorical 2-signatures is itself a category in which a morphism between 2-signatures is an ω-sequence of functors.

Note that there is an **underlying signature functor** from the category of 2-theories to the category of categorical 2-signatures. Applied to the 2-theory T, this functor produces the sequence of categories $(T(1,0), T(1,1), \ldots)$. We will be concerned with finding a left adjoint to the underlying signature functor from 2-theories, pointed 2-theories and iteration 2-theories.

3.1 Tree 2-theories defined

The set of finite sequences of positive integers is denoted $[\omega]^*$. If ν and ν' are in $[\omega]^*$, their concatenation is denoted $\nu\nu'$. In particular, if j is a positive integer, νj is the sequence ν followed by j.

Suppose that Σ is a 1-signature such that each set Σ_n, $n \geq 0$, is disjoint from the countable set $\{x_1, x_2, \ldots\}$ of "variables". A **Σ-tree** $t : 1 \longrightarrow p$ is a partial function

$$t : [\omega]^* \rightarrow \bigcup_n \Sigma_n \cup \{x_1, \ldots, x_p\}$$

which satisfies the following conditions [EBT78, BE93]:

1. The domain of t, $\mathrm{dom}\, t$, is a nonempty, prefix closed subset of $[\omega]^*$.
2. If $\nu \in [\omega]^*$ is in $\mathrm{dom}\, t$ and $\nu t = x_i$, for some $i \in [p]$, then ν is a leaf, i.e., $\nu j \notin \mathrm{dom}\, t$, for any $j \in [\omega]$.
3. If $\nu \in [\omega]^*$ is in $\mathrm{dom}\, t$ and $\nu t \in \Sigma_n$, then $\nu j \in \mathrm{dom}\, t$ iff $j \in [n]$.

If $t : 1 \longrightarrow p$ is a Σ-tree and $\nu \in \mathrm{dom}\, t$, we write t_ν for the Σ-tree defined by:

$$\nu' t_\nu := (\nu\nu')t, \quad \nu' \in [\omega]^*.$$

A **subtree** of t is a tree t_ν, for some $\nu \in \mathrm{dom}\, t$. A tree t is **regular** if t has only finitely many subtrees. When the domain of t is finite, we call t a finite tree.

If Σ is a 1-signature, let $\Sigma_\perp$ denote the 1-signature obtained from Σ by the addition of a new letter $\perp$ to Σ_0. For any 1-signature Σ, the collection of all $\Sigma_\perp$-trees forms a theory $\Sigma_\perp\mathbf{TR}$, in which a morphism $g : p \to q$ is a p-tuple $g = (g_1, \ldots, g_p)$ of $\Sigma_\perp$-trees $1 \to q$. The composite of $t : 1 \to p$ with $(g_1, \ldots, g_p) : p \to q$ is, roughly, the tree obtained from t by attaching a copy of g_i, $i \in [p]$, to each leaf of t labeled x_i. The distinguished morphism $i_n : 1 \to n$ is the tree whose root is also a leaf labeled x_i. (As a partial function, the domain of i_n is only the empty word.) Except for the distinguished trees $1_{1+p} : 1 \to 1+p$, a dagger operation on all trees $f : 1 \to 1+p$ is determined by requiring that the fixed point identity holds: $f^\dagger = f \cdot \langle f^\dagger, 1_p \rangle$; we define $1_{1+p}^\dagger = \perp_p$. (See Section 7 below.) With this definition, it is well known that $\Sigma_\perp \mathbf{TR}$ is an iteration theory.

We will be concerned with 2-theories in which both horizontal and vertical morphisms are labeled trees. The labeling of both kinds of trees will be determined by a categorical 2-signature.

Each 2-signature $\Sigma = (\Sigma_0, \Sigma_1, \ldots)$ determines three 1-signatures:

$$H\Sigma := (\mathsf{ob}\,\Sigma_0, \mathsf{ob}\,\Sigma_1, \ldots)$$
$$V\Sigma := (\mathsf{ar}\,\Sigma_0, \mathsf{ar}\,\Sigma_1, \ldots)$$
$$|\Sigma| := (|\Sigma|_0, |\Sigma|_1, \ldots)$$

where $\mathsf{ob}\,C$ (respectively, $\mathsf{ar}\,C$) is the collection of all objects (respectively, arrows) in the category C, and where, for each $n \geq 0$, a letter in $|\Sigma|_n$ is a triple (x, f, y), where $f : x \to y$ in the category Σ_n:

$$|\Sigma|_n := \{(x, f, y) : f : x \to y \in \Sigma_n\}. \tag{1}$$

We use both $H\Sigma$ and $V\Sigma$ in our definition of the tree theory.

Given the 2-signature Σ, we define the 2-theory $\Sigma_\perp \mathbf{TR}$ of trees as follows.

Definition 3.2 *A 2-cell $(f, u, g) : n \to p$ in $\Sigma_\perp \mathbf{TR}$ consists of two $(H\Sigma)_\perp$-trees $f = \langle f_1, \ldots, f_n \rangle$, $g = \langle g_1, \ldots, g_n \rangle : n \to p$, and a $(V\Sigma)_\perp$-tree $u = \langle u_1, \ldots, u_n \rangle : n \to p$, which satisfy the following conditions. For each $j \in [n]$,*

- $\mathrm{dom}\, f_j = \mathrm{dom}\, u_j \subseteq \mathrm{dom}\, g_j$.
- *For $\nu \in \mathrm{dom}\, f_j$, if $\nu f_j = x_i$, then $\nu u_j = \nu g_j = x_i$.*
- *For $\nu \in \mathrm{dom}\, f_j$, if $\nu f_j = \perp$, then $\nu u_j = \perp$.*
- *For $\nu \in \mathrm{dom}\, f_j$, if $\nu f_j = \sigma \in H\Sigma_k$, for some $k \geq 0$, then $\nu g_j = \sigma' \in H\Sigma_k$ and νu_j is a morphism $\sigma \to \sigma'$ in Σ_k, so that νu_j is in $V\Sigma_k$.*

The **horizontal composite** *of $(f, u, g) : n \to p$ and $(f', u', g') : p \to q$ is done pointwise in the appropriate tree theories:*

$$(f, u, g) \cdot (f', u', g') := (f \cdot f',\ u \cdot u',\ g \cdot g').$$

To define vertical composition, assume that (f, u, g) and (g, v, h) are 2-cells $1 \to p$. The **vertical composite** *$(f, u, g) \star (g, v, h)$ is $(f, u \star v, h)$, where for $\nu \in \mathrm{dom}\, f$, if $\nu f \in \Sigma_k$, then $\nu(u \star u')$ is the composite in the category Σ_k*

$$\nu f \xrightarrow{\nu u} \nu g \xrightarrow{\nu u'} \nu h.$$

If $\nu f = x_j$, for some $j \in [p]$, or $\nu f = \perp$, then $\nu(u \star v)$ has the same value as νf. When (f, u, g) and $(g, v, h) : n \to p$, for $n > 1$, we define vertical composition componentwise.

Tree composition is known to be associative and the composition of vertical morphisms here is (pointwise) composition in the categories Σ_n. Since it is easy to see that the interchange law $(u \star v) \cdot (u' \star v') = (u \cdot u') \star (v \cdot v')$ holds, $\Sigma_\perp \mathbf{TR}$ is a 2-category. Lastly, the 2-cells $(x_i, x_i, x_i) : 1 \to n$, $i \in [n]$, are coproduct injections, as can be seen from the definition of tree composition. Thus $\Sigma_\perp \mathbf{TR}$ is a 2-theory.

Remark 3.3 Note that in $\Sigma_\perp\mathbf{TR}$, for any horizontal $g: 1 \to p$ in $H\Sigma_\perp\mathbf{TR}$, the tree $\perp$ in $V\Sigma_\perp\mathbf{TR}$ is the unique vertical morphism from the tree $\perp \in H\Sigma_\perp\mathbf{TR}$ to g. Thus, $\Sigma_\perp\mathbf{TR}$ is vertically pointed.

Two sub 2-theories of $\Sigma_\perp\mathbf{TR}$ are important for later purposes.

Definition 3.4 *The 2-theory $\Sigma_\perp\mathbf{TR}_{\mathrm{ri}}$ of* **rigid trees**, *is the sub 2-theory of $\Sigma_\perp\mathbf{TR}$ determined by the "rigid" 2-cells $(f,u,g): 1 \to p$ which satisfy the condition that, for $\nu \in \mathrm{dom}\, f$, $\nu g = \perp$ when $\nu f = \perp$, so that $\mathrm{dom}\, f = \mathrm{dom}\, u = \mathrm{dom}\, g$ and if $\nu f = \perp$ then $\nu g = \nu u = \perp$.*

Definition 3.5 *The 2-theory $\Sigma\mathbf{TR}$ of* **complete trees** *is the sub 2-theory of $\Sigma_\perp\mathbf{TR}_{\mathrm{ri}}$ determined by the 1-cells and 2-cells in which no tree contains an occurrence of $\perp$, i.e., if $(f,u,g): 1 \to p$ in $\Sigma_\perp\mathbf{TR}_{\mathrm{ri}}$, then for each $\nu \in \mathrm{dom}\, f$, $\nu f \neq \perp$.*

The collection of 2-cells $(f,u,g): n \to p$ in $\Sigma\mathbf{TR}$ in which *all* trees are finite determines a sub 2-theory of $\Sigma\mathbf{TR}$ denoted $\Sigma\mathbf{Tm}$. Similarly, the finite 2-cells in $\Sigma_\perp\mathbf{TR}$ determine a vertically pointed sub 2-theory of $\Sigma_\perp\mathbf{TR}$, denoted $\Sigma_\perp\mathbf{Tm}$.

The sub 2-theory of $\Sigma_\perp\mathbf{TR}$ in which all trees are regular is denoted $\Sigma_\perp\mathbf{tr}$; the sub 2-theory of $\Sigma_\perp\mathbf{TR}_{\mathrm{ri}}$ determined by the regular trees is denoted $\Sigma_\perp\mathbf{tr}_{\mathrm{ri}}$.

Below, it will be shown that $\Sigma\mathbf{Tm}$ is the 2-theory freely generated by Σ, and that $\Sigma_\perp\mathbf{Tm}$ is the vertically pointed 2-theory freely generated by Σ.

The following observation is quite useful. Recall the definition of the 1-signature $|\Sigma|$ in (1). For each 2-cell $(f,u,g): 1 \to p$ in $\Sigma_\perp\mathbf{TR}_{\mathrm{ri}}$, there is a $|\Sigma|$-tree $\tau = \tau(f,u,g): 1 \to p$ with the same domain as each of f,u,g, defined by:

$$\nu\tau := \begin{cases} x_i & \text{if } \nu f = x_i \\ \perp & \text{if } \nu f = \perp \\ (\nu f, \nu u, \nu g) & \text{otherwise.} \end{cases} \tag{2}$$

We extend τ to 2-cells $n \to p$ componentwise.

Proposition 3.6 *For each categorical 2-signature Σ, the function τ is a preiteration theory isomorphism from $\mathrm{Cell}\,\Sigma_\perp\mathbf{TR}_{\mathrm{ri}}$ to $|\Sigma|_\perp\mathbf{TR}$. By restriction, τ gives theory isomorphisms*

$$\begin{aligned} \mathrm{Cell}\,\Sigma\mathbf{TR} &\to |\Sigma|\mathbf{TR} \\ \mathrm{Cell}\,\Sigma_\perp\mathbf{tr}_{\mathrm{ri}} &\to |\Sigma|_\perp\mathbf{tr} \\ \mathrm{Cell}\,\Sigma_\perp\mathbf{Tm}_{\mathrm{ri}} &\to |\Sigma|_\perp\mathbf{Tm} \\ \mathrm{Cell}\,\Sigma\mathbf{Tm} &\to |\Sigma|\mathbf{Tm}. \quad \square \end{aligned}$$

4 Finite complete trees are the free 2-theory

In this section we use Proposition 3.6 to prove the following representation theorem.

Theorem 4.1 *The 2-theory $\Sigma\mathbf{Tm}$ of finite complete trees is freely generated by the 2-signature Σ in the class of all 2-theories.*

Proof. Suppose that T is a 2-theory and $\varphi = (\varphi_n : \Sigma_n \to T(1,n),\ n \geq 0)$ is a sequence of functors. The finite trees in $H\Sigma\mathbf{TR}$ form a free theory, so φ uniquely extends to a theory morphism from the 1-cells in $\Sigma\mathbf{Tm}$ to the 1-cells in T. We must show how φ extends to the 2-cells. Since the finite

$|\Sigma|$**TR**-trees form the theory freely generated by the 1-signature $|\Sigma|$, using τ there is a unique theory morphism

$$\varphi^{\#} : \mathbf{Cell}\,\Sigma\mathbf{Tm} \longrightarrow T$$

extending φ. We show that this map induces a 2-theory morphism. We show at the same time that $\varphi^{\#}$ determines maps φ_H and φ_V on the horizontal and vertical morphisms and that vertical composition is preserved.

Below, we will identify each morphism $|\Sigma|$**Tm** with the corresponding 2-cell in Σ**Tm**. Let $F : 1 \longrightarrow p$ be a finite tree in $|\Sigma|$**TR** which corresponds under τ to the 2-cell $(f, u, g) : 1 \longrightarrow p$ in Σ**Tm**. We show by induction on the "height" of F that there are maps φ_H, φ_V such that $F\varphi^{\#} = (f\varphi_H, u\varphi_H, g\varphi_H)$ and that if $F = (f, u, g) \star (g, v, h)$, then $F\varphi^{\#} = (f\varphi_H, u\varphi_V \star v\varphi_V, h\varphi_H)$.

When the height of F is zero, then the common domain of f, u, and g is the singleton consisting of the empty word λ. If $\lambda F = x_i$, then also $\lambda f = \lambda u = \lambda g = x_i$. Since the $|\Sigma|$**TR**-tree x_i maps under the theory morphism $\varphi^{\#}$ to the 2-cell $(i_p, i_p, i_p) : 1 \longrightarrow p$ in T, we may define $x_i\varphi_H = i_p$, and define $x_i\varphi_V$ as the vertical identity $i_p : i_p \longrightarrow i_p$. If λF is not a variable, then F factors through 0. Since $\varphi^{\#}$ preserves horizontal composition and the morphisms 0_p, we may assume that in this case $p = 0$. Thus, λu is a morphism in Σ_0 from λf to λg. Since $\varphi_0 : \Sigma_0 \longrightarrow T(1, 0)$ is a functor, λf and λg map under φ to horizontal morphisms $f\varphi_H, g\varphi_H : 1 \longrightarrow 0$ in T and λu maps to a vertical morphism $u\varphi_V : f\varphi_H \longrightarrow g\varphi_H$. For the same reason, φ preserves vertical composition of 2-cells of height 0.

Now assume that the $|\Sigma|$**TR**-tree $F : 1 \longrightarrow p$ has height at least 1. We may write F as the horizontal composite of an atomic tree $G = (h, w, h') : 1 \longrightarrow r$ with r trees H_i, each of height less than the height of F. Say that for $i \in [r]$, H_i corresponds to the 2-cell $(h_i, v_i, h_i') : 1 \longrightarrow p$. Thus, by induction, we may write

$$H_i\varphi^{\#} = (g_i\varphi_H, v_i\varphi_V, g_i'\varphi_H).$$

Now $G\varphi^{\#}$ is a 2-cell $(f', u', g') : 1 \longrightarrow r$ in T, and since $\varphi^{\#}$ preserves the horizontal structure,

$$\begin{aligned} F\varphi^{\#} &= (f', u', g') \cdot \langle H_1\varphi^{\#}, \ldots, H_r\varphi^{\#} \rangle \\ &= (f' \cdot \langle g_1\varphi_H, \ldots, g_r\varphi_H \rangle,\ u' \cdot \langle v_1\varphi_V, \ldots, v_r\varphi_V \rangle,\ g'\varphi_H \cdot \langle g_1'\varphi_H, \ldots, g_r'\varphi_H \rangle) \end{aligned}$$

This shows how to define φ_H and φ_V on the vertical and horizontal trees in F, namely

$$\begin{aligned} (h \cdot \langle g_1, \ldots, g_r \rangle)\varphi_H &:= f' \cdot \langle g_1\varphi_H, \ldots, g_r\varphi_H \rangle \\ (w \cdot \langle v_1, \ldots, v_r \rangle)\varphi_V &:= u' \cdot \langle v_1\varphi_V, \ldots, v_r\varphi_V \rangle \\ (h' \cdot \langle g_1', \ldots, g_r' \rangle)\varphi_H &:= g'\varphi_H \cdot \langle g_1'\varphi_H, \ldots, g_r'\varphi_H \rangle. \end{aligned}$$

We again use induction to show that vertical composition is preserved. Assume that $(f, u, g), (g, v, h)$ are 2-cells in which all trees have height at least 1. To show that $(u \star v)\varphi_V = u\varphi_V \star v\varphi_V$ in T, note that u and v factor as horizontal composites

$$\begin{aligned} u &= u' \cdot \langle u_1', \ldots, u_r' \rangle \\ v &= v' \cdot \langle v_1', \ldots, v_r' \rangle. \end{aligned}$$

Thus, by the interchange law,

$$u \star v = (u' \star v') \cdot (u'' \star v''),$$

where

$$\begin{aligned} u'' &= \langle u_1', \ldots, u_r' \rangle \\ v'' &= \langle v_1', \ldots, v_r' \rangle. \end{aligned}$$

Since φ_V preserves horizontal composition, and since the heights of u', v', u'', v'' are all less than that of u, v, it follows by induction that

$$\begin{aligned} (u \star v)\varphi_V &= (u' \star v')\varphi_V \cdot (u'' \star v'')\varphi_V \\ &= (u'\varphi_V \star v'\varphi_V) \cdot (u''\varphi_V \star v''\varphi_V) \\ &= (u'\varphi_V \cdot u''\varphi_V) \star (v'\varphi_V \cdot v''\varphi_V) \\ &= u\varphi_V \star v\varphi_V. \end{aligned}$$

In a similar way, it may be shown that φ_V preserves vertical identities. □

The preceding argument also establishes the following.

Theorem 4.2 *The subtheory of $\Sigma_\perp \mathbf{TR}_{ri}$ consisting of the finite rigid trees is freely generated by Σ in the class of all horizontally pointed 2-theories.*

5 Iteration 2-theories

When T is a 2-theory, and $n, p \geq 0$, we write $T(n,p)$ for the *category* whose objects are the 1-cells $f : n \longrightarrow p$ in T and whose morphisms are the vertical morphisms $u : f \longrightarrow g$, for $f, g : n \longrightarrow p$.

We extend the notion of a preiteration theory to 2-theories in two steps. First, we define a **2-theory with a dagger operation** as a 2-theory equipped with an operation mapping each 2-cell $(f, u, g) : n \longrightarrow n + p$ to a 2-cell $(f, u, g)^\dagger : n \longrightarrow p$.

Suppose that T is a 2-theory with a dagger operation. We say the dagger operation **is functorial** if there are dagger operations on both the horizontal and vertical morphisms such that

for each 2-cell $(f, u, g) : n \longrightarrow n + p$,

$$(f, u, g)^\dagger = (f^\dagger, u^\dagger, g^\dagger) : n \longrightarrow p$$
$$(\mathbf{I}_f)^\dagger = \mathbf{I}_{f^\dagger},$$

and, for any $(f, u, g),\ (g, v, h) : n \longrightarrow n + p$,

$$(u \star v)^\dagger = u^\dagger \star v^\dagger. \tag{3}$$

Definition 5.1 *A* **preiteration 2-theory** *is a 2-theory T with a dagger operation which is functorial. A* **morphism** *between preiteration 2-theories is a 2-theory morphism which preserves the dagger operation.*

Example 5.2 Suppose that T is an ordered theory equipped with a dagger operation $f \mapsto f^\dagger$ defined on each horizontal morphism $f : n \longrightarrow n + p$. When the dagger operation is monotonic, T is a preiteration 2-theory.

Definition 5.3 *An* **iteration 2-theory** *is a preiteration 2-theory T such that* Cell$T$ *is an iteration theory. A* **morphism** *of iteration 2-theories is a preiteration 2-theory morphism.*

Example 5.4 If T is an algebraically complete 2-theory satisfying the parameter identity (see below), then T is a preiteration 2-theory and T satisfies the axioms of iteration theories up to isomorphism. Thus, when T is skeletal, i.e., when any two isomorphic 2-cells are equal, T is an iteration 2-theory.

Definition 5.5 *If T_0 and T are iteration 2-theories, we say T_0 is a* **sub iteration 2-theory** *of T if T_0 is a sub 2-theory of T and if the dagger operation on T_0 is the restriction of that on T.*

An iteration 2-theory is naturally horizontally pointed when $\perp = 1_1^\dagger$. When each morphism $\perp_{1,p} = \perp \cdot 0_p$ is initial in the category $T(1,p)$, $p \geq 0$, we say that the iteration 2-theory is **vertically pointed**. (Any iteration 2-theory morphism between vertically pointed iteration 2-theories automatically preserves the initial vertical morphisms.)

In the next section, a class of examples of vertically pointed iteration 2-theories is discussed. Later, we will show that a 2-theory of regular trees is the free vertically pointed iteration 2-theory.

6 Algebraically complete 2-theories are vertically pointed iteration 2-theories

One of the motivations for studying iteration 2-theories is the fact that these algebraic structures arise when using initiality to solve fixed point equations in 2-theories. In this section, we recall the result of [EL96] that certain algebraically complete 2-theories are iteration 2-theories.

Definition 6.1 *Suppose that $f : n \longrightarrow n{+}p$ is a horizontal morphism in a 2-theory T. An **f-algebra** (g, u) consists of a horizontal morphism $g : n \longrightarrow p$ and a vertical morphism $u : f \cdot \langle g, \mathbf{1}_p\rangle \longrightarrow g$. Suppose that (g, u) and (h, v) are f-algebras. An **f-algebra morphism** $(g, u) \longrightarrow (h, v)$ is a vertical morphism $w : g \longrightarrow h$ such that*

$$u \star w = (f \cdot \langle w, \mathbf{1}_p\rangle) \star v.$$

Definition 6.2 *Suppose that $f : n \longrightarrow n + p$ is a horizontal morphism in the 2-theory T. The f-algebra (g, u) is an **initial f-algebra,** if for each f-algebra (h, v) there exists a unique morphism $(g, u) \longrightarrow (h, v)$.*

It is well known [Lam68] that if (g, u) is an initial f-algebra then u is a vertical isomorphism.

Definition 6.3 *An **algebraically complete 2-theory** is a 2-theory T such that each horizontal morphism $f : n \longrightarrow n + p$ has a specified initial f-algebra $(f^\dagger, \mu_f)$.*

Any algebraically complete category gives rise to an algebraically complete 2-theory. Indeed, if $(\mathcal{C}, \mathcal{F})$ is algebraically complete as defined in the Introduction, then the functors $\mathcal{F}$ and the natural transformations between these functors determine a 2-theory denoted $T = \mathbf{Th}(\mathcal{C}, \mathcal{F})$. Suppose that $f : n \longrightarrow n + p$ in T, so that f is a functor $\mathcal{C}^{n+p} \longrightarrow \mathcal{C}^n$. Then, since for each $y \in \mathcal{C}^p$, $(f^\dagger y, \mu_{f,y})$ is an initial f_y-algebra, and since by assumption the functor $f^\dagger$ is in $\mathcal{F}$, it follows that $(f^\dagger, \mu_f)$ is an initial f-algebra in T.

The definition of an algebraically complete 2-theory gives rise to a dagger operation on the horizontal morphisms:

$$f : n \longrightarrow n + p \mapsto f^\dagger : n \longrightarrow p.$$

This operation can be extended to vertical morphisms in the following way. Suppose that the 2-theory T is algebraically complete and $f, g : n \longrightarrow n + p$ in T. Suppose further that u is a vertical morphism $f \longrightarrow g$. Then the vertical composite $(u \cdot \langle g^\dagger, \mathbf{1}_p\rangle) \star \mu_g$,

$$f \cdot \langle g^\dagger, \mathbf{1}_p\rangle \xrightarrow{u \cdot \langle g^\dagger, \mathbf{1}_p\rangle} g \cdot \langle g^\dagger, \mathbf{1}_p\rangle \xrightarrow{\mu_g} g^\dagger$$

determines the f-algebra $(g^\dagger,\ (u \cdot \langle g^\dagger, \mathbf{1}_p\rangle) \star \mu_g)$. Since $(f^\dagger, \mu_f)$ is initial, there is a unique vertical morphism $v : f^\dagger \longrightarrow g^\dagger$ which is an f-algebra morphism $(f^\dagger, \mu_f) \longrightarrow (g^\dagger,\ (u \cdot \langle g^\dagger, \mathbf{1}_p\rangle) \star \mu_g)$. Let $u^\dagger$ denote this morphism v. The following square commutes.

$$\begin{array}{ccc}
f \cdot \langle f^\dagger, \mathbf{1}_p\rangle & \xrightarrow{\quad \mu_f \quad} & f^\dagger \\
{\scriptstyle f \cdot \langle u^\dagger, \mathbf{1}_p\rangle} \downarrow & & \downarrow {\scriptstyle u^\dagger} \\
f \cdot \langle g^\dagger, \mathbf{1}_p\rangle & \xrightarrow[\quad u \cdot \langle g^\dagger, \mathbf{1}_p\rangle \cdot \mu_f \quad]{} & g^\dagger
\end{array}$$

Proposition 6.4 [EL96] *Suppose that T is an algebraically complete 2-theory with a specified initial f-algebra $(f^\dagger, \mu_f)$, for each $f : n \longrightarrow n+p$. Then for any integers $n, p \geq 0$, the map $f : n \longrightarrow n+p \mapsto f^\dagger : n \longrightarrow p$ is the object map of a unique functor*

$$^\dagger : T(n, n+p) \longrightarrow T(n,p)$$

such that $\mu = (\mu_f)$, $f : n \longrightarrow n+p$, is a natural transformation (in fact, a natural isomorphism)

$$(-) \cdot \langle (-)^\dagger, \mathbf{1}_p \rangle \longrightarrow (-)^\dagger.$$

Below we will use the following notation. For any $f : n \longrightarrow n+p$ and $g : p \longrightarrow q$ in a theory or 2-theory, f_g denotes the morphism $f \cdot (\mathbf{1}_n \oplus g) : n \longrightarrow n+q$.

Definition 6.5 *Suppose that T is an algebraically complete 2-theory. We will say that the* **parameter identity holds in** *T, if for any $f : n \longrightarrow n+p$ and $g : p \longrightarrow q$, the f_g-algebra $(f^\dagger \cdot g, \mu_f \cdot g)$ is initial.*

There is an example on page 271 in [BE93] of an algebraically complete 2-theory which does not satisfy the parameter identity. On the other hand, when $(\mathcal{C}, \mathcal{F})$ is an algebraically complete category the algebraically complete 2-theory $\mathbf{Th}(\mathcal{C}, \mathcal{F})$ does satisfy the parameter identity.

Theorem 6.6 [EL96] *The dagger operation defined on an algebraically complete 2-theory T is functorial. Moreover, if T satisfies the parameter identity, T is an iteration 2-theory.*

In fact, an identity holds up to isomorphism in all skeletal algebraically complete 2-theories satisfying the parameter identity iff it holds in all iteration 2-theories (see [EL96]).

Example 6.7 Recall that a category is called an ω-category if it has initial object and colimits of all ω-diagrams. A 2-theory T is ω-continuous if each category $T(n,p)$, $n, p \geq 0$ is an ω-category, moreover, right composition with horizontal morphisms preserves initial objects, and horizontal composition preserves ω-colimits on either side. It is known that each ω-continuous 2-theory is algebraically complete and satisfies the parameter identity. In particular, if $\mathcal{C}$ is an ω-category and if $\mathcal{F}$ denotes the collection of all functors $\mathcal{C}^p \longrightarrow \mathcal{C}^n$, $n, p \geq 0$ that preserve the colimit of ω-diagrams, then $\mathbf{Th}(\mathcal{C}, \mathcal{F})$ is an ω-continuous 2-theory and hence an algebraically complete 2-theory satisfying the parameter identity. Other examples of ω-continuous 2-theories involve synchronization trees (see [BE93]). Further examples, including algebraically complete categories with a non-constructive dagger operation, may be found in [Fre91, Fre92, Esia].

7 Iteration 2-theories of trees

The dagger operation on trees $t : 1 \longrightarrow 1+p$ has a concrete description. If $t = x_1$, then $t^\dagger = \perp \cdot 0_p$. Otherwise, a sequence $\nu \in [\omega]^*$ is in the domain of $t^\dagger$ iff ν has a longest factorization as $\nu = \nu_1 \ldots \nu_k \nu'$, where ν' and each ν_j is in $\mathrm{dom}\, t$, and $\nu_j t = x_1$, $j \in [k]$. The value $\nu t^\dagger$ is $\nu' t$ if $\nu' t \neq x_j$; if $\nu' t = x_j$, then $\nu' t^\dagger = x_{j-1}$.

For a 1-signature Σ, the collection of all $\Sigma_\perp$-trees is equipped with the following order. For trees $f, g : 1 \longrightarrow p$ in $\Sigma_\perp\mathbf{TR}$, $f \leq g$ if $\mathrm{dom} f \subseteq \mathrm{dom}\, g$ and for all $\nu \in \mathrm{dom} f$, if $\nu f \neq \perp$, then $\nu f = \nu g$. When $f, g : n \longrightarrow p$, we define $f \leq g$ if $i_n \cdot f \leq i_n \cdot g$, for each $i \in [n]$. With respect to this ordering, for any tree $t : n \longrightarrow n+p$, $t^\dagger$ is the least solution to the fixed point equation (in the variable $\xi : n \longrightarrow p$)

$$\xi = t \cdot \langle \xi, \mathbf{1}_p \rangle.$$

Also, $t^\dagger$ is the least $\xi : n \longrightarrow p$ such that

$$t \cdot \langle \xi, \mathbf{1}_p \rangle \leq \xi.$$

The following is well-known (see [Esi80] and also [EBT78, Gin79, WTGW76] for closely related results.)

Theorem 7.1 *For any 1-signature Σ, the theory $\Sigma_\perp\mathbf{tr}$ of all regular $\Sigma_\perp$-trees is the iteration theory freely generated by Σ.* □

When Σ is a 2-signature, the dagger operation is extended to 2-cells in $\Sigma_\perp\mathbf{TR}$ as follows. Suppose that $(f,u,g) : n \longrightarrow n+p$. Then

$$(f,u,g)^\dagger := (f^\dagger, u^\dagger, g^\dagger), \tag{4}$$

where $f^\dagger$, $g^\dagger$ are in $H\Sigma_\perp\mathbf{TR}$ and $u^\dagger$ is in $V\Sigma_\perp\mathbf{TR}$.

In this way, the 2-theory $\Sigma_\perp\mathbf{TR}$ is a preiteration 2-theory. Since for any 1-signature, the regular trees form a sub preiteration theory of the theory of all trees, the 2-theories $\Sigma_\perp\mathbf{tr}$, $\Sigma_\perp\mathbf{tr}_{\mathrm{ri}}$ are sub preiteration 2-theories of $\Sigma_\perp\mathbf{TR}$.

8 Tree theories are algebraically complete

We omit the proof of the following theorem.

Theorem 8.1 *Each 2-theory $\Sigma_\perp\mathbf{TR}$, where Σ is any (categorical) 2-signature, is algebraically complete, and satisfies the parameter identity. The dagger operation determined by intiality is the same as that defined concretely above in (4).*

Thus, by Theorem 6.6 each 2-theory $\Sigma_\perp\mathbf{TR}$ is, up to isomorphism, an iteration 2-theory. By the next lemma, the iteration theory identities hold "on the nose", not just up to isomorphism. In this case, we will say that the iteration theory identities hold "exactly".

Lemma 8.2 *Suppose that T is an algebraically complete 2-theory such that the iteration theory identities hold exactly on the horizontal morphisms. They they hold exactly in* Cell *T.* □

Corollary 8.3 *Each 2-theory $\Sigma_\perp\mathbf{TR}$ is a vertically pointed iteration 2-theory.*

Thus, each 2-theory $\Sigma_\perp\mathbf{tr}$ is also a vertically pointed iteration 2-theory, since a sub 2-preiteration theory satisfies all identities true in the larger theory.

9 Regular rigid trees are the free iteration 2-theory

Proposition 3.6 is used to show that for any categorical 2-signature Σ, the iteration 2-theory of rigid regular $\Sigma_\perp$-trees is free. The proof is omitted.

Theorem 9.1 *Suppose that Σ is a categorical 2-signature. The theory $\Sigma_\perp\mathbf{tr}_{\mathrm{ri}}$ is freely generated by Σ in the class of iteration 2-theories.*

An *iteration 2-theory term* is a formal expression constructed in the usual way from sorted horizontal variables $n \longrightarrow p$ and sorted vertical variables $f \longrightarrow g$, where f and g are horizontal variables $n \longrightarrow p$, using horizontal and vertical composition and identities, and the cartesian operations and constants.

Corollary 9.2 *The equational theory of iteration 2-theories is decidable in polynomial time. In more detail, there is a polynomial time algorithm to decide whether a sorted equation between two iteration 2-theory terms holds in all iteration 2-theories.*

Proof. This follows from Theorem 9.1 and the fact that the equational theory of the regular trees (or of iteration theories) is decidable in polynomial time. See [BE93], Exercise 6.5.7. □

Corollary 9.3 *It is decidable in polynomial time whether a sorted equation between two iteration 2-theory terms holds up to isomorphism in all algebraically complete categories.*

Our last task is to show that the 2-theory $\Sigma_\perp \mathbf{tr}$ is freely generated by Σ in the class of vertically pointed iteration 2-theories. Since any 2-cell $(f, u, g) : n \longrightarrow p$ in $\Sigma_\perp \mathbf{tr}$ factors as the horizontal composite of a rigid 2-cell and an initial 2-cell $(\perp_{q,p}, \perp_h, h)$, for some q and h, it would seem an easy job to show how to extend any signature morphism $\Sigma \longrightarrow T$ to a morphism $\Sigma_\perp \mathbf{tr} \longrightarrow T$, using Theorem 9.1 and the fact that T is vertically pointed. Surprisingly, the details take up a bit of space, and will be omitted here.

10 The free vertically pointed iteration 2-theories

We state the main theorem of the paper here.

Theorem 10.1 *For any categorical 2-signature Σ, $\Sigma_\perp \mathbf{tr}$ is freely generated by Σ in the class of all vertically pointed iteration 2-theories.*

Restricting our attention to the sub 2-theory of finite trees, we obtain the following Corollary.

Corollary 10.2 *For any categorical signature Σ, the sub 2-theory $\Sigma_\perp \mathbf{Tm}$ of $\Sigma_\perp \mathbf{tr}$ consisting of the finite trees, is the 2-theory freely generated by Σ in the class of all vertically pointed 2-theories.* □

Corollary 10.3 *The equational theory of vertically pointed iteration 2-theories is decidable in polynomial time.*

11 Some applications

We give some hints of applications to computer science of the calculus of iteration 2-theories.

11.1 Data types

Consider the two ω-continuous functors F, G on the category of sets and functions, defined on objects by

$$F(A, X) := 1 + A \times X$$
$$G(A, X) := 1 + X \times A.$$

Then $F^\dagger(A)$ is all finite lists of elements of A; so is $G^\dagger(A)$, but how to show it? Let $\tau : F \stackrel{\cdot}{\rightarrow} G$ be the natural isomorphism, with inverse $\sigma : G \stackrel{\cdot}{\rightarrow} F$. Then, since $1_F = \tau \star \sigma$, $1_{F^\dagger} = (\tau \star \sigma)^\dagger = \tau^\dagger \star \sigma^\dagger$, and similarly $\sigma^\dagger \star \tau^\dagger = 1_{G^\dagger}$, showing that $F^\dagger$ and $G^\dagger$ are naturally isomorphic. This fact is intuitively obvious, but finding a formal system in which to prove it, and less trivial statements, has not been easy. See [HoogBack]. Similarly, consider the pair of functors

$$F'(A, X) := 1 + A \times X + A \times A \times X$$
$$G'(A, X) := 1 + X \times A + X \times A \times A,$$

and the obvious natural isomorphism $\sigma : F' \dot{\rightarrow} G'$. The fact that

$$\tau^\dagger = \sigma^\dagger$$

follows from the iteration 2-theory identities.

Now a functor may be thought of as a data type constructor, and a natural transformation between two functors is a translation or rather, an interpretation, of one data type in another. The operations of iteration 2-theories may be used to construct new translations from old, by means of horizontal and vertical composition, tupling and dagger. With these operations, we can build interpretations of lists of lists in trees, and lists of trees in trees of lists, etc. Using the iteration 2-theory identities, we may verify properties of these interpretations.

11.2 Rewriting

Given a rewriting system on trees or strings or other objects, we consider each rule as a vertical morphism whose source is the object on the left hand side of the rule and whose target is the object on the right hand side. By the 2-theory operations and dagger, we may perform operations on the rules to obtain compound rules. The operations include horizontal composition, pairing, etc, which result in compound rules that allow parallel applications of a finite number of perhaps distinct rules on different parts of the object at the same time. Some models also allow iterations of the rules. The iteration of a rule R replaces an "infinite rewriting sequence using R" with a single one. For lack of space, here we only include a simple example illustrating the iteration of a rule.

Consider the following recursive definition of the factorial function:

$$\mathrm{Fact}\,(x) = \textbf{if } x = 0 \textbf{ then } 1 \textbf{ else } \mathrm{Fact}\,(x-1) * x$$

The function Fact (x) can be obtained as the least fixed point of the functional F that takes a function f to

$$F(f) = \circ\,(\mathrm{Cond}, \mathrm{Id}, \mathrm{Const}_1, \circ\,(\star, \circ\,(f, \mathrm{Pred}), \mathrm{Id})) \tag{5}$$

where the conditional $\mathrm{Cond}(x, y, z)$ is **if** $x = 0$ **then** y **else** z, Id denotes the identity function, Const_1 the constant function with value 1, and Pred denotes the predecessor function. The sign $\circ$ denotes composition. Denoting this rule by R, the rule $R^\dagger$ rewrites the infinite tree $F^\dagger$ to the infinite tree $G^\dagger$, where G is the tree on the right hand side of (5). The tree $G^\dagger$, which is a formal representation of the computation of the factorial function, can be obtained from $F^\dagger$ by replacing each occurrence of F in $F^\dagger$ by the tree G.

For another class of examples concerning rewriting, consider (deterministic letter–to–letter) bottom-up tree transducers [GecSt]. These are a formal model of syntax directed translation [AhoUll]. Suppose that a tree transducer **A** has input signature Σ and output signature Δ and state set $A = \{a_1, \ldots, a_k\}$. The rules of the transducer determine, in a canonical way, functors $F, G : \mathbf{Set}^k \longrightarrow \mathbf{Set}^k$ (or $\mathbf{Set}^{k+p} \longrightarrow \mathbf{Set}^k$ if there are parameters) and a natural transformation $\tau : F \longrightarrow G$. For every $i \in [k]$, the ith component of τ determines the one step transformations ending in state a_i. It follows that for each $i \in [k]$, the ith component of $\tau^\dagger$ is just the tree transformation induced by **A** when a_i is the only final state. When **A** is given together with a specified set of final states, then this set determines a functor $\varphi : \mathbf{Set}^k \longrightarrow \mathbf{Set}$. The natural transformation $\varphi \star \tau$ is the **behavior** of **A**. Thus, in this context, the axioms of iteration 2-theories give an equational calculus for manipulating tree transformations, to show that two specifications give rise to the same transformation, etc.

References

[AhoUll] A. Aho and J. Ullman. *The theory of parsing, translation, and compiling. Vol. I: Parsing.* Prentice-Hall Series in Automatic Computation. Prentice-Hall, Inc., Englewood Cliffs, N. J., 1972.

[BEW80a] S.L. Bloom, C.C. Elgot and J.B. Wright. Solutions of the iteration equation and extension of the scalar iteration operation. *SIAM J. Computing*, 9(1980), 26–45.

[BEW80b] S.L. Bloom, C.C. Elgot and J.B. Wright. Vector iteration in pointed iterative theories. *SIAM J. Computing*, 9(1980), 525–540.

[BE93] S.L. Bloom and Z. Ésik. *Iteration Theories: The Equational Logic of Iterative Processes*. EATCS Monographs on Theoretical Computer Science. Springer–Verlag, 1993.

[Bor94] F. Borceux. *Handbook of Categorical Algebra 1, Basic Category Theory*. Encyclopedia of Mathematics and its Applications, Vol. 50, Cambridge University Press, 1994.

[EBT78] C.C. Elgot, S.L. Bloom and R. Tindell. On the algebraic structure of rooted trees. *Journal of Computer and System Sciences*, 16(1978), 362-399.

[Esi80] Z. Ésik. Identities in iterative and rational algebraic theories. *Computational Linguistics and Computer Languages*, 14(1980), 183-207.

[Esi88] Z. Ésik. The independence of the equational axioms of iteration theories. *Journal of Computer and System Sciences*, 36(1988), 66–76.

[Esia] Z. Ésik. Completeness of Park induction. *Theoretical Computer Science*, 177 (1997) 217–283.

[Esib] Z. Ésik. Group axioms for iteration. To appear.

[EL96] Z. Ésik and A. Labella. Equational properties of iteration in algebraically complete categories. in: proc. conf. *Mathematical Foundations of Computer Science '96*, LNCS 1113, Springer-Verlag, 1996, 336-347.

[GecSt] F. Gécseg and M. Steinby. *Tree Automata*. Akadémiai Kiadó, Budapest, 1984.

[HoogBack] P.F. Hoogendijk. Mathematics of Program Construction. 2nd International Conference, June/July 1992. LNCS 669, pages 163–190. Springer Verlag, 1993.

[Fre91] P. Freyd. Algebraically complete categories. in: Proc. of *Category Theory, Como 1990*, LNM vol. 1488, Springer–Verlag, 1991, 95–104.

[Fre92] P. Freyd. Remarks on algebraically compact categories. in: *Applications of Categories in Computer Science*, London Math. Society Lecture Notes Series, vol. 77, Cambridge University Press, 1992, 95–106.

[Gin79] S. Ginali. Regular trees and the free iterative theory. *Journal of Computer and System Sciences*, 18(1979), 228–242.

[KS74] G.M. Kelly and R. Street. Review of the elements of 2-categories. in: LNM 420, Springer–Verlag, 1974, 76–103.

[Lam68] J. Lambek. A fixed point theorem for complete categories. *Mathematische Zeitschrift*, 103(1968), 151–161.

[Lal79] G. Lallement. *Semigroups and Combinatorial Applications*. Wiley-Interscience, 1979.

[Law63] F.L. Lawvere. Functorial semantics of algebraic theories. *Proceedings of the National Academy of Sciences USA*, 50(1963), 869-873.

[Park81] D. Park. Concurrency and automata on infinite sequences. in: proc. conf. *Gesellschaft für Informatik*, LNCS 104, Springer-Verlag, 1981, 167-183.

[WTGW76] J.B. Wright, J. Thatcher, J. Goguen, and E.G. Wagner. Rational algebraic theories and fixed-point solutions. In *Proc. 17th IEEE Symposium on Foundations of Computing*, 1976, 147–158.

Model Checking and Fault Tolerance

Glenn Bruns and Ian Sutherland

Bell Labs, Lucent Technologies
{grb,ian}@research.bell-labs.com

Abstract. We present an algebraic approach to the model checking of fault-tolerant systems. Fault models and fault-handling mechanisms are modelled using special-purpose process operators. Besides providing for natural models, special-purpose operators allow systems with large state spaces to be verified using systems with small state spaces. To support this verification technique we show that a kind of simulation relation on processes preserves all process operators in tyft/tyxt format.

1 Introduction

Model checking – in which a system model is automatically checked to see if it satisfies a temporal logic formula – has two serious limitations. The *size problem* is that the state space of the model can grow exponentially with the state space of its components. Additionally, model checking algorithms for many logics have high time complexity. The *generality problem* is that model checking tells us only that some instance of a system satisfies a property. We usually want to know that a system works properly over a range of parameter values and initial conditions.

These limitations are especially serious in the application of model checking to fault-tolerant systems. By modelling failures of a system component one can increase its possible interactions with other components and thus dramatically increase the state space of the system. Furthermore, one usually wants to show that a fault tolerance mechanism is general purpose; in such cases it is not enough to show that it works for a particular underlying system.

Here we present an approach to the model checking of fault-tolerant systems based on process algebra. To model faults and fault-handling mechanisms we define new, special-purpose process operators. A faulty version of a process is modelled by applying a fault operator to it. For example, suppose process P models a system or system component. To obtain a crash-faulty version of P we define a new operator Cr and apply it to P. Similarly, a fault-tolerant or fault-detecting version of a process is defined by applying a process operator to it. This approach has modelling advantages because it is natural to understand faults and fault-handling mechanisms (e.g., triple-modular redundancy [19]) as behavior transformers that are independent of an underlying process or computation.

Defining faults and fault-handling mechanisms as process operators also has technical advantages. We show that if a temporal property holds of a fault-handling mechanism applied to a simple underlying process, then it holds of the mechanism applied to more complex underlying processes. In this way both the size and generality problems of model checking can be reduced. The technique is an application of a general abstraction principle for processes. To apply it here we have had to show that a kind of simulation relation on processes is preserved by every process operator that we might want to define.

Our work uses and extends results on rule formats for structured operational semantics [12, 5]. These results show that certain properties hold of every process built of operators defined in a specific format. The use of special-purpose process operators in specification is discussed by Bloom [4], but not specifically for modelling faults and fault-handling mechanisms. The use of the simulation relation in verification has been explored by Lynch [16], but not for the verification of temporal properties. Our work also draws on the new Process Algebra Compiler (PAC) [8], which takes a process language definition and produces a version of the Concurrency Workbench of North Carolina [9] that can analyze terms of the language.

Our verification approach is property-based: we verify that particular temporal properties hold of a system. This approach is more flexible than that used in [17], in which one shows that a fault tolerance mechanism applied to a faulty system yields behavior equivalent to a nonfaulty system. For example, consider a nuclear reactor protection system, which responds to faults in the reactor by shutting the system down. The protection system ensures safety, but does not ensure the other properties we expect of a normally operating reactor.

The paper is organized as follows. In the next section we show how faults and fault-handling mechanisms can be cleanly modelled using process operators. We then define the simulation relation on processes and show how it helps in verifying properties of complex systems. We illustrate the usefulness of our technique by using it to verify properties of British Rail's slow-scan design. Proofs of the theorems are given in the full version of the paper.

2 Modelling Faults

In hardware fault tolerance, a *fault* is "a physical defect which may or may not cause a failure" [14]. Software has no faults in this sense. We extend the notion of fault here to include design errors, and consider faults of both hardware and software.

Faults are rarely modelled directly, as that would require their precise nature and location to be known. Instead they are usually modelled by the way they transform the behavior of a system. For example, a crash fault extends the behavior of a system by allowing a crash to occur in any state. In this paper faults are modelled using process operators that conform to the *tyft/tyxt* rule format [12]. These rules, like the rules of CCS (see Appendix), are used to define the semantics of process operators. We do not have space to present the tyft/tyxt rule format here. However, we should point out that the format is very general: it has been used to describe the operators of CCS, ACP, and other process algebras, as well as the operators used in this paper.

Consider an operator *Cr* that models crash faults. A process with crash faults should be able to evolve silently in any state to a state in which no action is possible.

$$\frac{P \xrightarrow{\alpha} P'}{Cr(P) \xrightarrow{\alpha} Cr(P')} \qquad \frac{}{Cr(P) \xrightarrow{\tau} 0}$$

The rule on the left states that $Cr(P)$ can do whatever P can do. The rule on the right states that $Cr(P)$ can also crash. Notice that the behavior of $Cr(P)$ depends only on the behavior of P, not its structure. In our definition $Cr(P)$ need not eventually crash. This approach differs from that of [2], in which a crash-faulty system is one that has crashed, not one that may crash.

Since operators defined using tyft/tyxt rules can be regarded as behavior transformers, they are a natural way to capture fault models. Furthermore, they are modular in the sense that they are defined separately from any underlying process. Compare our modelling of crash faults to that used in [15], in which the modelling of crash faults is embedded in the system description. Other basic fault models, such as fail-stop faults, incorrect-computation faults, and byzantine faults, can also be described with process operators. Intermittent faults can also be modelled easily.

Fault-handling mechanisms are also modelled naturally with process operators. Consider a watchdog timer that detects a fault by performing action `det` ("detect") if n `tick` actions occur before action `cl` ("clear") occurs. The timer is modelled by operator WD.

$$\frac{P \xrightarrow{\alpha} P'}{\mathrm{WD}_{n,\mathtt{cl}}(i,P) \xrightarrow{\alpha} \mathrm{WD}_{n,\mathtt{cl}}(i,P')} \; \alpha \notin \{\mathtt{tick}, \mathtt{cl}\}$$

$$\frac{P \xrightarrow{\mathtt{tick}} P'}{\mathrm{WD}_{n,\mathtt{cl}}(i,P) \xrightarrow{\mathtt{tick}} \mathrm{WD}_{n,\mathtt{cl}}(i-1,P')} \; i > 0 \qquad \frac{P \xrightarrow{\mathtt{tick}} P'}{\mathrm{WD}_{n,\mathtt{cl}}(0,P) \xrightarrow{\mathtt{tick}} \mathtt{det}\,.P'}$$

$$\frac{P \xrightarrow{\mathtt{cl}} P'}{\mathrm{WD}_{n,\mathtt{cl}}(i,P) \xrightarrow{\mathtt{cl}} \mathrm{WD}_{n,\mathtt{cl}}(n,P')}$$

The first rule shows that actions not in $\{\mathtt{tick}, \mathtt{cl}\}$ are ignored by the timer. The second and third rules show that a `tick` action decrements the timer, and when time out occurs the action `det` is produced. The fourth rule shows that action `cl` will reset the timer.

3 Simulation

Our approach to the size problem involves the notion of one process *simulating* another. Roughly, process Q simulates process P if Q can perform any action that P can, and can continue to do so indefinitely. Simulation is useful in verification because if Q simulates P then many of the properties of Q will also hold of P. For example, if Q cannot perform certain undesirable actions, then neither can P. We verify that a process P with a large state space satisfies a property ϕ

by verifying that ϕ holds of a process Q that has a small state space and that simulates P.

When we use this technique, we show that the simulates relation holds between two processes that model the same system. Showing this can be expensive for systems with large state spaces. However, if the models are built out of components, one model can be shown to simulate the other by showing that a component of one simulates the corresponding component of the other. For this approach to work, it must be the case that replacing a subprocess of P by one that simulates it yields a new process that simulates P. We state this formally using the following terminology: If $\mathcal{R}$ is a binary relation on processes and O is a collection of process operators, O *preserves* $\mathcal{R}$ if, for every n-ary operator o in O and processes $P_1, \ldots, P_n$ and $Q_1, \ldots, Q_n$, $P_i \mathcal{R} Q_i$ for $1 \leq i \leq n$ implies $o(P_1, \ldots, P_n) \mathcal{R} o(Q_1, \ldots, Q_n)$. We need the simulation relation we adopt to be preserved by all process operators we use.

To avoid dependence on CCS, we define simulation here on an arbitrary *transition system* $(S, A, \{\xrightarrow{a} \mid a \in A\})$, where S is a set of states, A is a set of actions, and $\{\xrightarrow{a} \mid a \in A\}$ is a set of labelled transition relations.

Definition 1. A binary relation $\mathcal{R}$ on S is a *simulation* if $P \mathcal{R} Q$ implies that, for all a in A:

Whenever P $\xrightarrow{a}$ P', there exists Q' such that Q $\xrightarrow{a}$ Q' and $P' \mathcal{R} Q'$.

Process Q *simulates* P if there exists a simulation $\mathcal{R}$ such that $P \mathcal{R} Q$. Process Q *bisimulates* P if there exists a symmetric simulation $\mathcal{R}$ such that $P \mathcal{R} Q$.

We write $P < Q$ if Q simulates P and $P \simeq Q$ if P bisimulates Q. The relation $<$ is a preorder and $\simeq$ is an equivalence relation.

The transition systems we use, like that of CCS, have a distinguished action τ that represents internal activity of a process. "Internal" means that observers of a process P cannot tell how many τ actions P is performing along with its externally visible actions. This interpretation of τ requires that we adopt a slightly different notion of simulation. Let $(S, A, \{\xrightarrow{a} \mid a \in A\})$ be a transition system with $\tau \in A$. The corresponding *weak transition system* is $(S, A, \{\overset{a}{\Rightarrow} \mid a \in A'\})$, where $\overset{\tau}{\Rightarrow}$ is $(\xrightarrow{\tau})^*$ (the reflexive, transitive closure of $\xrightarrow{\tau}$), and $\overset{a}{\Rightarrow}$ is $\overset{\tau}{\Rightarrow} \circ \xrightarrow{a} \circ \overset{\tau}{\Rightarrow}$ (the composition of the relations $\overset{\tau}{\Rightarrow}$, $\xrightarrow{a}$, and $\overset{\tau}{\Rightarrow}$), for a in $A - \{\tau\}$.

If Q simulates P in the weak transition system then we write $P \ll Q$ and say that Q *weakly simulates* P. If P bisimulates Q in the weak transition system we write $P \approx Q$, and say that P and Q are *observation equivalent*. Weak simulation is a preorder and observation equivalence is an equivalence relation.

The operators of CCS preserve weak simulation, but we wish to extend CCS with new operators. If we wish to use weak simulation as our notion of "simulation", we must be able to show that the combination of the CCS operators and the new operators preserve weak simulation. The semantics of our new operators are defined using the tyft/tyxt rule format [12]. It is shown in [12] that the bisimulates relation (and, by a slight modification of the argument, the simulates relation) is preserved by any collection of operators defined in tyft/tyxt format that satisfy an additional condition called *well-foundedness*.

Weak simulation is *not* preserved by every collection of operators defined by well-founded tyft/tyxt rules. There is, however, a natural additional condition to impose on the rules that ensures that weak simulation is preserved.

Definition 2. A tyft/tyxt rule of the form

$$\frac{\{t_i \xrightarrow{a_i} t_i' \mid i \in I\}}{t \xrightarrow{a} t'}$$

is said to be *valid for weak transitions* if, whenever $t_i \overset{a_i}{\Rightarrow} t_i'$ for all $i \in I$, $t \overset{a}{\Rightarrow} t'$.

Theorem 3. *If R is a well-founded set of tyft/tyxt rules for a system with a τ action, and the rules of R are valid for weak transitions, then weak simulation and observation equivalence are preserved by the function symbols of R.*

Like the proof in [12], the heart of the proof is an induction on proofs of transitions from a set of tyft/tyxt rules, but using transitions of the weak transition system. The additional hypothesis that the rules are valid for weak transitions is needed to make the modified induction work.

Unfortunately, the rules for the CCS operator "+" are not valid for weak transitions, so instead we will use a slightly stronger definition of simulation. This notion of simulation is defined, like weak simulation, by describing a derived transition system. Let $(S, A, \{\xrightarrow{a} \mid a \in A\})$ be a transition system with $\tau \in A$. The corresponding *weak-plus transition system* is $(S, A, \{\overset{a}{\Rightarrow}_+ \mid a \in A\})$, where $\overset{a}{\Rightarrow}_+$ is $(\xrightarrow{\tau})^* \circ \xrightarrow{a} \circ (\xrightarrow{\tau})^*$. Informally, the weak-plus transition system corresponds to an interpretation of τ in which observers cannot tell the difference between the occurrence of many τ actions and few τ actions, but can tell whether a τ action has occurred at all.

We write $P \ll_+ Q$ if Q simulates P in the weak-plus transition system. If $P \ll_+ Q$ we say that Q *weakly-plus simulates* P. If P bisimulates Q in the weak-plus transition system, we write $P \approx_+ Q$, and say that P and Q are *observation-plus equivalent*. Weak-plus simulation is a preorder and observation-plus equivalence is an equivalence relation.

Proposition 4. *Weak-plus simulation implies weak simulation. Observational-plus equivalence implies observation equivalence.*

We define the notion of a set of tyft/tyxt rules being valid for weak-plus transitions exactly as in Definition 2, with "weak" replaced by "weak-plus". We can then obtain the following result.

Theorem 5. *If R is a well-founded set of tyft/tyxt rules for a system with a τ action, and the rules of R are valid for weak-plus transitions, then weak-plus simulation and observation-plus equivalence are preserved by the function symbols of R.*

All rules for the basic CCS operators are valid for weak-plus transitions, so this result allows us to use weak-plus simulation with CCS as the basic algebra.

Are there less restrictive notions of "simulation" than weak-plus simulation that have the properties we need? However we define simulation, we would at least like it to (1) imply weak simulation, and (2) be preserved by any collection of operators defined by well-founded tyft/tyxt rules, possibly with some additional condition as in the theorems above. The following result is relevant.

Theorem 6. *If $\leq$ is any binary relation on labelled transition systems with a τ action such that:*

- *$P \leq Q$ implies $P \ll Q$.*
- *$\leq$ is preserved by any set of function symbols defined by a well-founded set of tyft/tyxt rules for a system with a τ action that are valid for weak-plus transitions.*

then $P \leq Q$ implies that $P \ll_+ Q$.

This result shows that the only way to get an acceptable notion of "simulation" that is not just a special case of weak-plus simulation would be to remove or replace the requirement that the tyft/tyxt rules are valid for weak-plus transitions. While such notions of "simulation" may exist, it would seem to require a major modification of the proof in [12] to establish that such a notion of "simulation" is preserved by new operators defined by tyft/tyxt rules.

Tyft/tyxt is a fairly general format that can define the semantics of the basic CCS operators as well as our additional operators. The above theorem applies to all the operators we will use to construct models. In particular, if Q weakly-plus simulates P, then $Cr(Q)$ weakly-plus simulates $Cr(P)$.

4 An Abstraction Principle

Here we show that the weakly simulates relation preserves certain temporal properties. The preserved properties are those that can be expressed in a fragment of the modal mu-calculus [13], a simple but expressive temporal logic.

Formulas of the *diamond-free modal mu-calculus* have the following abstract syntax, where L ranges over sets of actions and X ranges over propositional variables:

$$\phi :== X \mid \phi \wedge \phi \mid \phi \vee \phi \mid [\![L]\!]\phi \mid \nu X.\phi \mid \mu X.\phi$$

The propositional connectives have their usual meaning. Formula $[\![L]\!]\phi$ holds of a process P if every weak transition from P leads to a process satisfying formula ϕ. The fixed-point operators allow properties to be defined recursively. They are binders; free occurrences of X in ϕ are bound in $\nu X.\phi$ and $\mu X.\phi$.

Falsity, written $\mathtt{ff}$, is an abbreviation for $\mu X.X$. We also write $[\![\alpha_1, \ldots, \alpha_n]\!]$ as an abbreviation for $[\![\{\alpha_1, \ldots, \alpha_n\}]\!]$, and $[\![-L]\!]$ as an abbreviation for $[\![Act - L]\!]$.

The semantics of a formula is given as the set of processes that it satisfies. Let $\mathcal{T} = (S, A, \{\xrightarrow{a} \mid a \in A\})$ be a transition system, with τ in A. Let $\mathcal{V}$ be a *valuation* that maps propositional variables to subsets of S. We write $()$ for the valuation that maps all variables to the empty set, and $\mathcal{V}[X := \mathcal{E}]$ for the valuation that is like $\mathcal{V}$ except that X is mapped to $\mathcal{E}$. Let f be a monotonic, set-valued function. By the Knaster-Tarski fixed-point theorem [18] we know that f has greatest and least fixed-points, written νf and μf respectively.

$$
\begin{aligned}
\|X\|_{\mathcal{V}}^{\mathcal{T}} &\stackrel{\text{def}}{=} \mathcal{V}(X) \\
\|\phi_1 \wedge \phi_2\|_{\mathcal{V}}^{\mathcal{T}} &\stackrel{\text{def}}{=} \|\phi_1\|_{\mathcal{V}}^{\mathcal{T}} \cap \|\phi_2\|_{\mathcal{V}}^{\mathcal{T}} \\
\|\phi_1 \vee \phi_2\|_{\mathcal{V}}^{\mathcal{T}} &\stackrel{\text{def}}{=} \|\phi_1\|_{\mathcal{V}}^{\mathcal{T}} \cup \|\phi_2\|_{\mathcal{V}}^{\mathcal{T}} \\
\|[\![L]\!]\phi\|_{\mathcal{V}}^{\mathcal{T}} &\stackrel{\text{def}}{=} \{E \in S \mid \forall E' \in S, a \in L. E \stackrel{a}{\Rightarrow} E' \text{ implies } E' \in \|\phi\|_{\mathcal{V}}^{\mathcal{T}}\} \\
\|\nu X.\phi\|_{\mathcal{V}}^{\mathcal{T}} &\stackrel{\text{def}}{=} \nu f, \text{ where } f(\mathcal{E}) \stackrel{\text{def}}{=} \|\phi\|_{\mathcal{V}[X:=\mathcal{E}]}^{\mathcal{T}} \\
\|\mu X.\phi\|_{\mathcal{V}}^{\mathcal{T}} &\stackrel{\text{def}}{=} \mu f, \text{ where } f(\mathcal{E}) \stackrel{\text{def}}{=} \|\phi\|_{\mathcal{V}[X:=\mathcal{E}]}^{\mathcal{T}}
\end{aligned}
$$

If ϕ is a closed formula and $P \in \|\phi\|_{()}^{\mathcal{T}}$ then we write $P \models \phi$ and say that P *satisfies* ϕ.

Formulas of the diamond-free modal mu-calculus can express safety properties [1]. However, the logic can also express weak liveness properties, which state that something will eventually happen in the absence of deadlock. The rough intuition of the following theorem is that nothing bad can happen in a process if nothing bad can happen in a process that simulates it.

Theorem 7. *Let $\mathcal{T} = (S, A, \{\stackrel{a}{\rightarrow} \mid a \in A\})$ be a transition system with τ in A, let P and Q be elements of S, and let ϕ be a formula of the diamond-free modal mu-calculus. Then*

$$(Q \models \phi \text{ and } P \ll Q) \Rightarrow P \models \phi.$$

Proof. This result is proved directly in the modal mu-calculus in [7], and proved using a logic with infinitary conjunction and disjunction in [3].

This theorem is useful because a process with many states can sometimes be simulated by a process with few states. Imagine that our goal is to show that $Cr(P)$ satisfies a formula ϕ of the diamond-free modal mu-calculus. Suppose that P' is a process that simulates P but has fewer states. Suppose also that $Cr(P')$ satisfies ϕ. Then $Cr(Q) \ll Cr(P)$ because Cr preserves weak simulation and $Cr(Q)$ satisfies ϕ by this theorem. Note that by Prop. 4 the weakly-plus simulates relation also preserves formulas of the diamond-free modal mu-calculus.

The following fact is a simple corollary of the theorem.

Proposition 8. *Let $\mathcal{T} = (S, A, \{\stackrel{a}{\rightarrow} \mid a \in A\})$ be a transition system with τ in A, let P and Q be elements of S, and let ϕ be a formula of the diamond-free modal mu-calculus. Then*

$$P \approx Q \Rightarrow (P \models \phi \Leftrightarrow Q \models \phi)$$

5 Analysis of the Slow-Scan System

Here we describe the slow-scan system and present three models of the system. The first model is written in CCS. The second model, written in CCS plus new operators, shows how special-purpose operators improve the modelling of faults and fault-handling mechanisms. The third model is like the second except that some components are modelled more realistically. We show that it satisfies some important properties by appealing to the simpler second model.

5.1 The Slow-Scan System

A railway signalling interlocking adjusts, at the request of the signal operator, the setting of colored light signals and direction controlling points in the railway to permit the safe passage of trains. An example of a modern interlocking is the *Solid State Interlocking* (SSI) [11], developed by British Rail in collaboration with GEC ALSTHOM Signalling and Westinghouse Signals. Figure 1 shows an SSI and the devices it controls. Operator commands are broadcast over a high-speed communication link to track-side functional modules (TFMs), which control signals and points.

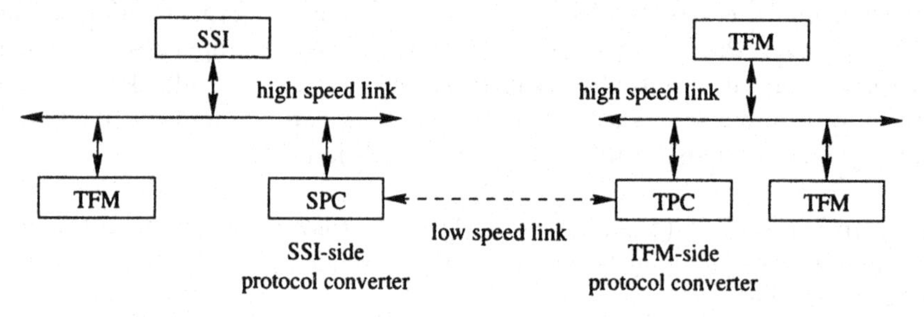

Fig. 1. The slow-scan system

It is important that TFM and communication link failures be detected quickly by the SSI. Instead of sending signal and point commands only as needed, the SSI sends a message of the form ⟨TFM-address, state⟩ to every attached TFM about once every second. The SSI then waits at most a few milliseconds for the addressed TFM to respond with the current state of its attached device. This command-cycling scheme provides fast failure detection, and allows the interlocking to take immediate action to maintain the system in a safe state.

In some rail networks the signals and points controlled by a single SSI lie many miles apart. The TFMs in such a network are connected by long high-speed links. A cheaper *low-grade link* (LGL) cannot directly replace a high-speed link because it does not have the bandwidth needed for the TFM command-cycling scheme. However, a low-speed link is feasible if used with a pair of *protocol converters*. The *slow-scan* system, shown in Figure 1, is built from a low-grade link and two protocol converters. The SSI-side protocol converter (SPC) accepts TFM commands once every second, and responds immediately with track-side device status, but only sends TFM commands along the low-grade link occasionally. The TFM-side protocol converter (TPC) sends a command to each attached TFM once every second. Responses from the TFMs are occasionally sent by the TPC to the SPC to update the SPC's device status information. The SPC appears to the SSI as a TFM and the TPC appears to a TFM as an SSI.

5.2 A CCS Model of the System

Our model is based on the model in [6]. The SSI and TFM's are taken as outside the scope of the model. The model therefore contains a process for the LGL, the TPC, the SPC, and a system clock that synchronizes the TPC and SPC.

We model the LGL as two unidirectional communication links, each with the capacity to buffer one message. Relabelling function f_c maps $\mathtt{in}$ to $\mathtt{c1}$, $\overline{\mathtt{out}}$ to $\overline{\mathtt{c2}}$, $\overline{\mathtt{out}_u}$ to $\overline{\mathtt{c2}_u}$, and all other actions to themselves. Relabelling function f_s maps $\mathtt{in}$ to $\mathtt{s1}$, $\overline{\mathtt{out}}$ to $\overline{\mathtt{s2}}$, $\overline{\mathtt{out}_u}$ to $\overline{\mathtt{s2}_u}$, and all other actions to themselves.

$$\begin{aligned}
Comm &\stackrel{\text{def}}{=} \mathtt{in}(m).Comm'(m) + \overline{\mathtt{out}_u}\,.Comm + \mathtt{fail}\,.CommF \\
Comm'(m) &\stackrel{\text{def}}{=} \overline{\mathtt{out}}(m).Comm + \mathtt{fail}\,.CommF \\
CommF &\stackrel{\text{def}}{=} \mathtt{in}\,.CommF + \overline{\mathtt{out}_u}\,.CommF \\
LGL &\stackrel{\text{def}}{=} Comm[f_c] \mid Comm[f_s]
\end{aligned}$$

Actions $\mathtt{in}$ and $\overline{\mathtt{out}}$ model the input and output ports of a link. The link can always read the input port but can only write on the output port if a message is buffered. However, the link can synchronize on $\overline{\mathtt{out}_u}$ when no message is buffered. Action $\mathtt{fail}$ models a link failure. The only failure we model is the spontaneous break of the communication medium. Once a link fails it no longer synchronizes on its output port.

The SPC is modelled as a parametrized process.

$$\begin{aligned}
SPC &\stackrel{\text{def}}{=} SPC(c_0, s_0, 0) \\
SPC(c,s,i) &\stackrel{\text{def}}{=} \mathtt{comm_in}(c').(\tau.SPC(c,s,i) + \tau.SPC(c',s,i)) + \\
&\quad \overline{\mathtt{stat_out}}(s).SPC(c,s,i) + \\
&\quad \overline{\mathtt{c1}}(c).SPC(c,s,i) + \mathtt{s2}(s').SPC(c,s',0) + \mathtt{s2}_u\,.SPC(c,s,i) + \\
&\quad \mathtt{mcs}\,.\overline{\mathtt{c1}}(c).(\text{if } i > n \text{ then } \mathtt{det}\,.SPCF \text{ else } SPC(c,s,i+1)) \\
SPCF &\stackrel{\text{def}}{=} \mathtt{comm_in}(c).SPCF + \mathtt{s2}(s).SPCF + \mathtt{s2}_u\,.SPCF + \mathtt{mcs}\,.SPCF
\end{aligned}$$

Actions $\mathtt{comm\_in}$ and $\overline{\mathtt{stat\_out}}$ model the command input and status output ports of an SPC. A command can be received and a status message can be output at any time. Actions $\overline{\mathtt{c1}}$, $\mathtt{s2}$, and $\mathtt{s2}_u$ model the ports on which interaction with the LGL takes place. Action $\mathtt{mcs}$ models the reception of a clock tick. After each clock tick occurs a command is sent to the LGL. Action $\mathtt{det}$ models the detection of an LGL failure by the SPC. It arises if n clock ticks have occurred without the reception of a status message over the LGL.

The TPC model is similar:

$$TPC \stackrel{\text{def}}{=} TPC(c_0, s_0, 0)$$

$$\begin{aligned} TPC(c,s,i) \stackrel{\text{def}}{=} & \overline{\texttt{comm\_out}}(c).(\tau.TPC(c,s,i) + \tau.TPC(c',s,i)) + \\ & \texttt{stat\_in}(s').TPC(c,s',i) + \\ & \overline{\texttt{s1}}(s).TPC(c,s,i) + \texttt{c2}(c').TPC(c',s,0) + \texttt{c2}_u\,.\,TPC(c,s,i) + \\ & \texttt{mct}\,.\,\overline{\texttt{s1}}(s).(\text{if } i > n \text{ then } \texttt{det}\,.\,TPCF \text{ else } TPC(c,s,i+1)) \end{aligned}$$

$$TPCF \stackrel{\text{def}}{=} \texttt{stat\_in}(s).TPCF + \texttt{c2}(c).TPCF + \texttt{c2}_u\,.\,TPCF + \texttt{mct}\,.\,TPCF$$

The TPC outputs commands and accepts status messages. It sends a status message to the LGL every clock tick. If n clock ticks occur without the reception of a command over the LGL then action det occurs.

Finally we model the clock process.

$$Clock \stackrel{\text{def}}{=} \texttt{tick}\,.\,\overline{\texttt{mcs}}\,.\,\overline{\texttt{mct}}\,.\,Clock$$

Action tick models a visible clock tick; actions $\overline{\texttt{mcs}}$ and $\overline{\texttt{mct}}$ model clock signals to the SPC and TPC.

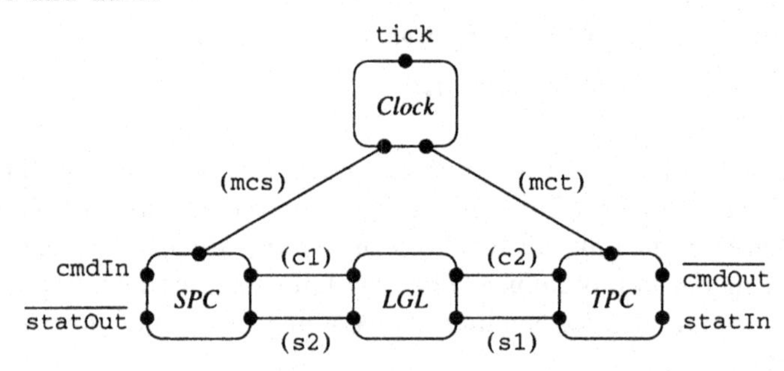

Fig. 2. Flow Diagram of the Slow-Scan System

The complete slow-scan model is obtained by putting the components together. Figure 2 is a flow diagram showing the components of the model and how they are connected through their ports. The model has about 26,000 states.

$$SS_1 \stackrel{\text{def}}{=} (SPC \mid LGL \mid TPC \mid Clock)\backslash\{\texttt{s1}, \texttt{s2}, \texttt{s2}_u, \texttt{c1}, \texttt{c2}, \texttt{c2}_u, \texttt{mcs}, \texttt{mct}\}$$

We are interested in knowing whether this model satisfies two main fault tolerance properties. First, are false alarms possible? In other words, can an LGL failure be detected before an LGL failure has occurred? Second, are failures always detected? These properties can be expressed as formulas of the diamond-free modal mu-calculus.

$$NoFalseAlarms \stackrel{\text{def}}{=} \nu X.[\![\texttt{det}]\!]\,\texttt{ff} \wedge [\![-\texttt{fail}]\!]X$$

$$\begin{aligned} FailuresDetected \stackrel{\text{def}}{=} & \nu X.[\![-\texttt{fail}]\!]X \wedge \\ & [\![\texttt{fail}]\!](\mu Y.\nu Z.[\![-\texttt{tick},\texttt{det}]\!]Z \wedge [\![\texttt{tick}]\!]Y) \end{aligned}$$

The property *NoFalseAlarms* can be understood recursively as "action **det** cannot occur, and after any non-fail action occurs, *NoFalseAlarms* holds". The property *FailuresDetected* is more difficult to understand because it incorporates the assumption that the clock continues to tick. The formula states that after any initial fail action occurs, there can be no path containing infinitely many tick actions and no **det** action.

Proposition 9. *SS_1 satisfies NoFalseAlarms and FailuresDetected.*

Proof. Verified with the Concurrency Workbench. □

The modelling of faults and of the fault detection mechanism is awkward here. In modelling the LGL we want to capture that a failure can occur in any state, so fail actions must be added to the model at several different points. The modelling of the nonfaulty LGL behavior and the modelling of faults are combined. Similarly, in the SPC and TPC models the modelling of the nonfaulty behavior and the modelling of the fault detection mechanism are combined.

Another problem with the model is that it has been simplified to make model checking feasible and to avoid committing to details that are not specified in the design of the system. For example, the model attempts to capture various SPC policies for sending commands along the low-grade link by allowing action $\overline{\texttt{c1}}$ to occur at any time. We have not shown that implementations of slow-scan will satisfy properties *NoFalseAlarms* and *FailuresDetected*.

In [10] the slow-scan system was modelled in a version of CCS extended with priorities. The use of priorities allows for more natural modelling and reduces the state space of the model. However, like the CCS model it suffers from awkward fault modelling and excessive simplification.

5.3 Modelling Slow-Scan with New Operators

We now show how the use of new operators improves the modelling of the slow-scan system. To model LGL faults we define new operator LF ("link failure"), which allows a failure to happen at any time, causing output actions of a link to be hidden.

$$\frac{P \xrightarrow{\alpha} P'}{\mathrm{LF}(P) \xrightarrow{\alpha} \mathrm{LF}(P')} \qquad \frac{}{\mathrm{LF}(P) \xrightarrow{\texttt{fail}} P \backslash\!\backslash \{\texttt{c2}, \texttt{s2}\}}$$

To revise the LGL model we first define a nonfaulty communications link. A faulty link is then defined as a nonfaulty link extended with a link failure. The advantage of using the fault operator LF would be greater if the LGL model was more complicated.

$$Comm \stackrel{\mathrm{def}}{=} \mathbf{in}(m).\overline{\mathbf{out}}(m).Comm + \overline{\mathbf{out}}_u\,.Comm$$

$$LGL \stackrel{\mathrm{def}}{=} \mathrm{LF}(Comm[f_c]) \mid \mathrm{LF}(Comm[f_s])$$

To model the failure detection mechanism used in the SPC and TPC we use two new operators. Operator ex ("exception") is an exception handler for action **det**. A process P ex Q evolves to Q when P performs action **det**.

$$\frac{P \xrightarrow{\alpha} P'}{P \text{ ex } Q \xrightarrow{\alpha} P' \text{ ex } Q} \; \alpha \neq \texttt{det} \qquad \frac{P \xrightarrow{\texttt{det}} P'}{P \text{ ex } Q \xrightarrow{\texttt{det}} Q}$$

We also use the watchdog timer operator $\mathrm{WD}_{n,\texttt{c1}}$ of Section 2. It produces action **det** if n clock ticks occur before action `c1` occur.

To revise the SPC model we first define a nonfaulty SPC and the SPC failure state. The SPC is then defined as a nonfaulty SPC that can time out and evolve to the failure state.

$$\begin{aligned}
SPCB &\stackrel{\text{def}}{=} SPCB(c_0, s_0)\\
SPCB(c,s) &\stackrel{\text{def}}{=} \texttt{comm_in}(c').(\tau.SPCB(c,s) + \tau.SPCB(c',s)) +\\
&\quad \overline{\texttt{stat_out}}(s).SPCB(c,s) +\\
&\quad \overline{\texttt{c1}}(c).SPCB(c,s) + \texttt{s2}(s').SPCB(c,s') + \texttt{s2}_u\,.SPCB(c,s) +\\
&\quad \texttt{mcs}\,.\,\overline{\texttt{c1}}(c).SPCB(c,s)\\
SPCF &\stackrel{\text{def}}{=} \texttt{comm_in}(c).SPCF + \texttt{s2}(s).SPCF + \texttt{s2}_u\,.SPCF + \texttt{mcs}\,.SPCF\\
SPC &\stackrel{\text{def}}{=} \mathrm{WD}_{2,\texttt{c2}}(2, SPCB) \text{ ex } SPCF
\end{aligned}$$

The new TPC definition is similar. We let the new definitions of *LGL*, *SPC*, and *TPC* replace the old ones, and call the new model SS_2. We have defined our new process operators with the PAC and verified automatically that processes SS_1 and SS_2 are observation equivalent.

Proposition 10. *SS_2 satisfies NoFalseAlarms and FailuresDetected.*

Proof. Process SS_1 satisfies the formulas. The Concurrency Workbench verifies that SS_1 and SS_2 are observation equivalent, so by Prop. 8 process SS_2 satisfies the formulas. □

5.4 A More Realistic Model

The models of the last two sections are highly simplified. They do not capture the contents of command and status messages or the local variables of the SPC and TPC. We now examine a more realistic slow-scan model and show how our modelling of faults helps in showing that it satisfies properties *NoFalseAlarms* and *FailuresDetected*.

In our previous SPC model we allowed commands to be transmitted over the LGL at any time. We can instead model that a command is transmitted only when it differs from the previous command.

$$\begin{aligned}
SPCB(c,s) &\stackrel{\text{def}}{=} \texttt{comm_in}(c').\,\overline{\texttt{stat_out}}(s).\\
&\quad (\text{if } c = c' \text{ then } \overline{\texttt{c1}}\,.SPCB(c',s) \text{ else } SPCB(c,s)) +\\
&\quad \texttt{s2}(s').SPCB(c,s') + \texttt{s2}_u\,.SPCB(c,s) +\\
&\quad \texttt{mcs}\,.\,\overline{\texttt{c1}}(c).SPCB(c,s)
\end{aligned}$$

To complete the model we make an analogous change to the SPC. The resulting model, which we call SS_3, has about 250,000 states. This example illustrates how sensitive the size of the model is to increases in the size of components.

To show that SS_3 satisfies *NoFalseAlarms* and *FailuresDetected* we need only show that the revised versions of *SPCB* and *TPCB* are weakly-plus simulated by the original versions. The following proposition is straightforward to prove by exhibiting a simulation relation.

Proposition 11. *Let $SPCB'$ and $TPCB'$ be the revised versions of processes SPCB and TPCB. Then $SPCB' \ll_{+} SPCB$ and $TPCB' \ll_{+} TPCB$.*

Proposition 12. *SS_3 satisfies NoFalseAlarms and FailuresDetected.*

Proof. SS_2 satisfies the formulas by Prop. 10. Let $SPCB'$ and $TPCB'$ be the revised versions of processes *SPCB* and *TPCB*. Then $SS_3 \ll_{+} SS_2$ by Prop. 11 and Theorem 5, since all operators of SS_3 are well-founded and valid for weak-plus transitions, and $SS_3 \ll SS_2$ by Prop. 4. Therefore by Theorem 7 SS_3 also satisfies the formulas. □

6 Future Work

One can define powerful new process operators for which implementation may be difficult. We have not described a general approach to implementing process operators or even what 'implementation' means. One notion of the implementation of an operator $\mathcal{O}$ is to find, for a process $\mathcal{O}(P)$, a CCS process P' such that $\mathcal{O}(P)$ and P' are observation equivalent. However, the implementation here might depend on P. A notion of the *modular* implementation of an operator $\mathcal{O}$ is to find a CCS process *context* C such that $C[P]$ is observation equivalent to $\mathcal{O}(P)$ for all CCS processes P. The proof that $C[P]$ and $\mathcal{O}(P)$ are observation equivalent could be done by exhibiting a bisimulation relation. This is the approach used by Bloom in [4]. We have not yet answered the interesting question: which tyft/tyxt operators have modular implementations in CCS?

A CCS

The terms of CCS represent processes that perform *actions*. The set *Act* of CCS actions contains *names* $(a, b, \ldots)$, *co-names* $(\overline{a}, \overline{b}, \ldots)$, and the special "silent" action τ. We let α, β range over *Act*. The set of *labels* contains all actions except τ. We let l range over labels. Complementation extends to all labels: $\overline{\overline{l}} = l$.

Processes are given as *agent expressions* having the following syntax, where A ranges over agent constants, L ranges over sets of labels, and f ranges over functions from actions to actions:

$$P ::= A \bigm| \alpha.P \bigm| \sum_{i \in I} P_i \bigm| P_1 \mid P_2 \bigm| P \backslash L \bigm| P[f]$$

We write $P_1 + P_2$ as an abbreviation for $\sum_{i\in\{1,2\}} P_i$, and 0 (the *inactive* agent) as an abbreviation for summation over the empty set. Constant definitions are of the form $A \stackrel{\text{def}}{=} P$. We refer to the set of all agents expressions and agent constants as simply ***agents***, denoted by $\mathcal{P}$. We let P, Q range over $\mathcal{P}$.

The meaning of agents is given as the transition system $(\mathcal{P}, Act, \{\stackrel{\alpha}{\rightarrow} \mid \alpha \in Act\})$, where $\stackrel{\alpha}{\rightarrow}$ is a labelled transition relation over agents. We write $P \stackrel{\alpha}{\rightarrow} P'$ if $(P, P') \in \stackrel{\alpha}{\rightarrow}$. The relation $\stackrel{\alpha}{\rightarrow}$ is defined as the least relation satisfying the following rules:

$$.: \quad \alpha.P \stackrel{\alpha}{\rightarrow} P$$

$$+: \frac{P_j \stackrel{\alpha}{\rightarrow} P'_j}{\sum_{i\in I} P_i \stackrel{\alpha}{\rightarrow} P'_j}\ j \in I$$

$$|: \frac{P \stackrel{\alpha}{\rightarrow} P'}{P \mid Q \stackrel{\alpha}{\rightarrow} P' \mid Q} \quad \frac{Q \stackrel{\alpha}{\rightarrow} Q'}{P \mid Q \stackrel{\alpha}{\rightarrow} P \mid Q'} \quad \frac{P \stackrel{l}{\rightarrow} P' \quad Q \stackrel{\bar{l}}{\rightarrow} Q'}{P \mid Q \stackrel{\tau}{\rightarrow} P' \mid Q'}$$

$$\backslash: \frac{P \stackrel{\alpha}{\rightarrow} P'}{P\backslash L \stackrel{\alpha}{\rightarrow} P'\backslash L}\ \alpha \notin L \cup \overline{L}$$

$$f: \frac{P \stackrel{\alpha}{\rightarrow} P'}{P[f] \stackrel{f(\alpha)}{\longrightarrow} P'[f]}$$

$$\text{def}: \frac{P \stackrel{\alpha}{\rightarrow} P'}{A \stackrel{\alpha}{\rightarrow} P'}\ A \stackrel{\text{def}}{=} P$$

A ***hiding*** operator, which effectively renames labels to τ actions, can be defined using CCS operators. For simplicity we instead define it directly:

$$\backslash\!\!\backslash: \frac{P \stackrel{\alpha}{\rightarrow} P'}{P\backslash\!\!\backslash L \stackrel{\alpha}{\rightarrow} P'\backslash\!\!\backslash L}\ \alpha \notin L \cup \overline{L} \quad \frac{P \stackrel{\alpha}{\rightarrow} P'}{P\backslash\!\!\backslash L \stackrel{\tau}{\rightarrow} P'\backslash\!\!\backslash L}\ \alpha \in L \cup \overline{L}$$

Value-passing CCS adds parametrized actions, parametrized agents, and conditional statements to CCS. These new features are defined by translation to CCS. Assume a fixed set V of data values and a notation for data expressions. Input action $a(x).P$ is defined to be $\sum_{v\in V} a_v.P[v/x]$, where $P[v/x]$ is the agent obtained by substituting v for all free occurrences of x in P. Output action $\overline{a}(e).P$ is defined to be $\overline{a}_v.P$, where v is the value obtained by evaluating data expression e. Parametrized agent definition $A(x_1, x_2, \ldots, x_n) \stackrel{\text{def}}{=} P$ is defined as the set of definitions $\{(A_{v_1,v_2,\ldots,v_n} \stackrel{\text{def}}{=} P[v_1/x_1, \ldots, v_n/x_n]) : (v_1, \ldots, v_n) \in V_{x_1} \times \cdots \times V_{x_n}\}$. Parametrized agent constant $A(e_1, \ldots, e_n)$ is defined to be $A_{v_1,\ldots,v_n}$, where v_i is the value obtained by evaluating data expression e_i. Finally, conditional statement *if* b *then* P *else* Q is defined to be P if the boolean expression b evaluates to true, else P. b

Acknowledgements

We would like to thank Stuart Anderson for helpful discussions and Steve Sims for help with the PAC and North Carolina Concurrency Workbench.

References

1. Bowen Alpern and Fred B. Schneider. Recognizing safety and liveness. *Distributed Computing*, 2:117–126, 1987.
2. Michael Barborak, Miroslaw Malek, and Anton Dahbura. The consensus problem in fault-tolerant computing. *ACM Computing Surveys*, 25(2):171–220, June 1993.
3. S. Bensalem, A. Bouajjani, C. Loiseaux, and J. Sifakis. Property preserving simulations. In *Proceedings of CAV '92, LNCS 663*, pages 260–273, 1992.
4. Bard Bloom. Structured operational semantics as a specification language. In *Proceedings of LICS '94*. IEEE Computer Society Press, 1994.
5. Bard Bloom, Sorin Istrail, and Albert R. Meyer. Bisimulation can't be traced. *Journal of the ACM*, 42(1):232-268, 1995.
6. Glenn Bruns. A case study in safety-critical design. In G.v. Bochmann and D.K. Probst, editors, *Proceedings of CAV '91, LNCS 575*, pages 220–233, 1991.
7. Glenn Bruns. *Process Abstraction in the Verification of Temporal Properties*. PhD thesis, University of Edinburgh, 1997.
8. R. Cleaveland, E. Madelaine, and S. Sims. Generating front ends for verification tools. In *Proceedings of TACAS '95, LNCS 1019*, pages 153–173, 1995.
9. R. Cleaveland and S. Sims. The NCSU concurrency workbench. In R. Alur and T. Henzinger, editors, *Proceedings of CAV '96*, 1996.
10. Rance Cleaveland, Gerard Lüttgen, V. Natarajan, and Steve Sims. Modeling and verifying distributed systems using priorities: A case study. *Software Concepts and Tools*, 15:50–62, 1996.
11. A.H. Cribbens. Solid-state interlocking (SSI): an integrated electronic signalling system for mainline railways. *IEE Proceedings*, 134(B3), 1987.
12. J. F. Groote and F. W. Vaandrager. Structured operational semantics and bisimulation as a congruence. *Information and Computation*, 100(2):202–260, 1992.
13. D. Kozen. Results on the propositional mu-calculus. *Theoretical Computer Science*, 27:333–354, 1983.
14. Parag K. Lala. *Fault Tolerant and Fault Testable Hardware Design*. Prentice Hall, 1985.
15. Patrick Lincoln and John Rushby. The formal verification of an algorithm for interactive consistency under a hybrid fault model. In *Proceedings of CAV '93*, 1993.
16. Nancy A. Lynch. Multivalued possibilities mapping. In J.W. de Bakker, W.-P. de Roever, and G. Rozenberg, editors, *Stepwise Refinement of Distributed Systems*, pages 519–543, 1989. LNCS 430.
17. Fred B. Schneider. Implementing fault-tolerant services using the state machine approach: A tutorial. *ACM Computing Surveys*, 22(4):299–320, 1990.
18. A. Tarski. A lattice-theoretical fixpoint theorem and its applications. *Pacific J. of Maths*, 5:285–309, 1955.
19. J. von Neumann. Probabilistic logics and synthesis of reliable organisms from unreliable components. *Annals of Mathematical Studies*, 34:43–98, 1956.

Deadlock Analysis for a Fault-Tolerant System

Bettina Buth*, Michel Kouvaras**, Jan Peleska***, and Hui Shi†

Abstract. This article presents an approach for the verification of communication properties in large-scale real-world embedded systems by means of formal methods. It is illustrated by examples and results obtained during an industrial verification project performed for a fault-tolerant system designed and implemented by Daimler-Benz Aerospace for the International Space Station ISS. The approach is based on CSP specifications and the model-checking tool FDR. The task is split into manageable subtasks by applying an abstraction technique for restricting the specifications to the essential communication behaviour, modularization according to the process structure, and a set of generic theories developed for the application.

1 Introduction

One of the essential obstacles for the acceptance of formal methods during the last years is their failure to scale up to realistic applications. In our experience this problem can only be overcome by a combination of methods and the use of suitable tools that are optimized for the efficient handling of well-defined subtasks. This article reports work performed over the last 1.5 years with an overall effort of about one man year which supports the above claims.

JP Software-Consulting in collaboration with the Bremen Institute for Safe System (BISS) were contracted by Daimler-Benz Aerospace (DASA) to perform an analysis of a fault-tolerant data management system for the International Space Station (ISS). The software was made available in form of occam pseudo code resp. occam code [4]. The main concern of the analysis described in this article was to ensure freedom from deadlock with regard to process communication. This analysis is the first layer of a full verification suite ranging from formal software verification of various correctness aspects to hardware-in-the-loop tests of the complete system.

The strong relation between occam and CSP as well as previous experiences with CSP and the model checker FDR suggested the following procedure:

- derive a CSP abstraction from the occam (pseudo) code

* BISS, Bremer Institute for Safe Systems, EMail bb@informatik.uni-bremen.de
** Daimler-Benz Aerospace, Bremen
*** JP Software-Consulting, Bremen, EMail jp@informatik.uni-bremen.de
† University of Bremen, EMail shi@informatik.uni-bremen.de

- use FDR to check that the abstraction is a refinement of a deadlock free process DF.

First studies soon showed that though in essence a sound approach it could not be used without further considerations. The main obstacle was the size of the software to be analyzed. Furthermore, the result "system is free of deadlocks" is too coarse to be of practical value. Instead more refined proof obligations like "none of the processes in the system will continuously block communication on their relevant input channels" should be investigated. A true abstraction catching all details of the given code would be by far too large to be submitted to the model checker in one piece: the state space would explode. This report describes our methodology how to overcome these problems by using abstraction, the compositional theory of CSP, algebraic transformations, generic theories, and last but not least refinement checks with the tool FDR in combination. The approach is illustrated by examples from the verification of the Fault Management Layer (FML) of the system which is responsible for all aspects of fault-tolerance in the system. In the following section an overview of the FML is given together with a more detailed description of the goal of the analysis. Section 3 contains information about the methods employed for the verification and their respective rôle. The technical results are summarized in Section 4, followed by a collection of experiences and goals for future work in the conclusion.

2 Technical Background: The Fault Management Layer

2.1 The Fault-Tolerant Computer

The FML software to be analyzed is part of a fault tolerant computer to be used in the International Space Station (ISS) to control space station assembly, reboost operations for flight control, and data management for experiments carried out in the space station. In order to understand the rôle of the FML an overview of the overall structure of this fault-tolerant computer is necessary.

The overall architecture consists of up to four communicating lanes, each providing services for the applications. Each of these lanes is structured into an application services layer (ASS), a fault management layer (FML), and the avionics interface (AVI). The ASS resides on the application layer board and contains table driven services for the application software and the operating system. The AVI is in charge of the MIL Bus protocol handling according to predefined timing slot allocations. These are defined in an input/output table. The FML is inserted between ASS and AVI, and is responsible for the detection of data failures and the isolation and reintegration of lanes. In each lane, the application layer plus ASS runs on a customized Matra board using a SPARC CPU. Both FML and AVI reside on separate transputer boards. The lanes communicate only at FML level using the transputer links. Each FML uses up to three links for communication with the other lanes, and one link (link 0) for communication with the AVI. Data transfer with the ASS is performed using a VME interface. See Figure 1 for the architecture of a full four-lane system.

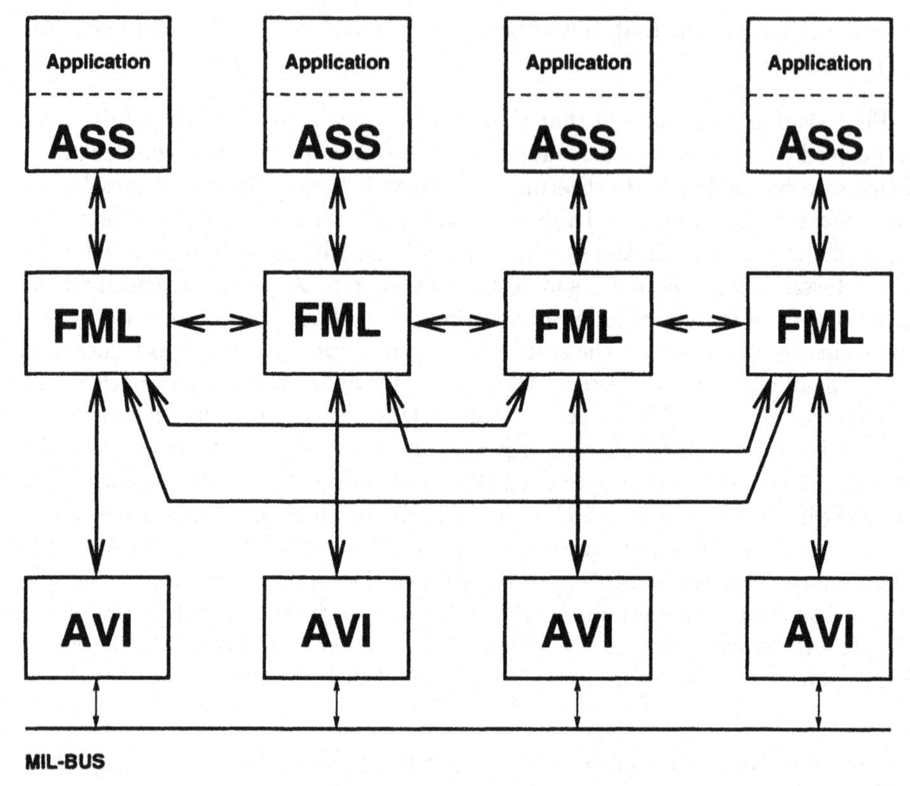

Figure 1. FTC architecure

The function of the FML is twofold: First, it provides the interface between the ASS and AVI of one lane, transferring messages from AVI to ASS and vice versa. Second, it performs the data transfer between lanes thus allowing communication between the fault management layers of all lanes.

The main task of the FML software is the fault management based on these communications. This task consists of error detection, error correction, lane isolation (in the case of an unrecoverable error), and lane reintegration.

Error detection is essentially based on a two round Byzantine distribution schema [9] where data are communicated between FMLs and voted using various specialized voters. The aim is to ensure that (1) all ASS instances of non-faulty lanes get identical messages from FML, (2) all AVI instances of non-faulty lanes get identical messages from FML, (3) for data calculated by all lanes (congruent source messages) all non-faulty lanes get the correct(ed) message, (4) for data calculated by one lane (single source messages) all non-faulty lanes get the correct(ed) message if the originator is not faulty. The implemented design allows detection of one Byzantine or deterministic fault in a four-lane system and recognition of a deterministic fault in a three-lane system.

2.2 FML Structure

The software architecture of the FML in one lane consists of a number of processes which communicate over a set of channels and jointly use a global memory and a separate global buffer. Figure 2 presents a simplified overview of this architecture. Each of the main processes itself is built from smaller subprocesses not shown in the figure, which communicate over local channels.

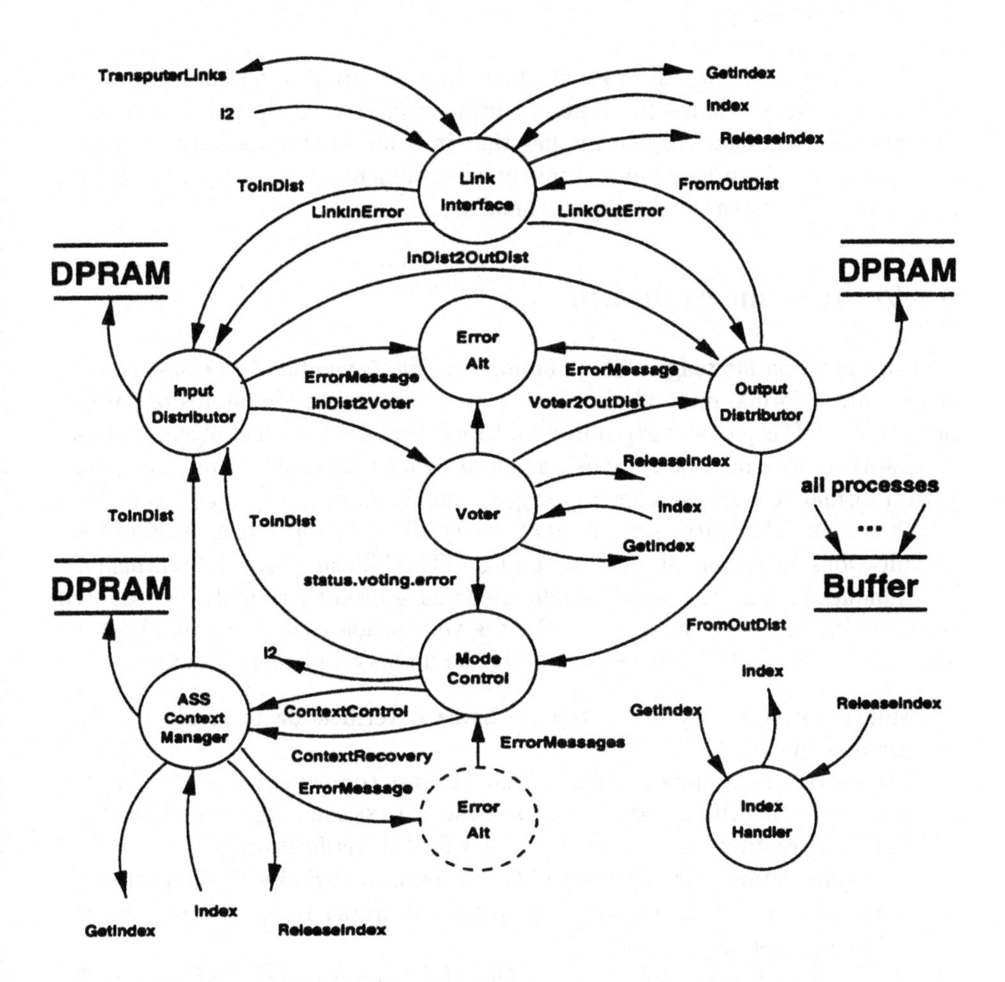

Figure 2. FML Processes

2.3 Deadlock Analysis

The overall goal of the analysis described in this article is to check whether none of the communicating system of processes that forms the FML software continuously blocks the communication on the vital channels. Precisely speaking, the following verification goal had to be investigated:

> In an environment that always accepts outputs from the system but may or may not refuse to provide inputs, the following assertion holds: Whenever the system reaches a stable state where all communications are blocked, all processes reading from vital channels are ready for input on these channels.

"Vital channels" are all those channels from Figure 2 which are still visible in Figure 3 below. Since the input transputer links used by the environment are vital, the verification goal implies that in a blocking situation the system is always ready for a new input from the environment, so this implies deadlock freedom of the system in the conventional sense.

3 Verification Approach

The specification language CSP (*Communicating Sequential Processes*) is associated with a formal method allowing to verify properties of systems of parallel processes. CSP is particularly suited for supporting the formal analysis of occam programs since it may be regarded as an abstract version of occam, associated with a formal semantics, allowing to give unambiguous interpretations of CSP specifications. The mathematical proof theory allows to verify properties of CSP specifications by means of logic reasoning. The CSP language, its mathematical foundations and its possible applications have been thoroughly investigated since the late sixties (see [7, 6, 5]). For the verification goal described above we apply five verification techniques that will be discussed in this section:

1. Model checking is used for the mechanized verification of small-size CSP components.
2. Abstraction is applied to "lift" occam process components to CSP components reflecting the essential aspects of the process communication behaviour while abstracting from details irrelevant for the verification goal.
3. The compositional proof theory of CSP is applied to derive global properties of the complete FML system from the local properties established for the isolated components.
4. Generic theories are applied to reduce the amount of proof obligations by showing that all process instances of a certain class inherit certain properties.
5. Algebraic reasoning is applied to transform CSP process specifications into equivalent ones better suited for the model checker.

3.1 Model-Checking with FDR

FDR (*Failures-Divergence Refinement*) is a model-checking tool for state machines, with foundations in the theory of concurrency based upon CSP. Except for the ability to check determinism [11], primarily for checking security properties, its method of establishing whether a property holds is to test for the refinement (in one of the semantic models of CSP) of a transition system capturing the required specification by the candidate machine. The main ideas behind FDR are presented in [10].

The notion of refinement is a particularly useful concept in many forms of engineering activity. If we can establish a relation between components of a system which captures the fact that one satisfies at least the same conditions as another, then we may replace a worse component by a better one without degrading the properties of the system. Refinement relations can be defined for systems described in CSP in several ways, depending on the semantic model of the language which is used. The relation to be used for goals as described here is *Failures Refinement* $P \sqsubseteq_F Q$, which is defined by the requirement that the failures (i. e., pairs of traces and associated refusal sets) of a refining process should be included in those of the refined process.

The FDR tool is well-established for verification purposes similar to the one described here, see [1].

3.2 Abstraction

For the analysis of deadlock freedom it is unnecessary to inspect every detail of the occam code, since only a subset of the statements of this code influences the communication behaviour. It is therefore possible to generate a CSP specification which represents an abstracted version of the original occam process P and shows only that amount of detail which is relevant for its communication behaviour. We call such a CSP specification $\mathcal{A}(P)$ a *valid abstraction* of the corresponding occam process P, if

> *Whenever P runs into a deadlock situation this implies that $\mathcal{A}(P)$ may run into a deadlock situation, too.*

If a valid abstraction $\mathcal{A}(P)$ is available, we only need to analyse $\mathcal{A}(P)$ instead of P: If $\mathcal{A}(P)$ is free of deadlocks, the same must hold for P.

The basic approach to construct valid abstractions uses four techniques in the translation from occam to CSP:

1. Every sequential algorithm whose results do not influence communication behaviour is deleted.
2. Each occam channel protocol is reduced to the set of values influencing the communication behaviour in a distinctive way.
3. Every occam IF-construct `IF condition THEN P ELSE Q` may be replaced by the equivalent if-construct in CSP or by the internal choice operator of CSP yielding $P \sqcap Q$.
4. If valid abstractions $\mathcal{A}(P)$, $\mathcal{A}(Q)$ for two processes P and Q are available and these interpretations use the same abstractions on their communication interface I, then $\mathcal{A}(P) \underset{I}{\|} \mathcal{A}(Q)$ is a valid abstract interpretation of P and Q

operating in parallel. Using this technique, larger abstractions can be build from existing ones.

The following table gives an overview of the translation between occam and CSP constructs.

occam-construct	**CSP-construct**
IF_THEN_ELSE	$\sqcap$ or if_then_else
PAR (PRIPAR)	$\vert\vert\vert$ or $\vert\vert$
ALT (PRIALT)	$\square$
WHILE	$P = \cdots \rightarrow P$ or $P =$ if b then $\cdots$ else SKIP
c?x	c or c?x
c!a	c or c!a
SEQ	; or $\rightarrow$

To show the applications of these techniques, we give an example including two parallel processes P and Q that communicate through the cannels a, b, and c, and have a common variable mc initialized to 0. At first, we present the occam definitions of P and Q.

P:

```
WHILE TRUE
  SEQ
    IF
      mc = 1
        a ! TRUE
      TRUE
        b ! FALSE
    c ? mc
```

Q:

```
WHILE TRUE
  SEQ
    IF
      mc = 1
        a ? x
        mc := 0
      TRUE
        b ? x
        mc := 1
    c ! mc
```

In the first abstraction, the occam IF-construct is simply converted to CSP internal choice $\sqcap$. Unfortunately, $S1$ is obviously not deadlock free, which can also be proved with FDR.

Abstraction 1:

$$P = a \rightarrow c \rightarrow P \sqcap b \rightarrow c \rightarrow P$$
$$Q = a \rightarrow c \rightarrow Q \sqcap b \rightarrow c \rightarrow Q$$
$$S1 = P \underset{\{c,a,b\}}{\parallel} Q$$

Since $S1$ is a valid abstraction of the occam process, two cases are possible: Either the occam process contains a deadlock or we have introduced too high a degree of nondeterminism in the construction of $S1$. Since we intuitively assume that the occam process should turn out to be deadlock free, we try to find another valid abstraction which is more deterministic than $S1$.

In the following abstraction, a new CSP process MC is introduced, which simulates the common variable mc of the occam process. Usually, two operations, *read* and *write*, can be applied to a variable. The channels *rp_mc*, *rq_mc* and *w_mc* implement these operations on the variable *mc*. The occam IF-construct is now interpreted as a CSP if-construct. It can be proved that $S2$ is deadlock free, which implies that the occam process ist deadlock free as well.

Abstraction 2:

$$
\begin{aligned}
MC &= MC1(0) \\
MC1(x) &= rp\_mc!x \rightarrow MC1(x) \\
&\quad [\,]\ rq\_mc!x \rightarrow MC1(x) \\
&\quad [\,]\ wq\_mc?y \rightarrow MC1(y)
\end{aligned}
$$

$$
\begin{aligned}
P &= rp\_mc?mc \rightarrow \\
&\quad \text{if } (mc == 1) \text{ then } a \rightarrow c \rightarrow P \\
&\quad \text{else } b \rightarrow c \rightarrow P \\
Q &= rq\_mc?mc \rightarrow \\
&\quad \text{if } (mc == 1) \text{ then } a \rightarrow wq\_mc!0 \rightarrow c \rightarrow Q \\
&\quad \text{else } b \rightarrow wq\_mc!1 \rightarrow c \rightarrow Q \\
S2 &= (P \underset{\{c,a,b\}}{\|} Q) \underset{\{|rp\_mc,rq\_mc,wq\_mc|\}}{\|} MC
\end{aligned}
$$

During generation of a CSP specification of an occam process, two important aspects have to be considered. On the one hand, the generated CSP specification should be a valid abstraction of the occam process; on the other hand, as many details which do not influence the communication behaviour of the occam process as possible should be omitted, in order to reduce the size of the state space of the CSP specification far enough to allow model-checking with FDR. This task requires considerable expertise from the person developing the abstraction, but large portions of the work can be automated using the translation heuristics described above.

3.3 Compositionality

CSP provides several high-level operators, such as parallel operator ($\|$) and interleaving operator ($|||$), that allow to construct new processes from existing ones. A crucial property of CSP is the fact that refinement is preserved under compositions involving these operators:

If $Q_i \sqsubseteq_F P_i$ for $i : 0..n$ and ω is an n-ary operator, then $\omega(Q_0, \ldots, Q_n) \sqsubseteq_F \omega(P_0, \ldots, P_n)$ holds.

This fact will be exploited for our analysis to partition the system state spaces that are too large to be represented by a single transition graph for model checking: If deadlock freedom of $\omega(P_0, \ldots, P_n)$ cannot be established because of the problem size, find simpler processes $Q_0, \ldots, Q_n$ such that $Q_i \sqsubseteq_F Q_i$ and $\omega(Q_0, \ldots, Q_n)$ is deadlock free. If this property can be established, compositionality combined with refinement implies the deadlock freedom of $\omega(P_0, \ldots, P_n)$ as well.

For our purpose, the compositionality of the parallel or interleaving operator is applied at two levels.

In order to proof that the overall system consisting of 8 main processes running in parallel is deadlock free we construct for each process P_i a valid abstraction $\mathcal{A}(P_i)$ and show that the parallel composition of these is deadlock free. Since even the system consisting of the abstractions is too large to be dealt with in the FDR model checker we find simpler processes Q_i such that each $\mathcal{A}(P_i)$ is a refinement of the corresponding Q_i. The Q_i are checked for deadlock individually; since they are deadlock free the refinement property ensures that the $\mathcal{A}(P_i)$ are deadlock free (internally), too. The essential proof now has to show that the parallel composition of the Q_i is deadlock free, which via the compositionality argument yields deadlock freedom of the system of $\mathcal{A}(P_i)$, and via abstraction and compositionality finally ensures the desired property of the original system.

In the next section we will introduce the Q_is and prove that the parallel composition

$$(Q_1 || \dots || Q_8)$$

of the simplified processes is deadlock free.

3.4 Generic Theories

To increase the efficiency of the verification process, we use generic theories stating properties of process classes that are inherited by each instance of the class. Concrete occam processes can be identified as refinements of certain class instances. Since the properties established in the generic theories are preserved under refinement, we can conclude that the occam process inherits the desired property as well.

To give an example, the following theorem states that a system which is deadlock free will still have this property if *concentrators or multiplexers* are added to its output channels, provided that the following conditions hold:

- Each concentrator or multiplexer operates in strict alternation between the following two phases:
  1. Output phase: produce a number of outputs on a (sub-)set of pre-defined output channels. This number may be zero, but must be limited by a constant *max*. Then start the input phase.
  2. Input phase: wait for an arbitrary input without blocking any input channel. After having received exactly one input, go back to the output phase.
- The environment never blocks an output channel of the concentrator or multiplexer.

Theorem 3.1. *Let MUX be a concentrator/multiplexer process defined as*

$$MUX =_{df} MUXOUT(max, IN, OUT)$$

$$\begin{aligned} MUXOUT(n, IN, OUT) =_{df} & \ \mathbf{if}\ (n = 0) \\ & \ \mathbf{then}\ MUXIN(IN, OUT) \\ & \ \mathbf{else}\ (MUXIN(IN, OUT) \\ & \qquad \sqcap \\ & \qquad (\sqcap_{y:OUT}\ y \\ & \qquad \to MUXOUT(n-1, IN, OUT))) \end{aligned}$$

$$MUXIN(IN, OUT) =_{df} \Box_{x:IN}\ x \to MUX$$

for a fixed max. Let X be a process which is deadlock free in the context $RUN(\Sigma)$[1]
and has a (sub-)set of outputs into IN. Let CON be the context

$$CON =_{df} RUN(OUT) \mid\mid\mid CHAOS(\Sigma - (\alpha(X) \cup IN \cup OUT))$$

Then

1. $(RUN(IN) \mid\mid\mid CHAOS(\Sigma - IN)) \sqsubseteq_F (MUX \underset{OUT}{\parallel} CON) \setminus OUT$ *holds.*
2. $(X \underset{IN}{\parallel} MUX) \underset{OUT}{\parallel} CON$ *is also deadlock free.*

This theorem is generic in the interfaces IN, OUT and in the maximum value max of consecutive outputs. It turns out that several of the processes shown in Figure 2 are refinements of the above multiplexer/concentrator process instantiated with different interfaces and maximum numbers.

3.5 Algebraic Reasoning

CSP possesses a proof theory which provides algebraic laws for the transformation of CSP processes into equivalent ones. Specifically, deadlock freedom is preserved under such term rewriting laws. Algebraic manipulations are useful to simplify process terms and reduce the state spaces of processes before model checking. Especially, after abstracting an occam process into a CSP specification, there are often situations in which several different occam cases are collapsed into one CSP case.

4 Verification Results: Deadlock Freedom of the FML

In this section we will present some results to prove that the FML of each isolated lane fulfills the verification goal stated in Section 2. The main result is stated in the following theorem.

[1] Σ denotes the set of all communications possible in the system, i.e. the union of all alphabets of subprocesses

Theorem 4.1. *In every context which never blocks outputs on transputer links, outputs to the ASS layer and outputs to the* AVI *layer, the following property holds:*

Whenever the FML *system reaches a stable state where no communications are possible, all processes reading from vital channels are ready for input on these channels.*

At first we will present two lemmas providing useful simplifications by structuring the FML of a lane into a number of sub-systems $S_1, S_2, \ldots, S_n$, such that the following conditions hold:

- S_{i+1} is a sub-system of S_i in the sense that there exist processes P_{i+1} such that $(S_{i+1} \parallel P_{i+1}) = S_i$.
- Let I_{i+1} be the interface between S_{i+1} and P_{i+1}. Then, if S_{i+1} is deadlock free in context CON_{i+1}, S_i will also be deadlock free in context CON_i.

Lemma 4.2. *Let S_1 be the* FML *sub-system of a lane consisting of all* FML *processes but* Index Handler *that is* FML $= (S_1 \parallel$ Index Handler$)$. *Define interface and context*

$$I_1 =_{df} \{\!|GetIndex[k], Index[k], ReleaseIndex[\ell] \mid k : 0..16, \ell : 0..7|\!\}$$

$$CON_1 =_{df} RUN(I_1)$$

Then, if $(S_1 \underset{I_1}{\parallel} CON_1)$ is free of deadlocks and no reader process permanently blocks its input channels, the same holds for the full FML *of one lane.*

According to this lemma, we need not consider the process Index Handler in proving the deadlock freedom of the whole system. Another lemma providing a useful simplification for the proof of Theorem 4.1 shows the possibility to delete the process Error ALT from the system without lossing the correctness of the theorem:

Lemma 4.3. *Let S_2 be the sub-system of S_1 consisting of all S_1-processes but* Error ALT *that is $S_1 = (S_2 \parallel$ Error ALT$)$. Define interfaces and context*

$$I_2 =_{df} I_1 \cup I_{21} \cup I_{22}$$
$$I_{21} =_{df} \{\!|ErrorMessages[k] | k : 0..6|\!\}$$
$$I_{22} =_{df} \{\!|AllErrorMessages|\!\}$$

$$CON_2 =_{df} (RUN(I_1 \cup I_{21}) \mid\mid\mid CHAOS(I_{22}))$$

Then, if $(S_2 \underset{I_2}{\parallel} CON_2)$ is free of deadlocks and no reader process permanently blocks its input channels, the same holds for $(S_1 \underset{I_1}{\parallel} CON_1)$.

The proofs of these lemmas follow from generic theories similar to the one described in the previous section.

There are two types of FML process behaviours regarding channel input:

- **Unconditional Input:** The process will always accept a new input on the channel, possibly after a bounded number of non-blocking internal communications. The acceptance of a new input does *not* depend on successful outputs to other channels prior to the next input. Unconditional input is provided whenever the corresponding process abstraction behaves as RUN on the input channel.
- **Bounded Conditional Input:** *Provided that the environment will not block process outputs*, the process will always accept a new input on the channel, possibly after a bounded number of non-blocking internal and external communications. This type of input behaviour is guaranteed whenever the corresponding abstraction behaves as $MUXOUT(max, IN, OUT)$ on its input channels IN and output channels OUT.

The occam processes Input Distributor and Output Distributor have only unconditional inputs. A valid abstraction of the occam process Input Distributor for example is a failures refinement of the following process:

$$(RUN(I_1) ||| CHAOS(I_2))$$

where

$$I_1 =_{df} \{| ToInDist[i], LinkInError[j] \mid i : 0..6, j = 0..4 |\}$$
$$I_2 =_{df} \{| InDist2Voter[i], InDist2OutDist \mid i : 0..3 |\}$$

All channels in I_1 are unconditional.

All other occam processes are failures refinements of some multiplexer/concentrator. ASS Context Manager, for instance, refines the following process:

$$MUXOUT(10, \{Context.recovery, Context.control\}, \{ToInDist[6]\}).$$

$Context.recovery$ and $Context.control$ are bounded conditional inputs. The similar processes are Voter, Link Interface, ASS Interface and Mode Control.

Proof sketch of Theorem 4.1.
The two preceding lemmas can be applied to conclude that the remaining channels and processes that are still to be analysed with respect to deadlock freedom are the ones depicted in Figure 3, where unconditional input is depicted by a dashed arrow and bounded conditional input is marked by a solid arrow, labelled by the channel name.

Analysis of the data flow diagram and the process behaviours regarding channel input shows that every cycle in the diagram contains at least one channel where the corresponding reader process provides unconditional input. Furthermore, every process provides at least bounded conditional input. As a consequence, a blocking situation on a cycle can never occur, as long as a process is still willing to output. Therefore a stable state without active communications implies that all the processes shown in Figure 3 are waiting for new inputs. These input channels include the set on vital channels. This completes the proof sketch of Theorem 4.1 (detailed proofs can be found in [3]).
□

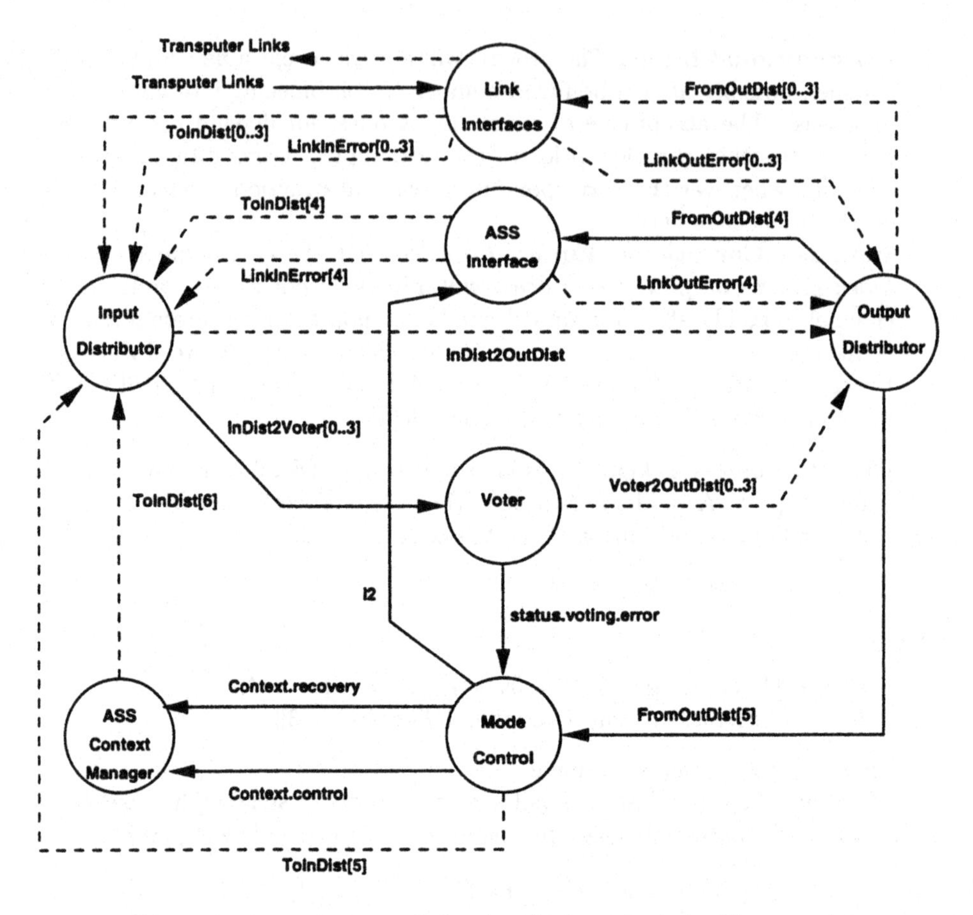

Figure 3. Data flow graph for deadlock analysis in Theorem 4.1

5 Conclusion

5.1 Experiences

The overall experience with this use of CSP specification and model-checking for the verification of realistic occam software is very positive. Despite the size and complexity of the object to be analyzed it was possible to use the approach by applying abstract interpretation and a suitable modularization for splitting the task into manageable subtasks. The result is a low cost/high quality verification of an important aspect of a real-world project. The following points justify this claim:

Real-world project: the collection of all relevant parts of the code accumulates to about 11,600 lines of occam code for FML. For the AVI layer

which has about the same size, a similar verification was performed.
Low cost: The effort for achieving the same verification results by means of conventional reviewing and testing techniques would have been at least four times the effort invested by the team applying our approach. At the same time we doubt whether the degree of trustworthiness achieved by the method described here would be reached at all using conventional techniques.
High quality: The verification of AVI and FML uncovered a number of deadlock situations that had neither been found nor could be retraced by testing.

5.2 Future Work

The main emphasis on our future work related to verification projects similar to the one described here is put on the following goals:

- Improve the degree of automation for the abstraction process occam to CSP.
- Improve the tool support for the proof of generic theories. This will be performed in the context of the UniForM project [13], based on the HOL/Isabelle tools [8, 12].
- Develop efficient verification suites using series of verification and test subgoals to cope with the complexity of the full verification task.

Acknowledgements. We would like to thank Rachel Cardell-Oliver for her extremely helpful suggestions related to the use of generic theories. Furthermore, we would like to thank the members of the UniForM project for providing a framework for the scientific aspects of this work. Discussions with the colleagues in the project helped to focus on essential points. Last but not least, we are grateful for the support of the development team at DASA Bremen, who were always ready to clarify details of the software and the overall design of FML. This work has been partially supported by the German Ministry of Education and Research (BMBF) as part of the project UniForM under grant No. FKZ 01 IS 521 B2.

References

1. N. A. Brock and D. M. Jackson: Formal Verification of a Fault Tolerant Computer. In *Proceedings of 1992 Digital Avionics Systems Conference.* (1992)
2. B. Buth and J. Peleska: *Daimler-Benz Aerospace - Project DMS-R, FTC Development - Verification of Avionics Interface AVI.* Technical Report, JP Software-Consulting, (1996).
3. B. Buth, J. Peleska and H. Shi: *Daimler-Benz Aerospace - Project DMS-R, FTC Development - Fault Management Layer (FML): Verification of Deadlock Freedom.* Technical Report, JP Software-Consulting, (1996).
4. Daimler-Benz Aerospace: *DMS-R FTC Detailed Design Document Volume 3 (FML Software)*
5. J. Davies: *Specification and Proof in Real-Time CSP.* Cambridge University Press (1993).

6. Formal Systemes: *Failures Divergence Refinement FDR2* Preliminary Manual. Formal Systems (Europe) Lts (1995).
7. C. A. R. Hoare: *Communicating Sequential Processes.* Prentice-Hall Internationaal (1985).
8. Kolyang, C. Lüth and B. Wolff: Generic Interfaces for Formal Development Support Tools. To appear in *Proceedings of the International Workshop for Tool Support in Verification and Validation.* LNCS (1997).
9. L. Lamport, R. Shostak, and M. Pease, *The Byzantine Generals Problem*, In: ACM Transactions on Programming Languages and Systems, Vol.4, Nr. 3, (1982)
10. A. W. Roscoe: *Model-Checking CSP.* In: A Classical Mind, Eassys in Honour of C.A.R. Hoare. Prentice-Hall Internationaal (1994).
11. A. W. Roscoe: *CSP and determinism in security modelling.* In: IEEE Symposium of Security and Privacy, (1995).
12. H. Tej and B. Wolff: A Corrected Failures-Divergence Model for CSP in Isabelle/HOL. To appear in *Proceedings of the Formal Methods Europe*, LNCS (1997).
13. B. Krieg-Brückner, J. Peleska, E.-R. Olderog, D. Balzer and A. Baer. Universal Formal Methods Workbench. In U. Grote and G. Wolf, editors, *Statusseminar Softwaretechnologie des BMBF, March 1996, Berlin*, Deutsche Forschungsanstanlt für Luft- und Raumfahrt, Berlin, 1996.

From Sequential to Multi-Threaded Java: An Event-Based Operational Semantics

Pietro Cenciarelli, Alexander Knapp, Bernhard Reus, and Martin Wirsing

Ludwig–Maximilians–Universität München
{cenciare,knapp,reus,wirsing}@informatik.uni-muenchen.de

Abstract A structural operational semantics of a non trivial sublanguage of Java is presented. This language includes dynamic creation of objects, blocks, and synchronization of threads. First we introduce a simple operational description of the sequential part of the language, where the memory is treated as an algebra with suitably axiomatized operations. Then, the interaction between threads via a shared memory is described in terms of structures, called "event spaces," whose well-formedness conditions formalize directly the rules given in the Java language specification. Event spaces are included in the operational judgements to develop the semantics of the full multi-threaded sublanguage, which is shown to extend the one for sequential Java conservatively. The result allows sequential programs to be reasoned about in a simplified computational framework without loss of generality.

1 Introduction

Java is an object-oriented programming language which offers a simple and tightly integrated support for concurrent programming. A concurrent program consists of multiple tasks that are or behave as if they were executed all at the same time. In Java tasks are implemented using *threads* (short for "threads of execution"), which are sequences of instructions that run independently within the encompassing program. Informal descriptions of this model can be found in several books (see e.g. [1], [4]). A precise description is given in the Java language specification [3].

This paper presents a formal semantics of a non-trivial sublanguage of Java which includes dynamic creation of objects, blocks, and synchronization of threads. The semantics is given in the style of Plotkin's structural operational semantics (SOS) [7]. This technique has been used e.g. for the semantics of SML [6] and earlier for ADA [5].

The thread model, and in particular the interaction between threads via shared memory, is described here in terms of structures called *event spaces.* These correspond roughly to *configurations* in Winskel's *event structures* [8], which are used for denotational semantics of concurrent languages. By using similar structures in operational semantics, a technique which is new, to our knowledge, we obtain an abstract "declarative" description of the Java thread model which is an exact formal counterpart of the informal language description [3] and which leaves maximal freedom for different implementations.

We present the semantics in two steps: First we introduce a simple operational description of the sequential part of the language, where the memory is treated as an algebra with suitably axiomatized operations. Then the thread model is developed and shown to be a conservative extension of sequential Java. For reasons of space we consider in this paper only the following subset of the Java language: access to local variables and instance variables, assignment, class instance creation, blocks, local variable declaration, threads and synchronization. We cut out, among other things, class declaration, method call and exceptions. However, what we include (whose BNF is given in Appendix A) is enough to describe the thread model in full generality.

Closely related work is the formal semantics of a sublanguage of Java in [2]. This paper focuses on the Java type system and develops an operational semantics for a *sequential* sublanguage of Java only. Therefore our semantics of threads is complementary.

The paper is organized as follows: In Section 2 the semantics of single-threaded (sequential) Java programs is given. Section 3 introduces the notion of event space and sets the rules for a correct interaction between main memory and threads. Section 4 describes the refinement of single-threaded Java to multi-threaded Java. The paper concludes with some remarks and future developments.

2 Sequential Java

The operational semantics of sequential Java is quite conventional. We give an overview by means of an example.

```
class Point {
  int x, y;

  Point() { }
}

class Sample {
  public static void main(String[] argv) {
    Point p = new Point();

    p.x = 1; p.y = 2;
    p.x = p.y;
  }
}
```

The sample program consists of two *class declarations* of `Point` and `Sample`. The *class* `Point` has two *attributes* `x` and `y`, the coordinates of a point, and provides only the standard *constructor* `Point()` that is called upon creation of a new *instance* (*object*) of class `Point`. The second class `Sample` has a single *method* `main(String[] argv)` (and a hidden standard constructor).

Programs start and end with the execution of the `main()` method, which must be defined in some (and only one) class. In our example this method creates a new instance of class `Point` by executing the expression `new Point()`; a *reference* to this object is assigned to the *local variable* `p`. Our program proceeds by assigning 1 and 2 to the coordinates of the object referenced by `p`, and then by setting the value of the `x` coordinate to the value of `y`.

Since the scope of local variables is determined by the block structure of the program, we keep them in a *stack* which grows and shrinks upon entering and exiting blocks. On the other hand, objects are permanent entities which survive the blocks in which they are created; therefore the collection of their *instance variables* (containing the values of their attributes) is kept in a separate structure: the *store*. Intuitively, stores can be thought of as mapping left-values (addresses of instance variables) to right-values (the primitive data of Java). Later on we shall see how different threads interact through the store. A formal description of stacks, stores and the configurations of the operational semantics is given below.

Stores. We use a semantic domain *Store* for abstract stores, a domain *Obj* for abstract objects and two domains *LVal* and *RVal* for left and right-values. Since references to objects can be assigned to variables in Java, we stipulate that $Obj \subseteq RVal$. Stores are axiomatized below by means of the following semantic functions:

$$\begin{aligned} new_C &: Store \rightarrow Obj \times Store \\ upd &: LVal \times RVal \times Store \rightarrow Store \\ lval &: Obj \times Identifier \times Store \rightharpoonup LVal \\ rval &: LVal \times Store \rightharpoonup RVal \\ this &: Store \rightarrow Obj \end{aligned}$$

where functions in the family *new* are indexed by class types $C \in ClassType$. As we do not deal with class declarations here, we assume that a function new_C "knows" how to initialize the instance variables of a newly created object of class C. In particular, we assume that initial values are returned by a family of partial functions

$$init_C : Identifier \rightharpoonup RVal$$

whose domain is the set of attributes of C.

In our example the evaluation of `new Point()` produces the object $o_{\mathtt{p}}$ of $new_{\mathtt{Point}}(\mu) = (o_{\mathtt{p}}, \mu')$ where μ is the current store. A new store μ' is also produced with two new left-values $l_{\mathtt{p.x}}$ and $l_{\mathtt{p.y}}$ suitably initialized.

The function *upd* updates a store. The function *lval* finds in the store the location pointed by expressions like `p.x`, where the evaluation of `p` yields an object in in *Obj*. In particular, as shown by the axioms below, $lval(o, i, \mu)$ is defined for those $i \in Identifier$ that are attributes of the class of o. The function *rval* gets the right-value associated in a store with a given left-value, and *this* gets the object whose code is being currently executed.

In the following, object are ranged over by the metavariable o, left values by l, right values by v and stores by μ. All these can be variously decorated. We write $\mu[l \mapsto v]$ and $\mu(l)$ for $upd(l, v, \mu)$ and $rval(l, \mu)$ respectively.

Abstract stores are axiomatized by using a unary predicate $\downarrow$ (written in postfix notation) and a binary predicate $\preceq$ (in infix notation). The meaning of $e\downarrow$ is that e is defined, i.e. it denotes a value, while $e_1 \preceq e_2$ means that if e_1 is defined, then so is e_2 and they denote the same value. By $e_1 \simeq e_2$ we mean that both $e_1 \preceq e_2$ and $e_2 \preceq e_1$ hold, and by $e_1 = e_2$ we mean that both $e_1 \preceq e_2$ and $e_1\downarrow$ hold. We write $\uparrow$ the negation of $\downarrow$. The axioms for abstract stores are listed in Table 1.

$$\begin{array}{rl}
\mu(l) \preceq \mu'(l) & (new_C(\mu) = (o, \mu')) \\
lval(o, i, \mu)\uparrow & (new_C(\mu) = (o, \mu')) \\
init_C(i) \preceq \mu'(lval(o, i, \mu')) & (new_C(\mu) = (o, \mu'))
\end{array}$$

$$\begin{array}{rl}
\mu[l \mapsto v](l) = v & \\
\mu[l' \mapsto v](l) \simeq \mu(l) & (l \neq l') \\
\mu[l \mapsto v'][l \mapsto v] = \mu[l \mapsto v] & \\
\mu[l' \mapsto v'][l \mapsto v] = \mu[l \mapsto v][l' \mapsto v'] & (l \neq l') \\
\mu[l \mapsto \mu(l)] \preceq \mu &
\end{array}$$

Table 1. Axiomatization of abstract stores

Environment stacks. *Environments* are pairs (I, ρ) where $I \subseteq \mathit{Identifier}$ is a *source* of identifiers and ρ is a partial function from I to right values:

$$Env = \textstyle\sum_{I \subseteq \mathit{Identifier}} I \rightharpoonup RVal\ .$$

Intuitively, I contains the local variables of a block. By abuse of notation, we write ρ for an environment (I, ρ) and indicate with $src(\rho)$ its source I. As usual, $\rho[i \mapsto v](j) = v$ if $i = j$ and $\rho[i \mapsto v](j) \simeq \rho(j)$ otherwise.

Let *S-Stack* be the domain of stacks of environments, ranged over by the metavariable σ. The empty environment and the empty stack are written respectively $\rho_\emptyset$ and $\sigma_\emptyset$. The operation $push : Env \times \textit{S-Stack} \rightarrow \textit{S-Stack}$ is the usual one on stacks. All other stack operations we use are recursively defined in Table 2.

In our example, the bindings of the block in `main()` yield the stack $push(\rho_\emptyset[\mathtt{p} \mapsto o_\mathtt{p}], \sigma_\emptyset)$.

Terms. The operational semantics of single-threaded Java works on a set *S-Term* of *single-threaded abstract terms.* We let the metavariable t range over *S-Term*. To each syntactic category of Java we associate a homonymous category of abstract terms. The well-typed terms of Java are mapped to abstract terms of corresponding category by a translation $(\_)^\circ$, which we leave implicit when no

$$\sigma[i = v] = \begin{cases} push(\rho[i \mapsto v], \sigma') & \text{if } \sigma = push(\rho, \sigma') \text{ and } i \in src(\rho) \\ undefined & \text{otherwise;} \end{cases}$$

$$\sigma[i \mapsto v] = \begin{cases} push(\rho[i \mapsto v], \sigma') & \text{if } \sigma = push(\rho, \sigma') \text{ and } i \in src(\rho) \\ push(\rho, \sigma'[i \mapsto v]) & \text{if } \sigma = push(\rho, \sigma') \text{ and } i \notin src(\rho) \\ undefined & \text{otherwise;} \end{cases}$$

$$\sigma(i) = \begin{cases} \rho(i) & \text{if } \sigma = push(\rho, \sigma') \text{ and } i \in src(\rho) \\ \sigma'(i) & \text{if } \sigma = push(\rho, \sigma') \text{ and } i \notin src(\rho) \\ undefined & \text{otherwise.} \end{cases}$$

Table 2. Operations on stacks

confusion arises. Abstract blocks are terms of the form $\{\, t \,\}_\rho$ where the environment ρ contains the local variables of the block. In our example, we have

$$\{\ \texttt{Point p = new Point(); p.x = 1; p.y = 2; p.x = p.y}\ \}^\circ =$$
$$\{\ \texttt{Point p} = \texttt{new Point( ); p.x} = 1;\ \texttt{p.y} = 2;\ \texttt{p.x} = \texttt{p.y};\ \}_{\rho_\emptyset[\texttt{p} \mapsto \texttt{null}]}\ .$$

Configurations and Rules. We call *configurations* elements of the domain *S-Term* × *S-Stack* × *Store*. We let γ range over this domain. The operational semantics is the binary relation $\rightarrow$ on configurations inductively defined by the rules that follow. Related pairs of configurations are written $\gamma_1 \rightarrow \gamma_2$ and are called *operational judgements*.

In the rule schemes (Tables 3–5), the metavariables (variously decorated) range as follows: $i \in$ *Identifier*, $k \in$ *Identifier* ∪ *LVal*, $e \in$ *Expression*, $\tau \in$ *Type*, $d \in$ *VariableDeclarator*, $D \in$ *VariableDeclarator*$^+$, $s \in$ *BlockStatement*, $S \in$ *BlockStatement** and $q \in$ *Block* (see Appendix A).

We understand statements, among which local variable declarations, as computations over the one-element domain $\{*\}$. Then, consistently with the type of the relation $\rightarrow$, we write $s, \sigma_1, \mu_1 \rightarrow \sigma_2, \mu_2$ for $s, \sigma_1, \mu_1 \rightarrow *, \sigma_2, \mu_2$.

Stacks and stores are omitted when not relevant; that is, we may write:

$$\frac{t_1 \rightarrow t_2}{t_3 \rightarrow t_4} \quad \text{for} \quad \frac{t_1, \sigma_1, \mu_1 \rightarrow t_2, \sigma_2, \mu_2}{t_3, \sigma_1, \mu_1 \rightarrow t_4, \sigma_2, \mu_2}\ .$$

The full set of rules can be found in Table 3 for expressions, Table 4 for local variable declarations, and Table 5 for statements.

For our example, a detailed run of (part of) the block in `main()` can be found in Figure 1. The annotations to the arrows indicate the rules applied. The object $o_{\texttt{p}}$, the locations $l_{\texttt{p.x}}$ and $l_{\texttt{p.y}}$, and the stores μ and μ' are defined as before.

3 Event Spaces

The execution of a Java program comprises many *threads* of computation running in parallel. Threads exchange information by operating on values and objects residing in a shared *main memory*. As explained in the Java language specification

[assign1]	$\dfrac{e_1 \rightarrow e_2}{e_1 = e \rightarrow e_2 = e}$	[assign2]	$\dfrac{e_1 \rightarrow e_2}{k = e_1 \rightarrow k = e_2}$
[assign3]	$l = v, \mu \rightarrow v, \mu[l \mapsto v]$	[assign4]	$i = v, \sigma \rightarrow v, \sigma[i \mapsto v]$
[unop1]	$\dfrac{e_1 \rightarrow e_2}{\mathtt{op}(e_1) \rightarrow \mathtt{op}(e_2)}$	[unop2]	$\mathtt{op}(v), \mu \rightarrow op(v), \mu$
[access1]	$\dfrac{e_1 \rightarrow e_2}{e_1 \, . \, i \rightarrow e_2 \, . \, i}$	[access2]	$o.i \, , \mu \rightarrow lval(o, i, \mu), \mu$
[this]	$\mathtt{this} \, , \mu \rightarrow this(\mu), \mu$	[pth]	$(e), \mu \rightarrow e, \mu$
[new]	$\mathtt{new} \; C \; (\,) \, , \mu \rightarrow new_C(\mu)$	[val]	$l \, , \mu \rightarrow \mu(l), \mu$
[var]	$i \, , \sigma \rightarrow \sigma(i), \sigma$		

Table 3. Expressions

[decl1]	$\dfrac{e_1 \rightarrow e_2}{i = e_1 \rightarrow i = e_2}$	[decl2]	$i = v, \sigma \rightarrow \sigma[i = v]$
[declseq1]	$\dfrac{d_1 \rightarrow d_2}{d_1 \; D \rightarrow d_2 \; D}$	[declseq2]	$\dfrac{d, \sigma_1 \rightarrow \sigma_2}{d \; D, \sigma_1 \rightarrow D, \sigma_2}$
[locvardecl1]	$\dfrac{D_1 \rightarrow D_2}{\tau \; D_1 \rightarrow \tau \; D_2}$	[locvardecl2]	$\dfrac{D, \sigma_1 \rightarrow \sigma_2}{\tau \; D \, , \sigma_1 \rightarrow \sigma_2}$

Table 4. Local variable declarations

[3], each thread also has a private *working memory* in which it keeps its own working copy of variables that it must use or assign. As the thread executes a program, it operates on these working copies. The main memory contains the master copy of each variable. There are rules about when a thread is permitted or required to transfer the contents of its working copy of a variable into the master copy or vice versa. Moreover, there are rules which regulate the *locking* and *unlocking* of objects, by means of which threads synchronize with each other. These rules are given in [3, Chapter 17] and formalized in this section as "well-formedness" conditions for structures called *event spaces.* In the next section event spaces are included in the configurations of multi-threaded Java to constrain the applicability of certain operational rules.

[statseq1]	$\dfrac{s_1 \rightarrow s_2}{s_1 \; S \rightarrow s_2 \; S}$	[statseq2]	$\dfrac{s, \mu_1 \rightarrow \mu_2}{s \; S, \mu_1 \rightarrow S, \mu_2}$
[expstat1]	$\dfrac{e_1 \rightarrow e_2}{e_1 \, ; \rightarrow e_2 \, ;}$	[expstat2]	$\dfrac{e, \mu_1 \rightarrow v, \mu_2}{e \, ; \; , \mu_1 \rightarrow \mu_2}$
[skip]	$; \; , \sigma \rightarrow \sigma$	[block1]	$\{ \; \}_\rho \, , \sigma \rightarrow \sigma$
[block2]	$\dfrac{S_1, push(\rho_1, \sigma_1) \rightarrow S_2, push(\rho_2, \sigma_2)}{\{S_1\}_{\rho_1}, \sigma_1 \rightarrow \{S_2\}_{\rho_2}, \sigma_2}$		

Table 5. Statements

$$\{\ \texttt{Point p} = \texttt{new Point()};\ \texttt{p.x} = 1;\ \texttt{p.y} = 2;\ \texttt{p.x} = \texttt{p.y};\ \}_{\rho_\emptyset[\texttt{p}\mapsto\texttt{null}]}, \sigma_\emptyset, \mu$$

$$\downarrow \text{[block2, statseq1, expstat1, locvardecl1, decl1, new]}$$

$$\{\ \texttt{Point p} = o_\texttt{p};\ \texttt{p.x} = 1;\ \texttt{p.y} = 2;\ \texttt{p.x} = \texttt{p.y};\ \}_{\rho_\emptyset[\texttt{p}\mapsto\texttt{null}]}, \sigma_\emptyset, \mu'$$

$$\downarrow \text{[block2, statseq2, expstat2, locvardecl2, decl2]}$$

$$\{\ \texttt{p.x} = 1;\ \texttt{p.y} = 2;\ \texttt{p.x} = \texttt{p.y};\ \}_{\rho_\emptyset[\texttt{p}\mapsto o_\texttt{p}]}, \sigma_\emptyset, \mu'$$

$$\downarrow \text{[block2, statseq1, expstat1, access1, var]}$$

$$\{\ o_\texttt{p}.\texttt{x} = 1;\ \texttt{p.y} = 2;\ \texttt{p.x} = \texttt{p.y};\ \}_{\rho_\emptyset[\texttt{p}\mapsto o_\texttt{p}]}, \sigma_\emptyset, \mu'$$

$$\downarrow \text{[block2, statseq1, expstat1, assign1, access2]}$$

$$\{\ l_{\texttt{p.x}} = 1;\ \texttt{p.y} = 2;\ \texttt{p.x} = \texttt{p.y};\ \}_{\rho_\emptyset[\texttt{p}\mapsto o_\texttt{p}]}, \sigma_\emptyset, \mu'$$

$$\downarrow \text{[block2, statseq2, expstat2, assign3]}$$

$$\{\ \texttt{p.y} = 2;\ \texttt{p.x} = \texttt{p.y};\ \}_{\rho_\emptyset[\texttt{p}\mapsto o_\texttt{p}]}, \sigma_\emptyset, \mu'[l_{\texttt{p.x}} \mapsto 1]$$

$$\ldots \downarrow \ldots$$

Figure 1. Sample run of `Sample.main()`

In accord with [3], the terms *Use*, *Assign*, *Load*, *Store*, *Read*, *Write*, *Lock*, and *Unlock* are used here to name actions which describe the activity of the memories during the execution of a Java program. *Use* and *Assign* denote the above mentioned actions on the private working memory. *Read* and *Load* are used for a loosely coupled copying of data from the main memory to a working memory and dually *Store* and *Write* are used for copying data from a working memory to the main memory.

For instance, a rule about the interaction of locks and variables [3, 17.6, p. 407] states for a thread θ, a variable V and a lock L:

> "Between an *assign* action by [θ] on V and subsequent *unlock* action by [θ] on L, a *store* action by [θ] on V must intervene; moreover, the *write* action corresponding to that *store* must precede the *unlock* action, as seen by the main memory. (Less formally: if a thread is to perform an *unlock* action on *any* lock, it must first copy *all* assigned values in its working memory back out to main memory.)"

We briefly recapitulate those rules by means of the example "Possible Swap" of [3, 17.10] where two threads θ_1 and θ_2 running in parallel want to manipulate the coordinates of the same point object $o_\texttt{p}$, referenced in both threads by the local variable p. The thread θ_1 wants to do `p.x = p.y`, while θ_2 wants to do `p.y = p.x`. These manipulations are to run under mutual exclusion; in Java this is obtained by a *synchronization* on a shared object:

$$(\theta_1,\ \texttt{synchronized(p)\{p.x=p.y;\}}) \mid (\theta_2,\ \texttt{synchronized(p)\{p.y=p.x;\}})$$

In order to enter the critical (`synchronized`) region both threads must perform a *Lock* action on $o_\texttt{p}$; by the rules of the Java language specification a *Lock* action of one thread on an object prevents any other thread to perform a *Lock* action on the same object. We assume that θ_1 is first. Now, θ_1 may proceed to obtain the y coordinate of the object referenced by p. By the rules for locks the value of `p.y`, which resides in the main memory, must be loaded first in θ_1's working memory. The language specification requires that such a *Load* action be preceded by a corresponding *Read* action of the main memory. Once this protocol is completed the requested value can be used by θ_1 with a *Use* action and assigned to the working copy of `p.x` with an *Assign* action.

Putting the new value of `p.x` back in the main memory reverses the chain of responsibilities: the working memory of θ_1 issues this value to the main memory by a *Store* action; then the main memory writes the value to the master copy of `p.x` by a *Write* action. This chain is again enforced by the *Unlock* action that ends the critical region. Now, θ_2 may proceed to achieve the lock on o_p, and so forth; the complete series of actions is depicted in Figure 2. Note that the omission of the synchronization would considerably liberalize the order of execution of the actions. Especially, a non-synchronized thread is not forced to write the contents of its working memory back to the main memory.

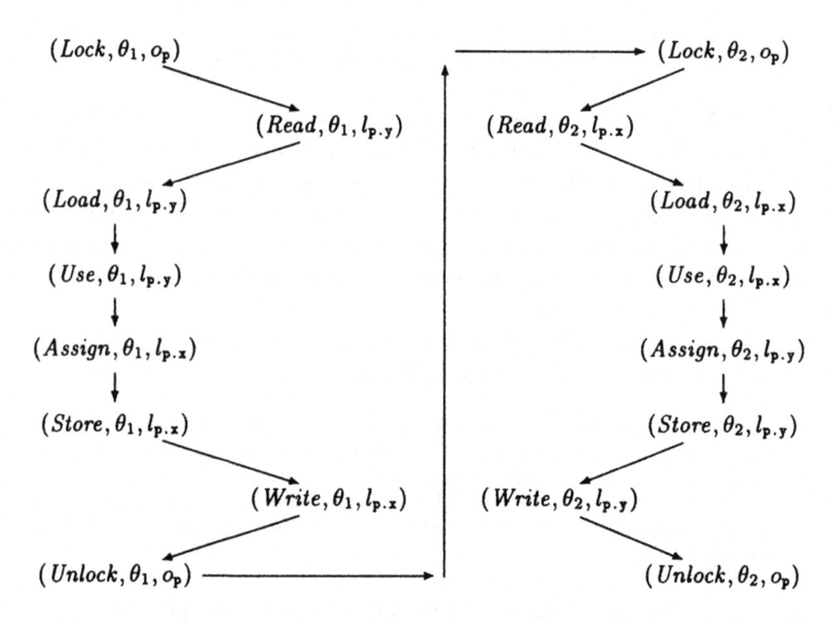

Figure 2. Event space of example "Possible Swap"

We proceed to formalize this behaviour. Let the metavariable A stand for a generic action name. Moreover, let B range over the set of thread actions and C over the set of memory actions, that is:

$$B \in \{Use, Assign, Load, Store, Lock, Unlock\} ,$$
$$C \in \{Read, Write, Lock, Unlock\} .$$

Let *Thread_id* be a set of thread identifiers. An *action* is either a 4-tuple of the form (A, θ, l, v) where $A \in \{Assign, Store, Read\}$, $\theta \in Thread\_id$, $l \in LVal$ and $v \in RVal$, or a triple (A, θ, l), where θ and l are as above and $A \in \{Use, Load, Write\}$, or a triple (A, θ, o), where $A \in \{Lock, Unlock\}$ and $o \in Obj$. A triple (A, θ, x) is read "θ performs an A action on x," for x a location or an object, while (A, θ, l, v) is read "(A, θ, l) with value v."

Events are instances of actions, which we think of as happening at different times during execution. We use the same tuple notation for actions and their instances (the context clarifies which one is meant) and let lower case letters stand for either. Sometimes we omit components of an action or event: we may write $(Read, l)$ for $(Read, \theta, l, v)$ when θ and v are not relevant.

An *event space* is a poset of events (thought of as occurring in the given order) in which every chain can be enumerated monotonically with respect to the arithmetical ordering $0 \leq 1 \leq 2 \leq \ldots$ of natural numbers, and which satisfies the conditions (1–15) below. These conditions, which formalize directly the rules of [3, Chapter 17], are expressed by clauses of the form:

$$\forall \boldsymbol{a} \in \eta \,.\, (\Phi \Rightarrow ((\exists \boldsymbol{b}_1 \in \eta \,.\, \Psi_1) \text{ or } (\exists \boldsymbol{b}_2 \in \eta \,.\, \Psi_2) \text{ or } \ldots\ (\exists \boldsymbol{b}_n \in \eta \,.\, \Psi_n)))$$

where $\boldsymbol{a}$ and $\boldsymbol{b}_i$ are lists of events, η is an event space and $\forall \boldsymbol{a} \in \eta \,.\, \Phi$ means that Φ holds for all tuples of events in η matching the elements of $\boldsymbol{a}$ (and similarly for $\exists \boldsymbol{b}_i \in \eta \,.\, \Psi_i$). Such statements are abbreviated by adopting the following conventions: quantification over $\boldsymbol{a}$ is left implicit when all events in $\boldsymbol{a}$ appear in Φ; quantification over $\boldsymbol{b}_i$ is left implicit when all events in $\boldsymbol{b}_i$ appear in Ψ_i. Moreover, a rule of the form $\forall \boldsymbol{a} \in \eta \,.\, (true \Rightarrow \ldots)$ is written $\boldsymbol{a} \Rightarrow (\ldots)$. We include some short, informal explanation of the rules and refer to [3] for more detail.

The actions performed by any one thread are totally ordered, and so are the actions performed by the main memory for any one variable [3, 17.2, 17.5].

$$(B, \theta), (B', \theta) \Rightarrow (B, \theta) \leq (B', \theta) \text{ or } (B', \theta) \leq (B, \theta) \tag{1}$$

$$(C, x), (C', x) \Rightarrow (C, x) \leq (C', x) \text{ or } (C', x) \leq (C, x) \tag{2}$$

Hence, the occurrences of any action (A, θ, x) are totally ordered in an event space. The term $(A, \theta, x)_n$ denotes the n-th occurrence of (A, θ, x) in a given space, if such an event exists, and is undefined otherwise. When two indices m and n are applied in a rule to instances of the same action, it is meant that $m \neq n$.

A *Store* action by θ on l must intervene between an *Assign* by θ of l and a subsequent *Load* by θ of l. Less formally, a thread is not permitted to lose its most recent assign [3, 17.3]:

$$(Assign, \theta, l) \leq (Load, \theta, l) \Rightarrow (Assign, \theta, l) \leq (Store, \theta, l) \leq (Load, \theta, l) \tag{3}$$

A thread is not permitted to write data from its working memory back to main memory for no reason [3, 17.3]:

$$\begin{aligned} &(Store, \theta, l)_m \leq (Store, \theta, l)_n \Rightarrow \\ &\qquad (Store, \theta, l)_m \leq (Assign, \theta, l) \leq (Store, \theta, l)_n \end{aligned} \tag{4}$$

Threads start with an empty working memory and new variables are created only in main memory and not initially in any thread's working memory [3, 17.3]:

$$(Use,\theta,l) \Rightarrow (Assign,\theta,l) \leq (Use,\theta,l) \text{ or } (Load,\theta,l) \leq (Use,\theta,l) \quad (5)$$
$$(Store,\theta,l) \Rightarrow (Assign,\theta,l) \leq (Store,\theta,l) \quad (6)$$

A *Store* action transmits the contents of the thread's working copy of a variable to main memory [3, 17.1]:

$$\begin{aligned}&(Assign,\theta,l,v)_n \leq (Store,\theta,l,v') \Rightarrow \\ &\quad v = v' \text{ or } (Assign,\theta,l,v)_n \leq (Assign,\theta,l)_m \leq (Store,\theta,l,v')\end{aligned} \quad (7)$$

Each *Load* or *Write* action is uniquely paired respectively with a matching *Read* or *Store* action that precedes it [3, 17.2, 17.3]:

$$(Load,\theta,l)_n \Rightarrow (Read,\theta,l)_n \leq (Load,\theta,l)_n \quad (8)$$
$$(Write,\theta,l)_n \Rightarrow (Store,\theta,l)_n \leq (Write,\theta,l)_n \quad (9)$$

The actions on the master copy of any given variable on behalf of a thread are performed by the main memory in exactly the order that the thread requested [3, 17.3]:

$$(Store,\theta,l)_m \leq (Load,\theta,l)_n \Rightarrow (Write,\theta,l)_m \leq (Read,\theta,l)_n \quad (10)$$

A thread is not permitted to unlock a lock it does not own. Only one thread at a time is permitted to lay claim to a lock, and moreover a thread may acquire the same lock multiple times and does not relinquish ownership of it until a matching number of unlock actions have been performed [3, 17.5]:

$$(Unlock,\theta,o)_n \Rightarrow (Lock,\theta,o)_n \leq (Unlock,\theta,o)_n \quad (11)$$
$$(Lock,\theta,o)_n \leq (Lock,\theta',o) \text{ and } \theta \neq \theta' \Rightarrow (Unlock,\theta,o)_n \leq (Lock,\theta',o) \quad (12)$$

If a thread is to perform an unlock action on any lock, it must first copy all assigned values in its working memory back out to main memory [3, 17.6] (this rule formalizes the quotation above):

$$\begin{aligned}&(Assign,\theta,l) \leq (Unlock,\theta) \Rightarrow \\ &\quad (Assign,\theta,l) \leq (Store,\theta,l)_n \leq (Write,\theta,l)_n \leq (Unlock,\theta)\end{aligned} \quad (13)$$

A lock action acts as if it flushes all variables from the thread's working memory; before use they must be assigned or loaded from main memory [3, 17.6]:

$$\begin{aligned}&(Lock,\theta) \leq (Use,\theta,l) \Rightarrow \\ &\quad (Lock,\theta) \leq (Assign,\theta,l) \leq (Use,\theta,l) \text{ or} \\ &\quad (Lock,\theta) \leq (Read,\theta,l)_n \leq (Load,\theta,l)_n \leq (Use,\theta,l)\end{aligned} \quad (14)$$
$$(Lock,\theta) \leq (Store,\theta,l) \Rightarrow (Lock,\theta) \leq (Assign,\theta,l) \leq (Store,\theta,l) \quad (15)$$

Discussion. Each of the above rules corresponds to one rule in [3]. Conversely, any rule in [3] which we have not included above can be derived in our axiomatization. In particular,

$$(Load, \theta, l) \leq (Store, \theta, l) \Rightarrow (Load, \theta, l) \leq (Assign, \theta, l) \leq (Store, \theta, l) \qquad (*)$$

of [3, 17.3] holds in any event space. In fact, by (6) there must be some *Assign* action before the *Store*; moreover, one of such *Assign* must intervene in between the *Load* and the *Store*, because otherwise, from (1) and (3), there would be a chain $(Store, \theta, l) \leq (Load, \theta, l) \leq (Store, \theta, l)$ with no *Assign* in between, which contradicts (4). Similarly, the following rule of [3, 17.3] derives from (8) and (9):

$$\begin{aligned} &\forall (Load, \theta, l)_n, (Store, \theta, l)_m, (Write, \theta, l)_m \in \eta \, . \\ &\qquad (Load, \theta, l)_n \leq (Store, \theta, l)_m \Rightarrow (Read, \theta, l)_n \leq (Write, \theta, l)_m \end{aligned}$$

The clauses (6) and (15) simplify the corresponding rules of [3, 17.3, 17.6] which include a condition $(Load, \theta, l) \leq (Store, \theta, l)$ to the right of the implication. This would be redundant because of $(*)$.

Note that the language specification requires any *Read* action to be completed by a corresponding *Load* and similarly for *Store* and *Write*. We do not translate such rules into well-formedness conditions for event spaces because the latter must capture incomplete program executions.

Usage in operational semantics. Event spaces serve two purposes: On the one hand they provide all the information to reconstruct the current working memories of all threads (which in fact do not appear in the configurations). On the other hand event spaces record the "historical" information on the computation which constrain the execution of certain actions according to the language specification, and hence the applicability of certain operational rules.

A new event $a = (A, \theta, x)$ is adjoined to an event space η by extending the execution order as follows: if A is a thread action, then $b \leq a$ for all instances b of (B, θ) in η; if a is a main memory action, then $c \leq a$ for all instances c of (C, x) in η. Moreover, if A is *Load* then $c \leq a$ for all instances c of $(Read, \theta, l)$ in η, and if A is *Write* then $c \leq a$ for all instances c of $(Store, \theta, l)$ in η. The term $\eta \oplus a$ denotes the space thus obtained, provided it obeys the above rules, and it is otherwise undefined. For example, by (5), the term $\eta \oplus (Use, \theta, l)$ is defined only if a suitable $(Assign, \theta, l)$ or $(Load, \theta, l)$ occurs in η. If η is an event space and $\boldsymbol{a} = (a_1, a_2, \ldots a_n)$ is a sequence of events, we write $\eta \oplus \boldsymbol{a}$ for $\eta \oplus a_1 \oplus a_2 \oplus \cdots \oplus a_n$.

4 Multi-Threaded Java

Stores assume in multi-threaded Java a more active role than they have in sequential Java because of the way the main memory interacts with the working memories: a "silent" computational step changing the store may occur without the direct intervention of a thread's execution engine. Changes to the store are subject to the previous occurrence of certain events which affect the state of computation. Event spaces are included in the configurations to record such historical information.

We first state the necessary extensions for the notions of terms, stacks, and configurations from the single-threaded to the multi-threaded case. Then we give the operational rules for multi-threaded Java and illustrate their use with the "Possible Swap" example. Finally we show that the multi-threaded semantics conservatively extends the semantics of Section 2.

Multi-threaded terms, stacks, and configurations. A multi-threaded Java configuration may include multiple S-terms, one for each running thread. An abstract term T of multi-threaded Java is a set of pairs (θ, t), where $\theta \in$ *Thread_id*, $t \in$ *S-Term* and no distinct elements of T bear the same thread identifier. The set of abstract terms of multi-threaded Java is called *M-Term*. M-terms $\{(\theta_1, t_1), (\theta_2, t_2), \dots\}$ are written as lists $(\theta_1, t_1) \mid (\theta_2, t_2) \mid \dots$ and pairs (θ, t) are written t when θ is irrelevant.

Each thread of execution of a Java program has its own stack. We call *M-Stack* the domain of multi-threaded stacks, ranged over by σ. More precisely, *M-Stack* = *Thread_id* $\rightharpoonup$ *S-Stack*. Given $\sigma \in$ *M-Stack*, the multi-threaded stacks $push(\theta, \rho, \sigma)$, $\sigma[\theta, i \mapsto v]$ and $\sigma[\theta, i = v]$ map θ' to $\sigma(\theta')$ when $\theta \neq \theta'$, and otherwise map θ respectively to $push(\rho, \sigma(\theta))$, $\sigma(\theta)[i \mapsto v]$ and $\sigma(\theta)[i = v]$.

The configurations of multi-threaded Java are 4-tuples (T, η, σ, μ) consisting of an M-term T, an event space η an M-stack σ and a store μ.

Multi-threaded rules. The operational rules make use of the following notation. We write $store_\eta(\theta, l)$ for the oldest unwritten value of l stored by θ in η. More formally: let an event $(Store, \theta, l)_n$ in η be called *unwritten* if $(Write, \theta, l)_n$ is undefined in η; then, $store_\eta(\theta, l) = v$ if there exists an unwritten $(Store, \theta, l, v)_n$ such that for any unwritten $(Store, \theta, l)_m$ we have $n \leq m$; if no such *Store* event exists, $store_\eta(\theta, l)$ is undefined. Similarly, we write $rval_\eta(\theta, l)$ for the latest value of l assigned or loaded (obtained by the corresponding *Read*) by θ in η.

The operational semantics for multi-threaded Java is given in Table 6. There is a "primed" version [x'] for of each rule [x] of Section 2; [x'] is omitted if it reads as [x] by the notational conventions.

Properly speaking, those of Table 6 are rule *schemes* whose instances are obtained by replacing the metavariables with suitable semantic objects. This point is crucial for a correct understanding of the rules [assign3', val', lock, unlock, read, load, store, write]. Indeed, suitably instances of such schemes can be found only if the operation $\oplus$ is defined for the given arguments, that is if the action being performed complies with the requirements of the language specification. By [assign3'] and [val'] *Assign* and *Use* actions are only added to an event space, when dictated by execution of the current thread [3, 17.3]. The rules [read, load, store, write] are applied spontaneously. The [store] rule "guesses" the value of the last *Assign*: axiom (7) ensures that the guess is right.

For a concrete example, consider the "Possible Swap" program of Section 3. Assume that $\sigma(\theta_1, \mathtt{p}) = \sigma(\theta_2, \mathtt{p}) = o_\mathtt{p}$ for a stack σ and that $\mu(l_{\mathtt{p.x}}) = 1$ and $\mu(l_{\mathtt{p.y}}) = 2$ for a store μ. Then any run of this program starting from an empty

[assign3']	$(\theta, l = v), \eta \to (\theta, v), \eta \oplus (Assign, \theta, l, v)$
[assign4']	$(\theta, i = v), \sigma \to (\theta, v), \sigma[\theta, i \mapsto v]$
[val']	$(\theta, l), \eta \to (\theta, rval_\eta(\theta, l)), \eta \oplus (Use, \theta, l)$
[var']	$(\theta, i), \sigma \to (\theta, \sigma(\theta, i)), \sigma$
[block2']	$\dfrac{(\theta, S_1), push(\theta, \rho_1, \sigma_1) \to (\theta, S_2), push(\theta, \rho_2, \sigma_2)}{(\theta, \{S_1\}_{\rho_1}), \sigma_1 \to (\theta, \{S_2\}_{\rho_2}), \sigma_2}$
[synchro1]	$\dfrac{e_1 \to e_2}{\texttt{synchronized}(e_1)\ q \to \texttt{synchronized}(e_2)\ q}$
[synchro2]	$\dfrac{q_1 \to q_2}{\texttt{synchronized}(o)\ q_1 \to \texttt{synchronized}(o)\ q_2}$
[lock]	$\dfrac{(\theta, e), \eta_1 \to (\theta, o), \eta_2}{(\theta, \texttt{synchronized}(e)\ q), \eta_1 \to (\theta, \texttt{synchronized}(o)\ q), \eta_2 \oplus (Lock, \theta, o)}$
[unlock]	$(\theta, \texttt{synchronized}(o)\ \{\ \}_\rho), \eta \to \eta \oplus (Unlock, \theta, o)$
[read]	$T, \eta, \mu \to T, \eta \oplus (Read, \theta, l, \mu(l)), \mu$
[load]	$T, \eta \to T, \eta \oplus (Load, \theta, l)$
[store]	$T, \eta \to T, \eta \oplus (Store, \theta, l, v)$
[write]	$T, \eta, \mu \to T, \eta \oplus (Write, \theta, l), \mu[l \mapsto store_\eta(\theta, l)]$
[par]	$\dfrac{t_1 \to t_2}{t_1 \mid T \to t_2 \mid T}$

Table 6. Multi-threaded Java

event space, stack σ, and store μ will eventually end up with $\mu(l_{\texttt{p.x}}) = \mu(l_{\texttt{p.y}}) = 1$ or $\mu(l_{\texttt{p.x}}) = \mu(l_{\texttt{p.y}}) = 2$. We detail a run where θ_1 is first in Figure 3. The event space of the end-configuration corresponds eventually to Figure 2, the final store is $\mu[l_{\texttt{p.x}} \mapsto 2][l_{\texttt{p.y}} \mapsto 2]$.

Conservativity. The operational semantics of multi-threaded Java extends conservatively the semantics given in Section 2 for the sequential part of the language. This is shown by Theorem 1 below, which exhibits a bisimulation between the two semantics where bisimilar configurations feature identical abstract terms. The significance of the theorem consists in showing that sequential programs can be reasoned about without loss of generality by using a simpler model of computation, free of working memories and forgetful of the past.

Below, a simple (unindexed) arrow $\to$ stands for the sequential Java semantics of Section 2 and $\to^=$ for its reflexive closure. We write $\to_\theta$ for the restriction of the multi-threaded Java semantics where the rules [read, load, store, write] involve actions of the thread θ only. The read/load extension $\rightsquigarrow_\theta$ of $\to_\theta$ to the left is inductively defined as follows: $\Gamma_1 \rightsquigarrow_\theta \Gamma_2$ when $\Gamma_1 \to_\theta \Gamma_2$ or $\Gamma_1 \to_\theta \Gamma_1'$

$$((\theta_1,\ \texttt{synchronized(p)}\ \{\ \texttt{p.x} = \texttt{p.y};\ \}_{\rho_\emptyset}) \mid (\theta_2,\ t),\ \emptyset, \sigma, \mu)$$

$\downarrow$ [lock,var']

$$((\theta_1,\ \texttt{synchronized}(o_\texttt{p})\ \{\ \texttt{p.x} = \texttt{p.y};\ \}_{\rho_\emptyset}) \mid (\theta_2,\ t),\ \{(Lock, \theta_1, o_\texttt{p})\}, \sigma, \mu)$$

[$\cdots$, $\downarrow$ $\cdots$]

$$((\theta_1,\ \texttt{synchronized}(o_\texttt{p})\ \{\ l_{\texttt{p.x}} = l_{\texttt{p.y}};\ \}_{\rho_\emptyset}) \mid (\theta_2,\ t),\ \{(Lock, \theta_1, o_\texttt{p})\}, \sigma, \mu)$$

$\downarrow$ [read]

$$((\theta_1,\ \texttt{sy}\ldots(o_\texttt{p})\ \{\ l_{\texttt{p.x}} = l_{\texttt{p.y}};\ \}_{\rho_\emptyset}) \mid (\theta_2,\ t),\ \{\cdots \leq (Read, \theta_1, l_{\texttt{p.y}}, 2)\}, \sigma, \mu)$$

$\downarrow$ [load]

$$((\theta_1,\ \texttt{sy}\ldots(o_\texttt{p})\ \{\ l_{\texttt{p.x}} = l_{\texttt{p.y}};\ \}_{\rho_\emptyset}) \mid (\theta_2,\ t),\ \{\cdots \leq (Load, \theta_1, l_{\texttt{p.y}})\}, \sigma, \mu)$$

[synchro2, block2, statseq1, expstat1, $\downarrow$ assign2, val']

$$((\theta_1,\ \texttt{sy}\ldots(o_\texttt{p})\ \{\ l_{\texttt{p.x}} = 2;\ \}_{\rho_\emptyset}) \mid (\theta_2,\ t),\ \{\cdots \leq (Use, \theta_1, l_{\texttt{p.y}})\}, \sigma, \mu)$$

[synchro2, block2, statseq2, expstat2, $\downarrow$ assign3']

$$((\theta_1,\ \texttt{sy}\ldots(o_\texttt{p})\ \{\ \}_{\rho_\emptyset}) \mid (\theta_2,\ t),\ \{\cdots \leq (Assign, \theta_1, l_{\texttt{p.x}}, 2)\}, \sigma, \mu)$$

$\downarrow$ [store]

$$((\theta_1,\ \texttt{sy}\ldots(o_\texttt{p})\ \{\ \}_{\rho_\emptyset}) \mid (\theta_2,\ t), \{\cdots \leq (Store, \theta_1, l_{\texttt{p.x}}, 2)\}, \sigma, \mu)$$

$\downarrow$ [write]

$$((\theta_1,\ \texttt{sy}\ldots(o_\texttt{p})\ \{\ \}_{\rho_\emptyset}) \mid (\theta_2,\ t), \{\cdots \leq (Write, \theta_1, l_{\texttt{p.x}})\}, \sigma, \mu[l_{\texttt{p.x}} \mapsto 2])$$

$\downarrow$ [unlock]

$$((\theta_1) \mid (\theta_2,\ t), \{\cdots \leq (Unlock, \theta_1, o_\texttt{p})\}, \sigma, \mu[l_{\texttt{p.x}} \mapsto 2])$$

Figure 3. Sample run of "Possible Swap"

by a *Read* or a *Load* action and $\Gamma_1' \leadsto_\theta \Gamma_2$. The store/write completion $\downarrow_\theta$ of $\rightarrow_\theta$ is defined as follows: $(\eta_1, \mu_1) \downarrow_\theta (\eta_2, \mu_2)$ when $(\eta_1, \mu_1) \rightarrow_\theta^* (\eta_2, \mu_2)$ by *Store* and *Write* actions only, and there is no Γ such that $(\eta_2, \mu_2) \rightarrow_\theta \Gamma$ by such an action. We write $(\eta_1, \mu_1) \downarrow_\theta \mu_2$ if there is an η_2 such that $(\eta_1, \mu_1) \downarrow_\theta (\eta_2, \mu_2)$. It is easy to verify that $\Gamma \downarrow_\theta \Gamma_1$ and $\Gamma \downarrow_\theta \Gamma_2$ imply $\Gamma_1 = \Gamma_2$. (Note that we use the same conventions as for the statement of the rules, i.e. we omit irrelevant configuration components.)

Let the binary relation $\sim_\theta$ between configurations of the sequential and multi-threaded Java semantics be defined as follows:

$$(t, \sigma_1, \mu_1) \sim_\theta (T, \eta, \sigma_2, \mu_2) \quad \text{iff} \quad T = (\theta, t) \text{ and } \sigma_1 = \sigma_2(\theta) \text{ and } (\eta, \mu_2) \downarrow_\theta \mu_1 \ .$$

Theorem 1. *For any configurations γ and Γ, if $\gamma \sim_\theta \Gamma$ then:*

(i) for all Γ', if $\Gamma \rightarrow_\theta \Gamma'$ then there exists γ' such that $\gamma \rightarrow^= \gamma'$ and $\gamma' \sim_\theta \Gamma'$;
(ii) for all γ', if $\gamma \rightarrow \gamma'$ then there exists Γ' such that $\Gamma \leadsto_\theta \Gamma'$ and $\gamma' \sim_\theta \Gamma'$.

Proof. By induction on the length of derivation of the operational judgements. The interesting cases involve the silent memory actions. We detail only some particularily involved cases for each direction.

(i) [val'] Let $l, \eta, \mu \rightarrow_\theta v, \eta \oplus (Use, \theta, l), \mu$, with $v = rval_\eta(\theta, l)$, and let $(l, \mu_1) \sim_\theta (l, \eta, \mu)$. It must be $(\eta, \mu) \downarrow_\theta \mu_1$. By rule (5), either an event $(Assign, \theta, l, v)$ is the most recent assignment to l by θ in η, or events $(Read, \theta, l, v) \leq (Load, \theta, l)$ occur in η and no assignment afterwards. In either cases $(\eta, \mu) \downarrow_\theta \mu_1$ imply $\mu_1(l) = v$. Hence, $l, \mu_1 \rightarrow v, \mu_1$ by [val]. Now, the store/write completion of η and $\eta \oplus (Use)$ is the same and we thus have $(\eta \oplus (Use, \theta, l), \mu) \downarrow_\theta \mu_1$. Therefore, $(v, \mu_1) \sim_\theta (v, \eta \oplus (Use, \theta, l), \mu)$ as required.

[store, write] Let $(T, \mu_1) \rightarrow_\theta \Gamma$ by a *Store* or a *Write* action, and let $(t, \mu_2) \sim_\theta (T, \mu_1)$. It must be $(T, \mu_1) \downarrow_\theta \mu_2$. If $\Gamma \downarrow_\theta \mu_3$ then, composing transitions, we have $(T, \mu_1) \downarrow_\theta \mu_3$ and hence $\mu_2 = \mu_3$. Therefore $(t, \mu_2) \sim_\theta \Gamma$ as required after an identity $\rightarrow^=$ transition.

(ii) [assign1] Let $(e_1 = e, \mu_1) \sim_\theta (e_1 = e, \eta, \mu_2)$. We have immediately $(e_1, \mu_1) \sim_\theta (e_1, \eta, \mu_2)$. Let $e_1 = e, \mu_1 \rightarrow e_2 = e, \mu_3$ by a derivation whose last step involves the rule [assign1]. It must be $e_1, \mu_1 \rightarrow e_2, \mu_3$ by a shorter derivation. Hence, by inductive hypothesis, $e_1, \eta, \mu_2 \leadsto_\theta e_2, \eta_1, \mu_4$ and $(e_2, \mu_3) \sim_\theta (e_2, \eta_1, \mu_4)$ where, by definition, the read/load extension can be split into $e_1, \eta, \mu_2 \rightarrow_\theta^* e_1, \eta_2, \mu_2$ by a possibly empty sequence of silent *Read* and *Load* actions, and $e_1, \eta_2, \mu_2 \rightarrow_\theta e_2, \eta_1, \mu_4$. It follows that $e_1 = e, \eta, \mu_2 \rightarrow_\theta^* e_1 = e, \eta_2, \mu_2$ by the same sequence of silent actions and $e_1 = e, \eta_2, \mu_2 \rightarrow_\theta e_2 = e, \eta_1, \mu_4$ by [assign1], that is $e_1 = e, \eta, \mu_2 \leadsto_\theta e_2 = e, \eta_1, \mu_4$. Moreover, since $(e_2, \mu_3) \sim_\theta (e_2, \eta_1, \mu_4)$, we have $(e_2 = e, \mu_3) \sim_\theta (e_2 = e, \eta_1, \mu_4)$ as required.

5 Conclusions and Future Work

In this paper we have presented a structural operational semantics of the concurrency model of Java and we have shown how it relates to sequential Java. Our semantics covers a substantial part of the dynamic behaviour of the language. Most notably method calls, exceptions, and type information (class, interface and method declarations) are missing. We plan to investigate those parts in a further study. Method calls can easily be included in our semantics by the usual SOS techniques. The inclusion of exceptions is slightly more complicated; it requires the definition of evaluation contexts in order to keep the number of rules small. Concerning type information, we expect that one can easily combine our semantics with the type system developed in [2].

We have also not covered the full concurrency model of Java. Especially wait sets and notification as described in [3, 17.14] have to be added. There are some more detailed rules for variables declared `volatile` and for the non-atomic treatement of `double` and `long` variables; these are easily incorporated.

Furthermore, we are studying the flexibility of our approach by means of an extension to the so-called "prescient" store actions [3, 17.8]. These actions "allow optimizing Java compilers to perform certain kinds of code rearrangements that preserve the semantics of properly synchronized programs [...]."

References

1. Ken Arnold and James Gosling. *The Java Programming Language.* Addison–Wesley, Reading, Mass., 1996.
2. Sophia Drossopoulou and Susan Eisenbach. Java is Type Safe — Probably. In Mehmet Aksit, editor, *Proc. 11th Europ. Conf. Object-Oriented Programming*, volume 1241 of *Lect. Notes Comp. Sci.*, pages 389–418, Berlin, 1997. Springer.
3. James Gosling, Bill Joy, and Guy Steele. *The Java Language Specification.* Addison–Wesley, Reading, Mass., 1996.
4. Doug Lea. *Concurrent Programming in Java.* Addison–Wesley, Reading, Mass., 1997.
5. Wei Li. An Operational Semantics of Multitasking and Exception Handling in Ada. In *Proc. AdaTEC Conf. Ada*, pages 138–151, New York, 1982. ACM SIGAda.
6. Robin Milner, Mads Tofte, Robert Harper, and David MacQueen. *The Definition of Standard ML (Revised).* MIT Press, Cambridge, Mass., 1997.
7. Gordon D. Plotkin. Structural Operational Semantics (Lecture notes). Technical Report DAIMI FN–19, Aarhus University, 1981 (repr. 1991).
8. Glynn Winskel. An Introduction to Event Structures. In Jacobus W. de Bakker, editor, *Linear Time, Branching Time and Partial Order in Logics and Models for Concurrency*, volume 354 of *Lect. Notes Comp. Sci.*, Berlin, 1988. Springer.

A Syntax

$$
\begin{aligned}
\mathit{Block} &::= \texttt{\{}\ \mathit{BlockStatement}^*\ \texttt{\}} \\
\mathit{BlockStatement} &::= \mathit{LocalVariableDeclaration} \mid \mathit{Statement} \\
\mathit{LocalVariableDeclaration} &::= \mathit{Type}\ \mathit{VariableDeclarator}^+ \\
\mathit{VariableDeclarator} &::= \mathit{Identifier}\ \texttt{=}\ \mathit{Expression} \\
\mathit{Statement} &::= \texttt{;} \mid \mathit{Block} \mid \mathit{ExpressionStatement}\,\texttt{;} \\
&\mid \texttt{synchronized(}\ \mathit{Expression}\ \texttt{)}\ \mathit{Block} \\
\mathit{ExpressionStatement} &::= \mathit{Assignment} \mid \texttt{new}\ \mathit{ClassType}\ \texttt{()} \\
\mathit{Assignment} &::= \mathit{LeftHandSide}\ \texttt{=}\ \mathit{AssignmentExpression} \\
\mathit{LeftHandSide} &::= \mathit{Name} \mid \mathit{FieldAccess} \\
\mathit{Name} &::= \mathit{Identifier} \mid \mathit{Name}\ \texttt{.}\ \mathit{Identifier} \\
\mathit{FieldAccess} &::= \mathit{Primary}\ \texttt{.}\ \mathit{Identifier} \\
\mathit{AssignmentExpression} &::= \mathit{Assignment} \mid \mathit{UnaryExpression} \\
\mathit{UnaryExpression} &::= \mathit{UnaryOperator}\ \mathit{UnaryExpression} \\
&\mid \mathit{Primary} \mid \mathit{Name} \\
\mathit{Primary} &::= \mathit{Literal} \mid \texttt{this} \mid \mathit{FieldAccess} \\
&\mid \texttt{(}\ \mathit{Expression}\ \texttt{)} \mid \texttt{new}\ \mathit{ClassType}\ \texttt{()} \\
\mathit{Expression} &::= \mathit{AssignmentExpression}
\end{aligned}
$$

Permissive Subsorted Partial Logic in CASL

Maura Cerioli[1], Anne Haxthausen[2], Bernd Krieg-Brückner[3], Till Mossakowski[3]

[1] DISI, Via Dodecaneso 35, I-16146 Genova
[2] Dept. of Information Technology, Techn. University of Denmark, DK-2800 Lyngby
[3] BISS, Universität Bremen, P.O. Box 330440, D-28334 Bremen

Abstract. This paper presents a permissive subsorted partial logic used in the CoFI Algebraic Specification Language. In contrast to other order-sorted logics, subsorting is not modeled by set inclusions, but by injective embeddings allowing for more general models in which subtypes can have different data type representations. Furthermore, there are no restrictions like monotonicity, regularity or local filtration on signatures at all. Instead, the use of overloaded functions and predicates in formulae is required to be sufficiently disambiguated, such that all parses have the same semantics. An overload resolution algorithm is sketched.

1 Introduction

During the past decades a large number of algebraic specification languages have been developed. The presence of so many similar specification languages with no common framework hinders the dissemination and application of research results in algebraic specification. In particular, it makes it difficult to produce educational material, to re-use tools and to get algebraic methods adopted in industry. Therefore, in 1995, an initiative, CoFI[4], to design *a Common Framework for Algebraic Specification and Development* was started [Mos97]. The goal of CoFI is to get a common agreement in the algebraic specification community about basic concepts, and to provide a family of specification languages at different levels, a development methodology and tool support. The family of specification languages will comprise a central, common language, called CASL[5], various restrictions of CASL, and various extensions of CASL (e.g. with facilities for particular programming paradigms). A tentative design [CoFI96] of CASL has already been completed by representatives of most algebraic specification language groups. Note that the concrete syntax used in this paper is a proposal and no decision about concrete syntax has yet been taken.

CASL provides constructs for writing structured requirement and design specifications as well as architectural specifications. Basic CASL specifications consist of declarations and axioms representing theories of a first-order logic in which predicates, total as well as partial functions, and subsorts are allowed. Predicate and function symbols may be overloaded.

[4] CoFI is an acronym for *Common Framework Initiative* and is pronounced like 'coffee'.

[5] CASL is an acronym for *CoFI Algebraic (or* Axiomatic*) Specification Language* and is pronounced like 'castle'.

In this paper we will present the subsorting approach used in CASL. The main novelties of our approach compared with the usual order-sorted approach [GM92] are:

- Functions may be partial.
- Predicates are allowed as in EqLog [GM86].
- Projection functions from supersorts to subsorts are naturally defined as partial functions, instead of total retract functions [GM92].
- Subsorting is not modeled by set inclusions, but by injective embeddings allowing for more general models in which subtypes may have different data type representations.
- There are no requirements like monotonicity, regularity or local filtration imposed on signatures.

We dropped the requirements like monotonicity, regularity or local filtration in order to avoid problems with modularity (as described in [HN96] and [Mos96]) and to allow overloading of constants. Instead, the use of overloaded functions and predicates in formulae is required to be sufficiently disambiguated, such that all parses have the same semantics. This means a more complicated definition of well-formed formulae, and requires a parsing algorithm which is more complex than the simple bottom-up least sort parsing algorithm by Goguen and Meseguer [GM92]. However, in cases where the signatures satisfy the mentioned requirements, the complexity of the two algorithms is the same.

The idea of dropping regularity (but not local filtration) has been proposed by Goguen and Diaconescu [GD94], and the idea of dropping local filtration (but not regularity) has been proposed by Haxthausen [Hax97] for a subsorting approach with implicit non-injective coercions. However, it is new that both requirements are dropped at the same time, and it is new that a parsing (overload resolution) algorithm is sketched.

First, in section 2, some well-known definitions from many-sorted partial logic are given, and, in section 3, the underlying subsorted partial logic of CASL is defined in terms of the many-sorted partial logic. Then, in section 4, the CASL subsorting language is presented, and in section 5, an overload resolution algorithm and the possibility of re-using existing theorem provers are briefly described. Finally, in section 6 a discussion is given. A longer version of this paper with all technical details will appear in a forthcoming report.

2 Many-sorted Partial Logic

This section defines the notions of signatures, models, and sentences of many-sorted partial first-order logic. For a full treatment of the topic, see e.g. [CMR97].

2.1 Signatures

Definition 2.1 A *many-sorted signature* $\Sigma = (S, TF, PF, P)$ consists of:

- a set S of *sorts*
- two $S^*{\times}S$-sorted families $TF = (TF_{w,s})_{w \in S^*, s \in S}$ and $PF = (PF_{w,s})_{w \in S^*, s \in S}$ of ***total function symbols*** and ***partial function symbols***, respectively, such that $TF_{w,s} \cap PF_{w,s} = \{\}$, for each $(w,s) \in S^*{\times}S$ (constants are treated as functions with no arguments)
- a family $P = (P_w)_{w \in S^*}$ of ***predicate symbols***

Signature morphisms are defined as usual, with the speciality that a partial function symbol may be mapped to a total function symbol (but not vice versa).

Note that function and predicate symbols may be overloaded, occurring in more than one of the above sets. To ensure that there is no ambiguity in sentences, however, symbols are always qualified by profiles when used. In the CASL language considered in section 4, such qualifications may be omitted when these are unambiguously determined by the context.

Notation. We write $f : w \rightarrow s \in TF$ for $f \in TF_{w,s}$, $f : w \rightarrow\!\!\!\!\!+ \; s \in PF$ for $f \in PF_{w,s}$ and $p : \P w \in P$ for $p \in P_w$.

For a function symbol $f \in TF_{w,s}$ or $f \in PF_{w,s}$, we call $w \rightarrow s$ or $w \rightarrow\!\!\!\!\!+ \; s$, resp., its ***profile***. For predicate symbols $p : \P w$, we call $\P w$ its ***profile***.

2.2 Sentences

Let a many-sorted signature $\Sigma = (S, TF, PF, P)$ and an S-sorted family of variables $X = (X_s)_{s \in S}$ be given.

Definition 2.2 The sets $T_\Sigma(X)_s$ of *many-sorted Σ-terms* of sort s, $s \in S$, with variables in X are the least sets satisfying the following rules:

1. $x \in T_\Sigma(X)_s$, if $x \in X_s$
2. $(f : w \rightarrow s)(t_1, \ldots, t_n) \in T_\Sigma(X)_s$, if $t_i \in T_\Sigma(X)_{s_i}$, $f \in TF_{w,s}$, $w = s_1 \ldots s_n$
3. $(f : w \rightarrow\!\!\!\!\!+ \; s)(t_1, \ldots, t_n) \in T_\Sigma(X)_s$, if $t_i \in T_\Sigma(X)_{s_i}$, $f \in PF_{w,s}$, $w = s_1 \ldots s_n$

Note that each term has a unique sort.

A many-sorted atomic Σ-formula with variables in X comprises (1) applications of qualified predicate symbols to terms of appropriate sorts, (2) existential equations between terms of the same sort, (3) strong equations between terms of the same sort, and (4) assertions about definedness of terms:

Definition 2.3 The set $AF_\Sigma(X)$ of *many-sorted atomic Σ-formulae* with variables in X is the least set satisfying the following rules:

1. $(p : \P w)(t_1, \ldots, t_n) \in AF_\Sigma(X)$, if $t_i \in T_\Sigma(X)_{s_i}$, $p \in P_w$, $w = s_1 \ldots s_n \in S^*$
2. $t \stackrel{e}{=} t' \in AF_\Sigma(X)$, if $t, t' \in T_\Sigma(X)_s$, $s \in S$
3. $t = t' \in AF_\Sigma(X)$, if $t, t' \in T_\Sigma(X)_s$, $s \in S$
4. $¿(t) \in AF_\Sigma(X)$, if $t \in T_\Sigma(X)_s$, $s \in S$

Definition 2.4 *Many-sorted Σ-sentences* are the usual closed many-sorted first-order logic formulae, built using quantification (over sorted variables), logical connectives and atomic Σ-formulae.

2.3 Models

Definition 2.5 Given a many-sorted signature $\Sigma = (S, TF, PF, P)$, a *many-sorted Σ-model M* consists of:

- a carrier set s^M for each sort $s \in S$
- a partial function f^M from w^M to s^M for each function symbol $f \in TF_{w,s} \cup PF_{w,s}$, the function being total if $f \in TF_{w,s}$
- a predicate $p^M \subseteq w^M$ for each predicate symbol $p \in P_w$.

Notation. We write w^M for the Cartesian product $s_1^M \times ... \times s_n^M$, when $w = s_1...s_n$.

Definition 2.6 A *many-sorted Σ-homomorphism* $h : M \to N$ consists of a family of functions $(h : s^M \to s^N)_{s \in S}$ such that

- for all $f \in TF_{w,s} \cup PF_{w,s}$ and $(a_1, \ldots, a_n) \in w^M$ with $f(a_1, \ldots, a_n)$ defined,

$$h_s(f^M(a_1, \ldots, a_n)) = f^N((h_{s_1}(a_1), \ldots, h_{s_n}(a_n))$$

- for all $p \in P_w$ and $(a_1, \ldots, a_n) \in w^M$

$$(a_1, \ldots, a_n) \in p^M \text{ implies } (h_{s_1}(a_1), \ldots, h_{s_n}(a_n)) \in p^N$$

2.4 Satisfaction Relation

The satisfaction of a Σ-sentence by a Σ-model M is defined as usual in terms of the satisfaction of its constituent atomic formulae w.r.t. assignments of values to all the variables that occur in them, the value assigned to variables of sort s being in s^M. Variable assignments are total, but the value of a term w.r.t. a variable assignment may be undefined, due to the application of a partial function during the evaluation of the term. Note, however, that the satisfaction of sentences is two-valued.

The application of a predicate symbol p to a sequence of argument terms holds in M iff the values of all the terms are defined and give a tuple belonging to p^M. A definedness assertion concerning a term holds iff the value of the term is defined. An existential equation holds iff the values of both terms are defined and identical, whereas a strong equation holds also when the values of both terms are undefined; thus both notions of equation coincide for defined terms. The value of an occurrence of a variable in a term is that provided by the given variable assignment. The value of the application of a function symbol f to a sequence of argument terms is defined only if the values of all the argument terms are defined and give a tuple in the domain of definedness of f^M, and then it is the associated result value.

3 Subsorted Partial Logic

This section defines the notions of signatures, models, and sentences of subsorted partial first-order logic, leading to an institution *SubPFOL* which is used in the semantics of CASL specifications.

The definitions are based on the many-sorted partial first-order logic given in section 2. Subsorted models, homomorphisms and sentences are defined to be certain many-sorted models, homomorphisms and sentences. This has the important consequence, that results like the existence of initial models carry directly over from the many-sorted case.

3.1 Signatures

The notion of subsorted signatures extends the notion of order-sorted signatures as given by Goguen and Meseguer [GM92], by allowing not only total function symbols, but also partial function symbols and predicate symbols:

Definition 3.1 A *subsorted signature* $\Sigma = (S, TF, PF, P, \leq_S)$ consists of a many-sorted signature (S, TF, PF, P) together with a reflexive transitive *subsort relation* $\leq_S$ on the set S of sorts.

Notation. The relation $\leq_S$ extends pointwise to sequences of sorts. We drop the subscript S when obvious from the context.

Note that the signatures are not required to be monotonic as in [GM92]. This decision was taken in order to allow constants to be overloaded and avoid problems with modularity. This is further discussed in section 6. However, whenever two overloaded symbols are in the monotonicity ordering defined below, their semantics are still required to be consistent, cf. the monotonicity axioms in section 3.3.

For a subsorted signature, $\Sigma = (S, TF, PF, P, \leq_S)$, we define *overloading relations* (also called *monotonicity orderings*), $\leq_F$ and $\leq_P$, for function and predicate symbols, respectively:

Definition 3.2 Let $f : w_1 \to_1 s_1, f : w_2 \to_2 s_2 \in TF \cup PF$ (where $\to_1, \to_2 \in \{\to, \rightarrow\!\!\!\!\!+\}$), then $f : w_1 \to_1 s_1 \leq_F f : w_2 \to_2 s_2$ iff $w_1 \leq w_2$ and there exists a common supersort of s_1 and s_2.

Let $p : \P w_1, p : \P w_2 \in P$, then $p : \P w_1 \leq_P p : \P w_2$ iff $w_1 \leq w_2$.

Note that two profiles of an overloaded constant declared with two different sorts are in the overloading relation iff the two sorts have a common supersort.

Definition 3.3 A *signature morphism* $\sigma : \Sigma \to \Sigma'$ is a many-sorted signature morphism that preserves the subsort relation and the overloading relations.

For modularity aspects, it is important that signatures can be combined. This is guaranteed by the following

Proposition 3.4 The category of subsorted CASL signatures and signature morphisms is cocomplete.

Definition 3.5 With each subsorted signature $\Sigma = (S, TF, PF, P, \leq_S)$ we associate a many-sorted signature $\Sigma^\#$, which is the extension of the underlying many-sorted signature (S, TF, PF, P) with

- a total *injection* function symbol $\mathtt{inj} : s \to s'$, for each pair of sorts $s \leq_S s'$
- a partial *projection* function symbol $\mathrm{pr} : s' \rightarrow\!\!\!\!\!+ \, s$, for each pair of sorts $s \leq_S s'$
- a unary *membership* predicate symbol $\in^s : \P s'$, for each pair of sorts $s \leq_S s'$

We assume that the symbols used for injection, projection and membership are not used otherwise in Σ.

3.2 Sentences

Definition 3.6 *Subsorted Σ-sentences* are ordinary many-sorted $\Sigma^\#$-sentences.

Note that in the sentences, injections from subsorts to supersorts must be explicit. In the CASL language considered in section 4 these are left implicit and must unambiguously be determined by the context.

Since terms are fully disambiguated, they have a unique sort. This implies that, at this institution level, there is no need at all to require signatures to be regular and locally filtered. However, for the parsing of CASL terms it makes a difference whether signatures satisfy these requirements or not.

3.3 Models

Definition 3.7 Subsorted Σ-models are ordinary many-sorted $\Sigma^\#$-models satisfying the following set of axioms $J(\Sigma)$ (where the variables are all universally quantified):

$(\mathtt{inj} : s \to s)(x) \doteq x$ ⟨identity⟩
$(\mathtt{inj} : s \to s')(x) \doteq (\mathtt{inj} : s \to s')(y) \Rightarrow x \doteq y$ for $s \leq_S s'$ ⟨injectivity⟩
$(\mathtt{inj} : s' \to s'')((\mathtt{inj} : s \to s')(x)) \doteq (\mathtt{inj} : s \to s'')(x)$
for $s \leq_S s' \leq_S s''$ ⟨transitivity⟩
$((\mathtt{inj} : s \to s')(x) \doteq y) \Leftrightarrow ((\mathrm{pr} : s' \rightarrow\!\!\!\!\!+ \, s)(y) \doteq x)$ for $s \leq_S s'$ ⟨projection⟩
$(\in^s : \P s')(x) \Leftrightarrow$ ¿$((\mathrm{pr} : s' \rightarrow\!\!\!\!\!+ \, s)(x))$ for $s \leq_S s'$ ⟨membership⟩
$(\mathtt{inj} : s \to s'')((f : w \to_1 s)(x_1, \ldots, x_n)) =$
$(\mathtt{inj} : s' \to s'')((f : w' \to_2 s')((\mathtt{inj} : s_1 \to s'_1)(x_1), \ldots, (\mathtt{inj} : s_n \to s'_n)(x_n)))$
for $f : w \to_1 s \leq_F f : w' \to_2 s'$, where $w' = s'_1 \times \ldots \times s'_n$ and
$w = s_1 \times \ldots \times s_n$ and $s, s' \leq s''$ ⟨function-monotonicity⟩
$(p : \P w)(x_1, \ldots, x_n) \Leftrightarrow (p : \P w')((\mathtt{inj} : s_1 \to s'_1)(x_1), \ldots, (\mathtt{inj} : s_n \to s'_n)(x_n))$
for $p : \P w \leq_P p : \P w'$, where $w' = s'_1 \times \ldots \times s'_n$ and
$w = s_1 \times \ldots \times s_n$ ⟨predicate-monotonicity⟩

Definition 3.8 Σ-homomorphisms are $\Sigma^\#$-homomorphisms.

The following result directly follows from the corresponding result for partial first-order logic (PFOL) stated in [Rei87]:

Proposition 3.9 Consider the restriction of *SubPFOL* to universally quantified positive conditional axioms. In this restriction, all theories have initial models and along all theory morphisms there exist free extensions.

3.4 Injections Versus Inclusions

In CASL, subsorting is modeled by (implicit) injections (i.e. injective embedding functions between the corresponding carriers), and not by set inclusions as in usual order-sorted algebra [GM92]. This extra generality means that it is possible to specify a sort $s1$ to be a subsort of another sort $s2$ without requiring that their implementations use the same data representation (i.e. there are models in which the carrier set of $s1$ is not a subset of the carrier set of $s2$), as it is often the case in imperative programming languages (for efficiency reasons). The injection functions are used to convert the data representation when passing from a subtype to a supertype. In cases where it is desirable not to have the cost of converting data representation, a model with subset inclusions should be used.

It is possible to pass from a model with injections to an isomorphic model with true subset inclusions. Goguen and Meseguer [GM92] proved that under the assumption that the signature is locally filtered. But this transition can be done also without the assumption of local filtration:

Theorem 3.10 Given a subsorted Σ-model A, there is a subsorted Σ-model B isomorphic to A which interprets the subsorting relation as true set inclusion.

Proof. First, generalize the colimit construction on page 250 of [GM92] to non-filtered diagrams by using corollary 19 on page 48 of [AM75]. Then also Lemma 4.1 of [GM92] can be generalized to non-filtered diagrams. With this, for each model (of a possibly non-locally filtered signature) we can find an isomorphic model where all injections are inclusions, using the construction of colimits above, and proceed as in [GM92]. □

3.5 Satisfaction Relation

Since subsorted Σ-models and Σ-sentences are just certain many-sorted $\Sigma^{\#}$-models and $\Sigma^{\#}$-sentences, the notion of satisfaction for the subsorted case follows directly from the notion of satisfaction for the many-sorted case.

4 CASL Subsorting Language

In this section we present the CASL subsorting language. We use an ad-hoc concrete syntax, as the concrete syntax for CASL has not yet been decided, and we give the semantics in terms of signatures, sentences and models of the underlying institution of subsorted partial logic defined in section 3. A description of the full CASL language is given in the tentative design proposal [CoFI96].

4.1 Basic Specifications

A *basic* CASL *specification* consists of a set of declarations and a set of axioms. In section 4.7 some examples of CASL specifications are given.

A specification is *well-formed* if the declarations (see section 4.2) determine a subsorted signature Σ and a possible empty set of subsorted Σ-sentences $E1$. Furthermore, the set of axioms (see section 4.3) must determine a set of subsorted Σ-sentences $E2$. The *semantics* of the specification is then the class of subsorted Σ-models satisfying $E1$ and $E2$.

CASL also provides facilities for writing structured specifications and architectural specifications, but these are not covered in this paper as they are institution independent and hence independent of the subsorting in basic specifications.

4.2 Declarations

A CASL declaration can be

- a declaration of a sort, s,
- a declaration of a total function symbol, $f : w \to s$ [6],
- a declaration of a partial function symbol, $f : w \to\!\!\!\!+ s$,
- a declaration of a predicate symbol, $p : \P w$, or,
- an assertion of a subsort relationship, $s1 \leq s2$

and contributes in the obvious way to the elements S, TF, PF, P and $\leq_S$ of a subsorted signature $(S, TF, PF, P, \leq_S)$.

Furthermore, a declaration can be a *predicative sort definition* of the form:

s: sort = { x : s′ • $\phi[x]$}

where s' is an existing sort and $\phi[x]$ is a formula. It declares the new sort s to be a subsort of the sort s', asserting that the values of the subsort s are precisely the projections of those values x from the supersort s' for which the given formula $\phi[x]$ holds. More formally, the predicative sort definition is a shorthand for the following declarations:

$$s : sort$$
$$s \leq s'$$
$$\forall x : s' \bullet \phi[x] \Leftrightarrow x \in s$$

4.3 Axioms

CASL *axioms*[7] are CASL *formulae* built from atomic CASL formulae using quantification (over sorted variables) and the usual logical connectives of first-order logic.

---

[6] We allow a declaration of the form $f : s$ as a shorthand for $f : \to s$, when w is empty

[7] In the full CASL language, it is also possible to state sort generation constraints.

An *atomic* CASL *formula* can have the following forms:

$p(t_1 \ldots t_n)$	(application of a predicate p to terms $t_1 \ldots t_n$)
$(p : \P w)(t_1 \ldots t_n)$	(application of a qualified predicate to terms $t_1 \ldots t_n$)
$¿(t)$	(the assertion that a term t is defined)
$t \doteq t'$	(existential equation between terms t and t')
$t = t'$	(strong equation between terms t and t')
$t \in s$	(the assertion that a term t is within a subsort s)

A CASL *term* can have one of the following forms[8]:

x	(variable)
$f(t_1, \ldots, t_n)$	(application of a function f to terms $t_1 \ldots t_n$)
$(f : w \rightarrow s)(t_1, \ldots, t_n)$	(application of a qualified total function to terms)
$(f : w \rightarrow\!\!\!\!\!+\; s)(t_1, \ldots, t_n)$	(application of a qualified partial function to terms)
$t \Downarrow s$	(casting a term t to a subsort s)
$t : s$	(sort disambiguation: force term t to have sort s)

Sort disambiguations and the qualification of function and predicate symbols with their profiles are used to avoid unintended interpretations of overloaded function and predicate symbols.

In section 4.4, we introduce the rules for *well-sortedness* of CASL formulae. These rules allow implicit embeddings in term formation (i.e. terms of a subsort can be used whenever terms of a supersort are expected). Well-sorted CASL formulae can be *parsed/expanded* to subsorted sentences of the underlying institution *SubPFOL* of subsorted partial logic by qualifying function and predicate symbols with their profiles, inserting implicit injection functions, replacing casts with corresponding applications of projection functions and removing sort disambiguations. Due to the overloading of function and predicate symbols and implicit injections, it turns out that a CASL formula may have several possible expansions. The expansion relation is defined in section 4.5. Finally, in section 4.6, we define a CASL formula to be *well-formed*, if it is well-sorted and can be sufficiently disambiguated (i.e. all its expansions have the same semantics).

A well-formed CASL formula then *determines* all the subsorted sentences it can be expanded into.

4.4 Well-sorted Terms and Formulae

The well-sortedness of a CASL formula is defined wrt. a subsorted signature $\Sigma = (S, TF, PF, P, \leq_S)$ (determined from the declarations in the specification in which the formula occur):

Definition 4.1 A CASL formula is *well-sorted* wrt. Σ, if each of its constituent quantifications uses S-sorted variables, and each of its constituent atomic formulae φ is well-formed wrt. Σ and X, where X is an S-sorted family of variables determined in the obvious way from those quantifications which enclose φ.

[8] We allow the term f as a shorthand for $f()$

Before defining which atomic formulae are well-sorted, we first define the sets of well-sorted terms:

Definition 4.2 The set $W_\Sigma(X)_s$ of *well-sorted* CASL terms of sort s wrt. Σ and X is defined inductively by the following rules:

1. $x \in W_\Sigma(X)_s$, if $x \in X_s$
2. $f(t_1,\ldots,t_n) \in W_\Sigma(X)_s$, if $t_i \in W_\Sigma(X)_{s_i}$, and $f \in TF_{w,s} \cup PF_{w,s}$, $w = s_1 \ldots s_n$
3. $(f : w \to s)(t_1,\ldots,t_n) \in W_\Sigma(X)_s$, if $t_i \in W_\Sigma(X)_{s_i}, f \in TF_{w,s}, w = s_1 \ldots s_n$
4. $(f : w \to\!\!\!\!\!\!\;\;+ s)(t_1,\ldots,t_n) \in W_\Sigma(X)_s$, if $t_i \in W_\Sigma(X)_{s_i}, f \in PF_{w,s}, w = s_1 \ldots s_n$
5. $t : s \in W_\Sigma(X)_s$, if $t \in W_\Sigma(X)_s$
6. $t \Downarrow s' \in W_\Sigma(X)_{s'}$, if $t \in W_\Sigma(X)_s$ and $s' \leq_S s$
7. $t \in W_\Sigma(X)_{s'}$, if $t \in W_\Sigma(X)_s$ and $s \leq_S s'$

The set of *well-sorted* CASL terms, wrt. Σ and X is the union of the sorted sets defined above: $W_\Sigma(X) = \cup_{s \in S} W_\Sigma(X)_s$.

Note that, due to function overloading and implicit injections, a CASL term may have several sorts.

Definition 4.3 The set $A_\Sigma(X)$ of *well-sorted* atomic CASL formulae wrt. Σ and X is the least set satisfying the following rules:

1. $p(t_1,\ldots,t_n) \in A_\Sigma(X)$, if $t_i \in W_\Sigma(X)_{s_i}, p \in P_{s_1 \ldots s_n}$
2. $(p : ¶w)(t_1,\ldots,t_n) \in A_\Sigma(X)$, if $t_i \in W_\Sigma(X)_{s_i}, p \in P_w, w = s_1 \ldots s_n$
3. $t \doteq t \in A_\Sigma(X)$, if $t, t' \in W_\Sigma(X)_s$
4. $t = t' \in A_\Sigma(X)$, if $t, t' \in W_\Sigma(X)_s$
5. $¿(t) \in A_\Sigma(X)$, if $t \in W_\Sigma(X)$
6. $t \in s \in A_\Sigma(X)$, if $t \in W_\Sigma(X)_{s'}, s \in S, s \leq_S s'$

4.5 Expansion of Terms and Formulae

In this section we define the *expansion* relation, $\leadsto$, between well-sorted terms or formulae of the CASL language and terms or formulae of the underlying institution *SubPFOL* of subsorted partial logic.

The expansion relation for formulae and terms is defined wrt. a subsorted signature $\Sigma = (S, TF, PF, P, \leq_S)$, and for atomic formulae and terms also wrt. an S-sorted set of variables X.

Definition 4.4 The expansion relation, $\leadsto \subseteq W_\Sigma(X) \times T_{\Sigma^\#}(X)$, from well-sorted CASL terms into subsorted Σ-terms is inductively defined by the following rules in which $t \leadsto_s t'$ is a shorthand for $t \leadsto t' \wedge t' \in T_{\Sigma^\#}(X)_s$:

1. $$\frac{t \leadsto_s t'}{t \leadsto (\texttt{inj} : s \to s')(t')}\; s \leq_S s'$$

2. $$\frac{}{x \leadsto x}\; x \in X$$

3. $$\frac{t_i \leadsto_{s_i} t'_i}{f(t_1,\ldots,t_n) \leadsto (f : w \to s)(t'_1,\ldots,t'_n)}\; f \in TF_{w,s}\;, w = s_1 \ldots s_n$$

4. $$\frac{t_i \rightsquigarrow_{s_i} t'_i}{f(t_1,\ldots,t_n) \rightsquigarrow (f : w \nrightarrow s)(t'_1,\ldots,t'_n)}\ f \in PF_{w,s}\ , w = s_1 \ldots s_n$$

5. $$\frac{t_i \rightsquigarrow_{s_i} t'_i}{(f : w \rightarrow s)(t_1,\ldots,t_n) \rightsquigarrow (f : w \rightarrow s)(t'_1,\ldots,t'_n)}\ f \in TF_{w,s}\ , w = s_1 \ldots s_n$$

6. $$\frac{t_i \rightsquigarrow_{s_i} t'_i}{(f : w \nrightarrow s)(t_1,\ldots,t_n) \rightsquigarrow (f : w \nrightarrow s)(t'_1,\ldots,t'_n)}\ f \in PF_{w,s}\ , w = s_1 \ldots s_n$$

7. $$\frac{t \rightsquigarrow_s t'}{t : s \rightsquigarrow t'}$$ 8. $$\frac{t \rightsquigarrow_{s'} t'}{t \Downarrow s \rightsquigarrow (\mathrm{pr} : s' \nrightarrow s)(t')}\ s \leq_S s'$$

Definition 4.5 The expansion relation, $\rightsquigarrow \subseteq A_\Sigma(X) \times AF_\Sigma(X)$, from well-sorted atomic CASL formulae into atomic subsorted Σ-formulae is inductively defined by the following rules:

1. $$\frac{t_i \rightsquigarrow_{s_i} t'_i}{p(t_1,\ldots,t_n) \rightsquigarrow (p : \P w)(t'_1,\ldots,t'_n)}\ p \in P_w\ , w = s_1 \ldots s_n$$

2. $$\frac{t_i \rightsquigarrow_{s_i} t'_i}{(p : \P w)(t_1,\ldots,t_n) \rightsquigarrow (p : \P w)(t'_1,\ldots,t'_n)}\ p \in P_w\ , w = s_1 \ldots s_n$$

3. $$\frac{t_1 \rightsquigarrow_s t'_1 \wedge t_2 \rightsquigarrow_s t'_2}{t_1 \doteq t_2 \rightsquigarrow t'_1 \doteq t'_2}$$ 4. $$\frac{t_1 \rightsquigarrow_s t'_1 \wedge t_2 \rightsquigarrow_s t'_2}{t_1 = t_2 \rightsquigarrow t'_1 = t'_2}$$

5. $$\frac{t \rightsquigarrow_s t'}{¿(t) \rightsquigarrow ¿(t')}$$ 6. $$\frac{t \rightsquigarrow_{s'} t'}{t \in s \rightsquigarrow (\in^s : \P s')(t')}\ s \leq_S s'$$

Well-sorted CASL formulae expand into subsorted Σ-formulae in the obvious way by expanding their constituent atomic CASL formulae.

4.6 Equivalent Expansions and Well-formedness of Formulae

Let ψ be an expansion of a CASL formula φ. By the definition of expansions, for each occurrence of a non-qualified function symbol f in φ we have a corresponding occurrence of a qualified function symbol $f : w \rightarrow s$ or $f : w \nrightarrow s$ in ψ, and for each occurrence of a non-qualified predicate symbol p in φ we have a corresponding occurrence of a qualified predicate symbol $p : w$ in ψ.

Definition 4.6 Let ψ and ψ' be two expansions of a CASL-formula φ. Inductively define ψ and ψ' to be *equivalent* (written $\psi \sim \psi'$), if

1. (a) for each occurrence of a non-qualified function symbol f in φ, for the corresponding occurrences of qualified function symbols $f : w \rightarrow_1 s$ in ψ and $f : w' \rightarrow_2 s'$ in ψ', we have either $f : w \rightarrow_1 s \leq_F f : w' \rightarrow_2 s'$ or $f : w' \rightarrow_2 s' \leq_F f : w \rightarrow_1 s$, where $\rightarrow_1 \in \{\rightarrow, \nrightarrow\}$, and $\rightarrow_2 \in \{\rightarrow, \nrightarrow\}$,

(b) and, for each occurrence of a non-qualified predicate symbol p in φ, for the corresponding occurrences of qualified predicate symbols $p : w$ in ψ and $p : w'$ in ψ', we have either $p : w \leq_P p : w'$ or $p : w' \leq_P p : w$,

2. or, there exists an expansion ψ'' of ϕ such that $\psi'' \sim \psi$ and $\psi'' \sim \psi'$.

The following theorem states that two equivalent expansions are satisfied by the same models.

Theorem 4.7 Let ψ_1 and ψ_2 be sub-sorted Σ-sentences, which are expansions of a CASL formula φ, and let m be a sub-sorted Σ-model. If ψ_1 and ψ_2 are equivalent, then m satisfies ψ_1 iff m satisfies ψ_2.

Definition 4.8 A CASL formula is *well-formed* wrt. Σ iff it is well-sorted wrt. Σ and all its expansions are equivalent.

Theorem 4.9 If a CASL formula φ is well-sorted wrt. a *regular* subsorted signature Σ, then φ is also well-formed wrt. Σ.

From definition 4.8 and theorem 4.7 it follows that all the expansions of a well-formed CASL formula are satisfied by the same models. Therefore, we can say that a well-formed formula *determines* any of its expansions.

4.7 Examples of CASL Specifications

Example 1
This example demonstrates the interplay between subsorting and partiality:

NAT =

$nat, pos : sort$
$pos < nat$
$even : sort = \{n : nat \bullet iseven(n)\}$
$0 : nat$
$succ : nat \to pos$
$pred : nat \twoheadrightarrow nat$
$pred : pos \to nat$
$iseven : ¶nat$
$\forall n : nat \bullet$
$\neg ¿(pred(0))$
$pred(succ(n)) = n$
$iseven(0)$
$iseven(succ(n)) \Leftrightarrow \neg iseven(n)$

Now the axiom $¿(pred(pred(succ(succ(0)))))$ can be parsed with the first *pred* being partial, while the second *pred* can have any of the two profiles. But since the two profiles are in the overloading relations, this ambiguity is harmless. If we omit the partial *pred* from the signature, the axiom becomes ill-formed, since no retracts are inserted automatically. We then have to insert an explicit projection:

$$¿(pred(\ pred(succ(succ(0))) \Downarrow pos\ ))$$

to make the axiom well-formed.

Example 2
This example (inspired by [GD94]) shows that in CASL it is possible to have multiple representations (for example, points are represented by both cartesian and polar coordinates), to switch between representations without invoking explicit conversion functions and even to have overloaded functions on different representations.

$$\vdots$$

$$atan : Float \to Angle$$
$$Point, Cart, Polar : sort$$
$$Cart, Polar < Point$$
$$origin : Cart$$
$$coord : Float \times Float \to Cart$$
$$origin : Polar$$
$$coord : PosFloat \times Angle \to Polar$$

$$\vdots$$

$$\forall x : PosFloat, y : Float \bullet coord(x, y) = coord(sqrt(x^2 + y^2), atan(y/x))$$

Above, it is assumed that *PosFloat* is a subsort of *Float*, and, *sqrt*, $\_^2$ and $+$ have been declared with sufficient profiles such that $sqrt(x^2 + y^2)$ has sort *PosFloat*. Furthermore, it is assumed that *Angle* is not a subsort of *Float*. This has the effect that the two profiles of *coord* are not in the overloading relation and thus can coexist as different functions. Otherwise, one would have to use two different names, say *coordPolar* and *coordCart*.

5 Tools

The design of CASL has been finished only recently, so it is clear that tools have to be developed yet. In this section, we briefly describe an overload resolution algorithm and the possibility to re-use existing theorem provers. Both together comprise a minimal set of tools which make the "in-the-small" part of CASL amenable to machine support. This will also be the basis for a shallow encoding of the "in-the-small" part of CASL into the HOL/Isabelle system, cf. the embedding of Z in HOL [Kol96].

5.1 Overload Resolution

Overload resolution for an arbitrary closed CASL formula proceeds inductively over the structure of the formula, while an environment with the sorts of the variables in the current scope is carried around. Thus it suffices to design an overload resolution algorithm for atomic formulae, which receives an atomic formula and an environment as input and which returns either an expansion of the atomic formula or the message "not resolvable".

There is a simple, naive overload resolution algorithm: just collect the set of all expansions of a given atomic formula, and check that they are all equivalent. But this bears a lot of redundancy. The "least sort parse" algorithm for regular signatures described in [GM92], p. 252, just picks *one* expansion (the one with minimal profiles) and forgets about all the other ones. Of course, regularity is defined in a such way precisely that this algorithm works. Since CASL does not impose any condition on signatures, we cannot expect to get such a simple algorithm here. But we can expect that our algorithm behaves as simple as the least sort parse if the signature ***happens*** to be regular.

Given an atomic formula φ and a context X of sorted variables, our overload resolution algorithm proceeds in the following steps:

- Inductively compute the set $MinExp(\varphi, X)$ of minimal expansions of φ in context X.
- Check that $MinExp(\varphi, X)$ is non-empty and all of its elements are equivalent. If so, return an arbitrary element of $MinExp(\varphi, X)$, otherwise return "not resolvable".

The set $MinExp(\varphi, X)$ is defined as follows:

- $MinExp(x, X) = \begin{cases} \{x : s\}, & \text{if } x \in X_s \\ \emptyset, & \text{if } x \notin \bigcup_{s \in S}(X_s \cup PF_{\lambda,s} \cup TF_{\lambda,s}) \end{cases}$
- $MinExp(f(t_1, \ldots, t_n), X) = \{(f : w \rightarrow_1 s)(u'_1, \ldots, u'_n) \mid$
  $u_i : s_i \in MinExp(t_i, X)$ for $i = 1, \ldots, n, w = s'_1, \ldots, s'_n$ and
  $w \rightarrow_1 s$ is minimal in $\{w \rightarrow_1 s \mid f : w \rightarrow_1 s \in \Sigma$ and $w \geq s_1 \ldots s_n\}$,
  where $u'_i = (\mathtt{inj} : s_i \rightarrow s'_i)(u_i)$, if $s_i \neq s'_i$, otherwise $u'_i = u_i\}$
- $MinExp(p(t_1, \ldots, t_n), X) = \{(p : \P w)(u'_1, \ldots, u'_n) \mid$
  $u_i : s_i \in MinExp(t_i, X)$ for $i = 1, \ldots, n$ and $w = s'_1, \ldots, s'_n$ is minimal in
  $\{w \mid p : \P w \in \Sigma$ and $w \geq s_1 \ldots s_n\}$
  where $u'_i = (\mathtt{inj} : s_i \rightarrow s'_i)(u_i)$, if $s_i \neq s'_i$, otherwise $u'_i = u_i\}$

Here, $u : s \in MinExp(\ldots)$ is shorthand for $u \in T_{\Sigma^\#}(X)_s$ and $u \in MinExp(\ldots)$. The application of $MinExpr$ to other forms of terms and predicates is defined in a similar way.

In the regular case, all the $MinExp$-sets are just singletons and consist of the least sort parse. Thus only in (rather exceptional) non-regular cases the algorithm becomes more complicated. The above algorithm should work in linear time for all practical cases, but it may be exponential for contrived examples. By doing a more complicated equivalence check at each inductive step, one can get an algorithm which runs in linear time for all cases.

5.2 Theorem proving

The traditional way to proceed would be to build a calculus and theorem prover for *SubPFOL*, the underlying institution of *CASL*, from scratch. Indeed, we believe that this is possible without great difficulties. But this approach has the disadvantages that much work has to be redone and that for *PFOL* (partial first-order logic with ***total assignments***) there can exist only calculi (like that in [Bur82]) that do not keep the simple substitution rule of FOL (total first-order logic).

It is already clear now that good theorem provers for $SubPFOL$ are available. This is because it is possible to translate a $SubPFOL$-theory to a first-order (FOL) theory and then just use any theorem proving tool for first-order logic. The translation is done in two steps: The first step is to translate subsorted partial first-order logic to partial first-order logic, as was indicated in section 3. The second step is the translation of partial first-order logic to total first-order logic, as described in [CMR97]. Both translation steps are particular cases of the ***borrowing*** technique proposed in [CM97].

Note that the translation to FOL allows one to use (among others) the usual substitution- and resolution-based theorem provers for FOL. In general, such theorem provers can be used directly only for partial logics with ***partial*** variable valuations, see also [Sco79].

6 Discussion

In this paper we have presented the subsorting approach of the CASL language. The main novelty is that there are no requirements like monotonicity, regularity or local filtration imposed on subsorted signatures.

The main argument against these requirements is that they give complications with modularity. In order to be able to combine specifications and to use the pushout-approach to parameterization, the signature category has to be cocomplete. To guarantee cocompleteness of the signature category, one either has to restrict the category of signatures in a rather complicated way [HN96] or to confuse the user with unexpected identifications of sorts and extra sorts in the colimit [Mos96].

A second argument against imposing monotonicity (or regularity, which entails monotonicity) is that monotonicity rules out overloading of constants, which we consider very useful. Many many-sorted frameworks with overloading already allow them, and these frameworks should be easily embeddable into CASL.

It turns out that the notions (of models) and results (about initiality and freeness) remain as simple as in the many-sorted case (and can even be directly carried over!). The only price for dropping the requirements is a more complicated definition of well-formed atomic formulae than in the regular case. However, our overload resolution algorithm sketched in section 5 shows that this does not add too much complexity, and in the case that a signature happens to be regular, even the least sort parse algorithm is simulated.

The idea to drop monotonicity and regularity is not new, it stems from Goguen and Diaconescu [GD94]. They point out that the result about existence of initial models also holds for non-regular signatures. However, they still assume local filtration, and they do not propose how overload resolution should be done.

Local filtration (in combination with regularity) is required by Goguen and Meseguer [GM92] in order to ensure that equational satisfaction is closed under isomorphism. This is necessary, because they define equations $t_1 = t_2$ to be well-formed if just the least sorts of t_1 and t_2 are in the same connected component. (Note, that this means that the least sorts are not required to have a common upper bound). This liberal definition has the advantage that well-formedness of $t_1 = t_2$ and $t_2 = t_3$ ensures well-formedness of $t_1 = t_3$.

The idea to drop local filtration has been proposed by Haxthausen [Hax97] for a subsorting approach with implicit non-injective coercions. However, regularity was still assumed. In order to ensure that equational satisfaction was still closed under isomorphism, it was proposed to use explicitly sorted equations $t_1 =_s t_2$, which were well-formed only if the least sorts of the terms had the sort s as a common upper bound. The price for this was that transitivity of well-formedness of equations only holds for equations over the same sort.

The same idea is adopted in CASL. However, here it was possible to leave the sort implicit. The following example illustrates how transitivity of well-formedness of equations in CASL only holds for equations over the same sort:

$s, t, u : sort, \quad t < s, t < u$
$a : s, b : t, c : u$
$\bullet\ a = b, b = c$

$a = b$ is well-formed with sort s, $b = c$ is well-formed with sort u, but $a = c$ is ill-formed. We can repair this by considering $a \Downarrow t = c \Downarrow t$, which is well-formed, but has a semantics different from $a = c$ in [GM92]. Note that the problem of satisfaction not being closed under model isomorphism does not arise in CASL.

The overloading relation (also called monotonicity ordering) leads to identification of related functions and predicates in the semantics. This implements the "same name – same meaning" principle that is pervasive in the CASL language (cf. e.g. unions of specifications). We have deliberately excluded strong overloading in the sense of [GD94]. An alternative notion of signature would provide the relations $\leq_F$ and $\leq_P$ explicitly instead of deriving them from the other information in the signature, thus allowing strong overloading. In [GD94] it is argued that this may be used, for example, to model overwriting in the object oriented paradigm. We are not convinced that this suffices really to model object orientation, so both object orientation and strong overloading are left for extensions of CASL.

Acknowledgements The authors would like to thank all the participants of CoFI, and in particular Peter Mosses and Olaf Owe, for their contributions of ideas for the subsorting approach.

References

[AM75] Arbib and Manes. *Arrows, Structures, and Functors - The categorical Imperative.* Academic Press Inc, 1975.

[Bur82] P. Burmeister. Partial algebras — survey of a unifying approach towards a two-valued model theory for partial algebras. *Algebra Universalis*, 15:306–358, 1982.

[CM97] M. Cerioli and J. Meseguer. May I borrow your logic? (transporting logical structures along maps). *Theoretical Computer Science*, 173:311–347, 1997.

[CMR97] M. Cerioli, T. Mossakowski, and H. Reichel. From total equational to partial first order. In E. Astesiano, H.-J. Kreowski, and B. Krieg-Brückner, editors, *Algebraic Foundations of Systems Specifications*. 1997. To appear[9].

[GD94] Joseph Goguen and Răzvan Diaconescu. An Oxford survey of order sorted algebra. *Mathematical Structures in Computer Science*, 4(3):363–392, September 1994.

[GM86] J. Goguen and J. Meseguer. Eqlog: Equality, types, and generic modules for logic programming. In Douglas DeGroot and Gary Lindstrom, editors, *Functional and Logic Programming*, pages 295–363. 1986.

[GM92] J. A. Goguen and J. Meseguer. Order-sorted algebra I: equational deduction for multiple inheritance, overloading, exceptions and partial operations. *Theoretical Computer Science*, 105:217–273, 1992.

[Hax97] A.E. Haxthausen. Order-sorted algebraic specifications with higher-order functions. *Theoretical Computer Science*, 183, 1997. To appear.

[HN96] A.E. Haxthausen and F. Nickl. Pushouts of order-sorted algebraic specifications. In *Proceedings of AMAST'96*, volume 1101 of *Lecture Notes in Computer Science*. Springer-Verlag, 1996.

[Kol96] B. Wolff Kolyang, T. Santen. A structure preserving encoding of Z in Isabelle/HOL. In *Proc. 1996 International Conference on Theorem Proving in Higher Order Logic (Turku)*, volume 1125 of *Lecture Notes in Computer Science*. 1996.

[Mos96] T. Mossakowski. *Representations, hierarchies and graphs of institutions*. PhD thesis, Bremen University, 1996.

[Mos97] Peter D. Mosses. CoFI: The common framework initiative for algebraic specification and development. Invited paper for TAPSOFT'97, 1997.

[Rei87] H. Reichel. *Initial Computability, Algebraic Specifications and Partial Algebras*. Oxford Science Publications, 1987.

[Sco79] D. S. Scott. Identity and existence in intuitionistic logic. In M.P. Fourman, C.J. Mulvey, and D.S. Scott, editors, *Application of Sheaves*, volume 753 of *Lecture Notes in Mathematics*, pages 660–696. Springer-Verlag, 1979.

[CoFI96] CoFI: The Common Framework Initiative for Algebraic Specification. CASL - the COFI Algebraic Common Language Tentative Design: Language Summary[10], 1996.

[9] See http://www.informatik.uni-bremen.de/~kreo/ifip_chapters/chapters.html

[10] Available at http://www.brics.dk/Projects/CoFI/DesignProposals/Summary

Specification of Timing Constraints within the Circal Process Algebra*

Antonio Cerone and George J. Milne

Advanced Computing Research Centre, School of Computer and Information Science, University of South Australia, Adelaide SA 5095, Australia
{cerone,milne}@cis.unisa.edu.au.

Abstract

We present a methodology for describing timing constraints within various time models. This methodology exploits the constraint-based modelling style available within Circal, a process algebra that permits a natural representation of time without any *ad hoc* extension. The methodology is illustrated through several examples in the area of communication protocols and asynchronous hardware.

1 Introduction

The increased use of digital computers to control complex real-time systems, communication protocols with time-dependencies, and the renewed interest in asynchronous hardware have highlighted the importance of an accurate representation of time within specification formalisms. The combination of process algebra and temporal logic through the technique of *model checking* [9, 13] has allowed the development of tools for the automatic verification of properties of systems. Time, however, cannot be directly modelled by some process algebras such as CSP [11], CCS [17] and LOTOS [2]. In order to overcome this problem, timed extensions to process algebras have been developed (see e.g. [10]). However, introducing time makes the semantics of such process algebras cumbersome.

In this paper we consider Circal (CIRcuit CALculus) [15, 16], a process algebra whose basic features permit a natural representation of time without any extension to the process algebra framework together with a *constraint-based modelling* mechanism, in which the behaviour of a process may be constrained simply by composing it with another process which represents the constraint. *Timing events* can be represented as ordinary actions, which follow the same rules as any other action. The use of this representation, on top of constraint-based modelling, results in a methodology for describing timing constraints within various time models. For each distinct class of application it is therefore possible to choose the most appropriate time model such that we may attempt to avoid the high level of detail that inflames the state explosion problem (see e.g. [6]). This paper presents several time models and illustrate them with examples.

* This work has been supported by a grant of the Australian Research Council

1.1 The Circal Process Algebra

In this section we give a brief description of the Circal operators and their semantics and refer the reader to [1, 15, 16, 18] for further explanations. The syntax of Circal processes is summarised by the following BNF expressions, where Γ is a guard, P is a process, D a process definition, $\mathcal{A}$ is the set of possible actions and $\mathtt{a}, \mathtt{b} \in \mathcal{A}$, and I is a process variable:

$$M ::= \mathtt{a} \mid \mathtt{a}\, M$$
$$\Gamma ::= \mathtt{a} \mid (M)$$
$$P ::= /\backslash \mid \Gamma P \mid P + P \mid P \,\&\, P \mid I \mid P * P \mid P - M \mid P\,[\mathtt{a}/\mathtt{b}]$$
$$D ::= I \texttt{<-} P$$

Each Circal process has a *sort* associated with it, which specifies the set of actions (ports) through which it may interact with other processes. Every sort will be a non empty subset of $\mathcal{A}$, the collection of all available actions.

The /\ constant represents a process which can participate in no communication. This is a process that has terminated or deadlocked.

In ΓP the P process may be guarded by sets of simultaneously occurring actions. This is a key feature of Circal which greatly enriches the modelling potential of the algebra in contrast to process algebras such as CSP [11], CCS [17] and LOTOS [2], which only permit a single action to occur at one computation instant.

A name can be given to a Circal process with the *definition* operator (<-). Recursive process definitions, such as P <- $\Gamma\, P$, are permitted.

The + operator defines an *external choice*, which is decided by the environment where the process is executed, whereas the & operator defines an *internal choice*, which is decided autonomously by the process itself without any influence from its environment. Internal choices appear to an external observer as *non-determinism*.

Given processes P and Q, the term $P * Q$ represents the process which can perform the actions of the subterms P and Q together (*composition*). Any synchronisation which can be made between two terms, due to some atomic action being common to the sorts of both subterms, must be made, otherwise the actions of the subterms may occur asynchronously.

The terms P-a and P[a/b] define *abstraction* and *relabelling*, respectively, in the usual way.

1.2 The Circal System

The Circal process algebra provides an ideal basis from which to build and reason about process models. In order to readily build large or complex models it is necessary to extend the algebra with data-types, functions and control structures. The Circal System implements the XCircal language, which is an extension of the basic process algebra [16]. The added features of XCircal that are used in this paper are the following:

Events An `Event` is a data-type corresponding to a Circal action set. Atomic events, which are events consisting of a single action, must be declared before the use. A shorthand for n nested guards consisting of the same event `a` is `(a` n`)`. For example `((a b) 2) Q` is a shorthand for `(a b) (a b) Q`.

Processes A `Process` is a data-type corresponding to a Circal term. It must be declared before the use. An array of processes may be declared. A process may be declared with an event parameter corresponding to its sort.

Process Generation Functions Processes may be generated by functions having events or other processes as parameters.

Control Structures They have a syntax immediately derived from the programming language C.

Testing Equivalence The Circal System

2 Constraint-based Modelling

The constraint-based modelling style [16, 20] is supported by the following distinctive features of the Circal process algebra:

- guarding of processes by sets of simultaneous actions;
- sharing of events over arbitrary numbers of processes;
- the particular nature of the composition operator which provides synchronisation between processes without removal of the synchronising events in the resultant behaviour.

The behaviour of a process may be constrained simply by composing it with another Circal process which represents the constraint. The sort of the constraint is a subset of the sort of the process to be constrained.

As an example, consider the process P of sort $\{a, b, c\}$ defined as follows:

```
Event a, b, c
Process P, A, B
P <- a B + b A + c P
A <- a B + c A
B <- b A + c B
```

Process `P` generates all the finite strings on the alphabet $\{\mathtt{a}, \mathtt{b}, \mathtt{c}\}$ that consist of alternating occurrences of `a` and `b` and arbitrary occurrences of `c`. Two constraints for process `P` are processes `C1` of sort $\{a, b, c\}$ and `C2` of sort $\{b, c\}$ defined as follows

```
Process C1, S, C2, C, D
C1 <- a S
S  <- a S + b S + c S
C2 <- b C + c D
C  <- c D
D  <- b C
```

Since P and C1 have the same sort and at the initial state C1 can perform only a, the composite process P*C1 must perform a as the first action. Then C1 evolves to S, which can perform every possible sequence of actions. Therefore, process C1 constrains the string to start with an occurrence of a with any arbitrary behaviour then following. Process C2 constrains b and c to occur in alternation, whereas it does not affect the occurrences of action a, which does not belong to its sort.

3 Models of Time

In all process algebras there is an implicit model of time. The guarding operator generates a term ΓP which represents the behaviour in which event Γ occurs followed by the behaviour denoted by the renewal process P. This implies that event occurrences are related by a temporal order relation and indeed occur relative to one another in time. The temporal order is in general a partial order, due to the presence of choice operators which induce a branching behaviour. However, while this permits a natural modelling of the temporal ordering of actions, a quantitative representation of time is not always possible.

In order to describe quantitative aspects of time in Circal, the above notion of time is augmented by using some actions as timing signals and defining the processes that constrain such timing signals to occur always in a particular relation with each other. Timing signals are new actions that are not used in modelling the untimed system, but they are not special actions and follow the same rules as any other action. Therefore time can be incorporated within Circal without any extension to the process algebra framework.

Depending on the granularity of the timing signals and on the relationships defined between different timing signals we can obtain various time models. We first introduce discrete models of time that allow the representation of delays, durations and timing constraints commonly used in the specification of real-time systems. Then, in Section 3.3, we show how to model dense time.

3.1 Delays and Durations

The most obvious way in which to incorporate time within a process algebra is to introduce a timing signal to represent a global tick. In most process algebras the critical point is to relate the signals describing time to the actions performed by other processes. In Circal, however, this can be done in a natural way, without any special extension to the formalism. The simple inclusion of a timing signal in a guard is used to describe the concept of *all* the actions in the guard occurring synchronously with the signal. Moreover, because of the particular nature of the composition operator when used to compose several processes, at every point-in-time in which a component performs synchronisations on a timing signal any other component that can perform that signal must also do it, and the signal occurrences are still visible after the synchronisation without removal.

In order to model discrete time we suppose that every action performed by the system occurs simultaneously with an occurrence of the global tick. If the `t` action represents the global tick, then the `P` process defined as follows

```
P <- (a t) t t t (b t) t t P
```

models an infinite sequence of alternating occurrences of `a` and `b` with a delay of 4 time units (3 ticks) between `a` and `b` and a delay of 3 time units (2 ticks) between `b` and `a`. In this special case an alternative interpretation of the `P` process is that action `a` has a duration of 4 time units and `b` has a duration of 3 time units. In general, durations can be modelled by splitting events into pairs defining the start and the end of the event. If `sa` and `sb` represent the start of `a` and `b`, respectively, and `ea` and `eb` represent the end of `a` and `b`, respectively, the same durations as above are modelled by the `Q` process defined as follows:

```
Q <- (sa t) t t (ea t) (sb t) t (eb t) Q
```

In the previous examples time is incorporated within the system specification. This can be the case of a physical clock. However, in several practical situations we are interested in verifying a system whose timing is an assumption about the environment or in analysing how time can modify the behaviour of an untimed system. In this case it is useful to have the (untimed) system specification and the system timing at two different levels. The untimed version of the `P` process above is the `UP` process defined as follows:

```
UP <- a b UP
```

We define the `Delay` process generation function to introduce delays between occurrences of events:

```
Process Delay(Event e1, e2, int n) {
        Process D[2]
        D[0] <- (e1 t) D[1] + (e2 t) D[0] + t D[0]
        D[1] <- (t (n-1)) (e2 t) D[0]
        return D[0]                   }
```

Using the Circal System we can verify the following equivalence:

```
P == UP * Delay(a,b,4) * Delay(b,a,3)
```

Analogously, durations of events can be introduced into the untimed version of the `Q` process above by the `Delay` process generation function by instantiating the first two parameters with the start and the end of the event, respectively.

3.2 Timing Constraints

In the specification of real-time systems we usually do not know the exact length of delays and durations. The specification, however, must contain timing constraints that bound delays and/or durations [3, 7, 8, 12]. Timing constraints are statically associated with points in the physical or logical structure that defines the system: in a physical structure such as a circuit they can be associated with wires [6], whereas in a logical structure such as a Petri net they can be associated with basic components of the structure (in a Petri net: places, transitions and arcs) [3, 7, 8].

Therefore, since in our framework only action occurrences can be timed, timing signals must be attached to actions that are associated with a unique point in the physical or logical structure that defines the system. For example in a digital circuit timing signals can be attached to the actions that correspond to ports on logic gates.

The Circal program in Figure 1(a) defines the finite state machine in Figure 1(b). We want to introduce between the e and e1 events a delay bounded by a time interval $I(\mathtt{e},\mathtt{e1}) = [\mathtt{l1},\mathtt{u1}]$ and between the e and e2 events a delay

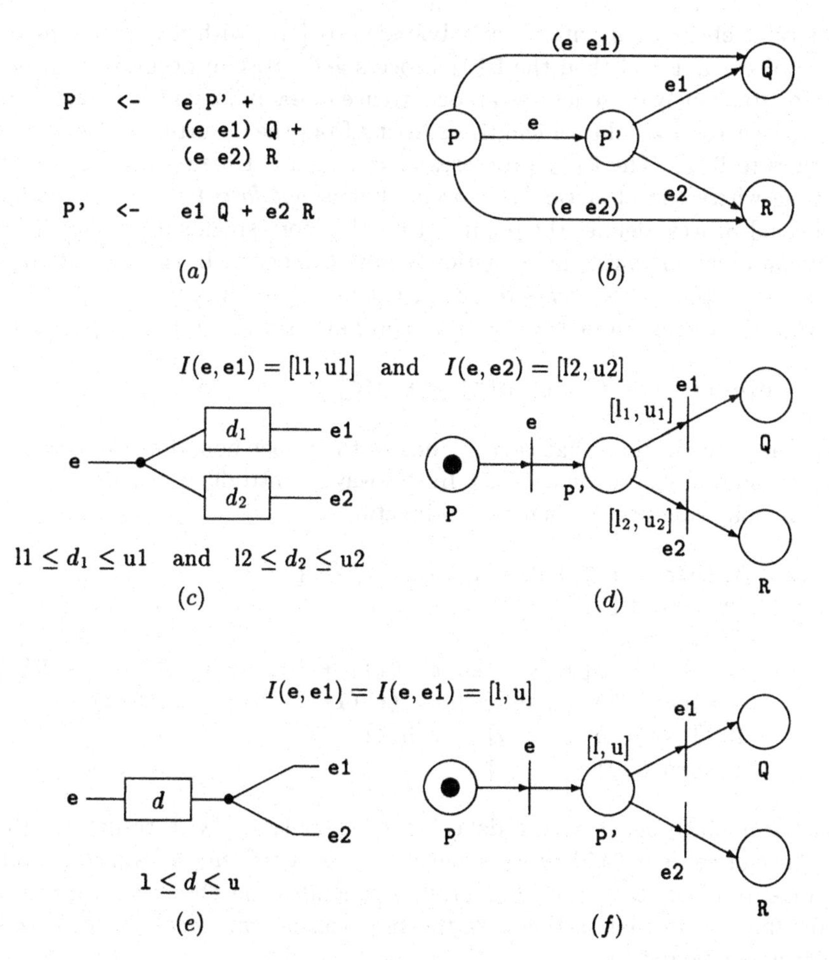

Fig. 1. Examples of timings and their interpretations in terms of circuits and Petri nets.

bounded by a time interval $I(\mathtt{e}, \mathtt{e2}) = [\mathtt{l2}, \mathtt{u2}]$. We consider only intervals with a positive upper bound. The following process generation function

```
Process TimeInt(Event ea, eb, int l, u) {
        Process D[u-l+2]
        if (l==0) { D[0] <- (ea t) D[1] + (ea eb t) D[0] + t D[0]
        } else      D[0] <- (ea t) (t (l-1)) D[1] + t D[0]
        for (i=1;i<=(u-l);i++)
            D[i] <- (eb t) D[0] + t D[i+1]
        D[u-l+1] <- (eb t) D[0]
        return D[0] }
```

constrains eb to occur with a delay bounded by $[\mathtt{l}, \mathtt{u}]$ with respect to the occurrence of ea. If $\mathtt{l} = 0$ then the D[0] process generates an occurrence of ea and eb simultaneously or generates an occurrence of ea and changes to D[1], otherwise it generates a delay of length l starting from the occurrence of ea and then changes to D[1]. The D[i] processes, $\mathtt{i} = 1, ..., \mathtt{u} - \mathtt{l}$, defines the $\mathtt{u} - \mathtt{l}$ points in time where the eb action *can* occur, but is *not forced* to occur; finally the D[u-l+1] process defines the point in time that corresponds to the upper bound of the interval, in which the eb action is *forced* to occur. In this way *strong time* [7, 8, 14], which forces events to occur, has been introduced.

If in the definition of TimeInt the D[u-l+1] process state is replaced by

```
D[u-l+1] <- (eb t) D[0] + t D[0]
```

then the point in time that corresponds to the upper bound of the interval can pass without any occurrence of eb. In this way we introduce *weak time* [7, 8, 21].

The following process generation function

```
Process TimeIntInf(Event ea, eb, int l) {
        Process D[2]
        if (l==0) {
                  D[0] <- (ea t) D[1] + (ea eb t) D[0] + t D[0]
        } else    D[0] <- (ea t) (t (l-1)) D[1] + t D[0]
        D[1] <- (eb t) D[0] + t D[1]
        return D[0]        }
```

constrains eb to occur with a delay bounded by $[\mathtt{l}, \infty[$ with respect to the occurrence of ea. The D[0] process generates a delay of length l starting from the occurrence of ea; then the D[1] process generates the eb action after an arbitrary time. Note that in this case the time can be only weak since there is no finite upper bound.

The timed behaviour such that the occurrences of e, e1 and e2 in the process P in Figure 1(a) are constrained by the time intervals $I(\mathtt{e}, \mathtt{e1}) = [l1, u1]$ and $I(\mathtt{e}, \mathtt{e2}) = [l2, u2]$ is obtained through the composition

```
P * TimeInt(e,e1,l1,u1) * TimeInt(e,e2,l2,u2)
```

If we interpret the P process as a fork in a circuit, then we have the situation described in Figure 1(c), where the distinct wire branches have different delays. If we interpret it as a time Petri net, then we have the net described in Figure 1(d), where timing constraints are associated with arcs incoming into transitions.

If $I(\mathtt{e},\mathtt{e1}) = I(\mathtt{e},\mathtt{e2}) = [l,u]$, then the corresponding timed behaviour is obtained through the composition

```
P * TimeInt(e,e1,l,u) * TimeInt(e,e2,l,u)
```

Such a situation is interpreted in Figure 1(e) as a fork in a circuit, with the delay occurring before the branch, and in Figure 1(f) as a time Petri net where timing constraints are associated with places.

In the Circal program in Figure 2(a) the e action is shared between the Q1

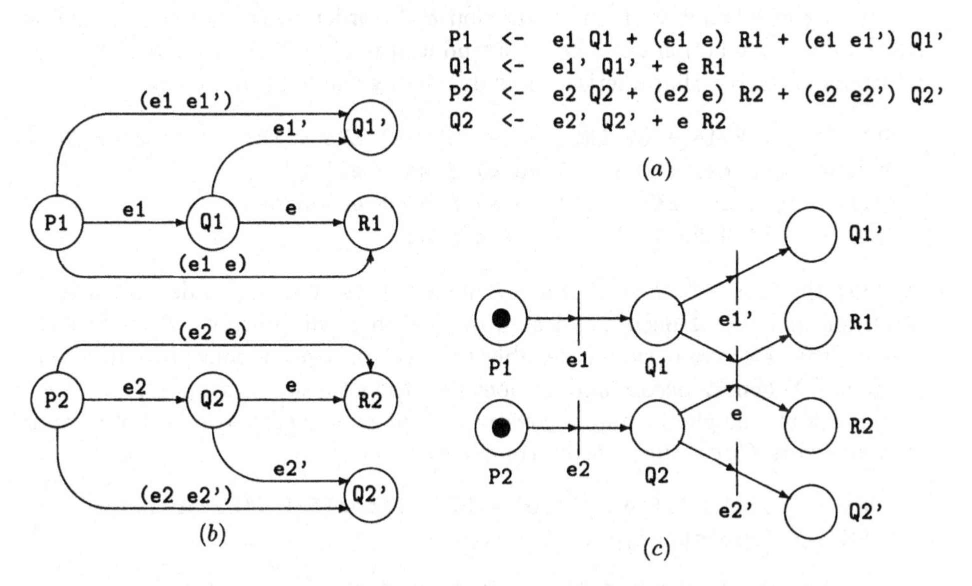

Fig. 2. Example of timing and its interpretation in terms of Petri nets.

and Q2 processes. When composing P1 and P2, whose behaviours are described by the finite state machines in Figure 2(b), the e action can occur only through a synchronisation between the two processes, either simultaneously with or after the occurrence of e1 and e2. This situation is described by the Petri net in Figure 2(c).

A delay between the e1 and e events that is bounded by a time interval $I(\mathtt{e},\mathtt{e1}) = [\mathtt{l1},\mathtt{u1}]$ and a delay between the e2 and e events that is bounded by a time interval $I(\mathtt{e},\mathtt{e2}) = [\mathtt{l2},\mathtt{u2}]$ can be easily introduced through the composition

```
P1 * TimeInt(e1,e,l1,u1) * P2 * TimeInt(e2,e,l2,u2)
```

where TimeInt(e1,e,l1,u1) and TimeInt(e2,e,l2,u2) are local timing constraints for P1 and P2, respectively. However, when modelling a system it is more useful to measure the delay of an event from the time when such an event is enabled rather than from the occurrence of events which are necessary, but not sufficient for its enabling. This is a *global* timing constraint that is defined on the whole system rather than on its components. Timing constraints often depends on assumptions about the environment, whose interactions with the overall system are not easily decomposable in interactions with the single components. This kind of global timing constraint has been introduced in [14] and has been frequently used in the modelling of real-time systems, in particular with safety-critical systems [12].

In the example in Figure 2, the occurrence of both `e1` and `e2` causes an occurrence of `e`. Therefore, we want to introduce a timing constraint $I(\mathtt{e}) = [\mathtt{l}, \mathtt{u}]$ that bounds the delay between the time when `e` is enabled to occur and the time when it occurs. In the Petri net in Figure 2(c) this corresponds to associating the timing constraint with the transition `e`. In order to specify such a timing constraint a new action `ee` must be introduced to characterise when `e` starts to be enabled. Such a characterisation is defined by the following process:

```
SENe <- e1 EN1e + e2 EN2e + (e1 e2 ee) ENe + (e1 e2 ee e) SENe
EN1e <- (e2 ee) ENe + (e2 ee e) SENe + e1' SENe
EN2e <- (e1 ee) ENe + (e1 ee e) SENe + e2' SENe
ENe  <- e1' SENe + e2' SENe + e SENe
```

In `SENe` the preconditions `e1` and `e2` of `e` may occur either independently or simultaneously. If `e1` occurs and `e2` does not, then the process evolves to `EN1e` where either `e2` may occur and enable `e` or `e1'` may occur and prevent `e` from occurring. When `e2` occurs and `e1` does not, the situation is symmetric.

Therefore, the global timing constraint that is defined above on the `e` event is modelled in Circal through the composition

```
P1 * TimedIntInf(e1,e1',0) * P2 * TimedIntInf(e2,e2',0) *
SENe * TimeInt(ee,e,l,u)
```

Notice that the `TimedIntInf(e1,e1',0)` and `TimedIntInf(e2,e2',0)` processes do not bound the delay between `e1` and `e1'` and the delay between `e2` and `e2'` respectively, but force `e1'` and `e2'`, which do not appear in any other timing constraint, to occur simultaneously with an occurrence of t in order to meet the discrete time assumption.

3.3 Dense Time

In the previous two sections we have presented techniques for modelling discrete time within the Circal process algebra. If we remove the assumption that every action performed by the system occurs simultaneously with the occurrence of a global tick, then the events that occur between the n-th and the $(n+1)$-th occurrences of the global tick can be thought of as occurring at a time x, such that $n \cdot u < x < (n+1) \cdot u$, where u is the time between two successive occurrences of the global tick. This is based on an implicit assumption that the global tick occurs at regular intervals of length u. Therefore, the global tick models ***absolute*** time.

If the `t` action represents the global tick, then the `P` process defined as follows

```
P <- (a t) t t t b Q
```

models an occurrence of `a`, followed by an occurrence of `b` after a time x such that $3 \cdot u < x < 4 \cdot u$, followed by the behaviour of the `Q` process.

We can extend the model presented in the previous two sections to a dense time that ranges on the set of rational numbers. Since the number of the timing constraints that are associated with the specification of a system is finite, they can be defined by a finite set of rational numbers. The global tick may be chosen fine enough to define all timing constraints. For example we can introduce into the system modelled in Figure 2 the timing constraints $I_e = [\frac{3}{4}.\frac{5}{6}]$, $I_{e1'} = [\frac{2}{3}.1]$ and $I_{e2'} = [\frac{7}{10}.\frac{3}{5}]$ by choosing a time $u = \frac{1}{60}$ between two successive ticks and defining $I_e = [45 \cdot u, 50 \cdot u]$, $I_{e1'} = [40 \cdot u, 60 \cdot u]$ and $I_{e1'} = [42 \cdot u, 36 \cdot u]$. With such a resolution an event can occur simultaneously with the n-th occurrence of the global tick, that is at time $x = \frac{n}{60}$ or between the n-th and the $(n+1)$-th occurrence of the global tick, that is at a time x such that $\frac{n}{60} < x < \frac{n+1}{60}$. In the second case the time cannot be precisely characterised, but only approximated by an interval of time.

The `TimeInt` and `TimeIntInf` process generation functions must be modified to allow the asynchronous occurrences of events with respect to the global tick. However, such an extension is not sufficient. In fact, if an event is enabled by the asynchronous occurrence of one of its preconditions (the other preconditions having already occurred), with respect to the global tick, then the time between the occurrence of the enabling event and the occurrence of the enabled event cannot be measured precisely, but only approximated to by an interval.

This problem can be overcome by associating a *local clock* with every *sequential* component and one with every set of possible interacting components. The clock is then reset at each occurrence of an event that contains some action local to the component or is shared by the interacting components. Time between two successive events is then measured with respect to the ticks of the local clocks rather than with respect to a global tick. The example in Figure 2 consists of two sequential components, `P1` and `P2`. We associate the new `t1` and `r1` actions with `P1`, the new `t2` and `r2` actions with `P2`. and the new `tt` and `rr` actions with the interaction between `P1` and `P2`, with `t1`, `t2` and `tt` tick actions and `r1`, `r2` and `rr` reset actions. The `TimeInt` process generation function is modified as follows

```
Process TimeInt(Event t, r, ea, eb, int l, u) {
        Process S, D[u-l+2]
        S <- r D[0]
        if (l==0) { D[0] <- (ea r) D[1] + (ea eb r) D[0] + t D[0] +
                             (ea r t) D[1] + (ea eb r t) D[0]
        } else      D[0] <- (ea r) (t (l-1)) D[1] + t D[0] +
                             (ea r t) (t (l-1)) D[1]
```

```
for (i=1;i<=(u-1);i++)
    D[i] <- (eb r) D[0] + (eb r t) D[0] + t D[i+1]
D[u-1+1] <- (eb r) D[0] + (eb r t) D[0]
return D[0] }
```

and the TimeIntInf process generation function is modified analogously. Every occurrence of an action in the system resets the local tick via the r action in order to precisely measure the time between successive events. In general, ticks of different local clocks do not occur simultaneously. However, we must ensure that all the local clocks tick at the same rate. This constraint is modelled using the following process generation function:

```
Process Rel(Event ra, ta, rb, tb) {
        Process R, S, AB, BA
        R  <- (ra rb) S
        S  <- (ta tb) S + ra BA + rb AB +
              (ta tb ra) S + (ta tb rb) S + (ta tb ra rb) S
        AB <- ta BA + ra BA + rb AB +
              (ta ra) BA + (ta rb) S + (ta ra rb) S
        BA <- tb AB + rb AB + ra BA +
              (tb rb) AB + (tb ra) S + (tb rb ra) S
        return R                     }
```

which is applied to every possible pair of local clocks.

Therefore the timing constraints that we defined above are modelled in Circal through the composition

```
P1 * TimedInt(t1,r2,e1,e1',40,60) *
P2 * TimedInt(t2,r2,e2,e2',42,36) *
SENe * TimeInt(tt,rr,ee,e,45,50) *
Rel(r1,t1,r2,t2) * Rel(r1,t1,rr,tt) * Rel(r2,t2,rr,tt)
```

This modelling style is still limited by the unit of resolution, but has the important advantage that events occurring within a time period that is less than the unit of resolution are not represented as occurring simultaneously. Moreover, events can be associated with different clocks which are related to each other through external constraints. In the example above the Rel process constrains the local clocks to have the same rate. In that case clocks are abstract entities introduced in order to define timing constraints. In many cases, however, physical clocks explicitly or implicitly exist within real systems and they can also have different clocking rates. Such drifting clocks can be modelled by composing the system with a process that constrains the ratio between the rates of two different components to have a fixed value or even to vary within a fixed interval of time.

For example the process generation function

```
Process TwiceRate(Event r, ta, tb) {
        Process R[3]
```

```
R[0] <- r R[1]
R[1] <- ta R[2] + r R[1] + (r ta) R[1]
R[2] <- (ta tb) R[1] + r R[1] + (r ta tb) R[1]
return R[0]                    }
```

models two clocks having the same reset signal (`r`) and such that the tick of the first clock (`ta`) has a rate that is twice the rate of the tick of the second clock (`tb`).

Such an approach has been used in [4, 5] to specify and verify a simplified version of an audio control protocol developed by Philips. In this protocol messages consist of finite sequences of 0 and 1 bits and are encoded by a sender, according to a Manchester encoding, into timed transitions of the voltage between two levels on the single wire bus connecting the components. The end of a message is modelled by a sufficiently long time gap between the last transition that encodes the current message and the first transition that encodes the next message. Receivers in components attached to the bus interpret the voltage transitions and reconstruct the bitstream message.

The senders and receivers are run on different microprocessors and, since the microprocessors run code in addition to the protocol software, sender and receiver clocks may not be synchronised in frequency. The receiver clock tick (`tr`) is reset by a transition observed by the receiver on the bus (`trans`) or by an internal action of the receiver that is generated when the end of the message is detected (`end`). The `end` action resets to an idling state where it waits for the next transition, whereas the `trans` action resets to the state where the first tick of the receiver clock occurs.

Assuming that there is no delay on the bus, after composing the sender and the receiver the `trans` action will always occur simultaneously with the clock of the sender (`ts`). Therefore the occurrence of `trans` forces a synchronisation of `ts` and `tr`, whereas the occurrence of `end` stops the receiver clock. A given ratio between the sender and receiver clocks corresponds to a particular ordering between occurrences of the sender and receiver ticks, which is modelled by a process `Drift(ts,tr,trans,end)`, where occurrences of `trans` and `end` interrupt the ordered sequence of `ts` and `tr` through the same resetting game played by the receiver. The `Drift` process is described in detail in [4]. By imposing the `Drift` process that expresses a given ratio between the sender and receiver on the protocol specification as an external constraint the correctness of the audio control protocol is verified for that particular value of the ratio [4, 5].

3.4 Timing Constraints without explicit time

In the previous sections we have presented models of timing constraints that are based on the explicit representation of time in terms of clock ticks.

For some classes of systems, however, the exact timing of events is not necessary. This is the case of the design of bounded delay asynchronous circuits where the actual delays in the circuits are less important than the relationships between delays. For example, in a micropipeline [19] the major consideration for correct operation of the circuits is to ensure that the delay in the control path is longer than the delay in the data path. Thus it is natural to express delays as inequalities.

An approach suitable to this purpose has been developed in [6]. Instead of constraining delays to vary within an interval that is quantitatively defined, delays can be symbolically described as pairs of abstract events. These will be associated with the physical events occurring in the system behaviour through the composition of the process that specifies the system with processes that contain within the same action set both the physical and the corresponding abstract events. These processes are modelled through calls of the following process generation function:

```
Process SymbDelay(Event start,end,from,to) {
        Process D
        D <- (start from) D + (end to) D
        return D                          }
```

In this way constraints can be modelled in terms of processes having only the abstract events in their sorts, but which do not involve the physical events that occur in the system specification. Such constraints establish among the abstract events a time relationship that is then propagated by the `SymbDelay` processes to the physical events. An example of such a constraint is one where the length of a delay whose start and end are characterised by `d1s` and `d1e` respectively, is less than the length of a delay whose start and end are characterised by `d2s` and `d2e`. Such a constraint is modelled through calls of the following process generation function:

```
Process LessThan(Event d1s, d1e ,d2s, d2e) {
        Process L[3]
        L[0] <- (d1s d2s) L[1]
        L[1] <- d1e L[2]
        L[2] <- d2e L[0]
        return L[0]                        }
```

In the example in Figure 2 the delay between `e1` and `e1'` can be constrained to be less than the delay between `e2` and `e2'` through the composition

```
P1 * SymbDelay(d1s,d1e,e1,e1') * P2 * SymbDelay(d2s,d2e,e2,e2') *
LessThan(d1s,d1e,d2s,d2e)
```

This approach is explained in detail in [6], where it has been applied to the specification and verification of a hazard free combinational bounded delay asynchronous circuit.

4 Discussion

In this paper we have presented a methodology for introducing timing constraints into a system specification, according to various time models. This methodology exploits three distinctive features of the Circal process algebra: simultaneous event guards, sharing of events over arbitrary numbers of processes and the nature of the composition operator which provides synchronisation of processes without the removal of the synchronising events in the resultant behaviour. These permit a natural representation of time and support a constraint-based modelling style, which are the basis of our methodology. Since timing signals are new actions that follow the same rules as any other action, time is incorporated within Circal without any extension to the process algebra framework. Constraints are imposed on the system specification to define both the general time model and the specific timing properties of the system under analysis.

When timing constraints are fixed delays or durations defined in terms of the occurrences of a global tick, the definition of the time model does not require additional constraints. All constraints are defined through the `Delay` function introduced in Section 3.1 and are used only to model the specific lengths of the delays. Analogously, when time intervals are introduced as local constraints on a global tick all constraints are defined through the `TimeInt` and `TimeIntInf` functions defined in Section 3.2.

The use of time intervals as global constraints on a global tick requires an interface between the local view of the event occurrences and the global view of the event enablings. The `SENe` function defined in Section 3.2 provides such a global view, on which timing constraints are then applied.

The use of timing intervals on local ticks requires two levels of constraints. The `Rel` functions defined in Section 3.3 are the constraints used to characterise the time model, whereas the `TimeInt` and `TimeIntInf` functions characterise the timing constraints that are specific for the system under analysis. In some applications it is convenient to model both levels within the same constraint. For example, in the audio control protocol the two levels of constraints are modelled together by the `Drift` function.

Finally in the more abstract time model defined in Section 3.4 the `SymbDelay` function provides an interface between the system specification and the timing level whereas the `LessThan` function defines the specific timing constraints.

A key feature of this methodology is that the timing constraints are not included in the system specification. They are modelled at a different level of abstraction and imposed on the specification through the use of Circal composition.

References

1. A. Bailey, G. A. McCaskill, and G. J. Milne. An Exercise in the Automatic Verification of Asynchronous Designs. *Formal Methods in System Design*, 4(3), pp. 213–242, May 1994.
2. T. Bolognesi, and E. Brinksma. Introduction to the ISO specification language LOTOS. *Computer Networks and ISDN Systems*, 14(1), pp. 25–59, 1987.
3. A. Cerone, A Net-based Approach for Specifying Real-Time Systems, Ph. D. thesis, TD–16/93, University of Pisa, Department of Computer Science, Pisa, Italy, 1993.

4. A. Cerone, A. J. Cowie, G. J. Milne, and P. A. Moseley. Description and Verification of a Time-Sensitive Protocol. Technical Report CIS-96-009, University of South Australia, School of Computer and Information Science, Adelaide, Australia, October 1996.
http://www.cis.unisa.edu.au/cgi-bin/techreport?CIS-96-009
5. A. Cerone, A. J. Cowie, G. J. Milne and P. A. Moseley. Modelling a Time-Dependent Protocol using the Circal Process Algebra. In O. Maler (ed.), *Proc. of the International Workshop on Hybrid and Real-Time Systems*, Grenoble, France, March 1997, Lecture Notes in Computer Science 1201, pp. 124–138, Springer, Berlin, Germany, 1997.
6. A. Cerone D. A. Kearney and G. J. Milne. Verifying Bounded Delay Asynchronous Circuits using Time Relationship Constraints. Technical Report CIS-97-012, University of South Australia, School of Computer and Information Science, Adelaide, Australia, August 1997.
http://www.cis.unisa.edu.au/cgi-bin/techreport?CIS-97-012
7. A. Cerone and A. Maggiolo-Schettini. Time-based Expressivity of Timed Petri Nets. Technical IB 12/95, Goethe University, Department of Computer Science, Frankfurt am Main, Germany, July 1995.
http://www.cis.unisa.edu.au/staff/cerone.a./abstracts/frankfurt95.html
8. A. Cerone and A. Maggiolo-Schettini. Time-based Expressiveness of Timed Petri Nets for System Specification. To appear in *Theoretical Computer Science.*
9. E. M Clarke, E. A. Emerson and A. P. Sistla. Automatic Verification of Finite-state Concurrent Systems Using temporal logic specifications. *ACM Transactions on Programming Languages and Systems*, 8(2), pp. 244–263, 1986.
10. M. Hennessy and. T. Regan. A Process Algebra for Timed Systems. *Information and Computation*, 117, pp. 221–239, 1995.
11. C. A. R. Hoare. *Communication Sequential Processes.* International Series in Computer Science. Prentice Hall, 1985.
12. N. G. Leveson and J. L. Stolzy, Safety Analysis Using Petri Nets, *IEEE Transactions on Software Engineering*, 13, pp. 386–396, 1987.
13. K. L. McMillan. Symbolic model checking. Kluwer Academic Publishers, 1993.
14. P. M. Merlin and D. J. Farber, Recoverability of Communication Protocols — Implication of a Theoretical Study, *IEEE Transactions in Software Communications*, 24, pp. 1036–1043, 1976.
15. G. J. Milne. The Formal Description and Verification of Hardware Timing. *IEEE Transactions on Computers*, 40(7), pp. 811–826, July 1991.
16. G. J. Milne. *Formal Specification and Verification of Digital Systems.* McGraw-Hill, 1994.
17. R. Milner. *Communication and Concurrency.* International Series in Computer Science. Prentice Hall, 1989.
18. F. Moller. The Semantics of Circal. Technical Report HDV-3-89, University of Strathclyde, Department of Computer Science, Glasgow, UK, 1989.
19. I. E. Sutherland. Micropipelines. *Com. of ACM*, 32(6), pp. 720–738, Jun 1989.
20. C. A. Vissers, G. Scollo, M. van Sinderen and E. Brinksma. Specification Styles in Distributed Systems Design and Verification. *Theoretical Computer Science*, 89, pp. 179–206, 1991.
21. B. Walter, Timed Petri-Nets for Modelling and Analyzing Protocols with Real-Time Characteristics. In H. Rudin and C. H. West eds., *Proc. of the 3rd IFIP Workshop on Protocol Specification, Testing, and Verification*, pp. 149–159, North Holland, Amsterdam, The Netherlands, 1983.

On the Specification and Verification of Performance Properties for a Timed Process Algebra*

Xiao Jun Chen[1] and Flavio Corradini[2]

[1] School of Computer Science University of Windsor, xjchen@cs.uwindsor.ca
[2] Dip. di Mat. Pura ed Appl., Università di L'Aquila flavio@univaq.it

Abstract. We consider the problem of verifying properties in processes with durational actions. The properties are expressed in terms of a discrete-time extension of ACTL. The algorithm for model checking formulae in this logic over finite state timed transition systems is provided. We consider processes that have infinite models due to the increase of the value of the clock and show how to reduce the verification problem over the infinite models to the one over their compact finite representations.

1 Introduction

The analysis of system efficiency in the context of process algebras can be measured by way of the time consumed for the process executions [1, 8, 16, 17, 9]. This treatment relies on the assumption that actions have a *static duration*, chosen on the basis of the features of the abstract machine. More precisely, systems are distributed over the space where each sequential component is associated with a *local clock* whose elapsing is set dynamically during the execution of the actions by the corresponding component. Whenever an action a is executed by a sequential component E, the value n of the clock of E is incremented to n plus the duration of a, whilst the local clocks of those sequential components not involved in the execution of a are unaffected. By incorporating the duration of actions into the notion of process equivalence, we are able to discriminate processes not only according to the *functionality*, but also according to their *performance*.

In this paper we study performance properties of systems described in a timed process algebra [9] whose actions are of the form a_m^M meaning that an action a can be performed within the interval $[m + t, M + t]$, where t is the actual time. This permits expressing urgency, i.e. no delay between activation and execution of actions (by letting $m = M$), laziness, i.e. no upper bound on the delay of the execution (by letting $M = \infty$), as well as patient actions which can be delayed for a certain period. We concentrate on the subset of processes which can be described by finite state transition systems according to

* This work has been partially founded by EEC within the HCM Project EXPRESS, and by Italian CNR.

the standard untimed operational semantics. Even in this sublanguage, however, the timed transition systems describing the transitional semantics of such timed processes, usually have infinite states due to the increase of the clock values in the states. Since most approaches and implemented tools on system verification (either equivalence checking or model checking) are given on finite models, we introduce compact (finite) transition systems as alternative representations to the infinite models of these timed processes.

When timed processes have all clocks of their processors set to zero (which is the usual case of the experiments on processes), the compact transition systems are consistent with the original ones, in the sense that two processes are equivalent if and only if their compact transition systems are equivalent (cf. Figure 1(a)).

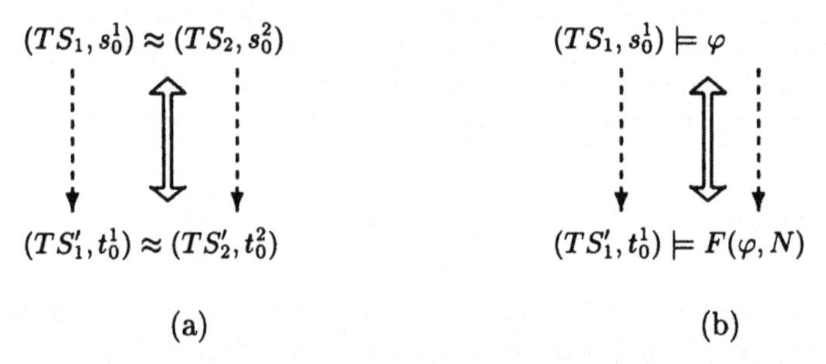

(TS_i, s_0^i) is a timed transition system with initial state s_0^i,
and (TS_i', t_0^i) is its compact transition system with initial state t_0^i (i=1,2)

Fig. 1. Reduction of verification problems

Our performance properties are expressed in terms of a logic called TAL, a discrete-time version of ACTL [10] (an action-based version of CTL [13, 15]). The algorithm can be obtained from the one for checking CTL formula over a finite state Kripke Structure. To deal with the infinite models, we prove that (i) for finitely branching transition systems, verifying the truth of a TAL formula over a timed transition system can be reduced to verifying the truth of the same formula over its compact transition system; (ii) in general, as Figure 1(b) illustrates, we can construct a formula transformation $\mathcal{F}$, so that verifying the truth of a TAL formula φ over a timed transition system TS_1 (which may also be infinitely branching) can be reduced to verifying the truth of $\mathcal{F}(\varphi, N)$, for certain number N related to TS_1, over its compact transition system TS_1'.

The paper is organized as follows: Section 2 presents the syntax of the language and Section 3 its behavioural semantics. Section 4 presents the compact finite representation while Section 5 introduces the logic TAL and a logical characterization of the behavioural equivalence. In Section 6, we discuss the model checking problem and show an applicative example for it. Section 7 is devoted to concluding remarks.

2 Syntax of Processes and States

The language used in the paper as a case study is a timed version of Milner's *CCS* [22]. Below we report its syntax [9]. As usual, the set of atomic actions is denoted by A (ranged over by a, b, ...), its complement by $\bar{A}$ (ranged over by $\bar{a}$, $\bar{b}$, ...) and *Act* (ranged over by α, β, ...) is defined as $Act = A \cup \overline{A}$. Complementation is extended to *Act* by $\bar{\bar{\alpha}} = \alpha$. As usual, τ ($\tau \notin Act$) denotes the invisible or internal action, and we use Act_τ (ranged over by μ, γ, ...) to denote $Act \cup \{\tau\}$. Let V (ranged over by v, v', ...) denotes a set of variables. The set $\mathcal{E}$ (E, $E' \in \mathcal{E}$) of *CCS processes*, is the set of closed (i.e. without free variables) and guarded (i.e. variable v in a rec $v.E$ term, can appear only within μ_m^M._ contexts) terms generated by the following grammar:

$$E ::= nil \;\Big|\; \mu_m^M.E \;\Big|\; E+E \;\Big|\; E|E \;\Big|\; E\backslash\{\alpha\} \;\Big|\; E[\Phi] \;\Big|\; v \;\Big|\; \text{rec } v.E$$

where, in $\mu_m^M.E$, $m \in \mathbf{N}^+$, $M \in \mathbf{N}^+ \cup \{\infty\}$ and $M \geq m$. *Sequential* processes (ranged over by $p, p', \ldots$) are terms in $\mathcal{E}$ of the form nil, $\mu_m^M.E$, $E+E$ or rec $v.E$.

Process $\mu_m^M.E$ can perform action μ and then behaves like E; m and M represent, respectively, the lower and the upper bounds for the time units needed to perform μ (e.g., its duration). This permits us to model two interesting situations: urgency and laziness. Urgency is obtained by requiring $m = M$: action μ can only take m time units to be performed. Laziness is obtained by requiring $M = \infty$: action μ can take as long as it wants to be performed.

The other operators are standard. *nil* denotes a terminated process; we often omit terminal *nil*'s. The alternative composition of E_1 and E_2 is denoted by $E_1 + E_2$, while $E_1|E_2$ denotes the parallel composition of E_1 and E_2 that can perform any interleaving of the actions of E_1 and E_2 or a synchronization whenever E_1 and E_2 can perform complementary actions. Process $E\backslash\{\alpha\}$ behaves like E except that actions $\alpha, \bar{\alpha}$ are forbidden, while $E[\Phi]$ stands for a process which can perform action $\Phi(\alpha)$ whenever E can perform action α. Φ is required to be a *renaming function* $\Phi : A \to A$; it is extended to Act_τ by requiring $\Phi(\bar{a}) = \overline{\Phi(a)}$ and $\Phi(\tau) = \tau$. Finally, rec $v.E$ is used for recursive definitions.

The states of the labelled transition system we are going to define are processes enriched by local clocks which record the local view of the elapsing of time together with the value of the global clock (corresponding to the maximum of local views). Formally, we introduce *extended processes*, obtained by equipping each sequential component of a process with a local clock. This is done, syntactically, via a *local clock prefixing* operator, $n \Rightarrow$ _. The set $\mathcal{D}$ (ranged over by d, d' ...) of extended processes is the set of terms generated by the following grammar:

$$d ::= n \Rightarrow p \;\Big|\; d|d' \;\Big|\; d\backslash\{\alpha\} \;\Big|\; d[\Phi].$$

where p is a sequential process and $n \in \mathbf{N}$. The *clock distribution equations*

$$\begin{aligned} n \Rightarrow (E \mid E') &= (n \Rightarrow E) \mid (n \Rightarrow E') \\ n \Rightarrow (E\backslash\{\alpha\}) &= (n \Rightarrow E)\backslash\{\alpha\} \\ n \Rightarrow (E[\Phi]) &= (n \Rightarrow E)[\Phi] \end{aligned}$$

show that a term $n \Rightarrow E$ can be reduced canonically to an extended process, when interpreting these equations as rewrite rules from left to right.

A *timed process* (or *state*) $d \triangleright n$ is an extended process d, equipped with a global clock n. The global clock represents the global observation time for the execution. Here, we require that $n \geq maxclock(d)$, where $maxclock(d)$ gives the maximum of clock values m occurring in subterms of d of the form $m \Rightarrow p$. We use $\mathcal{S}$ (ranged over by s, $s', \ldots$) to denote the set of timed processes.

3 Transitional and Behavioural Semantics

Processes are interpreted on *timed labelled transition systems* $\langle S, M, T\rangle$, where S is the set of timed processes, M a set of *timed actions* and $T = \{\xrightarrow{l} \subseteq S \times S \mid l \in M\}$ is the set of *transition relations*.[3] A timed action is a pair (μ, n) where $\mu \in Act_\tau$ and $n \in \mathbf{N}^+$. Intuitively, a label (μ, n) means that action μ has been completed exactly n time units after the computation began. As usual, the transition relations are given through a set of inference rules, see Table 1.

$$Act \; \frac{m \leq d \leq M, \; d < \infty, \; n + d \geq n'}{(n \Rightarrow \mu_m^M.E) \triangleright n' \xrightarrow{(\mu, n+d)} (n + d \Rightarrow E) \triangleright n + d}$$

$$Alt_1 \; \frac{(n \Rightarrow E_1) \triangleright n' \xrightarrow{(\mu,t)} d \triangleright t}{(n \Rightarrow E_1 + E_2) \triangleright n' \xrightarrow{(\mu,t)} d \triangleright t} \qquad Alt_2 \; \frac{(n \Rightarrow E_2) \triangleright n' \xrightarrow{(\mu,t)} d \triangleright t}{(n \Rightarrow E_1 + E_2) \triangleright n' \xrightarrow{(\mu,t)} d \triangleright t}$$

$$Rec \; \frac{(n \Rightarrow E[\mathrm{rec}\ v.\ E/v]) \triangleright n' \xrightarrow{(\mu,t)} d \triangleright t}{(n \Rightarrow \mathrm{rec}\ v.\ E) \triangleright n' \xrightarrow{(\mu,t)} d \triangleright t}$$

$$Par_1 \; \frac{d_1 \triangleright n \xrightarrow{(\mu,t)} d_1' \triangleright t}{(d_1 \mid d_2) \triangleright n \xrightarrow{(\mu,t)} (d_1' \mid d_2) \triangleright t} \qquad Par_2 \; \frac{d_2 \triangleright n \xrightarrow{(\mu,t)} d_2' \triangleright t}{(d_1 \mid d_2) \triangleright n \xrightarrow{(\mu,t)} (d_1 \mid d_2') \triangleright t}$$

$$Synch \; \frac{d_1 \triangleright n \xrightarrow{(a,t)} d_1' \triangleright t, \qquad d_2 \triangleright n \xrightarrow{(\bar{a},t)} d_2' \triangleright t}{(d_1 \mid d_2) \triangleright n \xrightarrow{(\tau,t)} (d_1' | d_2') \triangleright t}$$

$$Res \; \frac{d \triangleright n \xrightarrow{(\mu,t)} d' \triangleright t, \; \mu \notin \{\alpha, \bar{\alpha}\}}{d \backslash \{\alpha\} \triangleright n \xrightarrow{(\mu,t)} d' \backslash \{\alpha\} \triangleright t} \qquad Rel \; \frac{d \triangleright n \xrightarrow{(\mu,t)} d' \triangleright t}{d[\Phi] \triangleright n \xrightarrow{(\Phi(\mu),t)} d'[\Phi] \triangleright t}$$

Table 1. The Structural Rules for the Operational Semantics.

On top of this transitional semantics, an equivalence relation is proposed in [9] which is based on the branching-time semantics of bisimulation and relates two systems whenever they perform the same actions at the same time.

[3] As usual, we will write $s \xrightarrow{\mu} s'$ instead of $\langle s, s'\rangle \in \xrightarrow{\mu}$.

Definition 1. *(Performance Equivalence)*

1) A binary relation $\Re$ over $\mathcal{S}$ is an *R-bisimulation* iff for each $(d_1 \triangleright n, d_2 \triangleright n) \in \Re$:
   i) $d_1 \triangleright n \xrightarrow{(\mu,n')} d_1' \triangleright n'$ implies $d_2 \triangleright n \xrightarrow{(\mu,n')} d_2' \triangleright n'$ and $(d_1' \triangleright n', d_2' \triangleright n') \in \Re$;
   ii) $d_2 \triangleright n \xrightarrow{(\mu,n')} d_2' \triangleright n'$ implies $d_1 \triangleright n \xrightarrow{(\mu,n')} d_1' \triangleright n'$ and $(d_1' \triangleright n', d_2' \triangleright n') \in \Re$.
2) Two timed processes s_1 and s_2 are *f-performance equivalent*, written $s_1 \sim^f s_2$, iff there exists an *R-bisimulation* $\Re$ such that $(s_1, s_2) \in \Re$.
3) Two processes E_1, $E_2 \in \mathcal{E}$ are *f-performance equivalent*, written $E_1 \sim^f E_2$, iff $(0 \Rightarrow E_1) \triangleright 0 \sim^f (0 \Rightarrow E_2) \triangleright 0$. When f is clear from the context, we omit the superscript f, as in $d_1 \triangleright n \sim d_2 \triangleright n$ and $E_1 \sim E_2$.

Some interesting properties of this equivalence are studied in [9]. It has been shown that performance equivalence is preserved by all operators of the language and is decidable within the class of processes which have associated a finite state transition system according to the standard untimed operational semantics. Furthermore, it has been shown that within the only lazy fragment of the language, performance equivalence strictly implies (untimed) Milner's observational equivalence while, in general, it is incomparable with the standard untimed equivalences.

4 Compact Representations

A serious drawback of the operational semantics defined above is that the timed transition systems associated to timed processes are, in general, infinite state structures, due to the explicitly expressed global clock. In order to apply standard verification techniques (e.g. verification of bisimulation equivalence or verification of whether a process holds a certain property) on finite structures, we introduce compact transition systems as alternative representations of the models we discussed so far. When we confine ourselves to the comparison of processes with the same global clock (which is the case of the experiments on processes), we show that the compact transition systems are consistent with the original ones, in the sense that two processes are equivalent if and only if their compact transition systems are equivalent. In Section 6, we will discuss how to reduce the verification of the truth of a formula over these infinite structures to the verification over their compact structures.

To introduce the compact transition systems, the first change is on the time associated to the actions in the labels: instead of the actual global time of the ending state, it will now denote the increment in the value of the global clock passing from the source state to the target state of the transition. Formally, let $\_ \xrightarrow{-} \_$ be the transition relation defined in Section 3. Then we consider a new transition relation $\_ \stackrel{-}{\Longrightarrow} \_$ defined as: $d \triangleright m \stackrel{(\alpha,n-m)}{\Longrightarrow} d' \triangleright n$ *iff* $d \triangleright m \xrightarrow{(\alpha,n)} d' \triangleright n$.

The new relation: (i) facilitates our discussion on (finite) alternative representations, which will turn out clearer later; (ii) facilitates our model checking procedure because the timing constraints in logical formulas are specified on the basis of the (relative) time consumed between two states, rather than on the (absolute) time of the global clock; (iii) is sound in general, in the sense that the new transition relation $\Rightarrow$ preserves performance equivalences whenever we compare two processes with the same global clock:

Proposition 2. *Let $TS_i = \langle S_i, A, \rightarrow\rangle$ $(i = 1,2)$ be transition system for $d_1 \triangleright n$ and $d_2 \triangleright n$ respectively. Let $TS'_i = \langle S_i, A, \Rightarrow\rangle$ $(i = 1,2)$ where $\Rightarrow$ is defined as above. Then: $(TS_1, d_1 \triangleright n) \sim (TS_2, d_2 \triangleright n)$ iff $(TS'_1, d_1 \triangleright n) \sim (TS'_2, d_2 \triangleright n)$*

In order to introduce *compact timed states*, we need some auxiliary functions. The first one is $maxdelay(d)$ that gives the minimum time after which the behaviors of a process become uniform (cf. Proposition 7 below). We define $maxdelay(d) = 0$ if d does not contain μ_m^M-prefixings and

$$maxdelay(d) = max(\{M \mid \mu_m^M \text{ appears in } d, M < \infty\} \cup \{m \mid \mu_m^M \text{ appears in } d, M = \infty\}) + 1$$

otherwise. Function $\widehat{--}$ is applied to a state $d \triangleright n$ and returns an extended process that is an updating of d where the local clocks are possibly increased to the difference between the current value of the global clock and the maximal duration in the sequential agent. Formally:

$$\widehat{n \Rightarrow p \triangleright t} = max\{n, t - maxdelay(p)\} \Rightarrow p \qquad \widehat{d\backslash\{\alpha\} \triangleright t} = \widehat{d \triangleright t}\backslash\{\alpha\}$$

$$\widehat{d|d' \triangleright t} = \widehat{d \triangleright t}|\widehat{d' \triangleright t} \qquad \widehat{d[\Phi] \triangleright t} = \widehat{d \triangleright t}[\Phi]$$

Finally, let $minclock(d)$ denote the minimum of clock values n occurring in subterms of d of the form $n \Rightarrow p$, and let $addclock(d,n)$ denote d with all its local clocks augmented by n.

Definition 3. Given a state $d \triangleright n$, we define its *compact* state $[\![d \triangleright n]\!]$ as

$$[\![d \triangleright n]\!] = addclock(\widehat{d \triangleright n}, -minclock(\widehat{d \triangleright n})) \triangleright (n - minclock(\widehat{d \triangleright n}))$$

It is easy to see that

(i) $0 \leq n - minclock(\widehat{d \triangleright n}) \leq maxdelay(d)$;
(ii) every local clock in $addclock(\widehat{d \triangleright n}, -minclock(\widehat{d \triangleright n}))$ is in range $[0, n - minclock(\widehat{d \triangleright n})]$.

Furthermore, we have the following proposition on compact states stating the soundness of the translation w.r.t. the executions.

Proposition 4.

(i) $s \xRightarrow{(\alpha,t)} s'$ implies $\exists s''$. *s.t.* $[\![s]\!] \xRightarrow{(\alpha,t)} s''$ *and* $[\![s']\!] = [\![s'']\!]$;
(ii) $[\![s]\!] \xRightarrow{(\alpha,t)} s''$ implies $\exists s'$. *s.t.* $s \xRightarrow{(\alpha,t)} s'$ *and* $[\![s']\!] = [\![s'']\!]$.

Using compact timed states, we introduce the *compact transition system* w.r.t. a specific time t. A compact transition system w.r.t. t is a timed transition system whose states are compact timed states and the transition relation relates compact states to labels of the form (μ, n) where $n \leq t$.

Definition 5. *(compact transition system)*
Given transition system $\langle S, A, \Rightarrow\rangle$ associated to timed process $d \triangleright n$ and a specific time $t \geq maxdelay(d)$, the *compact transition system* of $d \triangleright n$ w.r.t. t is defined as $\langle S', A, \Rightarrow'\rangle$ where $S' = \{[\![s]\!] \mid s \in S\}$ and $\Rightarrow' = \{[\![s]\!] \overset{(\alpha,n)}{\Longrightarrow}{}' [\![s']\!] \mid s \overset{(\alpha,n)}{\Longrightarrow} s',\ n \leq t\}$

Proposition 6. *Let TS_1 be the compact transition system of $d \triangleright n$ w.r.t. t, and TS_2 the transition system associated to the untimed process $forget(d)$ according to the standard untimed operational semantics.*[4] *Then:*
$|TS_1| \leq |TS_2| \times maxdelay(d) \times N_d$, where $|TS|$ denotes the number of states of TS, and N_d denotes the maximum number of parallel composition d may have.

As a direct consequence, the compact transition system is finite, and thus we may use the verification techniques on finite state systems to reason about the timed transition systems by means of their compact ones.

The following results show the relationships on transition relations between transition systems and their compact representations. They are needed to reduce the verification of timed properties over transition systems into the verification over their compact systems.

Proposition 7. *Let $d \triangleright n$ be a timed state and $N \geq maxdelay(d)$. Then:*

i) $d \triangleright n \overset{(\mu,n'-n)}{\Longrightarrow} d' \triangleright n'$ *and* $n' - n \geq N$, *imply* $d \triangleright n \overset{(\mu,N)}{\Longrightarrow} d'' \triangleright N + n$ *and* $[\![d' \triangleright n']\!] = [\![d'' \triangleright N + n]\!]$.
ii) $d \triangleright n \overset{(\mu,N)}{\Longrightarrow} d'' \triangleright N + n$ *implies* $\forall n' \geq N + n$, $d \triangleright n \overset{(\mu,n'-n)}{\Longrightarrow} d' \triangleright n'$ *and* $[\![d' \triangleright n']\!] = [\![d'' \triangleright N + n]\!]$.

By Proposition 7 and by Definition 5, it follows that:

Corollary 8. *Let $TS = \langle S, A, \Rightarrow\rangle$ be a timed transition system for $d \triangleright n$, and $TS' = \langle S', A, \Rightarrow'\rangle$ its corresponding compact system w.r.t. $t = maxdelay(d)$. Then:*

i) $(n' - n > t, d \triangleright n \overset{(\mu,n'-n)}{\Longrightarrow} d' \triangleright n')$ implies $[\![d \triangleright n]\!] \overset{(\mu,t)}{\Longrightarrow}{}' [\![d' \triangleright n']\!]$
ii) $[\![d \triangleright n]\!] \overset{(\mu,t)}{\Longrightarrow}{}' s$ implies $\forall n'$ *s.t.* $n' - n > t$. $\exists d'$. *s.t.* $d \triangleright n \overset{(\mu,n'-n)}{\Longrightarrow} d' \triangleright n'$ *and* $[\![d' \triangleright n']\!] = s$.

When we consider two timed processes with the same global clock, equivalent transition systems are preserved equivalent in their compact transition systems:

Theorem 9. *Let $TS_1 = \langle S_1, A, \Rightarrow_1\rangle$ and $TS_2 = \langle S_2, A, \Rightarrow_2\rangle$ be timed transition systems associated to $d_1 \triangleright n$ and $d_2 \triangleright n$ respectively. Let $TS_1' = \langle S_1', A, \Rightarrow_1'\rangle$ and $TS_2' = \langle S_2', A, \Rightarrow_2'\rangle$ be the compact transition systems of TS_1 and TS_2 respectively, w.r.t. $max\{maxdelay(d_1), maxdelay(d_2)\}$. Then: $(TS_1, d_1 \triangleright n) \sim (TS_2, d_2 \triangleright n)$ iff $(TS_1', [\![d_1 \triangleright n]\!]) \sim (TS_2', [\![d_2 \triangleright n]\!])$*

[4] Here, function $forget(d)$ returns the untimed process obtained by forgetting all time prefixing $n \Rightarrow (\_)$ and all time bounds m and M in a μ_m^M-prefixing within d.

In some special cases, the compact transition system is equivalent to the original one.

Theorem 10. *Let $TS = \langle S, A, \Rightarrow \rangle$ be a timed transition system associated to $d \triangleright n$, and let $TS' = \langle S', A, \Rightarrow' \rangle$ be its associated compact transition system w.r.t. $maxdelay(d)$. If for any μ_m^M occurring in d, $M < \infty$, then: $(TS, d \triangleright n) \sim (TS', [\![d \triangleright n]\!])$.*

Note that Theorem 10 is not valid without the condition that for any μ_m^M occurring in d, $M < \infty$. For example, let $\langle S, A, \rightarrow \rangle$ be the transition system associated to $s = (0 \Rightarrow a_1^\infty.nil) \triangleright 0$, and $\langle S', A, \Rightarrow' \rangle$ its compact transition system with respect to 2. Then we have

$$s \xRightarrow{(a,3)} (3 \Rightarrow nil) \triangleright 3, \text{ but } \nexists s' \in S' \text{ such that } [\![s]\!] \xRightarrow{(a,3)}{}' s'.$$

5 Logical Characterizations

Many temporal and modal logics have been proposed in the literature for abstract specifications of concurrent systems [13, 19, 21], since they can be used to describe system properties, such as necessity, possibility, eventuality, etc.

Real-time temporal logics are suitable specification formalisms for systems with timing constraints, interpreted on either discrete or dense time models [2, 3, 14, 18]. For instance, one could express a property like *whenever p holds, a state satisfying q will eventually be reached within 5 time units.* Usually, these logics are natural extensions of certain temporal logics. For example, TPTL [4] extends linear-time propositional temporal logic PTL [23] with clocks on which a resettable quantification can be defined. In a similar way, TCTL [2] extends branching-time propositional temporal logic CTL [6, 13, 15].

In this paper, we discuss a discrete timed version of ACTL [10], denoted by TAL below. ACTL has a framework similar to CTL (interpreted on Kripke Structure), but it is interpreted on labelled transition systems, which is the semantic model of processes we consider.

Temporal and modal logics offer another way to characterize equivalences [5, 19, 11]: two processes are equivalent if they are not distinguishable by formulas of the logical language under consideration. For example, HML gives a logical characterization of bisimulation [19], while the equivalence deduced by HML extended with an *until* operator coincides with branching bisimulation [11]. Here we show that the equivalence deduced by TAL coincides with performance equivalence under the finitely branching condition.

5.1 TAL: A timed version of ACTL

As in ACTL, an auxiliary logic of actions is introduced. The *action formulae* over Act_τ is defined by the following grammar where χ, χ' range over action formulae and $\mu \in Act_\tau$:

$$\chi ::= \mu \mid \neg\chi \mid \chi \vee \chi$$

The satisfaction of χ by a timed action (μ, t), written $(\mu, t) \models \chi$, is defined inductively by

$$\begin{array}{lll} (\mu,t) \models \mu' & \textit{iff} & \mu = \mu' \\ (\mu,t) \models \neg\chi & \textit{iff} & (\mu,t) \not\models \chi \\ (\mu,t) \models \chi \vee \chi' & \textit{iff} & (\mu,t) \models \chi \textit{ or } (\mu,t) \models \chi' \end{array}$$

The syntax of TAL is generated by the following grammar, where ϕ, ϕ', ... range over TAL formulae, χ, χ' are action formulae, $c \in \mathrm{N}^+$ is a clock constant, and $\bowtie \in \{=, <, >, \leq, \geq\}$:

$$\begin{array}{l} \phi ::= tt \mid \neg\phi \mid \phi \wedge \phi' \mid \exists\rho \mid \forall\rho \\ \rho ::= X_\chi^{\bowtie c}\phi \mid \phi_\chi U^{\bowtie c}\phi' \mid \phi_\chi U_{\chi'}^{\bowtie c}\phi' \end{array}$$

Intuitively, the indexed *next* modality $X_\chi^{\bowtie c}\phi$ says that the next state of the run is reached by an action in χ with the time constrained by $\bowtie c$, and in the next state, formula ϕ holds. The indexed *until* modality $\phi_\chi U^{\bowtie c}\phi'$ says that along the run, all states satisfy ϕ and are reached by actions in χ, until a state that satisfies ϕ', and the total time until this state satisfying ϕ' is constrained by $\bowtie c$. Similarly, $\phi_\chi U_{\chi'}^{\bowtie c}\phi'$ says that along the run, all states satisfy ϕ and are reached by actions in χ, until a state that satisfies ϕ' reached by an action in χ', and the total time until this state satisfying ϕ' is constrained by $\bowtie c$.

The TAL formulae are interpreted on the timed transition systems. Let $(S, A, \Rightarrow)$ be a timed transition system. A *run* π starting from a state $d_0 \triangleright t_0$ of S is a (possibly infinite) sequence of alternative timed states and timed actions

$$(d_0 \triangleright t_0).(\mu_1, (t_1 - t_0)).(d_1 \triangleright t_1). \ldots .(\mu_n, (t_n - t_{n-1})).(d_n \triangleright t_n) \ldots$$

such that $(d_i \triangleright t_i) \xRightarrow{(\mu_{i+1}, (t_{i+1} - t_i))} (d_{i+1} \triangleright t_{i+1})$. We adopt the following notations:

1. $\pi_{|i}$, defined as $(d_0 \triangleright t_0).(\mu_1, (t_1 - t_0)).(d_1 \triangleright t_1). \ldots .(d_{i-1} \triangleright t_{i-1})$, denotes the prefix of π up to the i-th state;
2. $act(\pi, i)$, defined as μ_i, denotes the i-th action.
3. $aug(\pi, i, j)$, defined as $\Sigma_{k=i}^{j} t_k$, denotes the augmented global clock between the i-th and the j-th step;
4. $\Pi_S(q)$ denotes the set of all runs in S starting from q, and Π_S the set of all runs in S.

The semantics of TAL formulae is defined in terms of the satisfaction relation $\models$ between a state (represented by a run equipped with a number i for the position of this state in the run), and a formula, as shown in Table 2.

Obviously, TAL is a natural extension of ACTL: the ACTL formulae can be seen as the corresponding TAL formulae with ≥ 0 as timing constraints, since ≥ 0 is always satisfied. For instance, ACTL formula $\exists X_\chi tt$ is equivalent to TAL formula $\exists X_\chi^{\geq 0} tt$.

$(\pi, i) \models tt$		
$(\pi, i) \models \neg\phi$	*iff*	$(\pi, i) \not\models \phi$
$(\pi, i) \models \phi_1 \wedge \phi_2$	*iff*	$(\pi, i) \models \phi_1$ *and* $(\pi, i) \models \phi_2$
$(\pi, i) \models \exists\rho$	*iff*	$\exists\pi' \in \Pi_S$ *s.t.* $\pi'_{\vert i} = \pi_{\vert i}$, $(\pi', i) \models \rho$
$(\pi, i) \models \forall\rho$	*iff*	$\forall\pi' \in \Pi_S$. $\pi'_{\vert i} = \pi_{\vert i}$ *implies* $(\pi', i) \models \rho$
$(\pi, i) \models \phi_\chi U^{\bowtie c} \phi'$	*iff*	$\exists k \geq i$ *s.t.* $(\pi, k) \models \phi'$, $aug(\pi, i, k) \bowtie c$,
		$\forall i \leq j \leq k-1$. $(\pi, j) \models \phi$, $act(\pi, j) \models \chi$
$(\pi, i) \models \phi_\chi U_{\chi'}^{\bowtie c} \phi'$	*iff*	$\exists k > i$ *s.t.* $(\pi, k) \models \phi'$, $aug(\pi, i, k) \bowtie c$, $act(\pi, k) \models \chi'$
		$\forall i \leq j \leq k-1$. $(\pi, j) \models \phi$, $act(\pi, j) \models \chi$
$(\pi, i) \models X_\chi^{\bowtie c} \phi$	*iff*	$(\pi, i+1) \models \phi$, $act(\pi, i+1) \models \chi$, $aug(\pi, i, i+1) \bowtie c$

Table 2. Satisfaction Relation for TAL

Example 1.

1. $\neg\exists tt_{\neg a} U_b^{\geq 0} tt$ expresses that there is no run beginning by actions all different from a until b, i.e. b can only happen when a has happened;
2. $\neg\exists tt_{\neg a} U_a^{\geq 0} (\exists tt_{\neg b} U_b^{\leq 20} tt)$ expresses that after any action a, there must happen a b action within 20 time units.

Remark. We use $(TS, s) \models \varphi$ to denote that in system TS, $(\pi, 0) \models \varphi$, where π is a run beginning at s. When there is no confusion, we simply write $s \models \varphi$.

5.2 Logical characterization of performance equivalence

The equivalence deduced by TAL coincides with performance equivalence under finitely branching condition.

Theorem 11. *Let TS, TS' be finitely branching timed transition systems and s_1, s'_1 be states in TS, TS' respectively. $(TS, s_1) \sim (TS', s'_1)$ iff* $(\forall \varphi \in TAL,\ (TS, s_1) \models \varphi$ iff $(TS', s'_1) \models \varphi)$.

The proof technique of this theorem is standard. As we know, if for any μ_m^M appearing in d, $M < \infty$, then the transition system associated to $d \triangleright n$ is finitely branching. Hence we have

Corollary 12. *Let E_1, $E_2 \in \mathcal{E}$ such that for any μ_m^M appearing in $0 \Rightarrow E_1$ and $0 \Rightarrow E_2$, $M < \infty$. Then $E_1 \sim E_2$ iff $(\forall \varphi \in TAL,\ (0 \Rightarrow E_1 \triangleright 0) \models \varphi$* iff *$(0 \Rightarrow E_2 \triangleright 0) \models \varphi)$.*

6 Specifying and Verifying Performance Properties

In this section, we discuss the verification (model checking) of TAL formulae over timed processes. First, we give the algorithm to verify the truth of TAL formulae over finite state timed transition systems. Then we show that (i) verifying the truth of a TAL formula over a finitely branching timed transition system can be reduced to verifying the truth of the same formula over its compact transition system; (ii) in general cases, we can construct a formula transformation $\mathcal{F}$, so that verifying the truth of a TAL formula φ over a timed transition system can be reduced to verifying the truth of $\mathcal{F}(\varphi, N)$, for certain number N, over its compact transition system.

6.1 Model checking TAL in finite state timed transition systems

for $i = 1$ **to** **length**(φ_0)
  for each subformula φ **of** φ_0 **of length** i**, case on the form of** φ
    $(1)\varphi = tt$: **for each** $s \in S$, **let** $\varphi \in L(s)$;
    $(2)\varphi = \phi_1 \wedge \phi_2$: **for each** $s \in S$, **such that** $\phi_1 \in L(s)$, **and** $\phi_2 \in L(s)$, **let** $\varphi \in L(s)$;
    $(3)\varphi = \neg\phi$: **for each** $s \in S$, **such that** $\phi \notin L(s)$, **let** $\varphi \in L(s)$;
    $(4)\varphi = \exists X_{\chi}^{\bowtie c}\phi$: **for each** $s \in S$,
      if $\exists \mu, t, s'. \ (\mu, t) \models \chi, \ (s, (\mu, t), s') \in \Rightarrow, t \bowtie c, \ \phi \in L(s')$
      then let $\varphi \in L(s)$
    $(5)\varphi = \forall X_{\chi}^{\bowtie c}\phi$: **(analogous to (4))**
    $(6)\varphi = \exists \phi_{\chi} U^{\bowtie c} \phi'$:
      for each $s \in S$
        if $\phi' \in L(s)$
          then $cond(s, \varphi) := x \bowtie c$
          else $cond(s, \varphi) := ff$
      repeat
        for each $s \in S$ **such that** $\exists \mu, t, s'. \ (s, (\mu, t), s') \in \Rightarrow, \ (\mu, t) \models \chi, \ \phi \in L(s)$
          $cond(s, \varphi) := \bigvee \{cond(s', \varphi) - t \mid (s, (\mu, t), s') \in \Rightarrow, \ (\mu, t) \models \chi, \ \phi \in L(s)\}$
      until $\forall s \in S. \ (cond(s, \varphi)[x/0] \equiv tt$ **or** $cond(s, \varphi)[x/0] \equiv ff)$
      for each $s \in S$ **such that** $cond(s, \varphi)[x/0] \equiv tt$, **let** $\varphi \in L(s)$
    $(7)\varphi = \exists \phi_{\chi} U_{\chi'}^{\bowtie c} \phi'$: **(analogous to (6))**
    $(8)\varphi = \forall \phi_{\chi} U^{\bowtie c} \phi'$: **(analogous to (6))**
    $(9)\varphi = \forall \phi_{\chi} U_{\chi'}^{\bowtie c} \phi'$: **(analogous to (8))**

Table 3. Labelling procedure for model checking TAL

The model checker for the truth of TAL formula over finite timed transition systems follows the standard labelling procedure in the model checking of CTL formula over finite Kripke Structure [12]. The algorithm is sketched in Table 3. The main difference is the consideration of the timing constraints especially for labelling the truth of formulae with "until" operator. We explain it further below.

We use $cond(s, \varphi)$ to remember the timing constraint for φ to be true at s. $cond(s, \varphi)$ is a formula with unique variable x. It is constructed by tt, ff, $\wedge$, $\vee$, and $x \bowtie c$ for $c \in \mathbb{N}^+$ and $\bowtie \in \{=,<,>,\leq,\geq\}$. Let B be such a formula. $B[x/0]$ denotes the closed formula obtained by substituting x by 0. This condition $cond(s,\varphi)$ is constructed in a way that φ is true at s iff $cond(s,\varphi)[x/0]$ is equal to true (tt). We use $B - t$ to denote the formula obtained by substituting each $x \bowtie c$ (for any c and $\bowtie$) in B by $x \bowtie (c-t)$. For $\varphi = \exists\phi_\chi U^{\bowtie c}\phi'$, if ϕ is true at s, $s \xRightarrow{(\mu,t)} s'$ and $(\mu,t) \models \chi$, then φ may be true at s under timing constraint $cond(s',\varphi) - t$. In regards of the efficiency of the algorithm in Table 3, let S be the input transition system to the model checker. Let

- $|S|$ = the number of transitions in S;
- $C_{\varphi_0} = \max\ \{c \mid\bowtie c$ appears in $\varphi_0\}$;
- $|\varphi_0|$ = the length of φ_0;
- $l_S = \max\ \{|\rho| \mid \rho$ is a path in S with no time increase in the actions$\}$.

The **repeat** statement will be executed at most $(l_S + 1) \times |S| \times C_{\varphi_0}$ times. The combined two *for* statements at the beginning of the algorithm will be executed as many times as the number of subformulae in φ_0, which is $\mathcal{O}(|\varphi_0|)$, and thus the total algorithm will be executed in time $\mathcal{O}(l_S \times |S| \times C_{\varphi_0} \times |\varphi_0|)$. Now, if S is a timed transition system associated to $d \rhd n$. We know that $l_S \leq N_d$, where N_d is the maximum number of parallel composition d may have. So the algorithm will run in time $\mathcal{O}(N_d \times |S| \times C_{\varphi_0} \times |\varphi_0|)$.

6.2 Model checking in timed transition systems

Theorem 13. *(correctness of model checking in finitely branching compact systems) Let $TS = \langle S, A, \Rightarrow\rangle$ be the timed transition system associated to $d \rhd n$ and TS' its corresponding compact system. If TS is finitely branching, then for any state s in TS and φ in TAL, $(TS,s) \models \varphi$ iff $(TS', [\![s]\!]) \models varphi$*

When a transition system S is not finitely branching, however, TAL formulae may have different truth value in S and in its compact system. For example, $\exists tt_{tt} U_{\overline{a}}^{\geq 10} tt$ states that it is possible that an a action appears after 10 time units. [5] This property is true in the transition system of $(0 \Rightarrow a_5^\infty.nil) \rhd 0$, yet it is not true in its compact system. This is due to the fact that for infinitely branching systems, only Theorem 9 holds, but the stronger Theorem 10 doesn't.

However, a weaker form holds. We first provide below a transformation $\mathcal{F}$ constructed for each formula φ, so that for certain $N \in \mathbb{N}^+$, $\mathcal{F}(\varphi, N)$ holds the same truth value in the compact transition system, as φ does in the original system. This transformation $\mathcal{F}$ is given in Table 4. Note that the transformed formula is defined on a slight extension of TAL, using also auxiliary *until* operators $\bar{U}(N)$ and $\tilde{U}(N)$. The meaning of $\phi_\chi \bar{U}(N)^{\bowtie c}\phi'$ is defined as

$$\begin{array}{ll} (\pi,i) \models \phi_\chi \bar{U}(N)^{\bowtie c}\phi' \ \ \textit{iff} & \exists k \geq i\ s.t.\ (\pi,k) \models \phi',\ aug(\pi,i,k) \bowtie c, \\ & \forall i \leq j \leq k-1.\ (\pi,j) \models \phi,\ act(\pi,j) \models \chi \\ & \exists i \leq j \leq k-1.\ aug(\pi,j,j) \geq N \end{array}$$

[5] We use tt in the action formulae as an abbreviation of $\bigvee_{\alpha \in Act_\tau} \alpha$. Obviously, any action satisfies this formula.

with the additional condition $\exists i \leq j \leq k-1.\ aug(\pi, j, j) \geq N$ (w.r.t. $\phi_\chi U^{\bowtie c} \phi'$) whose intuition is that along the path until a state satisfying ϕ' is reached, there is an action with time $\geq N$ (formula $\phi_\chi \bar{U}(N)^{\bowtie c}_{\chi'} \phi'$ can be similarly defined). The meaning of $\phi_\chi \tilde{U}(N)^{\bowtie c} \phi'$, on the other hand, is defined as

$$
\begin{aligned}
(\pi, i) \models \phi_\chi \tilde{U}(N)^{\bowtie c} \phi' \ \textit{ iff } \ & \exists k \geq i \ s.t.\ (\pi, k) \models \phi',\ aug(\pi, i, k) \bowtie c, \\
& \forall i \leq j \leq k-1.\ (\pi, j) \models \phi,\ act(\pi, j) \models \chi \\
& \forall i \leq j \leq k-1.\ aug(\pi, j, j) < N
\end{aligned}
$$

with the additional condition $\forall i \leq j \leq k-1.\ aug(\pi, j, j) < N$.

Obviously, the model checking on finite state processes discussed previously can be easily extended to cope with these operators.

$$
\begin{aligned}
&(1)\ \mathcal{F}(tt, N) = tt \\
&(2)\ \mathcal{F}(\neg\phi, N) = \neg\mathcal{F}(\phi, N) \\
&(3)\ \mathcal{F}(\phi_1 \wedge \phi_2, N) = \mathcal{F}(\phi_1, N) \wedge \mathcal{F}(\phi_2, N) \\
&(4)\ \mathcal{F}(\exists X^{\bowtie c}_\chi \phi,\ N) = \begin{cases} \exists X^{=N}_\chi \mathcal{F}(\phi, N) & \bowtie \in \{>, \geq, =\},\ c > N \\ \exists X^{\bowtie c}_\chi \mathcal{F}(\phi, N) & \text{otherwise} \end{cases} \\
&(5)\ \mathcal{F}(\forall X^{\bowtie c}_\chi \phi,\ N) = \begin{cases} \forall X^{<N}_\chi \mathcal{F}(\phi, N) & \bowtie \in \{<, \leq\},\ c > N \\ \forall X^{\bowtie c}_\chi \mathcal{F}(\phi, N) & \text{otherwise} \end{cases} \\
&(6)\ \mathcal{F}(\exists \phi_\chi U^{\bowtie c} \phi',\ N) = \begin{cases} \exists \mathcal{F}(\phi, N)_\chi \bar{U}(N)^{\geq 0} \mathcal{F}(\phi', N) \vee \exists \mathcal{F}(\phi, N)_\chi U^{\bowtie c} \mathcal{F}(\phi', N) & \bowtie \in \{>, \geq, =\} \\ \exists \mathcal{F}(\phi, N)_\chi U^{\bowtie c} \mathcal{F}(\phi', N) & \text{otherwise} \end{cases} \\
&(7)\ \mathcal{F}(\forall \phi_\chi U^{\bowtie c} \phi',\ N) = \begin{cases} \forall \mathcal{F}(\phi, N)_\chi \bar{U}(N)^{\bowtie c} \mathcal{F}(\phi', N) & \bowtie \in \{<, \leq, =\} \\ \forall \mathcal{F}(\phi, N)_\chi U^{\bowtie c} \mathcal{F}(\phi', N) & \text{otherwise} \end{cases} \\
&(8)\ \mathcal{F}(\exists \phi_\chi U^{\bowtie c}_{\chi'} \phi',\ N) = \begin{cases} \exists \mathcal{F}(\phi, N)_\chi \bar{U}(N)^{\geq 0}_{\chi'} \mathcal{F}(\phi', N) \vee \exists \mathcal{F}(\phi, N)_\chi U^{\bowtie c}_{\chi'} \mathcal{F}(\phi', N) & \bowtie \in \{>, \geq, =\} \\ \exists \mathcal{F}(\phi, N)_\chi U^{\bowtie c}_{\chi'} \mathcal{F}(\phi', N) & \text{otherwise} \end{cases} \\
&(9)\ \mathcal{F}(\forall \phi_\chi U^{\bowtie c}_{\chi'} \phi',\ N) = \begin{cases} \forall \mathcal{F}(\phi, N)_\chi \bar{U}(N)^{\bowtie c}_{\chi'} \mathcal{F}(\phi', N) & \bowtie \in \{<, \leq, =\} \\ \forall \mathcal{F}(\phi, N)_\chi U^{\bowtie c}_{\chi'} \mathcal{F}(\phi', N) & \text{otherwise} \end{cases}
\end{aligned}
$$

Table 4. Formulae transformation

Theorem 14. *(correctness of model checking in compact systems)*
For any timed process $d \rhd n$, let $TS = \langle S, A, \Rightarrow \rangle$ be the timed transition system associated to $d \rhd n$, and TS' its corresponding compact system. Then for any state s in TS and any φ in TAL, $(TS, s) \models \varphi$ iff *$(TS', [\![s]\!]) \models \mathcal{F}(\varphi, N)$ where $N = maxdelay(d)$.*

7 Related Work and Concluding Remarks

While in [9] it has been discussed the problem of decidability of the equivalences in the theory of processes with durational actions, in this paper we have shown techniques to reduce the equivalence checking problem over the models that may be infinite due to the increase of the explicitly expressed clocks, to the one over their finite compact models. The existence of these finite compact models strongly relies on the well-timedness assumption (the execution time coincides with the observation time) of the system executions and on the discrete time domain. As an interesting line of further work we would like to see whether the symbolic technique in [20] can be exploited to extend the compact transition techinque when dealing with a dense time domain. We have also provided a formula transformation so that model checking a performance property (formula) over such a (possibly infinite) model can be reduced to model checking the transformed formula in its compact model. We have chosen TAL to study the model checking techniques in timed processes with durational actions. The required transformation $\mathcal{F}$ we used depends on the syntax and semantics of TAL. However, our method on reducing the model checking problem over infinite models to the one over finite models may work as well for other real-time temporal logics, and our transformation $\mathcal{F}$ actually shows the way for the construction of the corresponding transformations for other considered logical languages.

In [7] we discussed the model checking problem over transition systems associated to processes with *patient actions*. Comparing with this work: (i) The process language in [7] is a subset of the one we used in this paper. Moreover, the transition systems associated to the processes discussed in [7] are finitely branching and thus its model checking problem can be included in the actual work as a simple case without using formula transformation (cf. Theorem 13). (ii) The logical language in this paper is more expressive, in describing timing constraints, than the one in [7]. There, only global clocks (natural numbers) are allowed and thus we can only express properties referring to the absolute time between the execution of an action and the beginning of the total execution. For example, we can specify *a state satisfying q will eventually be reached within* 5 *time units (after the beginning of the execution)*. Using TAL, instead, we can describe properties referring to the relative time between the executions of two actions. For example, we can specify *whenever property p holds, (for that moment) a state satisfying q will eventually be reached within* 5 *time units.*

This extended abstract does not contain proofs. They can be found in its full version, where the reader can also find applicative examples of our theory.

Acknowledgments: We would like to thank Roberto Gorrieri for useful comments and suggestions on an earlier version of this paper. Monica Nesi and the anonymous referees also gave useful comments.

References

1. L. Aceto and D. Murphy. Timing and causality in process algebra. *Acta Informatica* **33** (4), pp.317-350, 1996.
2. R. Alur, C. Courcoubetis, and D. Dill. Model-checking for real-time systems. *IEEE LICS*, pp.414-425, 1990.

3. R. Alur, T. Feder and T.A. Henzinger. The benefits of relaxing punctuality. *10th ACM PODC*, 1991.
4. R. Alur and T. Henzinger. A Really Temporal Logic. *TCS* **126**, 1994.
5. S. Brooks and W. Rounds. Behavioural equivalence relations induced by programming logics. *LNCS* **154**, pp.97-108, Springer-Verlag, 1983.
6. M.C. Browne, E.M. Clarke, and O. Grumberg. Characterizing finite Kripke structure in propositional temporal logic. *TCS* **59**, pp.115-131, 1988.
7. X.J. Chen, F. Corradini, and R. Gorrieri. A Study on the Specification and Verification of Performance Properties. *AMAST'96*, *LNCS* **1101**, pp.306-320, 1996.
8. F. Corradini, R. Gorrieri, and M. Roccetti. Performance preorder: Ordering processes with respect to speed. In *MFCS'95*, *LNCS* **969**, pp.444-453, 1995. See also: Performance preorder and competitive equivalence. *Acta Informatica* **33** (11), 1997.
9. F. Corradini, and M. Pistore. Specification and Verification of Timed Lazy Systems. *MFCS'96*, *LNCS* **1113**, pp.279-290, 1996. See also: Specification and Verification of Timed Systems. Technical Report 107/96, Department of Pure and Applied Mathematics, University of L'Aquila, 1996.
10. R. De Nicola, A. Fantechi, S. Gnesi, and G. Ristori. An action-based framework for verifying logical and behavioural properties of concurrent systems. *Computer Networks and ISDN Systems*, **25**, pp.761-778, 1993.
11. R. De Nicola and F. Vaandrager. Three logics for branching bisimulation. *Journal of ACM* **42** (2), pp.458-487, 1995.
12. E. A. Emerson. Temporal and Modal Logic. *Handbook of Theoretical Computer Science*, volume B, chapter 16. Elsevier Science Publishers B.V., 1990.
13. E.A. Emerson and J.Y. Halpern. "Sometimes" and "Not Never" revisited: on branching time versus linear time temporal logic. *Journal of ACM* **33** (1), pp.151-178, 1986.
14. E.A. Emerson, A.K. Mok, A.P. Sistla and J. Srinivasan. Quantitative Temporal Reasoning. *2nd CAV, LNCS* **531**, Springer-Verlag, 1990.
15. E.A. Emerson and J. Srinivasan. Branching time temporal logic. *LNCS* **354**, pp.123-172. Springer-Verlag, 1989.
16. G-L. Ferrari and U. Montanari. Dynamic matrices and the cost analysis of concurrent programs. *AMAST'95* **936**, pp.307-321, 1995.
17. R. Gorrieri, M. Roccetti, and E. Stancampiano. A theory of processes with durational actions. *TCS*, **140** (1), pp.73-94, 1995.
18. E. Harel, O. Lichtenstein and A. Pnueli. Explicit Clock Temporal Logic. *5th IEEE LICS*, 1990.
19. M. Hennessy and R. Milner. Algebraic laws for nondeterminism and concurrency. *Journal of ACM*, **32** (1), pp.137-161, 1985.
20. U. Holmer, K. Larsen and W. Yi. Deciding Properties of Regular Real Timed Processes. *CAV'91* **575**, pp.443-453, 1991.
21. Z. Manna and A. Pnueli. The anchored version of the temporal framework. *LNCS* **354**, pp.201-284, Springer-Verlag, 1989.
22. R. Milner. *Communication and Concurrency*. Prentice Hall International, 1989. International Series on Computer Science.
23. A. Pnueli. The Temporal Logic of Programs. *IEEE FOCS'77*, 1977.
24. C. Stirling. Modal and temporal logics. *Handbook of Logic in Computer Science*, **2**, pp.477-563. Oxford University Press, 1992.

Abstract Interpretation of Algebraic Polynomial Systems
(Extended Abstract)

Patrick Cousot[1] and Radhia Cousot[2]

[1] LIENS, École Normale Supérieure, 45 rue d'Ulm, 75230 Paris cedex 05, France
cousot@dmi.ens.fr http://www.dmi.ens.fr/~cousot
[2] LIX, CNRS & École Polytechnique, 91140 Palaiseau cedex, France
rcousot@lix.polytechnique.fr http://lix.polytechnique.fr/~rcousot

Abstract. We define a hierarchy of compositional formal semantics of algebraic polynomial systems over $\mathcal{F}$-algebras by abstract interpretation. This generalizes classical formal language theoretical results and context-free grammar flow-analysis algorithms in the same uniform framework of universal algebra and abstract interpretation.

1 Introduction

We consider algebraic polynomial systems generalizing language-theoretic context-free grammars to $\mathcal{F}$-algebras [Courcelle, 1996; Mezei & Wright, 1967]. We provide a compositional fixpoint derivation tree semantics and show that by abstract interpretation [Cousot & Cousot, 1977, 1979], we can derive a hierarchy of formal fixpoint semantics generalizing results from the theory of formal languages e.g. [Ginsburg & Rice, 1962; Schützenberger, 1962] as well as grammar analysis algorithms e.g. [Möncke & Wilhelm, 1991; Jeuring & Swierstra, 1994, 1995]. We extend the results to infinite terms.

2 Algebraic Polynomial Systems

Let $\mathcal{S}$ be a set of *sorts*. An $\mathcal{S}$-*signature* is a set $\mathcal{F}$ of *function symbols* equipped with a mapping *type* $\in \mathcal{F} \longmapsto \mathcal{S}^* \times \mathcal{S}$. We write $f^{s_1 \times \ldots \times s_n \to s}$ for $type(f) = \langle s_1 \ldots s_n, s \rangle$ and $f^{\epsilon \to s}$ when $n = 0$. An $\mathcal{F}$-*algebra* [Meinke & Tucker, 1992; Wirsing, 1990] is a pair $\mathcal{A} = \langle \{\mathcal{A}_s\}_{s \in \mathcal{S}}, \{f_{\mathcal{A}}\}_{f \in \mathcal{F}} \rangle$ where the *domain* $\mathcal{A}_s$ of sort s of $\mathcal{A}$ is a non-empty set and for each $f \in \mathcal{F}$ of type $s_1 \times \ldots \times s_n \to s$, the *operation* $f_{\mathcal{A}}$ is a total mapping $\mathcal{A}_{s_1} \times \ldots \times \mathcal{A}_{s_n} \longmapsto \mathcal{A}_s$. Classical examples of $\mathcal{F}$-algebras are the monoids of words and traces, trees, graphs with sources, etc. [Courcelle, 1996].

Let $\mathcal{X}$ be an $\mathcal{S}$-sorted set of free *variables* x (disjoint from function symbols). We write x^s for $type(x) = s$. Let $\mathcal{M}^{s,\mathcal{X}}$ be the set of *monomials of type* s *over variables* $\mathcal{X}$ with the following syntax:

$$M^{s,\{x^s\} \cup Y} \to x^s, \qquad \text{monomial of type } s \text{ over variables } \{x^s\} \cup Y;$$
$$M^{s,Y} \to f^{\sigma \to s}(L^{\sigma,Y}), \quad f \in \mathcal{F}, \text{ (c() is written c for constants } c^{\epsilon \to s});$$

$L^{s \times \sigma, Y} \rightarrow M^{s,Y}, L^{\sigma,Y}$, list of monomials of type $s\sigma$ over variables Y;

$L^{s,Y} \rightarrow M^{s,Y}$, unary list.

Let $\mathcal{D}$ be an $\mathcal{S}$-sorted set of *derivation labels* d^s (disjoint from function symbols and variables). Let $\delta \in \mathcal{X} \longmapsto \wp(\mathcal{D})$ such that $\forall x^s \in \mathcal{X}^s : \forall d \in \delta(x^s) : d \in \mathcal{D}^s$ and $\forall x, y \in \mathcal{X} : x \neq y \Longrightarrow \delta(x) \cap \delta(y) = \emptyset$ be an *assignment of derivation labels to variables*. For each $d^s \in \mathcal{D}$, we let $\Delta(d^s) \in \mathcal{M}^{s,\mathcal{X}}$ be a monomial of type s over the variables $\mathcal{X}$ representing the *derivation* labeled $d^s \in \delta(x^s)$ for variable x^s. An $\mathcal{S}$-sorted *polynomial system* $\mathcal{P}$ is a tuple $\langle \mathcal{F}, \mathcal{X}, \mathcal{D}, \delta, \Delta \rangle$ defining the *system of equations* $\{x^s = \Delta(d^s) \mid s \in \mathcal{S} \wedge x^s \in \mathcal{X}^s \wedge d^s \in \delta(x^s)\}$.

Example 1 (Polynomial system). The polynomial system given by $\mathcal{S} = \{s\}$, $\mathcal{F} = \{b^{s \times s \rightarrow s}, a^{\epsilon \rightarrow s}\}$, $\mathcal{X} = \{A, B\}$, $\mathcal{D} = \{d_1, d_2\}$, $\delta(A) = \{d_1, d_2\}$, $\delta(B) = \emptyset$, $\Delta(d_1) = b(A, A)$ and $\Delta(d_2) = a$ with equations $\{A = b(A, A),\ A = a\}$ can be written as: $A = b(A, A)\ [d_1]\ +\ a\ [d_2],\ B = \Omega$. □

If $\mathcal{F}$ is an $\mathcal{S}$-signature then $\mathcal{F}_+$ is $\mathcal{F}$ enlarged for each sort $s \in \mathcal{S}$ with a new symbol $+_s$ of type $s \times s \rightarrow s$ and a new constant Ω_s of type $\epsilon \rightarrow s$. The syntax of an *$\mathcal{F}_+$-polynomial system $\mathcal{P}$ over $\mathcal{X}$ and $\mathcal{D}$* [Courcelle, 1996; Mezei & Wright, 1967] of type σ is given by the following context-free attribute grammar with axiom $S^{\sigma,\mathcal{X},\mathcal{X},\mathcal{D}}$, $\sigma \in \mathcal{S}^+$ (for short we often omit the derivation labels):

$S^{s \times \sigma, X, Y, D_1 \cup D_2} \rightarrow E^{s, x^s, Y, D_1}\ S^{\sigma, X \setminus \{x^s\}, Y, D_2}$,

polynomial system of type $s\sigma$ ($s \notin \sigma$) with left-variables $X \subseteq \mathcal{X}$, right-variables $Y \subseteq \mathcal{X}$ and labels $D_1 \cup D_2 \subseteq \mathcal{D}$ ($D_1 \cap D_2 = \emptyset$);

$S^{s,\{x^s\},Y,D} \rightarrow E^{s,x^s,Y,D}$, monoequational polynomial system;

$E^{s,x^s,Y,D} \rightarrow x^s = P^{s,Y,D}$, equation of type s;

$E^{s,x^s,Y,\emptyset} \rightarrow x^s = \Omega_s$, void equation;

$P^{s,Y,\{d^s\} \cup D} \rightarrow M^{s,Y}\ [d^s] +_s P^{s,Y,D}$, polynomial of type s over variables Y and derivation labels $\{d^s\} \cup D$ with $d^s \notin D$;

$P^{s,Y,\{d^s\}} \rightarrow M^{s,Y}\ [d^s]$, labeled derivation.

The corresponding label assignments and derivations are given by:

$$
\begin{aligned}
\delta[\![ES]\!] &= \delta[\![E]\!] \cup \delta[\![S]\!], & \Delta[\![ES]\!] &= \Delta[\![E]\!] \cup \Delta[\![S]\!],\\
\delta[\![x = P]\!] &= \{\langle x,\ \delta[\![P]\!]\rangle\}, & \Delta[\![x = P]\!] &= \Delta[\![P]\!],\\
\delta[\![x = \Omega]\!] &= \emptyset, & \Delta[\![x = \Omega]\!] &= \emptyset,\\
\delta[\![M\ [d] + P]\!] &= \{d\} \cup \delta[\![P]\!], & \Delta[\![M\ [d] + P]\!] &= \{\langle d,\ M\rangle\} \cup \Delta[\![P]\!],\\
\delta[\![M\ [d]]\!] &= \{d\}, & \Delta[\![M\ [d]]\!] &= \{\langle d,\ M\rangle\}\ .
\end{aligned}
$$

Context-free grammars can be considered as algebraic polynomial systems in several ways [Courcelle, 1996]. The meta-syntax of context-free grammars is given by the following meta-grammar[1]:

$G \rightarrow P\ G \mid P$,	Grammar;	$R \rightarrow V\ R \mid R$,		Right sides;
$P \rightarrow N$ '$\rightarrow$' A,	Production;	$A \rightarrow A$ '|' $R \mid R \mid$ 'ε',		Alternative right sides.
$V \rightarrow N \mid T$,	Vocabulary;			

[1] We omit attributes ensuring that all productions with the same left side nonterminal have their right sides grouped, with the alternative right sides separated by |.

In this meta-grammar the meta-terminals are {'$\longrightarrow$', '|', 'ε'} and the meta-nonterminals are $\{G, P, A, R, V, N, T\}$. The meta-productions for nonterminals $N \in \mathcal{N}$ and terminals $T \in \mathcal{T}$ (not containing $\longrightarrow$, | and ε) have been left unspecified. The meta-vocabulary $\mathcal{V}$ is $\mathcal{T} \cup \mathcal{N}$. A grammar G is usually presented as a triple $\langle \mathcal{T}, \mathcal{N}, \mathsf{P}[\![G]\!]\rangle$ or a quadruple $\langle \mathcal{T}, \mathcal{N}, \mathsf{A}, \mathsf{P}[\![G]\!]\rangle$, where the axiom $\mathsf{A} \in \mathcal{N}$ is a distinguished nonterminal, and the productions are:

$$\mathsf{P}[\![PG]\!] \triangleq \mathsf{P}[\![P]\!] \cup \mathsf{P}[\![G]\!], \quad \mathsf{P}[\![N \longrightarrow A]\!] \triangleq \{N \longrightarrow \mathrm{r} \mid \mathrm{r} \in \mathsf{A}[\![A]\!]\},$$

$$\mathsf{A}[\![A \mid R]\!] \triangleq \mathsf{A}[\![A]\!] \cup \mathsf{A}[\![R]\!], \qquad \mathsf{A}[\![R]\!] \triangleq \{\mathsf{R}[\![R]\!]\}, \qquad \mathsf{A}[\![\varepsilon]\!] \triangleq \{\varepsilon\},$$

$$\mathsf{R}[\![VR]\!] \triangleq \mathsf{R}[\![V]\!]\,\mathsf{R}[\![R]\!], \qquad \mathsf{R}[\![T]\!] \triangleq T, \qquad \mathsf{R}[\![N]\!] \triangleq N .$$

Example 2 (Sentence generating grammars). If grammars are understood as defining a set of sentences then there is only one sort *string*. The nullary function symbols are ε (empty string) and the terminals $T \in \mathcal{T}$. The only binary function symbol is the concatenation $\bullet$ of strings also denoted by juxtaposition. $\mathcal{F}_+$ includes $+$, also denoted | for alternative/language union and Ω which denotes the empty language. The nonterminals $N \in \mathcal{N}$ are the variables. For example, if $\mathcal{N} \triangleq \{\mathrm{x}, \mathrm{y}, \mathrm{z}\}$ and $\mathcal{T} \triangleq \{\mathrm{a}, \mathrm{b}\}$ then the grammar $\mathrm{x} \longrightarrow \mathrm{yx} \mid \mathrm{y}$, $\mathrm{x} \longrightarrow \mathrm{yx} \mid \mathrm{y}$ corresponds to $\mathrm{x} = \mathrm{y} \bullet \mathrm{x}\ [1] + \mathrm{y}\ [2]$, $\mathrm{y} = \mathrm{a}\ [3] + \mathrm{b}\ [4]$, $\mathrm{z} = \Omega$. The translation is given by:

$$\mathsf{P}[\![PG]\!]^{D_1 \cup D_2} \triangleq \mathsf{P}[\![P]\!]^{D_1}\ \mathsf{P}[\![G]\!]^{D_2} \quad \mathsf{P}[\![N \longrightarrow A]\!]^{D} \triangleq N = \mathsf{A}[\![A]\!]^{D}$$

$$\mathsf{A}[\![A \mid R]\!]^{D \cup \{d\}} \triangleq \mathsf{A}[\![A]\!]^{D} + \mathsf{A}[\![R]\!]^{d} \qquad \mathsf{A}[\![R]\!]^{d} \triangleq \mathsf{R}[\![R]\!]\ [d]$$

$$\mathsf{A}[\![\varepsilon]\!]^{d} \triangleq \varepsilon\ [d] \qquad \mathsf{R}[\![VR]\!] \triangleq V \bullet \mathsf{R}[\![R]\!] . \qquad \square$$

Example 3 (Parse tree generating grammars). We can also interpret grammars as generating parse trees, for example $\mathrm{x} \longrightarrow \mathrm{yx} \mid \mathrm{y}$, $\mathrm{x} \longrightarrow \mathrm{yx} \mid \mathrm{y}$ corresponds to $\bar{\mathrm{x}} = \mathrm{x}2(\bar{\mathrm{y}}, \bar{\mathrm{x}}) + \mathrm{x}1(\bar{\mathrm{y}})$, $\bar{\mathrm{y}} = \mathrm{y}1(\mathrm{a}) + \mathrm{y}1(\mathrm{b})$, $\bar{\mathrm{z}} = \Omega$. The translation is then:

$$\mathsf{P}[\![PG]\!] \triangleq \mathsf{P}[\![P]\!]\ \mathsf{P}[\![G]\!], \qquad \mathsf{P}[\![N \longrightarrow A]\!] \triangleq \overline{N} = \mathsf{A}[\![N, A]\!],$$

$$\mathsf{A}[\![N, A \mid R]\!] \triangleq \mathsf{A}[\![N, A]\!] + \mathsf{A}[\![N, R]\!], \qquad \mathsf{A}[\![N, R]\!] \triangleq N\ell[\![R]\!](\mathsf{R}[\![R]\!]),$$

$$\mathsf{A}[\![N, \varepsilon]\!] \triangleq N1(\varepsilon), \qquad \mathsf{R}[\![VR]\!] \triangleq \mathsf{R}[\![V]\!], \mathsf{R}[\![R]\!],$$

$$\mathsf{R}[\![T]\!] \triangleq T, \qquad \mathsf{R}[\![N]\!] \triangleq \overline{N},$$

$$\ell[\![VR]\!] \triangleq \ell[\![V]\!] + \ell[\![R]\!], \qquad \ell[\![V]\!] \triangleq 1 . \qquad \square$$

3 Small Step Operational Semantics: States and Transitions

The transition/small-step operational semantics associates a *discrete transition system* to each algebraic polynomial system that is a pair $\langle \Sigma, \tau \rangle$ where Σ is a (non-empty) set of states, $\tau \subseteq \Sigma \times \Sigma$ is the binary transition relation between a state and its possible successors. We write $\mathrm{s}\ \tau\ \mathrm{s}'$ or $\tau(\mathrm{s}, \mathrm{s}')$ for $\langle \mathrm{s}, \mathrm{s}' \rangle \in \tau$ using the isomorphism $\wp(\Sigma \times \Sigma) \simeq (\Sigma \times \Sigma) \longmapsto \mathbb{B}$ where $\mathbb{B} \triangleq \{\mathrm{tt}, \mathrm{ff}\}$ is the set of booleans. $\check{\tau} \triangleq \{\mathrm{s} \in \Sigma \mid \forall \mathrm{s}' \in \Sigma : \neg(\mathrm{s}\ \tau\ \mathrm{s}')\}$ is the set of *final/blocking states*. We formally define several transition systems $\langle \Sigma[\![\mathcal{P}]\!], \tau[\![\mathcal{P}]\!]\rangle$ associated with polynomial system $\mathcal{P}$ which generalize the term rewriting system and the derivation trees of [Courcelle, 1996].

Example 4 (Protosentence transition system). In order to generalize the protosentence derivation relation for context-free grammars, the set $\tau^s[\![\mathcal{P}]\!]$ of states for the polynomial system $\mathcal{P}$ defined by $A = b(A, A) + a$ is the language generated by the grammar $A' \rightarrow A'A' \mid a \mid A$ with terminals $\{a, A\}$ and nonterminals $\{A'\}$. More generally states can be chosen as protosentences that is sentences containing constants $c^{\epsilon \rightarrow s} \in \mathcal{F}$ and variables $x \in \mathcal{X}$. The set $\Sigma^s[\![\mathcal{P}]\!]$ of states of the $\mathcal{S}$-sorted *polynomial system* $\mathcal{P} = \langle \mathcal{F}, \mathcal{X}, \mathcal{D}, \delta, \Delta \rangle$ is the language generated by the grammar $G = \langle \mathcal{V}, \{x' \mid x \in \mathcal{X}\}, P \rangle$ where vocabulary is $\mathcal{V} \triangleq \{f \mid c^{\epsilon \rightarrow s} \in \mathcal{F}\} \cup \mathcal{X}$ and the productions are $P = \{x' \rightarrow x \mid x \in \mathcal{X}\} \cup \{x' \rightarrow \varphi'(\Delta(d)) \mid x \in \mathcal{X} \wedge d \in \delta(x) \wedge \Delta(d) \neq \Omega\}$ with $\varphi'(x) \triangleq x'$, $\varphi'(c^{\epsilon \rightarrow s}) \triangleq c$, $\varphi'(f^{\sigma \rightarrow s}(L)) \triangleq \varphi'(L)$ when $\sigma \neq \epsilon$ and $\varphi'(M, L) = \varphi'(M)\varphi'(L)$. The transition relation is then:

$$\tau^s[\![\mathcal{P}]\!] \triangleq \{\langle pxq,\ p\varphi(\Delta(d))q \rangle \mid x \in \mathcal{X} \wedge \exists d \in \delta(x) : \Delta(d) \neq \Omega\} \qquad (1)$$

with $\varphi(x) \triangleq x$, $\varphi(c^{\epsilon \rightarrow s}) \triangleq c$, $\varphi(f^{\sigma \rightarrow s}(L)) \triangleq \varphi(L)$ when $\sigma \neq \epsilon$ and $\varphi(M, L) = \varphi(M)\varphi(L)$. This one-step derivation $\langle s,\ s' \rangle \in \tau^s[\![\mathcal{P}]\!]$ is written as $s \stackrel{\mathcal{P}}{\Longrightarrow} s'$. □

Example 5 (Context transition system). For top-down analysis, it is convenient to consider the derivation sequence where all replacements are delimited by brackets. The transition system is: $\langle \Sigma^c[\![\mathcal{P}]\!],\ \tau^c[\![\mathcal{P}]\!] \rangle$ with:

$$\Sigma^c[\![\mathcal{P}]\!] \triangleq \mathcal{V}^\star \bullet \{[\} \bullet \mathcal{V}^\star \bullet \{]\} \bullet \mathcal{V}^\star \quad \text{where} \quad \mathcal{V} \triangleq \mathcal{X} \cup \{c^{\epsilon \rightarrow s} \mid c \in \mathcal{F}\}, \qquad (2)$$

$$\tau^c[\![\mathcal{P}]\!] \triangleq \{\langle p[qxq']p',\ pq[\varphi(\Delta(d))]q'p' \rangle \mid x \in \mathcal{X} \wedge d \in \delta(x) \wedge \Delta(d) \neq \Omega\}.$$

For the example polynomial system $\mathcal{P}$ defined by $A = b(A, A) + c(A) + d(a, A) + a$, two possible derivations sequences with delimited contexts would be $[A] \stackrel{\mathcal{P}}{\Longrightarrow} [aA] \stackrel{\mathcal{P}}{\Longrightarrow} a[A]$ and $[A] \stackrel{\mathcal{P}}{\Longrightarrow} [AA] \stackrel{\mathcal{P}}{\Longrightarrow} [a]A$. □

Example 6 (Parse tree transition system). Parse trees for context free grammar generalize to $\mathcal{F}$-algebras [Meinke & Tucker, 1992]. The states of the transition system $\langle \Sigma^p[\![\mathcal{P}]\!],\ \tau^p[\![\mathcal{P}]\!] \rangle$ for the polynomial system $\mathcal{P} = \langle \mathcal{F}, \mathcal{X}, \mathcal{D}, \delta, \Delta \rangle$ are parse trees in parenthesized form. They derive from the nonterminals x'', $x \in \mathcal{X}$ in the meta-grammar with productions:

$$\begin{aligned} x'' &\rightarrow [x'], && \text{for each } x \in \mathcal{X}, \\ x'' &\rightarrow x, && \text{for each } x \in \mathcal{X}, \\ x' &\rightarrow x : \phi'(\Delta(d)), && \text{for each } x \in \mathcal{X}, d \in \delta(x) \text{ and } \Delta(d) \neq \Omega, \end{aligned}$$

with $\phi'(x) \triangleq x'$, $\phi'(c^{\epsilon \rightarrow s}) \triangleq c$, $\phi'(f^{\sigma \rightarrow s}(L)) \triangleq f[\phi'(L)]$ when $\sigma \neq \epsilon$ and $\phi'(M, L) = \phi'(M), \phi'(L)$. For example the parse tree $[A : b[A : a, A]]$ is a state of the polynomial system $\mathcal{P}$ defined by $A = b(A, A) + a$. Transitions construct children of a variable node in a parse tree as given by the right-hand side of the polynomial system equations:

$$\tau^p[\![\mathcal{P}]\!] \triangleq \{\langle p[qxq']p',\ p[qx : \phi'(\Delta(d))q']p' \rangle \mid d \in \delta(x) \wedge \Delta(d) \neq \Omega \wedge q' \neq [q'']\}. \quad (3)$$

For the $A = b(A, A) + a$ example, a possible transition is $[A : b[A, A]] \stackrel{\mathcal{P}}{\Longrightarrow} [A : b[A : a, A]]$. □

Example 7 (Derivation tree transition system). More generally, we can built the parse tree and record which variables are expanded in parallel at each derivation step thus generalizing the *derivation trees* of [Courcelle, 1996]. For example, the states of the polynomial system $A = b(A, A)\ [d_1] + a\ [d_2]$ are given by $A' \to \langle A \rangle \mid A \mid A[d_1]b(A', A') \mid A[d_2]a$ where $\langle A \rangle$ is to be derived as in $\langle A \rangle \stackrel{\mathcal{P}}{\Longrightarrow} A[d_1]b(\langle A \rangle, \langle A \rangle) \stackrel{\mathcal{P}}{\Longrightarrow} A[d_1]b(A[d_1]b(\langle A \rangle, A), A[d_2]a) \stackrel{\mathcal{P}}{\Longrightarrow} A[d_1]b(A[d_1](A[d_2]a, \langle A \rangle), A[d_2]a) \stackrel{\mathcal{P}}{\Longrightarrow} A[d_1]b(A[d_1]b(A[d_2]a, A[d_2]a), A[d_2]a)$.

Given an $\mathcal{S}$-sorted polynomial system $\mathcal{P} = \langle \mathcal{F}, \mathcal{X}, \mathcal{D}, \delta, \Delta \rangle$, the set of state is the set $\Sigma^d[\![\mathcal{P}]\!]$ of *derivation trees* T^s of sort s defined by the following grammar:

$$\begin{array}{lll} T^s \to & x^s & \text{variable,} \\ \mid & \langle x^s \rangle & \text{substitution variable,} \\ \mid & f^{s_1 \times \ldots \times s_n \to s}(T^{s_1}, \ldots, T^{s_n}) & \text{node,} \\ \mid & c^{\epsilon \to s} & \text{leave,} \\ \mid & x^s[d^s] f^{s_1 \times \ldots \times s_n \to s}(T^{s_1}, \ldots, T^{s_n}) & \text{substituted node,} \\ \mid & x^s[d^s] c^{\epsilon \to s} & \text{substituted leave.} \end{array}$$

A *substitution* θ maps variables $x^s \in \mathcal{X}$ to sets $\theta(x)$ of monomials m^s of type s over the variables $\{x, \langle x \rangle \mid x \in \mathcal{X}\}$. The *identity substitution* ι satisfies $\forall x \in \mathcal{X} : \iota(x) = \{x, \langle x \rangle\}$. The *application* $T[\![\theta]\!]$ *of substitution* θ *for derivation label* d *to a tree* T is defined as follows:

$$\begin{aligned} x^s[\![\theta]\!]d^s &\triangleq \{x^s, \langle x^s \rangle\}, \\ \langle x^s \rangle[\![\theta]\!]d^s &\triangleq \{x^s[d^s]m^s \mid m^s \in \theta(x^s)\}, \\ f^{s_1 \times \ldots \times s_n \to s}(T^{s_1}, \ldots, T^{s_n})[\![\theta]\!]d^s &\triangleq \{f(m^{s_1}, \ldots, m^{s_n}) \mid \bigwedge_{i=1}^{n} m^{s_i} \in T^{s_i}[\![\theta]\!]d^s\}, \\ c^{\epsilon \to s}[\![\theta]\!]d^s &\triangleq \{c\}, \\ x^s[d_0^s] f^{s_1 \times \ldots \times s_n \to s}(T^{s_1}, \ldots, T^{s_n})[\![\theta]\!]d^s &\triangleq \{x^s[d_0^s]f(m^{s_1}, \ldots, m^{s_n}) \mid \bigwedge_{i=1}^{n} m^{s_i} \in T^{s_i}[\![\theta]\!]d^s\}, \\ x^s[d_0^s]c^{\epsilon \to s}[\![\theta]\!]d^s &\triangleq \{x^s[d_0^s]c\}. \end{aligned}$$

The transition relation consists in replacing all substitution variables in a derivation tree by corresponding right-hand side monomials and then in choosing substitution variables for the next step:

$$\tau^d[\![\mathcal{P}]\!] \triangleq \{\langle T, T' \rangle \mid \exists \theta : \forall x \in \mathcal{X} : \exists d \in \delta(x) : \theta(x) \subseteq \Delta(d)[\![\iota]\!] \wedge T' \in T[\![\theta]\!]d\}.$$

$\langle T, T' \rangle \in \tau^d[\![\mathcal{P}]\!]$ is written $T \stackrel{\mathcal{P}}{\Longrightarrow} T'$, $\stackrel{\mathcal{P}}{\Longrightarrow}{}^{\star}$ is the reflexive transitive closure. □

4 Fixpoint Semantics

A *fixpoint semantic specification* is a pair $\langle D, F \rangle$ where the *semantic domain* $\langle D, \sqsubseteq, \bot, \sqcup \rangle$ is a poset with partial order $\sqsubseteq$, infimum $\bot$ and partially defined least upper bound (lub) $\sqcup$ and the *semantic transformer* $F \in D \stackrel{m}{\longmapsto} D$ is a total monotone map from D to D assumed to be such that the transfinite *iterates of* F *from* $\bot$, that is $F^0 \triangleq \bot$, $F^{\delta+1} \triangleq F(F^\delta)$ for successor ordinals $\delta + 1$

and $F^{\lambda} \triangleq \bigsqcup_{\delta<\lambda} F^{\delta}$ for limit ordinals λ are well-defined (e.g. when $\langle D, \sqsubseteq, \bot, \sqcup \rangle$ is a directed-complete partial order or DCPO). By monotonicity, these iterates form an increasing chain, hence reach a fixpoint so that the *iteration order* can be defined as the least ordinal ϵ such that $F(F^{\epsilon}) = F^{\epsilon}$. This specifies the *fixpoint semantics* S as the $\sqsubseteq$-least fixpoint $S \triangleq \mathrm{lfp}^{\sqsubseteq} F = F^{\epsilon}$ of F.

5 Derivation Semantics, Its Fixpoint Characterization

The set Σ^{+} of finite derivations for the transition system $\langle \Sigma, \tau \rangle$ is the set $\tau^{\vec{*}} \triangleq \bigcup_{n>0} \tau^{\vec{n}}$ where the set of non-empty sequences of n states separated by transitions τ is $\tau^{\vec{n}} \triangleq \{\sigma_0 \ldots \sigma_{n-1} \mid \forall i \in [0, n-1[: \langle \sigma_i, \sigma_{i+1} \rangle \in \tau\}$.

Example 8. A possible maximal derivation for the polynomial system $A = b(A, A)\ [d_1] + a\ [d_2]$ is $\langle A \rangle \stackrel{\mathcal{P}}{\Longrightarrow} A[d_{d_1}]b(\langle A \rangle, A) \stackrel{\mathcal{P}}{\Longrightarrow} A[1]b(A[d_2]a, \langle A \rangle) \stackrel{\mathcal{P}}{\Longrightarrow} A[d_1]b(A[d_2]a, A[d_2]a)$. □

The set $\tau^{\vec{*}}$ of finite derivations for the transition system $\langle \Sigma, \tau \rangle$ can be characterized in fixpoint top-down/forward and bottom-up/backward form:

$$\begin{aligned} \tau^{\vec{*}} &= \mathrm{lfp}^{\subseteq} \vec{T} \quad \text{where} \quad \vec{T}(X) \triangleq \tau^{\vec{1}} \cup (X \,;\, \tau^{\vec{2}}) \quad \text{(top-down/forward)}, & (4)\\ &= \mathrm{lfp}^{\subseteq} \vec{B} \qquad\qquad\quad \vec{B}(X) \triangleq \tau^{\vec{2}} \,;\, (X \cup \tau^{\vec{1}}) \quad \text{(bottom-up/backward)}, & (5) \end{aligned}$$

where $\tau^{\vec{1}} \cong \Sigma$ is the set of state sequences $\sigma_0 \in \Sigma$ of length one and $X \,;\, Y \triangleq \{\sigma_0 \ldots \sigma_{n-1} \bullet \sigma'_1 \ldots \sigma'_{m-1} \mid \sigma_0 \ldots \sigma_{n-1} \in X \wedge \sigma_{n-1} = \sigma'_0 \wedge \sigma'_0 \ldots \sigma'_{m-1} \in Y\}$ is the sequential composition of sets of finite derivations. The transformers $\vec{T}$ and $\vec{B}$ are $\cup$-additive on the complete lattice $\langle \wp(\Sigma^{+}), \subseteq, \emptyset, \Sigma, \cup, \cap \rangle$ of sets of derivation sequences.

6 Fixpoint Semantics Transfer and Approximation

In abstract interpretation, the *concrete semantics* $S^{\natural}$ is approximated by a (usually computable) *abstract semantics* $S^{\sharp}$ via an abstraction function $\alpha \in D^{\natural} \longmapsto D^{\sharp}$ such that $\alpha(S^{\natural}) \sqsubseteq^{\sharp} S^{\sharp}$ [2]. The abstraction is *exact* if $\alpha(S^{\natural}) = S^{\sharp}$ and *approximate* if $\alpha(S^{\natural}) \sqsubset^{\sharp} S^{\sharp}$.

6.1 Fixpoint Semantics Approximation

To derive $S^{\sharp}$ from $S^{\natural}$ by abstraction or $S^{\natural}$ from $S^{\sharp}$ by refinement, we can use the following fixpoint approximation theorems (as usual, we call a function f *Scott-continuous*, written $f : D \stackrel{c}{\longmapsto} E$, if it is monotone and preserves the lub of any directed subset A of D):

Theorem 9 (S. Kleene fixpoint approximation). Let $\langle\langle D^{\natural}, \sqsubseteq^{\natural}, \bot^{\natural}, \sqcup^{\natural} \rangle, F^{\natural} \rangle$ and $\langle\langle D^{\sharp}, \sqsubseteq^{\sharp}, \bot^{\sharp}, \sqcup^{\sharp} \rangle, F^{\sharp} \rangle$ be concrete and abstract fixpoint semantic specifications. If the $\bot$-strict Scott-continuous abstraction function $\alpha \in D^{\natural} \stackrel{\bot, c}{\longmapsto} D^{\sharp}$ is such that for

[2] More generally, we look for an abstract semantics $S^{\sharp}$ such that $\alpha(S^{\natural}) \preceq^{\sharp} S^{\sharp}$ for the *approximation partial ordering* $\preceq^{\sharp}$ corresponding to logical implication which may differ from the *computational partial orderings* $\sqsubseteq$ used to define least fixpoints [Cousot & Cousot, 1994].

all $x \in D^\natural$ such that $x \sqsubseteq^\natural F^\natural(x)$ there exists $y \sqsubseteq^\natural x$ such that $\alpha(F^\natural(x)) \sqsubseteq^\sharp F^\sharp(\alpha(y))$ then $\alpha(\mathrm{lfp}^{\sqsubseteq^\natural} F^\natural) \sqsubseteq^\sharp \mathrm{lfp}^{\sqsubseteq^\sharp} F^\sharp$. □

Theorem 10 (A. Tarski fixpoint approximation). Let $\langle D^\natural, F^\natural\rangle$ and $\langle D^\sharp, F^\sharp\rangle$ be concrete and abstract fixpoint semantic specifications such that $\langle D^\natural, \sqsubseteq^\natural, \bot^\natural, \top^\natural, \sqcup^\natural, \sqcap^\natural\rangle$ and $\langle D^\sharp, \sqsubseteq^\sharp, \bot^\sharp, \top^\sharp, \sqcup^\sharp, \sqcap^\sharp\rangle$ are complete lattices. If the monotone abstraction function $\alpha \in D^\natural \stackrel{m}{\longmapsto} D^\sharp$ is such that for all $y \in D^\sharp$ such that $F^\sharp(y) \sqsubseteq^\sharp y$ there exists $x \in D^\natural$ such that $\alpha(x) \sqsubseteq^\sharp y$ and $F^\natural(x) \sqsubseteq^\natural x$ then $\alpha(\mathrm{lfp}^{\sqsubseteq^\natural} F^\natural) \sqsubseteq^\sharp \mathrm{lfp}^{\sqsubseteq^\sharp} F^\sharp$. □

6.2 Fixpoint Semantics Transfer

When the abstraction must be exact, that is $\alpha(S^\natural) = S^\sharp$, we can use the following fixpoint transfer theorem, which provide guidelines for designing $S^\sharp$ from $S^\natural$ (or dually) in fixpoint form [Cousot & Cousot, 1979, theorem 7.1.0.4(3)]:

Theorem 11 (S. Kleene fixpoint transfer). Let $\langle D^\natural, F^\natural\rangle$ and $\langle D^\sharp, F^\sharp\rangle$ be concrete and abstract fixpoint semantic specifications. If the $\bot$-strict Scott-continuous abstraction function $\alpha \in D^\natural \stackrel{\bot,c}{\longmapsto} D^\sharp$ satisfies the *commutation condition* $F^\sharp \circ \alpha = \alpha \circ F^\natural$ then $\alpha(\mathrm{lfp}^{\sqsubseteq^\natural} F^\natural) = \mathrm{lfp}^{\sqsubseteq^\sharp} F^\sharp$. Moreover the respective iterates $F^{\natural\delta}$ and $F^{\sharp\delta}$, $\delta \in \mathbb{O}$ of $F^\natural$ and $F^\sharp$ from $\bot^\natural$ and $\bot^\sharp$ satisfy $\forall\delta \in \mathbb{O}$: $\alpha(F^{\natural\delta}) = F^{\sharp\delta}$ and the iteration order of $F^\sharp$ is less than or equal to that of $F^\natural$. □

Observe that in theorem Theorem 11 (as well as in theorem Theorem 9), Scott-continuity of the abstraction function α is a too strong hypothesis since we only use the fact that α preserves the lub of the iterates of $F^\natural$ starting from $\bot^\natural$. When this is not the case, but α preserves glbs, we can use:

Theorem 12 (A. Tarski fixpoint transfer). Let $\langle D^\natural, F^\natural\rangle$ and $\langle D^\sharp, F^\sharp\rangle$ be concrete and abstract fixpoint semantic specifications such that $\langle D^\natural, \sqsubseteq^\natural, \bot^\natural, \top^\natural, \sqcup^\natural, \sqcap^\natural\rangle$ and $\langle D^\sharp, \sqsubseteq^\sharp, \bot^\sharp, \top^\sharp, \sqcup^\sharp, \sqcap^\sharp\rangle$ are complete lattices. If the abstraction function $\alpha \in D^\natural \stackrel{\sqcap}{\longmapsto} D^\sharp$ is a complete $\sqcap$-morphism satisfying the *commutation inequality* $F^\sharp \circ \alpha \sqsubseteq^\sharp \alpha \circ F^\natural$ and the *post-fixpoint correspondence* $\forall y \in D^\sharp : F^\sharp(y) \sqsubseteq^\sharp y \Longrightarrow \exists x \in D^\natural : \alpha(x) = y \wedge F^\natural(x) \sqsubseteq^\natural x$ then $\alpha(\mathrm{lfp}^{\sqsubseteq^\natural} F^\natural) = \mathrm{lfp}^{\sqsubseteq^\sharp} F^\sharp$. □

6.3 Semantics Abstraction

An important particular case of abstraction function $\alpha \in D^\natural \longmapsto D^\sharp$ is when α preserves existing lubs $\alpha\big(\bigsqcup^\natural_{i\in\Delta} x_i\big) = \bigsqcup^\sharp_{i\in\Delta} \alpha(x_i)$. In this case there exists a unique map $\gamma \in D^\sharp \longmapsto D^\natural$ (so-called the *concretization function* [Cousot & Cousot, 1977]) such that the pair $\langle\alpha, \gamma\rangle$ is a *Galois connection*, written$\langle D^\natural, \sqsubseteq^\natural\rangle \underset{\alpha}{\overset{\gamma}{\leftrightarrows}} \langle D^\sharp, \sqsubseteq^\sharp\rangle$, which means that $\langle D^\natural, \sqsubseteq^\natural\rangle$ and $\langle D^\sharp, \sqsubseteq^\sharp\rangle$ are posets, $\alpha \in D^\natural \longmapsto D^\sharp$, $\gamma \in D^\sharp \longmapsto D^\natural$, and $\forall x \in D^\natural : \forall y \in D^\sharp : \alpha(x) \sqsubseteq^\sharp y \Longleftrightarrow x \sqsubseteq^\natural \gamma(y)$. If α is surjective (resp. injective, bijective) then we have a *Galois insertion* written $\underset{\alpha}{\overset{\gamma}{\leftrightarrows\!\!\!\!\rightarrow}}$ (resp. *embedding*[3] written $\underset{\alpha}{\overset{\gamma}{\leftleftarrows\!\!\!\!\rightarrow}}$, *bijection* written $\underset{\alpha}{\overset{\gamma}{\leftleftarrows\!\!\!\!\twoheadrightarrow}}$). The use of

[3] If α and γ are Scott-continuous then this is an embedding-projection pair.

Galois connections in abstract interpretation was motivated by the fact that $\alpha(x)$ is the best possible approximation of $x \in D^{\natural}$ within $D^{\sharp}$ [Cousot & Cousot, 1977, 1979]. We often use the fact that Galois connections compose[4]. If $\langle D^{\flat}, \sqsubseteq^{\flat}\rangle \xleftrightarrow[\alpha_1]{\gamma_1} \langle D^{\natural}, \sqsubseteq^{\natural}\rangle$ and $\langle D^{\natural}, \sqsubseteq^{\natural}\rangle \xleftrightarrow[\alpha_2]{\gamma_2} \langle D^{\sharp}, \sqsubseteq^{\sharp}\rangle$ then $\langle D^{\flat}, \sqsubseteq^{\flat}\rangle \xleftrightarrow[\alpha_2\circ\alpha_1]{\gamma_1\circ\gamma_2} \langle D^{\sharp}, \sqsubseteq^{\sharp}\rangle$.

Example 13 (Elementwise subset abstraction). If $D^{\natural}$ is a set and $D^{\sharp} \subseteq D^{\natural}$ then the *subset abstraction* is $\langle \wp(D^{\natural}), \subseteq\rangle \xleftrightarrow[\alpha]{\gamma} \langle \wp(D^{\sharp}), \subseteq\rangle$ where $\alpha(X) \triangleq X \cap D^{\sharp}$ and $\gamma(Y) \triangleq X \cup \neg D^{\sharp}$ (where the *complement* of $\mathcal{E} \subseteq \mathcal{D}$ is $\neg\mathcal{E} \triangleq \{x \in \mathcal{D} \mid x \notin \mathcal{E}\}$).

If $@ \in D^{\natural} \longmapsto D^{\sharp}$, the *elementwise abstraction* is $\langle \wp(D^{\natural}), \subseteq\rangle \xleftrightarrow[\alpha]{\gamma} \langle \wp(D^{\natural}), \subseteq\rangle$, where:

$$\alpha \in \wp(D^{\natural}) \longmapsto \wp(D^{\sharp}), \qquad \alpha(X) \triangleq \{@(s) \mid s \in X\}, \tag{6}$$

$$\gamma \in \wp(D^{\sharp}) \longmapsto \wp(D^{\natural}), \qquad \gamma(Y) \triangleq \{s \mid @(s) \in Y\}\,. \tag{7}$$

Moreover, if $@$ is surjective then so is α.

If $\mathcal{S} \subseteq D^{\natural}$ and $@ \in \mathcal{S} \longmapsto D^{\sharp}$ then by composition, we get the *elementwise subset abstraction* $\langle \wp(D^{\natural}), \subseteq\rangle \xleftrightarrow[\alpha]{\gamma} \langle \wp(D^{\natural}), \subseteq\rangle$ where $\alpha(X) \triangleq \{@(x) \mid x \in X \cap \mathcal{S}\}$ and $\gamma \triangleq \{x \mid @(x) \in Y\} \cup \neg\mathcal{S}$. □

Example 14 (Transitive derivation relation). In order to illustrate fixpoint transfer Theorem 11, let us consider the reflexive transitive closure τ^* of the transition relation τ. It is the image $\alpha(\vec{\tau}^{*})$ of the derivation sequences for τ by the elementwise abstraction $\langle \wp(\Sigma^+), \subseteq\rangle \xleftrightarrow[\alpha]{\gamma} \langle \wp(\Sigma \times \Sigma), \subseteq\rangle$ defined by (6) for the abstraction mapping which records initial and final states of derivations:

$$@ \in \Sigma^+ \longmapsto \Sigma \times \Sigma, \qquad @(\sigma_0 \ldots \sigma_{n-1}) \triangleq \langle \sigma_0, \sigma_{n-1}\rangle\,. \tag{8}$$

The classical fixpoint characterization:

$$\tau^* = \operatorname{lfp} T^*, \qquad \text{where} \qquad T^*(\rho) \triangleq 1_{\Sigma} \cup (\rho \circ \tau) \tag{9}$$

and 1_{Σ} is the identity relation on states Σ, can be derived from the fixpoint characterization (4) of derivation sequences by fixpoint transfer Theorem 11 since $\alpha \circ \vec{T}(X) = T^* \circ \alpha(X)$. □

7 Examples of Abstractions

We now give a number of useful abstractions to relate different semantics of algebraic polynomial systems, at various levels of abstraction.

7.1 State Abstraction

Example 15 (Parse tree to protosentence abstraction). A protosentence is a less informative state than a parse tree since the details of the derivation process

---

[4] contrary to Galois's original definition corresponding to the semi-dual $\langle D^{\natural}, \sqsubseteq^{\natural}\rangle \xleftrightarrow[\alpha]{\gamma} \langle D^{\sharp}, \sqsupseteq^{\sharp}\rangle$.

are lost. The abstraction mapping $\alpha^{ps} \in \Sigma^p \longmapsto \Sigma^s$ flatten a parse tree to its tips. For example $\alpha^{ps}([A : b[A : a, A]]) = aA$. Formally:

$$\alpha^{ps}([\Theta]) \triangleq \alpha^{ps}(\Theta), \qquad \alpha^{ps}(x) \triangleq x, \qquad \alpha^{ps}(x : c^{\epsilon \to s}) \triangleq c, \tag{10}$$
$$\alpha^{ps}(x : f^{s_1 \times \ldots \times s_n \to s}[\Theta_{s_1}, \ldots, \Theta_{s_n}]) \triangleq \alpha^{ps}(\Theta_{s_1}) \bullet \ldots \bullet \alpha^{ps}(\Theta_{s_n}) . \qquad \square$$

Example 16 (Context to protosentence abstraction). The same way, the abstraction mapping:

$$\alpha^{cs} \in \Sigma^c \longmapsto \Sigma^s, \qquad \alpha^{cs}(p[r]q) \triangleq p \bullet r \bullet q$$

abstracts contexts to protosentences. The α^{cs} abstraction does <u>not</u> preserve blocking states (as shown by the counter example $\alpha^{cs}(a[A]) = \alpha^{cs}([a]A) = aA$ but $[a]A$ is a blocking state for $\tau^c[\![\mathcal{P}]\!]$ when $\mathcal{P}$ is $A = b(A, A)+c(A)+d(a, A)+a$ while $a[A]$ is not). It follows that in general $\{\alpha(\sigma) \mid \sigma \in \tau^{\vec{\star}}\} \neq \alpha(\tau)^{\vec{\star}}$ so that it is a priori not equivalent to reason on contexts and protosentences. However we observe that:

$$\langle s, s' \rangle \in \tau^c[\![\mathcal{P}]\!]^\star \Longrightarrow \langle \alpha^{cs}(s), \alpha^{cs}(s') \rangle \in \tau^s[\![\mathcal{P}]\!]^\star,$$

while the inverse implication does not hold. Nevertheless:

Theorem 17. If $x \in \mathcal{X}$, $V \in \mathcal{X} \cup \{c^{\epsilon \to s} \mid c \in \mathcal{F}\}$ and $\langle x, p \bullet V \bullet q \rangle \in \tau^s[\![\mathcal{P}]\!]^\star$ then $\langle x, p'[p'' \bullet V \bullet q'']q' \rangle \in \tau^s[\![\mathcal{P}]\!]^\star$, $\langle p' \bullet p'', p \rangle \in \tau^s[\![\mathcal{P}]\!]^\star$ and $\langle q'' \bullet q', q \rangle \in \tau^s[\![\mathcal{P}]\!]^\star$.

These abstractions can be extended to sets of states by (6). $\square$

7.2 Transition Abstraction

Given an abstraction mapping $\alpha \in \Sigma \longmapsto \Sigma^\sharp$, a concrete transition system $\langle \Sigma, \tau \rangle$ can be approximated by any abstract transition system $\langle \Sigma^\sharp, \tau^\sharp \rangle$ such that:

$$\langle s, s' \rangle \in \tau \Longrightarrow \langle \alpha(s), \alpha(s') \rangle \in \tau^\sharp . \tag{11}$$

The least such $\subseteq$-upper approximation is:

$$\alpha(\tau) \triangleq \{\langle \xi, \xi' \rangle \mid \exists s, s' : \xi = \alpha(s) \wedge \xi' = \alpha(s') \wedge \langle s, s' \rangle \in \tau\} . \tag{12}$$

Example 18. Applying (12) to the abstraction (10) of parse trees into protosentences, the parse tree transition system (3) is approximated by $\tau^s[\![\mathcal{P}]\!] = \alpha^{ps}(\tau^p[\![\mathcal{P}]\!])$ as defined in (1). $\square$

7.3 Derivation Abstraction

An abstraction mapping on states $\alpha \in \Sigma \longmapsto \Sigma^\sharp$ can be extended pointwise to derivation sequences (i.e. non empty sequences of states):

$$\alpha \in \Sigma^+ \longmapsto \Sigma^{\sharp +}, \qquad \alpha(\sigma_0 \ldots \sigma_{n-1}) = \alpha(\sigma_0) \bullet \ldots \bullet \alpha(\sigma_{n-1}) .$$

Example 19. According to (10), the parse tree derivation sequence $[A] \stackrel{\mathcal{P}}{\Longrightarrow} [A : b[A, A]] \stackrel{\mathcal{P}}{\Longrightarrow} [A : b[A : a, A]] \stackrel{\mathcal{P}}{\Longrightarrow} [A : b[A : a, A : a]]$ for the algebraic polynomial system $A = b(A, A) + a$ can be approximated by the protosentence derivation $A \stackrel{\mathcal{P}}{\Longrightarrow} AA \stackrel{\mathcal{P}}{\Longrightarrow} aA \stackrel{\mathcal{P}}{\Longrightarrow} aa$. $\square$

If $\langle \Sigma^\sharp, \tau^\sharp \rangle$ is an α-abstraction of $\langle \Sigma, \tau \rangle$ (i.e. satisfying (11)) then the abstraction process can only introduce more derivation sequences:

$$\{\alpha(\sigma) \mid \sigma \in \vec{\tau^\star}\} \subseteq \vec{\tau^{\sharp\star}} .$$

We say that the abstraction mapping α preserves blocking states for τ if and only if:

$$\forall s, s' \in \Sigma : [\alpha(s) = \alpha(s') \land \exists s'' : \langle s, s'' \rangle \in \tau] \Longrightarrow [\exists s'' : \langle s', s'' \rangle \in \tau]$$

In this case, the abstraction of the concrete derivation sequences for $\langle \Sigma, \tau \rangle$ is exactly the set of abstract derivation sequences for $\langle \Sigma^\sharp, \alpha(\tau) \rangle$:

$$\{\alpha(\sigma) \mid \sigma \in \vec{\tau^\star}\} = \vec{\alpha(\tau)^\star} . \tag{13}$$

8 Lattice of Semantics

A preorder can be defined on semantics $\tau^\natural \in D^\natural$ and $\tau^\sharp \in D^\sharp$ when $\tau^\sharp = \alpha^\sharp(\tau^\natural)$ and $\langle D^\natural, \leq \rangle \underset{\alpha^\sharp}{\overset{\gamma^\sharp}{\leftrightarrows}} \langle D^\sharp, \leqq \rangle$. The quotient poset is isomorphic to M. Ward lattice [Ward, 1942] of upper closure operators $\gamma^\sharp \circ \alpha^\sharp$ on $\langle \wp(\Sigma^+), \subseteq \rangle$, so that we get a lattice of semantics of algebraic polynomial systems which is part of the lattice of abstract interpretations of [Cousot & Cousot, 1977, sec. 8]. We illustrate a few abstract semantics in the lattice below.

9 Bottom-Up/Backward Abstract Semantics of Algebraic Polynomial Systems

For bottom-up analysis, we use a fixpoint semantics of the form:

$$\tau^\star = \operatorname{lfp} B^\star, \qquad \text{where} \qquad B^\star(\rho) \triangleq (\tau \circ \rho) \cup 1_\Sigma . \tag{14}$$

9.1 Compositional Bottom-Up Abstract Semantics

By refining the specification (14), the big-step semantics $\tau[\![\mathcal{P}]\!]^\star$ can be expressed in compositional form, that is by induction on the syntax of algebraic polynomial systems, as an instance of the following bottom-up abstract semantics:

$$S[\![\mathcal{P}]\!] \triangleq \operatorname{lfp}^{\sqsubseteq} B[\![\mathcal{P}]\!], \tag{15}$$

where $\langle \mathbf{L}, \sqsubseteq, \bot, \sqcup \rangle$ is a cpo, $\langle \mathbf{P}, \leq, \nabla \rangle$ is a poset and the $\sqsubseteq$-monotonic transformer $B[\![S]\!] \in \mathbf{L} \overset{m}{\longmapsto} \mathbf{L}$ and $B[\![P]\!] \in \mathbf{L} \overset{m}{\longmapsto} \mathbf{P}$ are defined compositionally by induction on the syntax S of systems $\mathcal{P}$ and P of polynomials, as follows:

$$\begin{aligned} B[\![ES]\!]r &\triangleq B[\![E]\!]r \sqcup B[\![S]\!]r, & B[\![x]\!]r &\triangleq x\langle r \rangle, \\ B[\![x = P]\!]r &\triangleq \langle 1 \rangle \sqcup \langle x \multimap B[\![P]\!]r \rangle r, & B[\![f^{\sigma \to s}(L)]\!]r &\triangleq f\langle r \rangle(B[\![L]\!]r), \\ B[\![\Omega]\!]r &\triangleq \langle \Omega \rangle, & B[\![M, L]\!]r &\triangleq B[\![M]\!]r \otimes B[\![L]\!]r, \\ B[\![M + P]\!]r &\triangleq B[\![M]\!]r \nabla B[\![P]\!]r, & B[\![c^{\epsilon \to s}]\!]r &\triangleq c\langle r \rangle . \end{aligned} \tag{16}$$

Example 20 (Big-step protosentence semantics). For $\tau^{s}[\![\mathcal{P}]\!]^{\star}$, we have (recall that $\mathcal{V} \triangleq \{c \mid c^{\epsilon \to s} \in \mathcal{F}\} \cup \mathcal{X}$):

$\mathbf{L}^{s}$	$\sqsubseteq^{s}$	$\perp^{s}$	$\sqcup^{s}$	$\mathbf{P}^{s}$	$\leq^{s}$	∇^{s}	$\langle\Omega\rangle^{s}$	$\langle 1\rangle^{s}$	$\langle x \multimap R\rangle^{s} r$	$\otimes^{s}$	$x\langle r\rangle^{s}$	$f\langle r\rangle^{s}(R)$	$c\langle r\rangle^{s}$
$\wp(\mathcal{V}^{\star} \times \mathcal{V}^{\star})$	$\subseteq$	$\emptyset$	$\cup$	$\wp(\mathcal{V}^{\star})$	$\subseteq$	$\cup$	$\emptyset$	$1_{\mathcal{V}^{\star}}$	$\dagger$	$\bullet$	$\ddagger$	R	$\{c\}$

$\dagger$ is $\{\langle pNq, p'mq'\rangle \mid \langle p, p'\rangle \in r \wedge m \in R \wedge \langle q, q'\rangle \in r\}$, $X \bullet Y$ is $\{xy \mid x \in X \wedge y \in Y\}$ and $\ddagger$ is $\{p \mid \langle x, p\rangle \in r\}$.

The proof relies on the fact that $\tau^{s}[\![\mathcal{P}]\!]^{\star}$ is a *relational morphism*, that is $r \subseteq \mathcal{V}^{\star} \times \mathcal{V}^{\star}$ such that:

$$\langle m \bullet p, q\rangle \in r \iff \exists m', p' : \langle m, m'\rangle \in r \wedge \langle p, p'\rangle \in r \wedge q = m' \bullet p', \tag{17}$$

which generalizes $\mathcal{F}$-homomorphisms [Meinke & Tucker, 1992]). □

Example 21 (Finitary Powerset $\mathcal{F}$-Algebra Semantics). The same way, the powerset $\mathcal{F}$-algebra semantics $S^{\star}[\![\mathcal{P}]\!]$ of [Courcelle, 1996] is given by choosing $\mathbf{L}^{\star} \triangleq \mathcal{X} \longmapsto \wp(\mathcal{M})$, $\mathbf{P}^{\star} \triangleq \wp(\mathcal{M})$ where $\mathcal{M} \triangleq \bigcup\{\mathcal{M}^{s,\emptyset} \mid s \in \mathcal{S}\}$ is the set of ground monomials, and:

$\sqsubseteq^{\star}$	$\perp^{\star}$	$\sqcup^{\star}$	$\leq^{\star}$	$\nabla^{\star}$	$\langle\Omega\rangle^{\star}$	$\langle 1\rangle^{\star} x$	$\langle x \multimap R\rangle L y$	$\otimes^{\star}$	$x\langle L\rangle^{\star}$	$f\langle L\rangle^{\star}(R)$	$c\langle L\rangle^{\star}$
$\dot{\subseteq}$	$\dot{\emptyset}$	$\dot{\cup}$	$\subseteq$	$\cup$	$\emptyset$	$\emptyset$	$(y = x \; ? \; R \; ¿ \; \emptyset)$	$\times$	$L(x)$	$f[R]$	$\{c\}$

where $f^{s_1 \times \ldots \times s_n \to s}[R] \triangleq \{f(x_1, \ldots, x_n) \mid \langle x_1, \ldots, x_n\rangle \in R\}$. □

9.2 Compositional Bottom-Up Abstract Interpretations

This compositional presentation is preserved by abstract interpretation. If we have defined a concrete semantics $S^{\flat} \in \mathbf{L}^{\flat}$ (15) compositionally (16), we may want, given an abstraction $\langle \mathbf{L}^{\flat}, \sqsubseteq^{\flat}\rangle \underset{\alpha}{\overset{\gamma}{\leftrightarrows}} \langle \mathbf{L}^{\sharp}, \sqsubseteq^{\sharp}\rangle$, to derive an abstract semantics $S^{\sharp} \triangleq \alpha(S^{\flat})$ which can be defined in the same compositional form (15), (16). By the fixpoint transfer theorem Theorem 11, $S^{\sharp} \triangleq \alpha(S^{\flat})$ can be defined in compositional form (15) and (16) if we can check the following conditions:

$$\begin{aligned}
&\langle \mathbf{L}^{\flat}, \sqsubseteq^{\flat}\rangle \underset{\alpha}{\overset{\gamma}{\leftrightarrows}} \langle \mathbf{L}^{\sharp}, \sqsubseteq^{\sharp}\rangle, && \alpha(\langle x \multimap R\rangle^{\flat} r) = \langle x \multimap \alpha'(R)\rangle^{\sharp} \alpha(r), \\
&\langle \mathbf{P}^{\flat}, \leq^{\flat}\rangle \underset{\alpha'}{\overset{\gamma'}{\leftrightarrows}} \langle \mathbf{P}^{\sharp}, \leq^{\sharp}\rangle, && \alpha'(r_1 \otimes^{\flat} r_2) = \alpha'(r_1) \otimes^{\sharp} \alpha'(r_2), \\
&\langle\Omega\rangle^{\sharp} = \alpha(\langle\Omega\rangle^{\flat}), && \alpha'(f\langle r\rangle^{\flat}) = f\langle \alpha'(r)\rangle^{\sharp}, \\
&\langle 1\rangle^{\sharp} = \alpha(\langle 1\rangle^{\flat}), && c\langle r\rangle^{\sharp} = \alpha'(c\langle r\rangle^{\sharp}) .
\end{aligned} \tag{18}$$

This generalizes the homomorphism result of [Mezei & Wright, 1967] for the case of power-set $\mathcal{F}$-algebra (also [Courcelle, 1996, proposition 3.7]).

When $\langle \mathbf{L}^{\sharp}, \sqsubseteq^{\sharp}\rangle$ satisfies the ascending chain condition, (15) and (16) can be understood as the specification of an abstract interpreter defined in terms of the abstract operations (18) and computing fixpoints iteratively. The abstract interpreter is generic and can be instantiated for particular applications as considered in the next section.

10 Examples of Bottom-Up Algebraic Polynomial Systems Abstract Interpretations

The following few examples are abstractions of bottom-up big-step polynomial system semantics and generalize classical results for context free grammars.

10.1 Examples of Bottom-Up Algebraic Polynomial Systems Semantics

Example 22 (Generated Protolanguage). The abstraction $\alpha(r) \triangleq \lambda x \cdot \{p \mid \langle x, p\rangle \in r\}$ of the big-step semantics $S^s[\![\mathcal{P}]\!] \triangleq \tau^s[\![\mathcal{P}]\!]^*$ provides the protolanguage $S^v[\![\mathcal{P}]\!]x$ generated for each variable $x \in \mathcal{X}$ by the polynomial system $\mathcal{P}$. α' is the identity. The corresponding compositional fixpoint definition is obtained from (15) and (16) with $\mathbf{L}^v \triangleq \mathcal{X} \longmapsto \wp(\mathcal{V}^*)$, $\mathbf{P}^v \triangleq \wp(\mathcal{V}^*)$ and:

$\sqsubseteq^v$	$\perp^v$	$\sqcup^v$	$\leq^v$	∇^v	$\langle\Omega\rangle^v$	$\langle 1\rangle^v x$	$\langle x \multimap R\rangle^v L y$	$\otimes^v$	$\langle x\rangle^v L$	$\langle f\rangle^v L(R)$	$\langle c\rangle^v L$
$\dot{\subseteq}$	$\dot{\emptyset}$	$\dot{\cup}$	$\subseteq$	$\cup$	$\emptyset$	$\{x\}$	$(y = x \mathrel{?} R \mathrel{¿} \emptyset)$	$\bullet$	$L(x)$	R	$\{c\}$

where the test $(b \mathrel{?} t \mathrel{¿} e)$ is t is b is true ($tt \in \mathbb{B}$) and e if b is false ($ff \in \mathbb{B}$) and $\langle \mathcal{X} \longmapsto \wp(\mathcal{V}^*), \dot{\subseteq}, \dot{\emptyset}, \lambda x \cdot \mathcal{V}^*, \dot{\cup}, \dot{\cap}\rangle$ is the pointwise extension of the complete lattice $\langle \wp(\mathcal{V}^*), \subseteq, \emptyset, \mathcal{V}^*, \cup, \cap\rangle$. □

Example 23 (Generated Language). Ginsburg & Rice [1962] and Schützenberger [1962] fixpoint characterization of the language generated by a context-free grammar is easily generalized to polynomial systems by the further abstraction $S^t[\![\mathcal{P}]\!] \triangleq \alpha(S^v[\![\mathcal{P}]\!])$ which consists in ignoring nonterminal sentences: $\alpha(L) \triangleq \lambda x \cdot \{p \mid p \in L(x) \cap \mathcal{T}^*\}$ where $\mathcal{T} \triangleq \{c \mid c^{\epsilon \to s} \in \mathcal{F}\}$. $S^t[\![\mathcal{P}]\!]$ is defined by (15) and (16) with $\mathbf{L}^t \triangleq \mathcal{X} \longmapsto \wp(\mathcal{T}^*)$, $\mathbf{P}^t \triangleq \wp(\mathcal{T}^*)$ and:

$\sqsubseteq^t$	$\perp^t$	$\sqcup^t$	$\leq^t$	∇^t	$\langle\Omega\rangle^t$	$\langle 1\rangle^t x$	$\langle x \multimap R\rangle^t L y$	$\otimes^t$	$\langle x\rangle^t L$	$\langle f\rangle^t L(R)$	$\langle c\rangle^t L$
$\dot{\subseteq}$	$\dot{\emptyset}$	$\dot{\cup}$	$\subseteq$	$\cup$	$\emptyset$	$\emptyset$	$(y = x \mathrel{?} R \mathrel{¿} \emptyset)$	$\bullet$	$L(x)$	R	$\{c\}$

This is also an abstraction of the powerset $\mathcal{F}$-algebra semantics of Example 21 by $\alpha(L) \triangleq \lambda x \cdot \{\mathbf{c}(m) \mid m \in L(x)\}$ where $\mathbf{c}(c) \triangleq c$ and $\mathbf{c}(f^{s_1 \times \ldots \times s_n \to}(m_{s_1}, \ldots, m_{s_n})) \triangleq \mathbf{c}(m_{s_1}) \bullet \ldots \bullet \mathbf{c}(m_{s_n})$. □

10.2 Examples of Bottom-Up Algebraic Polynomial Systems Analysis

Other classical examples of abstraction for grammars are also easily generalizable to algebraic polynomial systems such as variable productivity, the set $\textsc{First}[\![\mathcal{P}]\!](x)$ of constants c that begin the strings derived from x, etc. [Wilhelm & Maurer, 1995]. In this last case, empty grammatical production $N \to \varepsilon$ have no direct counterpart for algebraic polynomial systems, so that we can define $\textsc{First}[\![\mathcal{P}]\!](E)x$ as the set of constants c which can start a protosentence deriving from variable x when erasing all symbols in E or ε if the string resulting from this erasure is empty. Observe that the two definitions coincide when grammars are translated into polynomial systems as specified in Example 2 and $E = \{\varepsilon\}$. Formally, we define:

$$\textsc{First}[\![\mathcal{P}]\!](x) \triangleq \alpha_E(S^t[\![\mathcal{P}]\!]), \qquad \mathbf{c}_E(c \bullet p) \triangleq (c \in E \mathrel{?} \mathbf{c}_E(p) \mathrel{¿} x),$$

$$\alpha_E(r)x \triangleq \{\mathbf{c}_E(p) \mid \langle x, p\rangle \in r\}, \qquad \mathbf{c}(\epsilon) \triangleq \varepsilon\,.$$

In compositional form, $\textsc{First}[\![\mathcal{P}]\!](\mathrm{E})$ is defined by (15) and (16) where $\mathbf{L} \triangleq \mathcal{X} \longmapsto \wp(\mathcal{T})$, $\mathbf{P} \triangleq \wp(\mathcal{T})$ and:

$\sqsubseteq$	$\bot$	$\sqcup$	$\leq$	∇	$\langle\Omega\rangle$	$\langle 1\rangle x$	$\langle x \multimap R\rangle L y$	$X \otimes Y$	$x\langle L\rangle$	$f\langle L\rangle(R)$	$c\langle L\rangle$
$\dot{\subseteq}$	$\dot{\emptyset}$	$\dot{\cup}$	$\subseteq$	$\cup$	$\emptyset$	$\emptyset$	$(y = x \,?\, R \,¿\, \emptyset)$	†	$L(x)$	R	$\{c\}$

$\mathcal{T} \triangleq \{c \mid c^{\epsilon \to s} \in \mathcal{F}\} \setminus \mathrm{E}$ and † is $X \cup (X \cap E \neq \emptyset \,?\, Y \,¿\, \emptyset) \cup \{\varepsilon \mid X \cap E \neq \emptyset \wedge Y \cap E \neq \emptyset\}$.

11 Top-Down/Forward Compositional Abstract Semantics of Algebraic Polynomial Systems

Top-down/forward abstract semantics are abstractions of derivation sequence semantics (4), such as (9). The big-step semantics $\tau[\![\mathcal{P}]\!]^\star$ can be defined as an instance of the top-down abstract semantics:

$$\mathrm{S}[\![\mathcal{P}]\!] \triangleq \mathrm{lfp}^{\sqsubseteq}\, \mathrm{T}[\![\mathcal{P}]\!],$$

where $\langle \mathbf{L}, \sqsubseteq, \bot, \sqcup\rangle$ is a cpo, $\langle \mathbf{P}, \leq, \nabla\rangle$ is a poset, the $\sqsubseteq$-monotonic transformer $\mathrm{T}[\![\mathrm{S}]\!] \in \mathbf{L} \stackrel{\mathrm{m}}{\longmapsto} \mathbf{L}$ and $\mathrm{T}[\![\mathrm{P}]\!] \in \mathbf{P}$ are defined compositionally by induction on the syntax S of $\mathcal{P}$ and P of polynomials, as follows:

$$\begin{aligned}
\mathrm{T}[\![\mathrm{ES}]\!]r &\triangleq \mathrm{T}[\![\mathrm{E}]\!]r \sqcup \mathrm{T}[\![\mathrm{S}]\!]r, & \mathrm{T}[\![x]\!] &\triangleq \langle x\rangle,\\
\mathrm{T}[\![x = \mathrm{P}]\!]r &\triangleq \langle 1\rangle \sqcup \langle x \multimap \mathrm{T}[\![\mathrm{P}]\!]\rangle r, & \mathrm{T}[\![f^{\sigma \to s}(\mathrm{L})]\!] &\triangleq \langle f\rangle(\mathrm{T}[\![\mathrm{L}]\!]),\\
\mathrm{T}[\![\Omega]\!] &\triangleq \langle\Omega\rangle, & \mathrm{T}[\![\mathrm{M}, \mathrm{L}]\!] &\triangleq \mathrm{T}[\![\mathrm{M}]\!] \otimes \mathrm{T}[\![\mathrm{L}]\!], \quad (19)\\
\mathrm{T}[\![\mathrm{M}\ [d_o] + \mathrm{P}]\!] &\triangleq \langle d_o\rangle \mathrm{T}[\![\mathrm{M}]\!] \mathbin{\nabla} \mathrm{T}[\![\mathrm{P}]\!], & \mathrm{T}[\![c^{\epsilon \to s}]\!] &\triangleq \langle c\rangle\ .\\
\mathrm{T}[\![\mathrm{M}\ [d_o]]\!] &\triangleq \langle d_o\rangle \mathrm{T}[\![\mathrm{M}]\!], & &
\end{aligned}$$

For the big-step derivation tree semantics $\tau^{d}[\![\mathcal{P}]\!]^\star$, we choose $\mathbf{L}^d \triangleq \wp(\Sigma^d \times \Sigma^d)$, $\mathbf{P}^d \triangleq \mathcal{D} \longmapsto \wp(\Sigma^d)$ and:

$\sqsubseteq^d$	$\bot^d$	$\sqcup^d$	$\leq^d$	∇^d	$\langle d_o\rangle M$	$\langle\Omega\rangle^d$	$\langle 1\rangle^d$	$\langle x \multimap R\rangle^d r$	$\otimes^d$	$\langle x\rangle^d$	$\langle f\rangle^d R$	$\langle c\rangle^d$
$\subseteq$	$\emptyset$	$\cup$	$\dot{\subseteq}$	$\dot{\cup}$	†	$\lambda d_o \cdot \emptyset$	1_{Σ^d}	‡	$\times$	$\{x, \langle x\rangle\}$	$f^\star(R)$	$\{c\}$

‡ is $\{\langle T, T''\rangle \mid \langle T, T'\rangle \in r \wedge d_o \in \mathcal{D} \wedge R(d_o) \neq \emptyset \wedge T'' = T'[\![\lambda y \cdot (y = x \,?\, R(d_o) \,¿\, \emptyset)]\!]d\}$,

† is $\lambda d \cdot (d = d_o \,?\, M \,¿\, \emptyset)$ and $f^\star(M) \triangleq \{f(m_{s_1}, \ldots, m_{s_n}) \mid \langle m_{s_1}, \ldots, m_{s_n}\rangle \in M\}$.

For the big-step protosentence semantics $\tau^{s}[\![\mathcal{P}]\!]^\star$, we choose:

$\mathbf{L}^s$	$\sqsubseteq^s$	$\bot^s$	$\sqcup^s$	$\mathbf{P}^s$	$\leq^s$	∇^s	$\langle d_o\rangle R$	$\langle\Omega\rangle^s$	$\langle 1\rangle^s$	$\langle x \multimap R\rangle^s r$	$\otimes^s$	$\langle x\rangle^s$	$\langle f\rangle^s R$	$\langle c\rangle^s$
$\wp(\mathcal{V}^\star \times \mathcal{V}^\star)$	$\subseteq$	$\emptyset$	$\cup$	$\wp(\mathcal{V}^\star)$	$\subseteq$	$\cup$	R	$\emptyset$	$1_{\mathcal{V}^\star}$	‡	$\bullet$	$\{x\}$	R	$\{c\}$

where ‡ is $\{\langle p, qmq'\rangle \mid \langle p, qxq'\rangle \in r \wedge m \in R\}$.

For the big-step context semantics $\tau^{c}[\![\mathcal{P}]\!]^\star$, we choose:

$\mathbf{L}^s$	$\sqsubseteq^s$	$\bot^s$	$\sqcup^s$	$\mathbf{P}^s$	$\leq^s$	∇^s	$\langle d_o\rangle R$	$\langle\Omega\rangle^s$	$\langle 1\rangle^s$	$\langle x \multimap R\rangle^s r$	$\otimes^s$	$\langle x\rangle^s$	$\langle f\rangle^s R$	$\langle c\rangle^s$
$\wp(\Sigma^c \times \Sigma^c)$	$\subseteq$	$\emptyset$	$\cup$	$\wp(\Sigma^c)$	$\subseteq$	$\cup$	R	$\emptyset$	1_{Σ^c}	‡	$\bullet$	$\{x\}$	R	$\{c\}$

where ‡ is $\{\langle p, q[q'm\ell]\ell'\rangle \mid \langle p, q[q'x\ell]\ell'\rangle \in r \wedge m \in R\}$.

12 Examples of Top-Down Algebraic Polynomial Systems Analysis

We consider a few examples which are abstractions of the top-down semantics and are classical applications for context grammars [Wilhelm & Maurer, 1995].

Accessible Variables: Given an axiom $A \in \mathcal{X}$, a variable x is accessible (written $\text{Reachable}(x)$) if and only if $\langle A,\ pxq\rangle \in \tau^{s}[\![\mathcal{P}]\!]^{\star}$. It is not possible to use Kleene fixpoint transfer Theorem 11 or Tarski's fixpoint transfer Theorem 12 with the big-step protosentence semantics $\tau^{s}[\![\mathcal{P}]\!]^{\star}$. The abstraction would be $\text{Reachable}(x) = \alpha(\tau^{s}[\![\mathcal{P}]\!]^{\star})$ with $\alpha(r) = \lambda x \bullet \langle A,\ pxp'\rangle \in r$. For equation $x = P$, we would have:

$$
\begin{aligned}
&\alpha(\langle x \multimap R\rangle^{s} r) \\
&= \lambda x \bullet \langle A,\ pxp'\rangle \in \{\langle p,\ qmq'\rangle \mid \langle p,\ qxq'\rangle \in r \wedge m \in R\} \qquad (\text{defs. } \alpha \text{ \& } \langle x \multimap R\rangle^{s}) \\
&= \lambda x \bullet pxp' = qmq' \wedge \langle A,\ qxq'\rangle \in r \wedge m \in R\,.
\end{aligned}
$$

The difficulty is now that we have to consider the cases when x occur in q or q′ for which no inductive information is available. Fortunately, thanks to (17), we can avoid this phenomenon using the big-step context semantics $\tau^{c}[\![\mathcal{P}]\!]^{\star}$ in compositional form (19) where:

L	$\sqsubseteq$	$\bot$	$\sqcup$	**P**	$\leq$	∇	$\langle d_0\rangle X$	$\langle\Omega\rangle$	$\langle 1\rangle y$	$\langle x \multimap X\rangle r y$	$\otimes$	$\langle x\rangle$	$\langle f\rangle X$	$\langle c\rangle$
$\mathcal{X} \longmapsto \mathbb{B}$	$\dot{\Longrightarrow}$	$\dot{\mathrm{ff}}$	$\dot{\vee}$	$\wp(\mathcal{X})$	$\subseteq$	$\cup$	X	$\emptyset$	$y = A$	$r(x) \wedge y \in X$	$\cup$	$\{x\}$	X	$\emptyset$

Follow: The set $\text{Follow}[\![\mathcal{P}]\!](E)x$ of constants $c \in \mathcal{T}$ which, after erasure of the symbols belonging to E, can follow variable x in a protosentence derived from the axiom $A \in \mathcal{X}$ or $\dashv$ if x can appear at the end of such a protosentence. Again by (17), we can use the big-step context semantics $\tau^{c}[\![\mathcal{P}]\!]^{\star}$ with the abstraction.

$$
\begin{aligned}
\alpha_1(r) &\stackrel{\Delta}{=} \lambda x \bullet \{c \in \text{First}'(m'p') \mid \langle [A],\ p[mxm']p'\rangle \in r\}, \\
\text{First}'(p) &\stackrel{\Delta}{=} \text{First}(p) - \{\varepsilon\} \cup (\, \varepsilon \in \text{First}(p)\ ?\ \{\dashv\}\ ¿\ \emptyset\,)\,.
\end{aligned}
$$

This does not exactly lead to the classical algorithm [Aho et al., 1986] which relies on the fact that all nonterminals are assumed to be accessible. We get $\mathbf{L} \stackrel{\Delta}{=} \mathcal{X} \longmapsto \wp(\mathcal{T})$, $\mathbf{P} \stackrel{\Delta}{=} \wp(\mathcal{V}^{\star})$ and:

$\sqsubseteq$	$\bot$	$\sqcup$	$\leq$	∇	$\langle d_0\rangle M$	$\langle\Omega\rangle$	$\langle 1\rangle x$	$\langle x \multimap R\rangle r$	$\otimes$	$\langle x\rangle$	$\langle f\rangle R$	$\langle c\rangle$
$\dot{\subseteq}$	$\dot{\emptyset}$	$\dot{\cup}$	$\subseteq$	$\cup$	M	$\emptyset$	$(\, x = A\ ?\ \{\dashv\}\ ¿\ \emptyset\,)$	$\ddagger$	$\bullet$	$\{x\}$	R	c

where $\ddagger$ is $\lambda y \bullet (\,\text{Reachable}(x) \wedge pyq \in R\ ?$
$\text{First}(q) - \{\varepsilon\} \cup (\, \varepsilon \in \text{First}(q)\ ?\ r(x)\ ¿\ \emptyset\,)\ ¿\ \emptyset\,)\,.$

Since Follow makes use of Reachable, we can use the reduced product of the two abstractions [Cousot & Cousot, 1979] (whereas the lattice lifting technique used in [Jeuring & Swierstra, 1995] is specific to the combination with Reachable).

13 Generalization to Infinite Terms

Let $\mathcal{M}^{\star}_{s,\mathcal{X}}$ (respectively $\mathcal{M}^{\omega}_{s,\mathcal{X}}$) be the set of finite (resp. infinite) trees of root sort $s \in \mathcal{S}$ built with the function symbols $\mathcal{F}$ and variables $\mathcal{X}$. The finite trees are isomorphic with monomials $\mathcal{M}^{s,\mathcal{X}}$. Let $\mathcal{M}^{\infty}_{s,\mathcal{X}} \triangleq \mathcal{M}^{\star}_{s,\mathcal{X}} \cup \mathcal{M}^{\omega}_{s,\mathcal{X}}$. We drop the s subscript when considering the join for all sorts $s \in \mathcal{S}$ and the $\mathcal{X}$ subscript when $\mathcal{X} = \emptyset$ that is for ground trees. The infinitary powerset $\mathcal{F}$-algebra semantics $S^{\infty}[\![\mathcal{P}]\!]$ is defined compositionally by (15) and (16) when choosing $\mathbf{L}^{\infty} \triangleq \mathcal{X} \longmapsto \wp(\mathcal{M}^{\infty})$, $\mathbf{P}^{\infty} \triangleq \wp(\mathcal{M}^{\infty})$ and:

$\sqsubseteq^{\infty}$	$\perp^{\infty}$	$\sqcup^{\infty}$	$\leq^{\infty}$	∇^{∞}	$\langle\Omega\rangle^{\infty}$	$\langle 1\rangle^{\infty}x$	$\langle x \multimap R\rangle ry$	$\otimes^{\infty}$	$x\langle r\rangle^{\infty}$	$f\langle r\rangle^{\infty}(R)$	$c\langle r\rangle^{\infty}$
$\dot{\supseteq}$	$\lambda x^s \cdot \mathcal{M}^s$	$\dot{\cap}$	$\subseteq$	$\cup$	$\emptyset$	$\emptyset$	$(r = x\ ?\ R\ ¿\ \emptyset)$	$\times$	$r(x)$	$f[R]$	$\{c\}$

Define the finite projection $X^{\star} = X \cap \mathcal{M}^{\star}$ and the infinite projection $X^{\omega} = X \cap \mathcal{M}^{\omega}$. The abstraction to finite sentences defined by the Galois connection $\langle \mathcal{X} \longmapsto \wp(\mathcal{M}^{\infty}),\ \dot{\sqsubseteq}^{\infty}\rangle \underset{\alpha}{\overset{\gamma}{\leftrightarrows}} \langle \mathcal{X} \longmapsto \wp(\mathcal{M}^{\star}),\ \dot{\subseteq}\rangle$, where $\alpha(r) \triangleq \lambda x \cdot r(x)^{\star}$ and $\gamma(r) \triangleq \lambda x \cdot r(x) \cup \mathcal{M}^{\omega}$, yields to the finitary powerset $\mathcal{F}$-algebra semantics $S^{\star}[\![\mathcal{P}]\!]$ of [Courcelle, 1996] considered at Example 21 in greatest fixpoint form[5]. The abstraction to infinite terms defined by the Galois connection $\langle \mathcal{X} \longmapsto \wp(\mathcal{M}^{\infty}),\ \dot{\sqsubseteq}^{\infty}\rangle \underset{\alpha}{\overset{\gamma}{\leftrightarrows}} \langle \mathcal{X} \longmapsto \wp(\mathcal{M}^{\omega}),\ \dot{\supseteq}\rangle$, where $\alpha(r) \triangleq \lambda x \cdot r(x)^{\omega}$ and $\gamma(r) \triangleq \lambda x \cdot r(x) \cup \mathcal{M}^{\star}$, yields to a generalization $S^{\omega}[\![\mathcal{P}]\!]$ of Nivat's [1977, 1978] greatest fixpoint characterization of the infinite language generated by grammar to algebraic polynomial systems. We get $\mathbf{L}^{\omega} \triangleq \mathcal{X} \longmapsto \wp(\mathcal{M}^{\omega})$, $\mathbf{P}^{\omega} \triangleq \wp(\mathcal{M}^{\omega})$ and:

$\sqsubseteq^{\omega}$	$\perp^{\omega}$	$\sqcup^{\omega}$	$\leq^{\omega}$	∇^{ω}	$\langle\Omega\rangle^{\omega}$	$\langle 1\rangle^{\omega}x$	$\langle x \multimap R\rangle ry$	$\otimes^{\omega}$	$x\langle r\rangle^{\omega}$	$f\langle r\rangle^{\omega}(R)$	$c\langle r\rangle^{\omega}$
$\dot{\supseteq}$	$\lambda x^s \cdot \mathcal{M}^{\omega}_s$	$\dot{\cap}$	$\subseteq$	$\cup$	$\emptyset$	$\emptyset$	$(r = x\ ?\ R \cap \mathcal{M}^{\omega}\ ¿\ \emptyset)$	$\times$	$r(x)$	$f[R]$	$\{c\}$

The least fixpoint $\text{lfp}^{\dot{\supseteq}}\ B[\![\mathcal{P}]\!]$ in (15) is Nivat's greatest for $\dot{\subseteq}$.

14 Infinite Abstract Domains

As an example of infinite abstract domain, let us consider the abstraction of terminal sentences by the vector of number of instances of each terminal in the sentence: $\mathbb{O}(\varepsilon)T = 0$, $\mathbb{O}(T\sigma)T = 1 + \mathbb{O}(\sigma)T$, $\mathbb{O}(T\sigma)T' = \mathbb{O}(\sigma)T'$ when $T \neq T'$. The extension to languages is elementwise (6). By Parikh's theorem [1966], the abstraction of the generated language is the union of a finite number

[5] The complete lattice $\langle \wp(\mathcal{M}^{\infty}), \sqsubseteq^{\infty}, \perp^{\infty}, \top^{\infty}, \sqcup^{\infty}, \sqcap^{\infty}\rangle$ with generalized Scott's ordering $X \sqsubseteq^{\infty} Y \triangleq X^{\star} \subseteq Y^{\star} \wedge X^{\omega} \supseteq Y^{\omega}$, infimum $\perp^{\infty} \triangleq \mathcal{M}^{\omega}$, supremum $\top^{\infty} \triangleq \mathcal{M}^{\star}$, lub $\bigsqcup^{\infty}_{i \in \Delta} X_i \triangleq \bigcup_{i \in \Delta} X_i{}^{\star} \cup \bigcap_{i \in \Delta} X_i{}^{\omega}$ and glb $\bigsqcap^{\infty}_{i \in \Delta} X_i \triangleq \bigcap_{i \in \Delta} X_i{}^{\star} \cup \bigcup_{i \in \Delta} X_i{}^{\omega}$ introduced in [Cousot & Cousot, 1992] to provide a fixpoint characterization of the finite and infinite execution traces of a transition system cannot be *directly* generalized. A counter example is $x = a + b(x) + c(x,x)$ since the iterates start with $X^0 = \mathcal{M}^{\omega}$, so that $X^1 = \{a, b(x), c(x,y) \mid x, y \in X^0\}$, hence the limit, does not contain the infinite tree with equation $t = c(b(a)), t)$ with finite subtree $b(a) \notin X^0$. When least and greatest fixpoints may differ, we can resort to the traditional topological notions based on the prefix ordering [see e.g. de Bakker et al., 1983] which naturally generalizes to inverse limits [Meinke & Tucker, 1992] but then their is a "discontinuity" in the passage to the limit, all prefixes being finite objects while the limit is an infinite one. This causes problems when considering abstractions (which are not admissible in the sense of Scott-induction).

of linear sets. Another abstraction consists in taking the convex-hull of the semi-linear set, using a widening to speed-up convergence [Cousot & Halbwachs, 1978] that would allow us to determine relationships such as "the number of a's in a sentence is greater than twice the number of b's". This is not possible in the restricted framework of [Wilhelm & Maurer, 1995].

15 Conclusion

Traditional abstract interpretations have been mainly based on small step/big-step operational semantics or denotational semantics whereas algebraic semantics have been rather neglected, except may-be for Prolog. The difficulty is often that the proposed analyses are quite dependent on the considered programming language semantics. Since there is no universal semantics, the analyzes can be hard to generalize from one semantic framework to another. We think that the use of algebraic semantics could solve this problem since many analyzes can be expressed using the algebraic metastructure in a language independent way. As a first step, algebraic polynomial systems which generalize context-free grammars with their fixpoint semantics seem to be very well suited for expressing first-order fixpoint abstract semantics. To do this the semantics of algebraic polynomial systems must be extended to infinite terms, so as e.g. to be able to encode infinite execution paths. The program abstract semantics is then one of the semantics of the algebraic polynomial system representing the abstract equations e.g. the protosentence semantics where terminals correspond to atomic actions of the program while variables correspond to procedure calls or using the FOLLOW abstraction, the set of atomic actions which can follow a call to a given procedure.

Algebraic polynomial systems could themselves be used as abstract values in program analysis, the abstract program analysis equations being now algebraic polynomial system transformers. This would generalize grammar-based or set-based analysis abstract interpretations [Cousot and Cousot, 1995; Heintze, 1992; Jones and Muchnick, 1981; Uhl and Horspool, 1994]. It remains to explore the idea that abstract semantics of the algebraic polynomial system resulting from the abstract equations resolution would yield a hierarchy of information on the program executions abstracted by the algebraic polynomial system.

Acknowledgments

We thank A. Venet for his comments on a preliminary version of this paper.

Bibliography

A.V. Aho, R. Sethi & J.D. Ullman. *Compilers. Principles, Technique and Tools.* Addison-Wesley, 1986.

B. Courcelle. The monadic second-order logic of graphs X: Linear orders. *TCS*, 160:87–143, 1996.

P. Cousot & R. Cousot. Abstract interpretation: a unified lattice model for static analysis of programs by construction or approximation of fixpoints. *4th ACM POPL*, pp. 238–252, 1977.

P. Cousot & R. Cousot. Systematic design of program analysis frameworks. *6th ACM POPL*, pp. 269–282, 1979.

P. Cousot & R. Cousot. Inductive definitions, semantics and abstract interpretation. *19th ACM POPL*, pp. 83–94, 1992.

P. Cousot & R. Cousot. Higher-order abstract interpretation (and application to comportment analysis generalizing strictness, termination, projection and PER analysis of functional languages), invited paper. *Proc. 1994 ICCL*, pp. 95–112, 1994. IEEE Comp. Soc. Press.

P. Cousot and R. Cousot. Formal language, grammar and set-constraint-based program analysis by abstract interpretation. *Proc. 7th ACM FPCA*, pp. 170–181, 1995.

P. Cousot & N. Halbwachs. Automatic discovery of linear restraints among variables of a program. *5th ACM POPL*, pp. 84–97, 1978.

J.W. de Bakker, J.-J.Ch. Meyer & J.I. Zucker. On infinite computations in denotational semantics. *TCS*, 26:53–82, 1983. (Corrigendum: TCS 29:229–230, 1984).

S. Ginsburg & G. Rice. Two families of languages related to ALGOL. *J. ACM*, 9:350–371, 1962.

N. Heintze. *Set Based Program Analysis*. PhD thesis, CMU, Pittsburgh, 1992.

J. Jeuring & D. Swierstra. Bottom-up grammar analysis — a functional formulation —. *Proc. ESOP '94*, LNCS 788, pp. 317–332, 1994. Springer-Verlag.

J. Jeuring & D. Swierstra. Constructing functional programs for grammar analysis problems. *Proc. 7th ACM FPCA*, pp. 259–269, 1995.

N.D. Jones and S.S. Muchnick. Flow-analysis and optimization of Lisp-like structures. In S.S. Muchnick & N.D. Jones, editors, *Program Flow Analysis: Theory and Applications*, pp. 102–131. Prentice-Hall, 1981.

K. Meinke & J.V. Tucker. Universal algebra. In S. Abramsky, D.M. Gabbay & T.S.E. Maibaum, editors, *Background: Mathematical Structures*, vol. 1 of *Handbook of Logic in Com . Sci.*, ch. 3, pp. 189–411. Clarendon Press, 1992.

J. Mezei & J. Wright. Algebraic automata and context-free sets. *Inf. & Cont.*, 11:3–29, 1967.

U. Möncke & R. Wilhelm. Grammar flow analysis. *Proc. Int. Summer School SAGA*, LNCS 545, pp. 151–186, 1991. Springer-Verlag.

M. Nivat. Mots infinis engendrés par une grammaire algébrique. *RAIRO Informatique Théorique*, 11:311–327, 1977.

M. Nivat. Sur les ensembles de mots infinis engendrés par une grammaire algébrique. *RAIRO Informatique Théorique*, 12:259–278, 1978.

R.J. Parikh. On context-free languages. *J. ACM*, 13(4):570–581, 1966.

M.P. Schützenberger. On a theorem of R. Jungen. *Proc. Amer. Math. Soc.*, 13:885–889, 1962.

J.S. Uhl and R.N. Horspool. Flow grammars — a flow analysis methodology. *Proc. CC '94*, LNCS 786, pp. 203–217, 1994. Springer-Verlag.

M. Ward. The closure operators of a lattice. *Ann. Math.*, 43:191–196, 1942.

R. Wilhelm & D. Maurer. *Compiler Design*. Addison-Wesley, 1995.

M. Wirsing. Algebraic specification. In J. van Leeuwen, editor, *Formal Models and Semantics*, vol. B of *Handbook of TCS*, ch. 13, pp. 675–788. Elsevier, 1990.

Modular Refinement and Model Building

Martin de Groot and Ken Robinson
School of Computer Science and Engineering
martindg@cse.unsw.edu.au, k.robinson@unsw.edu.au

University of New South Wales
Sydney NSW 2052 Australia

Abstract. In this paper we show that formal program development can be viewed as a process of model building. Refinement diagrams are introduced and formally defined in terms of refinement developments. Hierarchical models are shown to be equivalent to modular refinement developments. Modular refinement developments are a subset of refinement developments and refinement diagrams. A function is defined to extract the corresponding model from any refinement development.

1 Introduction

We propose that formal program derivation effectively produces a hierarchical model of the system being derived. A specification can be seen as representing any one level, while refinement ($\sqsubseteq$) defines the ordering of the levels within the hierarchy. The specification defining any one level will be very complex for a realistically large system. Thus it is useful to advance formal program developments by decomposing larger specifications into a collection of smaller specifications, along with a program constructor to hold the whole system specification together. This decomposition process not only makes refinement manageable, it also defines the ultimate structure of the implemented system in terms of its constituent components. A layered description of a system's structure is a hierarchical model of that system.

All the information necessary to define the final structure is contained within the record of the refinement development. However, as sub-specifications are sometimes (re-)composed during refinement, the refinement development itself does not immediately give the ultimate system structure. This structure must be extracted from the refinement development. Below we will formally define a total function that performs hierarchical model extraction from refinement developments.

Although a program derivation is a formal process, program derivations themselves have not been formally defined. The clearest proposal of how such derivations are structured is given by Ralph Back in his paper *Refinement Diagrams* [1]. Refinement diagrams were the starting point for this investigation of the formal structure of refinement developments. For completeness, we show that refinement diagrams can also be formally defined in terms of refinement developments. Hence, models can also be extracted from refinement diagrams.

2 Notation

Two different, but widely used, formalisms are employed in this paper. We will use the Z notation of Abrial [7] to define refinement developments and diagrams. However, individual specifications will be given using the wide spectrum language of the refinement calculus of Morgan [6,4]. For a more detailed explanation please consult the references.

2.1 Z

Z is a specification language based on set theory and logic. The basic entity of a Z specification is the *schema.* A schema defines a named set of objects, in which each object has a set of named components. There are two equivalent forms of a schema definition

```
┌─ Name ──────
│ Signature
├──────────
│ Predicate
└────────────
```

or $Name \mathrel{\widehat{=}} [\,Signature \mid Predicate\,]$

where *Signature* is a set of variable declarations and *Predicate* is a predicate that expresses a constraint on those variables. For example:

```
┌─ add ─────────────────────────
│ in1, in2, sum : ℕ
├──────────
│ sum = in1 + in2
└───────────────────────────────
```

A schema calculus supports the building of new schemas using schema inclusion, conjunction, hiding, etc. For example,

```
┌─ arithmetic ──────────────────
│ add
│ diff : ℤ
├──────────
│ diff = in1 − in2
└───────────────────────────────
```

Abbreviations are defined using *new* == *old*, and constants are defined using an axiomatic definition, for example:

```
│ double : ℤ ⤖ ℤ
├──────────
│ ∀ n : ℤ • double(n) = n * 2
```

The following definition of a linked list of integers demonstrates how disjoint sets, or free types, are defined.

$$
\begin{aligned}
list &::= end \\
&\quad\mid\ link\langle\!\langle \mathbb{Z} \times list \rangle\!\rangle
\end{aligned}
$$

To introduce basic sets into a specification we use the following notation:

$$[Dog, Cat]$$

Z is used in this paper to define modular refinement diagrams because it is a very convenient language for building up complex specifications and is sufficiently expressive to describe the model extraction function.

2.2 Specifications

The specification statement [4] is used to specify an operation and has the following form:

$$frame : [\ precondition / postcondition\ ]$$

where *frame* is a vector of the variables that are allowed to be changed, *precondition* is a predicate specifying the state before the operation, and *postcondition* is a predicate specifying the state on termination of the operation. For example we could define an operation that adds two natural numbers by:

$$add \ = \ sum : [\ \{in1, in2\} \subset \mathbb{N}\ /\ sum = in1 + in2\ ]$$

In the refinement calculus of Morgan [5] the specification statement is embedded in Dijkstra's [3] guarded command language forming a wide spectrum language that can be used to represent everything from abstract specifications through to executable programs. Figure 1 shows a simple refinement sequence and demonstrates the use of embedded specification statements.

$$\begin{array}{l}
\quad x : [x \in \{2,3\}\ /\ x = x_0 * 2]\ ;\ \mathbf{skip} \\
\sqsubseteq x : [x \in \{2,3\}\ /\ x = x_0 * 2] \\
\sqsubseteq \mathbf{if}\ x = 2 \rightarrow x : [x = 2 \wedge x \in \{2,3\}\ /\ x = x_0 * 2] \\
\quad\ [\!]\ x = 3 \rightarrow x : [x = 3 \wedge x \in \{2,3\}\ /\ x = x_0 * 2] \\
\quad\ \mathbf{fi} \\
\sqsubseteq \mathbf{if}\ x = 2 \rightarrow x : [x = 2\ /\ x = x_0 * 2] \\
\quad\ [\!]\ x = 3 \rightarrow x : [x = 3\ /\ x = x_0 * 2] \\
\quad\ \mathbf{fi}
\end{array}$$

Fig. 1. Example refinement sequence

The combination of specification statements, guarded commands and code is used in the following discussion to describe programs and systems. These constructs will be referred to as *program specifications*, *system specifications* or often just as *specifications*.

3 Refinement diagrams

Refinement diagrams graphically represent formal program development. A system (or more usually a subsystem) is drawn as a box. Boxes drawn inside a box are subsystems of the system represented by the surrounding box. Boxes representing a subsystem must always be completely contained within another box. All the text and boxes within another box must give the complete specification for a program. Refinement relationships between components are shown by linking boxes with lines. A refinement link always begins on the right hand side of a box and terminates on the left hand side of another. (In Figure 2 this convention is emphasised by placing explicit arrows on the links.) The refinement diagram corresponding to the refinement sequence in Figure 1 is given in Figure 2.

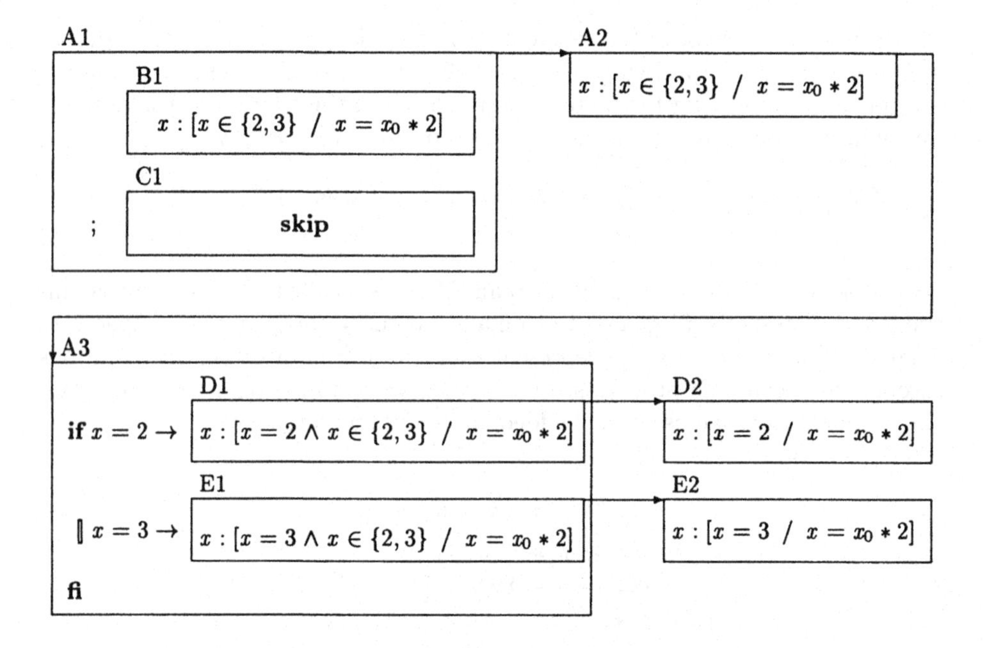

Fig. 2. Example refinement diagram

Refinement diagrams are invariably complex and quickly become too big to be viewed as a whole. Consequently a special tool called *Centipede* [2] has been developed to allow such diagrams to be managed and inspected. In the example refinement diagram in Figure 2 all boxes have been given an alphanumeric label. (The text immediately above any box on the left hand side.) This has been done to simplify discussion when referring to a particular box. Normally refinement diagrams contain very little text, often just a label in place of the actual expression.

The link between $A1$ and $A2$ shows refinement by *skip composition*, $A2$ to $A3$ is a case of *alternation introduction*, while $D1$ to $D2$ and $E1$ to $E2$ are instances of refinement by simplifying the precondition predicates. Being graphical, refinement diagrams make the program derivation very easy to follow.

4 Defining systems

To formally specify the structure of a refinement development we need a basic program specification type, for which we will use the set *Spec*.

$[Spec]$

Each component in a system will be identified by a unique label. The label distinguishes components on the basis of their position in the development not on their specification. We will assume a set of labels named *Label*.

$[Label]$

A refinement diagram consists of systems (or programs) which are identified with boxes, and refinement relations between those boxes. Systems are either atomic components, or composite systems consisting of several subsystems and some sort of glue to stick those subsystems together. We call the inter-box text a *harness*.

$$Harness == (Label \nrightarrow Spec) \nrightarrow Spec$$

The syntax of the contents of boxes is:

$$\begin{aligned} System ::= &\ comp \langle\langle Spec \rangle\rangle \\ |\ &\ subsys \langle\langle Harness \rangle\rangle \end{aligned}$$

The *comp* variant of the *System* type corresponds to a single specification. This construct is used to represent a unitary component that has no identified sub-components.

The *subsys* form of the *System* type resembles a harness which is populated by components. The harness consists of all the text in which the next layer of boxes is embedded. Harnesses can be thought of as lambda expressions that are parameterised by a set of labelled specifications—a catalogue. The equivalent single specification can be obtained by effectively applying the harness function to the catalogue of basic components.

We will use the terms *box*, *component*, *subcomponent*, *system* and *subsystem* to refer to anything of type *System*. A set of labelled components can be thought of as an inventory of parts.

$$Inventory == Label \nrightarrow System$$

A function (*build*) is required to assemble the highest level specification from a *System* type by populating all harnesses with the dereferenced component

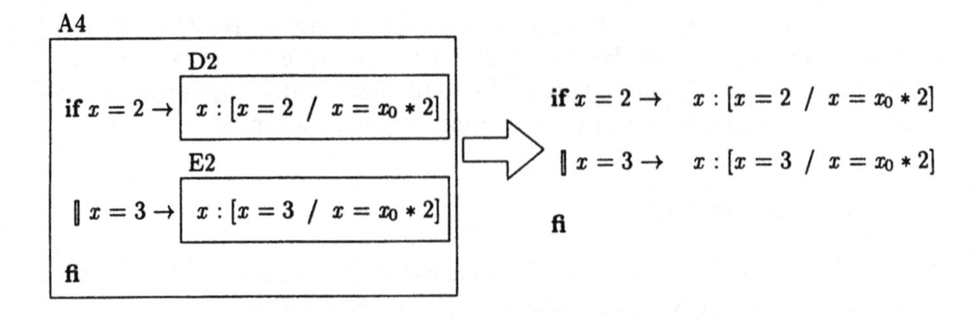

Fig. 3. Extracting the top level specification

labels (i.e. the available parts from a supplied inventory). Figure 3 shows the effect of applying *build* to a *System*.

Notice that the assembly function performs no simplification of the assembled specification. It simply dereferences the labels and unpacks the constituent systems into specifications. We define *build* as a curried function, taking an inventory and the particular system that is to be converted into a specification. The inventory is used to supply the components of the system to be converted and of all its subsystems.

$$
\begin{array}{|l}
build : Inventory \longrightarrow System \nrightarrow Spec \\
\hline
\forall i : Inventory; sy : System; sp : Spec \mid sy = (comp\ sp) \bullet build\ i\ sy = sp \\
\forall i : Inventory; sy : System; h : Harness \mid \\
\quad sy = (subsys\ h) \land ((build\ i) \circ i) \in \mathrm{dom}\, h \bullet build\ i\ sy = h((build\ i) \circ i)
\end{array}
$$

The following example shows how the specification of a complete subsystem can be produced from a *subsys* construction. For example, an alternation could be represented as:

$$harn1 = subsys\ (\lambda\, C.\mathbf{if}\ g_0 \rightarrow C(\ell_1) \ \| \ g_1 \rightarrow C(\ell_2)\, \mathbf{fi}\ )$$

Note that we can also define an empty harness (i.e. a box around another box with absolutely no intermediate text) with the following statement:

$$harn2 = subsys\ (\lambda\, C.C(\ell))$$

For convenience we define a corresponding *package* function which takes an inventory and a subsystem and encapsulates the built specification in a *comp* construct.

$$package == (\lambda\, i : Inventory \bullet (\lambda\, sy : System \bullet (comp\ (build\ i\ sy))))$$

Because *subsys* constructs require an inventory of parts to be converted into an equivalent specification, it will be useful to define a complete inventory. An inventory can be considered complete if it contains all the parts necessary to assemble any of its systems. This is like a construction kit that can be bought in a hobby store. It contains all the parts necessary to assemble the whole model or any part of the whole model. Hence we will use the name *Kit* to refer to the set of such complete inventories. An inventory is a kit if *build* can be applied to all elements of that inventory, using the same inventory as the set of parts from which the specification is built. For example, any inventory containing *harn*1 would also need to contain the parts defining components ℓ_1 and ℓ_2.

$$Kit == \{i : Inventory \mid (\forall s : \operatorname{ran} i \bullet s \in \operatorname{dom}(build\ i))\}$$

Lemma 1
Any element of a kit can be replaced by the already assembled version of that element without affecting the completeness of the kit.

$$\forall k : Kit;\ \ell : Label \mid \ell \in \operatorname{dom} k \bullet (k \oplus \ell \mapsto (package\ k\ (k\ \ell))) \in Kit$$

5 Refinement developments

For conciseness we will refer to refinement developments as just *developments* from now on. Before producing the development definition, one more utility definition is needed. Back proposed that refinement diagrams could be used for any partial ordering on programs (i.e. specifications), not just program refinement. Recall that a *poset* is a relation that is reflexive, transitive and anti-symmetric:

$$
\begin{array}{l}
[X] \\
poset : \mathbb{P}(X \leftrightarrow X) \\
\hline
\forall po : poset \bullet \\
\quad (\forall x : X \bullet x \mapsto x \in po) \land \\
\quad (\forall x_1, x_2, x_3 : X \mid x_1 \mapsto x_2 \in po \land x_2 \mapsto x_3 \in po \bullet x_1 \mapsto x_3 \in po) \land \\
\quad (\forall x_1, x_2 : X \mid x_1 \neq x_2 \bullet x_1 \mapsto x_2 \in po \Rightarrow x_2 \mapsto x_1 \notin po)
\end{array}
$$

Developments consist of three elements: list of components, list of derivation links and, definition of the refinement relation. Because a specification may appear in more than one place in a development, different instances of a specification must be distinguished by labels. However, the refinement relation is defined for programs (i.e. specifications), hence a label dereferencing function must be part of any development. This dereferencing function (called *boxes*) is effectively the catalogue of components that may be used to build the system. A development is an encapsulation of a formal program derivation. Refinement may proceed by either refining the whole specification or by *monotonic* refinement. Monotonic refinement occurs when a *subsys* construct is refined by refining one or more of its components. Monotonic refinement implies that system decomposition has been performed prior to the refinement step. The *refinements* relation of developments shows how the various instances of specifications are linked to give the development structure.

$$\begin{array}{l}
\textit{Development} \\
\hline
boxes : Kit \\
refinements : Label \leftrightarrow Label \\
refRel : poset[Spec] \\
\hline
\forall \ell_1, \ell_2 : Label \mid \ell_1 \mapsto \ell_2 \in refinements \bullet \\
\qquad (build\ boxes\ (boxes\ \ell_1)) \mapsto (build\ boxes\ (boxes\ \ell_2)) \in refRel \\
\hline
\end{array}$$

6 Modularity

The term *modular* is often used in computer science. Consequently it has a range of meanings. Common to most uses of the term is the notion that a module should be a self-contained unit. Refinement proceeds by transforming specifications. Sometimes a specification is decomposed into several independently refinable sub-specifications. It is also possible to re-compose sub-specifications. Any refinement step that does not compose specifications can be considered modular.

6.1 Examples of modular refinement

(1) $P \sqsubseteq (S\ ;\ T)$

(2) $x : [x > 2\ /\ x < 5]\ ;\ x : [x < 10\ /\ x = 0]$
$\sqsubseteq x : [x > 2\ /\ x < 3]\ ;\ x : [x < 15\ /\ x = 0]$

(3) $x : [x \in \{2, 3\}\ /\ x = x_0 * 2]$
$\sqsubseteq \mathbf{if}\ x_0 = 2 \rightarrow x : [x_0 = 2\ /\ x = 4]$
$\quad [\!]\ x_0 = 3 \rightarrow x : [x_0 = 3\ /\ x = 6]\ \mathbf{fi}$

(4) $\mathbf{do}\ x > 0 \rightarrow x : [x \in \mathbb{N}\ /\ x = x_0 - 1]\ \mathbf{od}$
$\sqsubseteq \mathbf{do}\ x > 0 \rightarrow |[\ \mathbf{var}\ y \bullet x, y : [x \in \mathbb{N}\ /\ y = x_0 - 1 \wedge x = y]\ ]|\ \mathbf{od}$

6.2 Examples of non-modular refinement

(5) $(S\ ;\ T) \sqsubseteq P$

(6) $\mathbf{var}\ y \bullet x, y : [true\ /\ y = x_0 + 1 \wedge x = y]$
$\sqsubseteq \mathbf{var}\ z \bullet x, z : [true\ /\ z = x_0 + 1 \wedge x = z]$

(7) $\mathbf{if}\ g_0 \rightarrow P\ [\!]\ g_1 \rightarrow Q\ \mathbf{fi}$
$\sqsubseteq \mathbf{if}\ g_0 \rightarrow P\ [\!]\ g_1 \wedge \neg g_0 \rightarrow Q\ \mathbf{fi}$

6.3 Components

The component list for any particular *subsys* construct is not explicit. We define a function *components* to help refer to the components of a *System*. *components* generates the set of labels corresponding to the components for any *System*.

$$
\begin{array}{l}
components : System \longrightarrow \mathbb{P}\ Label \\
\hline
\forall sy : System; i : Inventory \mid (sy \in \operatorname{dom}(build\ i) \land \\
\quad (\forall i' : Inventory \mid sy \in \operatorname{dom}(build\ i') \bullet \operatorname{dom} i \subseteq \operatorname{dom} i')) \bullet \\
\quad components(sy) = \operatorname{dom} i
\end{array}
$$

To refer to all the components of an inventory we define the function *allComps*:

$$allComps == \{i : Inventory \bullet i \mapsto \bigcup\{sy : \operatorname{ran} i \bullet components(sy)\}\}$$

6.4 Modular developments

We define modular developments to be developments containing only modular refinement steps. That means once a component has been created it will never be combined with other components. Thus every component in a modular development corresponds to a component, or composition of components, in all later stages of the development. Because the inventory of a modular development only contains actual components of the final design, it is synonymous with an accurate hierarchical model of the developed system. Modular developments are models. We can formally define a *Model* as a variation on a *Development*. The boxes of the development are renamed *parts* as they are all implemented. A further constraint is added requiring that all refined systems have no identified sub-components.

$$
\begin{array}{l}
\underline{\quad Model \quad} \\
Development[parts / boxes] \\
\hline
\forall \ell : \operatorname{dom} refinements \bullet components\ (parts\ \ell) = \varnothing
\end{array}
$$

7 Extracting models from developments

In order to define a model extraction function three conditions must be met: all refinement steps are modular; the original high level specifications are included, and; the model is the largest (most detailed) possible. To clearly demonstrate how these conditions are met, we define the modelling function in three stages.

7.1 Modular sub-developments

A relation *modular* can be defined to extract modular sub-developments from any development. The most important feature of this relation is that non-modular refinement steps must be made modular. Non-modular refinement steps can be transformed into modular refinement steps by absorbing the internal components (i.e. boxes) of the system being refined. Absorption can be performed without any loss of detail in the specification by applying the *package* function defined in Section 5. From Lemma 1 we know that replacing a subsystem with a pre-assembled (using *package*) version of that subsystem will always produce a *Kit*.

$$\mathit{modular} : \mathit{Development} \leftrightarrow \mathit{Model}$$

$$\begin{aligned}
&\mathit{modular} = \{d : \mathit{Development};\ m : \mathit{Model} \mid \\
&\quad m.\mathit{refinements} \subseteq d.\mathit{refinements} \land \\
&\quad m.\mathit{refRel} = d.\mathit{refRel} \land \\
&\quad m.\mathit{parts} \subseteq (d.\mathit{boxes} \oplus \{\ell : \mathrm{dom}(d.\mathit{boxes}) \mid \ell \in \mathrm{dom}(d.\mathit{refinements}) \bullet \\
&\qquad\qquad \ell \mapsto (\mathit{package}\,(d.\mathit{boxes})\,(d.\mathit{boxes}\,\ell))\})\}
\end{aligned}$$

7.2 Partial models

As we want to extract a model of the system derived in the development, we naturally require that the extracted modular refinements have the same set of original high level specifications. The high level specifications are the origins of the refinement development. A more specific version of the extract relation *partialModel* can be defined which is constrained to extract only those modular sub-developments which have the same origins as the original. Such developments can be considered partial models of the implemented system as they contain all the high level specifications but only a portion of the system structure.

$$\mathit{partialModel} : \mathit{Development} \leftrightarrow \mathit{Model}$$

$$\begin{aligned}
&\mathit{partialModel} = \{d : \mathit{Development};\ m : \mathit{Model} \mid \\
&\quad (d \mapsto m) \in \mathit{modular} \land \\
&\quad (\mathrm{dom}\, d.\mathit{boxes} \setminus (\mathit{allComps}\ d.\mathit{boxes}) \cup \mathrm{ran}\, d.\mathit{refinements})) = \\
&\qquad (\mathrm{dom}\, m.\mathit{parts} \setminus (\mathit{allComps}\ m.\mathit{parts}) \cup \mathrm{ran}\, m.\mathit{refinements}))
\end{aligned}$$

Lemma 2
A modular sub-development with the same high level specifications as the original can always be produced because a development consisting of just the origins is a partial model.

$$\mathrm{dom}\, \mathit{partialModel} = \mathit{Development}$$

7.3 Modelling

Finally we want to further restrict the extraction relation to return the best partial model, namely, the partial model that includes all of the lowest level components as well as the highest level specifications. We define the final extraction function *model* which returns the largest (most detailed) partial model. Lemma 2 shows that there is always a partial model for any development. The largest partial model will include all the other partial models as partial models of itself. Hence we define an extraction function *model* that is total.

$$
\begin{array}{l}
model : Development \twoheadrightarrow Model \\
\hline
model = \{d : Development;\ m : Model \mid \\
\qquad m \in partialModel(\!|\{d\}|\!) \wedge (\forall m' : partialModel(\!|\{d\}|\!) \bullet \\
\qquad m'.refinements \subseteq m.refinements \wedge m'.parts \subseteq m.parts)\}
\end{array}
$$

8 Refinement diagram definition

Development can now be used to build a refinement diagram definition schema.

$$
\begin{array}{l}
\textit{RefDiag} \\
\hline
Development \\
refineComp : Label \leftrightarrow Label \\
refineHarn : Label \leftrightarrow Label \\
newHarness : Label \leftrightarrow Label \\
monotonic : Label \leftrightarrow Label \\
\hline
refinements = refineComp \cup refineHarn \cup newHarness \cup monotonic \\
\forall \ell_1, \ell_2 : Label;\ L_1, L_2 : \mathbb{P}\, Label \mid \ell_1 \mapsto \ell_2 \in refinements \wedge \\
\qquad L_1 = (components\,(boxes\,\ell_1)) \wedge L_2 = (components\,(boxes\,\ell_2)) \bullet \\
\qquad (\ell_1 \mapsto \ell_2 \in refineComp \Leftrightarrow L_1 = \varnothing \vee L_2 = \varnothing) \wedge \\
\qquad (\ell_1 \mapsto \ell_2 \in refineHarn \Leftrightarrow L_1 \neq \varnothing \wedge L_1 = L_2) \wedge \\
\qquad (\ell_1 \mapsto \ell_2 \in newHarness \Leftrightarrow L_1 \neq \varnothing \wedge L_2 \neq \varnothing \wedge \\
\qquad\qquad L_1 \cap \operatorname{dom} refinements = \varnothing) \wedge \\
\qquad (\ell_1 \mapsto \ell_2 \in monotonic \Leftrightarrow (\exists F : Label \rightarrowtail\!\!\!\!\!\mapsto Label \bullet \\
\qquad\qquad F \subseteq \operatorname{id} Label \oplus refinements^+ \wedge F \cap refinements^+ \neq \varnothing \wedge \\
\qquad\qquad build\,(boxes \circ F)\,(boxes\,\ell_1) = build\ boxes\,(boxes\,\ell_2)))
\end{array}
$$

Monotonic refinement relations are not explicit in refinement diagrams. It is safe to leave these links out because they can be deduced from the the other links and the component catalogue. Also, it is quite easy to recognise such relations from a graphical representation of a program derivation when labels are used to identify the actual system definition text. Unfortunately, the formal definition of monotonic links is not so obvious. Monotonic links can only exist between *subsys* constructs. There must be a one-to-one function (F) between the components of those systems. Of the pairs of corresponding components, one pair at least ($F \cap refinements^+$) must actually be linked, either explicitly or monotonically. Because there may be multiple intermediate refinements (both explicit and monotonic) the closure of the set of links will contain the correct corresponding pair. Finally, the two harnesses must be functionally equivalent. A new list of components is constructed by prepending the component correspondence relation to the system list (*boxes*). Functional equivalence is established by populating the refined harness with the new catalogue and equating that to the second harness populated from the system component list.

9 Extracting modular refinement diagrams

All modular derivations will be elements of *refineComp*. The *refineHarn* and *newHarness* links are not modular refinements because they allow the internal structure of the boxes they link to differ. Links represented by *monotonic* will not be necessary because there is no need to refer to composite systems to refine them as a whole. Therefore, the single line connecting the tops of boxes (*refineComp* links) in refinement diagrams is the only modular link. In a modular refinement diagram *refinements* and *refineComps* would be identical, while *refineHarn*, *newHarness* and *monotonic* would all be empty. The *refineComp* links are still a superset of modular refinement as it includes links where components are absorbed as in Figure 4. Thus, only refinement of the lowest level components is permitted in modular developments. That is, modular links may only originate from the innermost boxes.

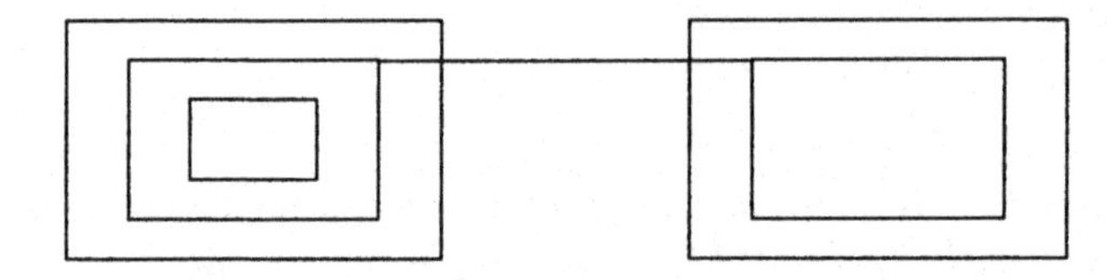

Fig. 4. Non-modular *refineComp* link

Because all modular refinements are the same kind of link there is no need to define a new modular refinement diagram type. The previously defined *Model* structure contains exactly the same information. We will therefore define modular refinement diagrams to be identical to modular developments (i.e. models). As refinement diagrams are augmented refinement developments with no extra constraints on the signature elements of the *Development*, the modelling function defined for developments can be adapted to model refinement diagrams. We define the modular refinement diagram extraction function *modelRD* as:

$$modelRD : RefDiag \twoheadrightarrow Model$$

$$\begin{aligned} modelRD = \{ & r : RefDiag;\ d : Development \mid d.refRel = r.refRel \land \\ & d.refinements = r.refinements \land d.boxes = r.boxes \bullet \\ & r \mapsto (model\ d)\} \end{aligned}$$

Returning to the sample refinement diagram in Figure 2, applying *modelRD* to $A1$ would produce the modular refinement diagram shown in Figure 5. In this extraction process, the highest level specification has been extracted from $A1$. This makes sense in terms of the final decomposition of the whole system into implemented components. Both subsystems $B1$ and $C1$ do not form part of the final system specification. Therefore their individual specifications are irrelevant to the implemented system's composition. That is not to say that

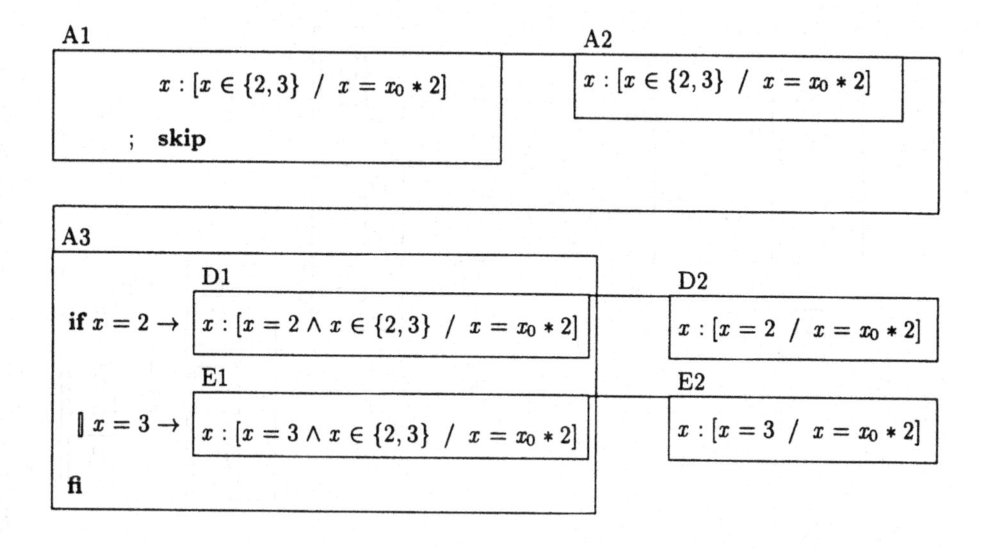

Fig. 5. Detailed modular refinement diagram

these components serve no purpose in the process of arriving at the final system, rather simply stating that they are not actually distinct subsystems of that final system.

Modular refinement diagrams are a very restrictive subset of refinement diagrams. Clearly it would be impractical to prohibit any other kind of program transformation in formal developments. Indeed, there may be very good reasons for doing non-modular refinement in order to actually achieve a proof of correctness. The development of a model extraction function which is total means that using program derivations as the basis for models places no extra restrictions on the system development process.

10 Modular refinement diagram extraction example

To further illustrate the effect of modular refinement diagram extraction we will include an example from a larger refinement development. In Figure 6 a program derivation is described that includes all the different kinds of refinement links defined for refinement diagrams. (Note that we have used alphanumeric strings to represent expression text. To indicate that these strings are not labels they have been placed inside the boxes and constructed from lower case letters.) From this (relatively) large development a modular refinement diagram has been extracted. The extracted diagram is shown in Figure 7.

This example shows that model extraction can be performed simply from the structure of a refinement history. We need very little knowledge about the actual systems being developed. It can also be seen that the extracted diagram includes the final version of all components and harnesses. There are no func-

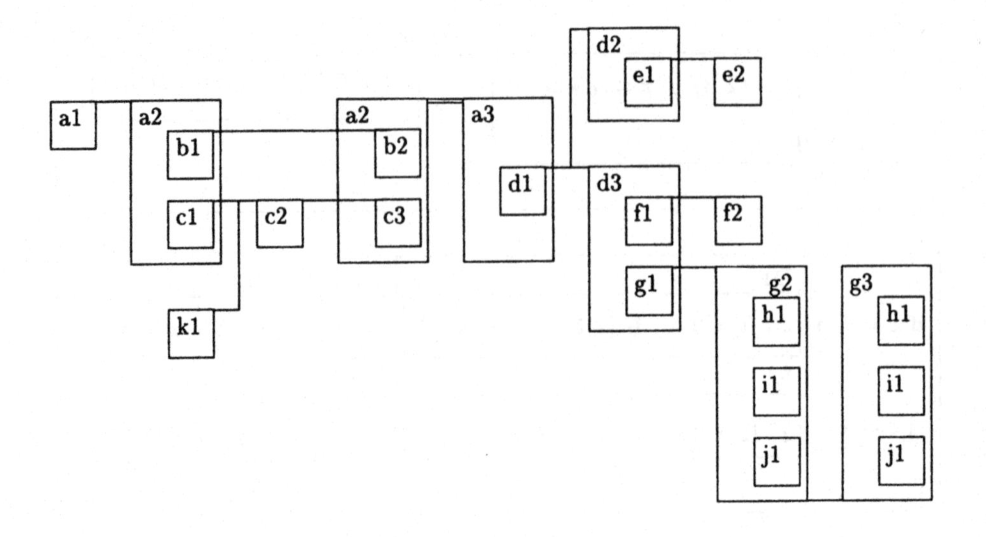

Fig. 6. Large refinement diagram

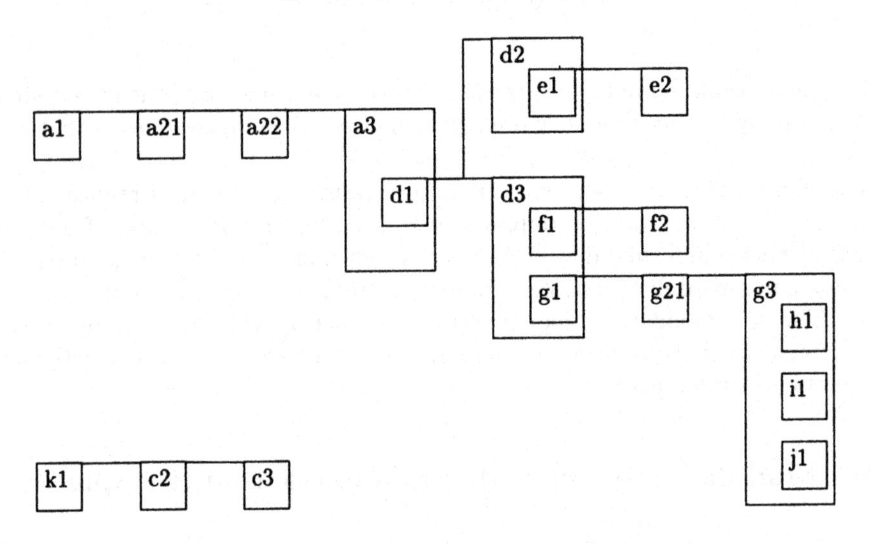

Fig. 7. Large modular refinement diagram

tional partitions to be found anywhere in Figure 7 that do not persist through to the implementation.

11 Conclusion

We have shown that a formal system development can itself be defined formally. A simple structure, which we have called a *Development*, can be used to record every refinement step. Back's refinement diagrams are a well known way to graphically encapsulate program derivations. Refinement diagrams have been shown to be a minor variation on *Developments*. Recording the refinement process in this way has absolutely no impact on the manner in which the development is performed; it does not direct or limit the proof steps taken in the derivation.

Having recorded the derivation in either a *Development* or a refinement diagram (*RefDiag*) a completely accurate hierarchical model of the implemented system can be generated. We have defined a total function (*model*) that extracts the largest model for any development. This function has then been used to give a corresponding total model extraction function for refinement diagrams. These modelling functions have been defined without complicating or restricting the original derivation.

Hierarchical models of systems are very useful once the system has been delivered to perform system monitoring tasks. Because model manipulation is often NP-hard, a hierarchical model is necessary to automate such tasks. There are many applications for models derived from the development process, like fault diagnosis and diagnostic test generation. It is generally accepted in the model-based diagnosis community [8] that modelling is often the hardest part of building monitoring or diagnostic systems. The proposal presented in this paper may provide a way to make model generation automatic for those systems which are formally derived. It may also provide an additional incentive to use formal software engineering methods.

References

1. R.J.R. Back. Refinement diagrams. In *4th BCS Refinement Workshop*, pages 125–137. Springer-Verlag, 1991.
2. R.J.R. Back, J. Hekanaho, and K. Sere. Centipede–a program refinement environment. Reports on Computer Science & Mathematics Series A–139, Åbo Akademi, Turku, Finland, September 1992.
3. E.W. Dijkstra. *A Discipline of Programming*. Academic Press, 1976.
4. Carroll Morgan. The specification statement. *ACM Transactions on Programming Languages and Systems*, 10(3), July 1988.
5. Carroll Morgan. *Programming from Specifications*. Prentice Hall, UK, 1994.
6. C.C. Morgan and K.A. Robinson. Specification statements and refinement. *IBM Journal of Research and Development*, 31(5):546–555, September 1987.
7. J.M. Spivey. *The Z Notation*. Prentice Hall, UK, 1992.
8. Luca Console Walter Hamscher and Johan de Kleer. *Readings in Model-based Diagnosis*. Morgan Kaufmann, San Mateo, CA, 1992.

A Linear Temporal Logic Approach to Objects with Transactions

Grit Denker[1], Jaime Ramos[2], Carlos Caleiro[2], and Amílcar Sernadas[2]

[1] Technische Universität Braunschweig, Informatik, Abt. Datenbanken
Postfach 3329, D–38023 Braunschweig, Germany
e–mail: G.Denker@tu-bs.de

[2] Instituto Superior Técnico, Departamento de Matemática
Av. Rovisco Pais, P-1096 Lisboa Codex, Portugal
e–mail: {jabr|ccal|acs}@math.ist.utl.pt

Abstract. Our concern is the high level specification of reactive software systems such as information systems. We adopt an object oriented, temporal logic based approach to specification. The notion of transaction incorporates various application domains, for instance transactions as abstractions from processes as known from refinement theory, transactions as abstractions from business processes as known in business process modelling or database transactions. In this paper we investigate object specifications with transactions. We illustrate the use of transactions by examples given in an object oriented style and introduce a linear temporal logic with transactions (TOSL) which serves as denotional model for such object specifications with transactions. We explain how TOSL is semantically defined in terms of life cycles and illustrate by example the translation of object specifications to TOSL. Using TOSL for system specification results in sets of formulae which are independent from the level of granularity.

Keywords: linear temporal logic, formal specification language, object orientation, specification method, refinement, transaction, reactive system

1 Introduction and related work

Applications of temporal logics can be found in various independent problem domains. Due to its natural expressiveness of dynamics it is especially suitable as a semantic domain for object oriented approaches. Objects are understood as units of structure and behaviour. Denotation of behaviour can be given in terms of temporal logics. We adopt a formal, object oriented, logic based approach to reactive system specification such as information systems. Information systems are understood as reactive systems with underlying databases and application programs for storage, manipulation, and retrieval of data. Object oriented modelling techniques are accepted as a promising approach to software design. This is the reason for new languages, methods and models emerging. The various existing design notations range from informal analysis methods to formal specification languages. Typical design issues include specification, verification, testing, refinement, etc. One of the requirements to handle these issues is formality. There are formal specification languages defined on top of different frameworks, including algebraic and process models, equational and temporal logics, and others. The specification languages TROLL [6,12] and GNOME [22] are being developed at TU Braunschweig and IST Lisbon, respectively. Both languages are supposed to be used in early phases of the design and modelling of information system. Theoretical investigations accompanied the design during the whole time. Object Specification Logic (OSL [23,24]) is the semantical basis for GNOME. It is a linear time temporal logic. Recently, TROLL and its underlying semantics are focussed towards specifying distributed systems. An appropriate Distributed Temporal Logic (DTL [8,7] based on n-agent logic [18]) has been developed.

In this paper we investigate the concept of transaction in object oriented specifications. We understand transactions as complex processes composed of smaller units, i.e., actions, by using operators like sequence, choice, and loop. The notion of transaction is not tied to a specific task. Firstly, transactions come along with refinement. Refinement is a technique often applied in the design process. A system is described as a sequence of specifications on different levels of abstraction, where each specification is implemented by its successor. Notions of refinement for structured programming, abstract data types, and process theory are well known. The object oriented framework puts additional complexity to this technique. In this case, refinement includes data refinement (structural refinement) as well as action refinement (behavioural refinement). Action refinement is understood as the principle of implementing abstract actions through complex processes using operators like sequence, choice, and loop. Such processes can be regarded as transactions. Secondly, the notion of transaction is supported by many database management systems. We aim at modelling information systems with object oriented techniques. Thus, the concept of transaction known from databases is important for our work. A database transaction follows the ACID-principle. It is executed atomically from the users viewpoint (ATOMICITY), it transforms the database from one consistent state to another consistent state (CONSISTENCY), its effect is the same as it would have taken place in isolation (ISOLATION), and its effect is persistent in the database (DURABILITY). Thirdly, business processes may be understood as transactions. Significant behavioural parts of an enterprise can be described as business processes. The behaviour of such processes is known a priori. That is the reason, why such processes are already specifiable in the design phase. A business process uses several resources and puts together different services to construct a new service. An appropriate concept of transaction could be used to give semantics to business processes.

The focus of this paper is to deal with transactions in an object oriented, temporal logic based setting. Work done in the field of temporal logics about refinement and change of granularity ([14,1,9,10,17]) is related to our work. One of the main problems in this area can be described as follows: temporal operators such as Y (yesterday,previous) and X (tomorrow,next) in a temporal formula are strongly connected to the underlying granularity. Thus, if the execution of an action takes one step, then Y refers to the state before the action execution, but if the execution takes several steps (as for a transaction), then Y refers to the penultimate state which is usually not the state before the transaction began. Thus, a formula like "Before the action occurred φ hold true" will change its meaning if the action is refined to a transaction. There are different solutions to this problem. Either the use of this operators together with refinement is forbidden (see eg TLA [15]), or others propose to specify different formulae for the different abstraction levels (eg [9]). Another solution is, to introduce different local clocks and associate formulae with these clocks (eg [17]). This way temporal operators are bound to different granularities and, thus, a next operator can refer to different states depending on the formula it belongs to. There has been done also work about refinement in the area of formal specification and object orientation (eg [2, 16, 9, 3, 25] to mention a few, most of which are based on algebraic techniques). The differences to our work are that either they do not work with temporal logics (eg [2, 3, 25]) or for those who use temporal logics [16, 9] they use one of the approaches mentioned above.

Our approach is different and innovative in the following sense. We aim to write only formulae which are independent of the level of granularity. That means, we do not want to change the formula because the granularity has changed, rather we would like to write formulae in such a way that possible changes of granularity are already taken into account. Thus, the formulae we intend to reach are those which are independent from the level of abstraction or granularity. The reason why this is possible is the following: The logic is used as an underlying semantics for object oriented specifications. Therefore, formulae are not just freely built, rather than they are derived by translating concepts of the specification language into logical expressions. Thus, if we find an appropriate, granularity-independent translation of the language constructs to temporal formulae, we succeeded. This is exactly what we are going to do in the rest of the paper. We investigate the main concepts needed in object oriented specification (such as communication, effects and preconditions of actions) and show how they are translated appropriately to temporal formulae which are preserved under refinement, i.e., which are granularity-independent. The logic we use for this purpose is a linear temporal logic which incoporates the concept of transaction, so-called Transactional Object Specification Logic (TOSL). This logic is the basis for formalizing dynamics. Together with an algebraic part which serves as semantics for structural aspects this constitutes a firm mathematical framework to give semantics to object specifications including transactions.

The rest of the paper is organized as follows. Section 2 illustrates the main problems when temporal logic is combined with different levels of granularity. We explain the problems by means of examples and propose a first solution. In section 3 we introduce TOSLand define its semantics. This establishes the basis for dealing with the problems as illustrated before. Thus, in section 4 we use TOSL as a tool and formalize our first solution. We translate object specifications with transactions into TOSL formulae and show that we yield formulae which are compatible with refinement. Finally, we give a short summary and point out future work.

2 The problem: temporal logic and levels of granularity

We demonstrate basic specification features using notations in the spirit of TROLL or GNOME. Especially for transactional parts we use an ad-hoc notation influenced by the intended semantics. The example does not exploit all features of object oriented specification (eg inheritance, etc.), rather we emphasize on the transactional aspect. But the theoretical framework is capable of dealing with fully object oriented models.

Example 1 (Casino – Abstract level). We specify part of a casino world in an object oriented way (cf. [11]). We start with an informal description of the Universe of Discourse (UoD) which has to be modelled.

Slot machines are very famous games in casinos. Players put money in the machine, pull the handle and wait for the reaction, i.e., winning money or not. Playing the machine implies that the pot of the slot machine is increased and a decision is made whether money is paid out to the player.

A first object oriented approach to model this may result in two types of objects: `player` and `slot_machine`.

```
object class player
  actions play(nat)
  behavior play(n)  synchronizes with move(n)
end
```

A player can play the slot machine. Whenever a player plays, he/she synchronises with the slot machine, i.e., `play` *synchronizes with* `move`. Thus, the behavior of a player is such that he/she synchronously communicates with the machine when playing it. `play` has a parameter which will be set by the action `move` of slot machine. Randomly the slot machine assigns a value to the parameter. A very rough specification of slot machine is:

```
object class slot_machine
  attributes pot:nat initialized 0
             lucky:bool
  actions move(n)
  behavior move(0) onlyIf  not lucky do pot=pot+1 od
           move(n) (n#0) onlyIf (lucky and pot=n-1) do pot=0 od
end
```

The slot machine has a `pot` as attribute to store the current amount of money. Attribute `lucky` presents the randomized selection whether money is paid off or not. The action move `move` will occurr with the parameter zero only if the player is not lucky (*onlyIf* clause of `move(0)`). In this case it will increase the pot (*do-od* clause of `move(0)`). The player gets no money because the synchronisation is done with parameter zero. The slot machine performs a move with a parameter `n` different from zero only if the player is lucky and the pot already stored the amount `n-1` of money (*onlyIf* clause of `move(n)`). Thus, by putting the coin, the pot is increased, all the money is given to the player, and the pot is afterwards set to zero (*do-od* clause of `move(0)`).

The given example illustrates the following concepts of object oriented approaches: Objects are units of structure (eg attributes) and behavior (eg actions plus behavior clauses). They are encapsulated in the sense that they change their state (represented by attributes) only through action execution. Objects communicate with each other by synchronous action calling.

Object specifications such as the one give above can be formalized as a pair $Spec = (\Sigma, \Phi)$, where Σ incorporates structural parts such as identities, attribute and action symbols, among others, and Φ is a set of temporal formulae derived from the specification. We adopt an algebraic approach for the structural part (for details see [8]). Concerning the dynamics each language concept is translated into a temporal formula. Thus, axioms about occurrences of actions, their effects on attributes and interactions between actions, respectively, are given.

Example 2 (Casino – Abstract level – Temporal formulae). The following natural language expressions about the casino behaviour can be derived from the specification: "`play(n)` synchronizes with `move(n)`, i.e., whenever `play(n)` happens also `move(n)` happens", and "moving the slotmachine increments the pot and depending on the value of lucky money is paid out or not", etc.

There are different possibilities to express such statements in logic: eg dynamic logic [20, 13], situation calculus [19, 21], among others. On the basis of temporal logic we introduced in former papers [23, 8] a special predicate on actions $\odot\alpha$ (occurrence of action α). $\odot\alpha$ is true in the state where α has just been executed. Thus, the given player specification could be translated to

$$\odot\mathtt{play(n)} \Rightarrow \odot\mathtt{move(n)}. \tag{1}$$

I.e., `play(n)` can only happen with `move(n)` happening synchronously. Analogously, the behaviour of slot machine could be formalized as

$$[\mathsf{Y}(\mathtt{lucky} = \mathtt{false} \wedge \mathtt{pot} = \mathtt{n}) \wedge \odot\mathtt{move(k)}] \Rightarrow (\mathtt{k} = 0 \wedge \mathtt{pot} = \mathtt{n} + 1) \tag{2}$$

$$[\mathsf{Y}(\mathtt{lucky} = \mathtt{true}) \wedge \odot\mathtt{move(n)}] \Rightarrow \mathtt{pot} = 0 \tag{3}$$

The first axiom says that if lucky does not hold then moving the machine will increase the pot and no money will be paid out (`k=0`). Y stands for the temporal logic operator *yesterday*. The second axiom states that after moving the slot machine from a state where `lucky` held implies that all money is paid out, i.e., `pot=0`.

What we have done so far is formalizing the semantics of an object specification by translation to temporal logic formulae. The former specification was a first rough approach to a formalization of the given UoD. To get a more concrete, closer to implementation description one might apply refinement techniques.

Example 3 (Casino – Refined level). The action move is refined to a transaction MOVE composed of two steps. First, the pot is incremented. The next step in the transaction depends on the value of attribute lucky. Either all the money is paid off (*then*-case) or nothing is paid (*else*-case).

```
object class slot_machine
  attributes pot:nat initialized 0
             lucky:bool
  actions inc
          payoff(nat)
          zeropay(nat)
  transactions MOVE(nat)
  behavior MOVE(n)=<inc;if(lucky,payoff(n),zeropay(n))>
            inc do pot=pot+1 od
            payoff(n) onlyIf pot=n do pot=0  od
            zeropay(n) onlyIf  n=0
end
```

MOVE is specified as a transaction composed of several actions. The first step increments the pot. The effect of the inc action is specified in a *do-od* clause. The second step deals with the paying off. The amount n can only be paid off (payoff(n)) if this amount has been stored in the pot before. Afterwards the pot will be reset to zero. The formalization is given in the behavior clause of payoff(n). A zeropay can only happen with the parameter zero.

Now we have a second specification which intuitively does the same as the previous. We also put some effort in formalizing the behavior of the abstract specification as temporal formulae. In real-size case studies the set of formulae increases rapidly. Thus, instead of re-doing the formalization one would wish to reuse the set of temporal formulae by just substituting transactions for the actions. But usually this does not yield the intended result.

Example 4 (Casino – Refined level – Temporal formulae). The temporal formulae given in example 2 are no longer meaningful in the presence of transactions. A substitution of the transaction MOVE(n) for the action move(n) yields the following formulae:

$$\odot\mathtt{play(n)} \Rightarrow \odot\mathtt{MOVE(n)}, \tag{4}$$

$$[\mathsf{Y}(\mathtt{lucky} = \mathtt{false} \wedge \mathtt{pot} = \mathtt{n}) \wedge \odot\mathtt{MOVE(k)}] \Rightarrow (\mathtt{k} = 0 \wedge \mathtt{pot} = \mathtt{n} + 1), \tag{5}$$

$$[\mathsf{Y}(\mathtt{lucky} = \mathtt{true}) \wedge \odot\mathtt{MOVE(n)}] \Rightarrow \mathtt{pot} = 0. \tag{6}$$

The following problem arise:

Synchronisation: The first problem concerns the interaction between player and slot_machine. What does it intuitively mean, that an action (play) and a transaction (MOVE) occur together? Does it mean that the action play(n) occurs simultaneously with the first (or the last) action of the transaction MOVE(n)? It seems that the translation of interaction statements to an implication between action occurrences, as done in equation (1), is too strict.

At least, it could be more appropriate to give another formalisation of interaction which will also be meaningful in the presence of transactions. For instance, synchronisation of two transactions is formalized as "they overlap during their execution".

Effects and preconditions of actions: The temporal operator Y always refers to the preceding state. But the expression "preceding state" has different meanings depending on the level of granularity. On the abstract level in equation (3) the temporal operator Y refers to the state *before the execution* of `move(n)`. This is what one expects to test a precondition. Whereas in (6) the temporal operator refers to the last state before the execution of `MOVE(n)` is finished. Intuitively, $\odot$`MOVE(n)` holds in a state where all actions belonging to the transaction have been performed one after each other. Thus, in (6) Y does not refer to the state before the execution started, rather than the state where `inc` has happened. Thus, temporal operators have to be used carefully when different levels of granularity are involved as it is the case of object specifications with transactions.
Similar investigations show that the formula for the effect of `MOVE(n)` (see (5)) is not appropriate.

Re-investigating the formulae of our example yields in the following more appropriate expressions: "There is an interaction between `play(n)` and `MOVE(n)`", "if `lucky=false` and `pot=n` in the state just before the execution of `MOVE(n)` started, and if `MOVE(n)` has finished then `pot=n+1`", and "if `lucky=true` in the state before the execution of `MOVE(n)` started, then `pot=0` holds in the state where `MOVE(n)` has just finished". Thus, an appropriate logic must be able to specify these subtle kind of expressions referring to states before and after the execution of transactions (for preconditions and effects) as well as it must be capable of specifying when two transactions interact, i.e., when they overlapp.

The conclusions we draw from these investigations are the following:

1. The formalization of system requirements is a time-consuming task. Therefore, we can only increase productivity by using refinement technique if that what has been specified once on a specific level of abstraction remain under refinement.
2. The formalization of object oriented system specifications is done by translation to temporal formulae. Therefore, we have to translate object oriented features in such a way that the resulting formulae are independent of the level of granularity.
3. An appropriate logic must be able to express statements about overlapping of transactions (for modelling synchronisation) as well as it must be able to refer to the beginning and the end of transactions to get the right states for expressing preconditions and effects.

Therefore, in the following we define TOSL a linear temporal logic enriched by the notion of transaction, in which such statements are expressible. Its semantics is based on life cycles, i.e., sequences of action occurrences. In section 4 we illustrate the use of TOSL by formalizing the casino example.

3 The logic: TOSL

TOSL is a linear temporal logic with added features for specifying transactions. As usual for defining a logic we first have to define what are the signatures from which one can built terms, and then how formulae are built. Since we are going to use TOSL as denotational semantics for object specifications, we need to talk about data signatures (eg for the domains of attributes), as well as object signatures (i.e., attribute, action, and transaction symbols of objects), and signatures of object communities. Every action can be understood as a transaction, i.e., that one which consists only out of one action, but not vice versa. Therefore, one may think that transactions are sufficient. But to define semantics of TOSL we will associate sequences of actions to objects. Therefore, we still have to distinguish between actions and transactions in our approach. Due to space limitations we will not go into all details concerning data-, object-, and object system signatures, terms, etc. Rather we will focus on the those points in which we differ from the classical stuff and which are innovative in our approch. The formal definitions for signatures, terms, etc. are straightforward once the main ideas have been made clear. Moreover, we want to emphasize that the way of specifying changes when transactions come into play. Thus, we decided to spend some space on illustrating specification with transaction by means of examples in section 4.

Let $\langle ACT, TRAC, ATT\rangle$ be an **object signature** which consists of sets of action symbols, transaction symbols and attribute symbols as defined in the specification. Thus, an **object community signature** is a pair $\Sigma = \langle ID, \{\Sigma^i\}_{id \in ID}\rangle$ where ID is a finite set of object identifiers and each Σ^i is an object signature. Because of space limitations we cannot detail how object community signatures are derived from object specifications such as TROLL or GNOME (for details concerning TROLL see [8]). Given a signature Σ and a set of variables X, terms in $T_\Sigma(X)$ are built as usual. Thus, in our approach we have **attribute terms, action terms**, and **transaction terms**. Those are constructed by applying attribute, action or transaction symbols, respectively, to terms. There is one special action term $i.\bot \in T_{\Sigma,act^i}(X)$ (act^i means action of object i) to indicate that an object is currently quiet, i.e., it is not performing an action. We need this because of the life cycle semantics where objects may be quiet while others perform actions (*stuttering*). Our focus is on transactions. Transactions are built by using operators such as sequence, choice or loop. Thus, $\langle t\rangle, \langle t_1; \ldots; t_n\rangle, \mathsf{if}(t_0, t_1, t_2), \mathsf{while}(t_0, t_1) \in T_{\Sigma,trac^i}(X)$ are transaction terms provided that t_k, $k = 1, \ldots, n$, are transaction terms, and t_0 is a boolean term.

As for **formulae** in $Tosl_\Sigma(X)$ we have the common things, i.e., equality on data terms, implication ($\Rightarrow$), negation ($\neg$), all-quantifier ($\forall$), since (S), until (U). With the help of these we can define the usual abbreviations such as $\vee, \wedge, \exists, \mathsf{X}, \mathsf{Y}, \ldots$. There are three special formulae which will provide the basis for giving semantics to object specification with transactions, namely

- $i.\mathsf{c} \in Tosl_\Sigma(X)$ provided that $i \in ID$;
- $\mathsf{B}(t), \mathsf{E}(t) \in Tosl_\Sigma(X)$ provided that $t \in T_{\Sigma,trac^i}(X)$ for some $i \in ID$.

Consistency of an object i ($i.$c) is a notion that comes along with transactions. Consistent states are those where a transaction has not begun or its execution has just finished, respectively. All states in-between a transaction execution are inconsistent. This is a widely used terminology in database theory. $\mathsf{B}(t)$ refers to the state just **before the execution of a transaction** t and $\mathsf{E}(t)$ refers to the state **after its execution**. We will use these formulae to formalize object specifications with transactions.

In the following we briefly sketch the semantics of this logic. As usual data signatures are interpreted by algebras. Applying an action symbol of an object i to values of appropriate sort from the algebra gives an **action of object** i. Analogously, **attributes and transactions of an object** are received. Thus, referring to the casino example actions of the slot machine are `move(0)`, `move(1)`, ..., and attributes are `pot=0`, `pot=1`, ... In what follows we write $\mathcal{A}_{act^i}, \mathcal{A}_{trac^i}$, and $\mathcal{A}_{att^i_s}$ for actions, transactions, and attributes, respectively, of object i.

Interpretation structures for TOSL formulae are life cycles, i.e., sequences of action occurrences. In every step a set of actions is assigned which are currently executed by the objects of the system. We assume that each object performs one action at the moment. Additionally, there is more information in every step of an objects life cycle. For each step we know, whether the object is currently in a consistent state or not and what are the values of the attributes. Moreover, we allowed for choice and loop operator in transactions. Therefore, the denotation, i.e., meaning of a transaction, depends on the current state of attributes. We illustrate this by means of an example.

Example 5 (Casino – Semantics). In figure 1 part of a slot machine life cycle is depicted. All states are labelled with the current attribute values and the actions that have just been performed. In state 1 attribute lucky holds, the pot equals n-1 and the object is quiet. From state 1 to state 2 the object started the execution of `MOVE` by incrementing the pot. In the following step `pot` is set to zero and the money is paid out. Moreover, a demon changed attribute lucky. Thus, the execution of transaction `MOVE(n)` started in state 1 and has been finished in state 3. State 1 and 3 are consistent objects states (black circle), whereas in state 2 the object is still executing the transaction and therefore is in an inconsistent state.

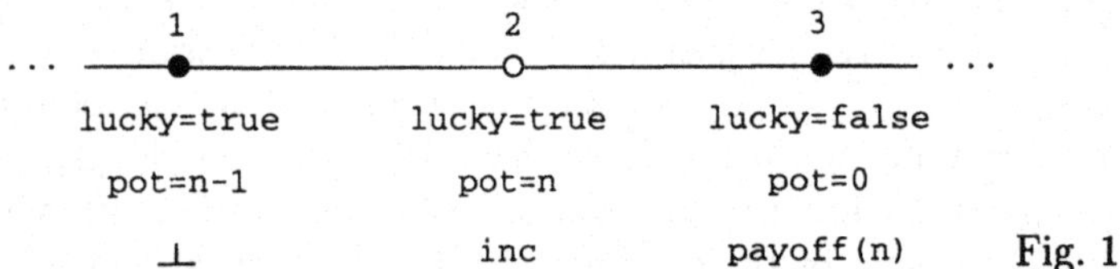

Fig. 1

The interpretation of a transaction that involves choices or loops depends on the state. Eg the denotation of `MOVE(n)=<inc;if(lucky,payoff(n),zeropay(n))>` in state 1 is the sequence `<inc;payoff(n)>` since lucky holds. In contrast, the denotation of `MOVE(n)` in state 3 is the sequence `<inc;zeropay(n)>` since lucky does not hold. Thus, the interpretation structure has to reflect the fact that transactions are interpreted depending on the state.

Formally, an interpretation structure for TOSL, so-called Σ-structure, is an ID-indexed family of maps $\lambda = \{\lambda^i\}_{i \in ID}$, where each λ^i is 4-tuple

$$\lambda^i : \mathrm{N}_o \to \mathcal{A}_{act^i} \otimes \{0,1\} \otimes [\mathcal{A}_{trac^i} \to \mathcal{A}^*_{act^i}] \otimes \{[\mathcal{A}_{att^i_s} \to \mathcal{A}_{DT_s}]\}_{s \in S_{DT}}.$$

For each object i an interpretation structure is a sequential life cycle. For each natural number the 4-tuple consists of the action which has just happened (first component), values of attributes (last component), sequences of actions corresponding to transactions (third component) and a flag stating whether the object is in a consistent state or not (second component).

Denotation of terms is given for a life cycle λ at a specific state k and a given assignment for variables. Let $\xi = \langle \lambda, k, \theta \rangle$ where $k \in \mathrm{N}_o$ and θ is an assignment, with the following conventions

- $\xi @ k' = \langle \lambda, k', \theta \rangle$, i.e., the same life cycle and the same assignment, but a different state;
- $\xi @ \theta' = \langle \lambda, k, \theta' \rangle$, i.e., the same life cycle at the same point in time, but a different assignment.

We will skip the detailed definition of denotation of terms. As already mentioned, the denotation of attribute terms is given corresponding to the last component of the interpretation structure. Analogously, the denotation of transactional terms refers to the third component of the interpretation structure. The intuitive idea is that a transaction term may always be interleaved by finitely many $\perp$ actions. Thus, the denotation of a sequential transaction term is given as the sequence of the denotations of the incorporated terms possibly extended by $\perp$ actions in-between the first and the last term. The denotation of a choice depends on the value of the boolean term t_0. Loop-terms are defined recursively.

We will directly go to the interesting features of our logic, i.e., the transactional concepts. As far as it concerns the normal elements satisfaction of formulae is given as usual. Satisfaction of the three new concepts we introduced (consistency, begin and end of transaction) are defined as follows:

- $\xi \Vdash i.\mathsf{c}$ iff $\lambda^i(k)_2 = 1$;
- $\xi \Vdash \mathsf{B}(t)$ iff exists $k' > k$ such that $\lambda^i[k+1, k'] \in [\![t]\!]_{\xi, trac^i}$;
- $\xi \Vdash \mathsf{E}(t)$ iff exists $k' < k$ such that $\lambda^i[k', k] \in [\![t]\!]_{\xi @ k', trac^i}$.

An object is in a consistent state if this state is labelled as consistent. This information is given in the second component of an interpretation structure λ.

To investigate whether $\mathsf{B}(t)$ holds for a transaction t at point k we have have to look at the denotation of that transaction. The denotation of a transaction is a specific sequence of actions depending on state k. In k all conditions which are part of the specification of t are evaluated. Thus, the denotation of t is a sequence of actions which have to be performed in order to perform t. Now, the formula $\mathsf{B}(t)$ holds for a transaction t at point k if there is a sequence of states starting from state $k+1$ which are labelled with the actions which correspond to the denotation of t. $\lambda^i[k+1,k']$ denotes the life cylce λ^i from state $k+1$ until state k'.

To decide for a state in a life cycle whether it is a state where a transaction has ended, we have to look back to a previous state k'. We get the denotation of the transaction at state k' (its starting point). This sequence of action must correspond to the labels of the life cycle between k' and k. Thus, $\mathsf{E}(t)$ holds at k iff there is a previous state k' such that the states of the life cycle from k' to k are labelled with the denotation of t.

We are almost done with syntax and semantics of our logic so that we can illustrate specification with transaction. There is only one thing missing which is due to the fact that $\mathsf{B}(t)$ and $\mathsf{E}(t)$ have been defined independent of consistent states. Intuitively one would expect, that the end of a transaction is a consistent state as well as the state before the transaction performs actions. All states in-between should be inconsistent. This leads us to the notion of "strong begin" $\mathbf{B}(t)$ and "strong end" $\mathbf{E}(t)$ of transactions. Thus, in a life cycle we are at the "strong begin of a transaction" $\mathbf{B}(t)$ if the necessary sequence of action will follow (i.e., $\mathsf{B}(t)$ holds), the state is consistent (i.e., $i.\mathsf{c}$), and there will be no consistent state until the transaction is finished. Analogously we can define $\mathbf{E}(t)$.

$$\mathbf{B}(t) \equiv \mathsf{B}(t) \wedge i.\mathsf{c} \wedge (((\neg i.\mathsf{c}) \wedge (\neg\, \mathsf{E}(t)))\ \mathsf{U}\ (i.\mathsf{c} \wedge \mathsf{E}(t))),$$
$$\mathbf{E}(t) \equiv \mathsf{E}(t) \wedge i.\mathsf{c} \wedge (((\neg i.\mathsf{c}) \wedge (\neg\, \mathsf{B}(t)))\ \mathsf{S}\ (i.\mathsf{c} \wedge \mathsf{B}(t))).$$

Note, that $\mathbf{B}(t)$ only holds if the whole transactions has been performed. Thus, the semantics of transaction guarantees atomicity. Consistency and isolation are no problems in this approach: (1) If there exists a life cycle model for a specification, then it fulfills all axioms by definition. Thus, it is consistent with the specification and all transition are therefore valid. (2) Isolation is not an issue since transactions operate sequentially on objects. There is no shared data. This will be future work, when we introduce transactions which incorporate different objects and which may perform concurrently. Durability is not an issue since we assume objects to be persistent.

Example 6 (Strong begin/end vs. weak begin/end). $\mathsf{B}(t), \mathsf{E}(t)$ are "weak forms of begin and end" in the sense that this does not imply that the transaction indeed happens. For instance, assume two transaction specifications `X=<a;b;c;d>` and `Y=<b;c>` of one object. The life cycle in figure 2 satisfies the following formulae: "`B(X)` holds at state 1", "`B(Y)` holds at state 2", "`E(Y)` holds at state 4", and "`E(X)` holds at state 5", respectively.

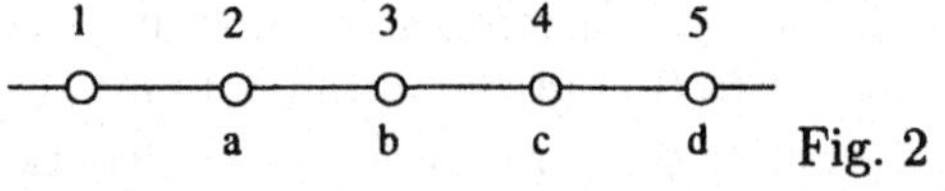

Fig. 2

But only one transaction can happen in one instance of time due to our assumption that objects are sequential. That is the reason for introducing consistency. There are various possibilities for valid life cycles. In figure 3 two such life cycles are illustrated. The first one corresponds to execution of transaction X whereas the second one corresponds to execution of transaction <a>, followed by transaction Y, followed by action <d>.

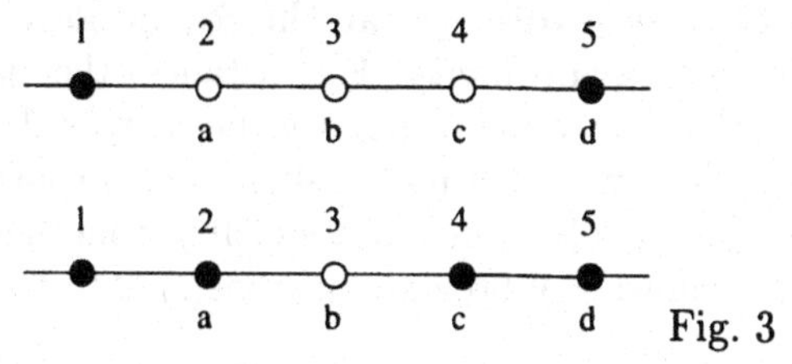

Fig. 3

For that reason we introduce the notions "strong begin" (**B**) and "strong end" (**E**) of a transaction. In figure 3 the following "strong" formulae hold. In the first life cycle "**B**(X) holds at state 1" and "**E**(X) holds at state 5". In the second life cycle of figure 3 "**B**(<a>) holds at state 1", "**E**(<a>) holds at state 2", "**B**(Y) holds at state 2", "**E**(Y) holds at state 4", "**B**(<d>) holds at state 4", "**E**(<d>) holds at state 5".

4 The solution: specifying with transactions

We start with synchronization of transactions. A transaction t_1 calls another transaction t_2 if the execution of t_1 *requires* in some sense the execution of t_2. As already pointed out in example 3 this may be appropriately formalized as "t_1 and t_2 overlap *during* their execution". In figure 4 four possibilities of transaction overlapping are illustrated.

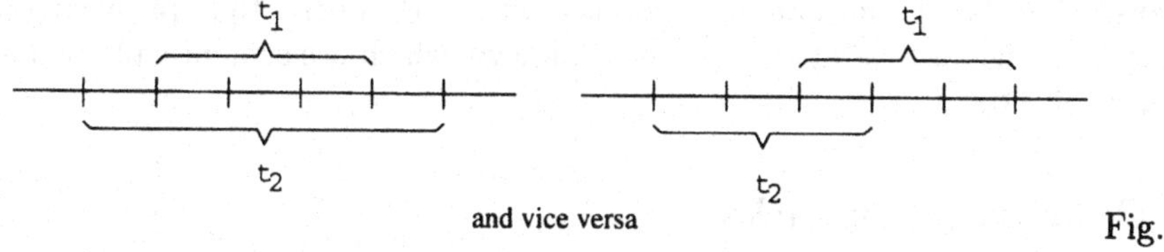

Fig. 4

Using the definitions for strong begin and end, we can define during(t) as an abbreviation:

$$\mathsf{during}(t) \equiv ((\neg\, \mathbf{E}(t))\ \mathsf{S}\ \mathbf{B}(t)) \vee \mathbf{E}(t).$$

during(t) incorporates all states where actions of the current transaction t are performed. Together with this notion we can now define t_1 requires t_2, $t_1 \gg t_2$, i.e., synchronization of transactions:

$$t_1 \gg t_2 \equiv \mathbf{E}(t_1) \Rightarrow [\mathsf{during}(t_2) \vee (\mathsf{during}(t_1)\ \mathsf{S}\ (\mathbf{E}(t_2) \wedge \mathsf{during}(t_1))))]).$$

Now we can formalize synchronisation in object systems with transactions.

Example 7 (Casino: synchronisation). The behavior of the player specification as given in example 1 is formalized as the following TOSL formula: `<play(n)>` $\gg$ `MOVE(n)`.

Effects of *actions* could be easily defined without TOSL. But since the granularity of an action may change through applying refinement techniques etc. we take a different approach. **The formalization is always given in terms of transactions. This guarantees that the formulae will hold independently of the level of granularity.** For instance, the specification `inc` *do* `pot=pot+1` *od* says that the value of pot will be increased by one (depending on the value of pot before incrementing). Using TOSL for formalization gives an appropriate formula which holds true independently from the granularity of `inc`.

We introduce the following abbreviation: $\mathsf{inside}(t) \equiv (\neg\,\mathbf{E}(t)\mathsf{S}\mathbf{B}(t)) \wedge (\neg\,\mathbf{E}(t))$.

Example 8 (Casino: effect and precondition). The behavior of example 3 is translated to the following TOSL axioms:

$$(\mathbf{B}(\texttt{<inc>}) \wedge \texttt{pot=n}) \Rightarrow [\mathsf{inside}(\texttt{<inc>})\ \mathsf{U}\ (\mathbf{E}(\texttt{<inc>}) \wedge \texttt{pot=n+1})]$$
$$\mathbf{E}(\texttt{<payoff(n)>}) \Rightarrow \texttt{pot=0}$$
$$\mathbf{B}(\texttt{<payoff(n)>}) \Rightarrow \texttt{pot=n}$$
$$\mathbf{B}(\texttt{<zeropay(n)>}) \Rightarrow \texttt{n} = 0$$

The third and fourth formulae describe preconditions for `<payoff>` and `<zeropay>`. These formulae refer to the beginning of those transactions. The first and second formulae correspond to effects of `inc` and `payoff`. In case of incrementing we have to refer to the value before the incrementing started.

We have illustrated by example that TOSL is very well suited for specifying object systems with transactions. Moreover, the given axioms are stable wrt to refinement in the sense that they are independent from the actual granularity of a transaction. We do not aim at specifying with TOSL rather than proposing intuitive language macros at the specification level which are semantically defined in terms of TOSL.

5 Concluding remarks

In this paper we investigated the concept of transaction in object oriented specification. We presented a linear temporal logic with transaction which serves as denotational semantics for object specifications with transactions. We extended Object Specification Logic (OSL) by the notion of transaction. Semantics of Transactional Object Specification Logic (TOSL) has been given in terms of life cycles and its use was illustrated by means of examples. One of the main advantages is that TOSL is capable of specifying formulae independently of the level of granularity.

Future work will be towards simulation and reification of object specification. The former deals with observational equivalence of objects. Abstract specifications are refined to more concrete ones by refining actions and transactions and specifying new axioms. In case of reification we only allow actions to be refined whereas transactions remain. The advantage of this approach is that refined formulae can be derived from abstract ones. Both cases are useful for high level specification. In the current framework, we restricted ourselves to sequential systems. There exists already work about extending DTL [7] with the notion of transaction (see [4, 5]). In this distributed framework serializability of transactions which share data as well as reification has been treated. A totally different way of dealing with transactions would be to provide a new semantics for our specification language. For instance, the work of Liu and Orgun about temporal logics with clocks seems very promising in this respect.

Acknowledgements: We would like to thank the referees for their valuable comments. The first author would like to thank her colleagues for internal discussions on the topic of the paper. Especially, the comments of Hans Dieter Ehrich and Juliana Küster Filipe helped to improve the paper.
This work was partially supported by DFG under Eh75/11-1, the PRAXIS XXI Program and JNICT, as well as by PRAXIS XXI Projects 2/2.1/MAT/262/94 SitCalc, PCEX/P/MAT/46/96 ACL plus 2/2.1/TIT/1658/95 LogComp, and ESPRIT IV Working Groups 22704 ASPIRE and 23531 FIREworks.

References

1. H. Barringer, R. Kuiper, and A. Pnueli. A Really Abstract Concurrent Model and its Temporal Logic. *ACM Symp. Principles of Programming Languages*, pages 173–183, 1989.
2. Bonner, A.J. and Kifer, M. Concurrency and Communication in Transaction Logic. In M. Maher, editor, *Proc. Joint Int. Conf. and Symp. on Logic Programming (JICSLP96), September 2-6, 1996, Bonn, Germany.* The MIT Press, 1996.
3. P. Borba and J. Goguen. On Refinement and FOOPS. Technical Report, PRG-TR-17-94 , Oxford University Computing Laboratory, Programming Research Group, 1994.
4. G. Denker. Reification – Changing Viewpoint but Preserving Truth. In M. Haveraan, O. Owe, and O.-J. Dahl, editors, *Recent Trends in Data Types Specification, Proc. 11th Workshop on Specification of Abstract Data Types joint with the 8th General COMPASS Meeting. Oslo, Norway, September 1995. Selected papers.*, pages 182–199. Springer, 1996. LNCS 1130.
5. G. Denker. Semantic Refinement of Concurrent Object Systems Based on Serializability. In B. Freitag, C. B. Jones, C. Lengauer, and H.-J. Schek, editors, *Object Orientation with Parallelism and Persistence*, pages 105–126. Kluwer Academic Publ., 1996.
6. G. Denker and P. Hartel. TROLL – An Object Oriented Formal Method for Distributed Information System Design: Syntax and Pragmatics. Technical Report 97–03, TU Braunschweig, 1997. `http://www.cs.tu-bs.de/idb/publications/pub_97`
7. H.-D. Ehrich. Object Specification. Technical Report 96–07, TU Braunschweig, 1996. `http://www.cs.tu-bs.de/idb/publications/pub_96`
8. H.-D. Ehrich and A. Sernadas. Local Specification of Distributed Families of Sequential Objects. In E. Astesiano, G. Reggio, and A. Tarlecki, editors, *Recent Trends in Data Types Specification, Proc. 10th Workshop on Specification of Abstract Data Types joint with the 5th COMPASS Workshop, S.Margherita, Italy, May/June 1994, Selected papers*, pages 219–235. Springer, Berlin, LNCS 906, 1995.
9. J.L. Fiadeiro and T. Maibaum. Sometimes "Tommorrow" is "Sometime" – Action Refinement in a Temporal Logic of Objects. In D. M. Gabbay and H. J. Ohlbach,

editors, *Proc. First Int. Conf. on Temporal Logic, ICTL, Bonn, Germany, July 1994*, pages 48–66. Springer, 1994. LNAI 827.
10. M. Huhn. Action Refinement and Property Inheritance in Systems of Sequential Agents. In *Proc. 7th Int. Conf. on Concurrency Theory, Concur'96, 26-29 August, Pisa, Italy.* Springer, 1996. LNCS 1119.
11. M. Huhn, H. Wehrheim, and G. Denker. Action Refinement in System Specification: Comparing a Process Algebraic and an Object-Oriented Approach. In U. Herzog and H. Hermanns, editors, *GI/ITG-Fachgespräch: "Formale Beschreibungstechniken für verteilte Systeme", 20/21. Juni 1996, Universität Erlangen, Germany*, number 29/9 in Arbeitsbericht des IMMD, pages 77–88, 1996.
12. R. Jungclaus, G. Saake, T. Hartmann, and C. Sernadas. TROLL – A Language for Object-Oriented Specification of Information Systems. *ACM Transactions on Information Systems*, 14(2):175–211, April 1996.
13. D. Kozen and J. Tiuryn. Logics of Programs. In J. Van Leeuwen, editor, *Handbook of Theoretical Computer Science B - Formal Models and Semantics*, chapter 789–840. 1990.
14. L. Lamport. Specifying Concurrent Program Modules. *ACM Trans. on Programming Languages and Systems*, 5:190–222, January 1983.
15. L. Lamport. The Temporal Logic of Actions. *ACM Trans. on Programming Languages and Systems*, 16(3):872–923, May 1994.
16. U. Lechner, C. Lengauer, and M. Wirsing. An Object-Oriented Airport: Specification and Refinement in Maude. In Astesiano, E. and Reggio, G. and Tarlecki, A., editor, *Recent Trends in Data Types Specification, Proc. 10th Workshop on Specification of Abstract Data Types joint with the 5th COMPASS Workshop, S.Margherita, Italy, May/June 1994, Selected papers*, pages 351–367. Springer, Berlin, LNCS 906, 1995.
17. C. Liu and M. A. Orgun. Dealing with Multiple Granularity of Time in Temporal Logic Programming. *Journal of Symbolic Computation*, 22(5 & 6):699–720, 1996.
18. K. Lodaya, R. Ramanujam, and P.S. Thiagarajan. Temporal Logics for Communicating Sequential Agents. *Int. Journal of Foundations of Computer Science*, 3(2):117–159, 1992.
19. J. McCarthy and P. Hayes. Some Philosophical Problems from the Standpoint of Artificial Intelligence. In B. Meltzer and D. Michie, editors, *Machine Intelligence 4*, pages 463–502. Edinburgh University Press, 1969.
20. V. R. Pratt. Semantical Considerations on Floyd-Hoare Logic. In *Proc. 17th Ann. IEEE Symp. on Foundations of Computer Science*, pages 109–121, 1976.
21. R. Reiter. Proving Properties of States in the Situation calculus. *Artificial Intelligence*, 64(2):337–351, 1993.
22. A. Sernadas and J. Ramos. The GNOME Language: Syntax, Semantics and Calculus. Technical Report, Instituto Superior Téchnico (IST), Dept. Mathemática, Av. Roviso Pais, 1096 Lisboa Codex, Portugal, 1994.
23. A. Sernadas, C. Sernadas, and J.F. Costa. Object Specification Logic. *Journal of Logic and Computation*, 5(5):603–630, October 1995.
24. A. Sernadas, C. Sernadas, and J. Ramos. A temporal logic approach to object certification. *Data & Knowledge Engineering*, 19:267–294, 1996.
25. E. Zucca. Implementation of data structures in an imperative framework. In E. Astesiano, G. Reggio, and A. Tarlecki, editors, *Recent Trends in Data Types Specification, Proc. 10th Workshop on Specification of Abstract Data Types joint with the 5th COMPASS Workshop, S.Margherita, Italy, May/June 1994, Selected papers*, pages 483–498. Springer, Berlin, 1995. LNCS 906.

Software Design, Specification, and Verification: Lessons Learned from the Rether Case Study*

Xiaoqun Du, Kevin T. McDonnell, Evangelos Nanos,
Y.S. Ramakrishna, Scott A. Smolka

Department of Computer Science
SUNY at Stony Brook
Stony Brook, NY 11794-4400, USA

Abstract. RETHER is a software-based real-time ethernet protocol developed at SUNY Stony Brook. The purpose of this protocol is to provide guaranteed bandwidth and deterministic, periodic network access to multimedia applications over commodity ethernet hardware. It has been implemented in the FreeBSD 2.1.0 operating system, and is now being used to support the Stony Brook Video Server (SBVS), a low-cost, ethernet LAN-based server providing real-time delivery of video to end-users from the server's disk subsystem.

Using local model checking, as provided by the Concurrency Factory specification and verification environment, we showed (for a particular network configuration) that Rether indeed makes good on its bandwidth guarantees to real-time nodes without exposing non-real-time nodes to the possibility of starvation. In the course of specifying and verifying Rether, we identified an alternative design of the protocol that warranted further study due to potential efficiency gains. Again using model checking, we showed that this alternative design also possesses the properties of interest.

1 Introduction

RETHER is a software-based real-time ethernet protocol developed at SUNY Stony Brook by Tzi-cker Chiueh and Chitra Venkatramani [CV95]. The purpose of this protocol is to provide guaranteed bandwidth and deterministic, periodic network access to multimedia applications over commodity ethernet hardware. It has been implemented in the FreeBSD 2.1.0 operating system, and is now being used to support the Stony Brook Video Server (SBVS), a low-cost, ethernet LAN-based server providing real-time delivery of video to end-users from the server's disk subsystem.

The MAC layer of ethernet uses the CSMA/CD protocol, which provides non-deterministic channel access to the nodes on the network. This form of access is unsuitable for real-time multimedia applications such as video conferencing. Rether is a datalink layer protocol that runs on top of CSMA/CD and requires no modification to the ethernet hardware. It accommodates real-time applications by using a token to regulate the transmission of packets in the network. At any time, only the node that holds the token is allowed to transmit. Therefore, nodes are provided deterministic and contention-free channel access.

* Research supported in part by NSF grants CCR-9505562 and CCR-9705998, and AFOSR grants F49620-95-1-0508 and F49620-96-1-0087.

In discussions with Rether's developers, it became clear that they would welcome some kind of formal assurance that their protocol does indeed deliver guaranteed bandwidth to real-time nodes without running the risk of starving non-real-time nodes. To this end, we set out to formally verify these properties of Rether using the *Concurrency Factory* specification and verification environment [CLSS96]. The primary features of the Factory are its graphical user interface for specification and simulation of hierarchical networks of communicating state machines; its VPL textual specification language for describing protocols involving complex data structures and value passing; and its suite of analysis routines for verifying properties of specifications.

One of the main analysis routines supported by the Factory is *model checking* [CE81, QS82, CES86], a verification technique for determining whether a system specification possesses a property expressed as a temporal logic formula. Model checking has enjoyed wide success in verifying, or finding design errors in, real-life systems. An interesting account of a number of these success stories can be found in [CW96]. A distinguishing aspect of the Factory's model checker is its use of *local model checking*, a technique aimed at combating state explosion by performing state space search in a need-driven fashion.

To carry out the proposed verification of Rether, we encoded the protocol in the Factory's VPL specification language and submitted this specification to the local model checker. A number of temporal logic properties were model checked, including the two mentioned above, and in all cases the specification was shown to possess the property of interest.

In the course of using the Factory to verify Rether, it occurred to us that an alternative design of the protocol might also be worth investigating. Rether, as it is currently implemented in FreeBSD, services the real-time nodes first during any given token rotation cycle; the period of a cycle is determined by the frequency of the real-time data transmissions. After servicing the real-time nodes, non-real-time requests are serviced until the cycle bandwidth is exhausted. We refer to this method as the *real-time first* (RTF) node servicing policy. In our alternative policy, nodes are serviced in sequential order (SQO) by their node ids. One of the benefits of the SQO policy is that, under certain reasonable assumptions, it incurs less token-passing overhead than RTF. This is because a node wishing to transmit real-time and non-real-time data within one cycle may do so in SQO during the same visit of the token. RTF, on the other hand, would require the token to make a second visit to the node in question in order for it to transmit its non-real-time data. SQO also requires less information to be stored in the token: in RTF, the token must maintain a bit vector indicating which nodes are in real-time mode.

In order to verify that the Rether developers could safely use our new policy, we submitted an SQO-based VPL specification of Rether to the Factory's local model checker. As in the original RTF-based protocol, the model checker revealed that all properties of interest were satisfied. Interestingly, our model checking experiments show that the size of the Rether state space goes down by a factor of four in moving from RTF to SQO.

In light of the above, the following lessons were learned from our Rether case study:

1. By requiring one to write an abstract and formally rigorous specification of a

system, specification and verification can have a positive (and perhaps unexpected) influence on software design. In our case, this was the discovery of the SQO node servicing policy. We believe this phenomenon is primarily one of being able to see the forest through the trees once an abstract specification is in hand. This view is consistent with that of Parnas in [Par96], who wrote on the topic of software jewels:

> [These] Programs were not just written; they had been planned, often in some pseudocode or a language other than the actual programming language.

2. Alternative software designs can be shown "equivalent" through verification.
3. An alternative software design may lead to a smaller state space, thereby facilitating model checking and other forms of verification.
4. Interesting properties of real-time protocols can be verified without the use of real-time formalisms, such as timed automata [AD94] or real-time logic [Mok91]. For our Rether case study, we abstracted real time into "time slots" and, in this context, it sufficed to use an untimed value-passing language (VPL) along with a non-real-time temporal logic (the modal mu-calculus [Koz83]). Our use of the time-slots abstraction to model the real-time behavior of the Rether protocol is discussed in greater detail in Section 5.

The structure of the rest of the paper is as follows. Sections 2 and 3 provide overviews of the Concurrency Factory and Rether protocol, respectively. Our alternative software design is the subject of Section 4. Section 5 describes how we specified the protocol in VPL, both for RTF and SQO. Our model checking results are presented in Section 6, and conclusions and directions for future work in Section 7.

2 The Concurrency Factory

The Concurrency Factory [CLSS96] is an integrated toolset for the specification, verification, and implementation of concurrent and distributed real-time systems such as communication protocols and process control systems. The main features of the Factory are: a *graphical user interface* that allows the non-expert to design and simulate concurrent systems using GCCS, a graphical process algebra; a *textual user interface* for VPL; a *suite of verification routines* that currently includes a local model checker with partial-order reduction [RS97] for the modal mu-calculus, a very expressive temporal logic, and a local model checker for a real-time extension of the modal mu-calculus [SS95]; and a *graphical compiler* that transforms GCCS and VPL specifications into executable Facile [TLK96] code.

We briefly describe here the components of the Factory that are most germane to our verification of the Rether protocol: VPL and the local model checker for the modal mu-calculus. VPL is well suited for specifying concurrent systems with non-trivial control structure and data structures, and which involve value passing (as opposed to pure synchronization). VPL-supported data structures include integers of limited size and arrays and records composed of such integers. Structural equivalence of data types is employed, i.e. two integer types are considered the same if their sizes are equal and two records are equivalent when they have fields of the same type appearing in the same order.

A system specification in VPL is a tree-like hierarchy of subsystems. A subsystem is either a *network* or a *process*. A network consists of a collection of subsystems running in parallel and communicating with each other through typed channels. Processes are at the leaves of the hierarchy. Each subsystem, be it a process or a network, consists of a header, local declaration and body. The header specifies a unique name for the subsystem and a list of "formal channels" (by analogy with formal parameters of procedures in programming languages). The names of the formal channels of a subsystem can be used in the body of the subsystem and represent events visible to an external observer.

Declarations local to a network include specifications of the subsystems of the network and channels for communication between subsystems, hidden from the outside world. The body of a network is a parallel composition of its subsystems. A subsystem declared within a network can be used arbitrarily many times; each time a new copy of the subsystem is instantiated with actual channels substituted for the formal ones. Actual channels must match the formal ones introduced in the header and must be declared either as local channels or formal channels of the network immediately containing the subsystem.

Declarations local to a process consist of variable and procedure declarations. Procedure bodies, like process bodies, are sequences of statements. Simple statements of VPL are assignments of arithmetic or boolean expressions to variables, and input/output operations on channels. Complex statements include sequential composition, `if-then-else`, `while-do`, and nondeterministic choice in the form of the `select` statement.

VPL programs can be verified using LMC, the Concurrency Factory's local model checker for the propositional modal mu-calculus. LMC first produces a graph representation of the logical formula under consideration and then computes the product of this graph with the labeled transition system (guaranteed to be finite-state) underlying the VPL program. This "product graph" is constructed on-the-fly: each product graph node has an associated boolean value (representing the value of a subformula in an LTS state) and the value of a node is computed based on the values of its successors. Values of the terminal nodes in the product graph can be decided immediately based on the node itself. Nodes are never constructed unless their values are needed to determine the value of a previously constructed node.

To further reduce the size of the product graph, LMC avoids interleaving process transitions whenever the order of interleaving cannot affect the truth of a logical formula. Intuitively, this is achieved by enlarging the granularity of process steps so as to avoid redundant interleavings. LMC is also equipped with a diagnostic facility that allows the user to request that the contents of the depth-first search stack be displayed whenever a certain "significant event" occurs—for instance, when the search first encounters a state at which a logical variable is determined to be either true or false. This technique can be used to great effect, for instance, to discover execution paths leading to deadlocked states, or to livelock cycles.

3 The Rether Protocol

Rether is a contention-free token bus protocol for the datalink level, designed to run on top of a CSMA/CD physical layer. A network running the protocol normally operates in CSMA/CD mode, transparently switching to Rether mode when one or more nodes generate requests for real-time (RT) connections. An initialization protocol is used to coordinate the switch to Rether mode. Once in Rether mode, a token is used to control access to the medium. That is, a node can transmit data on the network only when it has the token.

The token circulates the network in cycles, each of which is called a *token rotation cycle*. The period of a cycle, the *token cycle time*, is a configurable parameter determined by the frequency of real-time data transmissions. For instance, TCT (as this parameter is called) can be set to 33.3 ms for video applications, which typically transmit data at the rate of 30 frames per second. In each token cycle, all nodes that have successfully made a bandwidth reservation (the so-called "admitted nodes") can send out RT data in accordance with their reservations. In the time remaining in the cycle, nodes are permitted to send out non-real-time (NRT) data. To be fair to NRT transmission requests, part of each cycle, T_{nrt}, is set aside for NRT traffic.

An RT application is admitted into the system by the protocol only if there is sufficient bandwidth in the cycle. That is, suppose this application requests a reservation for an RT transmission of duration $THT_{RT_{new}}$ (where THT stands for "token holding time"). Then this request is granted only if the following inequality holds:

$$\left(\sum_{i \in RT\_set} THT_{RT_i} \right) + THT_{RT_{new}} + T_{nrt} \leq TCT$$

where RT_set is the set of admitted RT nodes, and THT_{RT_i} is the token holding time of the ith RT node. It is precisely this policy that enables the protocol to guarantee cycle bandwidth to RT applications.

Admitted RT nodes are serviced first in a cycle, and we refer to this policy as RTF. A newly admitted RT application adds its node id to RT_set, which is stored in the token as a bit vector. A node releasing RT bandwidth removes its id from RT_set before forwarding the token to the next node. The network reverts back to CSMA/CD mode when the last RT node releases its bandwidth. The token also carries a "residual time" counter, which records the amount of time remaining in a cycle. At the start of a cycle this field is initialized to TCT. Following a data transmission by the token-holding node, the residual time counter is decremented by that node's token holding time before the token is passed to the next node.

The admission policy ensures that at least T_{nrt} time remains in each cycle for NRT traffic. NRT transmissions are scheduled in a round-robin fashion to prevent the possibility of starvation. For this purpose, the token carries a field containing the id of the last node that failed to transmit its NRT data in a given cycle because of insufficient residual time.

To illustrate the behavior of the protocol, and the RTF node servicing policy, consider the example network depicted in Figure 1. RT_set contains 1, 3, and 5 and these nodes are serviced first during each token rotation cycle. Assuming that

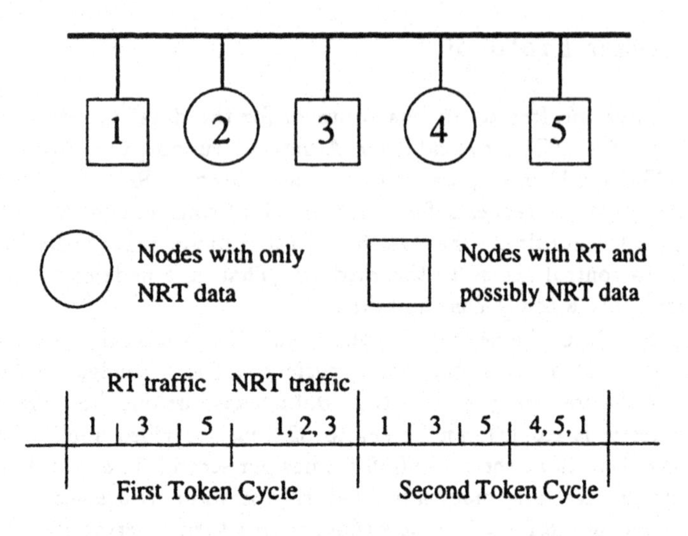

Fig. 1. A Sample Network Configuration.

each cycle can accommodate three NRT transmissions (in addition to the three guaranteed RT transmissions), and that each node has NRT data to transmit, it takes two successive cycles for the NRT transmissions to be serviced in round-robin fashion. In particular, the following sequences of node transmissions are possible in successive cycles:

$$1 - 3 - 5 - 1 - 2 - 3$$
$$1 - 3 - 5 - 4 - 5 - 1$$

4 SQO: An Alternative Node Servicing Policy

As mentioned in the Introduction, in the process of specifying and verifying Rether, we identified an alternative design of the protocol that warranted investigation because of potential efficiency gains. In this version, nodes are serviced in sequential order by their node ids, a policy we refer to as SQO. In order to ensure periodic access to the token by RT nodes, the node with the smallest node id number is the first to receive the token in each cycle. Upon receiving the token, a node will transmit its RT data if it has previously been admitted by the protocol as an RT node. It will also, during the same token visit, transmit a fixed amount of NRT data if: (1) it has NRT data to transmit, and (2) the "next" pointer, which is stored in the token and used to implement round-robin scheduling, indicates that sufficient NRT bandwidth remains in the current cycle to accommodate the node's transmission. The next-pointer is incremented when its value is i and node i has just completed an NRT transmission. Similarly, an NRT node (i.e. a node with only NRT data to transmit) transmits its data only if there is sufficient bandwidth. Otherwise, it simply passes the token to its neighbor. Note that, unlike RTF, there is no need in the SQO policy to store *RT_set* in the token.

To further illustrate the SQO strategy, consider once again the network of Figure 1. The following sequences of node transmissions are possible in successive cycles:

(1-1) – 2 – (3-3) – (4) – 5
(1-1) – (2) – 3 – 4 – (5-5)

where a sequence item of the form (i-i) means that node i transmits both RT and NRT data during the same token visit. Also, an item of the form (i) means that i is an NRT node that transmits no data but rather just passes the token along to its neighbor. At the beginning of the first sequence, the next-pointer is set to 1, which means that the NRT data transmissions of nodes 1, 2, and 3 can be accommodated during this cycle. The value of the next-pointer will be 4 at the beginning of the second sequence, allowing nodes 4, 5, and 1 to transmit NRT data. Comparing these sequences to the corresponding ones for RTF given above, we see that the token visits a total of five nodes per cycle in SQO, and six nodes per cycle in RTF.

In general, SQO will incur less token-passing overhead than RTF when the total number of per-cycle data transmissions (call this m) exceeds the number of nodes on the network (call this n). Moreover, the reduction in overhead increase linearly in $m - n$. If $m < n$, SQO could potentially require more token passing than RTF, depending on the relative ordering of RT and NRT nodes. In practice, though, the conditions favorable to SQO can be expected to occur frequently, and correspond to the situation where the network is not saturated by too many applications with RT demands.

5 VPL Specification of Rether

In this section, we describe how we specified the Rether protocol in VPL for both the original RTF version, and our alternative SQO version. The interested reader can find the VPL source code listings at `http://cs.sunysb.edu/~sas/rether.html`. The key to the specifications, and subsequent model checking, is our abstraction of time into "time slots." That is, each token cycle is divided into a fixed number of time slots, and each RT and NRT transmission consumes one time slot. Since the properties we wish to verify (admitted RT nodes receive their guaranteed cycle bandwidth and NRT transmissions are not starved) do not depend on the exact value of the token holding times, our time slot abstraction is sufficient for this purpose.

Both versions of the protocol are specified in VPL as a network of N+2 processes: `Node_0`, ..., `Node_N-1`, `Token`, and `Bandwidth`. The `Node_i` processes capture the behavior of the various nodes in the network, `Token` represents the Rether token, and `Bandwidth` is the process that nodes interact with to reserve or release cycle bandwidth. A separate process is set aside for the token in order to localize the token-passing logic deployed by the protocol. Modeling the token in this fashion decreases the size of the specification's state space.

Figure 2 depicts the network topology of the specification. In particular, it indicates the names of the channels that processes use to communicate with one another and with the outside world. To simplify the figure, only `Node_0` is depicted;

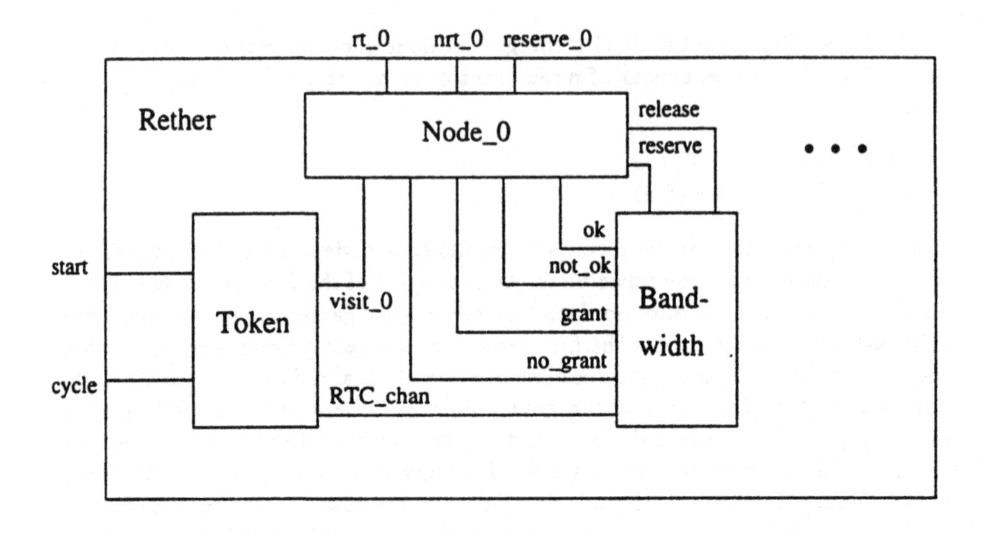

Fig. 2. **Network topology of the specification.**

the other nodes are connected to `Token`, `Bandwidth`, and the outside world in a similar fashion.

The connections to the outside world are for model-checking purposes. That is, actions over these channels will appear in the various modal mu-calculus formulas to be model checked. Each such action represents a pure synchronization and the significance of these actions is as follows:

`start:`	indicates the beginning of a token cycle
`cycle:`	indicates the end of a token cycle
`reserve_i:`	`Node_i` successfully makes a bandwidth reservation
`rt_i:`	`Node_i` performs an RT transmission
`nrt_i:`	`Node_i` performs an NRT transmission

Since the contents of the transmitted data is irrelevant to the correct operation of the protocol, it suffices to use the signals `rt_i` and `nrt_i` in their place.

Process `Bandwidth` is perhaps the simplest of the processes in the specification, and we start with it. It essentially behaves as a counting semaphore whose value should not exceed `RTSlots`, where `RTSlots` is the total number of time slots available in a token cycle for RT data transmissions. `RTSlots` is less then the total number of time slots (`Slots`) in a cycle since some slots are reserved for NRT traffic. An RT node requests a bandwidth reservation via the signal `reserve`. The request is granted if a time slot is available; i.e., if `RT_count` < `RTSlots` where `RT_count` is a local variable that keeps track of the number of RT nodes in the system.

When an RT node is ready to release its reserved bandwidth, it signals `Bandwidth` with `release`. It is ok for the node to release its bandwidth and become an NRT node as long as the system contains at least one RT node at all times. This is to ensure that the protocol remains in Rether mode: the protocol reverts back to

CSMA/CD mode when all RT connections terminate, and we do not model this mode of the protocol. Bandwidth also writes RT_count to channel RTC_chan when Token wants to read the number of RT nodes in the system.

Process Bandwidth is common to the RTF and SQO specifications. The difference in these versions of the protocol lies in the behavior of the other processes in the network. We consider first the behavior of these processes for the RTF version. The Token process determines the order in which the token visits the nodes in the network. It is also responsible for starting and ending the token rotation cycle and updating the information in the token at the beginning of each cycle. To perform these duties, it maintains a local data structure tok_value with the following fields: a bit-vector node[] used to encode *RT_set*; an integer NRT_count indicating the number of time slots available for NRT data transmissions in the current cycle (NRT_count is decremented each time an NRT data transmission occurs); an integer next, which points to the next node with NRT data to be serviced in round-robin fashion; and a boolean variable serving_rt, which indicates whether RT traffic or NRT traffic is currently being serviced.

Token starts a cycle by outputting the signal start to the outside world. It then passes the token to each of the nodes in *RT_set* in order by their node ids. Token passes the token to Node_i by writing the token data structure onto channel visit[i]; when Node_i is finished with the token it sends it back to Token over the same channel. After finishing with the RT nodes, Token circulates the token among the nodes in the system until all remaining time slots are consumed. At this point, Token terminates the cycle by outputting the signal cycle and setting NRT_count to Slots − RT_count (recall that RT_count is maintained by the bandwidth process). It then begins a new cycle.

In the RTF version of Rether, process Node_i first receives the token from process Token into the local variable local_tok. It then checks local_tok.serving_rt to determine if it should call procedure RT_action or NRT_action. (In the RTF model, only an RT node can get the token with serving_rt true.) Procedure RT_action simulates an RT data transmission by emitting signal rt_i, and then nondeterministically chooses to release its bandwidth. If its request to release bandwidth is successful, the node is deleted from *RT_set* and local_tok.node[i] is updated accordingly.

Node_i executes procedure NRT_action when it receives the token and local_tok.serving_rt is false. The following conditions are guaranteed to hold at this point: Node_i is being pointed to by local_tok.next and the value of local_tok.NRT_count is greater than zero. Therefore, it simulates an NRT transmission by emitting signal nrt_i, decrementing local_tok.NRT_count, and incrementing local_tok.next. NRT_action then checks local_tok.node[i] to see if it is an RT node; if not, it nondeterministically chooses to issue a request for bandwidth reservation. If granted, local_tok.node[i] is set to true, making Node_i an RT node, and signal reserve_i is emitted to the outside world, indicating that Node_i has successfully made a bandwidth reservation. Upon completion of NRT_action, Node_i outputs local.tok to Token.

Process Token is somewhat simpler in the SQO-based specification of the protocol than in the RTF-based one. It has simpler token-passing logic—the token is passed from one node to another in sequential order by their node ids—and the token carries less information in it since it no longer stores *RT_set*. In particular, tok_value has the following four fields: RT_count, NRT_count, next, and NRT_enabled. RT_count and NRT_count are the residual number of time slots for RT and NRT data transmissions, respectively, and next and NRT_enabled are used to implement round-robin scheduling of NRT transmissions.

NRT_enabled is set to true by Token if the NRT data transmission of the next node to receive the token can be accommodated during the current cycle. This is the case if the following (somewhat complicated looking) condition is met:

```
NRT_count > 0 & ( next = index | ( index <next &
                                   total_NRT > N - next + index ) )
```

Here index is the id of the next node to receive the token, total_NRT is the total number of time slots available in the current cycle for NRT transmissions, and N is the total number of nodes in the network. The reader is referred to the discussion of the SQO policy in Section 4 for the intuition underlying this logic.

Process Node_i in the SQO case has a local variable mode indicating whether or not the node is an RT node. Similar to the RTF case, once Node_i receives the token, it calls RT_action or NRT_action depending on the value of mode. In RT_action, it emits signal rt_i and decrements local_tok.RT_count to simulate an RT data transmission. If local_tok.NRT_enabled is true, it also emits signal nrt_i and decrements local_tok.NRT_count. Moreover, it increments local_tok.next if local_tok.next = i. As in the RTF case, it can then nondeterministically choose to release its bandwidth reservation; if successful, it switches to NRT_mode.

The SQO version of NRT_action also checks local_tok.NRT_enabled to decide if it can perform an NRT data transmission. If it can, it behaves as does RT_action in this case, after which it may nondeterministically choose to request a bandwidth reservation. If this request is granted, Node_i switches to RT_mode.

6 Model Checking the Rether Protocol

In this section, we summarize the results we obtained applying the Concurrency Factory's local model checker to our VPL specifications of the Rether protocol. To ensure that we are model checking a finite-state system, we fixed the following parameters of the specification at compilation time: the number of nodes in the system is chosen to be 4, i.e. the system contains Node_0 up to Node_3; the total number of time slots in each token rotation cycle (Slots) is 3; and one slot per cycle is reserved for NRT data transmission. Consequently, during each cycle there are either two RT transmissions plus one NRT transmission, or two NRT transmissions plus one RT transmission. Initially Node_0 is designated as an RT node and is pointed to by next. The remaining nodes are initially NRT nodes.

We model checked both versions of the protocol (RTF and SQO) against 14 formulas of the modal mu-calculus, expressing different properties of the system. The syntax of the modal mu calculus makes use of propositional constants *tt* and *ff*, logical variables X, Y and Z, standard logical connectives $\vee$ and $\wedge$, dual modal operators $\langle - \rangle$ and $[-]$, and dual fixed point operators μ (least fixed point) and ν (greatest fixed point). A formula of the form $\langle - \rangle \phi$ is true of a state s if it is possible

Name	Formula
DLF	$\nu X.([-]X \wedge \langle -\rangle tt)$
CC	$\nu X.([-]X \wedge [start]\mu Y.(\langle -\rangle tt \wedge [start]ff \wedge [-cycle]Y))$
RT0	$\nu X.([-]X \wedge [reserve_0]\mu Y.([-cycle]Y \wedge [rt_0]ff \wedge$ $[cycle]\mu Z.(\langle -\rangle tt \wedge [-rt_0]Z \wedge [cycle]ff)))$
RT1	$\nu X.([-]X \wedge [reserve_1]\mu Y.([-cycle]Y \wedge [rt_1]ff \wedge$ $[cycle]\mu Z.(\langle -\rangle tt \wedge [-rt_1]Z \wedge [cycle]ff)))$
RT2	$\nu X.([-]X \wedge [reserve_2]\mu Y.([-cycle]Y \wedge [rt_2]ff \wedge$ $[cycle]\mu Z.(\langle -\rangle tt \wedge [-rt_2]Z \wedge [cycle]ff)))$
RT3	$\nu X.([-]X \wedge [reserve_3]\mu Y.([-cycle]Y \wedge [rt_3]ff \wedge$ $[cycle]\mu Z.(\langle -\rangle tt \wedge [-rt_3]Z \wedge [cycle]ff)))$
NS0	$\nu X.([-]X \wedge [start]\nu Y.([-\{nrt_0, cycle\}]Y \wedge [cycle]\mu Z.([-nrt_0]Z \wedge \langle -\rangle tt)))$
NS1	$\nu X.([-]X \wedge [start]\nu Y.([-\{nrt_1, cycle\}]Y \wedge [cycle]\mu Z.([-nrt_1]Z \wedge \langle -\rangle tt)))$
NS2	$\nu X.([-]X \wedge [start]\nu Y.([-\{nrt_2, cycle\}]Y \wedge [cycle]\mu Z.([-nrt_2]Z \wedge \langle -\rangle tt)))$
NS3	$\nu X.([-]X \wedge [start]\nu Y.([-\{nrt_3, cycle\}]Y \wedge [cycle]\mu Z.([-nrt_3]Z \wedge \langle -\rangle tt)))$
RTT	$\nu X.([-]X \wedge [start]\mu Y.([cycle]ff \wedge \langle -\rangle tt \wedge [-S_{RT}]Y))$
NRT	$\nu X.([-]X \wedge [start]\mu Y.([cycle]ff \wedge \langle -\rangle tt \wedge [-S_{NRT}]Y))$
T3T	$\nu X_0.([-]X_0 \wedge [start]\mu X_1.([-S]X_1 \wedge [cycle]ff \wedge [S]\mu X_2.([-S]X_2 \wedge [cycle]ff \wedge$ $[S]\mu X_3.([-S]X_3 \wedge [cycle]ff \wedge [S]\mu X_4.([-cycle]X_4 \wedge [S]ff)))))$
RTF	$\nu X.([-]X \wedge [S_{NRT}]\mu Y.(\langle -\rangle tt \wedge [-cycle]Y \wedge [S_{RT}]ff))$

Table 1. Formulas we model checked. S is the set $\{rt_i, nrt_i \mid 0 \le i \le 3\}$, S_{RT} is the set $\{rt_i \mid 0 \le i \le 3\}$ and S_{NRT} is the set $\{nrt_i \mid 0 \le i \le 3\}$.

for s to perform an action and reach a state where ϕ holds. Dually, $[-]\phi$ is true of s if necessarily after s performs an action it reaches a state where ϕ holds. In place of '$-$' (any action) a specific action a or an expression of the form '$-a$' (meaning any action except a) can appear inside the modal operators. Fixed point formulas are of the form $\mu X \,.\, \phi(X)$ or $\nu X \,.\, \phi(X)$. Intuitively, μ formulas capture eventuality properties and ν formulas capture invariant properties.

The modal mu-calculus formulas we model checked are listed in Table 1. Their meaning can be understood as follows:

- DLF: Deadlock freedom.
- CC: Cycle completion. This formula states that each token rotation cycle must be completed. It requires that whenever the beginning of a cycle is seen ($[start]$), then eventually the end of the cycle must also be seen by observing the signal *cycle*, and that there cannot be another *start* before the *cycle* is observed.
- RT0 - RT3: Bandwidth guarantee for RT nodes. These formulas state that whenever `Node_i` successfully makes a bandwidth reservation during a token rotation cycle ($[reserve_i]$...$[cycle]$), then during the immediate following cycle (i.e. before a second *cycle* signal is seen), `Node_i` will transmit RT data ($[rt_i]$). Also no RT data transmission for this node is allowed during the cycle in which it made the reservation (the node is not yet an RT node in that cycle).

- NS0 - NS3: No Starvation for NRT traffic. If during a particular cycle, a `Node_i` does not transmit any NRT data (i.e. no nrt_i between *start* and *cycle*), then eventually an nrt_i signal will be observed, meaning that `Node_i` eventually transmits some NRT data.
- RTT: At least one RT data transmission in each cycle. Once a *start* is seen, at least one signal from the set $\{rt_i | 0 \leq i \leq 3\}$ must be observed before the *cycle* signal.
- NRT: At least one NRT data transmission in each cycle. Once a *start* is seen, at least one signal from the set $\{nrt_i | 0 \leq i \leq 3\}$ must be observed before the *cycle* signal.
- T3T: A total of three data transmissions in each cycle. Once a *start* is seen, there must be exactly three signals from the set $\{rt_i, nrt_i | 0 \leq i \leq 3\}$ before the *cycle* signal.
- RTF: RT-first property. This formula states that in each cycle, if an NRT data transmission is observed, no more RT data transmissions can be seen before the end of the cycle. This implies that all RT data transmissions must precede any NRT data transmissions in each cycle.

Our model checking results for the RTF and SQO models are summarized in Tables 2 and 3, respectively. All data is obtained from a Sun4m Sparc machine with 65MB RAM and 520MB swap space. All the formulas turn out to be true for the RTF model, as intended. For the SQO model, all formulas except RTF are true, again as intended.

Formula	Result	States (K)	Transitions (K)	Memory (MB)	Time (min)
DLF	True	49.2	53.4	11.0	80.6
CC	True	93.9	100.2	16.2	125.3
RT0	True	40.5	42.9	7.9	42.6
RT1	True	42.7	45.7	8.2	45.5
RT2	True	43.9	47.0	8.4	47.4
RT3	True	43.4	45.8	8.2	45.7
NS0	True	100.2	107.0	17.2	129.8
NS1	True	100.7	107.6	17.3	129.2
NS2	True	100.8	107.7	17.3	128.9
NS3	True	101.7	108.9	17.5	131.4
RTT	True	44.7	47.2	8.4	47.8
NRT	True	79.9	85.6	14.0	100.2
T3T	True	82.1	86.6	13.0	82.7
RTF	True	52.3	55.4	9.7	59.0

Table 2. Model cheking results for the RTF model.

Within each model, for the formulas RT0 through RT3, there are some small differences in their state count. This is due to the fact that our system is not strictly symmetric, since `Node_0` starts out as an RT node, while the others start out as

Formula	Result	States (K)	Transitions (K)	Memory (MB)	Time (min)
DLF	True	12.0	13.7	3.0	19.9
CC	True	22.6	25.1	4.2	25.4
RT0	True	10.9	12.0	2.3	10.7
RT1	True	11.3	12.7	2.4	12.4
RT2	True	11.5	12.9	2.4	12.1
RT3	True	10.4	11.5	2.2	10.3
NS0	True	19.4	21.4	3.6	22.8
NS1	True	21.8	24.1	4.0	26.2
NS2	True	21.9	24.3	4.0	25.7
NS3	True	25.0	27.8	4.5	31.0
RTT	True	13.7	15.2	2.8	15.1
NRT	True	14.7	16.5	3.0	17.3
T3T	True	19.8	21.7	3.4	18.8
RTF	False	1.8	1.8	0.9	2.6

Table 3. Model checking results for the SQO model.

NRT nodes. Also, the token visits the nodes in a specific order in each cycle. These reasons also explain the minor variation among the data obtained for formulas NS0 through NS3.

Owing to its simpler token-passing logic, the SQO model has a smaller state space than the RTF model: there is roughly a factor of four difference between the number of the states explored by the Concurrency Factory's local model checker. Consequently, the number of transitions, the memory usage, and the execution time are all down by roughly a factor of four in the SQO model.

7 Conclusion

We used the Concurrency Factory's local model checker to verify a number of key properties of the Rether real-time ethernet protocol. In the course of specifying and verifying Rether, we identified an alternative design of the protocol that warranted further study because of potential efficiency gains. Model checking was used to show that this alternative design also possessed the properties of interest.

As for future work, it would be interesting to implement the SQO node servicing policy in the FreeBSD kernel, so that its performance could be compared to the original protocol. It would also be interesting to observe its relative impact on the quality of service (e.g. jitter) in video applications.

Another research direction is to prove Rether correct for an arbitrary number of nodes and cycle time slots. This will require induction-based techniques, e.g. [MK95], symbolic techniques for parameterized systems, e.g. [KMM+97], or more general theorem-proving techniques, e.g. [RSS95].

References

[AD94] R. Alur and D. Dill. The theory of timed automata. *TCS*, 126(2), 1994.

[CE81] E. M. Clarke and E. A. Emerson. Design and synthesis of synchronization skeletons using branching-time temporal logic. In D. Kozen, editor, *Proceedings of the Workshop on Logic of Programs*, Yorktown Heights, volume 131 of *Lecture Notes in Computer Science*, pages 52–71. Springer-Verlag, 1981.

[CES86] E. M. Clarke, E. A. Emerson, and A. P. Sistla. Automatic verification of finite-state concurrent systems using temporal logic specifications. *ACM TOPLAS*, 8(2), 1986.

[CLSS96] R. Cleaveland, P. M. Lewis, S. A. Smolka, and O. Sokolsky. The Concurrency Factory: A development environment for concurrent systems. In R. Alur and T. A. Henzinger, editors, *Computer Aided Verification (CAV '96)*, volume 1102 of *Lecture Notes in Computer Science*, pages 398–401, New Brunswick, New Jersey, July 1996. Springer-Verlag.

[CV95] T. Chiueh and C. Venkatramani. The design, implementation and evaluation of a software-based real-time ethernet protocol. In *Proceedings of ACM SIGCOMM '95*, pages 27–37, 1995.

[CW96] E. M. Clarke and J. M. Wing. Formal methods: State of the art and future directions. *ACM Computing Surveys*, 28(4), December 1996.

[KMM+97] Y. Kesten, O. Maler, M. Marcus, A. Pnueli, and E. Shahar. Symbolic model checking with rich assertional languages. In *Proceedings of the 9th International Conference on Computer-Aided Verification*, Haifa, Israel, July 1997. Springer-Verlag.

[Koz83] D. Kozen. Results on the propositional μ-calculus. *Theoretical Computer Science*, 27:333–354, 1983.

[MK95] K. L. McMillan and R. Kurshan. A structural induction theorem for processes. *Information and Computation*, 117:1–11, 1995.

[Mok91] A. K. Mok. Toward mechanization of real-time system design. In A. van Tilborg and G. Koob, editors, *Foundations of Real-Time Computing: Formal Specifications and Methods*, pages 1–38. Kluwer Academic Publishers, 1991.

[Par96] D. L. Parnas. Why software jewels are rare. *IEEE Computer*, 29(2):57–61, February 1996.

[QS82] J. P. Queille and J. Sifakis. Specification and verification of concurrent systems in Cesar. In *Proceedings of the International Symposium in Programming*, volume 137 of *Lecture Notes in Computer Science*, Berlin, 1982. Springer-Verlag.

[RS97] Y. S. Ramakrishna and S. A. Smolka. Partial-order reduction in the weak modal mu-calculus. In *Proceedings of the Eighth International Conference on Concurrency Theory (CONCUR '97)*. Springer-Verlag, July 1997.

[RSS95] S. Rajan, N. Shankar, and M. K. Srivas. An integration of model checking with automated proof checking. In P. Wolper, editor, *Computer Aided Verification (CAV '95)*, volume 939 of *Lecture Notes in Computer Science*, pages 84–97, Liége, Belgium, July 1995. Springer-Verlag.

[SS95] O. Sokolsky and S. A. Smolka. Local model checking for real-time systems. In *Proceedings of the 7th International Conference on Computer-Aided Verification*. American Mathematical Society, 1995.

[TLK96] B. Thomsen, L. Leth, and T.-M. Kuo. A Facile tutorial. In *Proceedings of the Seventh International Conference on Concurrency Theory (CONCUR '96)*, Vol. 1119 of *Lecture Notes in Computer Science*, pages 278–298. Springer-Verlag, 1996.

Refinement Rules for Real-Time Multi-tasking Programs

C. J. Fidge

Software Verification Research Centre
School of Information Technology
The University of Queensland
Queensland 4072, Australia
cjf@it.uq.edu.au

Abstract. We present several formal program refinement rules for designing multi-tasking programs with hard real-time constraints.

1 Introduction

Practical theories of real-time task schedulability are now available, and are being supported by modern programming languages such as Ada 95. Nevertheless, methods for developing real-time multi-tasking programs, while well understood, still lack the degree of formality demanded by safety-critical applications.

Here we present a set of formal refinement rules for designing real-time multi-tasking programs. The rules introduce the computational components assumed by real-time scheduling theory, and can thus exploit a known schedulability test.

2 Real-time multi-tasking refinement rules

The rules are expressed using timed refinement calculus notation [11]. See Appendices A to C for the definitions used below. For brevity, the rules assume a single input and a single output, both of type integer. Generalisations to multiple variables and other types are straightforward.

2.1 Introduce reaction time

The first rule converts an 'instantaneous' output requirement, at every time t (vertical arrow in Figure 1), to one that permits the system to take up to rct time units to process inputs (horizontal arrow in Figure 1).

The programmer's intuition is to develop a system in which the latest output must always be some function $f : \mathbb{Z} \rightarrow \mathbb{Z}$ of the latest input. However, to be realistic, we accept that the system's view of inputs may be in error by up to $err : \mathbb{N}$ units (shaded area in Figure 1, assuming linear f). Furthermore, this requirement need apply only after some absolute starting time $strt : \mathbb{A}$.

One way to express this requirement is as follows.[1]

[1] For some number a and non-negative number b, $a \pm b$ is $\{c \mid a - b \leqslant c \leqslant a + b\}$.

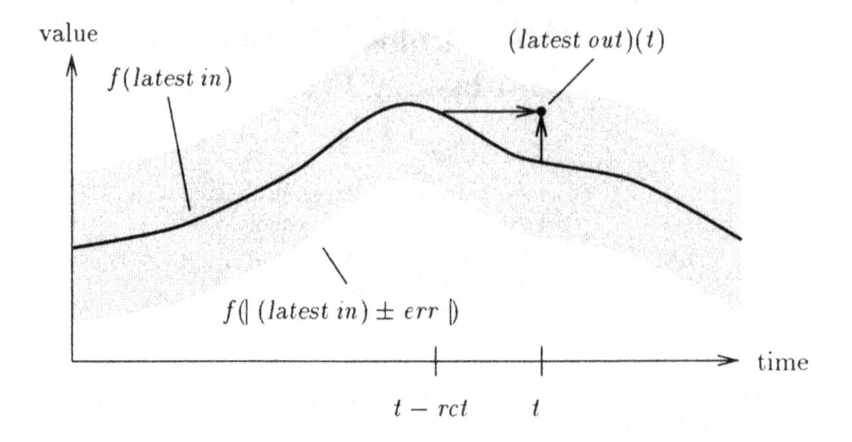

Fig. 1. Introduce reaction time.

OutputError

$in, out : \mathbf{dvar}[\mathbb{Z}]$

$\mathbf{henceforth}_{strt}((latest\ out) \in f(\!|\ (latest\ in) \pm err\ |\!))$

Using *latest out*, rather than *out*, means that we are not obliged to produce a continuously observable value. However there is still a requirement to produce new outputs before the 'latest' one becomes too stale. (An important variant of this predicate, when the rate of change of f is well understood, is to equivalently express the acceptable error on the output values, rather than inputs.)

Predicate *OutputError seems* to require the system to react instantaneously to changes in the input stream. However we know that any practical implementation will take some time to process inputs, so our goal is to devise a refinement rule that explicitly introduces this delay.

To make this possible some knowledge about the rate of change of inputs must be assumed. Let $\delta_{in} : \mathbb{R}$ be the maximum possible change of *in* per time unit. Also, since *in* is a partial function, we require that it may never remain undefined for more than $\mu_{in} : \mathbb{D}$ time units. Thus the input variable may not remain unobservable for too long, and may change value from x to y only at a bounded rate.

InputsBounded

$in : \mathbf{dvar}[\mathbb{Z}]$

$\mathsf{dur}_{\leqslant \mu_{in}}\ \mathbf{whenever}\ \mathsf{undef}\ in$

$\forall x, y : \mathbb{Z} \bullet$

$\quad \mathsf{dur}_{\geqslant |x-y|/\delta_{in}}\ \mathbf{whenever}\ \mathsf{initially}\ (\!-in = x-\!)\ \mathbf{and}\ \mathsf{finally}\ (\!-in = y-\!)$

Our goal is then to refine predicate *OutputError* to one which, more realistically, allows up to $rct : \mathbb{D}$ time units for the system to react to a new input.

The new predicate thus replaces worst-case error *err* with worst-case delay *rct*.

OutputDelay

$in, out : \mathbf{dvar}[\mathbb{Z}]$

$\mathbf{henceforth}_{strt}((latest\ out) \in f(\!|\ recent_{rct}\ in\ |\!))$

In other words, the latest value of *out* is required to be a function of a *recent* value of *in*, no more than *rct* time units out of date. In particular, note the liveness requirement implicit in this predicate. In order to guarantee this property (in the absence of further information about the behaviour of *in*) *out* must be updated at points no further apart than *rct* time units.

The refinement rule thus allows us to trade off acceptable data accuracy against an acceptable processing delay.

Rule 1 (Introduce reaction time) *If* $(rct + \mu_{in}) * \delta_{in} \leqslant err$, *then*

$$+out: [InputsBounded\ ,\ OutputError] \sqsubseteq +out: [\mathrm{true}\ ,\ OutputDelay]\ .$$

The proviso ensures that the introduced processing delay does not increase the data error. Each input processed may be up to $rct + \mu_{in}$ time units out of date in the worst case, so the error may be as great as $(rct + \mu_{in}) * \delta_{in}$. Assumption *InputsBounded* is not needed in any of the other rules below, so is removed.

Proof sketch

$$\begin{array}{l} \quad +out: [InputsBounded\ ,\ OutputError] \\ \sqsubseteq \text{`by law 2 (Appendix A), using rule 1's proviso'} \\ \quad +out: [InputsBounded\ ,\ OutputDelay] \\ \sqsubseteq \text{`by law 1'} \\ \quad +out: [\mathrm{true}\ ,\ OutputDelay] \end{array}$$

2.2 Introduce shared variable

The second rule allows a computation like that specified by *OutputDelay* above to be partitioned into two parts, communicating by a shared variable (Figure 2). Real-time multi-tasking applications use shared variables for internal communication to avoid unknown communication delays [1].

The first component reads input variable *in* and constructs a new variable *shrd*. At all times the latest value of *shrd* must be some function f_1 of the latest input, with a worst-case processing delay of up to rct_1 time units.

Writer

$in, shrd : \mathbf{dvar}[\mathbb{Z}]$

$\mathbf{henceforth}_{strt-rct_2}((latest\ shrd) \in f_1(\!|\ recent_{rct_1}\ in\ |\!))$

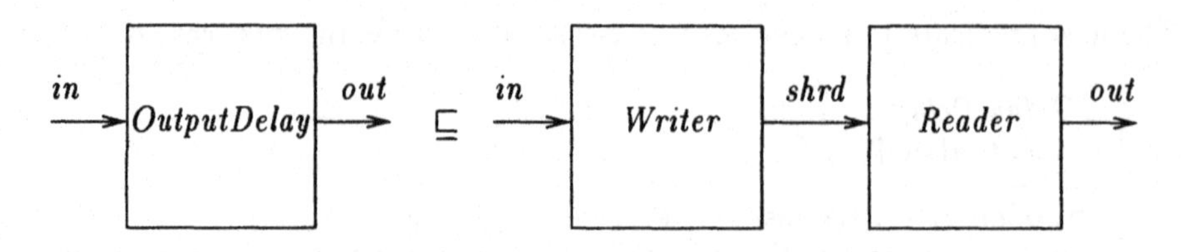

Fig. 2. Introduce shared variable.

Note that a starting time earlier than *strt* has been specified. Duration rct_2 is the acceptable worst-case delay for the *Reader* component below. Since it will take some time for data to move through the two-stage 'pipeline' illustrated in Figure 2, the first component must start *earlier* than the second to ensure that the initial output requirement is met.

The second component reads shared variable *shrd* and constructs required output *out* in the obvious way.

Reader

$shrd, out : \mathbf{dvar}[\mathbb{Z}]$

$\mathbf{henceforth}_{strt}((latest\ out) \in f_2 (\!|\ recent_{rct_2}\ shrd\ |\!))$

The refinement rule thus allows a single specification to be divided into two separate, but interacting, parts.

Rule 2 (Introduce shared variable) *If* $f = f_2 \circ f_1$, $rct_1 + rct_2 \leqslant rct$, *and variable shrd is fresh, then*

$$+out \colon [\mathrm{true}\ ,\ OutputDelay]$$
$$\sqsubseteq |[+out, shrd \colon [\mathrm{true}\ ,\ Writer \wedge Reader] \setminus \{shrd\}]| \,.$$

The first proviso ensures the resulting design has the same functional behaviour, and the second ensures that its end-to-end reaction time has not increased.

The rule generalises readily to multiple readers of the shared variable, or to the case where there are multiple outputs, each with different end-to-end reaction time requirements. Another variant is to use an existing output variable as the shared variable, in which case the hiding operator is not needed. Also it is easy to let f, f_1 and f_2 be relations, rather than functions.

Proof sketch

$$+out \colon [\mathrm{true}\ ,\ OutputDelay]$$
$$\sqsubseteq \text{`by law 3'}$$
$$|[+out, shrd \colon [\mathrm{true}\ ,\ OutputDelay] \setminus \{shrd\}]|$$
$$\sqsubseteq \text{`by law 2, using rule 2's proviso'}$$
$$|[+out, shrd \colon [\mathrm{true}\ ,\ Writer \wedge Reader] \setminus \{shrd\}]|$$

2.3 Introduce periodic behaviour

The next rule allows a 'continuous' output requirement (shaded area in Figure 3) to be replaced by one where outputs change at discrete points only ('staircase' line in Figure 3).

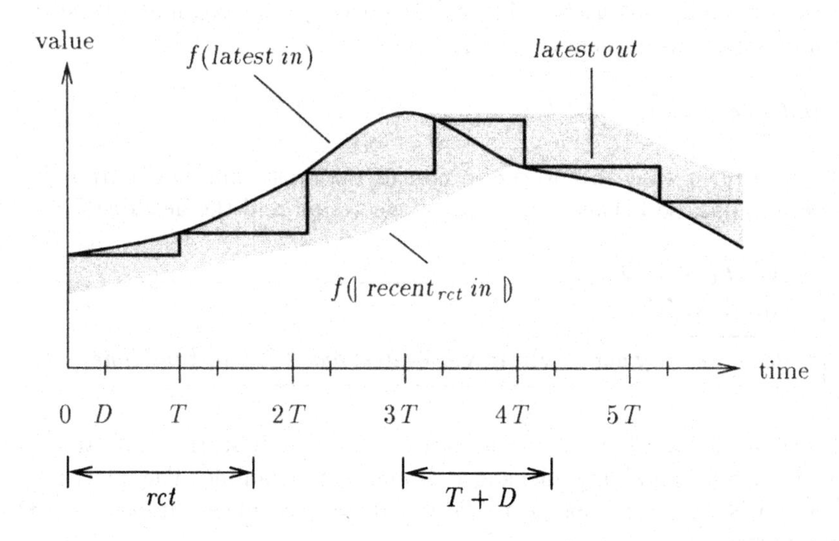

Fig. 3. Introduce periodic behaviour.

Our goal is to refine a predicate such as *OutputDelay* in Section 2.1 (or the identically-structured *Writer* and *Reader* predicates in Section 2.2) to one that produces new outputs at intervals determined by a *period* $T : \mathbb{D}$, within a *deadline* $D : \mathbb{D}$, where $D \leqslant T$ [1].

To ensure that the required output values are available at time *strt*, we must account for any delay in producing the *first* output. Since it may take up to D time units to produce each output, we must begin the periodic behaviour at least D time units *before* time *strt*. Let $B : \mathbb{A}$ mark the moment by which the process must begin its periodic behaviour, where $B \leqslant strt - D$. Therefore, the nth period extends from absolute time $B + n * T$ to $B + (n+1) * T$, and the nth deadline occurs at time $B + n * T + D$.

There are two requirements of interest. Firstly, given the above constants, let *atdeadline* be intervals starting after the beginning of the nth period, and ending at exactly the nth deadline.

$$atdeadline == \{n : \mathbb{N};\ t : \mathbb{D} \mid t < D \bullet (B + n * T + t) \mathrel{\circ\circ} (B + n * T + D)\}$$

Then the latest output must be up-to-date at each deadline.

$$
\begin{array}{|l}
\hline
\textit{OutputByDeadline} \\
in, out : \mathbf{dvar}[\mathbb{Z}] \\
\hline
\mathsf{finally}\ (\!-(\textit{latest out}) \in f(\!|\ \textit{recent}_D\ in\ |\!)\!-\!)\ \mathbf{whenever}\ \textit{atdeadline} \\
\hline
\end{array}
$$

The value of *latest out* at the time each deadline expires is thus defined using an input value no older than the beginning of the period, i.e., D time units ago.

Secondly, let *initdone* be all intervals starting *after* beginning time B. (We put no restrictions on behaviour *before* this time.)

$$initdone == \{a, z : \mathbb{A} \mid B \leqslant a \wedge a < z \bullet a \circ\circ z\}$$

Then we expect that the process produces (at most) one new output in each period and does so between the start of the period and the deadline.

$$
\begin{array}{|l}
\hline
\textit{OncePerPeriod} \\
out : \mathbf{dvar}[\mathbb{Z}] \\
\hline
\textit{atdeadline}\ \mathbf{fby}\ \mathsf{dur}_{>0}\ \mathbf{whenever}\ (\!|\textit{latest out} \in \mathbb{Z}|\!)\ \mathbf{and}\ \textit{initdone} \\
\hline
\end{array}
$$

In other words, *latest out* may exhibit a new value only starting at a time before a deadline, and remaining unchanged *beyond* that deadline. The latter property forces any subsequent change to *latest out* to take place after (at least) the beginning of the *next* period.

Together these two predicates define a periodic output behaviour.

$$PeriodicReq \mathrel{\widehat{=}} OutputByDeadline \wedge OncePerPeriod$$

The refinement rule then allows a specification that has a 'continuous' output requirement to be satisfied by one that produces outputs only periodically.

Rule 3 (Introduce periodic behaviour) *If* $T + D \leqslant rct$, *then*

$$+out\colon [\mathrm{true}\ , OutputDelay] \sqsubseteq +out\colon [\mathrm{true}\ , PeriodicReq]\,.$$

The proviso ensures that the separation between two outputs in adjacent periods is no greater than the required reaction time. The worst case is when an output occurs immediately after the start of the nth period and the next output does not appear until just before the $(n+1)^{\mathrm{th}}$ deadline [2].

The rule generalises easily for a specification containing the conjunction of several *OutputDelay* predicates, so that they can be individually refined to corresponding *PeriodReq* predicates. Each such predicate may have a different reaction time requirement and consequent period and deadline.

Proof sketch Immediate, via law 2, justified using rule 3's proviso.

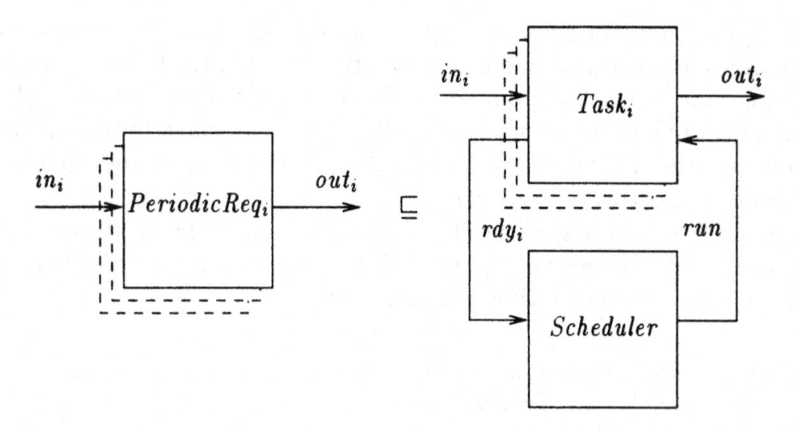

Fig. 4. Introduce scheduling policy.

2.4 Introduce scheduling policy

The final rule introduces a particular scheduling policy into the model. In this case we assume static-priority, non-preemptive scheduling [3]. The refinement both transforms periodic requirements into task specifications, and simultaneously introduces a specification of the scheduler itself (Figure 4) [4].

Let there be n $PeriodicReq_i$ requirements, as defined in Section 2.3, ordered by unique static *base priorities* [1], ranging from lowest priority 1 to highest n. Let identifier 0 denote 'no task'.

For some task i, define its periods as multiples of T_i starting from absolute time B_i.

$$period_i == \{n : \mathbb{N} \bullet (B_i + n * T_i) \circ\circ (B_i + (n+1) * T_i)\}$$

Ideally task i is ready to run at the start of every such period, as indicated via boolean variable rdy_i. Furthermore, i may *arrive*, i.e., become ready [1], only at the start of a period, *except* when the preceding ready interval overran, in which case the task becomes ready again immediately.

$ReadyPeriodically_i$

rdy_i : **fvar**$[\mathbb{B}]$

initially $(\!-\, rdy_i -\!)$ **whenever** $period_i$

after$_0$ $period_i$ **or** preceding$_0$($(\!-\, rdy_i -\!)$ **and** dur$_{> T_i}$) **whenever** $(\!\!\mid rdy_i -\!)$

Although allowing for the possibility of overruns makes this predicate complex, it means each task specification is robust enough not to need assumptions about other system components.

ReadyPeriodically$_i$ leaves the duration of each ready interval unbounded. To correct this we state each task's obligation not to consume more than $C_i : \mathbb{D}$ units of processor time at each invocation, its worst-case *computation time*, where $C_i \leqslant D_i$ [1]. For simplicity, let C_i incorporate the run-time kernel overheads associated with scheduling an invocation of task i [1]. For non-preemptive scheduling this is the time required for the scheduler to select i to run, plus the time required to resume execution of i, plus the time required to suspend i when it completes the invocation [3]. (Subsequent development of the task code [5] must confirm this timing behaviour.)

Thus, task i must *suspend* itself, i.e., become non-ready [3], whenever it has been ready and running for C_i time units. Variable *run*, constructed by the scheduler, denotes which task is running, if any.

$$\boxed{\begin{array}{l} \textit{WorstCaseExecTime}_i \\ \hline rdy_i : \mathbf{fvar}[\mathbb{B}];\ run : \mathbf{fvar}[0 \mathinner{..} n] \\ \hline \mathsf{sumdur}_{\leqslant C_i}\ (\!\!\vdash run = i \dashv\!\!)\ \mathbf{whenever}\ (\!\!\vdash rdy_i \dashv\!\!) \end{array}}$$

(The sumdur operator is general enough to allow for the possibility that i is preempted, although we never expect this to happen.)

We require the latest output to be up-to-date by the end of each invocation.

$$\boxed{\begin{array}{l} \textit{OutputByEndReady}_i \\ \hline out_i : \mathbf{dvar}[\mathbb{Z}];\ rdy_i : \mathbf{fvar}[\mathbb{B}] \\ \hline \mathsf{finally}\ (\!\!\vdash latest\ out_i \in f_i(\!|\ since_{rdy_i}\ in_i\ |\!) \dashv\!\!)\ \mathbf{whenever}\ (\!\!\vdash rdy_i \dashv\!\!\!\!\dashv) \end{array}}$$

In other words, task i may stop being ready only when it has guaranteed that the latest observable output is consistent with an observable input dating back no further than the time the task became ready. (The ultimate task implementation will be even more restrictive, using an input value dating back no further than the time the scheduler *released* [1] the task invocation.)

The task is expected to produce at most one new output per invocation. There may thus be only a single change to *latest* out_i during each ready interval. We define $initdone_i$, using B_i, as in Section 2.3.

$$\boxed{\begin{array}{l} \textit{OncePerInvocation}_i \\ \hline out_i : \mathbf{dvar}[\mathbb{Z}];\ rdy_i : \mathbf{fvar}[\mathbb{B}] \\ \hline (\!\!\vdash rdy_i \dashv\!\!\!\!\dashv)\ \mathbf{fby}\ \mathsf{dur}_{>0}\ \mathbf{whenever}\ (\!\!\vdash\!\!\!\!\vdash latest\ out_i \in \mathbb{Z} \dashv\!\!\!\!\dashv)\ \mathbf{and}\ initdone_i \end{array}}$$

(Again, subsequent task refinement will impose a further restriction that out_i can change only when task i is ready *and* running.)

Collectively these requirements specify the behaviour of a periodic task.

$$\begin{aligned} Task_i \mathrel{\widehat{=}} & \ ReadyPeriodically_i \wedge WorstCaseExecTime_i \\ & \wedge OutputByEndReady_i \wedge OncePerInvocation_i \end{aligned}$$

All timing constraints on outputs in our task model are now *relative* to times when a task invocation arrives or suspends itself. Compare predicates *OutputByDeadline* and *OncePerPeriod* from Section 2.3 with *OutputByEndReady* and *OncePerInvocation*, respectively. No absolute timing requirements remain. Proof that each task produces outputs at the correct *absolute* times is dependent on its interaction with other tasks, via the scheduler.

The other requirement for the refinement rule is a model of the scheduler itself. The goal of the scheduler is to construct schedule *run* using the various readiness indicators. It has four distinct properties.

At any time t, when all *rdy* flags are defined, let *highest* be the ready task with the highest priority, or 0 if no task is ready. Let vector $\tilde{rdy}$ denote $rdy_1, \ldots, rdy_n$.

$$highest == \lambda\, t : \mathbb{A} \mid t \in \operatorname{dom} \tilde{rdy} \bullet max(\{0\} \cup \{i : 1 \,..\, n \mid rdy_i(t)\})$$

The scheduler may *release* [1] task i, i.e., start it running, only if i is the highest-priority ready task.

ResumeReadyTasks

$$run : \mathbf{fvar}[0 \,..\, n];\ \tilde{rdy} : \mathbf{fvar}[\mathbb{B}]$$

$$\bigwedge_{i \in 0..n} \mathsf{initially} \lceil highest = i \rceil \ \mathbf{whenever} \lceil\!\lceil run = i \rceil$$

A ready task i may therefore initially suffer *interference* due to higher-priority tasks that are given precedence [1]. (Predicate *ResumeReadyTasks* reacts instantaneously because we have absorbed scheduling overheads into the task computation times. It should not be used to predict which task will be released at a particular moment. Scheduler models incorporating explicit run-time overheads [4] reveal the presence of nondeterministic *release jitter* [1].)

The scheduler must release *some* task whenever one or more is ready [7].

NoUnnecessaryIdling

$$run : \mathbf{fvar}[0 \,..\, n];\ \tilde{rdy} : \mathbf{fvar}[\mathbb{B}]$$

$$\lceil run \neq 0 \rceil \ \mathbf{whenever}\ \mathbf{or}_{i \in 1..n} \lceil rdy_i \rceil$$

Having started some task i running, the scheduler must let it continue, without preemption, until the task voluntarily *suspends* itself [3].

NoPreemption

$$run : \mathbf{fvar}[0 \,..\, n];\ \tilde{rdy} : \mathbf{fvar}[\mathbb{B}]$$

$$\bigwedge_{i \in 1..n} \lceil run = i \rceil \ \mathbf{whenever} \lceil rdy_i \rceil \ \mathbf{and}\ \mathsf{initially} \lceil run = i \rceil$$

Release of some ready task i may thus initially be *blocked* by a lower priority task which is already running when i arrives [1].

Finally, the scheduler may not allow a task to run when it is no longer ready.

SuspendNonReadyTasks

$run : \mathbf{fvar}[0 \mathinner{..} n];\ \tilde{rdy} : \mathbf{fvar}[\mathbb{B}]$

$\bigwedge_{i \in 1..n} (\!- run \neq i -\!)\ \mathbf{whenever}\ (\!- \neg\ rdy_i -\!)$

Collectively these requirements specify the behaviour of a non-preemptive, static-priority scheduler.

$$\begin{aligned} Scheduler \mathrel{\widehat{=}}\ & ResumeReadyTasks \wedge NoUnnecessaryIdling \\ & \wedge NoPreemption \wedge SuspendNonReadyTasks \end{aligned}$$

The refinement rule then allows a set of periodic requirements to be refined to a set of concurrent tasks controlled by a run-time scheduler. Let $\tilde{out}$ denote $out_1, \ldots, out_n$.

Rule 4 (Introduce scheduling policy) *If variables run and* rdy_1 *to* rdy_n *are fresh, and for each process requirement i, from* 1 *to n,*[2,3]

$$\begin{aligned} & R_i \leqslant D_i\,,\ \textit{where}\ R_i = r_i + C_i \\ & \qquad \textit{and}\ \ r_i = \max_{k=1}^{i-1} C_k + \sum_{j=i+1}^{n} \left(\left\lfloor \frac{r_i}{T_j} \right\rfloor + 1 \right) C_j\,, \end{aligned}$$

then

$$\begin{aligned} & +\tilde{out}\colon [\text{true}\,, (\wedge\, i : 1 \mathinner{..} n \bullet PeriodicReq_i)] \\ \sqsubseteq\ & |[\, (\|\ i : 1 \mathinner{..} n \bullet +out_i, rdy_i\colon [\text{true}\,, Task_i]) \\ & \quad \|\ +run\colon [\text{true}\,, Scheduler] \setminus \{run, \tilde{rdy}\}\,]|\,. \end{aligned}$$

The proviso is a real-time *schedulability test* [6]. For each task i it checks that i's worst-case *response time* R_i is less than its specified deadline D_i [3]. Under a non-preemptive scheduling policy, R_i is the worst-case computation time C_i of the current task invocation, plus the time spent waiting for the task to be released. The task's worst-case *release time* r_i is the worst-case blocking time due to a single invocation of a lower-priority task k, plus the worst-case interference due to arrivals of higher-priority tasks j during interval r_i (at least one for each higher-priority task) [3].

After applying this rule we are free to further develop each task in isolation, thanks to the monotonicity properties of parallel composition [10, p.8].

---

[2] For some number x, $\lfloor x \rfloor$ is $max\{y : \mathbb{Z} \mid y \leqslant x\}$.

[3] Let max and $\sum$ of the empty set both be 0.

Proof sketch

$$+\tilde{out}\colon [\text{true}\ , (\bigwedge i : 1\,..\,n \bullet \mathit{PeriodicReq}_i)]$$
$$\sqsubseteq \text{`by law 3'}$$
$$|[+\tilde{out}, \tilde{rdy}, run\colon [\text{true}\ , (\bigwedge i : 1\,..\,n \bullet \mathit{PeriodicReq}_i)] \setminus \{run, \tilde{rdy}\}]|$$
$$\sqsubseteq \text{`by law 2, using rule 4's proviso'}$$
$$|[+\tilde{out}, \tilde{rdy}, run\colon [\text{true}\ , (\bigwedge i : 1\,..\,n \bullet \mathit{Task}_i) \wedge \mathit{Scheduler}] \setminus \{run, \tilde{rdy}\}]|$$
$$\sqsubseteq \text{`by law 4, } n \text{ times'}$$
$$|[(\| \; i : 1\,..\,n \bullet +out_i, rdy_i\colon [\text{true}\ , \mathit{Task}_i]) \;\|\; +run\colon [\text{true}\ , \mathit{Scheduler}] \setminus \{run, \tilde{rdy}\}]|$$

In the second step we are required to prove that a set of periodically-arriving tasks, running under a non-preemptive scheduling policy, will always meet their specified deadlines. This is exactly the problem that scheduling theory answers. Therefore, as long as we are confident that our models of the tasks and scheduler accurately capture the computational assumptions used by the theory, we can appeal to the results in that field and conclude that, if the schedulability test appearing as a proviso to rule 4 is true [3], then all deadlines will indeed be met [1]. (See the work of Yuhua and Chaochen [14], Liu, Joseph & Janowski [9], and Liu & Joseph [8] for detailed proofs of schedulability in a formal setting.)

3 Conclusion

We have defined a set of refinement rules for designing real-time multi-tasking programs, corresponding to natural development steps. Elsewhere we show the resulting model's correspondence to Ada 95 code [4], and explain how the functional and timing requirements of individual tasks can be refined to sequential programming language statements [5].

Acknowledgements Thanks to Alan Burns, Ian Hayes, Peter Kearney, Brendan Mahony, Maris Ozols, Mark Utting and the anonymous referees for their many helpful corrections. This research is funded by the Information Technology Division of the Defence Science and Technology Organisation.

References

1. N. Audsley, A. Burns, M. Richardson, K. Tindell, and A. Wellings. Applying new scheduling theory to static priority pre-emptive scheduling. *Software Engineering Journal*, 8(5):284–292, September 1993.
2. A. Burns and A. J. Wellings. HRT-HOOD: A structured design method for hard real-time systems. *Real-Time Systems*, 6(1):73–114, January 1994.
3. A. Burns and A. J. Wellings. Simple Ada 95 tasking models for high integrity applications. Department of Computer Science, University of York, May 1996.

4. C. J. Fidge. Modelling real-time multi-tasking systems with timed traces. In *Proc. Third Australasian Conference on Parallel and Real-Time Systems*, pages 94–100, Brisbane, September 1996.
5. I. J. Hayes and M. Utting. Coercing real-time refinement: A transmitter. In D. J. Duke and A. S. Evans, editors, *BCS-FACS Northern Formal Methods Workshop, 1996*, Electronic Workshops in Computing. Springer-Verlag, 1997. http://www.springer.co.uk/ewic/workshops/NFM96/.
6. M. Joseph and P. Pandya. Finding response times in a real-time system. *The Computer Journal*, 29(5):390–395, 1986.
7. Z. Liu. Specification and verification in the duration calculus. In M. Joseph, editor, *Real-Time Systems—Specification, Verification and Analysis*, chapter 7, pages 182–228. Springer-Verlag, 1996.
8. Z. Liu and M. Joseph. Formalizing real-time scheduling as program refinement. In *Proc. 4th AMAST Workshop on Real-Time Systems, Concurrency and Distributed Software*, Mallorca, May 1997.
9. Z. Liu, M. Joseph, and T. Janowski. Verification of schedulability for real-time programs. *Formal Aspects of Computing*, 7(5):510–532, 1995.
10. B. Mahony. Using the refinement calculus for dataflow processes. Technical Report 94-32, Software Verification Research Centre, October 1994.
11. B. P. Mahony. The refinement calculus and data-flow processes. In *Proc. Second Australasian Refinement Workshop*, pages 1–28, Brisbane, September 1992.
12. B. P. Mahony and I. J. Hayes. A case-study in timed refinement: A mine pump. *IEEE Transactions on Software Engineering*, 18(9):817–826, September 1992.
13. C. Millerchip, B. Mahony, and I. J. Hayes. The generic problem competition: A whole system specification of the boiler system. Software Verification Research Centre, University of Queensland, June 1993.
14. Z. Yuhua and Z. Chaochen. A formal proof of the deadline driven scheduler. In H. Langmaack, W.-P. de Roever, and J. Vytopil, editors, *Formal Techniques in Real Time and Fault Tolerant Systems*, volume 863 of *Lecture Notes in Computer Science*, pages 756–775. Springer-Verlag, 1994.
15. C. Zhou. Duration calculi: An overview. In D. Bjorner, M. Broy, and I. Pottosin, editors, *Formal Methods in Programming and Their Applications*, volume 735 of *Lecture Notes in Computer Science*, pages 256–266. Springer-Verlag, 1993. Extended abstract.

A The timed refinement calculus

The *timed refinement calculus* [11] represents behaviour over time using traces, and defines specifications as trace-constructing predicate transformers.

A *timed specification statement* consists of three parts [11, p.7].

$$+\tilde{v}\colon [A \,,\, E]$$

The *frame* vector $\tilde{v}$ lists those variables *constructed* by this statement. The *assumption* predicate A defines the statement's environment; A may refer to external variables $\tilde{u}$, but not $\tilde{v}$. The *effect* predicate E defines the statement's behaviour; E may refer to both $\tilde{u}$ and $\tilde{v}$.

Each constructed variable v in $\tilde{v}$ is a *timed trace*, i.e., a function from the absolute time domain $\mathbb{A}$ to some type T, modelling the observable values of v over all time. (Gaps in the domain indicate no observable value at that time.)

$$v : \mathbb{A} \nrightarrow T$$

Specification statements can be *composed* in parallel [11, p.14].

$$+\tilde{x}:[A_1 , E_1] \parallel +\tilde{y}:[A_2 , E_2]$$

The first component constructs timed-trace variables $\tilde{x}$, assuming A_1, a predicate on $\tilde{u}$ and $\tilde{y}$, with effect E_1, a predicate on $\tilde{u}$, $\tilde{x}$ and $\tilde{y}$. Similarly for the second component, with the roles of $\tilde{x}$ and $\tilde{y}$ reversed. Vectors $\tilde{u}$, $\tilde{x}$ and $\tilde{y}$ must be mutually disjoint. Both parallel components thus contribute to the environment of the other.

Several fundamental refinement laws are then derived via the *refinement* relation '$\sqsubseteq$' [11, §4].

Law 1 (Weaken assumption) *If* $A_1 \Rrightarrow A_2$, *then* [11, p.10]

$$+\tilde{v}:[A_1 , E] \sqsubseteq +\tilde{v}:[A_2 , E] .$$

The $\Rrightarrow$ operator states that $A_1 \Rightarrow A_2$ is true for all variable values [11, p.4].

Law 2 (Strengthen effect) *If* $A \Rrightarrow (\forall \tilde{v} \bullet E_2 \Rightarrow E_1)$, *then* [11, p.10]

$$+\tilde{v}:[A , E_1] \sqsubseteq +\tilde{v}:[A , E_2] .$$

Law 3 (Introduce local constructions) *If variables in $\tilde{x}$ are fresh, then* [11, p.16]

$$+\tilde{v}:[A , E] \sqsubseteq |[+\tilde{v}, \tilde{x}:[A , E] \setminus \{\tilde{x}\}]| .$$

The $|[\cdots \setminus \{\tilde{x}\}]|$ operator scopes local constructed variables $\tilde{x}$ [11, p.16].

Law 4 (Introduce parallel composition) *If vectors $\tilde{x}$ and $\tilde{y}$ are disjoint, then* [12]

$$+\tilde{x}, \tilde{y}:[A_1 \wedge A_2 , E_1 \wedge E_2] \sqsubseteq +\tilde{x}:[A_1 , E_1] \parallel +\tilde{y}:[A_2 , E_2] .$$

The composition operator is associative [11, p.15] so this law readily generalises to arbitrary numbers of parallel processes. Variables $\tilde{x}$ and $\tilde{y}$ may be free throughout E_1 and E_2 [13, p.7].

B Interval notations

Interval operators are used in predicates on timed-traces to elide references to the absolute time domain. We use the following Z-based operators [13].

Let the absolute time domain $\mathbb{A}$, and durations of time $\mathbb{D}$, be continuous, as modelled by the reals.

$$\mathbb{A} == \mathbb{R} \qquad\qquad \mathbb{D} == \mathbb{R}_+$$

We represent an open interval from times a to z, exclusive, as follows.

$$a \circ\circ z == \{t : \mathbb{A} \mid a < t < z\}$$

A *timed history predicate* TH is a predicate on a number of time-indexed functions $\tilde{v}$ without time dereferencing. Let $times(TH)$ be the set of times when TH is true, i.e., points when all functions v in $\tilde{v}$ have a defined value, and expression 'TH' is true when each 'v' it contains is replaced by '$v(t)$' [13].

$$times(TH) = \{t : \mathbb{A} \mid t \in \operatorname{dom} \tilde{v} \wedge TH\left[\frac{\tilde{v}(t)}{\tilde{v}}\right]\}$$

Interval discriminator brackets construct sets of intervals during which a timed history predicate is true. For instance, the set of all open intervals during which TH is true, with the right-hand end maximal, is defined as follows [13].

$$(\!\!- TH \mid\!\!) == \{a, z : \mathbb{A} \mid a < z \wedge a \circ\circ z \subseteq times(TH) \wedge z \notin times(TH) \bullet a \circ\circ z\}$$

Similarly for other combinations of the discriminator brackets, $(\!\!-$, $-\!\!)$, $(\!\!\mid$, and $\mid\!\!)$.

We can refer to intervals during which a timed variable v is *not* defined.

$$\mathsf{undef}\ v == \{a, z : \mathbb{A} \mid a < z \wedge a \circ\circ z \cap \operatorname{dom} v = \varnothing \bullet a \circ\circ z\}$$

Logic-like operators are defined over interval discriminators ID using set operators [13].

$$ID_1 \ \mathbf{and}\ ID_2 == ID_1 \cap ID_2 \qquad ID_1 \ \mathbf{whenever}\ ID_2 == ID_1 \supseteq ID_2$$
$$ID_1 \ \mathbf{or}\ ID_2 == ID_1 \cup ID_2 \qquad ID_1 \ \mathbf{iff}\ ID_2 == ID_1 = ID_2$$

The "followed by" operator constructs those intervals where the end of an interval from ID_1 exactly meets the beginning of an interval from ID_2 [15].

$$ID_1 \ \mathbf{fby}\ ID_2 == \{a, m, z : \mathbb{A} \mid a \circ\circ m \in ID_1 \wedge m \circ\circ z \in ID_2 \bullet a \circ\circ z\}$$

A number of interval discriminator modifiers are available [13]. For instance, the $\mathsf{initially}$ ($\mathsf{finally}$) operator constructs all intervals that begin (end) with an interval from set ID, of duration d.

$$\mathsf{initially}_d\ ID == \{a, z, z' : \mathbb{A} \mid a \circ\circ z \in ID \wedge z - a = d \wedge z \leqslant z' \bullet a \circ\circ z'\}$$
$$\mathsf{finally}_d\ ID == \{a, z, a' : \mathbb{A} \mid a \circ\circ z \in ID \wedge z - a = d \wedge a' \leqslant a \bullet a' \circ\circ z\}$$

Similarly, the **after** (**preceding**) operator constructs all intervals that begin d time units before (after) an interval from ID begins (ends).

$$\mathsf{after}_d\ ID == \{a, z, a', z' : \mathbb{A} \mid a \mathrel{\circ\circ} z \in ID \wedge a - a' = d \wedge a' < z' \bullet a' \mathrel{\circ\circ} z'\}$$

$$\mathsf{preceding}_d\ ID == \{a, z, a', z' : \mathbb{A} \mid a \mathrel{\circ\circ} z \in ID \wedge a' - z = d \wedge a' < z' \bullet a' \mathrel{\circ\circ} z'\}$$

We also define two operators that allow us to refer to interval durations. Firstly, all open intervals of length d are defined as follows.

$$\mathsf{dur}_d == \{a, z : \mathbb{A} \mid z - a = d \bullet a \mathrel{\circ\circ} z\}$$

Secondly, we want to find the total time for which some property holds in an interval. Let *overlaps* define the set of *longest* intervals from interval discriminator ID that intersect some set of times A.

$$overlaps(ID, A) = \{a, z : \mathbb{A} \mid a \mathrel{\circ\circ} z \in ID \wedge a \mathrel{\circ\circ} z \subseteq A \wedge (\nexists B : ID \bullet B \subseteq A \wedge a \mathrel{\circ\circ} z \subset B)\}$$

This returns pairs consisting of the infimum a and supremum z of such intervals, rather than the intervals themselves. Then we define all intervals for which the total duration of time 'overlapped' by intervals from ID is d as follows.

$$\mathsf{sumdur}_d\ ID == \{a, z : \mathbb{A} \mid \textstyle\sum_{X \in overlaps(ID, a \circ\circ z)} (second\, X - first\, X) = d \bullet a \mathrel{\circ\circ} z\}$$

In all definitions above the "$= d$" test can be overridden by including an alternative comparator in the subscript. Omitting the subscript entirely admits any value of d [13].

We often want to assert that a timed history predicate TH is always true [13]. Below we qualify this requirement in two ways, however. Firstly, we expect TH to be true only after some absolute time a. This gives freedom during an initialisation period. Secondly, we expect TH to be true only when all variables $\tilde{v}$ it refers to are defined. This allows the predicate to be applied to partial functions.

$$\mathbf{henceforth}_a(TH) == \forall t : \mathbb{A} \mid t \geqslant a \wedge t \in \operatorname{dom} \tilde{v} \bullet TH \left[\frac{\tilde{v}(t)}{\tilde{v}}\right]$$

Finally, the variables in our model fall into two categories, both modellable using open intervals [13]. 'Digital' variables can change value only by becoming undefined.

$$
\begin{array}{l}
[T] \\
\hline
\mathbf{dvar} : \mathbb{P}(\mathbb{A} \mathrel{+\!\!\!\rightarrow} T) \\
\hline
\forall f : \mathbb{A} \mathrel{+\!\!\!\rightarrow} T \bullet \\
\quad f \in \mathbf{dvar}[T] \Leftrightarrow \\
\quad\quad \forall a, z : \mathbb{A} \mid a < z \wedge a \mathrel{\circ\circ} z \subseteq \operatorname{dom} f \bullet \# f(\!| a \mathrel{\circ\circ} z |\!) = 1 \\
\quad\quad \wedge \forall t : \operatorname{dom} f \bullet \\
\quad\quad\quad \exists b, y : \mathbb{A} \mid b < y \wedge b \mathrel{\circ\circ} y \subseteq \operatorname{dom} f \bullet t \in b \mathrel{\circ\circ} y
\end{array}
$$

In other words, in a contiguous interval from a to z where **dvar** function f is defined, f has only a single value, i.e., f exhibits a 'stepped' graph. Also, any point t for which f is defined must be part of some interval from b to y over which f is continuously defined, i.e., f cannot be defined at isolated points.

It is also often useful in specifications to use imaginary 'flag' variables in a specification that can change value *only* instantaneously [13].

$$
\begin{array}{l}
[T] \\
\hline
\mathbf{fvar} : \mathbb{P}(\mathbb{A} \nrightarrow T) \\
\hline
\forall f : \mathbb{A} \nrightarrow T \bullet \\
\quad f \in \mathbf{fvar}[T] \Leftrightarrow \\
\qquad \forall a, z : \mathbb{A} \mid a < z \wedge a \mathinner{\ldotp\ldotp} z \subseteq \operatorname{dom} f \bullet \# f(\!| a \mathinner{\ldotp\ldotp} z |\!) = 1 \\
\qquad \wedge \forall t : \mathbb{A} \setminus \operatorname{dom} f \bullet \\
\qquad\quad \exists d : \mathbb{D} \mid d > 0 \bullet (t - d \mathinner{\ldotp\ldotp} t + d) \setminus \operatorname{dom} f = \{t\}
\end{array}
$$

Again f exhibits a stepped graph. Also, any point t where f is undefined is separated by some non-zero duration d from any other such point, i.e., all state changes are instantaneous.

C Modelling input/output variables

We define several operators to abstract away from the particular communications model assumed. As shown in Figure 5, an input/output variable *io* may be represented as a partial function that exhibits a value only at certain times, e.g., when a new message-passing value is being sent, or when a hardware register is 'stable'.

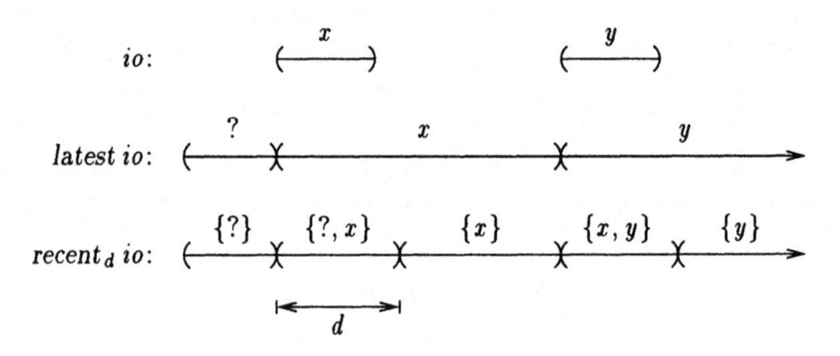

Fig. 5. Modelling input/output variables.

Let *latest* v be the most recently observable value of a timed variable v of type T.

$$\begin{array}{l} [T] \\ \hline \mathit{latest}\_ : \mathbf{dvar}[T] \rightarrow \mathbf{fvar}[T] \\ \hline \forall v : \mathbf{dvar}[T];\ x : T \bullet \\ \quad (\!\!- \mathit{latest}\ v = x -\!\!) \ \mathbf{whenever}\ (\!\!- v = x -\!\!) \ \mathbf{or}\ ((\!\!- v = x -\!\!) \ \mathbf{fby}\ \mathsf{undef}\ v) \end{array}$$

Thus, *latest* v equals x when v currently equals x, or when v is currently undefined but was previously equal to x. The value of *latest* v is unspecified before v has ever had a defined value. Figure 5 shows how this operator 'fills in' the undefined intervals for a communication variable, allowing us to refer to its 'latest' value during *any* interval. (Such a capability may require buffering of input values in an implementation.)

More generally, let $\mathit{recent}_d\ v$ be the *set of* most recently observable values of *latest* v, at any time in the last d time units.

$$\begin{array}{l} [T] \\ \hline \mathit{recent}\_\_ : (\mathbb{D} \times \mathbf{dvar}[T]) \rightarrow \mathbf{fvar}[\mathbb{P}\, T] \\ \hline \forall d : \mathbb{D};\ v : \mathbf{dvar}[T];\ x : T \bullet \\ \quad \mathsf{initially}\ (\!\!- x \in \mathit{recent}_d\ v -\!\!) \ \mathbf{iff}\ \mathsf{preceding}_{\leqslant d}\ (\!\!- \mathit{latest}\ v = x -\!\!) \end{array}$$

In other words, those intervals beginning with x a member of $\mathit{recent}_d\ v$ are exactly those where *latest* v was equal to x no more than d time units ago. Figure 5 shows the behaviour of $\mathit{recent}_d\ \mathit{io}$ for a particular d.

Similarly, let $\mathit{since}_{TH}\ v$ be the set of values that *latest* v has had since timed history predicate TH became true.

$$\begin{array}{l} [T] \\ \hline \mathit{since}\_\_ : ((\mathbb{A} \twoheadrightarrow \mathbb{B}) \times \mathbf{dvar}[T]) \rightarrow \mathbf{fvar}[\mathbb{P}\, T] \\ \hline \forall TH : \mathbb{A} \twoheadrightarrow \mathbb{B};\ v : \mathbf{dvar}[T];\ x : T \bullet \\ \quad (\!\!- x \in \mathit{since}_{TH}\ v -\!\!) \ \mathbf{iff}\ (\!\!- TH -\!\!) \ \mathbf{and}\ \mathsf{initially}\ (\!\!- \mathit{latest}\ v = x -\!\!) \end{array}$$

In other words, those intervals in which some value x is a member of $\mathit{since}_{TH}\ v$ are exactly those in which TH is currently true, and *latest* v equalled x since TH became true. When TH is false, $\mathit{since}_{TH}\ v$ is the empty set.

Rigorous Object-Oriented Modeling: Integrating Formal and Informal Notations

R. B. France[1*], J.-M. Bruel[2], M. M. Larrondo-Petrie[1], E. Grant[1]

[1] Department of Computer Science & Engineering
Florida Atlantic University
Boca Raton, FL-33431, USA.
[2] Laboratoire IRIT/SIERA, bat. 1R1
118, rte de Narbonne
31062 Toulouse Cedex, France
Contact: robert@cse.fau.edu

Abstract. The high-quality modeling experiences embedded in the more mature graphical OO methods (OOMs) makes their application to complex systems attractive, but the lack of firm semantic bases for the modeling notations can significantly hamper the development of such systems. One approach to making OOMs more precise and amenable to rigorous analysis is to integrate them with suitable formal modeling techniques. In this paper we describe a technique for integrating an OOM, the Fusion method, and a formal specification notation, Z.

1 Introduction

The more mature informal object-oriented (OO) modeling techniques (e.g., Fusion [6]) provide good support for developing concise, highly-structured, models of behavior from a variety of perspectives. These techniques are based on some of the best modeling experiences available, and consist of rich sets of structuring and abstraction mechanisms. A deterrent to the use of OO methods (OOMs) for the development of complex systems is their lack of support for rigorous analysis. This is a result of the loosely-defined semantics for the modeling notations.

An approach to making informal OO models more precise and amenable to rigorous analysis is to integrate them with suitable formal notations. Several studies in this area have been published (e.g., see [1, 9]). In our work, "integration" means providing a bridge from the informal OO modeling concepts to the formal notation. Our work differs from others in that our focus is on producing formalizations that can directly support verification and validation activities, and for which mechanical support is possible. For this reason, we have used only formal notations for which there exist sound sets of analysis tools. The Z notation [3, 14] we use is supported by typecheckers (e.g., ZTC [12]), animators (e.g., ZANS [11]), and theorem proving environments (e.g., Z/EVES [7]). We assume

* This work was partially funded by NSF grant CCR-9410396.

that the reader is familiar with the Z notation. For a detailed description of the Z notation see [14].

Our past work focused on the formalization of the analysis models of the Fusion method [6] and it resulted in a set of rules for transforming Fusion Object Models to Z specifications (e.g., see [1]). We built a prototype tool, FuZE [4], that automatically generates Z specifications from Fusion Object Models. Z analysis tools (ZTC and ZANS) can be called from within the tool to analyze the generated Z specifications. The tool has been applied by graduate students at Florida Atlantic University on non-trivial projects and case studies (e.g., see [8]). In general, our experiences indicate that formalization and analysis of informal models can uncover problems with the informal models, and lead to a deeper understanding of the problem. Our applications of the integrated methods on case studies also uncovered limitations of our previous rules. In this paper we present a technique for transforming Fusion Object Models (OMs) to Z specifications that improves upon our previous technique. The new technique supports the automated transformation of a wider range of OMs.

We have also extended our transformation technique to the design models of Fusion. We present some of our current work on formalizing Fusion design models in this paper. In section 2 we give an overview of the Fusion analysis and design modeling techniques. In section 3 we outline our technique for formalizing Fusion's analysis models, and in section 4 we present the results of our recent work on formalizing Fusion's design models. We conclude in section 5 with a summary of our work and an outline of ongoing work.

2 The Fusion Modeling Techniques

Fusion is an object-oriented software development methodology that combines and extends existing techniques, e.g., Rumbaugh's Object Modeling Technique (OMT) [13], Booch's technique [2], Wirfs-Brock's Class Responsibility Collaborator [15] (CRC) technique, and Jacobson's Objectory [10]. Fusion claims to take the best ideas from these methods and incorporate them into a single coherent method that covers analysis, design, and implementation.

2.1 Fusion Analysis Models

In Fusion's analysis phase the required behavior of the system is described by the following models.

Object Model. An *Object Model* (OM) defines the static structure of the information manipulated by the application in terms of classes and the relationships among them. An example of an OM for a petrol dispensing system is given in Fig. 1 (taken from [6]). In an OM a class is represented by a box that consists of a partition containing the name of the class, and another containing a list of attributes for the class. Type information for attributes may or may not be shown in an OM. Relationships are depicted as diamond adorned lines between

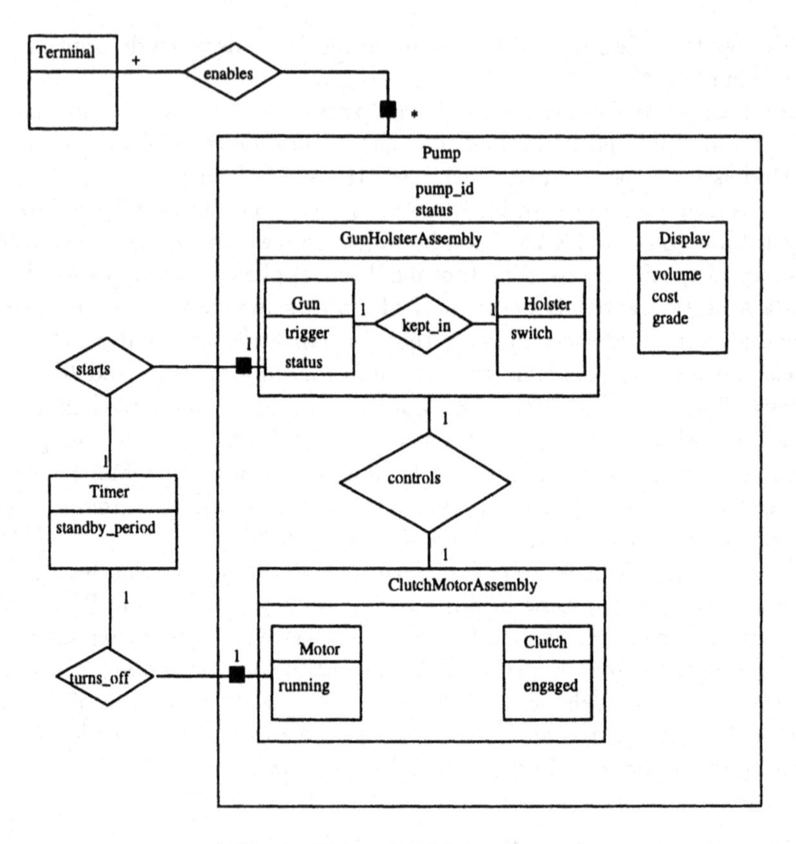

Fig. 1. Object Model for *Pump*

classes. In the diamond the name of the relationship and any attributes associated with it are given. In Fusion, relationships represent *optional* links between objects (class instances). Relationships are associated with cardinalities that restrict the number of class instances (objects) that can be linked to each other. A cardinality can be a single number, an integer range, '*' (0 or more), or '+' (1 or more). A black box attached to a relationship indicates that all existing objects of the adjacent class must be linked (i.e., it indicates mandatory links). For example, the relationship *enables* indicates that every existing *Pump* object must be linked to 1 or more *Terminal* objects, and an existing *Terminal* object may or may not be associated with (0 or more) *Pump* objects. In Fusion, classes that contain a class structure are called *aggregates*. The classes in an aggregate are called *components*. For example, *Pump* is an aggregate with components *GunHolsterAssembly*, *Display* and *ClutchMotorAssembly*. Fusion also provides constructs for building generalization/specialization structures. Additional constraints on class structures can be expressed as annotations in OMs.

Interface Model. This model defines the externally observable behavior of the application. It consists of two models: the Operation Model and the Lifecycle

Model. An *Operation Model* characterizes the observable effects of system operations. A system operation is one that can be invoked by users of the system. Each system operation is described by a Fusion *Operation Schema* (OS). A *Life-Cycle Model* characterizes the allowable sequences of system operation invocations for the application.

The Data Dictionary. The *Data Dictionary* provides information about the classes and operations not included in the previous models (e.g., attribute type information).

2.2 Fusion Design Models

In the Fusion design phase a system's behavior is modeled in terms of interactions between the objects of the system. The primary model of functional behavior is the *Object Interaction Graph* (OIG). An OIG is developed for each system operation described in the Operation Model, and it describes the object interactions that accomplish the operation.

Graphically, an OIG is a collection of boxes, each representing an object of the system to be implemented, connected by labeled arrows representing message passing between the objects (e.g., see Fig. 2). The order in which interactions can take place is constrained by sequence labels associated with the interactions. Interactions shown in an OIG do not indicate that they must take place; they indicate only the possibility of such an interaction taking place.

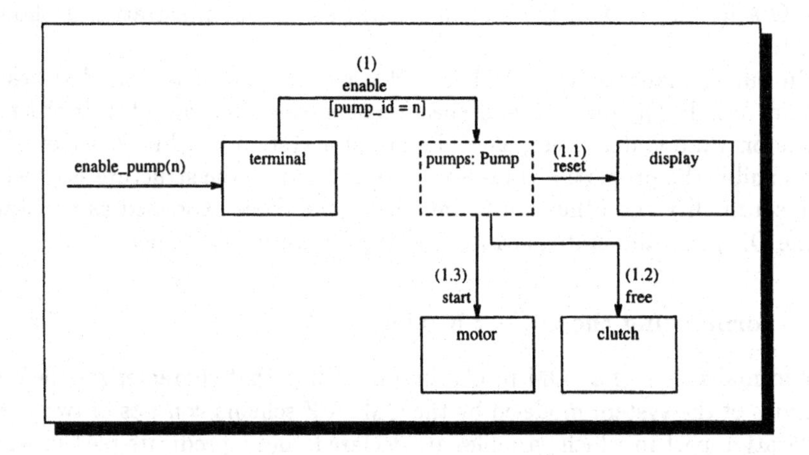

Fig. 2. The *enable_pump* Fusion OIG

An individual object is represented as a solid line box, and a collection of objects is represented as a broken line box. One object in an OIG is identified as the *controller* and all other objects are referred to as *collaborators*. The controller object is distinguished by being the only object with an arrow entering it that does not originate from another object (or collection of objects) in the OIG. A complete OIG model includes a descriptive text stating the conditions under which interactions take place.

An example of an OIG is shown in Fig. 2. The controller in the OIG is the object *terminal*. The message *enable* is sent to all objects in the collection *pumps* with $pump\_id = n$. Each selected object in *pumps* can then send messages *reset*, *free*, and *start* (in that order, as indicated by the interaction sequence labels).

The other models of the Fusion design phase are:

- a *Visibility Graph* that models access restrictions and lifetime bindings of objects,
- an *Inheritance Graph* that defines the inheritance structure of the solution, and
- a *Class Description* (CD) for each class in the system to be implemented.

The CDs provide a textual organization of the information found in the other Fusion Design Models.

3 Formalizing Fusion Analysis Models

In this section we outline a technique we developed for formalizing the Object and Operation Models of the Fusion Method. The Lifecycle Model is expressed formally in Fusion so there is no need to formalize it. We use models from the petrol system case study given in [6] to illustrate the formalization technique. The OM for the part of the system we will use in our illustration is shown in Fig. 1.

In our formalization, an OM is a characterization of the valid states of a system, and the Operation Model specifies operations in terms of their observable effects on valid states. Here, a valid state of a system is a linked set of objects that exhibit the properties expressed in the OM (i.e., the structure is consistent with cardinality and other constraints, including those expressed as annotations in the OM). A valid state is called a *configuration* in this paper.

3.1 Formalizing the Object Model

The formalization of an OM results in a Z schema that characterizes the configurations of the system modeled by the OM. A Z schema consists of two parts: a declaration part in which variables are declared, and a predicate part in which a predicate constraining the declared variables is given. A Z schema characterization of an OM consists of variables representing objects and links among objects in the declaration part, and constraints on the objects and links in the predicate part.

The formalization of an OM can be completely automated if the OM annotations are expressed formally in predicate logic. In practice, annotations expressed in predicate logic notation can be significantly longer than concise natural language annotations. A related problem is the sometimes lengthy Z specifications automatically produced by the OM-to-Z transformation process. We found that properties that are concisely expressed in natural language (e.g., "object identifiers are unique" and "subclasses are disjoint") often required lengthy formal statements. To alleviate this problem we developed a set of high-level Z definitional constructs, called *Z macros*, for some commonly occurring properties. Z macros can be automatically translated ('compiled') to Z specification elements. Whenever possible, the modeler can use the macros to express annotations. Properties not covered by the macros have to be expressed in predicate logic notation before complete Z specifications can be produced from OMs.

In transforming OMs to Z specifications, Z macros are used wherever possible in the result output to the modeler. These macros are transformed to 'raw' Z notation before they are analyzed by the Z analysis tools. Examples of macros are given throughout this section.

Below we outline the steps for formalizing a Fusion OM.

Step 1: Formalize Basic Classes. A basic class is a class that is not an aggregate or a subclass in a specialization hierarchy. For each basic class a Z schema called a *class schema* is produced. A class schema consists of a variable representing the identifier of a class object, and variables representing object attributes. Attribute and object identifier types are specified as Z *basic types* or as pre-defined Z types (e.g., $\mathbb{N}$, the natural number type). In Z a type is a set and a basic type is a set of primitive elements. The basic type declarations and the class schema for a basic class have the following forms:

$[CLASSNAME, ATTR1\_TYPE, \ldots]$

```
┌─ ClassName ──────────────────
│ ident : CLASSNAME
│ attr1 : ATTR1_TYPE; ...
├──────
│ [Constraints on attribute values]
└──────────────────────────────
```

In the above $CLASSNAME$, $ATTR1\_TYPE; \ldots$ are Z basic types. $CLASSNAME$ is the set from which identifiers of class objects are drawn and $ATTR1\_TYPE$, ... are attribute types. The predicate in the predicate part of the schema constrains attribute values. If the constraints are expressed in natural language in the OM then a human must provide their formal expressions. Note that the formalization forces a type to be associated with each attribute; if one is not given in the OM the FuZE tool uses the capitalized attribute name as the type of the attribute (the type is introduced as a basic type).

To illustrate the formalization of basic classes we formalize the *Holster*, *Gun*, *Clutch*, and *Motor* classes of the petrol system (see Fig. 1). The first step is to determine the attribute types. Type information not shown in the OM should be in the data dictionary. The data dictionary supporting the petrol system model (not given here for the sake of brevity), indicates that the attribute *status* of *Gun* can be one of the following values: *Enabled*, *Out_of_Service*, *Disabled*. It also indicates that the attributes *running* (in *Motor*), *engaged* (in *Clutch*), and *switch* (in *Holster*), can have one of two values: *on*, *off*. The basic types and class schemata for the classes are given below:

$[GUNID, HOLSTERID]$
$[MOTORID, CLUTCHID]$
$[TRIGGER]$
$STATUS ::= Enabled \mid Out\_of\_Service \mid Disabled$
$SETTING ::= on \mid off$

Holster
$ident : HOLSTERID$
$switch : SETTING$

Gun
$ident : GUNID$
$trigger : TRIGGER$
$status : STATUS$

Motor
$ident : MOTORID$
$running : SETTING$

Clutch
$ident : CLUTCHID$
$engaged : SETTING$

Step 2: Formalize Aggregate Classes and Subclasses. In this step, aggregates and subclasses are formalized. The class structure in an aggregate must be formalized before the aggregate can be completely formalized. The class structure is essentially an OM, and thus it can be (recursively) formalized using the OM formalization process we are outlining here. The class schema for an aggregate class has the following form:

$[AGGNAME, \ldots]$

AggName
InternalStruct
$ident : AGGNAME$
$attr1 : \mathbb{P}\, ATTR1\_TYPE; \ldots$

[*Constraints on attributes*]

InternalStruct defines the internal structure of the aggregate, that is, it defines the aggregate's components and relationships between the components. In the predicate part of *AggName* constraints on the attribute values are given.

To illustrate the formalization of aggregates we give the class schemata for *GunHolsterAssembly* and *Pump*. The *GunHolsterAssembly* aggregate is formalized below (the schema characterizing internal structure is on the left):

GunHolsterInternal
$gun : Gun$
$holster : Holster$
$kept\_in : Gun \leftrightarrow Holster$

$kept\_in \in 1 \twoheadleftarrow\!\!\!\twoheadrightarrow 1[\{gun\}, \{holster\}]$

$[GHAID]$

GunHolsterAssembly
GunHolsterInternal
$ident : GHAID$

The macro $1 \twoheadleftarrow\!\!\!\twoheadrightarrow 1$ specifies a mandatory 1-to-1 relationship (Fusion requires that component instances be linked via enclosed relationships).

The class schema for the *Pump* aggregate is given below:

$[PUMPID, PUMP\_ID]$

PumpInternal

$display : Display$
$gha : GunHolsterAssembly$
$cma : ClutchMotorAssembly$
$controls : GunHolsterAssembly \leftrightarrow ClutchMotorAssembly$

$controls \in 1 \leftrightarrow 1[\{gha\}, \{cma\}]$

Pump

$PumpInternal$
$ident : PUMPID$
$pump\_id : PUMP\_ID$
$status : STATUS$

Formalization of subclasses is done by including superclass class schemata in subclass class schemata.

SubClassName

$SuperClass$
$attr1 : ATTR1\_TYPE; \ldots$

[*Constraints on attributes*]

3. Specify Constraints on Specialization Hierarchies. In a specialization hierarchy subclasses can be disjoint (i.e., an instance cannot belong to more than one subclass), or not disjoint (i.e., multiple inheritance is possible). Also, the instances of a superclass may all be instances of depicted subclasses (in which case the superclass is said to be *abstract*), or there may be superclass instances that are not instances of any depicted subclass. Z macros are used to express these properties (not given here for lack of space).

Properties of specialization hierarchies are specified in a schema, called the *configuration schema* of the hierarchy. Such a schema has the following form:

SpecConfig

$supers : \mathbb{P}\, SuperClass$
$subs\_1 : \mathbb{P}\, SubClass\_1; \ldots; subs\_n : \mathbb{P}\, SubClass\_n$

[*One or more of the following Z macros included here :*]
$(subs\_1, \ldots, subs\_n)$ *partition supers*
$disjoint(subs\_i, \ldots, subs\_j)$
$abstract(supers, subs\_1, \ldots, subs\_n)$

4. Specify relationships and other constraints among classes. This last step results in the OM's *configuration schema*, that is, a characterization of the OM's configurations. Configuration schemata have the following form:

OMName

$Spec1Config; \ldots$ [*specialization config schemata*]
$classobjs\_1 : \mathbb{P}\, Class\_1; \ldots$ [*sets of class objects*]
$rel\_ij : Class\_i \leftrightarrow Class\_j; \ldots$ [*relationships*]

[*Cardinality and other constraints*]

The configuration schema for an OM expresses constraints on relationships, and restrictions on the sharing of components across aggregates. For example, the presence of a relationship in an aggregate is a reference to a larger relationship, that is, the relationship in the aggregate is a subrelation of a larger relation. This property is stated in the configuration schema for all relationships enclosed in an aggregate. We have defined the following Z macros for commonly occurring properties:

- *Relationship cardinalities:* We have defined macros that represent Z formalizations of cardinality constraints. These macros are of the form:

  $$p \longleftrightarrow q[domain, range]$$

  (if the relationship is mandatory black boxes are placed on the appropriate end(s)), where p and q are the cardinalities, *domain* is the domain of the relationship and *range* is the range of the relationship.
- *Object identifier uniqueness:* The property that object identifiers in a configuration are unique is captured by the following macro:

  $$unique\_ids[\{s1, s2, \ldots\}] == \forall\, i, j : s1 \bullet i.ident = j.ident \Leftrightarrow i = j \wedge \\ \forall\, i, j : s2 \bullet i.ident = j.ident \Leftrightarrow i = j \wedge \ldots$$

  In the above macro, $s1, s2, \ldots$, are sets of objects.
- *Constraints pertaining to sharing of aggregate components:* Modelers may want to restrict the sharing of components across aggregate instances. For example, the following Z macro is used to specify that components cannot be shared across aggregates (in the following, s is the set of instances of the aggregate *Agg* in a configuration):
  - $physical\_aggregate(s)$: This macro expands to a predicate that prohibits sharing of components of *Agg*. For example, if *aggs* is a set of objects of the aggregate *Agg* that has a single component class *comp* characterized by the schema *COMP* (i.e., $comp : COMP$), then $physical\_aggregate(aggs)$ expands to the following predicate:

    $$\forall\, a1, a2 : aggs \mid a1.comp = a2.comp \bullet a1 = a2$$

    The restriction as defined in the above is not recursive, for example, if *comp* is also an aggregate, then the above macro does not restrict it to be a physical aggregate.

For the pump system, the following restrictions are stated as OM annotations (not shown in model given in Fig. 1):

- The *GunHolsterAssembly* aggregate is a physical aggregate, that is, its components are not shared. The *ClutchMotorAssembly* and the *Pump* aggregates are also physical aggregates.

- All instances of component classes in a configuration must be a component of an aggregate in the configuration. For example, all instances of *Gun* in a configuration must be a component of one *GunHoslterAssembly* aggregate instance in the configuration.

The configuration schema for the pump system is given below:

PumpSystem

$terms : \mathbb{P}\, Terminal$ [*terminal instances in configuration*]
$pumps : \mathbb{P}\, Pump$ [*pump instances in configuration*]
$timers : \mathbb{P}\, Timer$ [*timer instances in configuration*]
$enables : Terminal \leftrightarrow Pump$
$keptin : Gun \leftrightarrow Holster$
$controls : GunHoslterAssembly \leftrightarrow ClutchMotorAssembly$
$starts : Timer \leftrightarrow Gun$
$turnsoff : Timer \leftrightarrow Motor$

$enables \in + \longleftrightarrow * [terms, pumps]$

$starts \in 1 \longleftrightarrow 1[timers, \{p : pumps \bullet (p.gha).gun\}]$

$turnsoff \in 1 \longleftrightarrow 1[timers, \{p : pumps \bullet (p.cma).motor\}]$
$keptin = \bigcup\{p : pumps \bullet (p.gha).kept\_in\}$
[*linked components form a subrelation keptin*]
$\bigcup\{p : pumps \bullet p.controls\} = controls$
[*linked components form a subrelation controls*]
$physical\_aggregate(pumps)$
$physical\_aggregate(\{p : pumps \bullet p.gha\})$
$physical\_aggregate(\{p : pumps \bullet p.cma\})$
$unique\_ids(\{terms, timers, pumps\})$
...[*unique_ids macros for the components of pumps*]

3.2 Formalizing Operation Models

In this section we formalize one of the system operations for the petrol system. The formalization of the Fusion Operation Model is only partially mechanizable because the operation descriptions are written mostly in natural language. Currently our tool, given a Fusion operation schema, generates only the declaration part of the corresponding Z operation schema. The formal relationship between the before and after states of the operation must be provided by a human developer. This relationship is stated in the predicate part of the Z operation schema.

The Fusion description of the operation *enable_pump* and its corresponding formalization in Z is given below:

Operation: *enable_pump*
Description: Enables the pump, that is, makes it ready to dispense petrol.

Reads: supplied n
Changes: p : *Pump* with $p.pump\_id = n$, *motor*, *clutch*, *display*
Sends:
Assumes:
Result: if p is enabled or out of service then no effect
otherwise:
Status of p is enabled.
Its *display* has been initialized.
its *motor* is running, and its *clutch* is not engaged.

enable_pump

$\Delta PumpSystem$
$n? : PUMP\_ID$ [*input declaration obtained from Reads section*]
$p, p' : Pump$ [*obtained from Changes section*]

$$
\begin{array}{l}
p \in pumps \land p.pump\_id = n? = p'.pump\_id \\
(p.status = Enabled \lor p.status = Out\_of\_service) \Rightarrow pumps' = pumps \\
p.status = Disabled \Rightarrow p'.ident = p.ident \land p'.gha = p.gha \land \\
\quad p'.status = Enbaled \land (p'.display).volume = 0 \land \\
\quad (p'.display).grade = (p.display).grade \land (p'.display).cost = 0 \land \\
\quad ((p'.cma).motor).running = on \land ((p'.cma).clutch).engaged = off \land \\
\quad pumps' = (pumps \setminus \{p\}) \cup \{p'\}
\end{array}
$$

ΔPumpSystem defines two pump system configurations, one representing a configuration before execution of the operation (represented by unprimed variables) and the other representing a configuration after execution (represented by primed variables). In the next section we formalize an OO design for this operation.

4 Formalizing Fusion Design Models

In [5] we presented a formalization of OIGs that used the promotion mechanism of Z. We found this particular approach to be cumbersome, and it introduced notation (the θ notation) that was not handled well by the static and dynamic analysis tools available in our environment. In this section we present another approach that does not require the use of the θ notation.

Design Formalization Example

At the design level, additional classes may be required to implement a solution to the problem, thus there may be some objects in an OIG that are not objects of any class described by the analysis-level Object Model. Though Fusion does not have a Design-level Object Model (DOM), we have found the use of such a model useful in our integrated approach. A DOM can be constructed from information in the Fusion Class Descriptions (CDs). Classes that have objects as attributes in CDs are modeled in a DOM as aggregates in which the components are the object attributes. Object attributes can be bound (i.e., their lifetimes are bound to the lifetime of the aggregate), constant (i.e., they cannot be replaced by another instance), and exclusive (i.e., only the aggregate class can access them). These properties are indicated in the DOM. Part of the DOM for the pump system is given in Fig. 3 (this was obtained from the Class Descriptions given in [6], pages 169-170).

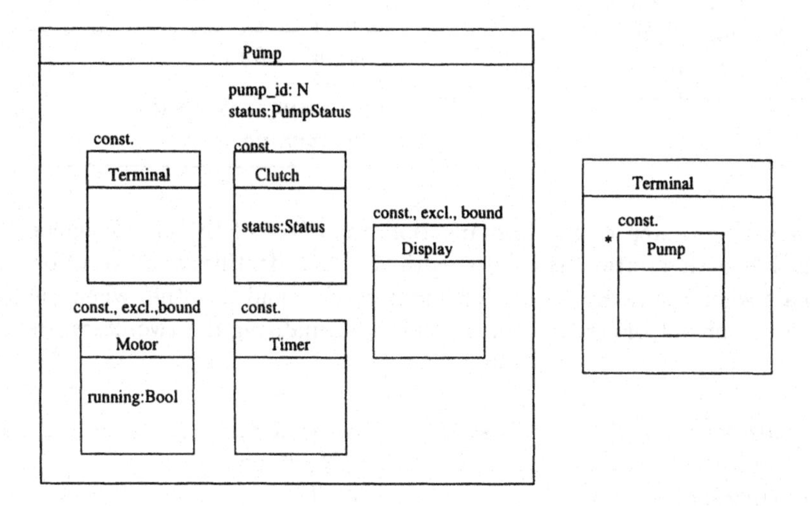

Fig. 3. Partial Design Object Model for *Pump*

A formalized DOM is a characterization of valid design-level states of a system. In our design formalization technique, design models of operations are formalized in terms of relationships between before and after (valid) design states.

In this section we outline the formalization of the OIG for the *enable_pump* system operation (see Fig. 2). The description associated with the OIG states:

> The invocation of *enable_pump* triggers the invocation of *enable* on a pump with identifier *n* (if there is no such pump then the operation halts, leaving the state unchanged). If the pump is in service and not already enabled then its display is reset, clutch is freed, and its motor is started (else the operation halts).

Our formalization of OIGs starts from the leaf objects (e.g., *display*), and works its way backward towards the controller object (e.g., *terminal*). Information about the effects of messages on objects is available from CDs (not given here). Below we give the formalizations of the *enable_pump* leaf messages.

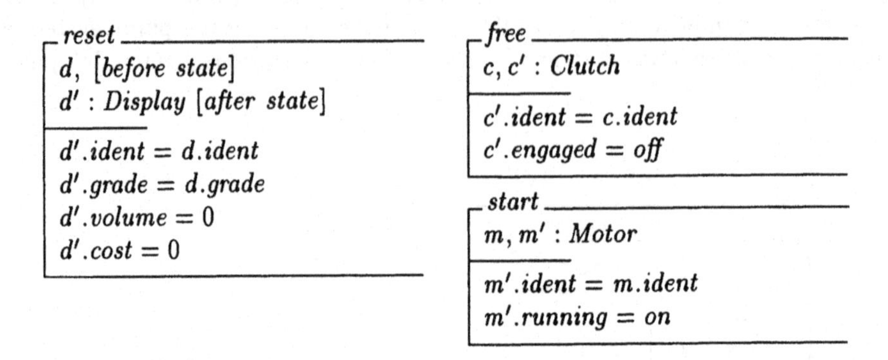

reset

d, [*before state*]
d' : *Display* [*after state*]

$d'.ident = d.ident$
$d'.grade = d.grade$
$d'.volume = 0$
$d'.cost = 0$

free

c, c' : *Clutch*

$c'.ident = c.ident$
$c'.engaged = off$

start

m, m' : *Motor*

$m'.ident = m.ident$
$m'.running = on$

In the next step of the formalization, the effect of the *enable* operation is defined. The description associated with the OIG identifies two execution cases: the case when the pump is disabled and in service, and the other when the pump is enabled or out of service. The schemata formalizing the two cases are given below:

$enablesub1 \mathrel{\widehat{=}} reset \wedge free \wedge start$

enable_OK

$enablesub1$
$p, p' : Pump$
$n? : \mathbb{N}$

$p.ident = p'.ident$
$p'.pump\_id = p.pump\_id = n?$
$d = p.display \wedge d' = p'.display$
$c = p.clutch \wedge c' = p'.clutch$
$m = p.motor \wedge m' = p'.motor$
$p.status = Disabled \wedge p'.status = Enabled$
$p'.timer = p.timer$

No_enable

$p, p' : Pump$
$n? : \mathbb{N}$

$p.pump\_id = n?$
$(p.status = Enabled \vee$
$\quad p.status = Out\_of\_Service)$
$p' = p$

The schema *enablesub*1 defines the combined effects of the suboperations. Note that in *enable_OK* no effect is defined for the *terminal* component of the pump. This is because the *terminal* component is an object in the OIG whose effect is not yet defined. On the other hand, the *timer* object does not take part in this operation and so its state is specified as unchanged here ($p'.timer = p.timer$).

The *enable* operation for the pump with identifier n can now be defined as:

$$enable \mathrel{\widehat{=}} enable\_OK \vee No\_enable$$

The formalization of the *enable_pump* operation is expressed as follows (there are two cases to consider: the pump is linked to the terminal, and the pump is not linked to the terminal):

enable_pump_OK
$$\begin{array}{l} enable \\ t, t' : Terminal \\ n? : \mathbb{N} \\ \hline p \in t.pumps \\ t'.pumps = (t.pumps \setminus \{p\}) \cup \{p'\} \\ p.terminal = t \land p'.terminal = t' \end{array}$$

enable_pump_notOK
$$\begin{array}{l} t, t' : Terminal \\ n? : \mathbb{N} \\ \hline \forall p : t.pumps \bullet p.pump\_id \neq n? \\ t = t' \end{array}$$

$enable\_pump \mathrel{\widehat=} enable\_pump\_OK \lor enable\_pump\_notOK$

The next step of the formalization is to promote the *enable_pump* operation to the system level. This is done below:

SYSenable_pump
$$\begin{array}{l} \Delta DesignPumpSystem \\ \hline \exists\, en : enable\_pump \bullet \\ \quad (en.t \in terminals \land terminals' = (terminal \setminus \{en.t\}) \cup \{en.t'\}) \\ \ldots \\ [conjuncts\ stating\ that\ all\ other\ configuration\ elements\ are\ unchanged] \end{array}$$

Using the above, and a refinement relationship between *DesignPumpSystem* (not given here) and *PumpSystem* (given in previous section), one can establish that the design is consistent with the analysis model of the operation. Verification techniques for Z can be used for this purpose. See [14] for more details on design verification with Z.

5 Conclusion and future works

In this paper we have illustrated the integration of an informal, graphical OOM with a formal specification technique. We used the formal models to tie together models produced in a particular phase of development, and across development phases. At the analysis level, the formalized Object Model characterizes the state affected by the operations specified in the formalized Operation Model. The formalized Object Model provides terms that can be used to express the effect of system operations precisely. Using the formalized models one can rigorously do internal consistency checks of models, as well as consistency checks across the models.

At the design level, the formalization of an OIG produces a model that can be formally verified against the formalized Operation Model.

We are currently developing rigorous refinement techniques for Fusion design. The intent is to develop an analysis and design development environment in which the complementary nature of formal and informal OO methods is exploited. We are also extending the prototype tool FuZE to support the techniques outlined in this paper.

References

1. Brian W. Bates, Jean-Michel Bruel, Robert B. France, and Maria M. Larrondo-Petrie. Formalizing Fusion Object-Oriented Analysis Models. In Elie Najm and Jean-Bernard Stephani, editors, *Proceedings of the First IFIP International Workshop on Formal Methods for Open Object-based Distributed Systems*, Paris, France. Chapman & Hall, London, UK, 4–6 March 1996.
2. Grady Booch. *Object-Oriented Analysis and Design with Applications.* Benjamin/Cummings, Menlo Park, CA, Second edition, 1994.
3. Stephen M. Brien and John E. Nicholls. Z base standard. Technical Monograph PRG-107, Oxford University Computing Laboratory, Wolfson Building, Parks Road, Oxford, UK, November 1992.
4. Jean-Michel Bruel, Robert B. France, Bharat Chintapally, and Gopal K. Raghavan. A Tool for Rigorous Analysis of Object Models. In *Proceedings of the* 20th *International Conference on Technology of Object-Oriented Languages and Systems (TOOLS'96)*, Santa Barbara, California, July 29–August 2 1996.
5. Jean-Michel Bruel, Robert B. France, Maria M. Larrondo-Petrie, Bharat Chintapally, and Gopal K. Raghavan. CASE-based Rigorous Object-Oriented Modeling. In *Proceedings of the Northern Formal Methods Workshop*, Bradford, UK, 23–24 September 1996.
6. Derek Coleman, Patrick Arnold, Stephanie Bodoff, Chris Dollin, Helena Gilchrist, Fiona Hayes, and Paul Jeremaes. *Object-Oriented Development: The Fusion Method.* Prentice Hall, Englewood Cliffs, NJ, Object-Oriented Series edition, 1994.
7. Dan Craigen, Sentot Kromodimoeljo, Irwin Meisels, Bill Pase, and Mark Saaltink. EVES: An Overview. In S. Prehn and W. J. Toetenel, editors, *VDM'91: Formal Software Development Methods*, volume 551 of *Lecture Notes in Computer Science*, pages 389–405. Springer-Verlag, 1991. Volume 1: Conference Contributions.
8. Robert B. France and Jean-Michel Bruel. The Role of Integrated Specification Techniques in Complex System Modeling and Analysis. In *Proceedings of the Workshop on Real-Time Systems Education (RTSE'96)*, Daytona Beach, Florida, 20 April 1996.
9. J. Anthony Hall. Specifying and Interpreting Class Hierarchies in Z. In Bowen and Hall editors *Z User Workshop, Cambridge 1994*, Workshops in Computing. Springer-Verlag, New York, 1994.
10. I. Jacobson. *Object oriented software engineering.* Addison-Wesley, 1992.
11. Xiaoping Jia. *An Approach to Animating Z Specifications.* Division of Software Engineering, School of Computer Science, Telecommunication, and Information Systems, DePaul University, Chicago, IL, USA, 1995.
12. Xiaoping Jia. *ZTC: A Z Type Checker, User's Guide, version 2.01.* Division of Software Engineering, School of Computer Science, Telecommunication, and Information Systems, DePaul University, Chicago, IL, USA, May 1995. Available via anonymous ftp at `ise.cs.depaul.edu`.
13. J. Rumbaugh, M. Blaha, W. Premerlani, F. Eddy, and W. Lorensen. *Object-Oriented Modeling and Design.* Prentice Hall, 1991.
14. J. Michael Spivey. *The Z Notation: A Reference Manual.* Prentice Hall, Englewood Cliffs, NJ, Second edition, 1992.
15. R. Wirfs-Brock and B. Wilkerson. *Designing object oriented software.* Prentice-Hall, 1990.

Completeness in Abstract Interpretation: A Domain Perspective

Roberto Giacobazzi* Francesco Ranzato**

*Dipartimento di Informatica, Università di Pisa
Corso Italia 40, 56125 Pisa, Italy
giaco@di.unipi.it

**Dipartimento di Matematica Pura ed Applicata, Università di Padova
Via Belzoni 7, 35131 Padova, Italy
franz@math.unipd.it

Abstract. Completeness in abstract interpretation is an ideal and rare situation where the abstract semantics is able to take full advantage of the power of representation of the underlying abstract domain. In this paper, we develop an algebraic theory of completeness in abstract interpretation. We show that completeness is an abstract domain property and we prove that there always exist both the greatest complete restriction and the least complete extension of any abstract domain, with respect to continuous semantic functions. Under certain hypotheses, a constructive procedure for computing these complete domains is given. These methodologies provide advanced algebraic tools for manipulating abstract interpretations, which can be fruitfully used both in program analysis and in semantics design.

1 Introduction

Abstract interpretation [8, 9] is a widely established methodology for programming language semantics approximation, which is primarily used for specifying and then validating static program analyses. Given a so-called concrete semantics defined by a concrete domain C (a complete lattice) and a semantic function $[\![\cdot]\!] : \mathit{Program} \to C$, an abstract interpretation is specified by an abstract domain A (a complete lattice) and an abstract semantic function $[\![\cdot]\!]^\sharp : \mathit{Program} \to A$, where the relationship between concrete and abstract objects is formalized by a pair of adjoint maps $\alpha : C \to A$ and $\gamma : A \to C$ such that $\alpha(c) \leq_A a$ means that a is a correct approximation of c. Then, a typical *soundness* theorem for an abstract interpretation goes as follows: For all programs P, $\alpha([\![P]\!]) \leq_A [\![P]\!]^\sharp$. It is well-known [8] that for the non-restrictive case of least fixpoint based semantics, i.e. where $[\![P]\!] = \mathit{lfp}(T_P)$ and $[\![P]\!]^\sharp = \mathit{lfp}(T^\sharp_P)$ for some monotone operators $T_P : C \to C$ and $T^\sharp_P : A \to A$ indexed over *Program*, soundness is implied by the following stronger, but nevertheless much easier to check, condition: $\alpha \circ T_P \leq_A T^\sharp_P \circ \alpha$.

While soundness is the basic requirement for any abstract interpretation, the dual notion of *completeness* is instead an ideal and quite rare situation. Completeness arises when no loss of precision occurs by approximating $\alpha([\![P]\!])$ with $[\![P]\!]^\sharp$, i.e. when $\alpha([\![P]\!]) = [\![P]\!]^\sharp$. Roughly speaking, this means that the abstract semantics is able to take *full* advantage of the power of representation of the abstract domain A. In this sense, complete abstract interpretations can be rightfully considered as optimal. As before, for least fixpoint based semantics, completeness is implied by the following stronger condition called *full completeness*: $\alpha \circ T_P = T^\sharp_P \circ \alpha$ (cf. [9]). For instance, the classical naïve "rule of signs" abstract interpretation is fully complete. In fact, the sign of a concrete integer multiplication can be exactly retrieved by the rule of signs applied to its arguments, i.e., by leaving out the details, $\mathit{sign}(n \cdot m) = \mathit{sign}(n) \cdot^\sharp \mathit{sign}(m)$, where $\cdot^\sharp$ is the obvious abstract multiplication between signs.

The problem of achieving the completeness for an abstract interpretation, by enhancing either the abstract domain or the abstract semantic operators, has been investigated by a number of authors (see Section 9). While this has been successfully solved for some specific abstract interpretations and analyses, the more general problem of making a generic abstract interpretation complete in the best possible way (i.e. involving the most simple abstract domains and operators), is still, to the best of our knowledge, open.

We attack this problem from a domain perspective, since we show that, fixed a concrete semantics, both completeness and fully completeness for an abstract interpretation only depend on the underlying abstract domain. Thus, we develop an algebraic theory of domain completeness within the classical abstract interpretation framework. We concentrate on the set of all the domains, in the lattice $\mathcal{L}_C$ of abstract interpretations of the fixed concrete domain C, which are complete and fully complete for a given family of semantic operators F, denoted resp. by $\Delta(C, F)$ and $\Gamma(C, F)$. In Section 4, we prove that both $\Delta(C, F)$ and $\Gamma(C, F)$ are always complete meet subsemilattices of $\mathcal{L}_C$. Moreover, while we show that, in general, $\Delta(C, F)$ is not a join subsemilattice of $\mathcal{L}_C$, even under very restrictive hypotheses on C and F, by contrast we prove that, when the functions in F are (Scott-)continuous, $\Gamma(C, F)$ is a complete join subsemilattice of $\mathcal{L}_C$, and therefore a complete sublattice. It should be remarked that this latter result is far from being trivial.

Based on these results, in Section 5, we introduce a family of operators acting on abstract domains, which transform non-complete domains into complete or fully complete ones. There are two possibilities for doing this: Either by refining domains, i.e. by enhancing their precision by adding new elements, or by simplifying them by taking out some information which may cause incompleteness. Thus, following the ideas on systematic abstract domain refinements and simplifications introduced in [14, 18], we define the *complete* and *fully complete kernel* operators $\mathbb{K}$ and $\mathcal{K}$, and the *least fully complete extension* operator $\mathcal{E}$. The first two are abstract domain simplifications which, given a set of concrete monotone functions F and an input abstract domain A, give as output the most concrete domains $\mathbb{K}(A)$ and $\mathcal{K}(A)$ which are more abstract than A and complete, resp. fully complete, for any $f \in F$. $\mathcal{E}$ is instead an abstract domain refinement which, given a set of concrete continuous functions F and A, returns the most abstract domain $\mathcal{E}(A)$ which is an extension (i.e. more precise) of A and fully complete for any $f \in F$. By the aforementioned negative findings on the structure of $\Delta(C, F)$, an analogous least complete extension operator is not generally definable. These operators satisfy a number of relevant algebraic properties; in particular, we show that the least fully complete extension of a domain can be always achieved by decomposing the input domain into simpler factors and then by refining these simpler domains. In Section 6, we present a constructive method for designing least fully complete extensions and fully complete kernels of abstract domains, under the hypotheses that the concrete semantic functions in F are additive.

As a relevant example, we reconstruct the Cousot and Cousot [8] abstract domain of integer intervals as the least fully complete extension for integer addition of the rule of signs domain. Clearly, to be an abstract domain is a relative notion. Thus, our systematic operators can be also applied to refine or simplify domains for analysis relatively to other more precise – but still approximated – ones. In Section 8, we show how to apply our operators to devise an intelligent strategy for improving the precision of abstract domains, which takes into account the efficiency/precision trade-off in a systematic refinement step. We apply this idea to compare the expressive power of some well-known abstract domains for ground-dependency analysis of logic programs.

2 Basic Notions

The structure $\langle uco(C), \sqsubseteq, \sqcup, \sqcap, \lambda x.\top, \lambda x.x\rangle$ denotes the complete lattice of all *upper closure operators* (shortly closures) on a complete lattice $\langle C, \leq, \vee, \wedge, \top, \bot\rangle$ (i.e., monotone, idempotent and extensive operators on C), where (i) $\rho \sqsubseteq \eta$ iff $\forall x \in C.\ \rho(x) \leq \eta(x)$, (ii) $(\sqcup_{i\in I}\rho_i)(x) = x \Leftrightarrow \forall i \in I.\ \rho_i(x) = x$; (iii) $(\sqcap_{i\in I}\rho_i)(x) = \wedge_{i\in I}\rho_i(x)$; (iv) $\lambda x.\top$ and $\lambda x.x$ are, respectively, the top and bottom. The complete lattice of all *lower closure operators* on C is denoted by $lco(C)$ and is dually isomorphic to $uco(C)$. Recall that each closure $\rho \in uco(C)$ is uniquely determined by the set of its fixpoints, which is its image, i.e. $\rho(C) = \{x \in C \mid \rho(x) = x\}$, that $\rho \sqsubseteq \eta$ iff $\eta(C) \subseteq \rho(C)$, and that a subset $X \subseteq C$ is the set of fixpoints of a closure iff X is meet-closed, i.e. $X = \mathcal{M}(X) = \{\wedge Y \mid Y \subseteq X\}$ (note that $\top \in X$). $\langle\rho(C), \leq\rangle$ is a complete meet subsemilattice of C, while it is a complete sublattice iff ρ is completely additive. Let us also recall that $uco(C)$ is dual-atomic, i.e., for any $\rho \in uco(C)$, $\rho = \sqcap_{x\in\rho(C)\setminus\{\top\}}\varphi_x$, where each closure $\varphi_x = \{\top, x\}$, for $x \in C \setminus \{\top\}$, is a dual-atom in $uco(C)$.

In the standard Cousot and Cousot abstract interpretation theory, abstract domains can be equivalently specified either by Galois connections (GCs) or by closure operators (see [9]). In the first case, the concrete domain C and the abstract domain A (both assumed to be complete lattices) are related by a pair of adjoint functions of a GC (α, C, A, γ). If (α, C, A, γ) is a Galois insertion (GI), each element in A is useful to represent the concrete domain C, being α onto. Any GC (α, C, A, γ) may be lifted to a GI by reduction of the abstract domain A, i.e. by identifying in an equivalence class those elements in A having the same concrete meaning. In the second case instead, an abstract domain is specified as (the set of fixpoints of) an upper closure on the concrete domain. These two approaches are completely equivalent: If $\rho \in uco(C)$ and $A \cong \rho(C)$ (with $\iota : \rho(C) \to A$ and $\iota^{-1} : A \to \rho(C)$ being the isomorphism) then $(\iota \circ \rho, C, A, \iota^{-1})$ is a GI; if (α, C, A, γ) is a GI then $\rho_A = \gamma \circ \alpha \in uco(C)$ is the closure associated with A such that $\rho_A(C) \cong A$; moreover, these two constructions are one the inverse of the other. Hence, we will identify $uco(C)$ with the so-called *lattice of abstract interpretations* of C, viz. the complete lattice of all abstract domains of the concrete domain C. Often, we will find convenient to identify closures with their sets of fixpoints, denoted as sets by capital Latin letters; instead, when viewing closures as functions, they will be denoted by Greek letters. We keep this soft ambiguity, since one can distinguish their use as functions or sets, according to the context. The ordering on $uco(C)$ corresponds precisely to the standard order used in abstract interpretation to compare abstract domains with regard to their precision: A_1 is *more precise* than A_2 iff $A_1 \sqsubseteq A_2$ in $uco(C)$. The *lub* and *glb* on $uco(C)$ have therefore the following meaning as operators on domains. Suppose $\{A_i\}_{i\in I} \subseteq uco(C)$: (i) $\sqcup_{i\in I}A_i$ is the most concrete among the domains which are abstractions of all the A_i's, i.e. it is their least common abstraction; (ii) $\sqcap_{i\in I}A_i$ is (isomorphic to) the well-known reduced product of all the A_i's, and, equivalently, it is the most abstract among the domains (abstracting C) which are more concrete than every A_i. Whenever C is a meet-continuous complete lattice (i.e., for any chain $Y \subseteq C$ and $x \in C$, $x \wedge (\vee Y) = \vee_{y\in Y}(x \wedge y)$), $uco(C)$ enjoys the lattice-theoretic property of *pseudocomplementedness* (cf. [17]). This property allowed to define the operation of *complementation* of abstract domains (cf. [6]), namely an operation which, starting from any two domains $D \sqsubseteq A$, where D is meet-continuous, gives as result the most abstract domain $D \sim A$, such that $(D \sim A) \sqcap A = D$. A (*conjunctive*) *decomposition* of an abstract domain $A \in uco(C)$ is any tuple of domains $\langle D_i\rangle_{i\in I} \subseteq uco(C)$ such that $A = \sqcap_{i\in I}D_i$. Complementation is important for decomposing abstract domains: If $D \sqsubseteq A$ then $\langle D \sim A, A\rangle$ is a (binary) decomposition for C, and more general decompositions can be obtained by complementation (see [6]).

3 Completeness in Abstract Interpretation

Let *Program* denote the set of (syntactically well-formed) programs. The concrete standard semantics is in general specified by a semantic function $[\![\cdot]\!] : \mathit{Program} \to C$, where C is a concrete semantic domain of denotations, which we assume to be a complete lattice. If an abstract interpretation is specified by a GI (α, C, A, γ) and by an abstract semantic function $[\![\cdot]\!]^\sharp : \mathit{Program} \to A$, then $[\![\cdot]\!]^\sharp$ is a *sound* abstract semantics, or *(correctly) approximates* $[\![\cdot]\!]$, if, for any program P, $\alpha([\![P]\!]) \leq_A [\![P]\!]^\sharp$, or, equivalently, $[\![P]\!] \leq_C \gamma([\![P]\!]^\sharp)$. The pattern of definition of $[\![\cdot]\!]$ obviously depends on the considered programming language and on the semantics style adopted. We follow here a customary *least fixpoint* semantic approach, which is general enough to subsume and include most kinds of semantic specifications (see [12]). In the following, for two complete lattices C and D, we denote by $C \xrightarrow{m} D$, $C \xrightarrow{c} D$, and $C \xrightarrow{a} D$, respectively, the set of all monotone, (Scott-)continuous and (completely) additive (i.e. preserving all *lub*'s) functions from C to D. A concrete semantics is therefore specified by a pair $\langle C, T\rangle$, where C is a complete lattice and $T : \mathit{Program} \to (C \xrightarrow{m} C)$. For $P \in \mathit{Program}$, we use T_P to denote more compactly $T(P)$. The least fixpoint semantics of any program P is then given by $[\![P]\!] = \mathit{lfp}(T_P) \in C$. On the abstract side, for some $T^\sharp : \mathit{Program} \to (A \xrightarrow{m} A)$, the abstract least fixpoint semantics is analogously defined by $[\![P]\!]^\sharp = \mathit{lfp}(T^\sharp_P)$.

Given a concrete semantics $\mathcal{S} = \langle C, T\rangle$ and an abstract semantics $\mathcal{S}^\sharp = \langle A, T^\sharp\rangle$, related by a GI (α, C, A, γ), $\mathcal{S}^\sharp$ is called a *sound* abstraction of $\mathcal{S}$ if for all $P \in \mathit{Program}$, $\alpha(\mathit{lfp}(T_P)) \leq_A \mathit{lfp}(T^\sharp_P)$. This soundness condition can be more easily verified by checking whether for all $P \in \mathit{Program}$, $\alpha \circ T_P \leq_A T^\sharp_P \circ \alpha$, or, equivalently, $\alpha \circ T_P \circ \gamma \leq_C T^\sharp_P$. We distinguish between these two forms of soundness and we say that $\mathcal{S}^\sharp$ is a *fully sound* abstraction of $\mathcal{S}$ if for all $P \in \mathit{Program}$, $\alpha \circ T_P \leq_A T^\sharp_P \circ \alpha$.

In abstract interpretation, the term completeness is used dually to the above notion of soundness [9, 11, 22]. Again, one distinguishes between a weaker form of completeness, involving least fixpoints only, and a stronger one (but easier to verify) involving semantic functions. We say that $\mathcal{S}^\sharp$ is a *(fully) complete* abstraction of $\mathcal{S}$ if for all $P \in \mathit{Program}$, $(T^\sharp_P \circ \alpha \leq_A \alpha \circ T_P)$ $\mathit{lfp}(T^\sharp_P) \leq_A \alpha(\mathit{lfp}(T_P))$. Because soundness is always required in abstract interpretation, in the following we abuse terminology and say that $\mathcal{S}^\sharp$ is (fully) complete for $\mathcal{S}$ if for all $P \in \mathit{Program}$, $(\alpha \circ T_P = T^\sharp_P \circ \alpha)$ $\alpha(\mathit{lfp}(T_P)) = \mathit{lfp}(T^\sharp_P)$. We also use such notions of completeness and full completeness locally for a given pair of semantic functions $T^\sharp_P$ and T_P.

Completeness as a Domain Property. For a pair of semantic functions $T_P : C \to C$ and $T^\sharp_P : A \to A$, when $\alpha \circ T_P \circ \gamma \leq_C T^\sharp_P$ holds, $T^\sharp_P$ is traditionally called a correct approximation of T_P [9]. It is also well-known since [9, Corollary 7.2.0.4], that the abstract domain A induces a *best* correct approximation of T_P given by $T^A_P = \alpha \circ T_P \circ \gamma$. Consequently, A always induces an (automatically) fully sound abstract semantics $\langle A, \lambda P.\, T^A_P\rangle$. By contrast, this is not true for completeness, i.e., for a given abstract domain A it may well happen that it is not possible to define a fully complete or merely complete abstract semantics based on A – on the contrary, this is the most frequent situation. Furthermore, if A admits a fully complete abstract semantic operator $T^\sharp_P$, then T^A_P is fully complete as well, and $T^A_P = T^\sharp_P$: $T^\sharp_P = T^\sharp_P \circ \alpha \circ \gamma = \alpha \circ T_P \circ \gamma = T^A_P$. Likewise, if $T^\sharp_P$ is complete then T^A_P is complete: $\alpha(\mathit{lfp}(T_P)) \leq_A \mathit{lfp}(T^A_P) \leq_A \mathit{lfp}(T^\sharp_P) = \alpha(\mathit{lfp}(T_P))$. Thus, we get the following important characterization of completeness as a domain property:

> *It is possible to define a (fully) complete abstract semantic operator on an abstract domain A if and only if the best correct approximation induced by A is (fully) complete.*

4 The Lattice of Complete Abstract Interpretations

We have seen that one can consider, without loss of generality, completeness and full completeness for best correct approximations only. Moreover, by the equivalence between the GI and closure operator approaches to abstract domain design, completeness and full completeness can be equivalently specified for closure operators: In fact, it turns out that for a GI (α, C, A, γ) and $f : C \xrightarrow{m} C$, the best correct approximation f^A is (fully) complete iff $\gamma(\alpha(\mathit{lfp}(f))) = \mathit{lfp}(\gamma \circ \alpha \circ f)$ $((\gamma \circ \alpha) \circ f = (\gamma \circ \alpha) \circ f \circ (\gamma \circ \alpha))$. Thus, in the following, we will study completeness and full completeness relatively to closure operators and generic (monotone) functions from a purely algebraic point of view, and say that A is (fully) complete for f if f^A is (fully) complete. We generalize full completeness to cope with generic (possibly nonmonotone) n-ary functions. If $\vec{o}$ denotes a generic tuple of objects, then $\vec{o}_i$ denotes its i-th component.

Definition 4.1 Let C be a complete lattice.
(i) Given $f : C^n \to C$ $(n \geq 1)$, $\rho \in uco(C)$ is *fully complete* for f if for any $\vec{x} \in C^n$, $\rho(f(\vec{x})) = \rho(f(\rho(\vec{x}_1), ..., \rho(\vec{x}_n)))$.
(ii) Given $f \in C \xrightarrow{m} C$, $\rho \in uco(C)$ is *complete* for f if $\rho(\mathit{lfp}(f)) = \mathit{lfp}(\rho \circ f)$. □

We denote the condition in (i) simply by $\rho \circ f = \rho \circ f \circ \rho$. Note that (i) encompasses also functions of type $C \to (C \to \cdots (C \to C) \cdots)$, by "Curryfying" them; moreover, $\mathit{lfp}(\rho \circ f)$ in (ii) could be equivalently replaced by $\mathit{lfp}(\rho \circ f \circ \rho)$.

For $f \in C^n \to C$, we define $\Gamma(C, f) \subseteq uco(C)$ to be the set of fully complete closures on C for f: $\Gamma(C, f) = \{\rho \in uco(C) \mid \rho \circ f = \rho \circ f \circ \rho\}$. If $f : C \xrightarrow{m} C$ then we define $\Delta(C, f) \subseteq uco(C)$ as the set of complete closures on C for f: $\Delta(C, f) = \{\rho \in uco(C) \mid \rho(\mathit{lfp}(f)) = \mathit{lfp}(\rho \circ f)\}$. Also, if $\eta \in uco(C)$ then $\Gamma^{\uparrow\eta}(C, f)$ and $\Delta^{\uparrow\eta}(C, f)$ are the set of closures on $\langle \eta(C), \leq_C \rangle$ that are, respectively, fully complete and complete (for f); since $\rho \in uco(\eta(C))$ iff $\rho \in uco(C)$ and $\rho \sqsubseteq \eta$, then, by denoting $\uparrow \eta$ the principal filter of $uco(C)$ generated by η, we have that $\Gamma^{\uparrow\eta}(C, f) = \Gamma(C, f) \cap \uparrow\eta$ and $\Delta^{\uparrow\eta}(C, f) = \Delta(C, f) \cap \uparrow\eta$. If (α, C, A, γ) is a GI such that $\gamma \circ \alpha = \eta$, then $\Gamma^{\uparrow A}(C, f)$ and $\Delta^{\uparrow A}(C, f)$ are alternative notations for $\Gamma^{\uparrow\eta}(C, f)$ and $\Delta^{\uparrow\eta}(C, f)$ respectively. We can also define completeness and full completeness relatively to any set of concrete functions: If $F \subseteq C^n \to C$ and $G \subseteq C \xrightarrow{m} C$ then $\Gamma(C, F) = \cap_{f \in F} \Gamma(C, f)$ and $\Delta(C, G) = \cap_{g \in G} \Delta(C, g)$ (obviously, $\Gamma(C, \emptyset) = \Delta(C, \emptyset) = uco(C)$). We can then restate the basic Cousot and Cousot [9] result on completeness using our notation as follows: If $F \subseteq C \xrightarrow{m} C$ then $\Gamma(C, F) \subseteq \Delta(C, F)$.

Example 4.2 Consider the classical "rule of signs" domain *Sign* in Fig. 1, which is an abstraction of $\langle \wp(\mathbb{Z}), \subseteq \rangle$ [8]. If ρ_s denotes the closure on $\langle \wp(\mathbb{Z}), \subseteq \rangle$ corresponding to *Sign*, i.e. $Sign \cong \rho_s(\wp(\mathbb{Z}))$, as noted by [22], it is easy to check that ρ_s is fully complete for the multiplication $* : \wp(\mathbb{Z})^2 \to \wp(\mathbb{Z})$ given by $X * Y = \{n \cdot m \mid n \in X, m \in Y\}$. Moreover, *Sign* (i.e. ρ_s) is not fully complete for integer addition $\oplus : \wp(\mathbb{Z})^2 \to \wp(\mathbb{Z})$: For instance, $\rho_s(\rho_s(\{-3, -1\} \oplus \rho_s(\{4, 7\})) = \rho_s(\mathbb{Z}) = \mathbb{Z}$, whereas $\rho_s(\{-3, -1\} \oplus \{4, 7\}) = \rho_s(\{1, 3, 4, 6\}) = 0+$. Also, consider the unary monotone function f that selects, e.g., even numbers, i.e. $f = \lambda X. X \cap \mathbb{Z}_{even}$. While *Sign* is not fully complete for f (e.g., $\rho_s(f(\{-1, 2\})) = 0+ \neq \mathbb{Z} = \rho_s(f(\rho_s(\{-1, 2\}))))$, it is instead complete for f: $\rho_s(\mathit{lfp}(f)) = \rho_s(\emptyset) = \emptyset = \mathit{lfp}(\rho_s \circ f)$. Consider now the lattice $uco(Sign)$ in Fig. 1 of all possible abstractions of *Sign*, and the monotone unary square operation $sq = \lambda X. X * X$. It is a routine task to check that the sets of complete and fully complete abstractions of *Sign* for sq are as follows:
(i) $\Delta^{\uparrow Sign}(\wp(\mathbb{Z}), sq) = uco(Sign) \setminus \{\rho_5\}$: In fact, $\rho_5(\mathit{lfp}(sq)) = \rho_5(\emptyset) = -0$, whilst $\mathit{lfp}(\rho_5 \circ sq) = \mathbb{Z}$, and this holds for ρ_5 only;

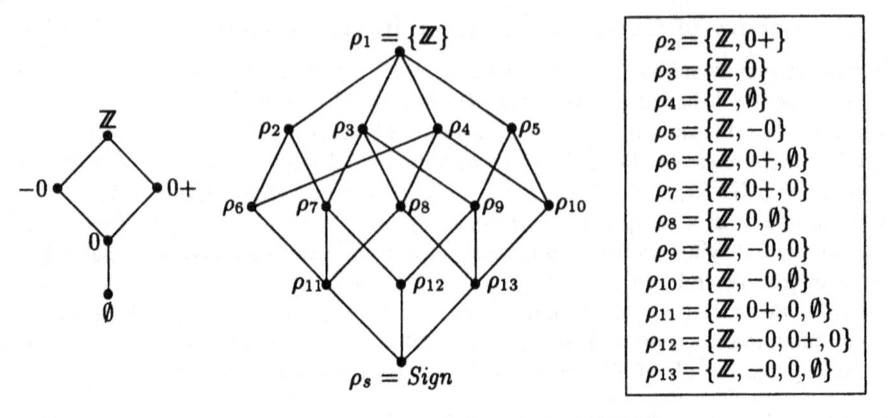

Fig. 1. The lattices *Sign* and *uco*(*Sign*).

(ii) $\Gamma^{\uparrow Sign}(\wp(\mathbb{Z}), sq) = uco(Sign) \setminus \{\rho_5, \rho_{10}\}$: For ρ_5 and ρ_{10}, just consider $X = \{0\}$. Observe that $\Delta(\wp(\mathbb{Z}), sq)$ is not a complete sublattice of $uco(\wp(\mathbb{Z}))$: In fact, $\rho_9, \rho_{10} \in \Delta(\wp(\mathbb{Z}), sq)$, whereas $\rho_9 \sqcup \rho_{10} = \rho_5 \notin \Delta(\wp(\mathbb{Z}), sq)$. Similarly, it is not difficult to check that $\Gamma^{\uparrow Sign}(\wp(\mathbb{Z}), *) = uco(Sign) \setminus \{\rho_2, \rho_5, \rho_6, \rho_{10}\}$. □

The following result summarizes some helpful basic properties of the set of complete and fully complete abstract domains.

Proposition 4.3 *Let* $f : C^n \to C$, $g : C \to C$, *and* $h : C \xrightarrow{m} C$.
(i) $\lambda x. \top_C, \lambda x. x \in \Gamma(C, f) \cap \Delta(C, h)$.
(ii) *For all* $c \in C$, $\Gamma(C, \lambda \vec{x}.\, c) = uco(C) = \Delta(C, \lambda x.\, c)$.
(iii) $\Gamma(C, \lambda \vec{x}.\, \vee_{i=1}^n \vec{x}_i) = uco(C)$.
(iv) $\rho \in \Gamma(C, \lambda \vec{x}.\, \wedge_{i=1}^n \vec{x}_i) \Leftrightarrow \forall X \subseteq C.\ |X| < \omega \Rightarrow \rho(\wedge X) = \wedge \rho(X)$.
(v) *If* $\rho \in \Gamma(C, \{f, g\})$ *then* $\rho \in \Gamma(C, g \circ f)$.
(vi) *If* $\rho, \eta \in \Gamma(C, f)$ *and* $\rho \circ \eta = \eta \circ \rho$ *then* $\rho \circ \eta \in \Gamma(C, f)$.
(vii) *For all* $i \in [1, n]$, $\Gamma(C, f) = \Gamma(C, \{\lambda \vec{x} \in C^{n-1}. f(\langle x_1, ..., x_{i-1}, c, x_i, ..., x_{n-1}\rangle)\}_{c \in C})$.

For $F \subseteq C^n \xrightarrow{m} C$ and $G \subseteq C \xrightarrow{m} C$, we now consider both $\Gamma(C, F)$ and $\Delta(C, G)$ equipped with the pointwise partial order $\sqsubseteq$ of relative precision of domains, inherited from the lattice of abstract interpretations $uco(C)$. Our first finding is that $\Gamma(C, F)$ and $\Delta(C, G)$ are always (the sets of fixpoints of) lower closures on $uco(C)$, i.e. complete meet subsemilattices of $uco(C)$. The fact that full completeness for monotone unary functions is preserved by *glb* was already observed in [6, Proposition 5.2.3].

Theorem 4.4 *If* $F \subseteq C^n \xrightarrow{m} C$, $G \subseteq C \xrightarrow{m} C$ *then* $\Gamma(C, F), \Delta(C, G) \in lco(uco(C))$.

As far as the *lub* is concerned, in Example 4.2 we observed that, in general, a subset of complete closures $\Delta(C, f)$ is not closed under *lub*'s.

Example 4.5 Let us consider the finite chain of five points $C = \{0 < 1 < 2 < 3 < 4\}$ and the function $f : C \to C$ defined as $f = \{0 \mapsto 0, 1 \mapsto 0, 2 \mapsto 0, 3 \mapsto 4, 4 \mapsto 4\}$. Note that f is monotone and hence it is both additive and co-additive, while $lfp(f) = 0$. Next, consider the closures $\rho_1, \rho_2 \in uco(C)$ given by $\rho_1 = \{1, 3, 4\}$ and $\rho_2 = \{2, 3, 4\}$. It is not difficult to verify that $\rho_1, \rho_2 \in \Delta(C, f)$: $\rho_k(lfp(f)) = k = lfp(\rho_k \circ f)$. It turns out that $\rho_1 \sqcup \rho_2 = \{3, 4\}$ does not belong to $\Delta(C, f)$. In fact, $(\rho_1 \sqcup \rho_2)(lfp(f)) = 3$, while $(\rho_1 \sqcup \rho_2) \circ f = \{0 \mapsto 3, 1 \mapsto 3, 2 \mapsto 3, 3 \mapsto 4, 4 \mapsto 5\}$, and hence $lfp((\rho_1 \sqcup \rho_2) \circ f) = 4$. □

In general, i.e. with no hypothesis on C and f, also $\Gamma(C,f)$ is not closed under *lub*'s, as the following example shows.

Example 4.6 Let the $\omega+1$ ordinal be C, and consider the upper closure $f \in uco(C)$ defined by $f(C) = \{x \mid x < \omega\} \cup \{\omega+1\}$ (thus, f is the identity on $C \setminus \{\omega\}$ whereas maps ω to the top $\omega+1$). Next, consider the closures $\rho_1, \rho_2 \in uco(C)$ defined by $\rho_1 = \{x < \omega \mid x \text{ is even}\} \cup \{\omega, \omega+1\}$ and $\rho_2 = \{x < \omega \mid x \text{ is odd}\} \cup \{\omega, \omega+1\}$. It is immediate to verify that $\rho_i \circ f = f \circ \rho_i$ $(i = 1, 2)$, and therefore, by Proposition 4.3 (vii), $\rho_1, \rho_2 \in \Gamma(C,f)$. Moreover, for the *lub* $\rho_1 \sqcup \rho_2 = \{\omega, \omega+1\}$, we have that $(\rho_1 \sqcup \rho_2) \circ f = \rho_1 \sqcup \rho_2$ whilst $(\rho_1 \sqcup \rho_2) \circ f \circ (\rho_1 \sqcup \rho_2) = \lambda x. \omega+1$, and therefore $\rho_1 \sqcup \rho_2 \notin \Gamma(C,f)$. □

Note that, in Example 4.6, f lacks of the continuity property. Indeed, the following key result shows that for continuous functions, *lub*'s of fully complete closures are still fully complete.[1] We already stated this fact, for continuous unary functions, in [18].

Theorem 4.7 *If* $F \subseteq C^n \xrightarrow{c} C$ *then* $\Gamma(C,F) \in uco(uco(C))$.

Continuity is a well-known and sufficiently weak hypothesis, which makes the above result widely applicable in programming language semantics and analysis.

Corollary 4.8 *If* $F \subseteq C^n \xrightarrow{c} C$ *then* $\Gamma(C,F)$ *is a complete sublattice of* $uco(C)$. *Moreover, if* $uco(C)$ *is pseudocomplemented then* $\Gamma(C,F)$ *is pseudocomplemented.*

In general, $\Gamma(C,F)$ is not a sub-pseudocomplemented lattice of $uco(C)$: In Example 4.2, the pseudocomplement of ρ_7 in $uco(Sign)$ is ρ_{10} while it is ρ_{13} in $\Gamma(\wp(\mathbb{Z}), sq)$.

5 Completeness by Domain Transformers

The notion of *abstract domain refinement* has been studied in [14], and more recently in [18], as a formalization and generalization for most of the systematic operators enhancing the precision of abstract domains (e.g. reduced product and disjunctive completion). For a fixed concrete domain C, a (unary) abstract domain refinement is defined as a mapping $\mathfrak{R} : uco(C) \to uco(C)$, such that $\mathfrak{R}$ is monotone, and, for any $A \in uco(C)$, $\mathfrak{R}(A)$ is more precise than A (i.e., $\mathfrak{R}$ is reductive: $\mathfrak{R}(A) \sqsubseteq A$). Moreover, most of the times, refinements are idempotent, i.e. they upgrade domains all at once. This last condition evidently defines *idempotent refinements as lower closure operators* on $uco(C)$, i.e. mappings in $lco(uco(C))$. A dual theory holds for abstract domain *simplifications*, that are defined as upper closures in $uco(uco(C))$ (cf. [18]). Following this framework and exploiting the results of Section 4, we introduce the *complete* and *fully complete kernel* simplifications, for a set F of monotone functions, and the *least fully complete extension* refinement, for a set F of continuous functions. The (fully) complete kernel of an abstract domain A is defined as the most concrete domain abstracting A which is (fully) complete for any $f \in F$, while the least fully complete extension of A is the most abstract domain which is more precise than A and fully complete for any $f \in F$; by the negative observations of Section 4, a similar least complete extension refinement is not in general definable.

Complete Kernel Operators. Let us introduce the following basic definitions.

Definition 5.1 For $F \subseteq C^n \to C$, $G \subseteq C \xrightarrow{m} C$, define $\mathcal{K}_F^C, \mathbb{K}_G^C : uco(C) \to uco(C)$ such that $\mathcal{K}_F^C(X) = \sqcap\{Y \in uco(C) \mid X \sqsubseteq Y,\ Y \in \Gamma(C,F)\}$ and $\mathbb{K}_G^C(X) = \sqcap\{Y \in uco(C) \mid X \sqsubseteq Y,\ Y \in \Delta(C,G)\}$. □

[1] Amato and Levi [1] have independently made an observation similar to Example 4.5, and stated an analogous but weaker result to Theorem 4.7 for additive functions.

When $F = \{f\}$, we write $\mathcal{K}_f^C$ and $\mathbb{K}_f^C$. By definition, $\mathcal{K}_F^C, \mathbb{K}_G^C \in uco(uco(C))$, i.e. both $\mathcal{K}_F^C$ and $\mathbb{K}_G^C$ are idempotent abstract domain simplifications (cf. [18]). We say that $\mathcal{K}_F^C$ ($\mathbb{K}_G^C$) is *safely defined* when for any $X \in uco(C)$, $\mathcal{K}_F^C(X) \in \Gamma(C, F)$ ($\mathbb{K}_G^C(X) \in \Delta(C, G)$). In this case, we call $\mathcal{K}_F^C$ and $\mathbb{K}_G^C$, respectively, the *fully complete kernel* operator for F (in C) and the *complete kernel* operator for G (in C). By Theorem 4.4, $\mathbb{K}_G^C$ is always safely defined, while monotonicity on F is enough for $\mathcal{K}_F^C$.

Example 5.2 The domain $\{\mathbb{Z}, -0, \emptyset\}$ in Example 4.2 is not fully complete for *sq* and $\{\mathbb{Z}, 0-\}$ is not even complete for *sq*. By Theorem 4.4, there exist their (fully) complete kernels, and from the diagram of $uco(Sign)$ in Fig. 1 we derive that $\mathcal{K}_{sq}^{\wp(\mathbb{Z})}(\{\mathbb{Z}, -0, \emptyset\}) = \{\mathbb{Z}, \emptyset\}$ and $\mathbb{K}_{sq}^{\wp(\mathbb{Z})}(\{\mathbb{Z}, -0\}) = \{\mathbb{Z}\}$. Let us also consider the following abstract domain $Sign^+$ depicted below, introduced by Mycroft in [22, Sect. 3.1]. With respect to *Sign* of Example 4.2, $Sign^+$ comprises a new element denoting the integer interval $[1, 9]$. ρ_s^+ denotes the closure associated with $Sign^+$ (i.e. such that $\rho_s^+(\wp(\mathbb{Z})) \cong Sign^+$). It is not difficult to check that $Sign^+$ is fully complete for $\lambda X. \{n\} * X$ iff $n \notin [2, 9]$: In fact, for any $n \in [2, 9]$, there exists $X \subseteq [1, 9] \subset \mathbb{Z}$ such that $\rho_s^+(\{n\} * X) \subset \rho_s^+(\{n\} * \rho_s^+(X))$ (if $n = 2$ then $X = [1, 2]$, and if $n = 9$ then $X = [1, 1]$). Note that only by removing $[1, 9]$ from $Sign^+$ we get a fully complete domain for all $n \in \mathbb{Z}$, viz. *Sign*. This observation implies that *Sign* is the fully complete kernel of $Sign^+$ for $\lambda X. \{n\} * X$ when $n \in [2, 9]$. Obviously, by the above considerations, $Sign^+$ is not fully complete for $*$, and indeed $\mathcal{K}_*^{\wp(\mathbb{Z})}(Sign^+) = Sign$. □

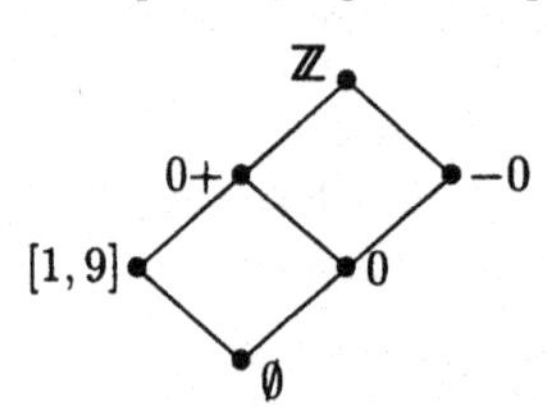

The Least Fully Complete Extension Operator. Dually to what done above, we give the following definition.

Definition 5.3 For $F \subseteq C^n \to C$, $G \subseteq C \xrightarrow{m} C$, define $\mathcal{E}_F^C, \mathbb{E}_G^C : uco(C) \to uco(C)$ as $\mathcal{E}_F^C(X) = \sqcup\{Y \in uco(C) \mid Y \sqsubseteq X,\ Y \in \Gamma(C, F)\}$ and $\mathbb{E}_G^C(X) = \sqcup\{Y \in uco(C) \mid Y \sqsubseteq X,\ Y \in \Delta(C, G)\}$. □

As before, when $F = \{f\}$ we write $\mathcal{E}_f^C$ and $\mathbb{E}_f^C$. By definition, both $\mathcal{E}_F^C$ and $\mathbb{E}_G^C$ are abstract domain refinements in the sense of [14], i.e. $\mathcal{E}_F^C, \mathbb{E}_G^C \in uco(uco(C))$. Similarly to what done above, we define $\mathcal{E}_F^C$ and $\mathbb{E}_G^C$ to be *safely defined* when their ranges are subsets of $\Gamma(C, F)$ and $\Delta(C, G)$, respectively. In this case, $\mathcal{E}_F^C$ and $\mathbb{E}_G^C$ are called, respectively, the *least fully complete extension* operator (for F) and the *least complete extension* operator (for G).

Recall that, in Examples 4.2 and 4.5, we have shown that even when the concrete domain is either an atomic complete Boolean algebra $\wp(X)$, or a finite chain and the concrete function is both additive and co-additive, a *lub* of complete closures is not necessarily still complete. Hence, this key observation precludes us the possibility of finding some reasonable conditions on C and/or G in order that $\mathbb{E}_G^C$ is safely defined. For instance, from the diagram of $uco(Sign)$ in Fig. 1 we derive that the least complete extension for *sq* of $\{\mathbb{Z}, -0\}$ does not exist: In fact, $\{\mathbb{Z}, -0\}$ just admits $\{\mathbb{Z}, -0, 0\}$ and $\{\mathbb{Z}, -0.\emptyset\}$ as minimal complete extensions, and therefore, wrongly, we would get $\mathbb{E}_{sq}^{\wp(\mathbb{Z})}(\{\mathbb{Z}, -0\}) = \{\mathbb{Z}, -0\}$. By contrast, when F consists of continuous functions, by Theorem 4.7, for any $X \in uco(C)$, $\mathcal{E}_F^C(X)$ is the least fully complete extension of X, i.e. in this case $\mathcal{E}_F^C$ is safely defined.

Example 5.4 Since *sq* in Example 4.2 is obviously continuous, by Theorem 4.7, every abstract domain of $\wp(\mathbb{Z})$ admits the least fully complete extension for *sq*. For instance, $\mathcal{E}_{sq}^{\wp(\mathbb{Z})}(\{\mathbb{Z}, -0\}) = \{\mathbb{Z}, -0, 0\}$ and $\mathcal{E}_*^{\wp(\mathbb{Z})}(\{\mathbb{Z}, 0+, \emptyset\}) = \{\mathbb{Z}, 0+, 0, \emptyset\}$. □

Algebraic Properties. We study now the basic algebraic properties of the above operators $\mathcal{K}$, $\mathcal{E}$, $\mathbb{K}$, and $\mathbb{E}$ with respect to the operations of reduced product and least common abstraction of domains. These results are particularly important in order to simplify the construction of complete domains.

Lemma 5.5 *Let $F \subseteq C^n \to C$ and $G \subseteq C \xrightarrow{\text{m}} C$. Then, $(\mathcal{K}_F^C, uco(C), uco(C), \mathcal{E}_F^C)$ and $(\mathbb{K}_G^C, uco(C), uco(C), \mathbb{E}_G^C)$ are Galois connections.*

The following relevant algebraic properties are consequences of the above result.

Proposition 5.6 *Let $F \subseteq C^n \to C$, $G \subseteq C \xrightarrow{\text{m}} C$, $X, Y \in uco(C)$ such that $X \sqsubseteq Y$.*
(i) $\mathcal{K}_F^C$ and $\mathbb{K}_G^C$ are additive, and $\mathcal{E}_F^C$ and $\mathbb{E}_G^C$ are co-additive.
(ii) If C is meet-continuous then $\mathcal{E}_F^C(X) = \mathcal{E}_F^C(X \sim Y) \sqcap \mathcal{E}_F^C(Y)$ and $\mathbb{E}_G^C(X) = \mathbb{E}_G^C(X \sim Y) \sqcap \mathbb{E}_G^C(Y)$.

By point (i), the least (fully) complete extension of a domain A can always be obtained by computing separately the least (fully) complete extensions of the factors in a decomposition of A. This decomposition can be obtained by complementation. For instance, by (ii), if C is meet-continuous then $\mathcal{E}_F^C(X) = \mathcal{E}_F^C(X \sim \mathcal{K}_F^C(X)) \sqcap \mathcal{K}_F^C(X)$.

The concrete domain C is not always the best place where completeness and full completeness for a semantic operator can be verified, as it might be far too concrete for this task. We show that one can always refine or simplify a domain A abstracting C by our operators, with the same result, on any (fully) complete abstraction D of C which is more concrete than A. We know that, for $A \in uco(C)$ and $f : C^n \to C$ (when needed, we assume $n = 1$), the best correct approximation of f for A is $f^A : A^n \to A$ defined as $f^A = \rho_A \circ f$, where ρ_A is the closure associated with A, and, on the right hand side, f is thought of being restricted to A^n. If F is a set of functions, then we denote by F^A the corresponding set of best correct approximations for A. The idea is that we can reason about completeness issues relatively to the concrete domain A and function f^A, instead of, resp., C and f. Note that when f is monotone then f^A is monotone as well. Thus, for $F \subseteq C^n \to C$ and $G \subseteq C \xrightarrow{\text{m}} C$, and for any $A \in uco(C)$, we can define the operators of Definitions 5.1 and 5.3 relatively to $\Gamma(A, F^A)$ and $\Delta(A, G^A)$, denoted by $\mathcal{K}_F^A$, $\mathbb{K}_G^A$, $\mathcal{E}_F^A$, and $\mathbb{E}_G^A$, where the superscript is intended to mean that the best correct approximations are considered. By Theorem 4.4, $\mathbb{K}_G^A$ is always a complete kernel operator, and, for $F \subseteq C^n \xrightarrow{\text{m}} C$, $\mathcal{K}_G^A$ is a fully complete kernel operator. Moreover, it is easy to prove that if $f : C^n \xrightarrow{\text{c}} C$ and $A \in \Gamma(C, f)$, then $f^A : A^n \xrightarrow{\text{c}} A$. Thus, if $F \subseteq C^n \xrightarrow{\text{c}} C$ and $A \in \Gamma(C, f)$ then also $\mathcal{E}_F^A$ is a safely defined least fully complete extension operator.

Theorem 5.7 *Let $F \subseteq C^n \to C$, $G \subseteq C \xrightarrow{\text{m}} C$, and $A \in uco(C)$.*
(i) $A \in \Gamma(C, F) \Leftrightarrow \forall X \in {\uparrow}A.\ \mathcal{K}_F^C(X) = \mathcal{K}_F^A(X) \Leftrightarrow \forall X \in {\uparrow}A.\ \mathcal{E}_F^C(X) = \mathcal{E}_F^A(X)$.
(ii) $A \in \Delta(C, G) \Leftrightarrow \forall X \in {\uparrow}A.\ \mathbb{K}_G^C(X) = \mathbb{K}_G^A(X) \Leftrightarrow \forall X \in {\uparrow}A.\ \mathbb{E}_G^C(X) = \mathbb{E}_G^A(X)$.

The following example shows how to practically exploit the properties in Proposition 5.6 and Theorem 5.7 to design the least fully complete extension of Mycroft's domain $Sign^+$ for integer multiplication.

Example 5.8 Consider the domain $Sign^+$ in Example 5.2. We constructively define the least fully complete extension of $Sign^+$ for integer multiplication. As we observed in Example 5.2, $Sign^+$ is fully complete for $f_n = \lambda X.\{n\} * X$ (which is obviously continuous) iff $n \notin [2, 9]$. Let $n \in [2, 9]$. As we have shown in Example 5.2, $\mathcal{K}_{f_n}^{\wp(\mathbb{Z})}(Sign^+) =$

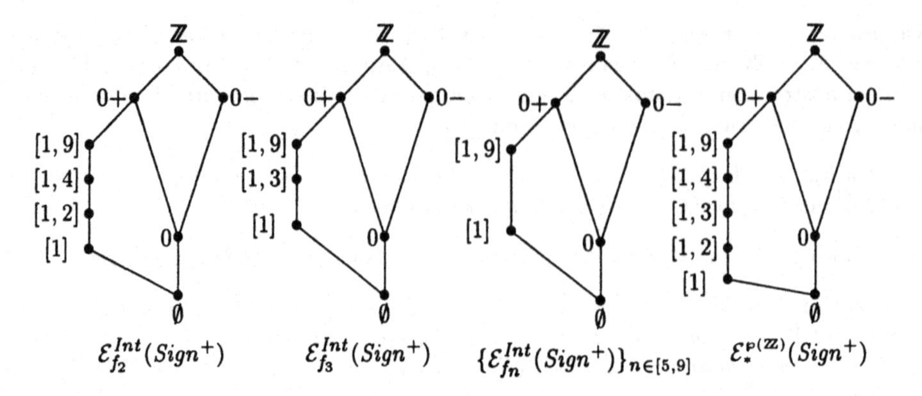

$\mathcal{E}_{f_2}^{Int}(Sign^+)$ $\mathcal{E}_{f_3}^{Int}(Sign^+)$ $\{\mathcal{E}_{fn}^{Int}(Sign^+)\}_{n\in[5,9]}$ $\mathcal{E}_*^{\wp(\mathbb{Z})}(Sign^+)$

Fig. 2. Least fully complete extensions of $Sign^+$.

Sign and $Sign^+ \sim Sign = \{\mathbb{Z}, [1,9]\}$. By Proposition 5.6 (ii), we get $\mathcal{E}_{fn}^{\wp(\mathbb{Z})}(Sign^+) = \mathcal{E}_{fn}^{\wp(\mathbb{Z})}(Sign^+ \sim \mathcal{K}_{fn}^{\wp(\mathbb{Z})}(Sign^+)) \sqcap \mathcal{E}_{fn}^{\wp(\mathbb{Z})}(\mathcal{K}_{fn}^{\wp(\mathbb{Z})}(Sign^+)) = \mathcal{E}_{fn}^{\wp(\mathbb{Z})}(\{\mathbb{Z},[1,9]\}) \sqcap Sign$. We compute the least fully complete extension $\mathcal{E}_{fn}^{\wp(\mathbb{Z})}(\{\mathbb{Z},[1,9]\})$ of the atomic domain $\{\mathbb{Z},[1,9]\}$ by a recursive computation. Consider the Cousot and Cousot [8] domain of integer intervals $Int \in uco(\wp(\mathbb{Z}))$ defined by

$$Int = \{[a,b]\}_{a\leq b} \cup \{(-\infty,b]\}_{b\in\mathbb{Z}} \cup \{[a,+\infty)\}_{a\in\mathbb{Z}} \cup \{(-\infty,+\infty)\} \cup \{\perp\}.$$

It is easy to prove that $Int \in \Gamma(\wp(\mathbb{Z}),*)$ and hence, for any $n \in \mathbb{Z}$, $Int \in \Gamma(\wp(\mathbb{Z}), f_n)$. Thus, by Theorem 5.7, for any $n \in \mathbb{Z}$ and A such that $Int \sqsubseteq A$, $\mathcal{E}_{fn}^{\wp(\mathbb{Z})}(A) = \mathcal{E}_{fn}^{Int}(A)$, and therefore we can consider the more abstract (and simple) domain *Int* as concrete domain of reference. The following proposition characterizes the least fully complete extension in *Int* of any atomic domain of the form $\{\mathbb{Z},[1,m]\}$. We assume that $m \geq 1$ and $n \in [2,m]$. An analogous result holds for $m \leq -1$, $\{\mathbb{Z},[m,1]\}$ and $n \in [m,2]$.

Proposition 5.9 $\mathcal{E}_{fn}^{Int}(\{\mathbb{Z},[1,m]\}) = \{\mathbb{Z},[1,m]\} \sqcap \mathcal{E}_{fn}^{Int}(\{\mathbb{Z},[1,\lfloor \frac{m}{n} \rfloor]\})$.

The above recursive definition has a solution which can be obtained finitely for any $n \leq m$. For $Sign^+$, i.e. $m = 9$, it provides the domains depicted in Fig. 2. In particular, if $F = \{f_n \mid n \in \mathbb{Z}\}$ then $\mathcal{E}_*^{\wp(\mathbb{Z})}(Sign^+) = \mathcal{E}_F^{\wp(\mathbb{Z})}(Sign^+) = \mathcal{E}_{\{f_2,f_3\}}^{Int}(Sign^+)$. □

6 Systematic Construction of Complete Domains

In Example 5.8 we have shown how to constructively design the least fully complete extension for integer multiplication of a simple domain for sign analysis. In this section, we show that under some hypotheses on the semantic functions, a similar methodology can be always defined and applied to finite abstract domains in order to construct their least fully complete extensions and kernels.

Constructing Least Fully Complete Extensions. The following result gives a useful characterization of full completeness for additive functions.

Theorem 6.1 *Let* $f : C \xrightarrow{a} C$. *Then, for all* $X \in uco(C)$, $X \in \Gamma(C,f) \Leftrightarrow \forall x \in X. \vee\{y \in C \mid f(y) \leq x\} \in X$.

Thus, when f is additive, it turns out that $\mathcal{E}_f^C(X)$ is the least meet-closed set Y containing X such that $x \in Y \Rightarrow \vee\{y \mid f(y) \leq x\} \in Y$. This domain can be constructively obtained as the greatest (viz. most abstract) solution in $uco(C)$, smaller or equal to X, of the recursive abstract domain equation $Y = Y \sqcap \mathcal{F}_f(Y)$, where

$\mathcal{F}_f = \lambda X.\mathcal{M}(\{\vee\{y \in C \mid f(y) \leq x\} \mid x \in X\})$. Note that $\mathcal{F}_f : uco(C) \to uco(C)$ is monotone, and therefore $\mathcal{E}_f^C(X)$ is the limit of the (possibly transfinite) iteration sequence $Y^0 = X$, $Y^{\alpha+1} = Y^\alpha \sqcap \mathcal{F}_f(Y^\alpha)$ if α is a successor ordinal, and $Y^\alpha = \sqcap_{\delta<\alpha} Y^\delta$ if α is a limit ordinal. Clearly, if C is finite, then this constructive method is terminating. It is not difficult to prove that if f is in addition extensive and $X = \{\top, x\}$, with $x \in C \setminus \{\top\}$, is an atomic domain, then each element Y^α of the above iteration sequence having $\mathcal{E}_f^C(\{\top, x\})$ as limit, is a chain. In this case, termination for an atomic domain $\{\top, x\}$ is ensured by assuming the weaker hypothesis that $\langle \downarrow x, \leq \rangle$ is a well-ordered sublattice (i.e. it does not contain infinite descending chains) of the (possibly infinite) concrete domain C. An analogous argument led us to the constructive characterization of Proposition 5.9. The interest in least fully complete extensions of atomic domains is justified by observing that, because $uco(C)$ is always dual-atomic, for any abstract domain there exists a canonical decomposition involving atomic domains only: If $X \in uco(C)$ then $\langle \{\top, x\} \rangle_{x \in X \setminus \{\top\}}$ is such a decomposition of X. Then, by Proposition 5.6 (i), for any $X \in uco(C)$ and $f : C \xrightarrow{c} C$, $\mathcal{E}_f^C(X) = \sqcap_{x \in X \setminus \{\top\}} \mathcal{E}_f^C(\{\top, x\})$. We also observe that the extension of the above constructive methods to a finite set of functions F is straightforward. In fact, if *Sol*(f, X) denotes the solution of the above equation for $f : C \xrightarrow{a} C$ and $X \in uco(C)$, then, independently from the order on which the function *Ref*, on the left, chooses f in F by *select*, for any finite set F of additive functions, *Ref*$(F, X) = \mathcal{E}_F^C(X)$.

```
fun Ref(F,X) = if F = ∅ then X
               else select f in F;
                    Ref(F, Sol(f,X)).
```

Constructing Fully Complete Kernels. The systematic construction of fully complete kernels relies on the above procedure for least fully complete extensions. As before, we consider atomic decompositions of the input domain, and the following result characterizes the fully complete kernel of a domain X in terms of the least fully complete extensions of the factors in the atomic decomposition of X.

Theorem 6.2 *If* $f : C \xrightarrow{c} C$ *then* $\mathcal{K}_f^C(X) = \sqcap\{\mathcal{E}_f^C(\{\top, x\}) \mid x \in X, \mathcal{E}_f^C(\{\top, x\}) \subseteq X\}$.

The above result hints a systematic constructive method to design fully complete of abstract domains. The correctness of the algorithm on the left follows by Theorem 6.2. The function *choose* selects and removes an arbitrary element from its input domain. Clearly, when f is additive, the least fully complete extension of the atomic domains can be obtained by the constructive method above.

```
Input : Finite domain X
Output : Fully complete kernel K of X
K := {⊤};
A := X;
while A ≠ {⊤} do
  x := choose(A \ {⊤});
  if E_f^C({⊤,x}) ⊆ X then
        K := K ⊓ E_f^C({⊤,x})
endwhile
```

7 Reconstructing the Integer Interval Domain

We observed in Example 4.2 that *Sign* is not fully complete for integer addition $\oplus$. Instead, it is an easy task to prove that the Cousot and Cousot integer interval domain *Int* of Example 5.8 is fully complete for addition, i.e. $Int \in \Gamma(\wp(\mathbb{Z}), \oplus)$. We can go beyond this expected result. Since $\oplus$ is additive, and therefore continuous, the least complete extension of *Sign* with respect to $\oplus$ does exist, and the following theorem actually proves that it coincides with *Int*.

Theorem 7.1 $\mathcal{E}_{\oplus}^{\wp(\mathbb{Z})}(Sign) = Int$.

Therefore, the domain *Int* for integer interval analysis can be reconstructed by a systematic domain refinement from the rule of signs domain *Sign*.

8 Intelligently Refining Domains: The Case of Groundness Analysis

We have seen that for a fixed concrete least fixpoint semantics $\mathcal{S} = \langle C, f\rangle$, any abstraction $D \in uco(C)$ and its corresponding best correct approximation $f^D : D \to D$ automatically induce a correct abstract semantics $\mathcal{I}^D = \langle D, f^D\rangle$. Clearly, being abstract or concrete is a relative notion, and therefore if $A \in uco(C)$ is a domain abstracting D, viz. $D \sqsubseteq A$, we can reason on the completeness relationships between A and D, where $\mathcal{I}^D$ plays the role of the relative concrete semantics for A. In such a scenario, we simply say that A is complete, resp. fully complete, for D when $A \in \Delta(D, f^D)$, resp. $A \in \Gamma(D, f^D)$. In particular, this situation arises whenever $\Re : uco(C) \to uco(C)$ is some (possibly nonidempotent) domain refinement, and therefore, for some abstract domain A, $C \sqsubseteq \Re(A) \sqsubseteq A$. In this case, we take into consideration the possible completeness relations of A wrt the relative concrete semantics $\langle \Re(A), f^{\Re(A)}\rangle$. Following the notation at the end of Section 5, we denote by $\mathcal{E}_f^{\Re(A)}$ the corresponding completeness transformer. This is a safely defined least fully complete extension operator under the weak hypothesis that the best correct approximation $f^{\Re(A)} : \Re(A) \to \Re(A)$ is continuous. In general, we have that $\Re(A) \sqsubseteq \mathcal{E}_f^{\Re(A)}(A) \sqsubseteq A$. We say that $\Re(A)$ is *too refined* when $\Re(A) \sqsubset \mathcal{E}_f^{\Re(A)}(A)$ holds. The intuition behind this definition is as follows. When, in the above scenario, it happens that A is fully complete for D, then we can reasonably consider the abstract interpretation $\mathcal{I}^A = \langle A, f^A\rangle$ as just thinly less precise than $\mathcal{I}^D$. In other terms, the gap of precision between the abstract interpretations $\mathcal{I}^A$ and $\mathcal{I}^D$ is very narrow, and therefore an efficiency/precision trade-off would suggest to prefer $\mathcal{I}^A$ to the more costly $\mathcal{I}^D$. In particular, whenever $\Re(A) \sqsubset \mathcal{E}_f^{\Re(A)}(A)$, one should prefer the thinly less refined domain $\mathcal{E}_f^{\Re(A)}(A)$ rather than the canonical refinement $\Re(A)$. Thus, under the weak hypothesis that each best correct approximation $f^{\Re(A)}$ is continuous, an intelligent "efficiency-oriented" version $\Re^*$ of a refinement $\Re$ can therefore be defined as $\Re^* = \lambda A. \mathcal{E}_f^{\Re(A)}(A)$. In the following, we illustrate a practical example of this idea in the field of ground-dependency analysis for logic programs.

The Intelligent Disjunctive Completion of *Def* is *Pos*. *Def* and *Pos* are two well-known finite abstract domains of propositional formulae widely used for ground-dependency analysis of logic programs [20]. We refer e.g. to [2] for the details of their definitions. These abstract domains can be viewed as abstractions of the standard concrete domain $\langle \wp(Atom), \subseteq\rangle$ used in a collecting bottom-up semantics for logic programs (as usual, the set of atoms *Atom* is considered up to renaming). It turns out that $\wp(Atom) \sqsubset Pos \sqsubset Def$. For instance, a pair $\langle p(x,y,z), x \wedge (y \leftrightarrow z)\rangle \in Def \subset Pos$ represents each atom $p(t_1, t_2, t_3)$ such that for any its instance $p(s_1, s_2, s_3)$: (i) s_1 is ground; (ii) $var(s_2) = var(s_3)$. In particular, $p(a,b,c)$ and $p(a, x, g(x))$ satisfy this property (where, as usual, $a, b, c, \ldots$ denote ground terms).

The *disjunctive completion* [9] is a well known abstract domain refinement that enhances an abstract domain so that it becomes disjunctive, i.e. so that the corresponding concretization map is additive. When the concrete domain C is completely distributive, as any powerset $\langle \wp(X), \subseteq\rangle$ is, the disjunctive completion $\mathbb{P}(A)$ of an abstract domain A can be obtained by quotienting the powerset of A for the equivalence relation $\{\langle S, T\rangle \mid S, T \subseteq \wp(A),\ \vee_C \gamma(S) = \vee_C \gamma(T)\}$ (see [15] for more details). The concretization of an equivalence class $[S]$ of the disjunctive completion $\mathbb{P}(A)$ is obviously defined as $\vee_C \gamma(S)$, while the abstraction of $[S]$ in A is given by $\vee_A S$. It has been shown in [15, Theorem 5.3] that *Pos* is not disjunctive, i.e. $\mathbb{P}(Pos) \sqsubset Pos$, while [19, Theorem 7.2] proved that $\mathbb{P}(Def) = \mathbb{P}(Pos)$. Thus, it turns out that $\mathbb{P}(Def) = \mathbb{P}(Pos) \sqsubset Pos \sqsubset Def$. For example, by considering the following abstract predicates $\langle p(x,y), x\rangle$ and $\langle p(x,y), x \to y\rangle$, one has $\gamma_{Def}(\langle p(x,y), x\rangle) \cup \gamma_{Def}(\langle p(x,y), x \to y\rangle) \subset$

$\gamma_{Def}(\langle p(x,y), x \vee (x \to y)\rangle) = \gamma_{Def}(\langle p(x,y), true\rangle)$ (it is enough to consider the atom $p(v,w)$), and this shows that *Def* and *Pos* are not disjunctive.

Following the standard bottom-up approach (e.g. [3]), we consider the well-known s-semantics $\mathcal{S} = \langle \wp(Atom), T_P^s\rangle$ of [13] as the concrete least fixpoint semantics of reference, which is fully abstract for the observable given by the computed answer substitutions of a logic program. Then, the abstract domains *Def*, *Pos* and their common disjunctive completion $\mathbb{P}(Def)$ induce the abstract semantics $Def^s = \langle Def, T_P^{Def}\rangle$, $Pos^s = \langle Pos, T_P^{Pos}\rangle$, $\mathbb{P}(Def)^s = \langle \mathbb{P}(Def), T_P^{\mathbb{P}(Def)}\rangle$, where each abstract semantic operator is defined as the best correct approximation of T_P^s on the corresponding abstract domain. Let us turn to discuss the completeness issues between these abstract semantics. It is known [20] that *Def* is not complete (and therefore fully complete) for *Pos* and $\mathbb{P}(Def)$, i.e. $Def \notin \Gamma(Pos, \{T_P^{Pos}\}_{P \in Program}) \cup \Gamma(\mathbb{P}(Def), \{T_P^{\mathbb{P}(Def)}\}_{P \in Program})$, while [15, Proposition 5.13] proved that *Pos* is fully complete (and hence complete) for $\mathbb{P}(Def)$, i.e. $Pos \in \Gamma(\mathbb{P}(Def), \{T_P^{\mathbb{P}(Def)}\}_{P \in Program})$.

Example 8.1 Consider the programs P and Q below.

$P:$	$p(x,y) :- q(x,y), r(x,y).$	$Q:$	$p(x,a) :- p(x,z), p(y,x).$
	$q(a,x) :-$		$p(x,x) :-$
	$q(x,a) :-$		$p(a,y) :-$
	$r(x,x) :-$		

It is easy to see that $\langle p(x,y), x \leftrightarrow y\rangle \in lfp(T_P^{Def})$, whilst $\langle p(x,y), x \wedge y\rangle \in lfp(T_P^{Pos}) = lfp(T_P^{\mathbb{P}(Def)})$. Thus, in P, by either *Pos* or $\mathbb{P}(Def)$, we are able to infer that any computed answer substitution for the predicate p will ground both its arguments, while in *Def* we can only conclude that the first argument is ground iff the second is ground. Moreover, the Kleene iterations for T_Q^{Pos} and $T_Q^{\mathbb{P}(Def)}$ are as follows: $(T_Q^{Pos})^0 = \langle p(x,y), false\rangle$, $(T_Q^{Pos})^1 = \langle p(x,y), y \to x\rangle$, $(T_Q^{Pos})^2 = \langle p(x,y), true\rangle$ (least fixpoint); $(T_Q^{\mathbb{P}(Def)})^0 = \langle p(x,y), false\rangle$, $(T_Q^{\mathbb{P}(Def)})^1 = \langle p(x,y), [x \leftrightarrow y, x]\rangle$, $(T_Q^{\mathbb{P}(Def)})^2 = \langle p(x,y), [x \leftrightarrow y, x, y]\rangle$ (least fixpoint). Thus, in Q, by $\mathbb{P}(Def)$ we are able to infer that in each computer answer substitution for p, either its first argument is ground or its second argument is ground or they are equivalent. Instead, by using *Pos* we get no ground-dependency information. Nevertheless, by abstracting in *Pos* the final output $\langle p(x,y), [x \leftrightarrow y, x, y]\rangle$ of $\mathbb{P}(Def)$ we get exactly the output $\langle p(x,y), true\rangle$ of *Pos*. □

We sharp the aforementioned result of [15, Proposition 5.13], and we show that *Pos* is the least complete and fully complete extension of *Def* in $\mathbb{P}(Def)$, i.e., by letting $F = \{T_P^{\mathbb{P}(Pos)}\}_{P \in Program}$, the following theorem holds.

Theorem 8.2 $\mathcal{E}_F^{\mathbb{P}(Def)}(Def) = \mathbb{E}_F^{\mathbb{P}(Def)}(Def) = Pos.$

To conclude, let us draw the practical consequences of Theorem 8.2, in view of the general observations made at the beginning of this section. If we want to systematically design an abstract domain for disjunctive ground-dependency analysis starting from the existing domain *Def*, then, according to the standard procedure of refining *Def* to its disjunctive completion, we should use the disjunctive domain $\mathbb{P}(Def)$. However, according to our definitions, $\mathbb{P}(Def)$ is too refined, since, by Theorem 8.2, $\mathcal{E}^{\mathbb{P}(Def)}(Def) = Pos$ is a proper abstraction of $\mathbb{P}(Def)$. By contrast, following the "efficiency-oriented" strategy of refinement outlined above, the intelligent disjunctive completion is defined as $P^\star = \lambda A.\mathcal{E}_F^{\mathbb{P}(A)}(A)$, and therefore we get $P^\star(Def) = Pos$. This still is a systematic step of refinement, and by doing this, it is important to remark that we dramatically gain in efficiency: While $\mathbb{P}(Def)$ has an exponential size wrt Def, i.e. $|\mathbb{P}(Def)| = O(2^{|Def|})$, by contrast, it is easy to verify that $|Pos| = O(|Def|)$ yet maintaining a relationship of full completeness between Pos and $\mathbb{P}(Def)$.

9 Related Work

The notion of completeness in abstract interpretation has been first considered by Cousot and Cousot in [9], where the basic properties of complete abstractions in the approximation of fixpoint-based semantics have been proved. Completeness arises typically among (concrete) semantics of programming languages at different levels of abstraction. Cousot and Cousot proved in [10] that some classical semantics of programming languages are (fully) complete abstractions of a generalized SOS operational semantics, and Cousot [7] formalized the relationships between some well known type inference systems as complete (called exact) abstract interpretations. In logic program semantics, Giacobazzi [16] proved that fully complete abstractions relating semantics provide a corresponding hierarchy of models for positive logic programs, while Comini and Levi [5] based their taxonomy of observables (perfect, denotational, and semi-denotational) on the notion of full completeness, applied to some basic operators for building SLD-trees. Recently, Amato and Levi [1] studied the lattice structure of these observables, which is basically the lattice of full complete abstractions of the above additive operators for building SLD-trees, and independently formulated an analogous but weaker result to our Theorem 4.7, for additive operators only. In program analysis, Sekar et al. [24] focussed on completeness of Mycroft's [21] strictness analysis of functional programs. Their approach is rather different from ours: They identified the greatest class Cl of programs such that the strictness analysis of P is complete iff $P \in Cl$. In our terminology, they have found the greatest set of programs Cl such that $Strictness \in \Delta(C, \{T_P\}_{P \in Cl})$, where C and T_P are, respectively, the concrete domain and the semantic transformer in the standard collecting denotational semantics of P. Reddy and Kamin [23] generalized [24] to first-order and typed higher-order functional languages. Steffen [25] is one of the first authors isolating completeness as a key property for analysis. His approach is "observation directed", in the sense that the design of a fully abstract (complete) abstract interpretation is directed by a certain observation level. This differs from our approach, which is, as the standard Cousot and Cousot theory of abstract interpretation, "semantics directed". A categorical generalization of Steffen's work has been successively studied in [26]. Colby [4] isolated the phenomenon of accumulated imprecision in abstract interpretation, which is essentially the same as the lack of full completeness. To overcome these problems, Colby proposes to consider a new enhanced so-called transfer relations language to express the net behavior of finite control paths in the operational semantics of programming languages, and he shows that this allows to solve the problem in some relevant examples. Colby's approach is therefore orthogonal to ours: The whole semantic metalanguage is changed to gain precision. Finally, the most related work is certainly that of Mycroft [22]. He considers a notion of completeness which is essentially equal to ours, except that he develops his theory using a predicate-based approach to abstract interpretation (a kind of logical view of classical abstract interpretation). Moreover, he argues that the well-known state minimization algorithm for finite deterministic automata can be used to produce a canonical (fully) complete abstract interpretation by removing useless domain elements. Although the technical approach followed by Mycroft is quite different from ours, the idea of systematically defining a canonical simplest complete abstract interpretation is basically the same idea of our complete kernel operators. This relationship certainly deserves further investigation in order to see if these two systematic methodologies actually have the same behavior. On the other hand, Mycroft does not consider the dual problem analogous to our least (fully) complete extension operators.

Acknowledgments. We are grateful to Francesca Scozzari for her contribution to Theorem 4.7.

References

1. G. Amato and G. Levi. Properties of the lattice of observables in logic programming. In *Proc. APPIA-GULP-PRODE'97*, pp. 175–187, 1997.
2. T. Armstrong, K. Marriott, P. Schachte, and H. Søndergaard. Two classes of Boolean functions for dependency analysis. To appear in *Sci. Comput. Program.*, 1997.
3. R. Barbuti, R. Giacobazzi, and G. Levi. A general framework for semantics-based bottom-up abstract interpretation of logic programs. *ACM TOPLAS*, 15(1):133–181, 1993.
4. C. Colby. Accumulated imprecision in abstract interpretation. In *Proc. 1st ACM AAS'97*, pp. 77–89, 1997.
5. M. Comini and G. Levi. An algebraic theory of observables. In *Proc. ILPS'94*, pp. 172–186, 1994.
6. A. Cortesi, G. Filé, R. Giacobazzi, C. Palamidessi, and F. Ranzato. Complementation in abstract interpretation. *ACM TOPLAS*, 19(1):7–47, 1997.
7. P. Cousot. Types as abstract interpretations. In *Proc. ACM POPL'97*, pp. 316–331, 1997.
8. P. Cousot and R. Cousot. Abstract interpretation: A unified lattice model for static analysis of programs by construction or approximation of fixpoints. In *Proc. ACM POPL'77*, pp. 238–252, 1977.
9. P. Cousot and R. Cousot. Systematic design of program analysis frameworks. In *Proc. ACM POPL'79*, pp. 269–282, 1979.
10. P. Cousot and R. Cousot. Inductive definitions, semantics and abstract interpretation. In *Proc. ACM POPL'92*, pp. 83–94, 1992.
11. P. Cousot and R. Cousot. Higher-order abstract interpretation (and application to comportment analysis generalizing strictness, termination, projection and PER analysis of functional languages). In *Proc. IEEE ICCL'94*, pp. 95–112, 1994.
12. P. Cousot and R. Cousot. Compositional and inductive semantic definitions in fixpoint, equational, constraint, closure-condition, rule-based and game-theoretic form. In *Proc. CAV'95*, LNCS 939, pp. 293–308, 1995.
13. M. Falaschi, G. Levi, M. Martelli, and C. Palamidessi. Declarative modeling of the operational behavior of logic languages. *Theor. Comput. Sci.*, 69(3):289–318, 1989.
14. G. Filé, R. Giacobazzi, and F. Ranzato. A unifying view of abstract domain design. *ACM Comput. Surv.*, 28(2):333–336, 1996.
15. G. Filé and F. Ranzato. The powerset operator on abstract interpretations. To appear in *Theor. Comput. Sci.*, 1998.
16. R. Giacobazzi. "Optimal" collecting semantics for analysis in a hierarchy of logic program semantics. In *Proc. STACS '96*, LNCS 1046, pp. 503–514, 1996.
17. R. Giacobazzi, C. Palamidessi, and F. Ranzato. Weak relative pseudo-complements of closure operators. *Algebra Universalis*, 36(3):405–412, 1996.
18. R. Giacobazzi and F. Ranzato. Refining and compressing abstract domains. In *Proc. ICALP'97*, LNCS 1256, pp. 771–781, 1997.
19. R. Giacobazzi and F. Ranzato. Optimal domains for disjunctive abstract interpretation. To appear in *Sci. Comput. Program.*, 1998.
20. K. Marriott and H. Søndergaard. Precise and efficient groundness analysis for logic programs. *ACM Lett. Program. Lang. Syst.*, 2(1-4):181–196, 1993.
21. A. Mycroft. *Abstract interpretation and optimising transformations for applicative programs*. PhD thesis, Univ. of Edinburgh, 1981.
22. A. Mycroft. Completeness and predicate-based abstract interpretation. In *Proc. ACM PEPM '93*, pp. 179–185, 1993.
23. U.S. Reddy and S.N. Kamin. On the power of abstract interpretation. In *Proc. IEEE ICCL '92*, 1992.
24. R.C. Sekar, P. Mishra, and I.V. Ramakrishnan. On the power and limitation of strictness analysis. *J. ACM*, 44(3), 1997.
25. B. Steffen. Optimal data flow analysis via observational equivalence. In *Proc. MFCS '89*, LNCS 379, 1989.
26. B. Steffen, C.B. Jay, and M. Mendler. Compositional characterization of observable program properties. *AFCET*, 26:403–424, 1992.
27. M. Ward. The closure operators of a lattice. *Ann. Math.*, 43(2):191–196, 1942.

Floating Point Verification in HOL Light: The Exponential Function

John Harrison

University of Cambridge Computer Laboratory
New Museums Site, Pembroke Street
Cambridge CB2 3QG, England

Abstract. Since they often embody compact but mathematically sophisticated algorithms, operations for computing the common transcendental functions in floating point arithmetic seem good targets for formal verification using a mechanical theorem prover. We discuss some of the general issues that arise in verifications of this class, and then present a machine-checked verification of an algorithm for computing the exponential function in IEEE-754 standard binary floating point arithmetic. We confirm (indeed strengthen) the main result of a previously published error analysis, though we uncover a minor error in the hand proof and are forced to confront several subtle issues that might easily be overlooked informally.

1 Introduction

Algorithms for performing floating point operations are often rather complex. It is difficult to make sure they are correct — for example, a bug in the floating-point division instruction of the Intel Pentium gained widespread publicity quite recently (Pratt 1995). We present here a machine-checked proof of a floating point algorithm, with the hope of illustrating the potential for theorem provers in this area. The present discussion is necessarily sketchy, and we refer the reader to an earlier technical report (Harrison 1997a) for a more detailed and discursive treatment.

Suppose we have a set $\mathbb{F}$ of floating point numbers. For the purposes of this general discussion, we will ignore special cases such as infinities and NaNs,[1] and suppose that each member of $\mathbb{F}$ has a corresponding real number value. We will use v to denote the valuation function $\mathbb{F} \to \mathbb{R}$.

We specify correctness of the floating point operation EXP by comparing its output with the true mathematical result, using the valuation function v to mediate between the realms of floating point and real numbers. That is, for each floating point number a, we compare $exp(v(a))$ and $v(\mathrm{EXP}(a))$; in algebraist's jargon, we are interested in how closely the following diagram 'almost commutes':

[1] NaN = Not a Number, a special value to represent the result of an erroneous calculation such as taking the square root of a negative number.

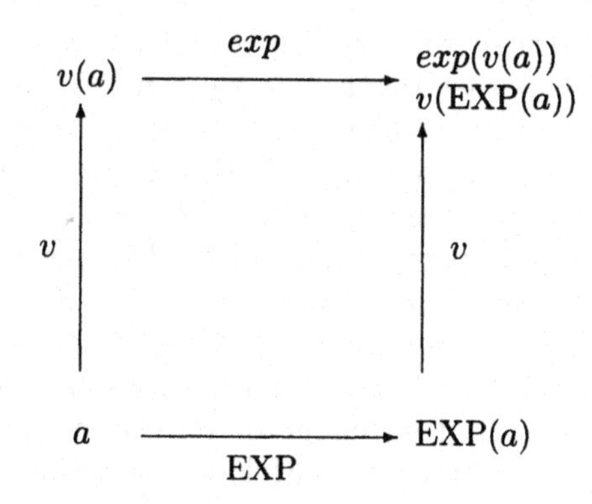

In the present verification, we quantify the relative error in the sense of 'units in the last place' (*ulp*). One *ulp* is the magnitude of the least significant bit of the value concerned. (When making formal statements we will follow our HOL formalization and regard *ulp* as a function of the relevant floating point number, writing $ulp(a)$ or ulp_a for one unit in the last place of a.) Note that perfect rounding would ensure that the error in the output was always ≤ 0.5 *ulp*, but owing to the 'table maker's dilemma' (Goldberg 1991) this is difficult for the transcendentals.

2 HOL Light

The verification described here is conducted using HOL Light (Harrison 1996a), a version of the HOL prover (Gordon and Melham 1993), itself descended from Edinburgh LCF (Gordon and Melham 1993). We cannot describe the system in detail here, and to help the reader unfamiliar with HOL, we will use standard symbols for the logical operators. Most of the operations on natural and real numbers should look familiar even in their HOL ASCII representations, but here are some of the less obvious ones together with renderings in standard mathematical notation and English:

HOL notation	Standard symbol	Meaning
`SUC(n)`	$n+1$	Successor operation on $\mathbb{N}$
`m EXP n`	m^n	Natural number exponentiation
`&`	*(none)*	Natural map $\mathbb{N} \to \mathbb{R}$
`--x`	$-x$	Unary negation of x
`inv(x)`	x^{-1}	Multiplicative inverse of x
`abs(x)`	$\|x\|$	Absolute value of x
`x pow n`	x^n	Real x raised to natural number power n
`root n x`	$\sqrt[n]{x}$	Positive n^{th} root of x
`Sum(n,d) f`	$\Sigma_{i=n}^{n+d-1} f(i)$	Sum of d terms $f(i)$ starting with $f(n)$

HOL's type system distinguishes natural numbers and reals, so `&` is used to map between them. It's mainly used as part of real number constants like `&0`, `&1`

etc. Note also that while one might prefer to regard 0^{-1} as 'undefined' (in some precise sense), we set `inv(&0) = &0` by definition.

The floating point algorithm is expressed in a simple imperative 'while language'. Following Gordon (1989), this is given a precise operational semantics inside HOL, while at the same time remaining a recognizable vehicle similar to a subset of typical programming or hardware description languages.

A HOL term '`correct` $p\ C\ q$' means that, if started in any state satisfying p, the command (program fragment) C will terminate in a state satisfying q. It is assertions of this form that we want to prove. In order to make this process easier, we use the standard technique of verification condition generation. The user presents a program together with loop annotations and possibly other assertions. HOL automatically processes this and produces a series of proof obligations. All these are purely concerned with facts in the underlying theories, and have no explicit connection with programming constructs. When they are all proved, HOL will reconstruct a proof that the program, stripped of its annotations if desired, obeys the required correctness criteria.

3 Formalizing IEEE arithmetic

We will therefore assume that our ultimate goal is to deal with IEEE-754 floating point numbers, and moreover, that where we use subsidiary floating point arithmetic operations such as addition and multiplication, they conform to the IEEE standard. Therefore, an important preliminary step in our work is to translate key parts of IEEE-754 into formal HOL specifications. We do not attempt an exhaustive exegesis of the standard — for some parts, e.g. the specification of trap handlers, this would be possible only as part of a more general specification of an ambient computing environment. We just aim to formalize enough to make it clear that any implementations we verify do in fact conform to the standard in the essential details. Our effort can be compared to a Z specification by Barratt (1989) and a PVS specification of IEEE-854 by Miner (1995). We have found the latter particularly valuable in our work; it is easy to read and the underlying logic is similar to HOL's.

The operations on floating point numbers are distinct from those on mathematical real numbers, natural numbers etc. However, HOL Light features operator overloading, so we use the conventional symbols for arithmetic operations on floats; HOL exploits types to disambiguate input, signalling an error if it is unable to do so. There is one exception: we cannot overload the equality operation as it is already polymorphic. Instead we use == for equality on floating point values, which should look familiar to C programmers. Arguably, using the conventional symbol for equality would be rather misleading, since the standard notion is neither reflexive ($x \neq x$ if x is a NaN) nor substitutive ($-0 = +0$ but $\frac{1}{+0} \neq \frac{1}{-0}$).

The reader may need to bear in mind this overloading in order to understand some of the HOL theorems that follow. It is usually easy to see what the type of an operation is by noting how it is combined with a function of known type such as the valuation function $Val : \mathbb{F} \rightarrow \mathbb{R}$ (this is in fact how HOL's typechecker does it). For example, in `Val(a + b)`, the addition operation must be a floating point operation, while in `Val(a) + Val(b)` the addition operator is mathematical real addition. Generally, overloading always makes some expressions more natural at the cost of requiring a certain alertness on the part of the reader. In informal explanations we may omit Val where we should properly write it.

As well as floating point numbers, the algorithm we are concerned with uses machine integers. We will not discuss the (straightforward) HOL formalization of these numbers in detail, but we will note that they are 2s complement 32-bit integers. Their behaviour on overflow is undefined, i.e. a fixed arbitrary value results. This seems the most pessimistic assumption that can reasonably be made about typical contemporary hardware. In fact, the correctness of the algorithm only requires a pretty limited range of integers.

There are coercions `Tofloat` and `Toint` for mapping between floats and ints, and these are of course subject to range restrictions in each case. We will just be explicit about two operations used later, to avoid any ambiguity. The integer modulus operation, written `%` as in C, always returns a positive answer whatever the sign of its arguments. The function `INTRND` is the composition of the round-to-integer-value operation on floating point numbers and the coercion function `Toint`. One further operation that we use, recommended but not mandated by the IEEE Standard, is `Scalb`, where `Scalb(a,N)` scales the floating point number a by 2^N for an integer N. This operation is performed atomically, so may avoid overflow even if 2^N itself would overflow.

4 Lemmas about floating point numbers

In order to perform error analysis reasonably smoothly, we try to arrive at fairly general theorems about the floating point operations. Occasionally we need to dive down to more specialized and intricate results — we will present an example later — but for the most part we can use a standard collection of lemmas. Following Tang (1989), we define the error resulting from rounding a real number x to a floating point value as `error(x)`. Now because of the regular way in which the operations are defined, they all relate to their abstract mathematical counterparts according to the same pattern for finite operands:

```
|- Finite(a) ∧ Finite(b) ∧
   abs(Val(a) + Val(b)) < threshold(float_format)
   ⟹ Finite(a + b) ∧
      (Val(a + b) = (Val(a) + Val(b)) + error(Val(a) + Val(b)))
```

The comparisons are even more straightforward, e.g.

```
|- Finite(a) ∧ Finite(b) ⟹ (a < b = Val(a) < Val(b))

|- Finite(a) ∧ Finite(b) ⟹ (a == b = (Val(a) = Val(b)))
```

We have several lemmas quantifying the error, of which the most useful is the following:

```
|- abs(x) < threshold(float_format) ∧
   abs(x) < (&2 pow j / &2 pow 125)
   ⟹ abs(error(x)) <= &2 pow j / &2 pow 150
```

The situation for numbers in the denormal range is slightly worse:

```
|- ∀x. abs x < inv (&2 pow 126) ⟹ abs(error x) <= inv (&2 pow 150)
```

There are many important situations, however, where the operations are exact, because the result is exactly representable. Trivially, for example, the negation and absolute value functions are always exact:

```
|- Finite(a) ⟹ Finite(abs(a)) ∧ (Val(abs(a)) = abs(Val(a)))
```

Also, if a result only has 24 significant digits (modulo some care in the denormal case), then it is exactly representable

```
|- (abs(x) = (&2 pow e / &2 pow 149) * &k) ∧
   k < 2 EXP 24 ∧ e < 254
   ⟹ ∃a. Finite(a) ∧ (Val(a) = x)
```

and the error in any calculation with an exactly representable result is zero, e.g.

```
|- Finite(a) ∧ Finite(b) ∧
   Finite(c) ∧ (Val(c) = Val(a) * Val(b))
   ⟹ Finite(a * b) ∧ (Val(a * b) = Val(a) * Val(b))
```

Another important case of exact operations is subtraction of nearby values with the same sign. This is a well-known result in floating point error analysis, similar to Theorem 11 of Goldberg (1991).

```
|- Finite(a) ∧ Finite(b) ∧
   &2 * abs(Val(a) - Val(b)) <= abs(Val(a))
   ⟹ Finite(a - b) ∧ (Val(a - b) = Val(a) - Val(b))
```

5 The algorithm

The algorithm we verify is one given by Tang (1989) for the exponential function. Tang gives a fairly detailed explanation of the algorithm together with an error analysis, which makes it a suitable target for formal treatment. It is based on a table of precomputed values with a polynomial used to interpolate between them. To achieve good accuracy, several values are split across two floating point number, one much larger than the other. Moreover, the ordering of certain operations is often critical. The following is a rendering of the algorithm in our while-language, embedded in the correctness assertion that is the ultimate conclusion of the work described here.

```
|- (Int_32          = Int(32)) ∧
   (Int_2e9         = Int(2 EXP 9)) ∧
   (Plus_one        = float(0,127,0)) ∧
   (THRESHOLD_1     = float(0,134,6056890)) ∧
   (THRESHOLD_2     = float(0,102,0)) ∧
   (Inv_L           = float(0,132,3713595)) ∧
   (L1              = float(0,121,3240448)) ∧
   (L2              = float(0,102,4177550)) ∧
   (A1              = float(0,126,68)) ∧
   (A2              = float(0,124,2796268)) ∧
   TABLES_OK S_Lead S_Trail
   ⟹
   correct
   T
   var X:float,E:float,R1:float,R2:float,R:float,P:float,Q:float,
       S:float, E1:float, N:Int,N1:Int,N2:Int,M:Int,J:Int;
     if Isnan(X) then E := X
     else if X == Plus_infinity then E := Plus_infinity
     else if X == Minus_infinity then E := Plus_zero
     else if abs(X) > THRESHOLD_1 then
       if X > Plus_zero then E := Plus_infinity
       else E := Plus_zero
     else if abs(X) < THRESHOLD_2 then E := Plus_one + X
     else
      (N := INTRND(X * Inv_L);
       N2 := N % Int_32;
       N1 := N - N2;
       if abs(N) >= Int_2e9 then
         R1 := (X - Tofloat(N1) * L1) - Tofloat(N2) * L1
       else
         R1 := X - Tofloat(N) * L1;
       R2 := Tofloat(--N) * L2;
       M := N1 / Int_32;
       J := N2;
       R := R1 + R2;
       Q := R * R * (A1 + R * A2);
       P := R1 + (R2 + Q);
       S := S_Lead(J) + S_Trail(J);
       E1 := S_Lead(J) + (S_Trail(J) + S * P);
       E := Scalb(E1,M)
      )
   end
   (Isnan(X) ⟹ Isnan(E)) ∧
   (X == Plus_infinity ∨
    Finite(X) ∧ exp(Val X) >= threshold(float_format)
    ⟹ E == Plus_infinity) ∧
   (X == Minus_infinity ⟹ E == Plus_zero) ∧
   (Finite(X) ∧ exp(Val X) < threshold(float_format)
   ⟹ Isnormal(E) ∧ abs(Val(E) - exp(Val X)) < (&54 / &100) * Ulp(E) ∨
       (Isdenormal(E) ∨ Iszero(E)) ∧
       abs(Val(E) - exp(Val X)) < (&77 / &100) * Ulp(E))
```

The constant TABLES_OK is used to abbreviate a large set of assumptions about the values of table entries. All the following values are taken from Tang's paper.

```
|- TABLES_OK S_Lead S_Trail =
       (S_Lead(Int 0)    = float(0,127,0)) ∧
       (S_Lead(Int 1)    = float(0,127,183680)) ∧
       ...
       (S_Lead(Int 31)   = float(0,127,8029056)) ∧
       (S_Trail(Int 0)   = float(0,0,0)) ∧
       (S_Trail(Int 1)   = float(0,106,5444997)) ∧
       ...
       (S_Trail(Int 31) = float(0,109,4943305))
```

6 The HOL verification

Following Tang, we split the error into three more or less independent parts and analyze them separately.

- The error in range reduction.
- The error in the polynomial approximation.
- The rounding error in the reconstruction of the result.

6.1 Checking of prestored constants

In several places, we need to prove mathematical results about the various prestored constants. Most of these constants bear a straightforward relationship to $ln(2)$, so first we obtain, by formal proof, an accurate approximation to $ln(2)$. We use $ln(2) = ln(1+\frac{1}{2}) - ln(1-\frac{1}{4})$, since each of the values on the right of this equation can be evaluated reasonably efficiently by truncating its Taylor series, using existing HOL theorems about the error in such situations. The numerical result is:

```
|- abs(ln(&2) - &544531980202654583340825686620847 /
               &785593587443817081832229725798400) < inv(&2 pow 51)
```

The other constants needed are approximations to $s_j = 2^{\frac{j}{32}}$ for $j = 0, \ldots, 31$. The easiest way to justify these is to measure the difference $s_j^{32} - 2^j$ and appeal to the following theorem, easily derived in HOL from the Mean Value Theorem for derivatives:

```
|- &0 < x ∧ x <= &2
   ⟹ abs(x - root 32 (&2 pow j))
      <= abs(x pow 32 - &2 pow j) /
         (if x pow 32 <= &2 pow j then &32 * x pow 32 / x
          else &16 * &2 pow j)
```

This allows us to deduce that the difference between the stored value s_j and the true mathematical figure $2^{\frac{j}{32}}$ is below 2^{-41} in all cases. This could be sharpened a little, but it is already much better than the accuracy we need later. There is one exception: we need later the fact that in the case $j = 0$ the error is zero, trivially so since s_0 is exactly 1.

6.2 Error in range reduction

The error analysis here is rather intricate, belying the simplicity of the code. We must establish that R_1 is calculated exactly. The stored values L_1 and L_2 have enough trailing zeros that multiplication by small enough integers is exact; this is a fairly straightforward application of earlier lemmas about the exact representability of values with few enough significant digits. More difficult is establishing that the subsequent subtractions, either $X - NL_1$ or both $X - N_1L_1$ and $(X - N_1L_1) - N_2L_1$ depending on the arm of the conditional, are exact by virtue of cancellation. We are tantalizingly close to being able to apply a previous lemma requiring that $2|X - NL| \leq |NL|$ or $2|X - NL| \leq |X|$. This always works for the subtraction $X - N_1L_1$, but the required preconditions are just missed in the other subtractions in the cases when $N = \pm 1$ or $N_2 = 1$ respectively. We need to analyze L_1's bit pattern more carefully to justify the exactness of subtraction over a larger range. This tedious reasoning is embedded in the following ad hoc lemma, which says that subtraction of NL_1 from any value within $\frac{1}{88}$ of it is exact.

```
|- (L1 = float (0,(121,3240448))) ∧
   Finite(X) ∧
   Finite(Tofloat(N) * L1) ∧
   (Val(Tofloat(N) * L1) = Ival(N) * Val(L1)) ∧
   abs(Val(X) - Val(Tofloat(N) * L1)) <= inv(&88)
   ⟹ Finite(X - Tofloat(N) * L1) ∧
      (Val(X - Tofloat(N) * L1) = Val(X) - Val(Tofloat(N) * L1))
```

6.3 Error in polynomial approximation

This is a matter of pure mathematics, and has no connection with floating point arithmetic. It is dismissed in a few lines of Tang's paper, since if one doesn't insist on a fully formal proof, then maximizing a smooth function over a closed interval is a straightforward matter for a numerical programmer. However, justifying such a result by a formal proof is much harder. We took several weeks of work, becoming diverted into the necessary proofs of various results about polynomial elimination. This is described in more detail in a separate paper (Harrison 1997b), but in summary the approach is as follows.

We want to arrive at reasonably sharp bounds for $e^x - (1 + p(x))$ over a suitable range. First, we find a truncated Taylor series to approximate e^x to an accuracy well beyond that we are interested in. Thus, the problem is reduced to bounding a *polynomial*, which is a tractable problem. We just need to locate the points of zero derivative. The main difficulty is that one must prove that *all* such points have been located; in general it may be fewer than the degree of the polynomial. Thus we need to prove formally how many (real) roots a polynomial has, and to do this we formalize Sturm's theorem on polynomial remainder sequences (Benedetti and Risler 1990).

It is worth noting that the only real error we have found in Tang's proof occurs here. He bounds the polynomial approximation accuracy over the interval $[-0.010831, 0.010831]$, with the implicit assumption that this is the limit of R, or to be precise, of $Val(R_1) + Val(R_2)$. However, in the case of single precision arithmetic this is not quite correct. For example if X has the hex representation $423708C0$ (real value about 45.76, and `float(0,132,3606720)` in the HOL formalization) the corresponding R already exceeds this slightly, while for $435C0524$ (value about 220.02, and HOL `float(0,134,6030628)`) the magnitude of R has risen to over 0.010833. (The latter example is only significant if one performs bias adjustment, since its exponential is out of range, but the first is well within range, and there are several other such counterexamples.) A naive error analysis gives a bound of 0.010844, which is the range we use; this could be improved by a more delicate analysis of how multiples of Inv_L round, but this hardly affects the overall error. We arrive at an error bound of $\frac{24}{27}2^{-33}$ rather than $\frac{23}{27}2^{-33}$ which could be proved over the narrower interval assumed by Tang. By the way, it may be the case that Tang's polynomial coefficients could be improved given the new interval.

6.4 Rounding errors

Though this occupies the largest part of Tang's error analysis, it is all a routine application of earlier lemmas. This is a little laborious since it has to be repeated for about a dozen arithmetic operations, but it is far from difficult. We organize things slightly differently from Tang, and exploit HOL's programmability to compose errors appropriately. For example, the calculation of P involves the composition of 41 error terms, many of which are the product of several others, and it would be quite tedious to do this by hand. Our analysis descends all the way to the rounding error in calculating Q, while Tang simply says that because of its small size, 'the rounding errors accumulated in its calculation are practically zero'. While this is quite true, justifying this intuition formally is harder than simply bounding that error in the usual way.[2] Anyway, one might argue that 'error bounds' should be just that — guaranteed upper bounds.

We arrive at a bound for the rounding error in P of $\frac{11}{20}2^{-30}$. Though this is larger than the error Tang assumed, the overall error bounds in $E1$ that we get are actually tighter. Tang derives bounds of $0.5267ulp$ and $0.5378ulp$ in $E1$, depending on the binary interval in which it lies, $[\frac{1}{2}, 1)$ or $[1, 2)$. Our bounds

[2] Arguably this is a general problem in trying to achieve a high level of formalization in applications of scientific theories — it can be harder to justify the simplifying assumptions rigorously than to avoid them. For example, think of some of the approximations commonly used in mechanics.

are $0.5125ulp$ and $0.5338ulp$ respectively (see the annotation given earlier for the HOL statement). The first is lower because we manually observed that in this case, we must have $Ival(J) = 0$ and then most of the arithmetic operations involved in calculating P in terms of Q are exact. The better bound for the second, however, results purely from HOL's mechanical application of the theorems about error bounds. It seems paradoxical that we get a better final result despite taking into account more errors, but the explanation seems to be that we avoid inserting any great 'safety margin' in results to compensate for neglected errors.

In some ways, our argument is also more natural than Tang's in that when deciding on the binary intervals in which results lie, we carefully separate abstract mathematical values from their floating point approximations and deal always with the ones that are actually relevant. For example, we case split over the binary intervals for the computed output $E1$, since this determines the value of an *ulp* in the result. We deduce that if $Val(E1)$ lies in $[\frac{1}{2}, 1)$ then $j = 0$ and $Val(S_{Lead}(J)) + Val(S_{Trail}(J) + (S_{Lead}(J) + S_{Trail}(J))P) < 1$, where $j = Ival(J)$. This is then used in the remaining error analysis. By contrast, Tang considers whether $j = 0$ first and then whether $r < 0$, where r is the exact variant of R, that is, $Val(X) - Ival(N)\frac{ln(2)}{32}$. This necessitates a nontrivial additional argument to see that, for example, r and $Val(R1) + Val(R2)$ always lie in the same binary interval.

The last line of the algorithm simply scales $E1$ by 2^M to yield the final result. This is close to being simple. If the result is normalized, then the scaling is exact and the maximum error is still $0.5338ulp$. If, on the other hand, the result is denormalized, we can get an extra error of $0.5ulp$ due to rounding, but the corresponding *ulp* is at least twice as large as it would be if the result could be scaled exactly. Thus the maximum error is $0.5 + \frac{0.5338}{2}ulp$. However there are subtleties lurking where overflow and underflow are concerned.

6.5 Overflow

Our specification makes quite a strong statement about the overflow behaviour of the algorithm.[3] We assert that overflow occurs (i.e. the result is $+\infty$) if and only if the true exponential exceeds the standard overflow threshold. (Tang doesn't make any similarly precise claim.) It is clear that overflow occurs precisely when our approximate exponential exceeds the overflow threshold, and we are left to prove that these are sufficiently close that either one overflows if the other does.

The proof proceeds by contradiction. If there is a disparity in the overflow behaviours, then $2^M Val(E1)$ and $e^{Val(X)}$ lie on opposite sides of the overflow threshold. This means that $2^M Val(E1)$ is at least as close to the overflow threshold as it is to $e^{Val(X)}$, that is, within about $0.54\ 2^M/2^{23}$. Thus $|threshold/e^{Val(X)} - 1| < 0.55/2^{22}$. Hence by appealing to the following theorem:

[3] We do not follow Tang in performing 'bias adjustment' in the case of overflow. This would be very easy to add, given that everything is tightly bounded until the final scaling by 2^M, but since this bias adjustment procedure is not specified in the IEEE standard, we don't bother.

```
|- abs(x - &1) <= e ∧ e <= inv(&4) ⟹ abs(ln(x)) <= e + e pow 2
```

we find that $|ln(threshold) - Val(X)| \leq 2^{-22}$. However by carefully approximating $ln(threshold)$, easily done using the known approximation to $ln(2)$, we discover that this is impossible: there is no such X. The reason is that $ln(threshold)$ is straddled by two floating point values, `float(0,133,3240471)` and `float(0,133,3240472)`, and is more than 2^{-22} from either of them, although not that much further from the latter. Quite naively, we could count ourselves unlucky if this property failed, since

$$e^{X(1+\delta)} = e^X e^{X\delta} \approx e^X(1 + X\delta)$$

In other words, the relative change in the output is about X times the relative change in the input. Since X at this point is around 2^6, we might expect a probability of about 2^{-5} that the true exponential lies dangerously close (within just over $0.5ulp$) to the overflow threshold.

6.6 Underflow

There is a similar dangerous case to be ruled out at the other end of the scale. We have said that the maximum error from scaling is $0.5ulp$, but in compensation an ulp is at least twice as large relative to the result as it would otherwise be. However our specification, following Tang, asserts that this situation only arises when the final result E is denormalized. We need to rule out the possibility that $E1$ loses a bit in scaling yet then rounds back up to a normalized result. This can only happen when the exact value of $2^M E1$ is $2^{-126}(1-2^{-24})$. Now $E1$ could not, in this case, lie in the interval $[1, 2)$, since we have proved earlier that it cannot exceed about $2 - 2^{-6}$ (see the annotation shown earlier). We must therefore have $E1 \in [\frac{1}{2}, 1)$ and so $M = -126$. The problem is reduced to showing that no floating point value X has an exponential within 2^{-150} of $2^{-126}(1 - 2^{-24})$.

This is susceptible to reasoning very similar to that in the case of overflow. Abbreviating $t = 2^{-126}(1 - 2^{-24})$, we want to show that $ln(t)$ is too far away from any representable value. In fact the situation is even better than before: $ln(t)$ is straddled by `float(1,133,3058767)` and `float(1,133,3058768)` and at least 2^{-19} from either of them; once again, a distance of 2^{-22} would suffice. Hence we get the final result.

7 Conclusions and methodological remarks

When describing verification efforts, there is a tension between impressing with our persistence, and demonstrating the maturity and usability of the tools chosen. While we are not averse to making such points, the main message we want to communicate is that verifications of this nature are, with a little effort, comfortably within the state of the art, and as such are well placed for industrial exploitation.

We believe that verifications of this sort are well worthwhile. Although we have found Tang's error analysis to be correct in essentials, we have found one small slip and have located a few subtle corners in the proof that a less careful worker than Tang might easily have overlooked. One of the commonest errors in postulated theorems is the forgetting of special or degenerate cases. (IEEE floating point is particularly rich in such cases, e.g. NaNs, negative zeros etc.) Using a mechanical theorem prover means we are never allowed to miss these things. On top of that, we derive the mathematics with the greatest rigour and integrate it with the verification, so it can be relied on that we have not misapplied some 'book' result such as the error in truncating a Taylor series.

Apart from standard real analysis, some parts of this correctness proof (Harrison 1997b) needed a lot of additional pure mathematics, e.g. Sturm's theorem. So it is a mistake to believe that to get concrete results, the only theorems about the reals needed are a few algebraic and order-theoretic banalities: sometimes one needs much more. Even so, these results are often quite concrete and combinatorial, in contrast to the clean, abstract results on often sees in mathematics texts, and are typically much harder to prove formally. To give an ad hoc comparison, the work here took about 100 times as much work as a HOL proof by us of M. H. Stone's theorem that a metrizable topological space is paracompact, a result arguably of greater mathematical depth.[4] However, while the result described here is the culmination of about 3 months of hard work, most of this was devoted to getting the IEEE-754 formalization right and proving general results on polynomial approximation and floating point error analysis. This is all re-usable, so we believe other verifications of this general type could now be cranked out reasonably quickly, say in one or two weeks each.

In this algorithm, we have taken IEEE-compliant addition, multiplication etc. as given. However, it would be perfectly possible to specify instead the kind of special extra precise arithmetic that might be implemented in hardware. For example, a simple CORDIC example we dealt with some time ago is based on this approach (Harrison 1996b). Indeed, we could attempt to verify some implementations of the IEEE primitives in terms of their low-level components. The proofs would presumably be quite simple compared with those tackled here.

Although the present algorithm could be verified by exhaustive testing, our proof scales straightforwardly to double, extended or perhaps even generic versions of the operation, whereas exhaustive testing seems not to. In particular, Tang sketches a proof for the double precision case, and it would be a straightforward mechanical process to adapt the present proof. (We might do this, but on reflection will probably make some improvements, as noted later.) This is an example of a general phenomenon: verification has more modularity than testing, i.e. it is often possible to re-use and modify proofs, or to link together proofs for submodules of a system, whereas this can be problematic for some other ap-

[4] This theorem was suggested on the QED mailing list on 17th June 1994 by Andrzej Trybulec as an interesting case study in the relative power and flexibility of theorem proving systems — see `ftp://ftp.mcs.anl.gov/pub/qed/archive/56` and `ftp://ftp.mcs.anl.gov/pub/qed/archive/66`.

proaches. However, testing does have the advantage, where it is applicable, of giving (in principle) tighter error bounds. That is, the various errors that are accumulated may be correlated in ways too subtle to analyze mathematically. However we don't believe that would make a substantial difference to the error bounds here.

We have assumed a correct algorithm. But is testing or verification better for detecting errors? Testing has the advantage of indicating counterexamples directly. By contrast, in verification, one simply finds that a proof does not go through as hoped, as in our attempts to prove Tang's bound on R. This doesn't (in this case or typically) constitute a *disproof*, but only motivates a more directed search for counterexamples. We found our counterexamples by testing numbers where the rounding to an integer leaves the greatest possible error of $0.5ulp$. On the other hand, while verification doesn't pinpoint *counterexamples*, it does pinpoint *mathematical errors* more directly. To go from a failure in testing to an analysis of the problem, one needs to trace through the counterexample to see where things go wrong. So we might say that testing is better for finding *when* things go wrong, and verification for finding *why and where* things (might) go wrong.

As for other theorem provers, there is hardly an alternative to some version of HOL for verifications of this kind at present. One needs available a large library of results from real analysis — for example we have used the mean value theorem, Taylor's theorem and common properties of the exponential function. One also needs a system that is reasonably 'heavyweight'; biased towards big, ugly verification proofs rather than the elegant solution of high-level mathematical problems. While some systems have one (e.g. Mizar) and some have the other (e.g. NQTHM), no other system that we are aware of combines these strengths. Probably the best alternative would be PVS, which has already benefited from some excellent work in formalized mathematics (Dutertre 1996) and floating point verification (Miner 1995; Miner and Leathrum 1996). Its type system offers some extra features over HOL's that might be helpful in giving a clear specification; for example, it is not necessary to distinguish between $\mathbb{N}$ and $\mathbb{R}$.

In future verifications, we can make better use of HOL's programmability. As it stands, we automated certain routine steps, e.g. the application of the valuation function Val to particular floating point values, the accumulation of rounding errors in expressions, and the evaluation of Taylor approximations. However, much more could be done and from the perspective gained as a result of this proof, we can identify the most important things to automate. We have used HOL's existing tools to prove innumerable trivial but tedious results of linear arithmetic automatically, and this was almost indispensable. But one of the most tiresome aspects of the proofs was that similarly simple results with a nonlinear component need to be proved manually. Similar experiences are reported by Miner and Leathrum (1996) when using PVS. However we have now implemented experimental tools to automate these steps, including the semi-automatic determination of the signs of product terms, many of which are of the form 2^k and are hence trivially strictly positive. We believe these tools would have been invaluable in this verification, and should streamline future efforts. We also intend to clean up, fill out and generalize the most useful-looking lemmas; in the present verification almost all of these were accreted 'by need' without any systematic plan.

Our insistence on reducing everything to logical first principles gives us the highest confidence in the final result, and has not been a disaster from the point of view of efficiency. There is one unfortunate exception: arithmetic. Performing arithmetic, particularly multiplication, of large numbers by proof is very time-consuming. So much so that the entire proof takes about 12 hours to run; this is cut to about 2 hours if addition and multiplication are performed as primitives using CAML's native bignums, rather than via logical decomposition. It might be a pragmatic *necessity* to do this for double precision or extended precision verifications; these are structurally identical and no harder for the user, but involve calculation with still larger numbers. The main problem areas are the evaluation of Sturm sequences and the accurate approximation of $ln(2)$ and $2^{\frac{i}{32}}$. On the other hand, most of the arithmetic operations could be done in a more sophisticated way using approximations tailored to the required accuracy rather than relying on exact rational arithmetic (Harrison 1996b).

There is an argument though, that forcing the user to think carefully about something as basic as arithmetic in order to make it acceptably efficient is not conducive to great productivity. Perhaps it should simply be made primitive. The ACL2 prover makes a virtue of its ability to mix efficient calculation in with the proof process. Our verification gives a good illustration of how important this can be. Of course ACL2 is hardly suited to verifications of this type since it has no notion of real number, and would therefore be unable to formalize some of the higher level details directly. However ACL2 has been used for interesting work in verifying a more elementary floating point operation, namely division (Moore, Lynch, and Kaufmann 1996; Brock, Kaufmann, and Moore 1996). This work in ACL2 was actually carried out in cooperation with the designer of the algorithm at AMD.

Acknowledgements

Thanks are due to Mark Aagaard, who suggested this algorithm for verification, and to Clemens Ballarin whose comments on a draft of this report have led to several improvements.

References

Barratt, M. (1989) Formal methods applied to a floating-point system. *IEEE Transactions on Software Engineering*, **15**, 611–621.

Benedetti, R. and Risler, J.-J. (1990) *Real algebraic and semi-algebraic sets.* Hermann, Paris.

Brock, B., Kaufmann, M., and Moore, J. S. (1996) ACL2 theorems about commercial microprocessors. See Srivas and Camilleri (1996), pp. 275–293.

Dutertre, B. (1996) Elements of mathematical analysis in PVS. See von Wright, Grundy, and Harrison (1996), pp. 141–156.

Goldberg, D. (1991) What every computer scientist should know about floating point arithmetic. *ACM Computing Surveys*, **23**, 5–48.

Gordon, M. J. C. (1989) Mechanizing programming logics in higher order logic. In Birtwistle, G. and Subrahmanyam, P. A. (eds.), *Current Trends in Hardware Verification and Automated Theorem Proving*, pp. 387–439. Springer-Verlag.

Gordon, M. J. C. and Melham, T. F. (1993) *Introduction to HOL: a theorem proving environment for higher order logic.* Cambridge University Press.

Harrison, J. (1996a) HOL light: A tutorial introduction. See Srivas and Camilleri (1996), pp. 265–269.

Harrison, J. (1996b) Theorem proving with the real numbers. Technical Report 408, University of Cambridge Computer Laboratory.

Harrison, J. (1997a) Floating point verification in HOL Light: The exponential function. Technical Report 428, University of Cambridge Computer Laboratory.

Harrison, J. (1997b) Verifying the accuracy of polynomial approximations in HOL. In Gunter, E. L. and Felty, A. (eds.), *Theorem Proving in Higher Order Logics: 10th International Conference, TPHOLs'97*, Volume 1275 of *Lecture Notes in Computer Science*, Murray Hill, NJ, pp. 137–152. Springer-Verlag.

Miner, P. S. (1995) Defining the IEEE-854 floating-point standard in PVS. Technical memorandum 110167, NASA Langley Research Center, Hampton, VA 23681-0001, USA.

Miner, P. S. and Leathrum, J. F. (1996) Verification of IEEE compliant subtractive division algorithms. See Srivas and Camilleri (1996), pp. 64–78.

Moore, J. S., Lynch, T., and Kaufmann, M. (1996) A mechanically checked proof of the correctness of the kernel of the $AMD5_K86$ floating-point division algorithm. Unpublished; available on the Web as `http://devil.ece.utexas.edu:80/~lynch/divide/divide.html`.

Pratt, V. R. (1995) Anatomy of the Pentium bug. In Mosses, P. D., Nielsen, M., and Schwartzbach, M. I. (eds.), *Proceedings of the 5th International Joint Conference on the theory and practice of software development (TAPSOFT'95)*, Volume 915 of *Lecture Notes in Computer Science*, Aarhus, Denmark, pp. 97–107. Springer-Verlag.

Srivas, M. and Camilleri, A. (eds.) (1996) *Proceedings of the First International Conference on Formal Methods in Computer-Aided Design (FMCAD'96)*, Volume 1166 of *Lecture Notes in Computer Science*. Springer-Verlag.

Tang, P. T. P. (1989) Table-driven implementation of the exponential function in IEEE floating-point arithmetic. *ACM Transactions on Mathematical Software*, **15**, 144–157.

von Wright, J., Grundy, J., and Harrison, J. (eds.) (1996) *Theorem Proving in Higher Order Logics: 9th International Conference, TPHOLs'96*, Volume 1125 of *Lecture Notes in Computer Science*, Turku, Finland. Springer-Verlag.

Verification of Distributed Real-Time and Fault-Tolerant Protocols

Jozef Hooman

Department of Computing Science, Eindhoven University of Technology
P.O. Box 513, 5600 MB Eindhoven, The Netherlands
e-mail: wsinjh@win.tue.nl
http://www.win.tue.nl/win/cs/tt/hooman/JH.html

Abstract. An assertional method to verify distributed real-time and fault-tolerant protocols is presented. To obtain mechanical support, the verification system PVS is used. General PVS theories are developed to deal with timing and failures. As a characteristic example, we verify a processor-group membership protocol, dealing with a dynamically changing network of processors and reasoning in terms of local clocks. Further we show some basic theories for the verification of the underlying synchronous atomic broadcast service.

1 Introduction

Safety-critical applications are often implemented using a hierarchy of protocols that provide a certain real-time and fault-tolerant service. For instance, starting from a network of processors with local clocks and a simple communication mechanism, usually some protocol is applied to achieve internally synchronized clocks. Based on synchronized clocks, a more powerful communication mechanism, such as multicast or atomic broadcast, can be implemented. This can then be used for higher-level services. Such a protocol stack usually forms the basis for numerous critical applications, and hence the correctness of the protocols is very important. On the other hand, the combination of distribution, local clocks, real-time, and fault-tolerance makes it extremely difficult to guarantee that these protocols indeed lead to the required service.

One method to increase the confidence in the correctness is the application of formal methods to verify (part of) the protocols. A large number of methods have been devised to specify and verify distributed real-time systems (see, e.g., [JP96]), but it is less clear how to deal with failures. A formal treatment of fault-tolerant, however, is important, since informal reasoning about failures is often based on hidden, implicit, assumptions and it is usually not clear whether all failures and combinations of failures have been covered. Moreover, given the complexity of the reasoning, it is clear that mechanical support is indispensable.

In this paper we use an assertional method to verify distributed protocols. That is, logical formulas (assertions) characterize the required service, the protocols, and assumptions about the underlying communication mechanism. Besides primitives to reason about timing, there are also primitives to express assumptions about the correctness of components and the failure hypothesis explicitly. To obtain mechanical support, we use the interactive proof checker PVS (Prototype Verification System) [ORS92,ORSvH95]. The PVS specification language is a higher-order typed logic and specifications can be structured into a hierarchy of (parameterized) theories. The tool contains a proof checker to construct proofs interactively and to rerun proofs automatically after small changes.

PVS is a very general tool with a rich specification language that can be used for a large number of applications. To guide the average user for a particular class of applications, it is convenient to have a clear sequence of steps to be performed and a number of re-usable theories and illustrative paradigms. Here we present our ideas in this direction on the verification of distributed protocols. The approach originates from previous manual verifications (e.g., for a distributed real-time arbitration protocol [Hoo94]). Mechanical support is obtained by defining general theories in PVS to reason about timing and failures.

To illustrate the approach, we consider a characteristic hierarchy of fault-tolerant protocols that should achieve a particular real-time computing service in spite of component failures. To achieve reliability, a group of servers is running on distinct processors. Processors may fail and servers should contain consistent service state information to redistribute workload. E.g., servers must agree on the identity of all correctly functioning processors, which is achieved by group membership services [Cri96]. As an example of such a protocol we consider a processor-group membership protocol of Cristian [Cri91] which is intended to achieve agreement on the identity of all correctly functioning processors in a dynamic network that can shrink with failures and grow with joins. We verify a basic version of the protocol, reasoning in terms of local clocks. For simplicity, we do not use the group identifiers mentioned in [Cri91] (assuming that the scheduling delay is zero). Further we assume fail-silent processors whereas in [Cri91] processors can suffer both crash and performance failures.

The membership algorithm uses a synchronous atomic broadcast service to communicate between processors. In [CASD95] it is shown that this broadcast service can indeed be implemented, using a lower-level point-to-point datagram service and internally synchronized local clocks. Here we indicate how to proceed with the verification of this atomic broadcast protocol in PVS. Interesting is the formulation of clock synchronization in terms of real-time, and the relation between reasoning with local clocks and real-time. Further, besides failures of processors, now also failures of links between processors are taken into account, re-using the theory that defines failure primitives. For details of the (manual) verification of the atomic broadcast protocol, we refer to [CASD95,ZH95].

In section 2 we define two general PVS theories for dealing with timing and failures. Our steps for protocol verification are presented in section 3. It is applied to a simple version of the membership protocol in section 4. In section 5 we show how the performance of this protocol can be improved, following [Cri91] more closely. A few basic ingredients of the verification of the underlying atomic broadcast protocol are presented in section 6. Finally, section 7 contains concluding remarks.

2 Basic Theories to deal with Timing and Failures

To reason about timing, we present below a general PVS theory *TimePrim* which has three parameters, a time domain *Time*, and two orders $<$ and $\leq$ on *Time* (the predicates *strict_order?* and *partial_order?* are pre-defined in the PVS prelude). Note that, instead of defining $\leq$, we add an assumption about the relation between the two orders. This makes it possible to import the theory with, e.g., the pre-defined relation $\leq$ on the reals and get more support from the decision procedures of the PVS proof checker.

We do not show all details of theory *TimePrim*, but indicate that intervals of time points are defined and that the boolean connectives are overloaded for predicates on *Time* (i.e., functions from *Time* to *bool*). Primitives are introduced to express that a predicate holds *inside* or *during* a set of time points (usually an interval). Finally we show a few simple lemmas, named *dur_inside* and *sub_dur*. All lemmas and theorems presented in this paper have been proved by means of the interactive proof checker of PVS. For instance, *dur_inside* can be proved automatically by one command, whereas *sub_dur* has been proved by eight commands.

$$\begin{array}{l}
\text{TimePrim[Time : TYPE}, < : (\text{strict_order?[Time]}), \\
\qquad\qquad\qquad\quad \leq : (\text{partial_order?[Time]})] : \text{THEORY} \\
\quad \text{BEGIN} \\
\quad \text{ASSUMING} \\
\qquad \text{leq_less} : \text{ASSUMPTION } \forall (t_1, t_2 : \text{Time}) : t_1 \leq t_2 \Leftrightarrow t_1 < t_2 \vee t_1 = t_2 \\
\qquad \text{ENDASSUMING} \\
\quad t, t_0, t_1, t_2, t_3, t_4 : \text{VAR Time} \\
\quad [t_0, t_1] : \text{setof[Time]} = \{t \mid t_0 \leq t \wedge t \leq t_1\} \\
\quad [t_0, t_1) : \text{setof[Time]} = \{t \mid t_0 \leq t \wedge t < t_1\} \\
\quad \ldots \\
\quad P, Q : \text{VAR pred[Time]} \\
\quad \neg P : \text{pred[Time]} = \lambda\, t : \neg P(t); \\
\quad P \wedge Q : \text{pred[Time]} = \lambda\, t : P(t) \wedge Q(t); \\
\quad \ldots \\
\quad I : \text{VAR setof[Time]} \\
\\
\quad P \textbf{ in } I : \text{bool} = \exists\, t : t \in I \wedge P(t) \\
\\
\quad P \textbf{ during } I : \text{bool} = \forall\, t : t \in I \Rightarrow P(t) \\
\\
\quad \text{dur_inside} : \text{LEMMA } \neg(P \textbf{ in } I) \Leftrightarrow (\neg P) \textbf{ during } I \\
\\
\quad \text{sub_dur} : \text{LEMMA} \\
\qquad (\exists\, t_1, t_2 : P \textbf{ during } [t_1, t_2] \wedge t_1 \leq t_3 \wedge t_4 \leq t_2) \Rightarrow P \textbf{ during } [t_3, t_4] \\
\text{END TimePrim}
\end{array}$$

Next we present a theory to reason about failures of a certain type of *Resources*. To express the timing of failures, we again assume given a time domain with two orders and import theory *TimePrim*. Based on the primitives *Start* and *Crash*, it is defined when a resource is correct. We also show an example of a general property that has been proved, where *dichotomous?* expresses that for all t_1, t_2 we have $t_1 \leq t_2$ or $t_2 \leq t_1$.

$$\text{FailPrim}[\text{Resources}: \text{TYPE}, \text{Time}: \text{TYPE}, <: (\text{strict\_order?}[\text{Time}]), \leq: (\text{partial\_order?}[\text{Time}])]: \text{THEORY}$$

BEGIN
ASSUMING
$\text{leq\_less}: \text{ASSUMPTION}\ \forall (t_1, t_2: \text{Time}): t_1 \leq t_2 \Leftrightarrow t_1 < t_2 \lor t_1 = t_2$
ENDASSUMING
IMPORTING $\text{TimePrim}[\text{Time}, <, \leq]$
$r: \text{VAR Resources}$
$t, t_0, t_1, t_2: \text{VAR Time}$

$\text{Start}, \text{Crash}: [\text{Resources} \rightarrow \text{pred}[\text{Time}]]$

$\text{Correct}(r)(t): \text{bool} = \exists\ t_0: t_0 \leq t \land \text{Start}(r)(t_0) \land \neg\text{Crash}(r)\ \textbf{during}\ [t_0, t]$

$\text{Correct\_start}: \text{LEMMA}$
$\text{Correct}(r)\ \textbf{during}\ [t_1, t_2] \land t_1 \leq t_2 \land \text{dichotomous?}[\text{Time}](\leq) \Rightarrow$
$\exists t_0: t_0 \leq t_1 \land \text{Start}(r)(t_0) \land \text{Correct}(r)\ \textbf{during}\ [t_0, t_2]$
END FailPrim

3 Approach to Protocol Verification

To verify a distributed protocol for a network of processors, we perform the following steps.

1. Model the application domain; describe the main primitives that are needed to express the service specification.
2. Specify the service that should be provided by the network.
3. Specify the communication mechanism between processors.
4. Specify the protocol performed by each processor (or each type of processor if there are processors with different roles in the protocol). The specification of the protocol performed by a processor should only refer to the local state and the external interface of the processor itself.
5. Verify the protocol by proving that the conjunction of the specifications of the processors (point 4) and the communication mechanism (point 3) leads to the required service (point 2).

The last step, where the conjunction of the specifications is taken, is justified by earlier work on compositional proof rules for concurrency (see, e.g., [Hoo91]).

Note that for a fault-tolerant protocol the specifications also include the failure hypothesis, i.e., assumptions about the correctness of components and about the consequences of failures.

4 Membership Protocol

Following the steps of the previous section, we verify the basic part of a membership protocol. Consider a network of processors, where processors can crash and might be recovered. Each processor maintains a local view on the set of processors that are considered to be correct. Further each processor has a local boolean variable *Joined* which indicates whether a processor has correctly joined the network and its view can be inspected. Since it will in general be impossible to guarantee that these views are the same at any point in real-time, the specification of the membership service is expressed in terms of local clocks. It is required that the view of a correct and joined processor p at time T *on the local clock of* p equals the view of any other correct and joined processor q at time T *on the local clock of* q. This matches nicely with the specification of the underlying synchronous atomic broadcast service which is also expressed in terms of local clocks. To express these specifications, we first introduce in the next section primitives to refer to local clocks and the correctness of processors.

4.1 Modeling of the application domain

The application domain is modeled in theory *Config*, parameterized by the type of *Processors*. Since the aim is to reason in terms of local clocks, we define a discrete domain of clock values (using integers for simplicity) and import theory *TimePrim*. A local clock value is defined by a pair consisting of a clock value and a processor. We define orders $<$ and $\leq$ on local clock values and import theory *FailPrim* (and hence implicitly *TimePrim*). When theory *Config* is type-checked, PVS generates so called Type Check Conditions, corresponding to the type constraints on the parameters of *FailPrim* and the assuming clause. E.g., it is required that relation $<$ is indeed a strict order on local clock values.

Config[Processors : TYPE] : THEORY
  BEGIN
  ClockValues : TYPE $=$ int
  IMPORTING TimePrim[ClockValues, $<, \leq$]

  $T, T_0, T_1, T_2, T_3, T_4$: VAR ClockValues
  NonNegClockValues : TYPE $= \{T \mid T \geq 0\}$

  LocalClockVals : TYPE $=$ [ClockValues, Processors]
  LT, LT_1, LT_2 : VAR LocalClockVals
  $LT_1 < LT_2$: bool $=$
    $\text{PROJ\_1}(LT_1) < \text{PROJ\_1}(LT_2) \wedge \text{PROJ\_2}(LT_1) = \text{PROJ\_2}(LT_2)$;
  LT1 $\leq$ LT2 : bool $=$ LT1 $<$ LT2 $\vee$ LT1 $=$ LT2
  IMPORTING FailPrim[Processors, LocalClockVals, $<, \leq$]

By theory *FailPrim* we obtain primitives such as $Start(p)(T, p)$ to express that processor p starts at local clock value (T, p). To avoid duplication of processor p in this notation, we abbreviate it as *start*$(p)(T)$. Similarly for the other primitives. Since the membership protocol can be verified in terms of clock values, only the abbreviations *start*, *crash*, etc., are used. The use of processors in local clock values will become relevant for the implementation of atomic broadcast.

To express membership properties, we define the view of a processor p at a local time LT, representing the set of processors that are considered to be correct by p at LT. Predicate *Joined* expresses whether a processor has joined the group of processors and its view can be inspected. Again we define a few suitable abbreviations.

p, q, r : VAR Processors
$\text{start}(p)(T)$: bool $=$ $\text{Start}(p)(T, p)$
$\text{crash}(p)(T)$: bool $=$ $\text{Crash}(p)(T, p)$
$\text{correct}(p)(T)$: bool $=$ $\text{Correct}(p)(T, p)$

$\text{View}(p)(LT)$: setof[Processors]
$\text{view}(p)(T)$: setof[Processors] $=$ $\text{View}(p)(T, p)$

V : VAR [ClockValues $\rightarrow$ setof[Processors]]
$p \in V$: pred[ClockValues] $= \lambda\, T : p \in V(T)$

$\text{Joined}(p)(\text{LT})$: bool
$\text{joined}(p)(T)$: bool $=$ $\text{Joined}(p)(T, p)$
END Config

Henceforth, declarations of variables are not repeated, using for instance variable T ranging over *ClockValues*, p ranging over *Processors*, etc.

4.2 Specification of the required service

Theory *Membership* specifies the required membership service. Recall that we have introduced abbreviations to avoid duplication of processors, and hence property *Agree* below expresses that the view of p at T *measured on the clock of* p equals the view of q at T *measured on the clock of* q. Given that local clocks are synchronized, as will be expressed later, views do not differ too much in real-time.

Membership[Processors : TYPE] : THEORY
BEGIN
IMPORTING Config[Processors]

Agree : bool $= \forall\, T, p, q$:
$\text{correct}(p)(T) \wedge \text{correct}(q)(T) \wedge \text{joined}(p)(T) \wedge \text{joined}(q)(T) \Rightarrow$
$\text{view}(p)(T) = \text{view}(q)(T)$

Note that agreement allows arbitrary views; e.g., all sets could be empty. Following [Cri91] such trivial solutions are avoided by requiring that a joined processor is a member of its own view. Moreover, timeliness requirements are added to specify that a started processor is joined and a crashed processor is deleted from the view of a correct processor within a bounded amount of time.

Recognition : bool $= \forall\, T, p :\ \text{correct}(p)(T) \wedge \text{joined}(p)(T) \Rightarrow p \in \text{view}(p)(T)$

JoinDelay : NonNegClockValues

Join : bool $= \forall\, T_1, T_2, p :\ \text{start}(p)(T_1) \wedge \text{correct}(p)$ **during** $[T_1, T_2] \Rightarrow$
joined(p) **during** $[T_1 + \text{JoinDelay}, T_2]$

DetectionDelay : ClockValues

Detect : bool $= \forall\, T_1, T_2, p, q :$
crash$(p)(T_1) \wedge \neg\text{correct}(p)$ **during** $[T_1, T_2] \wedge \text{correct}(q)$ **during** $[T_1, T_2] \Rightarrow$
$p \notin \text{view}(q)$ **during** $[T_1 + \text{DetectionDelay}, T_2]$

MembSpec : bool $=$ Agree $\wedge$ Recognition $\wedge$ Join $\wedge$ Detect
END Membership

To get more confidence in a specification, e.g. that it is not contradictory and indeed expresses the desired properties, it is advisable (see, for instance, [ORSvH95]) to try to prove some properties that ought to hold. Here we show, as an example, an alternative formulation of the join property.

JoinAlt : bool $= \forall\, T_1, T_2, p, q :$
start$(p)(T_1) \wedge \text{correct}(p)$ **during** $[T_1, T_2] \wedge \text{correct}(q)$ **during** $[T_1, T_2] \Rightarrow$
$p \in \text{view}(q)$ **during** $[T_1 + \text{JoinDelay}, T_2]$

join_equiv : LEMMA Agree $\wedge$ Recognition $\wedge$ Join $\Rightarrow$ JoinAlt

4.3 Specification of the underlying communication mechanism

To implement the membership service, it is assumed that processors can use an atomic broadcast service. We introduce primitives to express that a message can be broadcast by a processor and that it can be delivered at a processor. Again abbreviations are used to avoid duplication of processors and to reason with clock values. Next the properties of synchronous atomic broadcast are axiomatized. First we specify *Termination*, that is, a message that is broadcast by a correct processor at time T on its own clock is delivered by all correct processors at time $T{+}BroadcastDelay$ on their clocks.

Broadcast[Processors : TYPE, Messages : TYPE] : THEORY
BEGIN
IMPORTING Config[Processors]
m : VAR Messages
Broadcast$(p, m)(LT)$: bool
Deliver$(p, m)(LT)$: bool
broadcast$(p, m)(T)$: bool $=$ Broadcast$(p, m)(T, p)$
deliver$(p, m)(T)$: bool $=$ Deliver$(p, m)(T, p)$

BroadcastDelay : NonNegClockValues

$$\begin{array}{l}\text{Termination}: \text{ bool } = \forall\, p, m, T: \\ \quad \text{broadcast}(p,m)(T) \wedge \text{correct}(p) \textbf{ during } [T, T + \text{BroadcastDelay}] \Rightarrow \\ \quad\quad (\forall\, q: \text{correct}(q) \textbf{ during } [T, T + \text{BroadcastDelay}] \Rightarrow \\ \quad\quad\quad\quad \text{deliver}(q,m)(T + \text{BroadcastDelay}))\end{array}$$

Note that *Termination* only specifies the delivery of a message if the processor that broadcasts it stays correct. To restrict the possible behavior in case of a processor crash during the broadcast action, we specify two atomicity properties: *Agreement* expresses that if a correct processor delivers a message at time T on its clock then this message is delivered by all correct processors at T on their clocks; *Integrity* specifies that if a message is delivered at time T then it was indeed broadcast at time $T - BroadcastDelay$. We have omitted an order property, since it is not relevant for the correctness of the membership protocol.

$$\begin{array}{l}\text{Agreement}: \text{ bool } = \forall\, p, m, T: \\ \quad \text{deliver}(p,m)(T) \wedge \text{correct}(p) \textbf{ during } [T - \text{BroadcastDelay}, T] \Rightarrow \\ \quad\quad (\forall\, r: \text{ correct}(r) \textbf{ during } [T - \text{BroadcastDelay}, T] \Rightarrow \text{deliver}(r,m)(T))\end{array}$$

$$\begin{array}{l}\text{Integrity}: \text{ bool } = \forall\, p, m, T: \\ \quad \text{deliver}(p,m)(T) \wedge \text{correct}(p) \textbf{ during } [T - \text{BroadcastDelay}, T] \Rightarrow \\ \quad\quad \exists\, q: \text{ broadcast}(q,m)(T - \text{BroadcastDelay})\end{array}$$

$$\text{AtomicBroadcast}: \text{ bool } = \text{ Termination} \wedge \text{Agreement} \wedge \text{Integrity}$$

END Broadcast

4.4 Protocol specification

We specify a simple membership protocol where each correct processor p broadcasts a message *(p,present)* at least once every *PresentPeriod* time units, as expressed by *StartBcastPresent*.

$$\begin{array}{l}\text{MembProt[Processors : TYPE] : THEORY} \\ \quad \text{BEGIN} \\ \quad \text{IMPORTING Config[Processors]} \\ \quad \text{MessageTypes}: \text{ TYPE } = \text{ present}\} \\ \quad \text{Messages}: \text{ TYPE } = [\text{Processors, MessageTypes}] \\ \quad \text{IMPORTING Broadcast[Processors, Messages], Membership[Processors]} \\ \quad \text{StartBcastPresent}: \text{ bool } = \forall\, p, T_1, T_2: \text{start}(p)(T_1) \wedge \text{correct}(p) \textbf{ during } [T_1, T_2] \Rightarrow \\ \quad\quad \forall (T_3 \mid T_3 \in [T_1, T_2]): \\ \quad\quad\quad \exists\, (T_4 \mid T_4 \in [T_1, T_3]): T_3 - \text{PresentPeriod} \le T_4 \wedge \text{broadcast}(p, (p, \text{present}))(T_4)\end{array}$$

Using parameter *LocalJoinDelay*, we specify that a correct processor will be joined *LocalJoinDelay* time units after its start.

$$\begin{array}{l}\text{LocalJoinDelay}: \text{ VAR NonNegClockValues} \\ \text{ProcJoin(LocalJoinDelay)}: \text{ bool } = \forall\, p, T_1: \text{joined}(p)(T_1) \wedge \text{correct}(p)(T_1) \Leftrightarrow \\ \quad \exists T_0: T_0 + \text{LocalJoinDelay} \le T_1 \wedge \text{correct}(p) \textbf{ during } [T_0, T_1]\end{array}$$

Next we specify that q is a member of the view of p if a *(q,present)* message has been received not longer than *PresentPeriod* time units ago (measured on the clock of p). Further only *present* messages after the start of p are used.

$$\text{LocalView}: \text{bool} = \forall\, p, T_1, T_2 : \text{start}(p)(T_1) \wedge \text{correct}(p)\ \textbf{during}\ [T_1, T_2] \Rightarrow$$
$$\forall (T_3 \mid T_3 \in [T_1, T_2]), q :$$
$$q \in \text{view}(p)(T_3) \Leftrightarrow$$
$$\exists\, (T_4 \mid T_4 \in [T_1, T_3]) :$$
$$T_3 - \text{PresentPeriod} \leq T_4 \wedge \text{deliver}(p, (q, \text{present}))(T_4)$$

Clearly processes should only broadcast their own identity. Moreover it is required that incorrect processors do not broadcast messages.

$$\text{OwnIdentityOnly}: \text{bool} = \forall\, p, q, T : q \neq p \Rightarrow \neg\text{broadcast}(p, (q, \text{present}))(T)$$

$$\text{FailSilent}: \text{bool} = \forall\, p, m, T : \text{broadcast}(p, m)(T) \Rightarrow \text{correct}(p)(T)$$

$$\text{MembProtSpec}(\text{LocalJoinDelay}): \text{bool} = \text{StartBcastPresent} \wedge$$
$$\text{ProcJoin}(\text{LocalJoinDelay}) \wedge \text{LocalView} \wedge \text{OwnIdentityOnly} \wedge \text{FailSilent}$$

END MembProt

4.5 Protocol verification

Next the PVS interactive proof checker is used to prove that the specification of the membership protocol together with the properties of atomic broadcast lead to the membership service. As usual, some constraints on the timing constants have to hold. E.g., to obtain *Agree*, the *LocalJoinDelay* should be greater than the *PresentPeriod* plus the *BroadcastDelay*, because this is the time needed to be sure that all *present* messages have been received. Since the *LocalJoinDelay* should be smaller than the *Joindelay*, this also gives the bound on *JoinDelay*.

MembVerif[Processors : TYPE] : THEORY
BEGIN
IMPORTING MembProt[Processors]

agree_verif : LEMMA $\text{LocalJoinDelay} \geq \text{PresentPeriod} + \text{BroadcastDelay} \wedge \text{LocalView} \wedge \text{Agreement} \wedge \text{ProcJoin}(\text{LocalJoinDelay}) \Rightarrow \text{Agree}$

recogn_verif : LEMMA $\text{LocalJoinDelay} \geq \text{BroadcastDelay} \wedge \text{ProcJoin}(\text{LocalJoinDelay}) \wedge \text{StartBcastPresent} \wedge \text{LocalView} \wedge \text{Termination} \Rightarrow \text{Recognition}$

join_verif : LEMMA $\text{LocalJoinDelay} \leq \text{JoinDelay} \wedge \text{ProcJoin}(\text{LocalJoinDelay}) \Rightarrow \text{Join}$

detect_verif : LEMMA $\text{DetectionDelay} \geq \text{BroadcastDelay} + \text{PresentPeriod} \wedge \text{LocalView} \wedge \text{OwnIdentityOnly} \wedge \text{FailSilent} \wedge \text{Integrity} \Rightarrow \text{Detect}$

memb_correct : THEOREM $\text{JoinDelay} \geq \text{PresentPeriod} + \text{BroadcastDelay} \wedge \text{DetectionDelay} \geq \text{BroadcastDelay} + \text{PresentPeriod} \wedge \text{MembProtSpec}(\text{JoinDelay}) \wedge \text{AtomicBroadcast} \Rightarrow \text{MembSpec}$

END MembVerif

Not shown are seven auxiliary lemmas used to structure the proof. On the average, the proofs of lemmas and theorems required around twenty user interactions.

5 Improving the join delay

To improve the join delay, [Cri91] introduces *(p,new)* messages to indicate the start of processor p. Property *StartUp* expresses that a processor broadcasts a *new* message when it starts. A started processor receives its own *new* message and then, as long as it is correct, periodically broadcast a *present* message. Further all correct processors respond to a *new* message by immediately broadcasting a *present* message. Property *BroadcastReason* expresses that there are no other *present* messages, so all correct processors broadcast at the same local clock value.

$\text{PeriodProt}[\text{Processors} : \textsc{type}] : \textsc{theory}$
$\quad\textsc{begin}$
$\quad\textsc{importing}\ \text{Config}[\text{Processors}]$
$\quad\text{MessageTypes} : \textsc{type} = \{\text{new}, \text{present}\}$
$\quad\text{Messages} : \textsc{type} = [\text{Processors}, \text{MessageTypes}]$
$\quad\textsc{importing}\ \text{Broadcast}[\text{Processors}, \text{Messages}],\ \text{Membership}[\text{Processors}]$

$\quad\text{StartUp} : \text{bool} = \forall\, p, T : \text{start}(p)(T) \wedge \text{correct}(p)(T) \Leftrightarrow \text{broadcast}(p, (p, \text{new}))(T)$

$\quad\text{deliver\_new}(p)(T) : \text{bool} = \exists\, q : \text{deliver}(p, (q, \text{new}))(T)$
$\quad\text{deliver\_present}(p)(T) : \text{bool} = \exists\, q : \text{deliver}(p, (q, \text{present}))(T)$

$\quad\text{PresentPeriod} : \text{NonNegClockValues}$
$\quad\text{PeriodPoint}(T_1, T_3) : \text{bool} = \exists\, (k : \text{nat}) : T_3 = T_1 + k \times \text{PresentPeriod}$

$\quad\text{BroadcastPresent} : \text{bool} = \forall\, p, q, T_1, T_2, T_3 :$
$\quad\ \text{deliver}(p, (q, \text{new}))(T_1) \wedge \text{correct}(p)\ \textbf{during}\ [T_1, T_2] \wedge$
$\quad\quad \neg\text{deliver\_new}(p)\ \textbf{during}\ (T_1, T_2] \wedge T_3 \in [T_1, T_2] \wedge \text{PeriodPoint}(T_1, T_3) \Rightarrow$
$\quad\ \ \text{broadcast}(p, (p, \text{present}))(T_3)$

$\quad\text{BroadcastReason} : \text{bool} = \forall\, p, T : \text{broadcast}(p, (p, \text{present}))(T) \Rightarrow$
$\quad\ \exists q, T_0 : T_0 \leq T \wedge \text{deliver}(p, (q, \text{new}))(T_0) \wedge$
$\quad\ \ \text{correct}(p)\ \textbf{during}\ [T_0 - \text{BroadcastDelay}, T] \wedge$
$\quad\quad \neg\text{deliver\_new}(p)\ \textbf{during}\ (T_0, T] \wedge \text{PeriodPoint}(T_0, T)$

Next we specify that the local view corresponds to the last delivered *present* messages and that a processor becomes joined when it receives its own *present* message. As before, we have *OwnIdentityOnly* and *FailSilent*.

$\quad\text{lastdelivered}(p, q)(T) : \text{bool} = \exists\, T_0 : T_0 \leq T \wedge \text{deliver}(p, (q, \text{present}))(T_0) \wedge$
$\quad\ \neg\text{deliver\_present}(p)\ \textbf{during}\ (T_0, T] \wedge \text{correct}(p)\ \textbf{during}\ [T_0 - \text{BroadcastDelay}, T]$

$\quad\text{LocalView} : \text{bool} = \forall\, p, T : \text{correct}(p)(T) \Rightarrow$
$\quad\ (\forall\, q : q \in \text{view}(p)(T) \Leftrightarrow \text{lastdelivered}(p, q)(T))$

$\quad\text{ProcJoin} : \text{bool} = \forall\, p, T_1 : \text{joined}(p)(T_1) \wedge \text{correct}(p)(T_1) \Leftrightarrow$
$\quad\ \exists T_0 : T_0 \leq T_1 \wedge \text{deliver}(p, (p, \text{present}))(T_0) \wedge$
$\quad\ \ \text{correct}(p)\ \textbf{during}\ [T_0 - \text{BroadcastDelay}, T_1]$

Then again the membership properties can be verified. Interesting is that now the *JoinDelay* should be greater or equal than two times *BroadcastDelay*, because a new processor first sends a *new* message; all correct processors receive this message after *BroadcastDelay*, and then immediately send a *present* message, which is received by any correct processor after another period of *BroadcastDelay* time units.

agree_verif : LEMMA
  LocalView ∧ Agreement ∧ ProcJoin ∧ Integrity ∧ OwnIdentityOnly ∧
    BroadcastReason ∧ StartUp ∧ Termination ∧ BroadcastPresent ⇒ Agree

join_verif : LEMMA JoinDelay ≥ 2 × BroadcastDelay ∧
  ProcJoin ∧ StartUp ∧ Termination ∧ BroadcastPresent ⇒ Join

6 Implementation of Atomic Broadcast

An implementation of the atomic broadcast service assumed in the previous section can be found in [CASD95]. To verify this protocol, we can again follow the steps of section 3, now using the theory of section 4.3 as a specification of the required service. Here we only show a few basic theories for such a verification in PVS, indicating how to deal with different notions of time and failing links between processors.

6.1 Local clock synchronization

Recall that the properties of atomic broadcast express the timing of actions of a processor in terms of the local clock of the processor itself. For instance, a broadcast action on processor p at local time T, measured on the clock of p, leads to a deliver action on another processor q at local time $T+$*BroadcastDelay*, measured on the clock of q. To be able to verify a protocol which realizes this on top of a simple point-to-point datagram service, we have to make some assumption about the relation between local clocks. A common assumption is that local clocks of correct processors are *internally synchronized*, that is, at any point in real-time they differ at most ϵ. To formulate this in PVS we define a domain *RealTime*, equal to the real numbers, and postulate for each processor p the existence of a surjective function $C(p)$ from *RealTime* to *ClockValues*.

LocalClockSynchr[Processors : TYPE] : THEORY
  BEGIN
  IMPORTING Config[Processors]
  RealTime : TYPE = real
  $C(p)$: (surjective?[RealTime, ClockValues])

Since we would like to express that predicates (e.g., about the correctness of processors) hold at certain points in real-time, we define a function *rt* which converts a predicate P on local clock values to one on real-time. By postulating this as a *conversion* in PVS, we can write $P(t)$, for $t \in RealTime$, which is interpreted as $rt(P)(t)$. Using surjectivity of $C(p)$ we can show that if a predicate holds on a local clock value, then it also holds at a point in real-time. To obtain the other direction we have to introduce axiom *real_to_local*. This leads to the desired relation between local clock values and real-time, as expressed by lemma *local_real_conv*.

t : VAR RealTime
P : VAR pred[LocalClockVals]
$\text{rt}(P)(t)$: bool $= \exists\, p : P(C(p)(t), p)$
CONVERSION rt
local_to_real : LEMMA $P(T,p) \Rightarrow \exists\, t : C(p)(t) = T \wedge P(t)$
real_to_local : AXIOM $P(t) \Rightarrow P(C(p)(t), p)$
local_real_conv : LEMMA $P(T,p) \Leftrightarrow \exists\, t : C(p)(t) = T \wedge P(t)$

Next we formulate the usual axiom expressing internal clock synchronization, where *abs* yields the absolute value. Note that $Correct(p)(t)$ is interpreted by means of conversion *rt*.

ε : ClockValues
local_clock_synch : AXIOM
$\text{Correct}(p)(t) \wedge \text{Correct}(q)(t) \Rightarrow \text{abs}(C(p)(t) - C(q)(t)) < \varepsilon$

Since the specification of the atomic broadcast service is written in terms of local clock values, the aim is to verify the protocol using local clock values only, avoiding real-time. Important part of such a proof is that we can transform a property in terms of the local clock of one processor into a property in terms of the local clock of another processor. Therefore we have proved the following two theorems which are based on the internal clock synchronization axiom, but do not refer to real-time.

clock_synchr : THEOREM
$P(T,p) \wedge \text{Correct}(p)(T,p) \wedge \text{Correct}(q)(T,p) \Rightarrow P \textbf{ in } [(T-\varepsilon, q), (T+\varepsilon, q)]$

clock_change : THEOREM
$P \textbf{ in } [(T_1,p),(T_2,p)] \wedge$
$\text{Correct}(p) \textbf{ during } [(T_1,p),(T_2,p)] \wedge \text{Correct}(q) \textbf{ during } [(T_1,p),(T_2,p)] \Rightarrow$
$P \textbf{ in } [(T_1-\varepsilon, q), (T_2+\varepsilon, q)]$
END LocalClockSynchr

6.2 Specification of datagram service

The atomic broadcast protocol of [CASD95] is based on a datagram service which allows the transmission of messages along links between pairs of nodes. Corresponding to step 3 of our approach, we specify this communication mechanism in theory *Datagram*, with a type *Links* as one of the parameters. Since links might crash, we import theory *FailPrim*, now with *Links* as a parameter. Assume given a function *links* which gives the set of links of a processor. We define primitives to express that a processor p starts sending or receiving a message m along a link l at local clock value LT, together with the usual abbreviations for clock values. Note that we require that link l is member of the links of p.

Datagram[Processors : TYPE, Links : TYPE, Messages : TYPE] : THEORY
  BEGIN
  IMPORTING LocalClockSynchr[Processors], FailPrim[Links, LocalClockVals, <]
  l : VAR Links

  links(p) : setof[Links]

  $\text{Send}(p, m, (l \mid l \in \text{links}(p)))(LT)$: bool
  $\text{Receive}(p, m, (l \mid l \in \text{links}(p)))(LT)$: bool
  $\text{send}(p, m, (l \mid l \in \text{links}(p)))(T)$: bool $=$ $\text{Send}(p, m, l)(T, p)$
  $\text{receive}(p, m, (l \mid l \in \text{links}(p)))(T)$: bool $=$ $\text{Receive}(p, m, l)(T, p)$

Property *BoundedCommunication* below expresses that, for a correct link l, any message that has been sent by p will be received by any processor q that is connected to p via l, between lower bound L and upper bound U. Following [CASD95], these time bounds are expressed in terms of clock values measured on the clock of any arbitrary correct processor r.

  L, U : NonNegClockValues
  LleqU : AXIOM $L \leq U$

  BoundedCommunication : bool $= \forall\, p, q, r, l, T, m$:
   $l \in \text{links}(p) \wedge l \in \text{links}(q) \wedge$
    $\text{correct}(q)$ **during** $[T + L, T + U] \wedge \text{correct}(r)$ **during** $[T + L, T + U] \wedge$
     $\text{Correct}(l)$ **during** $[(T, r), (T + U, r)] \wedge$
      $\text{Send}(p, m, l)(T, r) \Rightarrow$
       $\text{Receive}(q, m, l)$ **in** $[(T + L, r), (T + U, r)]$

When a link fails, there are several possible failure assumptions. For instance, messages might get lost (omission failures), messages might be received outside the specified time bounds (timing failures), messages might be corrupted, or spontaneous messages might be generated. To prove correctness of the atomic broadcast protocol, it is assumed that only omission failures occur.

  OnlyOmissionFailures : bool $= \forall\, q, r, l, T, m$:
   $l \in \text{links}(q) \wedge \text{correct}(r)(T) \wedge \text{Receive}(q, m, l)(T, r) \Rightarrow$
    $\exists\, p : p \neq q \wedge l \in \text{links}(p) \wedge \text{Send}(p, m, l)$ **in** $[(T - U, r), (T - L, r)]$

  Datagram : bool $=$ BoundedCommunication $\wedge$ OnlyOmissionFailures
 END Datagram

The next step in the verification is the formulation of properties representing the protocol of [CASD95]. Finally, it can be proved that this protocol and the specification of the datagram service lead to the atomic broadcast properties specified before. The proof proceeds by induction on the distance between the sender and the receiver, assuming that the network remains connected.

7 Concluding Remarks

An assertional method for the verification of distributed real-time and fault-tolerant protocols has been presented. To obtain mechanical support, two general theories concerning timing and failures have been defined for the verification system PVS. Our approach has been illustrated by the verification of a membership protocol, reasoning in terms of local clocks only. We also showed some basic theories for the verification of an atomic broadcast protocol to indicate, for instance, how to deal with real-time and local clock synchronization in relation to local clock reasoning. Note that failures of processors and links have been treated in a uniform way.

A good overview of related mechanical verifications can be found in [ORSvH95], where mainly applications related to aircraft flight control and their influence on the design of PVS are described. Relevant is also an extensive treatment of clock synchronization protocols in PVS by Shankar [Sha92]. A classical example of a hierarchical verification is the "CLI short stack", which has been verified using Nqthm [BHMY89].

Most of the literature mentioned above does not give a clear methodology that can easily be used by others. Sometimes the use of a formal framework structures the specification and the verification; see for instance the use of TLA for a treatment of the Byzantine generals problem [LM94]. Interesting in [AH97] is the formulation of a template for specifying Lynch-Vaandrager timed automata in PVS. Generic PVS theories to verify well-known algorithmic techniques such as divide-and-conquer have been formulated by Dold [Dol95]. Specific algorithms can be obtained by adding details to a general scheme.

To make our method more accessible, the aim is to formulate a general template of theories that has to be completed by the verifier of a particular protocol. In future work we also intend to work on the formulation of general proof principles that can be used to prove the correctness of classes of protocols. For instance, for protocols that are based on information diffusion, a general diffusion induction principle [CASD95] could be formulated in PVS. Closely related to our aim is an interesting recent paper by Rushby [Rus97] where a general transformation from an untimed synchronous system into a time-triggered implementation of fault-tolerant algorithms is presented. It provides a useful methodology for a particular class of applications

Acknowledgments

This paper has been inspired by earlier work with Ed de Gast and Ping Zhou on the manual verification of the protocols considered here. Many thanks goes to Flaviu Cristian for valuable and stimulating comments on this earlier work and on a previous version of the current paper.

References

[AH97] M. Archer and C. Heitmeyer. Verifying hybrid systems modeled as timed automata: A case study. In *Hybrid and Real-Time Systems (HART'97)*, pages 171–185. LNCS 1201, Springer-Verlag, 1997.

[BHMY89] W.R. Brevier, W.A. Hunt, J.S. Moore, and W.D. Young. An approach to systems verification. *Journal of Automated Reasoning*, 5(4):411–428, 1989.

[CASD95] F. Cristian, H. Aghili, R. Strong, and D. Dolev. Atomic broadcast: From simple message diffusion to Byzantine agreement. *Information and Computation*, 118:158–179, 1995.

[Cri91] F. Cristian. Reaching agreement on processor-group membership in synchronous distributed systems. *Distributed Computing*, 4:175–187, 1991.

[Cri96] F. Cristian. On the semantics of group communication. In *Formal Techniques in Real-Time and Fault-Tolerant Systems*, pages 1–21. LNCS 1135, Springer-Verlag, 1996.

[Dol95] A. Dold. Representing, verifying and applying software development steps using the PVS system. In *Algebraic Methodology and Software Technology (AMAST'95)*, pages 431–444. LNCS 936, Springer-Verlag, 1995.

[Hoo91] J. Hooman. *Specification and Compositional Verification of Real-Time Systems*. LNCS 558, Springer-Verlag, 1991.

[Hoo94] J. Hooman. Compositional verification of a distributed real-time arbitration protocol. *Real-Time Systems*, 6(2):173–205, 1994.

[JP96] B. Jonsson and J. Parrow, editors. *Formal Techniques in Real-Time and Fault-Tolerant Systems*. LNCS 1135. Springer-Verlag, 1996.

[LM94] L. Lamport and S. Merz. Specifying and verifying fault-tolerant systems. In *Formal Techniques in Real-Time and Fault-Tolerant Systems*, pages 41–76. LNCS 863, 1994.

[ORS92] S. Owre, J. Rushby, and N. Shankar. PVS: A prototype verification system. In *11th Conference on Automated Deduction*, volume 607 of *Lecture Notes in Artificial Intelligence*, pages 748–752. Springer-Verlag, 1992.

[ORSvH95] S. Owre, J. Rushby, N. Shankar, and F. von Henke. Formal verification for fault-tolerant architectures: Prolegomena to the design of PVS. *IEEE Transactions on Software Engineering*, 21(2):107–125, 1995.

[Rus97] J. Rushby. Systematic formal verification for fault-tolerant time-triggered algorithms. In C. Meadows and W. Sanders, editors, *Dependable Computing for Critical Applications 6*, pages 191–210, 1997.

[Sha92] N. Shankar. Mechanical verification of a generalized proctocol for byzantine fault tolerant clock synchronization. In *Proceedings Formal Techniques in Real-Time and Fault-Tolerant Systems*, pages 217–236. LNCS 571, Springer-Verlag, 1992.

[ZH95] P. Zhou and J. Hooman. Formal specification and compositional verification of an atomic broadcast protocol. *Real-Time Systems*, 9(2):119–145, 1995.

Invariants, Bisimulations and the Correctness of Coalgebraic Refinements

Bart Jacobs

Dep. Comp. Sci., Univ. Nijmegen, P.O. Box 9010, 6500 GL Nijmegen, The Netherlands.

Email: bart@cs.kun.nl Tel: ++31 - 24 - 3652236 Fax: ++31 - 24 - 3553450

Abstract. *Coalgebraic specifications are used to formally describe the behaviour of classes in object-oriented languages. In this paper, a general notion of refinement between two such coalgebraic specifications is defined, capturing the idea that one "concrete" class specification realises the behaviour of the other, "abstract" class specification. Two (complete) proof-techniques are given to establish such refinements: one involving an invariant (a predicate that is closed under transitions) on the concrete class, and one involving a bisimulation (a relation that is closed under transitions) between the concrete and the abstract class. The latter can only be used if the abstract class is what we call totally specified. Parts of the underlying theory of invariants and bisimulations in a coalgebraic setting are included, involving least and greatest invariants and connections between invariants and bisimulations. Also, the proof-principles are illustrated in examples (which are fully formalised and verified in* PVS*).*

1 Introduction

This paper is part of a recent research line of applying coalgebraic and coinductive notions and techniques in the formalisation of object-oriented concepts, see [26, 14, 11, 13, 15, 5, 6], building on earlier work [30, 2, 17]. Coalgebras consist of a state space together with a transition function and can be used to describe various kinds of dynamical systems, including automata, transition systems and hybrid systems, see *e.g.* [28, 22, 12] (or [16] for an introduction to the theory of coalgebras). A coalgebraic specification (as developed in [14]) formally captures several crucial aspects of classes in object-oriented languages: it consists of a (hidden) state space (typically written as X) to which a client only has limited access, together with several operations (or methods) which act on X. These operations may be attributes $X \to A$ taking values in a (constant) set A and giving some information about elements of X, or they may be procedures for modifying states. The effect of such modification is not directly visible, but only indirectly via the attributes. Procedures may be of the form $X \times B \to X$, but also of the more complicated form $X \times B \to A + (C \times X)$, where $+$ is a disjoint union (or variant) type constructor. In this case the outcome of a procedure application (with parameter from B) can either be an observable value in A, or a pair consisting of an observable value in C together with a next state (in X). In a typical situation, A is a singleton set so that we have a partially defined operation. Besides these methods, a coalgebraic specification consists of two parts: assertions (or constraints) describing the meaning of the operations, and creation conditions describing constraints for initial states (typically written as new). We refer the reader to [14, 13, 15] for more background information. Hopefully, the example specifications in this paper are self-explanatory.

The work that we are about to describe leans heavily on our earlier paper [11] (and extends the approach of [15]). There we described how to obtain terminal coalgebras satisfying constraints (and proved a "comonadicity" result). It took us some time to get the right perspective on (and see the further importance of) the notions and techniques developed there. The terminal coalgebras satisfying constraints were obtained in [11] via special predicates on state spaces of coalgebras that were closed under transitions of the coalgebra. At the time they were called "mongruences", in analogy with congruences (which are relations that are closed under operations). Only now we realise that they are best called "invariants". The terminal coalgebras satisfying constraints were constructed via greatest invariants implying the constraints (see also Section 4 below). These greatest invariants are in essence greatest fixed points of suitable form. Another recent insight is that these greatest invariants come with a proof-rule, which can be exploited to prove the correctness of refinements. This will be the main topic of the present paper. It will require us to further develop the theory of invariants, and to establish some (standard) connections between invariants and bisimulations, see Section 3.

Invariants have a long tradition in computer science. For example, as loop invariants in correctness proofs in the style of Floyd and Hoare. But also in automata-based verification, see *e.g.* [21]. And they occur in an object-oriented setting in [20] in the form of "representation invariants" for implementations of data abstractions in CLU. There is some variation in what precisely constitutes an invariant: it can be (1) a predicate which is closed under transitions (this is what we shall use); or (2) a predicate which holds for all reachable states; or sometimes also (3) a predicate which is closed under transitions and holds for all initial states. Clearly, (3) implies (2), and (2) implies (1). Invariants are well-established as a proof-method for refinements (or implementations) between automata, see *e.g.* [18] for a discussion. Here we extend this approach to a coalgebraic setting, thereby giving it a firm semantical basis.

The present work on refinement, with its invariant and bisimulation proof-principles, shows that the theory of coalgebraic specifications has reached a certain level of maturity and applicability. The following two points appear as advantages of coalgebraic specifications. (1) On the one hand, their formalism is reasonably close to actual object-oriented programming: it is not hard to recognise attributes $X \to A$ as instance variables (of type A), and methods $X \times B \to X$ (or even $X \times B \to A + (C \times X)$) as procedures (possibly with exceptions). The assertions in a coalgebraic specification describe the observable effect of a state change caused by a procedure invocation in a precondition-effect like style. (2) On the other hand, it is also relatively straightforward to describe coalgebraic specifications in a formal (logical) system, like that of the proof-tool PVS [25]. The main refinement example in this paper (Propositions 5.4) has been fully checked in PVS. A systematic approach to such formal, tool-assisted reasoning about class specifications (and refinements between them) will be described elsewhere.

The paper is organised as follows. We start in Section 2 with an illustration of a refinement between coalgebraic specifications, which is meant to convey the main ideas. Subsequently in Sections 3 and 4 we describe the semantics of coalgebraic specifications involving (polynomial) functors (capturing signatures of methods), natural transformations (corresponding to transformations of signatures), coalgebras (models, consisting of state spaces with methods), terminal coalgebras as minimal realisations, invariants and bisimulations. This will be used for a classification of coalgebraic specifications into three categories: they can be inconsistent, totally specified or underspecified. Part of these Sections 3 and 4 are somewhat technical, and readers may wish to first have a look at the definition of refinement and the associated proof-principles in Section 5.

2 An illustration

We present a very simple example of a "concrete" class specification, refining an "abstract" class specification, see Figure 1. First we explain the abstract specification. It has a value attribute val taking real numbers as values, and an increment procedure inc. The latter is not perfect, as becomes clear from the assertion: for an arbitrary state s, the value s.inc.val after an increment is not precisely the original value s.val plus one, but all that we are told is that it lies in the (real number) interval $[\mathsf{s.val} + \frac{3}{4}, \mathsf{s.val} + \frac{5}{4}]_{\mathbb{R}}$. Hence inc can be understood as having tolerance $\frac{1}{4}$ with respect to the perfect increment operation. The initial state new, which is the object that is returned when a new instance of the class is created, satisfies the "creation" condition that its value is between 0 and 1. We clearly have an example of an *underspecified* class, since the behaviour of its objects is not fully determined by the specification.

class spec: Abstract **methods:** val: $X \longrightarrow \mathbb{R}$ inc: $X \longrightarrow X$ **assertions:** $\mathsf{s.inc.val} \in [\mathsf{s.val} + \frac{3}{4}, \mathsf{s.val} + \frac{5}{4}]_{\mathbb{R}}$ **creation:** $\mathsf{new.val} \in [0, 1]_{\mathbb{R}}$ **end class spec**	**class spec:** Concrete **methods:** val: $X \longrightarrow \mathbb{R}$ inc: $X \longrightarrow X$ dec: $X \longrightarrow X$ **assertions:** $\mathsf{s.dec.val} \in [\mathsf{s.val} - \frac{5}{4}, \mathsf{s.val} - \frac{3}{4}]_{\mathbb{R}}$ $\mathsf{s.val} < 0 \vdash \mathsf{s.inc.val} \in [\mathsf{s.val} + \frac{1}{2}, \mathsf{s.val} + \frac{3}{2}]_{\mathbb{R}}$ $\mathsf{s.val} \geq 0 \vdash \mathsf{s.inc.val} \in [\mathsf{s.val} + \frac{7}{8}, \mathsf{s.val} + \frac{9}{8}]_{\mathbb{R}}$ **creation:** $\mathsf{new.val} = 2\frac{1}{2}$ **end class spec**

Figure 1: An abstract and a concrete class specification

The concrete specification in Figure 1 has one attribute val and two procedures inc and dec for incrementing and decrementing the value. Both of them are imperfect, with the imprecision of the increment operation depending on the value of the state on which it operates. This is also a case of underspecification.

Suppose we are in a situation where we need a class which behaves as described in the "abstract" specification, but all we have is a class satisfying the "concrete" specification. Then we do not really have a problem, since this available concrete class provides us with the required "abstract" behaviour: if we take $\mathsf{r} = \mathsf{new.dec.dec}$ in the concrete class as initial state (for the abstract specification that we are trying to realise), and if we only use the increment operation (of the concrete specification), then we get the required behaviour. This is because by using only the increment operation starting from this state r (with value $\mathsf{r.val} \in [0, 1]_{\mathbb{R}}$), the value will always be positive, so that the inc procedure is sufficiently precise. We conclude that the concrete class specification *refines* (sometimes also called *implements*) the abstract specification.

The informal argument that we have just given can be formalised as follows: the operations of the abstract specification also exist in the concrete specification. This is obvious in this situation, by the choice of names, but it may require an actual translation. Further, there is a predicate P on the states of the concrete specification which satisfies the following three properties.

(i) P is closed under the "abstract" procedures (in this case only the inc operation);

this expresses that P is an *invariant*.

(ii) there is a special, "reachable" state r in P which satisfies the creation condition of the abstract specification;

(iii) the states in P satisfy the assertion of the abstract specification.

The predicate P which satisfies these conditions is given by $P(\mathsf{s}) \Leftrightarrow \mathsf{s.val} \geq 0$. These three points will be developed into a (complete) proof-method for refinements in the next few sections.

3 Logical preliminaries: invariants and bisimulations for a polynomial functor

Invariants and bisimulations are special predicates and relations on state spaces (of state-based dynamical systems, in general). We start by recalling some basic facts from the logic of predicates and relations on sets. The main subsequent achievement is the definition for an arbitrary predicate P of the least (or weakest) invariant $\overline{P}$ implied by P and of the greatest (or strongest) invariant $\underline{P}$ implying P. These predicates $\overline{P}$ and $\underline{P}$ will play an important rôle in our proof principles.

We shall be working in the (ordinary) universe of discourse given by the category **Sets** of sets and functions. Of primary importance will be the structure given by Cartesian products $X \times Y$ (with projections $X \overset{\pi}{\leftarrow} X \times Y \overset{\pi'}{\rightarrow} Y$), coproducts (or disjoint unions) $X + Y$ (with coprojections $X \overset{\kappa}{\rightarrow} X + Y \overset{\kappa'}{\leftarrow} Y$), and exponents X^Y (with evaluation maps $\mathrm{ev}: X^Y \times Y \rightarrow X$). We often write 1 for a singleton set (with typical element $*$), and 0 for the empty set.

For an arbitrary set X we shall write $\mathcal{P}(X)$ for the poset (category) of subsets of X, ordered by inclusion. Such subsets will be identified with predicates on X, and the inclusion between them with implication. For a function $f: X \rightarrow Y$ we get a monotone function (*i.e.* a functor) $f^*: \mathcal{P}(Y) \rightarrow \mathcal{P}(X)$ by $(Q \subseteq Y) \mapsto (\{x \mid f(x) \in Q\} \subseteq X)$, which is commonly called ***substitution along*** f. It preserves the propositional connectives, like $\top, \wedge, \bot, \vee, \neg$. A basic observation is that this f^* has both a left and a right adjoint $\coprod_f \dashv f^* \dashv \prod_f$ in a situation:

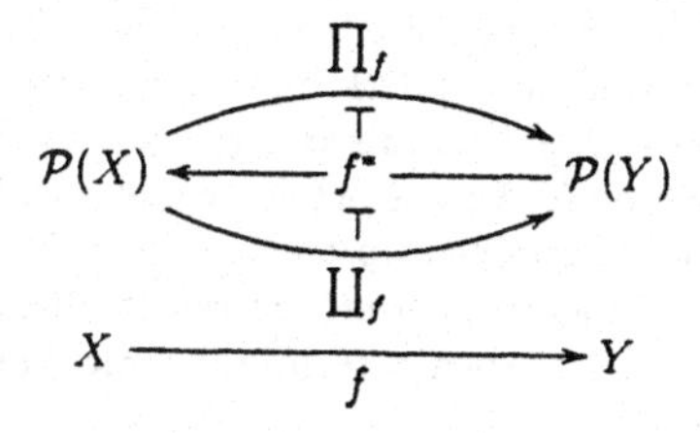

The adjoints $\coprod_f$ and $\prod_f$ are given by the formulas:

$$\begin{aligned} \coprod_f(P \subseteq X) &= (\{y \mid \exists x \in X\ f(x) = y \,\&\, x \in P\} \subseteq Y) \\ \prod_f(P \subseteq X) &= (\{y \mid \forall x \in X\ f(x) = y \Rightarrow x \in P\} \subseteq Y). \end{aligned}$$

The adjunctions $(\coprod_f \dashv f^*)$ and $(f^* \dashv \prod_f)$ are in essence Galois connections, and boil down to the following equivalences:

$$\coprod_f(P) \subseteq Q \Leftrightarrow P \subseteq f^*(Q) \qquad \text{and} \qquad f^*(Q) \subseteq P \Leftrightarrow Q \subseteq \prod_f(P).$$

It is not hard to see that for composable functions f, g one has $(g \circ f)^* = f^* \circ g^*$, $\coprod_g \circ \coprod_f = \coprod_{g \circ f}$ and $\prod_g \circ \prod_f = \prod_{g \circ f}$.

We restrict our attention to so-called polynomial (endo)functors $T\colon \mathbf{Sets} \to \mathbf{Sets}$ on the category **Sets**. These functors are defined inductively, as the elements of the least class of functors $\mathbf{Sets} \to \mathbf{Sets}$ containing[1]:

1. the identity functor $\mathrm{id}\colon \mathbf{Sets} \to \mathbf{Sets}$;
2. the constant functors $K_A\colon \mathbf{Sets} \to \mathbf{Sets}$ (for each set A), mapping $X \mapsto A$;
3. the product $X \mapsto T_1(X) \times T_2(X)$ and coproduct $X \mapsto T_1(X) + T_2(X)$ functors, for functors T_1, T_2 already belonging to the class;
4. the exponent functors $X \mapsto T(X)^A$ (for each set A), for a functor T in the class.

A (T-)*coalgebra* of a (polynomial) functor $T\colon \mathbf{Sets} \to \mathbf{Sets}$ consists of two things: a set X together with a function $\alpha\colon X \to T(X)$. The set X is often called the *state space* or *carrier*, and the function α the *operation* or *transition function*. The important point to realise is that the functor T determines the shape of the operation α. It corresponds to what is called a signature in algebra, see [16]. For example, a coalgebra $\alpha\colon X \to T(X)$ of the polynomial functor $T(X) = A \times X^B$ consists of two operations $\alpha_1\colon X \to A$ and $\alpha_2\colon X \to X^B$. This map α_1 may be called an *attribute*, giving us some information (in terms of values in A) about the states in X. And α_2 can be identified with a procedure operation $X \times B \to X$; it maps a state together with a (parameter) element in B to a next state. These two attribute and procedure operations are most common in our investigations, but more general operations, for example of the form $X \to (A + (C \times X))^B$ can be useful (as in [14]).

If we understand functors as describing signatures of operations, then natural transformations between functors can be understood as maps (or translations) between signatures. Indeed, given a natural transformation $\tau\colon T \Rightarrow S$ between two functors $T, S\colon \mathbf{Sets} \rightrightarrows \mathbf{Sets}$, one can transform every coalgebra $\alpha\colon X \to T(X)$ "of shape T" into a coalgebra $\tau_X \circ \alpha\colon X \to S(X)$ which is "of shape S". An easy example, arising in the setting of [15], involves functors $T(X) = C \times X^D$ and $S(X) = A \times X^B$. Two functions $f\colon C \to A$ and $g\colon B \to D$ (called translation functions in [15]) give rise to a natural transformation $T \Rightarrow S$ with components $f \times \mathrm{id}^g\colon C \times X^D \to A \times X^B$ given by $(c \in C, \varphi \in X^D) \mapsto (f(c) \in A, \varphi \circ g \in X^B)$.

A *homomorphism* of (T-)coalgebras, say from $\alpha\colon X \to T(X)$ to $\beta\colon Y \to T(Y)$ consists of a function $f\colon X \to Y$ between the underlying state spaces which commutes with the operations: $\beta \circ f = T(f) \circ \alpha$. One calls this coalgebra β on Y *terminal* (or also *final*) if for each set X and coalgebra α on X there is precisely one such homomorphism f. Terminal coalgebras, if they exist[2], are determined up-to-isomorphism. Therefore one often speaks of *the* terminal coalgebra of a functor. A standard result, due to Lambek, tells us that the transition function $\beta\colon Y \to T(Y)$ of such a terminal coalgebra is an isomorphism. It is a fixed point of the functor T.

Polynomial functors T as defined above gives rise to two adjoint operations on predicates:

$$\mathcal{P}(X) \underset{(-)_T}{\overset{(-)^T}{\rightleftarrows}} \mathcal{P}(T(X)) \qquad (\top)$$

The operation $(-)^T$ is written as $\mathrm{Pred}(T)(-)$ in [8, 11, 9], but here we choose to use a shorter notation with superscripts. Its left adjoint operation $(-)_T \dashv (-)^T$ is new. We shall

[1] There are at least two reasonable additional clauses imaginable, allowing (finite) powersets, and fixed points of existing functors (see [7] for the latter); such extensions are not needed for what follows.

[2] The polynomial functors T on **Sets** that we use here, all have a terminal coalgebra, which can be obtained via standard techniques [19, 29] as limit of the chain $1 \leftarrow T(1) \leftarrow T^2(1) \leftarrow \cdots$. See [14] for a concrete description of the terminal coalgebras of the kind of functors used below.

define both $(-)^T$ and $(-)_T$ simultaneously, by induction on the structure of the functor T. For predicates $P \subseteq X$ on X and $Q \subseteq T(X)$ on $T(X)$, we define $P^T \subseteq T(X)$ and $Q_T \subseteq X$ as:

$$\begin{array}{rclcrcl} P^{\mathrm{id}} & = & P & \qquad & Q_{\mathrm{id}} & = & Q \\ P^{K_A} & = & A\ (\subseteq A) & & Q_{K_A} & = & \emptyset\ (\subseteq X) \\ P^{T_1 \times T_2} & = & \pi^*(P^{T_1}) \cap \pi'^*(P^{T_2}) & & Q_{T_1 \times T_2} & = & (\coprod_\pi Q)_{T_1} \cup (\coprod_{\pi'} Q)_{T_2} \\ P^{T_1 + T_2} & = & \prod_\kappa (P^{T_1}) \cap \prod_{\kappa'} (P^{T_2}) & & Q_{T_1 + T_2} & = & (\kappa^* Q)_{T_1} \cup (\kappa'^* Q)_{T_2} \\ P^{T^A} & = & \prod_\pi \mathrm{ev}^*(P^T) & & Q_{T^A} & = & (\coprod_{\mathrm{ev}} \pi^* Q)_T. \end{array}$$

Some illustrations of these definitions[3,4] will be given below.

3.1. Lemma. *These newly defined predicates satisfy*
(i) $Q \subseteq P^T \Leftrightarrow Q_T \subseteq P$;
(ii) $(f^* P)^T = T(f)^*(P^T)$ *and* $\coprod_f (Q_T) = (\coprod_{T(f)} Q)_T$ *and* $\prod_f (Q_T) = (\prod_{T(f)} Q)_T$.

Proof. (i) By induction on the structure of the functor T, using the adjunctions described earlier. For example in the coproduct case:

$$\begin{array}{rll} Q \subseteq P^{T_1+T_2} = \prod_\kappa (P^{T_1}) \cap \prod_{\kappa'} (P^{T_2}) & & \\ \Leftrightarrow & Q \subseteq \prod_\kappa (P^{T_1}) \text{ and } Q \subseteq \prod_{\kappa'} (P^{T_2}) & \\ \Leftrightarrow & \kappa^* Q \subseteq P^{T_1} \text{ and } \kappa'^* Q \subseteq P^{T_2} & \\ \Leftrightarrow & (\kappa^* Q)_{T_1} \subseteq P \text{ and } (\kappa'^* Q)_{T_2} \subseteq P & \text{by induction hypothesis} \\ \Leftrightarrow & Q_{T_1+T_2} = (\kappa^* Q)_{T_1} \cup (\kappa'^* Q)_{T_2} \subseteq P. & \end{array}$$

(ii) The first statement is proved by induction on the structure of T. The other two then follows easily by the adjunctions. □

3.2. Definition. Let $\alpha: X \to T(X)$ be a coalgebra of a polynomial functor T and let $P \subseteq X$ be a predicate on its state space.
(i) Put

$$P^+ \stackrel{\text{def}}{=} \alpha^*(P^T) \subseteq X \qquad \text{and} \qquad P^- \stackrel{\text{def}}{=} (\coprod_\alpha P)_T \subseteq X.$$

The way to think of P^+ is as the predicate which holds of states whose "direct successors" satisfy P, and of P^- as the predicate of states which are "direct successors" of states satisfying P. Briefly, P^+ is NextTime P (or $\bigcirc P$), and P^- is LastTime P from temporal logic[5] (see *e.g.* [3]). Notice that we leave the dependence on α implicit.
(ii) Call the predicate $P \subseteq X$ an (α-)*invariant* if $P \subseteq P^+$, or equivalently, if $P^- \subseteq P$.

The equivalence mentioned in (ii) holds because $P \subseteq P^+ = \alpha^*(P^T) \Leftrightarrow \coprod_\alpha P \subseteq P^T \Leftrightarrow (\coprod_\alpha P)_T = P^- \subseteq P$. We illustrate these definitions in two examples.

---

[3] In earlier work [8, 11, 9] the formulation $P^{T_1+T_2} = \coprod_\kappa (P^{T_1}) \cup \coprod_{\kappa'} (P^{T_2})$ was used instead of the one above. These two formulations are equivalent, and the one we have chosen is easier when we consider the left adjoint $(-)_T$ to $(-)^T$, see the proof of the subsequent lemma.

[4] It is easy to extend these definitions to include (finite) powersets, namely by $P^{\mathcal{P}} = \mathcal{P}(P)$ and $Q_{\mathcal{P}} = \bigcup Q$.

[5] One can also use these definitions to introduce correctness specifications (in the style of Floyd and Hoare) for coalgebras: for predicates $P_1, P_2 \subseteq X$ on the state space of a coalgebra $\alpha: X \to T(X)$ define $\{P_1\}\alpha\{P_2\}$ as $\coprod_\alpha P_1 \subseteq P_2^T$. Then P^+ is by construction the weakest precondition wpr(α, P), and P^- is the strongest postcondition spo(α, P).

3.3. Examples. (i) Consider the (polynomial) functor $T(X) = A \times X$, with a coalgebra structure $(\mathsf{head}, \mathsf{tail})\colon X \to A \times X$. For a predicate $P \subseteq X$ we compute both P^+ and P^-:

$$\begin{aligned}
P^+ &= \{x \in X \mid (\mathsf{head}(x), \mathsf{tail}(x)) \in P^{K_A \times \mathrm{id}}\} \\
&= \{x \in X \mid \mathsf{head}(x) \in P^{K_A} \;\&\; \mathsf{tail}(x) \in P^{\mathrm{id}}\} \\
&= \{x \in X \mid \mathsf{head}(x) \in A \;\&\; \mathsf{tail}(x) \in P\} \\
&= \{x \in X \mid \mathsf{tail}(x) \in P\}. \\
P^- &= (\textstyle\coprod_{(\mathsf{head},\mathsf{tail})} P)_{K_A \times \mathrm{id}} \\
&= (\textstyle\coprod_{\pi} \coprod_{(\mathsf{head},\mathsf{tail})} P)_{K_A} \cup (\coprod_{\pi'} \coprod_{(\mathsf{head},\mathsf{tail})} P)_{\mathrm{id}} \\
&= \emptyset \cup \textstyle\coprod_{\mathsf{tail}} P \\
&= \{x \in X \mid \exists y \in P\; x = \mathsf{tail}(y)\} \\
&= \{\mathsf{tail}(y) \mid y \in P\}.
\end{aligned}$$

The predicate P is thus an invariant if and only if $\mathsf{tail}(x) \in P$ for all $x \in P$.

(ii) We consider a more complicated functor $X \mapsto (A + (C \times X))^B$ with a coalgebra $\alpha\colon X \to (A + (C \times X))^B$. For a predicate $P \subseteq X$ we compute:

$$\begin{aligned}
P^+ &= \textstyle\prod_{\pi} \mathrm{ev}^*(\prod_{\kappa}(A) \cap \prod_{\kappa'}(\pi^*(C) \cap \pi'^* P)) \\
&= \{x \in X \mid \forall b \in B\; \forall c \in C\; \forall y \in X\; \alpha(x)(b) = \kappa'(c, y) \Rightarrow y \in P\} \\
P^- &= \textstyle\coprod_{\pi'} \kappa'^* \coprod_{\mathrm{ev}} \pi^* \coprod_{\alpha} P \\
&= \{x \in X \mid \exists y \in P\; \exists b \in B\; \exists c \in C\; \alpha(y)(b) = \kappa'(c, x)\}.
\end{aligned}$$

The power of these definitions $(-)^T$ and $(-)_T$ is that they lead to a uniform notion of invariant, in which the (polynomial) functor T is a parameter. This ensures a wide applicability. Also, the abstract formulations in terms of $\coprod, \prod$ and $(-)^*$ allow us to reason conveniently with the adjointness (or Galois) properties. Moreover, these definitions can be given in an arbitrary (but sufficiently expressive) logical system of first order logic (containing $\exists, \forall$ and equality $=$), using induction on the functor T.

3.4. Fact. It can be shown that a predicate $P \subseteq X$ on the state space of a coalgebra $\alpha\colon X \to T(X)$ is an invariant (as defined above) if and only if P, as a subset of X, carries a *subcoalgebra* structure. The latter means that there is a (unique) transition function $\alpha_P\colon P \to T(P)$ making the inclusion function $P \hookrightarrow X$ a homomorphism of coalgebras:

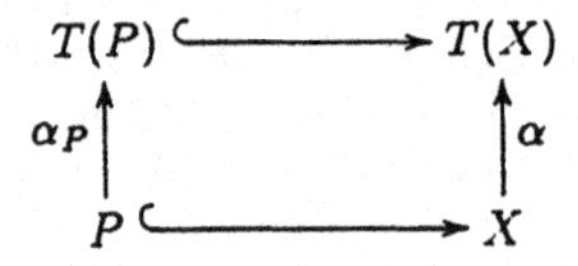

(Uniqueness follows from the fact that polynomial functors (on **Sets**) preserve injections.)

This subcoalgebra property seems simpler than the property $P \subseteq P^+$ (or equivalently, $P^- \subseteq P$) as used above to define invariants. The earlier definition however has the big advantage that it can be given (by induction) in an arbitrary predicate logic, as used for example by a proof-tool. The subcoalgebra property depends on the fact that predicates on sets can be identified with subsets (and thus are sets themselves). In general, predicates are not identified with subsets.

The following results follow directly from the adjointness properties.

3.5. Lemma. *Invariants are closed under conjunctions $\wedge$ and under universal quantification $\forall$.* □

3.6. Lemma. *The function $P \mapsto P^+$ is monotone and preserves meets $\bigcap_n P_n$ of descending chains ($P_0 \supseteq P_1 \supseteq P_2 \supseteq \cdots$). And the function $P \mapsto P^-$ is also monotone and preserves joins $\bigcup_n P_n$ of ascending chains ($P_0 \subseteq P_1 \subseteq P_2 \subseteq \cdots$).* □

3.7. Proposition. *For a predicate $P \subseteq X$ on the state space of a coalgebra $\alpha: X \to T(X)$ we define a descending chain $(P_n)_{n \in \mathbb{N}}$ of predicates by:*

$$P_0 = P, \qquad P_{n+1} = (P_n)^+ \cap P_n \qquad \text{and} \qquad \underline{P} = \bigcap_n P_n.$$

And similarly, an ascending chain $(P^n)_{n \in \mathbb{N}}$ by:

$$P^0 = P, \qquad P^{n+1} = (P^n)^- \cup P^n \qquad \text{and} \qquad \overline{P} = \bigcup_n P^n.$$

Then: $\underline{P}$ is the greatest invariant contained in P and $\overline{P}$ is the least invariant containing P.

Sometimes we write $\underline{P}_\alpha$ for $\underline{P}$ and $\overline{P}^\alpha$ for $\overline{P}$ if we wish to see the dependence on α explicitly. The predicate $\overline{P}$ captures the states which are reachable from P (via α). In [28] the existence of $\underline{P}$ and $\overline{P}$ (written as $\langle P \rangle$ and $[P]$ there) follows from the observation that invariants (or: subsystems, as used there) form a complete lattice. Here we show how $\underline{P}$ and $\overline{P}$ can be obtained by iteration.

Proof. By construction we have $\underline{P} \subseteq P \subseteq \overline{P}$. The predicate $\underline{P}$ is an invariant since $(\underline{P})^+ = (\bigcap_n P_n)^+ = \bigcap_n (P_n)^+ \supseteq \bigcap_n P_{n+1} = \underline{P}$. And if Q is an invariant with $Q \subseteq P$, then $Q \subseteq P_n$, by induction on n, and so $Q \subseteq \bigcap_n P_n = \underline{P}$. A similar argument shows that $\overline{P}$ is an invariant and that every invariant Q with $P \subseteq Q$ satisfies $\overline{P} \subseteq Q$. □

It is not hard to show that $\underline{P}$ is the greatest fixed point X in $X = P \cap X^+$. Hence we may write $\underline{P}$ as future-tense necessity $\Box P$, like in temporal logic, see [3]. Similarly, $\overline{P}$ is the least fixed point X in $X = P \cup X^-$, so that we can understand $\overline{P}$ as the past-tense eventuality $\Diamond P$. These connections with temporal logic are not fully explored yet.

In the sequel we shall meet the following situation.

3.8. Proposition. *Consider two polynomial functors S, T with a natural transformation $\tau: S \Rightarrow T$ between them. Let $\beta: Y \to S(Y)$ and $\alpha: X \to T(X)$ be two coalgebras with a homomorphism of T-coalgebras $f: Y \to X$ from the translation $(\tau_Y \circ \beta)$ of β to α. Assume further that $Q \subseteq Y$ is a $(\tau_Y \circ \beta)$-invariant and that $P \subseteq X$ is an arbitrary subset. Then: if $f(y) \in P$ for all $y \in Q$, then $f(y) \in \underline{P}_\alpha$ for all $y \in Q$.*

Proof. We may assume $Q \subseteq Q^+$ and $\coprod_f Q \subseteq P$ and have to show that $\coprod_f Q \subseteq \underline{P}_\alpha$. This follows if we can show that the predicate $\coprod_f Q \subseteq X$ is an α-invariant, *i.e.* if it satisfies $\coprod_f Q \subseteq (\coprod_f Q)^+$. Therefore we compute:

$$(\textstyle\coprod_f Q)^+ = (\coprod_\alpha \coprod_f Q)_T = (\coprod_{T(f)} \coprod_{\tau_Y \circ \beta} Q)_T = \coprod_f (\coprod_{\tau_Y \circ \beta} Q)_T = \coprod_f (Q^+) \supseteq \coprod_f (Q).$$

□

We conclude this section with bisimulations with respect to a polynomial functor T. Along the lines described above (and in line with [11, 9]) we define a bisimulation on two coalgebras $\alpha: X \to T(X)$, $\beta: Y \to T(Y)$ of the same functor as a relation $R \subseteq X \times Y$ on their sets of states such that $R \subseteq (\alpha \times \beta)^{*}(R^T)$, where the relation R^T (also written as

$\mathrm{Rel}(T)(R))$ on $T(X) \times T(Y)$ is defined by induction on the structure of T as:

$$
\begin{array}{rcl}
R^{\mathrm{id}} & = & R \\
R^{K_A} & = & \mathrm{Eq}(A) = \{(a,a) \mid a \in A\} \\
R^{T_1 \times T_2} & = & (\pi \times \pi)^*(R^{T_1}) \cap (\pi' \times \pi')^*(R^{T_2}) \\
 & = & \{(\langle x_1, x_2\rangle, \langle y_1, y_2\rangle) \mid R^{T_1}(x_1, y_1) \ \&\ R^{T_2}(x_2, y_2)\} \\
R^{T_1+T_2} & = & \prod_{\kappa\times\kappa}(R^{T_1}) \cap \prod_{\kappa'\times\kappa'}(R^{T_2}) \;=\; \coprod_{\kappa\times\kappa}(R^{T_1}) \cup \coprod_{\kappa'\times\kappa'}(R^{T_2}) \\
 & = & \{(\kappa x_1, \kappa y_1) \mid R^{T_1}(x_1, y_1)\} \cup \{(\kappa' x_2, \kappa' y_2) \mid R^{T_2}(x_2, y_2)\} \\
R^{T^A} & = & \prod_\pi \langle \mathrm{ev} \circ \pi \times \mathrm{id}, \mathrm{ev} \circ \pi' \times \mathrm{id}\rangle^*(R^T) \\
 & = & \{(f_1, f_2) \mid \forall a \in A\ R^T(f_1(a), f_2(a))\}.
\end{array}
$$

Bisimulations have received a lot of attention in process theory (see *e.g.* [24]), but also in coalgebra (*e.g.* in [1, 27, 28]). The greatest bisimulation on two coalgebras is usually written as $\leftrightarrow$. It captures behavioural indistinguishability. A standard result is that elements of the state spaces of two arbitrary T-coalgebras are bisimilar if and only if they are mapped to the same element of the terminal T-coalgebra. If we speak about bisimulation on a single coalgebra $\alpha: X \to T(X)$, then we mean bisimulation as above with $(Y, \beta) = (X, \alpha)$.

An aside: let δ be the diagonal function $\delta(x) = (x, x)$, so that for a predicate P, $\coprod_\delta(P)$ is the relation $\{(x,y) \mid P(x) \wedge x = y\}$. It is not hard to see that $P^T = \delta^*((\coprod_\delta(P))^T)$, where $(-)^T$ on the left hand side applies to a predicate, and $(-)^T$ on the right hand side to a relation. Hence the lifting $(-)^T$ of the functor T to predicates can be obtained from the lifting of T to relations. Also, P is an invariant, if and only if $\coprod_\delta(P)$ is a bisimulation (see *e.g.* [9, 28]). Hence one can argue that the lifting to relations is more fundamental. But our explicit treatment of predicates will be convenient in many situations.

The following technical result will be of importance later; it provides (folklore) connections between invariants and bisimulations.

3.9. Lemma. *Consider two coalgebras $\alpha: X \to T(X)$ and $\beta: Y \to T(Y)$ of the same polynomial functor T, together with a bisimulation $R \subseteq X \times Y$ and an invariant $Q \subseteq Y$ (for β). Then:*

(i) $\pi'^*(Q) \cap R = \{(x,y) \mid Q(y) \ \&\ R(x,y)\} \subseteq X \times Y$ *is a bisimulation;*
(ii) $\coprod_\pi(R) = \{x \mid \exists y \in Y\ R(x,y)\} \subseteq X$ *is an invariant (for α);*
(iii) $\coprod_\pi(\pi'^*(Q) \cap R) = \{x \mid \exists y \in Y\ Q(y) \ \&\ R(x,y)\} \subseteq X$ *is an invariant (for α).*

Proof. The last point follows from the first two. For (i) and (ii) the main steps are to prove $(\pi'^*(Q) \cap R)^T = \pi'^*(Q^T) \cap R^T$ and $(\coprod_\pi R)^T = \coprod_\pi(R^T)$, by induction[6] on the structure of T. The results then follow by calculation. □

Bisimulations of the form $\pi'^*(Q) \cap R$ as in (i) are called "weak" in [21].

4 The terminal model of a coalgebraic specification

In this section we describe terminal models of coalgebraic specifications via invariants, following [11]. In terms of these models we can define what it means for a class to be *underspecified*, *totally specified* or *inconsistent*.

Typical coalgebraic specifications are described in Figures 1, 2 and 3. They consist of three sections, describing the methods (or operations), assertions (or constraints) and

[6] The easiest way is simply to write out the definitions given earlier. Using the adjunctions is not straightforward, since some additional laws of categorical logic, like Beck-Chevalley and Frobenius, have to be used. In (ii), the case where T is an exponent functor requires the Axiom of Choice (which we assume to hold in the logic of sets, and which can be proved in the logic of PVS).

the creation conditions which are required to hold for an initial state new. We write s (for state of self) for an arbitrary inhabitant of the state space X. What is typically coalgebraic about these specifications is that nothing is told about what is inside X (or how it is built up, like in algebra). We are only given some information about the observable behaviour of elements of X. Using the bisimilarity sign $\leftrightarrow$ in assertion or creation clauses is justified, since $\leftrightarrow$ is determined by the functor associated with the signature of the (earlier given) methods of the specification, see the explanation in (i) below.

```
class spec: Stack(A)
  methods:
    push: X × A ⟶ X
    pop: X ⟶ X
    top: X ⟶ 1 + A
  assertions:
    s.push(a).top = a
    s.push(a).pop ↔ s
    s.top = * ⊢ s.pop ↔ s
  creation:
    new.top = *
end class spec

class spec: FreshStack(A)
  inherts from: Stack(A)
  methods:
    fresh_push: X × A ⟶ X
    occurs?: X × A ⟶ {0, 1}
  assertions:
    ∃n s.pop^(n).top = a ⊢ s.occurs?(a) = 1
    ¬∃n s.pop^(n).top = a ⊢ s.occurs?(a) = 0
    s.occurs?(a) = 0 ⊢ s.fresh_push(a) ↔ s.push(a)
    s.occurs?(a) = 1 ⊢ s.fresh_push(a) ↔ s
end class spec
```

Figure 2: Two stack specification Stack and FreshStack, where the latter has an extra method fresh_push which only pushes fresh (not already occurring) elements on the stack

A model of such a class specification consists basically of two parts: a set S serving as state space, together with suitable functions acting on S which interpret the methods; this interpretation should be such that (a) the assertions are satisfied, and (b) the subset of S consisting of those states for which the creation conditions hold is non-empty. Below we shall construct a particular model for a class specification, namely the terminal one. This construction involves three steps, which we shall illustrate for the stack specification in Figure 2.

(i) A functor T is extracted from the specification, which captures the signature of the methods. This functor is given by the Cartesian product of the output types of the methods, where the output type of an operation $X \times B \longrightarrow S(X)$ is defined as the exponent type $S(X)^B$. For example the functor associated with the stack methods is $T(X) = X^A \times X \times (1 + A)$. (The first two factors X^A and X resulting from push and pop can be combined into a single factor $X^{(A+1)}$, since $X^A \times X \cong X^{(A+1)}$, leading to further simplication.)

Coalgebras $X \to T(X)$ are models of the methods in the specification. Among these models the terminal coalgebra $Z \xrightarrow{\cong} T(Z)$ will play a special rôle. In the case of the stack specification, this terminal coalgebra can be identified with the set $Z = (1 + A)^{(A+1)^\star}$ of functions from $(A + 1)^\star$ to $1 + A$, with methods acting on $\varphi \in Z$ as:

$$\begin{aligned} \mathsf{push}(\varphi, a) &= \lambda\sigma \in (A+1)^\star\ \varphi(\sigma \cdot (\kappa a)) \\ \mathsf{pop}(\varphi) &= \lambda\sigma \in (A+1)^\star\ \varphi(\sigma \cdot (\kappa' *)) \\ \mathsf{top}(\varphi) &= \varphi(\langle\rangle). \end{aligned}$$

(ii) Once we have interpretations of the methods of a coalgebraic specification in some coalgebra $X \to T(X)$, we can consider the assertions. They give rise to a subset[7] $E \subseteq$

[7] We get a subset (instead of a relation, as in algebra), because the assertions are required to contain only one variable ranging over states (which is typically written as s), see [11].

X describing the states which statisfy the assertions. We can then simply say that the assertions hold in this coalgebra if this subset $E \subseteq X$ is all of X.

In the stack example we get the following subset E of the terminal coalgebra[8].

$$\begin{aligned} E = \{\varphi \in Z \mid & (\forall a \in A\ \varphi(\langle \kappa a \rangle) = \kappa' a \ \&\ \lambda\sigma\ \varphi(\sigma \cdot (\kappa a) \cdot (\kappa' *)) = \varphi) \\ & \&\ \varphi(\langle\rangle) = \kappa * \Rightarrow \lambda\sigma\ \varphi(\sigma \cdot (\kappa' *)) = \varphi\}. \end{aligned}$$

This subset E does not carry a coalgebra structure, but in the previous section we have seen how it can be provided with such structure, by taking $\underline{E}$ or $\overline{E}$. The set $\underline{E}$ is what we are interested in: it is the terminal model which satisfies the assertions (since $\underline{E} \subseteq E$).

We describe the set $\underline{E}$ explicitly for the stack example with E as above.

$$\begin{aligned} \underline{E} = \{\varphi \in Z \mid & \forall a \in A \forall \sigma, \sigma' \in (A+1)^*\ \varphi(\sigma \cdot (\kappa a)) = \kappa' a \\ & \&\ \varphi(\sigma \cdot (\kappa a) \cdot (\kappa' *) \cdot \sigma') = \varphi(\sigma \cdot \sigma') \ \&\ \varphi(\sigma) = \kappa * \Rightarrow \varphi(\sigma \cdot (\kappa' *) \cdot \sigma') = \varphi(\sigma \cdot \sigma')\} \end{aligned}$$

On close inspection we see that functions $\varphi \in \underline{E}$ are completely determined by their values $\varphi((\kappa' *)^n)$, where $(\kappa' *)^n$ is the sequence $(\kappa' *) \cdots (\kappa' *)$ of length n. Furthermore, these values $\varphi((\kappa' *)^n)$ are such that if $\varphi((\kappa' *)^n) = \kappa *$, then $\varphi((\kappa' *)^{n+1}) = \kappa *$. Hence such a $\varphi \in \underline{E}$ may be identified with a finite or infinite sequence of elements from A. Thus $\underline{E} \cong A^\infty$, where $A^\infty = A^* + A^{\mathbb{N}}$ is the set of both finite and infinite sequences of elements of A. The induced methods on $\sigma \in A^\infty$ are

$$\sigma.\mathsf{push}(a) = a \cdot \sigma \qquad \sigma.\mathsf{pop} = \begin{cases} \langle\rangle & \text{if } \sigma = \langle\rangle \\ \sigma' & \text{if } \sigma = a \cdot \sigma' \end{cases} \qquad \sigma.\mathsf{top} = \begin{cases} \kappa * & \text{if } \sigma = \langle\rangle \\ \kappa' a & \text{if } \sigma = a \cdot \sigma' \end{cases}$$

It is not hard to verify that the stack assertions hold in this coalgebra. By construction, A^∞ (with these operations) is the terminal coalgebra satisfying the assertions, see [11]. It is the *minimal realisation* (in automata theoretic terminology) of the specified behaviour[9].

(iii) In a final step, the creation conditions in the specification determine a subset $I \subseteq \underline{E}$ of "initial" states that can be used as interpretations of **new**. In the stack example,

$$I = \{\sigma \in A^\infty \mid \sigma.\mathsf{top} = \kappa *\} = \{\langle\rangle\}.$$

so that the interpretation of new is determined as the empty sequence. This corresponds to our intuition.

Recapitulating, we obtain the terminal model of a coalgebraic specification by successively carving out appropriate subsets $I \subseteq \underline{E} \subseteq E \subseteq Z$ of the terminal coalgebra $Z \xrightarrow{\cong} T(Z)$ of the functor T capturing the signature of methods.

The set $I \subseteq A^\infty$ of initial states in the terminal coalgebra A^∞ satisfying the assertions is a singleton. This need not be the case in general, and this leads us to the following classification of coalgebraic specifications.

4.1. Definition. Consider an arbitrary coalgebraic specification $\mathcal{A}$, for which we determine the terminal model as $I_{\mathcal{A}} \subseteq \underline{E}_{\mathcal{A}}$ as above, with set of initial states $I_{\mathcal{A}}$. We call $\mathcal{A}$

(i) *inconsistent* if $I_{\mathcal{A}}$ is the empty set;
(ii) *totally specified* if $I_{\mathcal{A}}$ is a singleton:
(iii) *underspecified* if $I_{\mathcal{A}}$ is neither empty nor a singleton.

---

[8] On the terminal coalgebra, the bisimilarity relation $\underline{\leftrightarrow}$ is simply equality; on an arbitrary coalgebra we have to use the bisimilarity relation on that coalgebra as interpretation of $\underline{\leftrightarrow}$ in the specification.

[9] The occurrence of the set A^* of finite sequences in the minimal Stack realisation is probably clear. We also get the infinite sequences $A^{\mathbb{N}}$ in this model since nothing in the specification tells us that the sequence of observations s.top, s.pop.top, s.pop.pop.top, ... must eventually lead to an element $*$ (indicating that the stack s is empty).

Hence, an inconsistency means that there is no (initial) state displaying the required behaviour; total specification means that there is precisely one such state, and underspecification means that there may be many such states[10]. The stacks in Figure 2 are totally specified, as we have seen. (The 'fresh' stacks are also totally specified, since they have the same models as stacks: the additional methods fresh_push and occurs? are defined in terms of the stack methods.) The store specification in Figure 3 gives an example of underspecification. Intuitively this may be clear, since it is not layed down after how many **delete_one** invocations a stored element is actually deleted.

class spec: Store(A)
  methods:
    occurs?: $X \times A \longrightarrow \{0, 1\}$
    put: $X \times A \longrightarrow X$
    delete_one: $X \longrightarrow X$
  assertions:
    s.occurs?(a) $= 1 \vdash$
      $\exists n$ s.delete_one$^{(n)}$.occurs?(a) $= 0$
    $a_1 = a_2 \vdash$ s.put(a_1).occurs?(a_2) $= 1$
    $a_1 \neq a_2 \vdash$ s.put(a_1).occurs?(a_2) $=$ s.occurs?(a_2)
    $\exists a$ s.occurs?(a) $= 1 \vdash$
      $\exists a$ (s.occurs?(a) $= 1 \wedge$ s.delete_one.occurs?(a) $= 0$
      $\wedge \forall b \neq a$ s.delete_one.occurs?(b) $=$ s.occurs?(b))
    $\neg\exists a$ s.occurs?(a) $= 1 \vdash$
      s.delete_one.occurs?(b) $= 0$
  creation:
    new.occurs?(a) $= 0$
end class spec

Figure 3: A specification of a class in which one can store elements from A, which reappear at some unspecified later stage

5 Refinements with invariant and bisimulation proofs

A refinement establishes a relation between two specifications. Usually one says that an *abstract* specification is refined by a *concrete* one, see [10, 23, 4] (and also Section 2). This means that the behaviour that is specified in the abstract specification can be realised by the concrete specification. The latter often contains more details about how to realise this behaviour. Typically, it is more deterministic (*i.e.* less underspecified) than the abstract specification (as stressed in [6]), see the stack specification refining the store specification later in this section. We start with the definition of refinement, and with two associated proof principles, involving invariants and bisimulations.

5.1. Definition. Consider two coalgebraic specifications: $\mathcal{A}$ for abstract, and $\mathcal{C}$ for concrete, with associated (polynomial) "signature" functors $T_{\mathcal{A}}$ and $T_{\mathcal{C}}$. We say that $\mathcal{C}$ *refines* $\mathcal{A}$ (or equivalently, that $\mathcal{A}$ is *refined by* $\mathcal{C}$) if

(i) there is a translation of methods from the abstract to the concrete specification in the form of a natural transformation $\tau: T_{\mathcal{C}} \Rightarrow T_{\mathcal{A}}$;

[10] The initial state new occurring in the specification may be understood in this case as an arbitrary element of this set.

(ii) for each model $\mathcal{M}_{\mathcal{C}}$ of the concrete specification $\mathcal{C}$, there is a reachable (in $\mathcal{C}$) state r, such that

(a) r satisfies the creation conditions from $\mathcal{A}$ (when they are suitably translated via τ);

(b) the predicate $RS = \overline{\{r\}}^{\mathcal{A}}$ of reachable states from r (with respect to the translated methods from $\mathcal{A}$) implies the assertions from $\mathcal{A}$ (translated via τ). This requirement makes sense, because RS, considered as subset of the model $\mathcal{M}_{\mathcal{C}}$, carries an $\mathcal{A}$-coalgebra structure by Fact 3.4 (using τ again).

The translation τ allows us to re-interpret the abstract assertions and creation conditions in the induced $T_{\mathcal{A}}$-structure on the concrete state space. The intuition behind the definition is the following: in order to realise the behaviour of the abstract class specification $\mathcal{A}$ we need first of all a translation τ of the methods of $\mathcal{A}$ to the methods of some other class specification $\mathcal{C}$. Then, in each model of $\mathcal{C}$, there should be a reachable state r which can play the rôle of the initial state new in $\mathcal{A}$, and all the states which are reachable from r via the translated methods from $\mathcal{A}$ should satisfy the assertions from $\mathcal{A}$. Hence on this subset RS of reachable states from r we realise the behaviour of $\mathcal{A}$. This suffices since by working in $\mathcal{C}$ (via τ) we will never get beyond the reachable states. In brief: $\mathcal{C}$ refines $\mathcal{A}$ if every model of $\mathcal{C}$ contains some reachable part which is a model of $\mathcal{A}$ (after suitable translation).

5.2. Theorem. *Consider abstract and concrete class specifications $\mathcal{A}$ and $\mathcal{C}$ as in the previous definition, with translation $\tau: T_{\mathcal{C}} \Rightarrow T_{\mathcal{A}}$. Then: $\mathcal{C}$ refines $\mathcal{A}$ if and only if for each model $\mathcal{M}_{\mathcal{C}}$ of $\mathcal{C}$ there is a reachable state r satisfying (a) above, and a predicate P on $\mathcal{M}_{\mathcal{C}}$ which satisfies:*

(i) *P is an $\mathcal{A}$-invariant*, i.e. *is closed under the translated operations of $\mathcal{A}$;*

(ii) *P contains r;*

(iii) *the (translated) assertions from $\mathcal{A}$ hold on P.*

Proof. The (only-if) part is easy, since by definition $\overline{\{r\}}^{\mathcal{A}}$ satisfies the conditions in the theorem. Conversely, if P is predicate as described in (i)–(iii), then $\overline{\{r\}}^{\mathcal{A}}$ is contained in P, by definition of $\overline{(-)}$. Hence all the assertions of $\mathcal{A}$ also hold on $\overline{\{r\}}^{\mathcal{A}}$. □

The advantage of reasoning with invariants is that they reduce global arguments to local ones which only involve reasoning with single steps.

There is an alternative proof method involving bisimulations in case the abstract class $\mathcal{A}$ is totally specified (see Definition 4.1). This proof technique is used in [15].

5.3. Theorem. *Consider again the abstract and concrete class specifications $\mathcal{A}$ and $\mathcal{C}$ with $\tau: T_{\mathcal{C}} \Rightarrow T_{\mathcal{A}}$ as in the previous theorem, but this time assume that the abstract class $\mathcal{A}$ is totally specified. Then: $\mathcal{C}$ refines $\mathcal{A}$ if and only if for all models $\mathcal{M}_{\mathcal{C}}$ of $\mathcal{C}$ and $\mathcal{M}_{\mathcal{A}}$ of $\mathcal{A}$ there is a reachable state r in $\mathcal{M}_{\mathcal{C}}$ (satisfying (a) in Definition 5.1) and a bisimulation relation R on $\mathcal{M}_{\mathcal{C}} \times \mathcal{M}_{\mathcal{A}}$ with $R(\mathsf{r}, \mathsf{new})$.*

The bisimulation R in this situation is associated with the functor $T_{\mathcal{A}}$ describing the abstract signature. The states of the concrete specification carry a $T_{\mathcal{A}}$-coalgebra structure via the translation τ.

Proof. First assume that $\mathcal{C}$ refines $\mathcal{A}$, and that models $\mathcal{M}_{\mathcal{C}}$ and $\mathcal{M}_{\mathcal{A}}$ are given, with a reachable state r in $\mathcal{M}_{\mathcal{C}}$. We may assume an invariant P on $\mathcal{M}_{\mathcal{C}}$ as in Theorem 5.2. Then $R = \{(\mathsf{s}, \mathsf{t}) \in \mathcal{M}_{\mathcal{C}} \times \mathcal{M}_{\mathcal{A}} \mid P(\mathsf{s}) \;\&\; \mathsf{s} \underline{\leftrightarrow} \mathsf{t}\}$ is our required relation. It is a bisimulation by Lemma 3.9 (i), and it satisfies $R(\mathsf{r}, \mathsf{new})$ because $P(\mathsf{r})$ and because $\mathcal{A}$ is totally specified: both r and new are mapped to the same element of the terminal $\mathcal{A}$-model, so that $\mathsf{r} \underline{\leftrightarrow} \mathsf{new}$.

In the reverse direction, assume we have an arbitrary model $M_{\mathcal{C}}$ of $\mathcal{C}$ with an appropriate reachable state r. Consider the terminal mode $M_{\mathcal{A}}$ of $\mathcal{A}$. By assumption, there is a bisimulation R on $M_{\mathcal{C}} \times M_{\mathcal{A}}$ with $R(\mathsf{r}, \mathsf{new})$. Now we can define a predicate P on $M_{\mathcal{C}}$ as $P(\mathsf{s}) \Leftrightarrow \exists \mathsf{t} \in \overline{\{\mathsf{new}\}}\ R(\mathsf{s}, \mathsf{t})$. It is an invariant by Lemma 3.9 (iii), and clearly satisfies $P(\mathsf{r})$. Further, all the assertions from $\mathcal{A}$ hold on P by the following argument. If $P(\mathsf{s})$, say with $R(\mathsf{s}, \mathsf{t})$ for $\mathsf{t} \in \overline{\{\mathsf{new}\}}$, then $\mathsf{s} \underline{\leftrightarrow} \mathsf{t}$ because R is a bisimulation. Since the assertions hold for t, they also hold for s. □

We conclude with an illustration of these notions and techniques in an example, involving a refinement of the Store specification (in Figure 3) by the FreshStack specification (in Figure 2). This refinement will be proved via an invariant. Examples of bisimulation refinement proofs occur in [15].

A store object, as characterised by the class specification Store, can store elements from some data set A. The occurs? method (or attribute) with interface $X \times A \longrightarrow \{0,1\}$ tells us of a particular element $a \in A$ if it is stored in a state (or object) s, namely if $\mathsf{s.occurs?}(a) = 1$. The procedure put: $X \times A \longrightarrow X$ allows us to put elements from A into a store, and the procedure delete_one: $X \longrightarrow X$ will delete an unspecified element from the store, provided the store is not empty. The first assertion of the specification tells us that if an element is stored, then it will be deleted after a finite number of invocations of the delete_one method. Notice that, as a result, only denumerably many elements from A can be stored in a single state.

There is an obvious way to realise the behaviour required for stores via stacks. Putting an element into a store-as-stack means pushing it onto the stack, where some care is needed to ensure that only elements which are not already on the stack are actually pushed; others are discarded. The fresh_push procedure in the FreshStack specification does precisely this. Deleting an element from a store-as-stack is simply popping an element off the stack. Notice that we hereby make a specific choice which element is deleted, namely the one which was last put on the stack. This illustrates the point that refinement reduces implementation freedom. But the store specification allows us to make such decisions. The invariant that has to be maintained for such stores-as-stacks is that there are no multiply occuring elements on the stack.

In the previous paragraph we have informally described a translation from the signature of Store to the signature of FreshStack. According to Definition 5.1, we formally have to define a natural transformation from the functor T_{FS} describing the signature of the FreshStack methods to the functor T_{St} capturing the signature of the Store methods. These (polynomial) functors are given by

$$T_{\mathrm{FS}}(X) = \{0,1\}^A \times X^A \times X^A \times X \times (1 + A) \quad \text{and} \quad T_{\mathrm{St}}(X) = \{0,1\}^A \times X^A \times X$$

where the first X^A component in $T_{\mathrm{FS}}(X)$ is the output type of fresh_push, and the second component X^A comes from push. The required natural transformation $\tau: T_{\mathrm{FS}} \Rightarrow T_{\mathrm{St}}$ is $\tau(f, g, h, x, y) = (f, g, x)$. It formally captures the translation of methods from Store to FreshStack, so that every T_{FS}-coalgebra gets translated into a T_{St}-coalgebra (via τ) in which delete_one is pop, put is fresh_push and occurs? is occurs?. Usually it is clear enough to describe such a translation at an informal level.

5.4. Proposition. *The Store specification in Figure 3 is refined by the FreshStack specification in Figure 2 via the invariant P (on each model of FreshStack) given by*

$$P(\mathsf{s}) \stackrel{\mathrm{def}}{\Leftrightarrow} \forall n \in \mathbb{N}\ \mathsf{s.pop}^{(n)}.\mathsf{top} \neq * \Rightarrow \forall m > 0\ \mathsf{s.pop}^{(n)}.\mathsf{top} \neq \mathsf{s.pop}^{(n+m)}.\mathsf{top}$$

and via the initial stack new *as representation of the initial store.*

Proof. Essentially this is straightforward reasoning. First, one has to show that $P(\mathsf{new})$ holds, and that P is an invariant: $P(\mathsf{s})$ implies both $P(\mathsf{s.pop})$ and $P(\mathsf{s.fresh\_push}(a))$ (for all $a \in A$). Then that the Store assertions follow from P. We shall do the first one. Assume therefore that $P(\mathsf{s})$ and that $\mathsf{s.occurs?}(a) = 1$. We have to show that for some $n \in \mathbb{N}$, $\mathsf{s.pop}^{(n)}.\mathsf{occurs?}(a) = 0$. The assumption $\mathsf{s.occurs?}(a) = 1$ means that we can pick an n with $\mathsf{s.pop}^{(n)}.\mathsf{top} = a$. We claim that $n + 1$ does what we want. If not, *i.e.* if $\mathsf{s.pop}^{(n+1)}.\mathsf{occurs?}(a) = 1$, say via m with $a = \mathsf{s.pop}^{(n+1)}.\mathsf{pop}^{(m)}.\mathsf{top} = \mathsf{s.pop}^{(n+1+m)}.\mathsf{top}$, then we have a contradiction with $P(\mathsf{s})$. □

6 Concluding remarks

We have developed a general theory of refinement in a coalgebraic setting, with associated proof principles based on invariants and bisimulations. This theory aims at proving the correctness of refinements between classes in object-oriented languages, using modern proof tools. We expect that this theory scales up smoothly to the hybrid setting of [12], since the underlying concepts are of the same (coalgebraic) nature.

Current research (in collaboration with Hensel, Huisman and Tews) focusses on the development of a (front-end) tool for reasoning about coalgebraic class specifications. The idea is that the tool should automatically translate such specifications into appropriate PVS theories, giving us a setting for PVS-assisted reasoning about the specifications. Proving refinements via invariants (as described here) forms an essential ingredient.

Acknowledgements

Thanks are due to Andrea Corradini, Joseph Goguen, Ulrich Hensel, Marieke Huisman, Jan Rutten and Frits Vaandrager for helpful comments and discussions.

References

1. P. Aczel and N. Mendler. A final coalgebra theorem. In D.H. Pitt, A. Poigné, and D.E. Rydeheard, editors, *Category Theory and Computer Science*, number 389 in Lect. Notes Comp. Sci., pages 357–365. Springer, Berlin, 1989.
2. M.A. Arbib and E.G. Manes. Parametrized data types do not need highly constrained parameters. *Inf. & Contr.*, 52:139–158, 1982.
3. E.A. Emerson. Temporal and modal logic. In J. van Leeuwen, editor, *Handbook of Theoretical Computer Science*, volume B, pages 997–998. Elsevier/MIT Press, 1990.
4. J.A. Goguen. An algebraic approach to refinement. In D. Bjørner, C.A.R. Hoare, and H. Langmaack, editors, *VDM '90. VDM and Z—Formal Methods in Software Development*, number 428 in Lect. Notes Comp. Sci., pages 12–28. Springer, Berlin, 1990.
5. J.A. Goguen and G. Malcolm. Proof of correctness of object representations. In A.W. Roscoe, editor, *A Classical Mind. Essays in honour of C.A.R. Hoare*, pages 119–142. Prentice Hall, 1994.
6. J.A. Goguen and G. Malcolm. An extended abstract of a hidden agenda. In J. Meystel, A. Meystel, and R. Quintero, editors, *Proceedings of the Conference on Intelligent Systems: A Semiotic Perspective*, pages 159–167. Nat. Inst. Stand. & Techn., 1996.
7. U. Hensel and B. Jacobs. Proof principles for datatypes with iterated recursion. In *Category Theory and Computer Science*, Lect. Notes Comp. Sci., Springer, Berlin, 1997.
8. C. Hermida and B. Jacobs. An algebraic view of structural induction. In L. Pacholski and J. Tiuryn, editors, *Computer Science Logic 1994*, number 933 in Lect. Notes Comp. Sci., pages 412–426. Springer, Berlin, 1995.
9. C. Hermida and B. Jacobs. Structural induction and coinduction in a fibrational setting. Full version of [8], 1996.
10. C.A.R. Hoare. Proof of correctness of data representations. *Acta Informatica*, 1:271–281, 1972.

11. B. Jacobs. Mongruences and cofree coalgebras. In V.S. Alagar and M. Nivat, editors, *Algebraic Methods and Software Technology*, number 936 in Lect. Notes Comp. Sci., pages 245–260. Springer, Berlin, 1995.
12. B. Jacobs. Coalgebraic specifications and models of deterministic hybrid systems. In M. Wirsing and M. Nivat, editors, *Algebraic Methods and Software Technology*, number 1101 in Lect. Notes Comp. Sci., pages 520–535. Springer, Berlin, 1996.
13. B. Jacobs. Inheritance and cofree constructions. In P. Cointe, editor, *European Conference on Object-Oriented Programming*, number 1098 in Lect. Notes Comp. Sci., pages 210–231. Springer, Berlin, 1996.
14. B. Jacobs. Objects and classes, co-algebraically. In B. Freitag, C.B. Jones, C. Lengauer, and H.-J. Schek, editors, *Object-Orientation with Parallelism and Persistence*, pages 83–103. Kluwer Acad. Publ., 1996.
15. B. Jacobs. Behaviour-refinement of coalgebraic specifications with coinductive correctness proofs. In M. Bidoit and M. Dauchet, editors, *TAPSOFT'97: Theory and Practice of Software Development*, number 1214 in Lect. Notes Comp. Sci., pages 787–802. Springer, Berlin, 1997.
16. B. Jacobs and J. Rutten. A tutorial on (co)algebras and (co)induction. *EATCS Bulletin*, 62:222–259, 1997.
17. S. Kamin. Final data types and their specification. *ACM Trans. on Progr. Lang. and Systems*, 5(1):97–123, 1983.
18. L. Lamport. Verification and specification of concurrent programs. In J.W. de Bakker, W.P. de Roever, and G. Rozenberg, editors, *A Decade of Concurrency*, number 803 in Lect. Notes Comp. Sci., pages 347–374. Springer, Berlin, 1994.
19. D.J. Lehmann and M.B. Smyth. Algebraic specification of data types: A synthetic approach. *Math. Systems Theory*, 14:97–139, 1981.
20. B. Liskov and J. Guttag. *Abstraction and Specification in Program Development.* The MIT Press, Cambridge, MA, 1986.
21. N. Lynch and F. Vaandrager. Forward and backward simulations. I. Untimed systems. *Inf. & Comp.*, 121(2):214–233, 1995.
22. E.G. Manes and M.A. Arbib. *Algebraic Appoaches to Program Semantics.* Texts and Monogr. in Comp. Sci.,. Springer, Berlin, 1986.
23. R. Milner. An algebraic definition of simulation between programs. In *Sec. Int. Joint Conf. on Artificial Intelligence*, pages 481–489. British Comp. Soc. Press, London, 1971.
24. R. Milner. *A Calculus of Communicating Systems.* Lect. Notes Comp. Sci. Springer, Berlin, 1989.
25. S. Owre, S. Rajan, J.M. Rushby, N. Shankar, and M. Srivas. PVS: Combining specification, proof checking, and model checking. In R. Alur and T.A. Henzinger, editors, *Computer Aided Verification*, number 1102 in Lect. Notes Comp. Sci., pages 411–414. Springer, Berlin, 1996.
26. H. Reichel. An approach to object semantics based on terminal co-algebras. *Math. Struct. in Comp. Sci.*, 5:129–152, 1995.
27. J. Rutten and D. Turi. On the foundations of final semantics: non-standard sets, metric spaces and partial orders. In J.W. de Bakker, W.P. de Roever, and G. Rozenberg, editors, *Semantics: Foundations and Applications*, number 666 in Lect. Notes Comp. Sci., pages 477–530. Springer, Berlin, 1993.
28. J.J.M.M. Rutten. Universal coalgebra: a theory of systems. CWI Report CS-R9652, 1996.
29. M.B. Smyth and G.D. Plotkin. The category theoretic solution of recursive domain equations. *SIAM Journ. Comput.*, 11:761–783, 1982.
30. M. Wand. Final algebra semantics and data type extension. *Journ. Comp. Syst. Sci*, 19:27–44, 1979.

On Bisimulation, Fault-Monotonicity and Provable Fault-Tolerance

Tomasz Janowski

The United Nations University
International Institute for Software Technology
P.O. Box 3058, Macau
tj@iist.unu.edu

Abstract. We introduce a necessary test for the claims about provable fault-tolerance: having proved to tolerate several faults, we must tolerate (provably) any combination of them. One notable failure to pass this test is bisimulation. The paper presents a class of bisimulations which are fault-monotonic and within CCS support compositional design of component specifications by stepwise refinement, each step increasing or at least preserving the current level of fault-tolerance.

1 Introduction

With growing complexity of computer systems and despite the progress in the technology of the basic components (software or hardware), the possibility that such systems are affected by faults is ever present. This pessimistic (but realistic) view requires that we are able to build systems tolerant of the failures of their components; to build reliable systems from unreliable components. The main concern of this paper are methods of justifying claims about this property.

A common approach is to reduce provable fault-tolerance to provable correctness. When we claim fault-tolerance for a given implementation *Impl* relative to a fault assumption *Faults* and a specification *Spec*, we only proceed to prove correctness of an implementation $\mathcal{T}(Impl, Faults)$, representing syntactically how *Impl* behaves in the presence of *Faults* [12, 13, 7]; this reduction is most common without introducing the transformation $\mathcal{T}$ explicitly [5, 4, 10, 18, 14, 15, 17, 11, 3, 19]. Although attractive for many reasons, e.g. reuse of a variety of tools and techniques already available for proving correctness, the method also raises some questions about its feasibility and applicability.

Feasibility: correctness under all anticipated faults is necessary for provable fault-tolerance but is it sufficient? After all, faults are unpredictable and even if we assume their presence, as we did within $\mathcal{T}(Impl, Faults)$, they may never actually occur. Our claim should therefore be invariant under some, perhaps even all of such faults being removed from the assumptions. Consider a preorder $<$ on the fault assumptions which represents the relative severity of faults: $Fault_1 < Fault_2$ representing that $Fault_1$ is less severe than $Fault_2$; say $Fault_2$ represents that a communication medium may both omit and permute messages and $Fault_1$ represents only omission. Then we would expect that verifying *Impl* as tolerant of $Fault_2$ would immediately imply that it is tolerant of $Fault_1$ alone. We may also invent $NoFault$ representing the strongest assumption (no faults) and expect that *Impl*, if tolerant of any $Fault$, would also be tolerant of $NoFault$ ($NoFault < Fault$ for any $Fault$); tolerance with respect to $NoFault$ could reasonably coincide with 'plain' correctness. Claims about fault-tolerance based on the implicit verification must be justified with respect to fault-monotonicity [8]!

Applicability. Formal reasoning can be (should be) considered as a means to analyse as well as support design of 'correct' systems. How to support design of systems tolerant of faults? There are many issues in this case that do not appear in the broader context: design of a system which is correct with respect to its specification, without taking faults into account. A theory for provable fault-tolerance which is based on reducing fault-tolerance to correctness in the presence of all faults, may not bring effective help into such design issues. Among the issues is the growing complexity of a system for an increasing number of tolerated faults, along the chain $NoFault < Fault_1 < \ldots < Fault_n$. Supporting this dimension we may like to have design techniques as follows:

1. Preservation rules that allow to modify design of a system while preserving (provably) the set of tolerated faults. Given *Impl* which is tolerant of $Fault$ relative to *Spec*, it should be possible to modify *Impl* into *Impl'*, following the rules, and still be able to claim this property. This may help to simplify design, for given level of fault-tolerance, as well as tolerate more faults.
2. Incremental refinement towards an increasing number of tolerated faults. We start with a system which is only correct with respect to its specification, then introduce faults incrementally, say given $Fault_1 < Fault_2$ and $Impl_1$, tolerant of $Fault_1$ with respect to *Spec*, we refine $Impl_1$ into $Impl_2$, following the preservation rules, which also becomes tolerant of $Fault_2$.
3. Separate development: deducing fault-tolerance of an overall system from fault-tolerance of its components. Suppose $|$ is an operator of the language and $Fault_1 \vee Fault_2$ is the least upper bound of $Fault_i$ $(i = 1, 2)$ with respect to $<$. If $Impl_i$ is tolerant of $Fault \vee Fault_i$ with respect to $Spec_i$, if neither $Impl_1$ is affected by $Fault_2$ nor $Impl_2$ by $Fault_1$, then $Impl_1 | Impl_2$ is tolerant of $Fault \vee \bigvee_{i=1,2} Fault_i$ with respect to $Spec_1 | Spec_2$.

We shall explore both issues (fault-monotonicity and development support) as they arise for bisimulations [16, 14]. Fault-tolerance for bisimulations means that no observer can distinguish between two processes despite an implementation process being affected by faults. First the bad news: we could apply bisimulations to verify a fault-affected process but this will not imply that the original process is provably fault-tolerant; this is shown in Section 2. Then the good news: fault-monotonicity is a property of a class of bisimulations, parameterised with fault assumptions and able to verify fault-tolerance explicitly; they are introduced in Section 3. Sections 4, 5 and 6 relate to specification, verification and development respectively, showing how such bisimulations can support the issues (1-3) in the design of fault-tolerant systems: separate design of components by stepwise refinement, each step increasing or at least preserving the current level of fault-tolerance. Section 7 contains some conclusions.

2 Motivating Example

To facilitate comparisons consider (again) the alternating bit protocol. The task is to provide reliable communication over a medium which may omit messages and using suggestive notation [14] can be specified as the process P.

$$P = in.\overline{out}.P$$

The protocol, depicted in Figure 1, consists of the sender S and the receiver R and applies bit values i and $\neg i$ to control the flow of messages and acknowledgements along the internal channels $L =_{def} \{a, b, c, d\}$. We define S as $S(0)$ and R as $R(1)$, where $S(i)$ and $R(i)$ are as described below.

$$S(i) = in.S'(i) \qquad S'(i) = \overline{a}(i).S'(i) + d(i).S(\neg i) + d(\neg i).S'(i)$$
$$R(i) = \overline{c}(i).R(i) + b(i).R(i) + b(\neg i).R'(\neg i) \qquad R'(i) = \overline{out}.R(i)$$

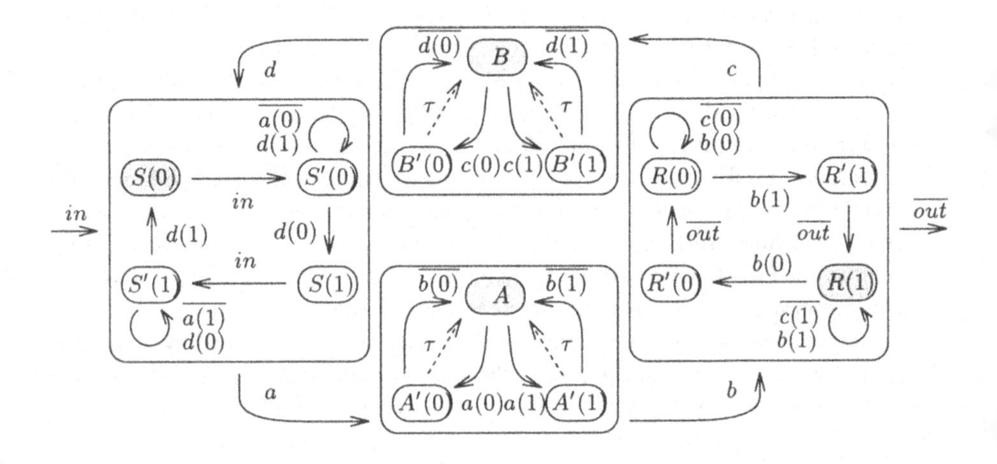

Fig. 1. Alternating-bit protocol.

Let us follow the 'usual' way of proving this protocol. Suppose A represents a fault-free transmission of messages along the channels $\overline{a}$ and b, and A_o is like A but can additionally decide to omit a message (τ is an internal action).

$$A \;= a(i).A'(i) \qquad A'(i) \;= \overline{b}(i).A$$
$$A_o = a(i).A'_o(i) \qquad A'_o(i) = \overline{b}(i).A_o + \tau.A_o$$

B and B_o are similar, except they use action c instead of a and d instead of b. Then we can compose S, R, A_o and B_o in parallel and, after restricting the actions L, verify the resulting process by proving bisimilarity [16, 14]:

$$P \approx (S|A_o|B_o|R)\backslash L$$

Does this allow claims that the protocol tolerates omission? Reconsider transitions of the sender and receiver by which they decide to ignore repeated messages:

$$S'(i) \xrightarrow{d(\neg i)} S'(i) \text{ and } R(i) \xrightarrow{b(i)} R(i)$$

One could argue that since both media loose messages such transitions are not needed – what we want to ignore will be lost anyway. The argument is clearly wrong as it stipulates that anticipated faults must occur when in fact we can only assume that faults (being outside of our control) may or may not occur. To carry out this argument anyway we would receive the following new versions $S_f =_{def} S_f(0)$ and $R_f =_{def} R_f(1)$ of S and R:

$$\begin{array}{ll} S_f(i) = in.S'_f(i) & S'_f(i) = \overline{a}(i).S'_f(i) + d(i).S_f(\neg i) \\ R_f(i) = \overline{c}(i).R_f(i) + b(\neg i).R'_f(\neg i) & R'_f(i) = \overline{out}.R_f(i) \end{array}$$

The result of this revision can still be shown correct, i.e. bisimilar with P in the presence of all anticipated faults but is no longer bisimilar with P in the absence of faults (contradicting faults being unpredictable) [2]:

$$\begin{array}{l} P \approx (S_f|A_o|B_o|R_f)\backslash L \\ P \not\approx (S_f|A|B|R_f)\backslash L \end{array}$$

Is it possible to carry out both proofs, in the absence of any faults and in the presence of all anticipated faults, and still not be able to claim fault-monotonicity? Consider A_c which can create messages and A_{oc} which can both loose and create messages; we represent created messages by $\surd$:

$$\begin{array}{ll} A_c = a(i).A'_c(i) + \tau.A'_c(\surd) & A'_c(i) = \overline{b}(i).A_c \\ A_{oc} = a(i).A'_{oc}(i) + \tau.A'_{oc}(\surd) & A'_{oc}(i) = \overline{b}(i).A_{oc} + \tau.A_{oc} \end{array}$$

B_c and B_{oc} are similar but use action c instead of a and d instead of b, as before. Take the original alternating-bit protocol S and R. The protocol can be shown correct when messages are lost and created, it can also be shown correct when media are completely free of any communication faults:

$$\begin{array}{l} P \approx (S|A|B|R)\backslash L \\ P \approx (S|A_{oc}|B_{oc}|R)\backslash L \end{array}$$

Yet the protocol will fail the proof if we only assume creation of messages. Unprepared to receive (only to ignore) messages $\surd$ the protocol will deadlock.

$$P \not\approx (S|A_c|B_c|R)\backslash L$$

We could only prove $P \approx (S|A_{oc}|B_{oc}|R)\backslash L$ because of one fault (omission) which compensates for the effects of another fault (creation). Of course we could never claim that this protocol is able to tolerate both!

3 Bisimulation and Fault-Tolerance

Let $\mathcal{P}$ be a set of processes and $\mathcal{A}$ a set of actions. We use P to range over $\mathcal{P}$, α over $\mathcal{A}$ and a over $\mathcal{A} - \{\tau\}$ where τ is a designated internal action. We shall write $P \stackrel{\alpha}{\longrightarrow} P'$ if a process P performs action α and thereafter behaves like P', and take $\longrightarrow \subseteq \mathcal{P} \times \mathcal{A} \times \mathcal{P}$ to denote the fault-free semantics of $\mathcal{P}$. We also anticipate that there are faults affecting $\mathcal{P}$ by introducing some additional τ-labelled transitions $\stackrel{\tau}{\cdots\rightarrow} \subseteq \mathcal{P} \times \mathcal{P}$ into its semantics. Then $\longmapsto$ is used to denote the union of both sets and represents the fault-affected semantics.

We shall base our study on the notion of weak bisimulation, a kind of invariant between the states of two processes for them to be deemed behaviourally equivalent [16, 14]; the relevant behaviour expressed in terms of transitions $\longrightarrow$.

Definition 1. A bisimulation is a binary relation $B \subseteq \mathcal{P} \times \mathcal{P}$, such that for all $\alpha \in \mathcal{A}$, $(P,Q) \in B$ iff:

$$\begin{array}{l} \text{whenever } P \stackrel{\alpha}{\longrightarrow} P' \text{ then } \exists_{Q',s}\, Q \stackrel{s}{\longrightarrow} Q' \wedge \widehat{s} = \widehat{\alpha} \wedge (P',Q') \in B \\ \text{whenever } Q \stackrel{\alpha}{\longrightarrow} Q' \text{ then } \exists_{P',s}\, P \stackrel{s}{\longrightarrow} P' \wedge \widehat{s} = \widehat{\alpha} \wedge (P',Q') \in B \end{array}$$

where s is a sequence of actions, $Q \stackrel{s}{\longrightarrow} Q'$ a corresponding sequence of transitions (labelled by the elements of s) and $\widehat{s}$ a sequence s with all τ's removed. We let $P \approx Q$ iff there exists a bisimulation B such that $(P,Q) \in B$.

Suppose P is a specification process and Q a fault-affected implementation process. There are two principles that we apply to prove that Q is fault-tolerant. The first is the observational principle: no observer can distinguish between P and Q despite transitions $\stackrel{\tau}{\cdots\rightarrow}$ affecting Q. The second is the principle of fault-monotonicity: having proved to tolerate transitions $\stackrel{\tau}{\cdots\rightarrow}$, we must be certain to tolerate any subset of them. In order to satisfy the first principle we could follow the original definition of bisimulation but let $\longmapsto$ as the semantics of the implementation process: if $(P,Q) \in B$ then

$$\begin{array}{l} P \stackrel{\alpha}{\longrightarrow} P' \Rightarrow \exists_{Q',s}\, Q \stackrel{s}{\longmapsto} Q' \wedge\ \widehat{s} = \widehat{\alpha} \wedge (P',Q') \in B \\ Q \stackrel{\alpha}{\longmapsto} Q' \Rightarrow \exists_{P',s}\, P \stackrel{s}{\longrightarrow} P' \wedge\ \widehat{s} = \widehat{\alpha} \wedge (P',Q') \in B \end{array}$$

This definition will not satisfy the second principle: it allows transitions $\stackrel{\tau}{\cdots\rightarrow}$ of Q to match transitions of P (specification process), making the concept rely on such transitions to occur. The second try:

Definition 2. A fault-tolerant bisimulation is a binary relation $B \subseteq \mathcal{P} \times \mathcal{P}$, such that for all $\alpha \in \mathcal{A}$, $(P,Q) \in B$ iff:

$$\begin{array}{l} \text{whenever } P \stackrel{\alpha}{\longrightarrow} P' \text{ then } \exists_{Q',s}\, Q \stackrel{s}{\longrightarrow} Q' \wedge \widehat{s} = \widehat{\alpha} \wedge (P',Q') \in B \\ \text{whenever } Q \stackrel{\alpha}{\longmapsto} Q' \text{ then } \exists_{P',s}\, P \stackrel{s}{\longrightarrow} P' \wedge \widehat{s} = \widehat{\alpha} \wedge (P',Q') \in B \end{array}$$

We let $P \sqsubseteq Q$ iff $(P,Q) \in B$ for some fault-tolerant bisimulation B.

The relation $P \sqsubseteq Q$ is fault-monotonic in the following sense: for any subset of the faulty transitions $\overset{\tau}{\dashrightarrow}$, the corresponding relation $\sqsubseteq$ would still hold between P and Q; the property will receive a more elegant formulation later in the paper. One consequence of this property is that $P \sqsubseteq Q$ implies $P \approx Q$.

But many properties that we would normally expect from an algebraic theory will not be possible here, paying the price for the power of fault-monotonicity. In particular, $\sqsubseteq$ is not in general reflexive or symmetric. This is related to the dual semantics appearing in the reasoning about fault-tolerance. Depending on the role played by a process Q, as an implementation in $P \sqsubseteq Q$ or a specification in $Q \sqsubseteq R$, it will have two different semantics and neither $Q \sqsubseteq Q$ can hold in general, nor $P \sqsubseteq Q$ can in general imply $Q \sqsubseteq P$. On the positive side:

- If the specification process P is not affected by faults, technically $P \overset{\tau}{\not\dashrightarrow}$, then verifying $P \sqsubseteq Q$ will indeed imply $Q \sqsubseteq P$. This is because $P \sqsubseteq Q$ implies $P \approx Q$ and $Q \approx P$ implies $Q \sqsubseteq P$ provided P is not affected by faults. Thus $\sqsubseteq$ is symmetric in the restricted sense:

$$P \sqsubseteq Q \text{ then } Q \sqsubseteq P \text{ provided } P \overset{\tau}{\not\dashrightarrow}$$

- The relation is transitive and left-transitive with $\approx$: $P \approx Q \sqsubseteq R$ implies $P \sqsubseteq R$. Thus bisimilarity allows to modify the specification process while preserving fault-tolerance. In contrast, modifying the implementation process may in general violate fault-tolerance; not unexpected given that $\approx$ is not taking transitions $\overset{\tau}{\dashrightarrow}$ into account.

$$\begin{array}{l} P \approx Q \sqsubseteq R \text{ then } P \sqsubseteq R \\ P \sqsubseteq Q \approx R \text{ then not always } P \sqsubseteq R \end{array}$$

- If $P \sqsubseteq Q$ then we have $P \approx Q$ and therefore $Q \approx P \sqsubseteq Q$ and $Q \sqsubseteq Q$. Thus $\sqsubseteq$ is reflexive in the restricted sense: for all fault-tolerant processes. Moreover, $P \approx Q \sqsubseteq Q$ implies $P \sqsubseteq Q$ and so an equivalence holds:

$$P \sqsubseteq Q \text{ iff } P \approx Q \sqsubseteq Q$$

Knowing more about the algebraic properties of this relation, we can also produce its logical characterisation, following $\approx$ and Hennessy-Milner logic [6]. This is elaborated in [8], including how to make the logic itself fault-monotonic.

4 Specification: CCS and Faults

The goal of this section is to introduce a simple notation that could help us formulate requirements, assumptions and process descriptions for claiming and verifying fault-tolerance, all embedded in the bisimulation semantics introduced in Section 3. We first define a process language which is basically CCS [14] but is given different semantics $\underset{\Psi}{\longmapsto}$, depending on the assumption Ψ about faults; we introduce a special language to specify and combine such assumptions.

First, let actions $\mathcal{A}$ be partitioned between a representing "input actions" and their complements $\overline{a}$ representing "output actions"; an action has exactly one complement, $\overline{\overline{a}} = a$, and the complement of τ is itself, $\overline{\tau} = \tau$. Moreover, let L be a set of actions without τ, $f : \mathcal{A} \to \mathcal{A}$ be a complement-preserving function on actions ($f(\tau) = \tau$ and $f(\overline{a}) = \overline{f(a)}$) and X be a process constant. The process language comprises three syntactic categories: process expressions E; declarations Δ; and processes $P \in \mathcal{P}$. They are as follows:

$$\begin{aligned} E &::= 0 \mid a.X \mid \alpha.E \mid E + E \\ \Delta &::= [\,] \mid \Delta[X \mathrel{\hat{=}} E] \mid \alpha \odot \Delta \mid \Delta \oplus \Delta \\ P &::= 0 \mid \mu X.\Delta \mid \alpha.P \mid P + P \mid P|P \mid P\backslash L \mid P[f] \end{aligned}$$

We have the familiar operators: prefix $\alpha.P$, summation $P+Q$, concurrency $P|Q$, restriction $P\backslash L$, renaming $P[f]$ and $\mu X.\Delta$: a solution X of the equations given by Δ [14]. We let $\mathcal{X}(P)$ contain all constants in P and assume that in $\mu X.\Delta$, both X and all constants in Δ are also declared in Δ.

The semantics of Δ is the assignment $[\![\Delta]\!]$ of process expressions to process constants. It is defined in Table 1, applying $dom(\Delta)$ as the constants declared in Δ. Constructions include: $[]$, the empty declaration; $\Delta[Y \mathrel{\hat{=}} E]$, introducing $Y \mathrel{\hat{=}} E$ into Δ; $\alpha \odot \Delta$, α-prefix on the right sides of all declarations in Δ; $\Delta \oplus \nabla$, summation on the right sides of the corresponding declarations in Δ and ∇. We abbreviate $[][X \mathrel{\hat{=}} E]$ as $[X \mathrel{\hat{=}} E]$ and $[X \mathrel{\hat{=}} E \mid p]$ as all declarations $X \mathrel{\hat{=}} E$ such that the predicate p holds.

Table 1. Semantics of declarations.

$$dom([\,]) =_{def} \emptyset$$

$$[\![\alpha \odot \Delta]\!](X) =_{def} \alpha.[\![\Delta]\!](X) \qquad \text{if } X \in dom(\Delta)$$

$$[\![\Delta[Y \mathrel{\hat{=}} E]]\!](X) =_{def} \begin{cases} E & \text{if } X = Y \\ [\![\Delta]\!](X) & \text{if } X \neq Y,\ X \in dom(\Delta) \end{cases}$$

$$[\![\Delta \oplus \nabla]\!](X) =_{def} \begin{cases} [\![\Delta]\!](X) & \text{if } X \in dom(\Delta) - dom(\nabla) \\ [\![\Delta]\!](X) + [\![\nabla]\!](X) & \text{if } X \in dom(\Delta) \cap dom(\nabla) \\ [\![\nabla]\!](X) & \text{if } X \in dom(\nabla) - dom(\Delta) \end{cases}$$

$\mathcal{P}$ is given the operational semantics in Table 2, by induction on the structure of a process, as usual; $[\![\Delta]\!](X)\{\widetilde{\mu Y.\Delta}/\widetilde{Y}\}$ denotes simultaneous substitution of all constants Y in $[\![\Delta]\!](X)$ by their corresponding fixed points $\mu Y.\Delta$.

The set $\overset{\tau}{\dashrightarrow} \subseteq \mathcal{P} \times \mathcal{P}$ provides a liberal approach to describing the effects of faults, with no relation to the structure of a fault-affected process Q; it is possible, for instance, that $\overset{\tau}{\dashrightarrow}$ affects Q but none of its components, or affects all components but not Q itself. For a tractable theory such abnormalities must be removed. To specify faults we shall use declarations Ψ:

$$\Psi \ ::= \ \tau \odot \Delta \mid \Psi \oplus \Psi$$

Table 2. Semantics of processes.

$$\frac{}{\alpha.P \xrightarrow{\alpha} P} \quad \frac{P \xrightarrow{\alpha} P'}{P+Q \xrightarrow{\alpha} P'} \quad \frac{Q \xrightarrow{\alpha} Q'}{P+Q \xrightarrow{\alpha} Q'} \quad \frac{P \xrightarrow{\alpha} P'}{P|Q \xrightarrow{\alpha} P'|Q} \quad \frac{Q \xrightarrow{\alpha} Q'}{P|Q \xrightarrow{\alpha} P|Q'} \quad \frac{P \xrightarrow{a} P' \;\; Q \xrightarrow{\overline{a}} Q'}{P|Q \xrightarrow{\tau} P'|Q'}$$

$$\frac{P \xrightarrow{\alpha} P'}{P[f] \xrightarrow{f(\alpha)} P'[f]} \quad \frac{P \xrightarrow{\alpha} P' \;\; \alpha, \overline{\alpha} \notin L}{P \backslash L \xrightarrow{\alpha} P' \backslash L} \quad \frac{[\![\Delta]\!](X)\{\widetilde{\mu Y.\Delta / Y}\} \xrightarrow{\alpha} P'}{\mu X.\Delta \xrightarrow{\alpha} P'}$$

Table 3. Ψ-affected semantics of processes.

$$\frac{}{\alpha.P \overset{\alpha}{\underset{\Psi}{\longmapsto}} P} \quad \frac{P \overset{\alpha}{\underset{\Psi}{\longmapsto}} P'}{P+Q \overset{\alpha}{\underset{\Psi}{\longmapsto}} P'} \quad \frac{Q \overset{\alpha}{\underset{\Psi}{\longmapsto}} Q'}{P+Q \overset{\alpha}{\underset{\Psi}{\longmapsto}} Q'} \quad \frac{P \overset{\alpha}{\underset{\Psi}{\longmapsto}} P'}{P|Q \overset{\alpha}{\underset{\Psi}{\longmapsto}} P'|Q} \quad \frac{Q \overset{\alpha}{\underset{\Psi}{\longmapsto}} Q'}{P|Q \overset{\alpha}{\underset{\Psi}{\longmapsto}} P|Q'} \quad \frac{P \overset{a}{\underset{\Psi}{\longmapsto}} P' \;\; Q \overset{\overline{a}}{\underset{\Psi}{\longmapsto}} Q'}{P|Q \overset{\tau}{\underset{\Psi}{\longmapsto}} P'|Q'}$$

$$\frac{P \overset{\alpha}{\underset{\Psi}{\longmapsto}} P'}{P[f] \overset{f(\alpha)}{\underset{\Psi}{\longmapsto}} P'[f]} \quad \frac{P \overset{\alpha}{\underset{\Psi}{\longmapsto}} P' \;\; \alpha, \overline{\alpha} \notin L}{P \backslash L \overset{\alpha}{\underset{\Psi}{\longmapsto}} P' \backslash L} \quad \frac{[\![\Delta]\!](X)\{\widetilde{\mu Y.\Delta / Y}\} \overset{\alpha}{\underset{\Psi}{\longmapsto}} P'}{\mu X.\Delta \overset{\alpha}{\underset{\Psi}{\longmapsto}} P'} \quad \frac{[\![\Psi]\!](X)\{\widetilde{\mu Y.\Delta / Y}\} \overset{\alpha}{\underset{\Psi}{\longmapsto}} P'}{\mu X.\Delta \overset{\alpha}{\underset{\Psi}{\longmapsto}} P'}$$

A Ψ-affected semantics of $\mathcal{P}$ is called $\underset{\Psi}{\longmapsto}$ and is defined in Table 3, introducing a rule where transitions of $\mu X.\Delta$ follow the transitions of $[\![\Psi]\!](X)$, in addition to $[\![\Delta]\!](X)$; since $[\![\Psi]\!](X)$ may introduce constants which are not declared in Δ, we assume that $\underset{\Psi}{\longmapsto}$ is defined on the suitable subclass $\mathcal{P}_\Psi$ of $\mathcal{P}$ [8]. Clearly, $\underset{\Psi}{\longmapsto}$ forms the superset of $\longrightarrow$ and we define:

Definition 3.
$Q \overset{\tau}{\underset{\Psi}{\dashrightarrow}} Q'$ iff $Q \overset{\tau}{\underset{\Psi}{\longmapsto}} Q'$ and $Q \overset{\tau}{\not\rightarrow} Q'$.

With well-known extensions of the language to introduce value-passing [14], we can now describe the protocol as follows:

$$\begin{array}{lll}
P =_{def} \mu X. & [X & \mathrel{\widehat{=}} in.X'][X' \mathrel{\widehat{=}} \overline{out}.X] \\
S =_{def} \mu X(0). & [X(i) & \mathrel{\widehat{=}} in.X'(i)] \\
 & [X'(i) & \mathrel{\widehat{=}} \overline{a}(i).X'(i) + d(i).X(\neg i) + d(\neg i).X'(i)] \\
R =_{def} \mu X(1). & [X'(i) & \mathrel{\widehat{=}} \overline{out}.X(i)] \\
 & [X(i) & \mathrel{\widehat{=}} \overline{c}(i).X(i) + b(i).X(i) + b(\neg i).X'(\neg i)] \\
A =_{def} \mu Y. & [Y & \mathrel{\widehat{=}} a(i).Y'(i)][Y'(i) \mathrel{\widehat{=}} \overline{b}(i).Y] \quad \Psi_o =_{def} \tau \odot [Y'(i) \mathrel{\widehat{=}} Y] \\
B =_{def} \mu Z. & [Z & \mathrel{\widehat{=}} c(i).Z'(i)][Z'(i) \mathrel{\widehat{=}} \overline{d}(i).Z] \quad \Phi_o =_{def} \tau \odot [Z'(i) \mathrel{\widehat{=}} Z]
\end{array}$$

One last obstacle to verification is the presence of two faults representing omission of messages and acknowledgements. We could overcome this introducing semantics $\underset{\Psi,\Phi}{\longmapsto}$ in the presence of Ψ and Φ (with additional rules for each of the faults), but the same effect can be represented by $\Psi \oplus \Phi$:

$$Q \overset{\alpha}{\underset{\Psi,\Phi}{\longmapsto}} Q' \text{ iff } Q \overset{\alpha}{\underset{\Psi \oplus \Phi}{\longmapsto}} Q'$$

5 Verification: Transformations and Multiple Faults

The task is to verify the process $(S|A|B|R)\setminus L$ as a $\Psi_o \oplus \Phi_o$-tolerant implementation of the process P. It can be fulfilled directly. We take an instance of fault-tolerant bisimilarity where transitions $\overset{T}{\dashrightarrow}$ are $\underset{\Psi}{\overset{T}{\dashrightarrow}}$, as specified by Ψ. The resulting relation $\sqsubseteq_\Psi$ is explicitly defined below:

Definition 4. A Ψ-tolerant bisimulation is a binary relation $B \subseteq \mathcal{P} \times \mathcal{P}_\Psi$, such that for all $\alpha \in \mathcal{A}$, $(P,Q) \in B$ iff:

$$\begin{array}{l} \text{whenever } P \xrightarrow{\alpha} P' \text{ then } \exists_{Q',s}\, Q \xrightarrow{s} Q' \wedge \widehat{s} = \widehat{\alpha} \wedge (P',Q') \in B \\ \text{whenever } Q \underset{\Psi}{\overset{\alpha}{\longmapsto}} Q' \text{ then } \exists_{P',s}\, P \xrightarrow{s} P' \wedge \widehat{s} = \widehat{\alpha} \wedge (P',Q') \in B \end{array}$$

We let $P \sqsubseteq_\Psi Q$ iff $(P,Q) \in B$ for some Ψ-tolerant bisimulation B.

Indeed, about the following relation, described schematically to avoid displaying all pairs of states, we can prove that it is a $\Psi_o \oplus \Phi_o$-tolerant bisimulation:

$$\begin{array}{rl} B =_{def} \{ & (P,\ (S\ |\cdot|\cdot|R)\setminus L), \\ & (P,\ (S\ |\cdot|\cdot|R')\setminus L), \\ & (P',(S'\,|\cdot|\cdot|R)\setminus L), \\ & (P',(S'\,|\cdot|\cdot|R')\setminus L)\} \end{array}$$

Therefore $P \sqsubseteq_{\Psi_o \oplus \Phi_o} (S|A|B|R)\setminus L$ what implies $P \approx (S|A|B|R)\setminus L$ and proofs all other combinations of the transitions introduced by $\Psi_o \oplus \Phi_o$. Only now, given the fault-monotonic power of the relation, the protocol is verified.

We now study how such proofs, directly dependent on the number of faults, can be made modular in this respect. To what extent we could help proving fault-tolerance for multiple faults by proving fault-tolerance for each fault in separate? First define a transformation $\mathcal{T}(\cdot,\Psi)$:

Definition 5.

$$\begin{array}{ll} \mathcal{T}(0,\Psi) & =_{def} 0 \\ \mathcal{T}(\alpha.Q,\Psi) & =_{def} \alpha.\mathcal{T}(Q,\Psi) \\ \mathcal{T}(Q\setminus L,\Psi) & =_{def} \mathcal{T}(Q,\Psi)\setminus L \\ \mathcal{T}(Q[f],\Psi) & =_{def} \mathcal{T}(Q,\Psi)[f] \\ \mathcal{T}(Q_1+Q_2,\Psi) & =_{def} \mathcal{T}(Q_1,\Psi)+\mathcal{T}(Q_2,\Psi) \\ \mathcal{T}(Q_1|Q_2,\Psi) & =_{def} \mathcal{T}(Q_1,\Psi)|\mathcal{T}(Q_2,\Psi) \\ \mathcal{T}(\mu X.\Delta,\Psi) & =_{def} \mu X.(\Delta \oplus \Psi) \end{array}$$

The resulting process $\mathcal{T}(Q,\Psi)$ represents syntactically how the process Q behaves in the presence of faults, specified by Ψ. In other words: Ψ-affected semantics of Q is "the same" as the semantics of $\mathcal{T}(Q,\Psi)$ in the absence of faults.

Proposition 6.
$Q \underset{\Psi}{\overset{\alpha}{\longmapsto}} Q'$ *iff* $\mathcal{T}(Q,\Psi) \xrightarrow{\alpha} \mathcal{T}(Q',\Psi)$.

But despite this, applying $\mathcal{T}(Q,\Psi)$ to verify $P \approx \mathcal{T}(Q,\Psi)$ gives a notion which is properly weaker than needed to ensure fault-monotonicity, even complemented by $P \approx Q$ (Section 2). Likewise, verifying $P \sqsubseteq_{\Psi} Q$ and $P \sqsubseteq_{\Phi} Q$ together is still insufficient for claiming $P \sqsubseteq_{\Psi \oplus \Phi} Q$. We shall compensate for both problems by extending $\mathcal{T}(\cdot,\Psi)$ to transform bisimulations themselves:

Definition 7.
$\mathfrak{T}(B,\Psi) =_{def} \{(P, \mathcal{T}(Q,\Psi)) \mid (P,Q) \in B\}$

This relational transformation allows us to formulate the necessary and sufficient condition for B to be a Ψ-tolerant bisimulation or a $\Psi \oplus \Phi$-tolerant bisimulation, expressed in terms of original bisimulations:

Proposition 8.
Consider a binary relation B:

- B is a Ψ-tolerant bisimulation iff B and $\mathfrak{T}(B,\Psi)$ are bisimulations.
- B is a $\Psi \oplus \Phi$-tolerant bisimulation iff it is simultaneously a Ψ-tolerant bisimulation and a Φ-tolerant bisimulation.

With help of $\Psi \oplus \Phi$ to represent the presence of multiple faults we can now formulate precisely what it means for relations $\sqsubseteq_{\Psi}$ to be fault-monotonic. Given that $P \sqsubseteq_{\Psi \oplus \Phi} Q$ iff $(P,Q) \in B$ for B which is a $\Psi \oplus \Phi$-tolerant bisimulation, therefore B must be a Ψ-tolerant bisimulation and a Φ-tolerant bisimulation, we have $P \sqsubseteq_{\Psi} Q$ and $P \sqsubseteq_{\Phi} Q$. A simple corollary:

Corollary 9.
If $P \sqsubseteq_{\Psi \oplus \Phi} Q$ then $P \sqsubseteq_{\Psi} Q$ and $P \sqsubseteq_{\Phi} Q$.

Thus for the protocol we need to check that B above is a bisimulation together with $\mathfrak{T}(B,\Psi_o)$ and $\mathfrak{T}(B,\Phi_o)$. And we can check B for each fault separately! We can also extend our claim, that the protocol is also tolerant of replication $\Psi_r \oplus \Phi_r$:

$$\Psi_r =_{def} \tau \odot [Y'(i) \mathrel{\widehat{=}} \overline{b}(i).Y'(i)] \qquad \Phi_r =_{def} \tau \odot [Z'(i) \mathrel{\widehat{=}} \overline{d}(i).Z'(i)]$$

Then it remains to check that $\mathfrak{T}(B,\Psi_r)$ and $\mathfrak{T}(B,\Phi_r)$ are also bisimulations, and conclude that $(S|A|B|R)\backslash L$ is tolerant of both kinds of faults:

$$P \sqsubseteq_{\Psi_{or} \oplus \Phi_{or}} (S|A|B|R)\backslash L$$

where $\Psi_{or} =_{def} \Psi_o \oplus \Psi_r$ and $\Phi_{or} =_{def} \Phi_o \oplus \Phi_r$. We have an implicit grouping: $(\Psi_o \oplus \Psi_r) \oplus (\Phi_o \oplus \Phi_r)$, but does it matter? Let us define an equivalence between fault descriptions: $\Psi \Leftrightarrow \Phi$ iff Ψ and Φ induce the same notion of fault-tolerance.

Definition 10.
$\Psi \Leftrightarrow \Phi$ iff for all P and Q, $P \sqsubseteq_{\Psi} Q$ iff $P \sqsubseteq_{\Phi} Q$.

With respect to $\Leftrightarrow$, $\oplus$ can be shown commutative, associative and idempotent. Thus the grouping of faults is irrelevant for the claims about fault-tolerance and $(S|A|B|R)\backslash L$ is effectively tolerant of $\Psi_o \oplus \Psi_r \oplus \Phi_o \oplus \Phi_r$.

6 Development

After showing how to specify (Section 4) and verify (Section 5) fault-tolerance, we now aim at techniques that facilitate formal development. We concentrate on the separate development of components and on two ways of refinement: preserving and increasing the current level of fault-tolerance.

6.1 Incremental Refinement

The more faults are anticipated, the more difficult it is to ensure that they all are tolerated. We could first design a process which is correct in the absence of faults and then refine this process to tolerate an increasing number of faults:

$$\begin{aligned} P &\sqsubseteq_{\Psi_1} P_1 \\ &\sqsubseteq_{\Psi_1 \oplus \Psi_2} P_2 \\ &\dots \\ &\sqsubseteq_{\Psi_1 \oplus \cdots \oplus \Psi_n} P_n \end{aligned}$$

The result is $P \sqsubseteq_{\Psi_1 \oplus \cdots \oplus \Psi_n} P_n$, following the proposition:

Proposition 11.
If $P \sqsubseteq_{\Psi} Q \sqsubseteq_{\Psi \oplus \Phi} R$ then $P \sqsubseteq_{\Psi \oplus \Phi} R$.

As an example, suppose the protocol should also tolerate corruption of messages, in addition to omission and replication.

$$\Psi_c =_{def} \tau \odot [Y'(i) \mathrel{\widehat{=}} \overline{b}(\surd).Y] \qquad \Phi_c =_{def} \tau \odot [Z'(i) \mathrel{\widehat{=}} \overline{d}(\surd).Z]$$

We apply a simple refinement of S and R by which they detect and omit all received values $\surd$. The result, the sender S_1 and the receiver R_1 are given below.

$$\begin{aligned} S_1 =_{def} \mu X(0).&[X(i) \mathrel{\widehat{=}} in.X'(i) + d(\surd).X(i)] \\ &[X'(i) \mathrel{\widehat{=}} \overline{a}(i).X'(i) + d(i).X(\neg i) + d(\neg i).X'(i) + d(\surd).X'(i)] \\ R_1 =_{def} \mu X(1).&[X'(i) \mathrel{\widehat{=}} \overline{out}.X(i) + b(\surd).X'(i)] \\ &[X(i) \mathrel{\widehat{=}} \overline{c}(i).X(i) + b(i).X(i) + b(\neg i).X'(\neg i) + b(\surd).X(i)] \end{aligned}$$

As $\surd$ represents the value of a corrupted message, ignoring this value has the effect of loosing the original message. But the protocol is already able to tolerate the loss of messages. Given $\Psi_{orc} =_{def} \Psi_{or} \oplus \Psi_c$ and $\Phi_{orc} =_{def} \Phi_{or} \oplus \Phi_c$ we can show that the resulting protocol tolerates all anticipated faults:

$$P \sqsubseteq_{\Psi_{orc} \oplus \Phi_{orc}} (S_1 | A | B | R_1) \backslash L$$

We can do this by constructing a bisimulation between the states of P and $(S_1|A|B|R_1)\backslash L$ which is checked, again, for each fault separately.

6.2 Preservation Refinement

Although within incremental refinement each step is easier than if many faults are tolerated at once, we should not underestimate such steps. One aspect is the 'size' of the processes involved, likely to increase with each new fault. Another are properties about faults we can tolerate already, to protect in refinement. When incremental refinement will not allow for many general rules to follow (not depending on the faults themselves), some help would be possible if the steps are built using the rules that preserve fault-tolerance.

It is sufficient to limit ourselves to the CCS laws for bisimilarity; bisimilarity must be implied by fault-tolerance. We could safely apply such laws to the specification process but not to the implementation process:

$$P' \approx P \sqsubseteq_\Psi Q \text{ implies } P' \sqsubseteq_\Psi Q$$
$$P \sqsubseteq_\Psi Q \approx Q' \text{ but possibly } P \not\sqsubseteq_\Psi Q'$$

Nevertheless, many laws will still enjoy the property, for example $P \sqsubseteq_\Psi Q_1|Q_2$ iff $P \sqsubseteq_\Psi Q_2|Q_1$, and an important issue is to study the limits of such transformations. Let us define $Q_1 \Rightarrow Q_2$ if proving Q_1 fault-tolerant, for any specification process P and any fault description Ψ, implies that Q_2 is fault-tolerant, for the same P and Ψ. We write $Q_1 \Leftrightarrow Q_2$ if $\Rightarrow$ holds symmetrically.

Definition 12.
$Q_1 \Rightarrow Q_2$ iff $P \sqsubseteq_\Psi Q_1$ implies $P \sqsubseteq_\Psi Q_2$, for all Ψ and P.
$Q_1 \Leftrightarrow Q_2$ iff $Q_1 \Rightarrow Q_2$ and $Q_2 \Rightarrow Q_1$, symmetrically.

Most CCS laws $Q_1 \approx Q_2$ will actually imply $Q_1 \Leftrightarrow Q_2$. Among exceptions are the expansion law and the recursion unfolding law, both changing the "number" of states that can be potentially affected by faults (process constants); we can only preserve fault-tolerance while decreasing this number. Some selected laws are given by the following proposition:

Proposition 13.

1. $Q+R \Leftrightarrow R+Q$
2. $Q+(R+S) \Leftrightarrow (Q+R)+S$
3. $Q \Leftrightarrow \tau.Q$
4. $Q+\tau.Q \Leftrightarrow \tau.Q$
5. $\mu X.\Delta \Rightarrow [\![\Delta]\!](X)\{\widetilde{\mu Y.\Delta}/\widetilde{Y}\}$
6. $a.Q|\bar{a}.R \Rightarrow \tau.(Q|R)+a.(Q|\bar{a}.R)+\bar{a}.(a.Q|R)$
7. $Q|(R|S) \Leftrightarrow (Q|R)|S$
8. $Q[f]\backslash L \Leftrightarrow Q\backslash f^{-1}(L)[f]$

We also have a proposition that helps to derive new laws from the existing ones, using the structure of the implementation process.

Proposition 14.

1. If $Q_1 \Rightarrow Q_2$ then $\alpha.Q_1 \Rightarrow \alpha.Q_2$, $Q_1\backslash L \Rightarrow Q_2\backslash L$ and $Q_1[f] \Rightarrow Q_2[f]$.
2. If $Q_1 \Rightarrow Q_2$, $\mathcal{X}(R) \cap dom(\Psi) = \emptyset$ then $Q_1+R \Rightarrow Q_2+R$ and $Q_1|R \Rightarrow Q_2|R$.
3. If $Q_1 \Rightarrow Q_2$ and $R_1 \Rightarrow R_2$ then $Q_1 + Q_2 \Rightarrow R_1 + R_2$ and $Q_1|Q_2 \Rightarrow R_1|R_2$.

Consider one more fault: creation of messages, again represented by $\surd$.

$$\Psi_e =_{def} \tau \odot [Y'(i) \widehat{=} \bar{b}(\surd).Y'(i)] \qquad \Phi_e =_{def} \tau \odot [Z'(i) \widehat{=} \bar{d}(\surd).Z'(i)]$$

We can show that the protocol $(S_1|A|B|R_1)\backslash L$, already able to tolerate omission, replication and corruption, is also tolerant of messages being created. This property is again demonstrated by a bisimulation which is checked for each fault separately. Given $\Psi_{orce} =_{def} \Psi_{orc} \oplus \Psi_e$ and $\Phi_{orce} =_{def} \Phi_{orc} \oplus \Phi_e$, we have:

$$P \sqsubset_{\Psi_{orce} \oplus \Phi_{orce}} (S_1|A|B|R_1)\backslash L$$

The laws can also help us simplify this protocol. Given the laws of transformation, among them (3) and (6), and composition we can show that:

$$\begin{array}{lll} (S_1|A|B|R_1)\backslash L \Rightarrow (S_2|A|B|R_2)\backslash L & & \\ \text{where} \quad S_2 =_{def} \mu X(0).[X(i) \widehat{=} in.X'(i)] & & \\ \qquad\qquad [X'(i) \widehat{=} \bar{a}(i).X'(i) + d(i).X(\neg i) + & & \\ \qquad\qquad\qquad d(\neg i).X'(i) + d(\surd).X'(i)] & & \\ \qquad\quad R_2 =_{def} \mu X(1).[X'(i) \widehat{=} \overline{out}.X(i)] & & \\ \qquad\qquad [X(i) \widehat{=} \bar{c}(i).X(i) + b(i).X(i) + & & \\ \qquad\qquad\qquad b(\neg i).X'(\neg i) + b(\surd).X(i)] & & \end{array}$$

Unlike S_1, S_2 is not ready to accept values $\surd$ while waiting for input, and unlike R_1, R_2 is not ready to accept $\surd$ when waiting to output. Informally, this additional behaviour would only become necessary if the protocol were to accept the next message before the previous one is sent, like in the sliding window protocol for the window size greater than two. For the alternating bit protocol we can effort the simplification. The result preserves the current level of fault-tolerance: omission, replication, corruption and creation of messages.

$$P \sqsubset_{\Psi_{orce} \oplus \Phi_{orce}} (S_2|A|B|R_2)\backslash L$$

6.3 Separate Development

Ideally, we would like refinement be driven by the structure of the implementation process, components of which are refined separately and the product, composed together, guaranteed to preserve refinement. In the presence of faults, however, this is not always possible: $P \sqsubset_\Psi Q$ will not in general imply $P|R \sqsubset_\Psi Q|R$ if R is affected by Ψ. Another problem is the well-known preemptive effect of τ on $+$. Let us first follow the standard solution to the second problem [14]:

Definition 15.

$$\begin{array}{ll} P \sqsubseteq_\Psi Q \text{ iff} & \text{whenever } P \xrightarrow{\alpha} P' \text{ then } \exists_{Q', s \neq \varepsilon}\, Q \xrightarrow{s} Q' \wedge \hat{s} = \hat{\alpha} \wedge P' \sqsubset_\Psi Q' \\ & \text{whenever } Q \underset{\Psi}{\overset{\alpha}{\mapsto}} Q' \text{ then } \exists_{P', s \neq \varepsilon}\, P \xrightarrow{s} P' \wedge \hat{s} = \hat{\alpha} \wedge P' \sqsubset_\Psi Q' \end{array}$$

Here initial transitions of each process must be matched by a non-empty sequence of transitions of another process; before we allowed for the empty sequence to match τ-labelled transitions. Like $\sqsubseteq_\Psi$, $\underline{\sqsubseteq}_\Psi$ supports incremental refinement but is also preserved by all fault-free and fault-tolerant contexts:

Proposition 16.

1. If $P \underline{\sqsubseteq}_\Psi Q$ then $\alpha.P \underline{\sqsubseteq}_\Psi \alpha.Q$, $P\backslash L \underline{\sqsubseteq}_\Psi Q\backslash L$ and $P[f] \underline{\sqsubseteq}_\Psi Q[f]$.
2. If $P \underline{\sqsubseteq}_\Psi Q$, $\mathcal{X}(R) \cap dom(\Psi) = \emptyset$ then $P+R \underline{\sqsubseteq}_\Psi Q+R$ and $P|R \underline{\sqsubseteq}_\Psi Q|R$.
3. If $P_1 \underline{\sqsubseteq}_\Psi Q_1$ and $P_2 \underline{\sqsubseteq}_\Psi Q_2$ then $P_1 + P_2 \underline{\sqsubseteq}_\Psi Q_1 + Q_2$ and $P_1|P_2 \underline{\sqsubseteq}_\Psi Q_1|Q_2$.

An example of this technique, here described informally, is design of a database which supports atomic transactions despite some failures of the underlying hardware, following the steps for sequential, concurrent and distributed databases.

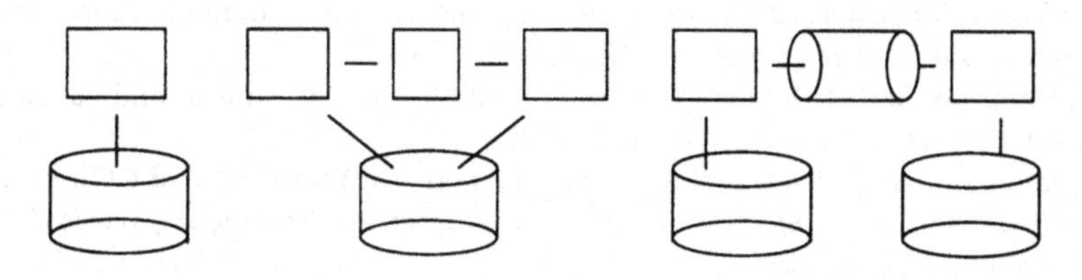

The first step is design of a stable storage for the disk that suffers from various problems like e.g. corruption of sectors. This proceeds by incremental refinement and ultimately produces an implementation of the sequential database. Second, sequential database plus the protocol for mutual exclusion, proven correct but itself not affected by faults, gives an implementation of the concurrent database. Finally, two or more concurrent databases, connected by a reliable medium (as in this paper but two-directional), with two- or three-phase commit protocol running on top, proven correct but not affected by faults, gives an implementation of a distributed database. All steps and claims about fault-tolerance making intensive use of the techniques described in this section. For the details see [8].

7 Conclusions

Unlike real-time, proving fault-tolerance is rarely thought to merit special treatment. It is mostly reduced to proving correctness of a system in the presence of all anticipated faults. This work provides a necessary test for the claims about provable fault-tolerance – fault-monotonicity, and one important case where such a reduction will fail this test – bisimulation. It also shows a class of bisimulations which are fault-monotonic and within CCS support reasoning and design of reactive systems under weak assumptions about faults. The timed extension of this work is in [9]. Some directions for future work include proving completeness of the preservation laws, extending the framework to specify and reason about graceful degradation and relating the notions of realisability [1] and fault-monotonicity.

Acknowledgements

I wish to thank Mathai Joseph for valuable comments on this work. I am grateful to Zhou Chaochen and Chris George for support.

References

1. M. Abadi, L. Lamport, and P. Wolper. Realizable and unrealizable specifications of reactive systems. *LNCS*, 372:1–17, 1989.
2. A. Borjesson, K.G. Larsen, and A. Skou. Generality in design and compositional verification using TAV. *Formal Methods in System Design*, 6(3):239–258, 1995.
3. G. Bruns. Applying process refinement to a safety-relevant system. Technical report, Lab. for Foundations of Computer Science, University of Edinburgh, 1994.
4. K.M. Chandy and J. Misra. *Parallel Program Design*. Addison-Wesley, 1988.
5. F. Cristian. A rigorous approach to fault-tolerant programming. *IEEE Transactions on Software Engineering*, 11(1):23–31, 1985.
6. M. Hennessy and R. Milner. Algebraic laws for nondeterminism and concurrency. *Journal of the ACM*, 32(1):137–161, 1985.
7. T. Janowski. Stepwise transformations for fault-tolerant design of CCS processes. In *Proc. 7th Int. Conference on Formal Description Techniques*, pages 505–520. Chapman and Hall, 1994.
8. T. Janowski. *Bisimulation and Fault-Tolerance*. PhD thesis, Department of Computer Science, University of Warwick, 1995.
9. T. Janowski and M. Joseph. Dynamic scheduling in the presence of faults: Specification and verification. In *Proc. 4rd Int. Symposium on Formal Techniques in Real-Time and Fault-Tolerant Systems*, volume 1135 of *LNCS*, pages 279–297, 1996.
10. He Jifeng and C.A.R. Hoare. Algebraic specification and proof of a distributed recovery algorithm. *Distributed Computing*, 2:1–12, 1987.
11. K.G. Larsen and R. Milner. A compositional protocol verification using relativized bisimulation. *Information and Computation*, 99:80–108, 1992.
12. Z. Liu. *Fault-Tolerant Programming by Transformations*. PhD thesis, University of Warwick, 1991.
13. Z. Liu and M. Joseph. Transformations of programs for fault-tolerance. *Formal Aspects of Computing*, 4:442–469, 1992.
14. R. Milner. *Communication and Concurrency*. Prentice-Hall International, 1989.
15. K. Paliwoda and J.W. Sanders. An incremental specification of the sliding-window protocol. *Distributed Computing*, 5:83–94, 1991.
16. D. Park. Concurrency and automata on infinite sequences. *LNCS*, 104, 81.
17. J. Peleska. Design and verification of fault tolerant systems with CSP. *Distributed Computing*, 5:95–106, 1991.
18. K.V.S. Prasad. *Combinators and Bisimulation Proofs for Restartable Systems*. PhD thesis, Department of Computer Science, University of Edinburgh, 1987.
19. H. Schepers. *Fault Tolerance and Timing of Distributed Systems*. PhD thesis, Eindhoven University of Technology, 1994.

Span(Graph): A Categorical Algebra of Transition Systems

Piergiulio Katis[1], N. Sabadini[2] and R.F.C. Walters[1]

[1] School of Mathematics and Statistics,
University of Sydney, N.S.W. 2006, Australia
[2] Dipartimento di Scienze dell'Informazione,
Università di Milano, Via Comelico 39/41, I-20135 Milano MI, Italy

1 Introduction.

Structured transition systems, or non-deterministic automata, have been widely used in the specification of computing systems, including concurrent systems [A94],[Z85]. We describe here an algebra of transition systems, an algebra in fact already known to category theorists but without any consciousness of its relation to concurrency. The algebra is closely related to, and may be regarded as an extension of, the algebra of Arnold and Nivat [A94] (which book contains comparisons with other models of concurrency - Petri nets, process algebras). What it has in addition to Arnold and Nivat's algebra is that there is a geometry associated with the new algebra along the lines of Penrose's algebra of tensors [P71] (a subject much developed of late in relation to the geometry of manifolds, and quantum field theory [JS91], [JS93], [S95], [T95], [M95]). In this paper we demonstrate how this geometry reflects the geometry of distributed systems.

For category theorists we can say in a line what the algebra is: it is the discrete cartesian bicategory structure [CW87] on **Span(Graph)** [B67]. (The category of relations also has this structure and, in the equivalent form of allegories, it has been used in [BJ94] to give a semantics of Ruby [JS90].) The second section of the paper is devoted to describing the operations (though not the equations) of this algebra, and their geometric interpretation. In the third section we show how traditional transition systems fit into the algebra, and we describe a specification of a distributed system using the algebra. In the fourth section we prove some language theoretic results about the effect of operations in **Span(Graph)** on behaviours; we study special systems (linearizable spans) for which interleaved behaviour is reasonable, and we give a semantics to Hoare's parallel operation as a derived operation in our algebra. The final section of the paper contains a precise definition of discrete cartesian bicategory, and we derive relations between feedback, composition, tensor and parallel (in the sense of Hoare) in such a bicategory.

Further developments of this algebra - an analogue of bisimulation [P81], model-checking, a semantics of CCS, and specific applications to concurrent systems will appear elsewhere. This work arose out of earlier study of bicategories of processes [BSW96], [KSW97], [K96], [SWW93], [SWW94] which itself arose from the study of distributive categories and imperative programming [W89],

[W92a], [W92b], [KW93]. A computer program [GKW96] has been written by Robbie Gates for computing in **Span(Graph)** and hence for checking properties of concurrent systems expressed in this way.

Much of the notation in this paper originates in category theory; for this the reader may consult a text such as [M70] or [W92a].

We acknowledge the support for this project by the Australian Research Council, Italian MURST 40% and the Italian CNR.

2 Span(Graph).

2.1 Objects and arrows of Span(Graph).

The objects of **Span(Graph)** are (finite) directed graphs. Given graphs X and Y an arrow from X to Y consists of a graph R and two graph morphisms $\partial_0 : R \to X, \partial_1 : R \to Y$. Such an arrow is called a span of graphs. It is often denoted as follows:

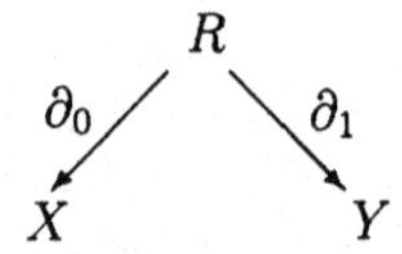

We call the graph R the head of the span and the morphisms ∂_0 and ∂_1 the two legs of the span. We will, by abuse of notation, denote the two legs of any span by the same symbols ∂_0 and ∂_1. We will often denote the span simply as $R : X \to Y$. We call X and Y the domain and codomain, respectively, of R; or the boundaries of R.

We may also picture a span in another way. If the objects are given as products of graphs, for example $X = X_1 \times X_2$, $Y = Y_1 \times Y_2 \times Y_3$ we picture the span as:

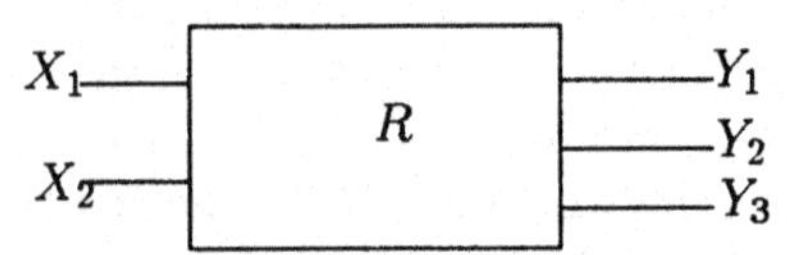

In this case we may call each of X_1, X_2, Y_1, Y_2, Y_3, boundaries of R.

2.2 Operations of Span(Graph).

Composition of spans.

The composite of spans $R : X \to Y$ and $S : Y \to Z$ is the span $R; S : X \to Z$ whose head is the graph with vertex set

$$\{(r, s); r \text{ is a vertex of } R, s \text{ is a vertex of } S, \partial_1(r) = \partial_0(s)\}$$

and with edge set

$$\{(\rho, \sigma); \rho \text{ is a edge of } R, \sigma \text{ is a edge of } S, \partial_1(\rho) = \partial_0(\sigma)\}.$$

Beginnings and ends of edges have the obvious definitions. (Technically, $R;S$ is the pullback $R \times_Y S$).

The pictorial representation of the composition of two spans R and S is as follows (with the obvious modification if the objects are products of graphs!):

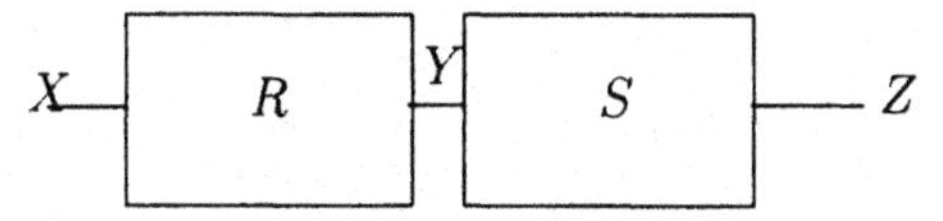

Tensor of spans.

The tensor of two spans $R : X \to Y$ and $S : Z \to W$ is the span denoted $R \otimes S : X \times Z \to Y \times W$, and defined by: the head of $R \otimes S$ is $R \times S$; the legs of $R \otimes S$ are $\partial_0 \times \partial_0$ and $\partial_1 \times \partial_1$. The pictorial representation of the tensor of two spans is:

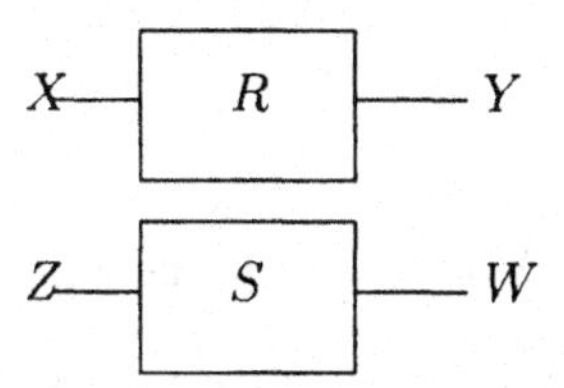

In addition to these operations there are the following constants of the algebra.

The identity of X.

The identity span $1_X : X \to X$ has head X and two legs $1_X, 1_X$. It is denoted by a plain wire.

The diagonal and the reverse diagonal of X.

The span with head X and legs $1_X : X \to X, \Delta_X : X \to X \times X$ is called the diagonal of X, and is denoted also $\Delta : X \to X \times X$.

The span with head X and legs $\Delta_X : X \to X \times X, 1_X : X \to X$ is called the reverse diagonal, and is denoted $\Delta^* : X \times X \to X$.

The two spans are pictured thus:

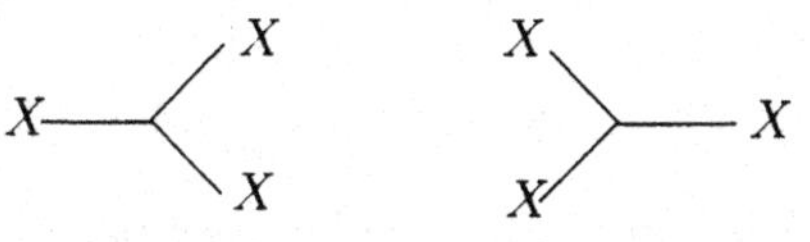

Diagonal Reverse diagonal

Projections and reverse projections.

The span with head $X \times Y$ and legs $1_{X \times Y} : X \times Y \to X \times Y, p_X : X \times Y \to X$ is denoted p_X and is called a projection, and is pictured by the termination of the wire Y. There is also a similarly defined reverse projection denoted p_X^*.

The spans $\eta_X : I \to X \times X$ and $\varepsilon_X : X \times X \to I$.

The terminal graph, denoted I, has one vertex and one edge, by necessity a loop. The span with head X and legs $! : X \to I, \Delta : X \to X \times X$ is called η_X.

The span with head X and legs $\Delta : X \to X \times X, ! : X \to I$ is called ε_X.

The two spans are pictured thus:

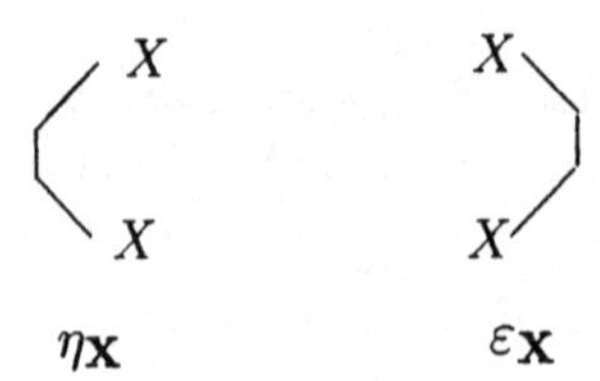

Technically, η and ε are the unit and counit of the self-dual compact-closed structure on **Span(Graph)**. It will become clear that their role in the context of this paper is to permit a feedback operation on distributed systems.

The correspondence between constants and operations, and the geometric representations given above, result in the fact that expressions in the algebra have corresponding circuit or system diagrams. We illustrate this by an example.

2.3 Example.

Given spans $S : X \to X \times X, C : X \to I$, the expression

$$\eta_X ; (S \otimes 1_X); (C \otimes 1_X \otimes 1_X); (S \otimes 1_X); (C \otimes 1_X \otimes 1_X); (S \otimes 1_X); (C \otimes 1_X \otimes 1_X); \varepsilon_X$$

has system diagram:

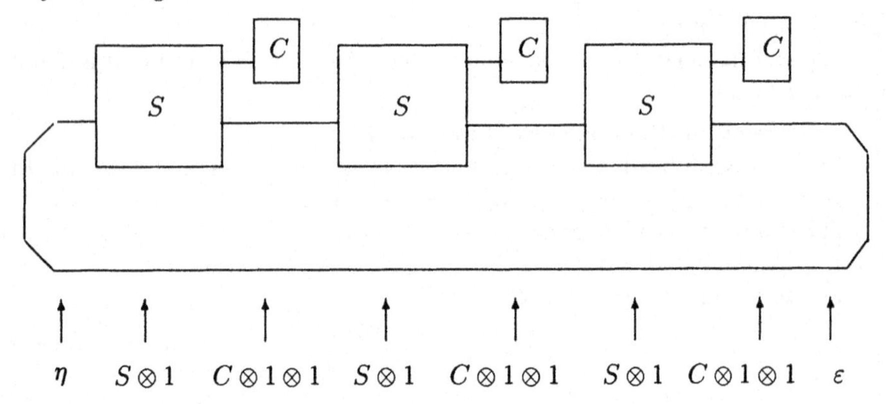

$\eta \quad S \otimes 1 \quad C \otimes 1 \otimes 1 \quad S \otimes 1 \quad C \otimes 1 \otimes 1 \quad S \otimes 1 \quad C \otimes 1 \otimes 1 \quad \varepsilon$

We have indicated the correspondence between parts of the expression and of the diagram using arrows. This diagram might be (with specific interpretation of the components S (server) and C (client)) a specification of a simple token ring.

Remark.

The reader may have noticed that apart from the fact that wires are distinguished as appearing on the left or right of components we have not indicated an orientation on the wires, by placing for example an arrowhead. The reason is that in this algebra no such orientation is possible, and this will be reflected later in discussing concurrent systems by the fact that at this level of abstraction wires represent input/output, and not either input or output channels.

2.4 Behaviours of a span.

Definition.

A behaviour π of a span $R : X \to Y$ is a finite path in the graph R, the head of the span.

Notice that applying the legs of the span to a behaviour π yields two paths, one $\partial_0(\pi)$ in X and the other $\partial_1(\pi)$ in Y. The graphs X and Y may be thought of as the (left and right) boundaries of the system R. Then $\partial_0(\pi)$, $\partial_1(\pi)$ may be thought of as the behaviour of the boundaries of the system corresponding to the behaviour π, or the behaviour of the system reflected on the boundaries.

The following result is straightforward.

Proposition.

(i) A behaviour of the composite $R;S$ of two spans is a pair of behaviours, one ρ of R, the other σ of S, such that $\partial_1(\rho) = \partial_0(\sigma)$. That is, a behaviour of $R;S$ consists of a behaviour of R and a behaviour of S which agree (synchronize) on the common boundary.

(ii) A behaviour of the tensor $R \otimes S$ of two spans is just a pair of behaviours, one ρ of R, the other σ of S.

(iii) A behaviour of $\eta_X : I \to X \times X$ is a path in X reflected (synchronously and equally) on the two boundaries. The behaviours of ε are similarly described.

(iv) A behaviour of $\Delta_X : X \to X \times X$ is a path in X reflected (synchronously and equally) on the three boundaries. The behaviours of Δ_X^* are similarly described.

3 Finite labelled transition systems.

The aim of this section is to relate traditional transition systems/automata [A94] to (arrows in) **Span(Graph)** .

3.1 Labelled transitions systems and Span(Graph).

Given an alphabet $\mathcal{A} = \{a_1, a_2, ...\}$ we may construct a graph, which we denote A, as follows: the graph A has one vertex, usually denoted '$*$', and a loop on this vertex for each element of the alphabet $\mathcal{A}$.

Proposition.

A span of graphs $R : A \to I$ is the same thing as a labelled transition system on the alphabet $\mathcal{A}$, in the sense of Arnold-Nivat.

proof.

A span consists of a graph R and two graph morphisms $\partial_0 : R \to A, \partial_1 : R \to I$. Since I is the terminal graph there is no information in ∂_1. The information in ∂_0 is precisely the assignment to each edge of R of a loop in A – since every vertex of R must be assigned to the single vertex $*$ of A. But this is exactly a labelling of the graph R by letters of the alphabet A.

Remark. If $\mathcal{A}$ and $\mathcal{B}$ are alphabets and A and B are the corresponding one vertex graphs then a general span of graphs $R : A \to B$ is a transition system labelled by the product alphabet $\mathcal{A} \times \mathcal{B}$. More generally, if $\mathcal{A}_1, \mathcal{A}_2, \ldots, \mathcal{A}_m$, $\mathcal{B}_1, \mathcal{B}_2, \ldots, \mathcal{B}_n$, are alphabets then a span of graphs $R : A_1 \times A_2 \times \ldots \times A_m \to B_1 \times B_2 \times \ldots \times B_n$ is a transition system labelled by the product alphabet $\mathcal{A}_1 \times \mathcal{A}_2 \times \ldots \times \mathcal{A}_m \times \mathcal{B}_1 \times \mathcal{B}_2 \times \ldots \times \mathcal{B}_n$. The separation of the alphabet into a left- and right-hand part seems to be a very minor change from the formalism of Arnold and Nivat but it is exactly this separation which makes the algebra we describe in this paper possible.

Proposition.

Let $\mathcal{A}_1, \mathcal{A}_2, \ldots, \mathcal{A}_m$ be alphabets and $R_1 : \mathcal{A}_1 \to I, R_2 : \mathcal{A}_2 \to I, \ldots, R_m : \mathcal{A}_m \to I$ be spans of graphs. Then $R_1 \otimes R_2 \otimes \ldots \otimes R_m$ is the free product in the sense of Nivat-Arnold of the corresponding labelled transition systems.

proof. Clear.

Remark.

The key to the calculus of Arnold and Nivat are subsystems of the free product called the synchronous products in which one is allowed to restrict the transitions that occur by specifying that they must be labelled by certain given synchronization vectors in the product alphabet. We will show how in **Span(Graph)** this may be achieved by the composition of spans.

3.2 A notation for spans of graphs.

We introduce a simplified notation for spans of graphs which it is easiest to describe by giving an example.

Example.

Consider the span of graphs:

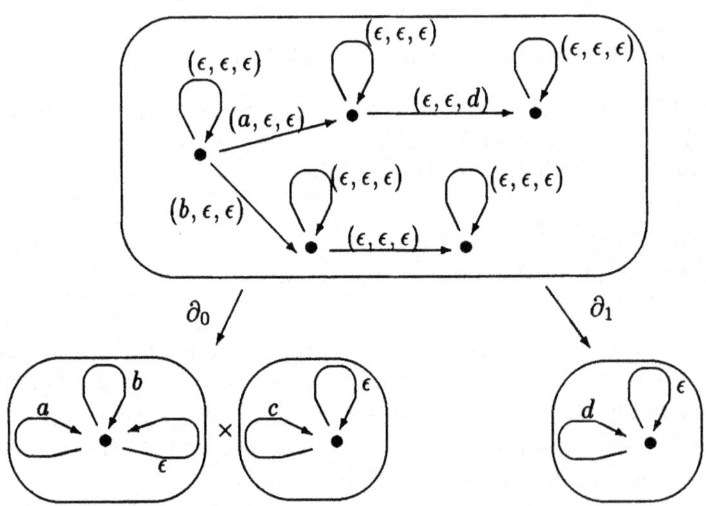

We will represent this graph by the following picture:

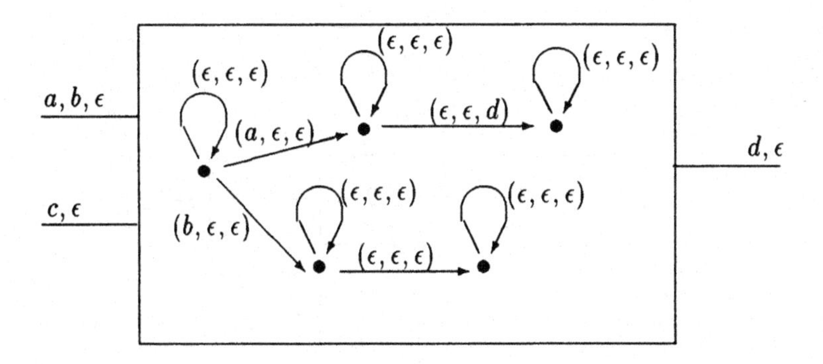

3.3 Systems with null actions.

Many systems, of which this last is an example, have the special form that all the graphs involved have a designated loop at each vertex called the null loop, denoted always ϵ. Further the morphisms involved preserve the null loops. Such graphs are called reflexive graphs. Properly speaking when dealing with such systems we are working in another category **Span(ReflexiveGraphs)**. For such systems we often omit, when unambiguous, mention of the null action. For example, the system in 3.2 may be concisely denoted:

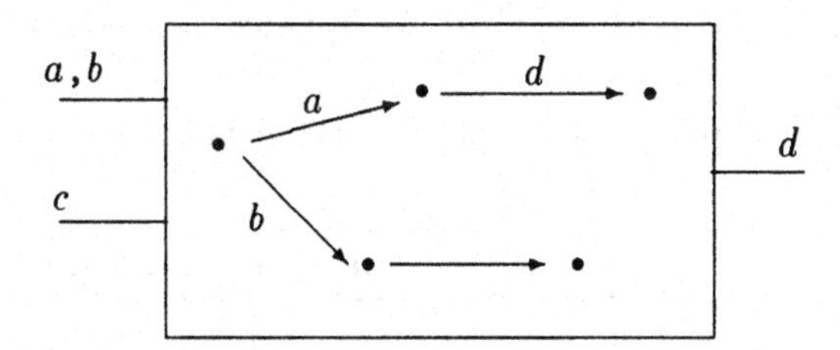

3.4 The Peterson mutual exclusion algorithm.

We give a description of Peterson's mutual exclusion algorithm for two processes. We choose to do this since it is the first example in [A94] and the reader should thus be in a position to compare our mode of description with that of Arnold-Nivat. All the spans below are reflexive.

Peterson's algorithm concerns two processes P_0, P_1 each of which has a critical section, and only one of the processes may be in this critical section at a time. In order to accomplish this the two processes communicate through three (parallel) shared binary variable, called D_0, T and D_1. The geometry of the system is therefore of the following form:

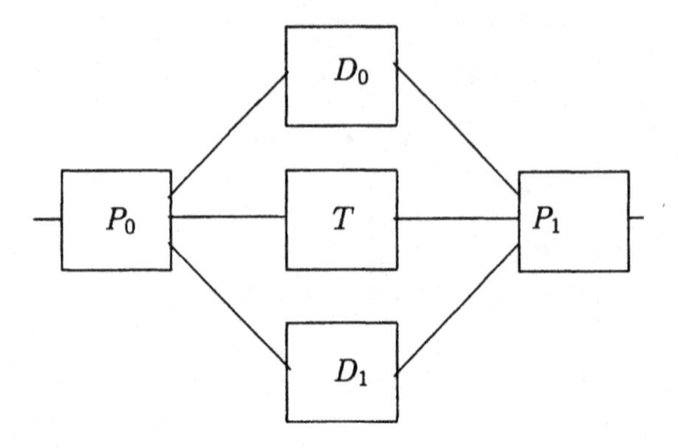

Hence we would expect to be able to represent the system by an expression in **Span(Graph)** of the form

$$P_0; (D_0 \otimes T \otimes D_1); P_1.$$

Each of the processes cycles goes through a cycle as follows: non-critical section; some communication actions with D_0, T and D_1; the critical section; further communication actions; and then the non-critical section again, and so on. The communication actions involve the processes writing or 'reading' the binary variables d_0, t, or d_1. We apostrophize the word 'reading' here because, although that is what the action is often called, we feel that it is a misnomer at this level of abstraction.

We now describe precisely the process P_0. It is the span of graphs pictured as follows.

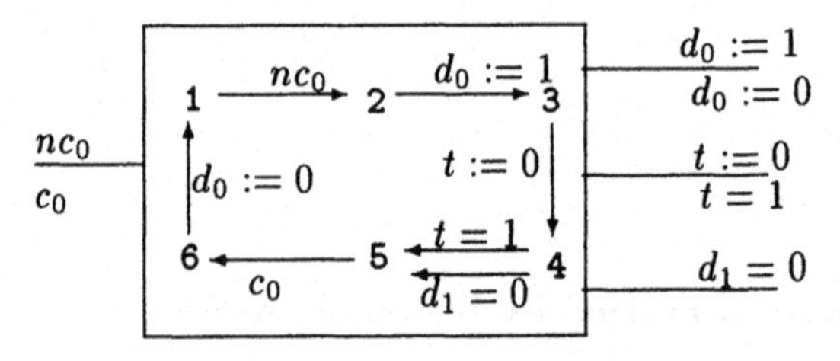

P_0

The actions nc_0 and c_0 are the non-critical and critical actions, respectively, of P_0. The actions $d_0 := 0$, $d_0 := 1$, $t := 0$ are write actions to the variables indicated. The actions $t = 1$, $d_1 = 0$ are actions enabled when the variables have the indicted values – these are the read actions, but notice that there are no read actions $t = 0$ or $d_1 = 1$ in P_0. These actions (and similar ones for P_1) in synchronization vectors on page 30 of Arnold need to be omitted.

The process P_1 has a similar description.

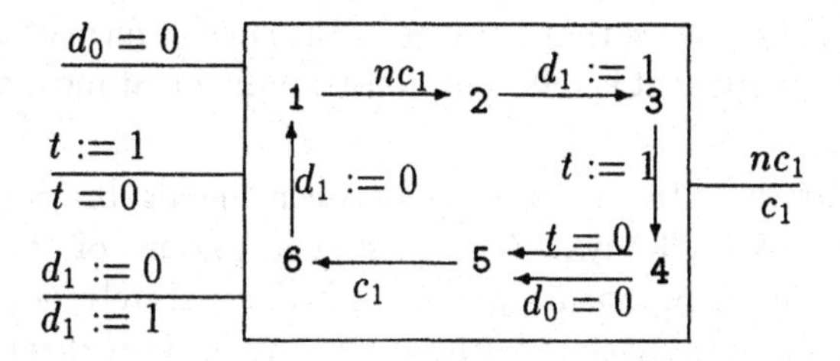

P_1

The three binary variables D_0, T and D_1 are defined as follows:

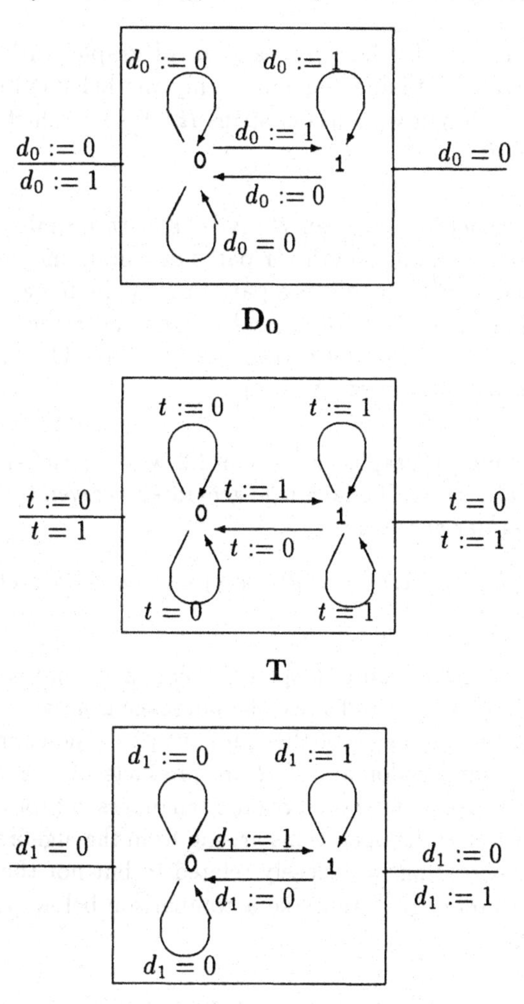

D_0

T

D_1

An action of the composed algorithm $P_0; (D_0 \otimes T \otimes D_1); P_1$ is an action of each of the components P_0, D_0, T, D_1, P_1, that is a 5-tuple of edges, which agree on connecting wires. Notice that because of the special form of the span involved each action of a component is reflected non-trivially on at most one input/output wire.

Remark. A remark on the comparison between the algebra **Span(Graph)** and the formalism of Arnold-Nivat. Our geometric picture of the system clarifies the algorithm. The components are described separately, and the operations allow a description of the system without needing to write down synchronization constraints for the system as a whole.

4 The language generated by a span.

One way of abstracting further from a span of graphs with initial vertex, is to forget the internal state and remember only the behaviours reflected on the boundaries. In this section we consider spans $R : X \to Y$ which have an assigned initial vertex $r_0 \in R$.

Definition.

The language generated by span $R : X \to Y$ with initial vertex r_0 is the set of pairs of paths of the same length (or paths of pairs), one in X and one in Y, of the form $(\partial_0(\pi), \partial_1(\pi))$ where π is a path in R beginning at the initial vertex. We denote the language of R by $Lang(R)$. We denote the set of all paths in $X \times Y$ commencing in the initial vertex as $(X \times Y)^*$. The language of a span from X to Y is thus a subset of $(X \times Y)^*$.

Example.

Consider the span of graphs in section 3.2 with the left-most vertex being taken as the initial vertex. The language generated is given by the prefix closure of the classical regular expression

$$(\epsilon,\epsilon,\epsilon)^*(a,\epsilon,\epsilon)(\epsilon,\epsilon,\epsilon)^*(\epsilon,\epsilon,d)(\epsilon,\epsilon,\epsilon)^* + (\epsilon,\epsilon,\epsilon)^*(b,\epsilon,\epsilon)(\epsilon,\epsilon,\epsilon)^*.$$

Remarks.

The reason the abstraction of a span to a language makes sense is that it is possible, as we show below, to deduce the language generated by an expression of spans knowing the languages of the components of the expression. It is clear that if the domain and codomain of R are products of one vertex graphs the languages that arise are prefix-closed regular languages in tuples of actions. What is interesting however is the operations arising from the algebra on these regular languages. These operations are closely related to but not the same as existing operations in the literature - we make a comparison below with operations on the traces of Hoare.

Theorem.

Consider spans $R : X \to Y, S : Y \to Z, T : Z \to W$.

(i) $Lang(R;S) = \{(x,y);$ there exists $l \in Lang(R), m \in Lang(S)$, so that $proj_1(l) = x, proj_2(l) = proj_1(m)$ and $proj_2(m) = y\}$;
(ii) $Lang(R \otimes T) = \{(l,m); length(l) = length(m)$ and $l \in Lang(R), m \in Lang(S)\}$.

proof.

(i) The path (x, y) lies in $Lang(R; S)$ iff there is a path t in $R; S$ such that $(\partial_0(t), \partial_1(t)) = (x, y)$. That is, by the definition of $R; S$, iff there are paths r in R, s in S, such that $\partial_0(r) = x, \partial_1(r) = \partial_0(s)$, and $\partial_1(s) = y$. That is, if and only if there is a path $n (= \partial_1(r) = \partial_0(s))$ in Y such that (x, n) is in $Lang(R)$, and (n, y) is in $Lang(S)$.

(ii) Straightforward.

4.1 Linearizable systems.

A large part of concurrency is based on the presumption that it is reasonable to consider *interleaved* actions in analysing systems. For a large subclass of reflexive spans, what we call *linearizable* spans, this is indeed the case, at least for checking certain properties like deadlock. For reasons of space the results in this section are stated without proof – the proofs are rather straightforward and will be given in an expanded version of the paper.

Definition.

Consider a reflexive span $R : X = X_1 \times X_2 \times ..X_m \to X_{m+1} \times ...X_{m+n} = Y$. Denote a label of the form $(\epsilon, \epsilon, \ldots, \epsilon)$ (only ϵ's) as $\tilde{\epsilon}$, and a label of the form $(\epsilon, \epsilon, \ldots, \epsilon, x_i, \epsilon, \ldots, \epsilon)$ (at most one non-ϵ label) as $\tilde{x}_i$. A path in R is said to be linear if each edge is labelled either $\tilde{\epsilon}$ or $\tilde{x}_i$ for some i, $x_i \in X_i$.

The span R is said to be linearizable if it satisfies the following property: given any edge $\rho : r \to s$ in R labelled $(x_1, x_2, \ldots, x_{m+1}, \ldots, x_{m+n})$, and any order on the numbers $1, 2, 3, \ldots, m+n$, there is a linear path also from r to s in R whose edges, apart from null-labelled ones, are precisely $\tilde{x}_1$, $\tilde{x}_2$, $\ldots$, $\tilde{x}_{m+n}$ in the given order.

Theorem.

If R is linearizable then so are $R; S$ and $R \otimes S$.

Note.

A reflexive span $R : X_1 \times \ldots \times X_m \to Y_1 \times \ldots \times Y_n$ with the property that each action is labelled non-null on at most one wire is linearizable. Hence the Peterson algorithm is linearizable since its components are, and it is formed from them using composition and tensor.

Note.

The identity, diagonal, η and ε are not linearizable, and hence linearizable systems do not form a subalgebra of **Span(Graph)**. Nevertheless various derived operations, for example the parallel operation described below, do yield linearizable spans when applied to linearizable spans. It is the fact that these derived operations, but not the constants Δ, η, ε, are linearizable which leads to the operations in such process algebras as CSP of Hoare.

Definition.

If $R : X \times Y \to I$, $S : Y \times Z \to I$ are spans of graphs then $R||_Y S : X \times Y \times Z \to I$ is the span defined by

$$R||_Y S = (1_X \otimes \Delta_Y \otimes 1_Z); (R \otimes S).$$

The geometry of this operation is:

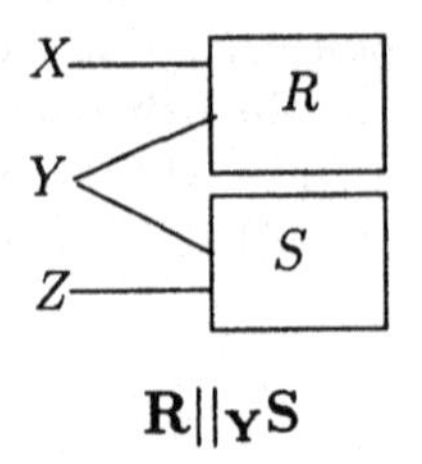

$\mathbf{R||_Y S}$

Theorem.
If $R : X \times Y \to I$ and $S : Y \times Z \to I$ are linearizable then so is $R||_Y S$.

Definition.
Consider a linearizable span $R : X = X_1 \times X_2 \times \ldots \times X_m \to X_{m+1} \times \ldots \times X_{m+n} = Y$ with an intial vertex r_0. Let $N(X_i)$ denote the non-null edges in X_i. For a linear behaviour of R we may consider that the labelling lies in

$$[N(X_1) + N(X_2) + \ldots + N(X_{(m+n)})]^*$$

(where + denotes disjoint union) rather than $(X_1 \times \ldots \times X_{(m+n)})^*$, since we may look just at the non-null actions which occur in a behaviour. We define $Trace(R)$ to be the subset of $[N(X_1) + N(X_2) + \ldots + N(X_{(m+n)})]^*$ arising as labellings of linear behaviours of R commencing at r_0. We may also restrict a trace t to a summand U of $[N(X_1) + N(X_2) + \ldots + N(X_{(m+n)})]$ by omitting letters which are not in the summand; we denote the result by $t|_U$.

The connection with Hoare's parallel operation is evident from the following theorem.

Theorem.
Consider linearizable spans $R : X_1 \times \ldots X_m \times Y_1 \times \ldots Y_n \to I$ and $S : Y_1 \times \ldots Y_n \times Z_1 \times \ldots \times Z_p \to I$. Let

$$U = N(X_1) + N(X_2) + \ldots + N(X_m) + N(Y_1) + N(Y_2) + \ldots + N(Y_n),$$

$$V = N(Y_1) + N(Y_2) + \ldots + N(Y_n) + N(Z_1) + N(Z_2) + \ldots + N(Z_p),$$

$$W = N(X_1) + \ldots + N(X_m) + N(Y_1) + \ldots + N(Y_n) + N(Z_1) + \ldots + N(Z_p).$$

Then

$$Trace(R||_{Y_1 \times \ldots \times Y_n} S) = \{t \in W^*; t|_U \in Trace(R) \text{ and } t|_V \in Trace(S)\}.$$

Remark. Ebergen [E87] and others have used parts of CSP to specify asynchronous circuits. The geometry we have given for expressions in our algebra makes precise the relation between process algebras and circuit diagrams as used in Ebergen. There are advantages to using our algebra in the specification of asynchronous circuits - a single wire, the diagonal, η and ε are very natural primitives in building circuits; using only linearizable components prevents the use of these primitives. In [E87] there is no such *component* as an instantaneous wire, or instantaneous fan-out.

5 Discrete cartesian bicategories

We give a concise definition of discrete cartesian bicategory (relying for basic categorical concepts on [M70], [B67]). We describe without proof some consequences of the definition and sketch the geometric meaning of these consequences. The proofs are relatively straightforward and will be given in an expanded version of the paper.

Let $\mathbf{B}$ be a bicategory with objects denoted X, Y, ..., arrows R, S, ..., and 2-cells α, β, ..., composition of arrows $R; S$. Let $Map(\mathbf{B})$ be the subbicategory of arrows with right-adjoints; we denote arrows of $Map(\mathbf{B})$ by f, g, ..., and their right adjoints by f^*, g^*, ... For simplicity we will assume that $Map(\mathbf{B})$ is a category.

Definition

$\mathbf{B}$ is a discrete cartesian bicategory if

(i) $Map(\mathbf{B})$ has finite products, the operation of product being denoted $\times$, the terminal object I, the diagonals denoted Δ, and the projections p;

(ii) For each pair of objects X, Y the category $\mathbf{B(X,Y)}$ has finite products, the operation of product being denoted $\wedge$; further, 1_I is terminal in $\mathbf{B(I,I)}$.

(iii) If $R : X \to Y, S : Z \to W$, the formula

$$R \otimes S = (p_X; R; p_Y^*) \wedge (p_Z; S; p_W^*) : X \times Z \to Y \times W$$

defines a tensor product on $\mathbf{B}$;

(iv) (discreteness axioms)

$$\Delta^*; \Delta = (1_X \otimes \Delta); (\Delta^* \otimes 1_X) : X \times X \to X \times X; \quad \text{and} \quad \Delta; \Delta^* = 1_X.$$

It is straightforward to show that **Span(Graph)** is a discrete cartesian bicategory. The 2-cells, which we have not mentioned to this point, are defined as follows: a 2-cell α from span $R : X \to Y$ to span $S : X \to Y$ is a graph morphism $\alpha : R \to S$ such that $\partial_0 \alpha = \partial_0$ and $\partial_1 \alpha = \partial_1$. Further an arrow of $Map(\mathbf{Span(Graph)})$ is a span $R : X \to Y$ in which $R = X$ and $\partial_0 = 1_X$ and hence $Map(\mathbf{Span(Graph)})$ is essentially **Graph**.

Notice the geometry of the discreteness axiom; using the rules above for drawing pictures of expressions we see that the first axiom is pictured as:

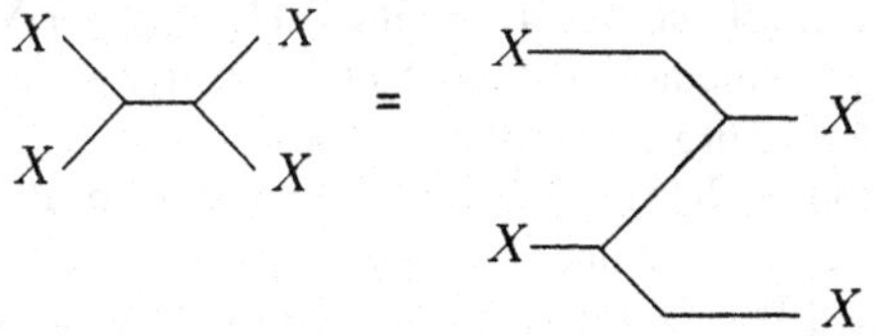

Definition of η and ε.

Though we gave η and ε independently in section 2 (for their use in describing feedback) they are in fact derived operations of the algebra, as the pictures suggest, namely

$$\eta_X = p_I^*; \Delta_X \text{ and } \varepsilon_X = \Delta_X^*; p_I.$$

Equation relating ⊗ and composition and feedback.

The following important equation holds:

$$R; S = (1 \otimes \eta); (R \otimes 1 \otimes S); (\varepsilon \otimes 1),$$

pictured as

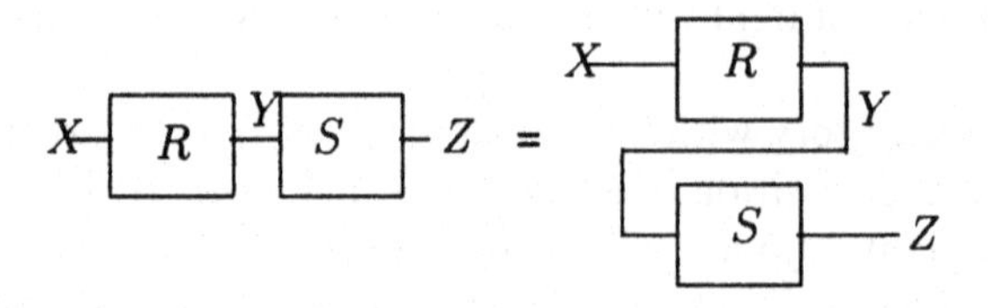

Equation relating ⊗ and || and composition.

We have described || in terms of ⊗, Δ, and composition, but in fact general composition of $R : X \to Y$ and $S : Y \to Z$ can be constructed using || as follows:

$$R; S = (1_X \otimes p_I^* \otimes \eta_Z); [((R \otimes 1_Y); \varepsilon_Y) || ((S \otimes 1_Z); \varepsilon_Z)] \otimes 1_Z)).$$

6 Conclusions.

We have shown that a natural algebraic structure on **Span(Graph)** allows the compositional specification of concurrent systems. Hoare's parallel operation appears as a derived operation in this algebra. The simpler basic operations of our algebra are possible because we do not insist on interleaving semantics: interleaving prevents consideration of the identity span, as well as other natural constants such as the diagonal. We have given some examples of transforming systems using the equations of the algebra. Associated to the algebra there is a geometry which expresses the distributed nature of a concurrent system. This relation between algebra and geometry makes precise the relation between process algebras and circuit diagrams as used, for example, in Ebergen [E87].

7 Bibliography.

[A94] A. Arnold, Finite transition systems, Prentice Hall, 1994.
[B67] J. Bènabou, Introduction to bicategories, Reports of the Midwest Category Seminar, Lecture Notes in Mathematics 47, pages 1–77, Springer-Verlag, 1967.
[BSW96] S. Bloom, N. Sabadini, R.F.C Walters, Matrices, machines and behaviors, Applied Categorical Structures, 4: 343-360, 1996.
[BJ94] C. Brown C. and A. Jeffrey, Allegories of circuits, in: Proc. Logical Foundations of Computer Science, St Petersburg, 1994.
[CW87] A. Carboni and R.F.C. Walters, Cartesian Bicategories I, Journal of Pure and Applied Algebra, 49, pages 11-32, 1987.
[E87] J.C. Ebergen, Translating Programs into Delay-insensitive Circuits, PhD thesis, Eindhoven University of Technology, 1987.
[GKW96] Robbie Gates, P. Katis and R.F.C. Walters, A program for computing with the cartesian bicategory **Span(Graph)**, School of Mathematics and Statistics, University of Sydney, 1996.

[H85] C.A.R. Hoare, Communicating sequential processes, Prentice Hall, Englewood Cliffs, NJ,1985.
[JS90] G. Jones and M. Sheeran, Circuit design in Ruby, in: Formal methods for VLSI design, North-Holland, 1990
[JS91] A. Joyal and R. Street, An introduction to Tanaka duality and quantum groups, Category Theory 1990, Como, Lecture Notes in Mathematics 1488, Springer Verlag, 1991.
[JS93] A. Joyal and R. Street, Braided tensor categories, Advances in Mathematics, 102: 20-78, 1993.
[K95] C. Kassel, Quantum Groups, Graduate Texts in Mathematics, Springer-Verlag, New York, 1995.
[KSW94] P. Katis, N. Sabadini, R.F.C. Walters, The bicategory of circuits, Computing: Australian Theory Seminar, UTS, Sydney, 1994.
[KSW97] P. Katis, N. Sabadini, R.F.C. Walters, Bicategories of processes, Journal of Pure and Applied Algebra, 115, no.2, pp 141 - 178, 1997
[K96] P. Katis, Categories and bicategories of processes, PhD Thesis, University of Sydney, 1996.
[KW93] W. Khalil and R.F.C. Walters, An imperative language based on distributive categories II, Informatique Thèorique et Applications, 27, 503-522, 1993.
[M70] S. Mac Lane, Categories for the working mathematician, Springer Verlag, 1970.
[M95] Majid, Foundations of quantum field theory, Cambridge 1995.
[P81] D. Park, Concurrency and automata on infinite sequences, in 5th GI Conference on theoretical computer science, 167-183, LNCS 104, Springer, 1981.
[P71] R. Penrose, Applications of negative dimensional torsors, in Combinatorial Mathematics and its applications, (D. J. A. Welsh, Ed.) pp. 221-244, Academic Press, New York, 1971.
[RSW] R. Rosebrugh, N. Sabadini, R.F.C. Walters, Minimal realization in bicategories of automata, to appear, Journal of Pure and Applied Algebra.
[SVW96] N. Sabadini, S. Vigna, R.F.C. Walters, A note on recursive functions, Mathematical Structures in Computer Science, 6, 127-139, 1996.
[SW93] N. Sabadini and R.F.C. Walters, On functions and processors: an automata-theoretic approach to concurrency through distributive categories, School of Mathematics and Statistics Research Reports, University of Sydney, (93-7), 1993.
[SWW93] N. Sabadini, R.F.C. Walters, Henry Weld, Distributive automata and asynchronous circuits, Category Theory and Computer Science 5, Amsterdam, 28-32, 1993.
[SWW94] N. Sabadini, R.F.C. Walters, Henry Weld, Categories of asynchronous circuits, Computing: Australian Theory Seminar, UTS, Sydney, 1994.
[S95] R.H. Street, Higher categories, strings, cubes and simplex equations, Applied Categorical Structures, 3, 29- 77, 1995.
[T95] Turaev, Quantum invariants of knots and 3-manifolds, Featured review in Mathematical Reviews MR:95k 57014.
[W89] R.F.C. Walters, Data types in a distributive category, Bull. Austr. Math. Soc., 40:79–82, 1989.
[W92a] R.F.C. Walters, Categories and Computer Science, Carslaw Publications 1991, Cambridge University Press 1992.
[W92b] R.F.C. Walters, An imperative language based on distributive categories, Mathematical Structures in Computer Science, 2:249–256, 1992.
[Z85] W. Zielonka, Notes on Finite Asynchronous Automata, RAIRO, 27, 99-135, 1985.

Representing Place/Transition Nets in Span(Graph)

Piergiulio Katis[1], N. Sabadini[2] and R.F.C. Walters[1]

[1] School of Mathematics and Statistics,
University of Sydney, N.S.W. 2006 , Australia
[2] Dipartimento di Scienze dell'Informazione,
Università di Milano, Via Comelico 39/41, I-20135 Milano MI, Italy

Abstract. The compact closed bicategory **Span** of spans of reflexive graphs is described and it is interpreted as an algebra for constructing specifications of concurrent systems. We describe a procedure for associating to any Place/Transition system Ω an expression Ψ_Ω in the algebra **Span**. The value of this expression is a system whose behaviours are the same as those of the P/T system. Furthermore, along the lines of Penrose's string diagrams, a geometry is associated to the expression Ψ_Ω which is essentially the same geometry as that usually associated to the net underlying Ω.

1 Introduction

This article is part of a project to study bicategories of processes ([KSW97a], [KSW97b],[BSW96],[K96],[KSW94],[SWW93]) in order to develop the algebraic foundations of concurrency. Much of this work has focused on deterministic systems and is closely related to the notion of a distributive automaton ([SW93]); in fact, a construction of elemetary nets using functional pulse circuits and synchronizers was given in [MSSW95]. This paper concerns itself only with nondeterministic systems. Though closely related, the resulting algebraic structures are not the same as in the deterministic case.

In the following section we describe an algebra **Span** for constructing specifications of communicating systems; the structure studied in this paper is that of a self-dual compact closed category ([KL80]). The algebra **Span** is actually a bicategory ([B67]) rather than a category. For the purposes of this paper, however, we will ignore the 2-cell structure; in particular, many of the equalities we state are in fact isomorphisms. A more detailed study of **Span** is given in [KSW97b], wherein other algebraic structures borne by this bicategory are described. Along the lines of Penrose's tensor diagrams ([P71]), we will associate a geometry to each expression of this algebra; such a geometry is to be interpreted as a depiction of the spatial distribution of a communicating system. For a detailed study of the geometry of tensor algebras, the reader is referred to [JS91] and [JSV96] – those familiar with these papers will notice that our diagrams are to be read from left to right rather than up the page.

In Section 3 the basic definitions concerning Place/Transition systems are recalled, after which two classes of spans are described: one that corresponds to the places of a P/T system and another that corresponds to the transitions. Given a P/T system Ω we define an expression Ψ_Ω in **Span** constructed from these two classes of spans such that the (states and) behaviours of Ψ_Ω are precisely those of Ω; furthermore, the geometry of the expression Ψ_Ω is equivalent to the geometry usually associated to the net underlying the P/T system Ω. Of course, not every expression constructed from these two classes of spans can be interpreted as a P/T system; we do, however, identify a class of expressions which do admit such interpretations. (Note that this use of algebra is different from the way monoidal categories were used in [MM90] to model Petri nets. In the aforementioned paper a net was defined to be a certain monoidal category; this paper uses a compact closed category to construct general nets.)

2 The algebra of spans

Recall that a reflexive graph is a directed graph with the extra structure that to each vertex v there is associated an edge $v \to v$; we call this edge the identity edge at v. Morphisms of reflexive graphs are morphisms of directed graphs which preserve identities. Let **RGraph** be the category of reflexive graphs.

We now begin describing the algebra **Span**. Its objects are one-vertex graphs – the reader may think of a one-vertex graph as an alphabet with a null symbol (the null symbol corresponding to the identity edge). Given two one-vertex graphs A and B, an arrow in **Span** from A to B is a diagram in **RGraph** of the form $A \xleftarrow{l} G \xrightarrow{r} B.$ This is called a *span* of graphs from A to B: the graph G (which is not necessarily a one-vertex graph) is called its *head* and l and r are respectively referred to as its left and right *legs*; we denote this arrow of **Span** by $G : A \to B$. Often a span will be given in the form where its domain and codomain are products of one-vertex graphs; for example, consider a span of the form $G : A \times B \to C \times D \times E$. We draw such a span as follows.

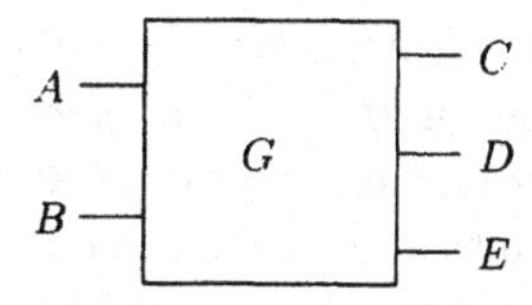

The objects A and B are called the *left boundaries* and C, D and E the *right boundaries* of G. Note that the span $G : A \times B \to C \times D \times E$ is just a labelling of G by $A \times B \times C \times D \times E$; in other words, it is a labelled transition system ([A94]) whose labelling is distributed among five alphabets. A more detailed comparison with existing work on transition systems is given in [KSW97b].

A *behaviour* of a span $G : A \to B$ is a finite path in the graph G. Notice that for each behaviour β of G there are corresponding behaviours (that is, sequences of letters) $l(\beta)$ and $r(\beta)$ of the boundaries A and B.

The first simple example of an 'agent' considered in [M89] is that of a message passer which can hold one datum. We would specify such a system by the span $M : A \to A$ pictured below. (Here, A is the one-vertex graph which has only one non-identity edge a.)

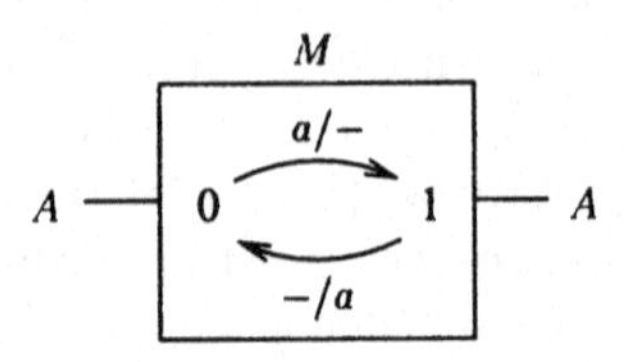

Notice that in depicting graphs we do not draw the identity edge at each vertex. The left and right legs are defined by the labelling of the edges. The symbol '−' denotes a labelling by the identity edge. The vertices (or states) 0 and 1 respectively correspond to the system having no data and having a datum. The edges $a/-$ and $-/a$ respectively correspond to the system receiving and sending a datum.

The first operation we define is *composition* (or series) of spans. Given two spans $G : A \to B$ and $H : B \to C$ their composite $G; H : A \to C$ is defined as follows. First form a diagram

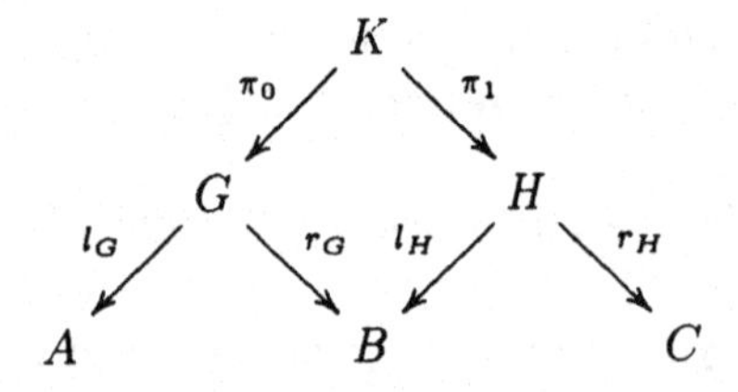

in **RGraph** having a pullback as its central square. The composite $G; H$ is $A \xleftarrow{l_G \cdot \pi_0} K \xrightarrow{r_H \cdot \pi_1} C.$ Explicitly, a vertex of $G; H$ is a pair (v, w) of vertices – a vertex v of G and vertex w of H. An edge of $G; H$ is a pair of edges (g, h) – g is an edge of G and h is an edge of H – which agree on their common boundary B. In this case, it would be reasonable to call B an interface between G and H. Later in this section we will introduce a more general notion of interface.

Composites are drawn in series. For example, the expression $M; M$ (that is, two message passers in series) is drawn as follows.

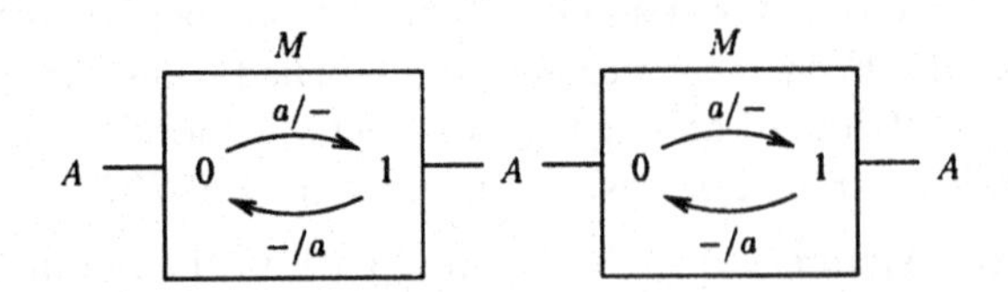

The value of the expression $M; M$ is the span depicted below.

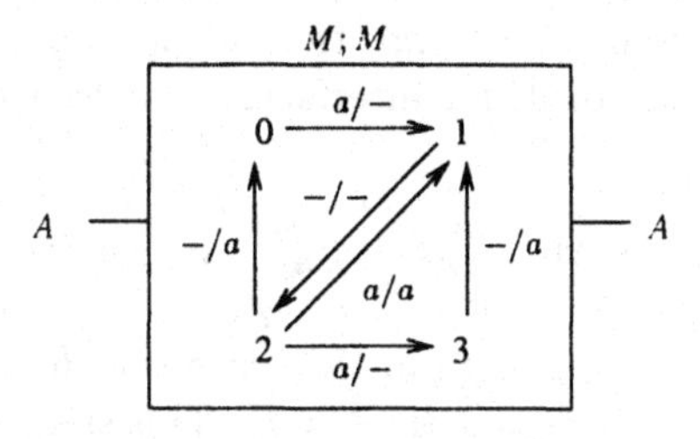

The states $0 = (0,0)$, $1 = (1,0)$, $2 = (0,1)$ and $3 = (1,1)$ respectively correspond to the system having no data, one datum in its first component, one datum in its second componenet and, lastly, two data items – one in each component. One interpretation of this system is that it specifies a bounded buffer of capacity two (that is, a message passer whose memory is a queue of length two).

It is perhaps worthwhile to point out that in general there is a distinction between an expression in an algebra and its value; in particular, many expressions may yield the same value. Most often, of course, we will want to record both the expression and its value.

The other operation we are going to define is the *tensor product* (or parallel). If A and B are objects of **Span** then their tensor product $A \otimes B$ is defined to be the product $A \times B$ of graphs in **RGraph** (this is, of course, also a one vertex graph). If $G : A \to B$ and $H : C \to D$ are spans, their tensor product $G \otimes H : A \otimes C \to B \otimes D$ is the span

$$A \times C \xleftarrow{l_G \times l_H} G \times H \xrightarrow{r_G \times r_H} B \times D.$$

Tensor products of spans are drawn in parallel. For example, the expression $M \otimes M : A \otimes A \to A \otimes A$ is drawn as follows.

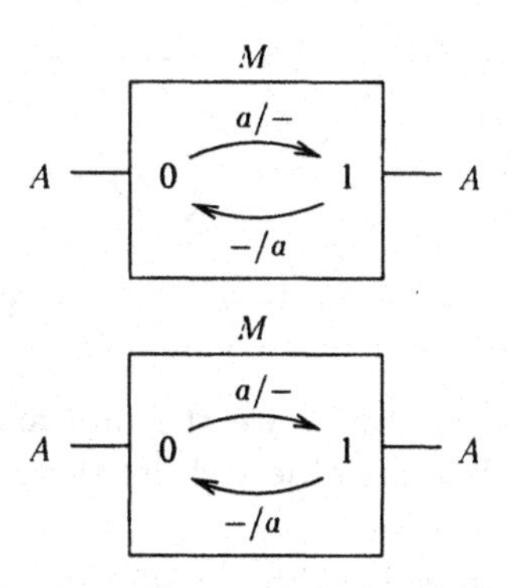

Let I be the terminal object of **RGraph**; that is, it is the one-vertex graph whose only edge is the identity edge. This object satisfies the property that $A \otimes I = A = I \otimes A$ and it plays the role of the 'null' boundary; note that to give a span $G : I \to I$ is just to give a graph G (since there is no information involved in giving the unique graph morphism $!_G : G \to I$). If a boundary of a span is I we usually omit it from the diagram.

We now introduce some constants; that is, special classes of spans. These constants will allow us to construct interfaces between more general spans.

For any object A, the span $A \xleftarrow{1_A} A \xrightarrow{1_A} A$ is denoted $1_A : A \to A$ or merely A. It is the *identity* for composition in the sense that for any $G : A \to B$ or any $H : C \to A$, we have $A; G = G$ and $H; A = H$. This span is drawn as a line from A to A.

The second type of constant we are going to define is a *permutation*. For any pair of objects A and B, there is a graph morphism tw $: A \times B \to B \times A : (a, b) \mapsto (b, a)$. The permutation $\pi_{A,B} : A \otimes B \to B \otimes A$ is defined to be the span

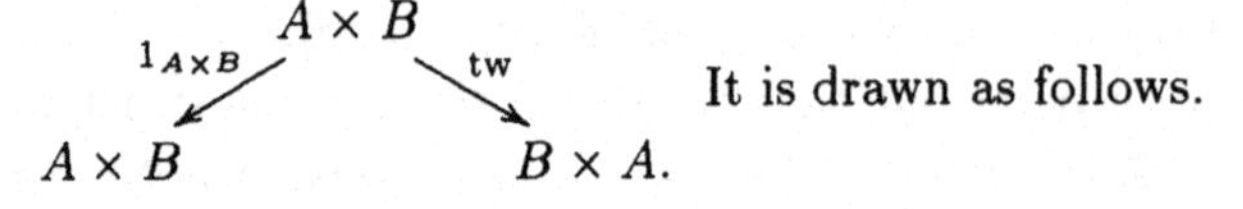

It is drawn as follows.

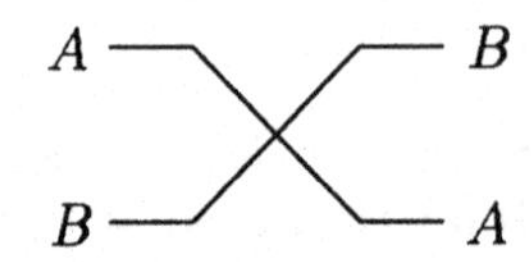

The crossing of the lines is not supposed to indicate that the boundaries A and B are in contact.

Given a bijective function $\pi : \{1, \ldots, n\} \to \{1, \ldots, n\}$ and objects $A_1, \ldots, A_n$, we can use spans of the form $\pi_{A,B}$ to construct a more general permutation $\pi : A_1 \otimes \ldots \otimes A_n \to A_{\pi(1)} \otimes \ldots \otimes A_{\pi(n)}$ in **Span**. For example, the following diagram depicts such a permutation.

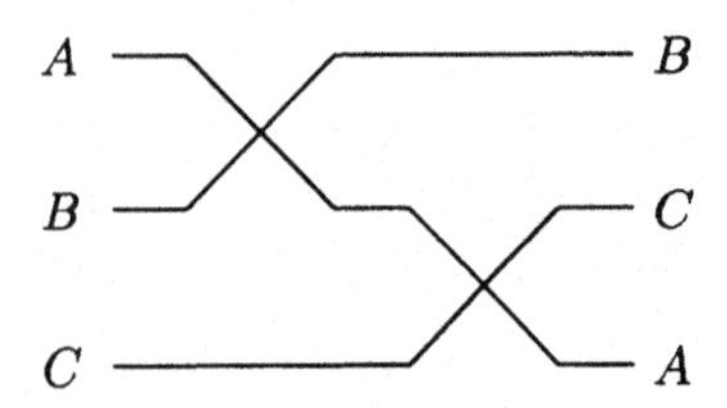

The final two types of constants are the *unit* and *counit* for the self-dual compact closed structure. For any object A, let the unit $\eta_A : I \to A \otimes A$ be the span $I \xleftarrow{!_A} A \xrightarrow{\Delta_A} A \times A$, where $!_A$ is the unique map to the terminal graph and $\Delta_A : A \to A \times A : a \mapsto (a, a)$ is the diagonal; also, let the counit $\epsilon_A : A \otimes A \to I$ be the span $A \times A \xleftarrow{\Delta_A} A \xrightarrow{!_A} I$. The spans η_A and ϵ_A are respectively drawn as follows.

In describing the compact closed structure of **Span** we have defined two operations and four types of constants. We will not give the axioms that these data must satisfy. (For this, the reader can see [KL80].) A remarkable consequence of these axioms is that any two expressions are equal if their geometries are equivalent. (Defining what is meant by geometrical equivalence would take us too far afield; the reader interested in pursuing this notion is referred to [JS91].) For example, for any $G : A \to B$ and $H : B \to C$, the equality $(A \otimes \eta_B); (G \otimes 1_B \otimes H); (\epsilon_B \otimes C) = G; H$ can be derived. In terms of diagrams we have the following equality. (The reader can check that they are the same in **Span**.)

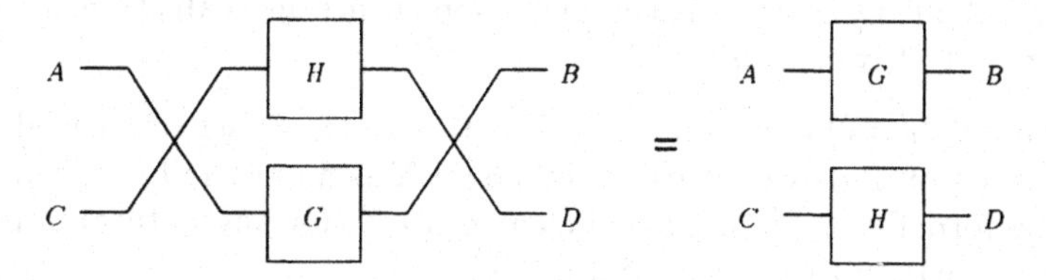

Another example of an equation that can be derived from the axioms is $\pi_{A,C}; H \otimes G; \pi_{D,B} = G \otimes H$. The corresponding equality of diagrams is depicted below.

A *concurrent system* comprising the spans $M_1, \ldots, M_n$ is defined to be an expression constructed from $M_1, \ldots, M_n$ and the constants described above using the operations composition and tensor product. Roughly speaking, the *interfaces* of a concurrent system are those parts of the system constructed from only the constants. We will not make this notion precise but give an example. In the concurrent system comprising G, H and K depicted below

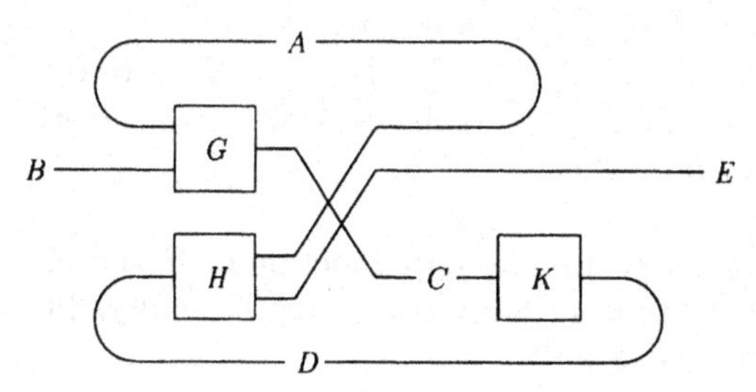

B and E are external interfaces (in fact, they are boundaries of the value of the concurrent system) and A, C and D are internal interfaces. A vertex of this system is a triple $(u, v, w) \in G \times H \times K$ of vertices; and an edge is a triple $(g, h, k) \in G \times H \times K$ of edges such that i) k and h agree on the interface D, ii) h and g agree on A and iii) g and k agree on C.

The reader may have noticed that our notion of interface is limited in that a boundary of a span can be in contact with at most one other boundary. In order to express a more general type of communication – in which a boundary can be in contact with several other boundaries – we need to consider the discrete Cartesian structure ([CW87]) of **Span** (from which the compact closed structure can be recaptured). This is described in [KSW97b].

3 Place/Transition systems and their representations

The following definition of a net is taken from [T86].

Definition 1. A *net* N is a quadruple (S, T, F, G) where
- S and T are non-empty finite sets and
- $F \subseteq S \times T$ and $G \subseteq T \times S$ are subsets

such that
- for all $s \in S$ there exists $t \in T$ such that $(s, t) \in F$ or $(t, s) \in G$ and
- for all $t \in T$ there exists $s \in S$ such that $(s, t) \in F$ or $(t, s) \in G$.

The set S is called the set of *places* of N (sometimes also called the set of states) and T, the set of *transitions* of N.

We adopt the following notation: $\aleph$ is the (ordered) set of natural numbers; $\aleph^{>0}$ is the set of positive natural numbers; if X is an ordered set then $X \cup \infty$ is formed by formally adjoining a top element to X; for any natural number n let $[n] = \{0, \ldots, n\}$; and we define $[\infty]$ to be $\aleph$.

The following definition is taken from [R86]; the reader will notice that we have not included the specification of an initial marking in our defintion of a P/T system.

Definition 2. A *Place/Transition* system Ω (often abbreviated to P/T system) is a sextuple (S, T, F, G, K, W) where
- the quadruple (S, T, F, G) is a net and
- $K : S \to \aleph^{>0} \cup \infty$ and $W : S \times T + T \times S \to \aleph$ are functions such that for all $s \in S$ and $t \in T$ we have i) $W(s, t) > 0 \Leftrightarrow (s, t) \in F$ and ii) $W(t, s) > 0 \Leftrightarrow (t, s) \in G$.

The function K is called the *capacity* function of Ω and W is called the *weight* function of Ω. Note that suitably restricting W will yield two functions $W_F : F \to \aleph^{>0}$ and $W_G : G \to \aleph^{>0}$.

An *elementary net* is a P/T system (S, T, F, G, K, W) such that K is the constant function whose value is 1 and W is bounded above by 1 (in other words, the value of W is always less than or equal to 1).

The following definitions introduce the concepts needed to define behaviours of a P/T system $\Omega = (S, T, F, G, K, W)$.

A *marking* M of Ω is a function $M : S \to \aleph$ such that for all $s \in S$ we have the inequality $M(s) \leq K(s)$.

A subset $R \subseteq T$ of transitions is said to be *enabled* at a marking M if for all $s \in S$

$$\sum_{t \in R} W(s,t) \leq M(s) \leq K(s) - \sum_{t \in R} W(t,s). \tag{1}$$

(Of course, the empty sum equals $0 \in \aleph$.)

A marking M is said to have been *produced* from a marking L by the *occurrence* of $R \subseteq T$ if

- the marking L enables R and
- for all $s \in S$ we have the equality

$$M(s) = L(s) + \sum_{t \in R} (W(t,s) - W(s,t)). \tag{2}$$

Notice that requiring L to enable R guarantees that M is a marking. In the case of such an occurrence of R, it is usually said that the transitions $r \in R$ have *concurrently fired.*

The *state-space* of Ω is the reflexive graph $\mathcal{S}_\Omega$ defined as follows: its set of vertices is the set of markings of Ω; and an edge from L to M is a triple (L, R, M) where M is produced from L by the occurrence of $R \subseteq T$. The identity edge at M is $(M, \emptyset, M)$.

A behaviour of Ω is a finite path in $\mathcal{S}_\Omega$ – that is, a behaviour of the span $\mathcal{S}_\Omega : I \to I$ (as defined in the previous section).

Most often, P/T systems are given with a specified marking; this marking is interpreted as the initial state of the system. Of course, behaviours of such systems are paths beginning at the specified marking.

For any P/T system Ω we will construct a concurrent system Ψ_Ω (that is, a term in the algebra **Span**) such that the span $\mathcal{S}_\Omega : I \to I$ equals the value of Ψ_Ω.

First, we define a class of spans which will play the role of the places of a P/T system.

Let $\mathcal{N}$ be the one vertex reflexive graph whose set of edges is $\aleph$, the element $0 \in \aleph$ being the identity edge of $\mathcal{N}$.

Let U and V be finite sets and suppose $n \in \aleph^{>0} \cup \infty$. Define the reflexive graph $X_{U,V,n}$ as follows. Its set of vertices is $[n]$. An edge from the vertex $i \in [n]$

to the vertex $j \in [n]$ is a quadruple $(i, \mathbf{x}, \mathbf{y}, j)$ where $\mathbf{x} = (x_u)_{u \in U} \in \aleph^U$ and $\mathbf{y} = (y_v)_{v \in V} \in \aleph^V$ are tuples of natural numbers such that

$$\sum_{v \in V} y_v \leq i \leq n - \sum_{u \in U} x_u \tag{3}$$

and

$$j = i + \sum_{u \in U} x_u - \sum_{v \in V} y_v . \tag{4}$$

We define the span $\mu_{U,V,n} : \mathcal{N}^U \to \mathcal{N}^V$ to be

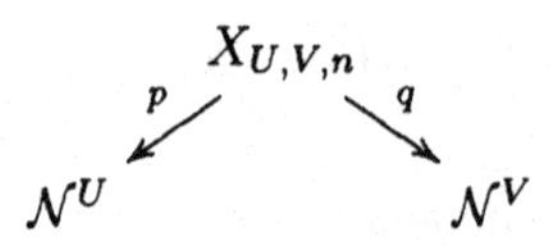

where $p(i, \mathbf{x}, \mathbf{y}, j) = \mathbf{x}$ and $q(i, \mathbf{x}, \mathbf{y}, j) = \mathbf{y}$.

We will draw these spans as circles. For example, the following is a depiction of an edge in such a system where $|U| = 2$ and $|V| = 3$.

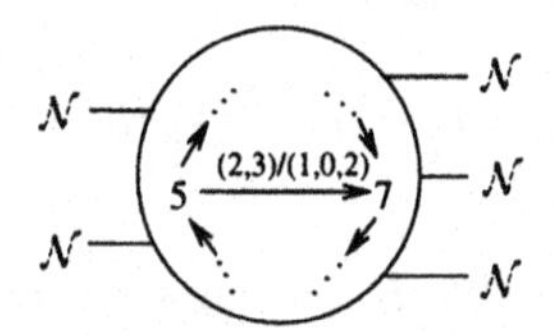

Notice that if $|U| = 1$ and $|V| = 1$ then $X_{U,V,1}$ is (the head of) the message passer M defined in the previous section.

We now define a class of spans which will play the role of the transitions in a P/T system.

Let E be the one vertex graph with only one non-identity edge e. Given finite sets U and V as well as tuples of natural numbers $\mathbf{x} \in \aleph^U$ and $\mathbf{y} \in \aleph^V$, let $\tau_{U,V,\mathbf{x},\mathbf{y}} : \mathcal{N}^U \to \mathcal{N}^V$ be the span

$$\mathcal{N}^U \xleftarrow{\;p\;} E \xrightarrow{\;q\;} \mathcal{N}^V$$

where $p(e) = \mathbf{x}$ and $q(e) = \mathbf{y}$.

When drawing such spans we will use squares and their boundaries will be labelled with the vectors $\mathbf{x}$ and $\mathbf{y}$. For example, if $\mathbf{x} = (1, 2)$ and $\mathbf{y} = (3, 4, 5)$ then we would draw $\tau_{U,V,\mathbf{x},\mathbf{y}}$ as follows.

$\mathcal{N}$ —1— [ ] —3— $\mathcal{N}$
$\mathcal{N}$ —2— [ ] —4— $\mathcal{N}$
—5— $\mathcal{N}$

Let $\Omega = (S, T, F, G, K, W)$ be a P/T system.

In order to facilitate describing Ψ_Ω we make the following definitions: for all $s \in S$ let $F(s,-) = \{t \in T \mid (s,t) \in F\}$ and $G(-,s) = \{t \in T \mid (t,s) \in G\}$; and for all $t \in T$ let $F(-,t) = \{s \in S \mid (s,t) \in F\}$ and $G(t,-) = \{s \in S \mid (t,s) \in G\}$.

For each place $s \in S$ let μ_s be the span

$$\mu_{G(-,s),F(s,-),K(s)} : \mathcal{N}^{G(-,s)} \rightarrow \mathcal{N}^{F(s,-)}.$$

For each transition $t \in T$ let $\mathbf{x} \in \aleph^{F(-,t)}$ be the tuple given by the function $F(-,t) \rightarrow \aleph : s \mapsto W_F(s,t)$ and let $\mathbf{y} \in \aleph^{G(t,-)}$ be the tuple determined by the function $G(t,-) \rightarrow \aleph : s \mapsto W_G(t,s)$. Define τ_t to be the span

$$\tau_{F(-,t),G(t,-),\mathbf{x},\mathbf{y}} : \mathcal{N}^{F(-,t)} \rightarrow \mathcal{N}^{G(t,-)}.$$

Let σ denote the permutation $\prod_{s \in S} \mathcal{N}^{F(s,-)} \cong \prod_{t \in T} \mathcal{N}^{F(-,t)}$ and let σ' denote the permutation $\prod_{t \in T} \mathcal{N}^{G(t,-)} \cong \prod_{s \in S} \mathcal{N}^{G(-,s)}$.

Let $n = |\sum_{s \in S} G(-,s)|$, $\eta = \eta_{\mathcal{N}^n} : I \rightarrow \mathcal{N}^n \otimes \mathcal{N}^n$ and $\epsilon = \epsilon_{\mathcal{N}^n} : \mathcal{N}^n \otimes \mathcal{N}^n \rightarrow I$. The concurrent system Ψ_Ω is defined to be the expression

$$\eta; (\mathcal{N}^n \otimes ((\prod_{s \in S} \mu_s); \sigma; (\prod_{t \in T} \tau_t); \sigma')); \epsilon \ : \ I \rightarrow I.$$

Theorem *The state-space $S_\Omega : I \rightarrow I$ is the value of the expression Ψ_Ω. Hence the behaviours of the net Ω and the concurrent system Ψ_Ω coincide.*

Before proving this theorem, let us consider an example. Below we depict the elementary net Ω (called mutex) which is often used to model a situation of mutual exclusion.

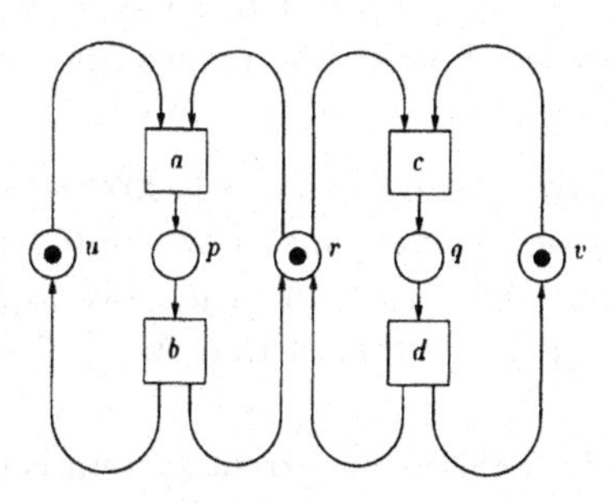

In this picture, the squares correspond to transitions and the circles to places. All the arcs are weighted by 1 and the dots represent the initial marking. The places u and v represent two users trying to gain access to the same resource r; when the place p is marked, u is using the resource, and when q is marked, v has access to it. We now draw the expression Ψ_Ω. (Some liberty has been taken in depicting the constants.)

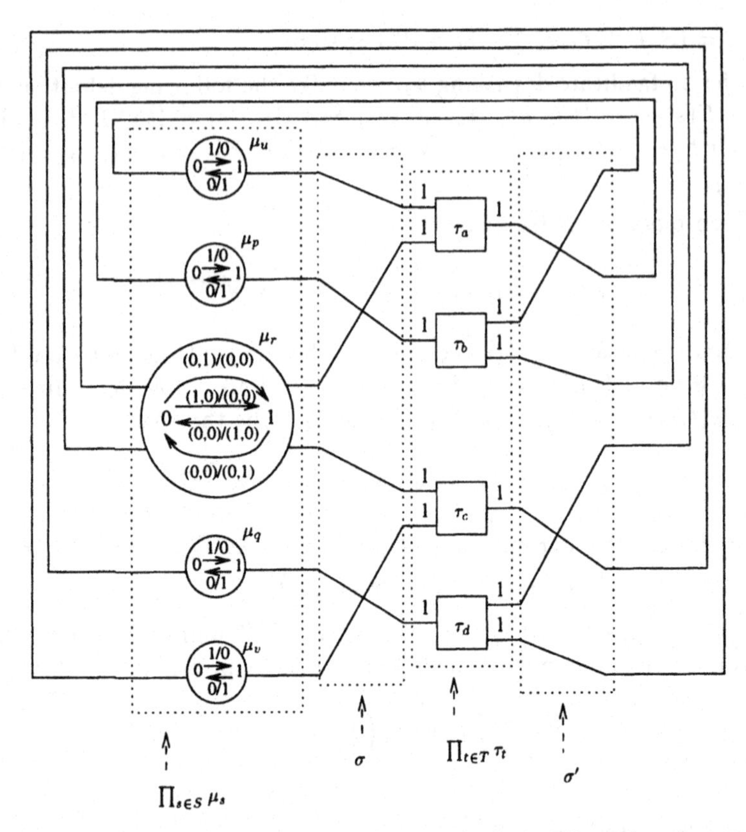

The geometries of the two pictures are equivalent. That the picture for Ψ_Ω appears more complicated is because, in order to state a theorem such as the one above, the geometry of the system must be in a normal form. Of course, the picture of a P/T system has extra information in that it describes a marking – that is, a state of the system. For instance, the initial marking of mutex corresponds to the state $(u, p, r, q, v) = (1, 0, 1, 0, 1)$ of Ψ_Ω.

When reading the following proof, the reader may wish to particularize the argument to the above example.

Proof of Theorem To give a vertex of Ψ_Ω is to give a vertex of each component of the system. The only components which have more than one vertex are those of the form μ_s. Recall that the vertex-set of μ_s is $[K(s)]$. So to give a vertex of Ψ_Ω is to give a function $M : S \to \aleph$ such that $M(s) \leq K(s)$. This is, of course, a marking of Ω.

Recall that to give an edge of a concurrent system is to give a family of edges (e_c) – one edge for each component c of the system – which are compatible on the interfaces. Consider a candidate for an edge of Ψ_Ω; that is, a family of edges $e = (e_c)_{c\in S+T}$. Let $T(e) \subseteq T$ comprise those transitions $t \in T$ such that e_t is a non-identity edge; recall that (the head of) τ_t has one identity edge and one non-identity edge.

The claim is that a family of edges $e = (e_c)_{c\in S+T}$ defines an edge in Ψ_Ω from L to M if and only if M is produced from L by the occurrence of $T(e) \subseteq T$.

Suppose $e = (e_c)_{c \in S+T}$ defines an edge in Ψ_Ω from L to M. For each $t \in T(e)$ the edge e_t of $\tau_t : \mathcal{N}^{F(-,t)} \to \mathcal{N}^{G(t,-)}$ is labelled $((W(s,t))_{s \in F(-,t)}/(W(t,s))_{s \in G(t,-)})$. For all other $t \in T \setminus T(e)$, the edge e_t is the identity and hence labelled by only zeros.

Let $s \in S$. Recall that the edge $e_s \in \mu_s$ is labelled $\mathbf{x}/\mathbf{y} : L(s) \to M(s)$ where $\mathbf{x} = (x_t) \in \mathcal{N}^{G(-,s)}$ and $\mathbf{y} = (y_t) \in \mathcal{N}^{F(s,-)}$. The family of edges $e = (e_c)_{c \in S+T}$ must be compatible on the interfaces; therefore, $x_t = W(t,s)$ and $y_t = W(s,t)$ if $t \in T(e)$, while $x_t = y_t = 0$ if $t \in T \setminus T(e)$. So, $\sum_{t \in G(-,s)} x_t = \sum_{t \in T(e)} W(t,s)$ and $\sum_{t \in F(s,-)} y_t = \sum_{t \in T(e)} W(s,t)$. It is clear then that conditions 3 and 4 (given in the definition of μ) imply the conditions 1 and 2 ensuring that the occurrence of $T(e)$ produces M from L.

Now suppose that M is produced from L by the occurrence of $R \subseteq T$. Define a family of edges $e = (e_c)_{c \in S+T}$ as follows. For each $t \in T$ the edge $e_t \in \tau_t$ is the non-identity edge if and only if $t \in R$. For each $s \in S$, the edge e_s is labelled $(x_t)_{t \in G(-,s)}/(y_t)_{t \in F(s,-)}$ where $x_t = W(t,s)$ if $t \in R$, $x_t = 0$ if $t \in T \setminus R$, $y_t = W(s,t)$ if $t \in R$ and $y_t = 0$ if $t \in T \setminus R$. Conditions 1 and 2 guarantee that there is such an edge $e_s : L(s) \to M(s)$ in μ_s. It is straightforward to see this family of edges is compatible on the interfaces and that $T(e) = R$.

□

Of course, there are expressions in **Span** which will not admit interpretations as P/T systems; for example, consider a single place $\mu_{U,V,n}$. It is easy, however, to identify a class of expressions for which such an interpretation is possible. Let Φ be a concurrent system comprising only spans $\mu_{U,V,n}$ (places) and $\tau_{U,V,\mathbf{x},\mathbf{y}}$ (transitions) such that each boundary of a place is in contact with the boundary of a transition and each boundary of a transition is in contact with the boundary of a place. It is clear that there is a net Ω such that the value of Ψ_Ω equals (actually, is isomorphic to) the value of Φ.

4 Final Remarks

Although we have shown how P/T systems can be constructed in a modular (that is, compositional) fashion from spans, we do not propose that **Span** be used to model concurrent systems in this way. The theory of Petri nets and the later developed P/T systems do not make a distinction between the places of a system and the states of a system – indeed, they are consciously blurred. In contrast to this, the calculus of spans does make a distinction between the *underlying geometry* of a system – which depicts the components of a system and their interfaces – and the *state-space* of each part of the system.

As an example, we would model the instance of mutual exclusion by the following expression Υ in **Span**. (The object A has non-identity edges a and b, and the object C has non-identity edges c and d.)

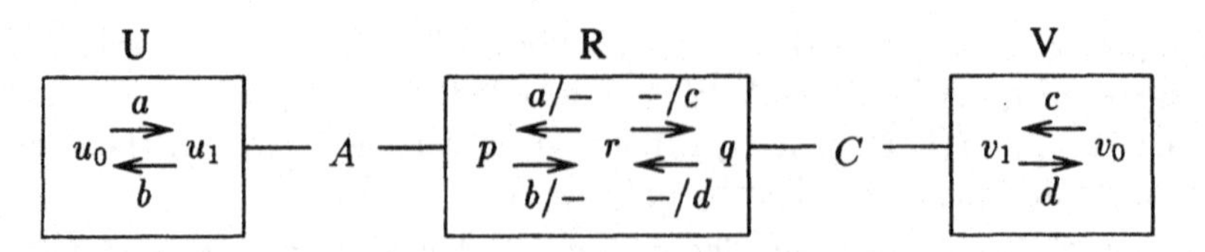

In the system there are three components: $U : I \to A$, $R : A \to C$ and $V : C \to I$. The interpretation of the states are as follows. When users U or V are respectively in states u_0 or v_0 they are not using the resource, while when in states u_1 or v_1 they do have access to it. When resource R is in state r, it is being used by no-one; when it is in state p, it is being used by some user connected to its left boundary – in Υ this user is U; and when R is in state q, it is being used by a user attatched to its right boundary – in this case, the user V. Here, a component plays the role of a place and an edge in the state-space of a component (which may have to synchronise on a boundary) plays the role of a transition. Notice that if Υ begins in state (u_0, r, v_0) then it has the same set of behaviours as mutex.

Compare the above picture with the net depicting mutex. The diagram of Υ has two levels of structure: one depicting the underlying geometry of the system (which is particularly simple) and the other, the state-spaces of the components. The picture of the net mutex can be thought of as a flattened version of the 'two-level geometry' depicting the concurrent system Υ. Also notice that the size of the state-space of (the value of) Υ is $2 \times 3 \times 2$, while the size of the state-space of mutex is 2^5.

The bicategorical structure of **Span** has not been discussed in this paper; it is, however, a fundamental part of the algebra's structure. In particular, it permits the development of a compositional theory of refinement and abstraction. This aspect of the theory will be treated by the authors elsewhere, wherein a comparison with bisimulation ([A93], [CS94], [JNW93]) will be given.

An important concept in net theory is that of hierarchy: roughly speaking, a hierarchical structure associates a net to a transition of a net. Though this is related to the notion of refinement mentioned in the preceeding paragraph, we would like express hierarchy in terms of the operations of our algebra. Given an expression in **Span**, built from the operations described in Section 2, we can replace any component of it by another expression. By doing this we are refining the underlying space of the system. We would like to do more: namely, refine both the underlying space as well as the state-space. This can be done by introducing more operations, the relevant operations coming from the algebra of *cospans* of graphs. (A cospan in a category $\mathbf{E}$ is a span in $\mathbf{E}^{\mathrm{op}}$.) An algebra which combines spans and cospans in order to express hierarchy will be defined in a future paper.

A span of graphs is a very abstract specification of a system, just as is a net. In modelling any real system one needs to specify quantities such as data-types. Two ways of achieving this in net theory are to use Predicate/Transition nets ([G86]) or coloured nets ([J86]). The bicategory **Span**, however, is closely related to the notion of a bicategory of processes in a distributive category, as defined in [KSW97a] – these processes in a distributive category being closely related to distributive automata ([SW93]) which have been constructed from data-types in a distributive category ([W92a],[W92b]). The way in which **Span** can be used to specify concurrent systems constructed from such data-types will also be described elsewhere.

5 Bibliography

[A93] Abramsky S., Interaction Categories (extended abstract), in: Theory and Formal Methods Workshop, Springer-Verlag (1993).

[A94] A. Arnold, Finite transition systems, Prentice Hall, 1994.

[B67] J. Bènabou, Introduction to bicategories, in: Reports of the Midwest Category Seminar, Lecture Notes in Mathematics 47, pages 1–77, Springer-Verlag, 1967.

[BSW96] Bloom S., Sabadini N, Walters RFC, Matrices, machines and behaviors, Applied Categorical Structures 4 (1996) 343-360.

[CS94] Cockett J.R.B. and Spooner D.A., SProc Categorically, in: Proceedings of CONCUR '94, Springer-Verlag (1994).

[CW87] A. Carboni and R.F.C. Walters, Cartesian Bicategories I, Journal of Pure and Applied Algebra, 49, pages 11-32, 1987.

[G86] Genrich H.J., Predicate/Transition nets, in: Petri nets, LNCS 254 Springer-Verlag (1986) 207-247.

[J86] Jensen K., Coloured Petri nets, in: Petri nets, LNCS 254 Springer-Verlag (1986) 248-299.

[JNW93] Joyal A., Nielsen M. and Winskel G., Bisimulation and open maps, in: Proceedings of the Eight Symposium on Logic in Computer Science, IEEE (1993).

[JS91] Joyal A. and Street R., The geometry of tensor calculus I, in: Advances in Math. 88 (1991) 55-113.

[JSV96] Joyal A., Street R. and Verity D., Traced monoidal categories, in: Math. Proc. Camb. Phil. Soc. 119 (1996) 447-468.

[K96] Katis P., Categories and bicategories of processes, PhD Thesis, University of Sydney (1996).

[KSW94] Katis P, Sabadini N, Walters RFC, The bicategory of circuits, Computing: Australian Theory Seminar, UTS, Sydney (1994).

[KSW97a] Katis P, Sabadini N, Walters RFC, Bicategories of processes, Journal of Pure and Applied Algebra, 115, no.2, pp 141 - 178, 1997.

[KSW97b] Katis P, Sabadini N, Walters RFC, Span(Graph): A categorical algebra of transition systems, LLNCS (this volume).

[KL80] Kelly G.M. and Laplaza M.L., Coherence for compact closed categories, in: Journal of Pure and Applied Algebra 19 (1980) 193-213.

[M70] S. Mac Lane, Categories for the working mathematician, Springer Verlag, 1970.

[M89] Milner R., Communication and Concurrency, Prentice Hall International (1989).
[MM90] Meseguer J. and Montanari U., Petri nets are monoids, in: Information and Computation, 88 (2) 105-155 (1990).
[MSSW95] Mauri G., Sabadini N., Shammah S. and Walters R.F.C., On distributive automata, asynchronous automata and Petri nets, Preprint, 1995.
[P71] R. Penrose, Applications of negative dimensional torsors, in Combinatorial Mathematics and its applications, (D. J. A. Welsh, Ed.) pp. 221-244, Academic Press, New York, 1971.
[R86] Reisig W., Place/Transition systems, in: Petri nets, LNCS 254 Springer-Verlag (1986) 117-141.
[SW93] Sabadini N. and Walters R.F.C., On functions and processors: an automata-theoretic approach to concurrency through distributive categories, School of Mathematics and Statistics Research Reports, University of Sydney, (93-7), 1993.
[SWW93] Sabadini N., Walters R.F.C., Weld Henry, Distributive automata and asynchronous circuits, Category Theory and Computer Science 5, Amsterdam, 28-32, 1993.
[SW93] N. Sabadini and R.F.C. Walters, On functions and processors: an automata-theoretic approach to concurrency through distributive categories, School of Mathematics and Statistics Research Reports, University of Sydney, (93-7), 1993.
[T86] Thiagarajan P. S., Elementary net systems, in: Petri nets, LNCS 254 Springer-Verlag (1986) 26-59.
[W92a] R.F.C. Walters, Categories and Computer Science, Carslaw Publications 1991, Cambridge University Press 1992.
[W92b] R.F.C. Walters, An imperative language based on distributive categories, Mathematical Structures in Computer Science, 2:249–256, 1992.

Invariants of Parameterized Binary Tree Networks as Greatest Fixpoints

David Lesens
VERIMAG *
Centre Equation - 2, avenue de Vignate, F-38610 Gières, France
e-mail: David.Lesens@imag.fr

Abstract. This paper describes a method to verify safety properties of parameterized binary tree networks of processes. The method is based on the construction of a network invariant, defined as a fixpoint. Since least fixpoints did not give satisfactory results, backward computation of greatest fixpoints is explored, and a technique of computation based on heuristics is proposed. This technique has been implemented and two examples are presented.

Keywords: computer-aided verification, parameterized networks, synchronous observers.

1 Introduction

After the very first success of automatic verification of finite state systems [QS82, CES86], Apt and Kozen [AK86] have shown that these techniques cannot be applied to infinite sets of processes. More formally, given a family $\mathcal{F} = \{P_i\}_{i=1}^{\infty}$ of processes, the problem of verifying that every $P_i \in \mathcal{F}$ satisfies a property φ is undecidable [AK86], even if it is decidable for each $P_i, i \geq 1$.

Decidable subcases have been identified [EN95, EN96], but they are quite restrictive. Several attempts [KM89, WL89, HLR92] were made to solve the general case, using the following induction principle: let $\preceq$ be a pre-order relation over processes, such that

$$(P \preceq Q \wedge Q \models \varphi) \implies P \models \varphi$$

Find a process I, called a *network invariant*, such that $\forall i \geq 1,\ P_i \preceq I$. Then, $I \models \varphi \implies \forall P_i \in \mathcal{F}, P_i \models \varphi$. The drawback of this technique is that the invariant I has generally to be constructed manually.

For some subcases, techniques have been developed to compute automatically invariants. In [MG91, SG89], *context-free network grammars* are used to generate infinite families with multiple repetitive components. Such a grammar is a tuple $\mathcal{G} = < T, N, \mathcal{P}, S >$ where:

- T is a set of terminals, i.e., a set of finite state processes.
- N is a set of non-terminals. Each non-terminal defines a network.
- $\mathcal{P}$ is a set of production rules of the form $A \rightarrow B \times C$, where $A \in N$, and $B, C \in T \cup N$, and $\times$ is a composition operator.
- $S \in N$ is the start symbol that represents the network generated by the grammar. The set $\mathcal{F}$ of processes generated by the grammar is equal to the set of processes generated by the non-terminal S.

In this framework, the induction principle is the following: for each non-terminal $P \in N$, find an invariant I_P such that, for each production rule $A \rightarrow B \times C$, one has

$$I_B \times I_C \preceq I_A$$

(where $I_P = P$ when P is terminal). Then, $I_S \models \varphi \implies \forall P \in \mathcal{F}, P \models \varphi$.

In [CGJ95], each production rule is seen as a least fixpoint equation. Then, they propose an extrapolation method, based on the construction of the syntactic monoid [Eil74] of a regular language, to compute each invariant.

In [LHR97], we considered the linear case where, for each production rule $A \rightarrow B \times C$, either B or C is terminal. To avoid the state explosion of the forward computation, each production rule is seen

*Verimag is a joint laboratory of CNRS, Institut National Polytechnique de Grenoble, Université J. Fourier and Verilog SA associated with IMAG. http://www.imag.fr/VERIMAG/PEOPLE/David.Lesens

as a greatest fixpoint equation. Then, we proposed an extrapolation technique, based on automata and inspired by Cousot's widening operators [CC77, CC92], to compute each invariant.

In this paper, we extend the backward computation to *binary tree networks*. Let $\{P_1, \ldots, P_k\}$ be a finite multi-set of processes, and $\times$ be a binary composition operator over processes. A binary tree network is a family $\mathcal{F}$ of processes generated by:

$$(\forall i = 1 \ldots k,\ P_i \in \mathcal{F}) \quad \text{and} \quad (P', P'' \in \mathcal{F} \Longrightarrow P' \times P'' \in \mathcal{F})$$

Following [LHR97], we have to search for a network invariant I such that

$$(\forall i = 1 \ldots k,\ P_i \preceq I) \quad \text{and} \quad (I \times I \preceq I)$$

The invariant I will be expressed as a greatest fixpoint, which will be computed with the help of extrapolation techniques. For the time being, we restrict ourselves to safety properties, and we use trace inclusion pre-order. Notice that our method can be easily extended to the general case of network grammars.

The paper is organized as follows. In section 2, we define the basic notions, including network observers. Section 3 extends the forward computation of least fixpoints to tree networks. Section 4 and 5 state and solve this problem as the backward computation of greatest fixpoints. In section 6, our method is applied to some examples.

2 Basic Definitions

2.1 Traces and Processes

The model of process we have in mind is that of synchronous languages [Hal93], like ESTEREL [BG92], ARGOS [Mar92], STATECHARTS [Har87], or LUSTRE [HCRP91]. A behavior of a process is a sequence of steps, each step resulting in an *event*, i.e., a set of present *signals*[1]. So, if X is a set of signals, we define a *trace* on X to be a (finite or infinite) sequence $\tau = (\tau_0, \ldots, \tau_n, \ldots)$ of subsets of X. Let Θ_X denote the set of traces on X.

We will not define a very precise notion of process. We just need to define the semantics of a process P to be the set T_P of its traces. Since we are only interested in safety properties, we will assume T_P to be prefix-closed. P is *regular* if T_P is a regular language.

Let X and X' be two disjoint sets of signals, and $\tau \in \Theta_X$ and $\tau' \in \Theta_{X'}$ be two traces of the same length. Then, $\tau \odot \tau'$ is a trace on $X \cup X'$, defined by

$$\tau \odot \tau' = (\tau_0 \cup \tau'_0, \ldots, \tau_n \cup \tau'_n, \ldots)$$

This operation is extended to sets of traces: let $T \subseteq \Theta_X$ and $T' \subseteq \Theta_{X'}$ be two sets of traces, then

$$T \odot T' = \{\tau \odot \tau' \mid \tau \in T, \tau' \in T', |\tau| = |\tau'|\}$$

For instance, $T_{P'} \odot T_{P''}$ will be the set of traces of the synchronous composition of two independent (i.e., not sharing signals) processes P' and P''. We will often write $T \odot \Theta_{X'}$ to consider T as a subset of $\Theta_{X \cup X'}$, where the signals of X' are left unconstrained.

Let X and X' be two sets of signals of the same cardinality related to each other by a one-one mapping ϕ. Then, for each trace $\tau = (\tau_0, \ldots, \tau_n, \ldots)$ on X, $\tau[X/X']$ is the trace $(\tau'_0, \ldots, \tau'_n, \ldots)$ on X' defined by $\tau'_i = \{\phi(x) \mid x \in \tau_i\}$. This operation is also extended to sets of traces.

Let X and X' be two sets of signals, $T \subseteq \Theta_X$, $T' \subseteq \Theta_{X'}$ be two sets of traces. Then

$$T \otimes T' = (T \odot \Theta_{(X' \setminus X)}) \cap (T' \odot \Theta_{(X \setminus X')})$$

i.e., $T \otimes T'$ is the set of traces that agree on signals in $X \cap X'$. For instance, $T_{P'} \otimes T_{P''}$ represents the traces of the synchronous product of two processes P' and P'', possibly communicating (by means of shared signals). We define also

$$T \oplus T' = (T \odot \Theta_{(X' \setminus X)}) \cup (T' \odot \Theta_{(X \setminus X')})$$

i.e., the union of T and T' as subsets of $\Theta_{(X \cup X')}$.

Let $T \subseteq \Theta_X$ be a set of traces, and Y be a subset of X. Then $\exists Y, T$ and $\forall Y, T$ are sets of traces on $X \setminus Y$ defined by

[1] In practice, these signals are partitioned into *input* signals (emitted by the environment) and *output* signals, emitted by the process, but, in general, we will not need to make this distinction.

$$\exists Y, T = \{\tau \in \Theta_{X \setminus Y} \mid \exists \tau' \in \Theta_Y \text{ such that } \tau \odot \tau' \in T\}$$
$$\forall Y, T = \{\tau \in \Theta_{X \setminus Y} \mid \forall \tau' \in \Theta_Y, (|\tau| = |\tau'|) \Rightarrow (\tau \odot \tau' \in T)\}$$

For instance, $\exists Y, T_P$ is the set of traces of a process P where all signals in Y are considered internal (hiding). $\forall Y, T$ will be considered for duality, as $\forall Y, T = \Theta_X \setminus (\exists Y, \Theta_X \setminus T)$.

Example: Let $X = \{a, b\}$. Let us use boolean notations to write sets of subsets of X — e.g., writing $\overline{a}$ for $\{\ \{\}, \{b\}\ \}$ — and the standard notations of regular expressions to denote sets of traces on X. Let $T = (\overline{a})^* + (\overline{a}\overline{b}.ab)^*$. Then

$$\exists b, T \;=\; (\overline{a})^* + (\overline{a}.a)^* \quad \text{and} \quad \forall b, T \;=\; (\overline{a})^*$$

□

2.2 Properties and Network Observers

A *safety property* φ on the set of signals X is also a prefix-closed subset of Θ_X. With such a property φ, we associate a process Ω_φ, called an *observer* [HLR93] of φ. Intuitively, Ω_φ can read all the signals in X, and emits an "alarm signal" $\alpha \notin X$ whenever the input trace received so far does not belong to φ. Thus a process P satisfies the property φ if and only if its synchronous product with Ω_φ never emits α.

Observers are naturally extended to networks in the following way [LHR97]: with each process in the network one associates an observer, reading the input/output behavior of the process together with observations provided by a finite number of other observers in the network. For instance, let us consider a binary tree network of identical processes, each of which emitting some signal u when it uses some resource. Assume we want to express the mutual exclusion property, that at most one process uses the resource at a given instant.

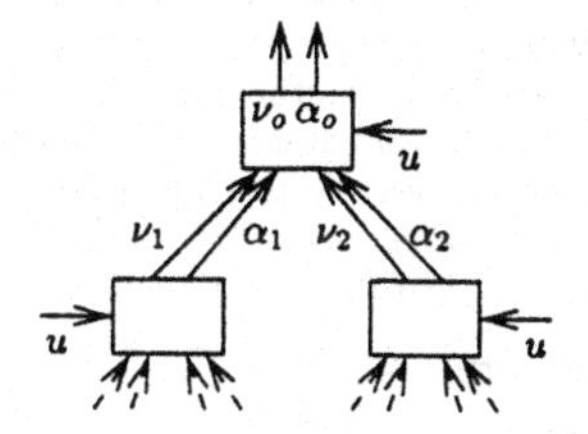

Figure 1: Network observers

Each process is given an observer, receiving the u signal of the process and the signals emitted by its "child observers" (see Fig 1). Each observer emits two signals: α is emitted whenever a violation of the mutual exclusion is detected, and ν is emitted whenever the resource is used either by the process or by one of its children. Such an observer can be described by the following system of Boolean equations:

$$\alpha_o \;=\; \alpha_1 \vee \alpha_2 \vee (\nu_1 \wedge \nu_2) \vee ((\nu_1 \vee \nu_2) \wedge u) \quad \text{and} \quad \nu_o \;=\; \nu_1 \vee \nu_2 \vee u$$

3 Network Invariants as Least Fixpoints

Thanks to the preceding section, we can assume that each P_i contains its local observer, and that all the networks in the family have the same set of external signals, say X (with $\alpha \in X$).
Let $C \subseteq \Theta_{X \cup X' \cup X''}$ be a set of traces such that

$$T_{P' \times P''} = \exists X', \exists X'', C \otimes T_{P'}[X/X'] \otimes T_{P''}[X/X'']$$

where X' and X'' are two sets of signals in one-one correspondence with X, and X, X', X'' are pairwise disjoint. Intuitively, C expresses the relation between the external signals of P' (renamed as X'), the external signals of P'' (renamed as X'') and the external signals X of $P' \times P''$.

Let $S = \Theta_{X \setminus \{\alpha\}}$ be the set of traces which never emit the "alarm" signal α. Our parameterized verification problem consists in showing: $\forall P \in \mathcal{F}$, $T_P \subseteq S$. Following [WL89, LHR97], we can look for a process I, called a *network invariant*, satisfying

[SAT] $T_I \subseteq S$
[INIT] $\forall i = 1 \ldots k,\ T_{P_i} \subseteq T_I$
[INDUC] $T_{I \times I} \subseteq T_I$ or, equivalently,
$(\exists X', \exists X'',\ C \otimes T_I[X/X'] \otimes T_I[X/X'']) \subseteq T_I$

Proposition 1 *There is a least set of traces T_I^m satisfying both* [INIT] *and* [INDUC]*. T_I^m is the least fixpoint of a monotone function F_1.*

Proof: Let us rewrite *[INDUC]* as: $f(T_I) \subseteq T_I$. The conjunction with *[INIT]* gives

$$F_1(T_I) \triangleq f(T_I) \cup \bigcup_{i=1}^{k} T_{P_i} \subseteq T_I$$

This means that T_I is a post-fixpoint of the (monotone) function F_1. There is a least solution, T_I^m, which is the least fixpoint of F_1. □

So, our verification problem is equivalent to showing $T_I^m \subseteq S$, where

$$T_I^m = \bigcup_{n \geq 0} F_1^{(n)}(\emptyset) \quad \text{and} \quad F_1 = \lambda T. \left(\bigcup_{i=1}^{k} T_{P_i} \right) \cup (\ \exists X', \exists X'',\ C \otimes T[X/X'] \otimes T[X/X''] \ )$$

Example: We present here a very simple algorithm on a binary tree network, for which an invariant can easily be computed as a least fixpoint. Let us consider a binary tree, each leaf of which is associated with a binary value. This algorithm computes the parity of the leaves values as follows [Ull84, CGJ95]. The root process initiates a wave by sending the *ready_down* signal to its children. Every internal node transmits this signal to its children. As soon as the *ready_down* signal signal reaches a leaf process, the leaf sends the *ready_up* signal and its value to its parent. When an internal node receives the *ready_up* signal from both of its children, it sends the *ready_up* signal and the *xor* of the values of these children to its parent (see Fig 2). The root cannot send an other wave before it receives the *ready_up* signal.

In the following description, both signals and states are represented by boolean variables. If x is a variable, **next** x represents its value in the next state. All variables are supposed to be initially false. We note *ru* for *ready_up* and *rd* for *ready_down*.

With these notations, the behavior of a leaf process is described by the following boolean equations:

$$\begin{array}{llllll} \textbf{next}\ iv & = & iv; & \textbf{next}\ ru & = & rd; \\ v & = & ru \wedge iv; & ov & = & iv; \end{array}$$

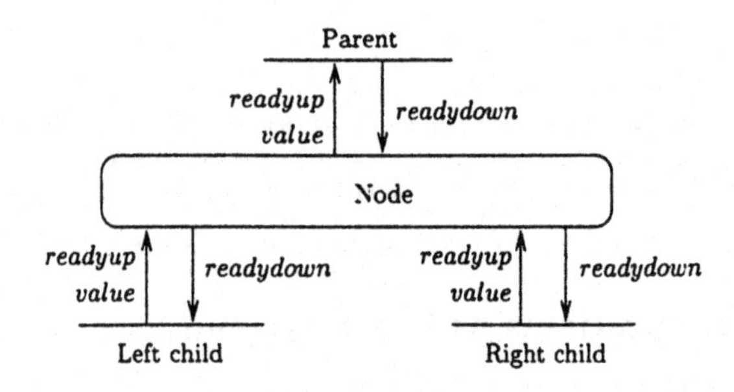

Figure 2: Internal node of the parity tree

iv (for *internal value*) is initialized randomly. *ov* (for *observed value*) is an observation signal. Of course, this is for specification only, and does not change the system itself.
A node is described by the following equations:

$$\begin{array}{llllll} \textbf{next}\ Lru & = & \neg(\textbf{next}\ rd) \wedge (lru \vee Lru); & \textbf{next}\ lrd & = & rd; \\ \textbf{next}\ Rru & = & \neg(\textbf{next}\ rd) \wedge (rru \vee Rru)); & rrd & = & lrd; \\ \textbf{next}\ Lv & = & (\textbf{next}\ lru) \wedge (\textbf{next}\ lv) \vee \neg(\textbf{next}\ lru) \wedge Lv; & v & = & ru \wedge (Lv \otimes Rv); \\ \textbf{next}\ Rv & = & (\textbf{next}\ rru) \wedge (\textbf{next}\ rv) \vee \neg(\textbf{next}\ rru) \wedge Rv; & ov & = & olv \otimes orv; \\ \textbf{next}\ ru & = & \textbf{next}\ (Lru \wedge Rru) \wedge \neg(Lru \wedge Rru); & & & \end{array}$$

lru (for *left ready_up*) and *lrd* (for *left ready_down*) respectively denote the *ready_up* signal received from the left child and the *ready_down* signal sent to the left child. In the same way, *rru* (for *right ready_up*) and *rrd* (for *right ready_down*) are defined for the right child. State variables *Lru* and *Rru* are true as soon as the node receives the *ready_up* signal, from respectively its left and right child. In the same way, *Lv* (for *left value*) and *Rv* (for *right value*) are the values received respectively by its left and right child, at the moment where the node receives a *ready_up* value.

The forward computation of the least invariant does not converge, but in this case, the limit can easily be extrapolated, using a technique similar to the one presented in [LHR97]. The invariant has 23 states and 90 transitions. □

Of course, the undecidability of our verification problem results from the fact that T_I^m cannot be computed, in general (the iterations are infinite, and the limit is an infinite state process). Notice that T_I^m is the set of all possible traces of all the networks in $\mathcal{F}$; intuitively, it is very unlikely to be generated by a finite state automaton.

In [CGJ95], a powerful technique to compute a upper-approximation of T_I^m is proposed. The great advantage of this method is its generality. It can be applied to general network grammars and can deal with complex properties. Nevertheless, most of the time, the forward computation leads to a state explosion that backward computation can avoid (see example of section 6): in fact, the previous example is one of the few, for which an approximation of the least fixpoint can be computed. This is the reason why we investigate the computation of a greatest fixpoint. Indeed, one can expect that the size of the greatest fixpoint will be more dependent on the property to check (which is usually quite small) than on the system size (which is almost always infinite).

4 Network Invariants as Greatest Fixpoints

4.1 Problem

As in [LHR97], we can rewrite *[INDUC]* as

$$T_I \subseteq (\ \forall X, X'.\ (\Theta_{X \cup X' \cup X''} \setminus C) \ominus (\Theta_X \setminus T_I)[X/X'] \ominus T_I\ )\,[X''/X] \quad \text{or}$$
$$T_I \subseteq (\ \forall X, X'',\ (\Theta_{X \cup X' \cup X''} \setminus C) \ominus (\Theta_X \setminus T_I)[X/X''] \ominus T_I\ )\,[X'/X]$$

i.e., $T_I \subseteq F_2(T_I)$. Unfortunately, the function F_2 is no longer monotone, because of the complementations of T_I. Thus, one cannot, as in [LHR97], come to a conclusion about the existence of a greatest fixpoint.

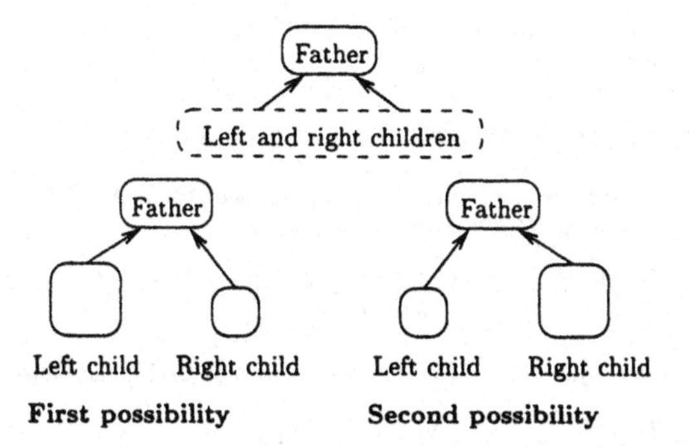

Figure 3: Intuition for the computation of a tree network invariant. Left and right children can be asymmetrically constrained, so that the father satisfies a given property

Intuition: The non existence of a greatest fixpoint can be intuitively understood in the following way (see Fig 3): The induction consists in finding a condition on the child nodes in such a way that the node satisfy a given property. Thus, it is possible to strongly constrain the left child behavior, and less the one of the right child, or to strongly constrain the right child behavior, and less the one of the left child. The ideal solution would be to find a unique property for the two children. In practice, this seems to be impossible, since the problem is not exactly symmetrical. Thus, in the example of section 6.1, the father can transmit the token to its left child, before it transmits it to its right child. In the next section, we will take advantage of the idea that properties of the left and of the right children have to be distinguished.

4.2 Induction principle with two invariants

Let us consider the induction inequation $I \times I \preceq I$. This inequation means that if the left and the right children of the node both satisfy the invariant I, then the whole subtree must satisfy the invariant I. Now, if we consider separately the left child and the right one, it is sufficient to find two invariants L (for left child) and R (for right child) such that

[SAT]	$L \models \varphi$ and $R \models \varphi$
[INIT]	$\forall i = 1...k,\ P_i \preceq L$ and $P_i \preceq R$
[INDUC]	$L \times R \preceq L$ and $L \times R \preceq R$

Recall $\mathcal{S} = \Theta_{X \setminus \{\alpha\}}$. In our trace semantics, these inequations can be written as

[SAT]	$T_L \subseteq \mathcal{S}$ and $T_R \subseteq \mathcal{S}$
[INIT]	$\forall i = 1...k,\ T_{P_i} \subseteq T_L$ and $T_{P_i} \subseteq T_R$
[INDUC]	$(\exists X', \exists X'', C \otimes T_L[X/X'] \otimes T_R[X/X'']) \subseteq T_L$ and
	$(\exists X', \exists X'', C \otimes T_L[X/X'] \otimes T_R[X/X'']) \subseteq T_R$

Let us note *[PROOF]=[SAT]*$\wedge$*[INIT]*$\wedge$*[INDUC]* the set of all these inequations.

4.3 Vector of invariants

The use of two invariants instead of one follows intrinsically from the problem of binary tree networks. Nevertheless, a greatest fixpoint computation is only possible with only one invariant. In order to overcome this difficulty, let us assume that our problem is solved i.e., we know two invariants L and R satisfying the previous inequations, and let us define $V \subseteq \Theta_{X' \cup X''}$ as the composition of $T_L[X/X']$ and $T_R[X/X'']$:

$$V = T_L[X/X'] \odot T_R[X/X'']$$

Notice that T_L and T_R can be easily retrieved from V by projection

$$T_L = (\exists X'', V)[X'/X] \quad \text{and} \quad T_R = (\exists X', V)[X''/X]$$

Let us now rewrite inequations *[PROOF]* with the help of V.

[SAT]: $V \subseteq \mathcal{S}[X/X'] \odot \mathcal{S}[X/X'']$.

[INIT]: First, rewrite the first inequation of *[INIT]* on $X \cup X' \cup X''$.

$$\forall i = 1 \ldots k,\ T_{P_i} \odot \Theta_{X'} \odot \Theta_{X''} \subseteq T_L \odot \Theta_{X'} \odot \Theta_{X''}$$

Since $T_L[X/X'] \subseteq \Theta_{X'}$ and $T_R[X/X''] \subseteq \Theta_{X''}$, this is equivalent to

$$\forall i = 1 \ldots k,\ T_{P_i} \odot T_L[X/X'] \odot T_R[X/X''] \subseteq T_L \odot \Theta_{X'} \odot \Theta_{X''}$$

Then, we use the following property. If A, B and C are sets, then $(A \cap B \subseteq C) \Leftrightarrow (A \cap B \subseteq C \cap B)$. Then the first inequation of *[INIT]* can be rewritten as

$$\forall i = 1 \ldots k,\ T_{P_i} \odot T_L[X/X'] \odot T_R[X/X''] \subseteq T_L \odot T_R[X/X''] \odot \Theta_{X'}$$
$$\text{i.e.,} \quad \forall i = 1 \ldots k,\ T_{P_i} \odot V \subseteq V[X'/X] \odot \Theta_{X'}$$

In the same way, the conjunction of the two inequations of *[INIT]* can be rewritten as

$$\forall i = 1 \ldots k,\ T_{P_i} \odot V \subseteq V[X'/X] \otimes V[X''/X]$$

[INDUC]: Let us use once again the property $(A \cap B \subseteq C) \Leftrightarrow (A \cap B \subseteq C \cap B)$. Then, *[INDUC]* is rewritten as

$$C \otimes T_L[X/X'] \otimes T_R[X/X''] \subseteq T_L \odot T_R[X/X''] \odot \Theta_{X'} \quad \text{and}$$
$$C \otimes T_L[X/X'] \otimes T_R[X/X''] \subseteq T_L[X/X'] \odot T_R \odot \Theta_{X''}$$
$$\textit{i.e.,} \quad C \otimes V \subseteq V[X'/X] \otimes V[X''/X]$$

To summarize, if V can be written $V = T_L[X/X'] \odot T_R[X/X'']$, inequations *[SAT]*, *[INIT]* and *[INDUC]* are respectively equivalent to inequations *[SAT']*, *[INIT']* and *[INDUC']* defined by

[SAT']	$V \subseteq \mathcal{S}[X/X'] \odot \mathcal{S}[X/X'']$
[INIT']	$\forall i = 1 \ldots k,\ T_{P_i} \otimes V \subseteq V[X'/X] \otimes V[X''/X]$
[INDUC']	$C \otimes V \subseteq V[X'/X] \otimes V[X''/X]$

Let us note *[PROOF']=[SAT']∧[INIT']∧[INDUC']* the set of all these inequations.

Proposition 2 *There is a greatest set of traces V^M satisfying* [PROOF'].

Proof: It is easy to show that the inequations *[INIT']* and *[INDUC']* can be rewritten as

$$\begin{array}{ll} [INIT'] & \forall i = 1...k,\ V \subseteq \forall X, (\ (\Theta_X \setminus T_{P_i}) \oplus (V[X'/X] \otimes V[X''/X])\ ) \\ [INDUC'] & V \subseteq \forall X, (\ (\Theta_{X \cup X' \cup X''} \setminus C) \oplus (V[X'/X] \otimes V[X''/X])\ ) \end{array}$$

This means that V is a pre-fixpoint of the (monotone) function F_3 where F_3 is defined by

$$F_3 = \lambda V. \forall X, \ (\ S[X/X'] \odot S[X/X'']\ ) \otimes \left((\Theta_{X \cup X' \cup X''} \setminus (C \otimes \bigcup_{i=1}^{k} T_{P_i})) \oplus (V[X'/X] \otimes V[X''/X]) \right)$$

There is a greatest solution, V^M, which is the greatest fixpoint of F_3. □

Proposition 3 *If V^M is empty,* all *the processes generated by the binary tree network do not satisfy the property φ.*

Proof: Proposition 1 shows that there exists a minimal set of traces T_I^m satisfying both *[INIT]* and *[INDUC]*. Suppose that the tree network satisfies the property φ. Since T_I^m represents the set of traces of all possible tree network, T_I^m must satisfy the property φ. Let $V = T_I^m[X/X'] \otimes T_I^m[X/X'']$. Then V is non empty and must satisfy the inequations *[PROOF']*, i.e., $V \subseteq V^M$. This is impossible, thus no process generated by the binary tree network satisfies the property φ. □

V^M cannot be computed in general (the iterations are infinite and V^M is a infinite state process). In [LHR97], we proposed heuristics to compute under-approximations of V^M using Cousot's extrapolation techniques [CC77, CC92]. In that way, we can obtain a vector $V \subseteq V^M$ satisfying *[PROOF']*.

If we find such a non-empty vector V, is the property φ necessarily satisfied by the binary tree network ? One can answer this question only if one is able to compute two invariants L and R from V. This is not always possible since inequations *[PROOF]* are equivalent to *[PROOF']* only if V can be written $V = T_L[X/X'] \odot T_R[X/X'']$ (which is not always the case). In the next section, we will propose heuristics to find two languages T_L and T_R such that the vector $T_L[X/X'] \odot T_R[X/X'']$ satisfies *[PROOF']*.

5 Computation of invariants L and R

Let V be a vector satisfying *[PROOF']*. V expresses a property that the tuple (L, R) must satisfy to verify equations *[PROOF]*. Intuitively, the fact that it cannot be decomposed in the form $V = T_L[X/X'] \odot T_R[X/X'']$, means that L and R are ***dependent*** (some behavior of L implies a specific reaction of R). The goal of the next section is to find independent L and R.

5.1 Approximations of L and R

5.1.1 Upper-bound

Let T_L^M and T_R^M be two sets of traces defined by

$$T_L^M = (\ \exists X'', V\ )[X'/X] \quad \text{and} \quad T_R^M = (\ \exists X', V\ )[X''/X]$$

All solutions (T_L, T_R) of inequations *[PROOF]* will be such that $T_L \subseteq T_L^M$ and $T_R \subseteq T_R^M$. (T_L^M, T_R^M) can be considered as a upper-bound.

5.1.2 Lower-bound

If we choose $T_L = T_L^M$, in order to satisfy the inequation $T_L[X/X'] \odot T_R[X/X''] \subseteq V$ one has to choose

$$T_R \supseteq (\ \forall X', (\Theta_X \setminus T_L^M)[X/X'] \oplus V\ )[X''/X]$$

Thus, let T_L^m and T_R^m be two sets of traces defined by

$$T_L^m = (\ \forall X'', (\Theta_X \setminus T_R^M)[X/X''] \oplus V\ )[X'/X] \cup \bigcup_{i=1}^{k} T_{P_i}$$

$$T_R^m = (\ \forall X', (\Theta_X \setminus T_L^M)[X/X'] \oplus V\ )[X''/X] \cup \bigcup_{i=1}^{k} T_{P_i}$$

All solutions (T_L, T_R) of inequations *[PROOF]* will be such that $T_L^m \subseteq T_L$ and $T_R^m \subseteq T_R$. (T_L^m, T_R^m) can be considered as a lower-bound. Generally, T_L^m, T_L^M, T_R^m and T_R^M do not satisfy *[PROOF]*. The next section will propose an algorithm based on heuristics to compute suitable invariants.

5.2 Decomposition of V with respect to a lower-bound

Our goal is to compute two sets of traces T_L and T_R, satisfying

$$T_L[X/X'] \odot T_R[X/X''] \subseteq V \quad (1)$$

This problem has no maximal unique solution. Intuitively, in order for T_L and T_R to satisfy *[PROOF]*, the product $T_L[X/X'] \odot T_R[X/X'']$ must be as close as possible to V. This section proposes heuristics allowing the computation of a solution of (1) which satisfies also *[PROOF]*.

5.2.1 Principle

We propose an algorithm based on automata: if $\mathcal{A}$ is a process, i.e., a deterministic Mealy machine with 2^X as input alphabet, let us note $T_\mathcal{A}$ the set of traces of $\mathcal{A}$. Now, let $\mathcal{A}_L^0$ and $\mathcal{A}_R^0$ be two automata on X such that $T_{\mathcal{A}_L^0}[X/X'] \odot T_{\mathcal{A}_R^0}[X/X''] \not\subseteq V$. The principle of our algorithm is to remove some transitions of $\mathcal{A}_L^0$ or of $\mathcal{A}_R^0$ in order to obtain two new automata $\mathcal{A}_L$ and $\mathcal{A}_R$ such that $T_{\mathcal{A}_L}[X/X'] \odot T_{\mathcal{A}_R}[X/X''] \subseteq V$.

This way, if $T_{\mathcal{A}_L^0}[X/X'] \odot T_{\mathcal{A}_R^0}[X/X''] \not\subseteq V$, there exist two traces $\tau_L, \tau_R \in \Theta_X$ respectively accepted by $\mathcal{A}_L^0$ and $\mathcal{A}_R^0$, and such that $\tau_L[X/X'] \odot \tau_R[X/X'']$ is not in V. We can either remove a transition of $\mathcal{A}_L^0$ to make it refuse τ_L, or remove a transition of $\mathcal{A}_R^0$ so that τ_R be refused. One can remove any transition, as long as inclusions $T_{P_i} \subseteq T_{\mathcal{A}_L}$ and $T_{P_i} \subseteq T_{\mathcal{A}_R}$ are satisfied. More generally, following inclusions must be preserved:

$$T_L^m \subseteq T_{\mathcal{A}_L} \quad \text{and} \quad T_R^m \subseteq T_{\mathcal{A}_R} \quad (2)$$

5.2.2 Choice of $\mathcal{A}_L^0$ and $\mathcal{A}_R^0$

Theoretically, any pair of automata $\mathcal{A}_L^0$ and $\mathcal{A}_R^0$ satisfying $T_{\mathcal{A}_L^0}[X/X'] \odot T_{\mathcal{A}_R^0}[X/X''] \not\subseteq V$ is suitable. In practice, the structure of these automata must be derived from the one of V. Automata $\mathcal{A}_L^M$ and $\mathcal{A}_R^M$, which recognize respectively T_L^M and T_R^M, satisfy these properties.

Moreover, in order to preserve inclusions (2), we propose to mark transitions of $\mathcal{A}_L^M$ and of $\mathcal{A}_R^M$ which cannot be removed. Thus, one can choose $\mathcal{A}_L^0$ as the automaton recognizing T_L^M such that any trace of T_L^m is recognized by marked transitions, and any trace of $(T_L^M \setminus T_L^m)$ is recognized by transitions at least one of which is not marked. $\mathcal{A}_R^0$ will be chosen in the same way. Let $\mathcal{A}_L^m$ and $\mathcal{A}_R^m$ be automata recognizing respectively T_L^m and T_R^m. Let us assume that each of them has a sink state such that the alarm signal α is emitted only by transitions reaching this state, and let us mark all transitions of $\mathcal{A}_L^m$ and $\mathcal{A}_R^m$. Thus, one states $\mathcal{A}_L^0 = \mathcal{A}_L^m \| \mathcal{A}_L^M$ and $\mathcal{A}_R^0 = \mathcal{A}_R^m \| \mathcal{A}_R^M$, where $\|$ denotes the synchronous product and where alarm signals of $\mathcal{A}_L^0$ and $\mathcal{A}_R^0$ are respectively the ones of $\mathcal{A}_L^M$ and $\mathcal{A}_R^M$.

5.2.3 Heuristics

In this section, we propose heuristics to remove some transitions of $\mathcal{A}_L^0$ or of $\mathcal{A}_R^0$ in order to satisfy the inclusion (1). Let τ_L and τ_R be two traces on X such that

$$\tau_L[X/X'] \odot \tau_R[X/X''] \in (T_{\mathcal{A}_L^0}[X/X'] \odot T_{\mathcal{A}_R^0}[X/X'']) \setminus V$$

There are two paths π_L and π_R respectively in $\mathcal{A}_L^0$ and $\mathcal{A}_R^0$ corresponding to traces τ_L and τ_R. In order to satisfy the inclusion (1), one has to choose two indexes k_L and k_R such that, either the k_L^{th} transition on the path π_L or the k_R^{th} transition on the path π_R, is removed. One can choose either k_L or k_R *maximal* (intuitively, this comes to remove all traces with a particular suffix), or k_L or k_R *minimal* (intuitively, this comes to remove all traces with a particular prefix). Experiments showed that only the second choice gives good results. In order to formalize the algorithm, let us introduce the function f_m taking as argument a trace τ and returning the minimal index k such that the kth transition of the path corresponding to τ is not marked. Thus, our decomposition algorithm is the following:

Algorithm 1

$\mathcal{A}_L = \mathcal{A}_L^m \| \mathcal{A}_L^M$; $\mathcal{A}_R = \mathcal{A}_R^m \| \mathcal{A}_R^M$;

While $T_{\mathcal{A}_L}[X/X'] \odot T_{\mathcal{A}_R}[X/X''] \not\subseteq V$

Let $\tau_L \odot \tau_R \in (T_{\mathcal{A}_L}[X/X'] \odot T_{\mathcal{A}_R}[X/X'']) \setminus V$

Let $k_L = f_m(\tau_L)$ *and* $k_R = f_m(\tau_R)$

if $k_L \leq k_R$ *then one removes the* k_L^{th} *transition on the path of* $\mathcal{A}_L$ *corresponding to* τ_L

else one removes the k_R^{th} *transition on the path of* $\mathcal{A}_R$ *corresponding to* τ_R

End of while

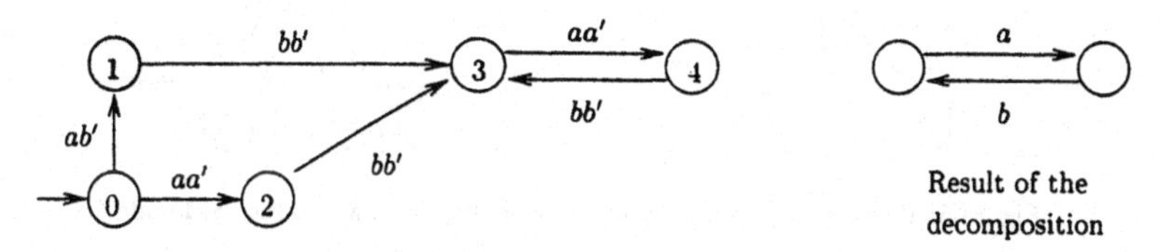

Figure 4: Example of an automaton recognizing the language V. The grey state has to be removed to make this automaton symmetrical

Example: Let us consider the set of signals $\{a, b\}$. The automaton of Fig.4 recognizes the language V defined by

$$V = ab'.(bb'.aa')^* + (aa'.bb')^*$$

The word $(aa'.bb')^*$ is symmetrical, in that if the prime and non prime variables are exchanged, the obtained words belong to the language V. In contrast, if $ab'.(bb'.aa')^*$ belongs to V, the symmetrical word $ba'.(bb'.aa')^*$ does not. This word is "removed" in forbidding the transition $0 \to 1$. Thus, we obtain as invariant the language $(a.b)^*$. □

The previous algorithm is not exactly symmetrical with respect to L and R, since the tests $k_L \leq k_R$ and $k_R < k_L$ are computed. A dual algorithm can be defined, where the tests $k_L < k_R$ and $k_R \leq k_L$ would be computed. It is not possible *à priori* to find the best solution.

6 Examples

Our method has been implemented in a tool, taking LUSTRE [HCRP91] programs as input, and computing invariants. We present here two problems, which have been automatically verified on a **Sun Ultra Sparc 1** with 256 Mb. Sources are available at [Les97].

In the following descriptions, both signals and states are represented by boolean variables. If x is a variable, **next** x represents its value in the next state. All variables are supposed to be initially false.

6.1 A token tree

Let n units $P_1, P_2, \ldots, P_n$ share a resource in mutual exclusion. They are connected as a binary tree, along which a token travels in depth. A process P_i can only use the resource when it has the token. It has one input signal tk_{in} (token in) and two output signals tk_{out} (token out) and use (resource used). The behavior of a unit can be represented by the following system of Boolean equations:

$$use = has\_tk \wedge req; \qquad tk_{out} = has\_tk \wedge \neg req;$$
$$\textbf{next}\ has\_tk = tk_{in} \vee (has\_tk \wedge \neg tk_{out});$$

Intuitively, the first equation tells that the unit uses the resource whenever it has the token and requests the resource. The second equation tells that the unit transmits the token if it has it and does not request it. The last equation states that the unit will have the token at the next step if either it receives it now, or it already has it and does not transmit it. The internal signal req is left unspecified.

6.1.1 Processes are connected with the leaves

Let us first consider the case, where each node of the tree is connected to such a unit (see Fig 5). Each node has 3 input signals and 3 output signals, corresponding to the communication with its father, its left child and its right child. When a node receives the token from its father, it transmits it to its left child. When it receives the token from its left child, it transmits it to its right child. And finally, when it receives the token from its right child, it gives it back to its father (see Fig 5).

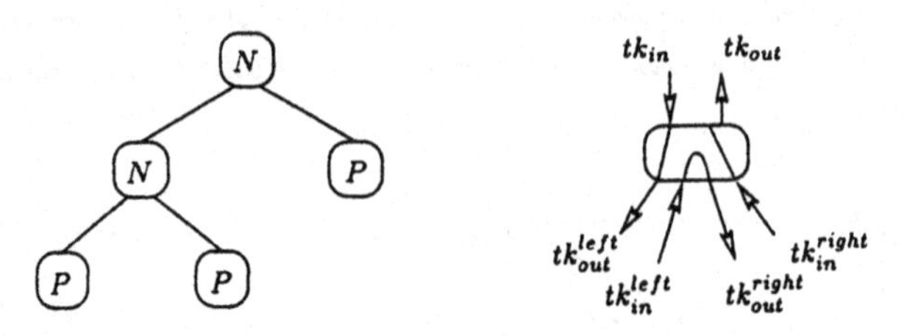

Figure 5: Processes are connected to the leaves. P is a process, N a node.

The mutual exclusion observer of a node has 4 input signals: ν_l (the resource is used in the left branch), α_l (mutual exclusion is violated in the left branch), ν_r (the resource is used in the right branch) and α_r (mutual exclusion is violated in the right branch). It emits the two signals α (the mutual exclusion property is violated) and ν (the resource is used by its unit or one of its children).

A node behavior is defined as follows (see Fig 5)

$$\begin{aligned} \textbf{next } tk_{out}^{left} &= tk_{in}; & \nu_{out} &= \nu_{left} \vee \nu_{right} \vee tk_{in}^{left} \vee tk_{in}^{right}; \\ \textbf{next } tk_{out}^{right} &= tk_{out}^{left}; & \alpha &= \alpha_{left} \vee \alpha_{right} \vee (\nu_{left} \wedge \nu_{right}); \\ \textbf{next } tk_{out} &= tk_{out}^{right}; \end{aligned}$$

The forward computation of invariant saturates the memory after 2 steps taking several hours. In contrast, the invariant V^M is exactly computed backward in 5 iterations in 9 minutes and 57 seconds. It has 829 states and 74013 transitions. This invariant is then decomposed into two invariants L and R which have respectively 32 states and 276 transitions, and 7 states and 57 transitions.

6.1.2 Processes are connected to the nodes

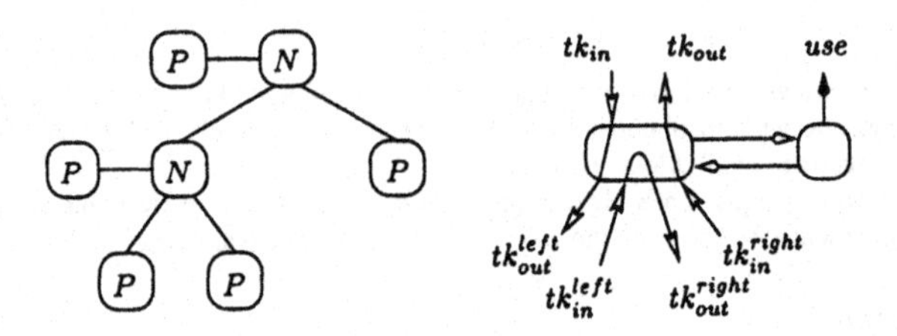

Figure 6: Processes are connected to the nodes. P is a process, N a node.

Let us consider a more complicated version of the previous algorithm, where each node of the binary tree is connected with a unit with which it can communicate (see Fig 6). Thus, each node has 4 input signals and 4 output signals, corresponding to the communications with its father, its left child, its right child and its associated unit. Each time the token reaches the node, it is transmitted also to the unit associated with the node, which can keep it for some time in order to use the resource. The mutual exclusion observer of a node has then one input signal more: *use* (the resource is used by the node unit). ν_{out} and α are then defined by

$$\begin{aligned} \nu_{out} &= \nu_{left} \vee \nu_{right} \vee tk_{in}^{left} \vee tk_{in}^{right} \vee use; \\ \alpha &= \alpha_{left} \vee \alpha_{right} \vee (\nu_{left} \wedge \nu_{right}) \vee (\nu_{left} \wedge use) \vee (\nu_{right} \wedge use); \end{aligned}$$

The invariant V^M is exactly computed backward in 5 iterations in 19 minutes and 15 seconds. It has 928 states and 72379 transitions. This invariant is then decomposed in two invariants L and R which have respectively 27 states and 266 transitions, and 15 states and 111 transitions.

6.2 Network in petals

Our second example shows that the technique of invariant computation on binary tree networks can be applied to asymmetrical networks (where left and right children are defined differently).

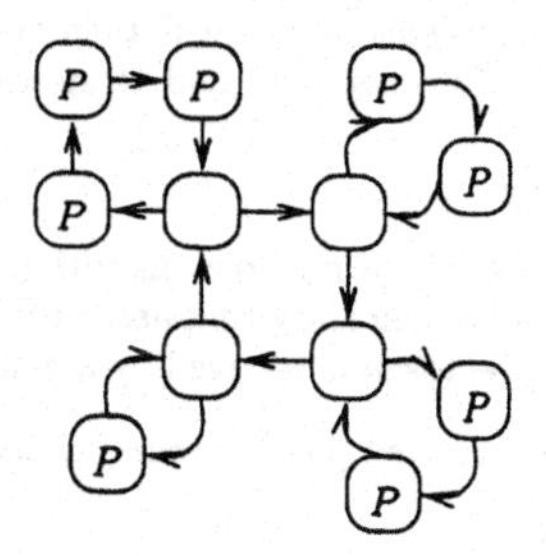

Figure 7: Network in petals

Let us consider a main ring, composed of nodes (called main nodes) which are associated with secondary rings (see Fig 7). This kind of networks can be generated by the following grammar (see

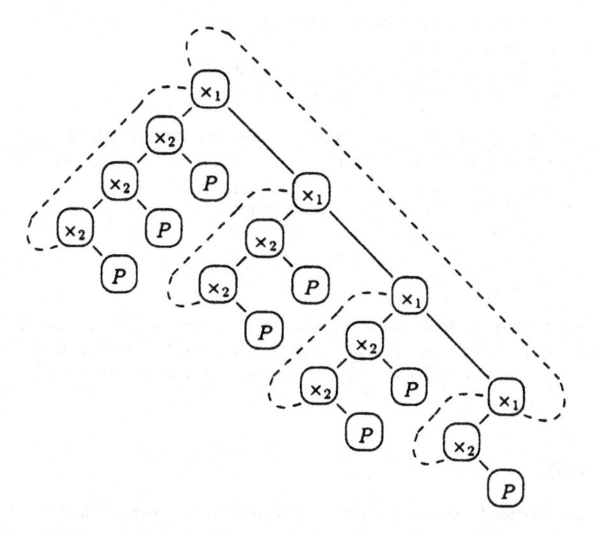

Figure 8: Construction of a network in petal by a binary tree grammar

Fig 8):

$$S \rightarrow L \times_1 R \qquad L \rightarrow L \times_2 P \qquad R \rightarrow L \times_1 R$$
$$L \rightarrow P \qquad R \rightarrow P$$

6.2.1 Without arbitration device

Let us first consider a token traveling in depth in all tree branches. Each process has 1 input signal tk_{in}, for "token in" (the process receives a token) and 1 output signal tk_{out}, for "token out" (the process emits a token) A process is formally defined by

$$\begin{array}{lcl}\textbf{next } \mathit{has\_token} & = & \neg(\textbf{next } tk_{out}) \wedge ((\textbf{next } tk_{in}) \vee \mathit{has\_token});\\ \textbf{next } tk_{out} & = & \mathit{has\_token} \wedge \mathit{release};\end{array}$$

The variable *has_token* is true as long as the process has the token. The input *release* is left unspecified.

As soon as a main node $\times_1$ receives the token, it transmits it to its left child (i.e., a secondary associated ring), then to its right child (i.e., the following main node). When a secondary node $\times_2$ receives the token, it transmits it to its right child (i.e., an elementary process), then to its left child (i.e., the following secondary node). That way, the token visits all network processes in turn.

The forward computation of invariant saturates the memory after 2 steps taking several hours. In contrast, the invariant V^M is exactly computed backward in 3 iterations. It has 612 states and 50782 transitions in 18 minutes and 3 seconds. This invariant is then decomposed in two invariants L and R which have respectively 32 states and 284 transitions, and 16 states and 127 transitions.

6.2.2 With an arbitration device

We propose the following improvement of the previous algorithm, to avoid useless token passing in a secondary ring. As soon as a process of a secondary ring needs the resource, it sends a request signal to the corresponding main node. When the token is received by a main node:

- Either a request signal has been received (i.e., a process of the ring asks for the resource), and the token is sent in this secondary ring.
- Or no request signal has been received, and the token is transmitted to the following main node.

Each process has 1 input signal tk_{in}, for "token in" (the process receives a token), and 2 output signals tk_{out}, for "token out" (the process emits a token) and sg_{out}, for "signal out" (the process emits a request signal). It has 2 internal signals *req* and *rel* for the token request and the token release. A process is described by the following equations:

$$\begin{array}{lcl}\textbf{next } \mathit{wait} & = & (\mathit{req} \vee \mathit{wait}) \wedge \neg tk_{in} \wedge \neg \mathit{has\_tk};\\ \textbf{next } \mathit{has\_tk} & = & (\mathit{has\_tk} \vee tk_{in}) \wedge \neg tk_{out};\\ tk_{out} & = & (tk_{in} \vee \mathit{has\_tk}) \wedge \neg \mathit{wait} \wedge \neg(\mathit{req} \vee \mathit{rel});\\ sg_{out} & = & \neg(\mathit{has\_tk} \vee tk_{in}) \wedge \neg \mathit{wait} \wedge \mathit{req};\end{array}$$

The composition operator $\times_1$ is defined in such a way that the token is sent in a secondary ring only if a request signal has been received. It is defined by

$$\begin{array}{lcl}\textbf{next } \mathit{has\_sig} & = & (\textbf{next } sg_{in}^{left}) \vee (\mathit{has\_sig} \wedge \neg tk_{out}^{left});\\ \textbf{next } tk_{out}^{left} & = & (\textbf{next } \mathit{has\_sig}) \wedge tk_{in};\\ \textbf{next } tk_{out}^{right} & = & tk_{in}^{left} \vee (\neg(\textbf{next } \mathit{has\_sig}) \wedge tk_{in});\\ tk_{out} & = & tk_{in}^{right};\end{array}$$

We find an invariant on an abstract network, where the request signal is abstracted. V^M is computed in 3 steps in 3 hours and 18 minutes. It has 777 states and 51711 transitions. This invariant is then decomposed in two invariants L and R which have respectively 28 states and 219 transitions, and 22 states and 157 transitions.

7 Conclusion

In this paper, we have extended the computation of invariant from linear parameterized networks [LHR97] to networks generated by context-free grammars. To avoid the non convergence of the least fixpoint computation, a technique of computation of greatest fixpoint is proposed, which takes care of the two children of a node at the same time. Heuristics have been proposed to decompose a vector of invariants and have been implemented in a tool.

For the time being, we have only very few elements for comparing our method with the one proposed in [CGJ95]. By the way, we believe that the least and the greatest fixpoint are complementary. For the parity-tree example (which is the only one used in [CGJ95]), the computation of the greatest fixpoint is much longer than the one of the least fixpoint. In contrast, in all the examples of section 6, the least fixpoint computation saturates the memory after only two steps, while the one of greatest fixpoint converges rapidly.

References

[AK86] K. R. Apt and D. C. Kozen. Limits for automatic verification of finite-state concurrent systems. *Information Processing Letters*, 22:307–309, 1986.

[BG92] G. Berry and G. Gonthier. The Esterel synchronous programming language: Design, semantics, implementation. *Science of Computer Programming*, 19(2):87–152, 1992.

[CC77] P. Cousot and R. Cousot. Abstract interpretation: a unified lattice model for static analysis of programs by construction or approximation of fixpoints. In *4th ACM Symposium on Principles of Programming Languages, POPL'77*, Los Angeles, January 1977.

[CC92] P. Cousot and R. Cousot. Comparing the Galois connection and widening/narrowing approaches to abstract interpretation. In M. Bruynooghe and M. Wirsing, editors, *PLILP'92*, Leuven (Belgium), January 1992. LNCS 631, Springer Verlag.

[CES86] E. M. Clarke, E. A. Emerson, and A. P. Sistla. Automatic verification of finite-state concurrent systems using temporal logic specifications. *ACM TOPLAS*, 8(2), 1986.

[CGJ95] E. M. Clarke, O. Grumberg, and S. Jha. Verifying parameterized networks using abstraction and regular languages. In *CONCUR'95*. LNCS 962, Springer Verlag, August 1995.

[Eil74] S. Eilenberg. *Automata, Languages, and Machines*. Academic Press, 1974.

[EN95] E. A. Emerson and K. S. Namjoshi. Reasoning about rings. In *Proc. 22th ACM Conf. on Principles of Programming Languages, POPL'95*, San Francisco, January 1995.

[EN96] E. A. Emerson and K. S. Namjoshi. Automatic verification of parameterized synchronous systems. In R. Alur and T. Henzinger, editors, *8th International Conference on Computer Aided Verification, CAV'96*, Rutgers (N.J.), 1996.

[Hal93] N. Halbwachs. *Synchronous programming of reactive systems*. Kluwer Academic Pub., 1993.

[Har87] D. Harel. Statecharts: A visual approach to complex systems. *Science of Computer Programming*, 8(3), 1987.

[HCRP91] N. Halbwachs, P. Caspi, P. Raymond, and D. Pilaud. The synchronous dataflow programming language LUSTRE. *Proceedings of the IEEE*, 79(9):1305–1320, September 1991.

[HLR92] N. Halbwachs, F. Lagnier, and C. Ratel. An experience in proving regular networks of processes by modular model checking. *Acta Informatica*, 29(6/7):523–543, 1992.

[HLR93] N. Halbwachs, F. Lagnier, and P. Raymond. Synchronous observers and the verification of reactive systems. In M. Nivat, C. Rattray, T. Rus, and G. Scollo, editors, *Third Int. Conf. on Algebraic Methodology and Software Technology, AMAST'93*, Twente, June 1993. Workshops in Computing, Springer Verlag.

[KM89] R. P. Kurshan and K McMillan. A structural induction theorem for processes. In *8th ACM Symposium on Principles of Distributed Computing*, pages 239–247, Edmonton (Alberta), August 1989.

[Les97] D. Lesens. The boolean automaton network grammar checker home page. http://www.imag.fr/VERIMAG/PEOPLE/David.Lesens/BANG, 1997.

[LHR97] D. Lesens, N. Halbwachs, and P. Raymond. Automatic verification of parameterized linear networks of processes. In *24th ACM Symposium on Principles of Programming Languages, POPL'97*, Paris, January 1997.

[Mar92] F. Maraninchi. Operational and compositional semantics of synchronous automaton compositions. In *CONCUR'92*, Stony Brook, August 1992. LNCS 630, Springer Verlag.

[MG91] R. Marelly and O. Grumberg. Gormel-grammar oriented model checker. Technical report, The Technion, 1991.

[QS82] J. P. Queille and J. Sifakis. Specification and verification of concurrent systems in CESAR. In *International Symposium on Programming*. LNCS 137, Springer Verlag, April 1982.

[SG89] Z. Shtadler and O. Grumberg. Network grammars, communication behaviors and automatic verification. In *Workshop on Automatic Verification Methods for Finite State Systems, Grenoble.* LNCS 407, Springer Verlag, June 1989.

[Ull84] J. D. Ullman. Computational aspects of VLSI. *Computer Science Press*, 1984.

[WL89] P. Wolper and V. Lovinfosse. Verifying properties of large sets of processes with network invariants. In *International Workshop on Automatic Verification Methods for Finite State Systems, Grenoble.* LNCS 407, Springer Verlag, 1989.

Modelling Specification Construction by Successive Approximations

Nicole Lévy and Jeanine Souquières

LORIA, BP. 239, F-54506 Vandœuvre-les-Nancy
{Nicole.Levy, Jeanine.Souquieres}@loria.fr

Abstract. Software development lacks tools supporting the steps actually followed by developers, e.g. with successive approximations. The Proplane framework aims at modelling specifications construction. In this framework, a development step is composed of a workplan denoting both the history of goals and the decisions taken, a product denoting the specification being defined, and the links between them. These links are expressed by means of a meta-program. Each step is obtained by the application of a development operator. Operators enable developments with successive approximations to be captured. The use of the framework is illustrated by some steps of the development of the production cell case study.

1 Introduction

Developing specifications is one of the most difficult activities which software engineers have tried to cope with for decades. The use of any formalism or formal technique is not sufficient to guarantee writing correct and adequate specifications. A major drawback of formal techniques is that they are not easy to apply. Users have to deal with lots of details, and often they are left alone without any guidance on how to use the formalism. Some guidance can rely on the availability of process knowledge, the nature of which ranges from informal guidelines to formal derivations.

Our research aims to capture the process of developing specifications, whatever the formalism and underlying methods are. It applies in particular to the development of a first specification. We propose a model, Proplane, to capture developments. It allows formal specifications to be built by successive approximations [LS96], starting from informal or semi-formal requirements. Operators are a key notion in our model, capturing strategies and design concepts. They enable the user to develop specifications in an intuitive fashion by separating the use of design concepts from the technical details of how they are captured in the specification language. Operators offers flexibility since it is possible to define libraries of operators capturing alternative definitions of particular concepts and strategies.

The Proplane approach is related to process modelling. According to [JvL94], process modelling approaches can be classified into rule-based, blackboard-based, coordination-based, plan-based, and multi-paradigm approaches (examples of those can be found in [FKN94]). They mostly concern management activities spreading over the entire life cycle. Our approach is complementary: it addresses the processes followed by developers to achieve their assigned objectives, e.g. to develop a specification, on both the methodological and technical levels.

The Proplane notion of operator can be compared with the notions of software paradigm, style [HL97] and pattern [GHJV95,BMR+96]. For example, [Sha95] presents a paradigm motivated by process control loop and recommends the definition of some elements of a pattern such as computational elements or data elements. Our operators use parameterised patterns.

On the one hand, introducing methodological aspects in languages makes them grow more and more. On the other hand, for comprehensibility, readability, learn-ability, ... concerns, languages with a small kernel are preferred. A good compromise is not easy to find.

With Proplane, methodological aspects are expressed outside the language by way of development operators. Operators are applied to development steps. A development step is composed of both a workplan describing the followed reasoning and the product, i.e. the specification under development. The workplan and the product are linked by means of a meta-program.

This paper is structured as follows. Section 2 presents an intuitive view of the Proplane model. Some steps of the development of the production cell case study [LL95], using the **Z** specification language [Spi89] are outlined. Section 3 gives the definition of the meta-program, intermediary between the workplan and the product. Two development steps by successive approximations are then developed in section 4.

2 The Specifier Point of View

We consider the production cell case study [LL95]. The system to be specified processes metal blanks which are conveyed to a press by a feed belt. A robot takes each blank from the feed belt and places it into the press. A table has to be introduced between the feed belt and the robot to bring the blanks into the right position for the robot to pick them up. Vertical movement is necessary for the table because the robot arm is located at a different level than the feed belt and because it cannot perform vertical translations. A rotation movement is also required because the robot arm's gripper is not rotary. The press forges blanks and the robot takes metal plates from the press and puts them on a deposit belt. In this paper, we will concentrate on the definition of the rotary elevating table. The chosen specification language is **Z** [Spi89].

2.1 Some Development Steps

We describe three steps resulting in the development state of Figure 1. At each step, an operator is applied.

A system made of sub-systems. To specify the production cell system, we first apply the operator ***system made of sub-systems*** decomposing the problem into three sub-problems:

- specify the sub-systems composing the production cell;
- specify the constraints between these sub-systems;
- specify the operations making the production cell evolve.

This operator considers that the system defined as a composition of various sub-systems will not have any specific attribute: the schema of the production cell will be just the inclusion of the various sub-systems composing it and some global constraints.

Introducing the Table sub-system. The sub-systems can be introduced one after the other. To do so, the operator ***introducing a system*** is applied repeatedly, taking as interactive parameter the name of a sub-system, *Table* for example.

Once introduced, a sub-system has to be defined. This can be done from scratch, or by reusing an existing system from the component library.

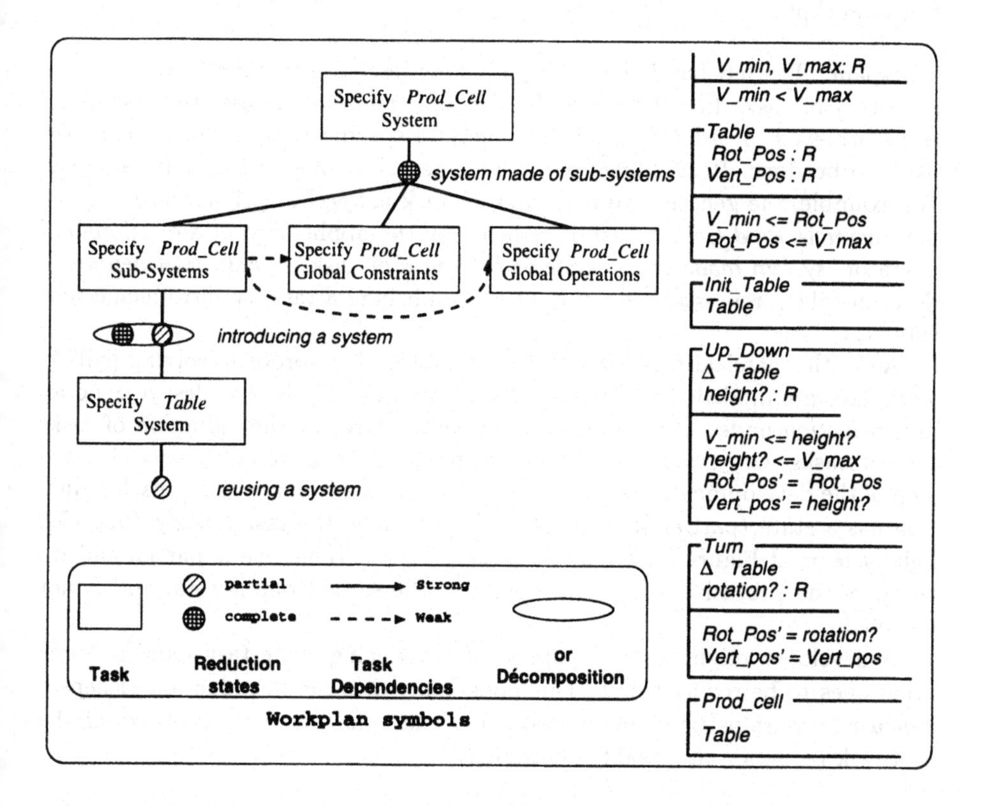

Fig. 1. A development state

Reusing the Table system. We want to reuse a table system from our component library. To do so, we apply the operator ***reusing a system*** which asks interactively the name of the system to be reused belonging to the library. The table reused, as shown in Figure 1, has two attributes corresponding to its vertical and rotational position. It has an initial state described by the *Init_Table* schema and two operations *Up_Down* and *Turn*. Two global constants are used, *V_min* and *V_max*, denoting the minimum and maximum height of the table.

2.2 The Proplane Model Description

The Proplane model defines a development process as composed of development states, steps and operators [Sou93,SL93]. More precisely, the development of a specification is defined as a sequence of steps. Each step maps some development state to the next one in sequence by applying an operator. From a specifier's point of view, a development state consists of two consistent and related viewpoints, a workplan describing the reasoning followed and a product or specification under development. Figure 1 shows the development state obtained after the three steps described in Section 2.1 with the meaning of the graphical symbols associated to the workplan.

Workplan. The left-hand side of Figure 1 represents a workplan state. It is a collection of tasks linked through a *reduction relation*. A *task* denotes a goal to be achieved in order to produce a piece of specification, or more generally, work to be done. It is characterised by a generic name and task parameters. For example, the generic name of the root task is Specify System and the some parameter is *Prod_Cell*. A task is reduced by the application of a development operator, ***system made of sub-systems*** for the root task. A *reduction* denotes a decision taken, representing a way of accomplishing a task by introducing new subtasks.

As in the classical top-down reduction approach to problem solving [Nil71], workplans are modelled by *and/or* -graphs with two kinds of nodes: *task* nodes and *reduction* nodes. *And* -graphs are used to represent the reduction of tasks into subtasks. *Or* -graphs are used to represent alternative reductions. At each step of the development, only one reduction of a task is *current*, and each reduction has a state (partial or complete). For example, the task Specify *Prod_Cell* Sub-Systems of Figure 1 has two reductions : the current one is partial and introduces the subtask Specify *Table* System ; the second one is total and is not depicted.

A developer might wish to express that reducing some task requires some other ones to be reduced first. This point motivates the introduction of *dependency relationships* between subtasks. For example, the three subtasks of the root task reduction are weakly dependent.

Product. The product consists of a text in a given formal language. During the development of a specification, an incomplete or not yet defined part of the product has a default value. For example, in Figure 1, the predicate of the

Prod_Cell schema, to be defined by the task Specify *Prod_Cell* Global Constraints is valued to true and therefore not written in the specification.

Meta-program and Workplan–Product Links. Figure 1 gives the specifier's point of view of a development. An intermediary, the meta-program, has been introduced to connect tasks and product and to describe how to construct the product [Lév95]. More details about the meta-program are given in Section 3.

Development Operator. A development operator works in parallel on both the workplan and the product to reduce tasks and either construct or modify the product text. The operator parameters are acquired interactively from the specifier and some data is computed from the current development state. An operator consists of (i) an application precondition related to the current development state, (ii) a description of the action on the workplan, and (iii) a meta-program to be instantiated, describing the product definition. Such a meta-program describes a parameterised pattern [GHJV95].

In Figure 1, the task Specify *Prod_cell* System has been reduced by application of the development operator ***system made of sub-systems***. The decision taken is to follow a bottom-up approach, requiring a first approximation of some subsystems before the definition of global constraints and operations.

Libraries of development operators support the formalisation of methods and strategies.

Development Step. At each development step, the specifier chooses a task among those to be reduced (tasks which are not reduced yet or partially reduced) and an operator among those that can be applied to the task. Next, operator parameters are instantiated and the operator is applied. A step description keeps track of the different operators that could have been used at this step, the interactive parameters given by the specifier and an informal rationale of the choice.

Prototype Tool. A prototype tool consisting of a plan editor connected to a product manager has been implemented [SL96]. The main activity of the specifier consists no longer in writing down the specification, but in applying predefined operators to make the specification evolve. This approach relieves him/her of many humdrum activities and enables him/her to focus on the underlying reasoning of the specification elaboration. The tool, equipped with a graphical interface, is parameterised by the specification language (Glider, Z or Lotos) and by development operator libraries [LL96].

3 The Meta-Program

A development step, as seen in Section 2, consists of both a workplan and a product. Tasks of the workplan denote some work to be done in order to produce a piece of specification represented by variables of a meta-program. Figure 2 shows the variables associated to the tasks of the workplan of Figure 1.

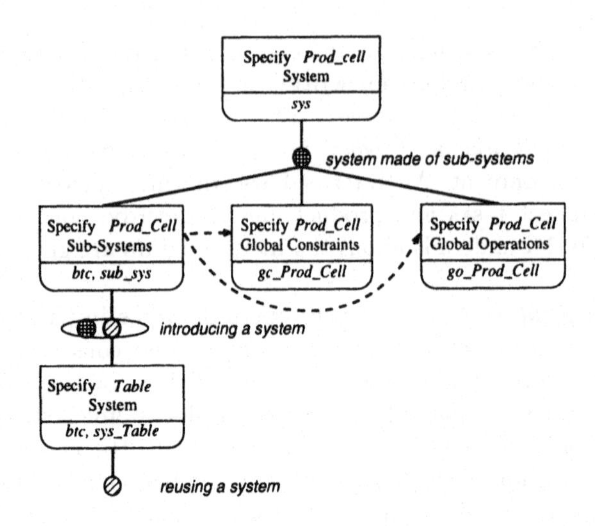

Fig. 2. Workplan of the Figure 1 with the variables associated to the tasks

A meta-program is a set of variable definitions describing the specification construction. Figure 3 gives the current meta-program associated to Figure 1. The specification itself (the product) is obtained by evaluation of the meta-program. The right hand part of Figure 1 corresponds to the evaluation of the meta-program of Figure 3.

Variable. A variable represents information concerning the construction of some part of the specification. For example, the whole system is associated to the variable *sys*. A variable may also denote information that will not be a piece of the final product. A variable can be associated to a task if its definition is to be given when reducing the task. It can also be an intermediate variable completely defined, such as *parl_Prod_Cell.* This variable represents the paragraphs preceding the *Prod_Cell* schema. It is decomposed into two part : basic type and constant declarations denoted by *btc* and the sub-systems to be defined, such as *Table*, denoted by *sub_sys*.

Variable Definitions. One of the advantages of the meta-program is to allow any piece of the specification to be defined by successive approximations. In the above example, the Table system is defined by reusing a component. In Section 4, we will add a new attribute to its schema state, modifying the reused component.

To capture these successive approximations, a list of definitions is associated to each variable. When introduced, a variable has at first a default definition, for example:

$$sys\_Table = \quad \langle\rangle \qquad : \mathsf{PAR\bot IST} \;\; \mathsf{I}$$

and then a new one is added when its associated task is reduced:

$$= \langle par\_Table \rangle ^\wedge \langle par\_Init\_Table \rangle ^\wedge op\_Table \qquad : \mathsf{PAR\bot IST} \;\; \mathsf{T}$$

```
sys_name              = "Prod_Cell"                                        : NAME        G
sys                   = init                                               : ANY         I
                      = <parl_Prod_Cell, par_Prod_Cell, go_Prod_Cell>      : PAR_LIST    T
parl_Prod_Cell        = btc ^ sub_sys                                      : PAR_LIST    T
btc                   = <>                                                 : PAR_LIST    I
                      = <cst_decl_Table>                                   : PAR_LIST    P
cst_decl_Table        = make(cst_decl_list_Table, cst_pred_Table)          : G_PAR       T
cst_decl_list_Table   =<make(cst_name1_Table,cst_type1_Table),             : DECL_LIST   P
                           make(cst_name2_Table,cst_type2_Table)>
cst_name1_Table       = "V_min"                                            : NAME        T
cst_type1_Table       = "R"                                                : TYPE        T
cst_name2_Table       = "V_max"                                            : NAME        T
cst_type2_Table       = "R"                                                : TYPE        T
cst_pred_Table        = inf(cst_name1_Table, cst_name2_Table)              : PRED        P

sub_sys               = <>                                                 : PAR_LIST    I
                      = sys_Table                                          : PAR_LIST    P
sys_name1             = "Table"                                            : NAME        G

sys_Table             = <>                                                 : PAR_LIST    I
                      = <par_Table> ^ <par_Init_Table > ^ op_Table         : PAR_LIST    P
par_Table             = make(sys_name1, att_Table, pred_Table)             : PAR         T
att_Table             = <att_decl1,_Table , att_decl2_Table>               : DECL_LIST   P
att_decl1_Table       = make(att_name1_Table, att_type1_Table)             : DECL        T
att_name1_Table       = "Rot_Pos"                                          : NAME        T
att_type1_Table       = "R"                                                : TYPE        T
att_decl2_Table       = make(att_name2_Table, att_type2_Table)             : DECL        T
att_name2_Table       = "Vert_Pos"                                         : NAME        T
att_type2_Table       = "R"                                                : TYPE        T
pred_Table            = infeg(cst_name1_Table, att_name2_Table) and        : PRED        I
                        infeg(att_name2_Table, cst_name2_Table)
par_Init_Table        = make("Init"^sys_name1, <Delta(sys_name1)>,         : PAR         P
                                 par_Init_Table_pred)
par_Init_Table_pred   =True                                                : PRED        I

op_Table              = <par_Up_Down, par_Turn>                            : PAR_LIST    P
op_name1_Table        = "Up_Down"                                          : NAME        T
op_name2_Table        = "Turn"                                             : NAME        T

par_Up_Down           = make(op_name1_Table, decl_Up_Down,                 : PAR         T
                                 pred_Up_Down)
decl_Up_Down          = <Delta(sys_name1), make("height?", "R")>           : DECL_LIST   P
pred_Up_Down          =  infeg(cst_name1_Table, "height?") and             : PRED        P
                         infeg("height?", cst_name2_Table) and
                         eq(prime(att_name1_Table),att_name1_Table) and
                         eq(prime(att_name2_Table), "height?")
par_Turn              = make(op_name2_Table, decl_Turn, pred_Turn)         : PAR         T
decl_Turn             = <Delta(sys_name1), make("rotation?", "R")>         :DECL_LIST    P
pred_Turn             = eq(prime(att_name1_Table),"rotation?") and         :PRED         P
                         eq(prime(att_name2_Table),att_name2_Table)

par_Prod_Cell         = make(sys_name, nl_Prod_Cell, gc_Prod_Cell)         : PAR         T
nl_Prod_Cell          = names_of(sub_sys)                                  : NAME_LIST   T
gc_Prod_Cell          = <>                                                 : PRED_LIST   I
go_Prod_Cell          = <>                                                 : PAR_LIST    I
```

Fig. 3. The meta-program corresponding to Figure 1 development state

A variable with several definitions can therefore be associated to several tasks, each of which has as objective to define the variable partially. In fact, to be more precise, a task is associated to the variable definitions. For example, the variable *btc* representing the definitions of all basic types and constants of the specification, is associated to both the tasks Specify *Prod_Cell* Sub-Systems and Specify *Table* System. It will as well be associated to all tasks whose objective is to define a sub-system of the *Prod_Cell* system.

Definition. Let us take as example the definition of the variable *sys* denoting the whole system. Its definition says that the system is composed of a list of paragraphs[1] corresponding to the production cell sub-systems, a paragraph representing the global state and a list of operation paragraphs:

sys $=$ $<$ *parl_Prod_Cell, par_Prod_Cell, go_Prod_Cell* $>$: PAR_LIST T

As shown in this example, a variable definition is composed of a type (PAR_LIST) denoting the type of the information associated to the variable, a functional expression ($<$ *parl_Prod_Cell, par_Prod_Cell, go_Prod_Cell* $>$) and a definition state (T). These three parts are detailed below.

Type. The type of a variable is the type of the piece of specification it represents, i.e. the type of the node of the abstract syntax tree of the specification. All types are predefined. Some are language dependent such as the type of a Z paragraph PAR and others are basic and language independent such as NAME. Types are related by a compatibility or inheritance relation which defines a lattice on the set of types. For this relation, the most general type is ANY.

Variables are typed when introduced, and then compatibly retyped when defined. For example, the first definition of the variable *sys* gives it the type ANY and the second one, the type list of paragraphs PAR_LIST.

Expression. A variable is defined by a functional expression. The functions, also called product operators, such as *init* or *make*, are associated to the types and predefined. A variable interactively defined will have the given value as expression, for example *"Table"* for *sys_name1*, the name of the first introduced sub-system.

State. A variable definition is characterised by a state:

- **G** when the value has been given interactively by the specifier, such as *sys_name1*;
- **I** when just introduced, not yet defined and associated to a task, such as the default definition of *btc*;
- **T** when provided with a definition, such as *parl_Prod_Cell*;
- **P** when the definition is partial, such as *sub_sys*.

[1] Any Z specification is composed of a list of paragraphs ; a paragraph can either be a declaration or a schema.

4 Development by Successive Approximations

In the development steps outlined in Section 2.1, the *Table* system has been defined reusing a component. Let us suppose now that we have specified the operation *From_Feed_Belt_To_Table*, in which the movement of a blank from the feed belt to the table is described. This operation can be performed when a blank has entered the final part of the feed belt and the table has the correct position, w.r.t. to its rotation and vertical movement.

When defining this global operation, it appears that several new attributes have to be introduced, for example *Loaded* and *Can_Receive* related to the *Table* system. In order to add these two attributes, we extend the *Table* system definition.

4.1 Extending the Reused Component.

The goal of the operator ***extending state*** applied to the task Specify *Table* System is to add two new attributes: *Loaded* and *Can_Receive* whose names, types and predicates are given interactively. *Loaded* indicates whether a blank is on the table or not and *Can_Receive* whether the table is not loaded and is in the correct position to receive a blank. Both attributes will be of boolean type $\mathbb{B}$.

The task Specify *Table* System has already a current reduction which is partial. The new reduction will be a composition of ***reusing a system*** and ***extending state***. It appears that *Can_Receive* is a constrained attribute, depending completely on *Rot_Pos*, *Vert_Pos* and *Loaded*. To denote the correct position, two constants are introduced, *FB_Rot* for the rotation (the table is turned towards the feed belt) and *FB_Vert* for the vertical position (the table is at the feed belt height).

The definition of the two attributes *Loaded* and *Can_receive* has several effects concerning the tasks to be achieved as shown in Figure 4:

- specify the constants *FB_Rot* and *FB_Vert*,
- propagate the introduction of the attribute *Loaded* throughout the Table system specification: each operation has to be revisited in order to indicate its precondition and postcondition in terms of the *Loaded* attribute (the attribute *Can_receive* being completely defined in the predicate, its introduction does not need to be propagated).

Concerning the meta-program, the application of the operator ***extending state*** will redefine the two variables *btc* and *sys_Table* associated to the task Specify *Table* System.

To add the attributes to the table system, the product operator *adj_att* is used. This operator has as parameters, the old definition of the Table system, the declarations of the attributes to be added and the new predicate:

sys_Table = *adj_att(old(sys_Table), <att_decl3_Table, att_decl4_Table>, new_pred_Table)* : PAR P

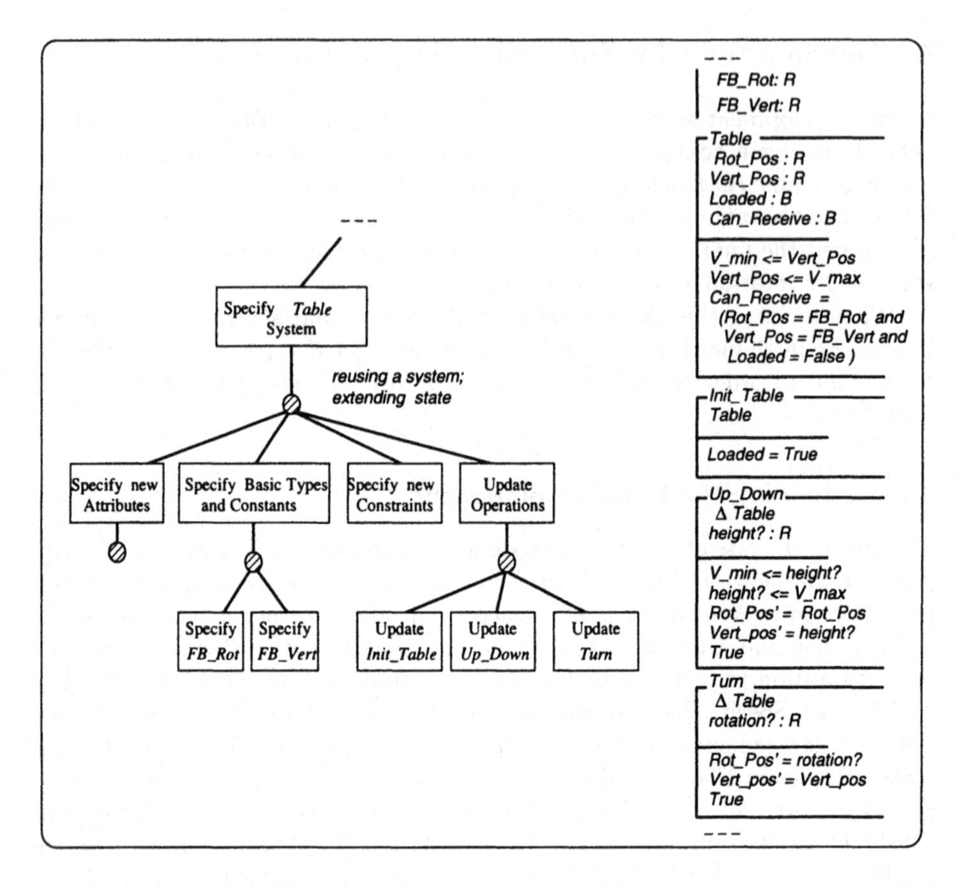

Fig. 4. The Table system definition revisited

The two variables *att_decl3_Table* and *att_decl4_Table* are introduced together with their intermediates variables. The names are given interactively, as are the types:

att_decl3_Table	= *make(att_name3_Table, att_type3_Table)*	: DECL	T
att_decl4_Table	= *make(att_name4_Table, att_type4_Table)*	: DECL	T
att_name3_Table	= *"Loaded"*	: NAME	G
att_type3_Table	= *B*	: TYPE	G
att_name4_Table	= *"Can_Receive"*	: NAME	G
att_type4_Table	= *B*	: TYPE	G

These attributes are constrained by a predicate given interactively as the value of the variable *new_pred_Table*:

new_pred_Table	= *eq(Can_Receive, eq(Rot_Pos, FB_Rot) and eq(Vert_Pos, FB_Vert) and eq(Loaded, False))*	: PRED	G

The operator ***extending state*** also modifies the variable *btc*. As the predicate *new_pred_Table* introduces two new constants, *FB_Rot* and *FB_Vert* to be defined by the tasks Specify *FB_Rot* and Specify *FB_Vert*, their declarations are added to the variable *btc* and their definitions initialised:

btc	= *old(btc)* ^ *<const_FB_Rot, const_FB_Vert>*	: PAR_LIST	P
const_FB_Rot	= *make(const_name1, const_type1, const_pred1)*	: G_DECL	T
const_name1	= *"FB_Rot"*	: NAME	G
const_type1	= *induce_type(sys_Table, const_name1)*	: TYPE	P
const_pred1	= *true*	: PRED	I
const_FB_Vert	= *make(const_name2, const_type2, const_pred2)*	: G_DECL	T
const_name2	= *"FB_Vert"*	: NAME	G
const_type2	= *induce_type(sys_Table, const_name2)*	: TYPE	P
const_pred2	= *true*	: PRED	I

Let us note that the type of the two constants is induced but can still be modified. The evaluation of the resulting meta-program gives the product part of Figure 4.

4.2 Backtracking in Order to Get a New Definition

Let us suppose that we want now to reuse another table system definition from the specification library. We can backtrack to a previous development state and propose another version for this sub-system. Figure 5 shows the development step obtained when backtracking to the Specify *Table* System reduction. The information concerning the Table system disappear from the current development state. The old version is kept and can be brought back again as current if necessary.

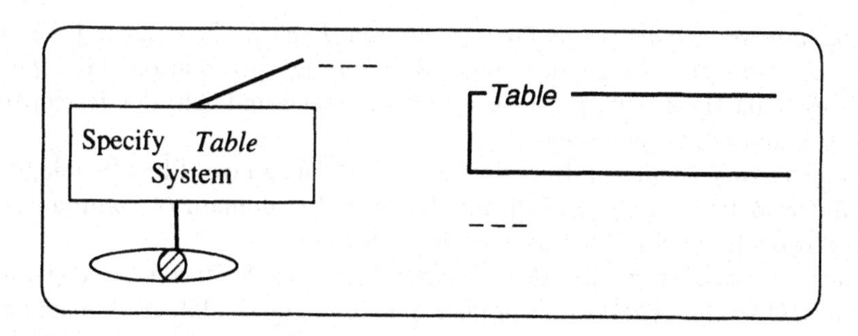

Fig. 5. Towards a new definition for the Table system

In the meta-program obtained after backtracking, all the definitions concerning the Table system are hidden as shown in Figure 6.

sys_name	= *"Prod_Cell"*	: NAME	G
sys	= *init*	: ANY	I
	= *<parl_Prod_Cell, par_Prod_Cell, go_Prod_Cell>*	: PAR_LIST	T
parl_Prod_Cell	= *btc ^ sub_sys*	: PAR_LIST	T
btc	= <>	: PAR_LIST	I
sub_sys	= <>	: PAR_LIST	I
	= *sys_Table*	: PAR_LIST	P
sys_name1	= *"Table"*	: NAME	G
sys_Table	= <>	: PAR_LIST	I
par_Prod_Cell	= *make(sys_name, nl_Prod_Cell, gc_Prod_Cell)*	: PAR	T
nl_Prod_Cell	= *names_of(sub_sys)*	: NAME_LIST	T
gc_Prod_Cell	= <>	: PRED_LIST	I
go_Prod_Cell	= <>	: PAR_LIST	I

Fig. 6. Current state of the meta-program after backtracking

5 Conclusion

With the concepts of workplan, meta-program and operators, we have introduced a way of organising the work that has to be carried out when developing specifications. The purpose of the operators is to capture the knowledge of the specifiers. The introduction of the meta-program, intermediate between the workplan and the product, makes it possible to define operators expressing different kinds of approaches. In particular, operators not directly influencing the current product state, and whose goal is to prepare the future work to be done, can be described. The use of notions not necessarily present in specification languages is possible, making easier the definition of approaches which are not syntactically driven. With the manipulation of variables in the meta-program, it is easy to operate at different product levels, making evolve in one step several parts of the specification. A variable can be defined by successive approximations, each definition detailing a bit more its associated product.

The benefits of the Proplane model devoted to specification modelling presented in this paper can be summed up as follows:

- *standardised acquisition and documentation [Par94].* The steps and the workplan record the design decisions taken during specification development. They make the specification easier to understand and help the developers to verify and refine the system ;
- *language-independency.* Experiments with the languages Pluss [Sou93,SL93], Glider, Z [DS93,LS94,Smi94] and Lotos in the domain of communication protocols [Lam96,LLS97] have been carried out ;
- *incremental construction of the specification, e.g. by successive approximations.* Operators enable the specifier to focus on methodological issues before addressing technical details related to the specification language [LS96] ;
- *support for guidance.* At any stage of the construction process, the specifier knows what remains to be done. In addition, operator preconditions restrain the set of applicable operators ;
- *support for backtracking.* Backtracking on decisions with the undoing of task side-effects is a basic construct in design processes which is rarely supported

in existing process models. Backtracking is supported by starting new reductions at appropriate places in the workplan;
- *replay*. Development decisions are recorded and thus a given development can be replayed [SS97].

Operators can be compared with specification templates introduced in [Tur96]. A template formalises a Lotos specification style for OSI as a fragment of specification text that can be conveniently recalled and inserted in a specification. To enhance the value of such templates and increase their generality, templates can be parameterised. Their instantiation is carried out by a macro processor, *m4* [KP76]. Operators in Proplane are more general than K. Turner's templates: (i) the history is recorded, (ii) operator composition is not pre-determined, (iii) the choice of operators is constrained by typing and preconditions and (iv) variables of the meta-program enable to take into account the development state.

References

[BMR+96] F. Buschmann, R. Meunier, H. Rohnert, P. Sommerlad, and M. Stal. *Pattern-Oriented Software Architecture, a System of Patterns.* J. Wiley and Sons, Inc, 1996.

[DS93] R. Darimont and J. Souquières. A Development Model: Application to Z specifications. In *Proc. of the IFIP WG 8.1 Working Conference on Information System Development Process*, Como, Italy, 1993. North Holland. September 1993.

[FKN94] A. Finkelstein, J. Kramer, and B. Nuseibeh, editors. *Software Process Modelling and Technology.* Wiley, 1994.

[GHJV95] E. Gamma, R. Helm, R. Johnson, and J. Vlissides. *Design Patterns - Elements of Reusable Object-Oriented Software.* Addison-Wesley, 1995.

[HL97] M. Heisel and N. Lévy. Using LOTOS patterns to characterize architectural styles. In *Proc. 7th International Joint Conference on the Theory and Practice of Software Development, (TAPSOFT'97-FASE)*, volume 1214 of *Lecture Notes in Computer Science*, April 1997.

[JvL94] P. Jamart and A. van Lamsweerde. A Reflective Approach to Process Model Customization, Enactment amd Evolution. *Proc. 3th Int. Conf. on Soft. Process, ICSP3*, pages 21–32, 1994.

[KP76] Brian W. Kernighan and P.J. Plauger. *Software Tools.* Reading. Addison-Wesley, Massachusetts, USA, 1976.

[Lam96] T. Lambolais. Development of Automata with LOTOS. In *Method Integration Workshop'96.* Leeds Metropolitan University, March 1996.

[Lév95] N. Lévy. Improving PROPLANE: a specifications development framework. In *Proc. Second IFAC Int. Workshop on Safety and Reliability in Emerging Control Technologies, Daytona Beach, Florida*, pages 229–240, November 1995.

[LL95] Claus Lewerentz and Thomas Lindner. *Formal development of reactive systems: case study production cell.* Number 891 in Lecture Notes in Computer Science. Springer-Verlag, 1995.

[LL96] T. Lambolais and N. Lévy. A Library of Development Operators to Specify Protocols. Technical report, CRIN-CNRS/CNET, 1996.

[LLS97] Th. Lambolais, N. Lévy, and J. Souquières. Assistance au développement de spécifications de protocoles de communication. In *Conférence AFADL, Approches formelles dans l'assistance au développement de logiciels*, Toulouse, Mai 1997.

[LS94] N. Lévy and G. Smith. A language-independent approach to specification construction. In *Proceedings of the ACM SIGSOFT'94: Symposium on the Foundations of Software Engineering, New Orleans, USA.*, pages 76–86, December 1994.

[LS96] N. Lévy and J. Souquières. A "coming and going" approach to specification construction: a scenario. In *Proceedings of the 8th International Workshop on Software Specification and Design (IWSSD-8)*, pages 155–158, Schloss Velen, Germany, March 1996.

[Nil71] N.-J. Nilsson. *Problem Solving Methods in Artificial Intelligence.* Computer Sciences Series. Mac Graw-Hill, 1971.

[Par94] D. L. Parnas. Software Aging. In *Proc. of ICSE-16*, pages 279–287. IEEE Press, May 1994.

[Sha95] M. Shaw. Beyond objects; a software design paradigm based on process control. *ACM SIGSOFT Software Engineering notes*, 20(1):27–38, January 1995.

[SL93] J. Souquières and N. Lévy. Description of Specification Developments. In *Proceedings IEEE International Symposium on Requirements Engineering*, San Diego (CA, USA), January 1993.

[SL96] J. Souquières and N. Lévy. PROPLANE : A Specification Development Environment. In *Fifth International Conference on Algebraic Methodology and Software Methodology AMAST'96*, volume 1101, Munich (G), July 1996. Lecture Notes in Computer Science.

[Smi94] G. Smith. A Development Framework for Object-Oriented Specification and Refinement. In B. Magnusson, B. Meyer, J.-M. Nerson, and J.-F. Perrot, editors, *Proceedings of TOOLS EUROPE'94*, March 1994.

[Sou93] J. Souquières. Aides au développement de spécifications. Thèse d'Etat de l'Université de Nancy 1, 1993.

[Spi89] J.M. Spivey. *The Z Notation: A Reference Manual.* Series in Computer Science. Prentice-Hall International, Englewood Cliffs, NJ, 1989.

[SS97] S. Sadaoui and J. Souquières. Quelques approches de la réutilisation en Proplane. In *Conférence AFADL, Approches formelles dans l'assistance au développement de logiciels*, Toulouse, Mai 1997.

[Tur96] K. J. Turner. Relating architecture and specification. *To appear in Computer Networks and ISDN Systems*, April 1996.

On Partial Validation of Logic Programs

Sébastien Limet[1] and Frédéric Saubion[1,2]

[1] LIFO, Université d'Orléans (France), { limet, saubion }@lifo.univ-orleans.fr
[2] LERIA, Université d'Angers (France), Frederic.Saubion@univ-angers.fr

Abstract. In this paper, we propose a method allowing us to compare the result of an execution of a logic program and a specification of the intended semantics. This approach is particularly interesting when the set of answers cannot be computed in finite time with usual prolog interpreters. We compute, using a special operational mechanism, a finite set of rewrite rules synthesizing the whole set of answers w.r.t. a goal. Then, we use some tree tuple grammar based techniques to express the languages of the computed answers. An algorithm allows us to compare this language with the intended semantics language which is extracted from a user's specification. This method can be considered as a partial validation mechanism for logic programs.

1 Introduction

Validation, partial validation and verification constitute central issues for full logic programming environment building [5]. By partial validation we mean here the comparison between the operational semantics of the program for a given goal, computed by an execution mechanism, and a specification of an user's intended semantics. The most common trend in verification is algorithmic debugging, based on [11], which consists in comparing the execution of the program with its formal specification. We may distinguish two different validation problems: soundness (i.e. each computed answer is correct w.r.t. the intended semantics) and sufficiency (i.e. each intended answer is computed by the mechanism). Of course, in order to perform such a comparison, we need to compute the full set of answers in finite time.

Unfortunately, with standard Prolog interpreters, some problems arise either because the set of computed answers is infinite or because the mechanism loops, providing no answer. In this context, since the operational semantics cannot be completely observed, it is not possible to check if it fits the intended semantics.

To overcome this problem, one needs tools to finitely compute, represent and compare infinite sets of solutions. In a logic programming framework, answers to a given problem are first-order terms. Therefore, a set of answers can be described by a tree grammar. With this approach, validation just consists in comparing the tree languages corresponding to the operational semantics and the intended one.

In this paper, we propose a partial validation method for logic programming relying on an integration of different rewriting based techniques. In fact, the first problem is the finite computation of infinite sets of answers. This can be achieved by using an alternative resolution mechanism based on an extension of the Knuth-Bendix completion procedure, called *Linear Completion (LC)* [2, 3] (see section 3). From a theoretical point of view, this mechanism is equivalent to Prolog but has a much more efficient behavior than standard SLD-resolution. It provides three main advantages : more frequent termination (by pruning unproductive loops), a synthesis ability (i.e. representation of infinite set of solutions by giving answers as a finite set of rewrite rules) and negation handling without any restriction.

In order to use this compact representation of solutions, we transform the set of answer rewrite rules into a new kind of grammar called tree tuple synchronized grammars (TTSG) (see section 4 and [8]). In this context, the operational semantics of P for the goal G corresponds to the language recognized by this grammar. At this step, we provide to the user two levels of description to define its intended semantics: either by a regular tree tuple grammar or by a term rewriting system (i.e. a set of oriented equations in the style of algebraic specifications) which we are able transform into a TTSG.

At this time, we provide a new algorithm (see section 5) to compare the operational and intended semantics languages based on the use of tree grammars. This method also allows us to test properties (like type checking) which is very useful for program verification. An example (see section 3.2) will be completely developed all along this paper to illustrate how partial validation of logic programs can be achieved in our framework.

2 Preliminaries

In this section, we recall the basic definitions related to logic programming and rewriting techniques. We refer the reader to [4, 9] for more details.

Let Σ be a finite set of symbols and V be an infinite set of variables, $T_{\Sigma \cup V}$ is the first-order term algebra over Σ and V. Σ is partitioned in two parts: the set $\mathcal{F}$ of function symbols, and the set $\mathcal{C}$ of constructors. A term is said linear if it does not contain several times the same variable. A term is said to be ground if it does not contain any variable.

Let t be a term, $O(t)$ is the set of occurrences of t, $t|_u$ is the subterm of t at occurrence u and $t(u)$ is the symbol that labels the occurrence u of t. $t[u \leftarrow s]$ is the term obtained by replacing in t the subterm at occurrence u by s. A substitution is a mapping from V into $T_{\Sigma \cup V}$, which extends trivially to a mapping from $T_{\Sigma \cup V}$ to $T_{\Sigma \cup V}$.

In the following x, y, z denote variables, s, t, l, r denote terms, f, g, h function symbols, c a constructor symbol, u, v, w occurrences, and σ, θ substitutions. In general, $\bar{t}$ will denote a list of terms $t_1, \ldots, t_n$, and $\bar{x}$, a list of variables.

We generalize the occurrences (as well as the above notations) to tuples in the following way: let $p = (p_1, \ldots, p_n)$ a tuple, $\forall i \in [1, n]$ $p|_i = p_i$, and when the p_i's are terms, $p|_{i.u} = p_i|_u$.

We consider now a set of predicate symbols Π. Atomic formulas are defined in the usual way (see [9]). A list of atoms $A_1, \cdots, A_n$ will be denoted as $\overline{A}$ (and this will mean their conjunction). A symbol $\neg$ denotes the negation : a literal is and atom or a negated atom.

A clause is a pair $(head, body)$ (written under the form : $head$: $-$ $body$.) where $head$ is an atom and $body$ is a conjunction of literals. If the body is empty, we have a $fact$. A logic program is just a set of clauses. Usual declarative and operational semantics can be found in [9].

A simplification ordering on terms is an irreflexive and transitive relation, which is stable under substitutions, and monotonic (i.e. stable under contexts) , and is such that any term is strictly bigger than any of its proper subterms ; this notion is extended to any first order signature. Such orderings are easily built over any specified precedence relation on the symbols.

A term rewrite system (TRS) is a finite set of oriented equations called rewrite rules or rules. lhs means left-hand-side and rhs means right-hand-side. For a TRS R, the rewrite relation is denoted by $\rightarrow_R$ and is defined by $t \rightarrow_R s$ if there exists a rule $l \rightarrow r$ in R, a non-variable occurrence u in t, and a substitution σ, such that $t|_u = \sigma l$ and $s = t[u \leftarrow \sigma r]$. The reflexive-transitive closure of $\rightarrow_R$ is denoted by $\rightarrow_R^*$, and the symmetric closure of $\rightarrow_R^*$ is denoted by $=_R$.

A TRS is said confluent if $t \rightarrow_R^* t_1$ and $t \rightarrow_R^* t_2$ implies $t_1 \rightarrow_R^* t_3$ and $t_2 \rightarrow_R^* t_3$ for some t_3. If the lhs (resp. rhs) of every rule is linear the TRS is said left-(resp. right-linear). If it is both left and right-linear the TRS is said linear. A TRS is constructor based if every rule is of the form $f(t_1, \ldots, t_n) \rightarrow r$ where the t_i's are data-terms.

t narrows into s, if there exists a rule $l \rightarrow r$ in R, a non-variable occurrence u of t, such that $\sigma t|_u = \sigma l$ where $\sigma = mgu(t|_u, l)$ and $s = (\sigma t)[u \leftarrow \sigma r]$. We write $t \leadsto_{[u, l \rightarrow r, \sigma]} s$, and the relation $\leadsto$ is called narrowing.

The next section present the first component of our validation scheme, i.e. the evaluation mechanism used to compute the operational semantics of the logic program.

3 Linear completion : a brief review

Application of term rewriting systems has been widely studied to provide new execution mechanisms for logic programs. Linear Completion is issued from the works of [3, 2] and has been extended in [1] to include constructive negation. By transforming clauses into logical equivalences considered as rewrite rules, logic programs are represented as rewrite programs whose operational mechanism is derived from the Knuth-Bendix completion procedure. One of the main contribution of rewrite techniques, introduced in this mechanism, is the fact that we gain a simplification rule which is essential for the loop avoiding and synthesis properties.

3.1 Program Transformation and Operational Semantics

We first transform logic programs into sets of rewrite rules thanks to the following function Ψ. We assume given a simplification ordering $\succ$.

Definition 1. Given a logic program P, we get a rewrite program $\Psi(P)$ by applying the following transformation rules:
- A fact A of P is transformed into the rewrite rule $A \rightarrow true$
- Any clause $A :- \overline{B}$ in P is transformed into the rewrite rule : $A, \overline{B} \rightarrow \overline{B}$, except when the ordering $\succ$ is such that $A \succ \overline{B}$ and no other head in P unifies with A : in such a case the clause gets transformed more simply into $A \rightarrow \overline{B}$.
- For each predicate $B(\overline{t})$ appearing in the body of a clause and not defined elsewhere in the program P, we add a rule : $B(\overline{x}) \rightarrow false$.
- For each predicate $C(\overline{t})$ appearing in the body of a clause, and defined elsewhere only with facts of the form $C(\overline{t_1}).,\ldots,C(\overline{t_p}).$, we add a constrained rewrite rule : $C(\overline{x}) \rightarrow false \; [\![\overline{x} \neq \overline{t_1}, \ldots, \overline{x} \neq \overline{t_p}]\!]$

This translation introduces new constants $true$ and $false$. Note that the constraints $[\![c]\!]$ are just unification constraints and can be mixed with usual substitution notions without adding any specific treatment. To describe the operational semantics of the rewrite program $\Psi(P)$, one needs to define what a goal will be in this context ; a special predicate Ans, assumed not defined elsewhere, is introduced, with arity equal to the number of free variables in the goal; the ordering $\succ$ is extended such that for every symbol s other than $true$ and $false$, we have $s \succ Ans \succ true \succ false$.

Definition 2. .
i) A goal rule is a rule of the form : $\overline{Q} \rightarrow Ans(\overline{x})$ where $\overline{x}$ denotes the set of free variables appearing in $\overline{Q}$.
ii) A state of computation is a triple $(P\,;G\,;M)$ where : P denotes a rewrite program, G denotes a rule (the current goal rule to process), M denotes a set of rules which are the ancestors of the current goal : M is the stored memory, containing the goal rules used to simplify the current goal rule.
iii) An initial state of a rewrite program $\Psi(P)$ is a triple $(\Psi(P)\,;\overline{Q} \rightarrow Ans(\overline{x})\,;\emptyset)$.

The mechanism is described as a transition system over the computation states. In comparison with standard SLD resolution mechanisms, if a σ substitution is an answer for a goal $\overline{Q}$ w.r.t. a pure logic program P, then our inference mechanism must be able to lead from an initial state $(P;\, \overline{Q} \rightarrow Ans(\overline{x});\, \emptyset)$ to a final state of the form $(P; \sigma(Ans(\overline{x})) \rightarrow true; M)$. The inference system LC is described by the following inference rules, more explanations can be found in [1, 2]

Delete

$$\frac{(\Psi(P)\,;\overline{A} \leftrightarrow \overline{A}\,;M)}{(\Psi(P)\,;-\,;M)}$$

Orient

$$\frac{(\Psi(P)\,;\overline{A} \leftrightarrow \overline{B}\,;M)}{(\Psi(P)\,;\overline{A} \rightarrow \overline{B}\,;M)} \text{ if } \overline{A} \succ \overline{B}$$

Simplify

$$\frac{(\Psi(P)\,;\overline{A},\overline{A}' \rightarrow \overline{B}\,;M)}{(\Psi(P)\,;\sigma\overline{C},\sigma\overline{A} \leftrightarrow \sigma\overline{B}\,;M)}$$

if $\overline{A}'' \rightarrow \overline{C} \in \Psi(P) \cup M$ and $\overline{A}' = \sigma\overline{A}''$

Resolve-Neg

$$\frac{(\Psi(P)\,;\,\neg B,\overline{L} \rightarrow \overline{R}\,;\,M)}{(\Psi(P)\,;\,\bigwedge_i \neg(\overline{C_i}\; [\![\sigma_i]\!]),\overline{L} \leftrightarrow \overline{R}\,;\,M \cup \{\neg B,\overline{L} \rightarrow \overline{R}\})}$$

for each rule $A_i, \overline{C_i} \rightarrow \overline{C_i} \in \Psi(P)$ and $\sigma_i B = \sigma_i A_i$

Overlap

$$\frac{(\Psi(P)\,;p(\overline{s}),\overline{A}\rightarrow\overline{B}\,;M)}{(\Psi(P)\,;\sigma\overline{C},\sigma\overline{A}\leftrightarrow\sigma\overline{C},\sigma\overline{B}\,;M\cup\{p(\overline{s}),\overline{A}\rightarrow\overline{B}\})}$$

if $p(\overline{t}),\overline{C}\rightarrow\overline{C}\in\Psi(P)\cup M$ and $\sigma s=\sigma t$

$\mathcal{NC}$-extract

$$\frac{(\Psi(P)\,;\,\neg(\overline{D}\,[\![\sigma\wedge C]\!]),\overline{L}\rightarrow\overline{R}\,;\,M)}{(\Psi(P)\,;\,\overline{L}\leftrightarrow\overline{R}\,[\![\neg\sigma]\!]\,;\,M\cup\{\neg(\overline{D}\,[\![\sigma\wedge C]\!]),\overline{L}\rightarrow\overline{R}\})}$$

$\mathcal{C}$-ripple

$$\frac{(\Psi(P)\,;\,\neg(\overline{D}\,[\![\sigma\wedge C]\!]),\overline{L}\rightarrow\overline{R}\,;\,M)}{(\Psi(P)\,;\,\neg(\sigma(\overline{D})),\sigma\overline{L}\leftrightarrow\sigma\overline{R}\,[\![C]\!]\,;\,M\cup\{\neg(\overline{D}\,[\![\sigma\wedge C]\!]),\overline{L}\rightarrow\overline{R}\})}$$

We write : $(P;Q;M)\vdash_{LC}(P;Q';M')$ if the latter state derives from the former, by an application of one or more of the linear completion inference mechanism. We can define clearly the notion of success in our context:

Definition 3. A *terminal rule* is a rule appearing in a terminal state and having one of the two following forms:
- $Ans(\overline{t})\rightarrow true$
- $Ans(\overline{t_1}),\cdots,Ans(\overline{t_i})\leftrightarrow Ans(\overline{t_{i+1}}),\cdots,Ans(\overline{t_n})$

The first type of rules constitutes basic answers while the second kind allows one to deduce new answers from these basic cases. The operational semantics is then defined as:

$$Synth(P,G)=\{\alpha\rightarrow\beta\text{ terminal rule }\mid(G\rightarrow Ans(\overline{x}),\emptyset)\vdash_{LC}(\alpha\rightarrow\beta,M)\}$$

The soundness and completeness of LC w.r.t. to usual logical semantics [9] are insured by theorems proven in [1, 2].

3.2 Example

We present here a complete example to illustrate our method all along this paper. We consider the following logic program defining alternate lists of even and odd integers using their symbolic representation with 0 and the successor function s.

```
even(0).
even(s(s(X))) :- even(X).
odd(X) :- not even(X).
evenl([]).
evenl([X|L]) :- even(X),evenl(L).
oddl([]).
oddl([X|L]) :- odd(X),oddl(L).
merge([],[],[]).
merge([X1,X2|L],[X1|L1],[X2|L2]) :- merge(L,L1,L2).
listealt(L) :- merge(L,L1,L2),evenl(L1),oddl(L2).
```

The lists, solutions for the goal `listalt(L)`, look like $[e,o,e,o,...]$ where e and o respectively denote even and odd integers. This is written in a fully declarative style by merging alternately a list of even integers and a list of odd integers. An usual prolog interpreter won't be able to compute all these answers for two reasons: this set is infinite and there is a negation in the definition of *odd* which cannot be treated (problem of floundering with non ground negative literal). Moreover, if the programmer defines the `listealt` predicate as `listealt(L) :- evenl(L1),oddl(L2),merge(L,L1,L2).`, the interpreter only provides the answer [ ] and goes into an infinite unproductive branch which occults the other answers. This is a well-known drawback of Prolog related to the resolution strategy. But the programmer should not cope with this kind of technical consideration. This problem is avoided with LC which allows to prune such unproductive loops thanks to simplification techniques. Using LC, we get the following operational semantics:

$$Synth(P, listealt(L)) = \begin{cases} Ans([]) \rightarrow true \\ Ans([0, s(0)|L]) \rightarrow Ans(L) \\ Ans([0, s(s(x))|L]) \rightarrow Ans([0, x|L]) \\ Ans([s(s(x)), s(0)|L]) \rightarrow Ans([x, s(0)|L]) \\ Ans([s(s(x_1)), s(s(x_2))|L]) \rightarrow Ans([x_1, x_2|L]) \end{cases}$$

These five rules describe an infinite set of solutions. Negation has been discarded and this set can now be treated as a usual TRS. The remaining question is : "How should we characterize and use the set of answers defined by this TRS ?" (i.e. the terms that can be rewritten into *true*). The solution proposed in this paper relies on the use of a particular type of grammar that we recall in the following section.

4 The Tree Tuple Synchronized Grammars

The Tree Tuple Synchronized Grammars (TTSG for short) have been introduced in [8] in order to solve unification modulo a TRS. Indeed, under some restrictions on the TRS, in one hand, TTSG's have good properties to represent infinite sets of R-unifier and to decide if the unification problem has at least one solution.

In the previous section, we have transformed a logic program and a goal into a TRS that represents the set of solutions. One way to enumerate the solutions of the goal consists in solving the equation $Ans(\overline{x}) = true$ with narrowing techniques. Fortunately the TRS $Synth(P, G)$ respects the restrictions imposed in [8], so the set of solutions it represents can be expressed by means of a TTSG. This new representation helps to compare the semantics of $Synth(P, G)$ with the intended semantics of the logic program.

In this section we briefly recall how a unification problem is transform into a TTSG (see [8] for more details) and give some formal definitions on TTSG. Note that the TTSG obtained from the goal $Ans(\overline{x}) = true$ is much more simpler than those usually obtained for R-unification problems because there is only one function call in this goal.

4.1 From a TRS to a TTSG

The idea behind this transformation is to consider the TRS as a kind of tree automaton (thus a tree grammar). This tree automaton simulates the rewrite resolution mechanism called narrowing. In this contexts the constructor symbols (i.e. all the function symbols but Ans) are the terminals.

First a non-terminal is associated to each occurrence of each term of the TRS and the goal $Ans(\overline{x}) = true$ thanks to a systematic numbering (see figure). Note that the occurrence ϵ of the lhs and the rhs of each rewrite rule have the same non-terminal to simulate the rewrite relation.

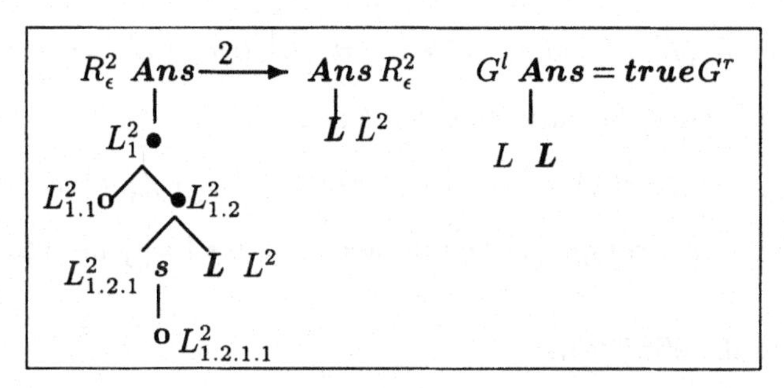

Once the non-terminals defined, we deduce productions from the TRS. The way the productions are computed is motivated by narrowing techniques. From the correspondence between rewriting and narrowing (lifting lemma [7]), the set of solutions of $Ans(x) = true$ is the set of the solutions computed by narrowing. This is why we look for narrowing possibilities. For instance, the right hand-side of rule 2 in our example, unifies with the left hand-side of the same rule. Therefore the narrowing step $Ans(L) \rightsquigarrow_{[\epsilon, r_2, L \mapsto 0 \bullet s(0) \bullet L']} Ans(L')$ is possible. This step achieves two operations: it maps the variable L to $0 \bullet s(0) \bullet L'$ and it sets the result of the narrowing step to $Ans(L')$.

From the TTSG point of view, this narrowing step is simulated as follows. The term $Ans(L)$ is represented by the non-terminal R^2_ϵ (see figure) and the variable L by L^2. Therefore the pair (R^2_ϵ, L^2) encodes $(Ans(L), L)$. The fact that $Ans(L)$ unifies with $Ans(0 \bullet s(0) \bullet L')$ (the renamed version of the left hand-side of rule 2) is encoded by the empty production $R^2_\epsilon \Rightarrow R^2_\epsilon$. The fact that the previous unification instantiates L is encoded by the empty production $L^2 \Rightarrow L^2_1$. In order to force these two operations to be achieved at the same time, the two productions are synchronized in the pack of productions $\{R^2_\epsilon \Rightarrow R^2_\epsilon,\ L^2 \Rightarrow L^2_1\}$. Thus when it is applied on (R^2_ϵ, L^2), we get (R^2_ϵ, L^2_1) which means that the unification is about to be done and therefore the narrowing step too, but the new constructors produced by the unification and the narrowing step have not appeared yet. This is the aim of the free productions deduced from subterm relationships. Back to example 3.2, the narrowing step does not produce any constructor but L is instantiated by $0 \bullet s(0) \bullet L'$ which is encoded by the free productions: $L^2_1 \Rightarrow \bullet(L^2_{1.1}, L^2_{1.2})$, $L^2_{1.1} \Rightarrow 0$, $L^2_{1.2} \Rightarrow \bullet(L^2_{1.2.1}, L^2)$, $L^2_{1.2.1} \Rightarrow s(L^2_{1.2.1.1})$, $L^2_{1.2.1.1} \Rightarrow 0$ The narrowing step is completely achieved by the derivation

$$(R^2_\epsilon, L^2_1) \Rightarrow^* (R^2_\epsilon, 0 \bullet s(0) \bullet L^2)$$

One can easily see that a second application of rule 2 on $Ans(L')$ can be simulated by applying again the pack of productions and then the free productions.

In fact, some other productions are deduced to compute the ground instances of the solutions but for lack of space we do not describe them.

The axiom of the grammar is defined by a tuple of initial symbols in order to describe the instance of each variable of the goal. For a goal $Ans(X_1,\ldots,X_n) = true$ the initial symbol is $(G^l, X_1,\ldots,X_n)$. In our example, it is (G^l, L).

One derivation of the TTSG of our example is

$$(G^l, L) \Rightarrow (R^2_\epsilon, L^2_1) \Rightarrow^* (R^2_\epsilon, 0 \bullet 1 \bullet L^2) \Rightarrow (R^1_\epsilon, 0 \bullet 1 \bullet L^1_1) \Rightarrow^* (true, 0 \bullet 1 \bullet [])$$

which simulates the narrowing derivation

$$Ans(L) \rightsquigarrow_{r_2, L \mapsto 0 \bullet 1 \bullet L'} Ans(L') \rightsquigarrow_{r_1, L' \mapsto []} true$$

This derivation computes the solution $\{L \mapsto 0 \bullet 1 \bullet []\}$ i.e. $\{L \mapsto [0,1]\}$.

4.2 Formal definitions

In the following, NT is a finite set of non-terminal symbols and recall that $\mathcal{C}$ is the set of constructor symbols (i.e. all the function symbols but Ans). Upper-case letters denote elements of NT.

Definition 4. A **production** is a rule of the form $X \Rightarrow t$ where $X \in NT$ and $t \in T_{\mathcal{C} \cup NT}$. A **pack of productions** is a set of productions denoted $\{X_1 \Rightarrow t_1, \ldots, X_n \Rightarrow t_n\}$. When the pack is a singleton of the form $\{X_1 \Rightarrow c(Y_1,\ldots,Y_n)\}$ where c is a constructor and $Y_1,\ldots,Y_n$ non-terminals, the production is said **free**, and is written more simply $X_1 \Rightarrow c(Y_1,\ldots,Y_n)$. When the pack is of the form $\{X_1 \Rightarrow Y_1, \ldots, X_n \Rightarrow Y_n\}$ where $Y_1,\ldots,Y_n$ are non-terminals, the productions of the pack are said **synchronized**.

Definition 5. A **TTSG** is defined by a 4-tuple $(\mathcal{C}, NT, PP, TI)$ where

- $\mathcal{C}$ is the set of constructors (terminals in the terminology of grammars),
- NT is the finite set of non-terminals,
- PP is a finite set of packs of productions,
- TI is the axiom of the TTSG. It is a tuple $((I_1, 0), \ldots, (I_n, 0))$ where every I_i is a non-terminal.

The 0 coupled to the non-terminals of the axiom of the TTSG are introduced because the TTSG described in previously does not take into account variable renamings which could leads to incorrect TTSG derivation. To solve this problem, an integer is coupled with any non-terminals in a derivation of the TTSG. This integer controls the synchronizations in the following way: a synchronized pack of derivation can be applied only on non-terminal whose control number are equal.

Definition 6. The set of **computations** of a TTSG $Gr = (Sz, \mathcal{C}, NT, PP, TI)$ denoted $\boldsymbol{Comp(Gr)}$ is the smallest set defined by:

- TI is in $Comp(Gr)$,

- if tp is in $Comp(Gr)$ and $tp|_u = (X, ct)$ and the free production $X \Rightarrow c(Y_1, \ldots, Y_n)$ is in PP then $tp[u \leftarrow c((Y_1, ct), \ldots, (Y_n, ct))]$ is in $Comp(Gr)$,
- if tp is in $Comp(Gr)$ and there exists n pairwise different occurrences $u_1, \ldots, u_n$ of tp such that $\forall i \in [1, n]$ $tp|_{u_i} = (X_i, ct_i)$ and $ct_1 = ct_2 = \ldots = ct_n$ and the pack of productions $\{X_1 \Rightarrow Y_1, \ldots, X_n \Rightarrow Y_n\} \in PP$, then $tp[u_1 \leftarrow (Y_1, b)] \ldots [u_n \leftarrow (Y_n, b)]$ (where b is a new integer) is in $Comp(Gr)$.

The symbol $\Rightarrow$ denoting also the above two deduction steps, a **derivation** of Gr is a sequence of computations $TI \Rightarrow tp_1 \Rightarrow \ldots \Rightarrow tp_n$. The language **recognized** by a TTSG Gr denoted $\boldsymbol{Rec(Gr)}$ is the set of tuples of ground data-terms $Comp(Gr) \cap T_C^n$.

In [8], we prove that the language recognized by the TTSG deduced from the TRS gives the solutions of the goal $Ans(\overline{x}) = true$. Here are some technical definitions and properties needed in the following.

Definition 7. Let $Gr = (C, NT, PP, TI)$ a TTSG.
- A set of non-terminals $\{X_1, \ldots, X_n\}$ of NT is a *synchronization* of Gr if there is a pack of synchronized production $\{X_1 \Rightarrow Y_1, \ldots, X_n \Rightarrow Y_n\}$ in PP. Note that for a TTSG built from a TRS, a non terminal belongs at most to one synchronization of the grammar.
- A computation of Gr is said in *simplified form* if no free production can be applied on it. We note $tp \Rightarrow\downarrow tp'$ the derivation from tp to a simplified form. Note that if Gr comes from a TRS, any computation as a unique simplified form.
- $Class(tp, u)$ for a computation tp of Gr and a non-terminal occurrence u of tp is the set of occurrences that may be synchronized with u. It is defined if $tp|_u = (X, a)$ by $Class(tp, u) = \{v \mid tp|_v = (Y, a)\}$. The set of non-terminals $NT - Class$ associated to $Class(tp, u)$ defined by $NT - Class(tp, u) = \{Y \mid tp|_v = (Y, a)\}$. Note that for a TTSG coming from a TRS, all non-terminals of a $NT - Class$ are different which means that the possible $NT - Class$ for this TTSG is finite.

5 Application to Program Partial Validation

In this section we expose our method for partial validation of logic programs (i.e. comparing the result of an execution with a formal specification of the intended semantics).

5.1 The Partial Validation Problem

The method proposed here is based on the the use of grammars, and more particularly TTSG introduced by [8], to describe both computed and intended semantics.

Starting from a logic program P and a goal G, LC (see section 3) allows to compute a set of answer rules $Synth(P, G)$ containing only one predicate Ans. This set is transformed into a TTSG (see section 4) defining the language of computed answers for the goal G and then simplified. It will be denoted $G_{Synth(P,G)}$.

Now, we have to describe how the user may specify the intended semantics of a program P for a given goal G (denoted $Int(P,G)$). Our approach provides two different levels of description that allows two kinds of representation:

- The user can give a term rewriting system using terminal rules, with Ans predicate (see definition 3), to describe $Int(P,G)$, which is the set of intended answers. For instance, to specify even numbers, the user will write $Ans(0) \rightarrow true$ and $Ans(s(s(X))) \rightarrow Ans(X)$. This set is then transformed into a simplified TTSG $G_{Int(P,G)}$ describing thus the language of intended answers. This allows the user to specify $Int(P,G)$ in the style of algebraic specifications.
- But the user may prefer to write directly a regular tree tuple grammar $G_{Int(P,G)}$ to define the intended answers. Such grammars are known to be a very simple and understandable way to describe languages. Moreover, it also allows to express program properties like type checking.

Therefore, validating the program P for a given goal G consists in comparing the language of computed answers with the one of intended answers. The following definition states the two validation aspects we are interested in.

Definition 8. Given a logic program P and a goal G, P is said to be:
- correct for G iff $Rec(G_{Synth(P,G)}) \subseteq Rec(G_{Int(P,G)})$
- sufficient (or complete) for G iff $Rec(G_{Int(P,G)}) \subseteq Rec(G_{Synth(P,G)})$

The full validation method may be summarized as follows:

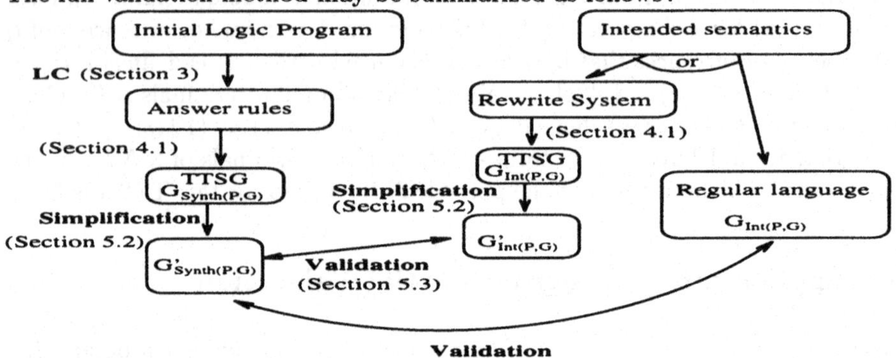

5.2 Simplifying a TTSG

In this subsection, we give two inference rules that simplify a TTSG that comes from a rewriting systems, eliminating useless productions. This enables to simplify test between grammars. The inference rules are inspired by simplification of regular tree grammars but are very different because of synchronizations. The productions that are eliminated are, on one hand, *unreachable productions* (i.e. productions that are not used in any derivation of the grammar) and, on the other hand, unproductive productions (i.e. productions that never lead to a tuple recognized by the grammar when they are applied).

Here is an algorithm that separates reachable and unreachable productions of a TTSG computed from a TRS. Let $Gr = (C, NT, PP, TI)$ be a TTSG.

```
ToDo=∅ ; Done={TI} ; PP_reach = ∅
while ToDo ≠ ∅ do
    Let (X_1,...,X_n) ∈ ToDo
    Done=Done ∪{(X_1,...,X_n)} ;     ToDo=ToDo \{(X_1,...,X_n)}
    for all p ∈ PP such that (X_1,...,X_n) ⇒ tp using p do
        PP_reach = PP_reach ∪ {p}
        Add to ToDo NT − Class of tp that are not in Done
     end for
end while
PP_unreach = PP \ PP_reach
```

This algorithm terminates because the number of possible $NT - Class$ is finite for TTSG coming from a TRS. The idea of the algorithm is the following, in a computation two $NT - Class$ are always derived independently (i.e. there are no possible synchronizations between two classes) because the application of a synchronized pack always divides a class into two classes and never merges two classes. Therefore the algorithm explores all the $NT - Classes$ that can be reached from the axiom, and for each $NT - Classes$ looks for applicable pack of productions. Thus at the end of the algorithm we get all the reachable productions.

Now let us give the inference rules that eliminates the useless production of a grammar.

Unreachable productions

$$\frac{PP \cup \{p\}}{PP} \text{ if } p \text{ is an unreachable pack of productions}$$

Unproductive synchronization

$$\frac{PP \cup \{\{X_1 \Rightarrow Y_1, \ldots, X_n \Rightarrow Y_n\}\}}{PP}$$

if $(Y_1, \ldots, Y_n) \Rightarrow\downarrow (t_1, \ldots, t_n)$ and one $NT - Class$ of $(t_1, \ldots, t_n)$ is not a synchronization of the grammar.

Obviously, when **Unreachable productions** is applied on PP, it does not modify the recognized language of the grammar because the production eliminated can never be used in a derivation. On the other hand, the application of **Unproductive synchronization** does not change the language too because, from the synchronization $(X_1, \ldots, X_n)$ we get the tuple $(t_1, \ldots, t_n)$ (from properties of TTSG coming from a TRS this tuple is unique) on which no more free productions can be applied. Moreover one $NT - Class$ of $(t_1, \ldots, t_n)$ is not a synchronization, this means that on this $NT - Class$ no more productions can be applied, so when $\{X_1 \Rightarrow Y_1, \ldots, X_n \Rightarrow Y_n\}$ is applied on a computation, the result can never produce a tuple of the language recognized by the grammar.

Simplifying a TTSG $G = (C, NT, PP, TI)$ coming from a TRS, consists in applying **Unproductive synchronization** on PP as long as it is applicable and then **Unreachable productions**. We obtain a pack of productions PP'. NT' is the set of non-terminals used in PP'. The *simplified version* of G is $G' = (\mathcal{C}, NT' \cup \{TI\}, PP', TI)$. A TTSG in simplified form has the following nice property.

Proposition 9. *Let $G = (\mathcal{C}, NT, PP, TI)$ be a TTSG in simplified form. If $TI \Rightarrow^* tp$ then $tp \Rightarrow^* tp'$ and $tp' \in Reg(G)$.*

In other words any derivation of G is successful. A consequence of this lemma is that if $Rec(G) = \emptyset$ then $PP = \emptyset$ because PP does not contain any unreachable productions and no derivations are successful.
Note that for a given TTSG G, the simplified form is unique but unfortunately when two TTSG, G_1 and G_2 are such that $Rec(G_1) = Rec(G_2)$, the simplified form of G_1 and G_2 are not always equal.
Now testing validity of a logic program P with a goal G wrt an intended semantics expressed by a TRS consists in simplifying $G_{Synth(G,P)}$ and $G_{Int(G,P)}$, then comparing the two grammars. If they are equal the program is correct and complete wrt to the intended semantics. If they are different we cannot say anything because of the previous remark. Note that due to synchronizations, it seems to be undecidable in general to test $Rec(G_1) = Rec(G_2)$ for two TTSG. That is why, in order to overcome this difficulty we propose to the programmer to define its intended semantics by means of a regular tree tuple grammar. Regular tree grammars are less expressive than equational specifications, but they are very simple to define and makes comparison much easier. Next section describes an algorithm to decide inclusions and equality between a regular tree language and a language recognized by a TTSG. This algorithm can be adapted to test inclusions of two TTSG loosing termination guaranty (for sake of simplicity we do not present it here).

5.3 Comparing TTSG with regular tree grammar

In this section, we suppose that the user gives its intended semantics by means of a regular tree language which makes possible to always compare the operation semantics with the intended one. Moreover, our method allows to prove properties on the logic program when testing only inclusion of the operational semantics into the intended one.
For example, the user may want to verify that for the predicate $plus(x, x, y)$, the property x is an integer implies that y is even. For that the programmer may express its intended semantics by the regular tree language $X \rightarrow s(X), X \Rightarrow 0, Y \Rightarrow s(s(Y)), Y \Rightarrow 0$. So, if the operational semantics is included in the intended one, the property is verified.

The algorithm we describe below, takes a TTSG $G = (\mathcal{C}, NT, PP, TI)$ in simplified form and a deterministic regular tree grammar $G' = (\mathcal{C}', NT', P', TI')$ in simplified form[3] (Any regular tree grammar can be transformed to be determin-

[3] This means that for any $tp' \in Rec(G')$ there exists one and only one derivation of G' that produces tp. See [6] chapter II for details on regular tree grammars and automata.

istic and simplified). It tests if $Rec(G) \subseteq Rec(G')$. A symmetric algorithm tests if $Rec(G') \subseteq Rec(G)$ (For lack of space we do not give it).

The idea of the algorithm is the following: if $Rec(G) \subseteq Rec(G')$ then for any derivation $TI \Rightarrow^* tp$ of G there exists a derivation $TI' \Rightarrow^* tp'$of G' such that $tp = tp'$ on the terminal occurrences. But it is impossible to test each derivation of G because they are infinitely many. So we will test for each $NT - Class$ reached by G and the corresponding set of non-terminals of G', that they can generate the same trees. Since there is a finite number of $NT - Class$ for G the algorithm terminates.

Let $G' = (\mathcal{C}, NT, PP, TI)$ be the simplified grammar computed from $Synth(P, G)$ and $G' = (\mathcal{C}', NT', Prod', TI')$ the simplified grammar that defines the intended semantics. The first function $New(tp, tp')$ associates to each $NT - Class$ of tp the corresponding set of non-terminals of tp' (tp begin equal to tp').

```
function New(tp,tp')
Result=∅
for each non-terminal occurrence u of tp do
    Result=Result∪{((X_1,...,X_n),(X'_1,...,X'_n))}
    where {X_1,...,X_n} = NT - Class(tp,u)} and
    if tp(u_i) = X_i, then tp'(u_i) = X'_i
end for
return Result

ToDo = {(TI,TI')}
Done=∅
while ToDo is not empty do
   Let (TI_1,TI_2) ∈ ToDo
    ToDo=ToDo\(TI_1,TI_2) ; Done=Done∪(TI_1,TI_2)
    for each tp such that TI_1 ⇒ tp
      if there exists a derivation TI_2 ⇒* tp' such that
         tp and tp' are equal on the terminal occurrences
      then ToDo=ToDo∪(New(tp,tp')\ Done)
      else return false
   end for
end while
return true
```

Proposition 10. *The previous algorithm terminates. When it answers* `true`, *$Rec(G) \subseteq Rec(G')$ otherwise $Rec(G) \not\subseteq Rec(G')$.*

Proof. The algorithm terminates because there is a finite number of possible $NT - Classes$ for G. To prove the second part of the proposition, we prove first that for each couple $((X_1, \ldots, X_n), (X'_1, \ldots, X'_n))$ examined by the algorithm there exists a derivation $TI \Rightarrow^* tp$ of G and a derivation $TI' \Rightarrow tp'$ of G' such that $tp = tp'$ on the terminal occurrences and $(X_1, \ldots, X_n)$ is a $NT - Class$ of tp and if $tp(u_i) = X_i$ then $tp'(u_i) = X'_i$. It is proven on induction on number n of iterations executed by the algorithm to examine $((X_1, \ldots, X_n), (X'_1, \ldots, X'_n))$.

If $n = 0$ then the couple is (TI, TI') so the property is obviously verified with empty derivations.
Else, let n' be the number of the iterations of the algorithm when $((X_1, \ldots, X_n), (X'_1, \ldots, X'_n))$ has been added to ToDo and $((Y_1, \ldots, Y_n), (Y'_1, \ldots, Y'_n))$ the couple examined at this iteration. $n' < n$ so from induction hypothesis, we have $TI \Rightarrow^* tp$ of G and $TI' \Rightarrow^* tp'_1$ of G' such that $tp = tp'$ on the terminal occurrences and if $tp(u_i) = X_i$ then $tp'(u_i) = Y_i$. As $X_1, \ldots, X_n), (X'_1, \ldots, X'_n))$ has been added to ToDo, $(Y_1, \ldots, Y_n) \Rightarrow (t_1, \ldots, t_n)$ and $(Y'_1, \ldots, Y'_n) \Rightarrow^* (t'_1, \ldots, t'_n)$ and $(t_1, \ldots, t_n) = (t'_1, \ldots, t'_n)$ on the terminal occurrences and $(X_1, \ldots, X_n)$ is a $NT\!-\!Class$ of $(t_1, \ldots, t_n)$ and $(X'_1, \ldots, X'_n)$ are the corresponding non-terminals in $(t'_1, \ldots, t'_n)$. So $tp \Rightarrow tp_1$ and $tp' \Rightarrow tp'_1$ (using the same productions as the one used in the algorithm). tp_1 and tp'_1 verifies the property we want to prove.
Now from the previous proof, if the algorithm answers `true` then for any derivation $TI \Rightarrow tp$ of G there exists a derivation $TI' \Rightarrow tp'$ of G' such that $tp = tp'$ on the terminal occurrences, so $Rec(G) \subseteq Rec(G')$. If the algorithm answers `false` then it means that there exists at least one derivation $TI \Rightarrow tp$ of G such that there is no corresponding derivation in G' so $Rec(G) \not\subseteq Rec(G')$.

Back to example 3.2, the intended semantics (i.e. all the alternate list of even and odd integers) can be described by the following regular tree tuple grammar:$\{L \Rightarrow P \bullet I \bullet L,\ L \Rightarrow [\,],\ \Rightarrow 0,\ P \Rightarrow s(s(P)),\ I \Rightarrow s(0),\ I \Rightarrow s(s(I))\}$[4]. This specification is completely different from the operational semantics $Synth(P, G)$. Thanks to our algorithm the programmer can verifies that the two semantics are equal.
Let us explain the algorithm only on a subset of the grammars of example 3.2 i.e. the consider productions for $G_{Synth(P,G)}$ are $\{G^l \Rightarrow R^1_\epsilon, L \Rightarrow L^1_1\}$, $\{G^l \Rightarrow R^2_\epsilon, L \Rightarrow L^2_1\}$, $\{R^2_\epsilon \Rightarrow R^1_\epsilon, L^2 \Rightarrow L^1_1\}$, $\{R^2_\epsilon \Rightarrow R^2_\epsilon, L^2 \Rightarrow L^2_1\}$, $R^1_\epsilon \Rightarrow true$, $L^1_1 \Rightarrow [\,]$, $L^2_1 \Rightarrow 0 \bullet s(0) \bullet L^2$. The axiom is (G^l, L). The productions for $G_{Int(G,P)}$ are $L \Rightarrow [\,]$, $L \Rightarrow 0 \bullet s(0) \bullet L$, $R \Rightarrow true$. The axiom is (R, L). Obviously $Rec(G_{Synth(P,G)}) = Rec(G_{Int(G,P)})$, they are pairs composed by the constant $true$ and a list of the form $[0, s(0), 0, s(0), \ldots,]$. Here is the trace of our algorithm

ToDo	Explanation
$((G^l, L), (R, L))$	$(G^l, R^1) \Rightarrow (R^1_\epsilon, L^1_1)$ and $(G^l, R^1) \Rightarrow (R^2_\epsilon, L^2_1)$
$((R^1_\epsilon, L^1_1), (R, L))$, $((R^2_\epsilon, L^2_1), (R, L))$	$(R^1_\epsilon, L^1_1) \Rightarrow (true, L^1_1)$ and $(R, L) \Rightarrow (true, L)$
	$(R^1_\epsilon, L^1_1) \Rightarrow (R^1_\epsilon, [\,])$ and $(R, L) \Rightarrow (R, [\,])$
(L^1_1, L), (R^1_ϵ, R), $((R^2_\epsilon, L^2_1), (R, L))$	$L^1_1 \Rightarrow [\,]$ and $L \Rightarrow [\,]$
(R^1_ϵ, R), $((R^2_\epsilon, L^2_1), (R, L))$	$R^1_\epsilon \Rightarrow true$ and $R \Rightarrow true$
$((R^2_\epsilon, L^2_1), (R, L))$	$(R^2_\epsilon, L^2_1) \Rightarrow (R^2_\epsilon, 0 \bullet s(0) \bullet L^2)$ and
	$(R, L) \Rightarrow (R, 0 \bullet s(0) \bullet L)$
$((R^2_\epsilon, L^2), (R, L))$	$(R^2_\epsilon, L^2) \Rightarrow (R^2_\epsilon, L^2_1)$

It terminates because $((R^2_\epsilon, L^2_1), (R, L))$ has already been explored. The algorithm answers `true`.

[4] In order to compare this grammar to $G_{Synth(P,G)}$ we need to add the production $R \Rightarrow true$ and the axiom is (R, L).

6 Conclusion and Future Works

In this paper, we have described a partial validation method for logic programs which is an attempt to solve problems related to termination. Given a logic program and a goal whose execution does not terminate, a complete observation of the operational semantics is not possible. Our approach, based on an alternative execution process, allows us to compute a finite representation of the set of solutions. We thus compare this finite set of equations with the intended semantics given either by an equational specification or a regular tree grammar. We propose an algorithm that allows us to compare the grammars of the intended and operational semantics.
Our approach could be adapted to constraint logic programs since *LC* already works for CLP programs [10]. It would also be interesting to determine some general classes of programs for which *LC* always terminates and therefore for which our scheme would be really effective. On the other hand, It would be interesting to provide to the programmer more expressive language recognizers to define its intended semantics (conditional TRS, disequations...).

References

1. S. Anantharaman and G. Richard. A Rewrite Mechanism for Logic Programs with Negation. In *Theoretical Computer Science.* Elsevier Science Publishers B.V., 1997. to appear (also Proceedings of RTA'95 LNCS 914 pp 163–178).
2. M.P. Bonacina and J. Hsiang. On Rewrite Programs : Semantics and Relationship with Prolog. *Journal of Logic Programming,* 14:155–180, 1992.
3. N. Dershowitz and N.A. Josephson. Logic Programming by Completion. In *Proceedings of the 2nd ICLP,* pages 313–320, 1984.
4. N. Dershowitz and J.P. Jouannaud. *Handbook of Theoretical Computer Science,* volume B, chapter Rewrite Systems, pages 243–309. J. Van Leeuwen, 1990.
5. M. Ducassé and J. Noyé. Logic Programming Environments: Dynamic Program Analysis and Debugging. *Journal of Logic Programming,* 19-20:351–384, 1994.
6. F. Gécseg and M. Steinby. *Tree Automata.* Akadémiai Kiadó- Budapest, 1984.
7. J.-M. Hullot. Canonical Forms and Unification. In W. Bibel and R. Kowalski, editors, *Proceedings 5th International Conference on Automated Deduction, Les Arcs (France),* volume 87 of *LNCS,* pages 318–334. Springer-Verlag, July 1980.
8. S. Limet and P. Réty. E-Unification by Means of Tree Tuple Synchronized Grammars. In *proc of the 6th Colloquium on Trees in Algebra and Programming,* 1997.
9. J.W. Lloyd. *Foundations of Logic Programming.* Symbolic Computation series. Springer Verlag, 1987 (revised version).
10. G. Richard and F. Saubion. Answer Synthesis for CLP Programs with Negation. *Journal of the Interest Group in Pure and Applied Logic,* 5(3), april 1997.
11. E. Shapiro. *Algorithmic Program Debugging.* MIT Press, Cambridge, MA, 1983.

Preservation and Reflection in Specification(*)

A.Lopes and J.L.Fiadeiro

Department of Informatics, Faculty of Sciences, University of Lisbon
Campo Grande, 1700 Lisboa, PORTUGAL
{mal,llf}@di.fc.ul.pt

Abstract. We extend the traditional notion of specification based on theories and interpretations between theories to model situations, typical of open, reactive systems, in which properties exhibited locally by an object no longer hold when that object is interconnected as a component of a larger system. The proposed notion of specification is based on the observation, due to Winskel, that while some assertions are *preserved* across morphisms of labelled transition systems, other are *reflected*. The distinction between these two classes of assertions leads us to the definition of two categories of specifications, one that supports horizontal structuring and another that supports vertical structuring, for which compositionality is proved.

1 Introduction

The notion of a specification as a collection of sentences in some logic (theory presentation) expressing the properties that the program is required to satisfy, and of specification morphism as a property preserving mapping (interpretation between theories), has served an important rôle in supporting software development, namely the process of stepwise refinement of high level descriptions of the functionality of the system [15]. These notions have also been useful for structuring specifications within a given layer of abstraction [4], giving rise to algebraic frameworks where both dimensions – *horizontal* (for structuring) and *vertical* (for refinement) – can be integrated [12].

Although these techniques were developed for supporting Abstract Data Type specification, i.e. for supporting the development of transformational programs, they seem to serve other programming paradigms namely those which, like object-oriented programming, adopt a "design-by-contract" style of development [17]. The contract (specification) consists of properties that the user, or client, of an object can rely on because any implementation is required to satisfy them.

However, when it comes to supporting the process of horizontal structuring in the context of reactive systems, i.e. of interconnecting objects to form a (complex) system, it seems that property preservation is not the right structural notion on which an algebraic approach can be based. For instance, typical clauses in an OO-contract are conditions under which methods are guaranteed to be available (pre-conditions in the sense of OO [17]). It is easy to understand that, in a synchronous mode of interconnection in which objects interact by sharing actions, the availability of an action (method) is determined by the intersection

(*) This work was partially supported by the project ARTS under contract to Equitel S.A., and through the contracts PRAXIS XXI 2/2.1/MAT/46/94 (ESCOLA) and PCSH/OGE/1038/95 (MAGO).

of the availability conditions of all the objects that synchronise in that action. Hence, the property of availability (readiness) is not preserved when moving from an individual object to a system.

The fact that certain properties do not carry forwards from components to systems is well known in open, reactive system development. The difficulty is, usually, to develop a specification formalism that is *compositional* with respect to a given program design formalism and, at the same time, accounts for all relevant classes of properties (e.g., [20, 14]). The "guilty" party in this context is usually the class of liveness properties (e.g., [2]). In the context of an algebraic approach to specification [8], this means that a functorial relationship between a category of programs (or lower-level specifications) and a category of specifications cannot be established [6].

In order to account for these phenomena, other styles of specification have been developed, mainly in the context of state-based approaches, which relativise the commitment to guarantee certain properties to certain assumptions on the behaviour of the environment [1, 5]. The crucial difference here with respect to "older" styles is the fact that the interference of an environment is taken into account in the specification.

Our aim in this paper is to incorporate these notions of interference of an environment in the algebraic approach to specification based on institutions [13]. Our approach is based on the fact, also observed in [19] in the context of local logics of labelled transition systems, that, whereas certain properties are *preserved* across morphisms, other can only be *reflected* in the sense that they will only be ensured as long as the environment of the component co-operates.

More specifically, in section 2, we propose that specifications include two sets of sentences: one expressing the properties that are ensured in any context, and the other expressing the properties that a component is willing to have when working as a component of a larger system, i.e. describing the degree of co-operation towards the environment. We call the latter *co-properties*.

In section 3, we formalise the difference between the rôles of these two sets of sentences by defining two different categories of specifications. One captures the component-of relationship, and supports horizontal structuring. Morphisms of this category preserve properties and reflect co-properties. The finite co-completeness of this category is proved and pushouts are characterised. The other category captures refinement (vertical structuring) by having morphisms that preserve both properties and co-properties, thus coinciding with the traditional specification morphisms as interpretations between theories. We then prove that the use of distinct morphisms for supporting horizontal and vertical composition is compositional.

2 Specification of Reactive Systems

2.1 The Specification Logic

The logic that we will use to illustrate the proposed revision of the notion of specification and specification morphism is a modal action logic (MAL) similar to the one that was developed in the context of the FOREST project [16] and to the basic propositional modal logics described in [18]. Notice that this use of modal logic is different from local logics of labelled transition systems in the style of Hennessy-Milner as used, for instance, in [19]. We present MAL in the style of institutions [13].

We denote by $\mathcal{SET}$ the category of sets and total functions and by $\mathcal{SET}_\perp$ the category of pointed sets: the objects are pairs $<A,\perp>$ where A is a set and $\perp$ is a distinguished element of A; a morphism σ from $<A',\perp'>$ to $<A,\perp>$ is a mapping $\sigma:A'\rightarrow A$ s.t. $\sigma(\perp')=\perp$.

Definition/Proposition 2.1. Signatures are pairs $<A,\Gamma>$ where A is a finite set and Γ is a finite pointed set. A signature morphism σ from $\Sigma=<A,\Gamma>$ to $\Sigma'=<A',\Gamma'>$ is a pair $<\sigma_{at}:A\rightarrow A',\sigma_{ac}:\Gamma'\rightarrow\Gamma>$ where σ_{at} is a mapping and σ_{ac} is a morphism in $\mathcal{SET}_\perp$. Signatures and signature morphisms constitute a category $\mathcal{SIGN}$. ∎

As in [8], a signature $<A,\Gamma>$ provides the (non-logical) symbols of the language used for specifying a system: *A* is the set of attribute symbols and Γ is the set of action symbols. In order to simplify the presentation we only consider Boolean attributes. As in [7], the distinguished action $\perp$ of Γ represents idle steps, that is, the steps performed by the environment, reflecting the fact that we are considering systems embedded in a wider environment.

A signature morphism σ from Σ to Σ' is intended to support the identification of a way in which a system (with signature Σ) is a component of, or is refined by, another system (with signature Σ'). Hence, such a morphism provides, for each attribute $a\in\Sigma$ of the component, the corresponding attribute $\sigma(a)\in\Sigma'$ of the system, and identifies the action of the component which is involved, or refined by, each action of the system, if ever. Notice that the condition $\sigma(\perp')=\perp$ states that the environment of Σ' is part of the environment of Σ. On the other hand, actions $a'\in\Sigma'$ of the system may be mapped to an idle step of the component – $\sigma(a')=\perp$ – meaning that σ identifies part of the environment of the component.

We shall see in section 3 at what level the crucial difference between refinement and composition is established. From the previous paragraph it is obvious that this distinction cannot be made at the signature level but at a more "semantic" level which considers the way systems behave.

Definition/Proposition 2.2. The grammar functor $\mathcal{MAL}:\mathcal{SIGN}\rightarrow\mathcal{SET}$ defines, for every signature $\Sigma=<A,\Gamma>$, the set of modal propositions $\mathcal{MAL}(\Sigma)$ as follows:

$$\phi ::= a \mid (\neg\phi) \mid (\phi\supset\phi') \mid \mathbf{beg} \mid [\gamma]\phi$$

for $a\in A$ and $\gamma\subseteq\Gamma$. A signature morphism $\sigma=<\sigma_{at},\sigma_{ac}>:\Sigma\rightarrow\Sigma'$ induces a translation $\mathcal{MAL}(\sigma):\mathcal{MAL}(\Sigma)\rightarrow\mathcal{MAL}(\Sigma')$, which we denote by $\underline{\sigma}$, defined as follows:

$$\underline{\sigma}(\phi) ::= \sigma_{at}(a) \mid (\neg\underline{\sigma}(\phi)) \mid (\underline{\sigma}(\phi)\supset\underline{\sigma}(\phi')) \mid \mathbf{beg} \mid [\sigma^{-1}_{ac}(\gamma)]\underline{\sigma}(\phi)$$ ∎

For each $\gamma\subseteq\Gamma$, the modal operator $[\gamma]$ is such that the formula $[\gamma]\phi$ expresses that, for every g in γ, ϕ holds after *g* occurs. The propositional constant **beg** denotes the initial state. (See the semantics below.)

We will also work with some derived operators. In particular, for each $\gamma\subseteq\Gamma$, the dual of $[\gamma]$ is the modal operator $<\gamma>$ defined by the abbreviation $<\gamma>\phi\equiv_{abv}$

$(\neg[\gamma](\neg\phi))$. The formula $<\gamma>\phi$ expresses that there exists an action g in γ that establishes ϕ. We also adopt the abbreviation of a singleton by its element, that is, for every $g\in\Gamma$, $[g]\phi \equiv_{abv} [\{g\}]\phi$ and $<g>\phi \equiv_{abv} <\{g\}>\phi$.

The translation of formulas induced by a translation of the non-logical symbols was defined inductively, in the usual way. Notice, however, the use of the pre-image in the translation of the modality: properties asserted on actions of the component are translated into properties of every action of the system that involves the component actions. As in [18], this modal language is interpreted on labelled transition systems.

Definition/Proposition 2.3. The model functor $\mathcal{MOD}:\mathcal{SIGN}\to\mathcal{SET}^{op}$ is defined as follows: for every signature $\Sigma=<A,\Gamma>$, a Σ-model consists of a quadruple $<\mathcal{W},\mathcal{R},\mathcal{V},w_0>$ where $\mathcal{W}$ is a set, $\mathcal{R}:\Gamma\to[\mathcal{W}\to 2^{\mathcal{W}}]$ and $\mathcal{V}:A\to 2^{\mathcal{W}}$ are mappings, and $w_0\in\mathcal{W}$, s.t., for every $w\in\mathcal{W}$, $\mathcal{R}(\perp)(w)\neq\emptyset$. We denote by $\mathcal{MOD}(\Sigma)$ the set of all Σ-models. A Σ-model $M=<\mathcal{W},\mathcal{R},\mathcal{V},w_0>$ is called a locus iff, for every $w\in\mathcal{W}$ and $w'\in\mathcal{R}(\perp)(w)$, $\mathcal{V}(w')=\mathcal{V}(w)$. Given a signature morphism $\sigma=<\sigma_{at},\sigma_{ac}>:\Sigma\to\Sigma'$, for every Σ-model $M=<\mathcal{W},\mathcal{R},\mathcal{V},w_0>$, its reduct $\mathcal{MOD}(\sigma)(M)$, which we denote by $M_{|\sigma}$, is defined by $<\mathcal{W},\mathcal{R}_{|\sigma},\mathcal{V}_{|\sigma},w_0>$ where $\mathcal{R}_{|\sigma}(g)(w)=\bigcup_{\sigma(g')=g}\mathcal{R}(g')(w)$ and $\mathcal{V}_{|\sigma}(a)=\mathcal{V}(\sigma_{at}(a))$. ∎

In a Σ-model $<\mathcal{W},\mathcal{R},\mathcal{V},w_0>$, $\mathcal{W}$ is the set of states, $\mathcal{R}$ provides, for every action, a transition relation, $\mathcal{V}$ is a valuation function providing, for each attribute, the set of states in which it holds, and w_0 is the initial state. We will also denote by $\mathcal{V}$ its dual, i.e. the mapping $\mathcal{W}\to 2^A$ that returns the set of the atributes that are true at each state.

Recalling that $\perp$ denotes an environment step, the condition $\mathcal{R}(\perp)(w)\neq\emptyset$ means that a system cannot prevent the environment from progressing on its own. This means that we are working with an *open* semantics of behaviour [3][1]. Moreover, the condition $\mathcal{V}(w')=\mathcal{V}(w)$, for every $w'\in\mathcal{R}(\perp)(w)$, means that a locus is a model in which the attributes remain unchanged whenever the component remains idle, i.e. attributes are local (encapsulation) [8].

Definition 2.4. For every signature $\Sigma=<A,\Gamma>$, the satisfaction relation is defined as follows: a Σ-proposition ϕ is said to be true in a Σ-model $M=<\mathcal{W},\mathcal{R},\mathcal{V},w_0>$ at state w (which we write $(M,w)\models_\Sigma\phi$) iff:

- $(M,w)\models_\Sigma a$ iff $w\in\mathcal{V}(a)$;
- $(M,w)\models_\Sigma\neg\phi$ iff $(M,w)\not\models_\Sigma\phi$;
- $(M,w)\models_\Sigma\phi\supset\phi'$ iff $(M,w)\models_\Sigma\phi$ implies $(M,w)\models_\Sigma\phi'$;
- $(M,w)\models_\Sigma$ **beg** iff $w=w_0$;
- $(M,w)\models_\Sigma[\gamma]\phi$ iff for every $g\in\gamma$, for every $w'\in\mathcal{R}(g)(w)$, $(M,w')\models_\Sigma\phi$.

A Σ-proposition ϕ is said to be true in M, which we denote by $M\models_\Sigma\phi$, iff $(M,w)\models_\Sigma\phi$ for every $w\in\mathcal{W}$. A Σ-proposition ϕ is said to be valid, which we denote by $\models_\Sigma\phi$, iff $M\models_\Sigma\phi$ for every locus M. ∎

Note that, by the notion of validity defined above, a valid formula is expected to hold at all states but only for the models which are loci. We consider that:

- $\Phi\models_\Sigma\varphi$ iff, for every Σ-locus M, if $M\models_\Sigma\phi$ for every $\phi\in\Phi$, then $M\models_\Sigma\varphi$;

---
[1] A similar property is used in state-based approaches, e.g. [1], for characterising open semantics.

- $\Phi \models_\Sigma \Psi$ iff, for every $\psi \in \Psi$, $\Phi \models_\Sigma \psi$;
- $\Phi^\bullet = \{\phi \in \mathcal{MAL}(\Sigma) : \Phi \models_\Sigma \phi\}$.

The definition of validity based only on the models which are loci gives rise to a logic for which the satisfaction condition of institutions does not hold. Following [10], in this case we obtain a "weakly-structural" logic, i.e., consequence is not preserved by translation, it depends on the the locality conditions which characterise the models which are loci.

Proposition 2.5. $\langle \mathcal{SIGN}, \mathcal{MAL}, \models \rangle$ is a weakly structural π-institution, i.e., given a signature morphism $\sigma : \Sigma \rightarrow \Sigma'$:

(1) for every $\phi \in \mathcal{MAL}(\Sigma)$ and $\Phi \subseteq \mathcal{MAL}(\Sigma)$, if $\Phi \models_\Sigma \phi$ then $\underline{\sigma}(\Phi), \underline{\sigma}(loc(\Sigma)) \models_{\Sigma'} \underline{\sigma}(\phi)$,

(2) $\models_\Sigma \phi$ for every $\phi \in loc(\Sigma)$,

(3) $\underline{\mu}(\underline{\sigma}(loc(\Sigma)), \underline{\mu}(loc(\Sigma')) \models_{\Sigma''} \phi$ for every $\phi \in \underline{\sigma;\mu}(loc(\Sigma))$,

(4) $\underline{\sigma;\mu}(loc(\Sigma)) \models_{\Sigma''} \phi$ for every $\phi \in \underline{\mu}(\underline{\sigma}(loc(\Sigma)))$,

where, given a signature $\Sigma = \langle A, \Gamma \rangle$, $loc(\Sigma) = \{a \supset [\perp]a, \neg a \supset [\perp]\neg a : a \in A\}$. ∎

2.2 Specifications

As already motivated in the introduction, we claim that open, reactive systems, should be described not only in terms of the properties that they ensure in any context but also of the properties that they are willing to have when working as a component of a larger system. We shall call the latter *co-properties* in the sense that they *reflect* the behaviour of the environment rather than induce behaviour on the environment. The use of the prefix *co* is also meant to suggest that these properties establish the degree of *co*-operation of a component in regard to its environment. Naturally, co-properties will be observed when the system runs in isolation but it is possible that they are not observed when the system is interconnected to other components in a larger system.

The nature of properties and co-properties is determined by the computation and interconnection models that are adopted: it is the discipline of component interconnection available at program design level that determines which formulas express properties, in the sense that they are preserved, and which formulas express co-properties, in the sense that they are reflected. In the specific case that we are using for illustration, for which interconnection is based on local, private attributes and global, shared actions, properties address the functionality ("partial correctness") of the transition system (invariants, pre-conditions, effects of the actions over the attributes) whereas co-properties are concerned with the readiness to perform certain actions (enabling conditions). The fact that the former are preserved results from locality of attributes. The fact that the latter cannot be preserved results from the fact that actions can be shared. Indeed, co-properties typically require the cooperation of the other components (environment) to be observed. This is, for instance, the case of readiness properties: a system is ready to execute an action only if the other components that are involved in the execution of that action are ready to execute it.

Properties and co-properties are supported by two sublanguages:

Definition 2.6. The mapping $\mathcal{STAT}$: $|\mathcal{SET}| \rightarrow |\mathcal{SET}|$ defines, for every set A, the set of state propositions $\mathcal{STAT}$(A) as follows:

$$\varphi \ := a \mid (\neg\varphi) \mid (\varphi\supset\varphi')$$

for $a\in A$. The mapping $\mathcal{PROP}$: $|\mathcal{SIGN}| \rightarrow |\mathcal{SET}|$ defines, for every signature Σ=<A,Γ>, the set of properties $\mathcal{PROP}(\Sigma)$ as follows:

$$\phi \ := \varphi \mid (\mathbf{beg}\supset\varphi) \mid (\varphi\supset[\gamma]\varphi')$$

for $\gamma\subseteq\Gamma$ and $\varphi,\varphi'\in\mathcal{STAT}(A)$. The mapping $co\text{-}\mathcal{PROP}$: $|\mathcal{SIGN}| \rightarrow |\mathcal{SET}|$ defines, for every signature Σ=<A,Γ>, the set of co-properties $co\text{-}\mathcal{PROP}(\Sigma)$ as follows:

$$\psi \ ::= \varphi \mid (\varphi\supset\langle g\rangle\mathbf{true})$$

for $g\in\Gamma$ and $\varphi\in\mathcal{STAT}(A)$. ∎

As already motivated, properties capture invariants (φ), initialisation conditions ($\mathbf{beg}\supset\varphi$), effects of actions ($\varphi\supset[g]\varphi'$), and restrictions to the occurrence of actions ($\varphi\supset[g]\mathbf{false}$). Co-properties capture the ability of actions to occur in certain states – readiness ($\varphi\supset\langle g\rangle\mathbf{true}$) – and also state propositions (φ). That is, state propositions can be used both as properties (guaranteeing that they will hold in any context) and as co-properties (expressing the fact that the component will reflect them).

Notice that formulas of type ($\varphi\supset\langle\gamma\rangle\mathbf{true}$), where γ is not a singleton, express internal nondeterminism and should not be considered as properties (they cannot be imposed on the environment) nor co-properties (they cannot be reflected because refinement is not required to preserve internal non-determinism – see section 3.3).

Definition 2.7. A specification is a triple <Σ,Φ,Ψ>, where Σ is a signature in $\mathcal{SIGN}$, $\Phi\subseteq\mathcal{PROP}(\Sigma)$ and $\Psi\subseteq co\text{-}\mathcal{PROP}(\Sigma)$. ∎

As an example, consider a vending machine that, once it accepts a coin, is ready to serve either a cake or a cigar, according to the selection made by its user; after delivering a cake or a cigar it only accepts a new coin; and is initialised so as to accept only coins. This object can be specified as follows.

specification vending machine **is**

attributes	ready		
actions	coin, cake, cigar		
axioms	**beg** ⊃ ¬ready	*co-axioms*	ready ⊃ <cake>**true**
	ready ⊃ [coin]**false**		ready ⊃ <cigar>**true**
	¬ready ⊃ [cake,cigar]**false**		
	[coin]ready		
	[cake,cigar]¬ready		

The absence of a co-axiom expressing the conditions under which *coin* is enabled implies that, whenever the machine is not ready, it can either accept or refuse a coin, depending on the result of an internal choice. As we shall see in section 3.3, this form of (allowed) non-determinism, modelled by underspecification, can be restricted during a refinement step, i.e. a choice can be imposed as a result of a refinement step. However, the property that the selection between delivering a cake or a cigar should be made by the user amounts to required non-determinism that is materialised in the specification through the two readiness (co-)axioms. These are properties that any refinement has to enforce.

In section 3, we will illustrate how the co-axioms of a component may not be preserved in the system, and how the co-axioms of the system are reflected in every component.

It is important to mention that the translations induced by signature morphisms preserve the category of state propositions and properties, that is:

Proposition 2.8. The mappings $\mathcal{STAT}$ and $\mathcal{PROP}$ defined in 2.6 extend to functors, considering that the translation induced by a signature morphism σ coincides with the translation $\mathcal{MAL}(\sigma)$ of these formulas. ∎

This does not hold, however, for co-properties because of the pre-image taken over the action that occurs in the modality: $(\underline{\sigma}(\varphi) \supset \langle \sigma_{ac}^{-1}(g) \rangle \underline{\sigma}(\varphi'))$ may not be a co-property because $\sigma_{ac}^{-1}(g)$ is not necessarily a singleton in which case, as already mentioned, the formula expresses internal non-determinism, which cannot be always reflected.

3 Categorical Approach to Specification

The formal justification for changing the notion of specification from theory presentations, as usual, to pairs of presentations over the same signature has to come from the fact that axioms and co-axioms behave differently when specification morphisms are considered. This was, indeed, the motivation for the proposed revision of the notion of specification: during horizontal composition, i.e. while structuring a complex system by interconnecting simpler components, axioms are preserved but co-axioms are reflected. We start by formalising and illustrating this behaviour through a new notion of specification morphism.

We then investigate how these new morphisms interact with the traditional notion of interpretation between theories (which supports refinement), and prove that the development framework that results from the use of distinct morphisms for supporting horizontal and vertical composition is compositional, meaning that, in this framework, systems can be specified independently of their environment and, since there is an explicit mechanism for putting systems together, they can be used (and reused) in several ways as components of larger systems.

3.1 The Component-of Relation

We investigate the kind of relationship that must exist between the specifications of two systems so that one can be considered as a component of the other.

As mentioned in the previous section, a specification $\langle\Sigma,\Phi,\Psi\rangle$ of a system S states that S guarantees to satisfy the set of properties $\Phi^\bullet$ in any context. More concretely, when S is working as a component of a system S', via a signature morphism σ from Σ to Σ', S guarantees to satisfy the properties $\underline{\sigma}(\Phi^\bullet)$ and, therefore, the properties that S' guarantees to satisfy include $\underline{\sigma}(\Phi^\bullet)$. In a weakly structural π-institution this corresponds to $\Phi' \vdash_{\Sigma'} \underline{\sigma}(\Phi)$ and $\Phi' \vdash_{\Sigma'} \underline{\sigma}(loc(\Sigma))$.

On the other hand, the set of co-axioms Ψ constrains the co-properties that a system S' may be willing to have in any context, given that S' includes S as a component. More specifically, for a system to be ready to perform an action g it is required that each of its components be ready to perform *the action in* g (if any) in which that component is involved (given by $\sigma_{ac}(g)$ for a component identified via σ). Because, as remarked after proposition 2.8, co-properties do not translate to co-properties, it seems clear that we need another way of accounting for the reflection, namely a different translation for co-properties. More precisely, we are going to define, for every signature morphism σ, a mapping $\bar{\sigma}$ (co-translation) such that, for any set Ψ of co-properties, $\bar{\sigma}(\Psi)$ is the set of co-properties that a system which includes S as a component via σ can be willing to have given that S is willing to have Ψ.

Just like the language of properties for a signature Σ is a subset of the language $\mathcal{MAL}(\Sigma)$, for which the morphisms satisfy the structural results typical of institutions (e.g. 2.5), the language of co-properties defined in 2.6 and the required co-translation mechanisms can be put in the context of a more general grammar – *co-*$\mathcal{MAL}$.

Definition/Proposition 3.1. The grammar functor *co-*$\mathcal{MAL}$:$\mathcal{SIGN}\to\mathcal{SET}$ defines, for every signature $\Sigma=<A,\Gamma>$, the set of modal co-propositions *co-*$\mathcal{MAL}(\Sigma)$ as follows:

$$\phi ::= a \mid (\neg\phi) \mid (\phi\supset\phi') \mid \mathbf{beg} \mid <[\gamma]>\phi$$

for $a\in A$, $\gamma\subseteq\Gamma$. A signature morphism $\sigma=<\sigma_{at},\sigma_{ac}>:\Sigma\to\Sigma'$ induces a (co)translation *co-*$\mathcal{MAL}(\sigma)$:*co-*$\mathcal{MAL}(\Sigma)\to$*co-*$\mathcal{MAL}(\Sigma')$, which we denote by $\bar{\sigma}$, defined as follows:

$$\bar{\sigma}(\phi) ::= \sigma_{at}(a) \mid (\neg\bar{\sigma}(\phi)) \mid (\bar{\sigma}(\phi)\supset\bar{\sigma}(\phi')) \mid \mathbf{beg} \mid <[\sigma_{ac}^{-1}(\gamma)]>\bar{\sigma}(\phi)$$ ∎

For each $\gamma\subseteq\Gamma$, the modal operator $<[\gamma]>$ is such that the formula $<[\gamma]>\phi$ expresses that, for some g in γ, ϕ holds after g occurs.

As before, we will also work with the dual operators. In particular, for each $\gamma\subseteq\Gamma$, the dual of $<[\gamma]>$ is the modal operator $[<\gamma>]$ defined by the abbreviation $[<\gamma>]\phi \equiv_{abv} (\neg<[\gamma]>(\neg\phi))$. We also adopt the abbreviation $[g]\phi \equiv_{abv} <[\{g\}]>\phi$ and $<g>\phi \equiv_{abv} [<\{g\}>]\phi$, for every $g\in\Gamma$.

At the level of models, the reflection of co-properties is captured in the reverse direction through an expansion of component models into system models (recall that preservation is captured through reducts of system models into component models). Due to space limitations, details will be presented elsewhere.

Definition 3.2. For every signature $\Sigma=<A,\Gamma>$, the satisfaction relation is defined as follows: a Σ-co-proposition ϕ is said to be true in a Σ-model $M=<\mathcal{W},\mathcal{R},\mathcal{V},w_0>$ at state w (which we write $(M,w)\models_\Sigma\phi$) iff:

- $(M,w)\models_\Sigma a$ iff $w\in\mathcal{V}(a)$;
- $(M,w)\models_\Sigma\neg\phi$ iff $(M,w)\not\models_\Sigma\phi$;
- $(M,w)\models_\Sigma\phi\supset\phi'$ iff $(M,w)\models_\Sigma\phi$ implies $(M,w)\models_\Sigma\phi'$;
- $(M,w)\models_\Sigma\mathbf{beg}$ iff $w=w_0$;
- $(M,w)\models_\Sigma<[\gamma]>\phi$ iff for some $g\in\gamma$, for every $w'\in\mathcal{R}(g)(w)$, $(M,w')\models_\Sigma\phi$.

A Σ-co-proposition ϕ is said to be true in M, which we denote by $M\models_\Sigma\phi$, iff $(M,w)\models_\Sigma\phi$ for every $w\in\mathcal{W}$. ∎

It is important to notice that state propositions, as defined in 2.6, are both propositions and co-propositions. It is easy to prove that they have exactly the same semantics under 2.4 and 3.2. The same holds for the co-propositions $[<\{g\}>]\varphi$

and the propositions $<\{g\}>\varphi$ which were both abbreviated to $<g>\varphi$.

Moreover, notice that the translation and the co-translation of state propositions coincide. The same does not hold, however, for formulae of the form $<g>\varphi$. Their translation $<\sigma_{ac}^{-1}(g)>\underline{\sigma}(\varphi)$ has a disjunctive flavour (allowed non-determinism) whereas their co-translation $[<\sigma_{ac}^{-1}(g)>]\overline{\sigma}(\phi)$ has a conjuntive flavour (required non-determinism). This difference captures, in fact, the whole point of having introduced the co-language (recall the remark after proposition 2.8). For co-properties, the translation $\overline{\sigma}$ induced by a signature morphism σ satisfies:

Proposition 3.3. Given a signature morphism $\sigma:\Sigma\rightarrow\Sigma'$, for every $\psi\in \mathit{co\text{-}PROP}(\Sigma)$, $\Psi\subseteq \mathit{co\text{-}PROP}(\Sigma)$, if $\Psi\models_{\Sigma}\psi$ then $\overline{\sigma}(\Psi),\overline{\sigma}(<\perp>\mathbf{true})\models_{\Sigma'}\overline{\sigma}(\psi)$. ∎

Finally, it is possible to define the set of co-properties that a component specified by $<\Sigma,\Phi,\Psi>$ is willing to have in a given context. This set is constituted by the set of co-properties which can be derived from $\overline{\sigma}(\Psi^{\bullet})$ and the state propositions that are ensured, as properties, in that context. Noticing that $\overline{\sigma}(\Psi^{\bullet})\models_{\Sigma'}\psi$ is equivalent to $\overline{\sigma}(\Psi),\overline{\sigma}(<\perp>\mathbf{true})\models_{\Sigma'}\psi$, the definition of a component-of morphism is immediate:

Definition/Proposition 3.4. Given specifications $S=<\Sigma,\Phi,\Psi>$ and $S'=<\Sigma',\Phi',\Psi'>$, a component-of morphism σ from S to S' is a signature morphism $\sigma:\Sigma\rightarrow\Sigma'$, s.t.

(1) $\Phi'\models_{\Sigma'}\underline{\sigma}(\Phi),\underline{\sigma}(loc(\Sigma))$

(2) $\Phi'^{\bullet}\cap \mathit{STAT}(A'),\overline{\sigma}(\Psi),\overline{\sigma}(<\perp>\mathbf{true})\models_{\Sigma'}\Psi'$,

where A' is the set of attributes of Σ'. Specifications and component-of morphisms constitute a category *c-SPEC*. ∎

It is interesting to notice the duality of conditions 1 and 2 of the definition above, in particular, the locality conditions which are associated to the translation of properties ($\underline{\sigma}(loc(\Sigma))$) and the co-translation of co-properties ($\overline{\sigma}(<\perp>\mathbf{true})$).

3.2 Interconnecting Specifications

The ability of the proposed framework to support the interconnection of components to make complex systems is, as in Goguen's approach to General Systems Theory, characterised by the finite co-completeness of the category of specifications. The specification of a composite system is given by the colimit of its configuration diagram which is guaranteed to exist by the following proposition.

Proposition 3.5. *c-SPEC* is finitely cocomplete. Its initial object is $<\Sigma_0,\emptyset, \mathit{co\text{-}PROP}(\Sigma_0)>$, where $\Sigma_0=<\emptyset,\{\perp\}>$ is the initial object in *SIGN*. The pushout of $\sigma_1:<\Sigma_0,\Phi_0,\Psi_0>\rightarrow<\Sigma_1,\Phi_1,\Psi_1>$ and $\sigma_2:<\Sigma_0,\Phi_0,\Psi_0>\rightarrow<\Sigma_2,\Phi_2,\Psi_2>$ is given by $\mu_1:<\Sigma_1,\Phi_1,\Psi_1>\rightarrow<\Sigma,\Phi,\Psi>$ and $\mu_2:<\Sigma_2,\Phi_2,\Psi_2>\rightarrow<\Sigma,\Phi,\Psi>$ where:

- μ_1 and μ_2 result from the pushout of σ_1 and σ_2 in *SIGN*;
- $\Phi=\underline{\mu}_1(\Phi_1)\cup\underline{\mu}_2(\Phi_2)\cup\underline{\mu}_1(loc(\Sigma_1))\cup\underline{\mu}_2(loc(\Sigma_2))$;
- $\Psi=\{\psi\in \mathit{co\text{-}PROP}(\Sigma):\ \Phi^{\bullet}\cap \mathit{STAT}(A),\overline{\mu}_1(\Psi_1),\overline{\mu}_1(<\perp>\mathbf{true})\models_{\Sigma}\psi$ and $\Phi^{\bullet}\cap \mathit{STAT}(A),\overline{\mu}_2(\Psi_2),\overline{\mu}_2(<\perp>\mathbf{true})\models_{\Sigma}\psi\}$

where A is the set of attributes of Σ. ∎

Informally, pushouts work as follows:

- Actions are synchronised according to the synchronisation points established by the channel and the morphisms. The synchronisation points defined by such an interconnection are the pairs $g_1 \mid g_2$ which are mapped to the same element of Γ_0, which are given in categorical terms by the limit of the underlying $\mathcal{SET}_\bot$ diagram. It is important to notice that independent behaviour of different components is non-stricted interleaved because actions can occur concurrently.
- The properties of the resulting system are given by the union of the translation of the properties and locality axioms of the components.
- The co-properties of the resulting system are the co-propositions that can be proved, separately, from the co-properties of both systems assuming the invariants (over the attributes) of the resulting system. Notice that since we take the translation of the closure of the co-properties of the components, the readiness for the actions that involve only one component consists of the local readiness of that component.

It is important to notice that axioms in Φ_0 and Ψ_0 add no relevant information to the interconnection. In fact, as in [11], it is possible to prove that any interconnection between two specifications can be made through a diagram of the form

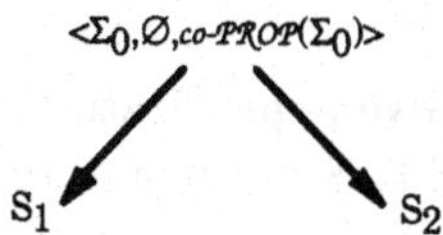

We designate the specifications of the form $\langle\Sigma,\emptyset,co\text{-}\mathcal{PROP}(\Sigma)\rangle$ by channels.

To illustrate composition, let us consider the following systems:

specification regulator **is**
attributes
actions action
axioms [action]**false**
co-axioms

specification accident **is**
attributes outoforder
actions action, breakdown
axioms $\mathbf{beg} \supset \neg$outoforder
[breakdown]outoforder
co-axioms $\neg$outoforder $\supset \langle$action$\rangle$**true**

The regulator, which has only one action that is never enabled, may be used to prevent an action of another system to occur. For instance, we can interconnect this system with the vending machine presented before in order to obtain a machine with the cigar option blocked. On the other hand, since every non-virtual machine may breakdown at any time, we will simultaneously compose our machine with a component which models this aspect of machine behaviour.

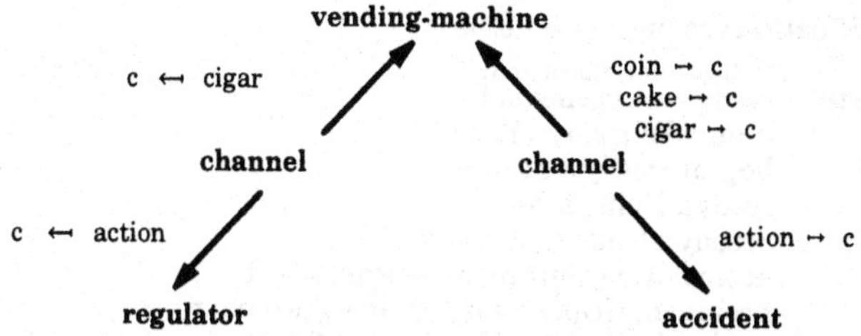

The architecture of the required system is given by the interconnection above, where the signature of channel is $\langle\emptyset,\{c,\bot\}\rangle$. The resulting specification is given, up to isomorphism, by the specification above. Notice that the readiness to accept the choice of cake is now restricted to the situations in which the machine is not out of order whereas the readiness to accept the choice of cigar is no longer true. On the other hand, notice that the last two axioms correspond to the translation of the locality axioms of the system components.

specification regulated vending machine **is**
attributes ready, outoforder
actions coin, cake, cigar, breakdown
axioms **beg** ⊃ ¬ready ∧ ¬outoforder
ready ⊃ [coin]**false**
¬ready ⊃ [cake]**false**
[cigar]**false**
[coin]ready
[cake]¬ready
[breakdown]outoforder
ready ⊃ [breakdown]ready
¬ready ⊃ [breakdown]¬ready
co-axioms (ready ∧ ¬outoforder) ⊃ <cake>**true**

3.3 Refinement and Compositionality

Considering that specifications describe the requirements which further developments must fulfill, the refinement of a specification must preserve its properties.

Definition/Proposition 3.6. Given specifications $S=\langle\Sigma,\Phi,\Psi\rangle$ and $S'=\langle\Sigma',\Phi',\Psi'\rangle$, a refinement morphism σ from S to S' is a signature morphism $\sigma:\Sigma\to\Sigma'$, s.t.

(1) $\Phi' \models_{\Sigma'} \underline{\sigma}(\Phi), \underline{\sigma}(loc(\Sigma))$,

(2) $\Phi'^{\bullet} \cap \mathcal{STAT}(A'), \Psi' \models_{\Sigma'} \underline{\sigma}(\Psi)$,

where A' is the set of attributes of Σ'. Specifications and refinement morphisms constitute a category *r-SPEC*. ∎

Refinement allows one to reduce underspecification, since it allows one to take decisions which were before left open and, thus, solved by internal choice.

Taking the semantics of a program P to be the specification ⟦P⟧ that consists of the properties it ensures and the co-properties it reflects, refinement morphisms allows us to formalise (and generalise) the usual notion of satisfaction relation between programs and specifications. More concretely, P is a realisation of S via the signature morphism σ iff $\sigma:S\to[\![P]\!]$ is a refinement morphism. The signature morphism can be seen to record the design decisions that lead from S to P.

In order to illustrate refinement, consider now the following vending machine:

specification vending machine2 **is**
data $\langle\Sigma_{bool\&nat},\Phi_{bool\&nat}\rangle$
attributes ready:bool, ncoins:nat
actions coin, cake, cigar, collect
axioms **beg** ⊃ (¬ready ∧ ncoins=0)
ready ⊃ [coin]**false**
¬ready ⊃ [cake,cigar]**false**
ncoins=n ⊃ [coin](ready ∧ ncoins=n+1)
ncoins=n ⊃ [cake,cigar](¬ready ∧ ncoins=n)
ready ⊃ [collect](ready ∧ ncoins=0)
¬ready ⊃ [collect](¬ready ∧ ncoins=0)
co-axioms (¬ready ∧ ncoins<lim) ⊃ <coin>**true**
ready ⊃ <cake>**true**
ready ⊃ <cigar>**true**

Notice that, in this example, we took the extension of the formalism which results from the use of the first order extension of *MAL* and the inclusion of data types in a system specification, more precisely, the inclusion of an algebraic specification of the data types used in each specification.

This specification refines the *vending machine* presented previously. It includes a new attribute (*ncoins*) which represents the actual number of coins inside the deposit of the machine, a new action (*collect*) representing the collection of coins and a readiness axiom for *coin* stating that *coin* is enabled whenever the machine is not ready and the number of coins (*ncoins*) is lower than a given limit (the deposit capacity). In this way, internal nondeterminism over the action *coin* is reduced to the states in which the machine is not ready and the number of coins is greater than the given limit. In these cases, the coin can either be accepted or refused.

It is worthwhile pointing out that the *regulated vending machine* is not a refinement of the initial *vending machine*, because it does not offer the same choices to its environment – more specifically, it does not offer the cigar option.

Refinement morphisms support the process of stepwise refinement of systems with the addition of detail (vertical composition). Given that system development also takes place at the horizontal level through the process of putting together a system from components, it is important to establish properties that relate these two processes (vertical and horizontal).

On the one hand, it is important to confirm that the notion of refinement is "congruent" with the notion of isomorphism in *c-SPEC*. That is, indistinguishable systems (as components of other systems) refine, and are refined exactly by, the same systems. Formally, this corresponds to the fact that isomorphisms in *c-SPEC* are also isomorphisms in *r-SPEC*. Actually, we have a stronger result:

Proposition 3.7. Let $\sigma:\Sigma\rightarrow\Sigma'$ be a signature morphism. $\sigma:S\rightarrow S'$ is an isomorphism in *c-SPEC* iff is an isomorphism in *r-SPEC*. ∎

On the other hand, it is important to investigate compositionality, i.e. the property according to which the refinement of a complex system can be obtained by putting together refinements of its components, what in [12] is called commutativity of horizontal with vertical composition. This is an essential property for supporting incremental development and the reuse of existing components.

Theorem 3.8. Consider the *c-SPEC* diagrams given by $\sigma_1:S_0\rightarrow S_1$, $\sigma_2:S_0\rightarrow S_2$, interconnecting specifications S_1 and S_2 via S_0 and $\sigma'_1:S'_0\rightarrow S'_1$, $\sigma'_2:S'_0\rightarrow S'_2$, interconnecting specifications S'_1 and S'_2 via S'_0. Given refinement morphisms $\eta_0:S_0\rightarrow S'_0$, $\eta_1:S_1\rightarrow S_1'$ and $\eta_2:S_2\rightarrow S_2'$ s.t. $\eta_{0_{ac}}$ is injective and $\eta_0;\sigma'_i=\sigma_i;\eta_i$, for i=1,2, there exists a unique refinement morphism $\eta:S\rightarrow S'$ s.t. $\mu_i;\eta=\eta_i;\mu'_i$, for i=1,2, where $\mu_1:S_1\rightarrow S$ and $\mu_2:S_2\rightarrow S$ result from the pushout of σ_1 and σ_2 and $\mu'_1:S'_1\rightarrow S$ and $\mu'_2:S'_2\rightarrow S$ result from the pushout of σ'_1 and σ'_2. ∎

Notice that, to achieve compositionality it is necessary to ensure that, for every synchronisation point $g_1 | g_2$ defined in the upper level, if g'_1 is a possible refinement of g_1 and g'_2 is a possible refinement of g_2 (i.e., $\eta_i(g'_i)=g_i$), then the interconnection specified in the lower level defines the synchronisation point

$g'_1 \mid g'_2$. The following lemma asserts that this is ensured when η_0 is injective.

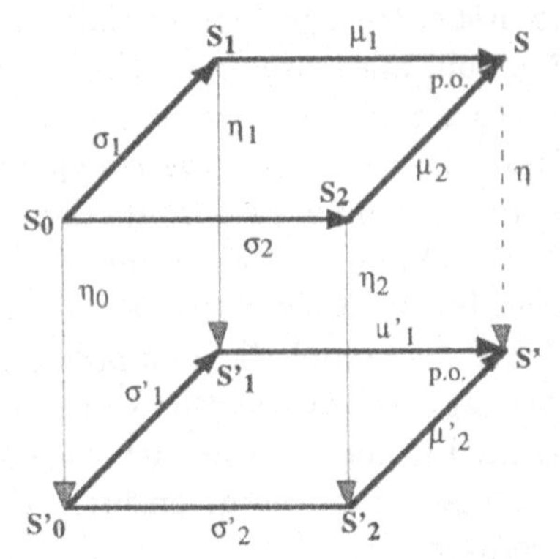

Lemma 3.9. Given two diagrams $<\sigma_1:\Gamma_1 \to \Gamma_0, \sigma_2:\Gamma_2 \to \Gamma_0>$ and $<\sigma'_1:\Gamma'_1 \to \Gamma'_0, \sigma'_2:\Gamma'_2 \to \Gamma'_0>$ in $\mathcal{SET}_\perp$, and morphisms $\eta_0:\Gamma'_0 \to \Gamma_0$, $\eta_1:\Gamma'_1 \to \Gamma_1$ and $\eta_2:\Gamma'_2 \to \Gamma_2$ also in $\mathcal{SET}_\perp$ s.t. $\sigma'_i;\eta_0 = \eta_i;\sigma_i$, for i=1,2; if η_0 is injective, then for every $g \in \Gamma$, $g'_1 \in \Gamma'_1$ and $g'_2 \in \Gamma'_2$, if $\eta_1(g'_1) = \mu_1(g)$ and $\eta_2(g'_2) = \mu_2(g)$ then there exists $g' \in \Gamma'$ s.t. $\mu'_1(g') = g_1$ and $\mu'_2(g') = g_2$ and $\eta(g') = g$, where $\mu_1:\Gamma \to \Gamma_1$ and $\mu_2:\Gamma \to \Gamma_2$ result from the pullback of σ_1 and σ_2, $\mu'_1:\Gamma' \to \Gamma'_1$ and $\mu'_2:\Gamma' \to \Gamma'_2$ result from the pullback of σ'_1 and σ'_2 and $\eta:\Gamma' \to \Gamma$ results from the universal property of pullbacks. ∎

Proposition 3.10. If C is a channel, $\sigma:C \to S$ is a component-of morphism and $\eta:S \to S'$ is a refinement morphism then $\sigma;\eta:C \to S'$ is a component-of morphism. ∎

From this proposition it follows the following corollary of the theorem 3.8:

Corollary 3.11. Consider the *c-SPEC* diagram given by $\sigma_1:C \to S_1$, $\sigma_2:C \to S_2$, interconnecting specifications S_1 and S_2 via the channel C. Given refinement morphisms $\eta_1:S_1 \to S_1'$ and $\eta_2:S_2 \to S_2'$, there exists a unique refinement morphism $\eta:S \to S'$ s.t. $\mu_i;\eta = \eta_i;\mu'_i$, for i=1,2, where $\mu_1:S_1 \to S$ and $\mu_2:S_2 \to S$ result from the pushout of $\sigma_1;\eta_1$ and $\sigma_2;\eta_2$ and $\mu'_1:S'_1 \to S$ and $\mu'_2:S'_2 \to S$ result from the pushout of σ'_1 and σ'_2. ∎

The corollary states that, given a composite system put together from components through channels, we obtain a system which refines it by using the same channels to interconnect arbitrary refinements of its components.

4 Concluding Remarks

In this paper, we have extended the traditional notion of specification as a theory presentation to include not only the set of sentences that express the properties that are guaranteed of the behaviour of the system but also the sentences (co-properties) that capture the willingness of the system to cooperate with its environment. The distinction between these two sets of sentences was also based on the fact, also observed in [19] in the context of local logics of labelled transition systems, that, whereas certain properties of systems are *preserved* across morphisms, other properties can only be *reflected* in the sense that they will only be ensured as long as the environment of the component cooperates. Morphisms were defined for the new notion of specification which behave in this way – properties are preserved whereas co-properties are reflected. The resulting category was proved to be finitely co-complete, thus supporting the operation of putting together a system from interconnected components. Another category of specifications was defined for which both properties and co-properties are preserved across morphisms. The morphisms of this category capture refinement relations between specifications, thus supporting vertical structuring. Compositionality (commutativity of horizontal composition wrt vertical composition in the sense of [12]) was also proved meaning that a refinement of a system is obtained by putting together refinements of its components.

The nature of properties and co-properties, i.e. of what is preserved and what is reflected, is determined by the computation and interconnection models that are adopted. In the case that we used for illustration, attributes are local (private). Hence, properties can include invariants proved locally about the attributes of a component, as well as initialisation conditions, effects of actions and restrictions to the occurrence of actions. On the other hand, actions are global (shared) which implies that readiness conditions (the availability of actions) are co-properties: they are directly related to the co-operation with the environment in the sense that an action is only ready to occur when all the components that synchronise in that action make it available. In the context of other interconnection mechanisms, we may have other classes of properties and co-properties. For instance, if local actions are also supported, than readiness for such actions will be treated as properties. If global (shared) attributes are allowed, invariants for those attributes should be treated as co-properties. We are currently working on a model-theoretic characterisation of properties and co-properties which can provide a systematic account of preservation and reflection that can then be incorporated in a generalisation of the notion of institution. This generalisation should then allow us to identify the nature of properties and co-properties in other logics, e.g. temporal logic.

One of the key points of the proposed extension of the notion of specification is the fact that it now reflects more directly the interference between the component and its environment. We are also investigating more closely the relationship between this approach and other styles of specification which, like assumption/commitment or rely/guarantee [1, 5], control the interplay between component and environment.

Finally, and although the paper focused almost exclusively on logical specifications, compositionality results have been proved for an extension of the parallel program design language COMMUNITY [9] that supports the specification of required non-determinism (readiness).

Acknowledgments

We would like to thank Michel Wermelinger and Tom Maibaum for many fruitful interactions.

References

1. M.Abadi and L.Lamport, "Composing Specifications", in *ACM Transactions on Programming Languages and Systems*, 15(1):73-132, January 1993.
2. R.Alur and T.Henzinger, "Local Liveness for Compositional Modeling of Fair Reactive Systems", in P.Wolper (ed), *CAV'95*, LNCS 939, Springer-Verlag 1995, 166-179.
3. H.Barringer, "The Use of Temporal Logic in the Compositional Specification of Concurrent Systems", in A.Galton (ed) *Temporal Logics and their Applications*, Academic Press 1987.
4. R.Burstall and J.Goguen, "Putting Theories Together to Make Specifications", in *Proc. 5th IJCAI*, 1977, 1045-1058.
5. P.Collette, "Design of Compositional Proof Systems Based on Assumption-Commitment Specifications: Application to UNITY", PhD thesis, Université Catholique de Louvain, 1994.
6. J.Fiadeiro, "On the Emergence of Properties in Component-Based Systems", in M.Wirsing and M.Nivat (eds), *AMAST'96*, LNCS 1101, Springer-Verlag 1996, 421-443.
7. J.L.Fiadeiro and J.F.Costa, "Mirror, Mirror in my Hand: a duality between specifications and models of process behaviour", in *Mathematical Structures in Computer Science* 6, 1996, 353-373.
8. J.Fiadeiro and T.Maibaum, "Temporal Theories as Modularisation Units for Concurrent System Specification", *Formal Aspects of Computing*, 4:239-272, 1992.
9. J.Fiadeiro and T.Maibaum, "Categorical Semantics of Parallel Program Design", *Science of Computer Programming*, 28:111-138, 1997.
10. J.Fiadeiro and T.Maibaum, "Generalising Interpretations Between Theories in the Context of π-institutions", in G.Burn, S.Gay and M.Ryan (eds), Theory and Formal Methods 1993, Springer-Verlag, 126-147.
11. J.L.Fiadeiro, A.Lopes and T.Maibaum, "Synthesising Interconnections", in Algorithmic Languages and Calculi, R.Bird and L.Meertens (eds), Chapman Hall, in print.
12. J.Goguen and R.Burstall, "CAT, a system for the structured elaboration of correct programs from structured specifications", *Technical Report CSL-118*, SRI International 1980.
13. J.Goguen and R.Burstall, "Institutions: Abstract Model Theory for Specification and Programming", *Journal of the ACM* 39(1):95-146, 1992.
14. B.Jonsson, "Compositional Specifiaction and Verification of Distributed Systems", in *ACM Transactions on Programming Languages and Systems*, 16(2):259-303, 1994.
15. T.Maibaum, "Rôle of Abstraction in Program Development", in H.-J.Kugler (ed) *Information Processing'86*, North-Holland 1986, 135-142.
16. T.Maibaum, "A Logic for the Formal Requirements Specification of Real-Time Embedded Systems", *Forest Research Report*, Imperial College 1987.
17. B.Meyer, "Applying Design by Contract", *IEEE Computer*, Oct.1992, 40-51.
18. C.Stirling, "Modal and Temporal Logics", *Handbook of Logic in Computer Science*, S.Abramsky, D.Gabbay and T.Maibaum (eds), Vol.2, 477-563, Oxford University Press 1992.
19. G.Winskel, "A Compositional Proof System on a Category of Labelled Transition Systems", *Information and Computation* 87:2-57, 1990.
20. S.Zhou, R.Gerth and R.Kuiper, "Transformations Preserving Properties and Properties preserved by Transformations", in E.Best (ed), CONCUR'93, LNCS 715, Springer-Verlag 1993, 353-367.

Case Studies in Using a Meta-Method for Formal Method Integration

Richard F. Paige

Department of Computer Science, University of Toronto, Toronto, ON, Canada, M5S 3G4. paige@cs.toronto.edu*

Abstract. We summarize the results of several experiments in applying a meta-method for formal method integration [18, 19]. We provide a small example of using an instance of integrated formal methods, and discuss properties and difficulties associated with applying the meta-method to combining and using several formal and semiformal methods.

1 Introduction

Method integration involves defining relationships between different methods so that they may be cooperatively used together. In software engineering, method integration has seen recent research on combining specific methods [15, 25], and on the formulation of systematic techniques [14, 18, 19]. In this paper, we follow the latter theme and describe several case studies in the application (and use of the products) of a meta-method for formal method integration [18, 19].

We commence with a very brief overview of method integration and the means we take to accomplishing it. Our lightweight technique is based on *heterogeneous notations*, combinations of formal and semiformal notations. After providing background for heterogeneous notations, we summarize a meta-method for integrations involving at least one formal method [19] used for system specification and design, and then describe several case studies in which the meta-method has been applied. With one case study, we provide a very small example using integrated methods, in order to give the flavour of the approach.

Due to space restrictions, this paper only summarizes the results of several case studies. The interested reader may find details in [18, 19, 20, 21].

1.1 Method integration

Method integration involves the resolution of incompatibilities between methods, so that the approaches can be safely and effectively used together [14]. Method integration in a software engineering context is of growing research interest. A reason for this is the low likelihood that one method will always suffice in the development of complex systems [5, 12]. Method integration has also been used and has been shown to be useful in practice in various forms, e.g., at BT [25], Westinghouse [9], Praxis [8], and elsewhere.

* *Current address:* Department of Computer Science, York University, North York, ON, Canada, M3J 1P3. paige@cs.yorku.ca

1.2 Heterogeneous notations and specifications

A notation is an important part of any method. Notations are used to specify system behaviour and to clarify requirements. Notations play an important role in how we carry out formal method integration. Specifically, we combine notations as a first step towards combining formal methods with other methods, all of which that are being used for system specification and design. A *heterogeneous notation* is a combination of notations that is used to write heterogeneous specifications.

Definition 1. A specification is *heterogeneous* if it is a composition of partial specifications written in two or more notations.

We do not place any constraints on what we mean by "composition". Useful compositions will depend on the problems to be solved, and the context in which the set of notations is to be used. Useful compositions may be specification combinators, shared state or names, or synchronization on events, for example.

Heterogeneous notations are useful for a number of reasons: for writing simpler specifications than might be produced using a single language [28]; for ease of expression [2]; and because they have been proven to be useful in practice [8, 29].

The formal meaning of a heterogeneous specification is given by defining the semantics of all the notation compositions. Formal meaning is provided by a heterogeneous basis.

Definition 2. A *heterogeneous basis* is a set of notations, translations between formal notations, and formalizations of semiformal notations.

The heterogeneous basis used in the work summarized in this paper is completely presented in [18]. We discuss it in the next section, and summarize the process of its construction in Section 2.

1.3 A heterogeneous basis

A heterogeneous basis supplies a formal semantics to a heterogeneous specification [18]. It is also used to provide the first step on which formal method integration is carried out. The basis used in the case studies in this paper consists of a set of languages with mappings defined between them. It is depicted in Figure 1.

The predicate notation is from [11]; Z is from [26]; specification statements (i.e., $w : [pre, post]$) are from [17]; and the Larch languages are from [6]. The remaining semiformal notations are from SA/SD [4], and Coad-Yourdon object oriented analysis and design [3]. More notations are considered in [18, 19].

In the diagram, the arrows represent translations. The translations in Figure 1 are described in detail in [18]. We will give a few examples of translations involving formalisms in Section 2, and will summarize some example formalizations involving semiformalisms. We will also describe the general approach we take to constructing a heterogeneous basis that consists of formal and semiformal notations.

A specification written using combinations of the notations from Figure 1 is given a semantics using only one of the formal notations of the basis. The user of the basis

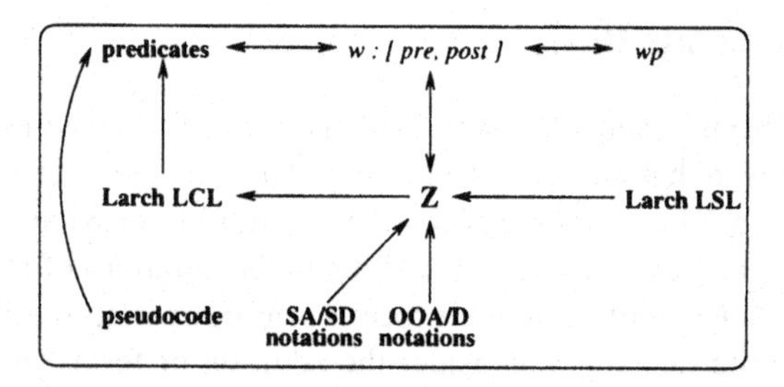

Fig.1. A heterogeneous basis

chooses the formal notation to use for their particular context, and defines the meaning of a heterogeneous specification in this formal notation. Syntactic complications must still be dealt with by the specifier, in particular, ensuring that combinations of different notations can be parsed.

1.4 Integrating methods with heterogeneous notations

Heterogeneous notations are used as a first step in formal method integration. In other words, we carry out formal method integration (for system specification and design methods) by *first combining the notations on which the methods rely.* The combination process occurs by constructing (or extending) a heterogeneous basis consisting of the notations of interest, and by resolving syntactic differences among the notations, so that combinations of notations can be unambiguously parsed. Once this is done, the method integration process can continue by generalizing method steps to use heterogeneous notations, and by embedding, ordering, interleaving (perhaps generalized) method steps from two or more different methods.

We do not claim that this is the only approach to combining formal methods with other methods. It is a lightweight technique that produces integrated methods with convenient properties (see Section 3, and the case studies) when applied to system specification and design methods, and has been used productively on a number of moderate-sized examples. One suggestion we make is that formal method integration can be partly systematized by using heterogeneous notations, since their use allows notation-related complications of method integration to be dealt with first, while the remainder of the integration process can concentrate on manipulating the steps of the methods to be combined.

1.5 Overview

We commence the paper by summarizing the process for constructing a heterogeneous basis. We then outline a meta-method for formal method integration, and clarify the role that heterogeneous notations play within it. We summarize the results of a number of example integrations involving only formal methods. One integration is applied to a very small example. Two larger integration case studies, involving semiformal methods, are outlined. We then discuss the benefits and limitations of each integration.

2 A Heterogeneous Basis

A heterogeneous basis is shown in Figure 1. This basis is created by translation: a set of mappings are given that transform a specification in one notation into a specification in a second notation. These mappings can then be used to provide a formal semantics to compositions of partial specifications written in the notations of the basis.

In this section, we summarize the process of constructing the heterogeneous basis of Figure 1. In particular, we consider the addition of formal notations to a basis (by translation), and the process of adding semiformal notations to an existing basis (by formalization). We only summarize the details here, due to space constraints; full translations, formalization procedures, and examples are given in [18].

2.1 Adding formal notations to a heterogeneous basis

A formal notation may be added to a heterogeneous basis by

- providing a translation from the formal notation into a notation already in a heterogeneous basis; and
- analyzing the expressive capabilities of each notation, viz., what can and cannot be translated with preservation of interpretation, and what is the effect of these notation differences on translation and on assigning a semantics to compositions.

In constructing the heterogeneous basis shown in Figure 1, we commenced with existing translations already presented in the literature. These included: the mapping of Z to specification statements [13]; the *wp* definition of specification statements [17]; and, the *wp* expression of an early version of a predicative programming specification [10]. To these translations, we added others. We provide several examples here, one mapping predicates without time variables into specification statements; a second mapping predicates with time variables into specification statements; and a third, mapping specification statements into Z. The translations are described as functions from notation to notation (we explain ways to handle expressive differences shortly). To simplify the process, we assume all translations use the primed/unprimed notation of Z for representing post and pre-state. More example translations are given in [18].

A predicate specification **frame** $w \bullet P$ that does not refer to the time variables t, t' [11] can be translated to a specification statement [17] using the mapping *PredToSS*.

$$\mathit{PredToSS}(\mathbf{frame}\ w \bullet P) \mathrel{\widehat=} w : [\, \mathit{true}, P \,]$$

Similar translations arise when dealing with predicate specifications that make reference to time variables t and t'. For a predicate specification **frame** $w \bullet P$ that includes references to t and t' in P, we translate it using *TimedPredToSS*.

$$\mathit{TimedPredToSS}(\mathbf{frame}\ w \bullet P) \mathrel{\widehat=} \\ w : [\, \forall t \bullet \exists n : \mathit{nat} \bullet \forall w' \bullet (P \Rightarrow t' \leq t + n), \exists t \bullet \exists t' \bullet (P \wedge t' \geq t) \,]$$

The specification statement $w : [\, \mathit{pre}, \mathit{post} \,]$ can be translated into Z using function *SSToZ*.

$$\mathit{SSToZ}(w : [\, \mathit{pre}, \mathit{post} \,]) \mathrel{\widehat=} [\, \Xi\rho;\ \Delta w \mid \mathit{pre} \wedge \mathit{post} \,]$$

ρ is all state variables not in the frame w. The user of *SSToZ* may identify input components (using a ?), or output (using a !) in the schema, instead of placing all state components in Δ or Ξ components. Miraculous specifications (i.e., terminating and establishing *false*) cannot be translated using this function.

We have not guaranteed that specific notations can be feasibly used together. There are still complications that must be resolved, e.g., syntactic ambiguity, how to write and define particular compositions, combining different viewpoints, etcetera. These are all issues that must be resolved on a specific-context level, i.e., when the notations to be combined and the compositions to be defined are known.

The translations between formalisms are all written as total functions. But some specifications expressible in one notation are inexpressible in a second language. To handle these language features while using translations, we have several options.

- Restrict the use of languages to only translatable elements. This can be described as an "intersection" approach to semantics, since only mutually expressible specifications are used in writing heterogeneous specifications.
- Extend languages (e.g., as is done in [10]) so as to be able to express all features of other languages. In contrast to the first approach, this might be called a "union" approach to semantics, since all expressible specifications can be used.
- Ignore the effect of differences in expressibility, and somehow account for the changes in interpretation when using notations in proof.

We used the first option in our case studies, and always checked for untranslatable elements in our specifications. Our case studies suggest that this lightweight approach to composition is feasible and useful in application. Alternative approaches are used, for example, in [28, 29].

A catalogue of untranslatable specifications is presented in [18]. This includes specifications like havoc, magic, and angelic nondeterminism.

2.2 Adding semiformal notations to a heterogeneous basis

The heterogeneous basis shown in Figure 1 contains semiformal notations, including those from Coad-Yourdon OOA/D [3] and SA/SD [4, 27]. To include a semiformal notation in the basis, we must *fix an interpretation* for it, and then express a general specification in this notation in one of the formalisms in the basis. This extends the heterogeneous basis to allow us to formally define the meaning of heterogeneous specifications that include parts written in (so-called) semiformalisms. Once formalization has occurred, the formal expression can thereafter be used to check for ambiguity at the semiformal level.

There are many interpretations we might take for a semiformalism. In particular, an interpretation will probably be useful only for a specific problem context or particular development context. Therefore, it is important that the approach to heterogeneous basis construction be extendible to new notations, interpretations, and formalizations. Our examples have convinced us that the basis is partwise extendible and changeable; that is, we can change formalizations without affecting the rest of the heterogeneous basis.

In [18], we provide a number of formalizations for semiformalisms, including:

- a formalization of data flow diagrams in Z, from [23], is used; a similar formalization of structure charts is also applied. This formalization does not permit expression of triggering or reactive behaviour. For such artifacts, formalizations from [15, 29] might be preferred.
- a formalization of Coad-Yourdon object oriented notations (e.g., object diagrams, assembly and classification diagrams, instance diagrams, etc.) is produced based on Hall's expression of objects in Z [7]. This formalization does not consider reactive behaviour of objects.
- a formalization of SADT diagram notations as sets and relations appears in [19].
- Jackson diagrams and pseudocode are also formalized, using predicates.

The formalizations we provide can easily be changed to fit new interpretations and domains. For example, the formalization of data flow diagrams from [15] could be used without much difficulty. Formalizations *should* be changed if they do not provide adequate interpretations for particular problems and contexts.

We now consider how heterogeneous notations are used in a meta-method for formal method integration.

3 A Meta-Method for Formal Method Integration

A meta-method for formal method integration (of system specification and design methods) was given in [18, 19]. The meta-method is based on the use of heterogeneous notations for defining compositions between notations, and thereafter on defining relationships between procedure steps. We briefly summarize the meta-method here, and then describe applications in the following sections.

The meta-method itself does not place constraints or restrictions on how the methods are to be used when integrated. This is the task of the method engineer, i.e., the user of the meta-method. The meta-method is designed to support the method engineer in placing constraints on using methods in combination. Whether particular methods are to be considered *complementary* is dependent on the context in which they are to be used.

The heterogeneous notation-based meta-method is summarized as follows.

1. *Fix a base method.* A base method gives a set of steps that is to be supported and complemented by other (invasive) methods. A base method may be formal or semiformal. It may support more of the software development cycle than other methods; it may also provide the steps that a developer may want to primarily use during development.
2. *Choose invasive methods.* Invasive methods will augment, be embedded, or be interleaved with the base method. The invasive methods complement the base method through notation, procedure, or user preference.
3. *Construct or extend a heterogeneous basis.* This is accomplished by constructing or adding notations from the base and invasive methods to a heterogeneous basis. A single formal notation from the heterogeneous basis (that is to be used to provide a formal semantics to system specifications that arise in the use of the integrated method) can be chosen and fixed at this point.

4. *Generalization and relation of method steps.* The method steps for the base and invasive methods are manipulated in order to define how they will work together in combination. Either one or both of the generalization and relation manipulations can be applied. In more detail, the manipulations are as follows.
   - *Generalization.* The steps of the base or invasive methods are generalized to use heterogeneous notations; effectively, new notations are added to a method, and the method steps are generalized to using the new notations.
   - *Relation.* Relation of method steps can follow generalization. Relationships between the (generalized) base steps and (generalized) invasive steps are defined. Steps of base and invasive methods may be ordered, mutually embedded, or interleaved to form a new set of steps. Examples of relationships are given in [19]; these include linking of sets of steps, replacing steps, extending and supplementing steps, and parallel use.

   The heterogeneous basis is used to support composition (and communication) of partial specifications. It also allows flexibility in how method steps are to be interrelated.
5. *Guidance to the user.* Hints, examples, and suggestions on how the integrated method can be used is provided.

The meta-method provides a systematic technique for combining formal methods with other formal and semiformal methods. It allows many different forms of (unintrusive and intrusive) integration, and supports the formal use of the formal methods in combination with semiformal methods. It does not provide a formal model of the steps and the methods being combined, e.g., as in [16]. It requires a fixed and formal semantics for all semiformalisms used in integrated methods, and it requires that the method engineer resolve syntactic ambiguities or incompatibilities across multiple notations and methods.

4 Case Study 1: Integrating Several Formal Methods

Our first small experiment with formal method integration involved combining several formal methods, selected from predicative programming, a Z "style", Morgan's refinement calculus, and Larch. The integrations were carried out at first in a pairwise fashion, by selecting specific pairs of methods and combining them using the meta-method; later, further methods were added to the results of these first integrations. Particular examples of integrations included: a combination of predicative programming, Morgan's refinement calculus, and the Z house style; a combination of the refinement calculus and predicative programming; and an integration of Z and Larch. We briefly summarize the process of integrating predicative programming and Z here as an example.

A Z house style and predicative programming can be considered as complementary: predicative programming is designed and has been shown to be useful for procedural or operational refinement, and is particularly convenient for developing recursive, concurrent, and real-time programs [11]. Z is useful for structuring large specifications, and has been shown to be a convenient notation in which to carry out data transformation [1]. In integrating the two methods, we chose the Z house style as the base method, and predicative programming as the invasive method. The heterogeneous basis shown in Figure 1 can be used to provide a formal semantics to compositions of specifications, by using predicative programming (we restricted use of Z to non-havoc specifications). The informal specification procedures of the Z style were generalized to also use predicative programming notations. Furthermore, the proof rules of Z were supplemented with predicative programming refinement rules.

We have applied this specific integrated method to a number of examples [18], ranging from very small (1-2 pages), to more substantial (10-15 pages). We found that predicative programming fits conveniently into the Z style of specification, especially with respect to a standard style of specification, where Z expressions are documented with informal text. We also found that the addition of predicative programming to the Z method makes procedural refinement much easier to do than with just pure Z. With a combination of both Z and predicative programming, we can build specifications to facilitate both data transformation and procedural refinement, and can build specification parts using the notation in which we want to carry out particular kinds of proof.

One complication with the approach was that syntactic differences in the notations had to be resolved in order to parse the compositions of syntaxes. For example, $\wedge$ and $\vee$ were overloaded operators, and so we used $\curlywedge$ and $\curlyvee$ to represent schema operators. Furthermore, we had to restrict the use of Z and predicative programming to only translatable specifications: therefore, we could not use the specification havoc in Z, or the specification magic in predicative programming.

In order to demonstrate the use of integrated formal methods, we briefly summarize a very small example. In this example, we use predicative programming and the refinement calculus to solve a problem. We choose to demonstrate this combination of methods because an example can be presented compactly. More interesting examples can be found in [18].

4.1 Example

The simple problem is as follows: we have an unordered, nonempty list of integers, L, and need to determine the minimum value s in the list and if a value x is in the list. A specification is as follows, using the parallel composition operator $\|$ of [11].

$$\mathit{findmin} \parallel \mathit{search},$$

findmin is:

$$\mathit{findmin} \mathrel{\widehat{=}} s' = \mathit{MIN}\ j : 0,..\#L \bullet Lj,$$

and the search is a specification statement as follows.

$$\mathit{search} \mathrel{\widehat{=}} i : [\ (0 \leq i' < \#L \wedge Li' = x) \vee (i' = \#L \wedge x \notin L[0,..\#L])\ ].$$

Integer i will be set to $\#L$ if and only if x is not in $L[0,..\#L]$.

To verify that the specification is satisfiable, we must show that:

$$\exists\, s', i' \bullet (\mathit{findmin} \parallel \mathit{search}).$$

This simplifies as follows:

$$\begin{aligned}
&\exists\, s', i' \bullet (\mathit{findmin} \parallel \mathit{search})\\
=\ &\exists\, s', i' \bullet (s' = \mathit{MIN}\ j : 0, ..\#L \bullet Lj) \wedge\\
&\qquad ((0 \le i' < \#L \wedge Li' = x) \vee (i' = \#L \wedge x \notin L[0, ..\#L]))\\
&\exists\, i' : 0, ..\#L \bullet Li' = x \vee \exists\, i' : \#L \bullet x \notin L[0;\ ..\#L]\\
=\ &x \in L[0, ..\#L] \vee x \notin L[0;\ ..\#L]\\
=\ &\top
\end{aligned}$$

We specify the minimum routine as a predicate, since we envision a tail-recursive implementation that is handled conveniently by predicate refinement. To demonstrate using two formal methods together, we specify the search and develop its implementation using the refinement calculus's invariant/variant approach.

Since predicate refinement (boolean implication) is monotonic over the combinator $\parallel$, we can refine the specification by parts. We first deal with the specification statement. It can be refined using $\sqsubseteq$ due to the result in [18] that says that monotonicity of *wp* refinement is preserved over all predicate combinators. Its development can be started as follows:

$$\begin{aligned}
\mathit{search} \sqsubseteq\ & i, L[\#L] := 0, x;\\
& i : [\, I \wedge i = 0, I' \wedge Li' = x \,] \qquad (i)
\end{aligned}$$

where invariant $I \mathrel{\widehat=} 0 \le i < \#L+1 \wedge \forall j : 0, ..i \bullet x \neq Lj$. The specification statement (i) is easily refined as follows, with variant $\#L - i$.

$$(i) \sqsubseteq \mathbf{do}\ Li \neq x \rightarrow i := i + 1\ \mathbf{od}$$

The refinement of the predicate is also straightforward (due to the monotonicity of $\Leftarrow$ over $\parallel$). It assumes that $+\infty$ is not an element of the list L.

$$\mathit{findmin} \Leftarrow i := 0.\ s := +\infty.\ s' = \mathit{min}(s, \mathit{MIN}\ j : i, ..\#L \bullet Lj) \qquad (1)$$

The predicate at the end of (1) is refinable to a selection.

$$\begin{aligned}
s' = \mathit{min}(s, \mathit{MIN}\ j : i, ..\#L \bullet Lj) \Leftarrow\ & \mathbf{if}\ i = \#L\ \mathbf{then\ ok\ else}\\
& i \neq \#L \Rightarrow s' = \mathit{min}(s, \mathit{MIN}\ j : i, ..\#L \bullet Lj)
\end{aligned}$$

And the **else** branch can be refined in the obvious way:

$$\begin{aligned}
i \neq \#L \Rightarrow s' = \mathit{min}(s, \mathit{MIN}\ j : i, ..\#L \bullet Lj) \Leftarrow\ & \mathbf{if}\ Li < s\ \mathbf{then}\ s := Li\ \mathbf{else\ ok}.\\
& i := i + 1
\end{aligned}$$

The resulting implementation is heterogeneous (involving the programming language of [11] and Dijkstra's guarded command language) and can be transliterated to a homogeneous form in either programming language subset.

5 Case Study 2: SA/SD and Predicative Programming

We combined Structured Analysis and Structured Design [4] with predicative programming in the second case study. More precisely, we carried out three different integrations: one, where predicative programming *supplemented* SA/SD; a second, where SA/SD was *linked* with predicative programming; and a third, where an SA/SD development was *extracted* from the aforementioned supplementation of SA/SD by predicative programming. Full details of the case studies and inter-relations appear in [21].

In the initial case study, we chose SA/SD as the base method (because of its modelling procedures), and predicative programming as the invasive method. We selected predicates to use as a basis notation. SA/SD procedures were generalized to use predicates, and then the predicative refinement rules were used to supplement the SA/SD procedures for decomposition, process specification construction, and implementation. This integration is shown in Fig. 2; the ellipses in the figure represent method steps, while the boxes represent method products. The arrows represent *generate* and *use* relations.

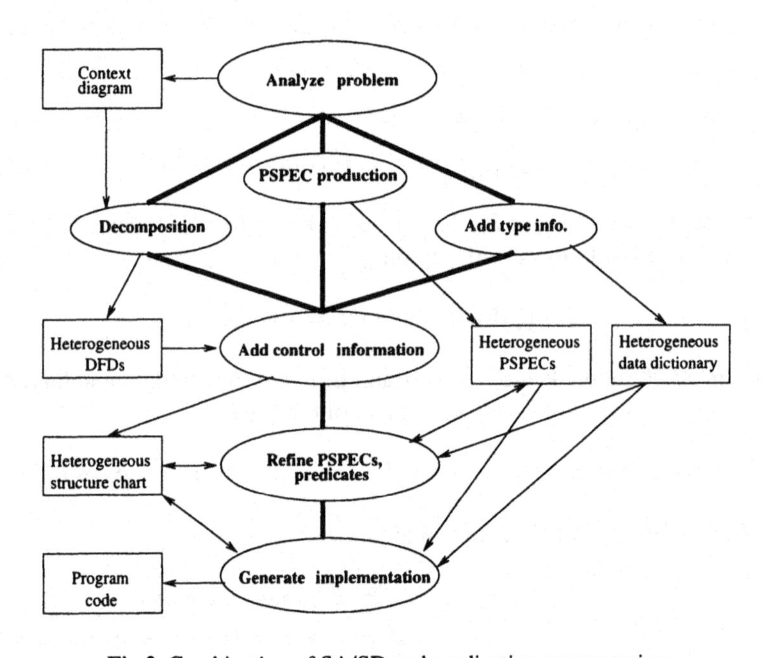

Fig.2. Combination of SA/SD and predicative programming

We applied this integrated method to a number of medium-sized examples, the largest being a construction of a simulator for a scheduler. The specification and (moderately detailed) development was approximately 20 pages long. The integration was particularly convenient to use: the predicative notation and procedures were *restrictable*, in that their use was confinable to the specification and development of a specific part of a system. In particular, we used predicative programming for specifying only those

PSPECs that seemed to have complex functionality at the requirement level; pseudocode and programming language specifications were used for the remaining PSPECs. This in turn leads us to suggest that it was possible to *gradually introduce* the predicative programming method into development, because of this restrictability feature.

The second integration of SA/SD and predicative programming mimicked the work of Semmens and Allen [25], and the SAZ project [22]. SA/SD was *linked* with predicative programming, by defining translations from SA/SD specifications to predicate specifications. The method was used by first applying standard SA/SD. Once a data flow diagram, PSPECs, and data dictionary had been produced, a pure predicative specification was constructed via the translations of Figure 1. Development could then continue, either by adding extra formal details and continuing with the predicative programming method, or by studying the produced specifications, analyzing what was missing, checking for consistency, and feeding back extra information into the standard SA/SD development.

The third integration was similar to what was described above. We commenced with a development using the SA/SD-predicative integration that is diagrammed in Fig. 2. After decomposition and PSPEC production, we *extracted* semiformal specifications from the formal specifications (e.g., following [23]), and continued the development using the semiformal specifications. This type of approach could be useful when changes in requirements occur, or when we find that during development the initial method to use in solving a problem is inappropriate.

A limitation with these approaches is that they required us to fix an interpretation and provide a formal semantics for semiformal SA/SD notations (e.g., DFDs, structure charts). This effectively fixes the domain of applicability of such notations. It must be possible to change such interpretations and formalizations, if other developers have other ideas on the meaning of the semiformal notations. Due to the partwise constructible nature of our heterogeneous basis, this seems possible. We might even envision the construction of heterogeneous bases for specific classes of applications and problems.

6 Case Study 3: Coad-Yourdon OOA/D and Z

The third application of the meta-method was to combine a Z house style with Coad-Yourdon object-oriented analysis and design [20]. The two methods are complementary: the Z house style offers formal specification techniques and proof rules; Coad-Yourdon offers procedures for the decomposition of requirements into objects and object structures.

In applying the meta-method, we selected Coad-Yourdon as the base method (since it supports a broader range of the software development process). The Z method was chosen as the invasive method. Coad-Yourdon procedures were generalized to use Z, and the Z proof procedures and specification style rules were used to supplement the Coad-Yourdon procedures. In particular, Z was used to specify particular objects of the system—objects that had complex functionality or data structures where a formal specification or development would prove to be justifiable. Z was also used to specify and develop implementations of object *methods* where the intended functionality of each method was complex. The integration is depicted in Fig. 3.

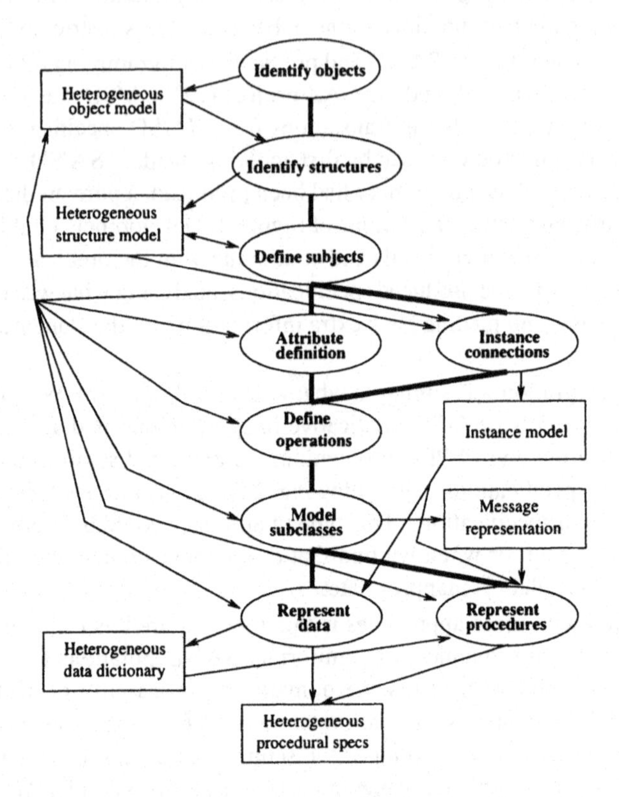

Fig.3. Integration of Coad/Yourdon OOA/D with Z method

We have applied this integrated method to a small collection of examples, the largest being the development of a text analyzer system with a graphical user interface. This required construction of X Windows code, text processing code, and statistics gathering code. Z was used in the formal development of the statistics gathering objects, and in providing a formal semantics to the specifications produced in the method. Coad-Yourdon was used in guiding the entire development. The entire specification was about 70 pages in length, resulting in approximately 4000 lines of C++ code.

We found that the combination of Z and Coad-Yourdon worked well, primarily because of the modular structure of specifications produced and required in both Z and Coad-Yourdon. That developers using this integrated method will be required to build specification parts with precise interfaces may help to make the process of using these specific multiple notations together much simpler. A further convenience using this approach is that the use of Z is again restrictable; we only used Z (and Z proof procedures) to develop those objects and methods that we felt necessary. Restrictability of formal methods may be important in allowing more wide-spread use of such techniques.

One particular difficulty in using Z and Coad-Yourdon arose when having to interface Z specifications with Coad-Yourdon specifications of object methods or attributes. At some point in a specification, it may be necessary to use semiformal attributes or methods in a formal specification (or vice versa). To avoid this problem, we made use of the heterogeneous basis. When using a semiformal method or attribute in a formal specification, we assumed that there existed a formal expression of the method or attribute in question. The interface to this method or attribute is acquired through the use of the formalization procedure in the heterogeneous basis; formalization of interfaces is inexpensive. Then, in the formal specification where we wanted to use the semiformal method or attribute, we simply used the formalization *interface*, even though we did not explicitly write down the entire formalization itself. This meant that we could not prove anything about the semiformal part, but we could use a formal *representation* of the part in a formal specification.

7 Conclusions

We have briefly described a general technique for integrating formal methods with other methods, all used for system specification and design. We have summarized the construction of a heterogeneous basis, and discussed some of the (syntactic and semantic) problems associated with using multiple notations together. We have detailed several case studies to which we have applied the integration techniques. While we have considered only a small number of studies, the evidence so far suggests to us that the lightweight approach to integration that we have taken is convenient and useful.

One issue we have not addressed so far is that of method compatibility. The meta-method itself provides a framework within which formal (and semiformal) methods can be put together and used. It does not directly address the issue of when methods can or cannot be combined. For particular methods, unresolvable incompatibilities in terms of model, syntax, or process may arise, and the meta-method may not be able to successfully integrate such methods. Future work will examine the problems of method compatibility, and will hopefully augment the meta-method to include such "soundness" constraints.

Further future work will encompass more and larger case studies, and will see us consider a wider spectrum of methods in integration. We will also look at constructing formal models of methods, in order to be able to speak precisely about the relationships we are defining between them. Finally, we will consider other approaches to giving semantics to heterogeneous specifications—particularly, union approaches, where the semantics of all specifications can be expressed in compositions.

Acknowledgements

Thanks to Rick Hehner, Pamela Zave, and the two anonymous referees for their suggestions and comments on this and other work.

References

1. R. Barden, S. Stepney, and D. Cooper. *Z in Practice,* Prentice-Hall, 1994.

2. J. Bowen and M. Hinchey. Ten Commandments of Formal Methods. Oxford University Computing Laboratory Technical Monograph, 1994.
3. P. Coad and E. Yourdon. *Object-oriented Analysis*, Prentice-Hall, 1990.
4. T. DeMarco. *Structured Analysis and System Specification*, Yourdon Press, 1979.
5. T. DeMarco. *Controlling Software Projects: Management, Measurement, and Estimation.* Yourdon Press, 1982.
6. J.V. Guttag and J.J. Horning. *Larch: Languages and Tools for Formal Specification*, Springer-Verlag, 1993.
7. A. Hall. Specifying and Interpreting Class Hierarchies in Z. In *Proc. Eighth Z User Meeting,* Cambridge, Springer-Verlag, 1994.
8. A. Hall. Using Formal Methods to Develop an ATC Information System. *IEEE Software,* March 1996.
9. J. Hammond. Producing Z Specifications from Object-Oriented Analysis. In *Proc. Eighth Z User Meeting,* Cambridge, Springer-Verlag, 1994.
10. E.C.R. Hehner and A.J. Malton. Termination Conventions and Comparative Semantics, *Acta Informatica*, 25 (1988).
11. E.C.R. Hehner. *A Practical Theory of Programming*, Springer-Verlag, 1993.
12. M.A. Jackson. *Software Requirements and Specifications*, Addison-Wesley, 1995.
13. S. King. Z and the refinement calculus. In *VDM '90: VDM and Z - Formal Methods in Software Development*, Third international symposium of VDM Europe, LNCS 428, Springer-Verlag, 1990.
14. K. Kronlöf, ed. *Method Integration: Concepts and Case Studies*, Wiley, 1993.
15. P. Larsen, J. van Katwijk, N. Plat, K. Pronk, and H. Toetenel. Towards an integrated combination of SA and VDM. In *Proc. Methods Integration Workshop*, Springer-Verlag, 1991.
16. Project MetaPHOR Group, MetaPHOR: Metamodeling, Principles, Hypertext, Objects and Repositories. Technical Report TR-7, University of Jyvaskyla, 1994.
17. C.C. Morgan. *Programming from Specifications*, Prentice-Hall, Second Edition, 1994.
18. R.F. Paige. *Formal Method Integration via Heterogeneous Notations,* PhD Dissertation, November 1997.
19. R.F. Paige. A Meta-Method for Formal Method Integration. In *Proc. Formal Methods Europe '97*, Lecture Notes in Computer Science, Springer-Verlag, 1997.
20. R.F. Paige. Using Heterogeneous Notations to Integrate a Formal and Object-Oriented Method. Submitted to *The Computer Journal,* 1997.
21. R.F. Paige. Integrating Predicative Programming and SA/SD using Heterogeneous Notations. Submitted to *PROCOMET '98.*
22. F. Polack, M. Whiston, and K.C. Mander. The SAZ Project: Integrating SSADM and Z. In *Proc. FME '93: Industrial-strength Formal Methods*, LNCS 670, Springer-Verlag, 1993.
23. G. Randell. Data flow diagrams and Z. In *Z Users Meeting '90*, Springer-Verlag, 1991.
24. K. Schoman and D. Ross. Structured Analysis for requirements definition, *IEEE Trans. on Software Engineering*, 3(1), 1977.
25. L.T. Semmens, R.B. France, and T.W. Docker. Integrated Structured Analysis and Formal Specification Techniques, *The Computer Journal* 35(6), June 1992.
26. J.M. Spivey. *The Z Notation: A Reference Manual*, Prentice-Hall, 1989.
27. E. Yourdon and L. Constantine. *Structured Design,* Prentice-Hall, 1979.
28. P. Zave and M. Jackson. Conjunction as Composition, *ACM Trans. on Software Engineering and Methodology*, 2(4), October 1993.
29. P. Zave and M. Jackson. Where do operations come from? An approach to multiparadigm specification, *IEEE Trans. on Software Engineering*, 12(7), July 1996.

The Update Calculus
(extended abstract)

Joachim Parrow[1] * and Björn Victor[2]

[1] Dept. of Teleinformatics, Royal Institute of Technology,
Electrum 204, S-164 40 Kista, Sweden.
[2] Dept. of Computer Systems, Uppsala University,
Box 325, S-751 05 Uppsala, Sweden.

Abstract. In the *update calculus* concurrent processes can perform update actions with side effects, and a scoping operator can be used to control the extent of the update. In this way it incorporates fundamental concepts both from imperative languages or concurrent constraints formalisms, and from functional formalisms such as the λ- and π-calculi. Structurally it is similar to but simpler than the π-calculus; it has only one binding operator and a symmetry between input and output. We define the structured operational semantics and the proper bisimulation equivalence and congruence, and give a complete axiomatization. The π-calculus turns out to be an asymmetric subcalculus.

1 Introduction

Theory of concurrent computation is a diverse field where many different approaches have been proposed and no consensus has emerged on the best paradigms. In this paper we take a step towards unifying two seemingly contradictory schools of thought: *global* vs *local* effects of concurrent actions. We define a calculus where an explicit scope operator regulates the extent of an action effect. The calculus is structurally simple and incorporates fundamental concepts both from imperative languages or concurrent constraints formalisms, and from functional formalisms such as the λ- and π-calculi.

A concurrent system consists of parallel processes that perform *actions*. "Globalists" and "localists" differ on how the effects of actions propagate through the system. For globalists, which typically deal with imperative languages or concurrent constraint formalisms, an action may update a global variable or unify a logical variable. In this case the effect of the action is immediately present in an unbounded part of the system, even in those processes which do not take part in the action. Formal semantics and proof methods using this paradigm can be found in, e.g., [CM88,BKS88,MP91] and normally use a separate "global state" encompassing all processes.

For a localist, on the other hand, an action may be to call a subroutine with actual parameters replacing formal parameters, or to send a message from one agent to another. The action is local to the interacting parties, and these must explicitly communicate with the rest of the system to spread the effect. Localists typically work with functional languages and formalisms such as the λ-calculus or the π-calculus [Bar84], [MPW92,Mil91,San92,PS95], [San96,San95a,PS96,Dam93]. Since these do not use a

* Work partially supported by ESPRIT BRA project No. 8130: LOMAPS, The Human Capital and Mobility Project EXPRESS, and the working group CONFER-2.

separate global state, proof methods are often conceptually simpler than for global formalisms, at the expense of some loss of expressiveness: in some ways the global paradigm is closer to many high-level programming languages.

It is well known that e.g. message-passing and shared variables can emulate each other. In general, a global state can be interpreted as just another process storing values and communicating with other processes; conversely, local interaction between processes is achieved by using a designated part of the global state as a temporary storage area. The global and local views do not entail absolute differences of expressiveness; rather, they differ in what phenomena can be modelled in a convenient and clear way. This has not prevented an occasionally fierce debate on which paradigm should be regarded as the most fundamental one.

The contribution of the present paper, the ***update calculus*** (or ***up-calculus***) is a step towards a unifying framework for actions with local and global effect. There will be ***update*** actions written $[y/z]$, meaning "z should everywhere be replaced by y" with a potentially unbounded extent, and a *scope* operator (z) explicitly controlling the extent of updates of z. By varying the scope we can localize the effects. There is no separate global state, instead the update actions affect all processes directly. In this way we mitigate the global vs local controversy and demonstrate how both are special cases of a more basic concept.

It is interesting to compare the up-calculus with the π-calculus, which is riddled by a few curious asymmetries. In π there are two binding operators, input binding $a(x).P$ meaning "receive something for x before continuing with P" and restriction $(\nu x)P$ meaning "x in P will always be distinct from other names". Other non derivable binding operators, such as delay input $a(x)P$, which does not imply a temporal precedence between the instantiation of x and the rest of P, have also been suggested. And since input actions must be accompanied by a binding there is a fundamental asymmetry between input and output. In the up-calculus there is only one binding operator, treatment of input and output is symmetric, and the π-calculus can be recovered as a subcalculus (formed by requiring all input actions to be enclosed by a scope as tightly as possible). This throws light on how some of the different versions of the π-calculus interrelate.

To give a taste of the up-calculus, consider two agents $\overline{a}y.P$ and $az.Q$. The first emits a name y along a port a, the second receives something for z along a. In the latter the scope of z is not specified, so an interaction between the two agents will result in a global update action:

$$\overline{a}y.P \mid az.Q \quad \xrightarrow{[y/z]} \quad P \mid Q$$

The fact that this action is "global" can be seen if we include a further parallel component, R, not part in the interaction:

$$\overline{a}y.P \mid az.Q \mid R \quad \xrightarrow{[y/z]} \quad P \mid Q \mid R$$

The update action will affect R as much as P and Q. The scope operator (z) determines the extent of the update action:

$$(z)(\overline{a}y.P \mid az.Q \mid R) \quad \xrightarrow{1} \quad (P \mid Q \mid R)\{y/z\}$$

Here **1** is an inert action, without any updating or communicating effect (cf τ in CCS) and the substitution y for z is performed on the right hand side. A further parallel component S outside the scope of z will not be affected by the substitution or update:

$$(z)(\overline{a}y\,.\,P \mid az\,.\,Q \mid R) \mid S \quad \xrightarrow{1} \quad (P \mid Q \mid R)\{y/z\} \mid S$$

We claim that this entails a clean way to model assignment to shared structures and resolution in concurrent constraint languages. For example, in a concurrent constraint formalism there will be existentially quantified logical variables with well defined scopes:

$$\exists z(P \wedge Q \wedge R) \wedge S$$

Resolution of the conjunct P may result in a new fact $z = y$, in other words $P \to P' \wedge z = y$. Then the whole expression will reduce:

$$\exists z(P \wedge Q \wedge R) \wedge S \quad \to \quad (P' \wedge Q \wedge R)\{y/z\} \wedge S$$

The update calculus is particularly well suited to model such reductions, as will be demonstrated in forthcoming papers. Of course, concurrent constraints can also be encoded in π by explicitly representing the logical variables as registers (see [VP96]). Proponents of concurrent constraints would presumably rather encode the π-calculus in one of their favourite formalisms. The purpose of the present paper is to demonstrate that both are particular cases of something more basic.

In the next section we present the syntax and semantics of the up-calculus. We also show how the π-calculus is isomorphic to an asymmetric subcalculus. In Section 3 we define the proper notion of bisimulation congruence, called hyperequivalence. It is strictly stronger than the bisimulation equivalences previously investigated for the π-calculus, and turns out to be the *only* reasonable candidate for a bisimulation-based congruence. In Section 4 we give a set of algebraic equalities which constitute a complete axiomatization for it. Section 5 contains conclusions and directions for further research.

2 Basic Definitions

2.1 Syntax

We begin by presupposing an infinite set $\mathcal{N}$ of *names* ranged over by $a, b, \ldots, y, z$. As in the π-calculus names will be used to represent all of communication ports, values, and placeholders for ports and values. A more refined version of the calculus would use a type system to distinguish between those, but that is not necessary for the development in the present paper.

Definition 1.
The *free actions*, ranged over by $\alpha, \beta, \ldots$ are defined by

$$\begin{array}{rll} \alpha ::= & ax & \text{(Input)} \\ & \overline{a}x & \text{(Output)} \\ & [x/y] & \text{(Update)} \end{array}$$

An input action ax means "input an object along the port a and replace x with that object." Contrary to the situation in the π-calculus this action does not bind x. In other words, the scope of x is not bounded by the action. The output action $\overline{a}x$ is familiar from the π-calculus and means "output the object x along the port a. The update action $[x/y]$ signifies an obligation to replace all y by x. It is not present in the π-calculus.

An action $[x/x]$, updating x to itself, is called an "inert" update and is often written $\mathbf{1}$, since the choice of x in $[x/x]$ will never matter. In all actions above (except in $\mathbf{1}$) x is called the *(free) object* of the action, written $\mathrm{obj}(\alpha)$. The inert update $\mathbf{1}$ has no object. In the input and output actions the name a is called the *subject* of the action, written $\mathrm{subj}(\alpha)$.

Definition 2. The *agents*, ranged over by $P, Q, \ldots$, are defined by

$$\begin{array}{lll} P ::= & \mathbf{0} & \text{(Inaction)} \\ & \alpha\,.\,Q & \text{(Prefix)} \\ & Q + R & \text{(Summation)} \\ & Q \mid R & \text{(Composition)} \\ & (x)Q & \text{(Scope)} \end{array}$$

The Prefix form means "first do α and then behave as Q." In a sense to be made precise below, update prefixes like $[x/y]\,.\,Q$ can be regarded as derived forms and are not strictly necessary in the definition, but admitting them simplifies the presentation. Summation is alternative choice and Composition is parallel execution, just as in the π-calculus. In examples to come we will often omit a trailing $\mathbf{0}$, therefore α will stand for the agent $\alpha\,.\,\mathbf{0}$ when no confusion is possible.

The Scope $(x)Q$ restricts the scope of the name x to Q. In a way this is a common denominator of π-calculus restriction $(\nu x)Q$ and input binding $a(x)\,.\,Q$. Restriction implies that no name will ever replace the bound names, while input binding requires that the bound name in immediately replaced by something received along a. Scope neither forbids nor insists on a replacement; it merely states the extent of the name. As we will see, restriction and input binding can be recovered as special cases of Scope.

The name x is said to be *bound* in $(x)P$. The *free names* in P, denoted $\mathrm{fn}(P)$, are the names in P with a non-bound occurrence. $\mathrm{n}(P)$ denotes all names occurring in P. As usual we will not distinguish between alpha-variants of agents, i.e., agents differing only in the choice of bound names.

Definition 3. The *substitution* of x for y in P, written $P\{x/y\}$, is the agent obtained by replacing all y by x in P, renaming bound names as necessary to avoid captures. We use σ to range over substitutions.

2.2 Semantics

We first define a structural congruence to equate agents that we never want to distinguish for any reason related to semantics, and using that we give the transition rules.

Definition 4. The *structural congruence*, $\equiv$, between agents is the least congruence satisfying the abelian monoid laws for Summation and Composition (associativity, commutativity and $\mathbf{0}$ as identity), and also the scoping laws

$$(x)\mathbf{0} \equiv \mathbf{0}, \quad (x)(y)P \equiv (y)(x)P, \quad (x)(P+Q) \equiv (x)P + (x)Q$$

and also the *scope extension* law $P \mid (z)Q \equiv (z)(P \mid Q)$ where $z \notin \mathrm{fn}(P)$.

Note that if $z \notin \text{fn}(P)$ then $(z)P \equiv (z)(P \mid 0) \equiv P \mid (z)0 \equiv P \mid 0 \equiv P$. Also note that after an alpha-conversion, any scope (x) not under a prefix can be pulled to the top level of an agent while preserving structural congruence.

The actions in the transition may be free or bound:

Definition 5. A *bound* action is of the form $(x)\alpha$ where x is the object of α. The *actions*, ranged over by γ, consist of the free actions and the bound actions. A *transition* is of the kind $P \xrightarrow{\gamma} Q$.

The meaning of a bound action is simply that the object is emitted out of its scope and must therefore not be confused with any similar name in the environment. There is no bound action corresponding to **1** since **1** has no object. We write $\text{n}(\gamma)$, $\text{fn}(\gamma)$ and $\text{bn}(\gamma)$ to mean all names, free names, and bound names respectively occurring in γ. For the inert update we define $\text{n}(\mathbf{1}) = \emptyset$.

Definition 6. The *transitions* $P \xrightarrow{\gamma} Q$ is the least family of transitions satisfying the laws in Table 1. In this definition structurally equivalent agents are considered the same, i.e., if $P \equiv P'$ and $Q \equiv Q'$ and $P \xrightarrow{\gamma} Q$ then also $P' \xrightarrow{\gamma} Q'$.

PREF $\dfrac{-}{\alpha\,.\,P \xrightarrow{\alpha} P}$	SUM $\dfrac{P \xrightarrow{\alpha} P'}{P + Q \xrightarrow{\alpha} P'}$
PAR $\dfrac{P \xrightarrow{\alpha} P'}{P \mid Q \xrightarrow{\alpha} P' \mid Q}$	COM $\dfrac{P \xrightarrow{az} P', \; Q \xrightarrow{\bar{a}y} Q'}{P \mid Q \xrightarrow{[y/z]} P' \mid Q'}$
SCOPE $\dfrac{P \xrightarrow{[y/z]} P', \; y \neq z}{(z)P \xrightarrow{\mathbf{1}} P'\{y/z\}}$	PASS $\dfrac{P \xrightarrow{\alpha} P', \; z \notin \text{n}(\alpha)}{(z)P \xrightarrow{\alpha} (z)P'}$
OPEN $\dfrac{P \xrightarrow{\alpha} P', \; \text{obj}(\alpha) = z, \; \text{subj}(\alpha) \neq z}{(z)P \xrightarrow{(z)\alpha} P'}$	

Table 1. The up-calculus: Laws of action.

No premise of any rule in Table 1 has a bound action, and the only rule for generating bound actions in transitions is OPEN. Using structural congruence, pulling the relevant scope to top level, we can still infer e.g. $P \mid (x)ax\,.\,Q \xrightarrow{(x)ax} P \mid Q$ using PREF and OPEN (provided $x \notin \text{fn}(P)$, otherwise an alpha-conversion is necessary). Note also that α cannot be **1** (or $[z/z]$) in OPEN, since **1** has no object.

It is illuminating to consider the COM and SCOPE rules in particular. COM results in an update action, signifying a requirement to replace z by y everywhere. The SCOPE rule produces the substitution and also changes the action to an inert action, so that no z outside the scope will be affected.

The gain in expressiveness over the π-calculus lies in this possibility to decouple the input action from the binding of the input object. As an example we can define an agent $(z)(az.\mathbf{0} \mid P)$ where the input is *delayed*, in the sense that it may happen at any time:

$$\begin{array}{llll} (z)(az.\mathbf{0} \mid P) & \xrightarrow{\gamma} & (z)(az.\mathbf{0} \mid P') & \text{if } P \xrightarrow{\gamma} P' \text{ and } z \notin \mathrm{n}(\gamma) \\ (z)(az.\mathbf{0} \mid P) & \xrightarrow{(z)az} & P & \text{for any } P \end{array}$$

This agent has all transitions from P not involving z, and in any derivative so obtained it has the bound input transition $(z)az$.

As a final example assume $z \notin \mathrm{fn}(P)$ and consider the agent

$$(z)az.bz.P$$

There are *two* inputs with object z under the same scope. The agent can interact with an environment that emits something along a,

$$(z)az.bz.P \mid \overline{a}u.Q \quad \xrightarrow{1} \quad bu.P \mid Q$$

and will proceed input something for u along b. In other words, the object to be *replaced* in an interaction along b is first transmitted along a. This has no immediate counterpart in the π-calculus.

Note in passing that update prefixes can be regarded as derived forms since $[y/z].P$ has exactly the same transitions as $(a)(\overline{a}y.\mathbf{0} \mid az.P)$ when $a \notin \mathrm{fn}(P)$. (In the same way the τ prefix can be regarded as derived in CCS and in the π-calculus.)

2.3 Subcalculi

Consider a version of the ordinary monadic π-calculus [MPW92] which differs from the update calculus in the following way: There are neither input nor update prefixes, instead there is a *bound input* prefix written $a(x).P$ with the transition $a(x).P \xrightarrow{(x)ax} P$. There is no scoping operator but a related *restriction* operator (νx), inheriting the laws PASS and OPEN. There is no SCOPE law since there are no update actions; instead the COM law is

$$\frac{P \xrightarrow{(z)az} P', \quad Q \xrightarrow{\overline{a}y} Q'}{P \mid Q \xrightarrow{1} P'\{y/z\} \mid Q}$$

(The notation for actions in π is usually slightly different. Bound actions $(z)az$ and $(z)\overline{a}z$ are usually written $a(z)$ and $\overline{a}(z)$, and the inert action $\mathbf{1}$ is written τ.)

The so defined π-calculus is isomorphic to a subcalculus of the up-calculus, formed by omitting update prefixes and by requiring that all input prefixes $ax.P$ occur immediately under a scope (x) of the object in the input prefix. Call this subcalculus the up$_\pi$-calculus. The isomorphy $\leftrightarrow$ between up$_\pi$ and π is simply the homomorphic extension of

$$\begin{array}{lll} (x)ax.P & \leftrightarrow a(x).P & \\ (z)P & \leftrightarrow (\nu z)P & \text{if } P \text{ is not a free input prefix} \end{array}$$

The rationale behind this is as follows. Consider a scope $(x)Q$ in up_π. If it is immediately over an input prefix, $Q = ax\,.\,P$, then before anything happens in P something must be received along a to replace x in P, precisely as the effect of a π-calculus input prefix $a(x)\,.\,P$. On the other hand, if it is not immediately over an input prefix, $Q \neq ax\,.\,P$, then there cannot be any input prefix inside Q for that particular x. Because of the syntactic restrictions in up_π, a free input ax not at the top level of Q must be enclosed by another scope (x), making the object different from the x in $(x)Q$. So this x cannot occur in an input and there are no updates, therefore x will remain distinct from other names throughout execution of the agent. This is precisely the effect of $(\nu x)Q$.

More formally, the result is (where $\circ$ is composition of relations):

Theorem 7. *For P a π-calculus agent and Q an up_π-calculus agent,*

1. *If $P \leftrightarrow Q$ and $P \xrightarrow{\gamma} P'$ then $Q \xrightarrow{\gamma} Q'$ and $P' \equiv \circ \leftrightarrow \circ \equiv Q'$.*
2. *If $P \leftrightarrow Q$ and $Q \xrightarrow{\gamma} Q'$ then $P \xrightarrow{\gamma} P'$ and $P' \equiv \circ \leftrightarrow \circ \equiv Q'$.*

The πI-calculus by Sangiorgi [San95b] is a subset of the π-calculus formed by requiring all output prefixes $\bar{a}x$ to occur immediately below a restriction (νx) of the object. Therefore that calculus is isomorphic to the subcalculus of up_π requiring that *all* prefixes — not merely input prefixes — occur under a scope of the object. As Sangiorgi has remarked the πI-calculus has a pleasing symmetry between input and output actions. The up-calculus has the same kind of symmetry, achieved by extending rather than restricting the π-calculus.

3 Equivalence and Congruence

Our notion of equivalence uses the well known idea of bisimulation. In essence, for two agents to be bisimilar, each transition from one agent must be mimicked from the other, reaching agents which are again bisimilar. In calculi where transitions can contain placeholders (such as variables) for values, care has been taken to properly define what "again bisimilar" means. For example, in the π-calculus there are varieties such as *early*, *late* [MPW92], and *open* [San96] bisimulation. These differ in the degree of universal quantification over the names, and each of these lead to a different congruence.

In the up-calculus this diversity is mercifully absent; there appears to be only one sensible bisimulation congruence. The reason is that the update actions allow us to formulate more powerful contexts than what is possible in the π-calculus. Update actions can enforce a global substitution of *any* name, and therefore the congruence must be closed under arbitrary substitutions in a way which will be made precise below.

Let us first consider the proper notion of bisimulation.

Definition 8. A *simulation* is a binary relation $\mathcal{S}$ between agents such that $P\;\mathcal{S}\;Q$ implies:

If $P \xrightarrow{\gamma} P'$ with $\text{bn}(\gamma) \not\in \text{fn}(Q)$ then

$$Q \xrightarrow{\gamma} Q' \text{ and } \begin{cases} P'\;\mathcal{S}\;Q' & \text{if } \gamma \text{ is an input or an output} \\ P'\{y/z\}\;\mathcal{S}\;Q'\{y/z\} & \text{if } \gamma \text{ is } [y/z] \text{ or } (y)[y/z] \end{cases}$$

A *bisimulation* is a relation $\mathcal{S}$ such that both $\mathcal{S}$ and $\mathcal{S}^{-1}$ are simulations. P is bisimilar to Q, written $P \dot{\sim} Q$, if $P\;\mathcal{S}\;Q$ for some bisimulation $\mathcal{S}$.

The interesting point in this definition is the treatment of update actions. An update $[y/z]$ represents an obligation to replace z by y everywhere. Therefore, if γ above is such an update, it only makes sense to relate P' and Q' when the substitution $\{y/z\}$ has been performed. Consider for example the following, where the objects of input and output prefixes are omitted for the sake of brevity (so $y\,.\,P$ means $yw\,.\,P$ for some fresh w, etc.)

$$\begin{aligned} y \mid \overline{z} &\stackrel{\cdot}{\sim} y\,.\,\overline{z} + \overline{z}\,.\,y \\ y \mid \overline{y} &\stackrel{\cdot}{\not\sim} y\,.\,\overline{y} + \overline{y}\,.\,y \\ y \mid \overline{y} &\stackrel{\cdot}{\sim} y\,.\,\overline{y} + \overline{y}\,.\,y + \mathbf{1} \\ [y/z]\,.\,(y \mid \overline{z}) &\stackrel{\cdot}{\sim} [y/z]\,.\,(y\,.\,\overline{z} + \overline{z}\,.\,y + \mathbf{1}) \end{aligned}$$

The third example implies the fourth even though $y \mid \overline{z}$ is not bisimilar to $y\,.\,\overline{z}+\overline{z}\,.\,y+\mathbf{1}$. In fact, we also have

$$[y/z]\,.\,y\,.\,\mathbf{0} \stackrel{\cdot}{\sim} [y/z]\,.\,z\,.\,\mathbf{0}$$

Bisimilarity is not a congruence. An easy example is that $y \mid \overline{z}$ is bisimilar to $y\,.\,\overline{z}+\overline{z}\,.\,y$, but prefixing both with $[y/z]$ will result in non bisimilar agents. We therefore look for a congruence included in bisimilarity. This is achieved by closing the definition of bisimulation under arbitrary substitutions.

Definition 9. A *hyperbisimulation* is a substitution closed bisimulation, i.e., a bisimulation $\mathcal{S}$ with the property that $P\ \mathcal{S}\ Q$ implies $P\{x/y\}\ \mathcal{S}\ Q\{x/y\}$ for any x, y. Two agents P and Q are *hyperequivalent*, written $P \sim Q$, if they are related by a hyperbisimulation.

Theorem 10. *Hyperequivalence is a congruence.*

Proof. Through a case analysis over the operators in the up-calculus. All cases are simple. □

Note that the special case for update actions in the definition of bisimulation is significant even though hyperbisimulation closes under all substitutions! The point is that $P'\ \mathcal{S}\ Q'$ would be a too *strong* requirement if $\gamma = [y/z]$, since it would require bisimulation also under the substitutions which do not replace z by y.

It is interesting to relate hyperequivalence to open equivalence, which is a congruence in the π-calculus and hence also in up_π. For a definition of open we refer to [San96], but even without the details of the definition a reader might appreciate the following arguments. Broadly speaking, for the purpose of hyperbisimulation, *all* names are considered universally quantified *after every transition.* That is, if we for a moment disregard the update actions (which are not part of the π-calculus), hyperbisimulation requires, if $P\ \mathcal{S}\ Q$ and $P \xrightarrow{\gamma} P'$, that $Q \xrightarrow{\gamma} Q'$ and $P'\sigma\ \mathcal{S}\ Q'\sigma$ *for all substitutions* σ. For late equivalence the corresponding requirement would be *for all substitutions* σ *involving a bound input name in* γ. For open equivalence the requirement would be *for all substitutions* σ *except those involving a bound output name in* γ.

In the π-calculus without the restriction operator the definitions of open and hyper would coincide. But with it hyper is strictly stronger, as evidenced by the up_π-calculus agents

$$(x)(y)\overline{a}x\,.\,\overline{a}y\,.\,(x \mid \overline{y}) \qquad \text{and} \qquad (x)(y)\overline{a}x\,.\,\overline{a}y\,.\,(x\,.\,\overline{y} + \overline{y}\,.\,x)$$

These are open equivalent but not hyperequivalent. To see this, after two bound output transitions the agents become

$$x \mid \overline{y} \qquad \text{and} \qquad x\,.\,\overline{y} + \overline{y}\,.\,x$$

and these are not bisimilar under the substitution $\{x/y\}$. Substitutions of names emitted as bound output objects are significant for hyper but not for open.

When we consider arbitrary up-contexts, this example can be used to demonstrate that open equivalence, though a congruence in π, is not a congruence in the up-calculus (which has more contexts and therefore puts a heavier burden on a congruence). Put the two agents in parallel with $(z)az\,.\,az$ (note that this agent is not in up_π because of the second non-bound input prefix az). There is then one more **1** transition from

$$(z)az\,.\,az \mid (x)(y)\overline{a}x\,.\,\overline{a}y\,.\,(x \mid \overline{y})$$

than from

$$(z)az\,.\,az \mid (x)(y)\overline{a}x\,.\,\overline{a}y\,.\,(x\,.\,\overline{y} + \overline{y}\,.\,x)$$

In essence, the parallel context $(z)az\,.\,az$ will enforce a unification of any two names emitted along a.

Even though open is not a congruence there might conceivably exist some other congruences larger than hyper, but our next theorem demonstrates that this is impossible. This result confirms that hyperequivalence is the only "interesting" congruence.

Theorem 11. *Hyperequivalence is the largest congruence in bisimilarity.*

We sketch the proof below. We construct a context which given a set of names N can perform any substitutions of names in N, and capture all bound names emitted on a name in N.

Let N be any finite set of names, and $\mathcal{F}_N = \{s_{xy}, r_x, q_x, e, d, u : x, y \in N\}$ consist of fresh names. We write $N + w$ for $N \cup \{w\}$ and $N - w$ for $N \setminus \{w\}$. Define $S_N^0 = \mathbf{0}$, and

$$\begin{aligned} S_N^k = & \sum_{\substack{x,y \in N \\ x \neq y}} s_{xy}\,.\,[x/y]\,.\,d\,.\,S_{N-y}^{k-1} \\ & + \sum_{x \in N} r_x\,.\,(u)xu\,.\,\overline{e}u\,.\,S_{N+u}^{k-1} \\ & + \sum_{x \in N} q_x\,.\,\overline{x}u\,.\,d\,.\,S_{N+u}^{k-1} \end{aligned}$$

The main Lemma states that if two agents are bisimilar in an S_N^k context, then they must also be hyperequivalent:

Lemma 12. $\mathcal{S} \equiv \{(P, Q) : \forall N : \text{fn}(P, Q) \subseteq N, \forall k : S_N^k \mid P \dot{\sim} S_N^k \mid Q\}$ *is a hyperbisimulation.*

Now Theorem 11 is a consequence of Lemma 12, using S_N^k contexts: If $\mathcal{R}$ is a bisimulation congruence, $(P, Q) \in \mathcal{R}$ implies that for all contexts C, $(C[P], C[Q]) \in \mathcal{R}$, so consider the family of contexts $C[\bullet] = S_N^k \mid \bullet$, for all k, $N = \text{fn}(P, Q)$, and then by Lemma 12, $\mathcal{R}$ is a hyperbisimulation. Thus there can not exist a larger (or "weaker") bisimulation congruence than hyperequivalence for the up-calculus.

4 Axiomatization

We now introduce two additional operators in the up-calculus: if P is an agent then so are $[x = y]P$, a *match*, and $[x \neq y]P$, a *mismatch*, with the laws of action

$$\text{MATCH}\ \frac{P \xrightarrow{\alpha} P'}{[x = x]P \xrightarrow{\alpha} P'} \qquad \text{MISM}\ \frac{P \xrightarrow{\alpha} P', x \neq y}{[x \neq y]P \xrightarrow{\alpha} P'}$$

These operators are found in earlier work on the π-calculus; match has been used for a sound axiomatization of late congruence [MPW92] as well as a complete axiomatization of open equivalence [San96], and mismatch has been used for complete axiomatizations of the late and early congruence [PS95]. We also use mismatch in our axiomatization, but we add it mainly in anticipation of its use for concurrent constraint modelling. A complete axiomatization of hyperequivalence without mismatch can be done along the lines of [San96]. Nevertheless, the axiomatization using mismatch displays the difference between scope and restriction in a clear way.

Here and in the following we use M, N to stand for a match or a mismatch operator, and define $\mathrm{n}([x = y]) = \mathrm{n}([x \neq y]) = \{x, y\}$. We add the scope law $(x)MP \equiv M(x)P$, *if* $x \notin \mathrm{n}(M)$ to the structural congruence. We write "match sequence" for a sequence of match *and* mismatch operators, ranged over by $\tilde{M}$, $\tilde{N}$, and we say that $\tilde{M}$ *implies* $\tilde{N}$, written $\tilde{M} \Rightarrow \tilde{N}$, if the conjunction of all matches and mismatches in $\tilde{M}$ logically implies all elements in $\tilde{N}$, and that $\tilde{M} \Leftrightarrow \tilde{N}$ if $\tilde{M}$ and $\tilde{N}$ imply each other. We write $(\tilde{x})$ for a sequence of scope operators $(x_1) \cdots (x_n)$, for $n \geq 0$, and $\sum_{i \in I} P_i$ for finite general summation, $P_1 + \cdots + P_n$.

For the axiomatization of hyperequivalence we subsume the fact that the equivalence is a congruence. We also subsume some of the laws for structural congruence (see Table 2) and the convention that $[x/x] . P = \mathbf{1} . P$. The axioms of the up-calculus are given in Table 3, and in Table 4 we present some derived rules (whose names start with **D**).

Summation		
S1	$P + 0 = P$	
S2	$P + Q = Q + P$	
S3	$P + (Q + R) = (P + Q) + R$	
Scope		
R0	$(x)0 = 0$	
R1	$(x)(y)P = (y)(x)P$	
R2	$(x)(P + Q) = (x)P + (x)Q$	
Match and Scope		
RM1	$(x)[y = z]P = [y = z](x)P$	if $x \neq y, x \neq z$

Table 2. Axioms from structural congruence.

Definition 13. A substitution σ *agrees with* a match sequence $\tilde{M}$, and $\tilde{M}$ agrees with σ, if for all x, y which appear in $\tilde{M}$ it holds that $\sigma(x) = \sigma(y)$ iff $\tilde{M} \Rightarrow [x = y]$.

Summation		
S4	$P + P = P$	
Match		
M1	$\tilde{M}P = \tilde{N}P$	if $\tilde{M} \Leftrightarrow \tilde{N}$
M2	$[x=y]P = [x=y](P\{x/y\})$	
M3	$MP + MQ = M(P+Q)$	
M4	$[x \neq x]P = \mathbf{0}$	
M5	$P = [x=y]P + [x \neq y]P$	
Scope		
R3	$(x)\alpha \,.\, P = \alpha \,.\, (x)P$	if $x \notin \mathrm{n}(\alpha)$
R4	$(x)\alpha \,.\, P = \mathbf{0}$	if $x = \mathrm{subj}(\alpha)$, α not upd.
Match and Scope		
RM2	$(x)[x=y]P = \mathbf{0}$	if $x \neq y$
Update		
U1	$[x/y] \,.\, P = [x/y] \,.\, [x=y]P$	
U2	$(z)[x/z] \,.\, P = \mathbf{1} \,.\, P$	if $z \neq x, z \notin \mathrm{fn}(P)$
Expansion		
E	for $P \equiv \Sigma_i M_i(\tilde{x}_i)\alpha_i.P_i$, $Q \equiv \Sigma_j N_j(\tilde{y}_j)\beta_j.Q_j$, $P \mid Q = \sum_i M_i(\tilde{x}_i)\alpha_i \,.\, (P_i \mid Q) + \sum_j N_j(\tilde{y}_j)\beta_j \,.\, (P \mid Q_j) + \sum_{\alpha_i \mathrm{opp} \beta_j} M_i N_j(\tilde{x}_i, \tilde{y}_j)[a_i = b_j][z_i/w_j] \,.\, (P_i \mid Q_j)$ where $\alpha_i \mathrm{opp} \beta_j$ means $\alpha_i \equiv \overline{a_i} z_i$ and $\beta_j \equiv b_j w_j$ or vice versa.	

Table 3. Axioms.

Match		
DM1	$[x=x]P = P$	
DM2	$[x=y]\alpha \,.\, P = [x=y]\alpha \,.\, [x=y]P$	
DM3	$\tilde{M}P = \tilde{M}(P\sigma)$	for σ agreeing with $\tilde{M}$
DM4	$M\mathbf{0} = \mathbf{0}$	
DM5	$MP + P = P$	
Match and Scope		
DRM1	$(x)[y \neq z]P = [y \neq z](x)P$	if $x \neq y, x \neq z$
DRM2	$(x)[x \neq y]P = (x)P$	if $x \neq y$
Update		
DU1	$[x/y] \,.\, P = [x/y] \,.\, (P\{x/y\})$	
DU2	$(z)[x/z] \,.\, P = \mathbf{1} \,.\, (P\{x/z\})$	if $x \neq z$

Table 4. Derived rules.

Of the derived rules, **DM2** follows from $[x=y]\alpha\,.\,P \overset{\mathbf{M2}}{=} [x=y](\alpha\,.\,P)\{x/y\} \overset{\mathbf{DM1}}{=} [x=y](\alpha\,.\,[x=y]P)\{x/y\} \overset{\mathbf{M2}}{=} [x=y]\alpha\,.\,[x=y]P$; **DM3** is derivable because we can write $\tilde{M}$ with the matches closest to P, and then apply **M2** repeatedly. The only worry is if the accumulated substitution becomes ambiguous, e.g. if $\{x/y\}\{z/y\}$ occurs. Since σ agrees with $\tilde{M}$, this means that $\tilde{M} \Rightarrow [x=y]$ and $\tilde{M} \Rightarrow [z=y]$, but then $\tilde{M} \Rightarrow [x=z]$ as well, and a corresponding substitution must occur in σ.

The derived rules **DRM** for match and scope correspond to the mismatch cases of the axioms **RM**, which apply to matches. **DRM1** is derived along the lines of [PS95], using **R2,M3,M4,M5,RM1** and the axioms for sum and congruence. **DRM2** follows from $(x)P \overset{\mathbf{M5,R1}}{=} (x)[x=y]P+(x)[x\neq y]P \overset{\mathbf{RM2,S1}}{=} (x)[x\neq y]P$. Finally, **DU1** follows from **U1** and **M2**, while **DU2** follows from **N2** and **DU1**.

It is interesting to note that all axioms except the two for update are well known from previous axiomatizations of the π-calculus. For example, all the axioms from Sangiorgi's axiomatization of open bisimulation equivalence for the π-calculus [San96] hold for hyperequivalence in the up-calculus, except the axiom treating restriction and the weaker form of congruence wrt input prefix. Please note also that our expansion law **E** is syntactically simpler than the corresponding laws for π-calculus equivalences.

Distinction relations between names have been used in axiomatizating π-calculus equivalences in [MPW92,San96], but are not needed in our axiomatization of up-calculus. In both calculi **RM2, DRM2** and **DM2** are valid, saying that a new name (by Scope or Restriction) is not equal to another name in the immediately following action (**RM2,DRM2**), and that if two names are equal they stay equal (**DM2**). However, in the π-calculus the law $[x\neq y]\alpha\,.\,P = [x\neq y]\alpha\,.\,[x\neq y]P$ holds for early and late congruence [PS95], while it is not valid for hyperequivalence.

In the rest of this section we outline the completeness proof for our axiom system, and briefly present the axiom system for up-calculus without mismatch. We begin with some basic definitions and one Lemma from [PS95].

Definition 14. The *depth* of an agent P, $\mathrm{d}(P)$, is defined inductively as follows: $\mathrm{d}(0)=0$, $\mathrm{d}(\alpha\,.\,P)=1+\mathrm{d}(P)$, $\mathrm{d}((\tilde{x})P)=\mathrm{d}(MP)=\mathrm{d}(P)$, $\mathrm{d}(P\mid Q)=\mathrm{d}(P)+\mathrm{d}(Q)$, $\mathrm{d}(P+Q)=\max(\mathrm{d}(P),\mathrm{d}(Q))$.

Definition 15. A match sequence $\tilde{M}$ is *complete on* a set of names V if for some equivalence relation $\mathcal{R}$ on V, called the equivalence relation *corresponding to* $\tilde{M}$, it holds that $\tilde{M} \Rightarrow [x=y]$ iff $x\,\mathcal{R}\,y$, and $\tilde{M} \Rightarrow [x\neq y]$ iff $\neg(x\,\mathcal{R}\,y)$

A complete match sequence $\tilde{M}$ is *maximally consistent* in the sense that adding something not already implied by $\tilde{M}$ makes $\tilde{M}$ inconsistent.

Lemma 16 ([PS95]). *Let V be a set of names and let $\tilde{M}$ be complete on V.*

1. *If $\tilde{N}$ is another match sequence with names in V, then either $\tilde{M}\tilde{N}$ is unsatisfiable or $\tilde{M}\tilde{N} \Leftrightarrow \tilde{M}$.*
2. *If $\tilde{N}$ is another match sequence complete on V such that $\tilde{M}$ and $\tilde{N}$ both agree with the same substitution σ, then $\tilde{M} \Leftrightarrow \tilde{N}$.*

The completeness of our axiom system says that if two agents are hyperequivalent, we can prove this using our axioms. We show that this is true in a standard way: first we define a head normal form for agents, and show that any agent can be written on this form. We can then find exactly which part of one agent that was used to simulate the transition of the other.

Definition 17. An agent P is in *head normal form (HNF) on V* (a finite set of names) if P is on the form

$$\sum_{i \in I} \tilde{M}_i(\tilde{x}_i)\alpha_i \,.\, P_i$$

where for all i, $\tilde{x}_i \cap V = \emptyset$, $\tilde{x}_i = \emptyset$ or $\tilde{x}_i = \{\mathrm{obj}(\alpha_i)\}$ and $\tilde{M}_i$ is complete on V.

Lemma 18. *For all agents P and finite V such that* $\mathrm{fn}(P) \subseteq V$*, there is an agent H such that* $\mathrm{d}(H) \leq \mathrm{d}(P)$*, H is in HNF on V, and $\vdash P = H$ from the axioms of Tables 2 and 3.*

Proof. By structural induction on P. □

Theorem 19. *If $P \sim Q$, then $\vdash P = Q$ from the axioms of Tables 2 and 3.*

Proof. By Lemma 18 we can assume P and Q to be in HNF on $\mathrm{fn}(P, Q)$. The proof is by induction on the depth of $P + Q$, showing that each summand of P is provably equal to a summand of Q.

If the depth is 0, $P \equiv Q \equiv \mathbf{0}$ and we are done. Otherwise, let $\tilde{M}(\tilde{x})\alpha \,.\, P'$ be a summand of P, σ a substitution agreeing with $\tilde{M}$, and $\sigma(w) = w$ for all $w \notin \mathrm{fn}(P, Q)$. Then $P\sigma \xrightarrow{((\tilde{x})\alpha)\sigma} P'\sigma$ (here $\tilde{x}$ contains one or zero names). By alpha-conversion $\tilde{x} \cap \mathrm{fn}(Q) = \emptyset$, and by $P \sim Q$, $Q\sigma \xrightarrow{((\tilde{x})\alpha)\sigma} Q''$, and

$$\begin{array}{lll} P'\sigma = Q'' & \text{by induction, if } \alpha \text{ not an update action} & (1) \\ P'\sigma\sigma_\alpha = Q''\sigma_\alpha & \text{by induction, if } \alpha \text{ an update action} & (2) \end{array}$$

where σ_α is $\{x/y\}$ if $\alpha\sigma$ is $[x/y]$.

By alpha-conversion, we can write the summand of Q used to simulate the action of $P\sigma$ as $\tilde{N}(\tilde{x})\beta \,.\, Q'$. Then $\tilde{N}$ agrees with σ and $(\tilde{N}(\tilde{x})\beta \,.\, Q')\sigma \xrightarrow{((\tilde{x})\beta)\sigma} Q'\sigma$, so $Q'' \equiv Q'\sigma$ and $((\tilde{x})\alpha)\sigma = ((\tilde{x})\beta)\sigma$, which implies

$$\alpha\sigma = \beta\sigma \qquad (3)$$

since σ is identity for names not free in P, Q.

$\tilde{M}$ and $\tilde{N}$ are complete, so by Lemma 16(2) we know $\tilde{M} \Leftrightarrow \tilde{N}$. Since σ agrees with $\tilde{M}$

$$\tilde{M}(\tilde{x})\alpha \,.\, P' \overset{\mathbf{DM3}}{=} \tilde{M}((\tilde{x})\alpha \,.\, P')\sigma$$

In the case that α is not an update action,

$$\begin{aligned} \tilde{M}((\tilde{x})\alpha \,.\, P')\sigma &= \tilde{M}(\tilde{x})(\alpha\sigma) \,.\, (P'\sigma) \overset{(3)}{=} \tilde{M}(\tilde{x})(\beta\sigma) \,.\, (P'\sigma) \\ &\overset{(1)}{=} \tilde{M}(\tilde{x})(\beta\sigma) \,.\, (Q'\sigma) \overset{\mathbf{M1}}{=} \tilde{N}(\tilde{x})(\beta\sigma) \,.\, (Q'\sigma) = \tilde{N}((\tilde{x})\beta \,.\, Q')\sigma \\ &\overset{\mathbf{DM3}}{=} \tilde{N}(\tilde{x})\beta \,.\, Q' \end{aligned}$$

In the case that α is an update action,

$$\begin{aligned}
&\tilde{M}((\tilde{x})\alpha\,.\,P')\sigma \overset{\mathbf{DU1}}{=} \tilde{M}(\tilde{x})(\alpha\sigma)\,.\,(P'\sigma\sigma_\alpha) \overset{(2)}{=} \tilde{M}(\tilde{x})(\alpha\sigma)\,.\,(Q'\sigma\sigma_\alpha)\\
&\overset{\mathbf{DU1}}{=} \tilde{M}(\tilde{x})(\alpha\sigma)\,.\,(Q'\sigma) \overset{(3)}{=} \tilde{M}(\tilde{x})(\beta\sigma)\,.\,(Q'\sigma) \overset{\mathbf{M1}}{=} \tilde{N}(\tilde{x})(\beta\sigma)\,.\,(Q'\sigma)\\
&= \tilde{N}((\tilde{x})\beta\,.\,Q')\sigma \overset{\mathbf{DM3}}{=} \tilde{N}(\tilde{x})\beta\,.\,Q'
\end{aligned}$$

Thus we have proven that each summand of P is provably equal to a summand of Q, and then it suffices to use the **S** rules to infer that P and Q are provably equal. □

By dropping axioms **M4** and **M5**, and promoting **DM5** to an axiom, we get an axiomatization of hyperequivalence for the up-calculus without mismatch, which can be proved complete along the lines of [San96].

5 Conclusion

We have presented a new calculus, the *update calculus*, which is a step towards a unifying framework for concurrent actions with local and global effect. The calculus is constructed by on the one hand adding to the π-calculus *update* actions written $[y/z]$, meaning "z should everywhere be replaced by y" with a potentially unbounded extent, and on the other hand simplifying the π-calculus by replacing the two binding operators by one *scope* operator (z) explicitly controlling the extent of updates of z. In the resulting calculus input and output are symmetric, and the π-calculus can be recovered as a subcalculus by simple syntactic restrictions.

By providing a framework for global updates without a separate global state, we hope that the update calculus is well suited to model the global updates of imperative languages, as well as assignment to shared structures in concurrent constraint languages and the local binding in functional concurrent languages and formalisms.

In the present paper we have defined a bisimulation congruence, called *hyperequivalence*. It is strictly stronger than bisimulation equivalences previously studied for the π-calculus, and we show that it is the *only* reasonable congruence for the up-calculus. We have also given equational laws constituting a complete axiomatization of hyperequivalence. The axiomatization highlights the semantic difference between the scope operator of the up-calculus and the restriction operator of the π-calculus.

The idea to separate scope from input has occurred independently to Fu in encodings of the λ-calculus and of cut elimination in linear logic [Fu97]. Fu's semantics is significantly more complex since it lacks update actions.

This paper is a starting point for much further work. To give confidence that the up-calculus is computationally feasible, we are working on a translation into the polyadic π-calculus. To use the new calculus for modelling concurrent constraint programming we are constructing type systems for differentiating between different uses of names; these systems can also be used to relate the up-calculus to other calculi such as the γ-calculus [Smo94]. A polyadic version of the up-calculus will also be constructed; here we anticipate the interesting task of defining the action, if any, from $a\langle xx\rangle \mid \overline{a}\langle bc\rangle$. On the more practical side, we want to construct a tool for reasoning about up-calculus. We aim at modifying the Mobility Workbench [VM94], an automated tool for the π-calculus, for this purpose.

References

[Bar84] H. P. Barendregt. *The Lambda Calculus. Its Syntax and Semantics*, volume 103 of *Studies in Logic and the Foundations of Mathematics*. Elsevier, 1984.

[BKS88] R. J. R. Back and R. Kurki-Suonio. Distributed cooperation with action systems. *ACM Transactions on Programming Languages and Systems*, 10(4):513–554, Oct. 1988.

[CM88] K. M. Chandy and J. Misra. *Parallel Program Design: A Foundation*. Addison-Wesley, 1988.

[Dam93] M. Dam. Model checking mobile processes. In E. Best, editor, *CONCUR'93: Concurrency Theory*, volume 715 of *Lecture Notes in Computer Science*, pages 22–36. Springer-Verlag, 1993.

[Fu97] Y. Fu. A proof theoretical approach to communication. In P. Degano and R. Gorrieri, editors, *ICALP'97: Automata, Languages and Programming*, volume 1256 of *Lecture Notes in Computer Science*, pages 325–335. Springer-Verlag, 1997.

[Mil91] R. Milner. The polyadic π-calculus: a tutorial. Technical Report ECS-LFCS-91-180, Laboratory for Foundations of Computer Science, Department of Computer Science, University of Edinburgh, UK, Oct. 1991.

[MP91] Z. Manna and A. Pnueli. *The Temporal Logic of Reactive and Concurrent Systems*. Springer-Verlag, 1991.

[MPW92] R. Milner, J. Parrow and D. Walker. A calculus of mobile processes, Parts I and II. *Journal of Information and Computation*, 100:1–77, Sept. 1992.

[PS95] J. Parrow and D. Sangiorgi. Algebraic theories for name-passing calculi. *Journal of Information and Computation*, 120(2):174–197, 1995.

[PS96] M. Pistore and D. Sangiorgi. A partition refinement algorithm for the π-calculus. In R. Alur and T. A. Henzinger, editors, *Proceedings of CAV'96*, volume 1102 of *Lecture Notes in Computer Science*. Springer-Verlag, 1996.

[PV97] J. Parrow and B. Victor. The update calculus (full version). Technical Report DoCS 97/93, Department of Computer Systems, Uppsala University, Sweden, Sept. 1997. URL: http://www.docs.uu.se/~victor/tr/upd-full.ps.gz.

[San92] D. Sangiorgi. *Expressing Mobility in Process Algebras: First-Order and Higher-Order Paradigms*. PhD thesis, Department of Computer Science, University of Edinburgh, UK, 1992.

[San95a] D. Sangiorgi. On the proof method for bisimulation (extended abstract). In J. Wiederman and P. Hájek, editors, *Mathematical Foundations of Computer Science 1995 (MFCS'95)*, volume 969 of *Lecture Notes in Computer Science*, pages 479–488. Springer-Verlag, 1995.

[San95b] D. Sangiorgi. π-calculus, internal mobility and agent-passing calculi. Rapport de Recherche RR-2539, INRIA Sophia-Antipolis, 1995.

[San96] D. Sangiorgi. A theory of bisimulation for the π-calculus. *Acta Informatica*, 33:69–97, 1996.

[Smo94] G. Smolka. A foundation for higher-order concurrent constraint programming. In J.-P. Jouannaud, editor, *Proc. 1st International Conference on Constraints in Computational Logics*, volume 845 of *Lecture Notes in Computer Science*, pages 50–72. Springer-Verlag, Sept. 1994.

[VM94] B. Victor and F. Moller. The Mobility Workbench — a tool for the π-calculus. In D. Dill, editor, *CAV'94: Computer Aided Verification*, volume 818 of *Lecture Notes in Computer Science*, pages 428–440. Springer-Verlag, 1994.

[VP96] B. Victor and J. Parrow. Constraints as processes. In U. Montanari and V. Sassone, editors, *CONCUR'96: Concurrency Theory*, volume 1119 of *Lecture Notes in Computer Science*, pages 389–405. Springer-Verlag, 1996.

Selective Attribute Elimination for Categorical Data Specifications

Frank Piessens*, Eric Steegmans

Department of Computer Science, Katholieke Universiteit Leuven,
Celestijnenlaan 200A, B-3001 Belgium

Abstract. Semantic data specifications are important components of most object oriented software development methodologies. When making a semantic data specification, one has to classify the different kinds of entities that occur in the part of the real world one wants to specify. This classification can be done in two semantically equivalent ways: by putting them in different entity types, or by putting them in one entity type and distinguishing them by means of an attribute. This redundancy, which exists in almost all semantic data specification systems, leads to problems during the view integration process. If two software engineers have chosen to do this classification in a different way, it is hard to integrate their specifications.
In this paper we develop and prove correct a transformation which, given a specification that models the real world in one of these ways, computes a new specification that models the real world in the other way. Such a transformation can be very useful during the view integration process.

1 Introduction

Semantic data specifications (also called semantic data models) have been used for a long time in the early stages of database design. They are also important components of object oriented software development methodologies ([CY90, VBLSVR91]). A very wide variety of semantic data specification systems has been described in the literature. The most well-known examples are undoubtedly the Entity Relationship Model ([Che76]), and its many extensions.

One of the most challenging problems that has been considered in the literature on semantic data specifications is the so-called *view integration problem*, i.e. the problem of combining a number of different data specifications into one large specification. Difficulties arise, because the different specifications to be combined may overlap partly: certain parts of the real world are specified in more than one of the specifications. Moreover, the same real world situation can often be specified in syntactically widely different ways. Roughly speaking, view integration requires:

1. recognizing the overlapping parts,

* Postdoctoral Fellow of the Belgian National Fund for Scientific Research (N.F.W.O.)

2. verifying whether the overlapping parts are indeed semantically equivalent and correcting them if they are not,
3. choosing one particular syntactic representation for each of the overlapping parts,
4. overlaying the data specifications (which now have isomorphic overlapping parts) resulting in one large integrated specification.

The approaches to view integration that have been proposed in the literature usually require a lot of work from the database designer or the software engineer ([BLN86, SP91]), and this is unavoidable if one works with data specifications that have no formal semantics. A number of authors have proposed categorical formal semantics for data specifications ([JD92, JD93, CD94, Tui94, PS95, Pie96, JRW97]). In this paper, we will attack one aspect of the view integration process using mathematical methods, based on such a categorical formal semantics. One of the steps in the view integration process is verifying the semantical equivalence of overlapping parts. Hence, a formal definition of semantical equivalence, and algorithms to decide semantical equivalence are needed to automate the view integration process.

In [PS94], a formal definition of semantical equivalence was proposed. Moreover, an algorithm was given to decide equivalence of specifications for a large family of categorical data specifications. However, the algorithm did not work for specifications with infinite attribute sets, or for specifications where connectivity constraints and attribute sets interacted in an unclean way.

More recently ([PS95]), the algorithm was extended so that it now works for all data specifications with finite attribute sets: the unclean interaction between attributes and connectivity constraints described in [PS94] is no longer a problem.

In this paper, we address data specifications with infinite attribute sets. We have not succeeded in developing an algorithm to decide equivalence, but we do prove correct a powerful kind of *equivalence preserving transformation*[2] on data specifications. The software engineer or database designer faced with the problem of having to verify the semantical equivalence of two data specifications can apply such equivalence preserving transformations to both data specifications to try to make them equal. If one can make both specifications equal through a number of applications of such an equivalence preserving transformation, one has proven the semantical equivalence of the specifications.

The structure of this paper is as follows. First, in section 2, we define categorical data specifications, and we give a number of examples. In section 3, we discuss the selective elimination of attributes, which is an equivalence preserving transformation on data specifications. In section 4, we discuss related work. Finally, in section 5, we summarize the main contributions of this paper.

[2] A transformation T is called equivalence preserving here, if, for any specification S, S and $T(S)$ are equivalent.

2 Data Specifications

In this section, we define data specifications and their models, and we define when two data specifications are semantically equivalent. These definitions are a generalization of the definitions in [PS95]. The generalization consists of the fact that infinite attribute sets are now allowed. Our definition is very close to definitions given by other authors ([JD92, CD95]). The main difference is that our specifications have less expressive power (but still enough expressive power to encompass classical ER-diagrams): the chosen level of expressive power is a compromise between ease of use, and ease of mathematical analysis.

2.1 Definition and Examples

Definition 1. A *source* in a category $\mathcal{C}$ is a pair $(X, (f_i)_{i \in I})$ consisting of an object X of $\mathcal{C}$ and a family of morphisms $f_i : X \to Y_i$ of $\mathcal{C}$, indexed by some set I.

We will use the notations $(X, (f_i)_{i \in I})$ and $f_i : X \to Y_i$ interchangeably.

A source $(X, (f_i)_{i \in I})$ is a mono source if $f_i \circ x = f_i \circ y$ for all $i \in I$ implies that $x = y$.

Definition 2. A *data specification* is a triple $(\mathcal{S}, \mathcal{M}, \mathcal{A})$, where

1. $\mathcal{S}$ is a finite category.
2. $\mathcal{M}$ is a finite set of sources in $\mathcal{S}$.
3. $\mathcal{A} : \mathcal{S}_0 \to \mathbf{Set}$ is a functor, where $\mathcal{S}_0$ is the discrete category whose set of objects is the set of objects of $\mathcal{S}$.

Essentially, $\mathcal{A}$ is just a function from the objects of $\mathcal{S}$ to the class of sets.

Definition 3. A *model* of a data specification $(\mathcal{S}, \mathcal{M}, \mathcal{A})$ is a pair (M, λ), where

1. $M : \mathcal{S} \to \mathbf{FinSet}$ is a functor taking every $\mu \in \mathcal{M}$ to a mono-source.
2. $\lambda : J \circ M \circ I \to \mathcal{A}$ is a natural transformation, where functors $I : \mathcal{S}_0 \to \mathcal{S}$ and $J : \mathbf{FinSet} \to \mathbf{Set}$ are the obvious inclusions.

The following examples are taken from [PS95]. The category $\mathcal{S}$ of the specification is often given as a graph $\mathcal{G}$, and a set $\mathcal{E}$ of equations. The category $\mathcal{S}$ is defined to be the free category on $\mathcal{G}$, divided by the congruence generated by the equations in $\mathcal{E}$. Of course, when presenting the category in this way, one has to check whether the resulting category is indeed finite, as is required by the definition of a data specification. We begin with a few examples for which the functor $\mathcal{A}$ is the constant functor on 1, the terminal set.

Example 1. If $\mathcal{S}$ is a discrete category (no non-identity arrows), the models are just typed sets. Let $\mathcal{S}$ be the discrete category with two objects (call them COMPUTER and PRINTER) and no arrows, and let $\mathcal{M}$ be empty. This specification says that the part of the world we want to specify consists of two kinds of entities (computers and printers), and that is all it says.

Example 2. Arrows in the category specify existential dependencies. Consider for instance:

$$\mathcal{G} = \begin{array}{c} \text{COMPUTER} \\ \downarrow l \\ \text{LOCATION} \end{array}, \quad \mathcal{E} = \emptyset, \quad \mathcal{M} = \emptyset$$

Since the arrow must be taken to a function in a model, this specifies that every computer must have a location associated with it. (An entity of type COMPUTER is always associated with an entity of type LOCATION.)

Example 3. A source with n arrows in the category can be seen as an n-ary multirelation:

$$\mathcal{G} = \text{COMPUTER} \xleftarrow{c} \text{CONNECTION} \xrightarrow{p} \text{PRINTER}, \quad \mathcal{E} = \emptyset, \quad \mathcal{M} = \emptyset$$

This specification says that connection is a multirelation between computers and printers: every entity of type CONNECTION is associated with a couple of entities (x, y) with x of type COMPUTER and y of type PRINTER. It is possible that two different entities of type CONNECTION are associated with the same couple. Hence CONNECTION is a *multi*-relation over COMPUTER and PRINTER. For example, a printer could be connected twice to a computer, once with a serial cable, and once with a parallel cable.

Example 4. A multi-relation is an ordinary relation (no duplicates allowed) if and only if the corresponding source is a mono-source. The specification:

$$\mathcal{G} = \text{COMPUTER} \xleftarrow{c} \text{CONNECTION} \xrightarrow{p} \text{PRINTER}, \quad \mathcal{E} = \emptyset, \quad \mathcal{M} = \{(\text{CONNECTION}, (c, p))\}$$

says that CONNECTION is an ordinary relation over COMPUTER and PRINTER. A printer can be connected only once to a computer.

With this example in mind, the similarity of our data specifications with traditional Entity Relationship diagrams should be obvious.

Example 5. By requiring certain equations to be valid in $\mathcal{S}$, we can express equality constraints:

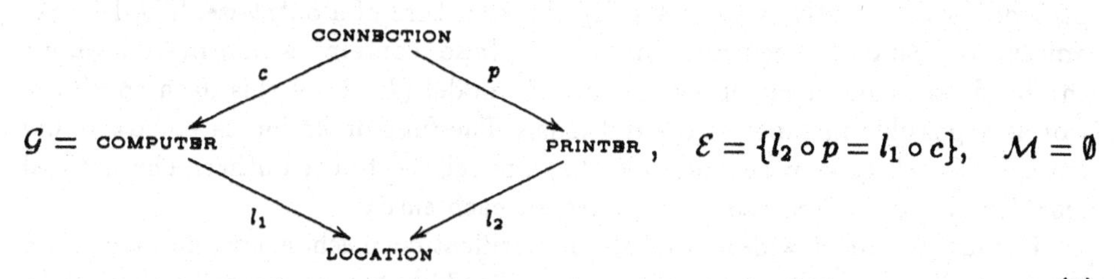

(1)

This specification says that computers and printers can be connected only if they have the same location. This kind of constraint occurs very often in practice.

In the examples we have discussed up to now, the functor $\mathcal{A}$ was always the constant functor 1. A data specification with $\mathcal{A} = 1$ only specifies the types of entities that exist in the part of the world we want to specify, and some structural constraints (e.g. a computer is always associated with a location, a printer can only be connected to a computer if they share the same location). In a database, we also want to store attributes of the entities. For example, for a printer, we might want to store whether it is a laserprinter or a matrixprinter (i.e. an attribute Type), and for a computer, we might want to store its amount of memory (i.e. an attribute MemorySize). Every such attribute a has an associated attribute set $S(a)$, which is the set of values that the attribute can attain. E.g. $S(\text{Type}) = \{\text{matrix, laser}\}$, and $S(\text{MemorySize}) = \mathbf{N}$, the set of natural numbers. Let $a_1, \ldots, a_n$ be the attributes of entity type C, with associated attribute sets $S(a_i)$. Then, the functor $\mathcal{A}$ is defined by:

$$\mathcal{A}(C) = \prod_{i=1,\ldots,n} S(a_i)$$

Looking at the definition of a model of a data specification, it is easy to see that in every model M, all entities of type C (i.e. all elements of the set $M(C)$) will be labelled with an element of $\mathcal{A}(C)$. The function which takes each entity to its label is the component of the natural transformation λ at C. If $\mathcal{A}$ is of the above kind, an element of $\mathcal{A}(C)$ is itself a tuple of values, one for each attribute of entity type C.

Example 6. Consider for example specification (1). Suppose computers have attributes MemorySize and DiskSize, printers have an attribute Type, and connections have an attribute TransferSpeed. We denote this as follows:

$$\begin{array}{lll} \mathcal{A} = & \text{COMPUTER} & \mapsto \text{MemorySize} : \mathbf{N} \\ & & \text{ DiskSize} : \mathbf{N} \\ & \text{PRINTER} & \mapsto \text{Type: \{matrix, laser\}} \\ & \text{CONNECTION} & \mapsto \text{TransferSpeed: } \mathbf{N} \end{array}$$

In a model of specification (1), with the attribute functor defined as above, every entity of type COMPUTER for example, will be labelled with two natural numbers: the memory size and the disk size of the computer.

With these examples in mind, it should be clear that data specifications provide for an intuitive way to specify the structure of a database. The last example, for instance specifies a (small) database, containing information about the hardware equipment of a company. A model (M, λ) of this data specification is a possible instance of the database. The functor M indicates how many entities of each type exist, and how they are related to each other. The natural transformation λ gives attribute values for each entity.

In fact, the most widely used data specification mechanisms, namely those based on Entity-Relationship diagrams ([Che76]), are very close to our data specifications. For more details on how to convert Entity-Relationship diagrams to our data specifications, consult [PS94].

Definition 4. A *homomorphism* between two models (M, λ) and (M', λ') of a data specification $(\mathcal{S}, \mathcal{M}, \mathcal{A})$ is a natural transformation $\alpha : M \to M'$ such that $\lambda' \circ J\alpha I = \lambda$.

In other words, it is a natural transformation between M and M' that is compatible with the labelling.

Models and homomorphisms of models of a specification $\mathcal{F} = (\mathcal{S}, \mathcal{M}, \mathcal{A})$ form a category, the *model category* of $\mathcal{F}$, which is denoted as $\mathrm{Mod}(\mathcal{F})$. Let $I : \mathcal{S}_0 \to \mathcal{S}$ be the inclusion, let $I^* : \mathrm{Fun}(\mathcal{S}, \mathbf{Set}) \to \mathrm{Fun}(\mathcal{S}_0, \mathbf{Set})$ be the functor of composition with I and let $\overline{\mathcal{A}} : 1 \to \mathrm{Fun}(\mathcal{S}_0, \mathbf{Set})$ be the functor picking out $\mathcal{A}$. Then,

Lemma 5. $\mathrm{Mod}(\mathcal{F})$ *is a full subcategory of the comma-category* $(I^* \downarrow \overline{\mathcal{A}})$.

The proof of this lemma is trivial. An object (F, α) of $(I^* \downarrow \overline{\mathcal{A}})$ belongs to $\mathrm{Mod}(\mathcal{F})$ iff the functor F factors through **FinSet** and takes all sources in $\mathcal{M}$ to mono-sources.

Lemma 6. *Let* $\mathcal{A}^! : \mathcal{S} \to \mathbf{Set}$ *be the right Kan extension of* $\mathcal{A}$ *along* I. $(I^* \downarrow \overline{\mathcal{A}})$ *is isomorphic to* $\mathrm{Fun}(\mathcal{S}, \mathbf{Set})/\mathcal{A}^!$.

The proof is a trivial modification of the proof given for the case of finite attribute sets in [PS95].

2.2 Equivalence of Data Specifications

We say that two data specifications are semantically equivalent iff their model-categories are equivalent.

Example 7. The following specification is equivalent to specification (1).

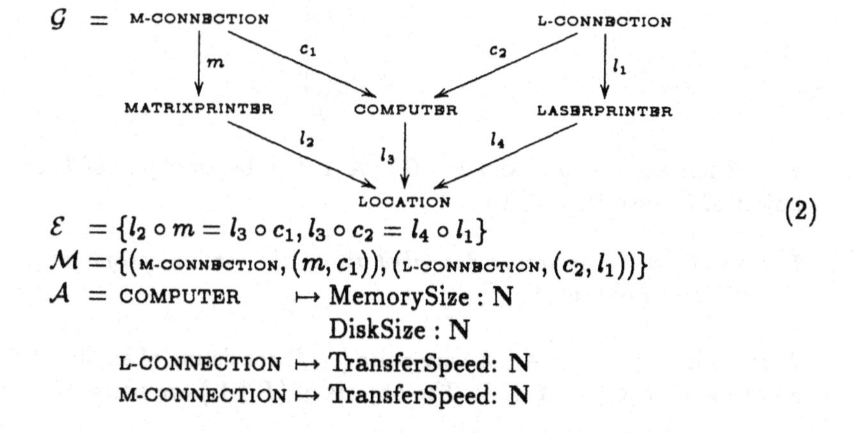

$$\mathcal{E} = \{l_2 \circ m = l_3 \circ c_1, l_3 \circ c_2 = l_4 \circ l_1\}$$

$$\mathcal{M} = \{(\text{M-CONNECTION}, (m, c_1)), (\text{L-CONNECTION}, (c_2, l_1))\}$$

$\mathcal{A}$ = COMPUTER $\mapsto$ MemorySize : $\mathbf{N}$
DiskSize : $\mathbf{N}$
L-CONNECTION $\mapsto$ TransferSpeed: $\mathbf{N}$
M-CONNECTION $\mapsto$ TransferSpeed: $\mathbf{N}$

Informally, it is not too hard to see that the two specifications are semantically equivalent. In the specification above, two different entity types are used for matrix-printers and laser-printers, instead of one entity type with an attribute. Further in this paper, we will prove that the model-categories are indeed equivalent.

The fact that the same real-world situation can be specified in a number of non-isomorphic ways is an important problem in database design and software engineering. Suppose for example, that a number of different data specifications exist, and that these different specifications overlap partly: certain parts of the real world are specified in more than one of the specifications. It is very likely that these parts are specified differently in each of the specifications, and that makes it hard to combine the given specifications into one large specification. This problem of combining data specifications is called the ***view integration*** problem in the database literature, and has been studied extensively. We refer the reader to [BLN86] for a survey. The usual approach is to develop heuristic algorithms which try to identify the equivalent subspecifications, and then leave it to a database designer to decide which subspecifications are indeed equivalent and which are not. A provably correct algorithm (in contrast with a heuristic algorithm) could minimize the amount of work that is left to the database designer. In the sequel of this paper, we will develop a class of ***equivalence preserving transformations***, and give algorithms to compute them. The database designer can apply these transformations to the given data specifications, to try to make them equal. If he succeeds, he has proven that the two given data specifications are indeed semantically equivalent.

3 Selective Attribute Elimination

We need the following technical result about comma categories. Consider the diagram of functors:

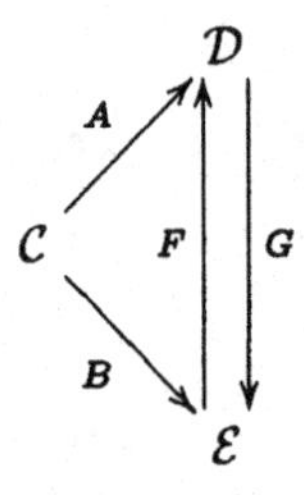

with F left adjoint to G and $F \circ B = A$. Let X be an object of $\mathcal{D}$ and Y be an object of $\mathcal{E}$, such that $G(X) = Y$.

Lemma 7. *In the situation described above, the comma categories $(A \downarrow X)$ and $(B \downarrow Y)$ are isomorphic.*

Proof. The objects of $(A \downarrow X)$ are pairs (C, f) consisting of an object C of $\mathcal{C}$ and an arrow $f : A(C) \rightarrow X$ of $\mathcal{D}$. The objects of $(B \downarrow Y)$ are pairs (C, g) consisting of an object C of $\mathcal{C}$ and an arrow $g : B(C) \to Y$ of $\mathcal{E}$. Since F is left adjoint to G, we have that:

$$\mathrm{Hom}(A(C), X) = \mathrm{Hom}(F(B(C)), X) \approx \mathrm{Hom}(B(C), G(X)) = \mathrm{Hom}(B(C), Y)$$

and hence, there exists a bijection between the objects of both comma categories.

Arrows in both comma categories are arrows h from $\mathcal{C}$. To be an arrow of $(A \downarrow X)$, they must satisfy commutativity of:

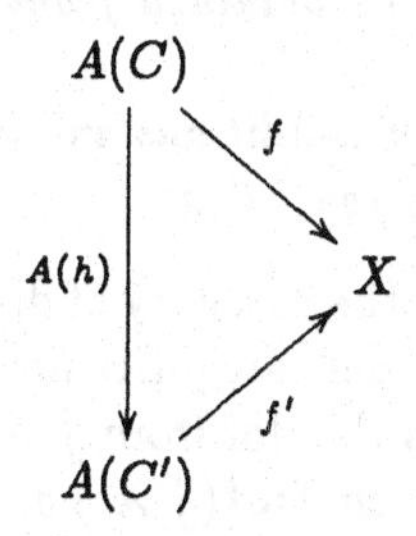

To be an arrow of $(B \downarrow Y)$, they must satisfy commutativity of:

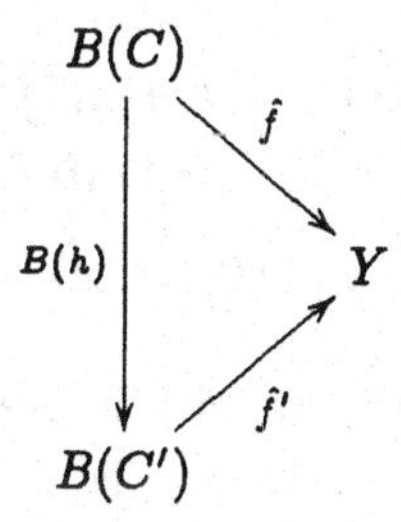

These two conditions are easily proved to be equivalent. □

Now, suppose we are given a data specification $(\mathcal{C}, \mathcal{M}, \mathcal{A})$, a functor $X : \mathcal{C}_0 \to$ **FinSet** (which we also sometimes consider as $X : \mathcal{C}_0 \to \mathbf{Set}$, i.e. as JX) and a natural transformation $\alpha : \mathcal{A} \to X$. Let, as usual, $I : \mathcal{C}_0 \to \mathcal{C}$ be the inclusion, $I^* : \mathrm{Fun}(\mathcal{C}, \mathbf{Set}) \to \mathrm{Fun}(\mathcal{C}_0, \mathbf{Set})$ the functor of composition with I, and $(-)^! : \mathrm{Fun}(\mathcal{C}_0, \mathbf{Set}) \to \mathrm{Fun}(\mathcal{C}, \mathbf{Set})$ the right adjoint to I^*. Hence $X^!$ will be the right Kan extension of X along I. We want to construct a new data specification $(\mathcal{C}', \mathcal{M}', \mathcal{A}')$. We define:

- $\mathcal{C}' = \int X^!$, where $\int F$ is the category of elements of a **Set**-valued functor F.
- $\mathcal{M}' = \{\mu \mid \Pi(\mu) \in \mathcal{M}\}$, where Π is the canonical projection of $\int X^!$ on $\mathcal{C}$.

It remains to define $\mathcal{A}'$. Note that $\mathcal{A}'$ must be a set, typed by the objects of $\int X^!$. Since the elements of $I^*(X^!)$ are in bijection with the objects of $\int X^!$, it suffices to give an arrow $\alpha' : \mathcal{A}' \to I^*(X^!)$ in $\mathrm{Fun}(\mathcal{C}_0, \mathbf{Set})$. We define this arrow to be the pullback of α along the counit ϵ of the adjunction between I^* and $(-)^!$. Hence, the following square is a pullback square:

$$\begin{array}{ccc} \mathcal{A}' & \longrightarrow & \mathcal{A} \\ {\scriptstyle \alpha'} \downarrow & & \downarrow {\scriptstyle \alpha} \\ I^*(X^!) & \xrightarrow[\epsilon_X]{} & X \end{array}$$

This defines the functor $\mathcal{A}' : \mathcal{C'}_0 \to \mathbf{Set}$ up to natural isomorphism.

We say that $(\mathcal{C}', \mathcal{M}', \mathcal{A}')$ is obtained from $(\mathcal{C}, \mathcal{M}, \mathcal{A})$ by elimination over α.

The functor X and the natural transformation α must be seen as the definition of a partition on the sets of attribute values. What attribute elimination does, is introducing a new entity type for each equivalence class in this partition, and this in such a way that the resulting specification is semantically equivalent.

Theorem 8. *Let $(\mathcal{C}', \mathcal{M}', \mathcal{A}')$ be obtained from $(\mathcal{C}, \mathcal{M}, \mathcal{A})$ by elimination over $\alpha : \mathcal{A} \to X$.*

If $X^!$ satisfies the monicity conditions in $\mathcal{M}$, then the model categories of $(\mathcal{C}, \mathcal{M}, \mathcal{A})$ and $(\mathcal{C}', \mathcal{M}', \mathcal{A}')$ are equivalent.

Proof. Let us write $\mathbf{Dof}(\mathcal{C})$ for the category of discrete opfibrations (dofs) over $\mathcal{C}$. First we prove that the two model categories are equivalent to full subcategories of $\mathbf{Dof}(\mathcal{C}')/\int \alpha^!$, where $\int \alpha^!$ is the dof from $\int \mathcal{A}^!$ to $\int X^! = \mathcal{C}'$ corresponding to $\alpha^!$ under the equivalence between $\mathbf{Dof}(\int X^!)$ and $\mathrm{Fun}(\mathcal{C}, \mathbf{Set})/X^!$.

The model category of $(\mathcal{C}, \mathcal{M}, \mathcal{A})$ is equivalent to a full subcategory of $\mathrm{Fun}(\mathcal{C}, \mathbf{Set})/\mathcal{A}^!$. Since

$$\begin{aligned} \mathrm{Fun}(\mathcal{C}, \mathbf{Set})/\mathcal{A}^! &\approx \mathbf{Dof}(\textstyle\int \mathcal{A}^!) \\ &\approx \mathbf{Dof}(\textstyle\int X^!)/\textstyle\int \alpha^! \end{aligned}$$

it follows that the model category of $(\mathcal{C}, \mathcal{M}, \mathcal{A})$ is equivalent to a full subcategory of $\mathbf{Dof}(\mathcal{C}')/\int \alpha^!$.

The model category of $(\mathcal{C}', \mathcal{M}', \mathcal{A}')$ is equivalent to a full subcategory of $\mathrm{Fun}(\mathcal{C}', \mathbf{Set})/\mathcal{A}'^!$. This last category is equivalent to $(J^* \downarrow \mathcal{A}')$, where $J : \mathcal{C'}_0 \to \mathcal{C}'$ is the inclusion, and J^* the functor of composition with J. This last category is easily seen to be equivalent with $(K \downarrow \alpha')$, where $K : \mathrm{Fun}(\mathcal{C}, \mathbf{Set})/X^! \to \mathrm{Fun}(\mathcal{C}_0, \mathbf{Set})/I^*(X^!)$ is the functor of composition with I, and where α' is the pullback of α along ϵ_X, as defined above. We can now use lemma 7 to prove that $(K \downarrow \alpha')$ is equivalent to $(L \downarrow \alpha)$, where $L : \mathrm{Fun}(\mathcal{C}, \mathbf{Set})/X^! \to \mathrm{Fun}(\mathcal{C}_0, \mathbf{Set})/X$ is the functor mapping an object $F \to X^!$ of $\mathrm{Fun}(\mathcal{C}, \mathbf{Set})/X^!$ to the object $I^*(F) \to X$ of $\mathrm{Fun}(\mathcal{C}_0, \mathbf{Set})/X$ according to the natural isomorphism between $\mathrm{Hom}(F, X^!)$ and $\mathrm{Hom}(I^*(F), X)$. An arrow h of $\mathrm{Fun}(\mathcal{C}, \mathbf{Set})/X^!$ is a commutative diagram:

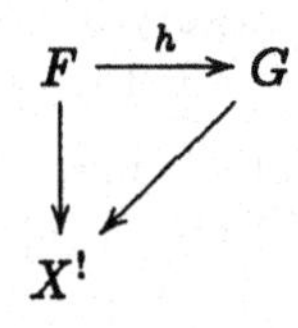

and this is mapped by L to the following commutative diagram which is an arrow of $\mathrm{Fun}(\mathcal{C}_0, \mathbf{Set})/X$:

$$\begin{array}{ccc} I^*(F) & \xrightarrow{I^*(h)} & I^*(G) \\ \downarrow & \swarrow & \\ X & & \end{array}$$

To prove that $(K \downarrow \alpha')$ and $(L \downarrow \alpha)$ are equivalent, it suffices to find an adjoint functor pair between the categories $\mathrm{Fun}(\mathcal{C}_0, \mathbf{Set})/X$ and $\mathrm{Fun}(\mathcal{C}_0, \mathbf{Set})/I^*(X^!)$ which satisfies the compatibility requirements requested in lemma 7. The reader can check that the following adjoint pair works. Let $\epsilon^* : \mathrm{Fun}(\mathcal{C}_0, \mathbf{Set})/I^*(X^!) \to \mathrm{Fun}(\mathcal{C}_0, \mathbf{Set})/X$ be the functor of composition with ϵ_X, and let $\epsilon_* : \mathrm{Fun}(\mathcal{C}_0, \mathbf{Set})/X \to \mathrm{Fun}(\mathcal{C}_0, \mathbf{Set})/I^*(X^!)$ be the functor which pulls back along ϵ_X. Then ϵ^* and ϵ_* are well-known to be adjoint, and it is straightforward to verify that they satisfy all the necessary requirements to apply lemma 7 to prove the equivalence of $(K \downarrow \alpha')$ and $(L \downarrow \alpha)$. Finally, $(L \downarrow \alpha)$ is easily seen to be equivalent to $\mathrm{Fun}(\mathcal{C}, \mathbf{Set})/\alpha^!$, and hence to $\mathbf{Dof}(\mathcal{C}')/\int \alpha^!$.

It remains to verify that an object of $\mathbf{Dof}(\mathcal{C}')/\int \alpha^!$ corresponds to a model of $(\mathcal{C}, \mathcal{M}, \mathcal{A})$ iff it corresponds to a model of $(\mathcal{C}', \mathcal{M}', \mathcal{A}')$. Consider an object of $\mathbf{Dof}(\mathcal{C}')/\int \alpha^!$:

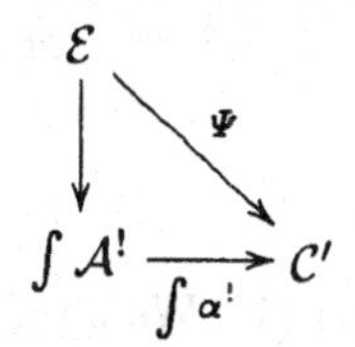

This object corresponds to a model of $(\mathcal{C}, \mathcal{M}, \mathcal{A})$ iff $\mathcal{E}$ is finite, and the functor $F : \mathcal{C} \to \mathbf{FinSet}$ corresponding to the dof $\Pi \circ \Psi$ satisfies all monicity conditions in $\mathcal{M}$. It corresponds to a model of $(\mathcal{C}', \mathcal{M}', \mathcal{A}')$ iff $\mathcal{E}$ is finite, and the functor $F : \mathcal{C}' \to \mathbf{FinSet}$ corresponding to the dof Ψ satisfies all monicity conditions in $\mathcal{M}'$. We prove that these two conditions are equivalent.

First, we investigate under what conditions on a dof $\Phi : \mathcal{E} \to \mathcal{C}$, the functor $F : \mathcal{C} \to \mathbf{Set}$ corresponding to Φ takes a source μ to a mono source.

Let $\mu = f_i : X \to Y_i$ be a source in $\mathcal{C}$ and suppose B and B' are nodes of $\mathcal{E}$ such that $\Phi(B) = \Phi(B') = X$. The arrow-lifting property of dofs ensures us the existence of two unique sources $g_i : B \to Z_i$ and $g_i' : B' \to Z_i'$ such that $\Phi(g_i) = \Phi(g_i') = f_i$. We say that $B \sim_\mu^\Phi B'$ iff $Z_i = Z_i'$ for all i. This situation is illustrated in the following picture:

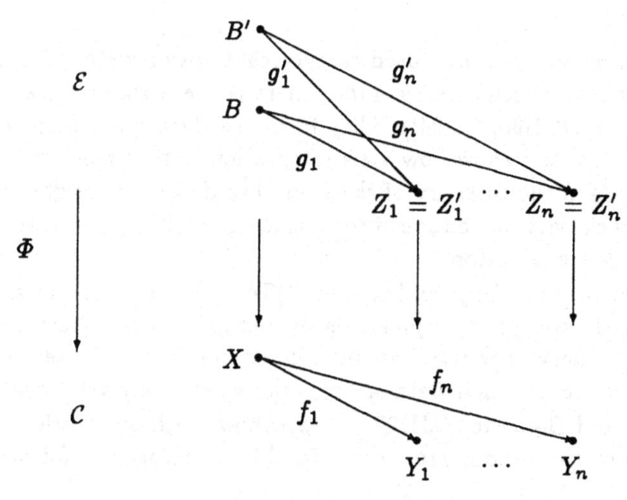

It is clear that the functor corresponding to Φ takes μ to a mono source iff $B \sim_{\mu}^{\Phi} B' \Rightarrow B = B'$.

Now, we turn to proving the equivalence of the two conditions.

1. Suppose the object corresponds to a model of $(\mathcal{C}, \mathcal{M}, \mathcal{A})$. Then we know that $B \sim_{\mu}^{\Pi \circ \Psi} B'$ implies that $B = B'$, for all $\mu \in \mathcal{M}$.
   Let μ' be an element of $\mathcal{M}'$ and suppose $B \sim_{\mu'}^{\Psi} B'$, then $B \sim_{\mu}^{\Pi \circ \Psi} B'$ where $\mu = \Pi(\mu')$, and hence $B = B'$. We conclude that all sources in $\mathcal{M}'$ are taken to mono sources.
2. Suppose, on the other hand, that the object corresponds to a model of $(\mathcal{C}', \mathcal{M}', \mathcal{A}')$.
   Let $\mu \in \mathcal{M}$ and suppose $B \sim_{\mu}^{\Pi \circ \Psi} B'$. Then $\Psi(B) \sim_{\mu'}^{\Pi} \Psi(B')$, and hence $\Psi(B)$ must be equal to $\Psi(B')$ since $X^!$ is assumed to satisfy all monicity conditions in $\mathcal{M}$. But that means that $B \sim_{\mu'}^{\Psi} B'$ for some μ' with $\Pi(\mu') = \mu$. Hence $B = B'$.

□

Example 8. Consider specification (1). We want to eliminate attribute Type from printers. Hence, we define a partition of $\mathcal{A}$(PRINTER) which puts the value matrix in one equivalence class and the value laser in another equivalence class. In other words, the functor X will take PRINTER to {matrix, laser}, and all other entity types to 1. The component of α at PRINTER is the identity, and the component at all other entity types is the unique function to 1. Computing the elimination over α leads to a specification isomorphic to specification (2). In this second specification, different entity types for matrixprinters and laserprinters have been introduced. The computation of the elimination over α requires the computation of the right Kan extension of X along I. An algorithm to compute such right Kan extensions can be found in Borceux' handbook ([Bor93]).

4 Related Work

A number of researchers have used categorical tools or methods in their theoretical study of data specifications. First, there is the work by Diskin, Cadish and Beylin ([CD95, DCB95, CD94]). They formalize data specifications by means of a general sketch, and show how view integration in that context corresponds to taking colimits in the category of sketches. The database designer must indicate manually which parts of the specifications are semantically equivalent, by means of correspondence equations.

Also in the work of Tuijn and Gyssens ([Tui94]) categorical data specifications are considered, but their emphasis is on designing data specification systems in which the query language can be defined completely in terms of universal constructions. Hence, their data specifications have only very weak constraints.

Johnson and Dampney ([JD92, JD93]) show, with real world examples, that category theoretic notions are very helpful in structuring information systems.

They propose an architecture for information systems (called Federated Information Systems), which encompasses both semantic data modelling and process modelling.

Johnson, Rosebrugh and Wood ([JRW97]) propose ER-sketches as a formal underpinning for classical ER-diagrams enhanced with commutativity constraints. They show that the category of updates of models of an ER-sketch is the category of spans of models, and that this category is itself a category of models of the ER-sketch.

Finally, Steve Vickers has proposed geometric logic as a specification language for databases ([Vic92, Vic93]) as a generalization of domain theoretic treatments of databases.

5 Conclusion

When giving a semantic data specification, one has to classify the different kinds of entities that occur in the real world. This classification can be done in two semantically equivalent ways: by putting them in different entity types, or by putting them in one entity type and distinguishing them by means of an attribute. This redundancy, which exists in almost all semantic data specification systems, leads to problems during the view integration process. If two software engineers have chosen to do this classification in a different way, it is hard to integrate their specifications.

In this paper we have proven correct a transformation which, given a specification that models the real world in one of these ways, computes a new specification that models the real world in the other way. Such a transformation can be very useful during the view integration process.

References

[BLN86] C. Batini, M. Lenzerini, and S. B. Navathe. A comparitive analysis of methodologies for database schema integration. *ACM Computing Surveys*, 15(4):323–364, 1986.

[Bor93] Francis Borceux. *Handbook of Categorical Algebra*, volume I, II and III. Cambridge University Press, 1993.

[CD94] Boris Cadish and Zinovy Diskin. Algebraic graph-oriented = category-theory-based: Categorical data modelling manifesto. Technical report, Frame Inform Systems, Database Design Laboratory, Latvia, July 1994.

[CD95] B. Cadish and Z. Diskin. Algebraic graph-based approach to management of multibase systems, I: Schema integration via sketches and equations. In *Next Generation of Information Technologies and Systems,NGITS'95*, pages 69–79, 1995.

[Che76] P. P. Chen. The entity-relationship model – towards a unified view of data. *ACM Transactions on Database Systems*, 1(1):9–36, 1976.

[CY90] P. Coad and E. Yourdon. *Object-Oriented Analysis*. Yourdon Press, New Jersey, 1990.

[DCB95] Z. Diskin, B. Cadish, and I. Beylin. Algebraic graph-based approach to management of multibase systems, II: Algebraic aspects of schema integration. To appear in the proceedings of the Moscow ACM Chapter Conference ADBIS'95, 1995.

[JD92] M. Johnson and C.N.G. Dampney. A mathematical foundation for era. In *Proceedings of the Institute for Mathematics and its Applications*, pages 77–84, 1992.

[JD93] M. Johnson and C.N.G. Dampney. Category theory and information systems engineering. In *Proceedings of AMAST'93*, pages 95–103, 1993.

[JRW97] M. Johnson, R. Rosebrugh, and R.J. Wood. Entity-relationship models and sketches. Preprint, 1997.

[Pie96] Frank Piessens. *Semantic Data Specifications: an Analysis Based on a Categorical Formalization.* PhD thesis, Katholieke Universiteit Leuven, Dept. of Computer Science, 1996. In preparation.

[PS94] Frank Piessens and Eric Steegmans. Canonical forms for data-specifications. In *Proceedings of Computer Science Logic 94*, number 933 in Lecture Notes in Computer Science, pages 397–411. Springer-Verlag, 1994.

[PS95] Frank Piessens and Eric Steegmans. Categorical data-specifications. *Theory and Applications of Categories*, 1:156–173, 1995.

[SP91] Stefano Spaccapietra and Christine Parent. Conflicts and correspondence assertions in interoperable databases. *SIGMOD Record*, 20(4):49–54, December 1991.

[Tui94] Chris Tuijn. *Data Modeling from a Categorical Perspective.* PhD thesis, Universitaire Instelling Antwerpen, 1994.

[VBLSVR91] Stefan Van Baelen, Johan Lewi, Eric Steegmans, and H. Van Riel. EROOS: An entity-relationship based object-oriented specification method. In G. Heeg, B. Magnusson, and B. Meyer, editors, *Technology of Object-Oriented Languages and Systems TOOLS 7*, pages 103–117. Prentice Hall, 1991.

[Vic92] Steve Vickers. Geometric theories and databases. In *Applications of Categories in Computer Science*, number 177 in London Mathematical Society Lecture Note Series, pages 288–314, 1992.

[Vic93] Steve Vickers. Geometric logic in computer science, 1993. Available by anonymous FTP from `theory.doc.ic.ac.uk` in directory `papers/Vickers`. The paper is called `GLiCS.dvi`.

ATM Switch Design: Parametric High-Level Modeling and Formal Verification

Sreeranga P. Rajan and Masahiro Fujita

Fujitsu Laboratories of America, Inc.
3350 Scott Blvd. #34
Santa Clara, CA 95054-3104
USA

Abstract. Asynchronous Transfer Mode (ATM) has emerged as a backbone for high-speed broadband communications networks. In this paper we present ATM switch design, starting from a parametric high-level model and debugging the model using a combination of formal verification and simulation. The parametric model is written in a language that supports concurrency and that can be used for both hardware and software design. The model has been used to synthesize ATM switches according to customers' choices, by choosing concrete values for each of the generic parameters. The difficulty in validating ATM switch design arises not only due to parametrization, but also due to delicate control module design arisiing from concurrent processes communicating through shared signals. ATM switch validation resulting from the exclusive use of either simulation or one of the formal verification methods such as theorem proving or finite-state model checking would be tedious and inefficient. We provide a pragmatic combination of simulation, model checking, and theorem proving to gain confidence in the ATM switch design correctness. We use a combination of theorem proving and model checking to discover bugs in the high-level model, which was presumed correct using simulation. Parametric design validation obviates the need to validate specific ATM switch designs derived from the parametric model. Our design methodology, in which begins with a reusable parametric model, to which formal verification is applied early in the design cycle, has a significant impact on drastically reducing design cost and time-to-market.

1 Introduction

Asynchronous Transfer Mode (ATM) technology has emerged as a backbone for high-speed broadband communications networks [CFFT96]. An ATM network backbone typically consists of a number of small ATM switches interconnected in a matrix topology. An ATM switch takes data from input ports and forwards the input data to the proper output ports in the same order as the input data. An ATM switch is typically designed as a RAM-embedded Application Specific Integrated Circuit (ASIC). Because of various applications of ATM switch as the core component of various ATM networks, advancement in technology, short product life-cycle, and changing standards demand an efficient methodology to modify the current design for a future product. High-level modeling and hardware synthesis has been shown to deliver good results in ATM switch design [LHCF96]. However, the high-level model presented earlier [LHCF96] works only for specific design requirements such as a fixed clock ratio and a fixed number of input/output ports. Furthermore, the model was presumed correct using simulation. However, by formal verification we discovered several bugs in the control part of the model. The difficulty in validation comes about because of complex control module design for a parametric number of concurrent processes, corresponding to an arbitrary number of input/output ports in the high-level model, communicating through shared signals. While simulation is efficient for validating portions of design that do not have many interacting concurrent processes, it is only by general purpose theorem proving that we can prove properties of designs with generic parameters, and model checking can efficiently handle the control part of the design with a small state space. Parametric ATM switch validation by exclusively using either simulation or one of the formal verification methods such as theorem proving and model checking would be tedious and inefficient. We employ a pragmatic combination of theorem proving and model checking [RSS95] in conjunction with small-scale conventional simulation.

There have been other efforts in ATM switch verification earlier [TZS+96, Cur94]. However, a major drawback with earlier efforts is that with any change of switch design requirements such as the clock ratio and the number of input/output ports, one needs to repeatedly iterate through high-level modeling, validation, and synthesis cycle until the design satisfies the design objectives. Furthermore, earlier efforts [CYF94, TZS+96, Cur94] do not introduce formal validation early in the design cycle, rather describe application of formal verification on a completed design *post-facto*. In order to cut down the modeling-validation-synthesis iteration cycle, the solution we propose in this paper is the development of a validated parametric high-level model that can be synthesized with concrete values for the generic parameters. The validation of the parametric model is done by a combination of simulation and formal verification early in the design cycle, before attempting high-level synthesis. The parametric model has been used to synthesize a family of ATM switches by simply supplying different concrete values for the generic parameters of the switch model.

We present a parametric model of an ATM switch in which

- The ratio of the internal switch clock to the external network clock is a generic value. The generic value can be instantiated with specific ratio numbers to produce corresponding switch models, which can then be piped into hardware synthesis.
- The number of input/output ports is a generic value. The generic value can be instantiated with specific numbers of ports to produce corresponding switch models. The specific switch models can then be input to hardware synthesis program.
- The buffer sizes of the ATM cell FIFO and the cell address FIFO units are generic values.

The parametric model is validated by simulation using a small number of test cases and formal verification of the properties of the model using Prototype Verification System (PVS) [ORR+96]. PVS provides an integrated environment for the development and analysis of formal specifications and has a powerful theorem prover with a high-degree of automation together with a Binary Decision Diagram (BDD)-based model checker.

The rest of the paper is organized as follows: Section 2 gives a brief overview of the ATM switch architecture. Section 3 presents the parametric model for the ATM switch. The formal verification process, using a combination of theorem proving and model checking with an outline of simulation, is discussed in Section 4. Finally, Section 5 presents the conclusions, work in progress, and directions for future work.

2 ATM Switch Architecture: Overview

An ATM switch forms the basic component of an ATM network, in which several switches could be connected in the form of a matrix for larger bandwidth. The modeling and functionality can be illustrated by a *small capacity ATM switch*, whose architecture is shown in Figure 1. The ATM switch has 2 input ports, 2 expanded ports, and 2 output ports. The incoming data are packed into 27 16-bit words called *cells*. The first 3 words of a cell form a `TAG`, which contains the switching information. The `TAG` includes the type of cell, the cell ID, and output routing information. ATM cells from the network arriving at the input ports `iHW0` and `iHW1` are collected by the `INPUT MODULE`. The cells are forwarded to the `CELL PROCESSING MODULE`, which stores the cells in the proper addresses and routes them to the corresponding output ports through the `OUTPUT MODULE`. The different formal verification methods applied to various modules are also shown in Figure 1.

The internal switch clock runs slower than the external network clock in order to reduce the cost of the different components within the ATM switch. Therefore, a serial-to-parallel (S/P) conversion module, as part of the `INPUT MODULE`, buffers the incoming words for processing multiple words in the buffer simultaneously. The S/P conversion ensures that the switching speed is maintained at the the original external network clock, notwithstanding switch clock speed reduction. The Write-Control (WC) unit belonging to the `CELL PROCESSING MODULE` obtains addresses from the Write-Address-FIFO (WAF) unit and stores the incoming cells from the S/P unit in the addresses obtained from WAF. The WAF, while providing the addresses to the WC, also provides the same addresses matching the corresponding cell TAGs to one of the two Read-Address-FIFOs: RAF0 and RAF1 depending on which output port (port 0 or 1) the cell should be switched. A cell can also be switched to more than one output port depending on the header information. In this case we call this cell the "copy cell" and a copy cell flag will be set. The expanded input ports, exHW0 and exHW1, send a Read-Request signal to the Read-Control (RC), which then obtains the addresses from RAF0/RAF1 and reads out the corresponding cells from the cell FIFO. A parallel-to-serial (P/S) conversion in the `OUTPUT MODULE` serializes the cell words to match the faster external network clock at the output ports. The address of the outgoing cell is recycled back to the WAF unit to be reused for the next incoming cell.

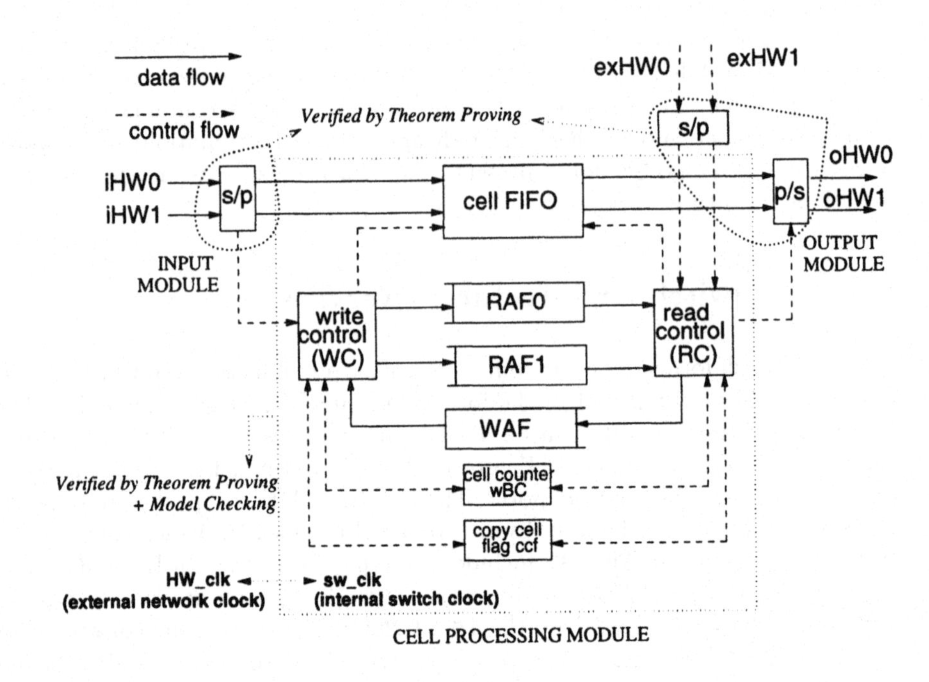

Fig. 1. Architecture of ATM switch with 2 input and 2 output ports

3 ATM Switch: Parametrized High-Level Model

A cycle-accurate behavior model of an ATM switch, shown in Figure 1 with 2 input ports, 2 output ports, and 2 expanded input ports has already been developed [LHCF96]. The ratio of the external network clock (`HW_clk`) to the internal switch clock (`sw_clk`) determines the size of the buffer for S/P conversion. A clock ratio of 3 fixes the buffer size to three 48-bit registers. Every 3 incoming 16-bit words are packed into a 48-bit word. At every (slower) internal switch clock cycle, i.e. at every third external clock cycle, 48 bits are fetched by the WC module described in Section 2. However, the two clocks (the switch clock and the network clock) may not be synchronized with respect to the clock rising/falling edges. Thus a S/P conversion which requires the buffer size to match the clock ratio restores the processing speed to the faster external network clock. We discuss the cycle-accurate behavior model with a parametric clock ratio in Section 3.1.

Typically, a number of ATM switches are arranged in the form of a matrix to obtain a larger bandwidth. In order to keep the cost of a single ATM switch low, the number of input/output ports of an ATM switch is a small fixed number. A model with 2 input and 2 output ports has been presented earlier [LHCF96]. However, under a different set of cost requirements, the switch design might demand a different number of input/output ports. A model with a fixed number of input/output ports is difficult and time-consuming to change for another number of ports. Thus a parametric model requiring that the designer supply the number of ports desired, and not requiring any modification to the model itself reduces the design cost enormously. Such a parametric model for an arbitrary number of input/output ports is discussed in Section 3.2.

First, in the parametric model of the ATM switch, the clock ratio parameter `n`, the number-of-ports parameter `m`, and the buffer size `b`, are declared at the top level. The model is then ready to be used for hardware synthesis and simulation with concrete instantiations of the generic parameters.

3.1 Parametric Clock Ratio

A parametric ratio entails a matching parametric size of the buffer for S/P conversion (see Section 3). Thus if we choose a ratio `n`, we need an `n x n` shift-register, i.e. `n` registers, each of which can store `n` words. Every external network clock cycle brings in a new incoming word to be stored in the first register. As shown in Figure 2, after every `n` external network clock cycles, i.e. at every internal switch clock cycle, all the contents of register `i` are shifted to register `i+1`, where `i` ranges from `1` to `n-1`. A generic `n`-bit counter is used to keep track of the next set of `n` words that need to be processed by the Write-Control (WC) for writing into the cell FIFO.

The S/P conversion module for a generic clock ratio `n` is modeled as a set of two concurrent processes. The processes `iHW_sp1` and `iHW_sp2` in Figure 2, both activated by the external network clock, execute as follows:

- Process `iHW_sp1` stores incoming cell words into the first register `iHW_bword(1)`. Thus the `i`th cell word is stored to the `i`th slot of register `1`, with `i` ranging from `1` to `n`. Every register is associated with a bit-vector for checking parity of the incoming cell words. Immediately after the incoming `n`th cell

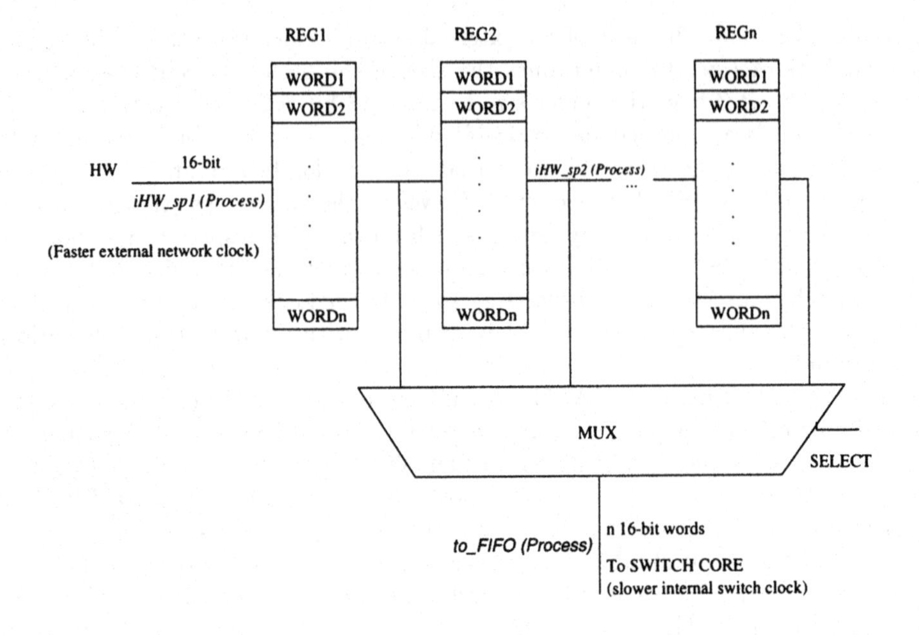

Fig. 2. Buffering for Serial-to-Parallel conversion with clock ratio n

word has been stored in the first register, the first bit of the `n`-bit counter `iHW_cycle_counter`, which keeps track of the register that contains set of words ready to be fetched by the next module, is set to bit value 1. Every other bit has the value 0. It should be noted that such a cycle counter is needed as a sentinel [LHCF96] because the internal switch clock (`sw_clk`) and the external network clock (`HW_clk`) may not be synchronized with respect to the rising/falling clock edges.

- Process iHW_sp2 shifts contents of register `i` to register `i+1` at every network clock cycle. The bit value 1 in `iHW_cycle_counter` is shifted to the left as the clock advances.
- Process `to_FIFO` is activated by the slower internal switch clock. The `i`th bit in `iHW_cycle_counter` is set to value 1, which indicates that the `i`th register contains the set of cell words ready to be fetched for further processing. Exactly one set of words is generated for every `n` external network clock cycles, or one internal switch clock cycle.

The parallel-to-serial (P/S) conversion module is modeled as a set of communicating processes similar to the S/P module, and is not discussed in this paper.

3.2 Parametrizing the number of ports

In the model of the ATM switch presented earlier [LHCF96], the two ports are each associated with a process, and each process communicates with other processes, such as the WC, using synchronization signals. In the parametric model, we must construct an arbitrary number of processes and corresponding synchronization signals corresponding to a generic number **m** of ports.

The communication between processes for an **m**-port ATM switch is shown in Figure 3. Each block contains **m** processes, one for each of the **m** ports. There are two kinds of inter-block communication:

- Communication between processes corresponding to a single port: process `i` in **iHW_sp** communicates only with process `i` in `to_FIFO`, where `i` ranges from 1 to **m**.
- Communication between a process (such as **RC**) in one block with every process in another block (such as **update_RAF**).

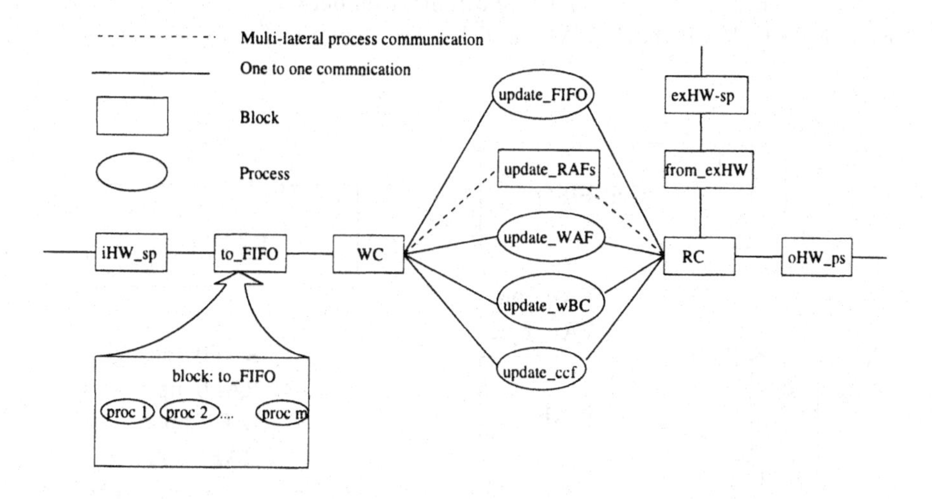

Fig. 3. The communication between processes for a m-port ATM switch

3.3 Address Recycling Control Module

At power-on or reset, the Write-Address FIFO (WAF) unit is initialized to consist of new addresses in which the incoming cells are to be stored. As a cell arrives from the input ports, the WAF unit supplies a new address in which the cell word must be stored, and supplies that same address to the RAF units. The new address in WAF is obtained from the pointer **WAF_hptr**, and the address is stored in RAFs in the location pointed to by **RAF_tptrs**. When a cell word is to be read out for output, the RAF units supply the address from which the cell word must be read. The pointer **RAF_hptrs** points to the address in RAFs from which the next cell word is to be read out. When the cell word is read out, the RAF units recycle the address back to the WAF unit. In the case of a copy cell, the cell must be read out of each RAF unit corresponding to an output port before the cell address is recycled back to the WAF. The recycling process in an ATM switch with 2 ports is shown in Figure 4. In summary,

- **WAF_hptr** points to the address in the WAF to be supplied to the current incoming cell word.
- **WAF_tptr** points to the WAF location in which the next recycled address must be stored.
- **RAF_hptr** points to the RAF location in which the cell word must be output next, and
- **RAF_tptr** points to the RAF location in which the cell word currently supplied by the WAF must be stored.

The pointers are incremented by 1 (modulus the buffer size) for accessing the next location in the FIFOs. The communication between various processes corresponding to WAF, RAFs, WC, and RC are shown in Figure 3.

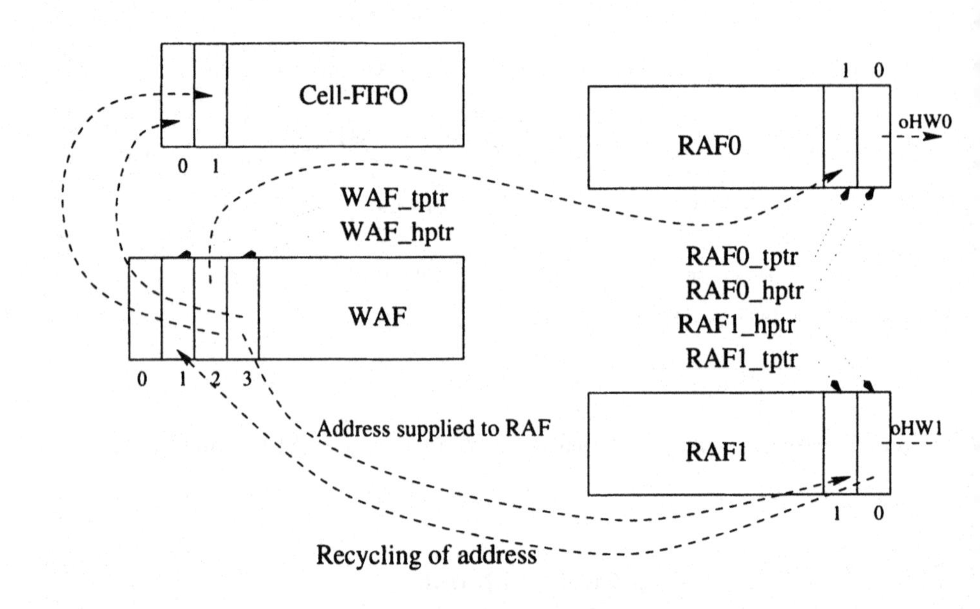

Fig. 4. Address Recycling in a 2-port ATM switch with generic buffer size for WAF, cell-FIFO, RAF0/1

4 Formal Verification

The goal of formal verification of the ATM switch model is to show the *overall functional correctness property* that the *input cells are switched to the proper output ports, and that the order of input cells is maintained upon output.* The overall correctness property subsumes the properties that input cells are not lost, and that the cells without a copy flag are not duplicated at the output. Furthermore, it should be noted that the overall correctness property for the parametric ATM switch model should hold for any arbitrary clock ratio, an arbitrary number of ports, and an arbitrary buffer size of FIFOs.

The parametric ATM switch model described in Section 3 is verified by first verifying the properties of its components. The verified component properties are then composed to show the overall correctness property. The components correspond to the processes of the high-level model. The model is first translated into the PVS specification language. Verification of the properties is performed by invoking appropriate built-in proof strategies, in particular a combination of induction, rewriting, and special-purpose decision procedures for linear arithmetic and model checking using BDDs provides a semi-automatic verification of the parametric ATM switch model.

There are essentially 3 modules in the ATM switch: input serial-to-parallel conversion (S/P), address recycling (AR), and output parallel-to-serial conversion (P/S). The overall correctness property can be shown by composing the correctness properties of each of the 3 components. First, Section 4.1 gives an overview of specification and verification using PVS. The verification of the correctness properties of the serial-to-parallel conversion module is discussed in Section 4.2, and the address recycling module in Section 4.3. The verification of the correctness of the output parallel-to-serial conversion is similar to the input module.

4.1 Overview of PVS

The Prototype Verification System (PVS) [ORR+96] is an environment for specifying entities such as hardware/software models and algorithms, and verifying properties associated with the entities. The specification language features common programming language constructs such as arrays, functions, and records. It has built-in types for reals, integers, naturals, and lists. The language also allows hierarchical structuring of specifications. Besides features such as subtyping and dependent typing, it permits overloading of operators, as in some programming languages and hardware description languages.

The PVS verifier is used to determine if the desired properties hold in the specification of the model. The user interacts with the verifier by a small set of commands. The verifier contains procedures for Boolean reasoning, arithmetic and (conditional) rewriting.
In particular, Binary Decision Diagram (BDD) [Bry92] based simplification may be invoked for Boolean reasoning. Model checking, in which properties are stated in fair-CTL and models are written as state transition relations, can be invoked within PVS as another proof rule. The PVS verifier also features a variety of general induction schemes to tackle large-scale verification. Moreover, different verification schemes can be combined into general-purpose strategies for similar classes of problems, such as microprocessor verification [Sha96].

4.2 Formal Verification of Serial-to-Parallel (S/P) conversion Module

The correctness property to be verified is that an incoming cell word from the network to an ATM input port appears at the output of the S/P buffer (i.e. the input to cell FIFO) at least after **n** (**n** is the clock ratio) external network clock cycles, i.e. 1 internal switch clock cycle and at most before **2n** external network clock cycles:

Theorem 1. *S/P Correctness Property*

```
∀ (t:time),(n > 0):
∃ m: {m | n ≤ m ≤ 2n}:
sp1_sp2(n,t) ∧ to_fifo(n,t)  %% Specification of the S/P modules
⟹ iHWO_cell_word(t) = iHWO_word(t+m)
%% iHWO_cell_word is the cell word at input port iHWO and iHWO_word
is input to cell FIFO
```

The proof in PVS follows by induction on clock ratio parameter "n", rewriting, arithmetic simplification, and propositional simplification using BDDs. The verification is semi-automatic with 5 interactive steps. The *run-time* of the proof on a Sparc-20 with 64 MB is **90 seconds**. The property could not have been checked using either simulation or finite-state model checking, because the clock ratio is a generic value.

4.3 Formal Verification of the Address Recycling (AR) Module

The address recycling module described in Section 3.3 consists of the WC, the WAF, the RC, and one RAF for each output port. In the parametric model, the sizes of the WAF and RAFs are arbitrary. The corresponding PVS model of the recycling module is a state machine parametrized with respect to the buffer-size of WAF/RAFs/cell-FIFO and number of input/output ports. The property that we would like to verify is that the cell contents of the address recycled from RAFs to WAF should be processed by the output module prior to recycling the address. The correctness of recycling depends on whether the concurrent processes WAF, RAF, WC, and RC, correctly update the shared signals corresponding to `RAF_hptrs`, `RAF_tptrs` and `WAF_hptr`, `WAF_tptr`.

The recycling correctness property can be recast as a property that the address supplied by the WAF unit to store the next incoming cell is not contained in any of the RAFs corresponding to the output ports. In the PVS state machine model, WAF and RAF buffer sizes are arbitrary (uninterpreted) and the number of ports is also arbitrary. Thus, we first instantiate the model with

- buffer size of 2 and
- number of input/output ports to 2

and verify the property that the address supplied from the WAF for the next incoming cell to be stored i.e. `iHWO_write_addr` or `iHW1_write_addr` corresponding to the 2 ports iHW0 and iHW1 is not contained in either of the 2 locations in either of the RAF buffers corresponding to the 2 output ports: oHW0 and oHW1 (see Figure 4). However, the verification did *not succeed* for our original model, and produced a counterexample in the form of a series of unprovable sub-properties. A closer examination of the sub-properties **revealed bugs** that the pointers to the WAF locations (`iHW0_WAF_hptr`, `iHW0_WAF_tptr`, `iHW1_WAF_hptr`, and `iHW1_WAF_tptr`) were not initialized to 0, and were not incremented at every clock step. The model was updated and the property was checked to hold in the model. Using CTL model checking in PVS, we specify the property using the **AG** modality to cover all the states and all the paths starting from the initial state as shown in Theorem 2:

Theorem 2. *Address Recycling (AR) Correctness Property*
$AG(\neg\ (\ (iHW0\_write\_addr\ =\ RAF0(1))\ \wedge\ (iHW0\_write\_addr\ =\ RAF0(0)))$
$\qquad \vee\ ((iHW1\_write\_addr\ =\ RAF1(1))\ \wedge\ (iHW1\_write\_addr\ =\ RAF1(0)))$

The state-space is small for a buffer size of 2, and the run-time for the verification is under **20 seconds** on Sparc-20 with 64 MB. We can characterize property 2 as a *safety* property.

Following earlier work on verification of Peterson's mutual exclusion algorithm for an arbitrary number of processes [Sha96], we can show using simple induction, rewriting, and arithmetic proof rules of general purpose theorem proving in PVS that property 2 holds for

- an arbitrary buffer size, and
- an arbitrary number of ports.

The verification is semi-automatic with a small number of interactive steps.

4.4 Verification of Overall ATM Correctness Property

In order to verify the overall correctness property that the cells are output in the same order as the input, we must verify 3 more properties corresponding to the RC and RAF units: "RC Liveness", which states that every RAF unit is read out eventually (i.e. no RAF unit is starved); "RAF Behavior", which states that every RAF unit behaves like a FIFO queue, and **Cell Tag Match** which asserts that the port tag bit of a cell word matches with the port number corresponding to the RAF unit in which the cell is stored. However, we employ a combination of theorem proving and model checking only for the first 2 properties, and check for **Cell Tag Match** by *simulation*. It is laborious to use formal verification for checking **Cell Tag Match** because of the data processing involved in extracting the proper TAG bits from the cell word. While simulation is efficient we can assert that the port tag bit of a cell word matches with the port number corresponding to the RAF unit in which the cell is stored.

Theorem 3. *RC Liveness* `AF(output_port_read_address = RAF(RAF_hptr))`

Theorem 4. *RAF Behavior* `AG(increment(RAF_hptr)` $\Rightarrow$
`AF(increment(RAF_tptr)))`

The verification of properties above are similar to that of property 2 and use a combination of theorem proving and model checking. By composing the individual correctness theorems 1, 2, 3, 4, and **Cell Tag Match** property checked by simulation, we obtain the following overall correctness property:

Theorem 5. *ATM Switch Correctness Property*
Every input cell is switched to the proper output port, and the order among the cells at an output port is identical to that at the corresponding input port.

5 Discussion, Summary and Future Work

In the ATM switch model [LHCF96], in order to achieve a lower design cost, the internal switch clock is slowed down by a fixed ratio with respect to the external clock. The slower clock entails buffering the input for serial-to-parallel conversion to avoid degrading the switching speed. Thus, a fixed clock ratio determines the size of the input buffer used for serial-to-parallel conversion. Therefore, the model must be largely rewritten for a different choice of clock ratio. Similarly new concurrent communicating processes must be added to the model for a different choice of the number of input/output ports, and communication between processes would have to be redesigned. Furthermore, the model must be revalidated when it undergoes modification. In earlier work [CYF94], a number of abstractions had to be manually applied without any computer-aided tool applied to formally verify an industrial ATM switch design using SMV-based model checking [McM93]. The verification successfully revealed some bugs and the design was corrected. However, such a post-facto verification would not be economically feasible in an industrial setting.

In this paper we have presented ATM switch design beginning with a parametric high-level model, using a combination of formal verification and simulation early in the design cycle to remove as many bugs as possible in the high-level model. The model has been used to obtain hardware implementations of customers' choice by hardware synthesis. We have presented a combination of simulation and semi-automatic formal verification methods of the parametric model, which obviates the need to validate specific ATM switch designs. An efficient proof strategy that needs to be selected for the verification of a module is done manually, whence the proof is fully automatic. We found bugs, among which two cell address pointers were not initialized in the model presumed correct by simulation. We have obtained ATM designs by hardware synthesis with different concrete values of the generic parameters of clock ratio, number of ATM switch ports, and buffer sizes. A slower clock rate for the internal switch core reduces the area of the switch. However, the optimal ratio of the network clock and the slower switch clock is dependent on the design goals (such as power consumption) corresponding to the ATM application. Similarly, a low-cost ATM switch with 2 ports could be used in a matrix to obtain a larger bandwidth. But, for many applications, increasing the number of ports would lead to lower overall cost of the ATM network system. It should be noted that verification of the model with generic parameters for clock ratio, cell-FIFO/WAF/RAFs buffer size, and number of input/output ports could not have been done using formal verification techniques, such as finite-state model checking or finite state reachability exploration [McM93, Dil96, Kur94] alone. Also, using general purpose theorem proving for the control part with a reduced state space is highly interactive, while model checking provides automatic verification for small state spaces.

Our work uses a pragmatic combination of theorem proving and model checking within a single framework, in conjunction with simulation for efficient verification of large industrial software/hardware designs. As part of future work, we are in the process of providing a formal method to compose verified properties of modules that form an ATM system to assert an overall system correctness property (eg: Property 5). We are investigating use of formal specification and verification for design trade-off/analysis to determine an efficient partitioning of the processes in the high-level model, and trade-offs with respect to clock ratio, number of input/output ports, and buffer size. Thus, a design methodology based on high-level parametric modeling coupled with the introduction of formal verification, in conjunction with small-scale simulation early in the design cycle, drastically reduces system design cost and time-to-market.

References

[AH96] R. Alur and T. A. Henzinger, editors. *Computer-Aided Verification, CAV '96*, volume 1102 of *Lecture Notes in Computer Science*, New Brunswick, NJ, July/August 1996. Springer-Verlag.

[Bry92] Randal E. Bryant. Symbolic boolean manipulation with ordered binary-decision diagrams. *ACM Computing Surveys*, 24(3):293–318, September 1992.

[CFFT96] Tom Chaney, J. Andrew Fingerhut, Margaret Flucke, and Jonathan Turner. Design of a gigabit ATM switching system. Technical Report WUCS-96-07, Computer Science Department, Washington University, St. Louis, Missouri, February 1996.

[Cur94] Paul Curzon. The formal verification of the fairisle ATM switching element. Technical Report 328 and 329, Computer Laboratory, University of Cambridge, Cambridge, UK, March 1994.

[CYF94] B. Chen, M. Yamazaki, and M. Fujita. Bug identification of a real chip design by symbolic model checking. In *Proceedings of the European Conference on Design Automation, the European Test Conference*, pages 132–136, Paris, France, February 1994. IEEE Computer Society.

[Dil96] David L. Dill. The Murϕ verification system. In Alur and Henzinger [AH96], pages 390–393.

[Kur94] R. P. Kurshan. *Computer-Aided Verification of Coordinating Processes—The Automata-Theoretic Approach.* Princeton University Press, Princeton, NJ, 1994.

[LHCF96] Mike T-C. Lee, Yu-Chin Hsu, Ben Chen, and Masahiro Fujita. Domain-specific high-level modeling and synthesis for ATM switch design using VHDL. In *Proceedings of the 33th Design Automation Conference.* Association for Computing Machinery, 1996.

[McM93] Kenneth L. McMillan. *Symbolic Model Checking.* Kluwer Academic Pub., Boston, MA, 1993.

[ORR+96] S. Owre, S. Rajan, J.M. Rushby, N. Shankar, and M.K. Srivas. PVS: Combining specification, proof checking, and model checking. In Alur and Henzinger [AH96], pages 411–414.

[RSS95] Sreeranga P. Rajan, N. Shankar, and M. Srivas. An integration of model-checking with automated proof checking. In *7th Conference on Computer-Aided Verification*, July 1995.

[Sha96] N. Shankar. PVS: Combining specification, proof checking, and model checking. In M. Srivas and A. Camilleri, editors, *Formal Methods in Computer-Aided Design (FMCAD '96)*, volume 1166 of *Lecture Notes in Computer Science*, pages 257–264, Palo Alto, CA, November 1996. Springer-Verlag.

[TZS+96] S. Tahar, A. Zhou, X. Song, E. Cerny, and M. Kangevin. Formal verification of an ATM switch fabric using mutiway decision graphs. In *Proceedings of IEEE Sixth Great Lakes Symposium on VLSI (GLS-VLSI'96)*, Ames, Iowa, March 1996. IEEE Computer Society.

The Hidden Function Question Revisited*

Arno Schönegge

Institut für Logik, Komplexität und Deduktionssysteme
Universität Karlsruhe, 76128 Karlsruhe, Germany
schoenegge@ira.uka.de

Abstract. While some common algebraic specification languages provide hiding mechanisms, others do not support hiding at all. The *hidden function question* asks whether hiding facilities are actually necessary for a specification method to be adequate.
Concerning the initial algebra approach this question of adequacy is answered for years [Maj79, TWW82, BT87]. Here we give the answer for the loose approach (and also for the final algebra approach).

1 Introduction

During the past 25 years of research, development and applications a large number of algebraic specification languages have been proposed. Some of them differ in only quite minor ways from each other. One distinguishing feature is the provision of hiding mechanisms which allow local definitions of sorts and functions that on the one hand facilitate the writing of the axioms, but on the other hand are hidden from the user of the data type. While some common specification formalisms provide explicit hiding facilities (e.g. CLEAR [BG80], ASL [SW83], PLUSS [Gau92], SPECTRUM [BFG+93], the language ASF of ASF+SDF [vDHK96], and the language CASL developed by the common framework initiative CoFI [Mos97]), others provide hiding facilities more implicitly (at the level of modules) (e.g. ACT TWO [Fey88], ABEL [DO91], and the RAISE specification language RSL [Geo91]), and others in turn do not provide any hiding mechanism at all (e.g. the LARCH shared language LSL [GH93], ACT ONE [Cla89], and the (more model-oriented) language Z [Spi92]). Naturally, the question arises whether hiding facilities are desirable or not.[2] On the one hand, they may be regarded as desirable for methodological reasons, e.g. to facilitate information hiding and to enhance modularity. However, this is not the point of the paper. Here we take a more theoretical point of view and ask whether hiding is necessary for reasons of expressive power.

* This research has been supported by the "Deutsche Forschungsgemeinschaft" within the "Schwerpunktprogramm Deduktion".

[2] Questions of this style are of topical interest: Since the wealth of languages is known as one of the obstacles for the use of algebraic methods in industrial contexts, a current collaborative effort (called CoFI [Mos97]) aims to design a common framework for algebraic specification and development of software. This design is based on a critical selection of concepts and constructs proven useful in existing algebraic frameworks.

It is well-known that, if equipped with hiding mechanisms, all the common algebraic specification methods are adequate for computable[3] data types, which are obviously the most important ones in the context of software development. Bergstra & Tucker [BT82, BT87] proved that any computable algebra A possesses an equational specification involving at most $3(n+1)$ hidden functions (where n is the number of sorts in A) which defines A under both its initial and final algebra semantics. I.e., allowing hidden mechanisms a monomorphic (equational) specification can be constructed for any computable algebra.[4] Thus the question is *whether the adequacy for computable data types is preserved if hiding is disallowed.*

For the initial algebra approach this "*hidden function question*", as it is called, is answered for years: Majster [Maj77, Maj79] gave an example of a computable data type (a traversable stack) which does not have an equational initial algebra specification. Further examples are given e.g. by Thatcher et al. [TWW82] and Bergstra & Tucker [BT87]. In [BT87] there is also an example of a computable data type which cannot be specified using finitely many conditional equations and initial algebra semantics.

In this paper we deal with the loose approach to algebraic specification. Of course, the examples just mentioned can also be interpreted in the loose setting: there is a computable data type which does not possess a monomorphic specification using finitely many conditional equations. However, in common loose formalisms one is usually not restricted to conditional equations but one often has all the first-order logic formulas at one's disposal. Thus the so-far known examples illustrating the inadequacy of the initial algebra specifications without hidden functions do not imply a corresponding inadequacy of the loose specifications. In fact, to our knowledge, the hidden function question for the loose approach is still unanswered. The aim of this paper is to give the outstanding answer. More precisely, we will prove the following.

Theorem 1. *There is a computable data type which does not have a monomorphic first-order specification (without hidden symbols).*

The computable data type as well as the proof technique we will use to establish this inadequacy result is quite different from the ones given to show the incompleteness of the initial algebra approach without hidden functions [Maj79, TWW82, BT87]. Surprisingly, we get by on an example which is both simple and non-artificial: the data type of integers.

The paper is organized as follows. Section 2 provides some basic definitions. In section 3, the data type of integers is presented. Then, in the section 4 we prove the existence of non-standard models for any possible first-order specification of integers. Section 5 states (as a corollary) that without hidden machinery the final algebra specification method is not adequate either. As a further (more

[3] Definitions of the notions of (computable) data types, initial and final algebra semantics, monomorphicity etc. are given in section 2.

[4] If one is additionally allowed to distinguish the constructor functions, even any hyperarithmetical algebra has a monomorphic specification [Wir90, THEOREM 5.3.9].

secondary) corollary, in section 6, we derive a decision procedure for first-order sentences over the integers. Section 7 shows that already little more additional (hidden) signature is sufficient to enable monomorphic specifications of integers. Finally, in the last section we draw conclusions and indicate directions for future work.

2 Preliminaries

We assume the reader to be familiar with the basic notions of algebraic specifications (cf. e.g. [EM85, Wir90]) like the notions of (many-sorted) *signature* $\Sigma = (S, F)$, (total) *Σ-algebra* $A = ((s^A)_{s \in S}, (f^A)_{f \in F})$, and *$\Sigma$-homomorphism*. $Alg(\Sigma)$ denotes the set of all Σ-algebras.

The set of *terms* $T(\Sigma, X)$ with variables taken from X is defined as usual. Terms without variables are called *ground terms*. A Σ-algebra A is called *term-generated* (or *reachable*) if for each of its carrier elements $a \in s^A$ ($s \in S$) there is a denotation, i.e. a ground term $t \in T(\Sigma, \emptyset)$ with $t^A = a$. The class of all term-generated Σ-algebras is denoted by $Gen(\Sigma)$.

Two Σ-algebras A, B are called *isomorphic* if there is a bijective Σ-homomorphism $h : A \to B$. The isomorphism class of a Σ-algebra A, also called the "abstract" data type, is denoted by $[A]$. For a class C of Σ-algebras an $A \in C$ is called *initial in* C (*final in* C) if for all $B \in C$ there exists a unique Σ-homomorphism $h : A \to B$ (or $h : B \to A$, respectively).

A Σ-algebra A is called *computable* if it is isomorphic to a *computable number algebra*, which is an algebra with all carrier sets decidable subsets of $\mathbb{N}$ and all functions computable (cf. [BT83, MG85]). For term-generated Σ-algebras computability is characterized by the decidability of the associated Σ-congruence.

Atomic Σ-formulas are Σ-equations $t_1 = t_2$ (with $t_1, t_2 \in T(\Sigma, X)$ terms of the same sort) and the boolean constant **false**. *First-order Σ-formulas* are built from the atomic ones with the logical connectives $\neg$ and $\wedge$, and the quantifier $\exists$. Further logical operators such as **true**, $\neq$, $\vee$, $\to$, $\leftrightarrow$, and $\forall$ are considered as abbreviations. As usual, we drop parentheses whenever possible; in particular we assume the quantifiers $\exists$ and $\forall$ to apply as little as possible.

A Σ-formula is said to be *closed*, and then is also called *Σ-sentence*, if it does not contain free variables. A *literal* is a formula which is atomic or the negation of an atomic formula. Is a signature $\Sigma = (S, F)$ clear from the context, the Σ-formulas in which at most the function symbols $\{f_1, \ldots, f_k\} \subseteq F$ occur are also called *$\{f_1, \ldots, f_k\}$-formulas* (or *$\{f_1, \ldots, f_k\}$-sentences* if closed).

By $A, v \models \varphi$ the usual *satisfaction* of a Σ-formula φ by a Σ-algebra A w.r.t. a valuation $v : X \to A$ is denoted. We write $A \models \varphi$, and say that φ is *valid in* A, if $A, v \models \varphi$ holds for all valuations v. For a set Φ of Σ-formulas we write $A \models \Phi$ if $A \models \varphi$ for all $\varphi \in \Phi$.

A *(first-order algebraic) specification* $SP = (\Sigma, \Phi)$ consists of a signature Σ and a finite set Φ of Σ-formulas, called *axioms*. If Φ consists of (conditional) Σ-equations we speak of *(conditional) equational specification*. According to the three main approaches three semantic functions are defined:

- *loose semantics:*
  $Mod(SP) := \{A \in Gen(\Sigma) \mid A \models \Phi\}$
- *initial algebra semantics:*[5]
  $I(SP) := \{A \in Mod(SP) \mid A \text{ initial in } Mod(SP)\}$
- *final algebra semantics:*[5]
  $Z(SP) := \{A \in Mod(SP) \mid A \text{ final in } Mod(SP)\}$

The elements of $Mod(SP)$ ($I(SP)$, $Z(SP)$) are called the *models* (*initial models*, *final models*, respectively) of SP. A specification SP is called *monomorphic* if any two of its models are isomorphic, i.e. if there is modulo isomorphism at most one[6] element in $Mod(SP)$. A specification $SP = (\Sigma, \Phi)$ is said to *specify* a Σ-algebra A (and also the corresponding abstract data type $[A]$)

- *under loose semantics* if $Mod(SP) = [A]$,
- *under initial algebra semantics* if $I(SP) = [A]$,
- *under final algebra semantics* if $Z(SP) = [A]$.

In particular, a specification SP specifies a Σ-algebra A under loose semantics if and only if SP is monomorphic and $A \in Mod(SP)$. A Σ-algebra A can be specified *with hidden symbols* (under loose, initial algebra, or final algebra semantics) if there is a super-signature $\Sigma' \supseteq \Sigma$ and a Σ'-algebra A' with A as its Σ-reduct, i.e. $A'|_\Sigma = A$, such that A' can be specified (under loose, initial algebra, or final algebra semantics, respectively).

3 The data type of integers

To prove theorem 1 an example of a computable data type has to be given which cannot be specified under loose semantics (using first-order axioms but no hidden functions). We choose the data type of integers. More precisely the signature $\Sigma_\mathbb{Z}$ with

$$
\begin{array}{lllll}
\textbf{sorts} & \texttt{int} & & & \\
\textbf{functions} & \texttt{zero} & : & & \to \texttt{int} \\
 & \texttt{succ} & : & \texttt{int} & \to \texttt{int} \\
 & \texttt{pred} & : & \texttt{int} & \to \texttt{int}
\end{array}
$$

is considered, and the $\Sigma_\mathbb{Z}$-algebra $A_\mathbb{Z}$ which interprets the symbols as intended:

$$
\begin{array}{lll}
\texttt{int}^{A_\mathbb{Z}} & := & \mathbb{Z} = \{\ldots, -1, 0, 1, \ldots\} \\
\texttt{zero}^{A_\mathbb{Z}} & := & 0 \\
\texttt{succ}^{A_\mathbb{Z}}(i) & := & i + 1 \\
\texttt{pred}^{A_\mathbb{Z}}(i) & := & i - 1
\end{array}
$$

[5] The results of the paper remain valid if in the definition of initial and final algebra semantics $Alg(SP) := \{A \in Alg(\Sigma) \mid A \models \Phi\}$ is used instead of $Mod(SP)$.

[6] Our definition of monomorphicity differs from the one given in [Wir90] where '*exactly one*' is demanded instead of '*at most one*'. According to the definition in [Wir90] any monomorphic specification is consistent, while according to the definition used here any inconsistent specification is monomorphic.

On the one hand the algebra $A_{\mathbb{Z}}$ is an initial model of the two equations:

$$\mathtt{succ}(\mathtt{pred}(\mathtt{x})) = \mathtt{x}$$
$$\mathtt{pred}(\mathtt{succ}(\mathtt{x})) = \mathtt{x}$$

I.e. the data type of integers has a very simple equational initial algebra specification.[7] On the other hand, we are going to prove the following

Theorem 2. *The $\Sigma_{\mathbb{Z}}$-algebra $A_{\mathbb{Z}}$ does not possess a monomorphic first-order specification (without hidden symbols).*

Notice that, since the algebra $A_{\mathbb{Z}}$ is obviously computable, theorem 1 is an immediate consequence of theorem 2. The proof of theorem 2 works by constructing non-standard models for any possible specification of integers.

4 Non-standard models of integer specifications

It is easily formalized that `succ` is the inverse operation of `pred`, and vice versa, e.g. using the two equational axioms given in the last section. Thus all the term-generated non-standard models of a possible integer specification worth considering exhibit a certain structure. A simple observation shows that they are isomorphic to some $\Sigma_{\mathbb{Z}}$-algebras A_m $(m \in \mathbb{N})$ defined by

$$\begin{aligned}
\mathtt{int}^{A_m} &:= \{0, \ldots, m\} \\
\mathtt{zero}^{A_m} &:= 0 \\
\mathtt{succ}^{A_m}(i) &:= \begin{cases} 0 & \text{if } i = m \\ i+1 & \text{otherwise} \end{cases} \\
\mathtt{pred}^{A_m}(i) &:= \begin{cases} m & \text{if } i = 0 \\ i-1 & \text{otherwise} \end{cases}
\end{aligned}$$

One can think of these models as finite cycles of the form illustrated in the following figure.

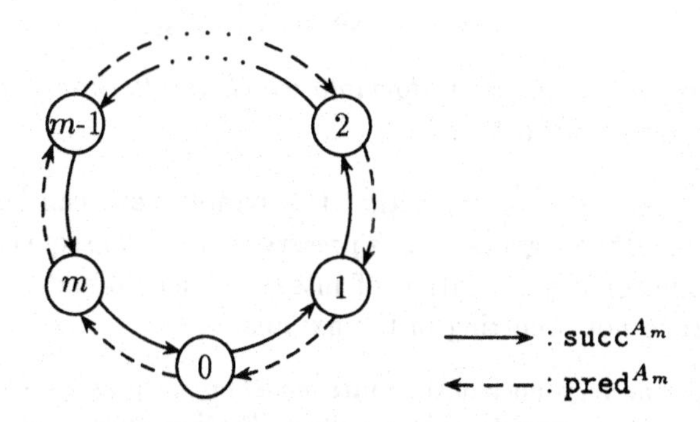

[7] For reasons of deductive weakness and lack of flexibility, initial algebra specifications using conditional equations are not appropriate for all applications, cf. e.g. [Rei92].

It remains to show that for any specification of integers a non-standard model of this kind actually exists, i.e. that for any $SP = (\Sigma_Z, \Phi)$ with $A_{\mathbb{Z}} \in Mod(SP)$ there is an $m_{SP} \in \mathbb{N}$ with $A_m \in Mod(SP)$. Since for term-generated algebras A it is

$$\begin{aligned} A \in Mod(SP) &\Leftrightarrow A \models \Phi \\ &\Leftrightarrow A \models \forall \overline{x} \bigwedge_{\varphi \in \Phi} \varphi \end{aligned}$$

(where $\overline{x}$ contains the variables free in Φ) we may consider closed formulas instead of specifications. Thus theorem 2 results immediately from the following lemma.

Lemma 3. (finite non-standard models)
For any $\{\mathtt{zero}, \mathtt{succ}, \mathtt{pred}\}$*-sentence* φ *there is an* $m_\varphi \in \mathbb{N}$ *such that*

$$A_{\mathbb{Z}} \models \varphi \;\Leftrightarrow\; A_{m_\varphi} \models \varphi.$$

This key lemma states the interesting phenomenon that for verifying validity of a $\{\mathtt{zero}, \mathtt{succ}, \mathtt{pred}\}$-sentence φ in the infinite standard model of integers it is sufficient to check validity in the finite model A_{m_φ}.[8] As we will see later (in section 6) this property suggests a decision procedure for the validity of $\{\mathtt{zero}, \mathtt{succ}, \mathtt{pred}\}$-sentences in the data type of integers.

Not surprisingly, it takes quite a lot of care and the rest of the current section to prove lemma 3. In particular, two further lemmas are formulated which are remarkable on their own.

For reasons of convenience we introduce some notations first. For a term $t \in T(\Sigma_{\mathbb{Z}}, X)$ and $k \in \mathbb{Z}$ the abbreviation $\mathtt{succ}^k(t)$ is used to denote the term $\underbrace{\mathtt{succ}(\cdots \mathtt{succ}(}_{k \text{ times}} t) \cdots)$ if $k \geq 0$; otherwise it denotes the term $\underbrace{\mathtt{pred}(\cdots \mathtt{pred}(}_{-k \text{ times}} t) \cdots)$. Furthermore, we define $\mathbb{N}_\infty := \mathbb{N} \cup \{\infty\}$ and $A_\infty := A_{\mathbb{Z}}$.

Lemma 4. (elimination of zero)
Let φ *a* $\{\mathtt{zero}, \mathtt{succ}, \mathtt{pred}\}$*-sentence,* x *a new variable, and* $m \in \mathbb{N}_\infty$*. Then*

$$A_m \models \varphi \;\Leftrightarrow\; A_m \models \varphi^x_{\mathtt{zero}}$$

where $\varphi^x_{\mathtt{zero}}$ *is the* $\{\mathtt{succ}, \mathtt{pred}\}$*-formula which results from replacing all occurrences of the symbol* **zero** *by* x*.*

Roughly speaking, it is stated that the symbol **zero** can be eliminated such that validity in all the algebras A_m is preserved. As a consequence, if there would exist a monomorphic specification of integers, there would also exist one with the symbol **zero** not occurring in the axioms.

[8] This reminds one very much of the *finite model property*, as it is called, (which comes up together with a proof technique called *filtration*) known in modal logic [BS84, Gab72, FL79]. Cf. also *correspondence theory* [vB84] which studies interrelations between modal and classical logic.

Proof of lemma 4. The implication "$\Leftarrow$" is trivial. For the other implication let $m \in \mathbb{N}_\infty$. We first claim that for any $\{\mathtt{zero}, \mathtt{succ}, \mathtt{pred}\}$-formula φ (not necessarily closed), $k \in \mathbb{Z}$, and any valuation $v : X \to A_m$ holds

$$A_m, v \models \varphi \quad \Leftrightarrow \quad A_m, v_k \models \varphi_{\mathtt{zero}}^{\mathtt{succ}^k(\mathtt{zero})}$$

where[9] $v_k := (\mathtt{succ}^{A_m})^k \circ v$. This can be shown with a rather straightforward (but quite technical) induction on the structure of the formula φ.

For the special case that φ is closed the claim implies that

$$A_m \models \varphi \;\Rightarrow\; A_m \models \varphi_{\mathtt{zero}}^{\mathtt{succ}^k(\mathtt{zero})} \qquad \text{for any } k \in \mathbb{Z}. \qquad (\star)$$

We now argue that all carrier elements $i \in \mathtt{int}^{A_m}$ of A_m can be denoted as a ground term of the (normal)form $\mathtt{succ}^k(\mathtt{zero})$, i.e. for each $i \in \mathtt{int}^{A_m}$ there is some $k_i \in \mathbb{Z}$ such that $i = \left(\mathtt{succ}^{k_i}(\mathtt{zero})\right)^{A_m}$.

Together with $(\star)$ it follows that

$$\begin{aligned} A_m \models \varphi \;&\Rightarrow\; A_m \models \varphi_{\mathtt{zero}}^{\mathtt{succ}^k(\mathtt{zero})} \text{ for all } k \in \mathbb{Z} \\ &\Rightarrow\; A_m \models \varphi_{\mathtt{zero}}^{x}. \end{aligned}$$

■

Lemma 5. (quantifier elimination)
For any $\{\mathtt{succ}, \mathtt{pred}\}$-formula φ there are a quantifier-free $\{\mathtt{succ}, \mathtt{pred}\}$-formula ψ (with all free variables in ψ also free in φ) and an $m_\varphi \in \mathbb{N}$ such that

$$A_m \models \psi \leftrightarrow \varphi \qquad \text{for all } m \in \mathbb{N}_\infty,\ m \geq m_\varphi.$$

The proof of lemma 5 is very much in the style of well-known quantifier elimination proofs, e.g. [End72, THEOREM 31G] where $\{\mathtt{zero}, \mathtt{succ}\}$-formulas interpreted in the algebra of natural numbers $\mathbb{N}$ are considered. The main difference is that our proof is done simultaneously for a whole class of algebras (viz. $\{A_m \mid m \text{ sufficiently large}\}$) instead of for a single fixed algebra. Notice further that we apply the proof technique of quantifier elimination to establish a "*negative*" result (viz. the *in*adequacy of specification methods) while usually it is applied to get "*positive*" results, like decidability (cf. section 6).

Proof of lemma 5. We carry out an induction on the structure of the formula φ. In the base case is φ an atomic formula and therefore quantifier-free. So we simply choose $\psi := \varphi$ and $m_\varphi := 0$.

In the induction step we first consider the case that $\varphi = \neg\varphi'$ for a certain formula φ'. The induction hypothesis supplies us with a quantifier-free formula ψ' and an $m_{\varphi'}$ such that $A_m \models \psi' \leftrightarrow \varphi'$ for all $m \geq m_{\varphi'}$. Thus, choosing $\psi := \neg\psi$ and $m_\varphi := m_{\varphi'}$ does the job.

The case that $\varphi = \varphi_1 \wedge \varphi_2$ is just as easy. By induction hypothesis there are quantifier-free formulas ψ_1, ψ_2 and $m_{\varphi_1}, m_{\varphi_2}$ such that $A_m \models \psi_1 \leftrightarrow \varphi_1$ for

[9] Here '$\circ$' denotes the usual concatenation of functions.

all $m \geq m_{\varphi_1}$ and $A_m \models \psi_2 \leftrightarrow \varphi_2$ for all $m \geq m_{\varphi_2}$. With $\psi := \psi_1 \wedge \psi_2$ and $m_\varphi := \max(m_{\varphi_1}, m_{\varphi_2})$ we get $A_m \models \psi \leftrightarrow \varphi$ for all $m \geq m_\varphi$.

It remains to consider the really interesting case that $\varphi = \exists x \varphi'$. Again the induction hypothesis supplies us with a quantifier-free formula ψ' and an $m_{\varphi'}$ such that $A_m \models \psi' \leftrightarrow \varphi'$ for all $m \geq m_{\varphi'}$. We transform ψ' in its logical equivalent disjunctive normal form (cf. e.g. [End72, COROLLARY 15C]) and get $\psi'_1 \vee \cdots \vee \psi'_n$ where the ψ'_i are conjunctions of literals. So, for all $m \geq m_{\varphi'}$ holds

$$A_m \models \exists x(\psi'_1 \vee \cdots \vee \psi'_n) \leftrightarrow \varphi$$

and therefore

$$A_m \models (\exists x \psi'_1) \vee \cdots \vee (\exists x \psi'_n) \leftrightarrow \varphi.$$

Thus, it suffices to replace the subformulas $\exists x \psi'_i$ by corresponding quantifier-free formulas ψ_i. We start with the claim, that we may assume without loss of generality that in ψ'_i do not occur equations of the form $x = \mathtt{succ}^k(x)$. The reason is that for $k = 0$ this formula is equivalent to **true** and otherwise it is $A_m \models x \neq \mathtt{succ}^k(x)$ for all $m \geq |k|$, i.e. for sufficiently large m we can replace the equation by **false**. Since any equation of the form $t_1(x) = t_2(x)$ is in each A_m equivalent[10] to some equation of the (normal)form $x = \mathtt{succ}^k(x)$ (for some appropriate k) we may even assume that in ψ'_i do not occur equations of the form $t_1(x) = t_2(x)$.

For the construction of a suitable quantifier-free formula ψ_i we first consider the case that ψ'_i contains a non-negated equation of the form $t_1(x) = t_2(y)$ (or of the form $t_1(y) = t_2(x)$) for some variable y. Is $x = \mathtt{succ}^k(y)$ the normal form of this equation the variable x does not occur in the formula $\psi_i := (\psi'_i)_x^{\mathtt{succ}^k(y)}$ (because y is different from x, due to the above claim) and it is easy to see that $(\exists x \psi'_i) \leftrightarrow \psi_i$ is valid in all A_m.

It remains to deal with the case that x does not occur in non-negated equations of ψ'_i but only in negated ones. These literals containing x can be transformed into their normal forms $x \neq t_1, \ldots, x \neq t_l$ for appropriate terms $t_1, \ldots, t_l$ (which due to the above claim do not contain x). If ψ_i denotes the remaining literals of ψ'_i we get for arbitrary m that

$$A_m \models (\exists x \psi'_i) \leftrightarrow \exists x(x \neq t_1 \wedge \cdots \wedge x \neq t_l \wedge \psi_i)$$

and since x does not occur in ψ_i, even

$$A_m \models (\exists x \psi'_i) \leftrightarrow \exists x(x \neq t_1 \wedge \cdots \wedge x \neq t_l) \wedge \psi_i. \qquad (\star\star)$$

---

[10] Notice, that the formulas

$$\mathtt{succ}(y) = x \leftrightarrow y = \mathtt{pred}(x)$$
$$\mathtt{succ}(\mathtt{pred}(x)) = x$$
$$\mathtt{pred}(\mathtt{succ}(x)) = x$$

are valid in each of the A_m.

On the other hand, it is $A_m \models \exists x(x \neq t_1 \wedge \cdots \wedge x \neq t_l)$ if only $m > l$: A simple consideration of cardinality reveals that for any l carrier elements of A_m, and in particular for the ones denoted by the terms $t_1, \ldots, t_l$, a carrier element different from these exists. Whenever $m > l$, this allows to simplify $(\star\star)$ to $A_m \models (\exists x \psi'_i) \leftrightarrow \psi_i$.

We have shown that for each ψ'_i a quantifier-free formula ψ_i can be constructed such that $A_m \models (\exists x \psi'_i) \leftrightarrow \psi_i$ for sufficiently large m. Thus, with $\psi := \psi_1 \vee \cdots \vee \psi_n$ and m_φ sufficiently large, we get $A_m \models \psi \leftrightarrow \varphi$ for all $m \geq m_\varphi$. ■

With the two strong lemmas at hand we are now able to perform a fancy proof of the key lemma.

Proof of lemma 3. Let a $\{\mathtt{zero}, \mathtt{succ}, \mathtt{pred}\}$-sentence φ be given. Due to lemma 4 we may assume that the symbol **zero** does not occur in φ; otherwise instead of φ the formula $\forall x \varphi^x_{\mathtt{zero}}$ is considered where x is a new variable.

Application of lemma 5 gives the existence of a quantifier-free $\{\mathtt{succ}, \mathtt{pred}\}$-sentence ψ and an $m_\varphi \in \mathbb{N}$ such that

$$A_m \models \psi \leftrightarrow \varphi \qquad \text{for all } m \geq m_\varphi. \qquad (\star\star\star)$$

As ψ is closed and quantifier-free it does not contain any variables at all. Furthermore also **zero** does not occur in ψ. Thus there are no terms, and consequently no equations contained in ψ. That is, ψ is built merely from the atom **false**, negation ($\neg$), and conjunction ($\wedge$), which implies that ψ is logical equivalent to either **false** or **true**. From $(\star\star\star)$ follows that either $A_m \models \varphi$ for all $m \geq m_\varphi$ or $A_m \not\models \varphi$ for all $m \geq m_\varphi$. In each case we get the equivalence

$$A_\infty \models \varphi \;\Leftrightarrow\; A_{m_\varphi} \models \varphi.$$

■

5 Inadequacy of the final algebra approach

In the previous section the data type of integers is shown to be an example manifesting the inadequacy of the loose approach to algebraic specification without the use of hidden symbols. The same example is applicable to prove the corresponding inadequacy of the final algebra approach.

Theorem 6. *There does not exist a first-order specification (without hidden symbols) with the $\Sigma_{\mathbb{Z}}$-algebra $A_{\mathbb{Z}}$ as its final model.*

Proof. By lemma 3, a specification SP with the algebra $A_{\mathbb{Z}}$ as one of its models possesses also a finite non-standard model A_m (for some $m \in \mathbb{N}$). Therefore the final model of SP, if existing at all, has to be finite too. In particular, it would be different from $A_{\mathbb{Z}}$. ■

Thus we have established the following inadequacy result.

Theorem 7. *There is a computable data type which cannot be specified using first-order axioms and final semantics (without hidden symbols).*

Of course, theorem 7 holds for any subset of first-order logic as well; e.g. one might syntactically restrict the form of axioms in order to guarantee existence of final models.

6 A decision procedure for integers

While the intention of lemma 3 was to prove that the integers cannot be specified monomorphically without the use of hiding, its proof has also the following interesting consequence:

Theorem 8. *For* $\{\mathtt{zero}, \mathtt{succ}, \mathtt{pred}\}$*-sentences validity in* $A_{\mathbb{Z}}$ *is effectively decidable.*

Proof. Validity of a given a $\{\mathtt{zero}, \mathtt{succ}, \mathtt{pred}\}$-sentence φ in $A_{\mathbb{Z}}$ can be decided as follows. First, using lemma 4, eliminate the symbol **zero** getting $\varphi' := \forall x \varphi^{x}_{\mathtt{zero}}$. Then, apply to φ' the (effective!) procedure of quantifier elimination implicit in the proof of lemma 5. This results in a quantifier-free $\{\mathtt{succ}, \mathtt{pred}\}$-sentence ψ with $A_{\mathbb{Z}} \models \varphi \leftrightarrow \psi$. As argued in the proof of lemma 3 the formula ψ is built merely from the atom **false**, negation ($\neg$), and conjunction ($\wedge$), which implies that validity of ψ is independent from $A_{\mathbb{Z}}$ and can be checked mechanically.

To summarize, for deciding validity of φ in $A_{\mathbb{Z}}$ construct the quantifier-free equivalent ψ, and check whether ψ is a tautology. ■

Notice, that lemma 3 also gives reason for a decision procedure of different nature: The quantifier elimination method implicit in the proof yields a value m_φ such that

$$A_{\mathbb{Z}} \models \varphi \;\Leftrightarrow\; A_{m_\varphi} \models \varphi.$$

Given this value, the only thing to do is to check validity of φ in the algebra A_{m_φ} which, due to the finiteness of the domain, can be performed effectively.

We have also done a (much more complicated) proof of the quantifier elimination which (due to space limitations is not presented here but) shows that one can choose $m_\varphi := |\varphi|$ where $|\varphi|$ is inductively defined (and can be easily computed) as follows:

$$\begin{array}{lcl}
|\mathbf{false}| & := & 0 \\
|t_1 = t_2| & := & \big|(|t_1|_{\mathtt{succ}} - |t_1|_{\mathtt{pred}} - |t_2|_{\mathtt{succ}} + |t_2|_{\mathtt{pred}})\big| \\
|\neg \varphi| & := & |\varphi| \\
|\varphi_1 \wedge \varphi_2| & := & \max(|\varphi_1|, |\varphi_2|) \\
|\exists x \varphi| & := & 2\,|\varphi| + 1.
\end{array}$$

Here $|t|_{\mathtt{succ}}$ denotes the number of **succ** symbols occurring in the term t, and analogously $|t|_{\mathtt{pred}}$ denotes the number of **pred** symbols in t.

7 Monomorphic specifications of integers

In theorem 2 we have shown that without the use of hidden symbols the data type of integers cannot be monomorphically specified. However, due to the completeness theorem of Bergstra & Tucker [BT82], a monomorphic specification of integers is enabled if only the signature is appropriately enriched. For example, adding the less predicate (<) (which should more accurately be written as boolean-valued function) to the signature, with the axioms

$$\begin{array}{l} \mathtt{succ(x)} = \mathtt{y} \;\leftrightarrow\; \mathtt{x} = \mathtt{pred(y)} \\ \mathtt{x} < \mathtt{succ(x)} \\ \neg\, \mathtt{x} < \mathtt{x} \\ \mathtt{x} < \mathtt{y} \;\wedge\; \mathtt{y} < \mathtt{z} \;\rightarrow\; \mathtt{x} < \mathtt{z} \end{array}$$

integers are (up to isomorphism) uniquely described.[11]

More surprisingly, adding plus (+) is already sufficient; the following axioms set up a somewhat tricky, but monomorphic integer specification:

$$\begin{array}{l} \mathtt{succ(x)} = \mathtt{y} \;\leftrightarrow\; \mathtt{x} = \mathtt{pred(y)} \\ \mathtt{zero} + \mathtt{x} = \mathtt{x} \\ \mathtt{succ(x)} + \mathtt{y} = \mathtt{succ(x+y)} \\ \mathtt{x} \neq \mathtt{zero} \rightarrow \mathtt{x} + \mathtt{x} \neq \mathtt{zero} \\ \mathtt{x} + \mathtt{succ(x)} \neq \mathtt{zero} \end{array}$$

The first three axioms are standard. The fourth axiom prevents all algebras A with

$$A \models \mathtt{succ}^{2n}(\mathtt{zero}) = \mathtt{zero} \qquad \text{for some } n \in \mathbb{N} \setminus \{0\}$$

from being models. Similarly, the last axiom prevents all algebras A with

$$A \models \mathtt{succ}^{2n+1}(\mathtt{zero}) = \mathtt{zero} \qquad \text{for some } n \in \mathbb{N}$$

from being models. Thus, none of the finite algebras A_m, $m \in \mathbb{N}$ is model of the specification.

8 Conclusions

We have provided an example of a non-artificial, computable data type which fails to possess a monomorphic first-order specification (without hidden symbols) (theorem 1). Thus (at least) for reasons of adequacy, in the loose approach to algebraic specification hiding facilities should be provided. The same holds for the final algebra approach (theorem 7).

While earlier work in this direction [Maj79, TWW82, BT87] has dealt with initial algebra semantics and (conditional) equations only, we have dealt with

[11] The monomorphicity of this specification is far from being obvious. To prove it one has to show (inductively) that for all ground literals φ either φ itself or its negation $\neg\varphi$ can be derived from the axioms (cf. [Wir90, FACT 2.3.2] or [Rei92]).

full first-order logic. Both, the example (of integers) we have chosen, as well as the proof method are completely different from the ones given in the context of initial semantics.

The integers are in some sense the "most simple" example of a data type which does not have a monomorphic specification. For the simpler signature $\Sigma = \{\mathtt{s};\ \mathtt{c} : \to \mathtt{s},\ \mathtt{f} : \mathtt{s} \to \mathtt{s}\}$ with one constant symbol c and only one unary function symbol f any term-generated Σ-algebra is either finite or freely generated and thus can be specified monomorphically.

Furthermore, all the operations (**zero**, **succ**, **pred**) of the data type are constructor functions. Thus, even facilities for distinguishing constructor functions from selector functions (e.g. through **generated by** clauses as provided e.g. in LSL [GH93] and SPECTRUM [BFG+93]) do not solve the problem of inadequacy.

Finally, notice that the hidden function question for initial algebra semantics is answered only for the case that the axioms are restricted to conditional equations [BT87]. A related question is, whether there is a computable data type which cannot be specified neither under initial algebra semantics nor under final algebra semantics. (Remember that the integers do possess an equational initial algebra specification.) In other words, does provision of both, initial and final constraints compensate for the lack of expressive power? In our most recent work [Sch97] we have answered this question negatively and thereby sharpened results from [BT87] and [TWW82]. The idea was to make use of the insight that with first-order logic formulas only "local properties" can be expressed [Han65, Gai82] (a phenomenon normally exploited to study the descriptive complexity in finite-model theory; see e.g. [FSV95]).

A remaining question is, whether first-order specifications are properly more expressive than conditional equational specifications (both without hiding facilities).[12] This means, is it possible to make up the inadequacy to some extend (but, of course, not completely) by allowing the axioms to be first-order (instead of conditional equations)?

Acknowledgments. I would like to thank A. Burandt van Schoor for valuable discussions and very useful hints.

References

[BFG+93] M. Broy, C. Facchi, R. Grosu, R. Hettler, H. Hußmann, D. Nazareth, F. Regensburger, and K. Stølen. The requirement and design specification language SPECTRUM — an informal introduction, version 1.0. Technical Report TUM-I9311, Technische Universität München, 1993.

[BG80] R.M. Burstall and J. Goguen. The semantics of Clear, a specification language. In *Proc. 1979 Copenhagen Winter School on Abstract Software Specification*, volume 86 of *LNCS*, pages 292–332. Springer, Berlin, 1980.

[12] It is already known that equations are properly more expressive than ground equations [BT87, LEMMA 4.5] and that conditional equations are properly more expressive than equations [TWW82, SECTION 3].

[BS84] R. Bull and K. Segerberg. *Basic Modal Logic*, volume II of *Handbook of Philosophical Logic*, pages 1–88. D. Reidel Publishing Company, 1984.

[BT82] J.A. Bergstra and J.V. Tucker. The completeness of the algebraic specification methods for computable data types. *Information and Control*, 54:186–200, 1982.

[BT83] J.A. Bergstra and J.V. Tucker. Initial and final algebra semantics for data type specifications: Two characterization theorems. *SIAM J. Comput.*, 12:366–387, 1983.

[BT87] J.A. Bergstra and J.V. Tucker. Algebraic specifications of computable and semicomputable data types. *Theoret. Comput. Sci.*, 50:137–181, 1987.

[Cla89] I. Claßen. Revised ACT ONE: categorical constructions for an algebraic specification language. In *Proc. Workshop on Categorical Methods in Computer Science with Aspects from Topology, Berlin*, volume 393 of *LNCS*, pages 124–141. Springer, Berlin, 1989.

[DO91] O.-J. Dahl and O. Owe. Formal development with ABEL. In *Proc. Workshop on Categorical Methods in Computer Science with Aspects from Topology, Berlin*, volume 552 of *LNCS*, pages 320–362. Springer, Berlin, 1991.

[EM85] H. Ehrig and B. Mahr. *Fundamentals of Algebraic Specification 1, Equations and Initial Semantics*, volume 6 of *EATCS Monographs on Theoretical Computer Science*. Springer, Berlin, 1985.

[End72] H.B. Enderton. *A Mathematical Introduction to Logic*. Academic Press, New York, 1972.

[Fey88] W. Fey. *Pragmatics, Concepts, Syntax, Semantics, and Correctness Notions of ACT TWO: An Algebraic Module Specification and Interconnection Language*. PhD thesis, Technische Universität Berlin, 1988.

[FL79] M.J. Fischer and R.E. Ladner. Propositional dynamic logic of regular programs. *Journal of Computer and System Sciences*, 18:194–211, 1979.

[FSV95] R. Fagin, L. Stockmeyer, and M. Vardi. On monadic NP vs. monadic co-NP. *Information and Computation*, 120:78–92, 1995.

[Gab72] Dov Gabbay. A general filtration method for modal logics. *Journal of Philosophical Logic*, 1:29–34, 1972.

[Gai82] H. Gaifman. On local and non-local properties. In J. Stern, editor, *Proc. of the Herbrand Symposium, Logic Colloquium'81*, pages 105–135. North-Holland, 1982.

[Gau92] M.-C. Gaudel. Structuring and modularizing algebraic specifications: the PLUSS specification language, evolutions and perspectives. In *STACS'92, 9th Annual Symposium on Theoretical Aspects of Computer Science*, volume 577 of *LNCS*, pages 13–18. Springer, Berlin, 1992.

[Geo91] C. George. The RAISE specification language: A tutorial. In S. Prehn and W.J. Toelenel, editors, *VDM'91, Formal Software Development Methods*, volume 551 of *LNCS*, pages 389–405. Springer, Berlin, 1991.

[GH93] J. Guttag and J. Horning. *Larch: Languages and Tools for Formal Specification*. Springer, Berlin, 1993.

[Han65] W. Hanf. Model-theoretic methods in the study of elementary logic. In J. Addison, L. Henkin, and A. Tarski, editors, *Symposium on the Theory of Models*, pages 132–145. North-Holland Publ. Co., Amsterdam, 1965.

[Maj77] M.E. Majster. Limits of the 'algebraic' specification of abstract data types. In *ACM SIGPLAN Notices*, volume 12, pages 37–42, 1977.

[Maj79] M.E. Majster. Data types, abstract data types and their specification problem. *Theoret. Comput. Sci.*, 8:89–127, 1979.

[MG85] J. Meseguer and J.A. Goguen. Initiality, induction, and computability. In M. Nivat and J. Reynolds, editors, *Algebraic Methods in Semantics*, pages 459–541. Cambridge University Press, 1985.

[Mos97] P. Mosses. CoFI: The Common Framework Initiative for algebraic specification and development. In *TAPSOFT'97: Theory and Practice of Software Development*, volume 1214 of *LNCS*, pages 115–137. Springer, Berlin, 1997.

[Rei92] W. Reif. Correctness of full first-order specifications. In *4th Conference on Software Engineering and Knowledge Engineering.* Capri, Italy, IEEE Press, 1992.

[Sch97] A. Schönegge. An answer to the hidden function question for algebraic specification methods (abstract), 4th Workshop on Logic, Language, Information and Computation, Fortaleza, Brazil. *Logic Journal of the Interest Group in Pure and Applied Logic, Oxford University Press*, 1997.

[Spi92] J.M. Spivey. *The Z Notation — A Reference Manual.* Prentice-Hall, 2nd edition, 1992.

[SW83] D.T. Sannella and M. Wirsing. A kernel language for algebraic specification and implementation. In *Proc. 1983 International Conference on Foundations of Computation Theory, Borgholm*, volume 158 of *LNCS*, pages 413–427. Springer, Berlin, 1983.

[TWW82] J.W. Thatcher, E.G. Wagner, and J.B. Wright. Data type specification: Parameterization and the power of specification techniques. In *ACM Transactions on Programming Languages and Systems*, volume 4, pages 711–732, 1982.

[vB84] J. van Benthem. *Correspondence Theory*, volume II of *Handbook of Philosophical Logic*, pages 167–247. D. Reidel Publishing Company, 1984.

[vDHK96] A. van Deursen, J. Heering, and P. Klint, editors. *Language Prototyping, An Algebraic Specification Approach*, volume 5 of *AMAST Series in Computing.* World Scientific Publishing Co., 1996.

[Wir90] M. Wirsing. *Algebraic Specification*, volume B of *Handbook of Theoretical Computer Science*, chapter 13, pages 675–788. Elsevier Science Publishers B. V., 1990.

Synchronization of Logics with Mixed Rules: Completeness Preservation

Amílcar Sernadas, Cristina Sernadas, Carlos Caleiro

Departamento de Matemática, Instituto Superior Técnico
Av. Rovisco Pais, 1096 Lisboa Codex, Portugal
email:{acs,css, ccal}@math.ist.utl.pt

Abstract. Several mechanisms for combining logics have appeared in the literature. Synchronization is one of the simplest: the language of the combined logic is the disjoint union of the given languages, but the class of models of the resulting logic is a subset of the cartesian product of the given classes of models (the interaction between the two logics is imposed by constraining the class of pairs of models). Herein, we give both a model-theoretic and a proof-theoretic account of synchronization as a categorial construction (using coproducts and cocartesian liftings). We also prove that soundness is preserved by possibly constrained synchronization and state sufficient conditions for preservation of model existence and strong completeness. We provide an application to the combination of dynamic logic and linear temporal logic.
Keywords: combination of logics, synchronization of logics, model existence, completeness, dynamic logic, temporal logic.

1 Introduction

There has been a recent growth of interest on the problem of combining logics and obtaining results about the preservation of logical properties like soundness, completeness, decidability, existence of finite models, *inter alia* (see for instance [14, 10, 4, 5, 2, 11]). Related work [13, 1, 3] motivated by applications in software engineering has addressed the problem of relating and combining institutions. The relevance to applications is very clear: the software development process is usually carried out in a heterogeneous environment of methods, languages, formalisms and platforms. For instance, we may use in the same project temporal logic and dynamic logic for specifying and verifying the envisaged software.

In a previous paper [12] we proposed two simple forms of combining logics: synchronization on formulae and synchronization on models. Herein, we continue the development of the latter mechanism by providing both proof and model theoretic categorial characterizations of synchronization. Furthermore, we prove that synchronizations preserve soundness and also model existence and completeness under suitable assumptions. This mechanism, though simple, is still useful as we explain via the example of combining dynamic logic and linear temporal logic. Indeed, synchronization seems to be the adequate form of combination in many cases when compared to other forms of combination, like temporalization [4] and fibring [6].

With synchronization, the language of the combined logic is the disjoint union of the given languages, but the class of models of the resulting logic is a subset of the cartesian product of the given classes of models: the interaction between the two logics is imposed by constraining the class of pairs of models.

In Section 2 we adopt the relevant notion of logic system as a tuple composed of language, models, satisfaction and inference rules, setting up the category we use in the rest of the paper.

In Section 3 we propose the basic mechanism of free synchronization of logic systems (with no interaction whatsoever). Synchronization without interaction is not interesting *per se*, but it is used in Section 4 in the definition of the useful mechanism of synchronization in the presence of interaction rules. We end Section 3 by showing that free synchronizations are coproducts.

In Section 4, before presenting the synchronization constrained by mixed inference rules, we first show how to extract a Hilbert system from a logic system by forgetting the semantic components. We show that the forgetful functor allows cocartesian liftings. These are used for the (categorial) definition of the constrained form of synchronization.

In Section 5 we concentrate on finding out sufficient conditions for proving that synchronizations preserve model existence and completeness since the preservation of soundness comes out already in Sections 3 and 4.

We illustrate the proposed combination mechanism by showing how to establish a useful combination of dynamic logic and linear temporal logic in Section 6 (remaining within the propositional context for the sake of economy of presentation).

2 Preliminaries

Since we are interested in both proof and model theoretic characterizations of synchronization, we need to work with a notion of logic system including both aspects. On one hand, we need models and satisfaction. On the other hand, we need inference rules. We also need an improper model that satisfies everything in order to be able to preserve completeness as we shall see. This implies no loss of generality because we can add to any logic such an improper model (if it does not exist already) without any impact on its semantic entailment. Moreover, we can assume that only one improper model exists (if there are several they can be collapsed). Therefore, we arrive at the following notion:

Definition 1. *A logic system is a tuple* $\langle L, M, \Vdash, R\rangle$ *where:*

- L *is a set;*
- M *is a pointed class with selected element* z*;*
- $\Vdash \subseteq M \times L$ *is a relation such that* $\{\varphi \in L : m \Vdash \varphi\} = L$ *iff* $m = z$*;*
- $R \subseteq \wp_{\mathrm{fin}} L \times L$.

Clearly, the elements of L are the *formulae* and the elements of M are the *models*, being z the *improper model*. Relation $\Vdash$ is the *satisfaction relation*. Each element $r = \langle Prem(r), Conc(r)\rangle$, of R is an inference *rule*: $Prem(r)$ is the (finite) set of premises and $Conc(r)$ is the conclusion. If $Prem(r) = \emptyset$ then r is said to be an *axiom*.

The entailment and derivation closures are defined as usual. We briefly review the basic definitions mainly to freeze the notation.

Definition 2. *Given a logic system, the entailment closure* $.^{\models} : \wp L \to \wp L$ *is defined as follows:* $\Psi^{\models} = \{\varphi \in L : m \Vdash \varphi \text{ whenever } m \Vdash \psi \text{ for every } \psi \in \Psi\}$.

Definition 3. *Given a logic system, we say that there is a derivation of* φ *from* Ψ *iff there is a sequence* $\psi_1, ..., \psi_m$ *of formulae such that:*

- ψ_m *is* φ;
- *for each* $i = 1, ..., m$, *the formula* ψ_i *is:*
  - *either an element of* Ψ;
  - *or* $Conc(r)$ *provided that* $r \in R$ *and every element of* $Prem(r)$ *occurs in the sequence* $\psi_1, ..., \psi_{i-1}$.

Definition 4. *Given a logic system, the derivation closure* $.^{\vdash} : \wp L \to \wp L$ *is defined as follows:* $\Psi^{\vdash} = \{\varphi \in L : \text{ there is a derivation of } \varphi \text{ from } \Psi\}$.

Definition 5. *A logic system is:*

- *sound iff* $\Psi^{\vdash} \subseteq \Psi^{\models}$ *for every* Ψ;
- *strongly complete iff* $\Psi^{\models} \subseteq \Psi^{\vdash}$ *for every* Ψ.

Definition 6. *A rule* r *in a logic system is said to be sound iff* $Conc(r) \in Prem(r)^{\models}$.

Proposition 7. A logic system is sound iff the rules are sound.

Proof:
Assume that the rules are sound and that $\varphi \in \Psi^{\vdash}$. We show that $\varphi \in \Psi^{\models}$ by induction on the length n of the derivation of φ from Ψ.
Base: $\varphi \in \Psi$. Then, of course $\varphi \in \Psi^{\models}$.
Step: φ is $Conc(r)$ for some $r \in R$. Then, $Prem(r) \subseteq \Psi^{\vdash}$ and so, using the induction hypothesis, $Prem(r) \subseteq \Psi^{\models}$. Moreover, $Conc(r) \in \Psi^{\models}$ using the soundness of r.
QED

In the sequel, we also need the notions of consistency and model existence.

Definition 8. *A set* Ψ *of formulae is said to be consistent (with respect to derivation) iff* $\Psi^{\vdash} \neq L$.

Definition 9. *A logic system is said to have the model existence property iff for every consistent set* Ψ *of formulae there is a proper model* m *such that* $m \Vdash \psi$ *for every* $\psi \in \Psi$.

Proposition 10. (Strong) completeness implies the model existence property.

Proof:
Assume that $\varphi \notin \Psi^{\vdash}$. Using completeness, there exists $m \in M$ such that $m \Vdash \Psi$ and $m \nVdash \varphi$. Thus, m is proper and the result follows. QED

We shall also need some results concerning logic systems with negation. We just require that negation has the usual semantics ($m \Vdash (\neg\varphi)$ iff $m \nVdash \varphi$, for every proper model m) and fulfils a usual metatheorem (if $\varphi \in (\Psi \cup \{(\neg\varphi)\})^{\vdash}$ then $\varphi \in \Psi^{\vdash}$).

Proposition 11. Let $\langle L, M, \Vdash, R\rangle$ be a logic system with negation, $\varphi \in L$ and $\Psi \subseteq L$. If $\varphi \notin \Psi^{\vdash}$ then $\Psi \cup \{(\neg\varphi)\}$ is consistent.

Proof:
Easily $\varphi \notin (\Psi \cup \{(\neg\varphi)\})^{\vdash}$. QED

Proposition 12. For logic systems with negation, completeness is equivalent to model existence.

Proof:
Assume that model existence holds and that $\varphi \notin \Psi^{\vdash}$. It follows that $\Psi \cup \{(\neg\varphi)\}$ is consistent and there exists a proper $m \in M$ such that $m \Vdash \Psi \cup \{(\neg\varphi)\}$. Therefore $m \nVdash \varphi$ and $\varphi \notin \Psi^{\vDash}$. QED

Proposition 13. Let $\langle L, M, \Vdash, R\rangle$ be a sound logic system with negation and $\Psi \subseteq L$. Ψ is consistent iff there is no $\varphi \in L$ such that $\varphi, (\neg\varphi) \in \Psi^{\vdash}$.

Proof:
If Ψ is inconsistent it is trivial that any formula and its negation are derivable from Ψ. On the other hand, if $\varphi, (\neg\varphi) \in \Psi^{\vdash}$ then, by soundness, Ψ cannot have proper models. Therefore, Ψ is inconsistent. QED

Proposition 14. Let $\langle L, M, \Vdash, R\rangle$ be a logic system with negation and $\{\Psi_n\}_{n \in \mathbb{N}}$ a chain of consistent sets. Then, $\Psi = \bigcup_{n \in \mathbb{N}} \Psi_n$ is consistent.

Proof:
Suppose Ψ is inconsistent. Then, for some $\varphi \in L$, $\varphi, (\neg\varphi) \in \Psi^{\vdash}$. Since derivations are finite sequences, $\Psi^{\vdash} = \bigcup_{n \in \mathbb{N}} \Psi_n^{\vdash}$. Thus, there exist $n, m \in \mathbb{N}$ such that $\varphi \in \Psi_n^{\vdash}$ and $(\neg\varphi) \in \Psi_m^{\vdash}$. Therefore, $\varphi, (\neg\varphi) \in \Psi_{max(m,n)}^{\vdash}$ and $\Psi_{max(m,n)}$ is inconsistent. QED

We conclude this section with the definition of the category of sound logic systems that we shall use in the rest of the paper.

Definition 15. *A logic system morphism* $h : \langle L, M, \Vdash, R\rangle \to \langle L', M', \Vdash', R'\rangle$ *is a pair* $\langle \overrightarrow{h}, \overleftarrow{h}\rangle$ *where:*

- $\overrightarrow{h} : L \to L'$;

– $\overleftarrow{h} : M' \to M$;

such that:

1. $\overrightarrow{h}(Conc(r)) \in \overrightarrow{h}(Prem(r))^{\vdash'}$ *for each* $r \in R$;
2. $\overleftarrow{h}(z') = z$;
3. $m' \Vdash' \overrightarrow{h}(\varphi)$ *iff* $\overleftarrow{h}(m') \Vdash \varphi$.

Condition 1. imposes the preservation of inference rules. Condition 2. states that the improper model is preserved. Condition 3. is known as the satisfaction condition [7]. Note that these morphisms preserve entailment and derivation:

Proposition 16. Let $h : \langle L, M, \Vdash, R\rangle \to \langle L', M', \Vdash', R'\rangle$ be a logic system morphism. Then:

– $\overrightarrow{h}(\Psi^{\vDash}) \subseteq \overrightarrow{h}(\Psi)^{\vDash'}$;
– $\overrightarrow{h}(\Psi^{\vdash}) \subseteq \overrightarrow{h}(\Psi)^{\vdash'}$.

Proof:
1. Assume that $\varphi \in \Psi^{\vDash}$ and that $m' \Vdash' \overrightarrow{h}(\psi)$ for every $\psi \in \Psi$. Then, $\overleftarrow{h}(m') \Vdash \psi$ for every $\psi \in \Psi$, hence $\overleftarrow{h}(m') \Vdash \varphi$, so $m' \Vdash' \overrightarrow{h}(\varphi)$ and therefore $\overrightarrow{h}(\varphi) \in \overrightarrow{h}(\Psi)^{\vDash'}$.
2. Assume that $\varphi \in \Psi^{\vdash}$. We prove the result by induction on the length n of the derivation of φ from Ψ.
Base: $n = 1$. Then, $\varphi \in \Psi$, hence $\overrightarrow{h}(\varphi) \in \overrightarrow{h}(\Psi)$ and so $\overrightarrow{h}(\varphi) \in \overrightarrow{h}(\Psi)^{\vdash'}$.
Step: φ is $Conc(r)$ for some $r \in R$. Then, $Prem(r) \subseteq \Psi^{\vdash}$, therefore, by the induction hypothesis $\overrightarrow{h}(Prem(r)) \subseteq \overrightarrow{h}(\Psi)^{\vdash'}$ and so $\overrightarrow{h}(Conc(r)) \in \overrightarrow{h}(\Psi)^{\vdash'}$. QED

Proposition 17. Sound logic systems and their morphisms constitute the category *Lsy*.

Note that we might work with all logic systems (instead of concentrating on the sound ones). However, some results below only hold for sound systems (namely, the cocartesian lifting in Section 4). And anyway we are not interested in unsound logic systems.

3 Free synchronization

Before presenting the main construction of the paper (synchronization of logic systems with additional mixed rules) it is worthwhile to look first at free synchronization (without any interaction between the given logic systems). The basic idea is as follows. The language is the disjoint union of the given languages and the class of models is the cartesian product of the given classes of models. Satisfaction is componentwise. The rules are just put together.

Definition 18. *The free synchronization of the logic systems* $\langle L', M', \Vdash', R' \rangle$ *and* $\langle L'', M'', \Vdash'', R'' \rangle$ *is the logic system*

$$\langle L', M', \Vdash', R' \rangle \oplus \langle L'', M'', \Vdash'', R'' \rangle = \langle L, M, \Vdash, R \rangle$$

where:

- $L = L' \oplus L''$ *(disjoint union) with injections* i', i'';
- $M = M' \otimes M''$ *(cartesian product) with projections* p', p'' *and the improper model* $\langle z', z'' \rangle$;
- $m \Vdash i'(\varphi')$ *iff* $p'(m) \Vdash' \varphi'$ *and* $m \Vdash i''(\varphi'')$ *iff* $p''(m) \Vdash'' \varphi''$;
- $R = i'(R') \cup i''(R'')$.

The notation we chose for the free synchronization is well justified by the following categorial characterization:

Proposition 19. Free synchronizations are coproducts in *Lsy*.

Proof:
1. Soundness. We just prove that each rule in R is sound. Let $r' \in R'$ and assume that $\langle m', m'' \rangle \Vdash Prem(i'(r'))$. Then, $m' \Vdash' Prem(r')$ and, using the soundness of r', we have $m' \Vdash' Conc(r')$ and so $\langle m', m'' \rangle \Vdash Conc(i'(r'))$.
2. Injections: $\langle i', p' \rangle : \langle L', M', \Vdash', R' \rangle \to \langle L', M', \Vdash', R' \rangle \oplus \langle L'', M'', \Vdash'', R'' \rangle$ and $\langle i'', p'' \rangle : \langle L'', M'', \Vdash'', R'' \rangle \to \langle L', M', \Vdash', R' \rangle \oplus \langle L'', M'', \Vdash'', R'' \rangle$.
3. Universal property: let $f' : \langle L', M', \Vdash', R' \rangle \to \langle L''', M''', \Vdash''', R''' \rangle$ and $f'' : \langle L'', M'', \Vdash'', R'' \rangle \to \langle L''', M''', \Vdash''', R''' \rangle$ be any morphisms in *Lsy*. Then, the unique morphism $k : \langle L', M', \Vdash', R' \rangle \oplus \langle L'', M'', \Vdash'', R'' \rangle \to \langle L''', M''', \Vdash''', R''' \rangle$ such that $k \circ \langle i', p' \rangle = f'$ and $k \circ \langle i'', p'' \rangle = f''$ is $\langle \overrightarrow{k}, \overleftarrow{k} \rangle$ where $\overrightarrow{k} : L' \oplus L'' \to L'''$ such that $\overrightarrow{k}(i'(\varphi')) = \overrightarrow{f'}(\varphi')$ and $\overrightarrow{k}(i''(\varphi'')) = \overrightarrow{f''}(\varphi'')$ and $\overleftarrow{k} : M''' \to M' \otimes M''$ such that $\overleftarrow{k}(m''') = \langle \overleftarrow{f'}(m'''), \overleftarrow{f''}(m''') \rangle$. QED

4 Synchronization constrained by mixed rules

The basic idea is to enrich a free synchronization with additional mixed rules imposing interaction between the given logic systems. We go directly to the categorial definition (cocartesian lifting) since it is more elegant. But, to this end, we need first to introduce the category of Hilbert systems and a forgetful functor from logic systems to Hilbert systems.

Definition 20. *A Hilbert system is a pair* $\langle L, R \rangle$ *where:*

- L *is a set;*
- $R \subseteq \wp_{\mathrm{fin}} L \times L$.

Clearly, as before, we can extract a *derivation closure* from a Hilbert system.

Definition 21. *A Hilbert system morphism* $h : \langle L, R\rangle \to \langle L', R'\rangle$ *is a map* $h : L \to L'$ *such that* $h(Conc(r)) \in h(Prem(r))^{\vdash'}$ *for each* $r \in R$.

Proposition 22. Hilbert systems and their morphisms constitute the category *Hsy*.

Proposition 23. The maps

- $N(\langle L, M, \Vdash, R\rangle) = \langle L, R\rangle$
- $N(\langle \vec{h}, \overleftarrow{h}\rangle) = \vec{h}$

constitute the functor $N : Lsy \to Hsy$.

Proposition 24. For each $\langle L, M, \Vdash, R\rangle$ in *Lsy* and each morphism $h : \langle L, R\rangle \to \langle L', R'\rangle$ in *Hsy* such that h is bijective, the morphism

$$\langle h\rangle : \langle L, M, \Vdash, R\rangle \to \langle L', M', \Vdash', R'\rangle$$

where

- M' is the subclass of all $m \in M$ such that, for each $r' \in R'$,
$$m \Vdash h^{-1}(Conc(r')) \text{ if } m \Vdash h^{-1}(Prem(r'))$$
- $m' \Vdash' \varphi'$ iff $m' \Vdash h^{-1}(\varphi')$
- $\langle h\rangle = \langle h, \overleftarrow{h}\rangle$ where $\overleftarrow{h}$ is an inclusion

is cocartesian by N for h on $\langle L, M, \Vdash, R\rangle$.

Proof:
1. $\langle L', M', \Vdash', R'\rangle$ is a sound logic system: comes directly from the definition of M'.
2. $\langle h\rangle$ is a morphism in *Lsy*. The satisfaction condition holds taking into account the definition of $\Vdash'$.
3. Universal property. Let $f : \langle L, M, \Vdash, R\rangle \to \langle L'', M'', \Vdash'', R''\rangle$ be any morphism in *Lsy* and $g : \langle L', R'\rangle \to \langle L'', R''\rangle$ be any morphism in *Hsy* such that $g \circ h = \vec{f}$. Then,
(a) $\langle g, \overleftarrow{f}\rangle$ is a morphism in *Lsy*. We have to show that $\overleftarrow{f}(m'') \in M'$. Assume that $\overleftarrow{f}(m'') \Vdash h^{-1}(Prem(r'))$. So, using the satisfaction condition for f, we get $m'' \Vdash'' \vec{f}(h^{-1}(Prem(r')))$. Therefore $m'' \Vdash'' g(Prem(r'))$ and, using the soundness of $g(r')$, we get $m'' \Vdash'' g(Conc(r'))$. Hence, $m'' \Vdash'' \vec{f}(h^{-1}(Conc(r')))$ and, using the satisfaction condition for f, we get $\overleftarrow{f}(m'') \Vdash h^{-1}(Conc(r'))$.
(b) $\langle g, \overleftarrow{f}\rangle$ is the unique morphism such that $\langle g, \overleftarrow{f}\rangle \circ \langle h\rangle = f$: direct consequence.
QED

We denote by $h(\langle L, M, \Vdash, R\rangle)$ the codomain of the cocartesian morphism above.

We are finally ready to introduce synchronization constrained by mixed rules. We start by making precise what we mean by a mixed inference rule.

Definition 25. *Within the context of a free synchronization of two logic systems* $s' = \langle L', M', \Vdash', R' \rangle$ *and* $s'' = \langle L'', M'', \Vdash'', R'' \rangle$*, a mixed* $s' \to s''$*-rule is a pair* $x = \langle Prem(x), Conc(x) \rangle$ *where* $Prem(x) \in \wp_{\text{fin}} i'(L')$ *and* $Conc(x) \in i''(L'')$.

Definition 26. *Let* $\langle L', M', \Vdash', R' \rangle$ *and* $\langle L'', M'', \Vdash'', R'' \rangle$ *be sound logic systems,* X *a set of mixed* $s' \to s''$*-rules and* Y *a set of mixed* $s'' \to s'$*-rules both within their free synchronization. Then, the synchronization of these logic systems constrained by* X *and* Y *is the sound logic system*

$$\langle L', M', \Vdash', R' \rangle \overset{XY}{\oplus} \langle L'', M'', \Vdash'', R'' \rangle = id(\langle L', M', \Vdash', R' \rangle \oplus \langle L'', M'', \Vdash'', R'' \rangle)$$

corresponding to the cocartesian lifting for the identity map id on $L' \oplus L''$ *taken as the morphism in Hsy*

$$id : \langle L' \oplus L'', i'(R') \cup i''(R'') \rangle \to \langle L' \oplus L'', i'(R') \cup i''(R'') \cup X \cup Y \rangle.$$

As we shall see, it is useful to distinguish the special case of *one-way* constrained synchronization when for instance $Y = \emptyset$. In this case all the mixed rules are of type $s' \to s''$.

5 Preservation results

We have already seen that soundness is preserved by synchronization (both free and constrained). Therefore we can state:

Theorem 27. Soundness is preserved by both free and constrained synchronization.

It remains to investigate the preservation of completeness. To this end, we start by looking at the preservation of the model existence property by free synchronization, after two lemmas.

Lemma 28. Let $\langle L, M, \Vdash, R \rangle = \langle L', M', \Vdash', R' \rangle \oplus \langle L'', M'', \Vdash'', R'' \rangle$. Then, we have $i'(\Psi'^{\vdash'}) = i'(\Psi')^{\vdash}$ and $i''(\Psi'^{\vdash''}) = i''(\Psi'')^{\vdash}$.

Proof:
Assume that $\varphi \in i'(\Psi')^{\vdash}$. We prove by induction on the length n of the derivation of φ from $i'(\Psi')$ that $\varphi \in i'(\Psi'^{\vdash'})$.
Base: $n = 1$. Then, $\varphi \in i'(\Psi')$, hence φ is $i'(\varphi')$ for some $\varphi' \in \Psi'$ and so $i'(\varphi') \in i'(\Psi'^{\vdash'})$.
Step: φ is $i'(Conc(r'))$ for some $r' \in R'$. Then, $i'(Prem(r')) \subseteq i'(\Psi')^{\vdash}$ and, using the induction hypothesis, $i'(Prem(r')) \subseteq i'(\Psi'^{\vdash'})$. Therefore, $Prem(r') \subseteq \Psi'^{\vdash'}$, hence $Conc(r') \in \Psi'^{\vdash'}$ and so $i'(Conc(r')) \in i'(\Psi'^{\vdash'})$. QED

Therefore, free synchronization is a conservative extension of the two components. As an immediate corollary we get:

Lemma 29. Let $\langle L, M, \Vdash, R \rangle = \langle L', M', \Vdash', R' \rangle \oplus \langle L'', M'', \Vdash'', R'' \rangle$. Then, we have $i'(\Psi'^{\vdash'}) \cup i''(\Psi''^{\vdash''}) = (i'(\Psi') \cup i''(\Psi''))^{\vdash}$.

We now prove that both model existence and completeness are preserved by free synchronization.

Proposition 30. Given two logic systems s', s'' with the model existence property, their free synchronization has the model existence property.

Proof:
Let $s' \oplus s'' = \langle L', M', \Vdash', R' \rangle \oplus \langle L'', M'', \Vdash'', R'' \rangle = \langle L, M, \Vdash, R \rangle$ and assume that $\Psi = i'(\Psi') \cup i''(\Psi'') \subseteq L$ is consistent. If $i'(\varphi') \notin \Psi^{\vdash}$ then, $\varphi' \notin \Psi'^{\vdash'}$ and, using model existence in s', there exists $m' \in M'$ such that $m' \Vdash' \Psi'$. Thus, $\langle m', z'' \rangle \Vdash \Psi$. Analogously if $i''(\varphi'') \notin \Psi^{\vdash}$. QED

A similar argument is used for completeness.

Proposition 31. Given two (strongly) complete logic systems s', s'', their free synchronization is (strongly) complete.

Proof:
Let $s' \oplus s'' = \langle L', M', \Vdash', R' \rangle \oplus \langle L'', M'', \Vdash'', R'' \rangle = \langle L, M, \Vdash, R \rangle$ and assume that $\Psi = i'(\Psi') \cup i''(\Psi'') \subseteq L$. If $i'(\varphi') \notin \Psi^{\vdash}$ then $\varphi' \notin \Psi'^{\vdash'}$ and, using completeness of s', there exists $m' \in M'$ such that $m' \Vdash' \Psi'$ and $m' \nVdash' \varphi'$. Thus, $\langle m', z'' \rangle \in M$ shows that $i'(\varphi') \notin \Psi^{\vDash}$. Analogously if $i''(\varphi'') \notin \Psi^{\vdash}$. QED

The constrained case is harder. We start by looking at the simpler case of one-way constrained synchronization.

Proposition 32. Given two logic systems s' and s'' with the model existence property and a set X of $s' \to s''$-rules, their synchronization constrained by X and $\emptyset$ has the model existence property.

Proof:
Let $s' \overset{X\,\emptyset}{\oplus} s'' = \langle L', M', \Vdash', R' \rangle \overset{X\,\emptyset}{\oplus} \langle L'', M'', \Vdash'', R'' \rangle = \langle L, M''', \Vdash''', R''' \rangle$ and assume that $\Psi = i'(\Psi') \cup i''(\Psi'') \subseteq L$ is consistent. We consider two cases.
1. $i'(L') \nsubseteq \Psi^{\vdash'''}$. Then, Ψ' is consistent in s' and, using the model existence property, there exists a proper $m' \in M'$ such that $m' \Vdash' \Psi'$. Thus, $\langle m', z'' \rangle \in M'''$ since z'' satisfies every conclusion of rule in X and $\langle m', z'' \rangle \Vdash''' \Psi$.
2. $i'(L') \subseteq \Psi^{\vdash'''}$. Clearly, $i''(L'') \nsubseteq \Psi^{\vdash'''}$. Since only $s' \to s''$-rules are added, $\Phi'' = \Psi'' \cup \{\varphi'' \in L'' : i''(\varphi'') \text{ is } Conc(x) \text{ for some } x \in X\}$ is consistent in s''. By model existence, there exists a proper $m'' \in M''$ such that $m'' \Vdash'' \Phi''$. Thus, $m'' \Vdash'' \Psi''$ and $\langle z', m'' \rangle \in M'''$ since m'' satisfies every conclusion of rule in X. Therefore, $\langle z', m'' \rangle \Vdash''' \Psi$. QED

As far as completeness is concerned we shall need to work with logics with negation (recall that, in this case, model existence is equivalent to completeness). We also require that the constrained logic satisfies, at least, the metatheorem required for negation, although it may not be a logic with negation. Furthermore, we require that the set of mixed rules introduced is countable.

Note that the same applies to two-way synchronization and so we shall only do the proof in the general case.

Proposition 33. Given two logic systems s' and s'' with negation and the model existence property, a set X of $s' \to s''$-rules and a set Y of $s'' \to s'$-rules such that $X \cup Y$ is countable and the metatheorem of negation is fulfilled by $s = s' \overset{XY}{\oplus} s''$, s has the model existence property.

Proof:
Let $s = s' \overset{XY}{\oplus} s'' = \langle L', M', \Vdash', R' \rangle \overset{XY}{\oplus} \langle L'', M'', \Vdash'', R'' \rangle = \langle L, M''', \Vdash''', R''' \rangle$ and assume that $\Psi = i'(\Psi') \cup i''(\Psi'') \subseteq L$ is consistent. We consider two cases.
1. If $i'(L') \subseteq \Psi^{\vdash'''}$ and $i''(L'') \not\subseteq \Psi^{\vdash'''}$ then the set $\Phi'' = \Psi'' \cup \{\varphi'' \in L'' : i''(\varphi'')$ is $Conc(x)$ for some $x \in X\}$ is consistent in s''. By model existence, there exists a proper $m'' \in M''$ such that $m'' \Vdash'' \Phi''$. Thus, $m'' \Vdash'' \Psi''$ and $\langle z', m'' \rangle \in M'''$ since every rule is satisfied. Therefore, $\langle z', m'' \rangle \Vdash''' \Psi$. Analogously if $i''(L'') \subseteq \Psi^{\vdash'''}$ and $i'(L') \not\subseteq \Psi^{\vdash'''}$.
2. If $i'(L') \not\subseteq \Psi^{\vdash'''}$ and $i''(L'') \not\subseteq \Psi \vdash'''$ then both Ψ' in s' and Ψ'' in s'' are consistent. Given an enumeration $r_1, r_2, \ldots$ of $X \cup Y$ we proceed as follows. Define $\Phi'_0 = \Psi'$ and $\Phi''_0 = \Psi''$ and then, inductively:

- if $r_{n+1} \in X$
  - $\Phi'_{n+1} = \Phi'_n$, $\Phi''_{n+1} = \Phi''_n \cup \{Conc(r_{n+1})\}$ if $Prem(r_{n+1}) \subseteq (\Phi'_n \cup \Phi''_n)^{\vdash'''}$;
  - $\Phi'_{n+1} = \Phi'_n \cup \{(\neg \psi')\}$, $\Phi''_{n+1} = \Phi''_n$ for a chosen $i'(\psi') \in Prem(r_{n+1})$ such that $i'(\psi') \notin (\Phi'_n \cup \Phi''_n)^{\vdash'''}$;
- *mutatis mutandis* if $r_{n+1} \in Y$.

Clearly, both $\Phi' = \bigcup_{n \in \mathbb{N}} \Phi'_n$ and $\Phi'' = \bigcup_{n \in \mathbb{N}} \Phi''_n$ are chains of consistent sets and hence consistent. By model existence on both s' and s'', there exist proper models $m' \in M'$ and $m'' \in M''$ such that $m' \Vdash' \Phi'$ and $m'' \Vdash'' \Phi''$. By construction, $\langle m', m'' \rangle \in M'''$ and $\langle m', m'' \rangle \Vdash''' \Psi$. QED

A similar argument is used to prove completeness preservation.

Proposition 34. Given two (strongly) complete logic systems s' and s'' with negation, a set X of $s' \to s''$-rules and a set Y of $s'' \to s'$-rules such that $X \cup Y$ is countable and the metatheorem of negation is fulfilled by $s = s' \overset{XY}{\oplus} s''$, s is (strongly) complete.

Proof:
Let $s = s' \overset{XY}{\oplus} s'' = \langle L', M', \Vdash', R' \rangle \overset{XY}{\oplus} \langle L'', M'', \Vdash'', R'' \rangle = \langle L, M''', \Vdash''', R''' \rangle$. Let $\Psi = i'(\Psi') \cup i''(\Psi'') \subseteq L$ and assume, without loss of generality, that $i'(\varphi') \notin \Psi^{\vdash'''}$. Again we have to consider two cases.
1. $i''(L'') \subseteq \Psi^{\vdash'''}$. Then, $\Phi' = \Psi' \cup \{\psi' : i'(\psi')$ is $Conc(y)$ for some $y \in Y\}$ is such that $\varphi' \notin \Phi'^{\vdash'}$. By completeness in s', there exists $m' \in M'$ such that $m' \Vdash' \Phi'$ and $m' \nVdash \varphi'$. Thus, $\langle m', z'' \rangle \in M'''$ since every rule is satisfied and $\langle m', z'' \rangle$ shows that $i'(\varphi') \notin \Psi^{\vDash'''}$.
2. $i''(L'') \not\subseteq \Psi^{\vdash'''}$. Then, both $\Psi' \cup \{(\neg \varphi')\}$ in s' and Ψ'' in s'' are consistent. Given an enumeration $r_1, r_2, \ldots$ of $X \cup Y$ we proceed as in the previous proof. Let $\Phi'_0 = \Psi' \cup \{(\neg \varphi')\}$ and $\Phi''_0 = \Psi''$ and then, inductively:

- if $r_{n+1} \in X$
  - $\Phi'_{n+1} = \Phi'_n$, $\Phi''_{n+1} = \Phi''_n \cup \{Conc(r_{n+1})\}$ if $Prem(r_{n+1}) \subseteq (\Phi'_n \cup \Phi''_n)^{\vdash'''}$;
  - $\Phi'_{n+1} = \Phi'_n \cup \{(\neg \psi')\}$, $\Phi''_{n+1} = \Phi''_n$ for a chosen $i'(\psi') \in Prem(r_{n+1})$ such that $i'(\psi') \notin (\Phi'_n \cup \Phi''_n)^{\vdash'''}$;
- *mutatis mutandis* if $r_{n+1} \in Y$.

Clearly, both $\Phi' = \bigcup_{n \in I\!N} \Phi'_n$ and $\Phi'' = \bigcup_{n \in I\!N} \Phi''_n$ are chains of consistent sets and hence consistent. By model existence on both s' and s'', there exist proper models $m' \in M'$ and $m'' \in M''$ such that $m' \Vdash' \Phi'$ and $m'' \Vdash'' \Phi''$. By construction, $\langle m', m'' \rangle \in M'''$, and $\langle m', m'' \rangle \Vdash''' \Psi$. QED

Theorem 35. Model existence is preserved by both free and one-way constrained synchronization, and also by two-way constrained synchronization of logics with negation with a countable set of rules when the metatheorem of negation holds.

Theorem 36. (Strong) completeness is preserved by free synchronization, and also by constrained synchronization of logics with negation with a countable set of rules when the metatheorem of negation holds.

6 Application

We now illustrate the proposed mechanism with the constrained synchronization of the weakest (propositional) dynamic logic (see for instance [9]) and the (propositional) linear temporal logic (see for instance [8]). For the sake of simplicity we remain within the propositional realm, although the problem is of greater practical significance within the first order setting.

We assume that we are given a set of propositional symbols Π and a finite set of action symbols $\Delta = \{\delta_1, ..., \delta_n\}$ such that $\Pi \cap \Delta = \emptyset$. The problem is to combine the following logic systems:

- $D = \langle L', M', \Vdash', R' \rangle$ the dynamic logic system over the signature $\langle \Pi, \Delta \rangle$;
- $T = \langle L'', M'', \Vdash'', R'' \rangle$ the linear temporal logic system over the signature $\Pi \cup \Delta$.

With respect to D, recall that:

- $L' = \Pi \mid (\neg L') \mid (L' \Rightarrow L') \mid ([\Delta]L')$;
- each proper model is a triple $\langle S', d', v' \rangle$ with S' a non empty set (of states), $d' : \Delta \to \wp(S' \times S')$ and $v' : S' \to \wp\Pi$;
- satisfaction is straightforward; just note that:
  - $\langle S', d', v' \rangle, s' \Vdash' ([\delta]\varphi)$ iff $\langle S', d', v' \rangle, k' \Vdash' \varphi$ for every $k' \in S'$ such that $\langle s', k' \rangle \in d'(\delta)$;
- the rules are straightforward; for instance normality is as follows:
  - $\langle \emptyset, (([\delta](\varphi \Rightarrow \psi)) \Rightarrow (([\delta]\varphi) \Rightarrow ([\delta]\psi))) \rangle$.

With respect to T, recall that:

- $L'' = \Pi \cup \Delta \mid (\neg L'') \mid (L'' \Rightarrow L'') \mid (\mathsf{X} L'') \mid (\mathsf{G} L'')$;
- each proper model is a map $m'' : \mathbb{N} \to \wp(\Pi \cup \Delta)$;
- satisfaction is straightforward; just note that:
  - $m'', n'' \Vdash'' (\mathsf{X}\,\varphi)$ iff $m'', n''+1 \Vdash'' \varphi$;
  - $m'', n'' \Vdash'' (\mathsf{G}\,\varphi)$ iff $m'', k'' \Vdash'' \varphi$ for every $k'' \geq n''$;
- the rules are straightforward; for instance induction is as follows:
  - $\langle \emptyset, (\varphi \Rightarrow ((\mathsf{G}(\varphi \Rightarrow (\mathsf{X}\,\varphi))) \Rightarrow (\mathsf{G}\,\varphi))) \rangle$.

The idea is to use T as a temporal action logic where $m'', n'' \Vdash'' \delta$ means that action δ happens at instant n''.

If we need to write specifications using formulae from both logics, we should work on the synchronization of D and T constrained by $D \to T$-rules such as (where α is a propositional formula over the signature Π):

- $\langle \{i'(\alpha)\}, i''(\alpha) \rangle$;
- $\langle \{i'(([\delta]\alpha))\}, i''((\delta \Rightarrow (\mathsf{X}\,\alpha))) \rangle$;
- $\langle \emptyset, i''((\delta_1 \vee \ldots \vee \delta_n)) \rangle$.

The first rule imposes that propositional assertions in D carry over to T. The second rule brings into T some properties of actions specified within D. The third rule has the nature of a closure rule and it is important when proving temporal invariants using properties imposed in D.

As an example, within the synchronization of D and T constrained as above, we can derive $i''((\pi_1 \Rightarrow (\mathsf{G}(\pi_1 \vee \pi_2))))$ from the set $\{i'(([\delta_k]\pi_1)) : k \text{ odd}\} \cup \{i'(([\delta_k]\pi_2)) : k \text{ even}\}$ of assumptions.

In the opposite direction, we might want to impose the following $T \to D$-rules (where α is again a propositional formula over the signature Π):

- $\langle \{i''(\alpha)\}, i'(\alpha) \rangle$;
- $\langle \{i''((\mathsf{X}\,\alpha))\}, i'((([\delta_1]\alpha) \wedge \ldots \wedge ([\delta_n]\alpha))) \rangle$.

Note that once we have rules in both directions, a proof in the combination of D and T may be carried out by reasoning alternatively in both logics.

7 Concluding remarks

Motivated by software engineering applications, we have been investigating alternative mechanisms for combining logics. Herein, we present in detail model-theoretic and proof-theoretic accounts of one of the simplest mechanisms: constrained synchronization. In this form of combination, the language of the combined logic is the disjoint union of the given languages, but the class of models of the resulting logic is a subset of the cartesian product of the given classes of models: the interaction between the two logics is imposed by constraining the class of pairs of models via mixed inference rules. We show the usefulness of synchronization in a plain but meaningful example (putting together propositional dynamic logic and propositional linear temporal logic). Of course, setting up the desired set of mixed rules depends on the particular desired interplay between the pair of logics being considered and on the particular intended application of the synchronized logic and is therefore out of the scope of this paper.

Along the way we give categorial characterizations of both free synchronization (coproduct) and constrained synchronization (cocartesian lifting). We also establish that both preserve soundness and give sufficient conditions for preservation of model existence and strong completeness.

The results are general since nothing is assumed about the given logic systems to be combined, with the exception of model existence and completeness preservation of general constrained synchronization. We found sufficient conditions but whether they are necessary or not is an open problem.

In a related effort we are investigating categorial characterizations of another widely known form of combination: fibring [6, 11]. It seems that no single form of combination will be sufficient to deal with the problems that practitioners face in software development. Therefore, we believe that a deep understanding of all forms of combination already identified in the literature is much needed. Later on, it will also be useful to establish results relating different forms of combination.

Another interesting line of research that we are following is aimed at the computability issues of combination of logics. Besides the obvious question concerning the preservation of (semi)decidability other computability problems appear, namely concerning morphisms relating logics.

Acknowledgments

We are grateful to our colleagues in the ACL initiative for many discussions on the role of categorial techniques in computing. We are also grateful to our colleagues in the FLIRTS group, namely Egidio Astesiano, Maura Cerioli, José Fiadeiro, Till Mossakowski, Wiesiek Pawlowski, Gianna Reggio, Antonino Salibra, Giuseppe Scollo, Andrzej Tarlecki, Uwe Wolter and Elena Zucca with whom we discussed the idea of combining logics within the institutional setting. This work was partially supported by the PRAXIS XXI Program and JNICT, as well as by PRAXIS XXI Projects 2/2.1/MAT/262/94 SitCalc, PCEX/P/MAT/46/96 ACL plus 2/2.1/TIT/1658/95 LogComp, and ESPRIT IV Working Groups 22704 ASPIRE and 23531 FIREworks.

References

1. M. Arrais and J. Fiadeiro. Unifying theories in different institutions. In M. Haveraaen, O. Owe, and O.-J. Dahl, editors, *Recent Trends in Data Type Specification*, pages 81–101. Springer-Verlag, LNCS 1130, 1996.
2. P. Blackburn and M. de Rijke. Why combine logics. *Studia Logica*, 58, 1997. In print.
3. M. Cerioli and J. Meseguer. May I borrow your logic? (Transporting logical structures along maps). *Theoretical Computer Science*, 173:311–347, 1997.

4. M. Finger and D. Gabbay. Adding a temporal dimension to a logic system. *Journal of Logic, Language and Information*, 1:203–233, 1992.
5. M. Finger and D. Gabbay. Combining temporal logic systems. *Notre Dame Journal of Formal Logic*, 37:204–232, 1996.
6. D. Gabbay. An overview of fibred semantics and the combination of logics. In F. Baader and K. Schulz, editors, *Frontiers of Combining Systems*, pages 1–55. Kluwer Academic Publishers, 1996.
7. J. Goguen and R. Burstall. Institutions: Abstract model theory for specification and programming. *Journal of the ACM*, 39(1):95–146, 1992.
8. R. Goldblatt. *Logics of Time and Computation*. CSLI, 1992. Second edition.
9. D. Harel. Dynamic logic. In D. Gabbay and F. Guenthner, editors, *Handbook of Philosophical Logic, vol II*, pages 497–604. Kluwer, 1984.
10. M. Kracht and F. Wolter. Properties of independently axiomatizable bimodal logics. *Journal of Symbolic Logic*, 56(4):1469–1485, 1991.
11. A. Sernadas, C. Sernadas, and C. Caleiro. Fibring of logics as a categorial construction. Research report, Section of Computer Science, Department of Mathematics, Instituto Superior Técnico, 1096 Lisboa, Portugal, 1997. Submitted for publication.
12. A. Sernadas, C. Sernadas, and C. Caleiro. Synchronization of logics. *Studia Logica*, 58, 1997. In print.
13. A. Tarlecki. Moving between logical systems. In M. Haveraaen, O. Owe, and O.-J. Dahl, editors, *Recent Trends in Data Type Specification*, pages 478–502. Springer-Verlag, LNCS 1130, 1996.
14. R. Thomason. Combinations of tense and modality. In D. Gabbay and F. Guenthner, editors, *Handbook of Philosophical Logic II*, pages 135–165. Kluwer Academic Publishers, 1984.

Symbolic Bisimulation for Full LOTOS

Carron Shankland[1]* and Muffy Thomas[2]

[1] Department of Computing Science and Mathematics, University of Stirling
[2] Department of Computing Science, University of Glasgow

Abstract. A *symbolic* semantics for Full LOTOS in terms of *symbolic* transition systems is defined, following the approach taken for message passing CCS in [HL95a], altered to take account of the particular features of LOTOS (multi-way synchronisation, value negotiation, selection predicates). Symbolic bisimulation over symbolic transition systems is defined, and symbolic bisimulation on ground behaviour expressions is shown to preserve the usual concrete (strong) bisimulation on the standard semantics. Finally, a modal logic based on symbolic transition systems is defined. All are illustrated with reference to examples.

1 Introduction

Full LOTOS[3] is a message passing process algebra which combines some features of both CSP [Hoa85] and CCS [Mil89]. In order to accommodate multi-way synchronisation, i.e. associative synchronisation between two or more processes, the standard semantics of LOTOS gives meaning only to processes with *ground* data; the semantics is in terms of structured labelled transition systems. This means that query events do not correspond to a single transition, but rather a set of transitions, one for each possible ground instance of the query variable(s). For example, when $B = g?x : S; B'$ then there is a transition $B \xrightarrow{gv} B'$ for each value v of sort S (i.e. each for each equivalence class in the associated initial algebra). The implication of this semantics is that a query event offer is equivalent (with respect to strong bisimulation) to an infinite choice over all values of the data type, e.g. $in?x : Nat; P$ is equivalent to $in!0; P \;[]\; in!1; P \;[]\; in!2; P \;[]\; \ldots$

While the advantage of this semantics is that it easily accomodates multi-way synchronisation between any number of processes (CCS only allows two-way synchronisation), it can result in infinite transition systems (both in depth and breadth) which are difficult to reason about. Moreover, by *embedding* the data values in the actions, any uniformities in the actions of the processes are lost and the semantics cannot be extended to partial specifications, i.e. open behaviour expressions; our experiences with LOTOS applications (e.g. [KT95, TO94]) confirm that this is highly desirable.

---

* This author was partially supported by a grant from the British Council enabling travel from Scotland to the Netherlands.

[3] Full LOTOS is Basic LOTOS plus algebraic data types. In the remainder of this paper the term LOTOS refers to Full LOTOS.

To overcome this, we define a *symbolic* semantics for LOTOS in terms of *symbolic* transition systems. To facilitate reasoning about these systems we define a related modal logic. The symbolic approach allows reasoning about data to be separated from reasoning about processes (the latter is our primary interest); we assume the existence of some oracle which will report the validity of predicates on the data. In reality this oracle will be implemented by some other proof system. Broadly, we follow the approach taken in [HL95a] for symbolic transition graphs and message passing CCS but our approach differs in several significant ways to accommodate the particular features of LOTOS (see below for details). We define symbolic bisimulation over symbolic transition systems and sketch the proof that symbolic bisimulation on ground behaviour expressions preserves the usual concrete (strong) bisimulation on the standard semantics. We define a modal logic based on symbolic transition systems.

Throughout, the semantics, bisimulation relation and logic are illustrated by application to a telephony example.

2 Preliminaries

In this section we give some basic definitions which are used throughout the paper. Some familiarity with LOTOS [ISO88, BB89] is assumed; only a brief overview of the distinguishing features is provided.

LOTOS LOTOS has three (related) features which distinguish it from most of the standard process algebras: value negotiation, multi-way (broadcast) synchronisation and selection predicates.

Value negotiation refers to the fact that there is no simple input–output model of value passing in LOTOS; rather, an event *offers* a single value, a type of values, or a set of values drawn from a type satisfying a selection predicate. For example, a single value offer is given by $g!succ(0)$. A type of values is being offered by $g?x : Nat$, meaning, informally, that any value of the type *Nat* is being offered, or is acceptable as a value for x. Finally, because of the selection predicate $x > 0$, $g?x : Nat[x > 0]$ offers only values from *Nat* which are greater than 0. The importance of selection predicates is that they may refer to variables which are being introduced in the current action. This differs from guards (also present in LOTOS) which may only refer to data introduced in previous actions. ! and ? offers can synchronise in any combination. For example, when u and v are ground terms, $g!u; P$ and $g!v; Q$ can synchronise iff $u \equiv v$, in the proof system associated with the data type specification.

Multi-way synchronisation means that when two actions synchronise, with possibly some data exchange taking place, the resulting action may be involved in further synchronisation. This is in contrast to, e.g. CCS, where two actions synchronise to give an unobservable τ action, which may not synchronise with any other action. So, in CCS, communication is strictly two-way and *not* associative, whereas in LOTOS synchronisation is multi-way and associative. For example,

$$(g!succ(0); P) \; |[g]| \; (g?x : Nat[odd(x)]; Q) \; |[g]| \; (g?y : Nat[y \geq 0]; R)$$

can synchronise, and is equivalent (with respect to bisimulation) to

$$g!succ(0); (P \; |[g]| \; Q[succ(0)/x] \; |[g]| \; R[succ(0)/y])$$

And this in turn can synchronise with, say,

$$g!pred(succ(succ(0))); S$$

all of which assumes an appropriate theory of *Nat*.

While LOTOS allows *multiple* data offers, e.g. $g!x!y?n : Nat; P$, we will, in order to simplify the definitions concerned with transition systems and bisimulation and without loss of generality, assume that only one event offer can occur at a gate/event.

Concrete Semantics and Bisimulation We refer to the standard semantics (as defined in [ISO88]) as the "concrete" semantics, and the standard strong bisimulation as "concrete" bisimulation. We write concrete bisimulation as $\sim$. (N.B. $\sim$ is defined only on closed behaviour expressions).

Variables and Substitutions σ denotes substitution of data names and is also written as $[z/x]$ where z is substituted for x. We assume a function **new-var** which generates fresh variable names. We call a unifier which generates new variables and uses those to unify terms a *renaming unifier*. For example, $[z/x, z/y]$ is a renaming unifier of x and y. We write the composition of two substitutions σ_1 and σ_2 as $\sigma_1\sigma_2$, where σ_2 has precedence over σ_1.

Free and Bound Variables The variables occurring in a data expression E are given by *vars(E)*. A behaviour expression may contain *free* and *bound* (data) variables; a closed behaviour expression is one with no free variables and a ground expression is one with no variables. Free variables arise in two ways: as formal process parameters, and as variables which have been introduced (and bound) earlier by a ? event. That is, ? is considered to be a binder; e.g. in $g?x; g!x; exit$, all occurrences of x are bound, but in $g!x; exit$, x is free. The free variables of a behaviour expression are denoted $fv(B)$.

3 Extended Transition Systems

Following [HL95a] *Symbolic transition systems* (STS) are transition systems which separate the data from process behaviour. STSs are essentially labelled transition systems with variables, both in states and transitions, and conditions, determining the validity of a transition.

Definition 1 *Let G be set of gate/event names. A Symbolic Transition System consists of*

a (nonempty) set of states with a distinguished initial state, s_0,
a set of transitions of the form $P \xrightarrow{b \quad gx} P'$, where
P is the source state,
b is a Boolean expression, or condition, which must hold for the transition to be valid,
g is a gate, or event name, $g \in G \cup \{\mathbf{i}, \delta\}$ where **i** *is the silent event in LOTOS, and δ is the special event produced by* **exit**,
x is a variable denoting data offer associated with g, $g \in G \cup \{\delta\}$,
P' is the destination state.

We give a symbolic semantics for LOTOS by associating a symbolic transition system with each LOTOS behaviour expression B, written STS(B). By an abuse of notation states are identified with their associated behaviour expression. We do not give a complete definition of the axioms and rules which define the symbolic semantics here; instead only some of the most important ones, i.e. those for action prefix, choice, guards and parallelism, are given in Figure 1. In the axioms and rules α is used to stand for gx when the particular g and x is not of interest.

Key features (and differences from [HL95a]) of this symbolic semantics are

- both kinds of data offer, i.e. both ? and !, are represented by a transition labelled by a gate/event, a variable and a condition. This is motivated by the observation that every offer is a *set* of values constrained by a condition – an equality in the case of a ! offer and an arbitrary predicate in the case of a ? offer. There is no distinction between ! and ? in this semantics.
- every transition introduces a new variable. This overcomes any potential variable name capture. For example, even if every ? variable in the expression is unique, it is possible that a process is invoked more than once, e.g. $P[g]\ |||\ P[g]$ where $P[g] = g?x : S; ....$
- synchronisation results in a new name being assigned to the value passed (with appropriate substitution in the subsequent processes) and conjunction of the transition conditions.
- guarding, prefix and parallelism are the only rules which alter transition conditions.
- nodes of the transition system are behaviour expressions, whereas in [HL95a] they are lists of free variables.

We illustrate STSs by example in the next section.

silent prefix axiom

$$i; B \xrightarrow{\text{tt} \quad \mathbf{i}} B$$

general prefix axiom

$$go[SP]; B \xrightarrow{SP\sigma \wedge b \quad gz} B\sigma$$

where $z \in$ **new-var**.

$$o = \begin{cases} !E & \text{then } b = (z \equiv E) \ \sigma = [\,] \\ ?x : S & \text{then } b = \text{tt} \qquad \sigma = [z/x] \end{cases}$$

exit axiom

$$\text{exit}(o) \xrightarrow{b \quad \delta z} \text{stop}$$

where $z \in$ **new-var**.

$$o = \begin{cases} E & \text{then } b = (z \equiv E) \\ \text{ANY } \mathit{sortname} & \text{then } b = \text{tt} \end{cases}$$

guard rule

$$\frac{B \xrightarrow{b \quad \alpha} B'}{([SP] \text{ -> } B) \xrightarrow{b \wedge SP \quad \alpha} B'}$$

choice rules

$$\frac{B_1 \xrightarrow{b \quad \alpha} B_1'}{B_1 \,[]\, B_2 \xrightarrow{b \quad \alpha} B_1'}$$

Similarly for $B2$.

general parallelism rules

$$\frac{B_1 \xrightarrow{b_1 \quad gu} B_1' \qquad B_2 \xrightarrow{b_2 \quad gw} B_2'}{B_1 |[A]| B_2 \xrightarrow{b_1[z/u] \wedge b_2[z/w] \quad gz} B_1'[z/u] |[A]| B_2'[z/w]}$$

where $z \in$ **new-var** and $g \in A \cup \{\delta\}$

$$\frac{B_1 \xrightarrow{b \quad gx} B_1'}{B_1 |[A]| B_2 \xrightarrow{b[z/x] \quad gz} B_1'[z/x] |[A]| B_2}$$

where $z \in$ **new-var** and $g \notin A \cup \{\delta\}$. Similarly for B_2.

instantiation rule

$$\frac{B' \xrightarrow{b \quad \alpha} B''}{p[g_1, \ldots, g_n](t_1, \ldots, t_m) \xrightarrow{b \quad \alpha} B''}$$

where $p[h_1, \ldots, h_n](x_1, \ldots, x_m) := B$ is a process definition,
$B' =$ relabel $[g_1/h_1, \ldots, g_n/h_n]$ in $B[t_1/x_1, \ldots, t_m/x_m]$

Fig. 1. Selected Axioms and Inference Rules for Symbolic Semantics for LOTOS

3.1 LOTOS Examples

Consider two specifications of user behaviour in a telephone network where users are forbidden to make and receive calls to/from particular users. The two specifications are given in Figures 2 and 4, and their respective STSs in Figures 3 and 5.

```
process Tel_I[dial,con,discon,unobt,on]
       (id:userid,bar_in:idlist,bar_out:idlist) :exit :=

(con?x:userid!id [not (x in bar_in)]; discon!x!id; on; exit)
[]
(dial?x:userid;
   ([x mem bar_out] -> unobt; on; exit
   []
   [not(x in bar_out)] -> con!id!x; discon!id!x; on; exit))
endproc
```

Fig. 2. LOTOS Description of Telephone I

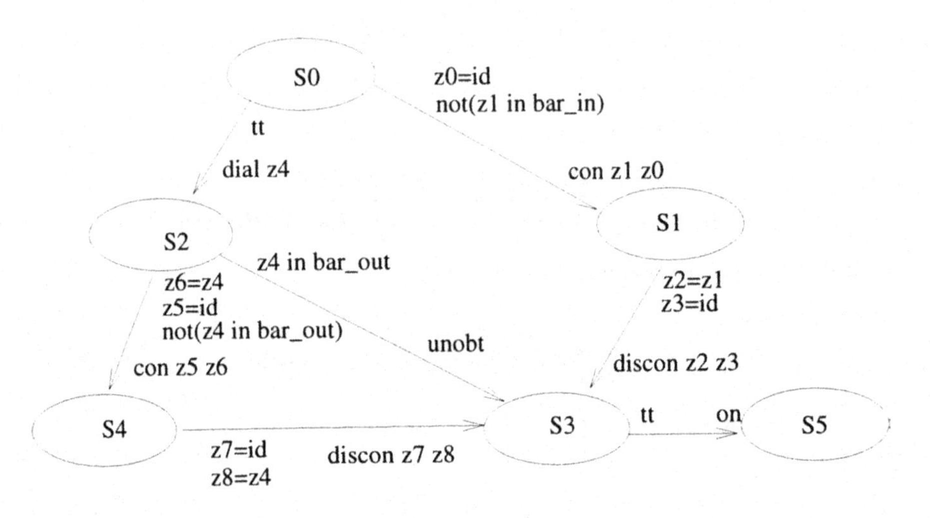

Fig. 3. STS for Telephone I

Each user process is parameterised by: the user id, the list of prohibited incoming callers, and the list of prohibited outgoing numbers. There are 5 events: the **con** (*connect*) and **discon** (*disconnect*) events, the **dial** (*dial*), **unobt** (*unobtainable*) and **on** (*on hook*) events. The first three events include data offers,

```
process Tel_II[dial,con,discon,unobt,on]
       (id:userid,bar_in:idlist,bar_out:idlist) :exit :=

con?x:userid!id [not (x in bar_in)]; discon!x!id; on; exit
[]
dial?x:userid [x in bar_out]; unobt; on; exit
[]
dial?x:userid [not(x in bar_out)]; con!id!x; discon!id!x; on; exit
endproc
```

Fig. 4. LOTOS Description of Telephone II

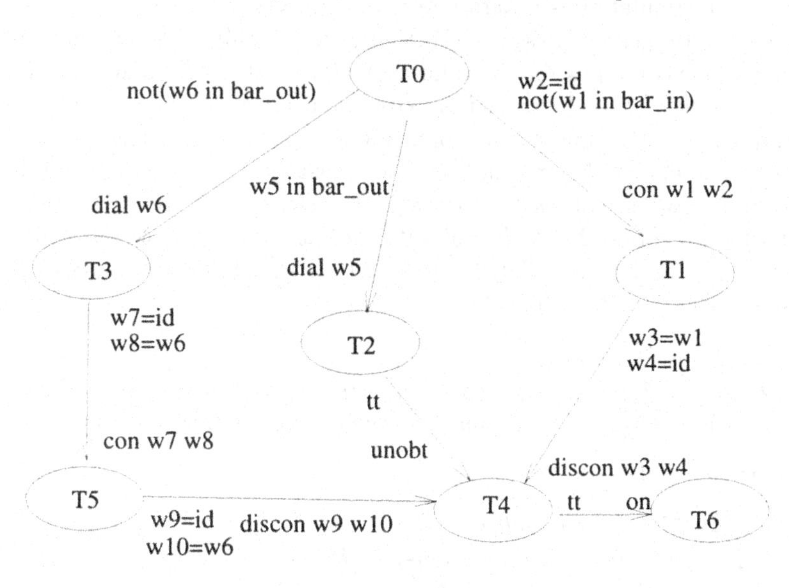

Fig. 5. STS for Telephone II

for example, **discon!x!y** denotes the event of disconnecting the call from user x to user y. Conditions are used both to guard processes (within a choice) and to qualify structured input events. For brevity, details of the datatype **userid** and **idlist** have been omitted. Also, we do not allow that phones are engaged, or unobtainable for reasons other than being in the **out** list.

The difference between **Tel_I** and **Tel_II** is essentially the points at which choices are made, rather than the criteria involved in those choices.

4 Bisimulation

The notion of bisimulation has proven to be useful in process algebra, to simplify specifications, and to show two specifications equivalent. We desire a similar notion for symbolic transition systems.

4.1 Symbolic Bismimulations on STS

As with symbolic transition systems, our main motivation here is to retain the separation between data and processes. When considering the equivalence of processes we must be very careful; obviously the particular value of a data variable can completely alter the behaviour of a process. Therefore, we must not discard this information.

The crux of the following definition of bisimulation is the notion that data can be partitioned according to some Boolean expressions, or predicates, e.g. $\{x < 0, x \geq 0\}$ and this may give enough information to accurately simulate a process, without assigning a particular value to the data variables. This also means that each bisimulation is a parameterised family of relations, where the parameters are the Boolean expressions. Furthermore, we only consider simulating transitions which could possibly be valid. Namely, given a particular Boolean expression, or "context" b, and a transition with condition b', we do not consider that transition at all if the context and condition are mutually inconsistent. For example, if b is $x = 0$, and b' is $x \neq 0$, then the transition can never be valid in this context, and so we do not need to consider the transition in the simulation. Hennessy and Lin do not do this; technically it is not necessary, but operationally it is desirable. The other main difference here is that we do not distinguish !, ? and neutral actions, while they must.

Definition 2 *(Symbolic Bisimulations)*
Let $\mathbf{S} = \{S^b | b \in BExp\}$ *be a parameterised family of relations over terms. Then* $\mathcal{SLB}(\mathbf{S})$ *is the* $BExp$*-indexed family of symmetric relations defined by:*

$(t_1, t_2) \in \mathcal{SLB}(\mathbf{S}^b)$ *if*

1. *whenever* $t_1 \xrightarrow{b_1 \;\; gx_1} t'_1$ *and* $b \wedge b_1\sigma$
   $\exists B$ *(a collection of Boolean expressions) such that* $b \wedge b_1\sigma \Rightarrow \bigvee B$.
   for each $b' \in B$ *there exists a* $t_2 \xrightarrow{b_2 \;\; gx_2} t'_2$ *such that*
   $b' \Rightarrow b_2\sigma \;\wedge\; (t'_1\sigma, t'_2\sigma) \in S^{b'}$
   where σ *is a renaming unifier of* x_1 *and* x_2.
2. *whenever* $t_2 \xrightarrow{b_2 \;\; gx_2} t'_2$ *and* $b \wedge b_2\sigma$
   $\exists B$ *(a collection of Boolean expressions) such that* $b \wedge b_2\sigma \Rightarrow \bigvee B$.
   for each $b' \in B$ *there exists a* $t_1 \xrightarrow{b_1 \;\; gx_1} t'_1$ *such that*
   $b' \Rightarrow b_1\sigma \;\wedge\; (t'_2\sigma, t'_1\sigma) \in S^{b'}$
   where σ *is a renaming unifier of* x_1 *and* x_2.

We use $\sim^b$ to denote the largest symbolic bisimulation, for a given b.

4.2 Example

Theorem 1 `Tel_I` *and* `Tel_II` *are symbolically bisimular under the trivial condition,* tt*; i.e.* `Tel_I` $\sim^{\mathrm{tt}}$ `Tel_II`.
Proof *There is a symbolic bisimulation consisting of the following relations (assuming the symmetric pairs in each set):*

$$\begin{aligned}
&\mathcal{S}^{tt} &&= \{(S0,\ T0)\}\\
&\mathcal{S}^{u6\equiv id \wedge not(u7\ in\ bar_in)} &&= \{(S1,\ T1)\}\\
&\mathcal{S}^{u6\equiv id \wedge not(u7\ in\ bar_in) \wedge u8\equiv u6 \wedge u9\equiv id} &&= \{(S3,\ T4),\ (S5,\ T6)\}\\
&\mathcal{S}^{u1\ in\ bar_out} &&= \{(S2,\ T2),\ (S3,\ T4),\ (S5,\ T6)\}\\
&\mathcal{S}^{not(u1\ in\ bar_out)} &&= \{(S2,\ T3)\}\\
&\mathcal{S}^{not(u1\ in\ bar_out) \wedge u2\equiv id \wedge u3\equiv u1} &&= \{(S4,\ T5)\}\\
&\mathcal{S}^{not(u1\ in\ bar_out) \wedge u2\equiv id \wedge u3\equiv u1 \wedge u4\equiv id \wedge u5\equiv u1} &&= \{(S3,\ T4),\ (S5,\ T6)\}
\end{aligned}$$

$$\begin{aligned}
\textit{where } \sigma = [&u1/z4, u1/w5, u1/w6, u2/z5, u2/w7, u3/z6, u3/w8, u4/z7, u4/w9,\\
&u5/z8, u5/w10, u6/z0, u6/w2, u7/z1, u7/1, u8/z2, u8/w3, u9/z3, u9/w4]
\end{aligned}$$

The proof relies on the partition induced by {u1 in bar_out, not (u1 in bar_out)}.

4.3 Relating Symbolic and Concrete Bisimulations

In [HL95a], concrete bisimulations are defined in terms of the symbolic transition systems, with concrete output events relating to symbolic output events, and concrete input events relating to symbolic input events. So, the relationship between the two semantics is reasonably straightforward. To illustrate the standard concrete semantics and the symbolic semantics defined here, Figures 6 and 7 contain portions of the respective transition systems for the behaviour expression $g?x : Nat[x < 10]; h?y : Nat; h!x; stop$. Note that whereas the concrete system has infinite branching, the symbolic system has finite branching.

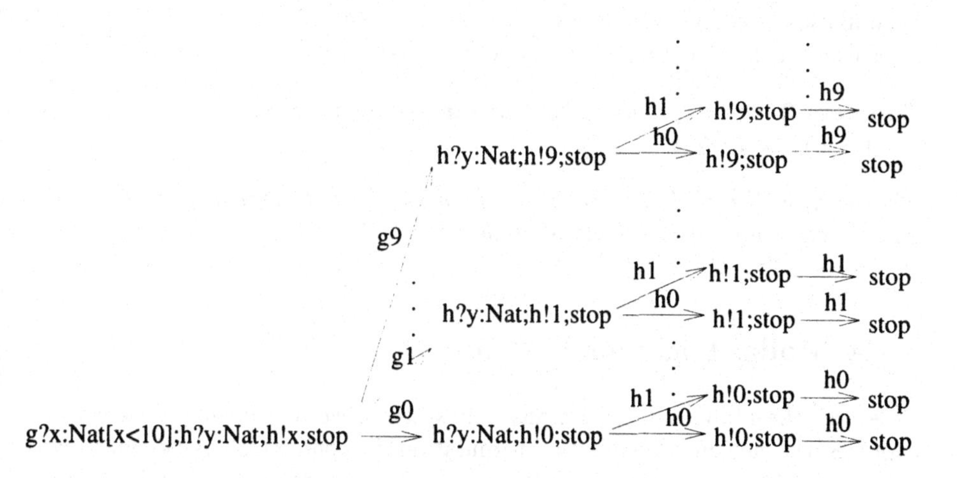

Fig. 6. Concrete Transition System

In the (concrete) semantics, query offers are instantiated by explicit data offers. Therefore, in Figure 6, the ? offers correspond to either many or an infinite number of transitions, each of which is labelled by an offer. Strictly speaking, the labels are the equivalence classes denoted by the ground terms.

$$\text{g?x:Nat[x<10];h?y:Nat;h!x;stop} \xrightarrow{\text{z0<10} \quad \text{g z0}} \text{h?y:Nat;h!z0;stop} \xrightarrow{\text{tt} \quad \text{gz1}} \text{h!z0;stop} \xrightarrow{\text{z2=z0} \quad \text{gz2}} \text{stop}$$

Fig. 7. Symbolic Transition System

In Figure 7, open terms label states, and transitions offer a single variable, under some conditions; these conditions determine the set of values which may be substituted for the variable.

The relationship between concrete and symbolic events is given by the following. The proofs, by induction on the structure of derivations, are omitted due to lack of space.

Lemma 1 *Relating Concrete Events to Symbolic Events.*
For all ground behaviour expressions t, t' events g and values v.
$t \xrightarrow{gv} t' \Rightarrow \exists z, B, u.u[v/z] = t' \wedge B[v/z] \wedge t \xrightarrow{B \quad gz} u.$

Lemma 2 *Relating Symbolic Events to Concrete Events.*
For all behaviour expressions t, t' events g, variables z, and Boolean expressions B.

$$t \xrightarrow{B \quad gz} t' \Rightarrow \quad \forall\ v, \textit{closed substitutions } \sigma \textit{ s.t. domain of } \sigma \textit{ is } fv(t).$$
$$B\sigma[v/z] \Rightarrow t\sigma \xrightarrow{gv} t'\sigma[v/z].$$

Now these relationships can be used to show the main result: that symbolic bisimulation is sound with respect to concrete bisimulation. The proofs are by induction on the structure of terms, and are omitted here.

Theorem 2 *For all ground behaviour expressions t and u.*
$(t \sim u) \;\Rightarrow\; t \sim^{\mathrm{tt}} u.$

Theorem 3 *For all boolean expressions b and substitutions σ such that $\sigma \models b$ and for all behaviour expressions t and u.*
$t \sim^{b} u \wedge \;\Rightarrow\; (t\sigma \sim u\sigma).$

5 A Modal Logic for LOTOS

Based on the above symbolic transition systems we now define a logic which captures the notion of symbolic bisimulation, i.e. one which is adequate with respect to symbolic bisimulation. Our ultimate aim is to give a modal μ-calculus in which to express properties of LOTOS; as a first step a modified version of HML [HM85] is presented. Quantifiers over data are added to the usual modalities to allow us to express properties of data in the logic.

The syntax of our logic is based on that presented in [HL95b]. Note that we allow lists of event offers in the quantifiers of the logic (rather than restricting to single offers as we have done, for simplicity, in the semantics).

Let G be a set of gate/event names. Then a logical formula is either a Φ or a Ψ, where

$$\Phi ::= B \mid \Phi_1 \wedge \Phi_2 \mid \Phi_1 \vee \Phi_2 \mid [a]\Phi \mid \langle a\rangle\Phi \mid [g]\Psi \mid \langle g\rangle\Psi$$

$$\Psi ::= \exists\overline{x}.\Phi \mid \forall\overline{x}.\Phi$$

where $a \in G \cup \{\mathbf{i}, \delta\}$, $g \in G \cup \{\delta\}$ and $\overline{x}$ denotes a list of variable names.

We define $S \models_C \Phi$, denoting when a state S in an STS satisfies a modal formula Φ in a context C. The relation is defined inductively over the syntax of the logic by the equations of Figure 8. These equations are mostly straightforward. For formulae involving $\langle\ \rangle$ *one* transition has to be found which will lead to a state which satisfies the rest of the formula, whereas for formulae involving $[\ ]$ *all* states reached by appropriately labelled transitions must satisfy the remainder of the formula. Note that the semantics treats modality/quantifier pairs together.

We assume that the length of all variable lists in both the transition system and the logical formula are identical. This allows us to match variables appropriately.

$$\begin{array}{lcl}
S \models_C B & = & B \wedge C \\
S \models_C \Phi_1 \wedge \Phi_2 & = & S \models_C \Phi_1 \text{ and } S \models_C \Phi_2 \\
S \models_C \Phi_1 \vee \Phi_2 & = & S \models_C \Phi_1 \text{ or } S \models_C \Phi_2 \\
S \models_C \langle a\rangle\Phi & = & \exists S'.S \xrightarrow{b \quad a} S' \ \wedge\ (C \wedge b)\ \wedge\ S' \models_{C\wedge b} \Phi \\
S \models_C \langle g\rangle\exists\overline{x}\Phi & = & \exists\overline{z}.\exists S'.S \xrightarrow{b \quad g\overline{y}} S' \ \wedge\ (C \wedge b[\overline{z}/\overline{y}]) \\
 & & \text{and } S'[\overline{z}/\overline{y}] \models_{C\wedge b[\overline{z}/\overline{y}]} \Phi[\overline{z}/\overline{x}] \\
S \models_C \langle g\rangle\forall\overline{x}\Phi & = & \forall\overline{z}.\exists S'.S \xrightarrow{b \quad g\overline{y}} S' \ \wedge\ (C \wedge b[\overline{z}/\overline{y}]) \\
 & & \text{and } S'[\overline{z}/\overline{y}] \models_{C\wedge b[\overline{z}/\overline{y}]} \Phi[\overline{z}/\overline{x}] \\
S \models_C [a]\Phi & = & \forall S'.(S \xrightarrow{b \quad a} S' \ \wedge\ (C \wedge b)) \Rightarrow S' \models_{C\wedge b} \Phi \\
S \models_C [g]\exists\overline{x}\Phi & = & \exists\overline{z}.\forall S'.(S \xrightarrow{b \quad g\overline{y}} S' \ \wedge\ (C \wedge b[\overline{z}/\overline{y}])) \\
 & & \Rightarrow S'[\overline{z}/\overline{y}] \models_{C\wedge b[\overline{z}/\overline{y}]} \Phi[\overline{z}/\overline{x}] \\
S \models_C [g]\forall\overline{x}\Phi & = & \forall\overline{z}.\forall S'.(S \xrightarrow{b \quad g\overline{y}} S' \ \wedge\ (C \wedge b[\overline{z}/\overline{y}])) \\
 & & \Rightarrow S'[\overline{z}/\overline{y}] \models_{C\wedge b[\overline{z}/\overline{y}]} \Phi[\overline{z}/\overline{x}]
\end{array}$$

Fig. 8. Relating the (General) Modal Formulae to Symbolic Transition Systems

We define $\langle\overline{x}, S\rangle \models \Psi$ in figure 9. This corresponds to cases where the STS contains free variables (i.e. it denotes a parameterised process or a partial specification) and the formula starts with a quantifier. In this event, we must explicitly relate the quantified variables of Ψ to the free variables of the behaviour expression (labelling the state).

All reasoning takes place with respect to a context C, usually initially tt. This context is the conjunction of the conditions generated by the transition

$$\langle fv(s_0), s_0\rangle \models_C \exists \overline{x}\Phi \quad = \quad \exists \overline{z}.(C[\overline{z}/fv(s_0)]) \wedge s_0[\overline{z}/fv(s_0)] \models_{C[\overline{z}/fv(s_0)]} \Phi[\overline{z}/\overline{x}]$$
$$\langle fv(s_0), s_0\rangle \models_C \forall \overline{x}\Phi \quad = \quad \forall \overline{z}.s_0[\overline{z}/fv(s_0)] \models_{C[\overline{z}/fv(s_0)]} \Phi[\overline{z}/\overline{x}]$$

Fig. 9. Relating Top-level Modal Formulae to Open Symbolic Transition Systems

system and by the logic. When the end of a proof is reached we look only for consistency in these conditions. This allows the flexibility to have a loose logical specification, or a loose process specification, and to generate the conditions under which a formula will hold during the construction of the proof.

Examples A number of properties can be defined which can be shown to hold of both the Telephony examples. We would expect this, because they are symbolically bisimilar. We omit the proofs here, due to lack of space.

1. $\forall id, bar\_in, bar\_out.\langle dial\rangle\exists v.not(v\ in\ bar\_out)$
   It is possible to dial a number which is not in the barred out list.
2. $\forall id, bar\_in, bar\_out.\langle dial\rangle\exists v.\langle unobt\rangle \mathrm{tt}$
   After dialling a number, the user might get unobtainable. The proof generates the condition under which this property holds, namely $v\ in\ bar\_out$. Alternatively, we could have specified this in the logic by
   $\forall id, bar\_in, bar\_out.\langle dial\rangle\exists v.(v\ in\ bar\_out) \wedge \langle unobt\rangle \mathrm{tt}$.
3. $\forall id, bar\_in, bar\_out.\langle dial\rangle\exists v_1.(v_1 = 999) \wedge \langle con\rangle\exists v_2, v_3.(v_3 = 999)$
   After dialling 999 the user will be connected to 999. The proof is made in the initial context that $not(999\ in\ bar\_out)$ (rather than the usual tt). Note that the variable v_2 must be introduced in order to force the matching between v_3 and the second offer of the *con* event (and we have no requirements of the first offer).
   This property only states that it is *possible* to be connected. A stronger statement would be $\forall id, bar\_in, bar\_out.$
   $\langle dial\rangle\exists v_1.(v_1 = 999) \wedge [dial]\exists v_1.((v_1 = 999) \wedge \langle con\rangle\exists v_2, v_3.(v_3 = 999))$
4. $\forall id, bar\_in, bar\_out.\langle dial\rangle\forall v.not(v\ in\ bar\_out) \vee (\langle unobt\rangle \mathrm{tt} \wedge [-unobt]\mathrm{ff})$
   After dialling a number in the barred list the user gets unobtainable (and no other action is possible). Here we use the shorthand $-unobt$ to mean "all actions except unobt".
   Sometimes it is quite difficult to get the right formulation of these properties. For example, an alternative way to express this property is
   $\forall id, bar\_in, bar\_out.\langle dial\rangle\exists v.(v\ in\ bar\_out) \wedge ((\langle unobt\rangle \mathrm{tt} \wedge [-unobt]\mathrm{ff}$.
   In this case, the proof relies on choosing the correct partition, whereas the proof of the first version does not. Clearly they say similar, but different, things about the systems; the version using $\forall$ is stronger because it says

there is no v (in *bar_out*) which doesn't do *unobt*, whereas the other version merely says that there is at least one v in *bar_out* which does *unobt*.
This alternative formulation can also be applied to the next two properties.

5. $\forall id, bar\_in, bar\_out.[dial]\forall v.not(v\ in\ bar\_out) \vee [con]\mathrm{ff}$
After dialling a number in the barred list, connection is not possible. Note here that we choose to ignore the data offers associated with the connection event.

6. $\forall id, bar\_in, bar\_out.[dial]\forall v_1.(v_1\ in\ bar\_out) \vee [con]\forall v_2, v_3.(v_1 = v_3 \wedge v_2 = id)$
After dialling a number not in the barred list, connection is possible (with the appropriate data offers). Unlike the previous example, here, if we omitted v_2 or v_3 we would merely be expressing that connection was possible (not necessarily between the desired parties).

7. $\forall id, bar\_in, bar\_out.[dial]\forall v.[-](\langle on\rangle \mathrm{tt} \vee [-]\langle on\rangle \mathrm{tt})$
After dialling, the second or third event will be an on hook event. Here we use $-$ as a shorthand for "all actions".

Adequacy of the Logic A desirable property of the logic is that it be *adequate* with respect to symbolic bisimulation, i.e.

$$\forall t, u, C, \Phi . t \sim^C u \Leftrightarrow (t \models_C \Phi \Leftrightarrow \ u \models_C \Phi).$$

This is the subject of a future paper.

Interesting variants of the logic may also be developed. For example, we can obtain a different version of the logic by allowing that the data partition takes place after the choice of transition. This gives a more elegant version of the semantics; see Figure 10.

$$
\begin{array}{ll}
S \models_C \langle a\rangle\Phi & = \exists S'.S \xrightarrow{b \quad a} S' \ \wedge \ (C \wedge b) \ \wedge \ S' \models_{C\wedge b} \Phi \\
S \models_C \langle g\rangle\Psi & = \exists S'.S \xrightarrow{b \quad g\overline{y}} S' \ \wedge \ (C \wedge b) \wedge (\overline{y}, S') \models_{C\wedge b} \Psi \\
S \models_C [a]\Phi & = \forall S'.(S \xrightarrow{b \quad a} S' \ \wedge \ (C \wedge b)) \Rightarrow S' \models_{C\wedge b} \Phi \\
S \models_C [g]\Psi & = \forall S'.(S \xrightarrow{b \quad g\overline{y}} S' \ \wedge \ (C \wedge b)) \Rightarrow (\overline{y}, S') \models_{C\wedge b} \Psi \\
(\overline{y}, S) \models_C \exists\overline{x}\Phi & = \exists\overline{z}.S[\overline{z}/\overline{y}] \models_{C[\overline{z}/\overline{y}]} \Phi[\overline{z}/\overline{x}] \\
(\overline{y}, S) \models_C \forall\overline{x}\Phi & = \forall\overline{z}.S[\overline{z}/\overline{y}] \models_{C[\overline{z}/\overline{y}]} \Phi[\overline{z}/\overline{x}]
\end{array}
$$

Fig. 10. Alternative Formulation of Logic Semantics

This means the logic is no longer adequate with respect to symbolic bisimulation, and we can therefore give properties which distinguish **Tel_I** and **Tel_II**. For example, **Tel_I** would satisfy $\forall id, bar\_in, bar\_out.[dial]\exists v.(v\ in\ bar\_out)$, while **Tel_II** would not. We observe that the change to the logic amounts to losing the difference between $[a]\exists v$ and $[a]\forall v$.

6 Conclusions and Further Work

We have defined a *symbolic* semantics for full LOTOS in terms of *symbolic* transition systems, symbolic bisimulation over those transition systems, and a symbolic modal logic. Broadly speaking, we have adopted the approach of [HL95a]; however, the features of LOTOS (especially the need to accomodate multi-way synchronisation, and the resulting model of value passing) mean that this is not a straightforward adaptation of the theory presented in [HL95a] and [HL95b].

The use of a symbolic semantics, relation, logic and proof system will allow us to reason about Full LOTOS processes, separating the data from the processes, but without losing essential information that the data supplies in terms of flow of control. Previous approaches to reasoning about Full LOTOS processes meant using considerable intuition about different representations of data, and data as processes [Got87] or using complex transformations [Bri92, Bol92], only some of which preserve the data information.

There are two main streams of further work: bisimulation-related and logic-related. We note that while we have a means of checking whether a given relation is a symbolic bisimulation we have not given here an effective method of constructing that relation. A particularly interesting case of state matching concerns recursive processes with query variables. These yield an infinite number of variables, and consequently conditions, and so we must be able to recognise the relationships between conditions.

For the logic, we have not shown here that the logic given is adequate with respect to symbolic bisimulation on finite processes. We will also extend the logic with fixpoint operators to give a more expressive language suitable for expressing properties of recursive processes.

Finally, in order to evaluate the effectiveness of our approach we need to carry out extensive case studies in a wide range of application areas.

Acknowledgements

The authors would like to thank Ed Brinksma for many fruitful discussions and the referees for their helpful comments.

References

[BB89] T. Bolognesi and E. Brinksma. Introduction to the ISO Specification Language LOTOS. In P.H.J. van Eijk, C.A. Vissers, and M. Diaz, editors, *The Formal Description Technique LOTOS*, pages 23–76. Elsevier Science Publishers B.V. (North-Holland), 1989.

[Bol92] T. Bolognesi, editor. Catalogue of LOTOS Correctness Preserving Transformations. Technical Report Lo/WP1/T1.2/N0045, The LOTOSPHERE Esprit Project, 1992. Task 1.2 deliverable. LOTOSPHERE information disseminated by J. Lagemaat, email `lagemaat@cs.utwente.nl`.

[Bri92] E. Brinksma. From Data Structure to Process Structure. In K.G. Larsen and A. Skou, editors, *Proceedings of CAV 91*, LNCS 575, pages 244–254, 1992.

[Eer94] H. Eertink. *Simulation Techniques for the Validation of LOTOS Specifications.* PhD thesis, University of Twente, 1994.

[Got87] R. Gotzhein. Specifying Abstract Data Types with LOTOS. In B. Sarikaya and G.V. Bochmann, editors, *Protocol Specification, Testing, and Verification, VI*, pages 15–26. Elsevier Science Publishers B.V. (North-Holland), 1987.

[HL95a] M. Hennessy and H. Lin. Symbolic Bisimulations. *Theoretical Computer Science*, 138:353–389, 1995.

[HL95b] M. Hennessy and X. Liu. A Modal Logic for Message Passing Processes. *Acta Informatica*, 32:375–393, 1995.

[HM85] M. Hennessy and R. Milner. Algebraic Laws for Nondeterminism and Concurrency. *Journal of the Association for Computing Machinery*, 32(1):137–161, 1985.

[Hoa85] C.A.R. Hoare. *Communicating Sequential Processes.* Prentice-Hall International, 1985.

[ISO88] International Organisation for Standardisation. *Information Processing Systems — Open Systems Interconnection — LOTOS — A Formal Description Technique Based on the Temporal Ordering of Observational Behaviour*, 1988.

[KT95] C. Kirkwood and M. Thomas. Experiences with LOTOS Verification: A Report on Two Case Studies. In *Workshop on Industrial-Strength Formal Specification Techniques*, pages 159–171. IEEE Computer Society Press, 1995.

[Mil89] R. Milner. *Communication and Concurrency.* Prentice-Hall International, 1989.

[TO94] M. Thomas and T. Ormsby. On the Design of Side-Stick Controllers in Fly-by-Wire Aircraft. In *Applied Computing Review, Special Issue: Safety-Critical Software*, pages 15–20. ACM Press, Volume 2, Number 1 Spring 1994.

Algebraic Composition and Refinement of Proofs

Martin Simons[1] and Michel Sintzoff[2]

[1] GMD Research Institute for Computer Architecture and Software Technology, and Technische Universität Berlin, Forschungsgruppe Softwaretechnik*
[2] Université catholique de Louvain, Department of Computing Science and Engineering**

Abstract. We present an algebraic calculus for proof composition and refinement. Fundamentally, proofs are expressed at successive levels of abstraction, with the perhaps unconventional principle that a formula is considered to be its own most abstract proof, which may be refined into increasingly concrete proofs. Consequently, we suggest a new paradigm for expressing proofs, which views theorems and proofs as inhabiting the same semantic domain. This algebraic/model-theoretical view of proofs distinguishes our approach from conventional type-theoretical or sequent-based approaches in which theorems and proofs are different entities. All the logical concepts that make up a formal system — formulas, inference rules, and derivations — are expressible in terms of the calculus itself. Proofs are constructed and structured by means of a composition operator and a consequential rule-forming operator. Their interplay and their relation wrt. the refinement order are expressed as algebraic laws.

1 Introduction

For a number of years, various proof-assistance systems have been designed and experimented with. They are mainly used for theorem proving and system verification. Recently, more and more attention is being paid to the recording, manipulation, and beautification of the proof objects, not just of the proof results. One symptom of this trend is the discussion of topics such as computation on proofs.

In this paper, we focus on the issue of proof objects, too. Our interest in this grew from a number of in-depth experiments with a proof-assistance system based on a generalized typed calculus (Weber, Simons & Lafontaine 1993). One original feature of this work, from the outset, was that it focused on software design rather than on classical theorem proving. In these experiments, the problems of proof representation, scalability, and readability became more and more important. Various techniques were therefore devised to alleviate some of these difficulties — for instance, the concept of implicit proofs in which details can be hidden (Weber 1993), and the support of literate proofs (Simons & Weber 1996, Simons 1997*b*) in the spirit of Knuth's literate programs. Here, we pursue two other lines of thought. First, we focus on modeling proofs algebraically rather than syntactically, which is the usual way. We believe that such an algebraic view greatly enhances understanding of the deep structure of proofs, and shows the essential relationships that exist between superficially different approaches.

* Technische Universität Berlin, Forschungsgruppe Softwaretechnik (FR5-6), Franklinstr. 28/29, D-10587 Berlin, Germany; e-mail: simons@cs.tu-berlin.de
** Université catholique de Louvain, Dept. of Computing Science and Engineering, Place Sainte-Barbe 2, B-1348 Louvain-la-Neuve, Belgium; e-mail: ms@info.ucl.ac.be

Second, we consider abstraction and its dual, viz. refinement, to be essential techniques in the case of proofs, too. We therefore wish to put these concepts at the very heart of our technique for modeling proof objects. Admittedly, the emphasis we place on an algebraic view and on the role of abstraction and refinement should not come as a surprise. It is well known that proofs are akin to programs, and that programs are better designed using algebra and refinement, e.g. (Bird & de Moor 1997). Moreover, algebraic views of proof objects have been considered before: Martin, Gardiner & Woodcock (1997) propose an algebraic theory of tactics and tacticals; Sintzoff (1993) models the composition of proof objects in an algebraic setting, using endomorphisms to abstract proof results from proof objects. In short, the main contribution of the present paper is simply to show how proof composition and refinement can be integrated smoothly and clearly in an algebraic style. As far as we know, proof abstraction and refinement have not yet been considered as such before. Previous work on understandable proof presentation has dealt with the re-expression of proofs in various ways, e.g. in a natural language or in a mathematical vernacular, but without changing the abstraction level of proofs.

The paper is organized as follows. First, we informally motivate a proof calculus built from composition, rule formation, and a refinement order. In Sect. 3, we give a brief overview of the mathematics, which are then employed in Sect. 4 to define a class of algebras for proofs and to derive some of their properties. In Sect. 5, the calculus is illustrated by proofs in a propositional logic. In Sect. 6, we review related work and discuss possible directions of further work. Finally, Sect. 7 contains our conclusions.

2 Motivation

Our aim is to devise a mathematical system for proof composition and refinement: a thesis is *refined* via a number of intermediate-level proofs to yield proof components whose validity is manifest, for instance by human understanding or machine verification. Such a stepwise organization of proofs can already be found in informal but rigorous and disciplined proof styles that have recently been recommended, such as Jones's (1990) "boxed proofs" or Lamport's (1994) "structured proofs".

We consider a formula to be itself an abstract *specification* of all its proofs. Such a specification is to be refined in a stepwise manner to obtain a sufficiently detailed proof:

$$\textit{formula} \sqsupseteq \cdots \sqsupseteq \textit{proof sketch} \sqsupseteq \cdots \sqsupseteq \textit{detailed proof}$$

This implies that theorems — or, more generally, formulas — and proofs inhabit the same structure. Thus, if we interpret this structure in the light of the refinement order, we find that a formula is a sketch of a proof that has not yet been refined; or, put differently, a proof with all details hidden. To illustrate these notions informally, let us consider the proof of the Knaster-Tarski fixpoint theorem.

Theorem (Knaster-Tarski) *Let L be a complete lattice and $\Phi : L \to L$ a monotonic map. Then, Φ has a fixpoint.* □

To prove this, one essentially shows that the l.u.b. of the set $M \triangleq \{x : x \in L : \Phi(x) \sqsupseteq x\}$ is a fixpoint of Φ. An essay proof taken from a textbook and a reasonably complete, hierarchically structured proof are given in Fig. 1.

Now, consider first the following very simple proof refinement: in order to prove $\Phi(\sqcup M) = \sqcup M$, we prove $\Phi(\sqcup M) \sqsupseteq \sqcup M$ and $\sqcup M \sqsupseteq \Phi(\sqcup M)$, and then use antisym-

Classical proof (Davey & Priestley 1990, 4.11). Let $M = \{x : x \in L : \Phi(x) \supseteq x\}$ and $\alpha = \sqcup M$. For all $x \in M$, we have $\alpha \supseteq x$, so $\Phi(\alpha) \supseteq \Phi(x) \supseteq x$. Thus, $\Phi(\alpha) \in M^u$, whence $\Phi(\alpha) \supseteq \alpha$. We now use this inequality to prove the reverse one (!) and thereby complete the proof that α is a fixpoint. Since Φ is order-preserving, $\Phi(\Phi(\alpha)) \supseteq \Phi(\alpha)$. This says $\Phi(\alpha) \in M$, so $\alpha \supseteq \Phi(\alpha)$. □

Hierarchical proof.

LET: $M \triangleq \{x : x \in L : \Phi(x) \supseteq x\}$
PROVE: $\Phi(\sqcup M) = \sqcup M$
1. $\Phi(\sqcup M) \supseteq \sqcup M$.
 1.1. $\Phi(\sqcup M)$ is an upper bound of M:
  ASSUME: $x \in M$
  PROVE: $\Phi(\sqcup M) \supseteq x$
  1.1.1. $\Phi(x) \supseteq x$
   PROOF: Def. of M.
  1.1.2. $\Phi(\sqcup M) \supseteq \Phi(x)$
   PROOF: Def. of $\sqcup$ and monotonicity of Φ.
  1.1.3. QED.
   PROOF: 1.1.1.,1.1.2.,transitivity.
 1.2. QED.
  PROOF: Def. of $\sqcup$ and 1.1.
2. $\sqcup M \supseteq \Phi(\sqcup M)$.
 2.1. $\Phi(\sqcup M) \in M$.
  PROOF: Def. of M, 1., and monotonicity of Φ.
 2.2. QED.
  PROOF: Def. of $\sqcup$ and 2.1.
3. QED.
 PROOF: 1., 2., and antisymmetry. □

Fig. 1. Classical and hierarchically structured proofs of the Knaster-Tarski theorem

metry of $\supseteq$. This is expressed by the following proof skeleton:

PROVE: $\Phi(\sqcup M) = \sqcup M$
1. $\Phi(\sqcup M) \supseteq \sqcup M$.
2. $\sqcup M \supseteq \Phi(\sqcup M)$.
3. QED.

The QED step states that steps 1. and 2. entail $\Phi(\sqcup M) = \sqcup M$. In the proposed proof algebra, this first-level refinement of the proof is expressed as

$$\{\Phi(\sqcup M) = \sqcup M\}$$
$$\sqsupseteq$$
$$\underbrace{\{\Phi(\sqcup M) \supseteq \sqcup M\}}_{1.} \fatsemi \underbrace{\{\sqcup M \supseteq \Phi(\sqcup M)\}}_{2.} \fatsemi \underbrace{\{\Phi(\sqcup M) = \sqcup M\}_{\text{QED}}}_{3.}$$

This formalization is obtained as follows: the change of proof level corresponds to the refinement $\sqsupseteq$; the concatenation of subproofs corresponds to proof composition, which we denote by $\fatsemi$. Formulas within braces denote basic objects of the proof algebra. The object of the third QED step is to justify the decomposition. More precisely, the composition of $\{\Phi(\sqcup M) \supseteq \sqcup M\}$ and $\{\sqcup M \supseteq \Phi(\sqcup M)\}$ must entail $\{\Phi(\sqcup M) = \sqcup M\}$. This is expressed as

$$(\{\Phi(\sqcup M) \supseteq \sqcup M\} \fatsemi \{\sqcup M \supseteq \Phi(\sqcup M)\}) \mapsto \{\Phi(\sqcup M) = \sqcup M\}$$

where the binary operator $\mapsto$ constructs a consequential derivation rule with a hypothesis and a conclusion. If $\{\Phi(\sqcup M) = \sqcup M\}_{\text{QED}}$ refines this entailment, then the first-level refinement given above is valid. The second step can, in turn, be refined to a proof of $\{\Phi(\sqcup M) \in M\}$ and a justification that this decomposition is valid:

$$\underbrace{\{\sqcup M \supseteq \Phi(\sqcup M)\}}_{2.} \quad \sqsupseteq \quad \underbrace{\{\Phi(\sqcup M) \in M\}}_{2.1.} \fatsemi \underbrace{\{\sqcup M \supseteq \Phi(\sqcup M)\}_{\text{QED}}}_{2.2.}$$

We have thus encountered two essential proof constructors: composition $\fatsemi$ and a consequential rule operator $\mapsto$. Let us now continue and refine the first substep:

$$
\begin{array}{ll}
& \underbrace{\{\Phi(\cup M) \supseteq \cup M\}}_{1.} \\
\sqsupseteq & \underbrace{\{\forall x \in M.\Phi(\cup M) \supseteq x\}}_{1.1.} \fatsemi \underbrace{\{\Phi(\cup M) \supseteq \cup M\}_{\text{QED}}}_{1.2.} \\
\sqsupseteq & (\forall x.\{x \in M\} \mapsto \underbrace{\{\Phi(x) \supseteq x\}}_{1.1.1.} \fatsemi \underbrace{\{\Phi(\cup M) \supseteq \Phi(x)\}}_{1.1.2.} \fatsemi \underbrace{\{\Phi(\cup M) \supseteq x\}_{\text{QED}}}_{1.1.3.}) \fatsemi \\
& \qquad\qquad\qquad\qquad\qquad\qquad\qquad\qquad \underbrace{\{\Phi(\cup M) \supseteq \cup M\}_{\text{QED}}}_{1.2.}
\end{array}
$$

What properties do we expect the two constructors to have? How do they interact and how do they behave with respect to the refinement order? Let us first note that, since the proof constructors are total operators, we need a way to distinguish valid proofs from invalid ones. To do so, we introduce a validity element $\mathbf{1}$ into our calculus and express the fact that a proof P is valid by $P \sqsupseteq \mathbf{1}$. This element forms, so to speak, the agglomeration of *all* true arguments: $\mathbf{1} = (\sqcap P : P \sqsupseteq \mathbf{1})$. It denotes abstract truth. Therefore, the relation $P \sqsupseteq Q$ states that P is more valid than Q. In other words, if Q is valid, i.e. $Q \sqsupseteq \mathbf{1}$, then P is valid as well. Conversely, $P \sqsupseteq Q$ states that Q is a valid attempt at refining P, which is successful if $Q \sqsupseteq \mathbf{1}$.

Composition builds sequences of mathematical reasoning steps. Arguments appearing later in the sequence may use information produced by earlier steps. With this intuition, we want composition to be associative but not commutative. Composition should also preserve refinements, i.e. arguments should be able to be refined independently of one another within a compound argument. Refining $P \fatsemi \mathbf{1}$ or $\mathbf{1} \fatsemi P$ should intuitively be equivalent to refining P

$$P \fatsemi \mathbf{1} \sqsupseteq Q \;\equiv\; P \sqsupseteq Q \;\equiv\; \mathbf{1} \fatsemi P \sqsupseteq Q$$

because $\mathbf{1}$, representing abstract truth, should not be involved in either refinement. Hence, we can expect $\mathbf{1}$ to be the left and right identity of composition.

The rule constructor should preserve the refinement of conclusions as follows:

$$P \sqsupseteq Q \;\Rightarrow\; R \mapsto P \sqsupseteq R \mapsto Q,$$

i.e., if we refine P to Q, then this should still count as a refinement if it takes place within the scope of some additional assumption R. An argument P should be refinable by composing an argument Q and an argument showing that Q entails P:

$$P \sqsupseteq Q \fatsemi (Q \mapsto P) \qquad (*)$$

This refinement corresponds nicely to a hierarchical decomposition as illustrated in the Knaster-Tarski example above: Q corresponds to the proof steps that make up the next level, and $Q \mapsto P$ to the closing QED step. Conversely, if one wants to refine the composition of P and Q under the assumption P, then all one should be left with is the refinement of Q, because one already has P:

$$P \mapsto (P \fatsemi Q) \sqsupseteq Q \qquad (**)$$

Put differently, P is canceled out in the expression $P \mapsto (P \fatsemi Q)$.

What we have just sketched forms the basic building blocks of our proof algebra $\mathcal{P}$: the algebra is basically a monoid $\langle \mathcal{P}; \mathbin{;}, \mathbf{1} \rangle$ equipped with a partial order $\langle \mathcal{P}; \sqsupseteq \rangle$. We will see in the next section that, together with the remaining properties we have just advocated, such as $*$ and $**$, this already determines a rich structure.

3 Mathematical Background

We refer to some already known results which will be used in Sect. 4. Here, we draw on Kleene (1971), Davey & Priestley (1990), Rosenthal (1990), and Vickers (1989).

Definition 1 (Formal Gentzen System) Let $\mathcal{L}$ be a formal language of well-formed *formulas*. A *sequent* is an element of $\mathcal{L}^* \times \mathcal{L}$ consisting of an *antecedent* and a *succedent*, written as $\Gamma_1, \ldots, \Gamma_n \vdash A$, where $\Gamma_i, A \in \mathcal{L}$, and $n \geq 0$. Let $\mathcal{S}$ denote the set of sequents. An *inference rule* is an element of $\mathcal{S}^* \times \mathcal{S}$, i.e. a pair consisting of a list of *premises* and a *conclusion*. An *axiom* is an inference rule without premises. A *formal Gentzen system* $\langle \mathcal{L} \mid A, S, L \rangle$ is given by a formal language $\mathcal{L}$ and three sets of inference rules: axioms A, structural rules S, and logical rules L. A *derivation* in a formal Gentzen system (wrt. assumptions $s_1, \ldots, s_n$) is a list of sequents (with prefix $s_1, \ldots, s_n$) such that each element in the sequent (except for the assumptions) is the conclusion of an inference rule all of whose premises appear earlier in the list. A *proof* of a sequent $\Gamma \vdash A$ (wrt. assumptions $s_1, \ldots, s_n$) is a derivation (with prefix $s_1, \ldots, s_n$) with last element $\Gamma \vdash A$. A sequent is *provable* if there is a proof of it. □

Definition 2 (Galois Connection) Let $\langle \mathcal{P}; \sqsupseteq_{\mathcal{P}} \rangle$ and $\langle \mathcal{Q}, \sqsupseteq_{\mathcal{Q}} \rangle$ be partial orders. A *Galois connection* between $\mathcal{P}$ and $\mathcal{Q}$ is a pair $\langle F, G \rangle : \mathcal{P} \rightharpoonup \mathcal{Q}$ where F and G are functions $F : \mathcal{P} \to \mathcal{Q}, G : \mathcal{Q} \to \mathcal{P}$ such that for all $x \in \mathcal{P}$ and $y \in \mathcal{Q}$,

$$G.y \sqsupseteq_{\mathcal{P}} x \;\equiv\; y \sqsupseteq_{\mathcal{Q}} F.x.$$

F is the *lower* or *left adjoint* to G, and G the *upper* or *right adjoint* to F. □

Definition 3 (Quantale) A structure $\langle \mathcal{P}; \sqcup, \mathbin{;}, \mathbf{1} \rangle$ is a *quantale* if $\langle \mathcal{P}; \sqcup \rangle$ is a complete join semilattice and $\langle \mathcal{P}; \mathbin{;}, \mathbf{1} \rangle$ is a monoid such that composition distributes from the left and from the right over arbitrary joins. A *homomorphism of quantales* is a map between two quantales that preserves arbitrary joins, composition and its unit. **Quant** denotes the category of quantales and their homomorphisms. A *congruence* on a quantale is an equivalence that is compatible with composition and arbitrary joins. A quantale $\mathcal{P}$ is called *commutative* if for every $x, y \in \mathcal{P}$, $x \mathbin{;} y = y \mathbin{;} x$. It is called *left-sided* or *right-sided* if for every $x \in \mathcal{P}$, $x \sqsupseteq \top \mathbin{;} x$ or $x \sqsupseteq x \mathbin{;} \top$, respectively. It is called *two-sided* if it is both left- and right-sided. It is called idempotent if for every $x \in \mathcal{P}$, $x = x \mathbin{;} x$. □

Hence, a quantale is a complete lattice and since the sections $x\mathbin{;}$ and $\mathbin{;}x$ preserve arbitrary joins, we know that they have upper adjoints, which we will denote by $x \mapsto$ and $\leftarrow\!\dashv x$, respectively. We thus have the following equivalent set of axioms for a quantale.

Fact 4 *A quantale can be presented as a structure* $\langle \mathcal{P}; \sqcap, \sqcup, \top, \bot, \mathbin{;}, \mathbf{1}, \mapsto, \leftarrow\!\dashv \rangle$ *such that*

(i) $\langle \mathcal{P}; \mathbin{;}, \mathbf{1} \rangle$ *is a monoid,*

(ii) $\langle \mathcal{P}; \sqcap, \sqcup, \top, \bot \rangle$ *is a complete lattice,*

(iii) $x \mapsto y \sqsupseteq z \;\equiv\; y \sqsupseteq x \mathbin{;} z$, *and*
$x \leftarrow\!\dashv y \sqsupseteq z \;\equiv\; x \sqsupseteq z \mathbin{;} y$, *for all* $x, y, z \in \mathcal{P}$.

By convention, $\mapsto$ and $\mapsfrom$ have lower precedence than $;$; $\mapsto$ associates to the right, and $\mapsfrom$ to the left. A homomorphism of quantales preserves arbitrary joins, composition and the unit, but not necessarily the remaining operations. □

Proposition 5 (Fundamental Theorem) *Let $\mathcal{P}$ and $\mathcal{Q}$ be quantales, let $h : \mathcal{P} \twoheadrightarrow \mathcal{Q}$ be a quantale homomorphism of $\mathcal{P}$ onto $\mathcal{Q}$ and define $x =_h y \triangleq h.x = h.y$ for all $x, y \in \mathcal{P}$ (read "x equals y modulo h"). Then, $=_h$ is a congruence on $\mathcal{P}$ and induces a quantale structure $\langle \mathcal{P}/{=_h}; \sqcap_h, \sqcup_h, [\top], [\bot], ;_h, [\mathbf{1}] \rangle$ on the set of equivalence classes, where, for all $A \subseteq \mathcal{P}$ and $x, y \in \mathcal{P}$, $(\sqcup_h x : x \in A : [x]) \triangleq [(\sqcup x : x \in A)]$ and $[x] ;_h [y] \triangleq [x ; y]$. The canonical map $[\cdot] : \mathcal{P} \to \mathcal{P}/{=_h}$, which maps elements to their equivalence classes, is a quantale homomorphism. Furthermore, there is a unique homomorphism $h' : \mathcal{P}/{=_h} \to \mathcal{Q}$ such that $h = h' \circ [\cdot]$. Moreover, h' is bijective.* □

Since quantale homomorphisms preserve arbitrary joins, we may write $x \sqsupseteq_h y$ for $h.x \sqsupseteq h.y$, which is equivalent to $[x] \sqsupseteq [y]$ with respect to the quotient order.

Proposition 6 (Free Construction) *Let* **Mon** *denote the category of monoids and homomorphisms. The functor $\mathfrak{P}$:* **Mon** $\to$ **Quant**

$$\begin{array}{ccc} \langle M; ;_M, \mathbf{1}_M \rangle & & \langle 2^M; \cap, \cup, M, \emptyset, ;'_M, \{\mathbf{1}_M\} \rangle \\ \downarrow h & \overset{\mathfrak{P}}{\longmapsto} & \downarrow A \mapsto \{a : a \in A : h.a\} \\ \langle N; ;_N, \mathbf{1}_N \rangle & & \langle 2^N; \cap, \cup, N, \emptyset, ;'_N, \{\mathbf{1}_N\} \rangle \end{array}$$

where $A ;' B \triangleq \{a, b : a \in A, b \in B : a ; b\}$, is left adjoint to the forgetful functor **Quant** $\to$ **Mon**. □

Together with the free monoid construction, we obtain free quantales over arbitrary sets.

Definition 7 (Generators and Relations) A *presentation by generators and relations in* ***Quant***, written as $\mathbf{Qu}\langle G \mid R \rangle$, is given by a set G of *generators* and a set R of *defining relations* of the form $e_1 = e_2$, where e_1 and e_2 are well-formed expressions in the language of quantales, i.e. expressions over G using the formal operators $\sqcup$, $;$ and $\mathbf{1}$. A *model* for $\mathbf{Qu}\langle G \mid R \rangle$ is a quantale $\mathcal{P}$ together with a map $[\![\cdot]\!] : G \to \mathcal{P}$ such that every relation $e_1 = e_2$ in R holds in $\mathcal{P}$, i.e. $[\![e_1]\!]' = [\![e_2]\!]'$, where $[\![\cdot]\!]'$ denotes the canonical extension of $[\![\cdot]\!]$ to well-formed expressions. The action of $[\![\cdot]\!]$ is called *injection of the generators*. A quantale $\mathcal{P}$ is *presented* by $\mathbf{Qu}\langle G \mid R \rangle$ iff it is a model for the presentation and the map $[\![\cdot]\!]_{\mathcal{P}}$ satisfies the following universal property: whenever $\mathcal{Q}$ is a model, there exists a unique homomorphism $h : \mathcal{P} \to \mathcal{Q}$ such that $[\![\cdot]\!]_{\mathcal{Q}} = h \circ [\![\cdot]\!]_{\mathcal{P}}$. □

Proposition 8 (Presentations Do Really Present) *In* **Quant**, *any presentation by generators and relations presents a quantale unique up to isomorphisms. Abusing notation,* $\mathbf{Qu}\langle G \mid R \rangle$ *denotes a quantale presented by this presentation.* □

Moreover, Abramsky & Vickers (1993) give a construction by means of *coverages*, which we use in Sect. 5 when constructing quantales for formal Gentzen systems.

4 An Algebraic Structure for Proofs

The algebraic structure in which we express proofs is that of a quantale. To emphasize this, we call quantales used for the purpose of expressing proofs *proof quantales*. As motivated in Sect. 2, proofs are composed sequentially by means of the operator

Unique characterization

$$x \mathbin{;} y = (\sqcap z : x \mapsto z \sqsupseteq y) \quad (1)$$
$$x \mapsto y = (\sqcup z : y \sqsupseteq x \mathbin{;} z) \quad (2)$$

Monotonicity laws

$$x \sqsupseteq x', y \sqsupseteq y' \Rightarrow x \mathbin{;} y \sqsupseteq x' \mathbin{;} y' \quad (3)$$
$$x \sqsupseteq x', y \sqsupseteq y' \Rightarrow x' \mapsto y \sqsupseteq x \mapsto y' \quad (4)$$

Distributivity laws

$$x \mathbin{;} (\sqcup y : y \in Y) = (\sqcup y : y \in Y : x \mathbin{;} y) \quad (5)$$
$$(\sqcup x : x \in X) \mathbin{;} y = \sqcup(x : x \in X : x \mathbin{;} y) \quad (6)$$
$$x \mapsto (\sqcap y : y \in Y) = \sqcap(y : y \in Y : x \mapsto y) \quad (7)$$
$$(\sqcup x : x \in X) \mapsto y = \sqcap(x : x \in X : x \mapsto y) \quad (8)$$

Refinement laws

$$x \sqsupseteq y \mathbin{;} (y \mapsto x) \quad (9)$$
$$x \mapsto z \sqsupseteq (x \mapsto y) \mathbin{;} (y \mapsto z) \quad (10)$$
$$x \mapsto x \mathbin{;} y \sqsupseteq y \quad (11)$$
$$x \mapsto y \mathbin{;} z \sqsupseteq (x \mapsto y) \mathbin{;} z \quad (12)$$

Identities

$$x \mathbin{;} (x \mapsto x \mathbin{;} y) = x \mathbin{;} y \quad (13)$$
$$x \mapsto x \mathbin{;} (x \mapsto y) = x \mapsto y \quad (14)$$
$$x \mapsto y \mapsto z = y \mathbin{;} x \mapsto z \quad (15)$$
$$\mathbf{1} \mapsto x = x \quad (16)$$
$$\bot \mapsto x = \top = x \mapsto \top \quad (17)$$
$$\bot \mathbin{;} x = \bot = x \mathbin{;} \bot \quad (18)$$

Fig. 2. Selected properties of quantales useful for proof refinement

$;$. Composition is associative but not commutative: the second operand may make assumptions about information provided by the first one. The identity **1** of composition captures abstract truth: composing an argument with it does not alter the argument in any way. Proofs are ordered by a lattice order $\sqsupseteq$ with meet $\sqcap$, join $\sqcup$, greatest element $\top$, and least element $\bot$. The order expresses refinement of proofs from abstract to concrete. With this interpretation, the join of two proofs denotes the least abstract proof that is refined by either one of the two proofs. The meet of two proofs denotes the most abstract proof that refines both proofs. The most abstract proof is denoted by $\top$ and is refined by any proof. The most concrete proof is denoted by $\bot$ and refines any proof. Thus, these two elements are merely technical entities. The rule arrows $\mapsto$ and $\leftarrow\!\!\!\mid$ construct proofs that use a hypothesis to derive a conclusion.

Fact 4 states a specific set of axioms for proof quantales. We chose this particular set of axioms in order to highlight the Galois connections in (iii). For elements x and y of $\mathcal{P}$, $x;$ and $;y$ are lower adjoints to $x \mapsto$ and $\leftarrow\!\!\!\mid y$, respectively. In fact, the arguments given earlier in Sect. 2 for what should constitute a proof-refinement calculus *enforce* these connections. From the theory of Galois connections, we know that monotonicity of composition and consequence, together with the refinements (*) and (**), determine (iii).

In Fig. 2, we list several properties that the reader can readily prove by simple calculations. Similar properties are listed, for instance, by Rosenthal (1990). Variables x, y and z range over arbitrary elements of a proof quantale $\mathcal{P}$, while X and Y range over arbitrary subsets of $\mathcal{P}$. Properties involving $\mapsto$ similarly hold for $\leftarrow\!\!\!\mid$, and we therefore only explicitly state the former.

Since lower adjoints uniquely determine upper adjoints and vice versa, we can define composition in terms of the rule arrow, and the rule arrow in terms of composition: (2) states that $x \mapsto y$ is the most abstract proof, which, composed with x, refines y. In this manner, (1) states that $x \mathbin{;} y$ is the most concrete proof, which, assuming x, is refined by y. Composition is monotonic in both of its arguments (3), the rule arrow in its second, and antitonic in its first (4). Incidentally, the latter is a direct consequence of monotonicity of composition or of a third implied Galois connection. Preservation of arbitrary joins by $x\,;$ and $;\,y$ and arbitrary meets by $x \mapsto$ is equivalent to the distributivity laws (5–8). The refinement laws that we stated in the introduction are consequences of the definition of proof quantales. In fact, (9) and (11), together with the monotonicity of $x\,;$ and $x \mapsto$, are equivalent to property 4 (iii). Although we are mainly interested in refinements, we can also establish some useful identities. First of all, we have the equalities that hold for all Galois connections (13–14). Next, we can prove a Curry-like law (15) that identifies nested assumptions with composition of assumptions, in reverse order. Moreover, $\mathbf{1}$ is a left unit of the rule arrow (16); $\bot$ is a left zero and $\top$ is a right zero of the rule arrow (17); and $\bot$ is both a left and right zero of composition (18). Last but not least, the following *deduction principle* holds:

$$x \sqsupseteq y \;\equiv\; y \mapsto x \sqsupseteq \mathbf{1} \tag{19}$$

If a proof x is refined by a proof y, then we certainly expect that the deduction that concludes x from y is valid. The converse also holds. This is only a small selection of the laws that hold in proof quantales. They provide, however, a useful basis for composing further rules. For instance, (10) and (15) can be combined to prove $y\,;\,x \mapsto z \sqsupseteq (x \mapsto a)\,;\,(y\,;\,a \mapsto z)$, a direct counterpart to the cut rule of Gentzen systems.

The deduction principle leads the way to a formulation of validity in proof quantales. When is an object of a proof quantale valid? In other words, when does it represent a valid deduction? By the deduction principle, we expect all objects above truth, or $\mathbf{1}$, to be valid. However, we wish to be more liberal when it comes to accepting the use of premises in the conclusion of a consequence: premises may be used in any order; a premise may be used any number of times; or a premise may not be used at all. In other words, the constructive, "operational" aspects of a proof term are irrelevant as far as validity is concerned. Were we to require formally that all proof objects that obey these three laws also be above $\mathbf{1}$, we would end up by requiring

$$x\,;\,y \sqsupseteq y\,;\,x \qquad \text{(commutativity)}$$
$$x\,;\,x \sqsupseteq x \qquad \text{(idempotence)}$$
$$x \sqsupseteq x\,;\,y \qquad \text{(weakening)}$$

for all objects x and y of a proof quantale. From the theory of quantales, we know that this forces the proof quantale to become a frame, where $; = \sqcap$, and we would lose all the structure which we use to express deductions. In fact, all valid deductions would be equal to $\top$. Hence, we check validity in a frame *quotient* of the proof quantale.

Definition 9 (Validity) An element x of a proof quantale $\mathcal{P}$ is *valid* iff $x \sqsupseteq_{Val} \mathbf{1}$ for all quantale homomorphisms, *Val*, from $\mathcal{P}$ to a frame, that also preserve the rule arrows. □

Prop. 5 implies that $x \sqsupseteq_{Val} \mathbf{1}$ is equivalent to $Val.x \sqsupseteq Val.\mathbf{1}$. In other words, validity amounts to being above $\mathbf{1}$ modulo commutativity, idempotence, and weakening.

5 Application to Positive Logic

We now illustrate the use of the proposed proof algebra. For this, we choose the setting of positive logic, i.e. intuitionistic logic without negation. Let us first specify what is meant by constructing proofs of positive logic within proof quantales. The only thing that is needed is a way of denoting formulas of positive logic within a proof quantale.

Definition 10 (Proof Quantale for Positive Logic) Let $\mathcal{L}$ denote a formal language of positive logic in the sense of Def. 1, i.e. a set of well-formed formulas generated by a set of atomic propositions and the connectives $\Rightarrow$, $\wedge$, and $\vee$. A proof quantale *for* $\mathcal{L}$ is a proof quantale $\langle \mathcal{P}; \sqcap, \sqcup, \top, \bot, \fatsemi, \mathbf{1}, \mapsto, \leftarrow\!\!\dashv \rangle$ together with an injection $[\![\cdot]\!] : \mathcal{L} \to \mathcal{P}$. When the parse of an expression is clear from the context, we omit $[\![\cdot]\!]$ around formulas in proof-quantale expressions. □

In the following discussion, let $\mathcal{P}$ be an arbitrary but fixed proof quantale for a language of positive logic $\mathcal{L}$. Furthermore, let *Val* range over all quantale homomorphisms in the sense of Def. 9. Let us recall from Sect. 2 that we use objects of $\mathcal{P}$ to denote formulas, rules of inference and proofs. We have just defined how formulas are handled. How can we capture rules of inference? Of course, we are only interested in the logical rules. The proof-quantale structure is intended to capture axioms and structural rules. Consider the natural-deduction style introduction rule for implication:

$$\frac{\begin{matrix}[A]\\ B\end{matrix}}{A \Rightarrow B} \Rightarrow \text{intro}$$

This rule is expressed in $\mathcal{P}$ as the object $\Rightarrow$_intro defined by

$$\Rightarrow\_\text{intro} \triangleq (\sqcap A, B : A, B \in \mathcal{L} : (A \mapsto B) \mapsto A \Rightarrow B)$$

and can be used in the following refinement for any $A, B \in \mathcal{L}$:

$$A \Rightarrow B \sqsupseteq (A \mapsto B) \fatsemi \Rightarrow\_\text{intro} \tag{20}$$

Fig. 3 illustrates how the remaining rules of positive logic are expressed in $\mathcal{P}$. Note, incidentally, that the expressions $\Rightarrow$_intro and $\Rightarrow$_elim directly reflect a natural symmetry, which is concealed by their natural-deduction- or sequent-style formulation. We can *calculate* important properties of these rules. To prove (21), for example, let $A, B \in \mathcal{L}$:

$$\begin{aligned}
& B \sqsupseteq A \fatsemi A \Rightarrow B \fatsemi \Rightarrow_\text{elim} \\
\equiv\ & \{\text{Galois connection}\} \\
& A \mapsto B \sqsupseteq A \Rightarrow B \fatsemi \Rightarrow_\text{elim} \\
\equiv\ & \{\text{Galois connection}\} \\
& A \Rightarrow B \mapsto (A \mapsto B) \sqsupseteq \Rightarrow_\text{elim} \\
\equiv\ & \{\text{meet, definition of} \Rightarrow_\text{elim}\} \\
& \text{true}
\end{aligned}$$

Armed with the two refinement laws (20,21) for implication, we can tackle a proof of the simple distribution property of implication: $(A \Rightarrow (B \Rightarrow C)) \Rightarrow ((A \Rightarrow B) \Rightarrow (A \Rightarrow C))$. During the development, we will make use of two purely syntactical conventions. To highlight the local window of refinement, we enclose a formula in angle brackets. To denote the intention that y refines x, we use the notation $y \therefore x$. More precisely, the notation $z \sqsupseteq \ldots (y \therefore x) \ldots$ stands for $z \sqsupseteq \ldots x \ldots \sqsupseteq \ldots y \ldots$; this notation helps to focus refinement steps and to avoid repeating copies of local contexts.

$$\begin{aligned}
& \langle (A \Rightarrow (B \Rightarrow C)) \Rightarrow ((A \Rightarrow B) \Rightarrow (A \Rightarrow C)) \rangle \\
\sqsupseteq\ \ & \{(20);\ \text{quantale calculus, e.g. (15)}\}
\end{aligned}$$

Axioms for Implication

$$\Rightarrow\_\text{intro} \triangleq (\sqcap A, B : A, B \in \mathcal{L} : (A \mapsto B) \mapsto A \Rightarrow B)$$

$$\Rightarrow\_\text{elim} \triangleq (\sqcap A, B : A, B \in \mathcal{L} : A \Rightarrow B \mapsto (A \mapsto B))$$

Axioms for Conjunction

$$\wedge\_\text{intro} \triangleq (\sqcap A, B : A, B \in \mathcal{L} : A \mathbin{;} B \mapsto A \wedge B)$$

$$\wedge\_\text{elim\_left} \triangleq (\sqcap A, B : A, B \in \mathcal{L} : A \wedge B \mapsto A)$$

$$\wedge\_\text{elim\_right} \triangleq (\sqcap A, B : A, B \in \mathcal{L} : A \wedge B \mapsto B)$$

Axioms for Disjunction

$$\vee\_\text{intro\_left} \triangleq (\sqcap A, B : A, B \in \mathcal{L} : A \mapsto A \vee B)$$

$$\vee\_\text{intro\_right} \triangleq (\sqcap A, B : A, B \in \mathcal{L} : B \mapsto A \vee B)$$

$$\vee\_\text{elim} \triangleq (\sqcap A, B, C : A, B, C \in \mathcal{L} : (A \mapsto C) \mathbin{;} (B \mapsto C) \mathbin{;} A \vee B \mapsto C)$$

Refinement laws for implication

$$A \Rightarrow B \sqsupseteq (A \mapsto B) \mathbin{;} \Rightarrow\_\text{intro} \tag{20}$$

$$B \sqsupseteq A \mathbin{;} A \Rightarrow B \mathbin{;} \Rightarrow\_\text{elim} \tag{21}$$

Refinement laws for conjunction

$$A \wedge B \sqsupseteq A \mathbin{;} B \mathbin{;} \wedge\_\text{intro} \tag{22}$$

$$A \sqsupseteq A \wedge B \mathbin{;} \wedge\_\text{elim\_left} \tag{23}$$

$$B \sqsupseteq A \wedge B \mathbin{;} \wedge\_\text{elim\_right} \tag{24}$$

Refinement laws for disjunction

$$A \vee B \sqsupseteq A \mathbin{;} \vee\_\text{intro\_left} \tag{25}$$

$$A \vee B \sqsupseteq B \mathbin{;} \vee\_\text{intro\_right} \tag{26}$$

$$C \sqsupseteq (A \mapsto C) \mathbin{;} (B \mapsto C) \mathbin{;} A \vee B \mathbin{;} \vee\_\text{elim} \tag{27}$$

Fig. 3. Positive logic in a proof quantale, with derived refinement laws

$$\begin{array}{ll}
& (A \mathbin{;} A \Rightarrow B \mathbin{;} A \Rightarrow (B \Rightarrow C) \\
& \quad \mapsto \langle C \rangle) \mathbin{;} \Rightarrow_\text{intro} \mathbin{;} \Rightarrow_\text{intro} \mathbin{;} \Rightarrow_\text{intro} \\
\sqsupseteq & \quad \{(21);\ \text{monotonicity}\} \\
& (A \mathbin{;} A \Rightarrow B \mathbin{;} A \Rightarrow (B \Rightarrow C) \\
& \quad \mapsto (\langle B \rangle \mathbin{;} \langle B \Rightarrow C \rangle \mathbin{;} \Rightarrow_\text{elim}) \therefore C \\
&) \mathbin{;} \Rightarrow_\text{intro} \mathbin{;} \Rightarrow_\text{intro} \mathbin{;} \Rightarrow_\text{intro} \\
\sqsupseteq & \quad \{(21)\ \text{twice};\ \text{monotonicity}\} \\
& (A \mathbin{;} A \Rightarrow B \mathbin{;} A \Rightarrow (B \Rightarrow C) \\
& \quad \mapsto (\ (A \mathbin{;} A \Rightarrow B \mathbin{;} \Rightarrow_\text{elim}) \therefore B \\
& \qquad \mathbin{;} (A \mathbin{;} A \Rightarrow (B \Rightarrow C) \mathbin{;} \Rightarrow_\text{elim}) \therefore B \Rightarrow C \\
& \qquad \mathbin{;} \Rightarrow_\text{elim}) \therefore C \\
&) \mathbin{;} \Rightarrow_\text{intro} \mathbin{;} \Rightarrow_\text{intro} \mathbin{;} \Rightarrow_\text{intro} \\
\sqsupseteq_{Val} & \quad \{\text{quantale/frame calculus}\} \\
& \Rightarrow_\text{intro} \sqcap \Rightarrow_\text{elim}
\end{array}$$

For the last refinement, recall that in *Val*.$\mathcal{P}$ we may calculate modulo commutativity, idempotence and weakening of $\mathbin{;}$. The complete refinement can be interpreted as a proof of the initial formula from the logical axioms of positive logic.

Correctness

We briefly sketch the sequence of arguments needed to show that this interpretation is sound. The full proof is given by Simons (1997*a*). Let Pl $\triangleq \langle \mathcal{L} \mid \bar{A}, \bar{S}, \bar{L} \rangle$ be a formal Gentzen system with inference rules as defined in Fig. 4 for a given formal language $\mathcal{L}$ of well-formed formulas of positive logic. The inference rules induce a set R of relations between lists of sequents of Pl in the sense of Def. 7 and as shown in Fig. 5; note that any term $x \sqsupseteq y$ amounts to an equation $x \sqcup y = x$. We add a set R' of relations

$$\frac{}{A \vdash A}\ \text{axiom}$$

Structural rules

$$\frac{\Gamma, A, B, \Delta \vdash C}{\Gamma, B, A, \Delta \vdash C}\ \text{interchange} \qquad \frac{A, A, \Gamma \vdash B}{A, \Gamma \vdash B}\ \text{contraction} \qquad \frac{\Gamma \vdash B}{A, \Gamma \vdash B}\ \text{thinning}$$

Logical rules

$$\frac{A, \Gamma \vdash B}{\Gamma \vdash A \Rightarrow B} \Rightarrow \text{intro} \qquad \frac{\Gamma \vdash A \quad \Delta \vdash A \Rightarrow B}{\Gamma, \Delta \vdash B} \Rightarrow \text{elim}$$

$$\frac{\Gamma \vdash A \quad \Delta \vdash B}{\Gamma, \Delta \vdash A \wedge B}\ \wedge\ \text{intro} \qquad \frac{\Gamma \vdash A \wedge B}{\Gamma \vdash A}\ \wedge\ \text{elim left} \qquad \frac{\Gamma \vdash A \wedge B}{\Gamma \vdash B}\ \wedge\ \text{elim right}$$

$$\frac{\Gamma \vdash A}{\Gamma \vdash A \vee B}\ \vee\ \text{intro left} \qquad \frac{\Gamma \vdash B}{\Gamma \vdash A \vee B}\ \vee\ \text{intro right} \qquad \frac{A, \Gamma \vdash C \quad B, \Delta \vdash C \quad \Theta \vdash A \vee B}{\Gamma, \Delta, \Theta \vdash C}\ \vee\ \text{elim}$$

Fig. 4. Gentzen-style rules of inference for positive logic

that enforce a frame structure:

$$(\Gamma \vdash A) ; (\Delta \vdash B) \sqsupseteq (\Delta \vdash B) ; (\Gamma \vdash A) \qquad \text{(commutativity)}$$
$$(\Gamma \vdash A) ; (\Gamma \vdash A) \sqsupseteq (\Gamma \vdash A) \qquad \text{(idempotence)}$$
$$(\Gamma \vdash A) \sqsupseteq (\Gamma \vdash A) ; (\Delta \vdash B) \qquad \text{(weakening)}$$

where again $A, B \in \mathcal{L}$ and $\Gamma, \Delta \in \mathcal{L}^*$. These relations, together with the set $\mathcal{S}$ of sequents over $\mathcal{L}$ as generators, present the quantale $\mathbf{Pl} \triangleq \mathbf{Qu}\langle \mathcal{S} \mid R \cup R' \rangle$, which — owing to the relations in R' — is a frame. Consider the construction of **Pl** by means of coverages, and let C denote the coverage induced by the relations. Let us recall that **Pl** is the set of C-ideals in the free monoid $\langle \mathcal{S}^*; ;, \mathbf{1} \rangle$. Specifically, the injection of the generators into **Pl** is determined by $[\![\Gamma \vdash A]\!] = C\text{-}\langle \Gamma \vdash A \rangle$. We can obtain a characterization of $C\text{-}\langle \Gamma \vdash A \rangle$. Let us interpret the relations, read from left to right, as a ground rewriting system over $\mathcal{S}^*$, and let $\stackrel{*}{\to}$ denote the induced derivability relation.

Lemma 11 *$C\text{-}\langle \Gamma \vdash A \rangle = \downarrow(\Gamma \vdash A)$, where $\downarrow s$ denotes the set of terms (lists of sequences) derivable from s, $\{t : t \in \mathcal{S}^* \text{ and } s \stackrel{*}{\to} t\}$.* □

Lemma 12 *A sequent $\Gamma \vdash A$ in Pl is provable with respect to assumptions $s_1, \ldots, s_n$ iff $s_1 ; \cdots ; s_n \in [\![\Gamma \vdash A]\!]$ in **Pl**.* □

Corollary 13 *A sequent $\Gamma \vdash A$ is provable iff $[\![\Gamma \vdash A]\!] \supseteq C\text{-}\langle \mathbf{1} \rangle$.* □

Thus, $\Gamma \vdash A$ is provable iff $[\![\Gamma \vdash A]\!]$ contains the cover of $\mathbf{1}$, viz. the quantale completion of the abstract-truth object $\mathbf{1}$.

Lemma 14 *In **Pl**, the objects corresponding to* ⇒_intro, ⇒_elim, ∧_intro, ∧_elim_left, ∧_elim_right, ∨_intro_left, ∨_intro_right, *and* ∨_elim *are valid:*

$$([\![\vdash A]\!] \mapsto [\![\vdash B]\!]) \mapsto [\![\vdash A \Rightarrow B]\!] \supseteq C\text{-}\langle \mathbf{1} \rangle \qquad [\![\vdash A \wedge B]\!] \mapsto [\![\vdash B]\!] \supseteq C\text{-}\langle \mathbf{1} \rangle$$
$$[\![\vdash A \Rightarrow B]\!] \mapsto ([\![\vdash A]\!] \mapsto [\![\vdash B]\!]) \supseteq C\text{-}\langle \mathbf{1} \rangle \qquad [\![\vdash A]\!] \mapsto [\![\vdash A \vee B]\!] \supseteq C\text{-}\langle \mathbf{1} \rangle$$
$$[\![\vdash A]\!] ; [\![\vdash B]\!] \mapsto [\![\vdash A \wedge B]\!] \supseteq C\text{-}\langle \mathbf{1} \rangle \qquad [\![\vdash B]\!] \mapsto [\![\vdash A \vee B]\!] \supseteq C\text{-}\langle \mathbf{1} \rangle$$
$$[\![\vdash A \wedge B]\!] \mapsto [\![\vdash A]\!] \supseteq C\text{-}\langle \mathbf{1} \rangle \qquad ([\![\vdash A]\!] \mapsto [\![\vdash D]\!]) ;_C ([\![\vdash B]\!] \mapsto [\![\vdash D]\!]) ;_C$$
$$[\![\vdash A \vee B]\!] \mapsto [\![\vdash D]\!] \supseteq C\text{-}\langle \mathbf{1} \rangle$$

for well-formed formulas $A, B, D \in \mathcal{L}$. □

$$A \vdash A \sqsupseteq \mathbf{1} \text{ (axiom)}$$

Structural rules

$$\Gamma, B, A, \Delta \vdash C \sqsupseteq \Gamma, A, B, \Delta \vdash C \text{ (interchange)} \qquad A, \Gamma \vdash B \sqsupseteq A, A, \Gamma \vdash B \text{ (contraction)}$$
$$A, \Gamma \vdash B \sqsupseteq \Gamma \vdash B \text{ (thinning)}$$

Logical rules

$$\Gamma \vdash A \Rightarrow B \sqsupseteq A, \Gamma \vdash B \text{ (}\Rightarrow\text{ intro)} \qquad \Gamma, \Delta \vdash B \sqsupseteq (\Gamma \vdash A) ; (\Delta \vdash A \Rightarrow B) \text{ (}\Rightarrow\text{ elim)}$$
$$\Gamma, \Delta \vdash A \wedge B \sqsupseteq (\Gamma \vdash A) ; (\Delta \vdash B) \text{ (}\wedge\text{ intro)}$$
$$\Gamma \vdash A \sqsupseteq \Gamma \vdash A \wedge B \text{ (}\wedge\text{ elim left)} \qquad \Gamma \vdash B \sqsupseteq \Gamma \vdash A \wedge B \text{ (}\wedge\text{ elim right)}$$
$$\Gamma \vdash A \vee B \sqsupseteq \Gamma \vdash A \text{ (}\vee\text{ intro left)} \qquad \Gamma \vdash A \vee B \sqsupseteq \Gamma \vdash B \text{ (}\vee\text{ intro right)}$$
$$\Gamma, \Delta, \Theta \vdash C \sqsupseteq (A, \Gamma \vdash C) ; (B, \Delta \vdash C) ; (\Theta \vdash A \vee B) \text{ (}\vee\text{ elim)}$$

Fig. 5. Quantale relations R for positive logic; $A, B, C \in \mathcal{L}$ and $\Gamma, \Delta \in \mathcal{L}^*$ (cf. Fig. 4)

The following theorem summarizes the previous arguments and provides the mathematical justification for the proof strategy outlined above.

Proposition 15 *Let $\mathcal{L}$ denote a formal language of positive logic. And let* $\mathbf{Pl} \triangleq \mathbf{Qu}\langle \mathcal{S} \mid R \cup R' \rangle$ *be a proof quantale for $\mathcal{L}$ with the insertion of formulas determined by mapping a formula $A \in \mathcal{L}$ to $[\![\vdash A]\!]$; note that, owing to the relations in R',* **Pl** *is a frame. The following laws hold in* **Pl** *for arbitrary $A, B, C \in \mathcal{L}$:*

$$(A \mapsto B) \mapsto A \Rightarrow B \sqsupseteq \mathbf{1} \qquad A \wedge B \mapsto B \sqsupseteq \mathbf{1}$$
$$A \Rightarrow B \mapsto (A \mapsto B) \sqsupseteq \mathbf{1} \qquad A \mapsto A \vee B \sqsupseteq \mathbf{1}$$
$$A ; B \mapsto A \wedge B \sqsupseteq \mathbf{1} \qquad B \mapsto A \vee B \sqsupseteq \mathbf{1}$$
$$A \wedge B \mapsto A \sqsupseteq \mathbf{1} \qquad (A \mapsto C) ; (B \mapsto C) ; A \vee B \mapsto C \sqsupseteq \mathbf{1}$$

A formula A is valid in **Pl**, *i.e. $A \sqsupseteq \mathbf{1}$, iff the sequent $\vdash A$ is provable in* Pl. □

Corollary 16 (Correctness) *Let* axioms *be the meet of the axioms in Fig. 3, i.e.*

$$\text{axioms} \triangleq \sqcap\{\Rightarrow\_\text{intro}, \Rightarrow\_\text{elim}, \wedge\_\text{intro}, \wedge\_\text{elim\_left}, \wedge\_\text{elim\_right}, \vee\_\text{intro\_left}, \vee\_\text{intro\_right}, \vee\_\text{elim}\}.$$

If, for all quantale homomorphisms, Val, to a frame, that preserve the rule arrows, $A \sqsupseteq_{Val}$ axioms *is a theorem of proof quantales for $\mathcal{L}$, then $\vdash A$ is provable in* Pl. □

Note that the elements of **Pl** are sets of (partial) derivations. With this interpretation, we can review the rule arrow from a slightly different perspective. Let x and y denote elements of **Pl**. Then, the inference $x \mapsto y$ turns out to be the union $(\cup \zeta : (\forall \chi : \chi \in x : \chi ; \zeta \in y))$ of all those derivations ζ which, combined with any derivation in x, complete to a derivation in y. This means that $x \mapsto y$ provides the answer to the question: Given a derivation specified by x, what is "the most abstract" derivation which, combined with x, yields a derivation specified by y? This is akin to the "weakest prespecification" introduced by Hoare & He (1987) for program refinement.

6 Related and Further Work

While investigating these semantic foundations, it became increasingly apparent to us that the essence of the problem is determining suitable abstractions for specifying various forms of *interactions* effected by *composing* objects. In proof quantales, interaction takes place during refinement. This question would appear to be fundamental, because it arises in a number of research areas, all of which are concerned with finding semantic foundations for expressing dynamic processes. In our context, a mathematical argument is viewed as such a process. It is an important goal to be able to characterize abstractly, or axiomatize, various forms of composition of two semantic entities by specifying the interaction effected by the act of composition. The forms of composition in question include, for instance, additive and multiplicative disjunction and conjunction of linear logic, sequential composition, and angelic or demonic parallel composition. Some recent contributions to this research, resulting from the study of semantics for linear logic and process calculi, include Chu spaces (Pratt 1995), interaction categories (Abramsky 1994), and weakly distributive categories (Cockett & Seely 1997).

Residuated lattices and related mathematical structures are well known and have been used to model substructural logics (Došen & Schroeder-Heister 1993). Ono (1993) gives an algebraic semantics for a class of substructural logics, which is based on a variant of quantales called complete full Lambek algebras, and uses it to prove a completeness theorem for the class of logics considered. Dunn (1990, 1993) investigates algebraic structures that are common to a variety of substructural logics. At the heart of these various approaches lie the Galois connections that bind composition and residuals together. They investigate logics, whether they are trying to exhibit algebraic properties of the connectives or to find semantic domains of an algebraic nature. To our knowledge, though, no approach considers proofs as such to be furnished with a quantale or related structure. Residuated lattices in the form of quantales have recently become prominent, following Yetter's (1990) discovery that they can serve as domains for algebraic semantics of linear logics. A related exposition of algebraic models of linear logic is given by Hesselink (1990). Troelstra (1992) gives a brief summary of these results, stating by way of introduction that quantales are for linear logic what frames are for intuitionistic logic. Basically, the tensor is interpreted by composition, and linear implication by the rule arrow. The storage modality ! is interpreted by a localic closure operator. Abramsky & Vickers (1993) use quantales to study various forms of process semantics. For this purpose, they equip the set of observations with a quantale structure: the join operation corresponds to nondeterministic choice.

Martin et al. (1997) present a tactic language and its denotational semantics and derive from there a number of algebraic laws. Abstractly, they investigate a calculus of list-producing functions (lists of subgoals), leaving the object language unspecified, and thus have no need for a notion of proof or validity. It would appear worthwhile adopting some of their tacticals in our proof algebra and determining whether fixing a concrete logical object language allows their calculus to be interpreted as a proof algebra.

Proof quantales are intended to provide an algebraic framework for proof refinement in various logics. The natural question then is: Does this framework really scale up to more expressive logics? To answer this question satisfactorily, further practical and theoretical investigations are needed. We believe that such investigations are worthwhile, because the overall approach is based on the paradigms of composition and refinement, which have proved most useful in software design.

As we have seen, it is a straightforward matter to translate a logical inference rule of a Gentzen calculus into its corresponding rule expression in a proof quantale. What should be investigated is a general theory of proof quantales for Gentzen calculi. Of particular interest would be a generalization of Lemma 14 that abstracts from the concrete form of the inference figures of positive logic. Quantification is another topic requiring investigation. One approach could be to look at higher-order logic as the generating basis of proof quantales. Another approach would be to abstract from object theories, in the style of institutions, while keeping enough properties to characterize validity. The calculus we present lacks more sophisticated means for "programming proofs". Thus, we intend to explore the design of a tactical language on top of the framework provided by proof quantales. One feature of such a language would be recursion or repetition, which leads us to study fixpoints in proof quantales. A simple yet fundamental fixpoint operator is a Kleene-like iterator: let x be an arbitrary element of a proof quantale $\mathcal{P}$; then the map $\lambda y.\, x \sqcap (x \,;\, y)$ is monotonic and hence has a greatest fixpoint x^+, which has the obvious properties:

$$x \sqsupseteq y \Rightarrow x^+ \sqsupseteq y^+ \qquad x \sqsupseteq \mathbf{1} \Rightarrow x^+ \sqsupseteq \mathbf{1} \qquad x \sqcap (x \,;\, y) \sqsupseteq y \Rightarrow x^+ \sqsupseteq y$$

$$x \sqsupseteq x^+ \qquad x \,;\, x^+ \sqsupseteq x^+$$

For instance, let $r = \mathit{rule}_1 \sqcap \cdots \sqcap \mathit{rule}_n$; then r^+ represents all finite compositions of the rules in r. Moreover, the second law means r^+ is valid if each rule_i is valid.

7 Conclusion

Our main aim in this paper has been to convince the reader of the usefulness of an algebraic modeling of proof composition and abstraction, and of the technical feasibility of such modeling. In order to focus the discussion on the essential issues, we presented a very simple model and a couple of quite elementary examples. Thus, the algebraic model we introduce only caters for a characteristic case of proof composition, viz. sequential concatenation, and for a typical case of proof-abstraction refinement, viz. a lattice-like order. The resulting model is minimalist and can be seen very much in the spirit of regular algebras with an explicit order. More elaborate algebras, i.e. those with finite and infinite products, can be accommodated easily. In the examples given, we focused on the role of proof refinement, which is usually given less attention than the issue of proof composition. This is why we developed the refinement paradigm in depth. The simplicity of the example considered (positive logic) allowed us to introduce our concept easily and to detail refinement steps carefully. In this paper, we concentrate on refinement processes, but the proposed framework can, of course, serve for abstraction activities as well. One possible application might be the reverse engineering of proofs: how to extract proof skeletons and schemas that are understandable to people from completely detailed proofs that are full of formal, low-level noise.

Acknowledgement. We wish to thank Phil Bacon for his help in polishing the English.

References

Abramsky, S. (1994), Interaction categories and communicating sequential processes, *in* A. W. Roscoe, ed., 'A Classical Mind: Essays in Honour of C.A.R. Hoare', Prentice Hall, pp. 1–16.

Abramsky, S. & Vickers, S. (1993), 'Quantales, observational logic and process semantics', *Mathematical Structures in Computer Science* **3**, 161–227.

Bird, R. & de Moor, O. (1997), *Algebra of Programming*, Prentice Hall.

Cockett, J. R. B. & Seely, R. A. G. (1997), 'Weakly distributive categories', *Journal of Pure and Applied Algebra* **114**(2), 133–173.

Davey, B. A. & Priestley, H. A. (1990), *Introduction to Lattices and Order*, Cambridge University Press.

Došen, K. & Schroeder-Heister, P., eds (1993), *Substructural Logics*, Oxford Science Publications.

Dunn, J. M. (1990), Gaggle theory: An abstraction of Galois connections and residuation, with applications to negation, implication, and various logical operators, *in* J. van Eijck, ed., 'European Workshop on Logics in AI (JELIA'90)', LNCS 478, Springer Verlag.

Dunn, J. M. (1993), Partial gaggles applied to logics with restricted structural rules, *in* Došen & Schroeder-Heister (1993), pp. 63–108.

Hesselink, W. J. (1990), 'Axioms and models of linear logic', *Formal Aspects of Computing* **2**, 139–166.

Hoare, C. A. R. & He, J. (1987), 'The weakest prespecification', *Information Processing Letters* **24**, 127–132.

Jones, C. B. (1990), *Systematic Software Development Using VDM*, second edn, Prentice Hall.

Kleene, S. C. (1971), *Introduction to Metamathematics*, sixth reprint edn, North Holland.

Lamport, L. (1994), 'How to write a proof', *American Mathematical Monthly* **102**(7), 600–608.

Martin, A. P., Gardiner, P. & Woodcock, J. C. P. (1997), 'A tactic calculus — abridged version', *Formal Aspects of Computing* **8**(4), 479–489.

Ono, H. (1993), Semantics of substructural logics, *in* Došen & Schroeder-Heister (1993), pp. 259–291.

Pratt, V. (1995), Chu spaces and their interpretation as concurrent objects, *in* J. van Leeuwen, ed., 'Computer Science Today: Recent Trends and Developments', LNCS 1000, Springer Verlag, pp. 392–405.

Rosenthal, K. I. (1990), *Quantales and their Application*, Longman Scientific & Technical.

Simons, M. (1997*a*), *The Presentation of Formal Proofs*, GMD-Bericht Nr. 278, Oldenbourg Verlag.

Simons, M. (1997*b*), Proof presentation for Isabelle, *in* E. L. Gunter & A. Felty, eds, 'Theorem Proving in Higher Order Logics — 10th International Conference', LNCS 1275, Springer Verlag, pp. 259–274.

Simons, M. & Weber, M. (1996), 'An approach to literate and structured formal developments', *Formal Aspects of Computing* **8**(1), 86–107.

Sintzoff, M. (1993), Endomorphic typing, *in* B. Möller, H. A. Partsch & S. A. Schumann, eds, 'Formal Program Development', LNCS 755, Springer Verlag, pp. 305–323.

Troelstra, A. S. (1992), *Lectures on Linear Logic*, number 29 *in* 'CSLI Lecture Notes', CSLI.

Vickers, S. (1989), *Topology via Logic*, Cambridge University Press.

Weber, M. (1993), 'Definition and basic properties of the Deva meta-calculus', *Formal Aspects of Computing* **5**, 391–431.

Weber, M., Simons, M. & Lafontaine, C. (1993), *The Generic Development Language Deva: Presentation and Case Studies*, LNCS 738, Springer Verlag.

Yetter, D. (1990), 'Quantales and (non-commutative) linear logic', *The Journal of Symbolic Logic* **55**, 41–64.

Ensuring Streams Flow*

Alastair Telford and David Turner

The Computing Laboratory, The University,
Canterbury, Kent, CT2 7NF, UK
E-Mail: `A.J.Telford@ukc.ac.uk`
Tel: +44 1227 827590 *Fax*: +44 1227 762811
`http://www.cs.ukc.ac.uk/people/staff/ajt/ESFP/`

Abstract. It is our aim to develop an elementary strong functional programming (ESFP) system. To be useful, ESFP should include structures such as streams which can be computationally unwound infinitely often. We describe a syntactic analysis to ensure that infinitely proceeding structures, which we shall term *codata*, are productive. This analysis is an extension of the check for *guardedness* that has been used with definitions over coinductive types in Martin-Löf's type theory and in the calculus of constructions. Our analysis is presented as a form of abstract interpretation that allows a wider syntactic class of corecursive definitions to be recognised as productive than in previous work. Thus programmers will have fewer restrictions on their use of infinite streams within a strongly normalizing functional language.

1 Introduction

We aim to develop an *Elementary Strong Functional Programming* (ESFP) system. That is, we wish to exhibit a language that has the strong normalization (every program terminates) and Church-Rosser (reduction strategies converge) properties whilst avoiding the complexities (such as dependent types, computationally irrelevant proof objects) of Martin-Löf's type theory [11,20]. We would like our language to have a type system straightforwardly based on that of Hindley-Milner [6,14] and to be similar in usage to a language such as Miranda[1] [22]. The case for such a language is set out in [25] — briefly, we believe that such a language will allow direct equational reasoning whilst being sufficiently elementary to be used for programming at the undergraduate level.

For such a language to be generally useful, it must be capable of programming input/output and, more generally, interprocess communication. The methods

* This work was supported by the UK Engineering and Physical Sciences Research Council grant number GR/L03279. We would also like to thank members of the Theoretical Computer Science group at the University of Kent at Canterbury for their discussions in connection with this work, particularly Andy King, Erik Poll and Simon Thompson. Eduardo Giménez, of INRIA, France, has also been most helpful in explaining his ideas and how they have been implemented within the Coq system.

[1] Miranda is a trademark of Research Software Limited.

of doing this in Miranda, Haskell [21] etc., typically involve infinite lists (or *streams*), or other non-well-founded structures.

However, in languages such as Miranda, the presence of infinite objects depends upon the use of the *lazy evaluation* strategy in that terms are only evaluated as far as is necessary to obtain the result of a program. In those languages, infinite objects are syntactically undifferentiated from their finite counterparts and, indeed, are of the same type. For example, in Miranda, the lists `[1]` and `[1..]` both have the type `[num]`, despite the fact that the latter is an infinite list (of all the positive integers).

It is apparent that such structures pose problems if we wish to construct a language that is strongly Church-Rosser. Firstly, how can we ensure that our programs reach a normal form? Secondly, how do we do so without relying on a particular evaluation method, as is the case with Miranda etc.? Finally, should infinite objects have the same type as their finite counterparts?

We have argued in [25] that infinite structures, which we call *codata*, should be kept in a separate class of types from the finite ones (*data*), reflecting the fact that they are duals of one another, semantically. We have formulated rules for codata in an elementary term language in [24]. These rules ensure that programs involving codata and corecursion will be strongly Church-Rosser. However, we would like the ESFP source language to permit more free-wheeling definitions, which it should then be possible to translate into the intermediate language. We now need a compile-time check to ensure that these definitions are well-formed in the sense that the extraction of any piece of data from the codata structure will terminate. This means that, for example, the heads of infinite lists must be well-defined. Or, to put it another way, there is a continuous "flow" of data from the stream. Coquand [2] in Type Theory, and Giménez [5], in the Calculus of (Inductive) Constructions, have used the idea of *guardedness*, first proposed by Milner in the area of process algebras [15], to produce methods for checking whether corecursive terms are normalizable.

We argue that their notion of guardedness is too restrictive for programming practice in that it precludes definitions such as:

$$evens \stackrel{def}{=} 2 \diamondsuit (comap\,(+2)\,evens) \tag{1}$$

Here, $\diamondsuit$ is the *coconstructor* for infinite lists and *comap* is the mapping function over infinite lists. Clearly, we can extract the nth positive even number from such a list, yet *evens* is unguarded according to the definitions used by Coquand and Giménez. Their notions of guardedness would appear to be sufficient for their purpose of *reasoning* about infinite objects, particularly within the Coq system [1], but are too limiting for programming in practice.

We have extended the idea of guardedness so that applications to the recursive call will not necessarily mean that they will be rejected as being ill-defined. To do this we have formulated the guardedness detection algorithm as an *abstract interpretation*. In particular, definitions of the form of (1) will be detected as being guarded. Conversely, our analysis is *sound* in that it will disallow definitions such as:

$$bh \stackrel{def}{=} 1 \Diamond (cotl\, bh)$$

Here *cotl* is the tail function over infinite lists.

Whilst it is undecidable whether a corecursive function is well-defined the extension to guardedness that we present here makes programming with infinite objects more straightforward in a strongly normalizing functional language.

Overview of this Paper. In Sect. 2 we give a summary of the theory behind infinite objects in strongly normalizing systems. We then show in Sect. 3 how the idea of guardedness can be extended by using an abstract interpretation. Examples of how the analysis detects whether a corecursive function is well-defined are given in Sect. 4. This is followed in Sect. 5 by a proof that our analysis is sound and in Sect. 6 we present our conclusions and suggestions for future work.

2 Infinite Objects

In this section we summarise how infinite objects have been represented in functional programming languages such as Miranda and Haskell and in systems based upon type theory. In general, infinite objects may be seen as the greatest fixed points of monotonic type operators. This, together with more details on the relationship between data and codata can be found in [17]. Here, however, we seek a concrete form of infinite data structures which does not rely upon the greatest fixpoint model and, moreover, does not rely on either a particular evaluation strategy or a type-theoretic proof system to have a sound semantics. We describe how we propose to represent infinite objects in an elementary strong functional language and why this requires the automatic syntactic check upon infinite recursive definitions that we present in the following sections.

2.1 Functional Programming and Infinite Data

Functional programming languages, such as Miranda, have exploited the idea of ***lazy evaluation*** to introduce the idea of infinite data structures. Hughes has pointed out the programming advantages of infinite lists in [9]. The disadvantages of these methods is that they rely upon a fixed evaluation strategy. In Miranda, definitions such as

```
ones = 1 : ones
```

only produce useful results with a lazy evaluation strategy (i.e. based upon call-by-name): a strict evaluation strategy (based upon call-by-value) would produce an undefined ("bottom") result for an evaluation of such a definition. There is also no guarantee that the streams will generate an arbitrary number of objects. For example, the following is a legal definition in Miranda:

```
ones' = 1 : tl ones'
```

However, it is only possible to evaluate the head of this list, whilst the rest is undefined. We have argued, in [25], that the existence of such partial objects greatly complicates the process of reasoning about infinite objects.

2.2 Guarded Infinite Objects

Coquand [2] in Type Theory and Giménez [5] in the Calculus of Constructions produced syntactic checks upon the definitions of infinite data structures which they called *guardedness*. (Giménez makes additional restrictions in order to cope with difficulties arising from impredicative types in the Calculus of Constructions.) The idea is similar to that formulated by Milner [15] for process algebras in that a check is made that recursive calls only occur beneath constructors. However, the work of both Coquand and Giménez is intended only to produce definitions of infinite structures that can be used within a proof system such as Coq [1] in order to prove coinductive propositions i.e. types of infinite structures. Their definitions of guardedness are, however, insufficient for a practical programming system. For example, we would not be allowed the following:

```
ints = 1 : map (+1) ints
```

This is due to the application of `map` to `ints`.

Conversely, the reasoning system of Sijtsma [18], being purely semantics-based, is not implementable as an automatic means of detecting whether a codata definition is productive.

2.3 Infinite Objects in ESFP

In ESFP, unlike in functional programming languages such as Haskell, we separate finite structures (*data*) from their infinite counterparts (*codata*). This is due to the fact that we cannot rely upon a lazy evaluation strategy to provide a computationally useful semantics for infinite structures. Indeed we seek *reduction transparency*. It is claimed that pure functional languages have the advantage of *referential transparency* over their imperative counterparts in that the meaning of expressions is independent of context. Reduction transparency goes further in that the semantics of expressions is independent of reduction order.

As in Coquand's approach for type theory [2], we have maintained the pivotal role of constructors in introducing codata. Thus, although we have separated codata from data, we have maintained similar syntactic forms to that of Haskell and Miranda. For example, the following is the type of infinite lists:

$$\mathsf{codata}\ Colist\ a \stackrel{def}{=} a \diamondsuit Colist\ a$$

Functions upon codata use *corecursion*: that is they recurse on their results rather than their inputs.

We need to check that an ESFP program will type check according to a set of rules that also serve to define an intermediate term language into which the

Introduction rule

$$\frac{s :: S;\ \{y :: S,\ x :: S \Rightarrow \&T\ \vdash\ X :: T\}}{\mathsf{Fix}\,(y = s)\,x.\,X :: \&T}$$

Side condition: X must be purely introductory with regard to x.
Write $\mathsf{Fix}\,y\,x.\,X$ for $\lambda y'.\,\mathsf{Fix}\,(y = y')\,x.\,X$

Elimination rule

$$a :: \&A\ \vdash \downarrow a :: A$$

Computation rule

$$\downarrow (\mathsf{Fix}\,(y = s)\,x.\,X) \rightarrow X[s/y,\ (\mathsf{Fix}\,y\,x.\,X)/x]$$

Normal form

$$\mathsf{Fix}\,s'\,F' :: \&T$$

where s' and F' are both normal forms.

Fig. 1. Rules for codata.

top-level language may be translated. These rules, given in natural deduction style, are shown in Fig. 1 and were first given in [24]. They are derived from those of Mendler and others [13] for the Nuprl system, a variant of type theory.

Briefly, recursive occurrences of a type are replaced with their *suspension* (denoted with a &). This terminology comes from the fact that each layer of the structure lies dormant ("in suspension") until the function is applied. We keep separate reductions upon elements of an infinite structure from the structure's construction. Data or codata used to construct parts of the structure is *state* information. An infinite data structure will consist of:

- The data at its topmost level.
- A function to generate the next level of the structure, given some state information.
  This is the suspended part of the structure.

Parts of a suspended structure can only be obtained by applying the *unwind* function ($\downarrow$) to produce a normal form of a type T, $C\,e_1 \dots e_n$, where each e_i is in normal form. Typically, some of the e_i will be the normal forms of suspensions of type T, $\&T$. We have, in effect, made the lazy evaluation strategy that was implicit in the Haskell definition above, explicit in our approach. This method thus is also similar to simulations of lazy evaluation that have been produced for strict languages such as ML, as may be seen in [16].

It is the problem of guaranteeing the side condition of "X must be purely introductory with regard to x" in the introduction rule that will concern us in the rest of this paper. Indeed, it is this condition that determines whether our codata definitions are "productive" or not in the sense that normal forms can be produced when they are unwound. In [24] the restriction is a purely syntactic one — only constructors and no destructors are permitted. This is similar to Coquand's definition of guardedness. It would be more convenient to extend this in a way that is driven by semantic considerations. Formally, we have the following definition:

Definition 1. Suppose that we have, $f :: A_1 \rightarrow \ldots \rightarrow A_n \rightarrow \&T$, where $n \geq 0$, and that T is a sum of product types (i.e. $T \stackrel{def}{=} \sum_{i=1}^{i=m} C_i\, T_i^1 \ldots T_i^{N(i)}$, where $N(i) \geq 0$). Then f is **productive** if and only if

$$(\forall a_1 :: A_1^r \ldots a_n :: A_n^r)\ ((\downarrow (f\ a_1 \ldots a_n)) \twoheadrightarrow C_i\ e_i^1 \ldots e_i^{N(i)})$$

where C_i is a constructor of type T, $\twoheadrightarrow$ is the reflexive, transitive closure of $\beta\eta$-reduction and each e_i^j is in normal form. Here, A_i^r denotes all the reducible elements of type A_i (see Definition 2 below). In addition, each e_i^j is reducible.

This definition of productivity can be extended to closed expressions in the obvious way.

In tandem with the above, we have a definition of what it means for an expression to be reducible.

Definition 2. An expression, e, is **reducible** if one of the following applies:-

1. e is data and is normalizable i.e. is convertible to normal form.
2. e is codata and is productive.

We ensure productivity (which is a property of the term model semantics of the ESFP rules) by defining an extension of Coquand and Giménez's idea of guardedness. This will serve as an abstraction of the property of productivity which is clearly undecidable.

3 Detecting Guardedness by Abstract Interpretation

In this section we define an abstract interpretation to detect whether a function definition is guarded. Rather than work with a *concrete* semantics[2] of infinite data structures (which may be expressed via our unwind function, for instance), we use a simpler, *abstract* semantics, whereby the meaning of a stream is given as a single ordinal. We do this by a form of *backwards analysis* which Hughes and others[3] have used to detect properties such as strictness within lazy functional programs. The point of a backwards analysis is that abstract properties, such as the guardedness levels that we shall define below, flow from the outputs of programs to the inputs. This reflects the intuitive way we think about infinite streams: the resulting list, *produced* rather than *analysed* by the function, is

[2] The Cousots [3] have shown how different semantic views of infinite structures may be related through abstract interpretation.

[3] [8] gives a good summary of abstract interpretation and backwards analysis in particular and [7] gives further details of backwards analysis.

neither guarded nor is it split up into its component parts. Therefore we know that the guardedness level of the *result* is 0. We thus use 0 as an input to our guardedness functions in order to determine whether the recursive call(s) is guarded. If it is safely guarded by a constructor then the resulting guardedness level will be greater than 0.

3.1 The Abstract Guardedness Domain, A

The abstract guardedness domain, **A**, is a complete lattice defined as the set, $\mathbb{Z} \cup \{-\omega, \omega\}$, where $-\omega$ and ω are the bottom and top points of the lattice, respectively. The usual ordering on $\mathbb{Z}$ applies to the rest of the lattice. We refer to elements of the lattice as **guardedness levels** and we call the greatest lower bound operator (which is necessarily both associative and commutative), min.

The guardedness levels represent the depth at which recursion occurs in the program graph. $-\omega$ indicates an unlimited or unknown number of destructions, whilst ω indicates that an infinite number of constructors will occur before a recursive call is encountered. No one program will use the whole lattice of guardedness levels since we will only have strictly finitary definitions in our source language.

We also have an associative and commutative addition operation, which is used to combine guardedness levels:

$$
\begin{aligned}
-\omega +_{\mathbf{A}} x &\stackrel{def}{=} -\omega \\
x +_{\mathbf{A}} \omega &\stackrel{def}{=} \omega && (x \in \mathbb{Z} \cup \{\omega\}) \\
x +_{\mathbf{A}} y &\stackrel{def}{=} x +_{\mathbb{Z}} y && (x, y \in \mathbb{Z})
\end{aligned}
$$

3.2 Guardedness Functions

We define mappings, called *guardedness functions*, which transform guardedness levels. This transformation is based upon the syntax of a function definition in the source language. We assume that codata in our source-level language is based upon a sugaring of the following abstract syntax of expressions:

$$e ::= x \mid c \mid \lambda x.e \mid Ce_1 \ldots e_n \mid f\, e \mid \mathsf{case}\; e\; \mathsf{of}\; (p_1 \to e_1) \ldots (p_n \to e_n)$$

Each c is a primitive constant and each p_i is a pattern match. Each source function definition will give rise to a number of guardedness functions. These functions are defined via an abstract semantic operator, $\mathcal{G}$, which maps from expressions to **A**.

Definition 3. Assume that a function definition has the form, $f\, x_1 \ldots x_n \stackrel{def}{=} E$. Then the **guardedness functions** of f are defined, relative to a vector $\boldsymbol{h}$ of actual parameter functions, as follows:

$$
\begin{array}{lll}
f_0^{\#}\ \boldsymbol{h}\, 0 \stackrel{def}{=} \mathcal{G}(f, E, \boldsymbol{h}) & \\
f_i^{\#}\ \boldsymbol{h}\, 0 \stackrel{def}{=} \mathcal{G}(x_i, E, \boldsymbol{h}) & (i > 0) \\
f_i^{\#}\ \boldsymbol{h}\, \omega \stackrel{def}{=} \omega & (i \geq 0) \\
f_i^{\#}\ \boldsymbol{h}\, g \stackrel{def}{=} g +_{\mathbf{A}} f_i^{\#}\ \boldsymbol{h}\, 0 & (g \notin \{0, \omega\}, i \geq 0)
\end{array}
$$

In the above, $f_0^{\#}$ is the *principal* (or *zeroth*) guardedness function of f. It measures the degree to which the recursive call of f is guarded by constructors within its own definition.

Definition 4. We say that a function f is **guarded** (relative to a vector, $\boldsymbol{h}$, of actual parameter functions) if and only if

$$f_0^{\#}\ \boldsymbol{h}\, 0 >_{\mathbf{A}} 0$$

The other guardedness functions, $f_i^{\#}$, where $i > 0$, reflect the extent to which the parameters of f are guarded within its definition. These *auxiliary* guardedness functions are important in that they allow us to determine whether functions passed as parameters to f will be guarded within f. It is by this mechanism of auxiliary guardedness functions that we can determine whether functions of the form, $f \ldots \stackrel{def}{=} \ldots (comap \ldots f) \ldots$, are guarded.

The set of guardedness functions thus produced will in general be recursive. However, since these functions operate upon a complete lattice, **A**, and can be shown to be continuous (see [19]), their *greatest fixed point* exists. This is found by forming a descending Kleene chain[4].

The $\mathcal{G}$ operator is used to define the guardedness functions over the syntactic form of expressions in the source language. In defining this operator, we also need, in general, a vector of actual parameter functions, $\boldsymbol{h}$. This reflects the fact that our function definitions may be *higher-order*, as is the case with *comap* which applies a function to every element of a list. In practice, however, we shall often omit this vector where it is inessential or empty.

Definition 5 (The $\mathcal{G}$ operator). Suppose that we have a named entity, f, which may be either a function or a variable name. We define the $\mathcal{G}$ operator, which produces the guardedness level of f relative to an expression in the source language, E, and a vector of actual parameter functions, $\boldsymbol{h}$, in Fig. 2. The definition of $\mathcal{G}$ involves the auxiliary operators, $\mathcal{S}$, $\mathcal{F}$ and $\mathcal{P}$, described below.

Commentary on the $\mathcal{G}$ Operator Definition. Clauses (8) and (9) extend the definitions of Guardedness given by Coquand and Giménez. (8) permits a function F (which may possibly be f itself) to be applied to an expression involving f. (9) allows the possibility of corecursion occurring within the switch expression of a case.

[4] This contrasts with most abstract interpretations which deal with *least* fixed points and *ascending* chains. However, we have used the definitions here to retain compatibility with Coquand's approach.

$$\mathcal{G}(f, f, \boldsymbol{h}) \stackrel{def}{=} 0 \tag{2}$$
$$\mathcal{G}(f, c, \boldsymbol{h}) \stackrel{def}{=} \omega \tag{3}$$
$$\mathcal{G}(f, x, \boldsymbol{h}) \stackrel{def}{=} \omega \tag{4}$$
$$\mathcal{G}(f, \mathit{fname}, \boldsymbol{h}) \stackrel{def}{=} \mathcal{S}(f, \mathit{fname}, \langle\rangle) \tag{5}$$
$$\mathcal{G}(f, \lambda x.E, \boldsymbol{h}) \stackrel{def}{=} \mathcal{G}(f, E, \boldsymbol{h}) \tag{6}$$
$$\mathcal{G}(f, C\, a_1 \ldots a_n, \boldsymbol{h}) \stackrel{def}{=} 1 + \min_{i=1}^{i=n} \mathcal{G}(f, a_i, \boldsymbol{h}) \tag{7}$$
$$\mathcal{G}(f, F\, a, \boldsymbol{h}) \stackrel{def}{=} \mathcal{F}(f, F, 1, \langle a \rangle, \boldsymbol{h}) \tag{8}$$
$$\mathcal{G}(f, \textsf{case}\ s\ \textsf{of}\ \langle p_1, e_1 \rangle \ldots \langle p_n, e_n \rangle, \boldsymbol{h}) \stackrel{def}{=} \min(\min_{i=1}^{i=n} \min(\mathcal{G}(f, e_i, \boldsymbol{h}), \mathcal{P}\,(p_i, e_i)\, \boldsymbol{h}\, g), g) \tag{9}$$
$$\text{where } g = \mathcal{G}(f, s, \boldsymbol{h})$$

Fig. 2. Definition of the $\mathcal{G}$ operator.

Function applications. In clause (8) $\mathcal{F}$ is the *guardedness function applicator*: it is a function which constructs a guardedness function application from the corresponding application in the source program. The basic idea is that the ith auxiliary guardedness function is applied to the guardedness level of the ith actual parameter. Where the ith auxiliary guardedness function does not exist, due to applications which return a function as their result, we must instead safely approximate using the $nom^{\#}$ function. This will return $-\omega$ on all inputs apart from ω.

We must also consider the possibility that the function, f, whose guardedness we are investigating, may occur in the body of the function F being applied. We thus have another operator, $\mathcal{S}$, the *substituted guardedness level* of f in F. It is intended to ensure that functions are guarded within mutually recursive definitions. If, $F\, y_1 \ldots y_p \stackrel{def}{=} E'$ then $\mathcal{S}(f, F, \boldsymbol{a}) \stackrel{def}{=} \mathcal{G}(f, E', \boldsymbol{a})$. Thus with the application of a named function, *fname*, say, we obtain the following:

$$\mathcal{G}(f, \mathit{fname}\, a_1 \ldots a_n, \boldsymbol{h}) = \min(\mathcal{S}(f, \mathit{fname}, \boldsymbol{b}), \min_{i=1}^{i=n} \mathcal{N}(f, \mathit{fname}, i, \boldsymbol{a}, \boldsymbol{h}))$$

Here, $\boldsymbol{b} = \boldsymbol{a}[\boldsymbol{h}/\boldsymbol{x}]$ and the auxiliary function, $\mathcal{N}$, produces the guardedness level of the application of a named function to a parameter:

$$\mathcal{N}(f, \mathit{fname}, i, \boldsymbol{a}, \boldsymbol{h}) \stackrel{def}{=} \begin{cases} \mathit{fname}_i^{\#}\, \boldsymbol{b}\, g & \mathit{if}\ i \leq \textbf{Arity}(\mathit{fname}) \\ nom^{\#}\, g & \mathit{otherwise} \end{cases}$$

Here, $g = \mathcal{G}(f, a_i, \boldsymbol{h})$. The substitution required to produce $\boldsymbol{b}$ consists of substituting actual parameters for their formal counterparts.

Similarly, we may obtain for corecursive applications:

$$\mathcal{G}(f, f\, a_1 \ldots a_n, \boldsymbol{h}) = \min(0, \min_{i=1}^{i=n} \mathcal{N}(f, f, i, \boldsymbol{a}, \boldsymbol{h}))$$

This means that f *can* be applied to a call of itself and still be guarded, provided that its auxiliary guardedness functions return appropriate results on the guardedness levels of the actual parameters.

In higher-order functions, the function applied may be one of the parameters to the function. This is dealt with by substituting the corresponding element of $\boldsymbol{h}$ for the variable, so that we have $\mathcal{F}(f, x_j, i, \boldsymbol{a}, \boldsymbol{h}) \stackrel{def}{=} \mathcal{F}(f, h_j, i, \boldsymbol{a}, \boldsymbol{h})$. Where we do not know the actual parameter functions that comprise $\boldsymbol{h}$, an abstraction will be constructed over $\boldsymbol{h}$. Examples of this will be seen in Sect. 4 where the second argument of *comap* is applied in the definition of the Hamming function. This method of dealing with general applications, including higher-order constructs, comes from [7] and is explained further in [19].

case *expressions.* (9) extends the class of definitions that are allowed in that the recursive call may conceivably occur in the switch, s, of the case expression. This means that the guardedness of s, relative to the recursive call is paramount when considering the guardedness of the whole expression: the case expression cannot be productive if the switch is not productive. This is why the resulting guardedness level is the minimum of the guardedness level of the switch together with the guardedness level of the rest of the components of the case expression. Even if the switch is productive, we have to ensure that each part of the structure that may be split up by this pattern matching process is in turn guarded. This is done by defining the *pattern guardedness function*, $\mathcal{P}$, for every pattern, expression pair in the case statement. $\mathcal{P}$ is defined as follows:

$$\mathcal{P}\,(p_i, e_i)\,\boldsymbol{h}\,0 \stackrel{def}{=} \min_{j=1}^{j=N(i)} (\mathcal{G}(v_i^j, e_i, \boldsymbol{h}) - \mathcal{D}(v_i^j, p_i))$$

Here, $\mathcal{D}$ is the *level of destruction* function of the infinite object, f i.e. the depth of a pattern matching variable where depth is measured by the number of constructors. It is defined as follows:

$$\begin{aligned}
\mathcal{D}(v, v) &\stackrel{def}{=} 0 \\
\mathcal{D}(v, x) &\stackrel{def}{=} -\omega \\
\mathcal{D}(v, C\, q_1 \ldots q_n) &\stackrel{def}{=} 1 + \max_{i=1}^{i=n} \mathcal{D}(v, q_i)
\end{aligned}$$

Here, max and $-$ are the dual operations to min and $+$, respectively. In the definition of $\mathcal{P}$, above, $v_i^j \in \mathrm{Var}(p_i)$ where $\mathrm{Var}(p_i)$ is the set of variables in the pattern, p_i. In addition, $N(i) \stackrel{def}{=} |\mathrm{Var}(p_i)|$.

4 Example of Guardedness Analysis

In this section we show how guardedness functions may be used to detect whether certain streams are well-defined or not. As a substantial example, we look at the Hamming function which, in the form that we give, cannot be detected as being guarded by the definitions of Coquand [2] or Giménez [5]. The Hamming function, *ham* is defined as the list of positive integers that have only 2 and 3 as their prime factors — further details on such a function can be found in [4]. It and functions used in its definition are given in a Haskell-like syntax in Fig. 3. The type *Colist* here consists of the streams of integers. Further examples of guardedness analysis, including a demonstration that both *comap* and *comerge* are guarded, may be found in [19].

```
ham :: Colist
ham ≝ 1◇(comerge (comap (×2) ham) (comap (×3) ham))

comap :: (Int → Int) → Colist → Colist
comap f (a◇y) ≝ (f a)◇(comap f y)

comerge :: Colist → Colist → Colist
comerge l@(a◇x) m@(b◇y) ≝
    case compare a b of
        LT → a◇(comerge x m)
        EQ → a◇(comerge x y)
        GT → b◇(comerge l y)
```

Fig. 3. Definition of the Hamming function.

In the analyses that follow we shall assume that the guardedness functions of purely recursive functions such as *compare* will be the identity guardedness function. We shall omit the vector of actual parameter functions except where necessary and refer to larger expressions by E, E', E'' etc. We shall also assume that definition via pattern matching is a sugaring of nested case statements.

Analysis of Auxiliary Guardedness Functions of *comap* and *comerge*. In order to analyse the *ham* function we shall need to know the level of guardedness of the second argument of *comap* and of both of the two arguments of *comerge*.

$$\begin{aligned}
comap_2^{\#}\,\langle h\rangle\,0 &= \mathcal{G}(l, \text{case } l \text{ of } (a\Diamond y) \to E') \\
&= \min(\mathcal{G}(l, E', \langle h\rangle), \mathcal{P}\,(a\Diamond y, E')\,\langle h\rangle\,0, 0) \\
\mathcal{G}(l, E', \langle h\rangle) &= \mathcal{G}(l, (f a)\Diamond(comap\ f\ y), \langle h\rangle) = \omega \\
\mathcal{P}\,(a\Diamond y, E')\,\langle h\rangle\,0 &= \min(\mathcal{G}(a, E', \langle h\rangle) - 1, \mathcal{G}(y, E', \langle h\rangle) - 1) \\
\mathcal{G}(a, E', \langle h\rangle) &= 1 + \mathcal{F}(a, f, 1, \langle a\rangle, \langle h\rangle) \\
&= 1 + h_1^{\#}\,0 \\
\mathcal{G}(y, E', \langle h\rangle) &= 1 + comap_2^{\#}\,\langle h\rangle\,0
\end{aligned}$$

It follows that,

$$comap_2^{\#}\ \langle h\rangle\, 0 = \min(h_1^{\#}\, 0, comap_2^{\#}\ \langle h\rangle\, 0, 0)$$

$$\begin{aligned} comerge_1^{\#}\ 0 &= \mathcal{G}(l, \text{case } l \text{ of } (a \Diamond x) \rightarrow E') \\ &= \min(\mathcal{P}\,(a \Diamond x, E')\, 0, 0) \end{aligned}$$

$$\begin{aligned} \mathcal{P}\,(a \Diamond x, E')\, 0 &= \min(\mathcal{G}(a, E') - 1, \mathcal{G}(x, E') - 1) \\ \mathcal{G}(a, E') &= \mathcal{G}(a, \text{case } m \text{ of } (b \Diamond y) \rightarrow E'') \\ &= \mathcal{G}(a, \text{case } compare\ a\, b \text{ of } E''') \\ &= \min(1 + \mathcal{G}(a, a), 1 + \mathcal{G}(a, a), \omega) = 1 \\ \mathcal{G}(x, E') &= \min(1 + comerge_1^{\#}\ 0, 1 + comerge_1^{\#}\ 0, \omega) \end{aligned}$$

Thus,

$$\begin{aligned} comerge_1^{\#}\ 0 &= \min(1 - 1, \min(1 + comerge_1^{\#}\ 0, 1 + comerge_1^{\#}\ 0, \omega) - 1, 0) \\ &= \min(0, comerge_1^{\#}\ 0, 0) \end{aligned}$$

The greatest fixpoint of the functional corresponding to this equation is 0.

Likewise, $comerge_2^{\#}\ 0 = \min(\mathcal{G}(b, E'') - 1, \mathcal{G}(y, E'') - 1, 0)$, and the solution to this is also 0.

Analysis of the Main Function, *ham*.

$$\begin{aligned} ham_0^{\#}\ 0 &= 1 + \mathcal{G}(ham, comerge\ (comap\ (\times 2)\ ham)\ (comap\ (\times 3)\ ham)) \\ &= 1 + \min(\mathcal{S}(ham, comerge), \\ &\qquad (comerge_1^{\#}\ \mathcal{G}(ham, (comap\ (\times 2)\ ham))), \\ &\qquad (comerge_2^{\#}\ \mathcal{G}(ham, (comap\ (\times 3)\ ham)))) \\ &= 1 + \min(\omega, \mathcal{G}(ham, comap\ (\times 2)\ ham), \mathcal{G}(ham, comap\ (\times 3)\ ham)) \end{aligned}$$

(The above follows since $comerge_1^{\#}$ and $comerge_2^{\#}$ both give 0 when applied to 0 and *ham* does not occur within the definition of *comerge* or any functions called through *comerge*.)

$$\mathcal{G}(ham, comap\ (\times 2)\ ham) = comap_2^{\#}\ \langle(\times 2)\rangle\, 0 = \mathbf{GFP}\ F^{\#}$$

where $F^{\#} = \lambda f.(\min((\times 2)_1^{\#}\, 0, f, 0))$. Now, $\mathbf{GFP}\ F^{\#} = 0$, since $(\times 2)_1^{\#}\, 0 = 0$, and so $\mathcal{G}(ham, comap\ (\times 2)\ ham) = 0$. Similarly, $\mathcal{G}(ham, comap\ (\times 3)\ ham) = 0$, and thus we obtain,

$$ham_0^{\#}\ 0 = 1 + \min(\omega, 0, 0) = 1$$

Therefore, *ham* **is guarded.**

5 Soundness and Completeness

It is necessary to show that any function that is detected as being guarded by our abstract interpretation will indeed be productive in the sense that it will be possible to obtain the normal form of any element of the structure within a finite time. The following result does indeed show that our analysis is *sound.*

Theorem 6 (Due to Coquand, 1993). *If we assume that all data terms are normalizable then a codata function, f, will be productive for any set of inputs if it is guarded and its definition includes only reducible functions apart from f.*

Proof. The proof is by structural induction over the forms of defining expressions. We shall give a sketch of part of the proof — further details are in [19].

The base cases over primitive constants and variables are trivial, as is the abstraction case given clause (6) in the definition of $\mathcal{G}$.

As an example of one of the extensions, we take the case of (named) function applications. Since the application is guarded, if $n \leq \mathbf{Arity}(\mathit{fname})$,

$$\begin{aligned} 0 &< \mathcal{G}(f, \mathit{fname}\ a_1 \ldots a_n, \boldsymbol{h}) \\ &= \min(\mathcal{S}(f, \mathit{fname}, \boldsymbol{b}), \min_{i=1}^{i=n} \mathcal{N}(f, \mathit{fname}, i, \boldsymbol{a}, \boldsymbol{h})) \\ &\leq \mathcal{G}(f, E[b_1/x_1 \ldots b_n/x_n], \boldsymbol{b}) \end{aligned} \tag{10}$$

Here, $\mathit{fname}\ x_1 \ldots x_n \stackrel{def}{=} E$, and $\boldsymbol{b}$ consists of $\boldsymbol{a}$ with the components of $\boldsymbol{h}$ substituted for corresponding free variables. The last inequality (10) is proved in [19]. Since $E[b_1/x_1 \ldots b_n/x_n]$ must, by assumption, include only reducible terms (including possibly *fname*) apart from f, $E[b_1/x_1 \ldots b_n/x_n]$ must be productive by the induction hypothesis. Consequently, the application must be productive.

Now, if $n > m$, where $m = \mathbf{Arity}(\mathit{fname})$, then, since the application is guarded, for all $1 \leq i \leq n-m$, $\mathit{nom}^{\#}\mathcal{G}(f, a_{m+i}, \boldsymbol{h}) = \omega$. Thus, $\mathcal{G}(f, a_{m+i}, \boldsymbol{h}) = \omega$. It follows that for any G, where we add the definition, $G x \stackrel{def}{=} (\mathit{fname}\, b_1 \ldots b_i)\, x$, with $\boldsymbol{b}$ as above, $G_1^{\#}$ must produce ω on this input too. It then follows similarly to the inequality (10) that $G b_{i+1}$ is reducible and so $\mathit{fname}\, a_1 \ldots a_n$ is productive.

Our Hamming function example showed that our analysis could detect a productive definition as being guarded which would not fulfil the Coquand definition. The following result shows that our analysis is a complete extension of Coquand's work.

Theorem 7 (Completeness). *For corresponding definitions in* ESFP *and Coquand's type theory [2], if the definitions are guarded by Coquand's algorithm then they will be detected as being guarded by our abstract interpretation.*

Proof. Coquand's definition of guardedness can be formalised as an abstract interpretation, mapping from expressions to the abstract semantic domain, **A**. We can show, by structural induction over expressions that the abstract value produced by Coquand's analysis will always be less than or equal to that of ours. Full details are given in [19].

6 Conclusions and Future Work

We have demonstrated that a form of abstract interpretation, which may be shown to be sound, can be used to extend the notion of guardedness for infinite data structures. Such a method can be incorporated within a compiler for an elementary strong functional programming language to detect whether infinite objects are productive or not.

We would expect to be able to perform a similar analysis for *data* i.e. the least fixed points of inductive type definitions. This would naturally follow since Giménez [5] defined the dual notion of *guarded by destructors* for recursive function definitions over data. Consequently, we would expect to be performing the dual analysis (with least fixed points rather than greatest fixed points) over the *same* abstract domain, **A**. It would also be worth comparing such an approach to that of Walther recursion where a decidable test for a broader class of definitions than primitive recursion has been established [12].

Another avenue for future research would be to investigate the meta-theoretic properties of this analysis. We have employed a backwards analysis in the style of Hughes [7] and it is unclear whether a forwards analysis would be sufficient to obtain the same results. A reason why forwards analysis may be inadequate for guardedness detection is that, for certain definitions, we have to determine whether the head of a *Colist* is guarded. It is known that, using a standard forward analysis, it is not possible to detect head-strictness of lists [10].

It also remains to show precisely the complexity of this abstract interpretation process. We have suggested in [19] that the overhead of performing this analysis should be polynomial in practice and so should not impact badly upon any future compiler for an elementary strong functional language.

We conclude that a syntactic check for productivity in a simply-typed yet expressive functional language is made feasible by the work presented.

References

1. The Coq project. World Wide Web page by INRIA and CNRS, France, 1996. URL: `http://pauillac.inria.fr/~coq/coq-eng.html`.
2. T. Coquand. Infinite objects in type theory. In H. Barendregt and T. Nipkow, editors, *Types for Proofs and Programs (TYPES '93)*, volume 806 of *Lecture Notes in Computer Science*, pages 62–78. Springer-Verlag, 1993.
3. P. Cousot and R. Cousot. Inductive definitions, semantics and abstract interpretation. In *Proceedings of the 19th ACM Symposium on Principles of Programming Languages*, pages 83–94. ACM press, 1992.
4. E.W. Dijkstra. *A Discipline of Programming.* Prentice Hall, 1976.
5. E. Giménez. Codifying guarded definitions with recursive schemes. In P. Dybjer, B. Nordström, and J. Smith, editors, *Types for Proofs and Programs (TYPES '94)*, volume 996 of *Lecture Notes in Computer Science*, pages 39–59. Springer-Verlag, 1995. International workshop, TYPES '94 held in June 1994.
6. J.R. Hindley. The principal type scheme of an object in combinatory logic. *Transactions of the American Mathematical Society*, 146:29–60, 1969.

7. R.J.M. Hughes. Backwards analysis of functional programs. In D. Bjørner, A.P. Ershov, and N.D. Jones, editors, *Partial Evaluation and Mixed Computation*, pages 187–208. Elsevier Science Publishers B.V. (North-Holland), 1988.
8. R.J.M. Hughes. Compile-time analysis of functional programs. In Turner [23], pages 117–155.
9. R.J.M. Hughes. Why functional programming matters. In Turner [23], pages 17–42.
10. S. Kamin. Head-strictness is not a monotonic abstract property. *Information Processing Letters*, 41(4):195–198, 1992.
11. P. Martin-Löf. An intuitionistic theory of types: predicative part. In H.E. Rose and J.C. Shepherdson, editors, *Proceedings of the Logic Colloquium, Bristol, July 1973*. North Holland, 1975.
12. D. McAllester and K. Arkoudas. Walther recursion. In M.A. Robbie and J.K. Slaney, editors, *13th Conference on Automated Deduction (CADE 13)*, volume 1104 of *Lecture Notes in Computer Science*, pages 643–657. Springer-Verlag, 1996.
13. P.F. Mendler, P. Panangaden, and R.L. Constable. Infinite objects in type theory. Technical Report TR 86-743, Department of Computer Science, Cornell University, Ithaca, NY 14853, 1987.
14. A.J.R.G. Milner. Theory of type polymorphism in programming. *Journal of Computer and System Sciences*, 17(3):348–375, 1978.
15. A.J.R.G. Milner. *A Calculus of Communicating Systems*, volume 92 of *Lecture Notes in Computer Science*. Springer-Verlag, 1980.
16. L.C. Paulson. *ML for the Working Programmer*. Cambridge University Press, second edition, July 1996.
17. J.J.M.M. Rutten. Universal coalgebra: a theory of systems. Technical Report CS-R9652, CWI, Netherlands, CWI, PO Box 94079, 1090 GB Amsterdam, The Netherlands, 1996.
18. B.A. Sijtsma. On the productivity of recursive list definitions. *ACM Transactions on Programming Languages and Systems*, 11(4):633–649, October 1989.
19. A.J. Telford and D.A. Turner. Ensuring the productivity of infinite structures. Technical report, University of Kent at Canterbury, 1997.
20. S.J. Thompson. *Type Theory and Functional Programming*. Addison-Wesley, 1991.
21. S.J. Thompson. *Haskell: The Craft of Functional Programming*. Addison-Wesley, 1996.
22. D.A. Turner. Miranda: A non-strict functional language with polymorphic types. In J.P. Jouannaud, editor, *Proceedings IFIP International Conference on Functional Programming Languages and Computer Architecture*, volume 201 of *Lecture Notes in Computer Science*. Springer-Verlag, September 1985.
23. D.A. Turner, editor. *Research Topics in Functional Programming*, University of Texas at Austin Year of Programming Series. Addison-Wesley, 1990.
24. D.A. Turner. Codata. Unpublished technical note (longer article in preparation), February 1995.
25. D.A. Turner. Elementary strong functional programming. In P. Hartel and R. Plasmeijer, editors, *FPLE 95*, volume 1022 of *Lecture Notes in Computer Science*. Springer-Verlag, 1995. 1st International Symposium on Functional Programming Languages in Education. Nijmegen, Netherlands, December 4–6, 1995.

Extending Process Languages with Time

Irek Ulidowski[1] and Shoji Yuen[2]

[1] Research Institute for Mathematical Sciences, Kyoto University, Japan
[2] Information Engineering Department, Nagoya University, Japan

Abstract. In recent years a large number of process languages with time have been developed as more realistic formalisms for description and reasoning about concurrent systems. We propose a uniform framework, based on the ordered structural operational semantics (SOS) approach, for extending arbitrary process languages with discrete time. The generality of our framework allows the user to select the most suitable timed process language for a task in hand. This is possible because the user can choose any operators, whether they are standard or new application-specific operators, provided that they preserve a version of weak bisimulation and all processes in the considered language satisfy the time determinacy property. We also propose several constraints on ordered SOS rules for the operators such that some other properties, which reflect the nature of time passage, are satisfied.

1 Introduction

Process languages, for example CCS [Mil89], CSP [Hoa85] and ACP [BW90], are well-known formalisms for specification and reasoning about concurrent systems. They are particularly successful in describing the functional behaviour of systems, represented by *actions*, but they lack the ability to express the *temporal* aspect of the behaviour. This inadequacy has been addressed and a large number of extensions of process languages with *time*, or simply *timed* process languages, have been proposed. These can be broadly divided into process languages with *discrete* time, for example [NRSV90, MT90, Jef91, Hen93, NS94, HR95, PU95, BB96], and process languages with *real* (dense) time, for example [RR88, Wan91, Sch95, BB91, Jef91, WG797, LL97].

We believe that in order to increase the usefulness of process languages in software technology we need to develop a theoretically justified framework for extending process languages with various user-friendly and application-specific features. E-LOTOS [WG797, LL97] is an excellent example of a successful specification formalism which is based on a process language extended with time and value passing. This paper proposes a framework for extending traditional process languages, like CCS and CSP, with user-defined and application-specific operators and with the notion of time. Since we intend our results to be general we make the following assumptions concerning the method for defining process languages, the preferred preorder on processes and the nature of time:

- There are many process operators which are best defined by SOS rules with negative premises, for example sequential composition, priority and action

refinement operators. Instead of rules with negative premises we will use equally expressive *ordered* SOS rules [UP97], an extension of the original SOS rules of Plotkin [Plo81], as our method for defining process languages.
- We shall consider a divergence sensitive version of weak bisimulation relation as our preorder on processes. For the compositionality reasons, we insist that all the considered operators preserve this preorder.
- After [NS94, HR95], we assume that timed concurrent systems function as collections of components which can either perform actions or let time pass. Actions of components are instantaneous and they can be either synchronous or independent. The passage of time is synchronous in all active components which are able to let time pass—there may be active components unable to let time pass but this will not block the passage of time in the whole system. This property is called *maximal time synchrony*. We will also consider several other properties which reflect the nature of time passage in systems. These properties are henceforth called the *timed properties*.

Timed process languages which can be defined within our framework have two important characteristics. Firstly, all process operators preserve a timed version of *eager bisimulation*, a divergence sensitive version of weak bisimulation. Secondly, all processes satisfy several timed properties. The most important of them is the *time determinacy* property and all our timed processes satisfy this property. We also consider other timed properties, including *weak timelock freeness, maximal progress* and *time persistence*, and discuss circumstances under which timed processes satisfy these properties.

Our work provides a powerful and flexible specification formalism for timed concurrent systems. Given a system to specify, the user is free to choose a timed process language, which is most suitable for the description of the system, by selecting both standard and new application-specific process operators. Compositionality of specifications is guaranteed by our congruence results. Moreover, the axiomatisation algorithms for GSOS and De Simone process languages [ABV94, Uli96] can be used, in conjunction with over techniques, to generate sound and complete axiom systems for the chosen timed process language. This may assist the verification stage of system's development.

Due to a limited space, we omit all the proofs. They can be found, together with further explanation and examples, in the full version of this work [UY97].

2 Preliminaries

2.1 Eager Bisimulation

We model timed concurrent systems by *processes* which are states in a *transition system*. The behaviour of systems is represented by transitions between states, where the functional behaviour is modelled by transitions labelled with standard visible or silent actions and the passage of time is represented by transitions labelled with a special *timed* action.

$\mathcal{P}$ is the set of processes and it is ranged over by $p, q, r, s, \ldots$. Vis is a finite set of visible actions and it is ranged over by a, b, c. τ is the silent action and σ is the timed action which denotes the passage of one time unit; $\tau, \sigma \notin \mathsf{Vis}$. $\mathsf{Act} = \mathsf{Vis} \cup \{\tau\}$ is ranged over by α, β and $\mathsf{Act}_\sigma = \mathsf{Act} \cup \{\sigma\}$ is ranged over by χ. A transition system is the structure $(\mathcal{P}, \mathsf{Act}_\sigma, \rightarrow)$, where $\rightarrow \subseteq \mathcal{P} \times \mathsf{Act}_\sigma \times \mathcal{P}$ is the *transition relation*. We will use the following abbreviations. We write $p \xrightarrow{\chi} q$ for $(p, \chi, q) \in \rightarrow$ and read it as process p performs χ and in doing so becomes process q. Expressions of the form $p \xrightarrow{\chi} q$ will be called *transitions*. We write $p \xrightarrow{\chi}$ when there is q such that $p \xrightarrow{\chi} q$, and $p \not\xrightarrow{\chi}$ otherwise. Expressions $p \overset{\tau}{\Rightarrow} q$ and $p \overset{\chi}{\Rightarrow} q$, where $\chi \neq \tau$, denote $p(\xrightarrow{\tau})^* q$ and $p(\xrightarrow{\tau})^* \xrightarrow{\chi} q$ respectively. $p\Uparrow$, read as p is divergent, means $p(\xrightarrow{\tau})^\omega$. We say p is convergent, written as $p\Downarrow$, if p is not divergent. We assume that, if $\chi = \tau$ then $p \xrightarrow{\widehat{\chi}} p'$ means $p \xrightarrow{\tau} p'$ or $p = p'$, else it is simply $p \xrightarrow{\chi} p'$.

Definition 1. Given $(\mathcal{P}, \mathsf{Act}_\sigma, \rightarrow)$, a relation $R \subseteq \mathcal{P} \times \mathcal{P}$ is an *eager bisimulation* if pRq implies

$$
\begin{array}{lll}
(a) \; \forall \chi.\, p \xrightarrow{\chi} p' & \text{implies} & (\exists q', q''.\, q \overset{\tau}{\Rightarrow} q' \xrightarrow{\widehat{\chi}} q'' \wedge p'Rq'') \\
(b) \; p\Downarrow & \text{implies} & q\Downarrow \\
(c) \; p\Downarrow & \text{implies} & [\forall \chi.\, q \xrightarrow{\chi} q' \text{ implies } (\exists p', p''.\, p \overset{\tau}{\Rightarrow} p' \xrightarrow{\widehat{\chi}} p'' \wedge p''Rq')]
\end{array}
$$

$p \sqsubsetapprox q$ if there exists an eager bisimulation R such that pRq.

Example 1. Consider processes p and q defined as follows: $p \xrightarrow{a} \mathbf{0}$, $q \xrightarrow{a} \mathbf{0}$ and $q \xrightarrow{\tau} q$. Process p can perform action a and evolve to the deadlocked process $\mathbf{0}$. Process q can perform a after any number of silent actions, but it can also compute internally by performing silent actions forever. Thus, $q \sqsubsetapprox p$ but $p \not\sqsubsetapprox q$. Moreover, consider CCS-like processes $r = a.(b + \tau.c)$ and $s = a.(b + \tau.c) + a.c$. Processes r and s are equivalent according to weak bisimulation of Milner [Mil89] (an instance of the third τ-law), but $r \not\sqsubsetapprox s$ since after $s \xrightarrow{a} c$ there is no r' such that $r \overset{\tau}{\Rightarrow}\xrightarrow{a} r'$ and $r' \sqsubsetapprox c$.

Relation $\sqsubsetapprox$ is a preorder. It is a divergence sensitive version of weak bisimulation relation studied in [Mil81, Abr87, Wal90, Uli94, UP97], where testing, modal logic and axiomatic characterisations were proposed and congruence results with respect to the ISOS and wbo formats were proved. $\sqsubsetapprox$ coincides with *delay* bisimulation [Wei89, vGW89] for processes with no divergence. We have chosen this finer version of weak bisimulation in preference to the standard one [Mil89] because formats for eager bisimulation have considerably simpler formulation [Uli94, UP97] than those for the standard weak bisimulation [Blo95]. Moreover, since we take divergence into account formats for eager bisimulation are much more general than those for the standard weak bisimulation [UP97, Blo95]. Finally, weak bisimulation, unlike eager bisimulation, is not preserved by some simple operators, for example, action refinement operators [UP97]. Having said that, we agree that both bisimulation relations are equally suitable for many process languages which do not require rules with negative premises and do not feature divergence.

We say that an n-ary process operator f preserves a preorder $\sqsubseteq$ if $\boldsymbol{p} \sqsubseteq \boldsymbol{q}$ implies $f(\boldsymbol{p}) \sqsubseteq f(\boldsymbol{q})$, for any n-ary vectors of processes $\boldsymbol{p}$ and $\boldsymbol{q}$. It is well known that eager bisimulation and many other weak process relations are not preserved by the CCS + and the ACP left-merge $\lfloor\!\lfloor$. We have $a \lesssim \tau.a$ but neither $a + b \lesssim \tau.a + b$ nor $a \lfloor\!\lfloor b \lesssim \tau.a \lfloor\!\lfloor b$. The usual solution is to use instead of the considered relation its *rooted* version [Mil89, BW90]. In our case we will use *rooted eager bisimulation* $\lesssim_r$. However, in the main part of the paper action σ is treated quite differently from other actions: it represents a synchronous passage of time. As a result, some operators, for example the timed version of the CCS +, do not preserve $\lesssim_r$. Thus, we will also use a stronger than $\lesssim_r$ relation which we call *timed rooted eager bisimulation* and denote by $\lesssim_{tr}$.

Definition 2. (a) $p \lesssim_r q$ if ($p \lesssim q$ and $p \xrightarrow{\tau}$ iff $q \xrightarrow{\tau}$).
(b) $p \lesssim_{tr} q$ if ($p \lesssim q$ and $p(\xrightarrow{\sigma})^k \xrightarrow{\tau}$ iff $q(\xrightarrow{\sigma})^k \xrightarrow{\tau}$, for all $k \in \mathbb{N}$).

Relations $\lesssim_r$ and $\lesssim_{tr}$ are preorders. In the next section we will show that $\lesssim_{tr}$ is preserved by all operators of timed process languages.

2.2 Ordered Process Languages

Let Var be a countable set of variables ranged by $X, X_i, Y, Y_i, \ldots$. A *signature* Σ is a set of pairs (f, n), where $n \in \mathbb{N}$ is the arity of operator f. The set of open terms over Σ with variables in Var, denoted by $\mathbb{T}(\Sigma)$, is ranged over by t and t'. The set of closed terms, written as $\mathrm{T}(\Sigma)$, is ranged over by $p, q, \ldots$. A *substitution* is a $\mathsf{Var} \rightarrow \mathbb{T}(\Sigma)$ mapping, it is ranged over by ρ and ρ'. Substitutions extend to $\mathbb{T}(\Sigma) \rightarrow \mathbb{T}(\Sigma)$ mappings in a standard way. The notion of transition is extended to expressions $t \xrightarrow{\chi} t'$.

Definition 3. A (transition) rule is an expression of the form

$$\frac{\{\, X_i \xrightarrow{\chi_{ij}} Y_{ij} \,\}_{i \in I, j \in J_i}}{f(\boldsymbol{X}) \xrightarrow{\chi} t},$$

where $(f, n) \in \Sigma$, $\boldsymbol{X}$ denotes the vector of process variables $X_1, \ldots, X_n$, all X_i and Y_{ij} are distinct, $I \subseteq \{1, \ldots, n\}$, all J_i are finite subsets of $\mathbb{N}$ and t is an open term with variables among $\boldsymbol{X}$ and all Y_{ij}.

Let r be the above rule. Then, f is the *operator* of r and *rules*(f) is the set of all rules with the operator f. The set of transitions above the horizontal bar in r is called the *premises*, written as *pre*(r). The transition below the bar in r is the *conclusion*, written as *con*(r). χ in the conclusion of r is the *action* of r, written as *act*(r), and t is the *target* of r. The set of all actions χ_{ij} in the premises of r is denoted by *actions*(r). If $\sigma = act(r)$ or $\sigma \in actions(r)$ then r is a *timed* rule. If $\sigma = act(r)$ and $actions(r) = \{\sigma\}$ then r is a *σ-rule*. If a rule is not a timed rule and not a τ-rule then it is an *action* rule.

Next, we introduce the notion of ordering on rules as in [UP97]. Let $<_f$ be a transitive relation on $rules(f)$. Expression $r <_f r'$ is interpreted as r' having higher priority than r when deriving transitions of terms with f as the outermost operator. Given a signature Σ, the ordering $<_\Sigma$, or simply $<$, is defined as $\bigcup_{f \in \Sigma} <_f$. An *ordered process language* is a tuple $(\Sigma, A, R, <)$, where Σ is a finite set of operators, $A \subseteq \mathsf{Act}_\sigma$, R is a finite set of rules for operators in Σ such that all actions mentioned in the rules belong to A, and $<$ is the ordering on the rules. Given $G = (\Sigma, A, R, <)$, we can define the transition relation $\rightarrow$ for G as described in [UP97]. Then, $(\mathrm{T}(\Sigma), A, \rightarrow)$ is the transition system for G and eager bisimulation, its rooted and timed rooted versions are defined over this transition system as in Definitions 1 and 2.

It is argued in [UP97] that ordered process languages and GSOS languages [BIM95] have the same expressive power. Hence, instead of GSOS rules with negative premises, i.e. rules with expressions of the form $X \stackrel{X}{\not\rightarrow}$ in the premises, we will use equally expressive ordered rules for defining process operators.

Example 2. We show that ordered rules have the same effect as rules with negative premises. We give an alternative definition of the sequential composition operator ; discussed in [BIM95]. The rules for operator ; are as follows:

$$\frac{X \stackrel{a}{\rightarrow} X'}{X;Y \stackrel{a}{\rightarrow} X';Y}\, r_{a*} \qquad \frac{X \stackrel{\tau}{\rightarrow} X'}{X;Y \stackrel{\tau}{\rightarrow} X';Y}\, \tau_1 \qquad \frac{Y \stackrel{\tau}{\rightarrow} Y'}{X;Y \stackrel{\tau}{\rightarrow} X;Y'}\, \tau_2 \qquad \frac{Y \stackrel{c}{\rightarrow} Y'}{X;Y \stackrel{c}{\rightarrow} Y'}\, r_{*c}$$

The ordering $<$ on rules is such that, for each action a and c, we have $r_{*c} < r_{a*}, \tau_1$ and $\tau_2 < r_{a*}, \tau_1$. So, $p;q$ can perform an initial action of q (by rule τ_2 or r_{*c}) if neither r_{a*} nor τ_1 are applicable, that is if $p \stackrel{\tau}{\not\rightarrow}$ and, for all c, $p \stackrel{c}{\not\rightarrow}$. When p is a totally divergent process then q will never start since τ_1 is always applicable.

Finally, we introduce a general class of ordered process languages whose operators preserve $\sqsubseteq_r$. Since an arbitrary ordered process language may contain operators which do not preserve $\sqsubseteq_r$ we define several conditions on the structure of rules and the orderings which guarantee that $\sqsubseteq_r$ is preserved. We will need the following notions of *active arguments* and *copies* in transition rules.

The ith argument X_i is *active* in a rule r, written as $i \in active(r)$, if it appears in the premises of r. Overloading the notation we write $active(f)$ instead of $\{i \mid i \in active(r) \text{ and } r \in rules(f)\}$. Consequently, the ith argument of $f(\boldsymbol{X})$ is active if it is active in some rule for f. The τ-rule for the ith argument of f, denoted by τ_i^f or simply by τ_i if f is clear from the context, is as follows:

$$\frac{X_i \stackrel{\tau}{\rightarrow} X_i'}{f(X_1,\ldots,X_i,\ldots,X_n) \stackrel{\tau}{\rightarrow} f(X_1,\ldots,X_i',\ldots,X_n)}$$

Given a rule r for f, the set of its τ-rules consists of all τ_i such that $i \in active(r)$. Thus, the set of τ-rules for f consists of all τ_i such that $i \in active(f)$.

Multiple occurrences of process variables in rules are called *copies*. They can be divided into *explicit* and *implicit* copies [Uli94]. Given a rule r as in

- (no τ actions in the premises except in τ-rules)

$$\textbf{if } \tau \in \mathit{actions}(r) \textbf{ then } r \text{ is a } \tau\text{-rule} \tag{1}$$

- (τ-rules for all active arguments)

$$i \in \mathit{active}(f) \textbf{ if and only if } \tau_i \in \mathit{rules}(f) \tag{2}$$

- (no rules above their τ-rules)

$$\textbf{if } r' < r \textbf{ and } i \in \mathit{active}(r) \textbf{ then } r' < \tau_i \tag{3}$$

- (rules and their τ-rules below a rule)

$$\textbf{if } \tau_i < r \textbf{ and } i \in \mathit{active}(r') \textbf{ then } r \neq \tau_i \textbf{ and } r' < r \tag{4}$$

- (rules above a τ-rule)

$$\textbf{if } \tau_i < r \textbf{ and } \mathit{active}(r) \cap \mathit{active}(r') \neq \emptyset \textbf{ then } \tau_i < r' \tag{5}$$

- (rules with implicit copies allowed only below their τ-rules)

$$\textbf{if } i \in \mathit{implicit\text{-}copies}(r) \textbf{ then } r < \tau_i \tag{6}$$

Fig. 1. Conditions for rebo process operators

Definition 3, explicit copies are the multiple occurrences of Y_{ij} and X_i, for $i \notin I$, in the target t. On the other hand, implicit copies are the multiple occurrences of X_i in the premises and the not necessarily multiple occurrences of X_i in t when $i \in I$. Implicit copies in r are denoted by *implicit-copies*(r).

Consider the conditions in Fig. 1, where f is any operator of an ordered process language, $<$ is the ordering and r and r' range over $\mathit{rules}(f)$.

Definition 4. An operator f is *τ-preserving* if the set of its rules satisfies (1)–(6), and it is *initial-τ-sensitive* if the set of its rules satisfies (3)–(6). An ordered process language is *rooted eager bisimulation ordered* (rebo) if it can be partitioned into τ-preserving and initial-τ-sensitive operators such that the targets of all rules contain only τ-preserving operators. Operators of rebo languages are called rebo operators.

rebo process languages are very similar to wbo process languages defined in [UP97]. The idea of partitioning operators in order to guarantee that the rooted versions of weak equivalences are preserved is due to Bloom [Blo95]. Almost all process operators are either τ-preserving or initial-τ-sensitive like the CCS + and the ACP left-merge which have no τ-rules. Thus, they are rebo operators. The exceptions are the Kleene star and Milner's interrupt operators.

Theorem 5. All rebo operators preserve rooted eager bisimulation.

3 Adding Time to Process Languages

In this section we show how to extend an arbitrary rebo process language with time. This is achieved by

time determinacy	if $p \xrightarrow{\sigma} p'$ and $p \xrightarrow{\sigma} p''$ then $p' = p''$
timelock freeness	$p \xrightarrow{\sigma}$
weak timelock freeness	if $p\Downarrow$ then $p \stackrel{\sigma}{\Rightarrow}$
maximal progress	if $p \xrightarrow{\tau}$ then $p \stackrel{\sigma}{\not\rightarrow}$
patience	if $p \stackrel{\tau}{\not\rightarrow}$ then $p \xrightarrow{\sigma}$
time persistence	if $p \xrightarrow{a}$ and $p \xrightarrow{\sigma} p'$ then $p' \xrightarrow{a}$, for any a
urgency	$q \stackrel{\tau}{\not\rightarrow}$ and $q \stackrel{\sigma}{\not\rightarrow}$, for some q

Fig. 2. Timed properties

- extending the definitions of untimed operators so that they preserve the passage of time; such operators will be called *time preserving* operators, and
- defining timed operators which introduce, alter or stop the passage of time in processes; these operators will be called *time altering* operators.

As a result, rebo process languages extended with time preserve timed rooted eager bisimulation and their processes are time deterministic. Moreover, we propose several conditions on operators such that other timed properties, given in Fig. 2 where p is an arbitrary process, are also satisfied. These and other timed properties, which reflect the nature of time, are studied in [Wan91, NS91, Sch95, Jef91, Hen93]. There are dependencies between some of these properties:

Lemma 6. The negation of the urgency property is equivalent to the patience property, and the patience property implies the weak timelock freeness property.

3.1 Time Preserving Operators

We propose a uniform method for extending untimed rebo operators with time so that they preserve the passage of time. Following [RR88, Wan91, NS91], one may expect that it is sufficient to extend the set of rules for each rebo operator f with the σ-rule

$$\frac{\{X_j \xrightarrow{\sigma} Y_j\}_{j\in J}}{f(X_1,\ldots,X_n) \xrightarrow{\sigma} f(Y_1,\ldots,Y_n)},$$

where $J = active(f)$ and $Y_i = X_i$ for $i \notin active(f)$. A σ-rule of the above form will be denoted thereafter by σ_J^f, where J indicates which arguments appear in the premises, or simply by σ_J when the operator is obvious from the context.

This method is correct for the CCS +, parallel operator and many other process operators: it guarantees that the maximal time synchrony property holds. But, it is not suitable for some operators which are defined by ordered rules. For example, this method incorrectly suggests adding the following rule for the sequential composition operator ; which we have defined in Example 2.

$$\frac{X \xrightarrow{\sigma} X' \quad Y \xrightarrow{\sigma} Y'}{X;Y \xrightarrow{\sigma} X';Y'}$$

The rule requires X and Y to synchronise on σ contrary to the intention that Y should only act when X is deadlocked and cannot pass time. Applying the rule, we deduce that $p;q$ cannot pass time if q cannot pass time, even though p may be able to pass time. This fails maximal time synchrony. Our solution is to add two σ-rules for ; (one for each of its arguments) and order them accordingly.

We will need the following notation in order to define time preserving versions of rebo process operators. Two active arguments X_i and X_j of f have the *same priority* if and only if neither $\tau_i < \tau_j$ nor $\tau_j < \tau_i$. Let $Levels(f) = \{I_1, \ldots, I_k\}$ be the disjoint partition of $active(f)$ such that members of any I_l have the same priority. Members of $Levels(f)$ are called the *priority levels* for f.

Definition 7. Given a rebo process language L with the set of actions not containing σ, the *time preserving extension* of L is obtained by extending
(a) $rules(f)$ with $\{\sigma_J \mid J \in Levels(f)\}$, for every operator f of L, and
(b) the orderings according to (3)–(6).
The operators of thus extended languages are called time preserving operators.

Example 3. Time preserving versions of popular process operators are obtained simply by adding the required σ-rules for each priority level. For example, for the CCS + and parallel operators we add the following σ-rules.

$$\frac{X \xrightarrow{\sigma} X' \quad Y \xrightarrow{\sigma} Y'}{X + Y \xrightarrow{\sigma} X' + Y'} \qquad \frac{X \xrightarrow{\sigma} X' \quad Y \xrightarrow{\sigma} Y'}{X \parallel Y \xrightarrow{\sigma} X' \parallel Y'}$$

Notice that time preserving versions of rebo operators are not necessarily rebo operators themselves. Time preserving + is not a rebo operator because it is not τ-preserving but it appears in the target of the conclusion of its σ-rule. Since sequential composition operator ; has two priority levels we add

$$\frac{X \xrightarrow{\sigma} X'}{X;Y \xrightarrow{\sigma} X';Y} \quad \text{and} \quad \frac{Y \xrightarrow{\sigma} Y'}{X;Y \xrightarrow{\sigma} X;Y'}.$$

The prefixing operators have no active arguments, so we obtain their time preserving versions by adding $\alpha.X \xrightarrow{\sigma} \alpha.X$, for each $\alpha \in \mathsf{Act}$. Similarly, the time preserving version of the deadlocked process operator $\mathbf{0}$ has one rule $\mathbf{0} \xrightarrow{\sigma} \mathbf{0}$.

There are only few timed versions of popular operators which are not time preserving. The examples are the ACP + in [Gro90] and $\oplus$ in [MT90]; the resulting transition systems are *not* time deterministic.

3.2 Time Altering Operators

In this subsection we propose a uniform method for defining time altering operators. We require that time altering operators preserve timed rooted eager bisimulation and the time determinacy property. These requirements considerably restrict the structure of timed rules and the orderings on rules for time altering operators. We motivate and derive these restrictions below.

We do not allow rules which change ordinary actions into timed actions or vice versa, i.e. rules with the action σ and visible or silent actions in the premises (or vice versa), because such rules can be used to define operators which do not preserve $\sqsubseteq_{tr}$ and time determinacy [UY97]. Thus, we demand that only σ actions can appear in timed rules of time altering operators. Next, we propose further restrictions on the timed rules and their orderings so that operators preserve time determinacy. Let an operator h be defined by the following rules.

$$\frac{X \xrightarrow{\sigma} X'}{h(X,Y) \xrightarrow{\sigma} X'}\; r_X \qquad\qquad \frac{Y \xrightarrow{\sigma} Y'}{h(X,Y) \xrightarrow{\sigma} Y'}\; r_Y$$

Consider $h(p,q)$ with $p \xrightarrow{\sigma} p'$, $q \xrightarrow{\sigma} q'$ and $p' \neq q'$. Clearly, if neither $r_X < r_Y$ nor $r_Y < r_X$ then $h(p,q)$ is not time deterministic. This example suggests that a given process $f(\boldsymbol{p})$ is time deterministic if, in the presence of ordered rules, either there is only one timed rule applicable to $f(\boldsymbol{p})$ or there are several applicable rules but with identical conclusions up to a change of process variables.

Definition 8. Given a rebo process language L with the set of actions not including σ, the *time altering extension* of L is obtained by extending
(a) the set of rules for each f with the set of σ-rules R_σ such that $R_\sigma \neq \{\sigma_J \mid J \in \mathit{Levels}(f)\}$ and all rules in R_σ satisfy (7) and (8) defined below, and
(b) the orderings according to (3)–(6).

For all $J \in \mathit{Levels}(f)$ and all r and r' in R_σ with active arguments in J

$$\textbf{if}\;\; \mathit{active}(r) \subset \mathit{active}(r') \;\;\textbf{then}\;\; r < r' \tag{7}$$

$$\textbf{if}\;\; \mathit{active}(r) \bowtie \mathit{active}(r') \;\;\textbf{then}\;\; \exists r''.\ \mathit{active}(r), \mathit{active}(r') \subset \mathit{active}(r'') \;\;\textbf{or}\;\; \forall \rho.\ \rho(\mathit{con}(r)) = \rho(\mathit{con}(r')), \tag{8}$$

where $\bowtie$ says that neither of its arguments is a proper subset of the other argument and r'' is a σ-rule with active arguments in J.

The operators of thus extended languages are called time altering operators.

Many of time altering operators have simple definitions, so the above conditions are trivially satisfied. Condition (7) says that if a σ-rule r' contains all the active arguments of another σ-rule r and some other active arguments then r' should have priority over r when deriving transitions of terms. If this condition is not satisfied then whenever r' is applicable r is also applicable. Hence, there is no guarantee that the application of r and r' will produce the same transition, so time determinacy may be lost. Condition (8) has been motivated above.

We need (8) because there are timed operators which do not satisfy it and thus fail time determinacy. The examples are the timed version of the ACP $+$ [Gro90] and the operator $\oplus$ in [MT90]. The σ-rules for the first operator are the same as the rules for the operator h above, of course with $X+Y$ replacing $h(X,Y)$. Although the sets of active arguments in the two σ-rules for $+$ are disjoint there is no third σ-rule with the active arguments X and Y and the conclusions of the two σ-rules for $+$ are not identical under all substitutions as (8) requires.

Example 4. All timed operators discussed in [RR88, Wan91, Sch95, BB91, Hen93, NS94, HR95, BB96] are essentially time altering operators provided that their definitions are slightly changed by including the required τ-rules and by using σ in transitions instead of t units of time. As an example, we give an alternative definition of the delay operator $\lfloor\ \rfloor(\ )$ of *Temporal Process Language* (TPL) of Hennessy and Regan [HR95]. We use ordered rules instead of rules with negative premises as used originally. The rules are as follows:

$$\frac{X \xrightarrow{a} X'}{\lfloor X\rfloor(Y) \xrightarrow{a} X'} \qquad \frac{X \xrightarrow{\tau} X'}{\lfloor X\rfloor(Y) \xrightarrow{\tau} X'}\ r_\tau \qquad \lfloor X\rfloor(Y) \xrightarrow{\sigma} Y\ \ \sigma_\emptyset$$

The ordering satisfies $\sigma_\emptyset < r_\tau$. We easily check that $\lfloor\ \rfloor(\ )$ is a time altering operator. It introduces the initial passage of one time unit only when its first argument is stable, i.e. cannot perform τ actions. Notice that $\lfloor\ \rfloor(\ )$ does not preserve $\underset{\sim}{\sqsubset}$. But, since $\lfloor\ \rfloor(\ )$ is a **rebo** operator it preserves $\underset{\sim}{\sqsubset}_r$, and hence $\underset{\sim}{\sqsubset}_{tr}$.

3.3 Timed Process Languages

We define a general class of timed process languages whose members preserve $\underset{\sim}{\sqsubset}_{tr}$ and satisfy time determinacy. Then, we identify several of its subclasses which additionally satisfy some other timed properties in Fig. 2.

Definition 9. A process language is called **timed rebo** if it can be partitioned into languages L_1 and L_2 with no common operators such that,
(a) L_1 is the time preserving extension of some **rebo** process language,
(b) L_2 is the time altering extension of another **rebo** process language, and
(c) the targets of all σ-rules in L_2 include only τ-preserving operators.
The class of all **timed rebo** languages is called the class of *timed process languages*.

The difference between **rebo** and **timed rebo** operators is that **timed rebo** operators may have rules with targets containing initial-τ-sensitive operators—such rules are forbidden for **rebo** operators. These rules are the σ-rules for time preserving operators which are initial-τ-sensitive as, for example, time preserving $+$. Thus, in general, **timed rebo** operators do not preserve rooted eager bisimulation. Consider time preserving $+$. We have $\sigma.a \underset{\sim}{\sqsubset}_r \sigma.\tau.a$ but $p = \sigma.a+\sigma.b \not\underset{\sim}{\sqsubset}_r \sigma.\tau.a+\sigma.b = q$ since $p \xrightarrow{\sigma} a+b$ and $q \xrightarrow{\sigma} \tau.a+b$, and clearly $a+b \not\underset{\sim}{\sqsubset} \tau.a+b$. However, because of the form of σ-rules for time preserving operators (Definition 7) and a suitably defined timed rooted eager bisimulation (Definition 2) we have the following.

Theorem 10. Let L be any timed process language and T be its transition system. Then, all operators of L preserve timed rooted eager bisimulation and T satisfies the time determinacy property.

Maximal Progress. A process satisfies maximal progress if whenever it passes time then it is stable.

Theorem 11. Let L be any timed process language and T be its transition system. If all operators f in L satisfy (9) defined below then T satisfies the maximal progress property.

For all rules r and σ-rules r' for f and all priority levels J for f

$$\textbf{if} \;\; act(r) = \tau \;\; \textbf{and} \;\; active(r) \cup active(r') \subseteq J \;\; \textbf{then} \;\; r' < r \tag{9}$$

Example 5. Consider a timed process language which is obtained by adding $\lfloor\,\rfloor(\,)$ from Example 4 to the time preserving extension of CCS. By Theorem 10, all processes in the language are time deterministic. We shall alter this language so it also satisfies maximal progress. We easily check that $\lfloor\,\rfloor(\,)$ satisfies (9). As for the time preserving versions of CCS operators, we put their σ-rules below their τ-rules and other rules with the action τ. So, for the prefixing with τ we have $\tau.X \xrightarrow{\sigma} \tau.X < \tau.X \xrightarrow{\tau} X$. Since $\tau.X \xrightarrow{\tau} X$ is always applicable its σ-rule is never applicable. As for the parallel operator, in order to satisfy (9) we put its σ-rule below its synchronisation rule. Thus, the resulting language, henceforth called TL, satisfies maximal progress.

Urgency, Patience and Weak Timelock Freeness. A process is urgent if it is able to perform some visible action without any delay or it is completely deadlocked. A transition system is urgent if it has an urgent process. We say that an n-ary operator f is *urgent* if, for some n-ary vector of non-urgent processes $\boldsymbol{p}$, we have $f(\boldsymbol{p}) \stackrel{\tau}{\not\rightarrow}$ and $f(\boldsymbol{p}) \stackrel{\sigma}{\not\rightarrow}$.

Example 6. Urgent prefixing $\alpha{:}X$ [MT90, NS94] is a time altering urgent operator. Its defining rule is $\alpha{:}X \xrightarrow{\alpha} X$ but there are no σ-rules. A completely deadlocked process operator called *timelock* [MT90, NS94], which has no defining rules, is also a time altering urgent operator.

In some situations time deadlock is undesirable. In order to avoid it we shall require the following two conditions.

For all rules r and σ-rules r' for f and all priority levels J for f

$$\textbf{if} \;\; act(r) \in \mathsf{Vis} \;\; \textbf{and} \;\; active(r) \cup active(r') \subseteq J \;\; \textbf{then} \;\; r' \not< r \tag{10}$$

For each priority levels J for f there exists a σ-rule r for f such that

$$active(r) \subseteq J \tag{11}$$

Condition (10) resembles in some sense (9). For the same r, r' and J as in (9), (10) insists that if the action of r is a visible action then r cannot be higher in the ordering than the σ-rule r'. Condition (11) says that for each level of priority for f there exists at least one σ-rule with active arguments in J.

It can be shown that if a time preserving f satisfies (9) and (10) then, for any non-urgent $\boldsymbol{p}$, we have either $f(\boldsymbol{p}) \xrightarrow{\tau}$ or $f(\boldsymbol{p}) \xrightarrow{\sigma}$, i.e. f is not urgent. This is roughly because either $f(\boldsymbol{p}) \xrightarrow{\tau}$ follows by some r with the action τ (due to (9)) or, if there is no such applicable rule, $f(\boldsymbol{p}) \xrightarrow{\sigma}$ follows by one of σ-rules since they are never blocked by any rule with visible actions (due to (10)). Similarly, if a time altering f satisfies (9), (10) and (11) then for any non-urgent $\boldsymbol{p}$, either $f(\boldsymbol{p}) \xrightarrow{\tau}$ or $f(\boldsymbol{p}) \xrightarrow{\sigma}$.

With help of Lemma 6 we have the following theorem.

Theorem 12. Let L be any general timed process language and T be the transition system generated by L. If all operators in L satisfy (9) and (10) and all time altering operators in L also satisfy (11) then T is *not* urgent and thus it satisfies the patience and weak timelock freeness properties.

Example 7. We show that the language TL from Example 5 is not urgent, and thus it satisfies the patience and weak timelock freeness properties. Condition (10) is satisfied because no operator of L has rules with visible actions which are above their σ-rules. Condition (11) holds because $\lfloor\ \rfloor(\ )$ has only one priority level $\{X\}$, $\sigma_\emptyset$ is the σ-rule for $\lfloor\ \rfloor(\ )$ and $active(\sigma_\emptyset) = \emptyset \subseteq \{X\}$.

Timelock Freeness and Time Persistence. Another interesting subclass of timed operators are *delay only* operators. A delay only operator f is an operator which is solely defined by σ-rules of the form

$$\frac{\{X_i \xrightarrow{\sigma} X_i'\}_{i \in I}}{f(X_1, \ldots, X_n) \xrightarrow{\sigma} t},$$

where $I \subseteq \{1, \ldots, n\}$ and $t = X_i'$, for some $i \in I$, or $t = f(X_1', \ldots, X_n')$ with $X_i' = X_i$ if $i \notin I$.

Many finite idling operators in [Wan91, HR95, MT90, Sch95] are essentially delay only operators, assuming that their τ-rules are included.

In the following theorem we will use a slightly stronger version of (10) which contains $act(r) \in \mathsf{Act}$ instead of $act(r) \in \mathsf{Vis}$. This version is denoted by (10') and it says that, for a given priority level J, no rule with active arguments in J can be above any σ-rule with active arguments in J. Hence, no time preserving operators which satisfy (10') can block the passage of time.

Theorem 13. Let L be any general timed process language and T be the transition system generated by L. If all time altering operators of L are delay only operators and all time preserving operators of L satisfy (10') then T satisfies the timelock freeness and time persistence properties.

4 Applications

In this section we examine three existing, but quite different, timed process languages and show how they can be represented in our framework.

The passage of time in *Algebra of Timed Processes* (ATP) of Nicollin and Sifakis [NS94] is introduced by the *unit-delay* operator $\lfloor\ \rfloor(\ )$. The operator is defined by

$$\frac{X \xrightarrow{\alpha} X'}{\lfloor X \rfloor(Y) \xrightarrow{\alpha} X'} \qquad \lfloor X \rfloor(Y) \xrightarrow{\chi} Y,$$

where χ, like σ, represents the passage of one time unit. We easily see that unit-delay (with σ instead of χ) is time altering. ATP has urgent prefixing and urgent $\mathbf{0}$ which are both time altering. But the choice, parallel and encapsulation operators are time preserving. The transition system generated by ATP is time deterministic but not timelock free due to urgent prefixing and **0**. The maximal progress property does not hold since parallel composition of two processes may pass time even when communication is possible. Also, time persistence does not hold: $\lfloor a \rfloor(b) \xrightarrow{a}$ but $\lfloor a \rfloor(b) \xrightarrow{\sigma} b \not\xrightarrow{a}$. Furthermore, [NS94] introduces four families of other timed operators: the timeout at t, the start delay within t, the unbounded start delay and the execution delay within t, where $t \in \mathbb{N}$. These operators can be expressed by families of time altering operators.

TPL [HR95] is a timed extension of CCS with two delay operators: simple delay σX defined by $\sigma X \xrightarrow{\sigma} X$ and the mentioned earlier $\lfloor\ \rfloor(\ )$ (same notation as the operator of ACP). TPL's $\lfloor\ \rfloor(\ )$ is defined by the following rules.

$$\frac{X \xrightarrow{\alpha} X'}{\lfloor X \rfloor(Y) \xrightarrow{\alpha} X'} \qquad\qquad \frac{X \not\xrightarrow{\tau}}{\lfloor X \rfloor(Y) \xrightarrow{\sigma} Y}$$

Clearly, σX is time altering and delay only. In Example 5 we have shown how $\lfloor\ \rfloor(\ )$ can be redefined as a time altering operator. Prefixing with τ is urgent and time altering since it has no σ-rules. But, the deadlocked operator **0**, prefixing with visible actions, choice and parallel operators are time preserving. The transition system for TPL is time deterministic and maximal progress holds because of urgent prefixing with τ and the following timed rule for the parallel operator.

$$\frac{X \xrightarrow{\sigma} X' \quad Y \xrightarrow{\sigma} Y' \quad X|Y \not\xrightarrow{\tau}}{X|Y \xrightarrow{\sigma} X'|Y'}$$

Also, the patience and weak timelock freeness properties hold for TPL. We have seen in Examples 5 and 7 that TPL can be equivalently expressed as the timed process language *TL*.

Moller and Tofts [MT90] defined another timed extension of CCS called *Temporal* CCS (TCCS). Unlike in ATP and TPL they used a family of delay operators (t): $(t).P$ behaves like P after t time units. These operators are essentially time altering delay only operators. Similarly as in ATP there is urgent prefixing and **0** does not let time pass. Instead of a general delay operator TCCS has two choice operators: a *strong* choice, which is essentially like the time preserving $+$ of CCS, and a *weak* choice $\oplus$. The latter allows to resolve the choice by the argument with a longer initial delay. A similar operator can be defined in our framework by the usual action rules for $\oplus$ and the σ-rules

$$\frac{X \xrightarrow{\sigma} X'}{X \oplus Y \xrightarrow{\sigma} X'}\,\sigma_X \qquad \frac{Y \xrightarrow{\sigma} Y'}{X \oplus Y \xrightarrow{\sigma} Y'}\,\sigma_Y \qquad \frac{X \xrightarrow{\sigma} X' \quad Y \xrightarrow{\sigma} Y'}{X \oplus Y \xrightarrow{\sigma} X' \oplus Y'}\,\sigma_{XY}$$

with $\sigma_X, \sigma_Y < \sigma_{XY}$. The transition system for TCCS is time deterministic, but due to urgent prefixing and $\oplus$ it fails time persistence, timelock freeness and maximal progress. In [MT91], a version of TCCS called *l*TCCS is proposed. Apart from the mentioned delay operators (which are delay only), *l*TCCS has only time preserving versions of CCS operators. Hence, its transition system satisfies time determinacy and, by Theorem 13, timelock freeness and time persistence.

5 Concluding Remarks

We have proposed a uniform framework for defining timed process languages which are compositional with respect to timed rooted eager bisimulation. As a result most process languages with discrete time can be represented in our framework. Moreover, the generality of our framework allows the user to choose any process operators for her/his favourite timed process language provided that two conditions are satisfied: all operators preserve $\underset{\sim}{\sqsubset}_{tr}$ and the time determinacy property holds. These conditions can be easily verified by checking whether or not the ordered rules for the operators satisfy several syntactical constraints.

In future we would like to generalise our results to an abstract time domain which would cover both discrete and real time.

Acknowledgments

We would like to thank the referees for constructive comments and suggestions, and Iain Phillips for discussions about extending process languages with time. The first author is partially supported by the Ministry of Education, Science and Culture of Japan grant no. 09780270, and the second author by the Hori Information Science Promotion Foundation.

References

[Abr87] S. Abramsky. Observation equivalence as a testing equivalence. *Theoretical Computer Science*, 53:225–241, 1987.

[ABV94] L. Aceto, B. Bloom, and F.W. Vaandrager. Turning SOS rules into equations. *Information and Computation*, 111:1–52, 1994.

[BB91] J.C.M Baeten and J.A. Bergstra. Real time process algebra. *Formal Aspects of Computing*, 3:142–188, 1991.

[BB96] J.C.M Baeten and J.A. Bergstra. Discrete time process algebra. *Formal Aspects of Computing*, 8:188–208, 1996.

[BIM95] B. Bloom, S. Istrail, and A.R. Meyer. Bisimulation can't be traced. *Journal of ACM*, 42(1):232–268, 1995.

[Blo95] B. Bloom. Structural operational semantics for weak bisimulations. *Theoretical Computer Science*, 146:27–68, 1995.

[BW90] J.C.M Baeten and W.P Weijland. *Process Algebra*, volume 18. Cambridge Tracts in Theoretical Computer Science, 1990.

[Gro90] J.F. Groote. Specification and verification of real time systems in ACP. In L. Logrippo, L.R. Probert, and H. Ural, editors, *Proceedings of PSTV'90*, Ottawa, 1990.

[Hen93] M. Hennessy. Timed process algebras: A tutorial. Technical Report 2/93, Dept. of Computer Science, University of Sussex, 1993.

[Hoa85] C.A.R. Hoare. *Communicating Sequential Processes.* Prentice Hall, 1985.

[HR95] M. Hennessy and T. Regan. A process algebra for timed systems. *Information and Computation*, 117:221–239, 1995.

[Jef91] A. Jeffrey. A linear time process algebra. In K.G. Larsen and A. Skou, editors, *Proceedings of* CAV'91, Aalborg, 1991. Springer-Verlag. LNCS 575.

[LL97] L. Léonard and G. Leduc. An introduction to ET-LOTOS for the description of time-sensitive systems. *Computer Networks and ISDN Systems*, 29(3):271–292, 1997.

[Mil81] R. Milner. A modal characterisation of observable machine behaviours. In G. Astesiano and C. Böhm, editors, *CAAP 81*, Berlin, 1981. Springer-Verlag. LNCS 112.

[Mil89] R. Milner. *Communication and Concurrency.* Prentice Hall, 1989.

[MT90] F. Moller and C. Tofts. A temporal calculus of communicating systems. In J.C.M. Baeten and J.W. Klop, editors, *Proceedings of* CONCUR'90, Amsterdam, 1990. Springer-Verlag. LNCS 458.

[MT91] F. Moller and C. Tofts. Relating processes with respect to speed. In J.C.M. Baeten and J.F. Groote, editors, *Proceedings of* CONCUR'91, Amsterdam, 1991. Springer-Verlag. LNCS 527.

[NRSV90] X. Nicollin, J.-L. Richier, J. Sifakis, and J. Voiron. ATP: an algebra for timed processes. In *Proceedings of the IFIP TC2 Working Conference on Programming Concepts and Methods*, Sea of Galilea, 1990.

[NS91] X. Nicollin and J. Sifakis. An overview and synthesis on timed process algebras. In K.G. Larsen and A. Skou, editors, *Proceedings of* CAV'91, Aalborg, 1991. Springer-Verlag. LNCS 575.

[NS94] X. Nicollin and J. Sifakis. The algebra of timed processes, ATP: Theory and application. *Information and Computation*, 114:131–178, 1994.

[Plo81] G. Plotkin. A structural approach to operational semantics. Technical Report DAIMI FN-19, Aarhus University, 1981.

[PU95] I.C.C. Phillips and I. Ulidowski. Stable and timed formats for process algebra. Technical Report, Imperial College, 1995.

[RR88] G.M. Reed and A.W. Roscoe. A timed model for communicating sequential processes. *Theoretical Computer Science*, 58:249–261, 1988.

[Sch95] S. A. Schneider. An operational semantics for timed CSP. *Information and Computation*, 116:193–213, 1995.

[Uli94] I. Ulidowski. *Local Testing and Implementable Concurrent Processes.* PhD thesis, Imperial College, University of London, 1994.

[Uli96] I. Ulidowski. Finite axiom systems for testing preorder and De Simone process languages. In M. Wirsing and M. Nivat, editors, *Proceedings of AMAST'96*, München, 1996. Springer. LNCS 1101.

[UP97] I. Ulidowski and I.C.C. Phillips. Formats of ordered SOS rules with silent actions. In M. Bidoit and M. Dauchet, editors, *Proceedings of TAPSOFT'97*, Lille, 1997. Springer. LNCS 1214.

[UY97] I. Ulidowski and S. Yuen. Towards general timed process languages. Available at http://www.kurims.kyoto-u.ac.jp/~irek/.

[vGW89] R.J. van Glabbeek and W.P. Weijland. Branching time and abstraction in bisimulation semantics. In G.X. Ritter, editor, *Information Processing 89*, pages 613–618. Elsevier Science Publishers, 1989. To appear in JACM.

[Wal90] D. Walker. Bisimulation and divergence. *Information and Computation*, 85(2):202–241, 1990.

[Wan91] Y. Wang. *A Calculus of Real Time Systems.* PhD thesis, Chalmers University of Technology, Göteborg, 1991.

[Wei89] W.P. Weijland. *Synchrony and Asynchrony in Process Algebra.* PhD thesis, University of Amsterdam, 1989.

[WG797] ISO/IEC JTC1/SC21 WG7. *Working Draft on Enhancements to LOTOS.* ftp://ftp.dit.upm.es/pub/lotos/elotos/Working.Docs/cd.ps, 1997.

Parametric Analysis of Computer Systems

Farn Wang Pao-Ann Hsiung

Institute of Information Science, Academia Sinica, Taiwan, ROC
+886-2-7883799 x 1717 FAX:+886-2-7824814 farn@iis.sinica.edu.tw

Abstract. A general parametric analysis problem which allows the usage of parameter variables in both the real-time automata and the specifications is proposed and solved. The analysis algorithm is much simpler and can run more efficiently in average cases than previous work.

1 Introduction

A successful real-world project management relies on the satisfaction of various timing and nontiming restraints which may compete with each other for resources. Examples of such restraints include timely responses, budget, domestic or international regulations, system configurations, environments, compatibilities, ... In this work, we define and algorithmically solves the *parametric analysis problem* of computer systems which allows for the formal description of system behaviors and design requirements with various timing and nontiming parameter variables and asks for a general conditions on all solutions to those parameter variables.

The design of our problem was influenced by previous work of Alur et al. [AHV93] and Wang [Wang96] which will be discussed briefly later. Our parametric analysis problem is presented in two parts : an automaton with nontiming parameter variables and a specification with both timing and nontiming parameter variables. The following example is adapted from the railroad crossing example and shows how such a platform can be useful.

Example 1. : **Railroad Gate Controller**
The popular railroad crossing example consists of a train monitor and gate-controller. In figure 1, we give a parametric version of the automaton descriptions of the monitor and controller respectively. The ovals represent meta-states while arcs represent transitions. By each transition, we label the transition condition and the clocks to be reset to zero on the transition. The global state space can be calculated as the Cartesian-product of local state spaces.

The safety requirement is that whenever a train is at the crossing, the gate must be in the D mode (gate is down). The more money you spend on monitor, the more precise you can tell how far away a train is approaching. Suppose we now have two monitor types, one costs 1000 dollars and can tell if a train is coming to the crossing in 290 to 300 seconds; the other type costs 500 and can tell if a train is coming to the crossing in 200 to 350 seconds.

We also have two gate-controller types. One costs 900 dollars and can lower the gate in 20 to 50 seconds and skip the U mode (gate is up) when a train is

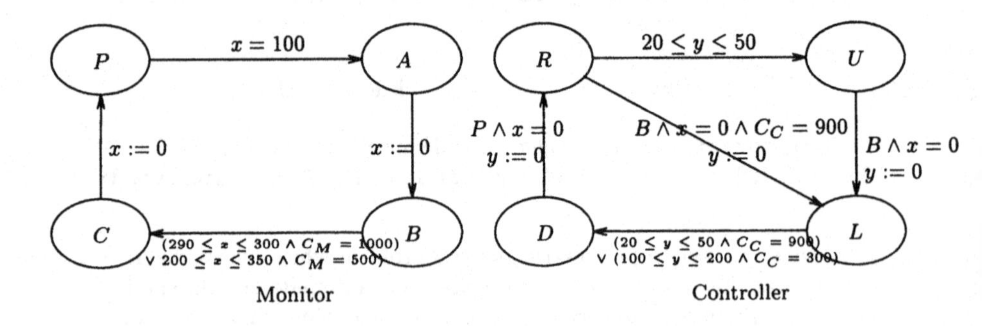

Fig. 1. Railroad Gate Controller Example

coming to the crossing and the controller is in the R mode (gate-Raising mode). The other type costs 300 dollars and can lower the gate in 100 to 200 seconds and cannot skip the U mode once the controller is in the R mode.

Suppose now the design of a rail-road crossing gate-controller is subjected to the budget constraint : the cost of the monitor ($\$_M$) and that of controller ($\$_C$) together cannot exceed 1500 dollars. We want to make sure under this constraint, if the safety requirement can still be satisfied. This can be expressed in our logic PCTL as $\$_M + \$_C \leq 1500 \wedge \forall\Box(C \rightarrow D)$. Here $\forall\Box$ is a modal operator from CTL [CE81, CES86] which means for all computations henceforth, the following statement must be true. ||

Our system behavior descriptions are given in *statically parametric automata (SPA)* and our specifications are given in *parametric computation tree logic (PCTL)*. The outcome of our algorithm are Boolean expressions, whose literals are linear inequalities on the parameter variables, and can be further processed with standard techniques like simplex, simulated annealing, ... to extract useful design feedback.

In the remainder of the introduction, we shall first briefly discuss related work on the subject, and then sketch an outline of the rest of the paper.

1.1 Related work

In the earliest development [CE81, CES86], people use finite-state automata to describe system behavior and check to see if they satisfy specification given in branching-time temporal logic CTL. Such a framework is usually called *model-checking.* A *CTL (Computation Tree Logic)* formula is composed of binary propositions $(p, q, \ldots)$, Boolean operators $(\neg, \vee, \wedge)$, and branching-time modal operators $(\exists\mathcal{U}, \exists\bigcirc, \forall\mathcal{U}, \forall\bigcirc)$. $\exists$ means *"there exists"* a computation. $\forall$ means *"for all"* computations. $\mathcal{U}$ means something is true "until" something else is true. $\bigcirc$ means *"next state."* For example, $\exists p\mathcal{U}q$ says there exists a computation along which p is true until q is true. Since there is no notion of real-time (clock time), only ordering among events are considered.

The following shorthands are generally accepted besides the usual ones in Boolean algebra. $\exists\Diamond\phi_1$ is for $\exists \mathit{true}\, \mathcal{U}\phi_1$; $\forall\Box\phi_1$ for $\neg\exists\Diamond\neg\phi_1$; $\forall\Diamond\phi_1$ for $\forall \mathit{true}\, \mathcal{U}\phi_1$; and $\exists\Box\phi_1$ for $\neg\forall\Diamond\neg\phi_1$. Intuitively $\Diamond$ means *"eventually"* while $\Box$ means *"henceforth."*

CTL model-checking has been used to prove the correctness of concurrent systems such as circuits and communication protocols. In 1990, the platform was extended by Alur et al. to *Timed CTL (TCTL) model-checking problem* to verify dense-time systems equipped with resettable clocks [ACD90]. Alur et al. also solve the problem in the same paper with an innovative state space partitioning scheme.

In [CY92], the problems of deciding the earliest and latest times a target state can appear in the computation of a timed automaton was discussed. However, they did not derive the general conditions on parameter variables.

In 1993, Alur et al. embark on the reachability problem of real-time automata with parameter variables [AHV93]. Particularly, they have established that in general, the problem has no algorithm when three clocks are compared with parameter variables in the automata [AHV93]. This observation greatly influences the design of our platform.

In 1995, Wang propose another platform which extends the TCTL model-checking problem to allow for timing parameter variables in TCTL formulae [Wang96]. His algorithm gives back Boolean conditions whose literals are linear equalities on the timing parameter variables. He also showed that his parametric timing analysis problem is PSPACE-hard while his analysis algorithm is of double-exponential time complexity. In comparision, our work provides a generalized framework for analysis of both timing and static parameter variables. Also our algorithm is based on cycle-reduction in dynamic programming style which is easier to understand, implement, and analyze. Moreover, since the cycles are implicitly represented in the succinct semilinear expressions,[1] our algorithm can run more efficiently with respect to time and space complexities in average cases.

Henzinger's HyTech system developed at Cornell also has parametric analysis power[AHV93, HHWT95]. However in their framework, they did not identify a decidable class for the parametric analysis problem and their procedure is not guaranteed to terminate. In comparison, our framework has an algorithm which can generate the semilinear description of the working solutions for the parameter variables.

1.2 Outline

Section 2 presents our system behavior description language : the *Statically Parametric Automaton* (SPA). Section 3 defines *Parametric Computation Tree Logic (PCTL)* and the *Parametric Analysis Problem.* Section 4 presents the algorithm, proves its correctness, and analyzes its complexity. Section 5 concludes the paper.

---

[1] A semilinear integer set is expressible as the union of a finite number of integer sets like $\{a + b_1 j_1 + \ldots + b_n j_n \mid j_1, \ldots, j_n \in \mathcal{N}\}$ for some $a, b_1, \ldots, b_n \in \mathcal{N}$.

We also adopt $\mathcal{N}$ and $\mathcal{R}^+$ as the sets of nonnegative integers and nonnegative reals respectively.

2 Statically parametric automata (SPA)

In an SPA, people may combine propositions, timing inequalities on clock readings, and linear inequalities of parameter variables to write the invariance and transition conditions. Such a combination is called a *state predicate* and is defined formally in the following. Given a set P of atomic propositions, a set C of clocks, and a set H of parameter variables, the syntax of a *state predicate* η of P, C, and H, has the following syntax rules.

$$\eta ::= \mathit{false} \mid p \mid x - y \sim c \mid x \sim c \mid \sum a_i\alpha_i \sim c \mid \eta_1 \vee \eta_2 \mid \neg\eta_1$$

where $p \in P$, $x, y \in C$, $a_i, c \in \mathcal{N}$, $\alpha_i \in H$, $\sim \in \{\leq, <, =, \geq, >\}$, and η_1, η_2 are state predicates. Notationally, we let $B(P, C, H)$ be the set of all state predicates on P, C, and H. Note the parameter variables considered in H are static because their value do not change with time during each computation of an automaton. A state predicate with only $\sum a_i\alpha_i \sim c$ type literals is called *static*.

Definition 1. : **Statically Parametric Automata**
A *Statically Parametric Automaton* (SPA) is a tuple $(Q, q_0, P, C, H, \chi, E, \rho, \tau)$ with the following restrictions.

- Q is a finite set of meta-states.
- $q_0 \in Q$ is the initial meta-state.
- P is a set of atomic propositions.
- C is a set of clocks.
- H is a set of parameters variables.
- $\chi : Q \mapsto B(P, C, H)$ is a function that labels each meta-state with a condition true in that meta-state.
- $E \subseteq Q \times Q$ is the set of transitions.
- $\rho : E \mapsto 2^C$ defines the set of clocks to be reset during each transition.
- $\tau : E \mapsto B(P, C, H)$ defines the transition triggering conditions. ||

An SPA starts execution at its meta-state q_0. We shall assume that initially, all clocks read zero. In between meta-state transitions, all clocks increment their readings at a uniform rate. The transitions of the SPA may be fired when the triggering conditon is satisfied. With different interpretation to the parameter variables, it may exhibit different behaviors. During a transition from meta-state q_i to q_j, for each $x \in \rho(q_i, q_j)$, the reading of x will be reset to zero. There are state predicates with parameter variables on the states as well as transitions. These parameters may also appear in the specifications of the same analysis problem instance.

Definition 2. : **State**
A *state* s of SPA $A = (Q, q_0, P, C, H, \chi, E, \rho, \tau)$ is a mapping from $P \cup C$ to $\{\mathit{true}, \mathit{false}\} \cup \mathcal{R}^+$ such that for each $p \in P$, $s(p) \in \{\mathit{true}, \mathit{false}\}$ and for each $x \in C$, $s(x) \in \mathcal{R}^+$, where $\mathcal{R}^+$ is the set of nonnegative real numbers. ||

The same SPA may generate different computations under different interpretation of its parameter variables. An *interpretation*, $\mathcal{I}$, for H is a mapping from $\mathcal{N} \cup H$ to $\mathcal{N}$ such that for all $c \in \mathcal{N}$, $\mathcal{I}(c) = c$. An SPA $A = (Q, q_0, P, C, H, \chi, E, \rho, \tau)$ is said to be interpreted with respect to $\mathcal{I}$, when all state predicates in A have their parameter variables interpreted according to $\mathcal{I}$.

Definition 3. : **Satisfaction of interpreted state predicates by a state**
State predicate η is satisfied by state s under interpretation $\mathcal{I}$, written as $s \models_{\mathcal{I}} \eta$, iff

- $s \not\models_{\mathcal{I}}$ *false*;
- $s \models_{\mathcal{I}} p$ iff $s(p) = true$;
- $s \models_{\mathcal{I}} x - y \sim c$ iff $s(x) - s(y) \sim c$;
- $s \models_{\mathcal{I}} x \sim c$ iff $s(x) \sim c$;
- $s \models_{\mathcal{I}} \sum a_i \alpha_i \sim c$ iff $\sum a_i \mathcal{I}(\alpha_i) \sim c$;
- $s \models_{\mathcal{I}} \eta_1 \vee \eta_2$ iff $s \models_{\mathcal{I}} \eta_1$ or $s \models_{\mathcal{I}} \eta_2$; and
- $s \models_{\mathcal{I}} \neg\eta_1$ iff $s \not\models_{\mathcal{I}} \eta_1$. ||

Now we are going to define the computation of SPA. For convenience, we adopt the following conventions.

An SPA $A = (Q, q_0, P, C, H, \chi, E, \rho, \tau)$ is *unambiguous* iff for all states s, there is at most one $q \in Q$ such that for some I, $s \models_{\mathcal{I}} \chi(q)$. Ambiguous SPA's can be made unambiguous by incorporating meta-state names as propositional conjuncts in the conjunctive normal forms of the $\chi()$-state predicate of each meta-state. For convenience, from now on, we shall only talk about unambiguous SPA's. When we say an SPA, we mean an unambiguous SPA.

Given an SPA $A = (Q, q_0, P, C, H, \chi, E, \rho, \tau)$, an interpretation $\mathcal{I}$ for H, and a state s, we let s^Q be the meta-state in Q such that $s \models_{\mathcal{I}} \chi(s^Q)$. If there is no meta-state $q \in Q$ such that $s \models_{\mathcal{I}} \chi(q)$, then s^Q is undefined.

Given two states s, s', there is a *meta-state transition* from s to s' in A under interpretation $\mathcal{I}$, in symbols $s \rightarrow_{\mathcal{I}} s'$, iff

- s^Q, s'^Q are both defined,
- $(s^Q, s'^Q) \in E$,
- $s \models_{\mathcal{I}} \tau(s^Q, s'^Q)$, and
- $\forall x \in C\ ((x \in \rho(s^Q, s'^Q) \Rightarrow s'(x) = 0) \wedge (x \notin \rho(s^Q, s'^Q) \Rightarrow s'(x) = s(x)))$.

Also, given a state s and a $\delta \in \mathcal{R}^+$, we let $s + \delta$ be the state that agrees with s in every aspect except for all $x \in C$, $s(x) + \delta = (s + \delta)(x)$.

Definition 4. : **s-run of interpreted SPA**
Given a state s of SPA $A = (Q, q_0, P, C, H, \chi, E, \rho, \tau)$ and an interpretation $\mathcal{I}$, a computation of A starting at s is called an *s-run* and is a sequence $((s_1, t_1), (s_2, t_2), \ldots\ldots)$ of pairs such that

- $s = s_1$; and
- for each $t \in \mathcal{R}^+$, there is an $i \in \mathcal{N}$ such that $t_i \geq t$; and
- for each integer $i \geq 1$, s_i^Q is defined and for each real $0 \leq \delta \leq t_{i+1} - t_i$, $s_i + \delta \models_{\mathcal{I}} \chi(s_i^Q)$; and
- for each $i \geq 1$, A goes from s_i to s_{i+1} because of
  - a meta-state transition, i.e. $t_i = t_{i+1} \wedge s_i \rightarrow_{\mathcal{I}} s_{i+1}$; or
  - time passage, i.e. $t_i < t_{i+1} \wedge s_i + t_{i+1} - t_i = s_{i+1}$. ||

3 PCTL and parametric analysis problem

Parametric Computation Tree Logic (PCTL) is used for specifying the design requirements and is defined with respect to a given SPA. Suppose we are given an SPA $A = (Q, q_0, P, C, H, \chi, E, \rho, \tau)$. A PCTL formula ϕ for A has the following syntax rules.

$$\phi ::= \eta \quad | \quad \phi_1 \vee \phi_2 \quad | \quad \neg\phi_1 \quad | \quad \exists\phi_1 \mathcal{U}_{\sim\theta}\phi_2 \quad | \quad \forall\phi_1 \mathcal{U}_{\sim\theta}\phi_2$$

Here η is a state predicate in $B(P, C, H)$, ϕ_1 and ϕ_2 are PCTL formulae, and θ is an element in $\mathcal{N} \cup H$.

Note that the parameter variable subscripts of modal formulae can also be used as parameter variables in SPA. Also we adopt the following standard shorthands : $\neg\phi_1$ for $(\phi_1 \rightarrow \mathit{false})$, true for $\neg\mathit{false}$, $\phi_1 \vee \phi_2$ for $(\neg\phi_1) \rightarrow \phi_2$, $\phi_1 \wedge \phi_2$ for $\neg(\phi_1 \rightarrow \neg\phi_2)$, $\exists\Diamond_{\sim\theta}\phi_1$ for $\exists \mathit{true}\, \mathcal{U}_{\sim\theta}\phi_1$, $\forall\Box_{\sim\theta}\phi_1$ for $\neg\exists\Diamond_{\sim\theta}\neg\phi_1$, $\forall\Diamond_{\sim\theta}\phi_1$ for $\forall \mathit{true}\, \mathcal{U}_{\sim\theta}\phi_1$, $\exists\Box_{\sim\theta}\phi_1$ for $\neg\forall\Diamond_{\sim\theta}\neg\phi_1$.

With different interpretations, a PCTL formula may impose different requirements. We write in notations $s \models_{\mathcal{I}} \phi$ to mean that ϕ is satisfied at state s in A under interpretation $\mathcal{I}$. The satisfaction relation is defined inductively as follows.

- If ϕ is a state predicate, then $s \models_{\mathcal{I}} \phi$ iff ϕ is satisfied by s as a state predicate under $\mathcal{I}$.
- $s \models_{\mathcal{I}} \phi_1 \vee \phi_2$ iff either $s \models_{\mathcal{I}} \phi_1$ or $s \models_{\mathcal{I}} \phi_2$
- $s \models_{\mathcal{I}} \neg\phi_1$ iff $s \not\models_{\mathcal{I}} \phi_1$
- $s \models_{\mathcal{I}} (\exists\phi_1 \mathcal{U}_{\sim\theta}\phi_2)$ iff there are an s-run $= ((s_1, t_1), (s_2, t_2), \ldots)$ in A, an $i \geq 1$, and a $\delta \in [0, t_{i+1} - t_i]$, s.t.
  - $t_i + \delta \sim t_1 + \mathcal{I}(\theta)$,
  - $s_i + \delta \models_{\mathcal{I}} \phi_2$,
  - for all $0 \leq j < i$ and $\delta' \in [0, t_{j+1} - t_j]$, $s_j + \delta' \models_{\mathcal{I}} \phi_1$, and
  - for all $\delta' \in [0, \delta)$, $s_i + \delta' \models_{\mathcal{I}} \phi_1$.
- $s \models_{\mathcal{I}} (\forall\phi_1 \mathcal{U}_{\sim\theta}\phi_2)$ iff for every s-run $= ((s_1, t_1), (s_2, t_2), \ldots)$ in A, for some $i \geq 1$ and $\delta \in [0, t_{i+1} - t_i]$,
  - $t_i + \delta \sim t_1 + \mathcal{I}(\theta)$,
  - $s_i + \delta \models_{\mathcal{I}} \phi_2$,
  - for all $0 \leq j < i$ and $\delta' \in [0, t_{j+1} - t_j]$, $s_j + \delta' \models_{\mathcal{I}} \phi_1$, and
  - for all $\delta' \in [0, \delta)$, $s_i + \delta' \models_{\mathcal{I}} \phi_1$.

Given an SPA A, a PCTL formula ϕ, and an interpretation $\mathcal{I}$ for H, we say A is a *model* of ϕ under $\mathcal{I}$, written as $A \models_{\mathcal{I}} \phi$, iff $s \models_{\mathcal{I}} \phi$ for all states s such that $s^Q = q_0$.

We now formally define our problem.

Definition 5. : **Statically Parametric Analysis Problem**
Given an SPA A and a specification (PCTL formula) ϕ, the *parametric analysis problem instance* for A and ϕ, denoted as *PAP*(A, ϕ), is formally defined as

the problem of deriving the general condition of all interpretation $\mathcal{I}$ such that $A \models_{\mathcal{I}} \phi$. $\mathcal{I}$ is called a *solution* to $PAP(A, \phi)$ iff $A \models_{\mathcal{I}} \phi$. ||

We will show that such conditions are always expressible as Boolean combinations of linear inequalities of parameter variables.

4 Parametric analysis

In this section, we shall develop new data-structures, *parametric region graph* and *conditional path graph*, to solve the parametric analysis problem. Parametric region graph is similar to the region graph defined in [ACD90] but it contains parametric information. A region is a subset of the state space in which all states exhibit the same behavior with respect to the given SPA and PCTL formula.

Given a parametric analysis problem for A and ϕ, a modal subformula ϕ_1 of ϕ, and the parametric region graph with region sets V, the *conditional path graph* for ϕ_1 is a fully connected graph of V whose arcs are labeled with sets of pairs of the form : (π, T) where π is a static state predicate and T is an integer set. Conveniently, we call such pairs *conditional time expressions (CTE)*. Alternatively, we can say that the conditional path graph J_{ϕ_1} for ϕ_1 is a mapping from $V \times V$ to the power set of CTE's. For a $v, v' \in V$, if $(\pi, T) \in J_{\phi_1}(v, v')$, then for all interpretation $\mathcal{I}$, $t \in T$, and $s \in v$, if π is satisfied by $\mathcal{I}$, then there is a finite s-run of time t ending at an $s' \in v'$ such that ϕ_1 is satisfied all the way through the run except at s'. In subsection 4.2, we shall show that all our modal formula evaluations can be decomposed to the computation of conditional time expressions.

The kernel of this section is a Kleene's closure procedure which computes the conditional path graph. Its computation utilizes the following four types of integer set manipulations.

- $T_1 \cup T_2$ means $\{a_1 \mid a_1 \in T_1 \text{ or } a_2 \in T_2\}$.
- $T_1 + T_2$ means $\{a_1 + a_2 \mid a_1 \in T_1; a_2 \in T_2\}$.
- T_1* means $\{0\} \cup \bigcup_{i \in \mathcal{N}} \sum_{1 \leq j \leq i} T_1$ where $\sum_{1 \leq j \leq i} T_1$ means the addition of i consecutive T_1.
- $\overline{T_1}$ is the complement of T_1, i.e., $\{a_1 \mid a_1 \in \mathcal{N}; a_1 \notin T_1\}$.

It can be shown that all integer sets resulting from such manipulations in our algorithm are semilinear.[2] Semilinear expressions are convenient notations for expressing infinite integer sets constructed regularly. They are also closed under the four manipulations. There are also algorithms to compute the manipulation results. Specifically, we know that all semilinear expressions can be represented as the union of a finite number of sets like $a + c*$. Such a special form is called *periodical normal form (PNF)*. It is not difficult to prove that given operands in PNF, the results of the four manipulations can all be transformed back into PNF. Due to page-limit, we shall skip the details here.

The intuition behind our algorithm for computing the conditional path graph is a vertex bypassing scheme. Suppose, we have three regions u, v, w whose con-

[2] A semilinear integer set is expressible as the union of a finite number of integer sets like $\{a + b_1 j_1 + \ldots + b_n j_n \mid j_1, \ldots, j_n \in \mathcal{N}\}$ for some $a, b_1, \ldots, b_n \in \mathcal{N}$.

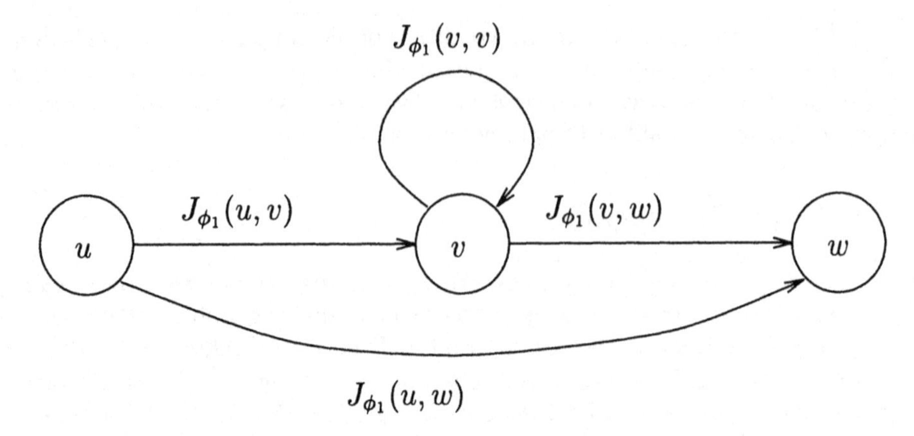

Fig. 2. Central operation in our Kleene's closure algorithm

nections in the conditional path graph is shown in Figure 2. Then it is clear that by bypassing region v, we realized that $J_{\phi_1}(u,w)$ should be a superset of

$$\left\{ (\pi_1 \wedge \pi_2 \wedge \bigwedge_{(\pi_3,T_3)\in D} \pi_3,\ T_1 + T_2 + \sum_{(\pi_3,T_3)\in D} T_3*) \middle| \begin{array}{l} (\pi_1,T_1) \in J_{\phi_1}(u,v); \\ (\pi_2,T_2) \in J_{\phi_1}(v,w); \\ D \subseteq J_{\phi_1}(v,v) \end{array} \right\}$$

Our conditional path graph construction algorithm utilizes a Kleene's closure framework to calculate all the arc labels.

In subsection 4.1, we kind of extend the regions graph concepts in [ACD90] and define parametric region graph. In subsection 4.2, we define conditional path graph, present algorithm to compute it, and present our labelling algorithm for parametric analysis problem. In subsections 4.3 and 4.4, we briefly prove the algorithm's correctness and analyze its complexity.

4.1 Parametric region graph

The brilliant concept of region graphs were originally discussed and used in [ACD90] for verifying dense-time systems. A region graph partitions its system state space into finitely many behavior-equivalent subspaces. Our parametric region graphs extend from Alur et al's region graph and contains information on parameter variable restrictions. Beside parameter variables, our parametric region graphs have an additional clock κ which gets reset to zero once its reading reaches one. κ is not used in the user-given SPA and is added when we construct the regions for the convenience of parametric timing analysis. It functions as a ticking indicator for evaluating timed modal formulae of PCTL. The reading of κ is always between 0 and 1, that is, for every state s, $0 \leq s(\kappa) \leq 1$.

The *timing constants* in an SPA A are the integer constants c that appear in conditions such as $x - y \sim c$ and $x \sim c$ in A. The timing constants in a PCTL formula ϕ are the integer constants c that appear in subformulae like $x - y \sim c, x \sim c, \exists\phi_1\mathcal{U}_{\sim c}\phi_2$, and $\forall\phi_1\mathcal{U}_{\sim c}\phi_2$. Let $K_{A:\phi}$ be the largest timing constant used in both A and ϕ for the given parametric analysis problem instance.

For each $\delta \in \mathcal{R}^+$, we define *fract*(δ) as the fractional part of δ, i.e. *fract*$(\delta) = \delta - \lfloor\delta\rfloor$.

Definition 6. : **Regions**
Given an SPA $A = (Q, q_0, P, C, H, \chi, E, \rho, \tau)$ and a PCTL formula ϕ for A, two states s, s' of A, $s \cong_{A:\phi} s'$ (i.e. s and s' are equivalent with respect to A and ϕ) iff the following conditions are met.

- For each $p \in P$, $s(p) = s'(p)$.
- For each $x - y \sim c$ used in A or ϕ, $s(x) - s(y) \sim c$ iff $s'(x) - s'(y) \sim c$.
- For each $x \in C$, if either $s(x) \leq K_{A:\phi}$ or $s'(x) \leq K_{A:\phi}$, then $\lfloor s(x)\rfloor = \lfloor s'(x)\rfloor$.
- For every $x, y \in C \cup \{0, \kappa\}$, *fract*$(s(x)) \leq$ *fract*$(s(y))$ iff *fract*$(s'(x)) \leq$ *fract*$(s'(y))$ where $s(0) = s'(0) = 0$.

$[s]$ denotes the equivalent class of A's states, with respect to relation $\cong_{A:\phi}$, to which s belongs and it is called a *region*. ||

Note because of our assumption of unambiguous SPA's, we know that for all $s' \in [s]$, $s'^Q = s^Q$. Using the above definition, parametric region graph is defined as follows.

Definition 7. : **Parametric Region Graph (PR-graph)**
The *Parametric Region Graph* (PR-graph) for an SPA $A = (Q, q_0, P, C, H, \chi, E, \rho, \tau)$ and a PCTL formula ϕ is a directed graph $G_{A:\phi} = (V, F)$ such that the vertex set V is the set of all regions and the arc set F consists of the following two types of arcs.

- An arc (v, v') may represent *meta-state transitions* in A. That is, for every $s \in v$, there is an $s' \in v'$ such that $s \rightarrow s'$.
- An arc (v, v') may be a *time arc* and represent passage of time in the same meta-state. Formally, for every $s \in v$, there is an $s' \in v'$ such that
  - $s + \delta = s'$ for some $\delta \in \mathcal{R}^+$;
  - there is no $\dot{s}$ and $\dot{\delta} \in \mathcal{R}^+$, $0 < \dot{\delta} < \delta$, s.t. $[\dot{s}] \neq v$, $[\dot{s}] \neq v'$, $s + \dot{\delta} = \dot{s}$, and $\dot{s} + \delta - \dot{\delta} = s'$.

Just as in [Wang96], propositional value-changings within the same meta-states are taken care of automatically.

For each (v, v') in F, we let $\epsilon(v, v') = \uparrow$ if going from states in v to states in v', the reading of κ increments from a noninteger to an integer; $\epsilon(v, v') = \downarrow$ if going from states in v to states in v', the reading of κ increments from an integer to a noninteger; otherwise $\epsilon(v, v') = 0$. Also $v \models$ *fract*$(\kappa) = 0$ iff for all $s \in v$, $s(\kappa)$ is an integer.

Also we conveniently write $v \models_{\mathcal{I}} \phi_1$ for some PCTL formula ϕ_1 when for all $s \in v(s \models_{\mathcal{I}} \phi_1)$. Similarly, we let v^Q be the meta-state such that for all $s \in v(v^Q = s^Q)$. ||

Since regions have enough informations to determine the truth values all propositions and clock inequalities used in a parametric analysis problem, we can define the mapping from state predicates to static state predicates through a region. Formally, given a region v and a state predicate η, we write $v(\eta)$ for the static predicate constructed according to the following rules.

- $v(false)$ is $false$.
- $v(p)$ is $true$ iff $\forall s \in v(s(p) = true)$; $v(p)$ is $false$ otherwise.
- $v(x-y \sim c)$ is $true$ iff $\forall s \in v(s(x) - s(y) \sim c)$; $v(x-y \sim c)$ is $false$ otherwise.
- $v(x \sim c)$ is $true$ iff $\forall s \in v(s(x) \sim c)$; $v(x-y \sim c)$ is $false$ otherwise.
- $v(\sum a_i \alpha_i \sim c)$ is $\sum a_i \alpha_i \sim c$.
- $v(\eta_1 \vee \eta_2) = v(\eta_1) \vee v(\eta_2)$.
- $v(\neg \eta_1) = \neg(\eta_1)$.

For convenience, we let $\langle\kappa\rangle v$ be the region in a PR-graph that agrees with v in every aspect except that for all $s' \in \langle\kappa\rangle v$, $s'(\kappa) = 0$. Given a PCTL formula ϕ and a path (cycle) $\Gamma = \langle v_1 v_2 \dots v_m\rangle$, Γ is called a *ϕ-path* (*ϕ-cycle*) iff there is an interpretation $\mathcal{I}$ such that for each $1 \le i < m$ and $s \in v_i$, $s \models_{\mathcal{I}} \phi$.

4.2 Labeling Algorithm

To compute the parametric condition for a parametric modal formula like $\exists\phi_1 \mathcal{U}_{\sim\theta}\phi_2$ at a region, we can instead decompose the formula into a Boolean combinations of path conditions and then compute those path conditions. For example, suppose under interpretation $\mathcal{I}$, we know there exists a ϕ_1-path $v_1 v_2 \dots v_n$ of time 5. Then a sufficient condition for all states in v_1 satisfying $\exists\phi_1 \mathcal{U}_{\le\theta}\phi_2$ is that $\mathcal{I}(\theta) \ge 5 \wedge v_n \models_{\mathcal{I}} \phi_2 \wedge \bigwedge_{1\le i<n} v_i \models \phi_1$. Now we define our second new

KClosure$_{\phi_1}(V, F)$
/* It is assumed that for all regions $v \in V$, we know the static state predicate condition $L^{\phi_1}(v)$ which makes ϕ_1 satisfied at v. */
{
(1) For each $(v, w) \in F$, if $\epsilon(v, w) = \uparrow$, {
  (1) then let $J_{\phi_1}(v, w) := \{(L^{\phi_1}(v) \wedge v(\chi(v^Q)) \wedge v'(\chi(v'^Q)) \wedge v(\tau(v^Q, v'^Q)), 1)\}$;
  (2) else let $J_{\phi_1}(v, w) := \{(L^{\phi_1}(v) \wedge v(\chi(v^Q)) \wedge v'(\chi(v'^Q)) \wedge v(\tau(v^Q, v'^Q)), 0)\}$.
  }
(2) Iteratively for each $v \in V$, do for each $u, w \in V$,
  let $J_{\phi_1}(u, w) := J_{\phi_1}(u, w) \cup$

$$\left\{ \left(\pi_1 \wedge \pi_2 \wedge \bigwedge_{(\pi_3,T_3)\in D} \pi_3,\ T_1 + T_2 + \sum_{(\pi_3,T_3)\in D} T_3 * \right) \middle| \begin{array}{l} (\pi_1, T_1) \in J_{\phi_1}(u, v); \\ (\pi_2, T_2) \in J_{\phi_1}(v, w); \\ D \subseteq J_{\phi_1}(v, v) \end{array} \right\}$$

}

Table 1. Construction of the conditional path graph

data structure : *conditional path graph* to prepare for the presentation of the algorithm.

Definition 8. : **Conditional path graph**
Given a region graph $G_{A:\phi} = (V, F)$ and a subformula ϕ_1 of ϕ, the *conditional path graph* for ϕ_1, denoted as J_{ϕ_1} is a mapping from $V \times V$ to the power set of conditional time expressions such that for all $v, v' \in V$, if $(\pi, T) \in J_{\phi_1}(v, v')$, then for all interpretation $\mathcal{I}$ satisfying π, $t \in T$, and $s \in v$, there is a finite s-run of time t ending at an $s' \in v'$ such that ϕ_1 is satisfied all the way through the run except at s'. ||

The procedure for computing $J_{\phi_1}()$ is presented in table 1. Once the conditional path graph has been constructed for ϕ_1 using $\text{KClosure}_{\phi_1}()$, we can then turn to the labeling algorithm in table 2 to calculate the parametric conditions for the modal formulas properly containing ϕ_1. However, there is still one thing which we should define clearly before presenting our labeling algorithm, that is : "How should we connect the conditional time expressions in the arc labels to parametric conditions ?" Suppose, we want to examine if from v to v', there is a run satisfying the parametric requirement of $\geq \theta$. The condition can be derived as $\bigvee_{(\pi,T)\in J_{\phi_1}(v,v')} \pi \wedge T \geq \theta$ where $T \sim \theta$ with semilinear expressions T in PNF and (numerical or variable) parameter θ is calculated according to the following rewriting rules.

- $a + c* \sim \theta \implies a + cj \sim \theta$ where j is a new integer variable never used before.
- $T_1 \cup T_2 \sim \theta \implies (T_1 \sim \theta) \vee (T_2 \sim \theta)$

Note since we assume that the operands are in PNF, we do not have to pay attention to the case of $+, *, -$.

Table 2 presents the labeling alogrithm for $L^{\phi}(v)$. This algorithm maps pairs of vertices and temporal logic formulas to a Boolean combination of linear inequalities with parameter variables as free variables. Also note the labeling algorithm relies on the special case of $\exists\Box_{\geq 0}\phi_j$ which essentially says there is an infinite computation along which ϕ_j is always true.

Also the presentation in table 2 only covers some typical cases. For the remaining cases, please check the appendix.

4.3 Correctness

The following lemma establishes the correctness of our labeling algorithm.

Lemma 9. *Given* PAP(A, ϕ), *an interpretation* $\mathcal{I}$ *for* H, *and a vertex* v *in* $G_{A:\phi}$, *after executing* $L^{\phi}(v)$ *in our labeling algorithm,* $\mathcal{I}$ *satisfies* $L^{\phi}(v)$ *iff* $v \models_{\mathcal{I}} \phi$.

proof : The proof follows a standard structural induction on ϕ, which we often saw in related model-checking literature, and very much resembles the one in [Wang96]. Due to page-limit, we shall omit it here. ||

4.4 Complexity

According to our construction, the number of regions in $G_{A:\phi}$, denoted as $|G_{A:\phi}|$, is at most $3|Q| \cdot (K_{A:\phi} + 1)^C \cdot (|C| + 1)!$ where coefficient 3 and constant +1

Label(A, ϕ) {
(1) construct the PR-graph $G_{A:\phi} = (V, F)$;
(2) for each $v \in V$, recursively compute $L^{\phi}(v)$;
}

$L^{\phi_i}(v)$ {
switch(ϕ_i){
case (*false*), $L^{false}(v) := false$;

case (p) where $p \in P$, $L^p(v) := true$ if $v \models p$, else $L^p(v) := false$;

case ($x - y \sim c$), if either x or y is zero in v, evaluate $x - y \sim c$ as in the next case; else $x - y \sim c$ is evaluated to the same value as it is in any region u such that $(u, v) \in F$.

case ($x \sim c$), $L^{\phi_i}(v) := true$ if $v \models (\phi_i)$, else $L^{\phi_i}(v) := false$;

case ($\sum a_i \alpha_i \sim d$), $L^{\sum a_i \alpha_i \sim d}(v) := \sum a_i \alpha_i \sim d$;

case ($\phi_j \vee \phi_k$), $L^{\phi_j \vee \phi_k}(v) := L^{\phi_j}(v) \vee L^{\phi_k}(v)$;

case ($\neg\phi_j$), $L^{\neg\phi_j}(v) := \neg L^{\phi_j}(v)$;

case ($\exists\Box_{\geq 0}\phi_j$), {
(1) KClosure$_{\phi_j}(V, F)$;
(2) $L^{\exists\Box_{\geq 0}\phi_j}(v) := \bigvee_{u \in V}\left(\left(\bigvee_{(\pi,T)\in J_{\phi_j}(\langle\kappa\rangle v, u)} \pi\right) \wedge \left(\bigvee_{(\pi,T)\in J_{\phi_j}(u,u)}(\pi \wedge T > 0)\right)\right)$
}

case ($\exists\phi_j \mathcal{U}_{\geq\theta}\phi_k$), {
(1) KClosure$_{\phi_j}(V, F)$;
(2) $L^{\exists\phi_j\mathcal{U}_{\geq\theta}\phi_k}(v) := \bigvee_{u\in V}\left(\left(\bigvee_{(\pi,T)\in J_{\phi_j}(\langle\kappa\rangle v,u)}(\pi \wedge T \geq \theta)\right) \wedge L^{\phi_k}(u) \wedge L^{\exists\Box_{\geq 0}\mathrm{true}}(u)\right)$
}

case ($\exists\phi_j\mathcal{U}_{\leq\theta}\phi_k$, $\exists\phi_j\mathcal{U}_{>\theta}\phi_k$, $\exists\phi_j\mathcal{U}_{<\theta}\phi_k$, or $\exists\phi_j\mathcal{U}_{=\theta}\phi_k$)
These cases are treated in ways similar to the above case and are left in the appendix at the end of the paper.

case ($\forall\phi_j\mathcal{U}_{\geq\theta}\phi_k$), {
(1) KClosure$_{\phi_j}(V, F)$;
(2) let $L^{\forall\phi_j\mathcal{U}_{\geq\theta}\phi_k}(v)$ be

$$\neg\left(\begin{array}{l} L^{\exists\Diamond_{<\theta}\neg\phi_j}(\langle\kappa\rangle v) \vee \left(\theta = 0 \wedge \left(L^{\exists\Box_{\geq 0}\neg\phi_k}(\langle\kappa\rangle v) \vee L^{\exists(\neg\phi_k)\mathcal{U}_{\geq 0}\neg(\phi_j\vee\phi_k)}(\langle\kappa\rangle v)\right)\right) \\ \vee\left(\theta > 0 \wedge \bigvee_{u_1,u_2\in V}\left(\begin{array}{l}\bigvee_{(\pi,T)\in J_{\phi_j}(\langle\kappa\rangle v,u_1)}\left(\begin{array}{c}\pi\wedge T = \theta - 1 \wedge L^{\phi_j}(u_1) \\ \wedge\epsilon(u_1,u_2) = \uparrow\end{array}\right) \\ \wedge\left(L^{\exists\Box_{\geq 0}\neg\phi_k}(u_2) \vee L^{\exists(\neg\phi_k)\mathcal{U}_{\geq 0}\neg(\phi_j\vee\phi_k)}(u_2)\right)\end{array}\right)\right)\end{array}\right)$$
}

case ($\forall\phi_j\mathcal{U}_{\leq\theta}\phi_k$, $\forall\phi_j\mathcal{U}_{>\theta}\phi_k$, $\forall\phi_j\mathcal{U}_{<\theta}\phi_k$, or $\forall\phi_j\mathcal{U}_{=\theta}\phi_k$),
These cases are treated in ways similar to above case and are left in in the appendix at the end of the paper.
}

Table 2. Labeling algorithm

reflect the introduction of ticking indicator κ. The inner loop of KClosure$_{\phi_1}$ will be executed for $|G_{A:\phi}|^3$ times. Each iteration takes time proportional to $|J_{\phi_1}(u,v)||J_{\phi_1}(v,w)|2^{|J_{\phi_1}(v,v)|}$. The conditional path graph arc labels, i.e. $J_{\phi_1}(u,v)$, roughly corresponds to the set of simple paths from u to v, although they utilize the succinct representation of semilinear expressions. Thus according to the complexity analysis in [Wang96], we find that procedure KClosure$_{\phi_1}$() has complexity doubly exponential to the size of $G_{A:\phi}$, and thus triply exponential to the size of input, assuming constant time for the manipulation of semilinear expressions.

We now analyze the complexity of our labeling procedure. In table 2, procedure $L^{\phi_i}()$ invokes KClosure$_{\phi_j}$() at most once. Label(A,ϕ) invokes $L^{\phi_i}()$ at most $|G_A||\phi|$ times. Thus the complexity of the algorithm is roughly triply exponential to the size of A and ϕ, since polynomials of exponentialities are still exponentialities.

Finally, PCTL satisfiability problem is undecidable since it is no easier than TCTL satisfiability problem[ACD90].

5 Conclusion

With the success of CTL-based techniques in automatic verification for computer systems [Bryant86, BCMDH90, HNSY92], it would be nice if a formal theory appealing to the common practice of real-world projects can be developed. We feel hopeful that the insight and techniques used in this paper can be further applied to help verifying reactive systems in a more natural and productive way.

Acknowledgements

The authors would like to thank Prof. Tom Henzinger. His suggestion to use dynamic programming to solve PTCTL parametric timing analysis problem triggered the research.

References

[ACD90] Alur, R., Courcoubetis, C., and Dill, D.L. (1993), Model-Checking in Dense Real-Time, *Information and Computation* **104**, Nr. 1, pp. 2–34.

[AD90] Alur, R. and Dill, D., (1990), Automata for modeling real-time systems, in "Automata, Languages and Programming: Proceedings of the 17th ICALP," Lecture Notes in Computer Science, **443**, pp. 332–335, Springer-Verlag, Berlin/New York.

[AH90] Alur, R. and Henzinger, T.A. (1990), Real-Time Logics : Complexity and Expressiveness, in "Proceedings, 5th IEEE LICS."

[AHV93] Alur, R., Henzinger, T.A., and Vardi, M.Y. (1993), Parametric Real-Time Reasoning, in "Proceedings, 25th ACM STOC," pp. 592–601.

[BCMDH90] J.R. Burch, E.M. Clarke, K.L. McMillan, D.L.Dill, L.J. Hwang. Symbolic Model Checking: 10^{20} States and Beyond, IEEE LICS, 1990.

[Bryant86] R.E. Bryant. Graph-based Algorithms for Boolean Function Manipulation, IEEE Trans. Comput., C-35(8), 1986.

[CE81] Clarke, E. and Emerson, E.A. (1981), Design and Synthesis of Synchronization Skeletons using Branching-Time Temporal Logic, in "Proceedings, Workshop on Logic of Programs," LNCS 131, Springer-Verlag.

[CES86] Clarke, E., Emerson, E.A., and Sistla, A.P., (1986) Automatic Verification of Finite-State Concurrent Systems using Temporal-Logic Specifications, *ACM Trans. Programming, Languages, and Systems*, **8**, Nr. 2, pp. 244–263.

[CY92] Courcoubetis, C. and Yannakakis, M. (1992), Minimum and Maximum Delay Problems in Real-Time Systems. *Formal Methods in System Design* **1**: 385-415, Kluwer Academic Publishers; also in "Proceedings, 3rd CAV," 1991, Springer-Verlag, LNCS 575.

[HHWT95] T.A. Henzinger, P.-H. Ho, and H. Wong-Toi. HyTech: the next generation. In proceedings of the 16th Annual Real-Time System Symposium, pages 56-65. IEEE Computer Society Press, 1995.

[HNSY92] T.A. Henzinger, X. Nicollin, J. Sifakis, S. Yovine. Symbolic Model Checking for Real-Time Systems, IEEE LICS 1992.

[Wang96] Wang, F. (1996). Parametric Timing Analysis for Real-Time Systems. Information and Computation, Vol. 130, Nr 2, Nov. 1996, Academic Press, ISSN 0890-5401; pp 131-150. Also in "Proceedings, 10th IEEE Symposium on Logic in Computer Science," 1995.

APPENDIX : Elaboration on cases in Label(A, ϕ)

{

(1) KClosure$_{\phi_j}(V, F)$;

(2) if ϕ_i is of the form $\exists\phi_j\mathcal{U}_{>\theta}\phi_k$, let $L^{\exists\phi_j\mathcal{U}_{>\theta}\phi_k}(v)$ be

$$\bigvee_{u\in V}\left(\begin{array}{l}\left(\bigvee_{(\pi,T)\in J_{\phi_j}(\langle\kappa\rangle v,u)}(\pi\wedge(T>\theta\vee(T=\theta\wedge u\models fract(\kappa)\neq 0)))\right)\\ \wedge L^{\phi_k}(u)\wedge L^{\exists\Box_{\geq 0}\mathrm{true}}(u)\end{array}\right)$$

(3) if ϕ_i is of the form $\exists\phi_j\mathcal{U}_{\leq\theta}\phi_k$, let $L^{\exists\phi_j\mathcal{U}_{\leq\theta}\phi_k}(v)$ be

$$\bigvee_{u\in V}\left(\begin{array}{l}\left(\bigvee_{(\pi,T)\in J_{\phi_j}(\langle\kappa\rangle v,u)}(\pi\wedge(T<\theta\vee(T=\theta\wedge u\models fract(\kappa)=0)))\right)\\ \wedge L^{\phi_k}(u)\wedge L^{\exists\Box_{\geq 0}\mathrm{true}}(u)\end{array}\right)$$

(4) if ϕ_i is of the form $\exists\phi_j\mathcal{U}_{<\theta}\phi_k$, let $L^{\exists\phi_j\mathcal{U}_{<\theta}\phi_k}(v)$ be

$$\bigvee_{u\in V}\left(\bigvee_{(\pi,T)\in J_{\phi_j}(\langle\kappa\rangle v,u)}(\pi\wedge T<\theta)\wedge L^{\phi_k}(u)\wedge L^{\exists\Box_{\geq 0}\mathrm{true}}(u)\right)$$

(5) if ϕ_i is of the form $\exists\phi_j\mathcal{U}_{=\theta}\phi_k$, let $L^{\exists\phi_j\mathcal{U}_{=\theta}\phi_k}(v)$ be

$$\bigvee_{u\in V}\left(\bigvee_{(\pi,T)\in J_{\phi_j}(\langle\kappa\rangle v,u)}(\pi\wedge T=\theta)\wedge u\models fract(\kappa)=0\wedge L^{\phi_k}(u)\wedge L^{\exists\Box_{\geq 0}\mathrm{true}}(u)\right)$$

(6) if ϕ_i is of the form $\forall\phi_j\mathcal{U}_{>\theta}\phi_k$, let $L^{\forall\phi_j\mathcal{U}_{>\theta}\phi_k}(v)$ be

$$\neg\left(\begin{array}{l}L^{\exists\Diamond_{\leq\theta}\neg\phi_j}(\langle\kappa\rangle v)\\ \vee\bigvee_{u_1,u_2\in V}\left(\begin{array}{l}\bigvee_{(\pi,T)\in J_{\phi_j}(\langle\kappa\rangle v,u_1)}(\pi\wedge T=\theta)\wedge L^{\phi_j}(u_1)\\ \wedge\epsilon(u_1,u_2)=\downarrow\wedge\left(L^{\exists\Box_{\geq 0}\neg\phi_k}(u_2)\vee L^{\exists(\neg\phi_k)\mathcal{U}_{\geq 0}\neg(\phi_j\vee\phi_k)}(u_2)\right)\end{array}\right)\end{array}\right)$$

(7) if ϕ_i is of the form $\forall\phi_j\mathcal{U}_{\leq\theta}\phi_k$, let $L^{\forall\phi_j\mathcal{U}_{\leq\theta}\phi_k}(v)$ be

$$\neg\left(\begin{array}{l}\left(\bigvee_{u_1,u_2\in V}\left(\begin{array}{l}L^{\neg\phi_k}(u_1)\wedge\epsilon(u_1,u_2)=\downarrow\wedge L^{\exists\Box_{\geq 0}\mathrm{true}}(u_2)\\ \wedge\bigvee_{(\pi,T)\in J_{\neg\phi_k}(\langle\kappa\rangle v,u_1)}(\pi\wedge T=\theta)\end{array}\right)\right)\\ \vee L^{\exists(\neg\phi_k)\mathcal{U}_{\leq\theta}\neg(\phi_j\vee\phi_k)}(\langle\kappa\rangle v)\end{array}\right)$$

(8) if ϕ_i is of the form $\forall\phi_j\mathcal{U}_{<\theta}\phi_k$, let $L^{\forall\phi_j\mathcal{U}_{<\theta}\phi_k}(v)$ be

$$\neg\left(\begin{array}{l}\left(\bigvee_{u_1,u_2\in V}\left(\begin{array}{l}L^{\neg\phi_k}(u_1)\wedge\epsilon(u_1,u_2)=\uparrow\wedge L^{\exists\Box_{\geq 0}\mathrm{true}}(u_2)\\ \wedge\bigvee_{(\pi,T)\in J_{\neg\phi_j}(\langle\kappa\rangle v,u_1)}(\pi\wedge T=\theta-1)\end{array}\right)\right)\\ \vee L^{\exists(\neg\phi_k)\mathcal{U}_{<\theta}\neg(\phi_j\vee\phi_k)}(\langle\kappa\rangle v)\end{array}\right)$$

(9) If ϕ_i is of the form $\forall\phi_j\mathcal{U}_{=\theta}\phi_k$, let $L^{\forall\phi_j\mathcal{U}_{=\theta}\phi_k}(v)$ be

$$\neg\left(\begin{array}{l}L^{\exists\Diamond_{<\theta}\neg\phi_j}(\langle\kappa\rangle v)\\ \vee\left(\theta=0\wedge\left(\begin{array}{l}\bigvee_{u_1,u_2\in V}\left(\begin{array}{l}L^{\neg\phi_k}(u_1)\wedge\epsilon(u_1,u_2)=\downarrow\wedge L^{\exists\Box_{\geq 0}\mathrm{true}}(u_2)\\ \wedge\bigvee_{(\pi,T)\in J_{\neg\phi_k}(\langle\kappa\rangle v,u_1)}(\pi\wedge T=0)\end{array}\right)\\ \vee L^{\exists(\neg\phi_k)\mathcal{U}_{=0}\neg(\phi_j\vee\phi_k)}(\langle\kappa\rangle v)\end{array}\right)\right)\\ \vee\bigvee_{u_1,u_2\in V}\left(\begin{array}{l}\theta>0\wedge\bigvee_{(\pi,T)\in J_{\phi_j}(\langle\kappa\rangle v,u_1)}(\pi\wedge T=\theta-1)\\ \wedge L^{\phi_j}(u_1)\wedge\epsilon(u_1,u_2)=\uparrow\\ \wedge\left(\begin{array}{l}\bigvee_{u_3,u_4\in V}\left(\begin{array}{l}L^{\neg\phi_k}(u_3)\wedge\epsilon(u_3,u_4)=\downarrow\wedge L^{\exists\Box_{\geq 0}\mathrm{true}}(u_4)\\ \wedge\bigvee_{(\pi,T)\in J_{\neg\phi_k}(\langle\kappa\rangle u-2,u_3)}\pi\wedge T=0\end{array}\right)\\ \vee L^{\exists(\neg\phi_k)\mathcal{U}_{=0}\neg(\phi_j\vee\phi_k)}(u_2)\end{array}\right)\end{array}\right)\end{array}\right)$$

}

CAMILA: Prototyping and Refinement of Constructive Specifications

J. J. Almeida, L. S. Barbosa, F. L. Neves and J. N. Oliveira

Computer Science Department
University of Minho
Largo do Paço — 4710 Braga
Portugal
{jj,lsb,fln,jno}@di.uminho.pt

Abstract. This paper accompanies the demonstration of CAMILA, an experimental platform for formal software development, rooted in the tradition of constructive specification methods. The CAMILA approach is an attempt to make available at software development level the basic problem solving strategy one got used to from school physics — *create, experiment and reason on a mathematical model.* Based on a notion of *formal software component*, it encompasses a set-theoretic language and an inequational *calculus* for classification and refinement. Its kernel is a functional prototyping environment, fully connectable to external applications, equipped with a classified component repository and distribution facilities.

Keywords Constructive specification, prototyping, program calculation.

1 An Overview

In the structure of an information system, Software Engineering distinguishes between *entities*, which represent information sources, and *transformations* upon them. The former originates the data structures, the later the algorithms. The fundamental observation behind *constructive* (or *model-oriented*) specification methods such as VDM [Jon86], Z [Spi89] or RAISE [Geo91], is that a similar duality appears in the definition of an algebra (sets and functions) or relational structure (sets and relations), making them suitable as a mathematical semantics for such systems.

CAMILA [1] development affiliates itself to the research in *constructive specification methods* as well as in exploring Functional Programming as a *rapid prototyping* environment for software models, a program whose origin can be traced back to Peter Hendersen's me too [Hen84]. The project main contributions may be summarized as follows:

[1] CAMILA is named after a Portuguese 19th-century novelist — Camilo Castelo-Branco (1825 - 1890) — whose immense and heterogeneous writings, deeply rooted in his own time controversies, mirrors a passionate yet difficult life.

1. As a (executable) specification language, CAMILA takes full advantage of the (Cartesian closed) structure of the category **Set** of sets and set-theoretical functions. In particular data sorts are regarded as endofunctors [2] over **Set**, transforming uniformly either sets and functions. This mirrors the intuition that (parametric) sorts are (some kinds of) functors and morphisms arise as natural transformations between them.
2. Traditionally, in the constructive style for software development design is factored in as many "mind-sized" steps as required. Every intermediate design is first proposed and then proved to follow from its antecedent. Such an "invent-and-verify" style is often impractical due to the complexity of the mathematical reasoning involved in real-life software problems. At the core of the CAMILA approach is a *calculus* — named SETS, after *Specification in* Set [Oli90,Oli92,Oli97] — which introduces explicit transformational rules in program data structuring. Here an intermediate design is drawn from a previous one according to some *law* available in the *calculus*, which is structural in the sense that model components can be refined in isolation (and, consequently, previous refinement results re-used). Proof discharge is achieved by replacing proofs from first principles by calculation. This is the point of a calculus, as witnessed elsewhere in the history of mathematics, and corresponds to a maturation stage emerging naturally after two decades of intensive research on the foundations of formal methods for software design.
3. CAMILA is particularly oriented to the development of systems involving some degree of distribution. Facilities are provided to prototype software components as communicating agents.

Last but not least, a major goal in CAMILA design has been to scale up formal development methods to the industrial practice. This has shaped the project as a collection of portable working tools, with simple interfaces but easily connectable to external applications (*e.g.*, databases, interface generators, document processors, etc.). Some real *case studies* include the development of reuse mechanisms for a CASE tool [Oli95b], the project of temporal databases and the design of a *building description language* [Oli95a]. The following section details the four main components of the CAMILA platform.

2 A "Guided Tour"

2.1 The Functional Prototyper

The *Functional Prototyper* animates Set as a mathematical space for building specifications as collections of parameterized data sorts and functions upon them.

The basic set constructors capture essential operations upon information:

[2] More rigorously, as combinations of polynomial functors plus the direct powerset functor $\mathbf{2}^{-}$.

- *Cartesian product* ($A \times B$) for aggregation in the spatial axis,
- *coproduct* ($A + B$), for choice (i.e., aggregation in the temporal axis) and
- *exponentiation*, or function space, (A^B) for functional dependence.

When processing data definitions, the prototyper generates automatically the constructors and selectors of each product type as well as the canonical embeddings associated to coproducts. Derived constructors, for finite A and B, are $\mathbf{2}^A$ (*finite subsets*), $A \hookrightarrow C$ (*finite mappings*), defined as $\sum_{K \subseteq A} C^K$, and A^* (*finite sequences*), defined as $\sum_{n \subseteq \mathbb{N}} A^n$, as well as recursive definitions in the form $X = \mathcal{F}(X)$, where $\mathcal{F}$ is a functor involving the above constructs.

By functoriality, those constructs also act upon functions (either primitive or user-defined) lifting its effect to the generated structure. For example, the expressions `(f-set)-seq` and `(f-seq)-set` correspond, respectively, to the action upon the function $f : A \longrightarrow B$ of the functors $(\mathbf{2}^-)^*$ and $\mathbf{2}^{(-^*)}$. These enables a particularly fruitful *modular calculus* in which *enrichment* and *specialization* amount to composition with suitable functors, respectively, on the right and on the left.

The operator repertoire in CAMILA is very rich and highly structured. Each operator is an arrow in Set, either *set-theoretic* (*e.g.*, $\mathbb{N} \xrightarrow{\lambda x.x^2} \mathbb{N}$), or *category-theoretic*. The last group includes arrows classified as *implicit* (*e.g.*, $A \times B \xrightarrow{\pi_1} A$), *functorial*, *i.e.* the action of some functor on another arrow (*e.g.*, $A \hookrightarrow X \xrightarrow{A \hookrightarrow f} A \hookrightarrow Y$), *universal*, *i.e.* arising as the unique arrow in an universal construction (*e.g.*, $A + B \xrightarrow{[f,g]} C$ or $C \xrightarrow{<f,g>} A \times B$) or *natural*, *i.e.* regarded as a component of a natural transformation (*e.g.*, $X^* \xrightarrow{\text{elems}} \mathbf{2}^X$). The SETS constructs, as well as the basic algebras associated with them, are directly expressible in the prototyper, from which a high level description is automatically generated (in the form of a LaTeX file). So are the propositional connectives and quantifiers, anonymous function definition, in the form of λ-expressions, and high-order functions.

Specifying in CAMILA is done in a stepwise-elaboration style, each stage of the model being immediately prototyped and quick feedback about its behavior being gathered within the design team. The prototyper type-checking filters primary syntactic errors and unexpected semantic behavior is likely to be spot and corrected. The tool is able to handle *lazy evaluation* and *partially defined functions*, i.e. functions whose signature has been declared but whose computation rule has not yet been supplied.

2.2 The SETS Animator

The reification phase, in the CAMILA life-cycle, is a systematic process of stepwise transformation of the original specification into another which can be eventually recognized as the formal semantics of a particular command, or program fragment, in the intended target technology. The purpose of the SETS *Animator* is to animate the calculus so that concrete data-structures modeling the specification sorts can be found by calculation, accompanied by the synthesis of abstraction functions and induced implementation-level invariants.

Different laws of SETS lead to different implementation structures and platforms. A typical example of a common target technology is that of relational databases, typically materialized by a particular SQL server. A database table is trivially formalized, in the SETS notation, by a relation in $\mathbf{2}^{A \times B}$ or a mapping in $A \hookrightarrow B$, for A,B arbitrary products of "atomic" types. Therefore, all SETS laws which somehow "lead" to such structures are welcome by such a target environment [3]. A SETS law is an (in)equation of the form $A \trianglelefteq_f^\phi B$, stating that every instance of A can be reified into the corresponding instance of B, by adopting abstraction function f and provided that concrete invariant ϕ is enforced over B. On the whole, the following abstraction invariant, using the terminology of [Mor90], is synthesized: $\lambda ab \,.\, (a = f(b)) \wedge \phi(b)$. For instance, law

$$A \hookrightarrow D \times (B \hookrightarrow C) \trianglelefteq_{\bowtie_n}^{dpi} (A \hookrightarrow D) \times ((A \times B) \hookrightarrow C)$$

states that finite mapping nesting of can be flattened. Repeated application of this law makes it possible to boil arbitrarily nested, intricate mapping-based data structures, down to products of atomic relation tables. The relevant abstraction function ($\bowtie_n$) computes a kind of "nested join" and invariant *dpi* will guarantee that such a join operation is effectively computed.

In the balance ***data vs algorithms***, CAMILA is strongly oriented to the data component as the refinement of data sorts induces by itself the ***simulations*** of the abstract operations in the reified context. Calculating a simulation for operation α amounts to prove (constructively) the commutativity of the refinement diagram for α. CAMILA does not claim any originality in this process, relying instead in other calculi such us the FOLD-UNFOLD [Dar82] or the Oxford REFINEMENT CALCULUS [Mor90] [4].

The animator is implemented with genetic algorithms [Mic94] which support a flexible, and surprisingly efficient, inequational term-rewriting. The "genetic engine" represents each potential solution as a chromosome of integer genes, whereas the size of each chromosome fixes the number of refinement steps to be applied. What is interesting is that, by modifying the evaluation function over SETS expressions, the user is able to bias the animator towards the target implementation technology [NO95].

---

[3] Should the target programming language be, for instance, C, then laws leading to structures of the $1 + A$ pattern (the "pointer to A abstraction") will become relevant, in particular recursive structures of the $X = 1 + \mathcal{F}(X)$ shape.

[4] In fact SETS and the REFINEMENT CALCULUS blend together nicely. The last is a weakest pre-condition (algorithmic) calculus in which change of representation is handed by choosing coupling invariants. SETS main purpose is that of *calculating*, rather than choosing, such coupling invariants.

2.3 The Repository

The CAMILA platform includes a *reusable components repository* which catalogues the available specifications as well as its implementations and the associated refinement calculations. In particular abstraction functions and induced invariants are recorded as CAMILA expressions allowing for the dynamic interconnection between different levels of abstraction.

The SETS *Animator* is used to classify and compare components (in a "classify-by-data" style). Furthermore architectural relationships such as *is-a*, *is-used-by*, *is-implementation-of*, *is-special-case-of* are formally decided and recorded, rather than fixed by intuition. In the *Repository* component aggregation can be expressed by "software-circuit" diagrams using a graphical notation suggestively resembling the conventional hardware design notation.

The *Repository* and the *Functional Prototyper* bears "full citizenship" at C/C++ programming level. A collection of libraries, enable both the processes of

- embedding CAMILA prototypes in (partial) implementations;
- enriching, either static or dynamically, the prototyping environment with modules supplied or already implemented in the target programming environments.

This leads to what may be called a "hybrid" prototype: some system components already fully reified may cohabit (and communicate) with other parts still in a prototyping phase. Such temporary configurations of the system, which may require abstraction functions explicit at run time, cannot be expected to be particularly efficient ones. But they provide for smooth, stepwise reification and testing.

2.4 The Process Prototyper

The specification of distributed systems is not only concerned with the components functionality, but also with the local and global *behavior patterns*, which entails the need to combine set-based specifications with some sort of process calculi over the set of declared operations.

The *Process Prototyper* allows for the annotation of CAMILA components with *behavioral patterns*, which can be simulated and further analyzed by a typical process algebra tool, like the CWB [MS96]. It also includes a small configuration language enabling the (eventually dynamic) association of each node of the system to an independent process (*e.g.*, a UNIX process), communication being achieved through a set of specific primitives. Application dependent constraints of the communication network are themselves prototyped as another system component.

On going work in this area includes the development of a calculus for process refinement dualising SETS results to a category of transition systems.

The idea is that, as specifications of functionality may be regarded as algebras of some **Set** functors, similarly behaviors emerge as co-algebras of other functors [Bar98]. CAMILA is expected to cope with this broader notion of refinement in the near future.

Acknowledgments

The CAMILA project has been supported by the JNICT council under PMCT contract nr. 169/90.

References

[Bar98] L. S. Barbosa. *Reification of Processes.* PhD thesis, Universidade do Minho (to appear), 1998.

[Dar82] J. Darlington. Program transformation. In *Funct. Prog. and Its Applications: An Advanced Course.* Cambridge Univ. Press, 1982.

[Geo91] C. George. The RAISE specification language: a tutorial. In *Proc. of VDM'91.* LNCS (551), 1991.

[Hen84] P. Hendersen. me too: A language for software specification and model building. Preliminary Report, University of Stirling, 1984.

[Jon86] Cliff B. Jones. *Systematic Software Development Using* VDM. Series in Computer Science. Prentice-Hall International, 1986.

[Mic94] Zbigniew Michalewicz. *Genetic Algorithms + Data Structures = Evolution Programs.* Springer-Verlag, 1994. Second, Extended Edition.

[Mor90] C. Morgan. *Programming from Specification.* Series in Computer Science. Prentice-Hall International, 1990. C. A. R. Hoare, series editor.

[MS96] F. Moller and P. Stevens. The edinburgh concurrency workbench (version 7). User's manual, LFCS, Edinburgh University, 1996.

[NO95] F. Luís Neves and José N. Oliveira. Software Reuse by Model Reification. *Seventh Annual Workshop on Software Reuse*, August 1995.

[Oli90] J. N. Oliveira. A reification calculus for model-oriented software specification. *Formal Aspects of Computing*, 2(1):1–23, 1990.

[Oli92] J. N. Oliveira. Software reification using the SETS calculus. In *Proc. of the BCS FACS 5th Refinement Workshop, Theory and Practice of Formal Software Development, London, UK*, pages 140–171. Springer-Verlag, 8–10 January 1992. (Invited paper).

[Oli95a] J. N. Oliveira. Formal specification and prototyping of a building description language. In *Proc. CIVIL-COMP'95, Cambridge*, August 1995.

[Oli95b] J. N. Oliveira. Fuzzy object comparasion and its application to a self-adaptable query mechanism. In *Proc. IFSA'95, S. Paulo*, July 1995.

[Oli97] J. N. Oliveira. Sets: A data structuring calculus and its application to program development. Technical Report Lecture Notes for the Macau Course, UNU/IIST, May 1997.

[Spi89] J. M. Spivey. *The Z Notation: A Reference Manual.* Series in Computer Science. Prentice-Hall International, 1989.

PAMELA+PVS

Bettina Buth

Universität Bremen - FB 3
P.O. Box 330 440, D - 28334 Bremen, Germany
email: bb@informatik.uni-bremen.de
URL: http://www.informatik.uni-bremen.de/~bb

1 Background

The system PAMELA (Proof Assistant for Meta IV-like Languages) was designed originally to check partial correctness of VDM-like specifications [3] of code generators with respect to implicit specifications given as sets of pre- and postconditions [1]. Explicit specifications in this framework essentially are systems of mutually recursive functions and procedures (in the following called *operations*) over a set of global variables. Operations are defined as sequential programs.

The goal of PAMELA is the calculation of a set of proof obligations for each operation that together ensure partial correctness of the overall system. An earlier version tried to discharge these obligations based on sets of rewriting and deduction rules provided by the user.

PAMELA+PVS is a modification of PAMELA that supports proofs for a larger class of specifications including non-deterministic sequential programs and uses PVS [5] as prover component for discharging proof obligations. Non-deterministic sequential programs are of interest for a development approach based on CSP [2] that was introduced in Peleska [4]. A certain subclass of CSP processes can be transformed into equivalent non-deterministic programs. The proof that such a CSP process satisfies a given trace specification can thus be transformed into an invariant proof for the equivalent non-deterministic program.

2 Generation of Proof Obligations

The generation of proof obligations in PAMELA+PVS is based on the splitting approach introduced by Buth [1]. The idea is to symbolically evaluate the code of operation bodies using the implicit specification as an interface to cope with recursive calls. The process corresponds to the calculation of strongest postconditions except for the treatment of calls. The result of splitting can thus be called a *relative strongest prostcondition.*

The name "splitting" refers to the process of splitting the code for which the obligations are to be generated into separate paths and generating obligations for the each individual path. The overall obligation then is that the disjunction of the obligations for each paths implies the postcondition that is stated for the operation under consideration, which is discharged by proving that the obligations for each path imply the postcondition.

3 PVS

PVS [5] is currently one of the most advanced specification and verification systems for software applications. The system consists of a specification language and a number of tools including a sophisticated prover.

A PVS specification consists of theories each of which may introduce types, constants and functions (which for PVS are higher level constants). Types are built from basic datatypes including boolean, integer and rational numbers, and type constructors, e.g. arrays, records, lists, sequences, and abstract datatypes. Specifications can use both algebraic style definitions and functional style definitions. Recursion is of particular interest, related to the philosophy to enforce use of total functions only. A large and still extending library of parameterized and special purpose theories including generic theorems allows specifications on a high level without bothering with details.

The prover itself uses sequent-style proofs. Proof strategies – user defined as well as powerful general purpose variants – help to structure the proof and to focus on the high level proof steps. The tedious task of a step by step application of simplification rules interactively is thus drastically simplified. The user can in this way choose a level of automation as seems appropriate for the proof at hand.

4 PAMELA+PVS

The interface between PAMELA and PVS is implemented as a set of Tcl/Tk applications grouped into two windows. This choice of interface is motivated by the different nature of the two systems. PAMELA is a file oriented, non-interactive system implemented in C and running in UNIX shells. Interaction is restricted to reactions to failing proofs and output reflecting the status of the generation of obligations and proofs. PVS on the other side is implemented in LISP and running as an interactive system in an Emacs-environment.

The aim was to find a way of generating the proof obligations successively and submitting them to PVS for examination, i.e. typechecking and/or proving. In this way it is possible to get feedback at the earliest possible time. This feedback comprises typecheck errors as well as the necessity to introduce further lemmata in order to proceed with the proof. A positive sideeffect is that the separate treatment of single obligations avoids the disadvantages of confronting PVS with a large theory containing all theorems. Such large theories can lead to very unsatisfactory response times for parsing and typechecking and an explosion of the prover state.

With the Tcl/Tk-interface it is now possible to investigate the individual obligations independently from each other after loading the common basic theory which is usually relatively small. Furthermore it is possible to interrupt and postpone the generation of proof obligations in favor of adding new lemmata or in general modifying the basic theory. Furthermore PAMELA+PVS generates the full theory containing all obligations as well as some information about the splitting process.

References

1. B. Buth: *Operation Refinement Proofs for VDM-like Specifications*, Dissertation; published as Technical Report 9501 Institut für Informatik und Praktische Mathematik, Christian-Albrechts-Universität Kiel 1995.
(see also: `http:\\www.informatik.uni-bremen.de/~bb`)
2. C.A.R. Hoare: *Communicating Sequential Processes*; Prentice Hall International, 1985
3. Cliff B. Jones: *Systematic Software Development using VDM*, Series in Computer Science. Prentice-Hall International, Second Edition, 1990.
4. J. Peleska: *Formal Methods and the Development of Dependable Systems*; *Habilitationsschrift*, Technical Report 9612, Institut für Informatik, Christian-Albrechts-Universität Kiel (1996); (see also: `http:\\www.informatik.uni-bremen.de/~jp`)
5. John Rushby: *A tutorial on specification and verification using PVS*, In: Tutorial Material for FME '93: Industrial-Strength Formal Methods. Proceedings of the First International Symposium of Formal Methods Europe, Odense, Denmark, 1993. (see also : `http://www.csl.sri.com/pvs.html`)

The Circal System

Antonio Cerone, Alex J. Cowie and George J. Milne

Advanced Computing Research Centre, School of Computer and Information Science,
University of South Australia, Adelaide SA 5095, Australia
{cerone,cowie,milne}@cis.unisa.edu.au.

The toolset is based on Circal (CIRcuit CALculus) [1, 8, 9], a process algebra with the following characteristics:

- Processes are guarded by sets of actions that are always performed simultaneously and an arbitrary number of processes can synchronize on the same action.
- There is no special action to describe a process that is evolving due to an internal (invisible) cause, but there are two different operators for an internal choice and an external choice.
- The concurrent composition operator allows the synchronization of actions with the same name and prevents actions belonging to both of the components from occurring independently.

The process algebra provides an ideal basis from which to build and reason about process models. In order to build large or complex models Circal has been embedded in the high level language XTC [7]. The resulting language, called XCircal (eXtended Circal), is equipped with data-types, functions and control structures, and has been implemented in the Circal System [9].

The Circal System exists in two versions: one uses an explicit representation of the state space, whereas the other uses an implicit representation in terms of OBDD's. The system also implements equivalence testing and several preorders on processes. Simulation can be carried out by composing test patterns (which can contain both input and output events) with a system behaviour.

The distinctive features of Circal support a constraint-based modelling style [9] and permit a natural representation of time without any extension to the process algebra framework [6]. The constraint-based modelling allows the characterization of both safety and liveness properties within the Circal process algebra. This makes the Circal System a verification tool with the significant feature that the verification procedure is entirely performed within the process algebra framework, without recourse to temporal logic or model checking techniques [3, 4]. The Circal System allows the specification and verification of real-time systems. Time is represented by using actions as timing signals and characterizing the relationships between timing signals in terms of constraints [3, 4, 5, 6]. The simple inclusion of a signal in a guard is used to describe the concept of *all* the actions in the guard occurring synchronously with the signal. Moreover, because of the particular nature of the composition operator, when used to compose several processes, every time a component performs synchronizations on a signal any other component that can perform that signal must also do it, and the signal occurrences are still visible after the synchronization without removal.

The Circal System supports also a hierarchical specification of systems at different level of abstractions. The abstraction levels of the modelled system are related through interface processes that define relationships among actions used at the different levels [5, 6]. This also allows the translation of properties proved at the lower level into assumptions at the higher level.

The Circal System has been extensively applied to the specification and verification of digital hardware (including both delay-insensitive and bounded-delay asynchronous circuits) [1, 5, 8, 9], safety-critical systems, communication protocol with real-time characteristics [3, 4], and to the simulation of traffic systems [2].

A graphical interface to a Circal model of the audio control protocol described in [3] has been developed. The user interface allows the input of messages and specification of relative clock timings both in the simulation and the automatic verification of the protocol operation.

The Circal System is available by anonymous ftp. Information can be obtained from: http://www.cis.unisa.edu.au/projects/circal/circal_system.html.

References

1. A. Bailey, G. A. McCaskill, and G. J. Milne. An Exercise in the Automatic Verification of Asynchronous Designs. *Formal Methods in System Design*, 4(3):213–242, May 1994.
2. M. Bate, A. Cowie, G. Milne and G. Russell. Process Algebras and the Rapid Simulation of Highly Concurrent System. *Australian Computer Science Communication*, 17(1):21–31, 1995.
3. A. Cerone, A. J. Cowie, G. J. Milne, and P. A. Moseley. Description and Verification of a Time-Sensitive Protocol. Technical Report CIS-96-009, University of South Australia, School of Computer and Information Science, Adelaide, Oct 1996. http://www.cis.unisa.edu.au/cgi-bin/techreport?CIS-96-009
4. A. Cerone, A. J. Cowie, G. J. Milne and P. A. Moseley. Modelling a Time-Dependent Protocol using the Circal Process Algebra. In *Proc. International Workshop on Hybrid and Real-Time Systems*, Grenoble, France, March 1997, Lecture Notes in Computer Science 1201, Springer, pages 124–138, Berlin, 1997.
5. A. Cerone D. A. Kearney and G. J. Milne. Verifying Bounded Delay Asynchronous Circuits using Time Relationship Constraints. Technical Report CIS-97-012, University of South Australia, School of Computer and Information Science, Adelaide, August 1997. http://www.cis.unisa.edu.au/cgi-bin/techreport?CIS-97-012
6. A. Cerone and G. J. Milne. Specification of Timing Constraints within the Circal Process Algebra. In *Proc. AMAST'97*, Sydney, Australia, December 1997, Lecture Notes in Computer Science, this volume.
7. G. A. McCaskill. The XTC Language Reference Manual. Technical Report HDV-14-91, University of Strathclyde, Department of Computer Science, Glasgow, 1991.
8. G. J. Milne. The Formal Description and Verification of Hardware Timing. *IEEE Transactions on Computers*, 40(7):811–826, Jul 1991.
9. G. J. Milne. *Formal Specification and Verification of Digital Systems.* McGraw-Hill, 1994.

A Refinement-Type Checker for Standard ML

Rowan Davies*

Carnegie Mellon University Department of Computer Science,
5000 Forbes Ave, Pittsburgh PA 15213, USA

One of the major benefits of statically-typed programming languages is that they significantly improve programmer productivity. An obvious reason for this is that they dramatically reduce the amount of time spent debugging by catching most common errors at compile time. A more fundamental reason is that programmers can use the types to guide understanding of the structure of a piece of code, both during the development of the code, and during code maintenance. One proposal for increasing the benefits of static typing is to extend an existing language so that each ordinary type is refined by a number of *refinement types*, which allow many common program properties to be expressed and checked. In the resulting system a part of a program which is assigned a particular type may also be assigned multiple refinements of that type.

We have designed an extension of the programming language Standard ML which includes refinement types, and have built a practical refinement-type checker for it which handles the full language, excluding modules. Our extension allows the programmer to define refinements of ML datatypes. For example, non-empty lists could be defined as a refinement of lists in order to express the invariant that a particular function always returns a non-empty list, thus allowing this invariant to be automatically checked by the compiler.

To better illustrate the use of refinement types (which we also call "sorts") in our extension, consider the following example. Suppose we are writing an application which manipulates simple arithmetic expressions. In some parts of this application we maintain the invariant that the expressions manipulated are sums of products, i.e. they do not contain additions as sub-terms of multiplications. Additionally, in some parts of the application only ground terms are manipulated, i.e. terms which contain no variables. The following small code sample shows how invariants like this can be captured with refinement types:

```
datatype exp =  Num of int | Var of string | Plus of exp * exp
              | Times of exp * exp
datasort prod = Num of int | Var of string | Times of prod * prod
datasort sum_pr = [prod] | Plus of sum_pr * sum_pr
datasort grnd = Num of int | Plus of grnd * grnd | Times of grnd * grnd

fun mult(Plus(st1a, st1b), st2) = Plus(mult(st1a, st2), mult(st1b, st2))
  | mult(st1, Plus(st2a, st2b)) = Plus(mult(st1, st2a), mult(st1, st2b))
  | mult(st1, st2) = Times (st1, st2)
withsort mult :> (sum_pr * sum_pr -> sum_pr) & (grnd * grnd -> grnd)
```

* Partially sponsored by the Advanced Research Projects Agency under the title "The Fox Project: Advanced Languages for Systems Software", ARPA Order No. C533.

In this example code we define a type **exp** for simple arithmetic expressions. Then we define some refinements of this type using **datasort** declarations, which are part of our extension to ML. These refinements correspond to the restricted forms required by the invariants of our application.

We then define an example function from our application, **mult**, which takes two expressions which are sums of products, and returns a sum of products expression for their product. Additionally, we have the invariant that if both input expressions are ground, it returns a ground expression. We express these invariants of the **mult** function by attaching a **withsort** clause to it, which is another one of our extensions to ML. This clause assigns a sort to the function which includes the symbol **&**, which intuitively means that the function must have both of the sorts on either side of the **&**, each of which corresponds to one of the invariants.

If we now run our refinement-type checker on this piece of code, it will succeed, thus verifying that the invariants hold. If instead there was an error in our code, such that these invariants did not hold, then refinement-type checking would fail with an appropriate error message, just like the error messages that would be generated by the compiler if there was an ordinary type error in the program.

The syntax of sorts exactly follows that of the existing ML types, with the addition that **&** may appear anywhere in a sort to conjoin two sorts which refine the same type. In order to make sorts manageable, we define a subsorting relation on them, similar to a subtyping relation. As an example of this, the sort **prod** is a subsort of **sum_pr**, and so the function **mult** can actually be applied to two variables which both have sort **prod**, to yield a result of sort **sum_pr**.

Our algorithms for refinement-type checking are quite different from ordinary type checking. Refinement-type inference is problematic, because programs often satisfy many accidental properties, all of which must be reflected in the inferred sorts. Thus, our algorithms depend on the programmer stating the important properties of a program using annotations such as **withsort**. These annotations are also very useful as reliable documentation for the code, particularly since they have been mechanically checked for correctness.

Our experience with adding refinement types to existing SML code indicates that our algorithms are efficient enough to be run every time a program is compiled. As an example of these experiments, we were able to check that an implementation of red-black balanced binary trees maintains the critical invariant that no red node appears immediately below another red node.

The refinement-type checker was built as part of the author's PhD thesis work, and he would like to give special thanks to his advisor, Frank Pfenning. For more information about refinement types, including a number of papers and some extended examples, see the web page:

http://www.cs.cmu.edu/~rowan/sorts.html

Recording HOL Proofs in a Structured Browsable Format

Jim Grundy[1] and Thomas Långbacka[2]*

[1] Department of Computer Science, The Australian National University
http://cs.anu.edu.au/~Jim.Grundy/
[2] Department of Computer Science, University of Helsinki
http://www.cs.helsinki.fi/~tlangbac/

1 Introduction

It is possible to discern two attitudes toward proof in the computer science community. Some regard a proof as a formal mathematical object, while the others view proof as a social process: a proof is an argument that convinces its reader. These views have been largely incompatible.

The goal of our work is to record proofs checked by the HOL theorem prover [4] in a readable format. Even experienced HOL users find it difficult to read proofs described using the HOL meta-language. Our idea is that such a record would constitute a convincing proof under both definitions by being both readable and machine checked.

We have attempted to address the readability problems of formal proofs by recording the steps and intermediate results of HOL proofs in a browsable format. This format hides unnecessary levels of detail in the proof from the reader, while allowing them to view as much of the proof as they feel is necessary to become convinced of its validity.

2 Window Inference

The window inference style of reasoning was originally proposed by Robinson and Staples [9], and later extended and implemented in HOL by Grundy [7]. Window inference is a transformational style of reasoning, where a proof begins with a term X, and proceeds by applying transformations that preserve some relationship R. The proof ends when X has been transformed into another term Y that has some desired property. The result is a theorem of the form $\vdash X \mathrel{R} Y$.

The distinguishing feature of window inference is that it allows users to transform a term by restricting attention to a subterm and transforming it. The remainder of the surrounding term is left unchanged. While transforming a subterm, it is possible to make assumptions based on its context. For example, suppose we wish to transform the term $A \wedge B$; this may be done by transforming the subterm A under the assumption that B is true. The assumption of B is valid

* **Second affiliation:** Turku Centre for Computer Science — TUCS

$$\begin{array}{ll} & A \wedge \boxed{(A \vee B \Rightarrow C \wedge A)} \\ = & \{\text{By simplifying the right conjunct.}\} \\ & A \wedge C \end{array}$$

$$\begin{array}{ll} & A \wedge \boxed{(A \vee B \Rightarrow C \wedge A)} \\ = & \{\text{By simplifying the right conjunct.}\} \\ & \quad 1\bullet \ \langle A \rangle \\ & \qquad A \vee B \Rightarrow C \wedge A \\ & \quad = \{\text{From the assumption that } A \text{ is true.}\} \\ & \qquad \top \vee B \Rightarrow C \wedge \top \\ & \quad = \{\text{By boolean algebra.}\} \\ & \qquad C \\ & A \wedge C \end{array}$$

Fig. 1. Two views of an example proof

because if B were false, the entire term would be false regardless of the value of A. In window inference parlance, the act of restricting attention to a subterm is referred to as *opening* a window on the subterm in question. Conversely, once a given subterm has been transformed into a suitable form, the window can be *closed* and the transformation is propagated into the original term. The term being transformed at a given moment is referred to as the *focus*.

3 A Notation for Presenting Proofs

Calculational proof, a style of reasoning popularised by Gries and Schneider [5], and others, offers an easy to read format for the presentation of short proofs. Back, Grundy and von Wright [1] have recently presented a structured extension to calculational proof that is well suited to the presentation of window inference reasoning.

A window inference proof without subproofs can, in fact, be written as a calculational proof. A window inference proof that contains a subproof can be presented as a calculational proof with a second calculational proof nested inside it. The nesting is indicated by indentation, and — for added clarity — the beginning of a subproof is marked with with a dot (•). In the extended notation of structured calculational proof, any assumptions local to a subproof are listed in brackets at its beginning. The right-hand side proof in Fig. 1. illustrates the notation. The box around the right conjunct indicates the subterm that forms the focus of the nested subproof.

4 ProofViews

The structured proof format described in the previous section admits the possibility of structured browsing to increase readability. A large proof containing many subproofs can appear daunting to a reader. Rather than presenting the

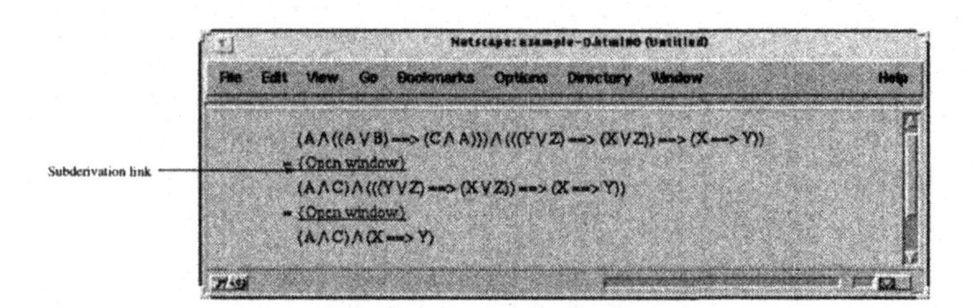

Fig. 2. Top level of browsable proof

whole proof at once, we can initially present the proof with all subproofs hidden. The left-hand side proof in Fig. 1. is an example of such an initial proof. If the reader is interested in a subproof, they can select the comment that describes it. The first layer of that subproof will then be revealed. In this way the reader can see not only the individual steps of a proof, but also the structure of the proof as a whole. Furthermore, the reader need only reveal as much of the proof as necessary to be convinced of its validity.

The ProofViews package[3] [6] adds support for additional macros to HTML, that can be used for formatting structured proofs. These macros can be used to format structured calculational proofs. For example, there are specific macros for handling transformations to a given term and commenting the transformation performed. The input to ProofViews is a document describing a structured calculational proof, like the one in Fig. 1., using the extended HTML notation. Processing the document creates a family of standard HTML documents. These documents give all the views of the proof described in the original, and contain hyper-links to navigate between them. Navigating between the documents using a web browser, like Netscape, allows the proof to be browsed without any specialised software.

5 TkWinHOL

TkWinHOL [8] is a graphical user interface to the HOL implementation of window inference. TkWinHOL is designed to simplify the task of work transforming terms. Most of the work is done by selecting regions of the display and choosing an operation from a button or menu. Thus, TkWinHOL works in a 'select-operate' fashion common to many graphical user interfaces.

The long term goal for TkWinHOL is to make it possible to use window inference with only a limited knowledge of the HOL system which lies beneath. One important step in this direction is the ability to record HOL proofs in a readable format. This is accomplished using the ProofViews system described above. When using TkWinHOL, every proof step is recorded. Most are recorded

[3] ProofViews is available at the following URL: `http://cs.anu.edu.au/~Jim.Grundy/proof_views/man.html`.

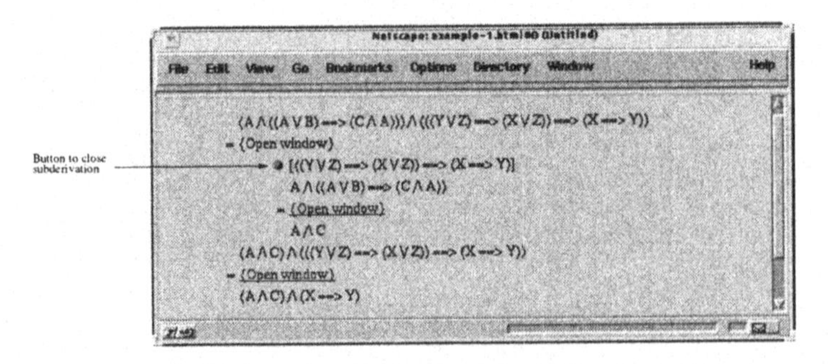

Fig. 3. Browsable proof partly expanded

---

using a simple ProofViews mark-up template, but some require more complex treatment. For example, starting and ending subproofs, where contextual information (among other things) has to be handled. Once a proof is finished, a complete record is saved in a file, where it can be processed by ProofViews to create a browsable version.

To further illustrate the browsable proofs constructed with TkWinHOL we will look at how the term

$$(A \wedge ((A \vee B) \Rightarrow (C \wedge A))) \wedge (((Y \vee Z) \Rightarrow (X \vee Z)) \Rightarrow (X \Rightarrow Y)) \qquad (1)$$

can be transformed to the much simpler term

$$(A \wedge C) \wedge (X \Rightarrow Y) \qquad (2)$$

while preserving equality, and how this is represented as a browsable proof.

The proof strategy for transforming (1) into (2) is straightforward. We begin by opening a window on the left conjunct of (1), creating the following focus:

$$A \wedge ((A \vee B) \Rightarrow (C \wedge A))$$

where we open another window, this time on the right conjunct. At this point one of the assumptions is A, and this assumption can be used to rewrite the focus $(A \vee B) \Rightarrow (C \wedge A)$ to C. This is achieved in the tool by selecting the assumption A with the mouse, and then choosing the 'rewrite' operation from a menu. After closing the two windows we opened, the original focus has been reduced to

$$(A \wedge C) \wedge (((Y \vee Z) \Rightarrow (X \vee Z)) \Rightarrow (X \Rightarrow Y)) \qquad (3)$$

which corresponds to the first step in the browsable proof shown in Fig. 2. This derivation is partly expanded in Fig. 3. The derivation is continued by concentrating on the right conjunct of (3) and transforming it into the form $X \Rightarrow Y$ in a similar way to that just shown, and we are done.

An interesting feature of the TkWinHOL tool is that it is designed to be extendable. The Refinement Calculator [3], a program refinement tool based on Back's refinement calculus [2], is one such extension. is an example of such an extension to TkWinHOL. Extensions to TkWinHOL inherit the ability to record proofs in a browsable format. This means that program derivations done using the Refinement Calculator can be turned into browsable proofs of the kind presented in Figs. 2 and 3.

6 Future Work

The tool we have just described for recording HOL proofs in a browsable format still requires further development before we may achieve our goal of creating readable, machine checked proofs. For example, the tool currently inserts only template comments into the proof record. These must be edited by a human to create a truly readable proof. We are considering two ways to improve on this. The first is for the tool to record the HOL commands associated with proof step, with hyper-linked cross references into the HOL documentation. The other is to consider the provision of machine generated natural language comments, like the proof descriptions generated by the MIZAR system [10].

At present the browsable proof record is generated offline, after a proof is complete. It is then viewed with a separate web browser. A HTML browser widget is now available for Tcl/Tk, the system in which TkWinHOL is implemented. This should allow us to extend the tool so that partially complete proofs can be browsed while they are being constructed.

References

1. R. Back, J. Grundy, and J. von Wright. Structured calculational proof. Joint Computer Science Technical Report TR-CS-96-09, The Australian National University, Department of Computer Science, Canberra ACT 0200, Australia, 1996.
2. R.-J. R. Back. On correct refinement of programs. *J. Comput. Syst. Sci.*, 23(1):49–68, 1981.
3. M. Butler, J. Grundy, T. Långbacka, R. Rukšėnas, and J. von Wright. The refinement calculator: Proof support for program refinement. In Groves and Reeves, editors, *Formal Methods Pacific'97: Proceedings of FMP'97*, Discrete Mathematics and Theoretical Computer Science, pages 40–61, Wellington, New Zealand, 1997. Springer-Verlag.
4. M. J. C. Gordon and T. F. Melham, editors. *Introduction to HOL: A theorem proving environment for higher order logic.* Cambridge University Press, Cambridge, England, 1993.
5. D. Gries and F. B. Schneider. *A Logical Approach to Discrete Math.* Texts and Monographs in Computer Science. Springer-Verlag, New York, 1993.
6. J. Grundy. A browsable format for proof presentation. *Mathesis Universalis*, 1(2), 1996.
7. J. Grundy. Transformational hierarchical reasoning. *Comput. J.*, 39(4):291–302, 1996.
8. T. Långbacka, R. Rukšėnas, and J. von Wright. TkWinHOL: A tool for doing window inference in HOL. In Schubert, Windley, and Alves-Foss, editors, *Higher Order Logic Theorem Proving and Its Applications: 8th International Workshop*, volume 971 of *LNCS*, pages 245–260, Aspen Grove, Utah, 1995. Springer-Verlag.
9. P. J. Robinson and J. Staples. Formalizing a hierarchical structure of practical mathematical reasoning. *J. Logic Comput.*, 3(1):47–61, 1993.
10. A. Trybulec and H. A. Blair. Computer aided reasoning. In Parikh, editor, *Logic of Programs*, volume 193 of *LNCS*, pages 406–412, New York, 1985. Springer-Verlag.

Analysing Multi-Agent System Traces with IDAF

C. K. Low

Department of Computer Science
University of Melbourne
Victoria 3052, Australia
clow@cs.mu.oz.au

Demonstration 1: ***dMARS***

IDAF can display execution traces of applications written in *dMARS*. The demonstrated application is a complicated multi-agent application called BIBSEARCH. It searches the World Wide Web for full bibliographic references using multiple concurrent agents which specialise in various domains. The agents can be dynamically selected to perform the search, for example, only agents specialising in computer science are selected for searching for computer science references. BIBSEARCH can also take advantage of proxy servers.

When the system was implemented, it was tested and debugged with the assistance of IDAF. The system was executed with test data and the execution trace collected. Figure 1 shows the start and the end of an actual execution. For clarity, the interactions in the middle have been removed and the long messages are shortened with ellipsis (...) in a legend. By using IDAF, errors were detected when the test data were executed and the execution traces were analysed. Some of the errors detected using IDAF were as follows.

- No results were being returned from *AltaVista*. The problem was with the interactions with *ScanPage*. Messages sent to *ScanPage* were not acted upon due to missing plans.
- Occasionally the system would not start searching. A race condition occurred when the agents received the ***search_for_citation*** message and the system ***initialise*** message (system messages are not shown) at the same time.
- For certain sequences of test cases, the system would not stop searching. It was in an infinite messaging sequence, where it started the search over and over again. This was caused by an incorrectly set belief that indicated the search had stopped.

Demonstration 2: ***SBA***

This second demonstration is to show IDAF used in a different multi-agent system called *SBA*. The demonstration application is a bank electronic access application written in *SBA*. It consists of two ATM agents and a bank agent. The interactions between the agents are bank operations such as ***query***, ***withdraw*** and ***deposit***. In this demonstration, we show the different message format in *SBA* as compared to *dMARS*. Figure 2 shows the execution trace of the system. IDAF reported a potential race condition between the seventh and eighth message, and the application had to be analysed to ensure that a race condition would not occur.

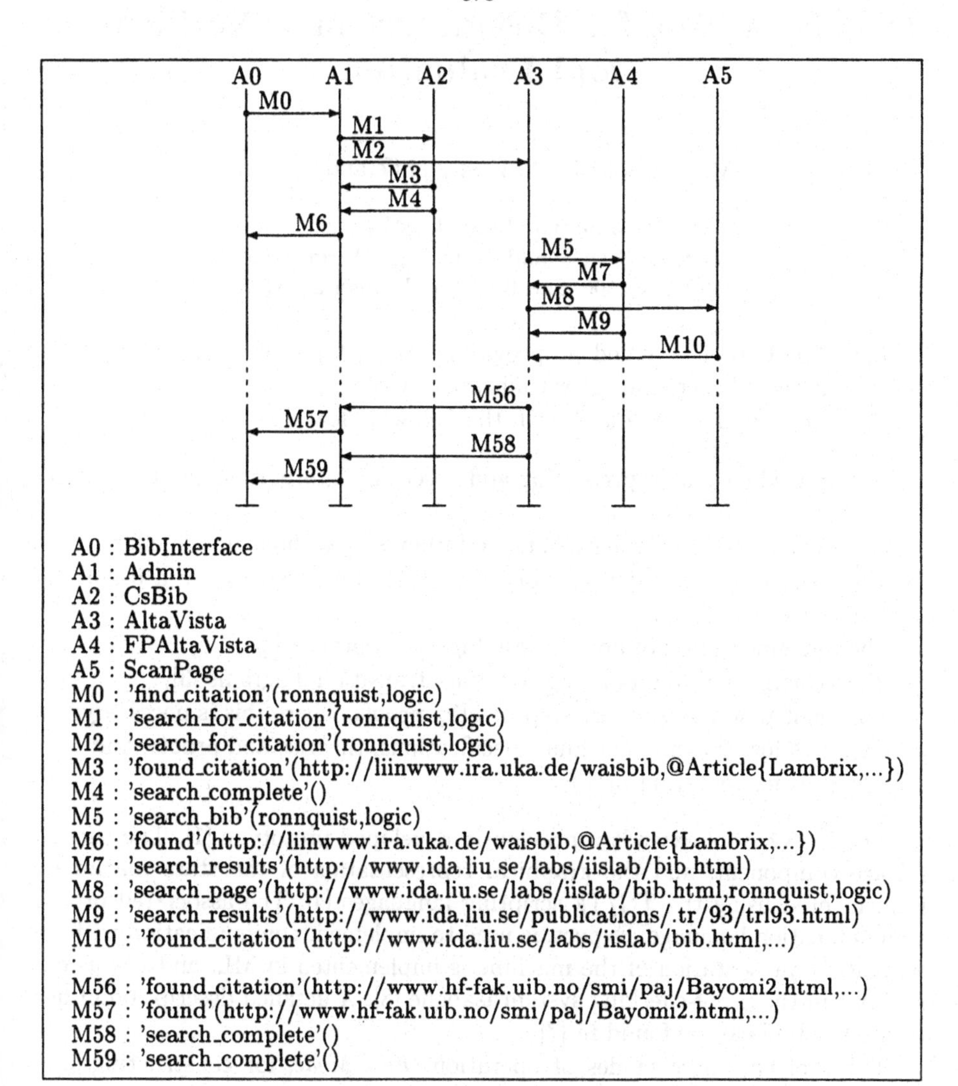
A0
A1
A2
A3
A4
A5
M0
M1
M2
M3
M4
M6
M5
M7
M8
M9
M10
M56
M57
M58
M59
A0 : BibInterface
A1 : Admin
A2 : CsBib
A3 : AltaVista
A4 : FPAltaVista
A5 : ScanPage
M0 : 'find_citation'(ronnquist,logic)
M1 : 'search_for_citation'(ronnquist,logic)
M2 : 'search_for_citation'(ronnquist,logic)
M3 : 'found_citation'(http://liinwww.ira.uka.de/waisbib,@Article{Lambrix,...})
M4 : 'search_complete'()
M5 : 'search_bib'(ronnquist,logic)
M6 : 'found'(http://liinwww.ira.uka.de/waisbib,@Article{Lambrix,...})
M7 : 'search_results'(http://www.ida.liu.se/labs/iislab/bib.html)
M8 : 'search_page'(http://www.ida.liu.se/labs/iislab/bib.html,ronnquist,logic)
M9 : 'search_results'(http://www.ida.liu.se/publications/.tr/93/trl93.html)
M10 : 'found_citation'(http://www.ida.liu.se/labs/iislab/bib.html,...)
M56 : 'found_citation'(http://www.hf-fak.uib.no/smi/paj/Bayomi2.html,...)
M57 : 'found'(http://www.hf-fak.uib.no/smi/paj/Bayomi2.html,...)
M58 : 'search_complete'()
M59 : 'search_complete'()

Fig. 1. Execution trace for BIBSEARCH

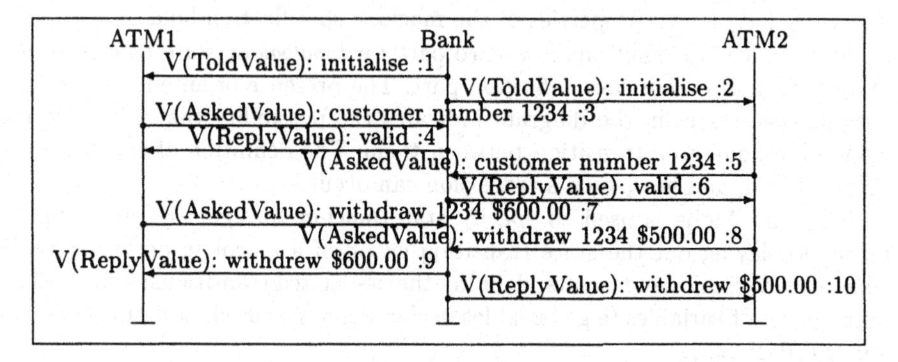
ATM1
Bank
ATM2
V(ToldValue): initialise :1
V(ToldValue): initialise :2
V(AskedValue): customer number 1234 :3
V(ReplyValue): valid :4
V(AskedValue): customer number 1234 :5
V(ReplyValue): valid :6
V(AskedValue): withdraw 1234 $600.00 :7
V(AskedValue): withdraw 1234 $500.00 :8
V(ReplyValue): withdrew $600.00 :9
V(ReplyValue): withdrew $500.00 :10

Fig. 2. An interaction diagram showing the execution trace

DOVE: A Tool for Design Oriented Verification and Evaluation

M. A. Ozols, K. A. Eastaughffe and A. Cant

Information Technology Division
Defence Science and Technology Organisation
PO Box 1500, Salisbury South Australia 5108

The DOVE tool is aimed at providing support for reasoning about state machine designs for critical software-based devices.

The aim is to develop a tool with the following features:

- a graphical means for presenting and accepting information about state machines;
- a means for critical properties to be formulated without undue effort;
- the combination of existing tools, notations and paradigms in a useful and smooth way;
- the implementation of appropriate high-level proof steps;
- the visualisation of proof steps on state transition diagrams [3];
- sufficient power to support step-by-step proofs, where this is necessary;
- facilities for browsing machine specifications, theories and proofs; and
- facilities for replaying proofs.

The DOVE tool extends a previously developed prototype [1]. The user interface component, and the graphical representation of the state machine is implemented using the Tcl/Tk scripting languages [4]. The associated process communication language, Expect, is used to implement communication with the semantic representation of the machine is implemented in ML, and proofs carried out in the proof-checking system Isabelle [8]. A detailed description of how to use the tool can be found in [7].

The tool has three modes of operation: *Edit Mode*, for constructing state machine specifications, including state transition diagrams; *Animation Mode*, for exploring symbolic execution of the machine; and a *Proof Mode*, for formally verifying that critical properties of the machine specification hold.

State machine definitions have two parts: a *topology* or *state transition diagram* part and a *transition definition* part. The presence of an edge(transition) between two states in the diagram indicates the possibility that the state machine may undergo a transition between them. The definition of the transition determines if, and how, such a transition can occur.

The Edit Mode is used to specify state machine designs by providing the means for laying out the state transition graph of a machine; declaring types, constants, variables and inputs; defining the associated transitions; and checking occurrences of variables (e.g. variables declared and not used, or idenitifiers used and not declared).

The Animation Mode is used to observe how variables and terms evolve during execution of the state machine. The basis of animation is the *animation path*, which is a path in the transition graph of the machine. Animations are carried out using the graph by selecting a final or initial node, proceeding through intermediate edges via back substitution or forwards animation and finishing at some initial or final state.

Proof Mode provides the means for defining, editing and browsing machine properties, including a check of the consistency of properties with different versions of machine specifications, and interactively proving a property. Once a state machine definition has been saved, such that all its transitions have been defined, an Isabelle theory for that machine can be automatically generated and a proof can be commenced.

A proof is carried out in a goal-directed fashion. The XIsabelle prover interface [5, 6] has been tailored to provide the interactive proof component for DOVE. Proof support includes the following:

- a *browser* that displays theory information in a form which is easy to read;
- high level tactics for carrying out *back substitution* steps, and reasoning about *execution paths* [2];
- a *tactic tree viewer* which graphically represents the overall structure of a proof in progress, and allows easy re-use of proof steps; and
- the recording of proof steps as a proof history, which can be displayed, saved, replayed, and re-used.

References

1. A. Cant, K. A. Eastaughffe and M. A. Ozols. A tool for practical reasoning about state machine designs. In *Proc. 1996 Australian Software Engineering Conference*, pages 16 – 26, Melbourne, July 1996. IEEE Computer Society Press.
2. K. A. Eastaughffe, M. A. Ozols and A. Cant. Proof tactics for a theory of state machines in a graphical environment. In *Proc. 14th Intenational Conference on Automated Deduction (CADE-14)*, Lecture Notes in Artificial Intelligence, Townsville, Australia, July 1997. Springer-Verlag.
3. K. A. Eastaughffe, M. A. Ozols and A. Cant. The visualisation of interactive proofs. In *Proceedings of 20th Australasian Computer Science Conference, Australian Computer Science Communications, Volume 19(1)*, pages 297–306, 1997.
4. J. K. Ousterhout. *Tcl and the Tk Toolkit.* Addison-Wesley, 1994.
5. M. A. Ozols, A. Cant and K. A. Eastaughffe. XIsabelle: A system description. In *Proc. 14th Intenational Conference on Automated Deduction (CADE-14)*, Lecture Notes in Artificial Intelligence, Townsville, Australia, July 1997. Springer-Verlag.
6. M. A. Ozols, A. Cant, K. A. Eastaughffe and V. Gajanayake. XIsabelle User Guide. 1997.
7. M. A. Ozols, K. A. Eastaughffe, A. Cant, V. Gajanayake and G. Tench. DOVE User Guide. 1997.
8. L. C. Paulson and T. Nipkow. *Isabelle: A Generic Theorem Prover*, Volume 828 of *LNCS.* Springer Verlag, 1994.

The B Method and the B Toolkit

Ken Robinson
School of Computer Science and Engineering
K.Robinson@unsw.edu.au

University of New South Wales
Sydney NSW 2052 Australia

Abstract. The B Method is a full spectrum formal software development method that covers the software process from specification to implementation. The method uses state machines, defined using logic and set theory with a notation similar to that of **Z**, that export operations. The method supports a notion of refinement and implementation, which is based on the notion of refinement in the refinement calculus with the exception that there is no distinction between procedural and data refinement. The B Toolkit is a configuration tool that manages developments under the B Method, generating proof obligations and supporting tools for the discharge of those proof obligations. There is also support for the generation of documentation, and for the browsing of developments.

1 Introduction

There are a number of formal specification techniques that are based on the building of mathematical models of the functionality of systems. The oldest and most prominent are VDM [4,5] and **Z** [10]. VDM consists of both a notation and a method that covers specification and refinement (called reification). **Z** was devised by J-R Abrial around 1980 and uses set theory and logic to build mathematical models for specification; refinement concepts have been introduced to allow refinement within **Z**. The B Method also involves mathematical modelling using set theory and logic and was developed within BP Research from about 1985 by J-R Abrial in collaboration with Ib Sørensen. The B Method matured around 1990 and two toolkits have been developed to support the method. Both the method and the toolkits have been used in a number of industrial projects from 1991.

2 The B Method

The B Method consists of a specification notation and a concept of refinement based on a development of Dijkstra's weakest precondition calculus [3] and Morgan's refinement calculus [9,8]. The method provides a framework in which specifications can be refined through to implementations, which can be translated into a programming language such as C or Ada. The B Method is the first single

```
MACHINE          MaxOfSet
VARIABLES        numset
CONSTANTS        max_val
PROPERTIES       max_val = 1000000
INVARIANT        numset <: NAT1
INITIALISATION   numset:={}
OPERATIONS
      enter(new) =  PRE new: NAT1 & new <= max_val
                    THEN numset :=  numset \/ {new}
                    END;

  mx <-- maximum =  PRE numset /= {}
                    THEN mx  := max(numset)
                    END
END
```

Fig. 1. A Simple Machine

```
REFINEMENT       MaxSoFar_1
REFINES          MaxOfSet
VARIABLES        maxnum
INVARIANT        maxnum : NAT &
                 maxnum = max({0} \/ numset)
INITIALISATION   maxnum := 0
OPERATIONS
      enter(new) =
          BEGIN
            maxnum := max({maxnum,new})
          END;
  mx <-- maximum =
          BEGIN mx := maxnum END
END
```

Fig. 2. A Refinement

formal method that encompasses all phases of the software development process from specification, through design to implementation. It even addresses some aspects of maintenance and re-use through the building of libraries of specifications and their associated implementation. The method has been used on a number of small to medium scale projects, for example [2]. The major reference for the B Method is J-R Abrial's *The B-Book: Assigning Programs to Meanings*[1] and there are another 3 books [7,6,11]

In the remainder of this paper we will use **B** to denote the B Method.

2.1 Machines

The principal construct in **B** is a *machine*. A machine encapsulates a state and a set of operations. The machines are expressed in an Abstract Machine Notation (AMN). AMN is based on set theory and logic, with a mathematical language similar—but not identical—to the mathematical notation for **Z**. Machines in **B** have a fixed structure, which is reminiscent of the structure of a program. A simple top level specification of a machine that maintains a set of numbers is shown in Figure 1. The machine has two operations that, respectively, add a value to the set and return the maximum value in the set. (Note: for technical reasons machine variable names must have at least two characters)

Substitutions The semantics of operations—and hence of machines—are given in terms of a generalised substitution, which is a re-expression of the notion of weakest precondition. If S is a substitution and P a predicate then $[S]P$ is a predicate produced by applying the substitution S to P. $[S]P$ is effectively the weakest precondition of S with respect to P.

2.2 Refinements

A machine is refined, generally, by replacing the variables by new variables, and the substitutions in the initialisation and the operations. The invariant of the refining machine enforces a relation between the refined machine and the refining machine. The operations in the refining machine must simulate the operations in the refined machine according to a semantics of refinement that is equivalent to that of the refinement calculus.

Figure 2 shows a refinement of the machine in figure 1.

2.3 Implementations

Implementation is a special case of refinement that can be done at any stage in a refinement sequence, but may be done only once. The implementation must be done according to very strict rules: the implementation cannot have any state of its own; the operations must be implemented using the *specified* operations of other machines that are imported into the implementation.

2.4 Machine inclusion and visibility

B has a number of mechanism for including, or viewing other machines. The capability ranges from full read/write inclusion: INCLUDES, EXTENDS, IMPORTS; to read only access: USES and SEES. These mechanisms come with various constraints that are beyond the scope of this paper to explain.

2.5 Layered development

The implementation step in **B** forces a machine to be implemented in terms of other machine specifications. If these machines have themselves been implemented, then the process is finished. However, in practice new machines will be specified to assist with the implementation of the current machine. Thus, we need to proceed with the refinement and implementation of the new machines. This gives rise to a layered development strategy as shown in figure 3. In this figure, circles represent specifications, boxes with rounded corners represent refinements and rectangles represent implementations.

3 The Toolkit

There are two toolkits that support the B Method. The B-Toolkit is distributed by B-Core (`http://www.b-core.com/`), and Atelier B is distributed by DIGILOG (`http://www.atelierb.societe.com/`). The toolkits support slightly different dialects of **B** and the one described in this paper is consistent with the B-Toolkit. The toolkit being demonstrated at AMAST also will be the B-Toolkit.

The B-Toolkit is a configuration management tool that helps with and in some cases automates the following steps in development:

Machine creation The toolkit initiates machine creation, presenting the developer with a template in their editor of choice. After editing the machine is subjected to a syntax check before being *committed.*

Analysis Before proceeding with any other phase of development a machine must be analysed for type correctness.

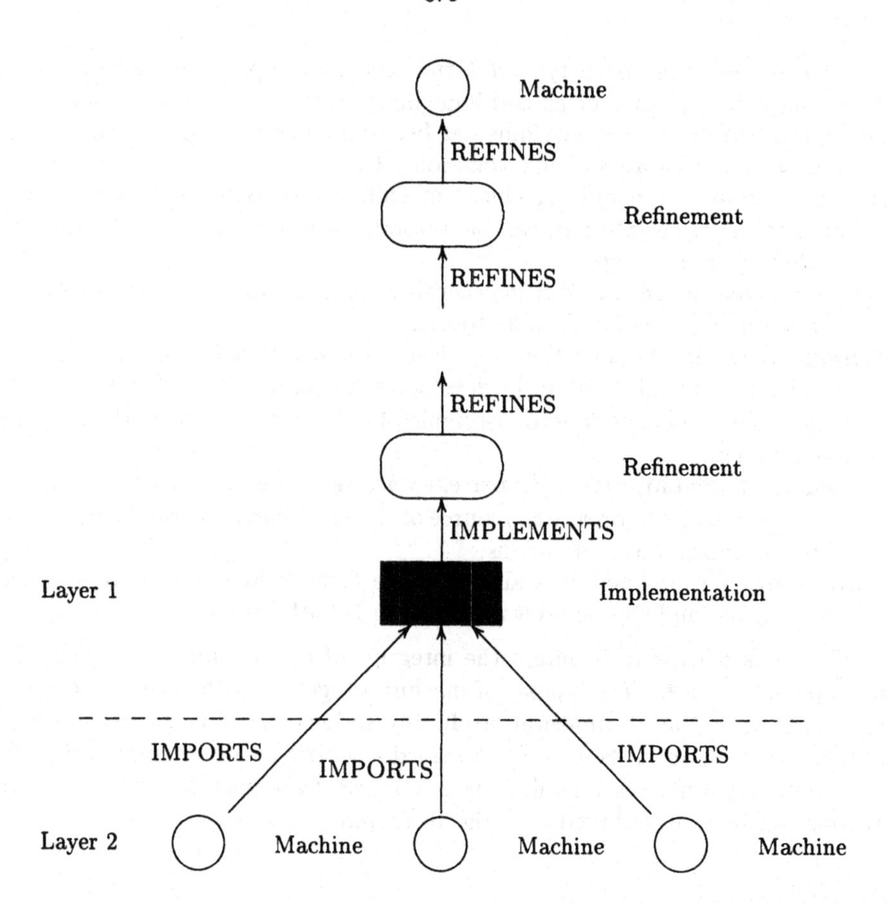

Fig. 3. Layered Development

Animation A specification machine may be symbolically executed (animated) to check the behaviour of the specification against the expected behaviour. This provides a facility for detecting requirements errors.

Proof obligation generation After analysis, the toolkit will generate the proof obligations for a machine.

Proof obligation discharge The toolkit provides two proof assistants: the automatic theorem prover that attempts to discharge the proof obligations against a library of proof theories. For proof obligations that the automatic theorem prover cannot discharge there is an interactive theorem prover that provides the developer with a view of the goals that cannot be proved. The developer can determine whether the proof obligations are valid and provide proof theories that will assist with the final proof.

Document generation and mark-up Documents also have an AMN syntax and it is possible to build documents that include marked-up versions of the machines, proof obligations, proofs and informal commentary. Independently of such documents, the machines can be marked up and viewed in the more appropriate publication typeset form. The mark-up process also provides automatic cross-referencing and indexing.

Code generation Once a machine has been implemented, the toolkit will automatically translate to code, commonly C.

Simple interface generation Once a machine has been implemented and translated to code, an interface can be automatically generated for running the machine as a prototype.

Base generation The toolkit can generate automatically all the machines needed to manipulate structured data objects.

Remake After any modification to a development a remake capability can be invoked to rerun all steps in the development that are affected by the modification. The toolkit is able to distinguish between documentary changes and mathematical.

Browsing of developments Hypertext versions of the machines are generated and it is possible to browse the source of the machines and also the overviews of the specifications and designs.

Online help On line help is available in the form of hypertext that is extensively linked and can be browsed using an HTML browser.

The toolkit helps to maintain the integrity of a development. In general a development consists of a number of machines together with their refinements, implementations and documentation. In any serious use of **B** the assistance of a toolkit is vital, and it is sensible to regard a toolkit as an essential part of **B**.

The example machines used in figures 1 and 2 are part of a set of demonstration machines distributed with the B-Toolkit.

References

1. J.-R. Abrial. *The B-Book: Assigning Programs to Meanings.* Cambridge University Press, 1996.
2. B. Dehbonei and F Mejia. *Applications of Formal Methods*, chapter Formal Development of Safety-critical Software Systems, pages 227–252. Prentice Hall, 1995.
3. Edsgar W. Dijkstra. *A Discipline of Programming.* Prentice-Hall, 1976.
4. C. B. Jones. Program specification and verification in VDM. Technical Report UMCS 86-10-5, University of Manchester, 1986.
5. C. B. Jones. *Systematic Software Development using VDM.* Prentice Hall International, 2nd edition, 1990. ISBN 0-13-880733-7.
6. K. Lano. *The B Language and Method - a guide to practical formal development.* Springer-Verlag, 1996.
7. K. Lano and H. Haughton. *Specification in B: an Introduction using the B-Toolkit.* Imperial College Press, 1996.
8. Carroll Morgan. *Programming from Specifications.* International Series in Computer Science. Prentice-Hall, 1990.
9. C.C. Morgan and K.A. Robinson. Specification statements and refinement. *IBM Journal of Research and Development*, 31(5):546–555, September 1987.
10. J.M. Spivey. *The Z Notation: A Reference Manual.* Prentice-Hall International, 2nd edition, 1992.
11. John B. Wordsworth. *Software Engineering with the B-Method.* Addison-Wesley, 1996.

An Algebraic Language Processing Environment

Teodor Rus, Tom Halverson, Eric Van Wyk, and Robert Kooima

Department of Computer Science, The University of Iowa, Iowa City, IA 52242

1 Introduction

Problem domains evolve, so it seems natural that the languages of problem solving need to evolve as well. The theme of our research is that the task of language design and implementation should be made a realistic endeavor for a larger group of computer users thus supporting the evolution of the language with the problem domain. This can be accomplished by creating a language processing environment in which methodologies and tools are provided that simplify and ultimately automate many of the language processing tasks. This reduces the effort necessary on the part of the language designer to develop a language and create language processing tools. Since the language itself is the key to problem solving, this is a prerequisite to further progress.

A language is a communication mechanism which provides a framework in which one can create statements which have meaning. In the realm of computer systems, a language is a notation used to express computations. The notation is referred to as the syntax, while the computation is the semantics. Computer language manipulation implies a specification aspect, a processing aspect, and a usage aspect: specification allows communicators to construct valid phrases that may be used to denote computing abstractions; processing concerns algorithms that recognize phrase validity, discover the computing abstractions denoted by a phrase, and perform meaning-preserving mappings of a phrase within a language and between languages; usage is the process of problem solving using computer languages. A *language processing environment* is a set of integrated tools that supports these aspects of computer language manipulation. Though these aspects of language manipulation are intimately related, historically they have been developed into software systems by different people using different approaches. Our project advocates a unifying framework for dealing with languages in which all aspects of language manipulation are formally specified. Specifications should formally define syntax and semantics by the same specification rules and should be used to automatically generate language processing tools, thus removing most of the usual programming burden from the developer. This simplifies the problem solving process and assures that correct specifications produce correct implementations. In addition, the language developer, as well as the language user, should be able to build processing systems incrementally and interactively.

Our vision of a language processing environment has resulted in the continuous development and evolution of the TICS (Technology for Implementing Computer Software) project. This project demonstrates many unique specification and processing components as well as new methods of integration which are based on the algebraic concepts of compositionality, incrementality, and modularity. Publications, tutorials, and demonstration materials may be found at http://www.cs.uiowa.edu/~rus. This methodology shows great promise: it has been applied to problems in a wide range of areas including syntactic[1] and semantic[2] analysis, language to language translation[3, 4], and the integration of model checking algorithms into the compiler as tools used for code optimization and parallelization[5, 6].

2 Specification

A language specification should formally describe the language syntax, semantics, and the relationship between them. In our framework, the signature of an operation in the source language algebra is described by a specification rule written in the well understood BNF notation $r : A_0 = t_0 A_1 t_1 A_2 t_2 \ldots A_n t_n$, where A_i, $0 \leq i \leq n$, are parameters called nonterminal symbols and t_i, $0 \leq i \leq n$, are fixed strings called terminal symbols. A collection of computation laws or interpretations of that signature which embeds the source algebra operations into various target algebras is attached to each specification rule. Thus, the syntax and the semantics of a language construct are specified by the same rule. While the BNF notation is common, our interpretation is not. We interpret each parameter A_i, both as a semantic domain, in which A_i is a set of computation objects denoted $[\![A_i]\!]$, and as a syntactic domain, in which A_i is the set of language phrases denoted $[A_i]$. Furthermore, each $w \in [A_i]$ represents a computation object $c_w \in [\![A_i]\!]$. Accordingly, each BNF rule is interpreted both as the signature of a syntactic operation $t_0 t_1 \ldots t_n : [A_1] \times [A_2] \times \ldots \times [A_n] \to [A_0]$ whose computation law is $t_0 t_1 \ldots t_n(w_1, w_2, \ldots w_n) = t_0 w_1 t_1 w_2 \ldots t_{n-1} w_n t_n \in [A_0]$, for each $w_i \in [A_i]$, $1 \leq i \leq n$, and as the signature of a semantic operation $t_0 t_1 \ldots t_n : [\![A_1]\!] \times [\![A_2]\!] \times \ldots \times [\![A_n]\!] \to [\![A_0]\!]$ whose computation law depends on the language processing purpose.

For each processing purpose, the computation specified by the semantic operation $t_0 t_1 \ldots t_n : [\![A_1]\!] \times [\![A_2]\!] \times \ldots \times [\![A_n]\!] \to [\![A_0]\!]$ is represented by a semantic macro associated with the BNF rule. Algebraically this macro is a derived operation embedding the language objects specified by the BNF rule into the language that supports the operations used in the macro-operation. In programming jargon, semantic macros are similar in form to conventional macros[7]. The difference results from the purpose of these macros. Conventional macros are used to extend the source language with user defined constructs; our macros are used to implement the source language by expressing the semantics of its valid constructs using parameterized constructs of the target language. The parameters of a semantic macro are valid target language constructs that implement the components of the source language constructs. Thus, the target image of a construct is built by the macro processor in a compositional manner as the source language construct is recognized. Consequently, semantic macros are automatic programming mechanisms that generate target programs from target components in a manner similar to that in which source language programs are generated as algebraic expressions by operations in the source language algebra. As an example, language translation operations are defined as computation laws performed by the operation $t_0t_1 \ldots t_n : [\![A_1]\!] \times [\![A_2]\!] \times \ldots \times [\![A_n]\!] \rightarrow [\![A_0]\!]$ where objects $c_i \in [\![A_i]\!]$ are target images of the constructs $w_i \in [A_i]$, $1 \leq i \leq n$, and the result is the target image of the construct $w \in [A_0]$ such that $w = t_0w_1 \ldots t_{n-1}w_nt_n$. Hence, this macro is a derived operation in the algebra of the target language and it embeds the language of $[A_0]$ into the target language by constructing the target image of w in terms of the target images of its components.

The macro-processor of semantic macros does not interfere with the parser of the source language because it is used for target image generation. Semantic macro-processors perform actions similar to those performed by the assembly language macro-processors since they produce correct pieces of target code from correct target code components. In addition, a semantic macro processor may check semantic properties of source and target language constructs, such as type, to determine exactly what should be produced as the result of the macro expansion. In other words, a semantic macro is more than just a substitution of the parameters. This has proven quite useful and powerful in a wide range of applications, as seen above.

Thus, the specification methodology we advocate is to combine a collection of compositional specification fragments into a specification rule. This takes the form of a syntactic rule and a group of zero or more macros, each for a particular language processing purpose such as mapping to a target language, defining the semantics of the construct in terms of the semantic of construct components, or constructing a graph representation of the computation.

3 Processing

Language processing tasks encompass such activities as recognizing the validity of language phrases, discovering the meaning of a message by creating an understandable representation of the intent of the communication, and mapping phrases or representations into other forms. As alluded to in the introduction, this takes the shape of extracting information from the specification rules to guide the activities of various algorithms. For example, the BNF rules are preprocessed to collect context information[1] which is used to guide the behavior of the parser to determine if its input is a construct of the language. As an aside, a jumping pattern matching parser[4] is used for construct recognition. It is a bottom up recognizer which may make reductions (rewriting) anywhere in the input as long as the validity of the input is maintained. Also, each macro in the specification is processed by the TICS system itself to create an internal, usable form. This processing produces the computation law that guides the semantic interpretation of the signature. When the macro is expanded, it will perform the intended language processing action such as translation or optimization.

This mechanism of developing language processing tools raises the issue of compositionally building a valid language phrase from valid subphrases. Since in our case, macros are used to map valid source language constructs to valid target language constructs, this issue becomes one of how to combine target language fragments while maintaining the validity of the result. This mechanism of target code generation ensures correct bootstrapping of language implementation where individual language processing tools are generated automatically from the specification rules.

4 Integration

The objective is to use a combination of the language processing tools to operate with language elements to achieve a given goal such as syntax analysis, semantic analysis, dataflow analysis, and program translation.

The BNF portion of a specification rule describes the syntax of source language constructs. It is used to generate the parser which we call a language recognizer because it can incrementally recognize the validity of any language construct in its input. When the parser recognizes the validity of a construct in the input using a rule r, it will perform a rewriting. Also, it communicates this information to other tools which deal with the macros. The integrating environment is a data structure we have tentatively termed an Abstract Parse Tree (APT) which is constructed by the recognizer. Each node in the APT is labeled by the rule r that was used to construct it, and its children are the APT nodes for the parameters on the right hand side of r. Each macro is provided with a hook on the APT so that it can attach the information generated during macro-expansion that is carried along for access during further processing activity. The APT node is given to a macro integration function to properly activate the macro processing and the recognizer may continue in parallel with the macro-processing since it does not partake in this activity. The integration function describes how to use various macros to achieve the goal.

The APT represents the syntactic structure of the input, while each macro creates a graph representation of the computation whose nodes are attached to the APT and whose edges are semantic relationships between the nodes as constructed according to the goal of the macro. For example, the semantic analysis macros generate a structure which hangs on the APT and represents the semantics of the construct recognized by the node. The interpretation of this structure is the transition system embodying the computation of the construct. The optimization macros generate another data structure superposed on the APT which represents a model of the computation encapsulated in the construct recognized by the APT node; the nodes of this structure are processes and the edges are dependences among these processes. The code generation macros superpose over the APT yet another structure whose nodes are the target code representing the computations at that node. In this way, all of the macros operate in a common environment, yet no restrictions are placed on what they do.

5 Demonstration

Our vision of a language processing environment becomes a unifying framework for dealing with languages. The TICS system provides tools and methodologies to simplify the task of developing a language and implementing language processing tools. A system demonstration, to be sketched below, will provide an insightful look at the advantages inherent in the use of our approach.

First the syntax of a simple block structure language will be developed. From this, we can construct a recognizer which decides the validity of a language phrase. Further, we associate a semantic macro with each rule developed so far to demonstrate the semantic analysis by mapping each construct into a representative transition system. This specification is used to generate a tool which performs the semantic analysis task. The two tools are then integrated and the result of this integrated tool will be a transition system superposed on the APT. Next, we associate another macro with each rule to describe a graph representation of the programs written in this language. We may now integrate the resulting tool with the recognizer and semantic analyzer obtaining a tool which creates the model of the program over which we may apply a model checking algorithm to discover program properties[5, 6]. Finally, yet another semantic macro may be attached to each rule to describe how to construct a target language image of the construct defined by the rule in terms of the target images of the construct's components. Automatically, we could create a tool to demonstrate all of the major language processing tasks: validation, understanding, and mapping.

The value of this experiment resides in the fact that the results can be reused in real-life language processing. We will show how is this carried out on subsets of such languages as C, Java, and Fortran.

References

1. T. Rus and T. Halverson. Algebraic tools for language processing. *Computer Languages*, 20(4):213–238, 1994.
2. T. Rus. Algebraic processing of programming languages. In A. Nijholt, G. Scollo, and R. Steetskamp, editors, *Twente Workshop on Language Technology*, pages 1–42, University of Twente, Enschede, The Netherlands, 1995.
3. T. Rus. Algebraic construction of compilers. *Theoretical Computer Science*, 90:271–308, 1991.
4. J.L. Knaack. *An Algebraic Approach to Language Translation*. PhD thesis, The University of Iowa, Department of Computer Science, Iowa City, IA 52242, December 1994.
5. T. Rus and E. Van Wyk. Integrating temporal logics and model checking algorithms. In *Lecture Notes in Computer Science 1231*, pages 95–110, May 21 1997.
6. T. Rus and E. Van Wyk. A formal approach to parallelizing compilers. In *SIAM Conference on Parallel Processing for Scientific Computation, Proceedings*, March 14 1997. Paper available at http://www.cs.uiowa.edu/~rus.
7. D. Weise and R. Crew. Programable syntax macros. *ACM SIGPLAN Notices*, 28(6), 1993.

The Cogito Development System

Owen Traynor, Dan Hazel, Peter Kearney,
Andrew Martin, Ray Nickson, and Luke Wildman

Software Verification Research Centre, School of Information Technology,
The University of Queensland

Abstract. The Cogito system provides comprehensive support for the development of specifications written in the Sum language (a modular extension of Z). The tool-set provides technology to aid in the construction, analysis and development of Sum specifications. Ada code is the final result of a development in Cogito.

1 Introduction

The Cogito project started in 1994 and since then has focused on the development of a methodology and associated support system which is capable of fully formal development of software systems.

In support of the Cogito methodology a variety of tools have been developed. These range from typecheckers and pretty printers for the Sum language to environments for verified algorithm refinement and the translation of refined Sum specifications to Ada. Parts of the Cogito System have already been used in an industrial pilot project [5].

This paper gives a brief overview of the Sum language framework and the Cogito methodology and describes the associated tool support for each phase of a Cogito development.

2 Introduction to Cogito

The intent of the Cogito 1 project [2,3,11,12] is to produce an integrated methodology and tool-set supporting formal program development. The Cogito methodology addresses specification, design and development, and construction of implementations. Verification is seen as a crucial activity, carried out as an integral part of all development phases.

At the heart of the Cogito methodology is the Z-based specification language Sum [12]. The Cogito development system revolves around the processing and analysis of Sum specifications. The result of a successful Cogito development is a program in some concrete programming language. Ada is currently the only supported target language.

2.1 The Sum language

While closely related to Z [9], Sum extends Z with various facilities that provide more comprehensive support for specification, validation, reasoning and refinement. In particular, Sum provides facilities at the specification level for:

- modular and parameterised specifications,
- distinguished state machines within a module (via distinguished *State*, *Init* and *Operation* schemas), and
- explicit preconditions in schemas.

In addition to these specification level facilities, Sum also includes an intermediate programming language. Since the implementation level constructs are part of the overall language framework the transition from specification to implementation is simplified.

2.1.1 Modules A module in Sum forms the basic unit of specification. Modules are collections of declarations that can be used in other modules via a reference mechanism (*import*).

Modules can be parameterised. Types, values and relations may be defined as parameters to modules. Parameterised modules must be fully instantiated when used (no partial parameterisation is permitted). The *import as* construct is used when referencing a parameterised module. Conceptually, *import as* creates a new instance of a module (with a new module identifier). This is also used when importing non-parameterised modules that have an encapsulated state component that we do not want to share with other importations of the module.

2.1.2 Defining state machines Modules can define an encapsulated state machine for the module. This involves defining a state schema (using the reserved identifier `state`), an initialisation schema (using `init`), a set of operation schemas (using `op`), and (perhaps) some auxiliary schemas. Each module may define only one such state machine.

Using importation and renaming, state machines from different modules can be combined within other modules to build more sophisticated state machines.

2.2 The Development Model

Figure 1 shows an abstract model of the Cogito development process. The phases of the model that are addressed by the Cogito development methodology are specification, development, implementation and (to an extent) evolution. The Cogito 1 methodology supports the formal development of software systems through:

- formal requirements specification in Sum;
- validation of these specification by animation and proof;
- construction of progressively more detailed designs, expressed in Sum, with proof that the detailed designs implement the specification;
- translation of the final detailed design to an Ada subset.

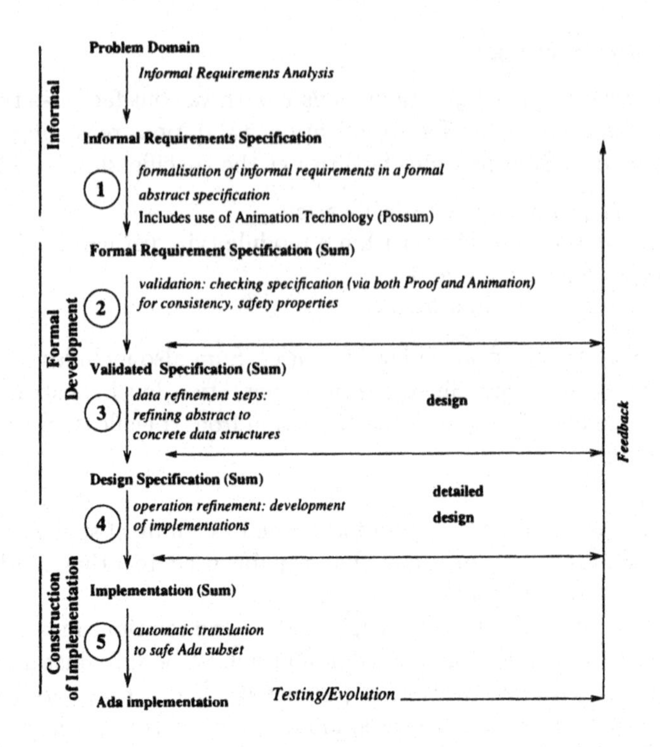

Fig. 1. A model of Cogito development process as applied to the development of Ada programs.

3 Tool Support for Cogito

3.1 The Cogito Tool Architecture

A model of the Cogito tool architecture [11] is given in Figure 2. At the core of Cogito is a repository management tool [10] that is used to integrate the various Cogito tools and to carry out configuration, version and development control tasks.

Another tool central to the Cogito system is the Ergo interactive theorem prover [1]. Ergo provides support for generating various kinds of proof obligation generation, discharging proof obligations, data refinement and algorithm refinement. At the core of the Ergo support for Cogito is a modelling of the Sum specification language[2]. This allows a relatively straightforward translation of specifications to theory level structures within the theorem prover. Ergo is capable of faithfully representing the structured nature of Sum specifications [8]. Ergo also provides a framework that enables reasoning about *generic* specifications [4].

Possum is an animator for the Sum language [6]. Possum interprets queries made in the Sum syntax and responds with simplifications of those queries. It can be used to test arbitrary Sum expressions and predicates or to step through

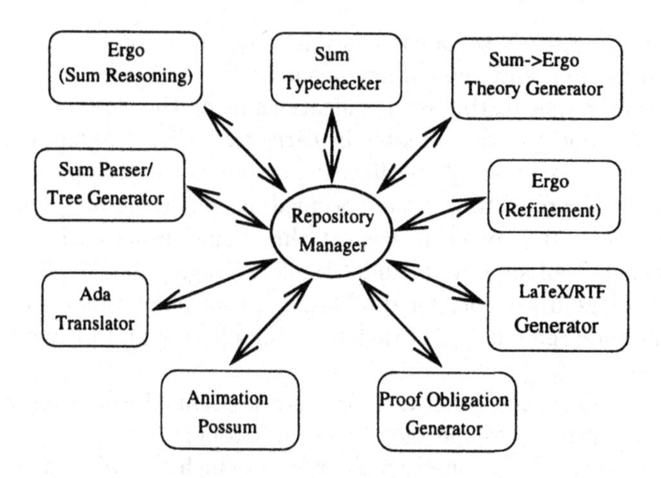

Fig. 2. The Cogito Tool Architecture.

consecutive states of a defined state machine by "executing" the operations of that machine.

Ergo and Possum have been implemented using the a variant of Prolog called Qu-Prolog [7]. The command-line interfaces of Ergo and Possum resemble that of many Prolog interpreters: responding to queries typed at a prompt. However, the user of these tools does not interact with specifications using this interface. Rather, a graphical user interface offers significantly improved functionality by providing the user the following facilities:

- *pull down menus* that allow the user to load Sum specifications, execution scripts and set a range of environmental properties;
- *context navigation* allowing the user to set the context for animation and proof relative to the Sum module structures currently active;
- *script creation and editing*, allowing the user to capture a session and subsequently re-run and edit that session interactively;
- *variable display and tracing* that track how the various state variables of designated schemas are changing during a session, and
- *query construction* providing the user with an interface that allows complex compound schema operations or proof commands to be built from the set of entities that are applicable within the current session.

3.2 Supporting a Cogito Development

The stages of a Cogito development (Figure 1) are as follows:

1. An abstract specification, written in Sum, captures the requirements formally. A system is specified as one or more modules, each module encapsulating a state, and a set of operations on that state. The system is specified using abstract, mathematical data structures. Support for this phase in the Cogito tool-set includes

   - Syntax and static semantic analysis of specifications.
   - Configuration and version management.
   - Animation and testing of specifications using the Possum tool.
2. The specification may be validated by carrying out formal consistency checks. This activity helps to find specification errors as early as possible. In addition, expected properties of the specified system (including safety and security properties) may be proven at this stage, as an early check on the specification. Tool support includes the following.
   - Sophisticated support for discharging proof obligations using Ergo, including a large number of tactics for simplifying and proving proof obligations.
   - A proof obligation generator (for both predefined validation criteria and required properties specified by the developer).
   - Theory generators construct theories in which formal reasoning about a specification can be carried out.
   - Further animation of the specification using Possum.
3. In one or more data refinement steps, the abstract data structures of the specification are mapped to more concrete data structures, with proof obligations to show that the more concrete specifications implement the more abstract. Intermediate specifications developed in this process are also checked for validity. At the final level of data refinement, the data structures are those of the intermediate programming language, but operations may still be expressed using pre- and post-conditions.
   Tool support for this phase includes
   - A data refinement environment (within Ergo) for undertaking refinement and discharging the obligations associated with the specified data refinement.
   - Configuration management support for defining the context for data refinement.
   - Animation - Possum may be used to animate refined specifications to increase the specifier's confidence that the correct design decisions have been made.
4. An operation is refined to the algorithmic constructs of Sum. Again, proof obligations are generated that guarantee correctness with respect to the operation's specification. Tool support for this phase includes
   - an algorithm refinement environment (based on Ergo's modelling of Sum) that allows arbitrary predicates to be refined to constructs in Sum's intermediate programming language.
   - a reasoning environment in which the obligations generated during algorithm refinement can be discharged.
   - a translation tool that allows specifications refined within the Ergo prover to be projected back to the Sum language level.
   - As in the previous stages, Possum may be used to animate any of the intermediate specifications.
5. Finally, the resulting detailed design is automatically translated to an Ada subset.

- An analysis tool constructs the context appropriate for this translation, including any Ada package structures and type declarations required (possibly generic). Statements of the intermediate language are then translated to Ada and embedded in the appropriate package context.

Various other tools are available throughout the development cycle, for example, pretty printers that generate LaTeX or Rich Text Format from Sum's ASCII representation enabling the developer to view or print specifications using the tradition Z graphical form. The Cogito front-end tools are available under Windows95/NT. Both the front-end tools and the other reasoning tools, including Ergo, are currently available for Sun Solaris and Linux (See http://svrc.it.uq.edu.au/).

References

1. Holger Becht, Anthony Bloesch, Ray Nickson, and Mark Utting. The ergo 4.1 reference manual. Technical Report 96-31, Software Verification Research Centre, Department of Computer Science, The University of Queensland, St. Lucia, QLD 4072, Australia, November 1996.
2. A. Bloesch, P. Kearney, E. Kazmierczak, J. Staples, O. Traynor, and M. Utting. A formal reasoning environment for Sum–a Z based specification language. In *Australasian Computer Science Communications, Vol18:1*, pages 45–54. ACSC96, 1996.
3. Anthony Bloesch, Ed Kazmierczak, Peter Kearney, and Owen Traynor. Cogito: A methodology and system for formal software development. *International Journal of Software Engineering and Knowledge Engineering*, (4):599–617, 1995.
4. Nicholas Hamilton, Ray Nickson, Owen Traynor, and Mark Utting. Interpretation and instantiation of theories for reasoning about formal specifications. In *Australasian Computer Science Communications, Vol19:1*, pages 37–45. ACSC97, 1997.
5. Tracey Hart, Fiona Linn, Roberto Morello, Greg Royle, Peter Kearney, Peter Lindsay, Kelvin Ross, and Owen Traynor. Formal methods pilot project. In *Proc. APSEC96*, pages 238–245. IEEE Computer Society Press, 1996.
6. Dan Hazel, Paul Strooper, and Owen Traynor. Possum: An animator for the sum language. Technical Report 97-17, Software Verification Research Centre, Department of Computer Science, The University of Queensland, St. Lucia, QLD 4072, Australia, March 1997.
7. P. Nickolas and P.J. Robinson. The Qu-Prolog unification algorithm: Formalisation and correctness. *Theoretical Computer Science*, 169:81–112, 1996.
8. Ray Nickson, Owen Traynor, and Mark Utting. Cogito Ergo Sum - providing structured theorem prover support for specification formalisms. In *Australasian Computer Science Communications, Vol18:1*, pages 149–158. ACSC96, 1996.
9. J.M. Spivey. *The Z Notation: a Reference Manual.* Prentice-Hall, New York, 1989.
10. Owen Traynor and Anthony Bloesch. The Cogito repository manager. In *Proc. APSEC94*, pages 356–367. IEEE Computer Society Press, 1994.
11. Owen Traynor and Anthony Bloesch. The Cogito tool architecture. In *Australasian Computer Science Communications, Vol18:1*, pages 97–106. ACSC96, 1996.
12. Owen Traynor, Peter Kearney, Ed Kazmierczak, Li Wang, and Einar Karlsen. Extending Z with modules. In *Australasian Computer Science Communications, Vol17:1*, pages 513–522. ACSC95, 1995.

Author Index

Springer and the environment

At Springer we firmly believe that an international science publisher has a special obligation to the environment, and our corporate policies consistently reflect this conviction.
We also expect our business partners – paper mills, printers, packaging manufacturers, etc. – to commit themselves to using materials and production processes that do not harm the environment. The paper in this book is made from low- or no-chlorine pulp and is acid free, in conformance with international standards for paper permanency.

Lecture Notes in Computer Science

For information about Vols. 1–1272

please contact your bookseller or Springer-Verlag

Vol. 1273: P. Antsaklis, W. Kohn, A. Nerode, S. Sastry (Eds.), Hybrid Systems IV. X, 405 pages. 1997.

Vol. 1274: T. Masuda, Y. Masunaga, M. Tsukamoto (Eds.), Worldwide Computing and Its Applications. Proceedings, 1997. XVI, 443 pages. 1997.

Vol. 1275: E.L. Gunter, A. Felty (Eds.), Theorem Proving in Higher Order Logics. Proceedings, 1997. VIII, 339 pages. 1997.

Vol. 1276: T. Jiang, D.T. Lee (Eds.), Computing and Combinatorics. Proceedings, 1997. XI, 522 pages. 1997.

Vol. 1277: V. Malyshkin (Ed.), Parallel Computing Technologies. Proceedings, 1997. XII, 455 pages. 1997.

Vol. 1278: R. Hofestädt, T. Lengauer, M. Löffler, D. Schomburg (Eds.), Bioinformatics. Proceedings, 1996. XI, 222 pages. 1997.

Vol. 1279: B. S. Chlebus, L. Czaja (Eds.), Fundamentals of Computation Theory. Proceedings, 1997. XI, 475 pages. 1997.

Vol. 1280: X. Liu, P. Cohen, M. Berthold (Eds.), Advances in Intelligent Data Analysis. Proceedings, 1997. XII, 621 pages. 1997.

Vol. 1281: M. Abadi, T. Ito (Eds.), Theoretical Aspects of Computer Software. Proceedings, 1997. XI, 639 pages. 1997.

Vol. 1282: D. Garlan, D. Le Métayer (Eds.), Coordination Languages and Models. Proceedings, 1997. X, 435 pages. 1997.

Vol. 1283: M. Müller-Olm, Modular Compiler Verification. XV, 250 pages. 1997.

Vol. 1284: R. Burkard, G. Woeginger (Eds.), Algorithms — ESA '97. Proceedings, 1997. XI, 515 pages. 1997.

Vol. 1285: X. Jao, J.-H. Kim, T. Furuhashi (Eds.), Simulated Evolution and Learning. Proceedings, 1996. VIII, 231 pages. 1997. (Subseries LNAI).

Vol. 1286: C. Zhang, D. Lukose (Eds.), Multi-Agent Systems. Proceedings, 1996. VII, 195 pages. 1997. (Subseries LNAI).

Vol. 1287: T. Kropf (Ed.), Formal Hardware Verification. XII, 367 pages. 1997.

Vol. 1288: M. Schneider, Spatial Data Types for Database Systems. XIII, 275 pages. 1997.

Vol. 1289: G. Gottlob, A. Leitsch, D. Mundici (Eds.), Computational Logic and Proof Theory. Proceedings, 1997. VIII, 348 pages. 1997.

Vol. 1290: E. Moggi, G. Rosolini (Eds.), Category Theory and Computer Science. Proceedings, 1997. VII, 313 pages. 1997.

Vol. 1291: D.G. Feitelson, L. Rudolph (Eds.), Job Scheduling Strategies for Parallel Processing. Proceedings, 1997. VII, 299 pages. 1997.

Vol. 1292: H. Glaser, P. Hartel, H. Kuchen (Eds.), Programming Languages: Implementations, Logigs, and Programs. Proceedings, 1997. XI, 425 pages. 1997.

Vol. 1293: C. Nicholas, D. Wood (Eds.), Principles of Document Processing. Proceedings, 1996. XI, 195 pages. 1997.

Vol. 1294: B.S. Kaliski Jr. (Ed.), Advances in Cryptology — CRYPTO '97. Proceedings, 1997. XII, 539 pages. 1997.

Vol. 1295: I. Prívara, P. Ružička (Eds.), Mathematical Foundations of Computer Science 1997. Proceedings, 1997. X, 519 pages. 1997.

Vol. 1296: G. Sommer, K. Daniilidis, J. Pauli (Eds.), Computer Analysis of Images and Patterns. Proceedings, 1997. XIII, 737 pages. 1997.

Vol. 1297: N. Lavrač, S. Džeroski (Eds.), Inductive Logic Programming. Proceedings, 1997. VIII, 309 pages. 1997. (Subseries LNAI).

Vol. 1298: M. Hanus, J. Heering, K. Meinke (Eds.), Algebraic and Logic Programming. Proceedings, 1997. X, 286 pages. 1997.

Vol. 1299: M.T. Pazienza (Ed.), Information Extraction. Proceedings, 1997. IX, 213 pages. 1997. (Subseries LNAI).

Vol. 1300: C. Lengauer, M. Griebl, S. Gorlatch (Eds.), Euro-Par'97 Parallel Processing. Proceedings, 1997. XXX, 1379 pages. 1997.

Vol. 1301: M. Jazayeri, H. Schauer (Eds.), Software Engineering - ESEC/FSE'97. Proceedings, 1997. XIII, 532 pages. 1997.

Vol. 1302: P. Van Hentenryck (Ed.), Static Analysis. Proceedings, 1997. X, 413 pages. 1997.

Vol. 1303: G. Brewka, C. Habel, B. Nebel (Eds.), KI-97: Advances in Artificial Intelligence. Proceedings, 1997. XI, 413 pages. 1997. (Subseries LNAI).

Vol. 1304: W. Luk, P.Y.K. Cheung, M. Glesner (Eds.), Field-Programmable Logic and Applications. Proceedings, 1997. XI, 503 pages. 1997.

Vol. 1305: D. Corne, J.L. Shapiro (Eds.), Evolutionary Computing. Proceedings, 1997. X, 307 pages. 1997.

Vol. 1306: C. Leung (Ed.), Visual Information Systems. X, 274 pages. 1997.

Vol. 1307: R. Kompe, Prosody in Speech Understanding Systems. XIX, 357 pages. 1997. (Subseries LNAI).

Vol. 1308: A. Hameurlain, A M. Tjoa (Eds.), Database and Expert Systems Applications. Proceedings, 1997. XVII, 688 pages. 1997.

Vol. 1309: R. Steinmetz, L.C. Wolf (Eds.), Interactive Distributed Multimedia Systems and Telecommunication Services. Proceedings, 1997. XIII, 466 pages. 1997.

Vol. 1310: A. Del Bimbo (Ed.), Image Analysis and Processing. Proceedings, 1997. Volume I. XXII, 722 pages. 1997.

Vol. 1311: A. Del Bimbo (Ed.), Image Analysis and Processing. Proceedings, 1997. Volume II. XXII, 794 pages. 1997.

Vol. 1312: A. Geppert, M. Berndtsson (Eds.), Rules in Database Systems. Proceedings, 1997. VII, 214 pages. 1997.

Vol. 1313: J. Fitzgerald, C.B. Jones, P. Lucas (Eds.), FME '97: Industrial Applications and Strengthened Foundations of Formal Methods. Proceedings, 1997. XIII, 685 pages. 1997.

Vol. 1314: S. Muggleton (Ed.), Inductive Logic Programming. Proceedings, 1996. VIII, 397 pages. 1997. (Subseries LNAI).

Vol. 1315: G. Sommer, J.J. Koenderink (Eds.), Algebraic Frames for the Perception-Action Cycle. Proceedings, 1997. VIII, 395 pages. 1997.

Vol. 1316: M. Li, A. Maruoka (Eds.), Algorithmic Learning Theory. Proceedings, 1997. XI, 461 pages. 1997. (Subseries LNAI).

Vol. 1317: M. Leman (Ed.), Music, Gestalt, and Computing. IX, 524 pages. 1997. (Subseries LNAI).

Vol. 1318: R. Hirschfeld (Ed.), Financial Cryptography. Proceedings, 1997. XI, 409 pages. 1997.

Vol. 1319: E. Plaza, R. Benjamins (Eds.), Knowledge Acquisition, Modeling and Management. Proceedings, 1997. XI, 389 pages. 1997. (Subseries LNAI).

Vol. 1320: M. Mavronicolas, P. Tsigas (Eds.), Distributed Algorithms. Proceedings, 1997. X, 333 pages. 1997.

Vol. 1321: M. Lenzerini (Ed.), AI*IA 97: Advances in Artificial Intelligence. Proceedings, 1997. XII, 459 pages. 1997. (Subseries LNAI).

Vol. 1322: H. Hußmann, Formal Foundations for Software Engineering Methods. X, 286 pages. 1997.

Vol. 1323: E. Costa, A. Cardoso (Eds.), Progress in Artificial Intelligence. Proceedings, 1997. XIV, 393 pages. 1997. (Subseries LNAI).

Vol. 1324: C. Peters, C. Thanos (Eds.), Research and Advanced Technology for Digital Libraries. Proceedings, 1997. X, 423 pages. 1997.

Vol. 1325: Z.W. Raś, A. Skowron (Eds.), Foundations of Intelligent Systems. Proceedings, 1997. XI, 630 pages. 1997. (Subseries LNAI).

Vol. 1326: C. Nicholas, J. Mayfield (Eds.), Intelligent Hypertext. XIV, 182 pages. 1997.

Vol. 1327: W. Gerstner, A. Germond, M. Hasler, J.-D. Nicoud (Eds.), Artificial Neural Networks – ICANN '97. Proceedings, 1997. XIX, 1274 pages. 1997.

Vol. 1328: C. Retoré (Ed.), Logical Aspects of Computational Linguistics. Proceedings, 1996. VIII, 435 pages. 1997. (Subseries LNAI).

Vol. 1329: S.C. Hirtle, A.U. Frank (Eds.), Spatial Information Theory. Proceedings, 1997. XIV, 511 pages. 1997.

Vol. 1330: G. Smolka (Ed.), Principles and Practice of Constraint Programming – CP 97. Proceedings, 1997. XII, 563 pages. 1997.

Vol. 1331: D. W. Embley, R. C. Goldstein (Eds.), Conceptual Modeling – ER '97. Proceedings, 1997. XV, 479 pages. 1997.

Vol. 1332: M. Bubak, J. Dongarra, J. Waśniewski (Eds.), Recent Advances in Parallel Virtual Machine and Message Passing Interface. Proceedings, 1997. XV, 518 pages. 1997.

Vol. 1333: F. Pichler. R.Moreno-Díaz (Eds.), Computer Aided Systems Theory – EUROCAST'97. Proceedings, 1997. XII, 626 pages. 1997.

Vol. 1334: Y. Han, T. Okamoto, S. Qing (Eds.), Information and Communications Security. Proceedings, 1997. X, 484 pages. 1997.

Vol. 1335: R.H. Möhring (Ed.), Graph-Theoretic Concepts in Computer Science. Proceedings, 1997. X, 376 pages. 1997.

Vol. 1336: C. Polychronopoulos, K. Joe, K. Araki, M. Amamiya (Eds.), High Performance Computing. Proceedings, 1997. XII, 416 pages. 1997.

Vol. 1337: C. Freksa, M. Jantzen, R. Valk (Eds.), Foundations of Computer Science. XII, 515 pages. 1997.

Vol. 1338: F. Plášil, K.G. Jeffery (Eds.), SOFSEM'97: Theory and Practice of Informatics. Proceedings, 1997. XIV, 571 pages. 1997.

Vol. 1339: N.A. Murshed, F. Bortolozzi (Eds.), Advances in Document Image Analysis. Proceedings, 1997. IX, 345 pages. 1997.

Vol. 1340: M. van Kreveld, J. Nievergelt, T. Roos, P. Widmayer (Eds.), Algorithmic Foundations of Geographic Information Systems. XIV, 287 pages. 1997.

Vol. 1341: F. Bry, R. Ramakrishnan, K. Ramamohanarao (Eds.), Deductive and Object-Oriented Databases. Proceedings, 1997. XIV, 430 pages. 1997.

Vol. 1342: A. Sattar (Ed.), Advanced Topics in Artificial Intelligence. Proceedings, 1997. XVII, 516 pages. 1997. (Subseries LNAI).

Vol. 1343: Y. Ishikawa, R.R. Oldehoeft, J.V.W. Reynders, M. Tholburn (Eds.), Scientific Computing in Object-Oriented Parallel Environments. Proceedings, 1997. XI, 295 pages. 1997.

Vol. 1344: C. Ausnit-Hood, K.A. Johnson, R.G. Pettit, IV, S.B. Opdahl (Eds.), Ada 95 – Quality and Style. XV, 292 pages. 1997.

Vol. 1345: R.K. Shyamasundar, K. Ueda (Eds.), Advances in Computing Science - ASIAN'97. Proceedings, 1997. XIII, 387 pages. 1997.

Vol. 1346: S. Ramesh, G. Sivakumar (Eds.), Foundations of Software Technology and Theoretical Computer Science. Proceedings, 1997. XI, 343 pages. 1997.

Vol. 1347: E. Ahronovitz, C. Fiorio (Eds.), Discrete Geometry for Computer Imagery. Proceedings, 1997. X, 255 pages. 1997.

Vol. 1349: M. Johnson (Ed.), Algebraic Methodology and Software Technology. Proceedings, 1997. X, 594 pages. 1997.

Vol. 1350: H.W. Leong, H. Imai, S. Jain (Eds.), Algorithms and Computation. Proceedings, 1997. XV, 426 pages. 1997.